Testing and Counseling Services

Bunting and Lyon, Inc., administers the Independent School Entrance Exam (ISEE) and the Secondary School Admission Test (SSAT) to small groups of students one or two weekday mornings throughout the year. We also counsel families in their search for private school placement, facilitating the research of appropriate schools for their children and guiding them through the admission process.

For further information, please contact us by telephone at 203-269-3333 or by e-mail at BuntingandLyon@aol.com.

Private Independent Schools

Bunting and Lyon, Inc., 238 North Main Street, Wallingford, Connecticut 06492

In 1936, at the height of the Great Depression, newlyweds James and Elizabeth Webster Lyon Bunting founded Bunting and Lyon, a small company that would become one of the leading publishers of reference books in the field of private education. *Private Independent Schools* first appeared in print in 1943 and featured description of 95 schools. From those modest beginnings, the Blue Book, as it is familiarly known, has carried information on thousands of schools, from nursery and preschool through Grade 12 and a postgraduate year. In 1948, Bunting and Lyon initiated counseling services for families seeking appropriate school placement for their children. In addition, for more than 10 years, we have administered on-site standardized admission tests in small groups of private school applicants.

Since the early '60s, our office has been housed in a historic homestead (photograph ca. 1860) on North Main Street in Wallingford, Connecticut, about halfway between Hartford and New Haven off Interstate 91 and the Merritt Parkway. The Davis Homestead was originally owned by cousins of Harriet Beecher Stowe, one of America's most renowned authors and civil rights advocates.

Private Independent Schools

2008
The Sixty-first Edition

Published and Distributed by
Bunting and Lyon, Inc.
238 North Main Street
Wallingford, Connecticut 06492
U.S.A.
Telephone: 1-203-269-3333
Fax: 1-203-269-5697
E-mail BuntingandLyon@aol.com
Web Site www.BuntingandLyon.com

238 North Main Street
Wallingford, Connecticut 06492
Telephone 1-203-269-3333
Fax 1-203-269-5697
Printed and Bound in U.S.A.

Library of Congress Catalog Card Number:
72-122324

International Standard Book Number:
0-913094-61-7

International Standard Series Number:
0079-5399

$115

Foreword

Preserving the Planet

In the 60+ years that Bunting and Lyon has published *Private Independent Schools,* we've chronicled many changes and innovations adopted by the thousands of schools whose descriptions have graced the pages of our directory.

From year to year, certain trends crop up with increasing frequency, mirroring new concerns and emphases, both within the independent school community and in the larger global community of the 21st century. Terms such as *diversity, multiculturalism, service learning,* and *social outreach* reflect the conscience and sensibilities of students, faculty, and families alike.

With world attention focused on the critical problem of global warming, hundreds of private schools are maximizing their efforts to avert the impending disaster predicted by many scientists and climate experts. From the National Association of Independent Schools (NAIS), sponsor of symposia, conferences, and workshops on the subject, to schools large and small across the country, the private educational world is tackling the problem head on.

This year, *sustainability* is the buzzword that has impelled many schools to take new initiatives in both curricular offerings and cocurricular activities. According to an online dictionary, *sustainability* is defined as "the conservation of ecological balance by avoiding the depletion of natural resources." To attain this goal, schools of all sizes, in cities as well as in rural and suburban areas, are becoming "green."

At its simplest level, sustainability involves cutting down on waste; increasing the efficiency of lighting, heating, and technological fixtures; learning about the benefits of recycling, composting, water conservation; emphasizing natural and organic food and materials as alternatives to current practices; and integrating relevant environmental education into science and other disciplines. At the other end, schools have incorporated the recommendations and principles set forth by Leadership in Energy and Environmental Design (LEED) as they undertake new construction of classrooms, buildings, and other facilities.

While virtually every school educates students about environmental stewardship and respect for nature, many incorporate specific topics into their regular curriculum beyond basic physical and earth science. Leafing through the pages of the Blue Book, readers encounter course offerings such as Environmental Science, Conservation Biology, Oceanography, Marine Biology, and a host of other subjects geared toward raising consciousness, imparting information, and inspiring students to take a proactive role in improving the quality of life on Earth.

In addition to course work in ecological subjects, students from around the country take school-sponsored expeditions to learn about and experience the rainforests of the Amazon, Ecuador, and Costa Rica; marine biology on Catalina Island; wildlife habitats in the Galapagos; and, closer to home, extended trips to such facilities as a research vessel in Long Island Sound, the New Jersey School of Conservation, Maine Coast Semester, and The Mountain School.

In Kent, Connecticut, Marvelwood School's science department has been recognized by the State for its innovative, hands-on programs as well as its contributions to state and local agencies such as the Department of Environmental Protection, the Audubon Society, and various local conservation commissions and land trusts. In addition, projects such as water quality testing, mapping vernal pools with GPS equipment, and operating one of only two licensed high school bird-banding stations in the U.S. illustrate Marvelwood's dedication to sustainability through experiential education.

In Ohio, Olney Friends School, a small Quaker boarding and day school, has a sustainability program that includes organic gardens that produce much of the fresh fruits and vegetables consumed by the school community.

Ranked by *The Green Guide* as the "second-greenest school" in the U.S., The Willow School recently completed two new buildings that incorporate all the essential elements of responsible, long-term environmental benefits. The Barn, which earned New Jersey's first LEED's Platinum certification, is constructed of materials recycled and salvaged from a historic barn in Connecticut and combined with those of an existing barn on the 34-acre campus. Willow's master plan calls for use of The Barn as a middle school, cafeteria, and performing arts and science center. A classroom building for students in Kindergarten through Grade 5 is made of wood, stone, and glass and carries LEED's Gold certification. Funds for this major undertaking came from donations and from Willow's budget, demonstrating a huge commitment by a tiny school to sustainability, from rainwater and daylight harvesting and on-site electric generation, to butterfly gardens and beautiful buildings designed for the future.

From coast to coast, private independent schools are making dramatic changes for the betterment of Planet Earth. Bunting and Lyon salutes the administration, staff, and students of these forward-thinking and courageous schools; we encourage others to follow their example.

Peter G. Bunting, *Publisher*
&
The Editors

On Applying

Now What?

Applying to a private independent school can be a lengthy, sometimes daunting, task. Ideally, you should begin the process several seasons in advance of the desired entry year. While procedures vary from school to school, the following overview is designed to give you the general timeline of what to do when.

September–October

- So many schools—so little time.
  Figure out your priorities and criteria. Research and narrow down school choices by using guides, brochures, view books, and web sites. Consult an educational counselor. Talk with alumni as well as current students and parents, if possible. Include a "stretch" and a "safety" school in your final list.

- The paper chase.
  Send for application forms and review them carefully for due dates, required materials, and admission testing requirements. Some schools have a preliminary form, which gets the candidate into the school's computer bank. And, yes, there is a fee to apply.

October–January

- What's the difference?
  Many schools hold open houses that showcase student-led tours, presentations by faculty members, discussion panels with current parents, and sample classes. Go. Get a feel for the school. Poke around. Ask questions.

- Put your best foot forward.
  Schedule an on-campus interview (usually required). This may include a tour of the school and class visitation, lasting from two hours to a full day, and involves parents and the candidate. Try to do this after some of your application material has been sent in. You and the admission officer will have a much more interesting conversation. Show interest and

be prepared to ask questions that are not answered in the school's promotional material. Look your best. It's better to dress conservatively than not. Respect the school you're visiting. When you get back home, write a thank-you note to your interviewer.

- Can't get there from here?
  If a visit to campus is impossible, schools can often arrange for an alumni representative to hold an interview near your home. Some schools also make telephone interviews available.

- Multiple choices.
  Register for and take any required standardized testing. Many schools require the Secondary School Admission Test (SSAT) or the Independent School Entrance Examination (ISEE). Other schools have their own test. Candidates for Grades 11–12 and a postgraduate year may have to submit PSAT or SAT scores. International students may have to take the Secondary Level English Proficiency Test (SLEP) or the Test of English as a Foreign Language (TOEFL). Make sure the score results will arrive before your schools' application due date.

- The five-paragraph theme.
  Finish your part of the application form, which usually includes student essays and a parent questionnaire. Don't leave this assignment until the last minute. Take your time; write out drafts; review, edit, rewrite. Be honest and enthusiastic. Dare to be different.

- Reach out and touch someone.
  Give recommendation forms to teachers, counselors, and others, as specified in the application packet, to fill out and return. Give transcript release forms to your school office. Provide everyone with stamped, addressed envelopes and a due date; then follow up! And be sure to thank your teachers.

- Where's the money?
  Don't let those tuition figures scare you off. All schools award financial aid, usually based on need, sometimes also on merit. Apply early, and, remember, your family will have to submit various personal financial records.

December–February

- The longest days.
  Be sure all application materials have been submitted. Some schools will send a postcard noting what is missing. Otherwise, call the school to check. Be proactive. Then wait while admission committees do their job.

March–April

- The good news.
  Schools send notifications of acceptance or denial. In many areas, school consortiums agree to the same mailing date and the same response deadline. You usually have a month to respond.

- Are we there yet?
  Some schools hold second visits for accepted students. Go if you can. Keep asking questions.

- Your final decision.
  Let the school of your choice know that you are coming. Your family must sign an enrollment agreement and send a deposit. And it is imperative to notify the other schools that accepted you that you are enrolling elsewhere, so they can offer the space to another candidate.

The timetable and procedures reflected in these guidelines are general in nature. No matter when you become interested in private independent education, you are encouraged to find appropriate schools and apply. It's never too late to follow your dream.

Standardized Testing Information

Most private independent schools require standardized testing as part of their admission procedure. The two most widely used admission tests are the Independent School Entrance Examination (ISEE) and the Secondary School Admission Test (SSAT). Some schools administer their own test. International students may be asked to take the Test of English as a Foreign Language (TOEFL); applicants for Grades 11–12 and a postgraduate year may have to submit ACT, SAT, or PSAT scores. You can receive information about these standardized tests through the contacts listed below.

Independent School Entrance Examination (ISEE)
Educational Records Bureau
220 East 42nd Street
New York, NY 10017
Telephone 212-672-9812; [Toll-free] 800-989-3721
E-mail isee@erbtest.org; Web Site www.iseetest.org

Secondary School Admission Test (SSAT)
CN 5399 (for regular mail)
Princeton, NJ 08543
862 Route 518 (for courier & express service)
Skillman, NJ 08558
Telephone 609-683-4440
E-mail info@ssat.org; Web Site www.ssat.org

Test of English as a Foreign Language (TOEFL)
Secondary Level English Proficiency Test (SLEP)
TOEFL Services
Educational Testing Services
P.O. Box 6151
Princeton, NJ 08541-6151
U.S.A.
Telephone 609-771-7100; [Toll-free] 877-863-3546
E-mail toefl@ets.org; Web Site www.ets.org/toefl

American College Test (ACT)
ACT
500 ACT Drive
P.O. Box 168
Iowa City, IA 52243-0168
Telephone 319-337-1000
Web Site www.act.org

SAT and PSAT
www.collegeboard.com

Seeking Financial Aid?

Many schools that offer financial assistance do so through the School and Student Service for Financial Aid, wholly owned by the National Association of Independent Schools. While you will find the best source of information about financial aid policies at the particular schools you are interested in, some general information may be found at http://nais.org/admission.

Underserved Minorities and Independent Education

A number of organizations and foundations exist to prepare minority students for placement in private and independent schools, primarily at the secondary level. These organizations seek out academically talented and motivated students who come from economically disadvantaged, low-income, and underserved segments of society. Some agencies specify that they serve African-Americans or children of color, which may include Black, Asian, Latino, and Native American.

Goals of the various organizations include equalizing the chances for opportunity and success, motivating and supporting qualified students, developing well-educated and capable leaders, and increasing the number of students of color in independent schools.

Many programs require a rigorous application process. Those students selected to participate commit to a year or more of preparation aimed at independent school placement, which is usually ensured upon a student's successful completion of the year's requirements. Preparation may include summer academic sessions, Wednesday afternoon and Saturday classes during the school year, and extra homework. Often these programs partner with a specific consortium of private schools in student placement.

Some programs provide exposure to the world of higher education and to professional entrepreneurship and business. Others concentrate on personal growth, leadership development, and community service.

All programs offer various services designed to help students apply and gain admission to private schools. These services, which involve student and family, consist of an introduction to specific schools through fairs and tours, help with the admission process (application paperwork, interview techniques, testing information), and guidance on financial aid and financial planning. Other support services may include tutoring and mentoring, transitional counseling, summer job assistance, college guidance, internships, reunions and recognition ceremonies, and parent workshops.

A few organizations make annual tuition grants; however, most families receive financial aid from the private school in which their child enrolls.

The following list of agencies is by no means exhaustive. These particular organizations have been in contact with Bunting and Lyon, and we have gleaned our informational overview from their materials. We are pleased to present them in hope that you will contact them about their programs.

A Better Chance
240 West 35th Street, 9th Floor
New York, NY 10001
Tel. 646-346-1310
Web Site www.abetterchance.org

Baltimore Educational Scholarship Trust (B.E.S.T.)
808 North Charles Street
Baltimore, MD 21201
Tel. 410-752-2225
Web Site www.besttrust.org

The Black Student Fund
3636 16th Street NW, 4th Floor
Washington, DC 20010-1146
Tel. 202-387-1414
Web Site www.blackstudentfund.org

The Boys' Club of New York
287 East 10th Street
New York, NY 10009
Tel. 212-533-2550
Web Site www.bcny.org

Early Steps
540 East 76th Street
New York, NY 10021
Tel. 212-288-9684

The Independent School Alliance for Minority Affairs
1545 Wilshire Boulevard, Suite 711
Los Angeles, CA 90017
Tel. 213-484-2411
Web Site www.thealliance-la.org

New Jersey SEEDS
494 Broad Street
Newark, NJ 07102
Tel. 973-642-6422
Web Site www.njseeds.org

Prep for Prep
328 West 71st Street
New York, NY 10023
Tel. 212-579-1390
Web Site www.prepforprep.org

Project Match
6303 Nelway Drive
McLean, VA 22101
Tel. 703-847-9677

Queen City Foundation
1 West 4th Street
Cincinnati, OH 45202
Tel. 513-241-1322

REACH Prep
2777 Summer Street
Stamford, CT 06905
Tel. 203-487-0750
Web Site www.reachprep.org

The Steppingstone Foundation
155 Federal Street, Suite 800
Boston, MA 02110
Tel. 617-423-6300
Web Site www.tsf.org

Summerbridge Manchester
2108 River Road
Manchester, NH 03104
Tel. 603-641-9426
Web Site summerbridge.derryfield.org

The Wight Foundation, Inc.
60 Park Place, 17th Floor
Newark, NJ 07102
Tel. 973-824-1195
Web Site www.wightfoundation.org

Contents

Index of the Schools

The following Index of the Schools includes the names and locations of the 1000 private schools described in our book. The schools have made this publication possible by subscribing for full Descriptive Articles and Listings.

Schools that have subscribed for Descriptive Articles are identified with an asterisk. These articles will give you a broad feeling for private schools in general as well as an objective, in-depth definition of individual schools, both day and boarding.

Index of the Schools

Asterisk indicates a Descriptive Article.

C

W

Y

The Schools

The Blue Book features descriptions of 1000 private schools in North America and abroad that meet our standards of acceptance. These educational institutions serve students ranging in grade levels from Nursery through Grade 12 and a postgraduate year.

For easy reference, schools in the United States are organized alphabetically within their respective states. Schools throughout the rest of the world follow and are listed alphabetically by country or territory.

The 20-line listings contain basic information and give a good idea of the philosophy and programs of the school. Descriptive Articles follow a set format and provide a school's characteristics in detail. All entries are written as "fact without opinion," allowing for clear comparisons between one school and another, from which readers may draw their own conclusions.

All entries in the book appear in their entirety online at **www.BuntingandLyon.com**. You can research schools by name, city, state, academic courses, arts offerings, sports teams, extracurricular activities, and personnel. Direct links to schools' web sites and an e-mail inquiry form are included.

If you are interested in any of these schools, we suggest that you contact the Director of Admission or the Head of the School, the names of whom appear in the entry.

ALABAMA

Advent Episcopal School 1950

2019 Sixth Avenue North, Birmingham, AL 35203
Tel. 205-252-2535; Fax 205-252-3023

ADVENT EPISCOPAL SCHOOL in Birmingham, Alabama, was founded in 1950. Since then, this independent, equal-opportunity institution has built a reputation for academic excellence, featuring an advanced curriculum for boys and girls in four-year-old Kindergarten through Grade 8. The School's location enables students to take advantage of such resources as the Alabama Civil Rights Institute, the Alabama Symphony Orchestra, Children's Theater, and the Alabama Jazz Hall of Fame. They also attend and participate in concerts in the park, parades, and festivals.

The Advent's credo declares a dedication to "Sharing the ADVENTure" of education, while its mission promises "to offer a superior, advanced, and enriched education in a Christian environment." At a time of unsettling events and circumstances, the School draws on its Christian heritage to help provide a safe, stable, wholesome, and caring atmosphere in which students can experience the total learning process with a sense of enthusiasm. In the belief that education is a continuing adventure to be shared with students and family, the faculty develops learning concepts from day to day, emphasizing basic skills and exploring the relationships among the various disciplines.

The Advent, a nonprofit institution, was the first elementary school in Birmingham and Jefferson County to be accredited by the Southern Association of Colleges and Schools and the first independent school to integrate. It holds membership in the National Association of Independent Schools, among other organizations. School policies are established by a 13-member Board of Trustees comprised of individuals from throughout the community.

THE CAMPUS. The School is set among the modern commercial towers of Birmingham, Alabama's largest city and a major medical, educational, business, and industrial center of the American South. The campus features shaded gardens, new and period buildings, a model outdoor playground, a gymnasium, and a newly constructed rooftop recreational facility. The music classroom/auditorium, constructed six years ago, has been nationally recognized for its excellent acoustical properties.

The School is adjacent to the historic Cathedral Church of the Advent where many school assemblies and special programs take place. The main, three-story building, with bright, airy rooms and art-filled halls, houses fully equipped Lower and Upper School science labs, a computer lab, a 15,000-volume library, classrooms, administrative offices, and an art room equipped with a printing press, a pottery wheel, a kiln, and a darkroom. A technology center is located in the McPhillips Library. Neal Gymnasium contains basketball and volleyball courts, while the paneled refectory offers a warm atmosphere for student dining.

THE FACULTY. Una Battles, appointed Headmistress in 1969, is a graduate of the University of Alabama (B.S., M.A.). Her previous experience includes service as a teacher in Alabama public schools. Mrs. Battles and her husband, Craig, have one son.

The 29 full-time faculty members hold baccalaureates, 20 master's degrees, and 2 doctorates representing study at Auburn, Birmingham-Southern, Emory, Furman, Gonzaga, Houston Baptist, Huntingdon, Judson, Louisiana State, Millsaps, Mississippi State, Northwestern, Samford, Spring Hill, Troy State, Tulane, Vanderbilt, and the Universities of Alabama, Mississippi, and Montevallo.

Six part-time instructors teach art; Lower School science, music, French, physical education, and literature/composition. A Red Cross-certified individual staffs the Health Room on a full-time basis.

Faculty benefits include long-term disability insurance, leaves of absence, cancer insurance, medical and life insurance, and a retirement plan.

STUDENT BODY. In 2007–08, the School enrolled a diverse group of 333 students from 50 zip codes located throughout the Birmingham Metropolitan area.

ACADEMIC PROGRAM. The Advent is organized into three components: Kindergarten, Lower School (Grades 1–4), and Upper School (Grades 5–8). Academics begin in four-year-old Kindergarten, and grades are departmentalized from Grade 5 upward. All children entering the Kindergartens and Grade 1 must meet the September 1 birthdate deadline. All children attend weekly chapel services.

Kindergartners have four hours of classroom instruction and play daily. Instruction consists of reading (with emphasis on phonics), mathematics, science, social studies, penmanship, art, music, French, and computer.

The schedule for Grades 1–8 is divided into 30-minute modules to accommodate approximately four morning and four afternoon class periods of varying lengths.

The basic curriculum for Grades 1–6 includes reading (with emphasis on phonics in Grades 1–3), language arts (vocabulary, composition, literature, critical thinking, and writing), penmanship (Grades 1–3), computer, French, social studies, mathematics, and science. Grades 1–4 have library periods with instruction in library skills. Social studies in Kindergarten–Grade 3 is designed to give students an awareness of the social and physical world around them. Grade 4 studies Alabama History; Grade 5, U.S. History; and Grade 6, Ancient World History. Literature and composition, emphasizing study of the novel, short story, drama, and poetry, are added in Grade 5, as are religion and the introduction of laboratory techniques in science. Special themes explored include migration (Grades 1–2), the dynamic earth (Grades 3–4), and oceans (Grade 5). Grade 6 studies earth and space science.

In Grade 7, language arts includes the study of English grammar, vocabulary, composition (including expository writing), and literature. Other subjects are French, world history and geography, modern mathematics (emphasizing geometry and the algebra of points and lines), basic life science, art, religion, and computer.

The eighth-grade curriculum consists of English grammar, composition, and literature as well as American History, French, civics, algebra, physical science, art, physical education, religion, and computer.

Regular art classes begin in Grade 3 and continue through Grade 8. All students participate in the music program, which aims toward musical literacy and appreciation as well as performance. The physical education program begins with directed play in Kindergarten and progresses to team games and dance activities for the older children. Sports included in the program are basketball, kickball, hockey, soccer, volleyball, and golf.

For students who require additional assistance, teachers are available to provide tutoring as needed for a charge.

Upon graduation from The Advent, most students elect to attend high school locally. Of these, the majority remain in independent schools. Others may choose boarding schools located throughout the eastern half of the United States.

STUDENT ACTIVITIES. The Student Council, made up of representatives from Grades 5–8 and elected by class, meets monthly with faculty advisers to discuss matters of student concern and to organize School-wide service projects for local charities. The Council also holds fund-raisers, sponsors the spring dance for Grades 7–8, and presents a leadership award to a graduating eighth grader. A Christmas Service Project is organized by the Student Council as well as a party day. A-Day activities, which include skits, sack and relay races, and a student-faculty talent show, are also planned by the Student Council.

Field trips are scheduled for all grades. Kindergarten and Lower School students have visited a bakery, a dairy, a local fire station, and the zoo. Destinations for older students may include Huntsville's Constitution Hall Village, the Birmingham-Southern planetarium, Oak Mountain State Park, McWane Science Center, City Hall, the county courthouse, and the Birmingham Museum of Art. In addition, Grades 4–8 take long trips each year to such places as the State Capitol in Montgomery, the Space Museum in Huntsville, the American Village in Montevallo, and Atlanta's CNN, World of Coke, and Aquarium. The fifth grade takes a five-day trip to Washington, D.C., while sixth graders participate in a three-day environmental program at Alabama's Camp McDowell. Seventh graders travel to Dauphin Island Sea Lab near Mobile for three days, and eighth graders visit the Museum of Natural History at the University of Alabama and the Warner-Westervelt Museum of Western American Art near Tuscaloosa.

Individual classes present plays and concerts periodically.

Traditional events for the school community are a parent/teacher Open House, parent/teacher Christmas luncheon, Grandparents' Day, Art Fair, Science Fair, Services of Lessons and Carols, and the May Festival.

Activities include basketball, volleyball, golf, French Club, Math Team, Chess Team, a student newspaper, choral ensemble, and Cross and Shield service organization.

ADMISSION AND COSTS. Advent Episcopal School admits students in all grades on the basis of a standardized, School-administered entrance examination, previous academic records, and recommendations from teachers and other adults. The School admits students without regard to race, creed, or national or ethnic origin. Students currently enrolled are given priority for registration until the first of February. At that time, new students are considered with the following priorities: siblings of current students, alumni children, members of the Cathedral Church of the Advent, and the earliest applicants. If vacancies exist, students may be enrolled at midyear. There is a $25 testing fee and a $275 registration fee.

In 2008–09, tuition is $4536 for Kindergarten and $7245 for Grades 1–8. There is a discount of $135 per year for kindergartners and $180 per year for Grades 1–8 for members of the Cathedral Church of the Advent. The cost of books and milk is included in the tuition; a Student Activities Fee, which is payable three times a year and varies with grade level, covers special events and materials such as novels, field trips, and seminars. The charge for before-school care is $15 per month or $1 per day; after-school care is $245 monthly or $10.25 per hour. A tuition insurance refund plan is offered.

Financial aid of approximately $90,000 is awarded annually on the basis of need and academic achievement.

Dean of Faculty: Mrs. Rosemary Ham
Alumni Secretary: Mrs. Lady Anne Buchanan
Director of Admissions: Mrs. Mary W. Hoffman
Director of Development: Mr. Craig Battles
Business Manager: Mr. Martin Johnson
Director of Athletics: Mr. John Brown
Director of Music: Mr. Richard Phillips

The Altamont School 1922

4801 Altamont Road, Birmingham, AL 35222
Tel. 205-879-2006; Fax 205-871-5666
Web Site www.altamontschool.org
E-mail sstevens@altamontschool.org

The Altamont School is a coeducational, college preparatory day school enrolling approximately 400 students in Grades 5–12. The School encourages students to think critically, communicate truthfully, and live honorably. The ultimate goal is the development of creative and imaginative students who are self-disciplined, honest, and hard-working and who also have a concern for making themselves useful citizens. All students take courses that follow a traditional liberal arts curriculum, and electives include Creative Writing, Photography, forensics, studio art, film making, instrument and choral music, Scholars Bowl, aerobics, and yoga. Students may take part in 25 athletic teams, orchestra, drama, school government, National Honor Society, publications, and environmental, history, music, French, Spanish, Latin, and science clubs. Community service at local organizations and Fall Project Week, during which students take field trips in the U.S. and abroad, also enhance the academic

program. Summer@Altamont provides academic and extracurricular enrichment. Tuition: $12,624–$15,696. Financial Aid: $621,000. Jimmy Wiygul is Director of Admissions; Sarah Whiteside is Interim Head of School. *Southern Association.*

Bayside Academy 1967

303 Dryer Avenue, Daphne, AL 36526
Tel. 251-626-2840; Fax 251-626-2899
Web Site www.baysideacademy.org
E-mail afoster@baysideacademy.org

Founded by parents to enable both average and gifted students to reach their potential, Bayside is a college preparatory day school enrolling 757 boys and girls in Pre-Kindergarten–Grade 12. The traditional academic program includes Advanced Placement courses as well as computer, fine arts, and foreign language in all grades. Teams are fielded in 11 sports; academic teams, drama, publications, and service clubs are also offered. Tuition: $6000–$8400. Extras: $1000. Financial Aid: $200,000. Alan Foster is Director of Admissions; Thomas Johnson (Valdosta State University, M.E. 1972) was appointed Head in 1998. *Southern Association.*

Highlands School 1958

4901 Old Leeds Road, Birmingham, AL 35213
Tel. 205-956-9731; Admissions Ext. 113; Fax 205-951-8127
Web Site www.highlandsschool.org
E-mail jladden@highlandsschool.org

Highlands is a coeducational day school enrolling 280 students from diverse backgrounds in Preschool–Grade 8. Its mission is to nurture each child's mental, physical, social, and emotional development and to instill self-confidence and a lifelong pursuit of learning. The curriculum is designed to meet individual learning styles while providing a strong base of understanding in the core disciplines. French and Spanish begin in preschool; keyboarding and computer skills are introduced in Grade 3. Among the activities are Student Council, community outreach, yearbook, scouting for girls and boys, and intramural athletics. A summer session offers enrichment and all-day care. Tuition:

$7360–$9350. Financial aid is available. Judy Ladden is Director of Admissions; Kathryn W. Barr is Head of School.

Randolph School 1959

1005 Drake Avenue, SE, Huntsville, AL 35802
Tel. 256-881-1701; Admissions Ext. 103; Fax 256-881-1784
Web Site www.randolphschool.net
E-mail nhodges@randolphschool.net

A National School of Excellence, Randolph is a coeducational, college preparatory day school dedicated to developing academic achievement, earned independence, and committed citizenship in its 876 students. The K–12 curriculum integrates the arts, sciences, and humanities with honors and Advanced Placement courses and a wide range of electives. Additional activities are available in athletics, student government, music, drama, clubs, and societies. Students in Grades 8–12 purchase personal laptops. Graduates are consistently admitted to competitive colleges and universities. Tuition: $10,375–$12,875. Financial aid is available. Nancy Hodges is Director of Admissions; Dr. Byron Hulsey is President and Head of School. *Southern Association.*

St. Luke's Episcopal School 1961

3975 Japonica Lane, Mobile, AL 36693
Tel. 251-666-2991; Fax 251-666-2996
Web Site www.sles.cc; E-mail leblen@sles.cc

St. Luke's Episcopal School, founded in 1961, is a college preparatory parish school seeking to provide educational excellence within a Christian environment. The 490 boys and girls in Pre-Kindergarten–Grade 8 are motivated to develop confidence and positive self-esteem through a challenging academic program, enhanced by Spanish, technology, and the arts. A variety of competitive sports, interest clubs, and extracurricular activities are offered. The trip curriculum includes excursions to the Tremont Institute in the Great Smoky Mountains, the Florida Keys, and Washington, D.C. Tuition: $1265–$5654. Financial aid is available. Leigh Eblen is Director of Admissions; W. Palmer Kennedy was appointed Head of School in 2006. *Southern Association.*

St. Paul's Episcopal School 1947

161 Dogwood Lane, Mobile, AL 36608
Tel. 251-342-6700; Admissions 251-461-2129; Fax 251-342-1844
Web Site www.stpaulsmobile.net
Admissions E-mail jtaylor@stpaulsmobile.net

This college preparatory Episcopal school enrolls approximately 1500 girls and boys as day students in Pre-Kindergarten through Grade 12. Chapel, an honor pledge, and community service are important elements of St. Paul's program. The Upper School provides Advanced Placement in the major disciplines, while the Middle and Upper Schools offer laptop computer sections in the core courses. The program also serves a modest number of students with learning differences. Approximately 50 percent of graduates are accepted by the "most competitive," "highly competitive," and "very competitive" colleges and universities. In sports, St. Paul's is ranked first for academic year 2006–07 and first overall in the state. The fine arts program includes portrait painting, chorus, and strings, among others. Tuition: $3632–$8180. Julie L. Taylor is Director of Admissions. *Southern Association.*

ARIZONA

All Saints' Episcopal Day School 1963

6300 North Central Avenue, Phoenix, AZ 85012
Tel. 602-274-4866; Fax 602-274-5032
Web Site www.allsaints.org; E-mail dwaage@allsaints.org

All Saints' Episcopal Day School in Phoenix, Arizona, is a church-affiliated, coeducational institution enrolling students in Pre Kindergarten through Grade 8. Phoenix (population 1,475,834) is the state capital and the fifth fastest-growing city in the United States. Most of Arizona's four-year colleges and universities are located within the greater Phoenix metropolitan area. The city is home to a symphony orchestra, Ballet Arizona, the nation's largest municipal park, and many theaters and museums.

All Saints' Episcopal Day School has nurtured the hearts and minds of students since 1963. As an outreach ministry of All Saints' Episcopal Church, the School expects and promotes the individual's active commitment to integrity, learning, and academic excellence. The challenging curriculum and close-knit, caring community reflect the traditional Anglican appreciation of cultural, racial, socioeconomic, and religious diversity. All children, regardless of their denomination, attend student-led chapel sessions twice a week and take part in religion classes. Religious education stresses morals, values, relationships, respect for others, and decision-making skills.

All Saints' is a nonprofit school under the auspices of All Saints' Episcopal Church. A 20-member Board of Trustees, including current and past parents, alumni, and representatives of the Vestry, governs the School. All Saints' is accredited by the Independent Schools Association of the Southwest and holds membership in the National Association of Independent Schools and the National Association of Episcopal Schools. The current endowment totals approximately $1,000,000. The Alumni Association represents the School's nearly 1200 alumni.

THE CAMPUS. Situated 10 minutes from downtown in the north central area of Phoenix, the campus is in a residential area of large homes along beautiful, tree-shaded streets. The 11-acre campus, which is shared with All Saints' Episcopal Church, is comprised of the David John Watson Academic Building, with science labs, computer labs, and 6 classrooms; the James M. Fail Library; and the Paul DeWitt Urbano and Florence Pearcy Thompson classroom buildings. The Manning Hall includes an activity center, kitchen, lobby, and 2 fine arts classrooms. In total, there are 38 classrooms. Athletic facilities include a playing field, basketball/volleyball courts, and the Father Carl G. Carlozzi Gymnasium, used for physical education, performances, and special events. The Administrative Facility houses offices and vital records. *The Campaign for All Saints'* funded construction of the academic building, the gymnasium, and Manning Hall, as well as the renovation of classrooms and the athletic fields.

THE FACULTY. John R. Hyslop, a graduate of McGill University (B.A.) and the University of Massachusetts (M.A.), was appointed Head of School in July 2006. He came to All Saints' with more than 40 years of experience as an educator. He has served as a teacher of mathematics and Director of Admissions at Berwick Academy in South Berwick, Maine, and was Head of the History Department, Director of Studies, and Founder of the English Language and Orientation Summer Program, which attracted students from around the world, at Cushing Academy in Ashburnham, Massachusetts. He was also Head of School at Shattuck-St. Mary's School in Faribault, Minnesota, and at Cheshire Academy in Cheshire, Connecticut. Prior to his present appointment, he served as Interim Head at All Saints' and Epiphany School in Seattle, Washington.

There are 62 full-time faculty members on staff, 9 men and 53 women. They hold baccalaureate degrees representing study at 40 colleges and universities as well as master's and doctoral degrees representing study at institutions such as Georgetown, Johns Hopkins, Marquette, Ohio University, Pennsylvania State, and the Universities of Colorado and Michigan. Faculty benefits include a retirement plan, leaves of absence, continuing professional education, and health, dental, and life insurance.

STUDENT BODY. In 2006–07, 485 students were enrolled in Pre Kindergarten–Grade 8. The majority reside in Phoenix and its suburbs, with some traveling an hour to attend the School. The Pre Kindergarten consists of two sections with 30 students. In Kindergarten–Grade 4, there are three sections of 15 students each; from Grade 5 upward, there are three to four classes, each with 12–22 students. All Saints' is committed to admitting children of all races and religions. Currently, the student body is 80.4 percent Caucasian, 2.2 percent Asian, 8.2 percent multiracial, 1.2 percent Middle Eastern, 1.4 percent African-American, 1.8 percent Hispanic/Latino, and 4.8 percent unreported or other. Twenty-one percent are Episcopalian; 43 percent are Protestant/Catholic; 9 percent are Christian; and 27 percent are unreported or other.

ACADEMIC PROGRAM. The school year, divided into semesters, begins in August and ends in late May. There are vacations at Thanksgiving, Christmas, and Easter, and a spring break. Classes are held five days a week from 8:00 A.M. to 3:00 P.M. An extended school program is available until 6:00 P.M.

Grades are posted on a quarterly basis with interim written progress reports. Report cards are mailed to the home or distributed at parent conferences, which are scheduled in the fall and spring and as needed throughout the year.

In Pre Kindergarten and Kindergarten, learning occurs in an atmosphere of fun and play. Classroom activities are structured in a relaxed, unhurried way to enable children to develop new skills and knowledge based on what they already know. Technology is introduced, using computers and audiovisual equipment in the computer laboratories. Spanish, music, art, religion, physical education, and library also begin in Pre Kindergarten.

In the Pre Kindergarten and Lower School, All Saints' considers two aspects of a child's development as important as cognitive development. One is that of a positive emotional climate. The School recognizes that the motivation to learn is influenced by emotional well-being, and learning is fostered through curiosity, excitement, laughter, enjoyment, and appreciation. The second aspect is that of social development. Compromise and cooperation are taught through work and play in small groups, and solutions are discussed in classroom meetings. By encouraging, stimulating, and nurturing enthusiasm about each new discovery, teachers kindle a love for learning that carries students through All Saints' and beyond. The curriculum for Grades 1–4 incorporates these developmental strategies in language arts, mathematics, science, social studies, Spanish, computers, physical education, library, religion, music, and art.

The departmentalized Middle School curriculum provides a well-rounded education, featuring courses in language arts, mathematics, social studies, science, and Spanish, with enrichment courses in music, art, physical education, computer, and religion. Electives may include Algebra II/Trig, Music Ensemble, Argument and Debate, Hands-on Art, Art, etc., Conditioning Workout, Cross-Country, Science Elective, Computer Elective, and Creative Writing. The Advisor Program enables each child to meet in a small group setting with the same teacher at the beginning and end of the school day. Students are welcome to visit with teachers for additional support before and after school.

Members of past graduating classes have enrolled in the following high schools and prep schools: Brophy College Preparatory, North High School IB Program, Notre Dame Preparatory, Phoenix Country Day School, and Xavier College Preparatory. Students take the Educational Records Bureau Tests on a regular basis, and the results are monitored to assess the progress and effectiveness of the School's academic programs.

A four-week summer program on campus enrolls students from All Saints' and nearby public schools.

STUDENT ACTIVITIES. All Saints' has an active school government with participation in a student council from Grades 5–8. One-third of Grades 7–8 students earn membership in the National Junior Honor Society, which recognizes outstanding efforts in academics, leadership, and service. The Builders Club provides opportunities for students in Grades 6–8 to serve others, learn and develop leadership skills, and have fun together while building the school community. Other activities include the yearbook, *Tiger's Tale*; the newspaper, *Tiger Tracks;* and a writing collection, *Colorful Collages*. Community service is an integral part of All Saints' life.

The School's strong fine arts program is evident at special events. Young Authors Night gives students the opportunity to display their writing and oratorical skills through presentations; the Art Show presents the wide array of art techniques that the children learn; and various dramatic and musical productions throughout the year showcase the students' performance skills.

A challenging interscholastic athletic program begins in Grade 6. All Saints' has basketball for boys and girls, volleyball and softball for girls, and baseball and flag football for boys. Students compete in the Catholic Youth Athletic Association program.

Traditional events include Special Persons Day, Book Fair, Tiger Breakfasts, Christmas Luncheon, Spring Fling, Harvest Fair, Young Authors Night, and the Art Show.

ADMISSION AND COSTS. All Saints' seeks academically talented and motivated students from diverse socioeconomic, ethnic, and religious backgrounds for enrollment in Pre Kindergarten–Grade 8. Candidates must fill out an application form, submit transcripts, and take tests appropriate to the grade level for which they are applying. Entry is possible when space is available. The greatest number of students enter in Kindergarten and Grade 5. However, as openings occur at other grade levels, students are admitted. Applications are accepted all year, and candidates are notified of their acceptance in March or when openings occur.

Tuition, including books, is $11,920 in Pre Kindergarten and $13,800 in Kindergarten–Grade 8. Deposits are ten percent of the tuition. A hot lunch program is available on a monthly basis. Uniforms and supplies are extra. Tuition insurance is provided. All Saints' subscribes to the School and Student Service for Financial Aid. For 2006–07, more than $315,000 in financial aid was awarded.

Head of School: John R. Hyslop
Head of Middle School: Irene Tseng
Head of Lower School: Shelley Campbell
Director of Development & External Affairs: Charles Norris
Director of Admissions & Financial Aid: Dan Waage
Chief Financial Officer: Steve Ward
Director of Athletics: Ami Beiriger

Phoenix Country Day School 1961

3901 East Stanford Drive, Paradise Valley, AZ 85253
Tel. 602-955-8200; Admissions Ext. 2256; Fax 602-381-4554
Web Site www.pcds.org; E-mail tom.sylvester@pcds.org

PHOENIX COUNTRY DAY SCHOOL is a college preparatory school enrolling 750 boys and girls in Pre-Kindergarten through Grade 12. The campus is located at 40th Street, north of East Camelback Road in Paradise Valley, a residential suburb of Phoenix. School bus service to and from most neighborhoods in the region is provided for students in Grades 1–12.

In 1960, a group of citizens led by Franz Talley and his wife, Dr. Mae Sue Talley, organized the effort to establish a coeducational school based on eastern models. A year later, Phoenix Country Day School opened with 93 students in Grades 3–9. Kindergarten and Grades 1 and 2 were added in the next year, and enrollment rose to 386 by the end of the decade. In 1982, an Upper School complex was added, and the current levels of enrollment were soon attained.

Phoenix Country Day School (PCDS) aims to provide a distinguished college preparatory, liberal arts program that fosters the growth of the whole person and establishes a foundation for success in college and in life. It strives to help students acquire a coherent body of knowledge; a range of academic, artistic, communication, and athletic skills; self-discipline; and sound moral and ethical values. This includes a respect for diversity and a culture of community service.

In the last three years, the School has enriched its offerings with the China Teacher and Student Exchange Program, through which PCDS and the Chengdu Experimental Foreign Languages School exchange teachers and up to two students for two months each term. The program has been beneficial to both schools and includes exchange visits by larger groups of students and faculty members. Preliminary exchanges have occurred with schools in Mexico and Germany to offer expanded opportunities for international experiences.

The School is incorporated as a nonprofit organization governed by a Board of 17 Trustees, including 14 regular members and 3 who serve on an *ex-officio* basis: the Head of School, the President of the Parents' Association, and the President of the Alumni Association. PCDS is a member of the Independent Schools Association of the Southwest, the North Central Association, the National Association of Independent Schools, and other professional organizations.

THE CAMPUS. The School has 24 separate buildings on 40 acres in Paradise Valley. The Lower, Middle, and Upper Schools have distinct facilities, and they share the use of others, including two auditoriums, music building, dining room, fields, gymnasium, and two swimming pools.

The west side of the campus accommodates the Lower and Middle Schools, administration building, music building, auditorium, and dining and maintenance facilities. The east side includes the Upper School, performing arts center, gymnasium, four tennis courts, and two outdoor swimming pools, with three diving platforms. Four athletic fields provide for regular team practices and games, physical education classes, and Lower and Middle School recess exercises.

In addition to the shared facilities and regular classroom space appropriate to the various grade levels, each division has its own library, computer facilities, art studios, and science laboratories.

THE FACULTY. Geoff Campbell, a graduate of Drew University (B.A. 1978) and Immaculata University (M.Ed. 2004), was appointed Head of School in 2006. Mr. Campbell has been a teacher and educational administrator for 30 years, 5 of them at PCDS.

The full-time teaching faculty includes 73 women and 32 men. They hold a total of 107 bachelor's degrees and 74 advanced degrees, including 4 doctorates, as well as many awards and citations for teaching from professional organizations.

A full-time nurse is on duty daily at the Ax Family Health Center to respond to health emergencies, administer medications, maintain health records, and teach health classes. Various faculty and staff members are trained in CPR and first aid and are prepared to act as first responders in the event of emergencies.

STUDENT BODY. Phoenix Country Day enrolls 365 boys and 385 girls as follows: 240 in the Lower School (Pre-Kindergarten–Grade 4), 250 in the Middle School (Grades 5–8), and 260 in the Upper School (Grades 9–12). The School seeks and accepts students without regard to race, creed, disability, gender, or ethnicity. Nearly one quarter of the students are from minority or international backgrounds, and 13 percent receive financial aid.

ACADEMIC PROGRAM. The academic year begins in late August and ends in early June. Vacations are scheduled for two weeks in late December and one week at the end of March in addition to several national holiday observances.

The Lower School provides small classes, a nurturing environment, and a curriculum of core academics taught by the homeroom teacher and supplemented by specialists in music, art, science, physical education, technology, library science, and Spanish. Middle School students follow a similar but more advanced curriculum and are encouraged to develop greater social skills and awareness through team sports, student council activities, class trips, and community service.

Alumna of the Year

Alumna of the Year Ana Maria Lopez

Ana Maria Lopez '78 is a medical doctor and associate professor at the University of Arizona College of Medicine She also directs the Rural Health Office at the UA College of Public Health, the Telemedicine Program, and the Women's Heath Initiative. She has been honored in Tucson for her work in providing medical care to women living in rural areas. PCDS has named her Alumna of the Year for 2007.

In the Upper School, students take a minimum of five courses each semester and must complete at least 23 credits to graduate. Because of the rigor of the program, most courses are taught at what is considered Honors Level in other schools. The credits must include:

Subject	Credits
English	4
History including Western Civilization, World History, and U.S. History	3
Mathematics including Algebra 1–2, Geometry, and a fourth course with Algebra 2 as a prerequisite	4
Laboratory Science including Biology, Chemistry, and Physics	3
Visual or Performing Arts	2
Physical Education	2
Electives	2

In addition, students must complete 10 hours of community service each year, and seniors must prepare and deliver a 7-minute speech before the Upper School faculty and student body.

Some of the courses offered are:

English
- Writing Seminar
- Art of Composition
- African American Literature
- Shakespeare
- American Literature
- British Literature
- World Literature

World and Classical Languages
- Chinese 1
- French 1–4
- Latin 1–4
- Spanish 1–5

History
- Western Civilization
- World History from 1500
- U.S. History
- American Government
- International Relations
- World Geography
- Holocaust Studies
- Art History
- Psychology
- Russian History through Literature
- America and Asia
- Modern Middle East History
- Cultural Anthropology

Mathematics
- Algebra 1–2
- Geometry
- Trigonometry
- Precalculus

Mathematics (cont.)
- Calculus
- Discrete Mathematics
- Statistics

Science
- Advanced Biology
- Chemistry 1–2
- Physics 1–2
- Anatomy and Physiology
- Environmental Science
- Human Evolution
- Astronomy

Visual Arts
- Art Exploration
- Drawing 2
- Photography 1–2
- Clay Studio 1–2
- Visual Literacy
- 3-D Design
- Painting
- Sculpture
- Printmaking

Performing Arts
- Theatre Arts 1–2
- Scene Study
- Advanced Acting and Directing
- Orchestra
- String Ensemble
- Choir
- Jazz Band
- Jazz Improvisation
- Woodwind Ensemble

Advanced Placement courses are offered in 14 subjects.

Students in the Upper School are briefed on the college application process by two experienced college counselors, and nearly all go on to higher education. Members of the Class of 2007 enrolled at the following institutions: Arizona State, Barnard, Boston University, Bryn Mawr, Calvin, Carnegie Mellon, Chapman, Claremont McKenna 2, Columbia, Davidson, Drew, Emory, Georgia Institute of Technology, Hamilton, Harvard, Haverford 2, Kenyon, Mount Holyoke, New York University, Northwestern, Parsons, Pomona, Princeton, Reed, Rensselaer, Rhodes, Santa Clara 2, Scripps, Southern Methodist 2, Stanford, Texas Christian, Trinity 3, Tufts 2, Washington University, Williams 2, Yale, and the Universities of Arizona 3, Denver, Pennsylvania, Southern California 2, and Virginia.

The Summer School and Arts Program offer courses in basic skills, enrichment and academic review, and drama, painting, and music workshops for Grades 1–12 in half-day sessions. The programs operate in three-week terms in June and July. Sports and day camps for Kindergarten–Grade 8 are also provided.

STUDENT ACTIVITIES. Middle and Upper School students channel their volunteer community service work through some two dozen local and national nonprofit organizations such as St. Mary's Food Bank, Habitat for Humanity, and the Desert Botanical Garden. Most of these efforts are coordinated by the Service and Awareness Club and the Student Council.

Aspiring journalists find outlets for expression through *The Phoenician,* the yearbook; *The Active Voice,* the school newspaper; *The Eagle's Nest,* a magazine covering school sports; and *En Este Momento,* published in Spanish by students interested in the cultures of Spanish-speaking countries. Students also perform in band, orchestra, small ensembles, choral concerts, and in plays and a winter musical production.

Students in Grades 5–12 play on more than 50 varsity and junior varsity teams in interscholastic competition for girls and boys. More than 80 percent of the students participate in team sports, competing in soccer, volleyball, cross-country, golf, swim and diving, basketball, baseball, softball, tennis, track, and lacrosse.

An active Parents' Association provides volunteers for school enrichment programs and fund-raisers.

ADMISSION AND COSTS. Phoenix Country Day School seeks to admit students who have the ability and desire to benefit from a rigorous academic program and who agree to abide by the standards of the school community. Candidates for Grades 1–12 must take a PCDS admissions test, complete the application, and come to the campus for a visit and a personal interview. Applications should be completed by March 1, and decisions are made in the last week of March. Later applications are considered on a rolling basis as vacancies become available.

Tuition fees for 2007–08 are as follows: $16,200 in Pre-Kindergarten; $18,000 in Kindergarten–Grade 1; $18,800 in Grades 2–4; $20,200 in Grades 5–8; and $20,700 in Grades 9–12. Lunch is included for Lower and Middle School students. The School provides $1,300,000 in financial aid and makes awards based on need.

Head of School: Geoff Campbell
Head of Lower School: Barbara Thommen
Head of Middle School: Liz Olson
Head of Upper School: Sharon Thompson
Director of Admissions: Tom Sylvester
Vice President for Development: Beverly Ax
Director of Alumni and Development: Karen M. Anderson
Chief Financial Officer: Kathy Peters
Director of Summer Programs: Tom Sylvester

Tesseract School 1988

4800 East Doubletree Ranch Road, Paradise Valley, AZ 85253
Tel. 480-991-1770; Fax 480-991-1954
Web Site www.tesseractschool.org
E-mail kjohnson@tesseractschool.org

Tesseract, a nonprofit private independent school, has emphasized the education and development of children in Preschool–Grade 8 for two decades. The School's inaugural ninth-grade class will open in 2008. Tesseract offers a challenging curriculum and small class sizes with a teacher-student ratio of 1:9. The School seeks to provide an environment that fosters the love of learning and joy of discovery in every child. Its mission is to educate the whole child by focusing on important core academic skills while enriching the PK–8 curriculum with performing and visual arts, foreign language, technology, physical education, and community service. In a climate of achievement, students enjoy a unique educational experience that develops inquisitive and reflective young adults with the maturity to meet academic, social, and emotional challenges. Tesseract graduates become confident individuals focused on discovering and achieving their dreams. Financial aid and extended day care are available. Tuition: $5900–$13,100. Nigel Taplin (University of Exeter [England], B.A.; California State, M.A.) is Head of School.

ARKANSAS

Episcopal Collegiate School 1996

1701 Cantrell Road, Little Rock, AR 72201
Tel. 501-372-1194; Admissions Ext. 406; Fax 501-372-2160
Web Site www.episcopalcollegiate.org
E-mail ahoneywell@episcopalcollegiate.org

Episcopal Collegiate School is an independent, college preparatory day school serving central Arkansas. As a school of fewer than 400 students in Grades 6–12, Episcopal strives to mentor and nurture each individual student to reach his or her full potential. Intellectual challenge is the foundation of the liberal arts curriculum. Episcopal offers 16 Advanced Placement courses, 12 sports, 3 foreign languages, and 24 clubs and organizations. With a state-of-the-art campus, the School's educational environment fosters academic rigor, character development, artistic and athletic enrichment, as well as spiritual growth. Episcopal also offers an extensive creative arts program. Tuition: $8650. Ashley Honeywell is Director of Admission; Dr. Mercer Neale is Headmaster.

CALIFORNIA

Abraham Joshua Heschel Day School 1972

17701 Devonshire Street, Northridge, CA 91325
Tel. 818-368-5781; Fax 818-360-6162
Web Site www.heschel.com; E-mail admissions@ajhds.com

Abraham Joshua Heschel Day School is an independent Jewish Community Day School serving 400 boys and girls from Transitional Kindergarten through eighth grade. AJHDS offers a "superior dual-curricular education" that focuses on individual learners achieving their highest potential in both general and Judaic studies, thereby enabling them to attain a love of learning, sound self-esteem, and a positive Jewish identification. The individualized, experiential program permits students to become active participants in the education process as they learn how to learn. In partnership with families, the School inspires students to become active, dedicated, ethical, and informed citizens and leaders. The School has two state-of-the-art science labs, fully equipped technology centers, SMART-boards in every classroom, an art studio, and an interscholastic sports program. Outdoor education and community service are important components of the educational experience. As they move into high school, graduates are ready to respond to the call to leadership and to apply the Jewish values with which they were imbued at AJHDS. Tuition: $10,000–$23,000. Gayle Baigelman is Director of Admission; Betty Winn is Head of School. *Western Association.*

All Saints' Episcopal Day School 1961

8060 Carmel Valley Road, Carmel, CA 93923
Tel. 831-624-9171; Admissions Ext. 12; Fax 831-624-3960
Web Site www.asds.org; E-mail admissions@asds.org

All Saints' Episcopal Day, affiliated with All Saints' Church parish, seeks to provide each child the opportunity to develop his or her highest potential to learn in a nurturing environment of spiritual growth and service to others. The School enrolls 215 students in Pre-kindergarten–Grade 8. The enriched curriculum includes language arts, math, science, social studies, history, French or Spanish, Latin, music, art, religion, art history, physical education, performing arts, outdoor education and an extensive outreach program. Students attend daily chapel services. After-school and summer programs are offered. Tuition: $12,869–$15,576. Financial aid is available. Michele M. Rench (University of California [Berkeley], B.A.; Notre Dame Belmont, M.A.) is Head of School; Anne Crisan is Admissions Director.

Barnhart School 1959

240 West Colorado Boulevard, Arcadia, CA 91007
Tel. 626-446-5588; Fax 626-574-3355
Web Site www.barnhartschool.org

Barnhart is an ecumenical, independent preparatory day school that enrolls 360 boys and girls in Kindergarten–Grade 8. It was founded to provide "an unparalleled educational experience in an atmosphere of caring and respect that fosters intellectual curiosity and a love of learning." The School's demanding curriculum focuses on the mastery of knowledge and skills in core subjects of reading and language arts, mathematics, social studies, Spanish, and science, complemented by music, art, and health and physical education. Computers are located in every classroom to facilitate learning, and students have access to a state-of-the-art computer lab. Lessons learned in the classroom are illustrated and experienced through educational field trips to such destinations as Catalina Island Marine Institute, Yosemite, and Washington, D.C. Sharing equal importance with academics is the Virtues Curriculum, which encourages ethnic, religious, and cultural diversity as a means of developing respectful, committed citizens of the world. Students take part in activities such as photography, band, choir, drama groups,

and interscholastic athletics. A summer adventure camp is optional. Tuition: $9188–$10,370. Virginia Watt is Admissions Director; Joanne Testacross (University of Washington, B.A.; M.Ed.) is Head of School.

The Bay School of San Francisco 2004

35 Keyes Avenue, The Presidio of San Francisco, San Francisco, CA 94129-1736
Tel. 415-561-5800; Fax 415-561-5808
Web Site www.bayschoolsf.org; E-mail admission@bayschoolsf.org

The Bay School of San Francisco, founded in 2004, is a coeducational, college preparatory high school located in the Presidio of San Francisco, overlooking San Francisco Bay and the Golden Gate Bridge. In 2007–08, the day school enrolled 245 students as freshmen and sophomores and has a faculty of 35 experienced educators. The challenging, broadly based curriculum places special emphasis on study of the sciences, technology, ethics, world religions, and cultures, having the mission of uniquely preparing students for their futures as engaged citizens and leaders of the 21st-century global community. Fine arts, music, and drama course offerings are integral to the curriculum in addition to comprehensive athletics, service learning, and extracurricular clubs and programs. Students are drawn from Bay Area public, parochial, and independent schools comprising an inclusive community that is racially, culturally, and economically diverse. Tuition: $28,350. Annie Tsang is Director of Admission; Malcolm H. Manson (Oxford University, B.A., M.A.) is Head of School.

Bellarmine College Preparatory 1850

960 West Hedding Street, San Jose, CA 95126-1215
Tel. 408-294-9224; Fax 408-297-2072
Web Site www.bcp.org; E-mail bcolucci@bcp.org

Now in its 157th year of educating young men, Bellarmine was the first Jesuit school west of the Mississippi. While distinctly Roman Catholic in philosophy and tradition, Bellarmine welcomes approximately 1570 young men from all faiths as day students in Grades 9–12. The school adheres to the Jesuit mission of developing "men for others," guiding the mind, spirit, heart, body, and imagination of its students through a challenging and comprehensive college preparatory curriculum, broad offerings in the arts and athletics, and opportunities for service and social outreach. Course work centers on the liberal arts, sciences, and humanities, enriched by religious studies, modern and classical languages, and cutting-edge technology. Honors and Advanced Placement opportunities are available in all major disciplines, and virtually all graduates go on to higher education. Activities encompass a wide range of interests, from student government, peer tutoring, Christian service, and social justice to publications, movies, fishing, snowboarding, theater arts, ethnic clubs, and interscholastic sports. Tuition: $12,800. Financial aid is available. Bill Colucci is Director of Admissions; Mark Pierotti is Principal; Rev. Paul Sheridan, S.J., is President. *Western Association.*

The Bentley School 1920

1 Hiller Drive, Oakland, CA 94618-2301
Tel. 510-843-2512; Admission Ext. 2460; Fax 510-845-6516
Web Site www.bentleyschool.net; E-mail nwhite@bentleyschool.net

The Bentley School serves 690 boys and girls in Kindergarten–Grade 12 in a program designed to develop essential skills and understanding of core subjects in a "climate of mutual trust and friendship." Bentley's challenging college preparatory curriculum focuses on the liberal arts and sciences, computer technology, modern languages, and the arts. It also emphasizes clear reasoning, good study and social skills, and acceptance of responsibility. The Upper School program includes honors and Advanced Placement courses, independent study/research projects, and off-campus senior internships. Among the activities are music groups, drama, student government, and interscholastic sports. Tuition: $18,000–$25,000. Nasi Maghsoudnia White is Admission Director; Richard P. Fitzgerald is Headmaster. *Western Association.*

Berkeley Hall School 1911

16000 Mulholland Drive, Los Angeles, CA 90049
Tel. 310-476-6421; Admissions Ext. 208; Fax 310-476-5748
Web Site www.berkeleyhall.org
E-mail nathaliemiller@berkeleyhall.org

Berkeley Hall School is committed to providing a strong, balanced education in a nurturing environment. Encompassing Preschool–Grade 8, the School enrolls 250 girls and boys. The curriculum is centered around language arts, math, science, and social studies, with numerous opportunities to develop creativity in music, drama, woodshop, photography, and studio art. Computer technology, field trips, and special cultural programs enrich and reinforce classroom instruction. Students take part in community service, sports, and student government. Character education is a vital thread running through the program. Tuition: $16,500–$19,500. Nathalie Miller is Director of Admissions; Craig Barrows is Headmaster. *Western Association.*

Besant Hill School of Happy Valley 1946

8585 Ojai-Santa Paula Road, P.O. Box 850, Ojai, CA 93024
Tel. 805-646-4343; [Toll-free] 800-900-0487; Fax 805-646-4371
Web Site www.besanthill.org; E-mail admission@besanthill.org

BESANT HILL SCHOOL OF HAPPY VALLEY in Ojai, California, is a coeducational, college preparatory school enrolling boarding and day students in Grades 9–12. Formerly known as Happy Valley School, Besant Hill is situated in an area of great natural beauty, surrounded by the Topa Topa Mountains about 5 miles from the resort village of Ojai, 40 miles from Santa Barbara, and 75 miles from Los Angeles.

The School was founded in 1946 under the auspices of the Happy Valley Foundation, a nonprofit cultural organization. The educational views of writer Aldous Huxley, an original trustee, are reflected in the School's policies and mission, which he helped formulate. In 2007, the School's official name was changed to honor visionary educator, feminist, and thinker Annie Besant, who was responsible for the 1927 acquisition of the campus Besant Hill School now occupies.

According to its mission statement, Besant Hill School, "where students learn how to think, not what to think," seeks to develop each individual's abilities and to encourage the pursuit of integrity and excellence in all aspects of life. In a community that celebrates diversity and respect for all cultures, students undertake a rigorous college preparatory curriculum, combined with experiential education, athletics, and 27 offerings in the visual and performing arts. Sound academic preparation and a Socratic, personal relationship between students and faculty help young people achieve well-balanced, fully developed personalities for future success in higher education and in life. The School's motto mirrors its philosophy: "I am still learning."

Besant Hill is a nonprofit institution owned by the Happy Valley Foundation and governed by a 12-member Board of Trustees. It is accredited by the Western Association of Schools and Colleges and holds membership in the National Association of Independent Schools and The Association of Boarding Schools, among other affiliations.

THE CAMPUS. Besant Hill's 500+-acre campus is set in a tranquil area of mountains, woodlands, and nature trails that serve as natural settings for both outdoor education and recreation. Boarding students reside in single-sex dormitories, two to a room. Each bedroom is equipped with Internet access and contains study and storage space, and each dorm has a common room and kitchen and laundry facilities. The dorms are supervised by resident staff assisted by student prefects. The newly renovated 8000-volume library doubles as a resource and technology center with fully networked computer stations. The Beatrice Wood Center for the Arts showcases the works of the noted artist and serves as a venue for workshops, special events, and changing exhibitions by contemporary artists. A 200-seat performing arts center, a modern dining hall, science and photo labs, an art studio, a music room, playing fields, and tennis, basketball, and volleyball courts complete the campus.

THE FACULTY. Paul Amadio was appointed Head of School in 2006. He had previously served for four years as Director of Institutional Advancement and External Affairs at Stoneleigh-Burnham School and several years in other administrative positions at Brewster Academy in New Hampshire and Chapel Hill-Chauncy Hall and Bancroft School, both in Massachusetts. Mr.

Amadio was also a founding partner of the consulting firm Independent Thinking, which provides strategic governance, management, coaching, and mentoring consultation services to over 25 independent schools and nonprofit organizations. Mr. Amadio and his wife, Donita Coburn-Amadio, have three children, two of whom attend Besant Hill School.

There are 20 full-time faculty, half of whom hold advanced degrees; 70 percent live on campus, many with their families.

A registered nurse oversees the Health Center and provides emergency care for minor problems; Ojai Valley Community Hospital is within easy access of the Besant Hill campus.

STUDENT BODY. In 2007–08, Besant Hill School enrolls 100 young men and women in Grades 9–12; approximately 80 percent are boarders. They come from across the U.S. and abroad, providing diverse racial, ethnic, religious, and socioeconomic backgrounds. In the current year, Cameroon, Canada, China, Hong Kong, Indonesia, Japan, Korea, Mexico, Taiwan, and Thailand are represented.

ACADEMIC PROGRAM. The school year is divided into semesters and extends from early September to late May, with Thanksgiving, winter, and spring recesses and the observance of several national holidays. Parents receive grade reports at the end of each quarter and semester. On a typical day, students attend classes from 8:00 A.M. to 2:00 P.M., with a lunch break and electives and sports occurring in the afternoon and evening. Boarders must report for evening study halls five nights a week. Classes are small, with an average enrollment of 10 and a 4:1 student-teacher ratio to permit individual attention, support, and participation in discussions.

Besant Hill's Director of Studies develops and oversees the college preparatory curriculum, which is designed to instill in every student a commitment to a lifetime of learning. The academic program is structured to develop students' cognitive growth and emphasizes skills of big-picture thinking, research, writing, and creative expression. All courses meet or exceed standard University of California requirements. There are Honors and Advanced Placement opportunities in English, Physics, and Calculus.

To graduate, students must complete 4 years of English, 3 years of social studies, 3 years of mathematics, 2 years of science, and 2 years each of Chinese or Spanish and fine arts, along with a variety of electives.

Courses in English focus on developing a true appreciation of written works and fostering a broader understanding of the world through literature and language. A thorough view of all genres of the written form—short stories, contemporary and classic novels, Shakespeare and other playwrights, poetry—links thoughtful expression of ideas with knowledge of historical and global perspectives.

In math, students concentrate on the concepts and skills they will require as they undertake more complex work as well as logical, analytical, and geometric thinking and problem solving. Typically, students progress from Algebra I, Geometry, and Algebra II to Pre-Calculus and AP Calculus.

Students choose from Chinese or Spanish as their foreign language requirement, advancing from fundamental skills to fluency, interpretation, comprehension, and oral and written communication.

The science program emphasizes process rather than a set body of knowledge through experimentation, observation, data analysis, and communicating and understanding scientific principles. Biology, chemistry, environmental studies, conceptual and advanced physics, and astronomy are available.

In social studies, students examine the history and political evolution of mankind as well as human relations, global responsibility, and the interdependence of all nations. Teachers encourage their students to question and challenge assumptions about historical events. Cultural Geography, Western Civilization, U.S. History, Comparative Religions, and Anthropology are among the courses offered.

English as a Second Language provides first-year international students with speaking, listening, and writing skills within the framework of regular classroom subjects. In subsequent years, ESL students are mainstreamed according to their proficiency. Preparation for the Test of English as a Foreign Language is provided, and the TOEFL is administered at the School three times a year.

Students have extensive opportunities to develop and nurture their talents in studio and digital arts, music, drama, ceramics, and photography. All students also take two one-week trips as part of the Outdoor Education program as a means of developing awareness of nature and their responsibility to improving and preserving the environment. The Experiential Education program allows students to pursue subjects in their natural environment by requiring them to travel and learn. For example, last year students traveled to Ecuador, a trip that taught Spanish, Latin American History, and current environmental science issues. Other special offerings include Campus & Land Sustainability and Windows to the World, a travel/study program.

A college counselor provides guidance in the selection and application process. Typically, all Besant Hill graduates matriculate to four-year colleges and universities such as Bentley, Berklee College of Music, Chicago Institute of the Arts, Columbia College, Goddard, Juilliard, New York University, Pepperdine, Sarah Lawrence, Seattle University, Smith, Stanford, and several branches of the California State University and University of California educational systems.

STUDENT ACTIVITIES. An elected school government and a Disciplinary Advisory Committee are among the opportunities for peer leadership experience at Besant Hill. All students, along with faculty, take part in two Project Days per year to improve and maintain the upkeep of school facilities, followed by an afternoon of fun and activities.

Clubs are based on interests in music, culinary arts, publications, computer programming, the arts, student activities, sustainable living, and astronomy.

Dances and social activities take place several times a year, and students have the opportunity to attend concerts, films, plays, guest lectures, and other events.

Besant Hill offers a fitness program featuring jogging, weight lifting, yoga, and hiking, among others. As a member of the Condor League, Besant Hill students compete interscholastically in cross-country, soccer, and volleyball for girls and basketball, baseball, tennis, cross-country, and volleyball for boys.

ADMISSION AND COSTS. Besant Hill School seeks young men and women of good character and academic promise. Acceptance is based on previous school transcripts, personal recommendations, parent and student questionnaires, and a personal interview. Early application is encouraged.

In 2007–08, tuition, room, and board is $37,400; day tuition is $19,900. The ESL program ranges from $2300, including books, to $6300. Instructional Support is available through the School's learning center, which is an extra fee. Need-based financial aid is available.

Head of School: Paul Amadio
Dean of Studies: Louis O'Prossack
Dean of Faculty: April Hendrix
Dean of Students: Barbara Bartok
Director of Residential Life: Kevin Henschel
Director of Communications: Donita Coburn-Amadio
Director of Development: Matt Storey
Director of Admissions: Randy Bertin
Information Coordinator: Terra Furguiel
Business Manager: Alex Smith
Director of Athletics: Tina Leslie

Bishop Montgomery High School 1957

5430 Torrance Boulevard, Torrance, CA 90503
Tel. 310-540-2021; Admissions Ext. 227; Fax 310-543-5102
Web Site www.bmhs-la.org; E-mail plynch@bmhs-la.org

This coeducational high school was founded by the Archbishop of Los Angeles to provide a quality academic program in the Roman Catholic tradition. Enrolling 1200 day students from diverse backgrounds in Grades 9–12, Bishop Montgomery High offers a rigorous college preparatory curriculum combined with positive discipline and Christian values. School-wide liturgies, retreats, religious studies, and community outreach strengthen spirituality in students of all faiths. Advanced Placement courses are offered in the major subjects, and 98 percent of graduates pursue higher education. School government, athletics, Key Club, publications, and clubs are among the activi ties. Tuition & Fees: $7000. Financial Aid: $142,000. Patricia Lynch is Director of Admissions; Rosemary Libbon is Principal. *Western Association.*

The Bishop's School 1909

7607 La Jolla Boulevard, La Jolla, CA 92037-4799
Tel. 858-459-4021; Fax 858-459-3914
Web Site www.bishops.com; E-mail admissions@bishops.com

The Bishop's School is a college preparatory day school, affiliated with the Episcopal Church, enrolling 725 boys and girls in Grades 7–12. The 11-acre campus includes a 32,000-square-foot science center, five tennis courts, an aquatic center, two athletic fields, gymnasium, a health and fitness center, library, resource and learning center, five computer laboratories and 350 computers, performing and visual arts facilities, and a parking structure. More than half of the faculty hold advanced degrees. The average class size is 14. The curriculum includes Advanced Placement courses for college credit. Summer programs are scheduled. Tuition: $24,400. Extras: $1350. Financial Aid: $2,300,000. Josie Alvarez is Director of Admissions; Michael W. Teitelman (Albright, A.B. 1960; Brown, M.A.T. 1962) is Headmaster. *Western Association.*

The Buckley School 1933

3900 Stansbury Avenue, Sherman Oaks, CA 91423-4618
Tel. 818-783-1610; Admission Ext. 709; Fax 818-461-6714
Web Site www.buckleyla.org; E-mail admissions@buckleyla.org

Buckley is the oldest coeducational day school in Los Angeles. The School's 4-Fold Plan of Education gives equal weight to academic training, creative self-expression, physical development, and moral education. The beautiful 19-acre campus in a wooded canyon is home to 750 students in Kindergarten–Grade 12. Blended into this natural setting is an academic community with comfortable classrooms, high-speed Internet connections, an indoor pool, and extensive music, art, and dance programs. Within this community, students are able to focus on learning in a physically and emotionally safe environment. Tuition: $23,100–$26,000. Financial Aid: $1,300,000. Carinne M. Barker is Director of Admission and Financial Aid; Larry W. Dougherty, Ph.D., is Head of School. *Western Association.*

Calmont School 1977

1666 Las Virgenes Canyon Road, Calabasas, CA 91302
Tel. 310-455-3725; Fax 310-455-7209
Web Site www.calmontschool.org; E-mail calmontschool@earthlink.net

Enrolling 150 boys and girls in 3-year-old Preschool through Grade 9, Calmont School provides "a personalized education in a magnificent natural setting." The School's mission is to establish a strong foundation in the arts and sciences and instill in the students a lifelong commitment to sustainability and environmental stewardship. An extensive community service program prepares students to make positive contributions to their world. Computer technology, Spanish, library, physical education, art, drama, and music enrich the core curriculum and are integrated into the program, which is carried out on a spacious

22-acre campus. Tuition: $18,500. Financial Aid: $300,000. Judith Chamberlain was appointed Head of School in 2001.

Calvary Christian School 1988

701 Palisades Drive, Pacific Palisades, CA 90272
Tel. 310-573-0082; Admission Ext. 128; Fax 310-230-9268
Web Site www.calvarychristian.org
E-mail admission@calvarychristian.org

Calvary offers a nurturing academic environment for 432 boys and girls in Preschool–Grade 8. It was founded as a ministry of Calvary Church to challenge students with a rigorous preparatory curriculum that emphasizes the "family" as a strong component of the school community. The goal is to guide each child in reaching his or her personal best intellectually, physically, and spiritually. Students receive a foundation in basic skills and move on to develop critical-thinking and problem-solving skills, along with creativity in music, art, and drama. Calvary is accredited by The California Association of Independent Schools and the Western Association of Schools and Colleges and is a member of the Association of Christian Schools International. Tuition: $6400–$13,100. Erwin T. Wong is Director of Admission and Community Relations; Teresa Roberson is Head of School. *Western Association.*

Campbell Hall 1944

4533 Laurel Canyon Boulevard, North Hollywood, CA 91607
Mailing Address: P.O. Box 4036, North Hollywood, CA 91617-0036
Tel. 818-980-7280
Web Site www.campbellhall.org; E-mail admissions@campbellhall.org

CAMPBELL HALL in North Hollywood, California, is a day school enrolling boys and girls in Kindergarten through Grade 12. The campus is located in a residential neighborhood of a major Los Angeles suburb.

Campbell Hall was founded in 1944 by the Reverend Alexander K. Campbell, D.D., to provide solid academic training within the context of the Judeo-Christian religious heritage. Believing that "students are persons of both faith and reason," the school endeavors to stimulate each one "to nurture a quest for knowledge and to fit this knowledge into a meaningful pattern of faith for daily living."

A nonprofit institution, Campbell Hall is governed by a self-perpetuating Board of Directors. It is affiliated with the Episcopal church through the Diocese of Los Angeles. Daily chapel attendance is required for Elementary students, while Junior High and High School students attend semiweekly services.

Campbell Hall is accredited by the Western Association of Schools and Colleges and The California Association of Independent Schools and holds membership in The Cum Laude Society, the National Association of Episcopal Schools, the National Association of Independent Schools, the Educational Records Bureau, The College Board, and the Commission on Schools of the Los Angeles Episcopal Diocese.

THE CAMPUS. A eucalyptus grove surrounds the 15-acre campus. At its hub stands The Academic Center and The Ahmanson Library, a three-story educational resource and teaching facility. The building encompasses 11 teaching spaces, four applications labs, an elementary science lab, a high school art studio, and a library with a 30,000-volume capacity. State-of-the-art technology is available for students and teachers throughout the facility, which also includes administrative offices. Other special facilities include the Fine Arts Building and the 22,000-square-foot Garver Gymnasium/Performing Arts/Classroom complex. A second gym, two athletic fields, and three outdoor basketball courts provide ample space for a variety of sports.

THE FACULTY. Julian Bull was appointed Headmaster in 2003. He is a graduate of Dartmouth (B.A. 1982), Boston College (M.A. 1988), and Virginia Theological Seminary (2007). Mr. Bull was formerly Head of School at Trinity Episcopal in New Orleans, Louisiana.

The full-time faculty includes 69 women and 37 men, while 6 instructors teach on a part-time basis. The faculty holds 65 baccalaureate degrees, 40 master's degrees, and 4 doctoral degrees representing study at such institutions as American River College, American University, Amherst, Art Center College of Design, Baylor, Boston University, California Institute of the Arts, California State, Calvin, Catholic University, Chapman, Claremont Graduate School, Columbia, Dartmouth, DePaul, Florida Southern, Georgetown, Harvard, Immaculate Heart College, Indiana University, King's College (England), Lehigh, Longwood, Loughborough College (England), Loyola Law School, Loyola Marymount, Middlebury, New York University, Ohio State, Pepperdine, San Francisco State, School of American Ballet, Southwestern, Stanford, Swarthmore, Temple, Tunghai (Taiwan), Ursinus, Washington and Lee, Wellesley, Wesleyan, Willamette, Yale, and the Universities of California,

Connecticut, Delaware, Massachusetts, Michigan, Minnesota, Montana, Pennsylvania, and Southern California.

The school infirmary, staffed by a registered nurse, is open daily.

STUDENT BODY. Campbell Hall enrolls approximately 1000 students in Kindergarten through Grade 12.

ACADEMIC PROGRAM. The school year is divided into semesters. The calendar includes Thanksgiving break, Christmas vacation, spring break, and observance of national holidays. The daily schedules vary with the grade level, with all Elementary School classes (Kindergarten–Grade 6) convening at 8:30 A.M. Kindergarten is dismissed at 2:15 P.M., Grades 1–2 at 2:30 P.M., Grades 3–4 at 2:45 P.M., and Grades 5–6 at 3:00 P.M. Junior and Senior High classes (Grades 7–12) are in session from 8:15 A.M. to 3:30 P.M. The schedule includes breaks for chapel, an activity period, nutrition, and lunch. On Fridays, all students are dismissed by 2:20 P.M.

Classes meet five days a week in the Elementary division; Grades 7–12 have a block/rotating schedule. The student-faculty ratio is 10:1 in Kindergarten–Grade 8 and 19:1 in Grades 9–12. Academic grade reports as well as work habits and cooperation ratings are mailed home twice a semester, and a mid-period report is sent four weeks before the regular report if a student is doing below-average work.

The Elementary School program emphasizes thorough preparation in reading, mathematics, spelling, grammar, composition, literature, science, social studies, handwriting, and Spanish. Art, music, computer, and physical education instruction are required. The Junior High curriculum requires seventh- and eighth-grade students to take six academic classes. Math honors is offered to qualified seventh graders. Spanish, French, and math honors courses are offered for qualified eighth-graders. Qualified students in the eighth grade may elect to begin high-school-level courses. Seventh graders take mini-courses in art, music, computers, theater, and study skills. Eighth graders are required to take two electives per year. They choose from offerings in art, music, study skills, stagecraft, film history, mock trials, yearbook, and music.

Students in Grades 7–12 study six academic solids each year plus elective courses. To graduate, High School students must complete the following: English 4, foreign language 3, social science 3, mathematics 3, laboratory science 3, music history 1/2, art appreciation 1/2, and 3 additional credits to be chosen from social science, English, advanced mathematics, laboratory science, foreign language, or fine arts. Two years of physical education and a one-semester senior humanities course are also required. Community service is incorporated into the curriculum.

The High School curriculum includes Modern World Literature and Composition, Ancient World Literature and Composition, American Literature and Composition, Senior English; Biology, Chemistry, Physics, Physiology; Ancient World History and Geography, Modern World History and Geography, United States History and Government; Ethics, Sociology; Algebra 1–2, Geometry, Pre-Calculus, Pre-Calculus Honors, Trigonometry, Trigonometry Honors, Calculus; French 1–4, Spanish 1–4, Japanese 1–3; Art History; and Music History. Typical electives include Ecology, Drawing, Sculpture, Printmaking, Chorus, Painting, Photography, Dance, Theater Arts, Programming and Multi-Media, Computer Applications, Yearbook, Physical Education, Weight Training, and Foundations of Visual Art. Tennis, volleyball, cross-country, 11-man tackle football, basketball, softball, baseball, soccer, and track teams are electives offered for C.I.F. competition.

Advanced Placement preparation is offered in 16 subjects. Qualified seniors participate in the UCLA Scholars Program.

Campbell Hall graduates have enrolled at such institutions as American University, Amherst, Bard, Baylor, Boston University, Brandeis, Brown, Bucknell, California State, Carnegie Mellon, Chapman, Claremont McKenna, Clark, Connecticut College, Cornell, Dartmouth, Drew, Duke, Emory, Georgetown, George Washington, Hartwick, Harvey Mudd, Hofstra, Johns Hopkins, Lake Forest, Lehigh, Massachusetts Institute of Technology, Morehouse, New York University, Northwestern, Pomona, Rice, Ripon, Rutgers, Saint Mary's, San Francisco Art Institute, Santa Clara, Skidmore, Smith, Southern Methodist, Stanford, Syracuse, Trinity, Tufts, Tulane, Vanderbilt, United States Military Academy, United States Naval Academy, Wake Forest, Wellesley, and the Universities of Arizona, California, Denver, Illinois, Massachusetts, Miami, Michigan, Northern Arizona, Oregon, the Pacific, Pennsylvania, Redlands, San Diego, Southern California, Texas, Virginia, and Wisconsin.

A six-week summer session offers preparatory and review as well as enrichment programs for students in Grades 7–12.

STUDENT ACTIVITIES. Campbell Hall has student governments at the Elementary and Secondary School. Elected and appointed representatives from each class serve on the Student Councils. Under the leadership of student body and class officers, students in Grades 2–12 assume responsibility for service and social activities.

Extracurricular organizations for Elementary School students include band, chapel aides, teacher aides, math teams, dance, chorus, and cheerleaders. Organizations and clubs available to Grades 7–12 include sound/video crew, honor societies, chapel aides, Junior Statesman, math teams, Science, Student Council, Thespian Society, and language and service clubs.

Varsity and junior varsity teams are organized in several sports, and team competition is introduced in Grade 4. Girls take part in softball, track and field, volleyball, tennis, and basketball; the boys participate in football, track and field, volleyball, tennis, baseball, and basketball. High School students also compete in soccer and cross-country. Elementary Olympics and Junior High field days, held in the spring, engage the students in intramural-type competition.

School-sponsored field trips to programs at the Los Angeles Music Center, Los Angeles County Art Museum, Children's Museum, Norton Simon Museum, and similar sites are scheduled frequently. Attendance at some plays and concerts is required for High School students. Holiday parties are planned for all classes. Junior High students have evening dances as well as special club trips, theme days, and student productions. The High School calendar includes holiday parties, Homecoming, alumni reunions, informal dances, and two formal dinner dances. The outdoor education program provides a week's study of environmental encounters with California's geography for students in Grades 4–11. Seniors participate in a College Week.

ADMISSION AND COSTS. In evaluating an applicant, three important considerations are his or her academic potential, citizenship record, and participation in school activities. Campbell Hall seeks students from a variety of ethnic and religious backgrounds.

New students are admitted in Kindergarten–Grade 11 but rarely in Grade 12. Application should be made in the year prior to expected admission. All candidates must submit school transcripts and recommendations from two current academic teachers. A personal interview with the applicant and his or her parents is also required, as is admissions testing for each applicant.

In 2007–08, tuition is $18,440 for Kindergarten–Grade 6 and $23,460 for Grades 7–12. There is an insurance fee for all grades and a one-time admissions charge of $2000 for processing new families. Additional fees for books, supplies, and activities (including environmental education trips) range from $500–$1000 in Kindergarten–Grade 6 to $700–$1300 in Grades 7–12. All students wear uniforms. Tuition payment plans, loans, and financial aid are available. In 2007, 220 students received financial aid.

Director of Admissions: Alice Fleming
Director of Development: Annie Block
Director of College Counseling: John Corona
Chief Financial Officer: Steven D. Tolbert
Directors of Athletics: Toya Holiday & Juan Velazquez (Grades 9–12)

The Carey School 1928

One Carey School Lane, San Mateo, CA 94403
Tel. 650-345-8205; Admissions 650-345-4410; Fax 650-345-2528
Web Site www.careyschool.com; E-mail etemple@careyschool.com

Enrolling 224 boys and girls as day students in Pre-Kindergarten (age 4)–Grade 5, Carey seeks to maximize each child's intellectual, social, creative, emotional, and physical potential. The student-centered curriculum is designed to instill a deep love of learning and provide a strong foundation for further education and for life. The academic program centers on reading, language arts, math, and social studies, enriched by science, technology, French, Spanish, library studies, physical education, and art. Teaching and learning are paced according to the individual student's capabilities. After-school programs are offered. Tuition: $12,720–$17,150. Financial aid is available. Lisa Fowler is Director of Admissions; Eric Temple (Columbia, M.Ed.; University of Massachusetts, M.A.) is Head of School.

Cathedral School for Boys 1957

1275 Sacramento Street, San Francisco, CA 94108
Tel. 415-771-6600; Admissions Ext. 113; Fax 415-771-2547
Web Site www.cathedralschool.net
E-mail madison@cathedralschool.net

Located adjacent to Grace Cathedral (Episcopal), Cathedral School for Boys enrolls 245 day students in Kindergarten–Grade 8. The School offers a rigorous curriculum for boys of all religious and ethnic backgrounds. Each child is encouraged to do his best, and the value of the individual and the development of mutual respect are emphasized. In Grade 2, students may audition for the Grace Cathedral Choir of Men

and Boys. Latin, Mandarin, Spanish, music, art, drama, sports, science and computer labs, and extended care up to Grade 5 are offered. Environmental education and community service are part of the program. Tuition: $20,600. Tuition assistance is available. Catherine Madison is Director of Admission; Michael Ferreboeuf is Canon Headmaster.

The Center for Early Education 1939

563 North Alfred Street, West Hollywood, CA 90048-2512
Tel. 323-651-0707; Fax 323-651-0860
Web Site www.centerforearlyeducation.org
E-mail hudnutd@cee-school.org

The Center for Early Education was founded by a group of parents who believed that children's emotional and social development were as important as their educational and academic growth. Enrolling 532 boys and girls in Preschool–Grade 6, The Center seeks to provide a stimulating, contemporary education and emphasizes a student body of different ethnic and socioeconomic backgrounds in a challenging, supportive setting. Team-taught curricular programs are designed to encourage students to become lifelong learners and to instill in them self-esteem, respect for each other, and commitment to the community beyond the school. The Preschool focuses on motor skills, self-mastery, creativity, communication, socialization, and logical and sequential thinking. The Elementary School offers classes and activities on literature, writing, math, science, social studies, art, music, physical education, computers, and library. Community service and service learning are also integrated into the academic curriculum. Day-care, after-school, and summer programs are offered. Financial aid is available. Tuition: $12,850–$18,750. Deedie Hudnut is Director of Admission; Reveta Bowers is Head of School. *Western Association.*

Chadwick School 1935

26800 South Academy Drive, Palos Verdes Peninsula, CA 90274
Tel. 310-377-1543; Admission Ext. 4025; Fax 310-377-0380
Web Site www.chadwickschool.org
E-mail judy.wolstan@chadwickschool.org

Chadwick, a nonprofit, nondenominational, coeducational day school, serves 825 culturally and economically diverse students in Kindergarten–Grade 12. Its mission encourages personal excellence; the mastery of academic, artistic, and athletic skills; and the development of social and individual responsibility. The curriculum emphasizes strong reading, writing, critical thinking, and problem-solving skills as well as effective use of technology in all disciplines. Field trips, international study and service, community service, outdoor education, and Advanced Placement courses enrich the core program. Activities include athletics, drama, music, art, school government, and publications. Tuition: $18,504–$22,850. Financial aid and transportation are available. Judith S. Wolstan is Director of Admission; Frederick T. Hill is Headmaster. *Western Association.*

Chandler School 1950

1005 Armada Drive, Pasadena, CA 91103
Tel. 626-795-9314; Admissions Ext. 177; Fax 626-795-6508
Web Site www.chandlerschool.org; E-mail info@chandlerschool.org

Thomas and Catherine Chandler founded this coeducational day school to provide children with "innovative, inspired academic programs taught by caring, dedicated faculty." Enrolling 420 students in Kindergarten through Grade 8, the mission of Chandler School is to provide each student with the highest quality and most academically challenging education in a nurturing, balanced, and diverse environment. Academic excellence shares equal emphasis with the development of character and values. Language arts, math, science, social studies, and modern language (Spanish) are enhanced by information technology, library, art, music, and physical education. The departmentalized Middle School (Grades 6–8) includes minicourses and diverse electives as well as personal development classes that focus on issues related to the challenges of adolescence. Students take part in activities such as Chess Club, competitive sports, and musical and dramatic presentations. After-school care and summer programs are available. Tuition: $14,320–$16,600. Financial Aid; $472,563. Gretchen Lurie is Director of Admissions; John Finch was appointed Head of School in 2001. *Western Association.*

Chatsworth Hills Academy 1977

21523 Rinaldi Street, Chatsworth, CA 91311
Mailing Address: P.O. Box 5077, Chatsworth, CA 31313
Tel. 818-998-4037; Fax 818-998-4062
Web Site www.chaschool.org; E-mail info@chaschool.org

Enrolling 272 day boys and girls in Early Childhood–Grade 8, Chatsworth Hills Academy's mission is to fulfill each child's intellectual, artistic, social, and physical potential in a positive, ethical, and supportive environment. Focusing on the "whole child," this college preparatory school in the liberal arts tradition is committed to selective enrollment to permit the involvement of each student in all school programs. Pursuing a spiral curriculum that continually introduces new materials while simultaneously reinforcing previous skills and content, the Early Childhood through Grade 4 programs focus on integrating all subjects, creating a comprehensive and expansive educational experience. Students in Grades 5–8 focus on both skills and

content presented throughout the major departments of liberal arts in a college preparatory program that includes English, mathematics, history, science, modern language, and the visual and performing arts. Based on the school's character education program, core values and principles of action have been identified and are practiced throughout the close-knit and supportive community. Tuition: $12,420–$13,300. F. Graham Brown is Head of School. *Western Association.*

Children's Day School 1983

333 Dolores Street, San Francisco, CA 94110
Tel. 415-861-5432; Admission Ext. 337; Fax 415-861-5419
Web Site www.cds-sf.org; E-mail dianel@cds-sf.org

Children's Day School enrolls 260 students in Preschool (2.8 years)–Grade 8. The School's curriculum promotes academic excellence, encourages creative exploration and critical thinking, and creates an enduring love of learning. Interdisciplinary projects involve students in problem-solving investigations that foster collaborative learning skills. Course work centers on language arts, mathematics, science, and social studies. Spanish, art and environmental education, physical education, and service learning round out the program. The School nurtures the development of the whole child—intellectually, personally, and socially—and measures success by the success of each individual student. Tuition: $1940–$19,400. Aimee Giles is Director of Admission; Rick Ackerly is Head of School.

Chinese American International School 1981
中美國際學校

150 Oak Street, San Francisco, CA 94102
Tel. 415-865-6000; Admission 415-865-6084; Fax 415-865-6087
Web Site www.cais.org; E-mail j_leiner@cais.org

This coeducational day school, enrolling 420 students in PreKindergarten–Grade 8, provides academic programs through immersion in American and Chinese language and culture. Written and spoken fluency in English and Mandarin are emphasized in all major subjects. A Chinese-speaking background is not required for admittance to PreKindergarten and Kindergarten. Multicultural experiences, creative thinking, and developing confidence in interaction with people from around the world are major themes. Art, music, movement, sports, Chinese calligraphy, and a student exchange program with China are offered. Extended care is available. Tuition & Fees: $18,900.

Financial aid is available. John Leiner is Director of Admission; Andrew W. Corcoran is Head of School. *Western Association.*

Clairbourn School 1926

8400 Huntington Drive, San Gabriel, CA 91775
Tel. 626-286-3108; Admissions Ext. 139; Fax 626-286-1528
Web Site www.clairbourn.org; E-mail admissions@clairbourn.org

Clairbourn School, an independent day school enrolling 405 boys and girls in Preschool–Grade 8, seeks to attain educational excellence in harmony with the teachings of Christian Science. Its basic elementary program is supplemented by the study of science, art, music, drama, and computers. League sports, Student Council, and scouting are scheduled after school. An academic summer program is also offered. Tuition: $8700–$14,400. Financial Aid: $150,000. Janna Windsor is Director of Admissions; Robert W. Nafie (University of Minnesota, B.S. 1970; University of Wisconsin, M.A.; The Claremont Graduate School, Ph.D. 1988) was appointed Headmaster in 1979.

The College Preparatory School 1960

6100 Broadway, Oakland, CA 94618
Tel. 510-652-0111; Admissions 510-652-4364; Fax 510-652-7467
Web Site www.college-prep.org
E-mail nettie@college-prep.org/jonathan@college-prep.org

The College Preparatory School is a coeducational day school enrolling 333 students in Grades 9–12. The School strives to prepare students for productive, ethical lives in college and beyond through a challenging and stimulating education in an atmosphere of consideration, trust, and mutual responsibility. The rigorous academic program prepares students for the most selective colleges, and the student-teacher ratio is low. There are specialized facilities for music, art, dance, drama, and sports. Debate, class retreats, an Intraterm program, and community service are integral features. Tuition: $26,850. Extras: $1000. Financial Aid: $1,320,000. Nettie Anthony-Harris and Jonathan Zucker are Directors of Admissions; Murray Cohen (Johns Hopkins, Ph.D.) is Head of School. *Western Association.*

Convent of the Sacred Heart Elementary School 1887

2222 Broadway, San Francisco, CA 94115
Tel. 415-563-2900; Admissions 415-292-3113; Fax 415-929-6928
Web Site www.sacredsf.org; E-mail thorp@sacredsf.org

An independent, Catholic day school enrolling 324 girls in Kindergarten–Grade 8, Convent Elementary School, one of the Schools of the Sacred Heart, is part of a four-school complex including Stuart Hall for Boys, Stuart Hall High School, and Convent High School. The School seeks to prepare students for entrance into college preparatory high schools and to develop spiritual and social responsibility. Foreign languages, chorus, art, music, computer science, community service, and interscholastic sports are offered. A coeducational summer school program is also available. Tuition: $20,200–$20,500. Financial aid is available. Pamela Thorp is Director of Admissions; Anne Wachter, RSCJ (St. Mary's College [Indiana], B.B.A.; University of San Francisco, M.A.), is Head. *Western Association.*

Convent of the Sacred Heart High School 1887

2222 Broadway, San Francisco, CA 94115
Tel. 415-563-2900; Admissions 415-292-3125; Fax 415-929-0553
Web Site www.sacredsf.org; E-mail ccurran@sacredsf.org

Convent of the Sacred Heart High School is part of a four-school complex including Convent Elementary School, Stuart Hall for Boys, and Stuart Hall High School. Named a National Exemplary School for a second time by the U.S. Department of Education, this Catholic, college preparatory day school enrolls 200 young women in Grades 9–12. Computer science, math, languages, science, art, music, sports, and community service are integral to the curriculum; 22 Advanced Placement courses are offered. Exchange programs with other Sacred Heart schools nationwide are available to qualified students. Tuition: $27,800. Financial aid is available. Caitlin Curran is Admissions Director; Douglas Grant (University of San Francisco, B.S.) is Head. *Western Association.*

Cornelia Connelly School 1961

2323 West Broadway, Anaheim, CA 92804
Tel. 714-776-1717; Admissions Ext. 34; Fax 714-776-2534
Web Site www.connellyhs.org; E-mail admissions@connellyhs.org

Cornelia Connelly School is a Catholic, independent, fully accredited, college preparatory high school enrolling 320 young women. Through small classes, attention to each individual, and a comprehensive educational program, Connelly creates a values-based learning culture that empowers students to become articulate and self-confident leaders and to use their gifts to contribute to a changing world. Honors and Advanced Placement courses are available in all core subjects. Cocurricular activities include an award-winning theater arts program, varsity sports, and numerous clubs and organizations. In addition to rigorous academics, students are encouraged to participate in community service and faith-building activities. Tuition: $10,700. Erin Mobley is Director of Admissions; Sr. Francine Gunther, SHCJ, is Head of School. *Western Association.*

The Country School 1948

5243 Laurel Canyon Boulevard, North Hollywood, CA 91607
Tel. 818-769-2473; Fax 818-752-1554
Web Site www.country-school.org; E-mail psinger@country-school.org

Enrolling 250 boys and girls of average to gifted ability, The Country School offers a developmentally appropriate program that emphasizes each student's needs within an environment of balanced freedom and structure. The curriculum, for youngsters age 2.6 through Grade 8, is designed to build a strong foundation of skills in language arts and mathematics. Core content areas are enriched with science, art, computer technology, music, and physical education. Field trips and coordinate projects with another school provide opportunities for learning beyond the classroom. Children take part in Student Council, informal athletics, and after-school classes in tae kwon do, music lessons, Shakespeare, cartooning or animation, and other activities. Tuition: $19,200–$22,500. Paul M. Singer is Head of School.

Crane Country Day School 1928

1795 San Leandro Lane, Santa Barbara, CA 93108-9986
Tel. 805-969-7732; Admission Ext. 105; Fax 805-969-3635
Web Site www.craneschool.org; E-mail dwilliams@craneschool.org

Crane Country Day School provides a traditional curriculum in which a thorough foundation in the fundamentals of English, mathematics, science, social studies, and Spanish is approached in an innovative manner. Visual arts, drama, music, athletics, and community service are essential parts of the program. Enrolling 250 boys and girls in Kindergarten through Grade 8, Crane seeks to provide a nurturing environment in which children may grow intellectually, realize personal creativity, develop self-assurance, and gain an appreciation of and respect for the diversity of the world around them. Tuition: $18,975–$19,975. Financial Aid: $750,000. Debbie Williams is Director of Admission; Joel Weiss (Harvard Graduate School of Education, M.Ed. 1983) was appointed Head of School in 2000.

Crespi Carmelite High School 1959

5031 Alonzo Avenue, Encino, CA 91316-3699
Tel. 818-345-1672; Fax 818-705-0209
Web Site www.crespi.org

Crespi Carmelite High School is a Catholic, college preparatory day school for 600 young men in Grades 9–12. The School seeks to provide a holistic model of education emphasizing the spiritual, intellectual, moral, and social development of students. English, mathematics, science, social studies, religion, foreign language, and fine arts courses are required each year. Nineteen honors courses, 18 Advanced Placement classes, and electives such as Film, International Relations, Web Design, World Music, and Law are also offered. The average class size is 26 students. School government, Campus Ministry, National Honor Society, California Scholarship Federation, Mock Trial, *The Celt,* the school newspaper, ethnic dinners, and cultural awareness, classics, debate, fishing, and biking clubs are among the extracurricular activities. Sports available include cross-country, water polo, soccer, tennis, swimming, golf, football, and wrestling. All students perform 100 hours of community service before graduation. One hundred percent of graduates are accepted to colleges and universities. Tuition and Fees: $10,600. Financial aid is available. Robert Kodama is Admissions Director; Fr. Tom Schrader is President. *Western Association.*

Crestview Preparatory School 1986

140 Foothill Boulevard, La Cañada, CA 91011
Tel. 818-952-0925; Fax 818-952-8470
Web Site www.crestviewprep.org; E-mail mkidd@crestviewprep.org

Enrolling 230 boys and girls in Kindergarten–Grade 6, Crestview Preparatory School seeks to provide a balanced and healthy learning environment where students can thrive intellectually, creatively, physically, and socially. The School emphasizes self-esteem and social awareness while instilling values of responsibility, integrity, and respect. The curriculum centers on building strong skills in reading, creative writing, spelling, language arts, social science, math, science, and critical thinking. Music, Spanish, art, computer technology, and physical education complete the program. Parental involvement demonstrates to children their commitment to education while providing important support of the School's mission. Extended day care and a summer program are optional. Tuition: $10,675–$11,450. Michele Poteet is Admissions Coordinator; Marie Kidd is Head of School.

Crystal Springs Uplands School 1952

400 Uplands Drive, Hillsborough, CA 94010
Tel. 650-342-4175; Admission Ext. 1511; Fax 650-342-7611
Web Site www.csus.com; E-mail admission@csus.com

Crystal Springs Uplands School is a college preparatory day school enrolling 350 boys and girls in Grades 6–12. It seeks to maintain an atmosphere of rigorous academics balanced by sensitive human support and trust and cultivates the desire for lifelong learning. Its traditional curriculum is complemented by fine arts, competitive interscholastic sports, and Advanced

Placement courses in all subjects. Student government, publications, drama, dance, and clubs are some of the activities. Tuition: $27,100. Financial Aid: $1,240,000. Abby Wilder is Director of Admission; Amy C. Richards (University of New Hampshire, B.A., 1982, M.A., 1992) was appointed Head of School in 2003. *Western Association.*

Curtis School 1925

15871 Mulholland Drive, Los Angeles, CA 90049
Tel. 310-476-1251; Fax 310-476-1542
Web Site www.curtisschool.org

Curtis School in Los Angeles, California, is an independent day school enrolling boys and girls in Developmental Kindergarten through Grade 6. The campus is situated in suburban Los Angeles, adjacent to the San Diego Freeway and the top of the Sepulveda Pass. The School takes advantage of the opportunities afforded in the Los Angeles area for field trips to sites of historical, cultural, and environmental interest. Students travel to and from school on buses provided by an independent company or in car pools arranged by parents.

Curtis School was founded in 1925 as a proprietary school by Carl Curtis and was continued after a 1937 reorganization by his nephew, Carl F. Curtis. In 1964, the School was purchased by Willard E. Badham, who had been the athletic director for 18 years, and two partners. Over the next 10 years, enrollment grew from 100 to 400 under his leadership. The School was reorganized as a nonprofit corporation in 1975, and Mr. Badham continued as Headmaster. Curtis School moved to the Mulholland site in 1981.

Since its founding, the goal of Curtis School has been to provide sound academic training and to develop young people who are thoughtful, creative, and responsible citizens. A standard dress or uniform is worn in all grades. Morals and values are emphasized in daily teaching. Students also organize service projects to help the needy or handicapped. Because of the value the School places on a sound body, physical education and athletics are vital to the program, and all students engage in physical education daily.

Curtis School is governed by a self-perpetuating Board of Trustees, which meets six times a year. The School holds membership in the National Association of Independent Schools and The California Association of Independent Schools, among other affiliations. The Parents' Association and the Alumni Association, which represents 3300 living graduates, assist the School in social, cultural, and fund-raising activities.

THE CAMPUS. The 27-acre campus, shaded by mature trees, is located in the Santa Monica Mountains and is normally cooled by breezes off the ocean. Athletic fields and grassy malls surround low-rise, Spanish mission-style buildings with red tile roofs and functional design.

In addition to regular classroom buildings, the main features are the Ahmanson Building, a multipurpose structure housing the auditorium and art, music, and science rooms; the library/administration facility; and the Pavilion, a performing arts/gymnasium complex. The library contains more than 16,000 volumes. In addition to fields for football, baseball, soccer, and track, athletic facilities include a 25-yard heated swimming pool, a volleyball court, a tennis court, a handball/racquetball court, and three basketball courts.

The School-owned plant is valued at $20,000,000.

THE FACULTY. Stephen E. Switzer was appointed Headmaster of Curtis School in 1997. A graduate of Hanover College (B.A.) and Oberlin College (M.A.), he had previously headed Le Jardin Academy in Kailua, Hawaii; Episcopal Day School in Jackson, Tennessee; The Lotspeich School in Cincinnati, Ohio; and Community School in St. Louis, Missouri. Mr. Switzer is the past president of the Hawaii Association of Independent Schools.

Faculty members are graduates of such institutions as Brigham Young, Bucknell, Connecticut College, Emory, Illinois State, Ohio State, Pennsylvania State, Scripps College, United States International, and the Universities of California, Colorado, and North Carolina.

Faculty benefits include health insurance, a retirement plan, Social Security, educational and personal development grants, and leaves of absence.

A health officer is on duty full-time at the School, and emergency facilities are available nearby at the UCLA Hospital.

STUDENT BODY. In 2007–08, Curtis School enrolled 498 day boys and girls in Pre-Kindergarten–Grade 6. The enrollments were distributed as follows: 34 in Developmental Kindergarten, 66 in Kindergarten, 67 in Grade 1, 64 in Grade 2, 67 in Grade 3, 68 in Grade 4, 66 in Grade 5, and 66 in Grade 6. Students represented Bel Air, Malibu, Marina del Rey, Pacific Palisades, Santa Monica, and other communities in the Los Angeles area.

ACADEMIC PROGRAM. Curtis School offers a well-balanced academic program, with necessary skills taught in lively and creative ways designed to teach students to read, write, speak, compute, and reason.

Most students enter Curtis in Developmental Kindergarten or Kindergarten. The Lower School (DK–Grade 3) aims to foster the natural curiosity and love of learning in young children. Reading is taught balancing elements of both phonics and whole language, and literature is a part of every classroom. The language arts curriculum stresses written and oral expression as well as the fundamental skills of grammar and spelling. The mathematics program also seeks a balance between conceptual understanding, problem solving, and the acquisition of basic skills. Social studies, a lab-based, hands-on science program, computers, and library round out the academic program.

The Middle School (Grades 4–6) focuses on the skills and attitudes needed for secondary school success. Writing, reasoning, and experiential and cooperative learning are emphasized. The English program continues to utilize literature with focus on comprehension and fluency. Writing remains at the core of the program, and students explore poetry and a variety of other genres. The formal written report is also a key part of the Middle School experience. The structure of language—grammar, syntax, and usage—increases in importance at these grade levels. Mathematics embraces a broad range of concepts and skills, incorporating the use of calculators and computers. The social studies and science programs become more project-oriented and are integrated with other subjects whenever possible. Students learn computer and technology skills appropriate to the age group. Many students go on to leading secondary schools at the conclusion of Grade 6.

The arts form an essential part of the Curtis curriculum. Holiday and Spring Concerts are annual events, and drama performances, poetry recitals, and dramatic readings are organized on a regular basis by individual teachers or through the after-school Curtis Extension Program.

STUDENT ACTIVITIES. Representatives from Grades 1 through 6 are elected to the Student Council, which organizes school activities, assists at various functions, and acts as a liaison among students, faculty, and administration.

Athletics are a major component of the Curtis program. Every Curtis student has a sports class each day, and more than 90 percent of students in Grades 4–6 participate in the extensive interscholastic sports program, which emphasizes sportsmanship and fair play. Girls' team sports include volleyball, basketball, soccer, and track, while boys' teams compete in flag football, soccer, baseball, basketball, and track. Students in all age groups swim and learn water safety skills in the Curtis pool. Middle School students may participate on the swim and debate teams as well as the award-winning orchestra and choir.

Field trips, many of them subject-related, are planned for all grades to take advantage of the cultural, historical, and community activities in the Los Angeles area. A wide range of performing arts events are scheduled for the entire School. Grades 5 and 6 take field trips to eastern cities, including Washington, D.C., during the spring break.

Special events on the school calendar include the Back to School Picnic, Curtis Fair, Holiday Program, Spring Event, Dad's Day, and Grandparent's Day.

ADMISSION AND COSTS. Curtis School seeks all-around students who will be good citizens. Students are accepted in all grades on the basis of entrance examinations and standardized test results, personal and teacher recommendations, and an interview at the School. A $100 fee is required with the application.

Tuition is $19,235 for Developmental Kindergarten–Grade 6. Uniforms, transportation, and field trip charges are extra. There is a one-time New Family Fee of $1500. Tuition insurance and payment plans are offered. The School awards more than $500,000 annually in financial aid on the basis of need.

Chief Operating & Financial Officer: Bob Kolb
Director of Admissions: Mimi Petrie
Director of Development: Patti Hartmann
Accounting Manager: Kate Fox
Director of Athletics: Mark Nott

Drew School 1908

2901 California Street, San Francisco, CA 94115
Tel. 415-409-3739; Admissions Ext. 107; Fax 415-346-0720
Web Site www.drewschool.org; E-mail et@drewschool.org

Drew School is a small, urban, college preparatory high school enrolling 250 boys and girls as day students in Grades 9–12. Its mission is to engage and support the academic talents, initiative, and self-confidence of all students while encouraging them to be respectful, responsible young adults. The School draws together a varied student body with diverse and emerging talents, providing a rigorous education in a friendly and cooperative environment "where every kid counts." Drew also aims to foster in each member of the school community the joy of active lifelong learning. Tuition: $27,000. Financial Aid: $800,000. Elizabeth Tilden is Director of Marketing and Enrollment; Samuel M. Cuddeback III is Head of School.

Ecole Bilingue de Berkeley 1977

1009 Heinz Avenue, Berkeley, CA 94710
Tel. 510-549-3867; Fax 510-845-3209
Web Site www.eb.org

In an environment where "multiculturalism is a fundamental way of life," Ecole Bilingue de Berkeley enrolls 530 boys and girls from 46 nationalities in Preschool–Grade 8; over 30 percent are students of color, and 63 percent of teachers are native speakers of French. The carefully structured curriculum, taught in French and English, is designed to develop and educate the whole child intellectually, physically, and socially. Basic skills are imparted through hands-on projects; reading and writing begin in Grade 1; Spanish and Chinese are introduced in the Middle School. The core program is enriched through technology, field trips, and extracurricular activities. EB is accredited by the French Ministry of Education. Tuition: $16,155–$18,692. Brigitte Bastrenta is Director of Admissions; Frédéric Canadas is Head of School. *Western Association.*

Flintridge Preparatory School 1933

4543 Crown Avenue, La Cañada Flintridge, CA 91011
Tel. 818-790-1178; Fax 818-952-6247
Web Site www.flintridgeprep.org

Flintridge Prep offers a rigorous, moral, and intimate learning environment for 500 day boys and girls in Grades 7–12. It seeks to nurture the skills, knowledge, and inspiration essential to a rewarding college experience, a lifelong embrace of education, devotion to community, and a full and responsible life. At Flintridge, ethical and emotional development share equal emphasis with intellectual development. A sense of community is fostered through senior mentoring, camping trips, and offerings in the visual and performing arts, student government, and interscholastic athletics. Graduates go on to "highly selective" colleges and universities. Tuition & Fees: $21,850–$22,500. Financial aid is available. G. Arthur Stetson is Director of Admissions; Peter Bachmann is Headmaster. *Western Association.*

Foothill Country Day School 1954

1035 West Harrison Avenue, Claremont, CA 91711
Tel. 909-626-5681; Admissions Ext. 12; Fax 909-625-4251
Web Site www.foothillcds.org; E-mail dzondervan@foothillcds.org

Foothill Country Day School, founded in 1954 by Howell and Betty Webb, aims to provide an exciting environment in which children can reach their full academic potential and develop character and values. The School enrolls 180 girls and boys in Kindergarten–Grade 8 and children ages 3–5 in an associated preschool, The Seedling School. The challenging curriculum emphasizes mastery of skills in core subjects, with enrichment in Spanish, Latin, technology, drama, music, art, library skills, and physical education. Students participate in community service projects, field trips, international travel, and daily chapel programs. After-school and summer programs are available. Tuition: $15,145–$15,580. Denise Zondervan is Admissions Director; Mark W. Lauria, Ph.D., is Headmaster.

Francis Parker School 1912

6501 Linda Vista Road, San Diego, CA 92111
Tel. 858-569-7900; Admission 858-874-3380; Fax 858-569-0621
Web Site www.francisparker.org; E-mail admission@francisparker.org

Francis Parker School seeks to offer a superior college preparatory education in a diverse, family-oriented environment to 582 boys and 638 girls enrolled as day students in Junior Kindergarten through Grade 12. The School provides a challenging curriculum that fosters independence, responsibility, and character education. Along with 25 Advanced Placement courses and an innovative curriculum, Francis Parker School provides its students with an extensive athletic program, a comprehensive arts program, and opportunities to grow through service, leadership, and community involvement. Tuition: $20,170. Financial Aid: $2,000,000. Judy Conner is Director of Admission; Dr. Richard M. Blumenthal (Harvard University, M.A., Ph.D.) is Head of School. *Western Association.*

Gateway School 1970

126 Eucalyptus Avenue, Santa Cruz, CA 95060
Tel. 831-423-0341; Admissions Ext. 302; Fax 831-479-8937
Web Site www.gatewaysc.org; E-mail admissions@gatewaysc.org

Gateway School is an independent, coeducational day school enrolling 275 students in Kindergarten through Grade 8. With its focus on active learning, small classes, and self-discovery, Gateway aims to develop confident, compassionate, articulate, and achieving students. In a theme-based curriculum, traditional core subjects are complemented by the visual and performing arts, music, physical education, and field trips. Spanish begins in Grade 1. Two hands-on science programs, Life Lab and MARE (marine science), teach environmental stewardship. Grades 6–8 engage in service projects for the greater community. Before- and after-care programs are available. Tuition: $11,600–$12,709. There is need-based financial aid. Colleen Sullivan is Director of Admissions; David Peerless is Head of School. *Western Association.*

The Gillispie School 1952

7380 Girard Avenue, La Jolla, CA 92037-5139
Tel. 858-459-3773; Fax 858-459-3834
Web Site www.gillispie.org

The Gillispie School arose from a commitment shared by Ada Gillispie and her husband, Samuel, a local pediatrician and prominent citizen, to care for and educate children in need. Today, the School has evolved into a dynamic community of teachers and learners who seek to grow intellectually, creatively, physically, and socially. Enrolling 305 boys and girls in Early Childhood–Grade 6, Gillispie's preparatory curriculum imparts the skills, comprehension, and knowledge students will need for success in middle school. Grade 3–6 use laptops for research and discovery. Reading, language arts, math, science, and social studies are enhanced by specialty classes in Spanish, art, writing, science, library skills, and physical education. Youngsters are introduced to musical concepts through singing, playing instruments, and movement, while older grades learn digital music recording, podcasting, and composition. Summer camps are offered. Tuition: $11,020–$15,390. Financial aid is available. Linda Moyer coordinates admissions; Margie Edwards is Interim Head of School. *Western Association.*

The Hamlin School 1863

2120 Broadway, San Francisco, CA 94115
Tel. 415-922-0300; Admission 415-674-5400; Fax 415-674-5445
Web Site www.hamlin.org; E-mail aquino@hamlin.org

The oldest nonsectarian day school for girls in the West, Hamlin enrolls 400 girls in Kindergarten–Grade 8. The School seeks to educate talented young women to meet the challenges of their times. It provides a balanced curriculum of humanities, science, mathematics, and fine arts in facilities that include the 13,000-volume Edward E. Hills Library, two science laboratories, two computer centers, art studios, and a theater. Extended-day care and after-school activities are offered and intermural sports are scheduled after classes. Summer and vacation camps are available. Tuition: $21,225. Financial Assistance: $1,000,000. Lisa Lau Aquino '81 is Director of Admission; Dr. Priscilla Winn Barlow (University of Liverpool, B.Sc., Ph.D.) is Interim Head of School.

Harbor Day School 1952

3443 Pacific View Drive, Corona del Mar, CA 92625
Tel. 949-640-1410; Fax 949-640-0908
Web Site www.harborday.org; E-mail dphelps@harborday.org

Harbor Day School, an elementary school enrolling 400 boys and girls in Kindergarten–Grade 8, is located on a 6-acre site overlooking the Pacific Ocean. The School has a challenging academic program, strong athletics, and an outstanding visual and performing arts program. Harbor Day School is committed to providing a warm environment conducive to the development of character and good citizenship. Facilities include a

library of more than 14,000 volumes, three fully equipped science laboratories, three computer science centers, two art studios complete with six pottery wheels and a kiln, a woodshop, a 400-seat performing arts center, a gymnasium, and athletic fields. Tuition: $14,885. Financial aid is available. Kristin H. Rowe is Director of the Lower School and Admissions; Douglas E. Phelps (Pepperdine University, B.A. M.S.) is Head of School. *Western Association.*

The Harker School 1893

Lower School (K–5): 4300 Bucknall Road, San Jose, CA 95130
Middle School (6–8): 3800 Blackford Avenue, San Jose, CA 95117
Upper School (9–12): 500 Saratoga Avenue, San Jose, CA 95129
Tel. 408-249-2510; Fax 408-984-2325
Web Site www.harker.org; E-mail admissions@harker.org

Harker provides a strong college preparatory curriculum for more than 1700 day students in Kindergarten–Grade 12. The core philosophy of the program is to develop intellectual curiosity, personal accountability, and a love of learning in all students. The curriculum includes state-of-the-art computer technology, AP courses, and challenging electives. Students participate in school government, athletics, award-winning performing arts, and numerous clubs. The diverse environment resulted in multiple college offers for 100 percent of the Class of 2007 and National Merit Recognition for 50 percent. Summer offerings are available. Tuition: $20,674–$29,894. Nan Nielsen is Director of Admissions & Financial Aid; Christopher Nikoloff is Head of School. *Western Association.*

Harvard-Westlake School 1989

Grades 7–9: 700 North Faring Road, Los Angeles, CA 90077
Tel. 310-274-7281; Admission 310-288-3200;
Fax 310-288-3212
Grades 10–12: 3700 Coldwater Canyon, North Hollywood, CA 91604
Tel. 818-980-6692; Fax 818-487-6631
Web Site www.hw.com

Harvard-Westlake is a college preparatory day school enrolling 1530 boys and girls in Grades 7–12. The School seeks able, interested students who reflect the diversity of Greater Los Angeles. It aims to provide an education that enables students to appreciate and develop their spiritual, intellectual, and emotional gifts. Music, arts, and publications are offered; Advanced Placement courses are available in all disciplines. Community service and sports are extracurricular activities. There are student exchanges with schools abroad and a summer program. Tuition: $25,000. Elizabeth Gregory is Director of Admission; Thomas C. Hudnut (Princeton, A.B. 1969; Tufts, A.M. 1970) is President; Jeanne Huybrechts (University of Detroit, B.A. 1972; California State [Northridge], B.S. 1986; University of California [Los Angeles], Ed.D. 1999) is Head. *Western Association.*

Head-Royce School 1887

4315 Lincoln Avenue, Oakland, CA 94602
Tel. 510-531-1300; Admissions Ext. 2113; Fax 510-530-8329
Web Site www.headroyce.org; E-mail cepstein@headroyce.org

Head-Royce School is an independent, coeducational day school enrolling 800 students in Kindergarten–Grade 12. Founded in 1887, the School seeks students committed to scholarship, diversity, and citizenship. Head-Royce offers a challenging program in the liberal arts and sciences in a supportive environment. Honors and Advanced Placement courses and accelerated programs are available in the Upper School. Tuition: $18,440–$25,590. Financial Aid: $2,204,000. Catherine Epstein is Director of Admissions and Financial Aid; Paul D. Chapman (Yale, B.A.; Stanford, M.A., Ph.D.) was appointed Head of the School in 1984. *Western Association.*

Idyllwild Arts Academy 1946

52500 Temecula Road, P.O. Box 38, Idyllwild, CA 92549-0038
Tel. 951-659-2171; Admissions Ext. 2223; Fax 951-659-2058
Web Site www.idyllwildarts.org; E-mail admission@idyllwildarts.org

IDYLLWILD ARTS ACADEMY in Idyllwild, California, is a boarding and day school offering preprofessional training in the arts in conjunction with a college preparatory academic program in Grades 9 through 12 and a postgraduate year. Located in the mountains above Palm Springs, the Academy is surrounded by more than 20,000 acres of protected forest and park land. Idyllwild is about 100 miles from San Diego, 125 miles from Los Angeles, and 50 miles from Palm Springs.

Dr. Max and Beatrice Krone established the Idyllwild Arts Foundation in 1946. The school opened in 1950 as a summer program with 100 students. The summer program, which reaches an enrollment of 2000 children, youth, and adults, was the core program for much of the school's history, including 19 years during which it operated under the auspices of the University of Southern California. In 1986, the year-round boarding Academy was established with a full academic program in addition to preprofessional training in the performing and visual arts. Graduates meet University of California admission standards.

The Academy seeks to prepare students for further education, for advanced arts studies, and for adult life as contributing, productive members of society.

Idyllwild Arts Academy is accredited by the Western Association of Schools and Colleges and is a member of the National Association of Independent Schools, California Association of Independent Schools, Network of Performing and Visual Arts Schools, Western Boarding Schools, and other professional organizations.

THE CAMPUS. The Academy's academic and arts facilities are situated on 206 acres at an elevation of more than 5000 feet in the midst of a pine forest.

Dormitories feature semiprivate rooms with en-suite bathrooms. The Max and Bee Krone Library, a state-of-the-art multimedia facility, opened in 2000; in 2001, a painting and drawing studio and an exhibition center for use by students and visiting artists was completed; and the Bruce Ryan Sound Stage opened in 2002. The Nelson Dining Hall opened in 2006.

THE FACULTY. William M. Lowman, a graduate of the University of Redlands (A.B.), is President of Idyllwild Arts Academy. A recipient of the Nevada Governor's Arts Award, Mr. Lowman founded the Nevada School for the Arts. He is a board member of the International NETWORK of Performing and Visual Arts Schools.

The Academy's 40 full-time and 40 adjunct faculty have distinguished themselves either as academic teachers or as professional artists by performance in music, dance, theater, or moving pictures in the United States and abroad, or by exhibition of their work in recognized galleries. They hold baccalaureate and graduate degrees from such institutions as Colby, Colgate, Harvard, Juilliard, Massachusetts Institute of Technology, Middlebury, Oberlin, Wayne State, Scripps, Southern Methodist, Stanford, Yale, and the Universities of California (Los Angeles), Pennsylvania, and Southern California. Prominent performing artists are in residence at various times during the academic year to conduct master classes and give performance examples.

STUDENT BODY. In 2006–07, the Academy enrolled 146 boarding girls, 90 boarding boys, and 30 day students in Grades 9–12 and a postgraduate year. The enrollments were distributed as follows: 67 chose to major in music, 60 in theatre, 50 in visual arts, 26 in dance, 26 in interdisciplinary arts, 20 in moving pictures, and 16 in writing. A majority of the students were from the Southwest; a total of 33 states and 21 countries were represented.

ACADEMIC PROGRAM. The academic year, divided into semesters, begins after Labor Day and ends in early June with vacations of one week at Thanksgiving, three weeks at Christmas, and two weeks in the spring. Academic classes are held Monday through Saturday mornings beginning at 8:00 A.M.; arts classes are scheduled Monday through Friday afternoons and on Saturday as needed.

To graduate, students must complete 14 academic units in addition to their regular arts curriculum. The academic units must include 4 units of English, 2 of foreign language, 3 of social studies, 3 of mathematics, 2 of sciences, 2 of physical education, and one semester of computer literacy.

In the arts program, students choose a major and complete the requirements for their discipline as determined by the department chair and the Vice President of the Academy. They choose among areas of study including music, dance, theater, technical theater, musical theater, visual arts, creative writing, interdisciplinary arts, and moving pictures (film and video). Each program incorporates courses in four categories: theory, history, and fundamentals of the form; creation, production, presentation, or performance; specialized master classes and private instruction; and field trips to arts communities of Southern California to observe professionals at work.

Postgraduates engage in a one-year intensive program in the arts. They must take at least four academic classes and present an audition or portfolio for admission.

Students are placed in arts courses according to levels of ability and experience and advance on the basis of performance. Among the regular courses offered are Dance 1–3, Dance Ensemble, Ballet, Modern Dance, Pointe, Jazz, Men's Class, Pas de Deux, Dance Composition; Music Fundamentals, Introduction to Music Literature, Ear Training/Sight Singing, Music Theory, Music History, Voice Class, Chamber Music, Musical Ensembles, Class Piano, Piano Proficiency, Accompaniment, Repertoire Class; Voice and Diction, Technical Theatre, Drama History and Literature, Movement, Playwriting, Directing, Stage Design; Drawing and Painting, Art History, Ceramics, Sculpture, Printmaking, Design and Aesthetics, Photography, Computer Graphics, Illustration; and Creative Writing courses in Fiction, Poetry, Short Stories, Literary Criticism, Playwriting, Acting for the Camera, Audio Techniques, Directing, Editing, Screenwriting, and Photography for Filmmakers.

Of the 93 graduates in the Class of 2006, 91 chose to continue their education. They matriculated at such colleges as

Bard, Boston University, California Institute of the Arts, Carnegie Mellon, Chicago Art Institute, Columbia, Cornish School of the Arts, DePaul, Eastman School of Music, Hartt Conservatory, Johns Hopkins, Juilliard, New York University, Oberlin Conservatory, Rhode Island School of Design, Rice, San Francisco Art Institute, Smith, Stanford, State University of New York (Purchase), Wesleyan, Yale, and the Universities of California (Los Angeles, San Diego, Santa Cruz), Michigan (Ann Arbor), Nevada (Las Vegas), and Southern California.

Idyllwild's summer program offers workshops of two days' to three weeks' duration for students of all ages and abilities. The Children's, Junior Artist's, Youth, and Adult Centers provide workshops in music, theater, dance, creative writing, and the visual arts.

STUDENT ACTIVITIES. Students elect a student government, which, with the help of faculty advisers, organizes entertainment and other activities.

Clubs are organized around the arts majors, and there are additional clubs for hiking, bicycling, and rock climbing. Dances, concerts, and dramatic performances are scheduled on a regular basis.

On weekends, students enjoy the cultural attractions of the Los Angeles and San Diego areas—museums, theaters, art galleries, and concert halls. They also have access to many world-famous recreational areas including Disneyland, Knott's Berry Farm, Magic Mountain, Sea World, and the San Diego Zoo and Wild Animal Park.

ADMISSION AND COSTS. The Idyllwild Arts Academy seeks dedicated, motivated, and talented arts students. They are admitted in Grades 9–12 and a postgraduate year on the basis of academic transcripts, recommendations, a personal interview, and a demonstration of potential through audition or portfolio. Application forms are available on request; the application fee is $50. Students can be admitted at midyear if space is available.

In 2007–08, boarding tuition is $42,500; day tuition is $27,950. The Academy subscribes to the School and Student Service for Financial Aid and awards approximately $3,300,000 in financial aid annually on the basis of talent and financial need. A tuition payment plan is available.

Vice President of the Academy: Dr. Karl Reiss
Dean of Academics: Anna-Karin Li
Dean of Students: John Newman
Dean of Admission: Karen Porter
Vice President for Advancement: Jolynn Reid
College Counselor: Jonathan Dunn
Vice President, Business & Finance: David Pittman

International School of the Peninsula 1979

151 Laura Lane, Palo Alto, CA 94303-3221
Tel. 650-251-8500; Admissions 650-251-8504; Fax 650-251-8501
Web Site www.istp.org

International School of the Peninsula was founded by Madame Charlotte de Géry to provide bilingual education within a warm, multicultural environment. Its mission is to educate children through a rigorous bilingual curriculum that promotes critical thinking, international awareness, and responsible global citizenship. Enrolling nearly 570 boys and girls from 30 nationalities as day students in Nursery–Grade 8, the School provides a dual-immersion program in French/English and Chinese/English up to Grade 5. Students in Grades 6–8 enroll in the International School. All languages are taught by internationally trained native-language instructors, and students graduate with AP-level proficiency in their second language. After-school activities include chess, Chinese dance, soccer, chorus, and cooking. A summer program provides additional language training, enrichment projects, and organized fun. Tuition: $15,750–$18,650. Philippe Dietz is Head of School.

The John Thomas Dye School 1929

11414 Chalon Road, Los Angeles, CA 90049
Tel. 310-476-2811; Fax 310-476-8675
Web Site jtdschool.com; E-mail jhirsch@jtdschool.com

THE JOHN THOMAS DYE SCHOOL in Los Angeles, California, is an independent, coeducational day school enrolling approximately 320 students from Kindergarten through Grade 6. The campus occupies 11 hilltop acres in Bel Air overlooking Santa Monica, Palos Verdes, and the Pacific Ocean. The homelike and inviting campus provides a country environment in the midst of the Greater Los Angeles urban area. Students enjoy easy access to the city's parks, zoo, museums, libraries, and performing arts centers. They are within reach of nearby beaches, mountains, and national parks.

In 1929, founders Cathryn Robberts Dye and her husband, John Thomas Dye II, started the Brentwood Town and Country School in their home for their only son, John Thomas Dye III, and his friends. Known to their students as Aunty Cathryn and Uncle John, the Dyes sought to nurture children in a loving atmosphere.

The School's reputation for academic excellence, strong ethics, and its unique learning environment attracted many new students. By 1949, the School had outgrown its home. A new, larger facility called The Bel Air Town and Country School was built on the present site. In 1959, the School was renamed in honor of John Thomas Dye III, who was killed in action during World War II. Mr. and Mrs. Dye served as Headmaster and Headmistress until they retired in 1963.

The vision of the founders is being carried into the 21st century by a new generation of leadership. Building on the history and core strength of the School, the present Headmaster, Raymond R. Michaud, Jr., and his elected 18-member Board of Trustees, strive to prepare children for a rapidly changing world. The basics—reading, writing, mathematics, science, history, the arts, athletics, problem solving, self-esteem, social skills, and respect for individuality—are still at the heart of the program. Because technology skills and the ability to gather and process information are vital to today's children, the entire School is linked by a state-of-the-art computer network to the Internet and the Worldwide Web.

The John Thomas Dye School, a nonprofit corporation, is accredited by the Western Association of Schools and Colleges and the California Association of Independent Schools. It is a member of the National Association of Independent Schools. One hundred percent of the School's endowment fund is actively invested. There are 2000 living alumni, many of whom continue their relationship with the School through a variety of supportive activities, including Development.

THE CAMPUS. At the center of the campus is John Dye Hall, which houses administrative offices, an assembly hall, a music room, and computer and science labs. Classrooms are located in two identical wings extending east and west from the main building. The Lower School (three Kindergarten classrooms and a K–3 Science Center) is located in a separate adjoining building. A multipurpose facility on the lower field furnishes a spacious gymnasium, an art studio, and a library with more than 13,000 volumes. Also on the grounds are two large outdoor play areas for the younger children, an athletic field for physical education and after-school sports program, and a 5-acre hiking canyon used as a living science classroom. The plant is owned by the School.

THE FACULTY. Raymond R. Michaud, Jr., has been affiliated with The John Thomas Dye School for 29 years and has been its Headmaster since 1980. He holds a bachelor's degree in History from the University of San Francisco, where he was also Assistant Director of Admissions. He received his M.A. in Educational Psychology from California Lutheran University and has held teaching and administrative positions at Harvard-Westlake School in Los Angeles.

All 46 men and women on the full-time faculty hold baccalaureates, and nearly half have earned advanced degrees. Faculty benefits include medical/dental/vision plans, life insurance, a retirement and flexible spending plan, Social Security, and long-term disability. All faculty and staff are trained in first aid and CPR by the Red Cross, and medical emergencies are handled at the nearby UCLA Medical Center.

STUDENT BODY. Students come primarily from West Los Angeles, but also from many different areas of the city and its suburbs. They are about evenly divided between boys and girls. There are three classes in Kindergarten and two each in Grades 1–6. One of the School's goals is to have its student body represent the cultural, economic, and ethnic diversity of the community.

ACADEMIC PROGRAM. The school year, from September to June, includes Thanksgiving, winter, and spring vacations and observances of several national and religious holidays. A typical day, including seven class periods, morning recess, and lunch, begins at 8:05 A.M. and ends at 3:05 P.M. for all students. Families may drop students off at school as early as 7:15 A.M. For an extra charge, an After-School Program lasting until 5:30 P.M. is also available.

Classes are small, with a 7:1 student-faculty ratio. Homework is part of the school program beginning in Kindergarten. Grades are sent to parents quarterly, and parent-teacher conferences are held at least twice a year. School-developed tests and Educational Records Bureau tests are conducted every spring to assess student progress.

The integrated curriculum focuses on the interrelationships among various disciplines. Problem solving and effective reading, writing, and oral communication skills are emphasized. Students are grouped heterogeneously to encourage them to learn from one another. In Kindergarten through Grade 4, classes are self-contained; fifth and sixth grades are departmentalized. Core subjects include reading, writing, and verbal skills; mathematics; social studies; and science. All students are taught by specialists in art, computers, library, music, and physical education.

After graduation, 100 percent of the Class of 2007 entered leading independent secondary schools in Los Angeles.

The John Thomas Dye School conducts a Summer School Program. Sessions are two, three, or five weeks in length. Summer School is open to students not enrolled in the regular yearlong program on a space-available basis.

STUDENT ACTIVITIES. Boys and girls in Grades 4–6 may develop leadership and initiative by serving on the elected student government. Officers and four representatives from each of these grades are chosen by their peers. Assisted by a faculty advisor, the group plans student activities, including community outreach projects. In recent years, John Dye students have held Thanksgiving drives for the needy, adopted Head Start families, and, in 2006, raised money for victims of Hurricane Katrina.

After-school athletics for Grades 4-6 include flag football, basketball, baseball, soccer, and track for boys. Girls compete in basketball, volleyball, soccer, and track. There are teams for every ability level, and everyone is encouraged to participate.

Students in Grades 4–6 also publish a school newspaper and a creative writing magazine. Older students mentor younger students; as an example, sixth graders act as Big Brothers and Sisters to first graders. Students may also serve on the Green Team, which takes responsibility for the school recycling program, and the Community Service Club. Frequent informal student variety shows, called Music for Lunch Bunch, entertain the school community. The sixth-grade musical is an annual success.

Guest artists and lecturers visit the School; the Parents' Association plans field trips to enrich the classroom experience. The Cultural Resource Project invites families to share their culture, traditions, and resources with the school community. The celebration of holidays and special events is a constant cycle in the life of the School. Back to School Night, Open House, Halloween, Thanksgiving, Hanukkah, Christmas, the Candle Lighting Ceremony, Grandparents' Day, the School Birthday, the fair, numerous festivals and feasts, and graduation provide lasting memories.

ADMISSION AND COSTS. John Thomas Dye welcomes bright, capable boys and girls who show promise of becoming strongly motivated, intellectually curious students capable of benefiting from the growth opportunities the School offers.

Acceptance of a candidate is based upon available space and upon an assessment of the child's readiness and academic ability. A study of his or her previous school record and of the results of School-administered testing helps determine readiness. Both standardized and teacher-developed tests are used. Children of alumni and siblings of current students are given priority once they have met the admissions requirements. Application, with a $125 fee, should be made one year prior to desired enrollment. The new Admissions cycle begins on August 1 and ends the third week in March, when notification of acceptance status is mailed out.

Tuition for the 2007–08 school year is $19,600 for Kindergarten–Grade 6. Required uniforms are extra. A $2000 one-time New Student Fee helps support the School's Financial Aid Program, which awards funds based on financial need. In 2006–07, the School distributed more than $325,000 in financial aid.

Assistant Headmaster: Andrew Taylor, Ed.D.
Director of Admissions: Judy Hirsch
Director of Development: Lisa Doherty
Business Manager: Robert E. Suppelsa

La Jolla Country Day School 1926

9490 Genesee Avenue, La Jolla, CA 92037
Tel. 858-453-3440; Admissions Ext. 132; Fax 858-453-8210
Web Site www.ljcds.org; E-mail kjohnson@ljcds.org

La Jolla Country Day School is a coeducational, college preparatory school committed to high standards. Enrolling nearly 1100 students in Nursery–Grade 12, Country Day has been developing scholars, artists, and athletes of character for more than 80 years. The 24-acre campus is in its third year of a comprehensive multimillion-dollar campus redevelopment. New buildings include a state-of-the-art Grades 5–8 middle school and library/academic center; an arts and science complex is scheduled for completion in August 2008. The School educates the whole child intellectually, physically, creatively, socially, and emotionally. A low student-teacher ratio enables faculty to enhance each student's innate talents and abilities within a dynamic educational environment. Tuition assistance, extended-day care, and transportation are available. Tuition: $14,490–$22,000. Vincent Travaglione is Director of Admissions; Christopher Schuck is Head of School. *Western Association.*

Laurence School 1953

13639 Victory Boulevard, Valley Glen, CA 91401
Tel. 818-782-4001; Fax 818-782-4004
Web Site www.laurenceschool.com
E-mail admissions@laurenceschool.com

Over the past five decades, Laurence School has provided an "outstanding learning environment" for children in Kindergarten–Grade 6 that focuses on their total development—social, emotional, physical, and the ever-important academic. Laurence's rich, well-balanced curriculum and state-of-the-art facilities motivate its 291 students to understand important concepts, refine higher-level thinking skills, explore their special interests and talents, engage in real-world discovery, and connect learning to their everyday environment. Laurence's nationally recognized character education and community service programs instill timeless values of good character and exemplary citizenship in each student. The integrated curriculum is enriched by Spanish, music, drama, art, physical education, computer technology, library, and science lab. Activities engage students in gardening, cooking, school governance, Kids' Court, Mandarin, and interscholastic sports. Tuition: $17,500. Marvin Jacobson is

Founder and Head of School; Associate Head Lauren Wolke is Director of Admissions. *Western Association.*

Lick-Wilmerding High School 1895

755 Ocean Avenue, San Francisco, CA 94112
Tel. 415-333-4021; Admissions 415-337-9990; Fax 415-239-1230
Web Site www.lwhs.org; E-mail lwadmit@lwhs.org

This coeducational, college preparatory day school enrolls 431 students in Grades 9–12. Lick-Wilmerding offers a rigorous curriculum in the liberal, technical, performing, and visual arts and views itself as a private school with a public purpose. L–W is the only independent school in the nation that offers a unique collection of shop classes in electronics, fabrications, glass, jewelry, and wood. The School seeks to educate and inspire students with diverse interests and experiences to develop qualities of the "head, heart, and hands," which will serve them well in life. Students are drawn from Bay Area charter, independent, public, and religious schools and are culturally, racially, economically, and ethnically diverse. Lick-Wilmerding is committed to sustaining a truly inclusive community where all students and families will thrive. Tuition: $28,980. Tuition Assistance: $3,000,000. Lisa Wu is Director of Admissions; Dr. Albert M. Adams II is Headmaster. *Western Association.*

Live Oak School 1971

1555 Mariposa Street, San Francisco, CA 94107
Tel. 415-861-8840; Admissions Ext. 220; Fax 415-861-7153
Web Site www.liveoaksf.org; E-mail admissions@liveoaksf.org

Live Oak, a day school enrolling 252 boys and girls in Kindergarten–Grade 8, supports the potential and promise in every child. Live Oak aims to provide an exemplary education in traditional disciplines while developing classical thinking skills, confidence, integrity, and compassion. Art, music, drama, Spanish, Advanced Spanish, physical education, intramural athletics, and frequent field trips support the core curriculum. Extended care and a summer program are also available. Located in the sunny Potrero Hill neighborhood of San Francisco, the School enjoys strong neighborhood relationships in its urban setting. Parent participation is an integral component of the school community. Live Oak admits a section of students in Kindergarten and Grade 6. Tuition: $18,800–$19,500. Need-based tuition assistance is available. Tracey Gersten is Director of Admissions; Holly Horton (Briarcliff, B.S.; Wheelock, M.S.) is Head of School.

Lycée Français La Pérouse 1967

PS–Grade 5: 755 Ashbury Street, San Francisco, CA 94117
Tel. 415-661-5232; Admissions Ext. 2100; Fax 415-661-0945
Web Site www.lelycee.org; E-mail admissions@lelycee.org
Grades 6–12: 1201 Ortega Street, San Francisco, CA 94122
Tel. 415-661-5232; Admissions Ext. 1100; Fax 415-661-0246
PS–Grade 5: 330 Golden Hind Passage, San Francisco, CA 94925
Tel. 415-661-5232; Admissions Ext. 3100; Fax 415-924-2849
Web Site www.lelycee.org; E-mail admissions@lelycee.org

The Lycée Français La Pérouse of San Francisco celebrated its 40th anniversary in 2007. The college preparatory school welcomes more than 835 children from pre-Kindergarten to Grade 12 on three campuses where all students follow the authentic French program of the National Education. Students from many nationalities evolve in a truly multicultural environment. The rigorous curriculum teaches students to think, opens their minds to other cultures, and prepares them for college. The Lycée Français La Pérouse is accredited by the California Association of Independent Schools and provides students with an American high school diploma, SATs, and Advanced Placement courses in addition to the French Baccalaureate. Tuition: $9400–$17,600. Isabelle Desmole is Director of Admissions; Alain Cuzin is Headmaster.

Marin Academy 1971

1600 Mission Avenue, San Rafael, CA 94901-1859
Tel. 415-453-4550; Admissions 415-453-2808; Fax 415-453-8905
Web Site www.ma.org; E-mail admissions@ma.org

Marin Academy, a college preparatory day school enrolling 400 students in Grades 9–12, asks students to think, question, and create as well as to accept the responsibilities posed by education in a democratic society. A demanding curriculum is complemented by extracurricular activities, a full interscholastic athletic program, a celebrated fine and performing arts program, and a week-long minicourse program for exploration of special areas of interest. Advanced Placement courses are offered in all subjects. Community service and a unique outings/wilderness program are among the many activities. Tuition: $29,245. Financial Aid: $1,700,000. Dan Babior is Director of Admissions and Financial Aid; Richard Drew (Amherst College, B.A.; Stanford University, M.A.; University of Colorado [Boulder], Ed.S.) is Interim Head of School.

Marin Country Day School 1956

5221 Paradise Drive, Corte Madera, CA 94925-2107
Tel. 415-927-5900; Admission 415-927-5919; Fax 415-924-2224
Web Site www.mcds.org; E-mail admission@mcds.org

Marin Country Day enrolls 540 boys and girls in Kindergarten–Grade 8 on its 35-acre waterfront campus. The curriculum, with an interdisciplinary, hands-on approach, includes English, Spanish, math, physical science, and social science. The arts, athletics, and outdoor education are integral to the program. Dedicated faculty, a low student-teacher ratio, and enrichment and extracurricular activities are designed to instill confidence, a joy for learning, and support of the School's core values: respect, responsibility, and compassion. After-school care and a multicultural summer program are offered. Tuition: $20,805–$24,095. Financial aid is available. Jeffrey Escabar and Ann Borden are Co-Directors of Admission; Dr. Lucinda Lee Katz is Head of School. *Western Association.*

Marin Horizon School 1977

305 Montford Avenue, Mill Valley, CA 94941
Tel. 415-388-8408; Fax 415-388-7831
Web Site www.marinhorizon.org
E-mail admissions@marinhorizon.org

Marin Horizon School offers a challenging academic program for 280 students, toddlers to Grade 8. Inspired by Montessori's philosophy, the program nurtures children's innate curiosity and love of learning through an integrated curriculum, small classes, a devoted faculty, and multiage classrooms. Mastery of the fundamentals in core subjects, emphasis on independent critical thinking, leadership, and strong communication and social skills are expected in graduates. Spanish, music, art, physical education, and library sciences are integrated into the multicultural and interdisciplinary academic program at all levels, enhanced by field trips and an outstanding outdoor education program. Enrichment classes and a summer camp are offered. Tuition: $12,510–$20,995. Tuition assistance is available. Rosalind Hamar is Head of School; Sharman M. Bonus is Director of Admissions.

Marin Primary & Middle School 1975

20 Magnolia Avenue, Larkspur, CA 94939
Tel. 415-924-2608; Admission Ext. 215; Fax 415-924-9351
Web Site www.mpms.org; E-mail info@mpms.org

Founded to encourage children and adults to work together to enjoy a lifelong pursuit of learning, Marin Primary & Middle School enrolls 350 boys and girls in Preschool–Grade 8. Project-based learning and team teaching aim to support a nurturing environment that includes a Library Media Center and an Outdoor Education Center. The core curriculum is enriched by woodworking, music, art, computer, and life skills. Students begin Spanish in Preschool and may continue through eighth grade. Before- and after-school care are offered. Tuition (K–8): $18,900–$20,550. Financial aid is available. Nicole Demaray Lavery is Director of Admission; Julie Elam is Head of School. *Western Association.*

Marlborough School 1889

250 South Rossmore Avenue, Los Angeles, CA 90004
Tel. 323-935-1147; Admissions 323-964-8450; Fax 323-933-0542
Web Site www.marlboroughschool.org
E-mail jeanette.woochitjian@marlboroughschool.org

The oldest independent school for girls in Southern California, Marlborough enrolls 530 students in Grades 7–12. The School is committed to providing a superior college preparatory education in an environment imbued with high ethical values. The curriculum offers 328 classes and 148 courses including 24 Advanced Placement and 15 Honors courses. Average SAT-I scores are 675 Critical Reasoning and 664 Math; graduates enroll in selective colleges nationwide. The campus offers state-of-the-art classroom facilities, performing arts space, and expanded athletic facilities for teams in nine interscholastic sports. Tuition: $26,750. Financial Aid: $1,900,000. Jeanette Woo Chitjian is Director of Admissions; Barbara E. Wagner (University of Colorado, M.M.E.) is Head of School. *Western Association.*

Marymount High School 1923

10643 Sunset Boulevard, Los Angeles, CA 90077
Tel. 310-472-1205; Admissions Exts. 220/306; Fax 310-440-4316
Web Site www.mhs-la.org; E-mail sstephens@mhs-la.org

Marymount High School, established in 1923 by the Religious of the Sacred Heart of Mary, is a Catholic, independent, college preparatory school for girls in Grades 9–12. Hallmarks of the highly personalized and student-centered program include extensive service outreach, a rigorous curriculum that offers 17 Advanced Placement and 9 Honors-level courses, comprehensive cocurricular opportunities, 23 sports teams, and numerous leadership opportunities. All Marymount seniors go on to attend college or university, and each year, outstanding students are admitted to some of the most selective academic institutions in the world. Tuition & Fees: $22,800. Mrs. Sharon Stephens is Director of Admission; Dr. Mary Ellen Gozdecki (Marymount College, B.A.; University of Southern California, MA., Ph.D.) is Head of School. *Western Association.*

Marymount of Santa Barbara 1938

2130 Mission Ridge Road, Santa Barbara, CA 93103
Tel. 805-569-1811; Admissions Ext. 131; Fax 805-569-0573
Web Site www.marymountsb.org
E-mail rwilcox@marymountsb.org

Marymount of Santa Barbara is an independent, nondenominational K–8 school enrolling 228 boys and girls. For nearly 70 years, the Marymount tradition of excellence has sought to instill a thirst for knowledge, develop core values, and create an intellectually engaging, supportive community. A 10:1 student-faculty ratio, commitment to diversity, accomplished teachers, and state-of-the-art facilites are enhanced by a picturesque, 10-acre campus along the Riviera. The rigorous curriculum encourages a love of learning while arts, athletics, and service prepare students to become global citizens possessing leadership skills and diverse talents. Academics include world-class language arts and math curricula, the Kaleidoscope program on world cultures and religions, and beginning in Kindergarten, technology and foreign language. Facilities include portable wireless computer labs, auditorium and stage, a swimming pool, athletic fields, rock-climbing wall, and basketball and tennis courts. Activities include moviemaking, drama, music, student ambassadors, study skills, scuba diving, basketball, soccer, volleyball, and track. Tuition: $15,438–$17,840. Financial Aid: $450,000. Deborah David is Head of School; Rageshwar Kaur Wilcox is Director of Admission.

Mayfield Junior School 1931

405 South Euclid Avenue, Pasadena, CA 91101
Tel. 626-796-2774; Fax 626-796-5753
Web Site www.mayfieldjs.org

Mayfield Junior School is a Catholic independent school founded by the Sisters of the Holy Child Jesus, enrolling 480 boys and girls as day students in Kindergarten through Grade 8. Its mission is to provide rich educational and cultural opportunities. The core curriculum, consisting of language arts, religion, mathematics, science, social studies, Spanish and French, computers, library, the arts, and physical education, is designed to promote a love of learning and a lifelong pursuit of knowledge. Classes enroll an average of 17 students, and the student-teacher ratio is 14:1. Intramural sports emphasize skills development, teamwork, and sportsmanship. Tuition: $14,235; New Student Fee: $2500. Averyl Thielen is Director of Admissions; Stephanie D. Griffin, M.A., is Head of School. *Western Association.*

Mayfield Senior School of the Holy Child 1931

500 Bellefontaine Street, Pasadena, CA 91105-2439
Tel. 626-799-9121; Admissions Exts. 210/287; Fax 626-799-8576
Web Site www.mayfieldsenior.org
E-mail clemmie.phillips@mayfieldsenior.org

Enrolling 300 young women in Grades 9–12, Mayfield Senior School offers a college preparatory curriculum designed to develop each student's full intellectual, spiritual, artistic, physical, emotional, and social potential. Catholic values and tradition guide the daily conduct of the School, which welcomes girls from all religious and cultural backgrounds. In addition to the liberal arts and sciences, Mayfield offers 23 Honors and Advanced Placement courses as well as in-depth training in dance, music, and other special areas through its Conservatory of the Arts. Community service, Student Council, athletics, publications, and plays and concerts are among the activities. Tuition: $18,200. Financial Aid/Merit Awards: $549,000. Clemmie Phillips is Director of Admissions; Rita Curasi McBride is Head of School.

Menlo School 1915

50 Valparaiso Avenue, Atherton, CA 94027
Tel. 650-330-2000; Admissions Ext. 2600; Fax 650-330-2012
Web Site www.menloschool.org
E-mail lschiavenza or *cshelburne@menloschool.org*

Located 25 miles south of San Francisco, Menlo is a coeducational, college preparatory day school enrolling 750 students in Grades 6–12. Its environment fosters self-reliance while striving to promote growth of mind, body, and spirit. The curriculum features Honors and Advanced Placement courses in all subjects, small class size, and individual attention that engages students in the life of the mind. More than 35 athletic teams provide opportunities for physical development. Visual arts, drama, music, dance, and extracurriculars, including community service, round out student growth. Tuition: $29,400. Financial Aid: $3,000,000. Cathy Shelburne (Upper School) and Lisa Schiavenza (Middle School) are Directors of Admissions; Norman Colb (Brandeis, B.A. 1964; Harvard, M.A.T. 1965) is Head of School.

Mid-Peninsula High School 1979

1340 Willow Road, Menlo Park, CA 94025
Tel. 650-321-1991; Fax 650-321-9921
Web Site www.mid-pen.com; E-mail info@mid-pen.com

Set on a state-of-the-art campus, Mid-Peninsula enrolls 145 young men and women in a college preparatory program designed to "help students find individual paths to their personal best." Individual academic programs provide maximum opportunities for youngsters to discover and expand their talents while understanding and overcoming impediments to success. The "Stages of Development" system enables faculty to assess and monitor students' progress based on their unique abilities. Technology-based learning is integrated throughout the curriculum. Graduates typically go on to four-year colleges and universities. Sports, music, drama, and clubs are among the activities. Tuition: $23,550. Molly McAuliffe is Admissions Director; Douglas C. Thompson, Ph.D., is Head of School.

The Mirman School for Gifted Children 1962

16180 Mulholland Drive, Los Angeles, CA 90049
Tel. 310-476-2868; Admissions 310-775-8411; Fax 310-775-8433
Web Site www.mirman.org; E-mail bfisher@mirman.org

One of the few schools in the country specifically dedicated to meeting the needs of highly gifted children with IQs of 145 or above, Mirman is a coeducational, ungraded school serving 340 students, ages 5–14. The School provides an educational setting in which children are encouraged to develop physically, socially, and emotionally. Located a short distance from UCLA, the campus includes two computer labs, two science labs, and specialized curricular programs in Spanish, Latin, French, choral and instrumental music, dramatic and visual arts, and athletics. The School was founded by Dr. and Mrs. Norman J. Mirman. Tuition: $19,000–$20,300. Need-based financial aid is available. Mrs. Becky Riley Fisher is Director of Admissions; John Thomas West is Headmaster.

Mount Tamalpais School 1976

100 Harvard Avenue, Mill Valley, CA 94941
Tel. 415-383-9434; Fax 415-383-7519
Web Site www.mttam.org

MOUNT TAMALPAIS SCHOOL in Mill Valley, California, is a coeducational day school enrolling children in Kindergarten through Grade 8. The suburban community of Mill Valley (population 13,000) is 12 miles north of San Francisco in Marin County. Students have access to the museums, theater, opera, symphony, and ballet of the city as well as the Pacific Ocean (6 miles from the campus) and Mount Tamalpais for hiking and nature study. Private bus service is available between the School and local communities; public bus stops are within walking distance of the campus.

Founder and Director Kathleen M. Mecca, Ph.D., Ed.D., established the School in 1976. From its original enrollment of 60 students in Kindergarten–Grade 6, the School has grown to an enrollment of 240.

Mount Tamalpais School seeks to provide students with a solid academic foundation and to foster a genuine enthusiasm for learning. The departmentalized, integrated curriculum focuses on concepts and research skills and permits each teacher to use a variety of methods and materials to strengthen individual skills. In addition, small-group instruction maximizes the inherent potential of each child and fosters respect for each student's interests and abilities.

A nonprofit organization, Mount Tamalpais School is governed by a Board of Trustees that includes parents, past parents, and community members. The Parent Council holds social and fund-raising events and coordinates family volunteer assistance to the School. The School holds membership in the National Association of Independent Schools, the California Association of Independent Schools, the Educational Records Bureau, the Secondary School Admission Test Board, the Educational Testing Service, and the Western Association of Schools and Colleges.

THE CAMPUS. The 12+-acre campus includes a large playing field and a playground with a variety of recreational structures. A 1.5-acre cypress grove is used for nature study. The four school buildings, which total more than 32,000 square feet, provide classrooms, a computer lab, an art studio, a faculty workroom, administrative offices, and the Rappaport Library Learning Center. Other facilities include a gymnasium-theater complex, tutorial rooms for individual instrumental instruction and learning assistance, two science laboratories, an art room, and a music room, and the MTSO, an observatory with a retractable roof and large-scale telescopes on adjustable piers. The value of the School-owned plant is more than $10,000,000.

THE FACULTY. Kathleen M. Mecca, Ph.D., Ed.D., has been Director of the School since its founding in 1976. A native of New Jersey, Dr. Mecca is a graduate of the University of California at Los Angeles (B.A. 1965, M.A. 1968, M.S.Ed. 1969), the University of California at Irvine (M.A. 1966), Stanford University (Ed.D. 1971), and the University of California at San Francisco (Ph.D. 1973). She has held teaching and administrative positions in public and private schools in California and has also worked as a reading specialist and child/adolescent psychologist. She was a mentor teacher and master teacher for the California State Department of Education. In addition, she has taught psychology and education at the college and graduate school levels.

The 32 full-time faculty hold baccalaureate and graduate degrees representing study at Brown, Bucknell, Columbia, Dartmouth, Dominican, Earlham, Harvard, Middlebury, Oberlin, Ohio State, Oregon State, Princeton, San Diego State, San Francisco State, Stanford, Trinity, Wellesley, and the Universities of California, Chicago, Michigan, Oregon, Pennsylvania, and Wisconsin. There are also part-time instructors who provide additional curricular support.

The School employs a full-time nurse/health instructor, and first aid is available on campus at all times. Paramedics are within 5 minutes of the School, and a hospital emergency room is 15 minutes away by car.

STUDENT BODY. The School enrolls 240 boys and girls in Kindergarten–Grade 8. The students reside in communities throughout Marin County and San Francisco.

ACADEMIC PROGRAM. The 180-day school year, from late August to mid-June, is divided into trimesters and includes a Thanksgiving recess, winter and spring vacations, a mid-winter recess, and all legal holidays. The daily schedule for Kindergarten–Grade 8, from 8:00 A.M. to 3:00 P.M. Monday–Thursday, includes morning and afternoon homeroom periods, eight 40- to 45-minute class periods, a morning recess, and a 40-minute lunch period. After-school care until 6:00 P.M. is available to students for an additional hourly fee. On Fridays, the schedule is adjusted to permit 2:15 P.M. dismissal for all students. In order to allow time for parent-teacher conferences in the fall, there is one week of noon dismissals.

An average grade-level homeroom, for which there are at least two teachers, enrolls two classes of 12–14 students, a total of 24–28 students. There is a supervised study hall every day from 3:15 to 4:00 P.M.; teachers are available to provide extra help during this time.

Students in Grades 4–8 receive grades each trimester in addition to narrative evaluations, and students in Kindergarten–Grade 3 receive narrative evaluations using a qualitative system. Written reports with teacher comments are sent to the parents of all students at the end of each trimester. The School encourages communication between parents and teachers, and formal parent/teacher/student conferences are scheduled at the end of the first trimester. Throughout the year, parents are urged to consult with the homeroom teachers, who act as the child's counselors, to discuss general progress or concerns.

Homework, ranging from 20 minutes four times a week for the youngest children to approximately an hour a day for students in Grades 6–8, is assigned to provide follow-up, reinforcement, and continuity.

The Kindergarten program is developmental and is designed to provide an introduction to the School's curriculum of departmentalized, experiential learning. Learning tasks offer opportunities for enjoyment and success as well as skill development. Students are placed according to developmental criteria that take into account each child's academic, social, and emotional maturation.

For Grades 1–8, the curriculum includes Language Arts (reading, literature, language, grammar, spelling, and writing), Geography, Spanish, French, social studies, mathematics, computer science, science, study skills, music, chorus, drama, art, art history, health, physical education, ceramics, woodworking, dance, movement, and sewing. An Enrichment program during the regular school day for Grades 6–8 provides elective opportunities for students to increase their skills in creative writing, music, drama, computers, dance, fine arts, current events, and film making. For Grades 4–8, values and family life are also offered. Students in Grades 6–8 study Latin in addition to either French or Spanish as well as special classes in Shakespeare, Current Affairs, and Public Speaking. Mandarin and Japanese are electives in Grades 7 and 8. All students receive basic instruction in special etiquette classes during their elementary years.

Outdoor Education experiences for Grades 4–8 complement the program of environmental study that begins in Kindergarten. Fourth and fifth graders spend a week at various California historic sites correlated with their social science curriculum. Sixth-grade students have a week at the Point Reyes National Seashore, followed by an all-day kayaking trip. Seventh graders spend a week rafting and camping in the American River wilderness. The eighth graders spend a week backpacking in Yosemite National Park.

Mount Tamalpais graduates have entered leading independent secondary schools in California and throughout the United States and have been accepted at such colleges and universities as Arizona State, Boston College, Boston University, Brown, Bucknell, Cornell, Dartmouth, Denison, Dominican, Duke, Georgetown, Harvard, Ithaca, Lewis & Clark, Loyola, Northeastern, Occidental, Pepperdine, Princeton, Reed, Smith, Stanford, Tufts, Tulane, Wellesley, Williams, and the Universities of Arizona, California, Chicago, Colorado, Michigan, Notre Dame, Oregon, Pennsylvania, Southern California, Virginia, and Washington, among others.

STUDENT ACTIVITIES. The Student Council is composed of two representatives, one boy and one girl, each from Grades 3–8. With parent volunteers who help coordinate activities, the Council arranges spirit days, dances, and community service projects. Extracurricular activities include Computer and the Literary Magazine and Yearbook Committees. After-school classes in sewing, woodworking, chess, ceramics, art, dance, drama, voice, yoga, cooking, science adventures, and instrumental music are available for a small fee.

Upper-grade students compete in basketball, soccer, volleyball, cross-country, and track and field with teams from other schools in San Francisco and Marin County. Soccer teams for Kindergarten–Grade 6 play in the Mill Valley Soccer League. Intramural sports include basketball, field hockey, gymnastics, lacrosse, softball, and volleyball.

School spirit days include Halloween, Teddy Bear Day, Gratitude Day, Hat Day, Hawaiian Day, Olympic Day, Field Day, International Day, and Angel Island Day. Traditional events include Grandparents' Day, Founder's Day Picnic, and the Gala Spring Auction.

ADMISSION AND COSTS. Mount Tamalpais School seeks to enroll a diverse group of students who are responsible, willing to learn, and who can reach their full potential in a challenging academic environment. New students are admitted to all grades on the basis of very competitive enrollment criteria: three recommendations (including one from a current teacher), a school visit with an interview, standardized testing, a transcript of grades, and, for Grades 3–8, a writing sample. Parents are encouraged to observe classes in session before submitting an application for the student. Application must be made prior to January 15, 2008. The nonrefundable application fee is $150. The Director and an Admissions Committee handle admissions.

In 2007–08, tuition is $19,950 for Kindergarten–Grade 8. Mount Tamalpais School subscribes to the School and Student Service for Financial Aid. The School offers financial assistance to approximately 17 percent of the students; in 2006–07, approximately $350,000 was awarded on the basis of need.

New Roads School 1995

Elementary School: 2000 Stoner Avenue, Los Angeles, CA 90025
Tel. 310-479-8500; Fax 310-479-8556
Middle School: 1238 Lincoln Boulevard
Santa Monica, CA 90401
Tel. 310-587-2255; Fax 310-587-2258
Middle School: 3504 Las Flores Canyon Road, Malibu, CA 90265
Tel. 310-456-1977; Fax 310-456-8027
High School: 3131 Olympic Boulevard, Santa Monica, CA 90404
Tel. 310-828-5582; Fax 310-828-2582
Web Site www.newroads.org; E-mail info@newroads.org

NEW ROADS SCHOOL in Santa Monica, California, is an independent educational community set on four campuses within Los Angeles County and currently serving 625 boys and girls in Pre-Kindergarten through Grade 12. Los Angeles County (population 10,000,000) is a region rich in cultural and natural resources, and both campuses enjoy easy access to beaches, canyons, recreation areas, and museums. Students travel to school via public bus and car pools.

New Roads School was established in 1995 as a model for education in an ethnically, racially, culturally, and socioeconomically diverse community. To prepare young people for the challenges and opportunities they face, the School aims to promote personal, social, political, and moral understanding and to instill in students a respect for the humanity and ecology of the world in which they live. The demanding college preparatory curriculum not only emphasizes strong reading and writing skills, effective expression, and critical thinking, but seeks to go beyond ordinary "schooling" with a concern for the whole person. Unique among independent schools, no less than 40 percent of the New Roads budget is devoted to need-based financial assistance.

A nonprofit, nondenominational institution, New Roads School is guided by a 30-member Board of Trustees. It holds membership in the National Association of Independent Schools, the California Association of Independent Schools, the Educational Records Bureau, The College Board, the Association for Curriculum Development, The Independent School Alliance for Minority Affairs, and the National Coalition of Educational Activists. New Roads is accredited by the Western Association of Schools and Colleges and the California Association of Independent Schools.

THE CAMPUSES. The Elementary School campus is located in West Los Angeles close to a public park. Comfortable classrooms, computerized science areas, and an art studio surround a playground. The Middle School in Santa Monica is conducted in a 27,000-square-foot facility owned by the Santa Monica Boys and Girls Club. It provides six spacious classrooms, an art room, a large gymnasium, meeting rooms, and outdoor playing fields. New Roads students take part in many after-school activities on the site, which is located near the beach, community arts resources, and the local library. The Middle School in Malibu is set on a lovely 3.5-acre campus. Surrounded by the Santa Monica Mountains and a nearby creek, the campus provides spacious classrooms, fully equipped playgrounds, basketball courts, a climbing rock, and a grass playing field. The High School is located on the West Side of Los Angeles.

THE FACULTY. David Bryan, a native of Brooklyn, New York, was appointed founding Head of School in 1995. He is a graduate of the State University of New York where he earned a B.A. at Stony Brook and J.D. and Ph.D. degrees at Buffalo. Dr. Bryan also holds an M.S. in kinesiology from the University of California at Los Angeles. His professional experience encompasses teaching in both public and independent schools and universities, including Crossroads School for Arts and Science, where he also served as Dean of Human Development.

In addition to the Head of School, there are 100 faculty who hold undergraduate and advanced degrees representing study at colleges and universities nationwide. Among these are Art Center for Design, Berklee College of Music, Boston University, Brown, California Institute of the Arts, California State (Long Beach, Los Angeles, Northridge), Columbia University, Dartmouth, Harvard, Loyola, Mary Washington, Pepperdine, Santa Clara State University, Santa Monica College, Simmons, Stanford, Williams, Yale, and the Universities of California, Colorado, Pittsburgh, Southern California, Tulsa, and Wisconsin (Madison).

Faculty benefits include medical and dental plans, disability insurance, and a retirement program. Medical and first-aid services are offered on campus, and Saint John's Medical Center and Santa Monica Hospital are available for emergencies.

STUDENT BODY. In 2007–08, New Roads School enrolled 625 students in Pre-Kindergarten–Grade 12, 324 boys and 301 girls. Students come from diverse backgrounds that reflect the multicultural heritage of the Greater Los Angeles area. Half the students are Caucasian, while the other half is comprised of Latino (15 percent), African-American (17 percent), Asian (10 percent), and Native American and others (8 percent).

ACADEMIC PROGRAM. The school year, divided into semesters, begins in early September and extends to mid-June, with Thanksgiving, winter, and spring breaks and days off for federal holidays. Grades and written progress reports are issued twice each semester, at eight weeks and at the end of the semester; marks are posted weekly for students who are experiencing difficulty. Classes, enrolling 15 to 20 students, are held five days a week from 8:00 A.M. to between 2:50 to 3:15 P.M., depending on the grade. Supervised study halls and writing and math labs are integrated into the daily schedule. Tutorials are available after school for students as needed.

New Roads School's fluid, individualized education and diverse community cultivate students who are college and life prepared, compassionate, and engaged in creating a just and sustainable future. New Roads offers an innovative college preparatory curriculum emphasizing traditional mathematics, English, social science, history, foreign language, and science as well as numerous courses in the visual and performing arts. *The Workshop for Social, Economic, and Ecological Action* enables students to apply their academic skills to solve such current issues as racism, sexism, population/overpopulation, stereotyping, and ecological regeneration and land use. Students write journals and research papers, design and collaborate on community projects, and make oral presentations to their peers and the larger community.

To earn a New Roads diploma, students must complete four years each of English and Social Science (including one year of American Studies); three years of mathematics (through Algebra II) and laboratory science; and three of the same foreign language, the arts, and Psycho-Physical Education. Students must also take one course each year in human development and Workshops/community service.

Among the colleges and universities to which the School's graduates have gained admission are Amherst, Bard, Barnard, Beloit, Bennington, Brown, California Institute of the Arts, California State (Northridge, San Diego, San Jose), Carleton, Colorado College, Dartmouth, Earlham, Georgetown, Grinnell, Hampshire College, Haverford, Kenyon, New York University, Northwestern, Oberlin, Pomona, Reed College, Sarah

Lawrence, Stanford, Wellesley, Wesleyan, and the Universities of California, Chicago, Colorado, Michigan, Pennsylvania, and Southern California.

New Roads conducts a small six-week summer program of academics and the arts.

STUDENT ACTIVITIES. A faculty-supervised Student Council is responsible for planning and implementing activities, representing the School at conferences and other events, and serving as liaison between the student body and the administration. Organizations on campus are formed according to student interest and include Amnesty International, a theater/improv group, school dancers, and debate, games, and science clubs. Parents are encouraged to teach after-school courses in a field of their expertise such as jewelry making, photography, computer building, and veterinary medicine.

New Roads athletes compete at the varsity and junior varsity level with other independent and public schools in the region in cross-country, track and field, soccer, flag football, golf, tennis, surfing, basketball, baseball, softball and volleyball. Middle School students play these sports as well as flag football. Intramural teams are organized in floor hockey, indoor soccer, and Ultimate Frisbee.

Traditional events on the calendar include Back-to-School Night, the Fall Drama Production, All School Celebration Feast, the Holiday Musical Celebration, Town Hall Meetings, the Midnite Special Reading, the talent show, the Spring Musical, and the All School Fund-Raiser, Kaleidoscope.

ADMISSION AND COSTS. New Roads welcomes students with grade-level skills who demonstrate a desire to become actively engaged in the School and greater community. Admission is offered based on the completed application, a student essay, previous academic transcripts, two teacher recommendations, an administrative evaluation, standardized test results, and an interview. The deadline for applying is early February, although late applicants may be considered if vacancies exist. The application fee is $100.

Tuition ranges from $19,000 to $24,000, depending on grade. Books and Fees ($400–$800) and a one-time Family Fee ($1,000) are additional. Financial aid in the amount of nearly $5,300,000 will be awarded to more than 60 percent of the student body.

Head of School: David Bryan, Ph.D., J.D., M.S.
Director, Elementary School: Patrick McCabe
Director, Middle School: Christine Elder
Associate Director, Malibu Middle School: Evan Beachy
Director, High School: William Webb
Director of Development: Amy Simons
Business Manager: Adrienne McCandless

The Nueva School 1967

6565 Skyline Boulevard, Hillsborough, CA 94010
Tel. 650-350-4600; Admissions 650-350-4528; Fax 650-348-3642
Web Site www.nuevaschool.org; E-mail admissions@nuevaschool.org

The Nueva School serves the academic, social, and emotional needs of 372 gifted and talented children in Pre-Kindergarten through Grade 8. Nueva is a child-centered, progressive school that focuses on integrated studies, inquiry-based learning, social-emotional learning, and real-world application of the curriculum. The program emphasizes a differentiated, theme-based approach to learning. Highlights of the program include the Menuhin Music Scholars, Japanese and Spanish language study with a culminating eighth-grade trip to Japan or Spain, and an Innovation Laboratory for design and engineering projects. Extended care and summer programs are also offered. Tuition: $16,835–$24,410. Financial Aid: $700,000. Taryn Clark is Admissions Director; Diane Rosenberg was appointed Director in 2001. *Western Association.*

The Oaks School 1986

6817 Franklin Avenue, Hollywood, CA 90028
Tel. 323-850-3755; Fax 323-850-3758
Web Site www.oaksschool.org; E-mail info@oaksschool.org

The Oaks, a day school enrolling 145 boys and girls in Kindergarten–Grade 6, provides a loving, safe, intellectually stimulating environment where students are free to be themselves, explore the world around them, and learn to make sense of it. The curriculum is designed to develop children's full potential as seekers, learners, independent thinkers, and problem solvers. The curriculum follows the California State Standards while also allowing individual creativity and spontaneous projects to develop. Student Council, an all-school campout, "Creative Athletics" circus, and an art show are among the activities. After-school enrichment programs are offered. Tuition: $14,925; New-Student Fee: $1000. Financial aid is available. Mary Fauvre, Ph.D., is Head of School. *Western Association.*

Ojai Valley School 1923

Lower School: 723 El Paseo Road, Ojai, CA 93023
Tel. 805-646-1423; [Toll-free] 800-433-4687
Fax 805-646-0362
Web Site www.ovs.org; E-mail admission@ovs.org
Upper School: 10820 Reeves Road, Ojai, CA 93023
Tel. 805-646-5593

Ojai Valley School was founded by Edward Yeomans, Sr., who believed that the beautiful surroundings and temperate climate of the region would "stimulate the interests of children in a natural, spontaneous way" and would prepare them for "intelligent, benevolent, and joyous participation" in their communities and the larger world. The coeducational college preparatory school enrolls nearly 360 students in Pre-Kindergarten (age 3)–Grade 12, with 160 five- and seven-day boarders from Grade 3 upward. The liberal arts "curriculum for life" emphasizes the mastery of those skills students need to achieve their maximum potential in college, careers, and throughout adulthood. Qualified scholars may take AP and Honors courses in English, English Literature, Computer Science, Biology, Chemistry, French, Spanish, United States History, Government, and Studio Art. International students ages 8–18 benefit from an extensive program in ESL intended to develop their reading, speaking, and writing skills. Activities include outdoor programs, student government, community service, publications, drama, music, and sports. Boarding Tuition: $39,900; Day Tuition: $17,150. Tracy Wilson is Director of Admissions; Michael Hermes is President. *Western Association.*

The Pegasus School 1984

19692 Lexington Lane, Huntington Beach, CA 92646
Tel. 714-964-1224; Fax 714-962-6047
Web Site www.pegasus-school.net; E-mail nconklin@pegasus-school.net

The Pegasus School, a coeducational day school enrolling 565 students in Preschool–Grade 8, offers a strong, challenging academic curriculum, taught by fully certified faculty. Small classes are limited to 18 students, each with a teacher and a teacher's assistant. In Kindergarten–Grade 8, the program is enriched with technology, science, Spanish, music, art, drama, and physical education. The campus features two state-of-the-art Technology Centers, Lower and Middle School science labs, an 18,000-volume library, and an Activities Center, which includes a gym, theater, and art studio. Camp Pegasus provides six weeks of summer enrichment. Tuition: $7000–$13,620. Financial aid is available. Nancy Conklin is Director of Admission; Dr. Laura Hathaway is Founder/Head of School.

The Phillips Brooks School 1978

2245 Avy Avenue, Menlo Park, CA 94025
Tel. 650-854-4545; Fax 650-854-6532
Web Site www.phillipsbrooks.org
E-mail clee@phillipsbrooks.org

Phillips Brooks, a coeducational day school enrolling 276 students in Preschool–Grade 5, is committed to a tradition of academic excellence along with an emphasis on preparing students to live creative, humane, and compassionate lives. Learning is nurtured by a team of talented faculty providing an academic curriculum that includes basic subjects, communications, art, technology, Mandarin or Spanish, library skills, music, physical education, and science. Chapel services are held twice weekly and emphasize universal values. The School emphasizes diversity and an understanding of world cultures. Extended day care is available in Kindergarten–Grade 5. Tuition: $11,700–$21,000. Financial aid is available. Amanda Perla is Director of Admissions; Kristi Kerins is Head of School.

Pilgrim School 1958

540 South Commonwealth Avenue, Los Angeles, CA 90020
Tel. 213-385-7351; Fax 213-386-7264
Web Site www.pilgrim-school.org
E-mail pkong@pilgrim-school.org

The First Congregational Church of Los Angeles founded Pilgrim School to provide an education that reflects the diversity and vitality of its urban setting. Enrolling 350 day students from many faiths in Preschool/PK–Grade 12, Pilgrim offers a college preparatory program in a challenging yet nurturing environment. The curriculum focuses on the traditional liberal arts and sciences and includes Advanced Placement courses and English as a Second Language classes. Students take part in school government, drama, dance, photography, Model UN, and interscholastic sports. An academic and recreational summer session is available. Tuition: $11,990–$18,450. Financial Aid: $200,000. Ms. Patricia Kong and Mrs. Laura Lee Everett are Co-Directors of Admissions; Mr. Jon Kidder is Secondary Director; Mrs. Sally Carr is Elementary Director; Dr. Mark A. Brooks is Head of School. *Western Association.*

Polytechnic School 1907

1030 East California Boulevard, Pasadena, CA 91106
Tel. 626-792-2147; Fax 626-449-5727
Web Site www.polytechnic.org; E-mail admissions@polytechnic.org

Polytechnic enrolls 850 students in Kindergarten–Grade 12 on a 15-acre campus with a state-of-the-art performing and fine arts center and professionally staffed libraries, computer rooms, and media centers. Students are encouraged to excel in academic, athletic, and artistic endeavors in an atmosphere that celebrates diversity and promotes community. The School emphasizes sound thinking and effective communication while fostering personal development, integrity, responsibility, and concern for others. Community service is integral to the curriculum; an extensive outdoor education program in Grades 6–12 enhances the Poly experience. Tuition: $17,575–$23,750. Financial Aid: $2,800,000. Sally Jeanne McKenna is Director of Admissions; Deborah Reed is Head of School. *Western Association.*

Ring Mountain Day School 1976

K–Grade 8: 70 Lomita Drive, Mill Valley, CA 94941
Tel. 415-381-8183; Admissions Ext. 35; Fax 415-381-8484
Web Site www.ringmountain.org
E-mail admissions@ringmountain.org
Preschool: 215A Blackfield Drive, Tiburon, CA 94920
Tel 415-381-8181; Admissions Ext. 31

RING MOUNTAIN DAY SCHOOL enrolls boys and girls in an academic program encompassing age 2 in Preschool through Grade 8. The School occupies two campuses in Marin County north of San Francisco. Mill Valley (population 13,557) is located at the foot of Mount Tamalpais, while Tiburon (population 8756) is a short ferry ride from San Francisco's Fisherman's Wharf. Both are charming residential communities that afford easy access to natural wonders such as Muir Woods as well as to the rich historic, cultural, aesthetic, and recreational attractions of the City by the Bay.

Ring Mountain Day School was established in 1976 by Gudrun Hoy, a leading educator who developed and implemented a progressive curriculum for early childhood and elementary education. At Ring Mountain, teachers are dedicated to enabling children to grow and mature in the creative, social, and emotional aspects of their young lives. The School actively seeks to achieve ethnic, racial, geographic, and socioeconomic diversity and to maintain gender balance. Ring Mountain's first Toddler Program was initiated in September of 2003, and its first class of eighth graders graduated in June of 2004.

Ring Mountain Day School Preschool is accredited by the National Association for the Education of Young Children; the Elementary/Middle School is currently in the process of accreditation by the California Association of Independent Schools.

In support of the school community, the Parent Association sponsors informational seminars, conducts the walkathon and other fund-raisers, and organizes numerous spirit-building activities.

THE CAMPUSES. The Mill Valley Campus, a former public school site leased from the Mill Valley Board of Education, is home to Kindergarten to Grade 8. Renovations to the existing building include a new science center, an expanded technology laboratory, library, darkroom, student publication center, a multipurpose room, an art studio with a low-fire kiln, and multimedia, science, and Spanish language labs. The facility is surrounded by grassy playing fields and will accommodate 155 elementary and middle school students. The campus also features a soccer field, basketball court, outdoor playground and play structure, and, in 2007, space for a community garden and courtyard amphitheater.

The Tiburon Campus accommodates the Toddler and Preschool Programs (ages 2–3) and Pre-Kindergarten (ages 4–5), offering classrooms, space for art, music, and movement, play areas, and, as its centerpiece, a children's learning garden.

THE FACULTY. Dr. Nancy Diamonti was appointed Head of School in 1999. She holds a B.A. degree from Caldwell College in New Jersey, an M.A. from the University of Wisconsin at Madison, and a Ph.D. in Child and Adolescent Psychology and Educational Leadership from Boston College. She has also completed doctoral course work in Curriculum and Instruction and Educational Policy Studies at the University of Wisconsin. Dr. Diamonti has more than 40 years of experience in the field of education, including 22 years as Principal/Head of School in private and public schools.

The 34 men and women on the Ring Mountain faculty hold undergraduate degrees or specialized certification as well as 12 advanced degrees. Among their representative colleges and universities are American Graduate School of International Management, Arizona State, Bank Street, Bowdoin, Brigham Young (Hawaii), Brooklyn College, California State, Chico State, Cornell, DePauw, Dominican, Gettysburg, Harvard, Lewis and Clark, Mills College, New College of California, North Park, Ohio State, Palm Beach Atlantic, St. Michael's, San Francisco State, Smith, Stanford, and the Universities of Arkansas, Birmingham (England), California (Berkeley, Irvine, Santa Barbara), Florida, Minnesota, Oregon, Toledo, and Western Ontario.

STUDENT BODY. In 2007–08, Ring Mountain Day School enrolled 220 children age 2 through Grade 8. They come from throughout the Bay Area and reflect the broad racial, ethnic, and cultural diversity of the region.

ACADEMIC PROGRAM. The school year begins the Tuesday after Labor Day and runs through the second week of June. Vacations are held at Thanksgiving and in December, February, and April, with days off for the observance of certain national and religious celebrations. Parent-teacher conferences are held in the fall and spring. The student-teacher ratio is 5:1 in the Two-Year-Old Program, 9:1 in Preschool, 10:1 in Kindergarten, and 12:1 in Grades 1–8. Student-to-student mentoring benefits those who need extra support in a specific area; specialized small-group learning centers provide a similar function. Before- and after-school care is available.

Ring Mountain Day School's progressive educational program is marked by structure and balance to provide each child with a strong foundation for future learning. The student-centered curriculum, from two-year-old Preschool through eighth-grade graduation, places equal emphasis on the sciences, humanities, and arts. Core subjects focus on reading and language arts, mathematics, science, Spanish, and social studies. Course work is designed to provide continuity and consistency as students progress from mastery of basic concepts in the early grades to more complex materials in the middle school.

Preschoolers' first experiences with learning revolve around play as a means of encouraging cognitive, social, and emotional growth. Students construct, design, build, choose, discuss, listen, question, experiment, and observe as they are introduced to central themes that expand as they move through the grades.

The elementary and middle schools extend the continuum of learning begun in Preschool. The language arts component focuses on reading, writing, and speaking, and children have many opportunities for self-expression, discussion, and the sharing of ideas. Students also read a wide range of age-appropriate fiction, nonfiction, and poetry as well as write daily in a variety of genres.

Math studies, including Algebra and Geometry in Grades 5–8, focus on the development of critical thinking, logic, and problem-solving skills and on the application of mathematical principles to everyday living.

In science, hands-on activities, lab experiments, and group and independent research provide lively demonstrations of key scientific processes in biology, physics, and physical and earth sciences. Environmental education is emphasized through activities such as composting, gardening, recycling, and caring for plant life.

The social studies curriculum makes use of children's experiences in their own families and communities as a means of understanding both the larger world around them and the people who make a difference in history.

Spanish language begins in Preschool and, by Kindergarten, is taught four or five times a week. The youngest children learn basic words and phrases through songs, games, and drama, while older students have more in-depth instruction in vocabulary, grammar, and conversation.

The use of technology is integrated into the teaching of core subjects beginning in Grade 1, while students in the upper grades use computers or laptops for Internet research, word processing, and data organization. The computer-student ratio is 1:2. Fifth- through eighth-grade students take part in the Just Think Foundation, a media literacy program that teaches them how to analyze media messages and become independent, critical thinkers.

In the middle school, students prepare for the Secondary School Admission Test as a core curricular component; they also attend workshops on such topics as the art of debate, conflict resolution, and appreciation for diversity.

Art, music, dance, drama, library skills, and physical education, taught by specialist instructors, enrich the program at all levels. Children from Kindergarten upward have the chance to take three classes a week in music, drama, and dance. At the conclusion of the classes, students participate in a dramatic presentation, sharing center stage with professional actors and musicians. Martin Charnin's *Annie* and a musical adaptation of William Goldman's *The Princess Bride* are representative productions.

Frequent field trips enliven the academic program for all students and extend the learning process beyond the classroom. Depending on the age, children take nature walks, attend Marin County Farm Day at the Civic Center, and enjoy week-long excursions to Washington, D.C., Mexico, and the Shakespeare conference in Ashland, Oregon.

Eighth graders from Ring Mountain were accepted to The Bay School, The Branson School, Hawaii Preparatory Academy, Marin Academy, Marin Catholic, The Marin School, Redwood High School, San Domenico School, San Francisco University High School, Sierra Lutheran High School (Nevada), and Tamalpais High.

In the summer, students in Preschool may enroll in a series of two-week specialty camps structured for fun and learning. Students entering Grade 8 may attend Phillips Exeter Academy for a five-week summer residential program, "Access Exeter."

STUDENT ACTIVITIES. Community service involves all Ring Mountain students in learning while helping others. They take part in Earth Day clean-up projects, support a local battered women's shelter, and help raise funds for worthy causes. Specific projects are determined by the wishes of the students and their teachers. Other activities include recycling and the "greening" of the campus.

Among the traditional events on the Ring Mountain calendar are Back to School Night, Open Houses, class Halloween parties, Walk-a-Thon, Book Fair, Holiday Sing, Spirit Week, the school play, the annual spring auction and dinner dance, the Step Up ceremony, and graduation.

ADMISSION AND COSTS. Ring Mountain Day School welcomes children from all racial, ethnic, religious, and socioeconomic backgrounds who have the interest and ability to succeed in its academic, artistic, athletic, and social programs. Admission is determined by the completed application, teacher recommendations, and previous school transcripts.

In 2007–08, monthly tuition in the Preschool ranges from $500 for two days to $1260 for five days. Tuition is $18,500 in Kindergarten through Grade 4, $19,000 in Grades 5–6, and $19,250 in Grades 7–8.

Head of School: Nancy Diamonti, Ph.D.
Preschool Director: Laura Di Stasi
Elementary/Middle School Director: Terry Bonn, Ed.D.
Director of Admissions: Mark Mabry
Director of Development: Suzanne Alpert
Business Manager: Rita Voss

Rolling Hills Preparatory School 1981

1 Rolling Hills Prep Way, San Pedro, CA 90732
Tel. 310-791-1101; Admissions Ext. 101; Fax 310-373-4931
Web Site www.rollinghillsprep.org

Rolling Hills Prep School provides an educational environment conducive to the development of disciplined minds, sound character, healthy bodies, and creative spirits. Enrolling 230 boys and girls in Grades 6–12, the School features small classes, proven teaching methods, and up-to-date technology to carry out its traditional college preparatory program. Among the activities are outdoor education, community service, clubs, and athletics. English as a Second Language and a recreational summer program are optional. Tuition: $19,200. Financial Aid: $733,000. Peter McCormack (York University, B.A. 1975; Exeter, P.G.C.E. 1976; Oxford, M.Sc. 1987) was appointed Head of School in 1993.

Sacramento Country Day School 1964

2636 Latham Drive, Sacramento, CA 95864
Tel. 916-481-8811; Fax 916-481-6016
Web Site www.saccds.org; E-mail info@saccds.org

Sacramento Country Day School is a coeducational, college preparatory school enrolling 540 students in Pre-Kindergarten–

Grade 12. "The Mission of Sacramento Country Day is to provide a traditional, college preparatory education to students from a variety of backgrounds who possess both strong academic potential and respect for others and to develop in them the qualities of self-confidence, creativity, integrity, and responsibility." The student-teacher ratio is 10:1. Fine arts, technology, and educational field trips enrich the curriculum at all levels. Extended-day care and summer programs are available. Tuition: $13,400–$16,300. Financial aid is offered. Lonna Bloedau is Director of Admission; Stephen T. Repsher (Union, B.A.; New York University, M.A.) is Headmaster. *Western Association.*

Sacred Heart Schools, Atherton 1898

150 Valparaiso Avenue, Atherton, CA 94027
Tel. 650-322-1866; Fax 650-326-2761
Web Site www.shschools.org; E-mail admission@shschools.org

These fully accredited, Roman Catholic, college preparatory day schools enroll 500 students in Grades 9–12 at Sacred Heart Preparatory High and 520 students in Preschool–Grade 8 at St. Joseph's School of the Sacred Heart. Located on a 62-acre campus, the Schools emphasize academic excellence, Christian values, and social awareness. Programs include required religious studies, challenging curricula, and competitive athletics as well as a wide range of cocurricular activities and summer camps. Sacred Heart Prep offers Advanced Placement in 20 subjects and exchange programs with Sacred Heart Schools worldwide. Tuition: $16,760–$26,885. Financial aid is available. Carl Dos Remedios (Grades 9–12) and Wendy Quattlebaum (Grades 1–8) are Directors of Admission; Richard A. Dioli is Director of Schools. *Western Association.*

Sage Hill School 2000

20402 Newport Coast Drive, Newport Coast, CA 92657
Tel. 949-219-0100; Admissions Ext. 1332; Fax 949-219-1399
Web Site www.sagehillschool.org; E-mail admission@sagehillschool.org

Parents and educators founded Sage Hill School to provide families in Orange County a choice in coeducational, independent, secondary day schools. Sage Hill currently enrolls 450 students in Grades 9–12. The challenging college preparatory curriculum includes Advanced Placement courses, Advanced Art Workshops, and service learning opportunities. Small classes ensure that each student receives individual attention and appreciation. More than 30 extracurricular activities include Model UN, Math Club, and Tutoring Club. Tuition: $23,750. Financial Aid: $974,000. Carol Inge Bernstein is Director of Admission; Judith Glickman, Ph.D., is Interim Head of School.

St. James' Episcopal School 1967

625 South St. Andrews Place, Los Angeles, CA 90005
Tel. 213-382-2315; Fax 213-382-2436
Web Site www.stjamesschool.net; E-mail admissions@stjamesschool.net

St. James' Episcopal School enrolls 300 girls and boys from diverse faiths and cultures in Kindergarten–Grade 6. The academic program is designed to provide a strong foundation for further education and daily life. Comprehensive reading and math programs form the basis of the core curriculum, complemented by science, music, art, physical education, religion, Spanish, computing, and library. Worship and religion are integral to the program. Children take part in school choir, bell choir, and athletics. An after-school program, including enrichment classes, study hall, and child care, is available. Tuition: $13,700. Financial aid is available. Stephen L. Bowers is Head of School. *Western Association.*

Saint Mark's School 1980

39 Trellis Drive, San Rafael, CA 94903
Tel. 415-472-8000; Admissions 415-472-8007; Fax 415-472-0722
Web Site www.saintmarksschool.org
E-mail bfinley@saintmarksschool.org

Saint Mark's is a nonsectarian day school enrolling 380 boys and girls in Kindergarten–Grade 8. It seeks to promote a love of learning in children of academic promise, to develop strong academic skills, and to promote character and self-confidence. Music, art, drama, technology, world languages, and physical education are required along with traditional subjects. Field trips, team sports, theater productions, the Headmaster's Reading Program, a national champion chess team, Computer Club, Science Fiction Club, and after-school enrichment classes are among the activities. Tuition: $18,758. Extras: $300–$1900. Financial Aid: $975,000. Barbara Finley is Director of Admissions; Damon H. Kerby (Kenyon, A.B. 1971; Stanford, M.A. 1999) was appointed Headmaster in 1987.

St. Matthew's Episcopal Day School 1953

16 Baldwin Avenue, San Mateo, CA 94401
Tel. 650-342-5436; Fax 650-342-4019
Web Site www.smeds.info; E-mail handalianl@smeds.info

St. Matthew's is a coeducational, independent, Episcopal school enrolling 230 students in Preschool–Grade 8. The School offers a challenging academic education and strives to help students become compassionate members of the community. The curriculum reflects an approach designed to enable children to understand the interconnectedness and interdependence of the disciplines they study. Students receive individual attention in an enriched, supportive environment that emphasizes the essential skills of reading, writing, mathematics, and critical thinking necessary for communication and problem solving. The program includes Spanish, state-of-the-art technology, music, drama, physical education, and after-school sports. Field study, community service, and student leadership are important elements of the school program. The average class size ranges from 15 to 22. St. Matthew's is fully accredited by the California Association of Independent Schools and the National Association of Episcopal Schools. Tuition: $8600–$19,425. Linda Handalian is Director of Admission; Mark McKee is Head of School.

St. Matthew's Parish School 1949

1031 Bienveneda Avenue, Pacific Palisades, CA 90272
Tel. 310-454-1350; Admission Ext. 150; Fax 310-573-7423
Web Site www.stmatthewsschool.com
E-mail lquiring@stmatthewsschool.com

Set near the ocean in a pastoral 33-acre campus, St. Matthew's is an Episcopal day school enrolling 325 boys and girls in Preschool–Grade 8. The School encourages each child's positive self-concept, sensitivity toward others, intellectual curiosity, and mastery of basic learning skills. In all grades, the curriculum includes laboratory science in two science centers and computer science in seven computer labs, plus art, music, drama, and foreign languages. A sports/performing arts complex houses the drama, physical education, and interscholastic athletic programs. A summer program is offered. Tuition: $11,610–$23,525. Financial Aid: $500,000. A. Lee Quiring is Director of Admission; Les W. Frost (University of California [San Francisco], D.Phar. 1968) is Headmaster.

St. Paul's Episcopal School 1975

116 Montecito Avenue, Oakland, CA 94610-4556
Tel. 510-285-9600; Admissions 510-285-9617; Fax 510-899-7297
Web Site www.spes.org; E-mail info@spes.org

St. Paul's Episcopal School offers a rigorous academic program that nurtures the whole child. Located in downtown Oakland near Lake Merritt, St. Paul's serves 360 boys and girls in Kindergarten through Grade 8; the middle school is in a renovated and expanded building that includes an all-new library. St. Paul's mission is twofold: the creation of future scholars and leaders and the inculcation of values of empathy, tolerance, and service to others. Children are encouraged to explore, to take risks, to solve problems, and to search out opportunities to indulge their loves of learning. The School's award-winning Service Learning Program, now in its 21st year, is a nationally recognized model of how to integrate community service into the academic program so that each serves as a complement to the other. Students and their families come from a wide variety of racial, ethnic, religious, and socioeconomic backgrounds, and the School prides itself in having one of the most comprehensive financial aid programs in the Bay Area. Tuition: $17,600–$19,000. Financial aid is available. Khadija Fredericks is Director of Admissions; Karan A. Merry is Head of School. *Western Association.*

Saklan Valley School 1978

1678 School Street, Moraga, CA 94556
Tel. 925-376-7900; Fax 925-376-1156
Web Site www.saklan.org; E-mail admissions@saklan.org

Saklan Valley, a day school enrolling 155 girls and boys in Preschool–Grade 8, is a learning community of students, teachers, and parents united to provide academic excellence and educate the whole child. Rigorous academics are combined with interdisciplinary and experiential learning opportunities. Saklan has a strong focus on community and the development of respect, responsibility, and integrity among its students, faculty, and families. All Saklan students and parents receive personal and individual attention in a nurturing environment. Tuition: $11,925–$16,650. Financial aid is available. Jonathan Martin (Harvard, B.A.; Starr King School for the Ministry, M.Div.; University of San Francisco School of Education, M.A.) is Head of School. *Western Association.*

San Francisco Friends School 2002

117 Diamond Street, San Francisco, CA 94114
Tel. 415-552-8500; Admissions Ext. 136; Fax 415-552-8501
Web Site www.sffriendsschool.org
E-mail admissions@sffriendsschool.org

San Francisco Friends School combines "outstanding academics" with Quaker values of simplicity, mutual respect, nonviolence, and service to others. Civic volunteers, educators, and business leaders founded this coeducational K–8 school, which currently serves 255 students in Kindergarten–Grade 5. The curriculum emphasizes mastery of foundational skills while fostering independence and critical thinking. Foreign language, the arts, and physical education are integrated into the core subjects of science and stewardship, language arts, math, and humanities. A welcoming, inclusive environment for families of all faiths and backgrounds is a touchstone of Quaker education. Tuition: $20,540. Financial aid is available. Catherine Hunter is Founding Head of School; Yvette Bonaparte is Director of Admissions.

San Francisco University High School 1973

3065 Jackson Street, San Francisco, CA 94115
Tel. 415-447-3100; Admission 415-447-3104; Fax 415-447-5801
Web Site www.sfuhs.org; E-mail karen.kindler@sfuhs.org

San Francisco University High School is a coeducational, college preparatory school enrolling 389 students in Grades 9–12. Created to serve young men and women of above-average intellectual ability, the School encourages in its students a love of learning so that graduates may enjoy full, meaningful lives and the community may benefit from the development of creative, capable leaders. The college preparatory curriculum emphasizes the acquisition of essential academic skills. At the same time, the School is committed to the students' total emotional, moral, physical, and intellectual growth. Tuition: $28,750. Financial Aid: $1,400,000. Karen N. Kindler is Director of Admission & Financial Aid; Dr. Michael Diamonti is Head of School. *Western Association.*

Santa Catalina School 1850

1500 Mark Thomas Drive, Monterey, CA 93940-5291
Tel. 831-655-9300; Admissions 831-655-9356; Fax 831-655-7535
Web Site www.santacatalina.org; E-mail admissions@santacatalina.org

SANTA CATALINA SCHOOL in Monterey, California, is dedicated to the education of young women. An independent, Catholic, college preparatory, boarding and day school encompassing Grades 9 through 12, Santa Catalina was founded in 1850 by Mother Mary Goemaere and established on its present site in 1950. The location of the School is convenient to the cultural and educational opportunities of the Monterey Peninsula and the San Francisco Bay Area.

The School's philosophy integrates spiritual values with life. Christian service is emphasized through community outreach, both locally and around the world. Santa Catalina seeks to encourage students to become lifelong learners, to strive for excellence, and to develop their fullest spiritual, personal, and academic potential.

Strong science, computer science, and mathematics programs enable students to grasp the technological principles shaping modern civilization. The Santa Catalina curriculum provides courses in the classical tradition of the liberal arts, enhanced by vigorous programs in the arts, athletics, and student leadership.

A nonprofit institution, Santa Catalina School is governed by a Board of Trustees. Through annual giving, the Board endeavors to implement the School's goal of maintaining academic excellence, supporting an outstanding faculty, and ensuring suitable growth. Santa Catalina is accredited by the Western Association of Schools and Colleges and is a member of the National Association of Independent Schools, California Association of Independent Schools, the National Coalition of Girls' Schools, and the Western Boarding Schools Association.

THE CAMPUS. The hacienda that served as the original school building is now encircled by classrooms, dormitories, and other facilities in a blend of traditional and contemporary Spanish-style architecture. The 36-acre campus, a mile from the Pacific Ocean, is graced by gardens, shaded walks, and California live oaks.

There are three classroom buildings, an athletic complex, a central library, a two-story science center, a performing arts center, and a music center and dance studio. The Sister Mary Kieran Memorial Library is computerized for access to libraries and their materials worldwide. It is open seven days a week and houses more than 35,000 volumes, three listening rooms, a lecture room, and art rooms. Art facilities include a general art studio, a ceramics studio, and a photography studio with developing equipment. The Science Center contains a lecture amphitheater, a projection room, an observation deck equipped with a Questar telescope, and chemistry, physics, and biology laboratories. In 2001, Santa Catalina was awarded a $100,000 grant from the Edward E. Ford Foundation, which provided several salt-water aquarium systems used in Marine Science, AP Environmental Science, and Biology courses. The Sister Carlotta Performing Arts Center houses a 500-seat theater with professional lighting and sound equipment. The Mary L. Johnson Music Center offers soundproof practice rooms and a dance studio with a spring-loaded floor. Completed in 2002, a 150-seat recital hall, a music library, music office, and additional practice rooms enhance the School's music center. The campus-wide computer network provides Internet access used both in and out of the classroom. The foreign language classrooms, library, and science laboratories are equipped with computer technology for student use.

The Bedford Athletic Complex incorporates a gymnasium, tennis courts, field areas, and track. The Salyer Aquatic Center (2002) houses a 25-yard-by-30-meter pool. Health-care facilities include a 16-bed health center and nurse's office. All resident students attend Mass on Sunday in the Rosary Chapel. The chapel is also available for optional weekday services and individual visits.

Residents live in three dormitories, all with wireless Internet access. Most share double rooms, though single rooms are also available. Each dormitory contains living accommodations for resident faculty families and single women.

THE FACULTY. In 2002, Sr. Claire Barone became Head of School after serving as Santa Catalina's Head of Upper School for 20 years. With a degree from the University of San Francisco, she succeeded long-standing head Sr. Carlotta O'Donnell.

Among the 40 teaching faculty, 32 hold advanced degrees. Representative colleges and universities of the faculty include Boston University, Brown, California State Polytechnic, Cornell, Goucher, Harvard, Massachusetts Institute of Technology, Monterey Institute of International Studies, Oberlin, San Francisco State, San Jose State, Santa Clara University, Scripps, Simmons, Stanford, Tufts, Wellesley, Yale, and the Universities of California, Chicago, Colorado, Illinois, Kansas, Miami, North Carolina, Pennsylvania, San Diego, and Wisconsin.

STUDENT BODY. In 2007–08, the Upper School enrolled 138 resident students and 146 day students. Resident students come from California, 16 other states, and eight countries and represent diverse cultures and religious traditions.

ACADEMIC PROGRAM. The school year, which extends from late August to early June, includes a ten-day Thanksgiving recess, a Christmas vacation, a Winter break, an Easter/spring vacation, and one three-day vacation weekend in the fall.

The basic Upper School curriculum includes four years each of English and religious studies; three to four years each of history, mathematics, foreign language, and science; and four years of an elective in the arts. Honors and Advanced Placement courses are available in all disciplines.

The student-faculty ratio is 7:1. Students are placed according to individual ability levels, with an average of 12–15 per class. Students and parents receive written reports as well as grades.

Freshmen, sophomores, and juniors have faculty advisors. These individuals assist and advise students in the development of their talents and potential. Seniors work with a team of advisors in an arrangement similar to the collegiate setting. Individual college counseling begins in the junior year with regular appointments with the Director of College Counseling. Annual visits to Santa Catalina by college representatives and the extensive, individual college counseling program serve as a significant aid in the application process.

Institutions in which graduates are currently enrolled include Bates, Boston College, Brown, Bucknell, Carnegie Mellon, Claremont McKenna, Connecticut College, Cornell, Denison, Dominican University, Franklin and Marshall, George Washington, Goucher, Harvard, Harvey Mudd, Loyola Marymount, Middlebury, Mount Holyoke, Northwestern, Princeton, Santa Clara, Scripps, Stanford, Swarthmore, Trinity University, Tulane, Vanderbilt, Washington University, Wellesley, Williams, Yale, and the Universities of California, Colorado, Michigan, North Carolina, Oregon, the Pacific, Pennsylvania, Seattle, Virginia, and Washington.

Santa Catalina's Summer Camp provides girls entering Grades 3–9 the option of two-, three-, or five-week sessions. The program features a tennis clinic, musical theater workshop, riding, golf, and marine biology, along with a full range of recreational and outdoor activities.

STUDENT ACTIVITIES. Students publish the newspaper, yearbook, and school literary magazine. Activity groups include the Student Alumnae Organization, the Student-Faculty Senate, a rock-climbing club, Amnesty International, Peace and Justice, Senior Prefects, Accents (dance), Schola, and ecco! (a cappella). Among community outreach opportunities, girls serve at convalescent homes, the Salvation Army Day Care Center, the Boys and Girls Club, Meals on Wheels, and Habitat for Humanity. Students participate in beach clean-ups, raise funds for food baskets, and sponsor underprivileged children. In addition, the entire Santa Catalina community devotes three days of service to local organizations.

Students audition for fall and spring musicals and a midwinter drama. Recent productions include *Music Man, The Miracle Worker, Thoroughly Modern Millie, Annie, Carnival,* and *Charley's Aunt*.

Concerts, dances, lectures, and movies are a regular part of campus life. Periodic assemblies in the Performing Arts Center feature appearances from guest speakers and artists through funding by the Edwin L. Wiegand Trust.

Santa Catalina's athletic teams compete interscholastically in cross-country, volleyball, tennis, golf, field hockey, water polo, basketball, soccer, track and field, lacrosse, softball, and swimming and diving. Through its membership in the United States Lawn Tennis Association, Santa Catalina hosts an annual Fall Invitational Tennis Tournament that draws players from throughout the state. Physical education options include horseback riding and dance, and studio classes are offered in ballet, jazz, and tap.

Weekend activities are planned by the Assistant Dean of Students (a faculty member), the Activities Coordinator (a Student Senate officer), and class advisors. Traditional annual events include the Halloween Party, Winter Formal, Christmas events, Spirit Day, Spring Dance, Ring Dinner, Junior/Senior Prom, Parents' Weekend, Father-Daughter Weekend, Yearbook Dinner, and Class Night.

Throughout the year, there are trips to the San Francisco Bay area for museum visits, plays, ballet, symphony orchestra, opera, sightseeing, and shopping. Other off-campus trips are taken to theme parks, ski resorts, and state and national parks for rafting, hiking, and camping. In addition, the Monterey Peninsula offers many recreational and cultural opportunities.

ADMISSION AND COSTS. Santa Catalina School admits students of any race, creed, color, and national or ethnic origin. Students are selected on the basis of scholastic achievement, strong personal qualifications, a personal interview, Secondary School Admission Test scores, and a written essay. The Upper School accepts students in Grades 9–11.

In 2007–08, resident tuition is $37,500; day tuition is $24,000. There is an additional fee of $600 for a bookstore deposit. Financial aid, awarded on the basis of need as indicated by the School and Student Service for Financial Aid, is extended to more than 30 percent of the student body. A Merit Scholarship is offered to an outstanding freshman for a one-time award of up to 20 percent of tuition. In addition, the School offers a low-interest loan program, and several tuition payment plans are available.

Head of School: Sr. Claire Barone
Head of Upper School: Dr. John Murphy
Assistant Head of Upper School: Sr. Christine Price
Director of Admission: Louise B. Douglas
Director of Financial Aid: Heather Willis Daly
Dean of Students: Kristi Solt
Director of Athletics: Mark Zalin

The Seven Hills School 1962

975 North San Carlos Drive, Walnut Creek, CA 94598
Tel. 925-933-0666; Admissions Ext. 4984; Fax 925-933-6271
Web Site www.sevenhillsschool.org
E-mail sgoldman@sevenhillsschool.org

Accredited by the Western Association of Schools and Colleges and the California Association of Independent Schools, Seven Hills is a coeducational day school enrolling 375 students in Preschool through Grade 8. The School strives to provide a developmentally appropriate, integrated curriculum in a small-class setting. The program emphasizes the acquisition and application of academic skills in the liberal and fine arts, supplemented by Spanish, French, music, art, physical education, computers, and electives. Summer day camp, Middle School intramural sports, clubs, an Extended Day Program, bus service, and hot lunch are available. Tuition: $7100–$18,250. Financial Aid: $525,000. Susanne Goldman is Director of Admissions; William H. Miller (University of Notre Dame, B.A. 1970; University of San Francisco, M.A. 1980) was appointed Headmaster in 1992. *Western Association.*

Sierra Canyon School 1977

Lower School (EK–8): 11052 Independence Avenue, Chatsworth, CA 91311
Upper School (9–12): 19809 Nordhoff Place, Chatsworth, CA 91311
Tel. 818-709-0134; Fax 818-709-8184
Web Site www.sierracanyonschool.org
E-mail jskrumbis@sierracanyonschool.org

Set on two campuses totaling 21 acres in the heart of the San Fernando Valley, Sierra Canyon School is a college preparatory, coeducational day school that seeks to provide students in EK–Grade 12 with an academically rigorous curriculum taught by highly trained teachers in their fields. Enrolling 700 Lower and Middle School students and 200 Upper School students, Sierra Canyon emphasizes mastery of strong skills in core academic subjects along with a varied arts and athletic program. In the Upper School, students receive their education from a challenging traditional curriculum, interdisciplinary programs, individual and collaborative learning, and small class sizes. A pioneering service learning program and international and

domestic academic travel are integrated into the curriculum. Before- and after-school care and summer programs are offered. Sierra Canyon offers a dynamic educational experience in a safe, stimulating, and nurturing environment. Tuition: $12,000–$23,000. Financial Aid: $1,200,000. Jim Skrumbis is Head of School; Sanje Ratnavale is Associate Head. *Western Association.*

Sinai Akiba Academy 1968

10400 Wilshire Boulevard, Los Angeles, CA 90024
Tel. 310-475-6401; Admissions Ext. 3251; Fax 310-234-9184
Web Site www.sinaiakiba.org; E-mail info@sinaiakiba.org

Sinai Akiba Academy, a Solomon Schechter Conservative Jewish coeducational day school, enrolls up to 605 children in Pre-Kindergarten–Grade 8. Drawing on its Jewish heritage, the school is committed to nurturing the curiosity of children, joy in the adventure of learning, and confidence in their abilities while developing disciplined study habits. In both general and Judaic studies, Sinai Akiba strives for academic excellence as it promotes a strong sense of both personal worth and Jewish identity. A challenging curriculum in core academics complements an innovative Judaic studies program, music, art, physical education, library, computers, and an after-school enrichment program. Tuition: $15,746–$17,108. Rabbi Laurence Scheindlin is Headmaster; Barbara Goodhill is Admissions Director.

Sonoma Academy 2001

50 Mark West Springs Road, Santa Rosa, CA 95403
Tel. 707-545-1770; Fax 707-636-2474
Web Site www.sonomaacademy.org; E-mail info@sonomaacademy.org

Founded by 12 community and business leaders, Sonoma Academy is a nondenominational, college preparatory day school enrolling 196 students in Grades 9–12. Its mission is to inspire, challenge, and nurture students, instilling a lifelong love of learning and motivating them to achieve their potential as scholars and citizens. The curriculum emphasizes the humanities, math-science, world languages, and the arts, with technology integrated in every discipline. Each student uses an iBook in the classroom and at home and is linked through SA's wireless network to the Internet and to all students and teachers at the school. Small classes and dedicated teachers facilitate lively discussion and individual participation in the educational process. School-wide meetings and conferences with faculty advisors take place on a weekly basis. The CONNECTIONS program enables students to travel and study abroad, while a January "intersession" provides in-depth immersion in a subject of special interest. Individualized college counseling begins in the sophomore year, and historically, all graduates go on to higher education. Tuition: $26,300. Financial aid is available. Mary Jo Dale is Director of Admission; Janet Durgin is Head of School.

Stuart Hall for Boys 1956

2222 Broadway, San Francisco, CA 94115
Tel. 415-563-2900; Admissions 415-292-3113; Fax 415-929-6928
Web Site www.sacredsf.org; E-mail thorp@sacredsf.org

An independent, Catholic day school enrolling 324 boys in Kindergarten–Grade 8, Stuart Hall for Boys, one of the Schools of the Sacred Heart, is part of a four-school complex including Stuart Hall High School, Convent Elementary School, and Convent High School. Stuart Hall seeks to prepare students for entrance into college preparatory high schools and to develop spiritual and social responsibility. Foreign languages, art, music, computer science, outdoor education, community service, and interscholastic sports are integral to the curriculum. A coeducational summer school program is also offered. Tuition: $20,200–$20,500. Financial aid is available. Pamela Thorp is Director of Admissions; Jaime Dominguez (Princeton, B.A.; Michigan State, M.A.Ed.Admin.) is Head. *Western Association.*

Stuart Hall High School 2000

1715 Octavia Street, San Francisco, CA 94109
Tel. 415-345-5812; Fax 415-931-9161
Web Site www.sacredsf.org

Stuart Hall High School is a boys' school and member of Schools of the Sacred Heart San Francisco. Located in the heart of the city, "The Hall" offers single-sex education in a coeducational environment because of its coordinate relationship with its sister school, Convent of the Sacred Heart, located only blocks away. Enrolling 170 students in Grades 9–12, Stuart Hall High emphasizes serious study, sportsmanship, artistic discovery, social responsibility, and faith development in a small, close-knit community. In addition to a rigorous core curriculum, the School offers Advanced Placement and Honor courses. Tuition: $27,800. Financial aid is available. Anthony Farrell is Admissions Director; Gordon Sharafinski is Head.

Town School for Boys 1939

2750 Jackson Street, San Francisco, CA 94115
Tel. 415-921-3747; Admission Ext. 125; Fax 415-921-2968
Web Site www.townschool.com; E-mail mckannay@townschool.com

Town School for Boys is an independent day school enrolling 400 students in Kindergarten–Grade 8. The academic program is complemented by a state-of-the-art science center, a laptop learning program in Grades 5–8, a PC lab, classroom computers, and a media theater. A wide range of activities includes outdoor education, intramural sports, music, drama, publications, student government, special-interest clubs, and a strong commitment to community service. Tuition: $19,600. Tuition Assistance: $845,000. Lynn McKannay is Director of Admission; W. Brewster Ely IV (Ithaca, B.A. 1970; Middlebury, M.A. 1975) was appointed Headmaster in 1989. *Western Association.*

Turning Point School 1970

8780 National Boulevard, Culver City, CA 90232
Tel. 310-841-2505; Admission Ext. 128; Fax 310-841-5420
Web Site www.turningpointschool.org
E-mail mwright@turningpointschool.org

Turning Point School enrolls 365 girls and boys from diverse backgrounds as day students in Primary (2 years, 10 months)–Level 8. In an intimate, focused learning environment, faculty seek to develop youngsters into responsible, well-balanced adults capable of succeeding in a challenging and changing world. The integrated curriculum is designed to nurture creative, emotional, and social skills as well as nurturing the intellectual and physical strengths needed to flourish and mature in the 21st century. Classroom instruction forms the basis of a Turning Point education, offering a series of learning experiences that foster the student's natural curiosity and rewards individual ingenuity. Reading, language arts, mathematics, and social sciences are at the heart of the program, enhanced by languages, drama, science, music, art, and athletics. After graduating from Turning Point, students typically enroll in independent college preparatory schools throughout the Greater Los Angeles area. Study tours and team sports are among the activities. A summer camp program is optional. Tuition: $18,100–$22,550. Maggi Wright is Director of Admissions; Deborah Richman is Head of School. *Western Association.*

The Urban School of San Francisco 1966

1563 Page Street, San Francisco, CA 94117
Tel. 415-626-2919; Fax 415-626-1125
Web Site www.urbanschool.org; E-mail info@urbanschool.org

The Urban School of San Francisco seeks to ignite a passion for learning. Urban's teachers challenge students with a highly acclaimed academic program that combines a college preparatory curriculum with community service, fieldwork, and internships. Urban students are prepared for higher education and beyond through a mastery of subject matter and academic skills. The most enduring aspect of an Urban education is the ability for students to become self-motivated, enthusiastic participants in their education. With 340 day boys and girls in Grades 9–12, Urban sponsors many championship athletic teams and provides numerous extracurricular opportunities, including an outdoor education program and wide range of student-led clubs. A 1:1 laptop school since 2000, Urban shares its teaching expertise and curriculum development through its summer Center for Innovative Teaching professional workshop series. Tuition: $28,000. Financial Aid: $1,550,000. Bobby Ramos is Director of Admissions; Mark Salkind (Yale, B.A. 1974) is Head of School. *Western Association.*

Viewpoint School 1961

23620 Mulholland Highway, Calabasas, CA 91302
Tel. 818-340-2901; Admission 818-591-6560; Fax 818-591-0834
Web Site www.viewpoint.org; E-mail info@viewpoint.org

Viewpoint School in Calabasas, California, is a coeducational, college preparatory day school enrolling students in Primary School (Kindergarten–Grade 2), Lower School (Grades 3–5), Middle School (Grades 6–8), and Upper School (Grades 9–12). The campus is located in the San Fernando Valley, about 25 miles from downtown Los Angeles.

The School was founded in 1961 by a group of parents to provide students with a strong college preparatory program in a nurturing and wholesome environment.

Viewpoint provides a traditional, liberal arts curriculum and fosters ethical values. Students learn to appreciate the unique contributions that each person adds to the School's diverse community. This blend allows students to experience a successful transition to college and to become responsible adults in today's world. Viewpoint is one of two schools in the United States to offer the prestigious Duke of Edinburgh's Young Americans Challenge International Award.

The Viewpoint Educational Foundation is a nonprofit corporation governed by a Board of Trustees. The School is accredited by the California Association of Independent Schools and the Western Association of Schools and Colleges and is a member of the National Association of Independent Schools and A Better Chance, among others.

THE CAMPUS. Viewpoint School is located on a 25-acre campus with scenic vistas, rolling hillsides, and stately heritage oak trees.

The Primary School features a regulation-size swimming pool, several outdoor basketball courts, and multiple playgrounds. Additional facilities include the Primary School Library, art and music studios, and science and computer laboratories.

The Lower and Middle Schools feature a regulation-size swimming pool, outdoor basketball courts, a weight-training facility, batting cages, the Rasmussen Family Pavilion for athletics and assemblies, the Prinn Library, and ECOLET, an outdoor natural science center. The combined libraries of all divisions contain 20,000 volumes and offer access to the Los Angeles County Library collection, the *Los Angeles Times* Network, and ProQuest magazine collection.

The Upper School has classrooms in the new Gates Academic Center, which also houses the state-of-the-art, 406-seat Carlson Family Theater. Additional facilities include science and computer laboratories and music and art studios. Many classrooms are equipped with laptop computer carts with wireless capabilities.

The School recently completed construction of a CIF regulation-size athletic field. The Ring Family Field is a full-size athletic facility for soccer, football, and other outdoor field sports. Featuring a state-of-the-art synthetic turf surface, the field is playable every day of the school year.

THE FACULTY. Dr. Robert J. Dworkoski, appointed Headmaster in 1986, is a graduate of George Washington University (B.A.), New York University (M.A.), and Columbia University (M.A., Ph.D., European History). Prior to his appointment, Dr. Dworkoski taught history at Brooklyn College and was Department Chairman of Social Studies at Woodmere Academy in New York. A Fulbright Scholar in Europe and the recipient of a grant from the National Endowment for the Humanities, Dr. Dworkoski has been active in the California Association of Independent Schools and the National Association of Independent Schools. He sits on the Advisory Committee of the Will Geer Theatricum Botanicum.

Viewpoint's faculty, selected for their academic expertise, enthusiasm, and energy, consists of 150 full-time and several part-time teachers, including administrators with teaching responsibilities. They hold 81 advanced degrees, including 6 doctorates, from colleges and universities in the United States and abroad. Faculty members have received awards from the National Endowment for the Humanities, the Council for Basic Education, the National Science Foundation, the Klingenstein Summer Institute, and the J. William Fulbright Foreign Scholarship Board.

STUDENT BODY. The 2007–08 enrollment totaled 1205 students, with 200 students in Kindergarten–Grade 2, 200 in Grades 3–5, 325 in Grades 6–8, and 480 in Grades 9–12. They represent diverse backgrounds; 15 different languages are spoken in students' homes.

ACADEMIC PROGRAM. The academic year, divided into semesters, begins in early September and extends to early June. All students follow a six-day rotation schedule that includes periods of varying length. The student-teacher ratio is 10:1 throughout the School. With classes of 10–22 students, teachers work closely with students both in and out of class to help them reach their full potential. The School sends grades to parents four times a year and provides four additional interim reports for parents of students with grades of C+ or less.

Graduation requirements in the Upper School include four years of English; three of mathematics; three of a single foreign language; three and one-half years of social studies; three years of science including two years of laboratory science; one year of the same art; the technology and human development course; eight seasons of physical education; and 45 hours of community service along with one Grade 9 community service project.

Viewpoint offers a traditional liberal arts core curriculum as well as honors and 28 Advanced Placement courses. In the spring of 2007, 172 students sat for 432 examinations in 28 subject areas, with 92 percent receiving scores of 3 or above, 74 percent receiving scores of 4 or 5, and 45 percent receiving scores of 5. Some of the elective courses are Contemporary Short Fiction, Modern Drama, Creative Writing, Modern Latin American History, Contemporary Politics, Economics, Humanities, Psychology, Computer Science, Neuroscience, Oceanography, Speech, Drama, Chorus, Instrumental Music, Music Composition, Theater Workshop, Studio Art, Ceramics, Sculpture, Photography, and Film and Video.

All of Viewpoint's graduates receive admission to four-year colleges. Graduates from the Class of 2007 achieved mean SAT I scores of 639 Critical Reading, 657 Writing, and 642 Mathematics. Graduates of Viewpoint are currently attending such colleges and universities as Barnard, Columbia, Dartmouth,

Duke, Georgetown, Johns Hopkins, Massachusetts Institute of Technology, Northwestern, Stanford, Tufts, Wesleyan, Yale, and the Universities of California, Kentucky, and Southern California.

Viewpoint conducts a summer program of academic, athletic, and recreational opportunities.

STUDENT ACTIVITIES. Students in the Primary and Lower Schools participate in a variety of community service, leadership, and public speaking activities. After-school classes are provided in chorus, dance, and martial arts, among others. The Middle and Upper Schools elect Student Councils, which work with the Assistant Divisional Directors on school service, student activities, charitable projects, and school spirit.

Students choose from activities including publications, speech and debate competitions, drama and musical productions, foreign language presentations, student clubs, honor societies, dances, domestic and international trips, and foreign exchange programs. In recent years, Viewpoint students participated in foreign exchanges with sister schools in China, England, France, Germany, Japan, Russia, and Spain. These exchanges have enabled students to make friends, learn about other cultures, and improve their skills in foreign languages.

All students are required to participate in physical education, and 80 percent of Middle and Upper School students are involved in team sports. Upper School students compete interscholastically in cross-country, basketball, volleyball, baseball, softball, football, golf, soccer, tennis, equestrian events, and swimming. In 2007, Viewpoint boys won CIF championships in tennis and volleyball.

Educational trips to the outdoors provide additional learning opportunities. Fourth graders travel to the Orange County Marine Institute to enhance their study of California's history. Astrocamp, an environmental science program in Idyllwild, is the site of a three-day retreat for fifth graders. In January, sixth graders travel for three days to a mountainous area in California to learn about the environment and to participate in winter activities. Seventh graders study marine biology on Catalina Island, and eighth graders spend four days working through personal initiatives and team-building activities in Santa Cruz. Ninth graders spend three days in the early fall at Camp Surf in San Diego.

Additional trips include the Voyage of Discovery, a nine-day tour of historic sites on the East Coast, and a tour of East Coast college campuses for 11th graders.

Family, alumni, and friends are invited for special events such as Parents' Nights, Great Pumpkin Day, Homecoming, Open House, holiday programs, student performances, art exhibits, athletic events, and sports banquets.

ADMISSION AND COSTS. Viewpoint School seeks highly motivated, academically able students with diverse backgrounds, interests, and talents. The School admits students based on a review of entrance examinations, recommendations, transcripts from previous schools, and an interview for applicants to Grades 6–12. International students must demonstrate a strong command of English. Families should submit an application and a fee of $100 by January 10 for Kindergarten–Grade 12 for entrance the following fall. The School will consider later applications if openings are available.

Tuition for 2007–08 is $19,100 for Kindergarten–Grade 2, $19,500 for Grades 3–5, $20,800 for Grades 6–8, and $22,150 for Grades 9–12. There is a one-time New Family Fee of $1250. Uniforms, purchased by the students, are required for Kindergarten–Grade 8. There is a dress code in the Upper School. Tuition payment and insurance plans are offered. Financial aid is available in cases of demonstrated need.

Associate Headmaster/Chief Operating Officer: Paul Rosenbaum
Head of Upper School: Deborah Monroe
Head of Middle School: Judy Preisler
Head of Lower School: Claudia Antoine
Head of Primary School: Cathy Adelman
Associate Head for Academic Affairs: Margaret Bowles
Director of Communications: Joyce Smith
Director of Admission: Laurel Baker Tew
Director of Development: Amy Maentz
Head of College Counseling: Amy Calvert
Chief Financial Officer: Chad Tew
Athletic Director: Patrick Moyal

Village Christian Schools 1949

8930 Village Avenue, La Tuna Canyon, CA 91352
Tel. 818-767-8382; Admissions Ext. 209
Web Site www.villagechristian.org
E-mail patricias@villagechristian.org

This Blue Ribbon School was founded to provide an education that embodies the highest standards of academic excellence and spiritual development within a nondenominational Christian environment. Enrolling 1700 students in Junior Kindergarten–Grade 12, the Elementary, Middle, and High School divisions each have their own principal and facilities on a collegiate-style, secluded, 110-acre campus that provides academic, athletic, and artistic resources at all grade levels. Honors and AP courses are offered in all major departments. Village Christian encourages students and their families to develop a relationship with Jesus and "teaches discipleship through example and personal application." Bible studies, chapel, and community outreach develop moral and ethical maturity. Activities include leadership groups, publications, theater productions, instrumental and vocal groups, and a full range of varsity sports. Within the past five years, CIF division championships have been won in football, volleyball, and softball. League championships have been won in all other major sports. Summer camps and programs for all grades are offered. Tuition: $8053. Financial aid is available. Patricia Smart is Admissions Director; Ronald G. Sipus, Ph.D., is Superintendent. *Western Association.*

Village School 1977

780 Swarthmore Avenue, Pacific Palisades, CA 90272-4355
Tel. 310-459-8411; Admission Exts. 102, 117; Fax 310-459-3285
Web Site www.village-school.org; E-mail bwilliams@village-school.com

VILLAGE SCHOOL in Pacific Palisades, California, is a coeducational elementary school enrolling children in Transitional Kindergarten–Grade 6. Set in a beautiful suburban community, Village School's location enables children to enjoy the quiet neighborhood setting of Pacific Palisades and the clean air of the Pacific coast. Students use the School's bus service, carpool with other families, or walk to school.

Village School was established in 1977 by a group of parents who sought to provide a nurturing, academically strong program within the atmosphere of a neighborhood school. Village has remained faithful to its founding mission, which aims to support and celebrate families who place a high priority on educational excellence. The broad, balanced curriculum is taught in small classes in which each child is assured of receiving individual attention, nurturing, and challenge.

A nonprofit, nondenominational institution, Village School is governed by a 13-member Board of Trustees. Jointly accredited by the Western Association of Colleges and Schools and the California Association of Independent Schools, Village School is a member of the National Association of Independent Schools. The Village School Parent Association provides essential support through fund-raising, volunteering in the classrooms, and planning special events.

THE CAMPUS. The main campus is designed in a Spanish style, constructed around a large court that includes a playground, covered lunch area, and a "village green." There are separate classrooms for a Transitional Kindergarten and three sections of Kindergarten. Grades 1 through 6 occupy two classrooms each. Additional facilities include a 6000-volume library, a technology center, a science lab, and two classrooms for Spanish language instruction.

The Center for the Arts and Athletics has a gymnasium adjacent to a grassy playing field. The space also becomes an auditorium with multiple stages and balconies. A performing arts and music room and recording, art, and dance studios round out the creative spaces of this facility.

THE FACULTY. Nora Malone was named Head of School in July 1999, after serving two years as Village School's Assistant Head/Director of Admissions. A 20-year teaching veteran, Ms. Malone received a Bachelor of Arts degree in English, a Master's degree in Educational Administration, and her California teaching credential from California State University at Northridge.

The full-time faculty includes 19 women and 6 men, all of whom have earned college degrees. Most have teaching credentials, and many hold advanced degrees from institutions across the country. Professional development is encouraged through workshops and in-service seminars. In addition to the teaching staff, 18 teaching assistants provide support in the classroom as well as outside supervision of the students. Faculty receive health insurance, a retirement plan, and additional benefits.

STUDENT BODY. In 2007–08, Village School enrolled 290 students, 144 girls and 146 boys, ages 4½ to 12 years. There are 12 students in Transitional Kindergarten, 41 in Kindergarten, 44 in Grade 1, 39 in Grade 2, 44 in Grade 3, 43 in Grade 4, 36 in Grade 5, and 31 in Grade 6. Students come from Brentwood, Los Angeles, Malibu, Pacific Palisades, Santa Monica, and other communities.

ACADEMIC PROGRAM. The school year, divided into trimesters, begins in early September and ends in early June, with vacation breaks at Thanksgiving, in the winter, and in the spring as well as the observance of several national holidays. Grades are issued three times a year, and parent-teacher conferences are held at the end of the first two trimesters. Classes, enrolling between 15 and 22 children, meet five days a week, from 8:00 A.M. to 3:00 P.M.

The Village School curriculum combines traditional and progressive approaches, with an emphasis on providing a strong foundation in basic reading, language, and mathematical skills. Spanish begins in Transitional Kindergarten and continues through all grade levels. Science, social studies, information technology, art, music, and physical education are also integral to the core program. At the same time, emphasis is given to the development of values, responsibility, and good citizenship as members of the school and larger community.

After graduation, a majority of sixth graders enter independent secondary schools such as Brentwood, Crossroads School for Arts and Sciences, Harvard-Westlake, Marlborough, and Windward.

STUDENT ACTIVITIES. Children have the opportunity to serve their school and develop leadership qualities through membership on the Student Council, which consists of representatives in Kindergarten–Grade 6. The Council meets on alternate weeks.

The after-school enrichment program features journalism, yearbook, music, arts and crafts, science, and other areas of interest. Students stage two musical performances a year and take part in community service projects such as beach cleanup.

Village Viking teams compete in a sports league with six other schools. Athletes in Grades 4–6 play on teams in flag football, soccer, basketball, and volleyball. Students also receive training in track and field events.

Special events are the all-school picnic, Open House, School fund-raisers, Grandparents Day/Science Fair, and Art Show. Students who graduated in June are invited to return to the School for a day in the fall.

ADMISSION AND COSTS. Village School welcomes students of average to superior ability from all racial, ethnic, and religious backgrounds who demonstrate the potential to thrive in the School's nurturing environment and to benefit from its academic and extracurricular programs. Most students enter in the Transitional Kindergarten or Kindergarten levels, although admission is offered in any grade where vacancies exist. Students are accepted based on a school visit, recommendations, and the previous school record, as applicable. Application should be made a year in advance of the desired enrollment date. The deadline for submission of applications is December 31 for all grades. Occasionally, midyear enrollment is possible. The nonrefundable application fee is $125.

In 2007–08, the tuition is $19,800, plus a one-time New Student Fee of $1500. Financial aid is awarded on the basis of need. A tuition payment plan is available.

Assistant Head of School/Director of Admissions: Barbara Ruth-Williams
Director of Finance & Operations: RoseAnn Zarasua
Director of Advancement: Sue Slotnick

The Walden School 1970

74 South San Gabriel Boulevard, Pasadena, CA 91107
Tel. 626-792-6166; Fax 626-792-1335
Web Site www.waldenschool.net
E-mail admissions@waldenschool.net

Walden School, accredited by the California Association of Independent Schools and the Western Association of Colleges and Schools, enrolls 250 boys and girls as day students in Pre-Kindergarten through Grade 6. Walden teaches children to think critically, to discover the interrelatedness of what they learn, and to develop the skills of traditional scholarship. The developmentally appropriate curriculum encourages responsibility, initiative, child-led inquiry, ethical behavior, and personal excellence. Before- and after-school child-care is offered. Tuition: $12,525; New Student Fee: $500. Financial aid is available. Christena Barnes is Assistant Director/Admission Director; Matt Allio is Director. *Western Association.*

The Wesley School 1999

4832 Tujunga Avenue, North Hollywood, CA 91601
Tel. 818-508-4542; Admission 818-508-4717; Fax 818-508-4570
Web Site www.wesleyschool.org; E-mail vdenove@wesleyschool.org

The Wesley School, founded by dedicated parents and faculty as a successor to St. Michael and All Angels School, enrolls 199 day students from diverse backgrounds in Kindergarten–Grade 8. To enable children to reach their full personal and intellectual potential, Wesley offers challenging course work, athletics, and cultural studies. Language arts, math, science, and social studies form the core curriculum, enriched by the arts, foreign language, and technology. A nondenominational chapel program and service learning develop character and social responsibility, while study-related field trips reinforce classroom lessons. Drama, speech, and Mock Trial are among the activities. Wesley holds membership in the National Association of Independent Schools and the California Association of Independent Schools. Tuition: $15,475–$16,675. Financial Aid: $300,000. Verena Denove is Director of Admission; Ruth Huyler Glass is Head of School. *Western Association.*

Westridge School 1913

324 Madeline Drive, Pasadena, CA 91105
Tel. 626-799-1153; Fax 626-799-9236
Web Site www.westridge.org; E-mail hhopper@westridge.org

Established in 1913, Westridge is a college preparatory day school enrolling 500 girls in Grades 4–12. Designed to promote independence and self-reliance in a cooperative and interdependent community, the School's rigorous academic program is enhanced by offerings in art, music, drama, and computer science. Extracurricular activities include clubs, sports, and student government. There is a community service requirement for all Upper School students. Tuition: $21,000–$23,600. Financial Aid: $1,700,000. Helen V. Hopper is Admissions Director; Fran Norris Scoble (Baylor University, B.A.; Vanderbilt University, M.A.) was appointed Head of School in 1990. *Western Association.*

Westside Neighborhood School 1980

5401 Beethoven Street, Los Angeles, CA 90066
Tel. 310-574-8650; Fax 310-574-8657
Web Site www.wnsk8.com; E-mail admissions@wnsk8.com

Parents and interested citizens established Westside Neighborhood School to provide quality education in a safe, respectful, and stimulating environment. From its initial enrollment of 56 students, the School has grown to serve 315 boys and girls from diverse racial, cultural, and economic backgrounds as day students in Pre-Kindergarten–Grade 8. The challenging preparatory curriculum, which is accredited by the California Association of Independent Schools, is designed to develop each student's intellectual, social, emotional, and physical potential. A strong foundation in reading, writing, and math is at the core of the program, integrated with social studies, science, Spanish, visual and performing arts, music, and physical education. Electives may include outdoor adventure, film making, robotics, and acting. Computer technology is used as a learning and research tool across the disciplines, while field trips to destinations in the Greater Los Angeles area enhance classroom instruction. Among the activities is an elected student council with representatives from Grades 2 through 8. Students also take part in after-school sports and an optional summer program. Tuition: $14,800–$15,600. Robin Sills is Director of Admissions; Brenda Parker was appointed Head of School in 1995.

Wildwood School 1971

Elementary Campus (Kindergarten–Grade 5): 12201 Washington Place, Los Angeles, CA 90066
Tel. 310-397-3134; Fax 310-397-5134
Secondary Campus (Grades 6–12): 11811 Olympic Boulevard, Los Angeles, CA 90064
Tel. 310-478-7189; Fax 310-478-6875
Web Site www.wildwood.org; E-mail admission@wildwood.org

Enrolling 709 day boys and girls in Kindergarten–Grade 12, Wildwood provides a strong academic program in a noncompetitive environment where students learn from each other as well as their teachers. The Wildwood experience develops an appreciation of individual and group differences and competency to lead in an ever-changing world. The elementary program features small, multiage classes, while the college preparatory program includes a learner-centered curriculum, advisory program, and internships. Students take part in drama productions, a literary magazine, jazz and rock bands, and athletics. After-school enrichment is also offered. Tuition: $20,710–$26,135. Financial Aid: $1,504,000. Lisa Glassman is Director of Admission; Landis Green is Head of School. *Western Association.*

Windrush School 1976

1800 Elm Street, El Cerrito, CA 94530
Tel. 510-970-7580; Admission Ext. 203; Fax 510-215-2326
Web Site www.windrush.org; E-mail garmenta@windrush.org

Windrush enrolls 250 students from diverse backgrounds in Kindergarten–Grade 8 on a 4-acre campus in the San Francisco/East Bay area. The progressive curriculum focuses on the skills students will need to thrive in the fast-paced global society of the 21st century. An emphasis on learning by doing engages students, teaching them to work together to solve real-world problems. Windrush teachers honor the integrity of childhood by encouraging the range of talents and interests that children bring to the classroom. Windrush students respect one another and take pleasure in shared accomplishments. They become lifelong learners who have the academic skills and the emotional resilience to approach the future with optimism, to embrace challenge, and to take joy in finding creative solutions to intriguing questions. Spanish, art, and physical education are taught in all grades. Computer, music, drama, and service learning also enrich the curriculum. Tuition: $15,600–$17,900. Financial aid, extended care, and a summer program are available. Gilbert Juan Armenta is Admissions Director; Ilana Kaufman is Head of School. *Western Association.*

Windward School 1971

11350 Palms Boulevard, Los Angeles, CA 90066
Tel. 310-391-7127; Fax 310-397-5655
Web Site www.windwardschool.org

WINDWARD SCHOOL in Los Angeles, California, is a college preparatory day school enrolling boys and girls in Grades 7 through 12. The School is named for one of its founders, Shirley Windward, a well-known writer and educator who has been a teacher, counselor, and board member through three decades. Its strengths are indicated by the motto at its entrance: responsible, caring, ethical, well informed, prepared.

Windward moved to its present location in 1982. The School aims to challenge each student to achieve academic excellence within a nurturing environment. The School offers a rigorous curriculum with inviting options and sponsors exchange programs with sister schools in France, Japan, and Latin America. Community service involves all students in projects on and off campus.

A nonprofit institution governed by a Board of 20 Trustees, Windward School is accredited by the Western Association of Schools and Colleges and holds membership in the National Association of Independent Schools, the California Association of Independent Schools, the Independent School Alliance for Minority Affairs, the Educational Records Bureau, and other professional organizations.

THE CAMPUS. The 9-acre campus offers a parklike setting in two sections linked by the Leichtman-Levine Bridge. In addition to traditional classroom space, an innovative Classroom Building provides ten state-of-the-art rooms with ample natural light, high-speed Internet connections, and advanced educational technology. Currently under construction are a new library/learning center with performing arts studios and broadcast production center, and a science/math center. The Irene Kleinberg Theater for Performing Arts includes separate dance and choral rehearsal halls. A Fine Arts Center houses art and sculpture classrooms as well as a multimedia lab for photography and film.

Computers play an important role in academics and other school activities, and networks extend throughout the campus. Laptops are used in many subject areas.

Playing fields for practice and interscholastic competition are located on campus, while the Lewis Jackson Memorial Sports Center houses basketball and volleyball courts, a weight training facility, meeting space, and a trophy room.

THE FACULTY. Thomas W. Gilder, a graduate of the University of California at Santa Barbara (B.A., Political Science) and Pepperdine University (M.S., Educational Administration), was appointed Headmaster in 1987. He had joined the faculty in

1981 as a teacher and Assistant Head of the School. Earlier, Mr. Gilder had served as West Coast coordinator of Johns Hopkins University's CTY (Center for the Advancement of Academically Talented Youth) program.

The teaching faculty is comprised of 65 men and women, including administrators who teach. All have baccalaureate degrees, and 40 have advanced degrees, including ten doctorates. They are graduates of such institutions as Amherst, Boston University, Brigham Young, Brown, California State University, Claremont Graduate School, Eastman School of Music, Loyola Marymount, Michigan State, Ohio State, Pepperdine, San Francisco Art Institute, Smith, Southwestern University School of Law, Stanford, Tufts, Union, West Virginia, Yale, and the Universities of California (Los Angeles, Santa Barbara), Illinois, Notre Dame, Southern California, Washington, and Wisconsin.

STUDENT BODY. In 2006–07, Windward School enrolled 475 students in Grades 7–12. The School actively seeks to maintain socioeconomic diversity in its student body and maintains sufficient financial aid programs to support it.

ACADEMIC PROGRAM. The academic year, divided into trimesters, begins in early September and extends to mid-June. The School observes several national holidays and schedules two-week winter and spring vacations. Classes meet five days a week beginning at 8:00 A.M. and extending through seven 55-minute periods to 3:00 P.M. A 20-minute nutrition break and a 50-minute lunch period are included in the schedule. Grades are issued three times a year.

In the Middle School (Grades 7–8), students have a six-course workload. The School seeks to develop students' critical and creative thinking skills, strong work habits, willingness to question and take risks, and genuine love of learning. The fine and performing arts, physical education, and athletics complement the core curriculum.

Students in the Upper School carry a minimum course load of six. This may be altered with the approval of a class dean in Grades 11 and 12, but, generally, students are urged to take six or seven courses each term. To graduate from the Upper School, students must complete four years of English; Level III in one foreign language or Level II in each of two languages; four years of history or social science; three of mathematics; three of science, including one laboratory science; two of fine arts; and two of physical education. They are also required to finish two 20-hour community service projects before graduation. A feature of the senior year is a one-week trip, just before graduation, at Windward's expense.

Among the courses offered are American Voices, World Literature; Latin, French 1–5, Spanish 1–5, Japanese 1–5; American History 1–2, World History 1–2, Government, Music History, History of Religions, The Search for Meaning; Algebra, Geometry, Algebra 2/Trigonometry, Algebra 3/Statistics, Pre-Calculus, Calculus; Principles of Science, Biology, Chemistry, Physics, Conservation Biology, Environmental Science; Theater 1–3, Technical Theater 1–3, Play Production, Dance 1–3, Jazz Ensemble, Advanced Instrumental Ensemble, Chorus, Madrigal Singers, Music Theory and Composition, Studio Art 1–3, Computer and Graphic Art, Film and Video 1–2, and Photography 1–3. Honors sections are offered in most areas, and Advanced Placement courses are available in all disciplines.

Windward places the utmost importance upon each senior's having options for higher education. Increasingly drawn toward the top colleges in the nation, students in the last several classes chose to attend such diverse institutions as Brown, Carleton, Colby, Columbia, Emory, Harvard, Kenyon, Princeton, Rhode Island School of Design, Rice, Stanford, Vassar, Washington University (St. Louis), Yale, and the Universities of California (Berkeley) and Pennsylvania. College counseling begins in earnest in the fall of Grade 11, when the college counseling staff meets with students and families to map out strategies and provide advice for Subject Tests. Students are prepared for interviews with college representatives, more than 100 of whom visit the School. The School offers close guidance in the application processes, essay writing, and the developmental challenges of separation from family, friends, and Windward. During the junior year, college counselors also lead a week-long trip to visit colleges and universities on both coasts.

STUDENT ACTIVITIES. Sixteen students, chosen from nominees proposed by classmates, faculty, and members of the administration, are appointed as Prefects. They are selected on the basis of community respect, personal integrity, and leadership qualities and serve as liaisons between their peers, teachers, and administrators and organize many activities.

Community service projects, undertaken by individuals or groups, involve students in activities off campus. Middle School students engage in group and grade-level projects, assisting in a Head Start program or Heal the Bay, which involves keeping the environment clean. Grade 9 volunteers distribute food for the needy and hold oral history interviews with the elderly. Upper School students work with a variety of agencies, choosing those projects in which they can be most effective.

Extracurricular activities are recognized in the weekly schedule through periods set aside on Tuesday and Thursday afternoons. Students use these times to participate in extra arts or club programs including the yearbook, newspaper, and literary magazine and such interests as chess, debate, robotics, cooking, and language clubs.

Varsity and junior varsity competition against other schools in the region are offered in tackle football, lacrosse, baseball, softball, cross-country, basketball, soccer, tennis, golf, and volleyball. Middle School students compete in flag football, baseball, cross-country, lacrosse, softball, basketball, soccer, volleyball, and tennis.

Students plan a variety of activities throughout the year. Among these are the Junior/Senior Prom, ski trips, spirit days, and other community-building activities. Parents and grandparents participate in campus events, contributing to the sense of community. Parent education courses bring guest speakers and counselors to campus to discuss issues specific to each grade level.

ADMISSION AND COSTS. Windward School seeks to admit able students of diverse economic, social, ethnic, and racial origins who can make positive contributions to the community. Most students enter in Grades 7 or 9, although some vacancies may occur in Grades 8 and 10. Applicants must submit the results of the Independent School Entrance Examination (ISEE) and recommendations from the previous school; a personal interview with a Windward admissions officer is also required.

Tuition for 2007–08 is $28,081. Financial aid is awarded to about 12 percent of the student body on the basis of need.

Director of the Upper School: Art Nagle
Director of the Middle School: Eric Mandel
Directors of Counseling: David G. Unger, Ph.D. & Tammy Clem
Director of Admission: Sharon Pearline
Directors of College Counseling: Molly Ryan & Nikki Danos

Woodside Priory School 1957

302 Portola Road, Portola Valley, CA 94028
Tel. 650-851-8223; Fax 650-851-2839
Web Site www.woodsidepriory.com
E-mail azappelli@woodsidepriory.com

Seven Hungarian monks of the Benedictine order founded Woodside Priory School to provide Catholic education for the San Francisco Bay Area. Today, as California's only Benedictine college preparatory school, Woodside Priory enrolls approximately 350 day students in Grades 6–12 and 50 boarders from the U.S. and 21 other nations in Grade 9 upward. Christian values and Catholic tradition guide the conduct of daily life at the Priory, which welcomes young men and women from many faiths and cultures. The college preparatory curriculum features small classes, a 9:1 student-teacher ratio, diverse electives, honors courses, and Advanced Placement in 18 subjects. The 60-acre wooded campus is the setting for numerous activities including community service, academic honor societies, student government, art, vocal and instrumental music, drama, publications, and athletic teams. All seniors go to college; recent graduates are attending Brown, California Institute of Technology, Duke, Harvard, New York University, Santa Clara University, Tufts, the U.S. Naval Academy, and the University of California, among others. Boarding Fees: $38,950; Day Fees: $28,050. Financial Aid: $1,250,000. Al Zappelli is Director of Admissions; Timothy J. Molak is Headmaster. *Western Association.*

COLORADO

Alexander Dawson School 1970

10455 Dawson Drive, Lafayette, CO 80026
Tel. 303-665-6679; Fax 303-381-0415
Web Site www.dawsonschool.org; E-mail jmitchell@dawsonschool.org

Dawson, a coeducational college preparatory day school enrolling 420 students in Kindergarten–Grade 12, is accredited by the National Association of Independent Schools and the Association of Colorado Independent Schools. With small classes, committed teachers, and high standards, Dawson aims to develop potential, build character, and prepare students for robust, intellectual, physical, and ethical lives. A traditional program includes Honors and Advanced Placement courses, 15 sports, theater, outdoor education, and 15 arts electives. Dawson's average SAT scores are the highest in the area, and the graduating Class of 2007 earned nearly $2,000,000 in scholarships. Tuition: $16,950. Financial Aid: $600,000. James Irwin Mitchell is Director of Admissions; Brian Johnson is Headmaster. *North Central Association.*

Aspen Country Day School 1969

3 Music School Road, Aspen, CO 81611
Tel. 970-925-1909; Fax 970-925-7074
Web Site www.aspencountryday.org
E-mail admissions@aspencountryday.org

Aspen Country Day School is a coeducational preparatory school enrolling 200 students in Pre-Kindergarten–Grade 8. The School seeks to foster a culture of learning by which each child reaches his or her highest potential. In a setting of natural beauty, it offers a rigorous curriculum and individualized education while promoting personal growth and responsible citizenship. The traditional academic program is supplemented by Outdoor Education and arts enrichment programs. Tuition: $5250–$19,700. Financial Aid: $500,000. Carolyn Hines is Admission Director; John H. Suitor is Headmaster.

Colorado Academy 1906

3800 South Pierce Street, Denver, CO 80235
Tel. 303-986-1501; Admissions 303-914-2513; Fax 303-914-2589
Web Site www.coloradoacademy.org
E-mail info@coloradoacademy.org

Colorado Academy is a coeducational day school enrolling 900 students in Pre-Kindergarten–Grade 12. Located on a 95-acre campus in southwest Denver, the Academy provides a 9:1 student-faculty ratio and a program emphasizing a well-rounded college preparatory program. Each division (Lower, Middle, and Upper) has its own principal, faculty, and facility. Fine arts and athletics are offered at all levels. Publications, sports, drama, community service, and clubs are among the activities. A summer recreational camp with academic enrichment, arts, and sports is available. Tuition: $11,150–$18,100. Financial Aid: $1,750,000. Catherine Laskey is Director of Admission; Christopher Babbs (Stanford, B.A.; University of Colorado, M.A.) is Headmaster.

The Colorado Springs School 1962

21 Broadmoor Avenue, Colorado Springs, CO 80906
Tel. 719-475-9747; Fax 719-475-9864
Web Site www.css.org; E-mail esckolnik@css.org

This coeducational day school provides a solid college preparatory program for 450 students in Preschool–Grade 12. Liberal arts and science courses are enhanced in and out of the classroom by an experienced-based curriculum that accelerates and cements academic understanding. Students in Grade 8 participate in Walkabout and practice adult responsibilities and decision-making by organizing, solving problems, and providing for themselves in a small group for two weeks under the supervision of a facilitator. High school students participate in Experience Centered Seminars, interdisciplinary studies that involve fieldwork or community service locally, nationally, or globally. The School's dedicated teachers hold high expectations for their students, providing challenges and encouragement as needed while recognizing each young person as a unique individual. College counseling is personalized, preparing students for colleges and universities nationwide. Foreign language begins in Preschool. Extracurricular activities available include student government, music, drama, clubs, community service, and sports. Tuition: $3900–$15,510. Eve Sckolnik is Director of Admission; Kevin Reel (Stanford, B.A., M.S.) is Head of School.

Crested Butte Academy 1993

P.O. Box 1180, Crested Butte, CO 81224
Tel. 970-349-1805; Fax 970-349-0997
Web Site www.crestedbutteacademy.org; E-mail info@cbacademy.org

Set in the Rockies amid 2,000,000 acres of national wilderness preserve, Crested Butte Academy combines rigorous college preparation with a training program in snowboarding, alpine racing, distance running and freeride skiing. Enrolling 65 boarding and day boys and girls in Grades 6–Postgraduate, the Academy is dedicated to small classes, close cooperation among faculty, staff, and students in all areas of school life, and a strong relationship with its mountain community. A rigorous core curriculum features programs in leadership and ethics, electives in arts and humanities, independent studies, a full AP program, creative writing, digital photography, film production, and graphic design. The school offers world-class coaching in mountain sports and a comprehensive outdoor experience. Coaches and trainers provide instruction, skill development, and insight into snow sports and running as they prepare athletes for regional, national, and world competitions. The school's goal is to graduate students who are prepared to pursue higher education and athletic interests, to lead fulfilling lives, and to make positive contributions to their communities. Boarding Tuition: $39,000–$40,000; Day Tuition: $20,000–$25,000. Graham D. Frey is Head of School.

Fountain Valley School of Colorado 1930

6155 Fountain Valley School Road, Colorado Springs, CO 80911
Tel. 719-390-7035; Admission 719-391-5251; Fax 719-390-7762
Web Site www.fvs.edu; E-mail admission@fvs.edu

Dedicated faculty, rigorous college preparation, commitment to high intellectual and personal standards, and an 1100-acre campus define learning at Fountain Valley. The curriculum includes Advanced Placement and honors courses in all subjects, preparing students for selective colleges and universities. The arts, athletics, outdoor education, and horseback riding are hallmarks of the curriculum. New and renovated residence halls, campus-wide technology, and state-of-the-art science, art, and campus

centers are among the resources. The School enrolls 250 students from 11 nations and 23 states in Grades 9–12. Boarding Tuition: $35,950; Day Tuition: $19,500. Need-based and merit scholarships are available. Randy Roach is Director of Admission and Financial Aid; Craig W. Larimer, Jr., '69, is Headmaster.

Graland Country Day School 1927

30 Birch Street, Denver, CO 80220
Tel. 303-399-0390; Admission 303-399-8361; Fax 303-336-3762
Web Site www.graland.org; E-mail mperez@graland.org

Graland Country Day School, set on a 7-acre hilltop campus, was founded by interested parents and teachers to provide a strong foundation in academics, the arts, and athletics along with good character and high morals. Graland seeks to inspire creativity, confidence, knowledge, and respect among students, families, faculty, and administration. The curriculum accommodates 635 boys and girls from diverse backgrounds in Kindergarten–Grade 9. The 70 faculty members, 60 percent of whom hold advanced degrees, are committed to the teaching philosophy of educator John Dewey. Small classes enrolling an average of 17 and an 8:1 student-teacher ratio ensure that every student has the opportunity to be heard and to take an active role in the learning process. French and Spanish begin in Grade 4; Latin is introduced in Grade 5. Beginning in seventh grade, participation in a team sport is required. The comprehensive program, centered on English, language arts, math, social studies, and science, is enriched by art, technology, drama, life skills, music, service learning, and athletics. Tuition (including all nonoptional fees): $15,900–$17,600. Financial Aid: $1,000,000+. Dr. Carolyn Craig is Director of Admission and Financial Aid; Bill Waskowitz is Head of School.

The Lowell Whiteman School 1957

42605 County Road 36, Steamboat Springs, CO 80487
Tel. 970-879-1350; Admissions Ext. 15; Fax 970-879-0506
Web Site www.lws.edu; E-mail admissions@lws.edu

The Lowell Whiteman School, located in the heart of the Rocky Mountains, serves boarding and day students in Grades 9 through 12. Balancing a challenging traditional liberal arts curriculum with opportunities beyond the classroom, the School fosters students' personal and academic growth. With an average class size of 8 students, personal relationships between students and faculty are the foundation of the college preparatory education. Of the 105-member student body, 60 percent participate in a 4-week foreign travel curriculum at one of five unique destinations. The 2008 destinations were Vietnam/Cambodia, Peru, South Africa, Kamchatka in eastern Russia, and Bolivia. Forty percent of the student body skis or rides competitively in partnership with the award-winning Steamboat Springs Winter

Sports Club. Lowell Whiteman has graduated over a dozen U.S. Olympians. All students participate in an experiential outdoor program with offerings in kayaking, rock and ice climbing, backpacking, mountain biking, canoeing, camping, and skiing and riding. Boarding Tuition: $31,265; Day Tuition: $16,850. Financial aid is available. Jared Olson is Director of Admissions; Walt Daub is Headmaster.

St. Anne's Episcopal School 1950

2701 South York Street, Denver, CO 80210-6098
Tel. 303-756-9481; Fax 303-756-5512
Web Site www.st-annes.org; E-mail rkelly@st-annes.org

St. Anne's seeks to guide children toward personal development and fosters social responsibility and involvement. The School instills a genuine love of learning through a broad, challenging academic program in a supportive, nurturing environment. Committed to Judeo-Christian values, St. Anne's is a family school that embraces students of varied talents, abilities, and backgrounds. The 421 students in Preschool–Grade 8 are taught language arts, literature, math, computer, science, fine arts, and foreign language at all levels. Summer programs and extended day are available. Tuition: $7892–$14,030. Financial Aid: $809,000. Rose Kelly is Director of Admission; Alan Smiley

(Middlebury College, B.A. 1987; University of Virginia, M.Ed. 1988) was appointed Head of School in 2006.

Telluride Mountain School 1998

200 San Miguel River Drive, Telluride, CO 81435-8924
Tel. 970-728-1969; Fax 970-369-4412
Web Site www.telluridemtnschool.org
E-mail info@telluridemtnschool.org

Telluride Mountain School, accredited by the Association of Colorado Independent Schools and a member of the National Association of Independent Schools, was founded to provide a challenging academic program that combines college preparation with outdoor education and community service. From an initial enrollment of 6, the School today serves over 100 day boys and girls in Preschool to Grade 12. A newly renovated 14,000-square-foot building (2006) houses all grades. The values-based curriculum develops well-rounded young citizens of their global society. The Montessori preschool phases into a more traditional approach for the upper grades. The core curriculum centers on reading/writing, language arts, math, science, and social studies, with technology across the disciplines. Spanish, music, visual and dramatic arts, and physical education are also emphasized. The Winter Sports Program includes instruction for all ability levels, from recreational skier/snowboarders to aspiring Olympic competitors. Experiential learning trips are conducted locally, regionally, nationally, and internationally. Tuition: $4650–$17,775. Financial aid is available. Karen Walker is Admissions Director; Ernie Patterson is Head of School.

CONNECTICUT

Academy of Our Lady of Mercy, Lauralton Hall 1905

200 High Street, Milford, CT 06460
Tel. 203-877-2786; Admissions Ext. 125; Fax 203-876-9760
Web Site www.lauraltonhall.org
E-mail kshine@lauraltonhall.org

Connecticut's oldest Catholic college preparatory school for young women, known familiarly as Lauralton Hall, enrolls more than 400 students in Grades 9–12. Sponsored by the Sisters of Mercy, the school offers a rigorous, values-centered liberal arts curriculum designed to nurture the mind, heart, and spirit within a community of faith. Advanced Placement and honors courses are available, and religious studies and community service are required. Girls may participate in numerous activities, including a mentoring program, academic honor societies, publications, Youth and Government, school government, clubs, and more than 14 sports. One hundred percent of graduates enter college. Tuition: $12,025. Financial aid is available. Kathleen Shine is Director of Admissions; Barbara C. Griffin is President. *New England Association.*

Brunswick School 1902

100 Maher Avenue, Greenwich, CT 06830
Tel. 203-625-5800; Admissions 203-625-5842; Fax 203-625-5889
Web Site www.brunswickschool.org
E-mail jharris@brunswickschool.org

A college preparatory day school enrolling 894 boys in Pre-Kindergarten–Grade 12, Brunswick provides an integrated program of academics, arts, community service, and athletics. Advanced Placement and honors courses are offered. Students in Grades 9–12 have coordinate classes and activities with Greenwich Academy, a neighboring girls' school. Brunswick continues to expand its technology and laptop programs. A state-of-the-art campus for the lower and middle schools, located on the 104-acre King Street site, includes extensive athletic facilities and fields. Tuition: $22,500–$29,100. Financial Aid: $3,523,000. Jeffry Harris is Director of Admission; Thomas W. Philip is Headmaster. *New England Association.*

Canterbury School 1915

101 Aspetuck Avenue, New Milford, CT 06776
Tel. 860-210-3800; Admission 860-210-3832; Fax 860-350-1120
Web Site www.cbury.org; E-mail admissions@cbury.org

Canterbury School, a coeducational, college preparatory school in the Roman Catholic tradition, enrolls 220 boarding and 146 day students in Grades 9–12. Students are presented with a strong academic program and a staff ready to support, challenge, and inspire. The liberal arts curriculum emphasizes all subject areas, with 19 AP courses offered. The Canterbury League, the School's service club, provides a variety of opportunities for volunteerism. Other activities include student government, the Canterbury Choir, student publications, and varsity, junior varsity, and recreational athletics. Boarding Tuition: $38,000; Day Tuition: $29,000. Financial aid: $2,300,000. Keith R. Holton is Director of Admission; Thomas J. Sheehy III (Bowdoin College, B.A.; Pennsylvania State University, M.A.) is Headmaster. *New England Association.*

Chase Collegiate School 1865

565 Chase Parkway, Waterbury, CT 06708-3394
Tel. 203-236-9500; Admission 203-236-9560; Fax 203-236-9494
Web Site www.chasecollegiate.org; E-mail admissions@chasemail.org

Set on a 47-acre wooded campus, Chase Collegiate School offers college-bound students a challenging liberal arts program in an environment that values respect, responsibility, and kindness. The 515 day boys and girls in Pre-K3–Grade 12 receive instruction from master teachers committed to the full development of each student academically, artistically, physically, and socially. Lower, Middle, and Upper School divisions occupy separate buildings for classroom and laboratory activities. Younger children receive a strong grounding in language arts and math as a basis for Middle School course work, which emphasizes core subjects as well as the needs of the emerging adolescent. In the Upper School, the academic program includes modern and classical languages, fine and performing arts electives, honors sections, and 18 AP courses. All graduates enter four-year colleges and universities. Among the activities are student government, service learning, publications, musical and dramatic performances, outdoor education, field trips, and interscholastic and intramural sports. A summer session is available. Tuition: $3650–$25,240. Margaretta Foulk is Director of Admissions; John D. Fixx is Head of the School. *New England Association.*

Choate Rosemary Hall 1890

333 Christian Street, Wallingford, CT 06492
Tel. 203-697-2000; Admission 203-697-2239; Fax 203-697-2629
Web Site www.choate.edu; E-mail admission@choate.edu

CHOATE ROSEMARY HALL in Wallingford, Connecticut, is a coeducational, boarding and day, college preparatory school enrolling students in Grades 9–12 and a postgraduate year. Wallingford (population 41,000) is located off Interstate 91, 15 miles north of New Haven. New York and Boston are about two hours away; Bradley International Airport is 45 miles to the north.

Rosemary Hall (1890) was founded by Mary Atwater Choate and The Choate School (1896) by her husband, Judge William Gardner Choate, on the same site. Rosemary Hall moved from Wallingford to Greenwich in 1900 and returned to the Wallingford campus in 1971 as a coordinate school, completing the merger to coeducation in 1974.

Choate Rosemary Hall provides a rigorous academic curriculum and emphasizes the formation of character. The school encourages students to think critically and communicate clearly, understand various methods of intellectual inquiry, and develop global perspectives. Community service is mandatory.

Choate Rosemary Hall is a nonprofit corporation governed by a self-perpetuating Board of Trustees. The school is accredited by the New England Association of Schools and Colleges and holds membership in the National Association of Independent Schools, among other associations.

THE CAMPUS. The school is situated on 450 acres in a residential setting. More than 119 houses, dormitories, and classroom buildings are on campus, along with 13 athletic fields, 23 tennis courts, and the state-of-the-art Bruce '45 and Lueza Gelb Track.

The Carl C. Icahn Center for Science (1989), designed by I.M. Pei, houses classrooms, laboratories, and an auditorium. The Paul Mellon Arts Center (1972), also designed by Pei, houses two theaters, a recital hall, art galleries, studios, practice rooms, and a music production studio. The Paul Mellon Humanities Center contains the English and History, Philosophy, Religion and Social Sciences Departments, photography and digital video studios, and a computer center. The Andrew Mellon Library houses 68,000 volumes, including special collections and a wide range of electronic services. An International Learning Center with a 32-station digital language laboratory is located in Steele Hall. Students can access the campus computer network from dormitory rooms. All classroom buildings and student rooms are wired for Internet access.

The Johnson Athletic Center holds basketball courts, squash courts, weight rooms, wrestling room, a suspended 1/10-mile indoor track, and an addition with a fitness center (2002). Other athletic facilities include the 25-meter Larry Hart Pool, Remsen Arena and Hockey Rink, Macquire Gym with climbing wall, Torrence Hunt Tennis Center, and Sylvester Boat House.

THE FACULTY. Edward J. Shanahan, a graduate of St. Joseph's College (B.A. 1965), Fordham University (M.A. 1968), and the University of Wisconsin (Ph.D. 1982), was appointed Headmaster in 1991. Dr. Shanahan was Dean of the College at Dartmouth for eight years and was previously Dean of Students at Wesleyan University.

Ninety-two men and 75 women, including 46 administrators, comprise the faculty. Most reside on campus and act as advisers to students who live with them. In addition to bachelor's degrees, they hold 116 advanced degrees, including 6 doctorates, from such institutions as Bryn Mawr 2, Columbia 6, Dartmouth 2, Harvard 2, Middlebury 10, New York University 2, Rutgers 2, Southern Connecticut State University 5, Springfield 2, Wesleyan 12, Yale 10, and the Universities of California 2, Chicago 2, Connecticut 7, Massachusetts 3, and Michigan 4.

A full-time physician and staff nurses provide round-the-clock medical care in the Pratt Health Center. Full-service hospitals are nearby.

STUDENT BODY. In 2007–08, the school enrolled 616 boarders and 240 day students in Forms 3–6 (Grades 9–12). The male-female ratio is about 50:50. Students come from 42 states and 25 foreign countries; 30 percent receive financial aid.

ACADEMIC PROGRAM. The academic year, divided into trimesters, begins in early September and ends in early June, with vacations at Christmas and in the spring. Classes are held five days a week and on six Saturdays. They are scheduled in seven 50-minute periods between 8:00 A.M. and 2:50 P.M. on four days; on Wednesdays and Saturdays, classes are held in four 50-minute periods and the academic day ends at 12:30 P.M. On academic nights, study hours are 7:30 to 9:00 P.M. and 9:45 to 10:30 P.M. Reports are sent to parents three times a year.

To graduate, a four-year student must complete 12 terms of English; third-year level in a foreign language; one year each of U.S. History and World History; Algebra I & II and Geometry, in a total of 14 quantitative courses; one year each of physical science and biological science; one term each of philosophy, religion, and, beginning with the Class of 2010, global studies; and three terms of arts, including two areas of the arts.

Course offerings include Composition and Literature, American Studies, British Studies, Etymology, Contemporary American Fiction, Public Speaking, Modernism; Intensive Beginning Arabic, German, Italian, and Russian, French 1–5, French Civilization, German 1, Beginning Italian, Japanese 3–4, Latin 1–4, Russian 1, Chinese 1–5, Spanish 1–5, Spanish-American Studies; World History, British History, The Contemporary Middle East, U.S. History, American Political Institutions, Modern Japan, Modern China, Constitutional Law, Macroeconomics, Microeconomics; Algebra 1–2, Geometry, Trigonometry, Probability, Statistics, Calculus 1–3, Multivariable Calculus, Linear Algebra; Physics, Astronomy, Electronics, Modern Physics, Astrophysics, Chemistry, Environmental Science, Organic Chemistry, Human Anatomy and Physiology, Biology, Marine Biology, Cell Biology; Abnormal Psychology, Child Development, Judaism, Christianity and Islam, Hinduism, Buddhism and Taoism, Moral Reasoning; Printmaking, Photography, Drawing, Oil Painting, Sculpture in the Round, Ceramics,

Weaving, Art History, Acting, Directing, World Music, History of Jazz, Classical Giants, Music Production, Theory/Harmony, and Dance. Honors and Advanced Placement courses are offered in most areas. The School offers international study programs in China, France, and Spain as well as a term trimester in Rome. Seniors may undertake an independent study project under faculty direction. Special programs include Capstone Project, Science Research Program, and Arts Concentration Program.

Virtually all graduates go to college. Popular choices for the Class of 2007 include Tufts and Wesleyan University, 8 each; Columbia University and Georgetown University, 7 each; New York University and Yale, 6 each; and Brown, Cornell, Dartmouth, Williams, and the University of Pennsylvania, 5 each.

Summer Programs include the Writing Project, the John F. Kennedy Institute of Government, English Language Institute, Connecticut Scholars Program (a public/private collaboration), and programs for students of middle school age including FOCUS, CONNECT, and the Young Writers Workshop. Beginning Writers Workshop, a day program for students completing Grade 5 or 6, is also offered.

STUDENT ACTIVITIES. The Student Council provides a forum for student views. Students are also elected to the Judicial Committee, which aids the Dean of Students in cases of school rule violations.

Activities include the yearbook, newspaper, literary magazine, sports weekly, and campus radio station; language clubs, math team, tutoring society; and computer, science, and theater clubs. Community service programs allow students to volunteer locally. Choral groups, student orchestra, string ensembles, and the jazz ensemble provide performance opportunities. Six student theater productions are staged each year. Interest groups include Amnesty International, Gold Key (campus tour guides), International Club, and Film Society, among others.

All students participate in athletics, and the school fields varsity and junior varsity teams to compete in football, cross-country, field hockey, soccer, water polo, basketball, ice hockey, squash, swimming, volleyball, wrestling, archery, baseball, softball, crew, golf, lacrosse, tennis, and track. Intramural and noncompetitive sports include basketball, cycling, swimming, rock climbing, volleyball, tennis, weight training, dance, and others.

Theater productions, films, concerts, and dances are offered on campus, while field trips take students to museums and theaters in New York, Boston, and New Haven. Special events include Parents and Reunion weekends and programs sponsored by the Spears Endowment for Spiritual and Moral Education.

ADMISSION AND COSTS. Choate Rosemary Hall seeks to enroll students from diverse ethnic and social backgrounds who have the potential to do well with the school's resources. Applicants are admitted in all grades on the basis of previous academic performance and their ability to contribute to the community. Transcripts, standardized test results, and letters of recommendation are required along with a personal interview. The application fee is $50 for U.S. applicants and $100 for international students.

Boarding tuition for 2007–08 is $39,360; day tuition is $29,260. Tuition insurance is included in the tuition; payment plans are available. Choate Rosemary Hall subscribes to the School Scholarship Service and offers financial aid amounting to about $6,800,000 annually. The Icahn Scholars Program, an initiative made possible by the Icahn Charitable Foundation of New York City, identifies bright, motivated, and talented middle schoolers from disadvantaged backgrounds and provides them with a fully funded Choate Rosemary Hall education.

Assistant Headmaster & Dean of Faculty: Stephen C. Farrell
Assistant Headmaster & Dean of Academic Affairs: Kathleen Lyons Wallace
Assistant Headmaster & Dean of Students: John H. Ford
Director of Admission: Ray Diffley III
Director of Development & Alumni Relations: Daniel J. Courcey III '86
Director of College Counseling: Dean A. Jacoby '88
Chief Financial Officer: Richard Saltz
Director of Athletics: Ned Gallagher

Cold Spring School 1982

263 Chapel Street, New Haven, CT 06513
Tel. 203-787-1584; Admissions Ext. 216; Fax 203-787-9444
Web Site www.coldspringschool.org
E-mail asudmyer@coldspringschool.org

Cold Spring School enrolls 125 children from Preschool through Grade 6 in a richly diverse urban neighborhood adjacent to a city park. Multiage classrooms, each with a master teacher and an associate teacher, are designed to foster the intellectual and emotional needs of students and provide them with a strong sense of community. The project-based curriculum, enriched by art, music, Spanish, and physical education, develops strong academic skills, a positive self-image, and a sense of civic responsibility. An optional extended day program from 3:00 to 5:30 P.M. is $2400. Tuition: $12,000–$16,500. Financial aid is available. Amy Sudmyer is Director of Admissions; Jeff Jonathan (Middlebury College, B.A.; Columbia University, M.A.) is Head of School.

Convent of the Sacred Heart 1848

1177 King Street, Greenwich, CT 06831
Tel. 203-531-6500; Admissions 203-532-3534; Fax 203-532-3301
Web Site www.cshgreenwich.org; E-mail admission@cshgreenwich.org

Convent of the Sacred Heart is an independent, Catholic, college preparatory day school enrolling 722 girls in Preschool–

Grade 12. Part of the international Network of 200 Sacred Heart Schools, including 21 in the U.S., Sacred Heart provides a strong academic foundation appropriate to each student's individual talents and abilities within an environment that fosters spirituality and establishes a strong sense of personal values. More than 90 percent of the Class of 2007 earned admission to at least one college ranked "most competitive" or "highly competitive." The 110-acre campus includes a new Middle School

and Library/Media Center, technology centers, including a new broadcast journalism suite, theater and expanded space for the arts, and two new synthetic-turf fields. The laptop program is in use in Grades 7–12. Girls take part in varsity and junior varsity sports, Student Council, publications, music groups, Model UN, and community service programs. Tuition: $13,100–$28,500. Financial aid is available. Pamela R. McKenna is Director of Admission and Financial Aid; Sr. Joan Magnetti, RSCJ (Manhattanville, B.A. 1965; Union Theological Seminary, M.A. 1972), is Headmistress.

The Country School 1955

341 Opening Hill Road, Madison, CT 06443
Tel. 203-421-3113; Fax 203-421-4390
Web Site www.thecountryschool.org

The Country School in Madison, Connecticut, is a coeducational day school offering a traditional, classical education for students in PreKindergarten through Grade 8. The town of Madison (population 18,812) is a residential community on Long Island Sound, about 20 miles southeast of New Haven and approximately 90 minutes by car from New York City. Its location in the center of the "Northeast Corridor" provides easy access to a wealth of cultural, historic, and recreational opportunities.

The Country School was founded in 1955 to meet the academic, social, and emotional needs of children. In a family-like environment, students undertake a curriculum designed to develop character, promote self-reliance and individual growth, and prepare them for further education and the responsibilities of citizenship. Spirited teaching, hands-on learning, and a balanced program of academic, artistic, and athletic challenges are hallmarks of The Country School's educational experience.

Guided by a Board of Trustees, the School is approved by the State of Connecticut Department of Education. It holds membership in the National Association of Independent Schools and the Connecticut Association of Independent Schools, among other professional affiliations. Parent and alumni groups are organized to support the School's mission, assist in fund-raising, and planning and implementing special events.

THE CAMPUS. The Country School is set on a 23-acre rural campus in an area of winding roads, open spaces, woods, and attractive homes. The Farmhouse accommodates the School's main office; the Admissions, Development, Alumni Relations, and Communications offices; and a conference room. Classrooms for PreKindergarten, Kindergarten, and Lower School French are located in Clark House; Grades 1 and 2 occupy MacLane House. Robinson House provides classrooms for Grades 3 and 4, the Head of School's office, and the business office. The majority of classes for Grades 5, 6, 7, and 8 take place in Jones House. In addition to athletic facilities, the DeFrancis Gym provides space for a stage, music rooms, and art studio. The Blatchford Learning Center houses the library, science laboratories, history classrooms, and a technology lab. Other facilities include the cafeteria, playgrounds, and playing fields.

THE FACULTY. William E. Powers was appointed Head of School in 2005. He earned a B.A. from Fairfield University and an M.A. from Wesleyan University.

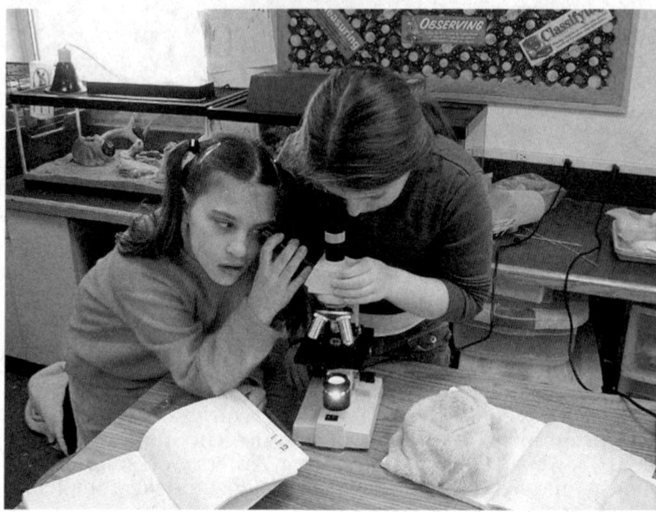

All faculty and administrators hold undergraduate degrees, and many have earned advanced degrees. Among the faculty colleges and universities are Albertus Magnus, Augustana, Berklee College of Music, Boston University, Brown, Catholic University, Central Connecticut State, Colgate, Columbia, Connecticut College, Dartmouth, Fairfield University, Franklin Pierce, Harvard, Lesley, New York University, Ohio University, Paris XIII University, Sacred Heart, Salve Regina, Southern Connecticut State, Springfield College, Trinity, Wesleyan, Wheelock, Yale, and the Universities of Connecticut, Hartford, Maine, Manchester (England), North Carolina, Rhode Island, Richmond, the South, and Vermont.

A registered nurse is on duty during the school day to provide medical attention as needed.

STUDENT BODY. In 2007–08, The Country School enrolled 270 students in PreKindergarten through Grade 8. Sections average 16 students. They come from Madison and 17 other shoreline and central Connecticut towns. The School prides itself on its commitment to diversity and welcomes youngsters from all racial, ethnic, and religious backgrounds. The student-teacher ratio is 9:1.

ACADEMIC PROGRAM. The school year, from September to June, is divided into quarters in the Lower School (PreK–Grade 4) and trimesters in the Middle School (Grades 5–8). Vacations are held at Thanksgiving, the December holidays, and in the spring, with observances of several national and religious holidays. A typical school day begins at 8:15 A.M. and ends between 3:00 and 3:09 P.M., depending on age. PreK is dismissed at 12:30 P.M., following lunch.

Younger students receive written comments, while Middle School students are evaluated through letter grades and effort ratings as well as teacher comments. Outstanding academic achievement is recognized on the Academic Honor Roll and Effort Lists. Homework is assigned beginning in Grade 2, and parent conferences for all grades take place in October and February. Before- and after-school care is offered through the Owl's Nest, which offers a safe, nurturing environment and periodic enrichment workshops and all-day programs.

In the early grades, the child-oriented curriculum introduces key concepts in core subjects through hands-on activities and subject-related projects. Language arts, arithmetic, science, and social studies are presented in age-appropriate content, enhanced by regular classes in music, French, art, and physical education. As students progress, academic material builds on the fundamental skills acquired, and subject matter increases in depth and breadth. Outdoor education and field trips are integrated into classroom learning at all levels.

In Grades 5–8, courses include English; foreign language (French and Spanish with Latin offered in Grades 7 and 8); History; Mathematics, including Pre-Algebra, Algebra, and Geometry; Science, including general science, Introductory Physical Science, Life Science, and Physics; Physical Education; Art; computer; chorus; and band. Private music lessons are also available. A core component of the Middle School curriculum is the Outdoor Education Program, which provides opportunities for students in Grades 5–8 to participate in hands-on outdoor experiences designed to strengthen qualities of character and citizenship, leadership skills, and notions of responsible stewardship of the environment. The program begins in Grade 5 with an overnight camping trip and culminates with a Grade 8 journey to the American Southwest for nine days of camping, hiking, and river rafting.

Through the Middle School advisor system, students receive regular guidance and monitoring of their progress. Groups of six or seven students meet regularly with their faculty advisors. In many cases, an advisor remains with the same students through their graduation.

Graduates have attended such schools as Cheshire Academy, Choate Rosemary Hall, Eaglebrook, The Gunnery, Hamden Hall Country Day School, Hopkins, Loomis Chaffee, The Masters School, Miss Porter's, Northfield Mount Hermon, Phillips Academy, Pomfret, Salisbury, Suffield Academy, Taft, Westminster, Westover, Westtown, Williams, Williston Northampton, and Xavier High School, among others.

STUDENT ACTIVITIES. After-school activities at The Country School are designed to complement the core curriculum while providing opportunities for leadership, service, enrichment, and fun. From Grade 5 upward, students, elected by their peers, may serve in the school government or as class officers. *Eureka,* the art and literary magazine, plays and musicals, interest clubs, and interscholastic and intramural athletics are other popular activities.

Traditional events on the school calendar include back-to-school night, the Halloween Parade, family picnics, book fairs, the MacLane Poetry Recitation, all-school concerts, the Middle School musical, Middle School Outdoor Education trips, Field Day, Grandparents and Special Friends Day, Prize Day, and Graduation.

ADMISSION AND COSTS. The Country School enrolls qualified children regardless of gender, race, color, national or ethnic origin, or financial need. Candidates must participate in a school visitation and classroom assessments and complete the School's admission form, including a writing sample. Parents who complete the application by February 15 are notified of the decision by March 10. When viable candidates exceed the number of openings in a class, the School gives preference to siblings of current students and to children of Country School alumni.

In 2007–08, tuition is $5685 for three-day PreKindergarten, $11,055 for five-day PreKindergarten, $17,495 in Kindergarten–Grade 4, and $20,300 in Grades 5–8. Transportation, hot lunch, before- and after-school care, and private music lessons are additional. Limited financial aid is available to qualified applicants, based on need; tuition payment and tuition refund plans are optional.

Head of School: William E. Powers
Lower School Director: Pam Glasser
Middle School Director: Terrie Hartsoe
Director of Admission: Jason Wainio
Director of Development & Alumni Relations: Jeanne Boyer Roy
Director of Technology: Harlan Brothers
Business Manager: Janet Tancreti
Facilities Manager: Edward Thomasi

Eagle Hill-Southport 1985

214 Main Street, Southport, CT 06890
Tel. 203-254-2044; Fax 203-255-4052
Web Site www.eaglehillsouthport.org
E-mail info@eaglehillsouthport.org

Eagle Hill-Southport is an ungraded, private day school for boys and girls with learning disabilities. Approximately 110 students, ages 6–16, are enrolled. Using tutorials and small group instruction, the school seeks to prepare students for traditional schools through a linguistically based language arts curriculum, adapted to each student's needs. An afternoon activities program provides soccer, cross-country, basketball, baseball, softball, art, and computers. A summer session offers skill enrichment for students who have experienced academic difficulties. Tuition: $36,500. Financial Aid: $244,200. Jeffrey Ruggiero is Director of Curriculum and Instruction; Leonard Tavormina (Boston University, B.A. 1969; Fairfield University, M.A. 1980) was appointed Headmaster in 1984.

The Ethel Walker School 1911

230 Bushy Hill Road, Simsbury, CT 06070
Tel. 860-658-4467; Fax 860-658-6763
Web Site www.ethelwalker.org
E-mail admission–office@ethelwalker.org

The Ethel Walker School is a college preparatory day and boarding school enrolling nearly 300 young women in Grades 6–12. A dedicated and academically gifted faculty strives to foster creativity, respect, confidence, responsibility, and compassion. A traditional liberal arts curriculum offers over 100 courses, including 18 AP courses, off-campus and independent study, exchange programs, and internships. An average class size of 11 and a 5:1 student-faculty ratio ensure individualized attention. Extracurricular options include school government, athletics, equestrian programs, dance, choir, drama, arts, and clubs, among others. Service learning and environmental stew ardship are key elements in curriculum and campus life. The 300-acre campus features a performing arts center, dormitories, extensive athletic fields and facilities, tennis courts, observatory, library, and a nondenominational chapel. Adjacent conservation acreage includes wetlands, meadows, streams, and hiking trails and offers experiential learning and outdoor education. Boarding Tuition: $39,500; Day Tuition: $24,900–$28,500. Financial aid is available. Clarissa Basch is Dean of Enrollment; Elizabeth Speers (Middlebury, B.A.; Johns Hopkins, M.L.A.) is Head of School. *New England Association.*

Fairfield Country Day School 1936

2970 Bronson Road, Fairfield, CT 06824
Tel. 203-259-2723; Fax 203-259-3249
Web Site www.fairfieldcountryday.org
E-mail andrew.holmgren@fcdsmail.org

Fairfield Country Day is an independent school for 270 boys in Kindergarten through Grade 9. All aspects of a Country Day education are designed to help each student expand his desire and ability to acquire knowledge, stimulate his curiosity and creativity, and enhance his self-esteem and respect for others. At every grade level, Country Day boys work in a curriculum constantly evolving to meet their needs. Emphasis and attention is devoted to the core subjects and fundamental skills integral to fostering the enjoyment of learning within each child and laying the foundation for academic success: reading, writing, and mathematics. Every student also has specialized instruction in science, foreign language, and technology. These curricular offerings prepare students to succeed in the most demanding secondary schools while identifying their personal passions and academic interests. Tuition: $25,700–$27,500. Financial aid is available. Andrew Holmgren is Director of Admissions; Christian G. Sullivan (Durham University, B.A.; University of Bath, M.A.) is Headmaster.

The Foote School 1916

50 Loomis Place, New Haven, CT 06511
Tel. 203-777-3464; Fax 203-777-2809
Web Site www.footeschool.org; E-mail laltshul@footeschool.org

The Foote School, enrolling 470 day boys and girls in Kindergarten–Grade 9, seeks to provide educational excellence in a child-centered environment by a grounding in basic skills with emphasis on the aesthetic and intellectual development of each student. Foote is committed to a multicultural curriculum, designed to foster an appreciation of human differences. Art, music, drama, French or Spanish, community service, and gym are taught in all grades. Computer literacy programs begin in Grade 1, Latin in Grade 7. Special activities and sports teams are offered in upper grades. A summer program serves ages 3–15. Tuition: $16,900–$19,650. Financial Aid: $1,200,000. Laura O. Altshul is Director of Admissions; C. Dary Dunham (University of Pennsylvania, B.A.; Boston University, M.Ed.) is Head of School.

Glenholme School 1969

81 Sabbaday Lane, Washington, CT 06793
Tel. 860-868-7377; Fax 860-868-7894
Web Site www.theglenholmeschool.org
E-mail admissions@theglenholmeschool.org

Set on a 100-acre campus in the foothills of western Connecticut, Glenholme offers a year-round academic and therapeutic program for youngsters with diagnosed learning and psychological disorders. The School enrolls 105 boys and girls ages 5–16, primarily boarders. Typically, these youngsters have struggled with challenges such as ADHD, Tourette's Syndrome, mood disorders, post-traumatic stress syndrome, and obsessive-compulsive disorders. Glenholme's mission is to unlock each child's potential and to provide a safe, supportive, highly structured environment in which students receive the specialized therapies and motivation they require to function and thrive in the larger community. Individual and small-group instruction and a Character Education program direct students toward success in their educational and personal endeavors. The academic program focuses on traditional courses in the liberal arts, sciences, and humanities, with classroom instruction enhanced by state-of-the-art information technology. The creative and performing arts, ESL, community service, and an equestrian program enhance the curriculum. Tuition: $105,774. Kathi L. Fitzherbert is Director of Admission; Gary L. Fitzherbert is Executive Director.

Greens Farms Academy 1925

P.O. Box 998, 35 Beachside Avenue, Greens Farms, CT 06838-0998
Tel. 203-256-0717; Admission 203-256-7514; Fax 203-256-7591
Web Site www.gfacademy.org; E-mail admission@gfacademy.org

Greens Farms Academy, a K–12, coeducational day school located in the Greens Farms section of Westport, enrolls 625 students of diverse backgrounds from more than 30 towns in Connecticut and New York. The school focuses on academic excellence and offers a broad arts program, wide-ranging athletics, and substantial community service at all levels. School life hinges on trust and close faculty-student relationships. Two new Middle and Upper School science and performing arts wings recently opened. In the Upper School, Advanced Placement and Honors courses are offered in all major disciplines. Summer programs are available. Tuition: $27,400–$29,980. Need-based Financial Aid: $1,800,000. Stephanie Whitney is Director of Admission; Janet M. Hartwell (University of Leeds, B.A.; Columbia, M.A.) was appointed Head of School in 2003. *New England Association.*

Greenwich Academy 1827

200 North Maple Avenue, Greenwich, CT 06830
Tel. 203-625-8900; Admission 203-625-8990; Fax 203-625-8912
Web Site www.greenwichacademy.org
E-mail awoodward@greenwichacademy.org
E-mail nhoffmann@greenwichacademy.org

Greenwich Academy, enrolling 793 girls in Pre-Kindergarten–Grade 12, emphasizes rigorous academics, active community service, and extensive programs in athletics and the arts. Lower School encourages a love of learning and mastery of basic skills. Middle School develops literary analysis, creative writing and research methods, and an understanding of math, world history, current events, and scientific principles. Upper School, coordinated with Brunswick School for boys, includes Honors and Advanced Placement courses in most disciplines. Laptop computers are required in all classes in Grades 7–12. Tuition: $24,500–$29,100. Financial Aid: $3,400,000. Ann B. Woodward is Dean of Admission and Financial Assistance; Molly H. King is Head of School. *New England Association.*

The Greenwich Country Day School 1926

P.O. Box 623, Old Church Road, Greenwich, CT 06836
Tel. 203-863-5600; Fax 203-622-6046
Web Site www.gcds.net

Enrolling 840 girls and boys in Nursery–Grade 9, Greenwich Country Day provides qualified students with opportunities for academic development, intellectual growth, and artistic and athletic appreciation. The traditional academic program is supplemented by computer education and foreign language beginning in Kindergarten, art, instrumental music, chorus, and physical education that includes 14 interscholastic sports for Grades 7–9. All students in Grades 7–9 have their own laptops. The student-teacher ratio is 7:1. Tuition: $17,400–$25,850. Financial Aid: $1,400,000. Kirby Williams is Director

of Admission; Adam C. Rohdie (Wesleyan University, B.A. 1989; Stanford University, M.A. 1992) was appointed Headmaster in 2004.

The Gunnery 1850

99 Green Hill Road, Washington, CT 06793
Tel. 860-868-7334; Fax 860-868-1614
Web Site www.gunnery.org; E-mail admissions@gunnery.org

The Gunnery is a coeducational college preparatory school enrolling 295 boarding and day students from 22 states and 14 nations in Grades 9–12 and Postgraduate. The liberal arts program is designed to promote academic excellence and build character. The curriculum includes honors and Advanced Placement courses, English as a Second Language, and the fine and performing arts. A Writing Lab assists students in strengthening skills and completing assignments. Among the activities are Community Council, publications, drama and musical theater, social outreach, interest clubs, and required athletics. Boarding Tuition: $39,600; Day Tuition: $29,600. Financial Aid:

$2,000,000. Thomas W. "Tommy" Adams is Director of Admissions; Susan G. Graham (Kent State, B.S.; Fordham, M.S.) is Head of School. *New England Association.*

Hamden Hall Country Day School 1912

1108 Whitney Avenue, Hamden, CT 06517
Tel. 203-752-2600; Admissions Ext. 610; Fax 203-752-2651
Web Site www.hamdenhall.org

HAMDEN HALL COUNTRY DAY SCHOOL in Hamden, Connecticut, is a coeducational college preparatory school enrolling 585 students in Pre-Kindergarten through Grade 12. Hamden (population approximately 55,000) is situated in south-central Connecticut, 3 miles north of New Haven.

Hamden Hall was founded in 1912 as a day school for boys by Dr. John P. Cushing, its first Headmaster. Coeducation was introduced in 1927 and, within seven years, the School was expanded to encompass Grades 9–12.

Hamden Hall's mission is to challenge students to develop a strong sense of personal integrity and social responsibility while preparing them for demanding academic programs at the collegiate level. Faculty serve as role models and mentors in the classroom, on the playing field, and in other areas of school life. With an 8:1 student-teacher ratio, the School aims to offer a nurturing environment in which young people can reach their full potential intellectually, physically, and socially.

A nonprofit institution, Hamden Hall is governed by a 20-member Board of Trustees. It is accredited by the New England Association of Schools and Colleges and holds membership in the National Association of Independent Schools and the Connecticut Association of Independent Schools.

THE CAMPUS. Hamden Hall is set on 12 acres overlooking Lake Whitney. The Dolven Admissions Center contains administrative and college counseling offices, a large art studio, and a computerized video production center. In front of Dolven, a colorful display of the flags of 35 nations represents the nationalities and ethnic backgrounds of the School's diverse student body. The three-story Joseph and Esther Schiavone Science Center houses classrooms, state-of-the-art facilities for science and the arts, Middle and Upper School computer labs, and the dining room. The Taylor Fine Arts Center features a fully equipped theater, music studios, and practice rooms. The Taylor Gymnasium includes basketball, wrestling, and weight-training facilities. Classrooms for the primary grades (Pre-Kindergarten–Grade 3) are located in the Ethyle R. Alpert Building, while the upper Elementary (Grades 4–6), Middle School (Grades 7–8), and Upper School (Grades 9–12) are housed in Whitson Hall. The Ellen and Charles Swain Library, with separate library facilities for the Lower and Middle/Upper Schools, houses a collection of more than 25,000 volumes, 60 periodicals, and extensive reference resources. Swain is linked electronically to computer networks via the Internet.

The campus has an athletic field, a challenging outdoors program, and a play area for younger children. An additional 30-acre sports facility is located 1.5 miles away, and students use golf and swimming facilities at Yale University and other local colleges.

THE FACULTY. Robert J. Izzo is Head of School. He earned a B.A. in Education from the University of Rhode Island in 1983 and an M.B.A. from Bryant University in 1987. Since joining Hamden Hall in 1989, Mr. Izzo has served as chief financial officer, mathematics teacher, and coach. Previously, he taught at the elementary-school level and served as a school administrator.

The faculty include 13 administrators and 80 teachers. They have earned 91 baccalaureate and 58 advanced degrees, including 7 doctorates, representing study at such institutions as Adelphi, Albertus Magnus, Amherst, Bates, Beirut College for Women, Boston College, Bowdoin, Brandeis, Brown, Bryant, Central Connecticut State, Clark, Colby, Colgate, College of William and Mary, Colorado State, Columbia, Cooper Union School of Art, Dartmouth, Denison, Eastern Connecticut State, Elizabeth Seton, Fairfield, Franklin College, Franklin and Marshall, George Mason, Gettysburg, Glassboro State, Hamilton/Kirkland, Hartt College of Music, Hartwick, Harvard, Hobart and William Smith, Illinois Wesleyan, Indiana University of Pennsylvania, Kings College (England), Knox, Manhattanville, Miami University, Middlebury, New York University, Northeastern, Northern Michigan, Oxford (England), Pennsylvania State, Princeton, Quinnipiac, Rollins, Rutgers, Sacred Heart, St. Lawrence, Simmons, Skidmore, Southern Connecticut State, Springfield, Temple, Thiel, Union, Vassar, Villanova, Wake Forest, Walden University, Weber State, Wesleyan, Western Connecticut State, Wheaton, Wheelock, Williams, Yale, Yeshiva, and the Universities of Bridgeport, Connecticut, Delaware, Guelph (Canada), Havana, Illinois, Kentucky, London, Miami, New Mexico, Paris IV and X, Pennsylvania, Rhode Island, Vermont, Virginia, and Wisconsin.

The staff also includes two librarians, reading and learning consultants, two computer resource specialists, a consulting psychologist, and an athletic trainer.

STUDENT BODY. In 2007–08, Hamden Hall enrolled 585 boys and girls, including 249 in the Upper School. They come from diverse racial, ethnic, and religious backgrounds and represent 34 towns within a 30-mile radius of the School.

ACADEMIC PROGRAM. The school year, from early September to early June, is divided into two semesters, with Thanksgiving, winter, and spring recesses and observances of several national and religious holidays. Parent-teacher conferences are held in November and April, or more often if needed. Written progress reports are issued four times a year, with interim reports sent home in the middle of each marking period.

Classes, enrolling an average of 15 students, are held five days a week from 8:10 A.M. to 3:00 P.M. Periods are 45 minutes long, and extra-help sessions are incorporated into the schedule.

The Lower School curriculum emphasizes reading and writing, comprehension, and critical thinking as well as the mastery of problem-solving and computational skills in mathematics. The introduction of laboratory sciences enables children to observe, experiment, research, and discuss scientific theories and concepts. Understanding other cultures from a global perspective is the focus of the social studies program, which utilizes regular field trips, guest lecturers, and group projects to reinforce classroom instruction. Specialists teach music, fine arts, computer activities, and physical education. Students in Grades 1–4 take Spanish and French for two years, followed by Latin in Grades 5–6. An Extended-Day program provides after-school enrichment for students in Pre-Kindergarten–Grade 6.

The Middle School program curriculum builds on the skills acquired in the early grades, combined with new challenges and techniques designed to maximize learning. English classes emphasize classical authors while providing students with opportunities to produce their own creative and expository essays. In mathematics, basic computational skills lead to the mastery of problem solving and a preview of algebraic concepts. Life science and physical science studies offer an overview of scientific vocabulary, concepts, and methods of investigation. French, Spanish, or Latin and participation in studio arts, music, and theater are required. Beginning in Grade 7, students work with a faculty advisor who meets with them regularly.

Students in the Upper School carry five courses each semester. To graduate, they must complete 19 credits as follows: four years of English; two and one-half years of history, including U.S. History; through the third level of a foreign language; mathematics through the junior year, including Geometry and Algebra II; two years of science, including Biology and a physical science; one year of fine arts; and four years of physical education, including participation in fall sports and winter or spring sports. Students must also demonstrate proficiency in computers.

Among the required and elective courses in the Upper School are English 9–12, British Fiction, Creative Writing, Modern American Fiction, American Literature, Shakespeare, Modern Poetry; African American History, Ethics, Constitutional Law, U.S. History, Vietnam; Meteorology and Oceanography, Geology, Astronomy, Zoology, Anatomy and Physiology, Physics, Electronics, Chemistry; Latin I–IV, Accelerated Italian, Spanish I–V, French I–V; Algebra I–II, Trigonometry, Pre-Calculus, Calculus AB/BC; and Introduction to Computers. Advanced Placement and honors courses are offered in most major disciplines. With the approval of the Director of Studies, students may undertake independent study projects.

In 2007, graduating seniors entered such institutions as Albertus Magnus, Bard, Bates, Boston College, Boston University, Brown, Bryn Mawr, Coastal Carolina University, Earlham, Eastern Connecticut State, Elmira, Holy Cross College at Notre Dame, Johns Hopkins, Lafayette, LaSalle, Mount Holyoke, Muhlenberg, Northwestern, Ohio Wesleyan, Parsons School of Design, Princeton, Rochester Institute of Technology, Sacred Heart, St. Peter's College, Santa Clara University, Skidmore, Smith, Union, Ursinus, Vassar, Wesleyan, Whitman, Worcester Polytechnic Institute, Yale, and the Universities of California, Santa Barbara, Hartford, Maryland, Massachusetts, Miami, Michigan, Nevada (Las Vegas), New Hampshire, North Carolina, Pennsylvania, Rochester, and Tampa.

Hamden Hall conducts a nine-week summer program of academics, arts, and sports.

STUDENT ACTIVITIES. Hamden Hall participates in The Princeton Peer Leadership Program, through which selected seniors undertake training to help their fellow students solve problems, seek alternatives, and improve communications on social and ethical issues. An elected Student Government provides further opportunities to develop leadership qualities and share responsibility for the quality of life at the School.

Middle and Upper School students publish their own literary magazines and newspapers, and the Upper School issues the yearbook. Among the groups organized to meet diverse interests are Thespians, debate clubs, tour guides, peer tutoring, environmental clubs, and Academic Decathlon. Students perform community service through the Jewish Home for the Aged and inner-city tutoring.

Interscholastic teams are formed in football, soccer, wrestling, basketball, baseball, lacrosse, and tennis for boys; and field hockey, soccer, basketball, lacrosse, tennis, softball, and volleyball for girls. Golf, ice hockey, and cross-country squads are coeducational.

ADMISSION AND COSTS. Hamden Hall seeks motivated students who are academically strong and eager to participate fully in the life of the School. Acceptance is based on the candidate's potential, previous record, math and English teacher recommendations, and the results of standardized testing. A campus tour is recommended; a personal interview is required.

In 2007–08, tuition, including lunch, ranges from $12,400 in Pre-Kindergarten to $24,900 in Grades 7–12. Hamden Hall awards financial aid to approximately 30 percent of its student body, based on need.

Head of School: Robert J. Izzo
Head of Lower School: Christine Aulicino
Head of Middle/Upper School: Robert H. Schroeder
Director of Admission: Janet B. Izzo
Director of Development & Alumni Relations: Jodi Amatulli
Director of College Counseling: Frederick B. Richter, Jr.
Director of Athletics: Bernard J. Kohler

Hopkins School 1660

986 Forest Road, New Haven, CT 06515
Tel. 203-397-1001; Admissions Ext. 211; Fax 203-389-2249
Web Site www.hopkins.edu; E-mail admissions@hopkins.edu

HOPKINS SCHOOL, in New Haven, Connecticut, is a coeducational, college preparatory day school enrolling 660 students in Grades 7–12. The campus offers a country setting with access to all that Yale University and New Haven offer, including museums, historical sites, theaters, orchestras, and dance companies.

Founded in 1660 with a bequest from Edward Hopkins, the first governor of Connecticut Colony, Hopkins Grammar School began as a one-room schoolhouse on the New Haven Green. Then a boys' school, Hopkins moved to the current site in 1925. The Day School (1938) and Prospect Hill School (1930) were prominent girls' schools that merged in 1960. Cooperative ventures between Hopkins Grammar and Day Prospect Hill led to the 1972 merger that formed the institution known today as Hopkins School.

Hopkins defines itself as a community of civility and learning, educating students from diverse backgrounds to a full measure of their talents and humanity. Hopkins seeks to instill a love of learning; the courage to live and think as responsible individuals; the creative vitality of the artist and competitive spirit of the athlete; the wisdom and goodwill necessary to gain confident self-reliance; and the character essential to a rich and purposeful life.

A nonprofit organization, Hopkins is governed by a self-perpetuating Committee of Trustees, which includes parents and alumni. Endowment totals more than $50,000,000. The Alumni Association, representing approximately 6000 living alumni, promotes participation in school events; *Views from the Hill* is published twice yearly, and an Annual Report of Giving is published annually. Hopkins is accredited by the New England Association of Schools and Colleges and holds membership in the National Association of Independent Schools and the Educational Records Bureau.

THE CAMPUS. The 108-acre campus offers 7 athletic fields, 11 tennis courts, and an outdoor adventure course. Baldwin Hall provides classrooms, a technology laboratory, a language lab, and offices; there are also classrooms in Hopkins House as well as the admissions, business, and college counseling offices. The Day Prospect Hill Building houses seventh- and eighth-grade classrooms, while Lovell Hall is home to the Drama Department. Also on campus are the Alumni House; the Walter Camp Athletic Center with basketball courts, wrestling room, trainer's room, lockers, and swimming pool; and the 25,000-square-foot Malone Science Center with ten laboratories, a student-faculty project room, and prep rooms. Heath Commons provides a 308-seat dining hall and commons space, a café, and two outdoor terraces. It also houses offices for the high school Head Advisers, the Director of Diversity, and Breakthrough-New Haven.

THE FACULTY. Barbara Masters Riley became Head of School in 2002. A 1973 graduate of Yale College, Ms. Riley earned M.A. and M.Phil. degrees in American Studies from Yale University in 1976. She joined the Hopkins faculty in 1996 after teaching history and English for five years at The Foote School in New Haven. Ms. Riley is the parent of three Hopkins graduates.

The full-time faculty numbers 111. There are also 8 part-time teachers. All hold undergraduate degrees; more than two-thirds have advanced degrees. Representative colleges and universities include Bowdoin, Colgate, Columbia, Cornell, Dartmouth, Georgetown, Harvard, Kenyon, Middlebury, Princeton, St. Lawrence, Wellesley, Williams, Yale, and the Universities of Michigan and Pennsylvania.

The support staff includes a full-time consulting psychologist and learning and reading specialists. Three full-time athletic trainers provide first aid, and emergency facilities are nearby.

STUDENT BODY. In 2007–08, the School enrolled 660 students from 49 Connecticut towns.

ACADEMIC PROGRAM. The school year, from early September to early June, is divided into semesters with Thanksgiving and midwinter recesses and December and March vacations. A typical day for Grades 7–12 is divided into six 55-minute periods, one of which is dedicated to athletics, from 8:20 A.M. to 3:30 P.M. The schedule is adjusted to permit early dismissal on Wednesday for athletic contests and club activities and, on Mondays and Fridays, for all-school assemblies.

The average class size is 14 students. There are supervised study halls for students in Grades 7–10; juniors and seniors may study in the Library or Heath Commons during free periods. Grades and comments are sent to parents four times a year; interim reports may be issued for students experiencing academic difficulties. Parent-teacher conferences are held once a year or as appropriate.

The prescribed curriculum for Grades 7–8 consists of English, Latin, History, Pre-Algebra (Grade 7), Elementary Algebra (Grade 8), Life Science (Grade 7), Physical Science (Grade 8), and art, drama, music, and woodworking. French or Spanish may be elected as a second language.

To graduate, students in Grades 9–12 must earn a total of 18 credits including 4 credits of English, 3 of a foreign language, 2 of history, 3 of mathematics, 2 credits of lab science, and 1 credit of arts. They must also fulfill athletics and community service requirements.

Among the courses offered are English courses such as The

Writing Semester, Heroic Figures in Literature, Dante, Political Shakespeare, Love in Shakespeare's Plays, About Poetry, Great Novels, Creative Writing, Russian Literature, and Philosophy, Wit and Wisdom. Other courses include French 1–6, Greek 1–3, Chinese 1–3, Italian 1–3, Latin 1–5, Spanish 1–6; Civics, Atlantic Communities I–III, African-American History, Asian Studies, Islam and the West, Urban Studies, Military History, The Holocaust and the Individual, Twenty-first Century Democracy; Algebra, Accelerated Algebra, Geometry, Accelerated Geometry, Advanced Algebra, Functions, Statistics and Trigonometry, Precalculus, Calculus AB, Calculus BC, Multivariable Calculus, Finite Mathematics, Introduction to Computers and Programming, HTML, Fractals and Chaos, Linear Algebra; Biology, Chemistry, Development & Applications of Technology, Physics, Contemporary Issues in Biology, Ecology, Physiology, Introduction to Organic Chemistry, Astronomy; and Studio Art 1–2, Photography 1–3, Pottery, History of Film, Classical Ensemble, Jazz/Rock Ensemble, Mixed Chorus, Music Theory, Performance Workshop, Video Production, Acting, and Graphic Design.

Advanced Placement and honors-level courses are offered in French, Latin, Spanish, United States History, European History, Human Geography, Linear Algebra, Dynamical Systems & Chaos, Differential Equations, Calculus, Probability and Statistics, Psychology, Biology, Environmental Science, Computer Science, Chemistry, Physics, Ecology, Art History, and Studio Art.

Colleges attended by Hopkins graduates in the past four years include Yale 38; Brown and the University of Connecticut, 18 each; University of Pennsylvania 17; Boston College, Cornell, and Georgetown, 16 each; and Middlebury, New York University, and Tufts, 13 each.

Entering its 107th year, the Hopkins Summer School offers two concurrent six-week programs, one academic, the other sports, for boys and girls in Grades 3–12. Breakthrough-New Haven provides a comprehensive academic enrichment program for public and parochial school students in Grades 7–8. Hopkins is also home to the Adam Kreiger Adventure Program, a state-of-the-art challenge course available to the Hopkins and Greater New Haven communities.

STUDENT ACTIVITIES. The Student Council, composed of elected representatives from Grades 9–12 and the President, elected by Grades 8–12, organizes school service and recreational activities. Council representatives and other students serve on faculty committees devoted to the examination of various school issues.

Students publish a newspaper, literary magazine, and a yearbook. Among the many other organizations and activities available are a Debate Team, Varsity and Junior Varsity Math teams, the Concert Choir, Model UN, the Hopkins Drama Association, three a cappella singing groups, Environmental Club, Amnesty International, GASP (Gay and Straight People), and SURE (Students United for Racial Equality). Hopkins has a thriving community service program. The majority of students become involved through programs sponsored by the Community Service office and the Maroon Key umbrella of student organization. Beginning with the class of 2007, seniors are required to participate in all four days of a School-sponsored community service project.

Hopkins teams compete with those of public and independent schools in Connecticut, Massachusetts, and New York. Boys' teams are organized in baseball, basketball, cross-country, football, golf, lacrosse, soccer, swimming and diving, tennis, track, fencing, water polo, and wrestling. Girls compete in basketball, cross-country, lacrosse, field hockey, golf, soccer, softball, swimming and diving, tennis, track, fencing, water polo, and volleyball. Junior School teams include baseball, basketball, field hockey, lacrosse, football, soccer, swimming and diving, tennis, and wrestling.

Dances and drama productions are held throughout the year. Traditional events for the school community include Pumpkin Bowl, Homecoming, Reunion Weekend, and various functions sponsored by the Student Council and the Parent Council.

ADMISSION AND COSTS. Hopkins seeks to enroll a diverse group of students who are eager to learn and willing to work hard. New students are admitted to all grades, although most often to Grades 7 and 9, on the basis of an application, a personal interview, results of the Secondary School Admission Test or the Independent School Entrance Examination, a writing sample, the transcript from the applicant's previous school, and two teacher references. Application should be made in the fall; the application deadline is January 20. There is a $50 application fee.

In 2007–08, tuition is $27,050. Tuition covers all costs except books ($300–$600), an activities fee ($350), student accident insurance, and trip and store charges. In the current year, Hopkins awarded more than $2,300,000 in financial aid to 128 students. Tuition payment plans and tuition insurance are available.

Chief Financial & Operating Officer: David E. Baxter
Assistant Head of School: R. John Roberts
Director of Admissions: Dana L. Blanchard '63
Dean of Academics: Rosemary O. Benedict
Dean of Faculty: Carla J. MacMullen
Dean of Students: Eric W. Mueller
Director of Athletics: Thomas A. Parr, Jr.
Director of Development: Barbara Price Monahan
Director of Development for Alumni & Parent Affairs: Deena Mack
Director of College Counseling: Susan Moriarty Paton
Director of Community Service: David Harpin
Director of Diversity: Veronica Guinazu
Director of Summer School: Thomas A. Parr, Jr.
Alumni Association President: Ronald P. Delfini '84

The Hotchkiss School 1891

11 Interlaken Road, P.O. Box 800, Lakeville, CT 06039
Tel. 860-435-2591; Admission 860-435-3102; Fax 860-435-0042
Web Site www.hotchkiss.org; E-mail admissions@hotchkiss.org

Hotchkiss, set on an 880-acre campus in northwestern Connecticut, is a coeducational college preparatory school enrolling 521 boarders and 57 day students from 42 states and 26 nations in Grade 9–Postgraduate. In a "small-school community with large-school resources," the academic program is designed to develop a life-long love of learning, citizenship, and integrity. The curriculum features more than 227 courses, including five languages, Advanced Placement in 21 subjects, independent study options, overseas travel/study exchanges, and summer

programs. Students have numerous choices in the arts, service outreach, leadership groups, and athletics. Boarding Tuition: $38,000; Day Tuition: $32,400. Financial Aid: $5,528,271. Christopher K. Downs is Dean of Admission and Financial Assistance; Malcolm H. McKenzie is Head of School. *New England Association.*

The Independent Day School 1961

115 Laurel Brook Road, P.O. Box 451, Middlefield, CT 06455
Tel. 860-347-7235; Fax 860-347-8852
Web Site www.idsmiddlefield.org; E-mail ids@idsmiddlefield.org

The Independent Day School, enrolling 190 boys and girls from Beginners (age 3) to Grade 8, offers an academically challenging program in a family-like environment. The School draws students from more than 30 towns. Balanced programs of academics, physical fitness, and studio and performing arts provide students with a well-rounded educational experience. Spanish is taught throughout the grades beginning in Pre-K. Community service is also an integral part of the IDS program, promoting an awareness of and empathy toward others in the world at large. Academically driven field trips, interscholastic sports, and class plays broaden students' experiences. After-school care programs, both after-school and summer theater and dance programs, and a summer camp are available. Tuition: $7375–$18,980. Mary Lou Stewart is Director of Admission; John Barrengos is Head of School.

Kent School 1906

P.O. Box 2006, Kent, CT 06757
Tel. 860-927-6000; [Toll-free] 800-538-5368
Admissions 860-927-6111; Fax 860-927-6109
Web Site www.kent-school.edu; E-mail admissions@kent-school.edu

KENT SCHOOL in Kent, Connecticut, is a coeducational college preparatory school enrolling boarding students and a limited number of day students in Grades 9–12 and postgraduate. The School is located on the Housatonic River in Kent about 80 miles north of New York City and 50 miles west of Hartford.

Kent School, which has been affiliated with the Episcopal Church since its inception, was established in 1906 by the Reverend Frederick Herbert Sill, a member of the monastic Order of the Holy Cross. Students of diverse religious and nonreligious backgrounds are welcome.

The School is dedicated to enabling students to develop intellectually, physically, and spiritually. Further, it structures the academic program and daily life to foster self-reliance and a sense of caring as an ethical foundation for living in the world.

Kent is accredited by the New England Association of Schools and Colleges and is a member of the National Association of Episcopal Schools, the National Association of Independent Schools, and the Connecticut Association of Independent Schools.

THE CAMPUS. The campus consists of approximately 1200 acres of woods and farmland traversed by Macedonia Brook. There are 13 outdoor tennis courts, 7 multipurpose fields for soccer, field hockey, and lacrosse, 2 for baseball and football, the John Phillips Field for soccer and lacrosse, Sanford Field for baseball, and a field for varsity football games. Other facilities include the Brainard Squash Racquet Courts, Nadal Hockey Rink, the Kent School Riding Stables, and the newly constructed B.W. Partridge Rowing Center. Kent crews train and compete on the Housatonic River.

Most buildings are of brick construction in the Georgian style. The Schoolhouse contains the 40,000-volume John Gray Park Library on three levels, five group study rooms, a Writing Center, classrooms, department offices, an audiovisual center, and Alumni and Development office. The Gifford T. Foley '65 Hall houses classrooms and offices. Fairleigh S. Dickinson Science Center holds classrooms, laboratories, and offices. Students reside in the Hadley Case '29 Dormitory (which also houses the Dickinson Health Center), the Bruce Robinson Field '81 Building (which also contains the art studios), North Dormitory, Dining Hall Dormitory containing the Student Center and store, and Middle Dormitory, which also houses a student lounge. Faculty live in dormitory apartments and in other on- and off-campus housing.

St. Joseph's Chapel—a Norman-style structure of slate and stone—includes a cloister, a garden, and a tower with ten bells used for change ringing. Magowan Field House contains a six-lane, 25-yard swimming pool, dressing rooms and showers, two basketball courts, and a weight-training room. The Frederick Herbert Sill Trophy Room is located in the Field House. The Indoor Tennis House provides four full-size lighted courts. Other facilities are the Administration Building, a Technology Center, the Auditorium, and the Old Main Admissions Office.

THE FACULTY. The Reverend Richardson W. Schell, appointed Headmaster and Rector in 1981, is a graduate of Kent School, Harvard (A.B. 1973), and Yale (M.Div. 1976). Previously, he served as a parish priest in Chicago and as Chaplain of Kent School (1980–81).

On the faculty are 75 full-time teachers. The average length of teaching experience is 14 years, and 8 faculty members are Kent graduates. Thirty-three faculty and administrators live on campus. The faculty hold 90 baccalaureate and 65 advanced degrees; 2 or more degrees were earned at Bowdoin, Colby, Columbia, Hamilton, Harvard, Kenyon, Middlebury, Princeton, Syracuse, Trinity, Wellesley, Williams, Yale, and the Universities of Pennsylvania and Vermont.

STUDENT BODY. In 2007–08, Kent enrolled 289 boarding boys, 28 day boys, 227 boarding girls, and 31 day girls. They come from 34 states and 24 foreign countries. More than one-fourth are children or siblings of Kent graduates.

ACADEMIC PROGRAM. The school year, from early September to early June, includes Thanksgiving, Christmas, and spring vacations. The daily schedule includes classes before and after lunch, free periods that may be used for conferences or study, regularly scheduled meetings with faculty advisors, afternoon sports, and evening study.

The average class size is 12, and the student-faculty ratio is approximately 7:1. Development of independent study habits is emphasized, although students are assigned to supervised study halls when necessary.

To graduate, students must complete four years of English, three years of a foreign language, American History, mathematics through Grade 11, two laboratory sciences, two terms of theology, and minor courses in art and music.

The curriculum includes yearlong courses in English; French, German, Spanish, Chinese, Latin; Classical Civilization, Ancient & Medieval World History, Modern European History, American History; Mathematics (Algebra through Calculus and Analytical Geometry); Biology 1–2, Chemistry 1–2, Physics 1–2, Environmental Science; and Art History, Studio Art Survey, and Harmony and Composition. Typical one-term topics are Astronomy, Meteorology, Ecology, Genetics, Biotechnology, Computer Programming, Asian Studies, Global Studies, History of Constitutional Law, Introduction to Attic Tragedy, Virgilian Epic, Religion and the Arts, Ethics, Design-Architecture, Painting-Color, Ceramics, Photography, Digital Photography, Music Fundamentals, and Music History.

All Third Formers take Third Form Seminar, which integrates the teaching of study techniques into a course in cultural history. Students needing individual attention may use the services of the Writing Center.

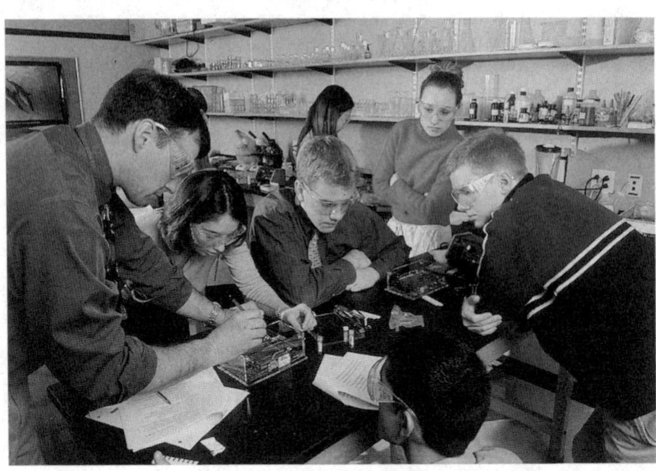

Advanced Placement is offered in English, French, German, Spanish, Latin, American history, European history, economics, mathematics, statistics, biology, chemistry, environmental science, art, computer science, psychology, and physics. An Independent Study Program allows students to pursue a specific topic in depth, usually in the Fifth or Sixth Form.

Kent's wiring infrastructure allows students to connect globally. Every student can plug into the School's Local Area Network and a direct Internet connection from his or her own room. Students may obtain individual Internet accounts by completing an orientation course. Kent School participates in the Microsoft Schoolbook Program, providing an affordable opportunity for every student to be equipped with a laptop computer and software. Students also have telephones in each room.

In 2007, all 158 graduates entered college. Some of the colleges entered are Boston University, Bryn Mawr, Carnegie Mellon, Colgate, Cornell, Davidson, Dickinson, Georgetown, New York University, Pennsylvania State, Princeton, Southern Methodist, United States Naval Academy, Vanderbilt, Yale, and the Universities of Michigan, North Carolina, Texas, and Virginia.

STUDENT ACTIVITIES. Students are expected to take responsibilities in many areas of school life. Every student at Kent participates in the jobs program. Underform students, supervised by Sixth Formers and teachers, help to clean the School and ensure smooth daily operation. Student leaders also serve as dormitory prefects and members of the Student Council.

Boys and girls organize clubs for French, Spanish, German, photography, and art. Other groups include Habitat for Humanity, Adopt-a-Grandparent, Math Team, Poets' Society, Youth Group, and Writers' and Theatre Clubs. Students may participate in drama through the Kent School Players and in music with the Bell Ringers Guild, Kentones, Kentettes, Choir, Concert Band, Jazz Band, String Orchestra, and other ensembles. Private music lessons are available, and recitals are given. Student publications include a literary magazine and the yearbook. Students work with faculty as disc jockeys at WKNT, the School FM radio station.

Individuals may select a faculty-sponsored Designed Extra-Curricular Activity. These long-term projects have been offered in journalism, creative writing, community service, music, art, photography, sports medicine, and bell ringing.

All physically fit students participate in interscholastic or intramural sports. Boys' teams are organized in football, soccer, riding, hockey, basketball, squash, swimming, lacrosse, cross-country, baseball, crew, golf, and tennis. Girls compete in field hockey, tennis, crew, cross-country, squash, swimming, basketball, lacrosse, softball, soccer, riding, golf, and ice hockey.

On weekends, Protestant students worship at Episcopal services. Roman Catholic students attend Mass, Jewish students attend services at synagogue in a nearby town, and Muslim students worship together in a prayer group. The Performing Arts and Lecture Series provides enrichment opportunities, and frequent art exhibits are displayed.

ADMISSION AND COSTS. Boys and girls are accepted in Grades 9–12 and postgraduate on the basis of academic accomplishment, character, and promise. Applicants must submit an academic transcript, references from three former teachers, a student application form, and the results of the Secondary School Admission Test. Candidates are asked to make an appointment for a campus visit and interview.

In 2007–08, tuition, room, and board is $39,900, and the cost for day students is $31,300. Additional mandatory fees for all students amount to $1205. Additional fees are charged for international students. Approximately $1700 will be necessary for personal expenditures. A tuition payment plan and tuition insurance are available. Approximately $5,000,000 is awarded annually in need-based financial aid.

Headmaster & Rector: Richardson W. Schell '69
Deans of Students: Cathe Mazza '76, Bettina Cloutier, Wayne Walton, Daniel Genck & Jeremy Sokolnicki
Alumni Director: Stacy Langa
Academic Dean: Tom Roney
Director of Studies: Diana Yammin
Director of Admissions: Kathryn F. Sullivan '94
Director of Development: Marc L. Cloutier
College Counselors: Claire Lerchen, John Lintner, Sarah Ross & Martin Walsh
Business Manager: Thomas L. Sides
Director of Athletics: Todd Marble

King & Low-Heywood Thomas School

1865

1450 Newfield Avenue, Stamford, CT 06905
Tel. 203-322-3496; Admission Ext. 350; Fax 203-504-6288
Web Site www.klht.org; E-mail admission@klht.org

KING & LOW-HEYWOOD THOMAS SCHOOL, familiarly known as KLHT in Stamford, Connecticut, is a coeducational, college preparatory day school enrolling students in Pre-Kindergarten through Grade 12. Students are drawn from Stamford and several surrounding towns in Fairfield and Westchester Counties, areas that provide numerous opportunities for discovery and learning and allow students to experience the culture of both urban and suburban environments.

The School's origins date back to Mrs. Richardson's School, an all-girls school founded in 1865. In 1883, Miss Louisa Low and Miss Edith Heywood purchased and renamed the School. Low-Heywood merged with Miss Thomas's School in 1973, and, in 1988, Low-Heywood Thomas merged with the all-boys King School.

The School seeks to develop each individual's talents and character by offering intellectual, creative, athletic, leadership, and service opportunities, thereby preparing its students for lives of learning in college and adulthood. Acquisition of communication skills, cultivation of intellectual ability, evolution of individual character, and attainment of personal growth are also emphasized.

Accredited by the New England Association of Schools and Colleges, the School is governed by a Board of Trustees. The Board appoints the Head of School and creates policies that enhance and underline the School's mission statement.

THE CAMPUS. The 36-acre campus is near both the Merritt Parkway and I-95, so parents can reach the School easily during visits, and field trip locations in surrounding areas are accessible.

A new state-of-the-art Middle School opened in September 2004. As students and faculty moved into that facility, renovations to the Lower School further enhanced the expanded space available for those students. The Upper School boasts updated library facilities, new science labs, expanded lounge areas for students, and state-of-the-art technology.

The Head of School's Office, Admission Office, and the Lower and Middle Schools are on the South Campus, while the Upper School and the College Counseling Office are on the North Campus.

THE FACULTY. Thomas B. Main was appointed Head of School in 2002. He matriculated at Bates College with a Bachelor of Arts in English and received a Master of Arts in Liberal Studies degree from Wesleyan University. Prior to moving to King & Low-Heywood Thomas School, he was a Middle School English teacher, coach, and advisor at King School, served in a variety of teaching and administrative positions at Rye Country Day School, and was Head of the Upper School at Cincinnati Country Day School.

King & Low-Heywood Thomas School's faculty is comprised of 136 teachers and administrators, with 69 holding master's degrees and 7 holding doctoral degrees. The faculty attended such colleges and universities as Bates College, Berklee College of Music, Boston College, Boston University, Bowdoin College, Columbia University, Cornell University, Dartmouth College, Duke University, Fairfield University, George Washington University, Harvard, Ithaca College, Johns Hopkins University, Lafayette College, New York University, Southern Connecticut State University, Trinity College, Wesleyan University, Williams College, Yale University, and the University of Pennsylvania.

STUDENT BODY. The School enrolls 206 students in the Lower School, 177 students in the Middle School, and 265 students in the Upper School. Students come from 31 towns in Fairfield and Westchester Counties and encompass a wide range of ethnic and racial backgrounds. Approximately 17 percent enrolled in the Upper School are students of color.

ACADEMIC PROGRAM. The school year is divided into semesters, with Thanksgiving, winter, and spring vacations. Day vacations include Rosh Hashanah, Columbus Day, Martin Luther King Day, and Presidents' Weekend. Each academic day begins at 8:00 A.M. and ends at 3:00 P.M. for students in the

Lower and Upper Schools and runs from 8:00 A.M. to 3:15 P.M. for the Middle School.

The Lower School teachers endeavor to build a foundation that will serve students in Pre-Kindergarten through Grade 5 for the remainder of their schooling and throughout their adult lives. The Lower School has a maximum class size of 15 and focuses on exploration and growth. Classes revolving around math, social studies, science, and language arts help students develop more abstract and complex thinking and problem-solving skills. Students in Grades 4 and 5 can begin instrumental instruction, and all students are introduced to Spanish culture, language, and history.

Because Grades 6–8 are a transition period, King & Low-Heywood Thomas School seeks to create a supportive yet challenging environment in which students can develop successfully and move on to the Upper School as thoughtful, perceptive, and sensitive young adults. With an average class size of 14, individual attention is guaranteed both academically and emotionally. Students take classes in English, mathematics, history, science, and French or Spanish along with various sports and arts programs. Teachers in the Middle School aim to hone the basic skills learned in the Lower School and encourage social responsibility and self-awareness.

The Upper School runs from Grade 9 to Grade 12. Although there is a maximum class size of 15, many classes are smaller, particularly at advanced levels. All courses are college preparatory, with Honors, Advanced Placement and Advanced Tutorial classes also available. Advanced Placement courses are offered in 17 subjects, and approximately 58 students of the Class of 2006 took 122 Advanced Placement exams, with 57 percent scoring 4 or higher.

Students must take a minimum of five full-year courses each year, and participation in two theater productions and four athletic seasons is also required. Upper School graduation requirements are as follows: four credits in English; three credits in history, science, mathematics, and modern languages; one credit in the arts; and a half credit in life skills.

Classes available include, among others, Fundamentals of Composition and Literary Study, Writing about Literature, American Literature, Literature of Social Reflections, Literature of Warrior Cultures, Poetry Writing, Fiction Writing, Literary Analysis; Algebra I and II, Geometry, Trigonometry, Discrete Mathematics, Statistics, Pre-Calculus, Calculus; World History, America, Vietnam, and the Sixties, United States History, European History, African-American Studies, Economics, Micro/Macro Economics, Philosophy; Biology, Chemistry, Organic Chemistry, Physical Anthropology, Physics, Meteorology, Forensics, Archaeology; Painting, Drawing, Clay Workshop, Printmaking, Art History; Computer Science; and French and Spanish. Chamber music, chorus, and a jazz ensemble are also provided.

College counseling begins in Grade 9 and becomes more involved as students progress through the Upper School. In Grades 9 and 10, students are urged to do their best academically and are introduced to the college application process, while sophomores are coached through all the steps of the PSAT. Students in Grade 11 visit several colleges during a class trip. The Office of College Counseling instructs seniors through the process of applying to college and assists them with deadlines, transcripts, and recommendations.

Members of the Class of 2007 enrolled in schools such as Boston College, Bucknell, Columbia, Cornell, Dartmouth, Dickinson, Fordham, Gettysburg, Hamilton, Harvard, Hobart, Lehigh, Mount Holyoke, New York University, Northeastern, Pepperdine, Rollins, Skidmore, Susquehanna, and the Universities of Colorado, Michigan, Pennsylvania, Rochester, and Virginia.

STUDENT ACTIVITIES. Sports available to Lower, Middle, and Upper School students include soccer, football, cross-country, field hockey, volleyball, cheerleading, ice hockey, basketball, lacrosse, baseball, softball, and tennis. Varsity teams belong to the Fairchester Athletic Association and compete against schools in the Western New England Prep School Athletic Association and the New England Prep School Athletic Council. Students in Grades 5 and 6 and in Grades 7 and 8 play on separate sports teams that foster skill building, sportsmanship, and teamwork.

Students also take part in extracurricular activities that enhance the academic, artistic, and athletic program. All students participate in community service and school government, and Upper School students form special-interest groups such as the A cafellas, A capella (singing groups), Amnesty International, Building with Books, Students Against Destructive Decisions, United Cultures Club, Student Council, Photography Club, Film Making Club, Creative Writing Club, Cooking Club, Debate Club, Business Club, Key Club, Math Team, and Model UN. Students in Grades 9–12 publish *Kaleidoscope*, a yearbook, and *The Standard*, a quarterly newspaper. Both Middle and Lower School students also publish magazines of their literary work. Middle School students can participate in drama, chorus, band, and art as extracurricular activities outside of athletics.

Special events include Homecoming, Upper and Middle School drama productions, holiday concerts, field trips and dances.

ADMISSION AND COSTS. King & Low-Heywood Thomas School seeks students who are academically motivated and who wish to become citizens who are involved in their communities. The application fee is $75; deadlines are January 1 for Pre-K and Kindergarten and January 15 for Grades 1–12. Candidates must visit the campus, complete the application and a Student Questionnaire, meet with a member of the admission committee, submit a transcript and teacher recommendations, and take an age-suitable standardized admission test.

Tuition ranges between $25,000 for Pre-K and $28,500 for Upper School students; activity fees are from $175 to $575, depending on the student's grade. Other expenses include lunch, snacks, tuition refund insurance, and student accident insurance. All parents are asked to contribute to the Annual Fund to improve the School and its ability to educate students well. Need-based financial aid is available.

Director of Admission and Financial Aid: Carrie Salvatore
Director of Development: Mary Vinton
Director of College Counseling: David Bonner
Assistant Head, Finance & Operations: Kimberly Leeker
Director of Athletics: Tom Decker

Kingswood-Oxford School 1969

170 Kingswood Road, West Hartford, CT 06119
Tel. 860-233-9631; Admission Ext. 2269; Fax 860-236-3651
Web Site www.kingswood-oxford.org; E-mail admission@k-o.org

Kingswood-Oxford is a coeducational, college preparatory day school enrolling 595 students in Grades 6–12. The School provides a challenging, supportive environment that nurtures relationships among young people, parents, and teachers. The traditional preliberal arts curriculum, which culminates in a rich array of Advanced Placement courses, emphasizes the development of analytical skills, critical thinking, intellectual independence, and confidence. Student government, publications, community service, and various athletics and clubs complete the program. Tuition: $28,200. Activity Fee: $325. Financial Aid: $2,275,536. James E. O'Donnell is Director of Enrollment Management; Dennis Bisgaard (Odense Universitet, B.S., M.A.; Teachers College Columbia University, M.A.) was named Head of School in 2006. *New England Association.*

The Long Ridge School 1938

478 Erskine Road, Stamford, CT 06903
Tel. 203-322-7693; Fax 203-322-0406
Web Site www.longridgeschool.org; E-mail mail@longridgeschool.org

The Long Ridge School is a coeducational day school with an enrollment of 150 boys and girls in Nursery–Grade 5, with a morning program for 2-year-olds. Offering "a child-centered education in a challenging, supportive atmosphere," the School seeks to nurture each student's academic, social, and emotional growth. Stressing a hands-on learning process through thematic studies, the School believes "a genuine caring and respect for children" is central to all activities. A new arts and athletic center opened in 2007. Tuition: $5550–$21,410. Financial Aid: $175,000. Ms. Kris Bria (Carnegie Mellon, B.A.; Teachers College, Columbia, M.A.; Bank Street College, M.Ed.) was appointed Head in 1989.

The Loomis Chaffee School 1914

4 Batchelder Road, Windsor, CT 06095
Tel. 860-687-6000; Admissions 860-687-6400; Fax 860-298-8756
Web Site www.loomis.org; E-mail admissions@loomis.org

A coeducational, college preparatory school enrolling 725 students in Grade 9–Postgraduate, Loomis Chaffee seeks to combine rigorous intellectual formation with sensitivity to the unique potential of each student. More than 200 courses are offered; off-campus internships and independent study are available to upperclassmen. The fully computerized 300-acre campus includes a 60,000-volume library, science center, a school center, and six international squash courts; all students have access to internal/external e-mail and the Internet. Boarding Tuition: $39,100; Day Tuition: $29,500. Financial Aid: $5,000,000. Thomas D. Southworth is Director of Admission; Russell H. Weigel (University of Colorado, Ph.D.) is Head of School. *New England Association.*

The Marvelwood School 1956

476 Skiff Mountain Road, P.O. Box 3001, Kent, CT 06757-3001
Tel. 860-927-0047; [Toll-free] 800-440-9107; Fax 860-927-0021
Web Site www.marvelwood.org; E-mail admissions@marvelwood.org

THE MARVELWOOD SCHOOL in Kent, Connecticut, is a coeducational college preparatory school enrolling a maximum of 165 boarding and day students in Grades 9 through 12. The School, located in the scenic northwest corner of the state, is situated in the foothills of the Berkshire Mountains and is easily accessible by public transportation and car. Marvelwood is 80 miles from New York City, 55 miles from Hartford, and 150 miles from Boston

Since its founding, Marvelwood has offered a guided journey to achievement for students who have not had success in traditional schools and who are willing to make an effort to turn things around. The environment is structured, caring, intense, and intimate; Marvelwood has a 51-year history of helping students improve their grades, develop self-confidence, and gain acceptance to appropriate colleges of their choice.

Marvelwood holds membership in the National Association of Independent Schools and is accredited by the New England Association of Schools and Colleges.

THE CAMPUS. The 83-acre campus is located on a mountaintop that provides sweeping views of the New England countryside. The main schoolhouse has classrooms and science labs. Wireless Internet access is available throughout the campus, and computers with e-mail and Internet access are located in the Bodkin Library, which contains a wide variety of books and periodicals. A second computer laboratory is located in a science room and has special software to graph scientific data. Art, photography, and filmmaking classes meet in five studios throughout the campus. The School's gymnasium has a performance stage, a music room, and indoor athletic facilities. A new athletic center includes a regulation-size basketball court, dance studio, weight room, and wrestling room. Other athletic facilities include playing fields and tennis courts. Small dormitories, supervised by faculty members, house students from all grade levels.

THE FACULTY. Scott E. Pottbecker was appointed Headmaster in 2005. Mr. Pottbecker, who holds a B.A. from the University of Connecticut and an M.P.A. from the University of Hartford, previously served as Assistant Head of School at The Forman School. He is assisted in his work by 51 experienced and supportive teachers, 25 with advanced academic degrees and several who are Marvelwood graduates. In addition to teaching duties, faculty members serve as advisers and coaches and live in dormitories.

STUDENT BODY. In 2007–08, Marvelwood enrolled 143 boys and girls as boarding and day students in Grades 9–12. Members of the diverse student body come from 18 states and 10 countries.

ACADEMIC PROGRAM. The academic program runs from September through June with vacations at Thanksgiving, in the winter, and in the spring. School days begin at 7:45 A.M. with breakfast. The first academic class begins at 8:30 A.M., with an all-school meeting at 10:00 A.M. Classes continue up to and after lunch, rounding out the day with sports practice, dinner, evening study hall, and staggered "lights out" times, depending on grade. Wednesdays are reserved for community service activities in the morning and athletic games in the afternoon. Academic classes are held on Saturday mornings, followed in the afternoon by athletic games.

Marvelwood's academic structure is designed to be "supportive, not rigid," in order to help students succeed. Accountability and self-confidence are emphasized in all tasks with the adviser/advisee relationship taking a central position in the student's well-being. An on-staff counselor and several outside professionals facilitate a variety of support groups that help students understand such issues as stress management, conflict resolution, and decision making.

The student-teacher ratio of 4:1 ensures individual attention, and the curriculum is a traditional college preparatory program that often uses hands-on, experiential learning techniques. Classes at each grade level are limited to no more than 12 students.

Specific course offerings include English 9–12; English as a Second Language; Strategies; Spanish I–IV, French I–III, Latin I–II; Pre-algebra, Algebra I–II, Geometry, Math Tutorial, Trigonometry, Precalculus, Calculus, AP Statistics, AP Calculus; Biology I–II, Environmental Science, Ethology, Applied Physics, Physics, Chemistry, Advanced Field Studies, Aquatic Ecology, Anatomy & Physiology, Psychology; World History I–II, U.S. History, Comparative Religion, Geography, Asian History, Art History, Modern European History; and Studio Art, Ceramics, Drama, Music Composition, Jazz, Rock & Broadway, Fundamentals of Acting, Introduction to Directing, Film, Musicianship, Photography, Creative Writing, Music Appreciation, and Yearbook.

Marvelwood's science department has been recognized by the State of Connecticut for its innovative, hands-on programs as well as its contributions to state and local agencies such as the Department of Environmental Protection, the Audubon Society, and various local conservation commissions and land trusts. In addition, projects such as guide dog training, water quality testing, mapping vernal pools with GPS equipment, and operation of one of only two licensed high school bird-banding stations in the country illustrate Marvelwood's dedication to experiential education through practical experiences that may significantly influence students' college and career choices.

Students enrolled in the English as a Second Language (ESL) program learn to develop solid proficiency in writing, speaking, reading, and listening to English while preparing for the Test of English as a Foreign Language (TOEFL). American roommates and special Wednesday morning activities provide international students with opportunities to learn about American culture on and off the campus and to practice communication skills.

About one-third of the student body take advantage of the optional Strategies and Math Tutorial programs at Marvelwood. Offered for credit, the programs help students with their reading comprehension and writing abilities or with math skills such as calculations, fractions, graphs, and word problems.

On Wednesday mornings, all students report to their community service assignments, which include helping the elderly, working at day care centers or elementary schools, assisting

Special Olympians as they prepare for regional athletic events, or volunteering at an animal rehabilitation shelter.

College counseling is intensive and is overseen by a director and one additional counselor. Marvelwood students attend such colleges and universities as Babson, Bard, Boston University, Clark, Colorado State, Connecticut College, Denison, Florida State, Fordham, Franklin Pierce, Gettysburg, Hamilton, Hartt School of Music, Hartwick, Hobart, Hunter, Johnson and Wales, Lake Forest, Marist, Michigan State, New York University, Northeastern, Ohio Wesleyan, Parsons School of Design, Pratt Institute, Providence, Purdue, Quinnipiac, Rochester Institute of Technology, Rollins, St. Lawrence, Salve Regina, Siena, Stonehill, Syracuse, Washington, Wellesley, Wheaton, and the Universities of Cincinnati, Colorado, Connecticut, Denver, Illinois, Washington, and Wisconsin.

Marvelwood's Summer Program offers four weeks of study in a variety of academic subjects. Classes may be taken for credit or enrichment. The Summer Program, based on the successful methods of the Salisbury Summer School, incorporates methodologies associated with Dr. Mel Levine's Schools Attuned program.

STUDENT ACTIVITIES. The Prefect System and Peer Mediation Program provide opportunities for leadership and growth as students mature. The arts are of central importance at Marvelwood. Students participate in a variety of dramatic productions each year including Shakespearean plays. Photography, painting, and ceramic exhibits are planned throughout the year.

All students take part in athletics including competitive team sports such as soccer, basketball, wrestling, baseball, lacrosse, and tennis for boys; soccer, volleyball, basketball, lacrosse, tennis, and softball for girls; and coeducational teams in cross-country, golf, snow skiing, and Ultimate Frisbee. Recreational mountain biking, rock climbing, wilderness ways, weight lifting, snowboarding, canoeing, dance, and yoga are also available. The Marvelwood boys' lacrosse, basketball, and tennis teams have won numerous championships, and the girls' volleyball and basketball teams are becoming strong championship contenders. The Athletic Director welcomes new ideas, and new teams or activities may be organized according to interest.

Student clubs are formed in photography, drama, literary magazine, yearbook, newspaper, student government, dance, chess, cooking, chorus, and cultural/social awareness. On- and off-campus activities are planned for every weekend including movies, skating, dances, trips to New York or Boston to see baseball games, plays or music at the Hartford Stage or Hartford Symphony, golf, mountain biking, and shopping.

ADMISSION AND COSTS. Marvelwood seeks boys and girls of "untapped potential," who will benefit from an environment that is structured, personalized, supportive, and challenging. A Marvelwood student is of average to above-average intelligence and may not have reached his or her full potential. These youngsters may also be gifted or talented in a particular area or may have different learning styles. Applicants are required to provide both parent and student applications, current transcripts, three recommendations, and the results of standardized test scores. An on-campus interview is required.

In 2007–08, day tuition is $23,600; boarding tuition is $39,000. The optional Strategies or Math Tutorial Program is an additional $6925 per year. Financial aid is available.

Headmaster: Scott E. Pottbecker
Assistant Head/Dean of Faculty: Blythe Everett
Director of Studies: Jamie Dwan
Dean of Students: Edward Banach
Director of Admissions: Katherine Almquist
Director of Development: Irene Hopkins
Director of Counseling Services: John Kennedy
Director of College Counseling: William Bingham
Athletic Director: Glenn Sanchez
Director of the Summer Program: Craig Ough

The Mead School 1969

1095 Riverbank Road, Stamford, CT 06903
Tel. 203-595-9500; Admissions Ext. 46; Fax 203-595-0735
Web Site www.meadschool.org; E-mail admissions@meadschool.org

The Mead School is a progressive learning environment committed to the development of the whole child. Enrolling approximately 170 boys and girls as day students in Nursery–Grade 8, the School combines developmentally appropriate academic programs with equal emphasis on the expressive arts and personal development. Honest and affectionate relationships, individualized programs, and the development of autonomous learners are priorities. Special-interest activities are incorporated into the regular curriculum. A summer program is available for children, ages 2–15. Tuition: $7195–$28,065. Financial Aid: $366,500. Brooke Wachtel is Director of Admissions; Karen Biddulph is Director.

The Montessori School 1964

34 Whipple Road, Wilton, CT 06897-4514
Tel. 203-834-0440; Admissions Ext. 36; Fax 203-761-9386
Web Site www.themontessorischool.com
E-mail info @themontessorischool.com
Middle School: 24 Lois Street, Norwalk, CT 06851
Tel. 203-840-1850; Fax 203-840-1852

Parents seeking a quality Montessori education for their young children founded this coeducational day school in 1964. Enrolling 232 boys and girls in PreKindergarten–Grade 8, The Montessori School is dedicated to helping each child develop confidence, competence, and respect for others. In a teacher-guided, self-directed learning environment, students work in small, multiage groups or independently to develop skills in language arts, math, science, social studies, and modern language. Lessons from nature are integrated into the academic program at all levels through outdoor projects such as gardening, composting, and camping. Art, chorus, foreign language, drama, and physical education enhance the core curriculum. A learning specialist assists children with special needs. Among the activities are sports and age-appropriate outreach and community service endeavors. The School is accredited by the Association Montessori International and holds membership in the Connecticut Association of Independent Schools. Before- and after-school care is available. Tuition: $10,500–$18,100. One-time Enrollment Fee: $2000. Financial Aid: $395,800. Steve Slaughter is Director of Admissions; Mary Zeman was appointed Head of School in 1988.

Mooreland Hill School 1930

166 Lincoln Road, Kensington, CT 06037
Tel. 860-223-6428; Admission Ext. 303; Fax 860-223-3318
Web Site www.mooreland.org; E-mail admissions@mooreland.org

Mooreland Hill School, founded by parents as a day middle school, is dedicated to the development of the child through the challenges of a strong, traditional academic curriculum with extensive opportunities for social and physical growth. Enrolled are 50 boys and girls in Grades 5–8 who follow a full academic schedule including French, Spanish, and Latin and enriched with programs in music, art, computer, and Human Growth and Development. All students participate in interscholastic sports. Extracurricular activities include drama, chorus, instrumental ensemble, student publications, and clubs and activities. Tuition & Fees: $17,900. Financial Aid: $139,000. Michael D. Dooman was appointed Headmaster in 2006.

New Canaan Country School 1916

545 Ponus Ridge, P.O. Box 997, New Canaan, CT 06840
Tel. 203-972-0771; Admission Ext. 204; Fax 203-966-5924
Web Site www.countryschool.net; E-mail admission@countryschool.net

Designated a National Exemplary "Blue Ribbon School" by the United States Department of Education, New Canaan Country School enrolls a diverse population of over 600 girls and boys in Beginners through Grade 9. The NCCS hands-on program combines creativity with high academic standards, reflecting the School's philosophy of educating the "whole child" through experiences designed to guide each student toward attaining his or her intellectual, creative, moral, and physical potential. The 75-acre campus includes seven major buildings, seven playing fields, two gymnasiums, a professional auditorium, and a 30-acre nature preserve. Tuition: $20,600–$26,240. Financial Aid: $2,630,000. Patricia F. Oakes is Director of Admission; Timothy R. Bazemore was appointed Head in 2000.

Notre Dame of West Haven 1946

24 Ricardo Street, West Haven, CT 06516-2499
Tel. 203-933-1673; Admission Ext. 501; Fax 203-933-2474
Web Site www.notredamehs.com
E-mail admissions@notredamehs.com

Founded and operated by the Brothers of Holy Cross, Notre Dame of West Haven is a Roman Catholic, college preparatory day school enrolling 700 young men in Grades 9–12. The school's mission is to assist parents in educating their sons, working to develop respect, dedication, and excellence in each student. The curriculum, which includes honors and Advanced Placement courses, accommodates a variety of learning abilities, and a 12:1 student-faculty ratio permits close, individualized attention. A strong athletic program, the fine arts, student government, publications, and interest clubs are among the activities. Tuition: $8500. Financial aid is available. Pasquale G. Izzo is Director of Admissions; Br. James Branigan, CSC, is President. *New England Association.*

Pear Tree Point School 1996

90 Pear Tree Point Road, Darien, CT 06820-0682
Tel. 203-655-0030; Fax 203-655-3164
Web Site www.ptpschool.org; E-mail info@ptpschool.org

Pear Tree Point School is a small, close-knit learning community enrolling over 200 boys and girls as day students in Pre-Kindergarten through Grade 5. As an official Core Knowledge School, Pear Tree Point School focuses on the development of cultural literacy through in-depth studies in history, geography, language arts, math, and science. Children learn in classrooms of 15 or fewer students, each staffed by a head teacher and an assistant; the overall faculty-student ratio is 1:4. Spanish, drama, technology, music, art, and physical education enrich the program at all levels. Students take part in after-school activities such as chess, crafts, cooking, photography, and team sports. Tuition: $23,500–$27,500. Financial aid is available. Janice Hawes is Director of Admissions; David Trigaux is Headmaster.

The Pine Brook School 1972

56 Stony Creek Road, Branford, CT 06405
Tel. 203-481-0363; Fax 203-488-3985
Web Site www.pinebrookschool.org
E-mail ssprague@pinebrookschool.org

Founded as Wightwood School in 1972, The Pine Brook School enrolls 90 children in PreK–Grade 8. Pine Brook aims to provide a challenging program in a learning environment that is responsive to individual needs while fostering intellectual curiosity, creativity, confidence, and social responsibility. The curriculum follows a thematic approach in which a single grade-appropriate topic integrates all the academic disciplines. Specialists teach art, music, physical education, Spanish, library, and multicultural studies at all levels. Small classes encourage strong relationships among students, faculty, and parents. Extended-day services, a flexible PreKindergarten schedule, and a full-day Kindergarten are offered. Tuition: $10,900–$14,300. Shelley Sprague is Head of School.

Pine Point School 1948

89 Barnes Road, Stonington, CT 06378
Tel. 860-535-0606; Admission Ext. 135; Fax 860-535-8033
Web Site www.pinepoint.org; E-mail admission@pinepoint.org

Pine Point, a coeducational day school on 25 wooded acres, enrolls 270 students in Preschool–Grade 9 from throughout Southeastern Connecticut and Rhode Island. It offers a strong, developmentally based curriculum with emphasis on hands-on learning and the importance of each student's social, emotional, and physical growth. All students participate weekly in dance, music, art, and physical education. The program in Grades 6–9 has advisory, community service, team sports, state-of-the-art science and technology labs, and an oceanology program with a School-owned research vessel. A summer day camp is offered for ages 3–15. Tuition: $3040–$18,510. Financial Aid: $500,000. Julie W. Abbiati is Admission Director; Paul G. Geise is Head of School.

Renbrook School 1935

2865 Albany Avenue, West Hartford, CT 06117
Tel. 860-236-1661; Fax 860-231-8206
Web Site www.renbrook.org; E-mail aclemons@renbrook.org

This coeducational day school encompassing preKindergarten through Grade 9 enrolls 525 students; 23 percent are children of color; the student-teacher ratio is 6:1. Renbrook's mission calls for the development of each child's academic and personal potential. The curriculum is enriched by the arts, athletics, science, and technology. French and Spanish start in Kindergarten, Latin in Grade 6. Opportunities include independent study, honors classes, performing arts, international travel, interscholastic sports, and community service. Renbrook offers child care services and Summer Adventure day camp sessions. Tuition: $6645–$25,895. Financial Aid: $1,905,201. Amy Clemons is Director of Admission; Jane C. Shipp (Rhodes College, B.A.; Brown, M.A.) is Headmistress.

Ridgefield Academy 1976

223A West Mountain Road, Ridgefield, CT 06877
Tel. 203-894-1800; Admissions Ext. 112; Fax 203-894-1810
Web Site www.ridgefieldacademy.com
E-mail lmattson@ridgefieldacademy.com

Ridgefield Academy, a coeducational day school enrolling 370 students in Pre-School–Grade 8 on the Ridgefield campus and 400 on the Westport and Redding Pre-School campuses, seeks to develop knowledgeable, independent thinkers who are eager to assume responsibility for their own education and for citizenship in the 21st century. In a close-knit learning community, students follow a sequential curriculum that encompasses language arts, math, social studies, science, French, art, technology,

library, and physical education. Classes are small with a maximum student-teacher ratio of 12:1. Students enjoy a variety of extracurricular activities such as community service, chorus, school newspaper, music and drama, and sports for boys and girls. Summer programs are available. Tuition: $8000–$19,800. Libby Mattson is Director of Admission; James P. Heus is Head of School.

Rumsey Hall School 1900

201 Romford Road, Washington Depot, CT 06794
Tel. 860-868-0535; Fax 860-868-7907
Web Site www.rumseyhall.org; E-mail admiss@rumseyhall.org

Rumsey Hall School in Washington Depot, Connecticut, is a coeducational boarding and country day school for students in Kindergarten through Grade 9. The boarding program begins in Grade 5. Situated in the southern range of the Berkshire Hills, Washington (population 4000) is 42 miles west of Hartford and 80 miles northeast of New York City. The region, which offers wooded countryside and access to several ski areas, is the site of numerous other independent schools and colleges.

Founded by Mrs. Lillias Rumsey Sanford in Seneca Falls, New York, in 1900, the School moved to larger quarters in Cornwall, Connecticut, in 1907, and to the present campus in 1948. Mrs. Sanford has been succeeded as Director by John F. Schereschewsky, Sr. (1941–1969), John F. Schereschewsky, Jr. (1969–1977), Louis G. Magnoli (1969–1985), and Thomas W. Farmen, the present Headmaster.

Since its inception in 1900, Rumsey Hall School has retained its original philosophy: to help each child develop "to his or her maximum stature as an individual, as a member of a family, and as a contributing member of society." The School aims to provide the support, nurture, and care that children need while presenting appropriate academic challenge and rigor. The basic curriculum is designed to teach students to read, write, and calculate proficiently and to establish the educational foundations that prepare them for success in secondary school and college. Rumsey Hall embraces the ideal of "honor through effort" and emphasizes effort more than grades as the criterion for achievement.

A nonprofit institution, Rumsey Hall School is directed by

a 24-member Board of Trustees, which meets quarterly. The School holds membership in the National Association of Independent Schools, the Connecticut Association of Independent Schools, Junior Boarding Schools Association, the Educational Records Bureau, the Secondary School Admissions Test Board, and Western Connecticut Boarding Schools Association.

THE CAMPUS. The 147-acre campus on the Bantam River provides landscaped and wooded areas, nine athletic fields, two skating ponds, and three outdoor tennis courts. The John F. Schereschewsky Center contains indoor athletic facilities, including three tennis courts.

The School is housed in 29 buildings, most of which have been constructed since 1950. Five structures provide a total of 27 classrooms, including the new Dicke Family Math and Science Centers. Other buildings house the study hall, two computer labs, and seven language skills classrooms.

The recently built Maxwell Sarofim '05 Performing Arts Center enhances the drama and music programs.

THE FACULTY. Thomas W. Farmen, appointed Headmaster in 1985, is a graduate of New England College (B.A.) and Western Connecticut State University (M.S.A.). He has also served at Rumsey Hall as a teacher, Director of Athletics, and Director of Secondary School Placement.

There are 50 full-time teachers, 25 men and 25 women. Thirty, including 11 with families, reside on campus. They hold 50 baccalaureate and 11 master's degrees, representing study at such institutions as Allegheny, Barnard, Bates, Bethany, Bowdoin, Colby, Connecticut College, Dartmouth, Elmira, Lafayette College, Long Island University, Lynchburg, Middlebury, New England College, Northern Kentucky, Randolph-Macon, Rollins, St. Lawrence, Springfield, Syracuse, Trinity, Tulane, Wesleyan, Western Connecticut State, Wheaton, Williams, Yale, and the Universities of Connecticut, Massachusetts, Michigan, and New Hampshire.

Five nurses staff the school infirmary, and a local doctor is on call. Emergency facilities are located in New Milford, 10 miles distant.

STUDENT BODY. In 2007–08, the School enrolled 303 students including 70 boarding boys, 43 boarding girls, 119 day boys, and 71 day girls in Kindergarten–Grade 9. In addition to Connecticut, resident students come from 20 other states and 12 countries.

ACADEMIC PROGRAM. The school year, from September to early June, provides 32 weeks of instruction, a Thanksgiving recess, and extended vacations at Christmas and in the spring. Classes, which have an average enrollment of 12, meet six days a week for the upper school and five days a week for the lower school. The daily schedule, from 8:00 A.M. to 4:30 P.M., includes a school meeting each morning, eight 40-minute class periods, lunch, extra-help sessions, and athletics in the afternoon. A supervised study hall is conducted from 7:00 to 8:30 P.M. each evening for boarding students. Clubs and activities meet each Monday.

All faculty members are available to provide special assistance during the afternoon extra-help period. Individualized language skills programs, administered by reading specialists, and English as a Second Language are offered at an additional cost.

Students have appropriate homework assignments, to be completed during study halls. Class assignments for the week are issued on Monday and graded each day. Faculty members meet once a week to review the work of each student and prepare reports, based on homework and class quizzes, that are issued biweekly to parents and students. Faculty members also compile a weekly effort list of students who the instructors feel have put forth maximum effort during that period. Both art and music are required in all grades.

In 2007, the School's graduates entered such independent secondary schools as Avon Old Farms, Cheshire Academy, Choate Rosemary Hall, Deerfield, The Hill School, Proctor Academy, St. Paul's, Salisbury, Suffield, and Taft.

Rumsey's five-week academic summer session enrolls approximately 75 boarding and day students in Grades 3–9. The program offers courses in English, elementary mathematics, algebra, and study skills. Classes are held five days a week.

STUDENT ACTIVITIES. Students in the Upper School may join such interest groups as community service, computer keyboarding, biking, fly fishing, school newspaper, chorus, rocketry, weight lifting, ceramics, yearbook, Ultimate Frisbee, golf, street hockey, a cappella, and drama clubs. In the Lower School, students can be involved in the creation of an original opera, either composing, writing, designing, set building, lighting, or performing. Student government organizations exist for students of all ages.

Interscholastic teams for students are organized in football, soccer, cross-country, hockey, skiing, wrestling, baseball, tennis, crew, and lacrosse for boys, and in field hockey, soccer, hockey, basketball, cross-country, volleyball, skiing, softball, tennis, and crew for girls. The student body is divided into Red and Blue teams, with intramural competition culminating in a Red and Blue Track Meet on Memorial Day. An equestrian program and recreational sports such as sledding, skiing, hiking, mountain biking, and fishing are also available.

Although boarding students have free time on weekends, they also participate in organized on-campus activities. Off-campus trips and various activities are planned each weekend, and day students are welcome to attend. Rumsey's location allows students to enjoy numerous cultural and entertainment activities in New Haven, Hartford, Boston, and New York City. Traditional annual events for the school community include

Parents' Days, the Holiday Carol Sing, a winter ski trip, Grandparents' Day, and Commencement.

ADMISSION AND COSTS. Rumsey Hall seeks to enroll students of good character and ability without regard to race, creed, or color. Students are admitted to Grades K–9 on the basis of an application form, a personal interview, recommendations from previous teachers, and an official school transcript.

In 2007–08, tuition is $36,520 for boarding students and between $13,840 and $17,440 for day students, depending on grade. In the current year, students received $630,000 in financial aid.

Associate Headmaster: Rick S. Spooner
Dean of Students: Clayton Ketchum
Assistant Headmaster for Enrollment Management: Matthew S. Hoeniger
Director of Development: Kim Pugh
Assistant Headmaster Secondary School Placement/Academic Affairs: Francis M. Ryan
Business Manager: Dorota Habib
Director of Athletics: Jay Przygocki
Director of Lower School: Rob Brenner
Coordinator of Girls' & Women's Issues: Allison Spooner-Linley

St. Luke's School 1928

377 North Wilton Road, P.O. Box 1148, New Canaan, CT 06840
Tel. 203-801-4833; Fax 203-972-3450
Web Site www.stlukesct.org; E-mail info@stlukesct.org

Now entering its 8th decade, St. Luke's School has sought to instill in students "a lifelong commitment to learning and social responsibility." St. Luke's is a nondenominational, coeducational school enrolling 500 day students from diverse backgrounds in a college preparatory program encompassing Grades 5–12. The School's programs are guided by an emphasis on academic excellence, service to others, and strong, healthy relationships among students and teachers. The curriculum features offerings in the liberal arts, sciences, and humanities designed to inspire active learning, critical thinking, and creative problem solving. In the Upper School, qualified students can earn college credit through AP courses in 18 subject areas. Students use state-of-the-art technology as learning tools throughout the disciplines. The 40-acre campus provides a natural classroom for scientific discovery and experimentation. Students are involved in social outreach, school government, four publications, drama, band, chorus, clubs, Model UN, and 12 team sports. Tuition: $27,900–$28,300. Samuel Gaudet is Director of Admission; Mark Davis is Head of School. *New England Association.*

St. Thomas's Day School 1956

830 Whitney Avenue, New Haven, CT 06511
Tel. 203-776-2123; Fax 203-776-3467
Web Site www.stthomasday.org; E-mail info@stthomasday.org

St. Thomas's is an Episcopal day school serving 155 children in Junior Kindergarten–Grade 6. As a mission of St. Thomas's Church, the School strives to educate students of all backgrounds by cultivating intelligence while engaging heart and spirit. It fosters academic excellence through a challenging, integrated curriculum with attention to each child's potential and learning style. St. Thomas's is characterized by a strong sense of community, a genuine commitment to children, and active parent participation. An extended-day program is available. Tuition: $15,694. Financial Aid: $298,486. Roxanne Turekian coordinates admissions; Fred Acquavita (Kansas State, B.S. 1968; Bank Street, M.S. 1981) was appointed School Head in 1981.

Salisbury School 1901

251 Canaan Road, Salisbury, CT 06068
Tel. 860-435-5700; Fax 860-435-5750
Web Site www.salisburyschool.org; E-mail admissions@salisburyschool.org

SALISBURY SCHOOL in Salisbury, Connecticut, is a college preparatory boarding and day school enrolling boys in Forms III through VI (Grades 9–12). The village of Salisbury is located in the foothills of the Berkshire Mountains. The campus is one hour from Hartford, two hours from New York, and two and a half hours from Boston, giving students access to the cultural and recreational resources of those cities and permitting shared activities with other private secondary schools and colleges in the region.

The Reverend George Emerson Quaile, an Episcopal clergyman, founded Salisbury School in 1901. From its inception, the School has sought to imbue young men with the self-confidence necessary to develop their maximum potential intellectually, morally, and physically. Salisbury seeks to foster trust, service to others, and faith based on Judeo-Christian values while promoting respect and appreciation for all backgrounds and beliefs.

The School is guided by a 30-member Board of Trustees and is accredited by the New England Association of Colleges and Secondary Schools. It holds membership in the National

Association of Independent Schools and the Connecticut Association of Independent Schools, among other organizations. The Alumni Association is active in fund-raising, recruitment, and other functions supportive of Salisbury's goals. The School's endowment is valued at approximately $42,000,000.

THE CAMPUS. Salisbury is situated on a 700-acre campus, bordered on the west by the Appalachian Trail and on the north by Twin Lakes. The Main Building (1901) houses the School's dining hall, the kitchen, bookstore, post office, and administrative and faculty offices. Academic facilities are centered in the Wachtmeister Mathematics and Science Building and the 40,000-square-foot Centennial Humanities Building, including The Phinny Library, which provides 25,000 volumes, 120 periodicals, and CD-ROM access to a wide range of reference materials in major library collections across the country. Other facilities include the Ruger Fine Arts Center, the Field Music Center, the Rudd Learning Center, and a photography laboratory.

Residential facilities include nine dormitories, twelve faculty houses, and the Headmaster's home. Salisbury School provides phone service, voice mail, a campus computer network, and Internet services to every student's room.

Among the School's athletic facilities are the Olympic-size Rudd Hockey Rink with an all-purpose playing surface for year-round use; the Myers gymnasium; eight outdoor tennis courts, three of which are covered by a dome; two heated platform tennis courts; a lake; miles of cross-country trails; soccer, baseball, lacrosse, and football fields; the Class of 2003 Fitness Center, a turf field (2007); and a three-bay boathouse (2008).

THE FACULTY. Appointed in 2003, Chisholm S. Chandler, the School's seventh Headmaster, attended The Hotchkiss School, Brown University (B.A.), and Harvard University (M.Ed.). During his 17 years at Salisbury, Mr. Chandler has served in a variety of capacities including Director of Admissions, Director of College Advising, and Assistant Headmaster for External Affairs. He also served as a dorm parent, a coach, and an advisor. Mr. Chandler resides on campus with his wife, Tracy, and their three children.

The Salisbury School faculty and administration consist of 63 members. Thirty-one members hold advanced degrees, including two doctorates. Colleges and universities represented by faculty members include Amherst, Bates, Boston University, Bowdoin, Brown, Colby, Dartmouth, Dickinson, Hamilton, Harvard, Middlebury, New York University, Northeastern, Pennsylvania State, Smith, Trinity, Tufts, Vassar, Wesleyan, Williams, Yale, and the Universities of Connecticut, Denver, Michigan, North Carolina, Texas, and Vermont.

The Health Center is staffed by a resident medical doctor, available 24 hours a day. Two full-time athletic trainers live on campus.

STUDENT BODY. In 2007–08, Salisbury School enrolled 296 boys, 93 percent of whom were boarders, distributed as follows: Form III—46, Form IV—80, Form V—77, and Form VI—93. The largest numbers came from New York and Connecticut, with 25 other states and 10 nations represented.

ACADEMIC PROGRAM. The school year, divided into trimesters, extends from early September to the end of May, with a Thanksgiving recess and Christmas, midwinter, and spring breaks. Each student is assigned an advisor who guides him and maintains contact with his parents regarding all aspects of school life. Written comments from teachers are sent home regularly, and grades are issued every five weeks as a gauge of academic progress. In addition, the entire faculty reviews each student's overall record periodically. Teachers and advisors are available for consultation whenever necessary. The student-teacher ratio is 6:1, with an average class enrolling 12 boys.

Students who need to develop reading, writing, time-management skills, and other academic areas may be tested and referred to the Rudd Learning Center for one-on-one tutoring. A fee is charged for this service.

Classes are held six days a week, with half days on Wednesday and Saturday. A typical schedule begins with breakfast from 7:00 to 8:00 A.M., followed by six 45-minute classes. All students take part in sports from 3:00 to 5:00 P.M. After dinner, evening study is held from 7:30 to 9:30 P.M., with boys back in their dorms by 10:15 P.M.

To earn the Salisbury diploma, a student must complete four years of English; three years of history, including U.S. History; three years of mathematics; three years of one foreign language or two years each of two languages; two years of laboratory science; two trimesters of art; and one year of Philosophy and Religion. Students must pass all their courses in the senior year to graduate.

Among the courses offered are English; Ancient History, World History, U.S. History, The History of Civil Rights, History of China, The World Since 1945, The Civil War/World War II/Vietnam, Economics; Algebra I and II, Algebra II and Trigonometry, Geometry, Pre-Calculus, Calculus, AB Calculus,

BC Calculus, Integrated Mathematics; French I–IV, Spanish I–V, Latin I–IV, Mandarin Chinese; Field Studies, Biology, Earth Science, Matter and Energy, Anatomy, Environmental Science, Physics, Chemistry, Forest Science, Geology, Fresh Water Ecology; Photography, Song Writing, Digital Illustration, Drawing & Painting, Sculpture, Drawing, Woodworking, Boat Building, Pottery, and The History of Jazz. Honors or Advanced Placement courses are available to qualified students. Students may also pursue a diploma with distinction in Entrepreneurial Studies. Additionally, there are opportunities to enroll in a postgraduate year in the United Kingdom through The English-Speaking Union.

College counseling begins in the Fifth Form, and representatives from colleges and universities throughout the United States visit the campus in the fall. Eighty percent of Salisbury's graduates are accepted to their first- or second-choice colleges, and, since 2000, eight or more have enrolled in such institutions as Boston College, Colgate University, Hobart College, St. Lawrence University, Trinity College, and Union College.

The Salisbury Summer School enrolls 105 boys and girls, ages 13 to 18, in a five-week program of reading, writing, and study skills.

STUDENT ACTIVITIES. Students may participate in a wide range of extracurricular activities designed to develop leadership skills as well as provide social interaction and physical well-being. The 14-member Student Council, elected from each of the four forms, works with the faculty in planning and implementing events and advising on disciplinary infractions. Students involved in the Vestry share in the planning and organization of chapel liturgies and spearhead the School's social outreach and community service projects.

Students publish a newspaper, a yearbook, and a literary magazine. There is a Gospel Choir, a Guitar Ensemble, and a Jazz Ensemble; and the Drama Club stages three plays each year. Other groups include The Cum Laude Society, the Key Society, Peer Counselors, Vestry, Radio Station, Music Technology, and the Science and Math Clubs.

On weekends, students take part in a variety of recreational and social activities, including dances, concerts, movies, and trips to New York or Boston. Many events are held in conjunction with nearby girls' schools. Popular outdoor pursuits include hiking, skiing, rock climbing, and flyfishing.

Athletic competition is organized at the varsity, junior varsity, and third levels, and the School's 31 interscholastic teams compete in cross-country, football, soccer, skiing, basketball, hockey, tennis, squash, wrestling, baseball, crew, golf, and lacrosse.

Special events on the calendar include Hilltop Day, Reunion Weekend, Parents Weekend, Christmas Service of Lessons and Carols, Fifth Form College Weekend, Awards Ceremony, and Graduation Day on the Quadrangle.

ADMISSION AND COSTS. Salisbury seeks young men of good character who demonstrate the ability to succeed in a college preparatory program and to contribute to the life of the School. Acceptance is based on an interview, previous academic records, a writing sample, recommendations from current teachers, personal references, and the results of standardized tests. A nonrefundable $750 deposit is due upon registration.

Tuition in 2007–08 is $29,700 for day students and $39,700 for boarders. Day students are assessed a general fee of $450, boarding students, $600. The technology fee is $200 for day students, $400 for boarders. Extra expenses for supplies, laundry, trips, and special tests may range from $800 to $1000. Salisbury belongs to the School and Student Service for Financial Aid and, in 2006, awarded approximately $2,200,000 to 30 percent of the student body.

Director of Admissions & Financial Aid: Peter B. Gilbert
Associate Directors of Admissions: Andrew O'Brien & Mark Leavitt
Assistant Director of Admissions: Matthew Corkery
Admissions Intern: Tim Randall

The Stanwich School, Inc. 1998

257 Stanwich Road, Greenwich, CT 06830
Tel. 203-542-0000; Admissions 203-542-0033; Fax 203-542-0025
Web Site www.stanwichschool.org
E-mail admissions@stanwichschool.org

Stanwich, a day school enrolling 436 boys and girls in Pre-Kindergarten–Grade 9, offers a rigorous and challenging college preparatory curriculum presented in a supportive way that encourages students to take increasingly greater responsibility for achieving their highest potential. It is balanced with creative fine and performing arts instruction and an athletic program that promotes healthy growth and teamwork. All faculty members hold advanced degrees and work closely with students in every aspect of school life, enriching, challenging, and encouraging them to be their best. A character culture is established through actively taught values and ethics classes founded on Judeo-Christian principles and tradition, meaningful community service, and a wide variety of enrichment activities. Small class sizes reinforce classroom lessons. Tuition: $17,500–$25,000. Financial Aid: $897,000. Kay Wall (Pre-K–Grade 3) and Ann Kroll (Grades 4–9) are Directors of Admission; Pat Young is Founding Headmistress.

The Taft School 1890

110 Woodbury Road, Watertown, CT 06795
Tel. 860-945-7777; Admissions 860-945-7700; Fax 860-945-7808
Web Site www.taftschool.org; E-mail admissions@taftschool.org

Taft is an independent, coeducational, college preparatory school enrolling 469 boarding and 108 day students in Grade 9–Postgraduate. The School fosters individual development through vigorous academic, athletic, and extracurricular programs, while providing the finest of liberal arts education through its 200-course curriculum. Advanced Placement courses are offered in every discipline. Over 40 clubs and organizations, a variety of sports, and summer enrichment courses are available. Boarding Tuition: $39,000; Day Tuition: $29,000. Financial Aid: $5,011,000. Peter A. Frew is Director of Admission; William R. MacMullen (Taft '78; Yale, B.A. 1982; Middlebury, M.A. 1989) was appointed Headmaster in 2001. *New England Association.*

The Unquowa School 1917

981 Stratfield Road, Fairfield, CT 06825
Tel. 203-336-3801; Admissions 203-367-3151; Fax 203-336-3479
Web Site www.unquowa.org; E-mail cgombos@unquowa.org

The Unquowa School is one of Connecticut's oldest independent coeducational day schools for students in PreK-3 through Grade 8. Enrolling 183 children, the School has a traditional high school preparatory curriculum with a progressive approach in a small classroom setting. All grades have studio art, music, Spanish, and daily physical education. After-school activities include Fairchester Athletic League team sports, chorus, string and guitar ensemble, and student government. Tuition: $6300–$20,750. Financial Aid: $490,000. Suellen Hansen is Admissions Director; Sharon Lauer is Head of School.

Watkinson School 1881

180 Bloomfield Avenue, Hartford, CT 06105
Tel. 860-236-5618; Fax 860-233-8295
Web Site www.watkinson.org; E-mail john_crosson@watkinson.org

Watkinson is a coeducational, college preparatory school for students in Grade 6–Postgraduate. Its mission is to help students develop the power to shape their lives and the world around them. A Lead Member of the Coalition of Essential Schools, Watkinson enrolls 280 day students from 40 towns and a wide range of academic, personal, and socioeconomic backgrounds. Special offerings include creative arts, technology, competitive and intramural sports, the Learning Skills Program, and classes at the adjacent University of Hartford. Homestays for international students and summer courses are also available. Tuition: $27,100. Financial Aid: $1,720,000. John J. Crosson is Director of Admissions; John W. Bracker (Haverford, B.A. 1984; Harvard, M.Ed. 1992) is Headmaster. *New England Association.*

Westminster School 1888

995 Hopmeadow Street, Simsbury, CT 06070-1812
Tel. 860-408-3060; Fax 860-408-3042
Web Site www.westminster-school.org
E-mail admit@westminster-school.org

Westminster is a college preparatory, coeducational, day and boarding school enrolling 375 students in Grade 9 through a postgraduate year. Students come from 22 states and 16 countries. The School's core values of community, character, balance, and involvement help students develop scholarship, leadership, citizenship, and sportsmanship. The rigorous liberal arts curriculum is supplemented by 23 Advanced Placement courses and electives such as Architecture. Gothic Fiction, Moral Philosophy, Latin, and Astronomy. Study-abroad opportunities in China, Italy, France, and England enhance the program. Extracurricular activities include community service, tour guides, choir, dance, band, tutoring, student council, Literary Society, publications, and outdoor education. Athletes are involved in over 50 sports teams, including squash, lacrosse, and field hockey. The 200-acre campus holds a 26,000-volume library, music and art studios, state-of-the-art athletic facilities, and theater. Boarding Tuition: $39,700; Day Tuition: $29,300. Financial Aid: $3,000,000. Jon Deveaux is Director of Admissions; W. Graham Cole, Jr. (Williams College, B.A.; Columbia University, M.A.), was appointed Headmaster in 1993. *New England Association.*

Westover School 1909

1237 Whittemore Road, P.O. Box 847, Middlebury, CT 06762
Tel. 203-758-2423; Admission 203-577-4521; Fax 203-577-4588
Web Site www.westoverschool.org
E-mail admission@westoverschool.org

Westover School, enrolling 122 boarding and 72 day students, challenges young women in Grades 9–12 to participate in all areas of academic, community, and athletic life. The School is diverse, with students from 19 countries and 15 states. Girls take advantage of numerous electives, 17 Advanced Placement courses, visual and performing arts, and outdoor activities. Three special programs enhance the curriculum: Women In Science and Engineering with Rensselaer Polytechnic Institute; a joint program with the Manhattan School of Music; and a program with the Brass City Ballet. Boarding Tuition: $37,650; Day Tuition: $26,100. Financial Aid: $2,000,000. Sara Lynn Renda is Director of Admission; Ann S. Pollina is Head of School.

Whitby School 1958

969 Lake Avenue, Greenwich, CT 06831
Tel. 203-869-8464; Admission Ext. 193; Fax 203-869-2215
Web Site www.whitbyschool.org; E-mail whitby@whitbyschool.org

Whitby, located in the Greenwich countryside, was founded in 1958 as the first Montessori school in the United States. Through the principles of Montessori education, Whitby provides opportunities for 345 children from Pre-School (18 months)–Grade 8 in a multiaged setting. Montessori-trained teachers work with students individually or in small groups in a warm, supportive classroom environment. French, Spanish, Mandarin, music, art, drama, and physical education enhance the core curriculum. The School is dedicated to building children's confidence and competency while nurturing their inherent joy of learning. Tuition: $15,700–$25,200. Financial Aid: $600,000. Dr. Michele Monson (Lesley, B.S., M.Ed.; Harvard, Ed.D.) is Head of School.

The Williams School 1891

182 Mohegan Avenue, New London, CT 06320-4110
Tel. 860-443-5333; Fax 860-439-2796
Web Site www.williamsschool.org; E-mail gayle_holt@williamsschool.org

THE WILLIAMS SCHOOL in New London, Connecticut, is a coeducational, college preparatory day school enrolling students in Grades 7 through 12. Located in the southeastern corner of the state on Long Island Sound and the Thames River, New London (population 23,869) is home to Connecticut College and the U.S. Coast Guard Academy.

Originally named The Williams Memorial Institute, the School was funded by an endowment created by Harriet Peck Williams. It opened in 1891 as a school "for the promotion and advancement of female education." For more than half a century, the Institute was the comprehensive high school for girls in New London. With the advent of a large city public high school in 1951, the School became preparatory in nature. In 1954, it moved to the grounds of Connecticut College. Boys were admitted to Grades 7–8 in 1971 and to all grades the following year.

The mission of The Williams School is to "foster the intellectual, moral, aesthetic, and physical development of young women and men" as they prepare for a life of learning and participation in a changing world. The School strives to be a thoughtful, vibrant community of adults and students who come together in the pursuit of knowledge and growth. Academic challenges and personal rewards take place in an environment of support and respectful, collaborative relationships.

This nonprofit institution is administered by the Head of School; a 21-member Board of Trustees establishes broad policies and oversees its financial health. Alumni and Parents Associations provide active support through volunteering, fundraising, and sponsoring programs and special events. Accredited by the New England Association of Schools and Colleges,

Williams is a member of the National Association of Independent Schools, the Connecticut Association of Independent Schools, and the Secondary School Admission Test Board.

THE CAMPUS. The Williams School occupies a tract of land on the Connecticut College campus. Erected in 1954, the school building contains 41 classrooms, including state-of-the-art science laboratories, a library/media center, four technology labs, a new fitness center, Performing Arts Center, two gymnasiums, a faculty room, and the Williams Room, used for receptions and special gatherings. Every classroom has Internet access.

Two miles from the main campus, a new athletic complex on 23 acres provides playing and practice fields, rest rooms, and parking.

THE FACULTY. Charlotte L. Rea (Lake Erie College, B.A.; New York University, M.A.; Columbia University, M.Ed.) was appointed Head of School in 1998. Before coming to Williams, she was Head of the Upper School at the Brearley School in New York City and Academic Dean at Northfield Mount Hermon School in Massachusetts.

Twenty-seven women and 17 men comprise the faculty, who hold 25 master's degrees and 5 doctorates. They studied at such institutions as Boston Conservatory, Boston University, Colgate, College of the Holy Cross, Connecticut College, Dartmouth, Durham University, Eastern Connecticut State, Fairfield University, Florida State, Fordham, George Washington University, Goddard, Hamilton, Harvard, Indiana State, Indiana University, London School of Economics, Middlebury, Ohio Wesleyan, Princeton, Rensselaer, St. Edmund Hall (Oxford), St. Petersburg University, Southern Connecticut State, State University of New York, Trinity College, Tufts, Union, Wellesley, Wesleyan University, Yale, and the Universities of Alabama, Bridgeport, Connecticut, Delaware, Michigan, Nebraska, and Vermont.

The School employs a nurse, a social worker, a health instructor, and an athletic trainer.

STUDENT BODY. In 2007–08, the School enrolled 314 students, of whom 45 percent are boys and 55 percent are girls, ages 12–18, as follows: 29 in Grade 7, 38 in Grade 8, 57 in Grade 9, 61 in Grade 10, 67 in Grade 11, and 62 in Grade 12. Students represent diverse backgrounds; 20 percent are of African-American, Asian, Hispanic, or Native American heritage. Students live in New London and surrounding communities and several towns in Rhode Island.

ACADEMIC PROGRAM. The school year begins in late August and ends in early June with Thanksgiving, winter, and spring breaks. The Upper School year is divided into two semesters, each two quarters in length. Letter grades and written comments are reported each quarter; final examinations are administered each semester.

The Middle School (Grades 7–8) focuses on a core curriculum that responds to the developmental needs and learning styles of the age group. Disciplines include English, mathematics, world languages, history, and science. An Enrichment Program provides opportunities in the creative arts, computer literacy, and physical education.

Upper School courses include English I–IV; Algebra I–II, Geometry, Honors Geometry, Intermediate Algebra, Pre-Calculus, Differential Calculus, Calculus, Introduction to Statistics, Senior Functions; Biology, Chemistry, Physics, Environmental Science; Ancient World History, Modern World History, U.S. History, Modern Germany, Music History, The Pursuit of Freedom, History of the Sixties, Government, Economics; French I–V, Spanish I–V, Latin I–II and Classical Languages III–IV, Virgil/Latin Literature, Classical Studies; Computer I–III; Acting Technique, Intermediate Acting, Advanced Acting, Musical Theater, Production; Beginning, Intermediate and Advanced Dance Technique I–II; Music Theory, and Music Composition. Honors courses begin in Grade 10, and preparation for various Advanced Placement courses is offered in English, calculus, history, the sciences, computer, art, music, and foreign languages. Classes range in size from 4 to 18 students, with a median enrollment of 13. The teacher-student ratio is 1:8.

To graduate, students must earn a minimum of 20 credits. These include 4 credits each in English, mathematics, foreign language (including three years of one language in the Upper School), at least one year of Latin, 2 credits each in history and laboratory science, 3 in electives, and 1 in the fine arts. The minimum course load is 5 credits annually; most students earn more. Qualified students, with faculty approval, may take independent study courses in connection with Connecticut College through the New London Scholars program.

During the last two weeks of the second semester, seniors are engaged in off-campus projects in order to explore career possibilities.

Beginning at 8:00 A.M. and ending at 3:30 P.M., classes operate on a seven-day rotation schedule, with major subjects meeting six of the seven days. Classes are 45 minutes long; each rotation has one double period of 75 minutes. Assigned study halls and an extra-help period are built into the daily schedule.

The advisor program facilitates communication among students, teachers, and parents. New students and Middle School students are assigned advisors, while returning students may select their own. Every faculty member serves as an advisor to 12 students. The groups meet weekly.

College counseling starts at the beginning of the junior year when parents and students meet with the counselor. Students undertake a number of writing tasks and conversations designed to clarify specific needs and interests. All graduates go on to four-year colleges. In the last three years, graduates have entered the following institutions: Amherst, Babson, Boston College, Boston University, Brown, Carnegie Mellon, Cornell, Fordham, Gettysburg, Hamilton, Harvard, Haverford, Hobart and William Smith, Ithaca, Johns Hopkins, Kenyon, Loyola College, Massachusetts Institute of Technology, New York University, Oberlin, Providence, St. Andrews (Scotland), Skidmore, Smith, Trinity, Trinity College (Dublin), Tufts, Tulane, Vassar, Wheaton, Yale, and the Universities of Aberdeen (Scotland), Connecticut, Edinburgh, Michigan, Pennsylvania, and Vermont.

The School hosts Summer Sticks, an evening lacrosse camp held during the last week of June, and a field hockey camp in August.

STUDENT ACTIVITIES. Students may develop interests and leadership skills through a variety of clubs and committees such as Student Council, Judiciary Committee, Ambassadors (tour guides), Spirit Committee, Chess Club, and *Legenda* (yearbook). The Multicultural Club plans programs and events throughout the year. Those interested in the arts may participate in Band, Jazz Band, String Ensemble, Chorus, and Thespians. Each year, three major productions are presented including a musical and two dance-music collaborations, Winterfest and Compchorea. The visual arts program also hosts an annual exhibit.

While there is no community service requirement, a majority of students participate in a range of volunteer activities coordinated by the service committee.

A majority of students participate in interscholastic sports, which begin in Grade 7. Most teams have varsity and junior varsity levels. Boys compete in soccer, basketball, baseball, tennis, and lacrosse; girls compete in field hockey, soccer, basketball, tennis, softball, and lacrosse. Coeducational teams are fielded in cross-country, golf, swimming, and sailing. The School belongs to the New England Preparatory School Athletic Conference and the Connecticut Independent School Athletic Conference. An athletic director, certified athletic trainer, and coaching staff oversee all facets of the program.

Among the traditional celebrations are Host Family Dinner, Spirit Week, Halloween Parade, Grandparents' Day, Holiday Ball, Upper School Prize Night, Diversity Day, Middle School Moving Up Night, and Commencement.

ADMISSION AND COSTS. The Williams School seeks students who have demonstrated solid work habits, show academic promise, and are committed to active participation in school life. Candidates must submit transcripts from the past two years, any standardized test scores, recommendations from an English and a math teacher, and results of the Secondary School Admission Test and writing sample. The application fee is $50. Upon submission of all relevant materials, candidates typically spend a full day on campus shadowing a host student.

In 2007–08, tuition is $21,505. The optional lunch plan is $750 for the year, while the cost of textbooks is approximately $500. In 2006–07, more than $1,250,000 in financial aid was awarded to greater than 28 percent of the student body. Williams subscribes to the School and Student Service for Financial Aid.

Assistant Head of School & Upper School Head: Mark Fader
Director of Admission & Middle School Coordinator: Gayle A. Holt
Director of Development: Ellen Spring
Director of Communications: Tim Reitz
Director of College Counseling: Meghan Ryan
Business Manager: Kathy Trammell
School Counselor: Loren Sterman
Diversity Director: Ana Ramirez

Wooster School 1926

91 Miry Brook Road, Danbury, CT 06810
Tel. 203-830-3900; Admissions 203-830-3916; Fax 203-790-7147
Web Site www.woosterschool.org
E-mail gary.taylor@woosterschool.org

Serving 400 students from Fairfield and Westchester Counties, Wooster is a coeducational, K–12 day school committed to its founding principles: Intellectual Excellence, Hard Work, Simplicity, and Religion. Central to its mission and values, Wooster has a long tradition of diversity; 25 percent of students receive financial aid, and 21 percent represent an ethnic minority. In Grades 9–12, the rigorous college preparatory curriculum offers Honors and AP courses in core subjects including computer science, music, and art; a year-long Study Abroad program in France or Spain; personalized college guidance; and emphasis on moral and ethical values, including community service. Tuition: $17,050–$26,490. Year Abroad: $33,240. Gary Taylor is Dean of Admission; Tim Golding is Headmaster. *New England Association.*

DELAWARE

Archmere Academy 1932

3600 Philadelphia Pike, P.O. Box 130, Claymont, DE 19703
Tel. 302-798-6632/610-485-0373
Admissions 302-798-6632, Ext. 703; Fax 302-798-7290
Web Site www.archmereacademy.org
E-mail jjordan@archmereacademy.org

This Roman Catholic, college preparatory day school enrolls approximately 500 boys and girls in Grades 9–12. Staffed by lay faculty and Norbertine priests, the Academy maintains a student-teacher ratio of 15:1. Curriculum requirements include math, science, foreign language, religion, history, and English; electives include music, art, computer, and speech. Advanced Placement courses cover 19 subjects. Computer, writing, and language labs; media and guidance centers; and a full range of sports and activities are offered. Tuition: $17,100. Extras: $250–$1300. Financial aid is available. John J. Jordan is Director of Admissions; the Rev. Joseph McLaughlin, O.Praem (University of Wisconsin, M.A.; Villanova University, M.A.), was appointed Headmaster in 2006; Paul J. Pomeroy, Jr. (University of Delaware, M.Ed.), was appointed Principal in 2007. *Middle States Association.*

The Independence School 1978

1300 Paper Mill Road, Newark, DE 19711
Tel. 302-239-0330; Admission 302-239-0332; Fax 302-239-3696
Web Site www.theindependenceschool.org
E-mail claire.brechter@theindependenceschool.org

This coeducational day school enrolling 804 students in PreSchool (age 3) through Grade 8 strives for academic excellence in a structured environment that reflects traditional Judeo-Christian values. The curriculum emphasizes strong academic skills and the arts. Foreign language study (French, German, Spanish) and computer technology begin in Grade 1; Latin is offered in Grades 5–8. Activities include jazz and concert bands, string instrumental music, chorus, 11 sports, yearbook, computer club, drama club, Science Olympiad, Math Counts, and Odyssey of the Mind. Twelve-month extended care and summer camp are offered. Tuition: $5748–$10,632. Claire Brechter is Director of Admission; Patricia A. Ireland (University of Pennsylvania, B.A.) is Head of School. *Middle States Association.*

St. Mark's High School 1969

Pike Creek Road, Wilmington, DE 19808
Tel. 302-738-3300; Fax 302-738-5132
Web Site www.stmarkshs.net

St. Mark's High School is a Roman Catholic, diocesan day school enrolling 1590 young men and women in Grades 9–12. The School aims to foster intellectual, spiritual, and social development according to each student's needs. The curriculum lists 300 courses on five ability levels, ranging from remedial to Advanced Placement. Extracurricular activities, including the Student Council, 47 boys' and girls' athletic teams, 19 clubs, 3 publications, drama, and music, are encouraged. Tuition: $8151. Financial Aid: $850,000. Thomas Lemon is Admissions Director; Mark J. Freund (Towson University, B.A.; Loyola College [Maryland], M.Ed.) was appointed Principal in 1998. *Middle States Association.*

Salesianum School 1903

1801 North Broom Street, Wilmington, DE 19802-2891
Tel. 302-654-2495; Fax 302-654-7767
Web Site www.salesianum.org; E-mail mwinchell@salesianum.org

SALESIANUM SCHOOL in Wilmington, Delaware, is a Roman Catholic, college preparatory day school enrolling boys in Grades 9 through 12. It is located at the intersection of Broom and 18th Streets, a few blocks from where Interstate 95 and Route 202 cross, and is easily accessible for those traveling by car. Many students commute to and from school by buses, some operated by companies contracted by Salesianum and other private schools, and some on public lines. The regularly scheduled buses cover routes in Delaware, Maryland, and parts of Pennsylvania and southwestern New Jersey.

Salesianum School was founded by the Oblate Fathers and Brothers of Saint Francis de Sales, the 17th-century teacher and spiritual writer who became known as "the Gentleman Saint." Three members of the Oblate order were the first faculty members, and 12 boys were enrolled when Salesianum opened in 1903. By 1957, when the School began a new era by relocating to its present site, 2312 young men had been graduated. Another era opened as the School approached its 2003 centennial celebration with major building and renovation projects that are still being implemented.

Salesianum continues to educate its students following the model of Saint Francis de Sales, who counseled that one should submit to the guidance of God-given reason, live with a mind open to learning and growth, serve the community, value brotherhood, and contribute positively to society. The love of learning is central to the School's aims, and the key to learning is study.

Salesianum School is governed by a Board of Trustees that includes members of the Oblate order, alumni, and parents. The School now has more than 13,000 alumni living in 48 states and around the world, and they provide financial and other support for the School.

Salesianum is fully accredited by the Middle States Association of Colleges and Schools.

THE CAMPUS. The School is situated on a 22-acre campus directly across North Broom Street from Wilmington's Brandywine Park.

A 34,000-foot science center is the most significant addition to the main academic building since 1999. Eight science laboratories occupy the top two floors, and the first floor contains seven "smart" classrooms for social studies. The spaces vacated by other science departments have been re-formed as the Fine Arts Center. The first floor is devoted to the music program, including classrooms and an auditorium for performances. The top floors were renovated for art and drafting. A technology corridor with 45 computer workstations and other equipment was established for training both students and faculty. The School also renovated the gymnasium and the faculty residence and built a conference center and memorial chapel. A new dining center was completed in 2007.

The campus includes six tennis courts, two baseball diamonds, two soccer fields, a lacrosse field, a football practice area, and facilities for jumping and weight events in track and field. Some varsity athletic contests are played across 18th Street at Wilmington's Baynard Stadium.

Secure parking is provided on the campus for students, faculty, staff, and visitors.

THE FACULTY. The faculty includes 12 priests and brothers of the Oblate order, 78 lay teachers, and a professional staff of 28. Approximately two-thirds of the faculty members hold master's degrees, and the average length of teaching experience is 23 years.

STUDENT BODY. Salesianum School enrolls 1040 boys of all faiths in Grades 9 through 12. The students come from four states, with the majority from Delaware and others from Maryland, Pennsylvania, and New Jersey.

ACADEMIC PROGRAM. The academic year begins at the end of August and extends to the first of June. Vacations are scheduled at Christmas and Easter with several individual holidays occurring through the year. Classes are scheduled on a rotating basis to provide depth in all subjects and are held in six 53-minute periods between 8:17 A.M. and 2:40 P.M., five days a week. Students are grouped by ability in each subject, based on their classroom performance. Grades are issued quarterly. A Director of Educational Support Services monitors the progress of students who have a diagnosed medical condition, learning disability, or Attention Deficit Disorder, and these needs are addressed as far as possible. Teachers are available to provide extra help during the day and up to an hour after the end of the school day.

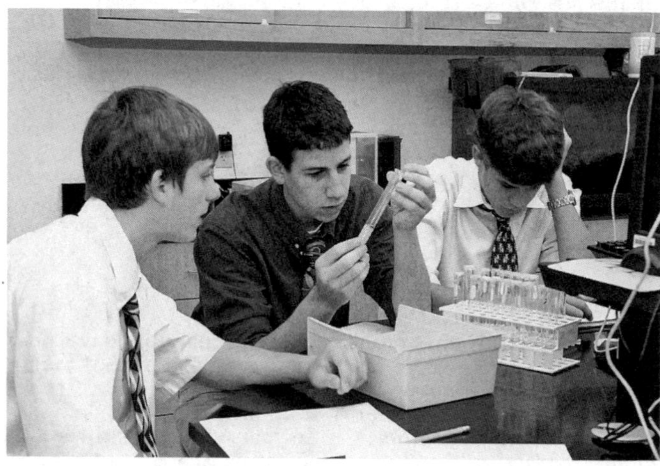

To graduate from Salesianum School, a student must complete the following credits: 4 each in Religious Studies, English, mathematics, and social studies; 3 credits in science; 2 in one foreign language; $1^1/_2$ in physical education and health; $^1/_2$ in fine arts; $^1/_2$ in technology skills; $^1/_4$ in driver education; $^1/_4$ for Junior Advisory; and 3 electives.

Some of the courses offered include Composition and Literature, American Literature, British Literature, The Novel and Drama, Western Literature, Shakespeare Theater, Journalism; French 1–5, German 1–5, Spanish 1–5, Latin 1–5; World History, U.S. History, Foreign Policy, Modern European History, Anthropology and Archaeology, Economics, Psychology; Catholic and Salesian Identity, Sacred Scripture, Morality and Social Justice, Christian Lifestyles, Senior Religion Seminar, Christian Service; Algebra, Geometry, Trigonometry, Probability/Statistics, Pre-Calculus, Introduction to Programming, Computer Science, Web Page Design; Biology, Macrobiology, Microbiology, Cell Biology, Chemistry, Physics, Advanced Physics, Biotechnology and Forensic Science, Human Anatomy/Physiology, Ecology, Environmental Science; Physical Education, Health, Sports Psychology; Concert Band, Wind Ensemble, Mixed Chorus, Music Appreciation, Music Technology, Art, Medium Exploration, Drafting, TV Production, Acting; and Accounting, Marketing, Business Law, and Consumer Economics. Advanced Placement courses are available in 23 subjects. Salesianum students participate in exchange courses with Ursuline and Padua Academies and have opportunities for independent study as well.

Virtually all graduates of Salesianum go on to further education. Some of the institutions where the most recent graduates are enrolled are Albright, American University, Boston College, Boston University, Bucknell, Carnegie Mellon, Colorado State, Cornell, Delaware College of Art and Design, De Sales, Dickinson, Drexel, Duquesne, Gettysburg, Goucher, Hamilton, Hofstra, Holy Family, Iona, James Madison, Johns Hopkins, La Salle, Lafayette, Lehigh, Loyola, Marist, Niagara, North Carolina State, Ohio State, Pennsylvania State University, Princeton, Purdue, Randolph-Macon, Rensselaer Polytechnic Institute, Rider, Saint Joseph's, Saint Vincent, Seton Hall, Vanderbilt, Villanova, and the Universities of Alabama, Colorado, Connecticut, Delaware, Indiana, Maryland, Michigan, North Carolina, Notre Dame, Pennsylvania, Richmond, Southern California, Vermont, Virginia, and Washington.

STUDENT ACTIVITIES. Students elect representatives to the Student Council, which plans and organizes social events and other activities and also serves as a forum for student views.

Service activities are central to student life and are required in the Religious Studies program. Some of the regular service activities are the Key Club, Minutemen, Peer Counselors, and SADD/Yell, which acts to curb destructive behavior both among their peers and in community groups. Many boys work through the Campus Ministry to become involved in peer counseling, tutoring at nearby grammar schools, and working with peace and justice groups such as Amnesty International. They also assist the Campus Minister in daily and special liturgies and morning prayer.

The National Honor Society, foreign language honor societies, Academic Challenge, Mathletes, Science Olympiad, and Model United Nations are academic activities that complement and enhance the classroom experience. Artistic outlets are found in five bands, chorus, theater programs, the student newspaper, and a literary and arts magazine. Students use Salesianum's television production facilities for news and special programs on a channel within the School.

The School's athletic programs are well known and have a

strong history of success. Salesianum athletes have earned more State Championships than any other school in Delaware. The School fields varsity teams in football, cross-country, soccer, basketball, ice hockey, indoor track, wrestling, swimming, tennis, golf, baseball, outdoor track and field, volleyball, and lacrosse. A strong intramural program draws participation by more than 300 students each year.

ADMISSION AND COSTS. Salesianum School is open to any young man who has the ability to take advantage of the academic opportunities it offers and the willingness to join in following the educational model of Saint Francis de Sales. The School administers its Entrance, Placement and Scholarship Examination to eighth graders in early December. Candidates should submit a completed application at least one week prior to the date of the exam to preregister for it. Seventh graders can take the exam as a practice test in the spring. The fee for the test is $55. Applicants are also invited to schedule visits to the School where they can attend classes. Admissions decisions are rendered in early February, based on exam results, elementary school record, and recommendations from teachers and principals.

Tuition for 2007–08 is $9880. Bus costs range from $1300 to $1600, and these are offset by state subsidies for residents of Delaware and Pennsylvania. Academic scholarships, based on merit, total $315,000 annually, and financial aid, based on need, totals $475,000.

President: Rev. James E. Dalton, OSFS
Principal: Rev. William T. McCandless, OSFS
Assistant Principal/Academic Dean: Mr. Jude M. Szczerba '96
Assistant Principal/Dean of Students: Mr. Michael Gallagher '69
Assistant Principal; Director of Activities: Rev. Michael C. Varnicola, OSFS
Director of Educational Support Services: Mrs. Susan Gardner
Director of Admissions: Mr. Mark Winchell '98
Director of Development: Mr. Daniel Sarkissian '97
Associate Director of Development/Alumni Affairs: Mr. Jon Allison '97

Sanford School 1930

6900 Lancaster Pike, P.O. Box 888, Hockessin, DE 19707-0888
Tel. 302-239-5263; Fax 302-239-5389
Web Site www.sanfordschool.org
E-mail admissions@sanfordschool.org

Sanford is an independent day school enrolling 701 boys and girls in Junior Kindergarten–Grade 12. The college preparatory curriculum offers performing and studio arts, foreign languages, humanities, reading programs, literature, writing, history, mathematics, sciences, computer studies, and physical education, with Advanced Placement courses in 14 subjects. Sports include soccer, field hockey, cross-country, volleyball, basketball, wrestling, baseball, tennis, lacrosse, and golf. A summer program offers enrichment and review courses. Tuition: $13,000–$19,500. Financial Aid: $1,120,000. Andrew R.N. Walpole is Director of Admissions and Financial Aid; Douglas MacKelcan, Jr. (Hobart, B.A. 1971; Wesleyan, M.A.L.S. 1979), was appointed Head of School in 1998. *Middle States Association.*

The Tatnall School 1930

1501 Barley Mill Road, Wilmington, DE 19807
Tel. 302-998-2292; Admissions 302-892-4285; Fax 302-998-7051
Web Site www.tatnall.org; E-mail admissions@tatnall.org

Tatnall, a college preparatory day school enrolling 710 boys and girls age 3–Grade 12, strives to provide the highest-level academic curriculum in a nurturing environment in which each student can grow in self-esteem and meet success. Art, music, drama, and athletics complement the academic program. Numerous Advanced Placement and college-credit courses are available. Situated on a beautiful 110-acre campus, Tatnall offers its students 23 sports and more than 30 clubs and activities. A year-round Extended Day Program provides care up to 6:00 P.M. Summer programs are offered. The School is accredited by the National Association for the Education of Young Children. Tuition: $9500–$19,980. Financial aid is available. Leon Spencer is Director of Enrollment and Financial Aid; Eric G. Ruoss (University of Virginia, Ed.D. 1992) is Headmaster. *Middle States Association.*

Ursuline Academy 1893

1106 Pennsylvania Avenue, Wilmington, DE 19806
Tel. 302-658-7158; Fax 302-658-4297
Web Site www.ursuline.org

Ursuline Academy is a Catholic, college preparatory day school, serving girls age 3–Grade 12 and boys age 3–Grade 3. Ursuline has preserved its tradition, established more than 470 years ago by foundress St. Angela Merici, of motivating students toward academic excellence. Embedded in that tradition is the school motto, *Serviam*, or "I will serve"; all Upper School students perform a minimum of 80 hours of service by the end of Grade 10, and National Honor Society students in Grades 11–12 perform 50 hours a year. All students and teachers in Grades 7–12 use a personal laptop as part of a networked wireless community that provides filtered Internet access, e-mail accounts, and technical support, integrating technology throughout the curriculum. Academic classes in liberal arts, sciences, and humanities are offered at college preparatory and honors levels; qualified scholars can earn college credits in 16 AP courses. Class size is no larger than 18 but often smaller. Ursuline offers both the Montessori and traditional Pre-Kindergarten–Kindergarten. Extended care and a summer camp are offered. Tuition: $6720–$13,940. Jamie Jones (Middle & Upper) and Jennifer Callahan (Lower) are Directors of Admission. *Middle States Association.*

Wilmington Friends School 1748

101 School Road, Wilmington, DE 19803
Tel. 302-576-2900; Admissions 302-576-2930; Fax 302-576-2939
Web Site www.wilmingtonfriends.org
E-mail admissions@wilmingtonfriends.org

This college preparatory, coeducational day school enrolls 830 students in Preschool–Grade 12. In the Quaker tradition of strong academics grounded in active learning and ethical discussion, students accept challenges, opportunities, and responsibilities as they prepare for those that lie ahead. The International Baccalaureate Diploma Programme is offered. Service is required in all divisions. Activities include athletics, cultural arts, and publications. After-school and summer camp programs are available. Tuition: $10,025–$18,650. Financial Aid: $1,500,000+. Kathleen Hopkins is Director of Admissions and Financial Aid; Dr. Bryan Garman (Bucknell University, B.A.; Emory University, M.A., Ph.D.) is Head of School. *Middle States Association.*

DISTRICT OF COLUMBIA

Beauvoir, The National Cathedral Elementary School 1933

3500 Woodley Road, NW, Washington, DC 20016
Tel. 202-537-6485
Web Site www.beauvoirschool.org

BEAUVOIR, THE NATIONAL CATHEDRAL ELEMENTARY SCHOOL in Washington, D.C., is an Episcopal, elementary day school enrolling boys and girls from Pre-Kindergarten through Grade 3. Beauvoir is situated within the 60-acre Close of the Washington National Cathedral, a magnificent Gothic structure begun in 1907 that has been the focal point of numerous significant events throughout its history. Students and faculty make frequent use of the many cultural and educational resources of the nation's capital. There is limited bus service to the School; however, most families use car pools or make their own transportation arrangements.

The Protestant Episcopal Cathedral Foundation established Beauvoir in 1933 as the elementary division of National Cathedral School; in 1939, it was recognized as an independent institution.

The School aims to provide an educational environment that will foster a lifetime enthusiasm for learning and growth while nurturing the spiritual, ethical, intellectual, emotional, physical, and social development of each child. Faculty teach basic skills through a broad-based, integrated curriculum enriched by offerings in science, the arts, technology, physical education, and Spanish. Developing students' understanding of themselves in relation to the larger community and establishing a diverse faculty and student body are integral to the program. The School also supports a strong relationship among parents, students, and faculty as a means of implementing its guiding mission and philosophy.

Beauvoir is guided by a self-sustaining Governing Board and is accredited by the Middle States Association of Colleges and Schools and the Association of Independent Maryland Schools. It holds membership in the National Association of Independent Schools, the Mid-Atlantic Episcopal School Association, and the Association of Independent Schools of Greater Washington. Beauvoir parents, as members of the Beauvoir Parents Association, participate actively in all aspects of school life such as raising significant funds for scholarships and other needs, sponsoring book fairs, organizing community service projects, and supporting the educational programs in many ways.

THE CAMPUS. Beauvoir is located within the Close of the Cathedral of St. Peter and St. Paul, known familiarly as Washington National Cathedral, and shares the grounds with the National Cathedral School for Girls and St. Albans School. In addition to the completely renovated main academic building, which houses classrooms for each grade level, there is an interior courtyard, landscaped playground, and fields for outdoor play.

THE FACULTY. Paula J. Carreiro was appointed Head of School in 1992. She holds a B.S. degree from Northeastern Oklahoma State University and a master's degree from Oklahoma State University.

There are 58 faculty members, including 22 classroom instructors and 16 associate teachers as well as 19 resource teachers and a school nurse. All faculty are trained and experienced in Early Childhood and Elementary Development and Curriculum, and a strong emphasis is placed on professional development.

STUDENT BODY. In 2007–08, Beauvoir enrolled 389 boys and girls. Students come from throughout the Greater Washington metropolitan area and represent a wide diversity of ethnic, racial, and religious backgrounds. The Governing Board has a proactive Outreach Committee charged with increasing the diversity of the applicant pool.

ACADEMIC PROGRAM. The school year, from early September to early June, includes a Thanksgiving recess, vacations in the winter and spring, and observance of national holidays. The full-day program extends from 8:15 A.M. to 3:00 P.M. Monday through Thursday, with dismissal at 2:30 P.M. on Fridays. An Extended Day option until 6:00 P.M. provides activities, snacks, a rest period, and time reserved for homework and outdoor play.

Recognizing that there are individual learning styles and paces, the School evaluates each child's progress in terms of individual development based on his or her potential as well as on specific academic accomplishments. Parent conferences are held in the early fall, the late spring, and at other times as needed. Parents receive written reports twice a year. There are three classes in Pre-Kindergarten and four each in Kindergarten through Grade 3. Classes range in size from 18 to 21, with an overall student-teacher ratio of 10:1.

Following completion of Grade 3 at Beauvoir, students enter the fourth grade at other private and public schools including St. Albans and National Cathedral School.

Summer Program sessions for children ages four to nine are conducted on campus from mid-June through early August. The summer program includes art, music, drama, sports, movement, crafts, science, and swimming. Academic programs are available for students ages six to ten.

ADMISSION AND COSTS. Beauvoir seeks students, ages four to eight, of varying backgrounds, personalities, and talents, regardless of race, creed, color, or national or ethnic origin. Applicants for Pre-Kindergarten must be four years old by September 1 of the desired year of enrollment. Tours of the School are scheduled for prospective parents from October through the middle of January. Individual testing and school visits are required. Parents are notified of admissions decisions in mid-March.

In 2007–08, tuition is $24,440. Financial aid is awarded on the basis of demonstrated need.

Capitol Hill Day School 1968

210 South Carolina Avenue, SE, Washington, DC 20003
Tel. 202-547-2244; Admissions Ext. 120; Fax 202-547-0510
Web Site www.chds.org; E-mail mbmoore@chds.org

Located in a historic District of Columbia school building, Capitol Hill Day serves approximately 230 students in Pre-Kindergarten–Grade 8. The School offers a strong academic program in a creative environment. Faculty make use of the resources in the metropolitan area to augment the curriculum. The art program is integrated into other subjects—math, literature, science, and social studies. French and Spanish are introduced at the early-childhood level, followed by a choice of French or Spanish in Grade 1. The selected language is continued through Grade 8. An after-school program and a summer camp are optional. Tuition: $18,540–$22,020. Financial aid is available. Mary Beth Moore is Admissions Director; Martha Shepardson-Killam was appointed Director in 2007.

Edmund Burke School 1968

4101 Connecticut Avenue, NW, Washington, DC 20008
Tel. 202-362-8882; Admissions Ext. 610; Fax 202-362-1914
Web Site www.eburke.org; E-mail admissions@eburke.org

Edmund Burke School, a coeducational, college preparatory day school, serves 300 students in Grades 6–12. Located conveniently near the Van Ness Metro stop, the School offers a rigorous curriculum in an informal environment. The student-teacher ratio of 7:1 and the small classes allow individual attention. Edmund Burke has a complete sports program and encourages participation in drama, music, and the arts. Advanced Placement and independent study courses are available. The Summer Programs feature academic courses, sports and arts programs, and a musical theater. Tuition: $26,695. Kai-Anasa George is Director of Admissions; David Shapiro (Oberlin, B.A.; Columbia, M.A.; Baruch College, M.S.) is Head of School.

The Field School 1972

2301 Foxhall Road, NW, Washington, DC 20007
Tel. 202-295-5800; Fax 202-295-5850
Web Site www.fieldschool.org; E-mail admissions@fieldschool.org

Enrolling 310 day boys and girls in Grades 7–12, The Field School offers a college preparatory program designed to provide a strong grounding in the liberal arts and sciences and to prepare students for responsible citizenship. The curriculum emphasizes the interrelationships among the diverse fields of knowledge, blending both traditional and innovative methods of teaching to accommodate various learning styles. Small classes ensure individualized attention; instruction is primarily through dialogue among students and teachers. The core academic program is enriched by an extensive studio arts program for all students and an annual two-week Winter Internship experience. Activities include varsity athletics and clubs. Tuition: $28,450. Will Layman is Director of Admission; Dale T. Johnson is Head of School. *Middle States Association.*

Georgetown Day School 1945

Lower/Middle School: 4530 MacArthur Boulevard, NW, Washington, DC 20007
Tel. 202-295-6200; Admissions 202-295-6210; Fax 202-295-6211
High School: 4200 Davenport Street, NW, Washington, DC 20016
Tel. 202-274-3200; Admissions 202-274-3210
Fax 202-274-3211
Web Site www.gds.org; E-mail info@gds.org

Georgetown Day, a coeducational, college preparatory school enrolling 1035 students in Pre-K–Grade 12, honors the integrity and worth of each individual within a diverse school community. It aims to provide a supportive atmosphere in which teachers challenge the abilities of its students and foster strength of character and concern for others. The High School offers 19 Advanced Placement courses. Each year, approximately 35 percent of seniors earn recognition in the National Merit and National Achievement Scholarship programs. Activities include athletics, performing arts, publications, clubs, and required community service. Tuition: $24,175–$27,665. Financial Aid: $3,000,000. Vincent Rowe is Director of Enrollment Management & Financial Aid; Peter M. Branch is Head of School.

Georgetown Visitation Preparatory School 1799

1524 35th Street, NW, Washington, DC 20007
Tel. 202-337-3350; Fax 202-342-5733
Web Site www.visi.org; E-mail jkeller@visi.org

Georgetown Visitation, a Roman Catholic day school for young women in Grades 9–12, offers a challenging college preparatory curriculum with Advanced Placement and honors courses in all disciplines. Visitation students perform at least 80 hours of Christian service before graduation. The athletic program includes varsity and junior varsity in 12 sports. Students also enjoy a lively performing arts program, including chorus, theater, and dance. More than 30 clubs such as Model UN, Great Books Club, three publications, and Booster Club enrich the student's experience. Tuition: $19,350. Sr. Mary Berchmans Hannan, VHM (University of St. Thomas, M.A.), is President Emerita; Daniel M. Kerns (George Mason University of Law, J.D.) is Head of School; Janet D. Keller is Director of Admissions. *Middle States Association.*

Gonzaga College High School 1821

19 Eye Street, NW, Washington, DC 20001
Tel. 202-336-7100; Admission 202-336-7101; Fax 202-454-1188
Web Site www.gonzaga.org; E-mail admissions@gonzaga.org

Gonzaga is a Catholic college preparatory day school for boys sponsored by the Society of Jesus. Drawing its inspiration from the spiritual vision of St. Ignatius of Loyola and the apostolic and educational tradition of the Jesuits, the School offers a challenging curriculum to 940 young men of diverse backgrounds in Grades 9–12. Gonzaga educates "Men for Others" who will seek to do justice in their world. The program requires the completion of 25 graduation credits including four years of English, history, math, and theology and three years of foreign language and laboratory science. AP courses are offered in 26 subjects. All students take part in community outreach and retreats. Ninety-nine percent of graduates enter a four-year college or university. With 17 varsity sports, Gonzaga competes in the Washington Catholic Athletic Conference. Activities include Student Council, drama, publications, music ensembles, and a production studio. Gonzaga is a member of the Jesuit Secondary Education Association and the Association of Independent Schools of Greater Washington. Tuition: $13,850. Financial aid is available. Andrew C. Battaile is Dean of Admissions; Michael J. Pakenham is Headmaster; Rev. Allen P. Novotny, S.J., is President. *Middle States Association.*

The Lab School of Washington 1967

4759 Reservoir, NW, Washington, DC 20007
Tel. 202-965-6600; Fax 202-944-3078
Web Site www.labschool.org

This nonprofit day school enrolls 330 learning-disabled children ages 5–18 with average to superior intelligence. The individualized Lower School program is enriched by skills taught in history clubs, music, dance, drama, film making, art, and woodwork. Sciences, Humanities, Student Council, the yearbook, and team sports augment the Junior High and High School programs. Summer School includes remediation and an arts program. There is a postsecondary night school, diagnostic and tutoring service, career counseling, college guidance, and a monthly lecture series for parents and professionals. The new Baltimore campus at 2220 St. Paul Street enrolls students ages 6–14. Tuition: $28,355–$30,510. Susan F. Feeley is Admission Director; Sally L. Smith is Founder/Director.

Lowell School 1965

1640 Kalmia Road, NW, Washington, DC 20012
Tel. 202-577-2000; Admissions 202-577-2004; Fax 202-577-2001
Web Site www.lowellschool.org; E-mail mbelton@lowellschool.org

Lowell School is a progressive school serving 315 students, age 3–Grade 6. The program reflects a philosophy that emphasizes the student's responsibility and expectation for attaining strong communication, collaborative, and academic skills, within a nurturing environment. Lowell's stimulating, thematic, integrated, project-oriented curriculum is enhanced by the arts, Spanish, physical education, field trips, and service learning. After-school and summer programs are offered. Tuition: $13,710–$22,850. Financial aid is available. Michelle Belton is Admissions Director; Debbie Gibbs (Pomona College, B.A.; University of Minnesota, B.S.; University of San Francisco, M.A.) is Head of School.

Maret School 1911

3000 Cathedral Avenue, NW, Washington, DC 20008
Tel. 202-939-8800; Admissions 202-939-8814; Fax 202-939-8845
Web Site www.maret.org; E-mail admissions@maret.org

This coeducational, college preparatory day school, founded by educator Louise Maret, enrolls 600 students in Kindergarten–Grade 12. Located on the Woodley Estate, Maret uses the nation's capital as an extension of classroom instruction. Small classes, an advisor system, and a learning skills program provide strong student support. The humanities, math, science, computer studies, and foreign languages form the basis of the demanding curriculum. Advanced Placement and independent study opportunities are offered as well as summer study on campus or in Florida, Costa Rica, or France. Tuition: $23,295–$26,820. Financial aid is available. Annie M. Farquhar is Admission Director; Marjo Talbott (Williams, B.A.; Harvard, M.Ed.) was named Head of School in 1994. *Middle States Association.*

National Cathedral School 1899

Mount St. Alban, Washington, DC 20016-5000
Tel. 202-537-6300; Admission 202-537-6374; Fax 202-537-2382
Web Site www.ncs.cathedral.org; E-mail ncs.admissions@cathedral.org

National Cathedral School is a college preparatory, Episcopal day school enrolling approximately 575 girls in Grades 4–12. The School aspires to excellence in education for girls, values the spiritual life of its students, and strongly supports a multicultural environment. A coordinate academic and social relationship is maintained with St. Albans School for boys. Extracurricular activities include sports, clubs, and the arts. Tuition: $28,905. Financial Aid: $1,600,000. Maureen V. Miller is Acting Director of Admission and Financial Aid; Kathleen O. Jamieson (University of Maryland, B.A. 1977; Columbia, M.Ed. 1997) was appointed Head of School in 2003. *Middle States Association.*

National Presbyterian School 1969

4121 Nebraska Avenue, NW, Washington, DC 20016
Tel. 202-537-7500; Admissions 202-537-7504; Fax 202-552-4200
Web Site www.nps-dc.org; E-mail agutman@nps-dc.org

National Presbyterian School is a coeducational, elementary day school enrolling 250 students in Nursery–Grade 6. The School's mission and program are focused exclusively on the intellectual, social, physical, and spiritual growth that occurs during the "decade of childhood," from ages 3–13. The lively, traditional curriculum is enhanced by science, foreign language, art, music, and physical education. After-school enrichment classes, interscholastic sports (Grades 5–6), extended day, and summer camp programs are offered. Chapel services are conducted weekly. Tuition: $12,000–$19,470. Financial aid is available. Anne Gutman is Director of Admissions; James T. Neill (Harvard University, B.A.; Northwestern University, M.B.A.) is Head of School.

St. Patrick's Episcopal Day School 1956

4700 Whitehaven Parkway, NW, Washington, DC 20007-1554
Tel. 202-342-2805; Admission 202-342-2807; Fax 202-342-2839
Web Site www.stpatsdc.org; E-mail admission@stpatsdc.org

A coeducational parish school serving 490 students in Nursery–Grade 8, St. Patrick's Episcopal Day balances tradition and innovation in an educational program emphasizing acquisition of essential skills, integration of disciplines, and active learning. It seeks to educate young people who will grow in intellectual and academic competence, personal integrity, openness to change, commitment to service, and confident and ethical involvement in the world. On two campuses, facilities include science labs, libraries, art studios, music rooms, a gymnasium, three play parks, and a playing field. After-school, sports, extended day, and summer programs are offered. Tuition: $12,984–$24,884. Financial Aid: $1,300,000. Jennifer S. Danish is Director of Admission and Financial Aid; Peter A. Barrett was appointed Head of School in 1994. *Middle States Association.*

St. Albans School 1909

Mount St. Alban, Washington, DC 20016
Tel. 202-537-6435; Admissions 202-537-6440; Fax 202-537-2225
Web Site www.stalbansschool.org
E-mail sta_admission@cathedral.org

This Episcopal, college preparatory school for boys enrolls 565 students in Grades 4–12, including 30 boarders in Grades 9–12. Set on the Close of the National Cathedral, St. Albans seeks to develop the spiritual, intellectual, and physical well-being of its students and to encourage participation in their School, church, and community. The School aims to teach students to think creatively and develop skills of analysis and expression through the core curriculum of the arts, sciences, and humanities. Students in the Lower School study the fundamentals of reading, writing, and math with an emphasis on logical thinking and powers of observation, while Upper School students take more focused higher-level classes. The program is enriched by six languages, Advanced Placement and Honors courses, and the resources of the nation's capital. Student Council, drama, publications, music, community service, 17 sports, and academic and special-interest clubs are among the activities. Many boys are acolytes and choir members at the Cathedral. A summer program is also available. Boarding Tuition: $40,824; Day Tuition: $28,860. Financial Aid: $2,500,000. Mason Lecky is Director of Admissions and Financial Aid; Vance Wilson is Headmaster.

Sheridan School 1927

4400 36th Street, NW, Washington, DC 20008
Tel. 202-362-7900; Admissions Ext. 103; Fax 202-244-9696
Web Site www.sheridanschool.org; E-mail jlewis@sheridanschool.org

Sheridan balances its city-based, academically challenging program for 215 boys and girls in Kindergarten–Grade 8 with a strong outdoor curriculum at the School's 130-acre mountain campus where students take overnight trips lasting one to four nights. Academic skills are taught through immersion in an inquiry/concept-based curriculum. The comfortable size of the student body and nurturing environment combine to build confidence and encourage risk taking. Extended day care, enrichment classes, vacation camps, and day and overnight summer programs are offered. Tuition: $21,738–$24,137. Financial Aid: $530,000. Ms. Julie C. Lewis is Director of Admission; C. Randall Plummer (University of Missouri, B.S.; Boston University, M.Ed.) is Head of School.

Sidwell Friends School 1883

3825 Wisconsin Avenue, NW, Washington, DC 20016
Tel. 202-537-8100; Admissions 202-537-8111; Fax 202-537-2401
Web Site www.sidwell.edu; E-mail admissions@sidwell.edu

Sidwell Friends School, founded by members of the Religious Society of Friends, is a college preparatory day school enrolling approximately 1100 boys and girls in Prekindergarten–Grade 12. The School follows a Quaker philosophy, seeking the uniqueness of each individual and emphasizing spiritual and human values. In addition to traditional subjects, the curriculum includes music, art, dance, Chinese language and studies, and a School Year Abroad program. Athletics and 20 clubs are among the activities. Tuition: $26,790–$27,790. Financial Aid: $4,350,000. Erby L. Mitchell is Director of Admissions and Financial Aid; Bruce B. Stewart (Guilford College, A.B.; University of North Carolina [Chapel Hill], M.Ed.) was appointed Head of School in 1998. *Middle States Association.*

Washington International School 1966

3100 Macomb Street, NW, Washington, DC 20008
Tel. 202-243-1800; Admissions 202-243-1815; Fax 202-243-1807
Web Site www.wis.edu; E-mail admissions@wis.edu

Washington International, a coeducational day school, serves 895 students in Pre-Kindergarten–Grade 12. The School offers a complete PK–12 International Baccalaureate curriculum in which children become functionally multilingual and receive rigorous preparation in math, science, world history, geography, literature, and cultures. Washington International prepares students for higher education worldwide, enabling some to enter universities in the United States with sophomore standing. The School's mission is to provide a demanding international education that will challenge students to become responsible and effective world citizens. Tuition: $22,765–$25,030. Financial Aid: $1,800,000. Dorrie Fuchs is Director of Admission; Clayton W. Lewis (Rhodes College, B.A.; Vanderbilt University, M.S.) is Head of School.

FLORIDA

Academy at the Lakes 1992

2220 Collier Parkway, Land O' Lakes, FL 34639
Tel. 813-948-6823; Fax 813-949-0563
Web Site www.academyatthelakes.org
E-mail info@academyatthelakes.org

Academy at the Lakes is a college preparatory day school serving 435 girls and boys from diverse backgrounds in Junior Kindergarten–Grade 12. Seeking to promote a "love of learning and joy in the journey," Academy at the Lakes is committed to the success of each student in a close-knit community of children and adults. Sixty percent of the 50-member faculty hold advanced degrees, and the student-teacher ratio is 9:1. The classical curriculum introduces students to key concepts in core subjects of math, reading, science, social studies, and languages. As they progress through the grades, students come to understand the interrelationships among the disciplines. The academic program uses technology as an important learning tool, and students have the opportunity to explore many facets of the arts, sciences, and humanities. Community service is an integral component of the overall curriculum, while athletic competition teaches teamwork, sportsmanship, and skills development. School government, honor societies, publications, clubs, and music groups are among the activities. A summer adventure program is open to ages 5–12. Tuition: $7910–$12,880. Julia B. Loncar is Director of Admission; Mark Heller is Head of School.

Academy of the Holy Names 1881

3319 Bayshore Boulevard, Tampa, FL 33629
Tel. 813-839-5371; Admission Ext. 307; Fax 813-839-1486
Web Site www.holynamestpa.org
E-mail mgorecki@holynamestpa.org

This Roman Catholic day school was established by the Sisters of the Holy Names of Jesus and Mary to provide spiritual and academic enlightenment and to motivate young people to their best personal potential. The Academy enrolls more than 870 students in its coeducational elementary division (PK–Grade 8) and college preparatory high school for young women. Religious formation is integrated into the program through liturgies and values education. Students are involved in activities such as National Forensics League, service organizations, publications, honor societies, athletics, and interest clubs. Tuition: $10,620–$13,200. Michelle Gorecki is Admission Director; Jacqueline L. Landry is President/CEO.

The Benjamin School 1960

Pre-K–Grade 8: 11000 Ellison Wilson Road, North Palm Beach, FL 33408
Tel. 561-626-3747; Fax 561-691-9017
Grades 9–12: 4875 Grandiflora Road, Palm Beach Gardens, FL 33418
Tel. 561-472-5998; Fax 561-691-8823
Web Site www.thebenjaminschool.org

Nancy and Marshall Benjamin founded this coeducational day school, which provides a diverse student body a challenging college preparatory education. Enrolling 1301 students in Pre-K through Grade 12, The Benjamin School combines academic excellence with a structured, nurturing community environment. Character education, modern languages, and the arts are integral to the curriculum. State-of-the-art computer technology, including a laptop program, enhances the acquisition of knowledge. Middle and Upper School students benefit from an advisor system as they further their development as independent and collaborative learners. Benjamin graduates enter leading colleges and universities throughout the country and worldwide. Student government, honor societies, dance, drama, chorus, band, visual arts, debate, SADD, RACE (Respecting All Cultures Equally), Political issues, Model UN, and 47 Buccaneer athletic teams are among the cocurricular opportunities. Tuition: $12,985–$18,800. Financial Aid: $1,985,162. Mary Lou Primm is Director of Admission; James B. Young is Interim Head of School. *Southern Association.*

Berkeley Preparatory School 1960

4811 Kelly Road, Tampa, FL 33615
Tel. 813-885-1673; Fax 813-886-6933
Web Site www.berkeleyprep.org; E-mail mcilvjan@berkeleyprep.org

BERKELEY PREPARATORY SCHOOL in Tampa, Florida, is a coeducational day school enrolling students in Pre-Kindergarten through Grade 12. The School's location allows convenient access for residents of the Tampa Bay and neighboring areas.

The Latin words *Disciplina, Diligentia,* and *Integritas* in the School's motto state the values underlying the rigorous college preparatory curriculum of Berkeley, founded in 1960 and opened for Grades 7–12 the next year. Kindergarten through Grade 6 were added in 1967 and Pre-Kindergarten, in 1988. The School's purpose is to enable students to achieve academic excellence in preparation for higher education and to instill in them a strong sense of morality, ethics, and social responsibility.

Incorporated as a nonprofit institution, Berkeley Preparatory School is directed by a Board of Trustees. The School is accredited by the Southern Association of Colleges and Schools and the Florida Council of Independent Schools and is a member of the National Association of Independent Schools, among other affiliations. In 1995 and again in 2000, Berkeley was designated a Blue Ribbon School by the U.S. Department of Education.

THE CAMPUS. The 76-acre campus in the Town 'n' Country suburb of Tampa features classrooms, a fine arts center, a science wing, two libraries, general convocation rooms, physical education fields, a Pre-Kindergarten and Kindergarten wing, a 19,000-square-foot student center, and administrative offices for Lower, Middle, and Upper Divisions.

Berkeley athletes participate in two gymnasiums, a junior Olympic swimming pool, a wrestling/gymnastics room, a weight-lifting room, a rock-climbing wall, tennis courts, baseball and softball diamonds, and a stadium for football, track, and soccer.

The arts program is enhanced by a 634-seat performing arts center, which also includes a gallery for visual arts displays, a flex studio for dance and small drama productions, dressing rooms, and an orchestra pit.

THE FACULTY. Joseph A. Merluzzi, appointed Headmaster in 1987, is a graduate of Western Connecticut State College and holds a master's degree in mathematics from Fairfield University. Previously, Mr. Merluzzi served as Head of the Upper School, Assistant Headmaster, and Dean of the Upper School at Cranbrook-Kingswood School in Michigan.

There are 171 teachers and administrators. They hold 78 graduate and 6 doctoral degrees from such colleges and universities as Agnes Scott, Amherst, Florida State, Furman, Indiana University, James Madison, Michigan State, Middlebury, Ohio State, Ohio University, Parsons School of Design, Pennsylvania State, Princeton, State University of New York, Vanderbilt, West Virginia University, Williams, Yale, and the Universities of California, Florida, Illinois, Maryland, Missouri, New Brunswick, North Carolina, Notre Dame, Oregon, Tampa, Texas, and Wisconsin.

STUDENT BODY. In 2007–08, the School enrolled approximately 1200 students in Pre-Kindergarten–Grade 12 as follows: 400 in the Lower Division (Pre-Kindergarten–Grade 5), 300 in the Middle Division (Grades 6–8), and 500 in the Upper Division (Grades 9–12).

ACADEMIC PROGRAM. The school year, from late August to early June, includes Thanksgiving, Christmas, and spring vacations.

The average class size in the Middle and Upper Divisions is 15–20. The day begins at 8:00 A.M. and ends at 3:15 P.M. An activity period and divisional convocations are scheduled into each class day. All Middle Division students, ninth graders, and other students who do not qualify for study hall exemptions attend supervised study halls when they do not have a scheduled class. Teachers are available for extra help during the activity period and at other times during the day. Grades are sent to parents four times a year.

In the Lower Division, students attend school from 8:00 A.M. to 3:10 P.M. Curricular emphasis is on the core subjects of reading and mathematics. Students receive a firm foundation in grammar and vocabulary development. Math skills are developed and used in problem-solving. Social studies and science curricula are designed to aid children in mastering the skills they need in a rapidly changing, technological society. An interdisciplinary approach is used in foreign language and social studies. Daily Spanish instruction exists at all Lower Division grade levels. Manipulatives are used extensively in both the science and mathematics programs. Music, art, drama, and physical education are integral parts of the Lower Division curriculum. Each student also receives instruction in library skills and computers.

Academic requirements in the Middle Division are English, English expression, mathematics, history, foreign language, science, computers, physical education, art, drama, and music. All students in Grades 6 and 7 take Latin in addition to Spanish, French, or Chinese. Continuing students in Grade 8 choose from Spanish, French, Chinese, or Latin.

In the Upper Division, students take four or five credit courses each year in addition to the fine arts and physical education requirements. To graduate, students must complete a total of 22 credits. Specific requirements are 4 credits in English; 3 each in mathematics, history, science, and foreign language; 2 electives; one year of personal fitness/health and an additional year of physical education; and two years of fine arts. In addition, Berkeley students are required to take a course in public speaking and to complete 76 hours of community service. Advanced Placement courses are offered including English, Spanish, Latin, French, Modern European History, U.S. History, Calculus (AB and BC), Microcomputers, Biology, Chemistry, Physics (B and C), Environmental Science, Economics, and Psychology. Advanced topics seminar courses are also available in English: literature; English: writing; history; and science.

Grades 4–12 use laptop computers to enhance their learning experience.

Traditionally, 100 percent of Berkeley graduates attend college. Members of the Class of 2007 were accepted at more than 130 colleges and universities throughout the United States; 90 percent were accepted at their first- or second-choice schools, including Boston College, Brown, Cornell, Dartmouth, Duke, Emory, Georgetown, Harvard, Johns Hopkins, New York University, Northwestern, Stanford, Vanderbilt, Villanova, and the Universities of Florida, Miami, Michigan, North Carolina, Pennsylvania, and Virginia. Scholarship offers totaling over $6,000,000 were made to 90 percent of the graduates. Twelve seniors were named National Merit Scholarship Finalists.

There is a six-week academic summer program for students in Pre-Kindergarten–Grade 12. Tuition ranges from $725 to $1500. Fine arts and sports camps are also offered in the summer.

STUDENT ACTIVITIES. The Student Forum is responsible for presenting student views to the Upper Division administration and the Headmaster for discussion, and for recommending new ideas to the administration. Other student leadership roles are given to 30 senior prefects who are selected each year by a faculty committee. The Student Guide organization assists the Director of Admissions in acquainting prospective families with Berkeley's campus and programs.

Students publish the *Fanfare*, the student newspaper; *Small Voices*, a literary magazine for Kindergarten–Grade 5; *Soundings*, a literary magazine for Grades 6–8; *Phoenix*, a literary magazine for Grades 9–12; and the *Buccaneer*, the student yearbook for Pre-Kindergarten–Grade 12. Qualified students may be invited to join The Cum Laude Society, the National Honor Society, or honor societies in French, Latin, Spanish, math, and drama. Opportunities are available for students to participate in the Latin Forum, and the Art, Photography, Social Services, Cheerleading, Drama, French, Mathematics, Music, Colloquium, Science and Environmental, Strategic Games, Amnesty International, Model United Nations, Latin, and Spanish clubs. Berkeley sponsors its own all-School philanthropy, Project Berkeley, which benefits a local food bank; students, faculty, administration, staff, and parents participate on a monthly basis.

Varsity sports for boys are baseball, basketball, cross-country, diving, football, golf, soccer, swimming, tennis, weight lifting, wrestling, track, lacrosse, and crew; sports for girls are basketball, cross-country, diving, soccer, softball, tennis, track, swimming, cheerleading, weight lifting, volleyball, and crew. Berkeley competes in the Upper Division with schools of the Bay Conference and in the Middle and Lower Divisions with schools in the Florida West Coast League or the Youth Sports League.

Seasonal sports award banquets, a homecoming football game, a spring field day, alumni day, grandparents' day, student retreats, Middle and Upper Division dances, and honors convocations are among the yearly events. The Berkeley Parents' Club and the Buccaneer Club hold fund-raising events for the School.

ADMISSION AND COSTS. Berkeley Preparatory School seeks students who are "able to compete in a college preparatory program" and who are "willing to accept a fairly structured program." The School has a policy of nondiscrimination regarding students on the basis of race, color, and national or ethnic origin or any other class protected by law.

The School uses the Secondary School Admission Test and its own testing program. Recommendations and transcripts from the previous school are required. Application should be made as early in the year as possible; most grades are on a wait-list basis by late spring. Students are enrolled during the school year if space is available. There is an application fee of $50.

Tuition is $13,880 for Pre-Kindergarten–Grade 5, $15,690 for Grades 6–8, and $16,980 for Grades 9–12. Books and uniforms are extra. Lower Division students wear a uniform daily. Middle and Upper Division students must comply with the school dress code Monday through Thursday and must wear a uniform on Friday. A required tuition payment plan with eight monthly payments is in effect. Scholarship funding and financial aid are available.

Headmaster: Joseph A. Merluzzi
Director of Admissions: Janie McIlvaine
Upper Division Director: Hugh Jebson
Middle Division Director: Cynthia Boss
Lower Division Director: M. Joanne Moore
College Counselor: Kemp Hoversten
Business Manager: Charlie Simpson
Director of Development: Laura Grams
Director of Athletics: Bobby Reinhart
Physical Plant Director: Hal Schaeffer
Technology Director: Mike Speer

Bishop Verot Catholic High School 1962

5598 Sunrise Drive, Fort Myers, FL 33919
Tel. 239-274-6700; Admissions 239-274-6784; Fax 239-274-6798
Web Site www.bvhs.org; E-mail information@bvhs.org

Bishop Verot, one of three Catholic high schools in the Diocese of Venice, enrolls 750 young men and women from many religious backgrounds in Grades 9–12. Under the guidance of the Oblates of Saint Francis de Sales, the School offers a "community of faith and learning devoted to educating minds and hearts, dedicated to service, and centered on Christ." The college preparatory curriculum enables students to earn up to 28 academic credits in religious studies, math, science, modern languages, social studies, the practical and performing arts, and physical education and fitness. Through the Campus Ministry, liturgies, retreats, and Christian outreach, students develop moral and spiritual values and deepen their understanding of faith. AP and honors courses are offered in the major disciplines, and virtually all graduates go on to higher education. Viking teams compete interscholastically in 22 sports; other activities include school government, chorus, band, Model UN, publications, and clubs devoted to service, the environment, acting, and language, among other pursuits. Tuition: $8225–$9225. Financial aid is available. Andrew Sicnolf is Director of Admissions; Rev. J. Christian Beretta, OSFS, is Principal. *Southern Association.*

Bolles 1933

7400 San Jose Boulevard, Jacksonville, FL 32217-3499
Tel. 904-733-9292; Admissions 904-256-5030
Fax 904-733-9929
Web Site www.bolles.org; E-mail admissions@bolles.org

BOLLES in Jacksonville, Florida, is a coeducational, college preparatory school enrolling day students in Pre-Kindergarten through Grade 12 and boarding students in Grade 7 through Postgraduate on four campuses: Upper School (Grades 9–12) on the San Jose Campus; Middle School (Grades 6–8) on the Bartram Campus; and two Lower Schools (Pre-Kindergarten–Grade 5) on the Whitehurst Campus and the Ponte Vedra Beach Campus. Boys' and girls' boarding programs are accommodated on the San Jose and Bartram campuses, respectively.

Bolles was founded in 1933 as a military boarding school by Col. Roger M. Painter and his wife, Agnes Cain Painter. In response to changing times, the School dropped the military programs in 1962 and adopted a comprehensive college preparatory program. Coeducation was instituted in 1971.

Bolles prepares students for the future by providing them with challenges that promote growth and development in academics, arts, activities, and athletics. Moral development is encouraged by an emphasis on respect for self and others, volunteerism, and personal responsibility.

A not-for-profit institution, Bolles is governed by a self-perpetuating Board of 31 Trustees. The Alumni Board and the Parent Association actively support the School and its programs through fund-raising, social events, and other endeavors. The School is accredited by the Southern Association of Colleges and Schools and the Florida Council of Independent Schools; it holds membership in the National Association of Independent Schools and the Council for Religion in Independent Schools, among other affiliations.

THE CAMPUSES. The Upper School and the Lower School Whitehurst Campus occupy 52 acres on the St. Johns River. Five miles to the northeast, the Middle School Bartram Campus is set on 23 acres at 2264 Bartram Road. Bolles Lower School Ponte Vedra Beach Campus is set on 12 acres off A1A in St. Johns County.

On the San Jose Campus, Bolles Hall houses classrooms, boys' dormitory rooms, a dining room and kitchen, offices, and three meeting rooms. Other Upper School academic buildings are Clifford G. Schultz Hall, with 17 classrooms; the Michael Marco Science Center, housing three science labs; the Joan W. and Martin E. Stein Computer Laboratory; the Hirsig Life Science Center; Ulmer Hall, including 15 classrooms, a language lab, and two science labs; and a marine science classroom along the St. Johns River.

The 16,000-volume Swisher Library houses the Meadow Multimedia Center with a large-screen television, two satellite dishes, and computer labs. Other facilities include the 600+-seat McGehee Auditorium; the Cindy & Jay Stein Fine Arts Center, providing the Independent Life Music Building and the Lucy B. Gooding Art Gallery; and the Lynch Theater.

Upper School athletic facilities include Collins Stadium at the Donovan Baseball Field, Hodges Field, the Bent Tennis Complex, the Baker-Gate Petroleum Company Track Facility, and Skinner-Barco Stadium. The Davis Sports Complex includes the Huston Student Center, basketball and volleyball courts, the 25-yard Lobrano and 50-meter Uible swimming pools, and the Garces Aquatic Center. The Agnes Cain Gymnasium features a wrestling room and athletic offices.

Middle School academic facilities include Murchison-Lane Hall for classrooms and administrative offices, the Art Barn, a marine science classroom along Pottsburg Creek, girls' dormitory rooms, the Pratt Library, and The Betsy Lovett Arts Center, opened in 2007.

Among the Middle School athletic facilities are the Conroy Athletic Center, a football and soccer field, Meninak Field including Collins Baseball Stadium, and a pool.

The Lower School Whitehurst Campus houses each grade separately in homelike classrooms set around a natural playground. The Lower School Ponte Vedra Beach Campus is a modern, self-contained facility that includes the McLauchlan-Evans Building and the River Branch Building, housing art and music rooms.

THE FACULTY. Dr. John E. Trainer, Jr., was appointed President and Head of School in July 2001. He holds a B.S. in Biology from Muhlenberg College, a master's degree in Biology from Wake Forest University, and a doctorate in Zoology from the University of Oklahoma.

Bolles has 159 full- and part-time faculty; 97 have earned master's degrees, and 11 hold doctorates. The average teaching experience is 14 years.

STUDENT BODY. Bolles enrolls 1745 students, 93 of whom are boarders who represent 23 countries and seven states.

ACADEMIC PROGRAM. The school year, from late August to late May, is divided into quarters with Thanksgiving, winter, and spring breaks. The daily schedule for the Upper School, from 8:00 A.M. to 3:45 P.M., includes seven 45-minute periods and "Zero Hour," a 30-minute period reserved for individual conferences and extra help. An average class enrolls 17, except for English classes, which average fewer than 15. Boarders have evening study in their rooms, with faculty available for extra help, and supervised study halls are provided for students needing more structured assistance. Grades, with narrative reports from faculty, are sent to parents twice each quarter.

The Middle School curriculum includes English, world cultures, world geography, United States history and government, mathematics through algebra, and science. Students may select from a varied fine and performing arts program and may choose from band, chorus, drama, dance, graphics, drawing and painting, ceramics and sculpture, computers, foreign language, and language arts as electives each year. Each student has an advisor, and a full-time, on-campus guidance counselor assists with decision-making skills, peer relations, and alcohol and drug abuse awareness.

Upper School students must earn 22 credits for graduation, with a college-certifying grade of C minus or above. Specific requirements are four years of English; two of a single foreign language; three of social studies including United States History and World History; three of mathematics through or beyond Algebra II; three of science including Biology and Chemistry; two years of physical education; one year of fine arts; one half-year of life management skills; and three and one-half years of additional electives.

Sequential courses are available in all college preparatory

subjects, and honors courses are offered in each discipline as well.

Advanced Placement courses are offered in American history, biology, calculus AB and BC, statistics, chemistry, physics B, American government and politics, comparative government and politics, computer science, English literature and English language, European history, French, Latin, Spanish, portfolio art, and art history.

The English Department offers strong literary analysis and composition experience at all levels. Electives include Creative Writing, Composition, and Public Speaking.

The Science Department provides college-level laboratory courses in Introduction to Physics and Chemistry, Biology, Psychology, Chemistry, and Physics. Human Anatomy, Marine Science, Environmental Science, Neurobiology Honors, and Life Management Skills are electives.

The Language Department offers sequential courses in Spanish, French, Latin, German, Japanese, and Mandarin Chinese.

The Mathematics Department requires Algebra I and II and Geometry. In addition, Pre-Calculus, Calculus, Algebra III, Trigonometry, Data Analysis, Computer Applications, and Web Site Development and Programming are offered.

The Fine and Performing Arts Department offers academic courses in Dance, Theatre, Vocal and Instrumental Music, and the visual arts, including Foundations in Studio Art, Sculpture, Ceramics, Painting, Drawing, and Photography.

Physical Education or an approved alternative is required of all students for two years in Grades 9–12.

All students who attend Bolles are college-bound. In the Class of 2007, 188 students were accepted to 148 colleges and universities, and 139 students, or 74 percent, were Florida Bright Futures Scholars candidates. The class had 2 National Merit Scholars, 5 National Merit Finalists, and 11 National Merit Commended Scholars. In addition, 146 students, or 78 percent of the class, qualified for academic, athletics, arts, leadership, or service scholarships.

STUDENT ACTIVITIES. The Student Council, including class representatives and the president of each class, meets weekly to organize extracurricular activities and to supervise the Honor Council.

Students publish a yearbook, a newspaper, and a literary magazine. There are also more than 40 extracurricular clubs. Private lessons are available with specialists in many musical disciplines. Community service opportunities are offered both on and off campus.

Bolles is a member of the Florida High School Athletic Association. Boys' varsity and junior varsity teams compete in football, swimming, cross-country, basketball, soccer, wrestling, baseball, track, tennis, volleyball, and crew. Varsity and junior varsity teams for girls are organized in volleyball, swimming, cross-country, basketball, soccer, softball, tennis, track, crew, and cheerleading. There are also boys' and girls' varsity teams in golf, sailing, and lacrosse. Middle School boys' teams compete in football, basketball, soccer, baseball, wrestling, swimming, and track, while Middle School girls' teams are formed in basketball, volleyball, soccer, softball, swimming, track, and cheerleading.

ADMISSION AND COSTS. Bolles seeks to admit academically qualified students with qualities of leadership and creativity. Students are admitted on the basis of the Bolles entrance examination, academic transcripts, and two academic recommendations. Resident students may submit the results of the Independent School Entrance Examination. Application should be made as early as possible after September 1 of the year prior to desired enrollment; midyear enrollment is possible if vacancies exist. There is a $45 application fee; a 10 percent deposit and a $500 facilities fee, nonrefundable but applicable toward tuition, are due upon acceptance.

In 2007–08, day tuition is $6900–$12,600 for Pre-Kindergarten–Grade 5, $16,000 for Grades 6–8, and $16,500 for Grades 9–12. Tuition is $34,250 for seven-day boarders. A tuition payment plan is available. Bolles, which subscribes to the School and Student Service for Financial Aid, awards need-based financial aid.

President & Head of School: Dr. John E. Trainer, Jr.
Associate Head of School/Academic Dean: Scott G. Smith
Associate Head of School/Student Life: Jack F. Milne
Associate Head of School/Elementary Education; Principal/Lower School Ponte Vedra Beach Campus: Frederick H. Scott
Associate Head of School/Finance: Ruth M. Hartley
Associate Head of School/Dean of Admission & Financial Aid: Bradford L. Reed

The Canterbury School 1964

8141 College Parkway, Fort Myers, FL 33919
Tel. 239-481-4323; Admissions 239-415-8945; Fax 239-481-8339
Web Site www.canterburyfortmyers.org
E-mail jpeters@canterburyfortmyers.org

The Canterbury School, located on 33 acres, is a coeducational, college preparatory day school committed to high standards. Enrolling 725 students in Pre-K through Grade 12, Canterbury balances academics with competitive athletics and the visual and performing arts. Activities include drama, sports, publications, and service groups. More than half of the faculty hold advanced degrees. With rigorous academic standards, the School strives to educate the whole child for a lifetime of intellectual exploration, personal growth, and social responsibility. Honors courses are offered in the Middle and Upper School. Advanced Placement courses are available for qualified upper-level students, and elective options are offered in all major disciplines as well as in the arts. College counseling is provided. Tuition:

$11,880–$16,495. Financial Aid: $1,010,000. Julie Peters is Director of Admission; Dr. Richard J. Dolven (Renssalaer Polytechnic Institute, B.S.; Yale University, Ph.D.) is Interim Head of School.

Carrollton School of the Sacred Heart 1962

3747 Main Highway, Miami, FL 33133
Tel. 305-446-5673; Fax 305-446-4160
Web Site www.carrollton.org; E-mail admissions@carrollton.org

Carrollton, established by the Society of the Sacred Heart, is a Roman Catholic college preparatory school enrolling 700 girls as day students in a Montessori three-year-old program to Grade 12. It aims to educate its students to a personal and active faith in God, respect for intellectual values, social consciousness, the building of community, and personal growth. A member of the Network of Sacred Heart Schools in 20 cities, all sharing the same traditions, the School conducts annual reviews of its programs and sets new directions accordingly. Tuition: $12,300–$18,850. Financial Aid: $1,000,000. Ana J. Roye is Director of Admissions; Sr. Suzanne Cooke, RSCJ (Manhattanville, B.A.; University of Chicago, M.A.), is Headmistress.

The Community School of Naples 1982

13275 Livingston Road, Naples, FL 34109
Tel. 239-597-7575; Admissions Ext. 205; Fax 239-598-2973
Web Site www.communityschoolnaples.org
E-mail jevans@communityschoolnaples.org

Located on 110-acres of greenspace in beautiful Naples on the Gulf, The Community School of Naples is an independent, coeducational, college preparatory day school where faculty, students, and parents are committed to the celebration of academic excellence. The Early Childhood (PK–K), Primary (1–3), Intermediate (4–5), Middle (6–8), and Upper (9–12) Schools provide more than 800 students with a curriculum that fosters the intellectual, artistic, and leadership potential of every child. An array of offerings in foreign language, the visual and performing arts, and technology begins in Pre-Kindergarten and broadens in number and scope throughout the grades. The Upper School offers courses in the liberal arts and sciences and more than 20 Advanced Placement courses. Students may participate in School Year Abroad, Mu Alpha Theta, Mock Trial, Model Congress, and competitive sports teams. Tuition: $16,140–$20,866. Judy Evans is Director of Advancement and Admissions; John E. Zeller, Jr., is Head of School.

The Cushman School 1924

592 North East 60th Street, Miami, FL 33137
Tel. 305-757-1966; Fax 305-757-1632
Web Site www.cushmanschool.org
E-mail admissions@cushmanschool.org

This Blue Ribbon School of Excellence was founded by Laura Cushman, who began teaching children on the front porch of her home in 1924. Today, The Cushman School enrolls 480 day students from diverse racial, religious, ethnic, and socioeconomic backgrounds in Nursery (age 3)–Grade 8. Offering a child-centered, liberal arts curriculum, Cushman focuses on building essential skills in literacy and numeracy in the earliest grades as a foundation for more complex subject matter as students progress. The core academic program is designed to develop understanding of key concepts in English, math, social studies, and science, enriched by classical and modern languages, technology, the fine arts, and physical education. The Laura Cushman Academy serves students in Pre-School through Grade 5 with specific learning disabilities. Students and faculty benefit from educational field trips to the many science, history, and art museums in Dade County. Student Council, sports, and interest clubs are among the activities. Summer programs are available. Tuition: $10,500–$14,660. Patricia Block is Director of Admissions; Dr. Joan D. Lutton (Rutgers, B.A.; Barry College, M.A.; University of Florida, Ed.D.) was appointed Head of School in 1981.

The Day School at Coral Springs 2000

9001 Westview Drive, Coral Springs, FL 33067
Tel. 954-255-0020; Fax 954-255-1336
Web Site www.thedayschoolatcoralsprings.com
E-mail debra.rowars@thedayschoolatcoralsprings.com

The mission of The Day School at Coral Springs is to create a caring community of lifelong learners through a standards-based, integrated academic program designed to develop the intellect and engage the spirit of its students. The School currently enrolls 300 boys and girls in Pre-Kindergarten 3–Grade 8. The traditional curriculum emphasizes core subjects, with Spanish instruction, music, and computer technology in all grades. Before- and after-school care, enrichment classes, and summer camp are options. Tuition: $5480–$11,890. Financial aid and merit scholarships are available. Debra Rowars is Director of Admission; Jerry Zank is Head of School.

Episcopal High School of Jacksonville 1966

4455 Atlantic Boulevard, Jacksonville, FL 32207
Tel. 904-396-5751; Admissions Ext. 1220; Fax 904-396-7209
Web Site www.episcopalhigh.org
E-mail admissions@episcopalhigh.org

Set on an 88-acre campus on the St. Johns River, Episcopal High School is a church-affiliated, coeducational day school enrolling 900 socially and culturally diverse students in Grades 6–12. Its mission is to offer educational excellence from a Christian perspective, developing the intellectual, spiritual, social, and leadership potential of every student. In addition to core college preparatory subjects, students have courses in theology, foreign languages, information technology, and the arts. Community service, student leadership programs, publications, drama, music groups, and interscholastic athletics are among the extracurricular activities. A summer session and financial aid are available. Tuition: $15,500–$16,200. Peggy Fox is Director of Admissions; Dale Regan is Head of School. *Southern Association.*

Gulf Stream School 1938

3600 Gulf Stream Road, Gulf Stream, FL 33483-7499
Tel. 561-276-5225; Fax 561-276-7115
Web Site www.gulfstreamschool.org
E-mail admissions@gulfstreamschool.org

Gulf Stream School, enrolling 250 day boys and girls in PreKindergarten 3–Grade 8, is located near the ocean a mile north of Delray Beach. The School is committed to meeting the academic, creative, and physical needs of each student and to encouraging success at each level. A close parent-school partnership creates a family atmosphere. Grades 5–8 are departmentalized. The curriculum includes Latin, Spanish, art, music, and computer. Among the activities are publications, drama, choral group, bell choir, and sports. Winter-season students are accommodated. Summer programs are available. Tuition: $10,000–$15,600. Need-based financial aid is available. Helen C. Burns is Director of Admission; Joseph Zaluski is Head of School.

Holy Comforter Episcopal School, Inc. 1955

2001 Fleischmann Road, Tallahassee, FL 32308
Tel. 850-383-1007; Fax 850-383-1021
Web Site www.holy-comforter.org

Established in 1955, Holy Comforter Episcopal School is a coeducational, independent day school enrolling 664 students in Pre-Kindergarten through Grade 8. In the conviction that each child is a unique creation of God, the School seeks to nurture the mind, spirit, and body through a challenging curriculum. Children of all faiths have weekly religious classes and take part in chapel devotionals, which are conducted on an interdenominational basis. A strong foundation in core subjects underscores the traditional curriculum centered on reading, language arts, science, math, and social studies. Technology, the arts, and modern languages complete the program. The 82-acre campus supports a wide range of extracurricular activities such as Outdoor Club, academic competitions, music, drama, community service, and, in Grades 4–8, interscholastic competition in nine sports. Before- and after-school care is optional. Tuition: $4800–$7975. Financial aid is available. Dr. Regan E. Rancourt is Director of Admission; Dr. Barbara Hodges is President/Head of School.

Independent Day School–Corbett Campus 1968

12015 Orange Grove Drive, Tampa, FL 33618
Tel. 813-961-3087; Admissions Ext. 306; Fax 813-963-0846
Web Site www.idsyes.com; E-mail pbarfield@idsyes.com

independent day school
Corbett Campus

Independent Day School—Corbett Campus provides a dynamic educational environment that uses innovative, proven strategies to incorporate joy and challenge in learning. Faculty, who are chosen for their lifelong learning focus, use interactive techniques to allow students to take an active role in their education. Implementation of M.O.R.E. (Multiple Options for Results in Education) promotes involvement in all aspects of student life through cooperative learning, high-level critical thinking skills, multiple intelligences, integrated curriculum, global perspectives, and an emphasis on character and community service. *It's All About Kids: Every Child Deserves a Teacher of the Year* describes how the School combines the best in academics with social, emotional, and physical well-being. This Blue Ribbon School, serving 550 boys and girls in PreK3–Grade 8, offers superior academic programs, International Baccalaureate Middle Years Program (MYP), state-of-the-art technology, competitive sports, an accomplished fine arts program, a community music and drama school, and a summer camp with academic and recreational programs. Tuition: $8930–$9880. Dr. Joyce Burick Swarzman is Headmaster; Pam Barfield is Director of Admissions.

Jacksonville Country Day School 1960

10063 Baymeadows Road, Jacksonville, FL 32256
Tel. 904-641-6644; Fax 904-641-1494
Web Site www.jcds.com; E-mail admiss@jcds.com

The mission of Jacksonville Country Day School is to empower students for a lifetime of intellectual exploration, development of character, and social responsibility. Enrolling 520 students in Junior Kindergarten–Grade 6, the academic program emphasizes mastery of reading and language arts and a strong basis in math, social studies, science, and the arts. More than 350 computers and a state-of-the-art science lab integrate technology into the curriculum. The 17-acre campus includes a Fine Arts Center with classrooms, an art gallery, and auditorium; a library with over 10,000 volumes and a story theater; athletic fields; two swimming pools; and an outdoor amphitheater. An eight-week summer day camp is offered. Tuition: $7900–$9800. Extras: $360–$750. Terry Bartow is Headmaster. *Southern Association.*

Julie Rohr Academy 1974

4466 Fruitville Road, Sarasota, FL 34232
Tel. 941-371-4979; Admissions 941-371-6099; Fax 941-379-5816
Web Site www.julierohracademy.com; E-mail jracademy@msn.com

Founded by Julie and Arthur Rohr to provide an academic private school for Sarasota County, the Julie Rohr Academy enrolls 150 boys and 156 girls as day students in Nursery–Grade 8. The school aims to provide a strong, individualized academic program geared to each student's rate of development. The curriculum emphasizes basic academics but also provides a performing arts program that seeks to teach poise, self-discipline, and expressiveness. Day-care services are available before and after school, and a recreational summer program is offered. Tuition: $5739–$7674. Extras: $500–$1500. Cecilia R. Blankenship is Admissions Director; Julie Rohr McHugh (University of Miami, B.M. 1968, M.M. 1969) has been Principal since 1974.

Maclay School 1968

3737 North Meridian Road, Tallahassee, FL 32312
Tel. 850-893-2138; Admission 850-893-7857; Fax 850-893-7434
Web Site www.maclay.org

Maclay is a college preparatory day school enrolling 1026 girls and boys in Preschool–Grade 12. It seeks to teach the liberal arts creatively and to help students realize their full potential through self-discipline and persistence. Computer studies, creative writing, music, and drama complement the traditional curriculum. Sports, student government, honor societies, publications, theater, and service clubs are among the activities. A summer session offers remedial and enrichment courses. Tuition: $8885. Financial Aid: $300,000. Michael Obrecht is Director of Admission; William W. Jablon (Boston College, B.A. 1968; Florida State, M.A. 1972) was appointed President/Headmaster in 1976. *Southern Association.*

The North Broward Preparatory Schools 1957

Pre-K–12: 7600 Lyons Road, Coconut Creek, FL 33073
Upper School Tel. 954-247-0011; Fax 954-247-0012
Lower School Tel. 954-941-4816; Fax 954-247-0177
Web Site www.nbps.org; E-mail faganj@nbps.org
Pre-K–5: 3251 NW 101 Avenue, Coral Springs, FL 33065
Tel. 954-752-3020; Fax 954-757-7590
Web Site www.nbps.org; E-mail cowanj@nbps.org

THE NORTH BROWARD PREPARATORY SCHOOLS (NBPS) are college preparatory schools enrolling boys and girls in Pre-Kindergarten through Grade 12. The Schools are located on two campuses: Coconut Creek, with both Lower School (Pre-Kindergarten–Grade 5) and Upper School (Grades 6–12) and at Coral Springs, a Pre-Kindergarten through Grade 5 program. The campuses are situated in adjacent communities within 10–20 miles of the coastal cities of Boca Raton, Deerfield Beach, and Fort Lauderdale. The area is served by express highways including Interstate 95, Florida's Turnpike, and the Sawgrass Expressway.

Dr. James Montgomery founded The North Broward School and Lighthouse Point Academy in 1957. After some years of growth and acquisitions, the Schools settled into their present format on two campuses in 2004. Lighthouse Point Academy provides a specialized program for students with mild learning differences in Grades 2–12 on a separate campus.

NBPS is a member of Meritas, a global family of schools that seek to set new standards in college preparatory education. Students in these schools are offered an unusual array of academic and extracurricular activities including study-abroad programs for a semester, summer, or entire year; sports tournaments for member schools in Europe, Mexico, and the United States; international band tours; two-week student and teacher exchanges with sister schools; and video-conferencing to discuss global issues and practice language skills in live situations. All Meritas Schools strive to foster self-discipline, cooperation, and responsible citizenship and rely on a student-written Honor Code to promote individual integrity and respect.

The North Broward Preparatory Schools are accredited by the Southern Association of Colleges and Schools and hold membership in the Florida Council of Independent Schools and the Florida Kindergarten Council.

THE CAMPUS. At Coconut Creek, students enjoy a campus of more than 80 wooded acres. The modern, low-rise academic buildings are grouped around a small lake with separate facilities for Lower, Middle, and Upper divisions. Athletic facilities include outdoor tennis courts, swimming pools, an all-weather track, and football, soccer, baseball, and softball fields. Boarding students live in three houses on campus, each with a suite for a faculty prefect. At Coral Springs, students enjoy a campus of more than 8 acres, including a gymnasium and swimming pool. Both campuses feature state-of-the-art technology and networking capabilities. Intranet and Internet resources are available to students and faculty around the clock from home as well as from classrooms and media centers.

THE FACULTY. David V. Hicks was appointed Headmaster in 2006. He is a graduate of Princeton University (A.B.) and Oxford University (M.A.) and holds a diploma in Russian from Moscow University.

NBPS maintains a student-teacher ratio of 8:1, a maximum class size of 18 in Grades 3 through 12, and a class size of 15 in Pre-Kindergarten through Grade 2. The full-time teaching faculty includes men and women who have up to 30 years of experience at NBPS. All faculty are qualified by degrees and/or certificates for grades and subjects they teach. More than half have earned advanced degrees, and all of those who work at the Lighthouse Point Academy receive specialized training in learning differences or related areas. Specialists in foreign languages, music, band, choir, visual arts, drama, computer technology, and library-media sciences are well qualified by both education and experience.

STUDENT BODY. The Schools enroll 1900 students on both campuses, of whom 50 are residential students living on the Coconut Creek campus or with host families. The Schools accept students of all races, religions, and national origins and award financial aid for qualifying students in all grades.

ACADEMIC PROGRAM. The academic year, divided into three 12-week terms, begins in late August and extends to late May. Vacations are scheduled for two weeks in December and one week in the spring. High school students have a two-week Interim Term beginning in late February when they break from their usual schedule and routines for intensive studies and experiential learning. These may involve international travel and field work in conjunction with students from other Meritas schools. Because all Meritas schools synchronize their calendars, students can sign up for courses at Meritas schools around the world.

The Lower School curriculum builds a strong foundation in mathematics, reading, science, social studies, foreign language, and writing. The overall program encourages students to be creative and explore new ideas while fostering respect for the ideas and ways of others. As students progress, the program is enriched with music, art, physical education, media, and computer science.

In Middle School, students take full-year courses in English, social studies, mathematics, and science. In Grade 7, they choose a foreign language for full-year study. Forty elective courses enrich the experience.

To graduate, high school students must complete the following requirements: 4 years of English; 3 of one foreign language or 2 each of two foreign languages; 4 of social studies; 4 of mathematics; and 3 of science. They must also complete 2 trimesters of Physical Education and 1 of Health, 6 trimesters of computers and/or fine arts, and 100 hours of community service.

In addition to standard courses in the core subjects, NBPS students can study such subjects as Film Analysis, Legal Studies, Marine Biology, Forensics, Physiology, Robotics, Animal Behavior, Online Journalism, Web Design, Dance History, Advanced Broadcast Production, and others. Honors courses are available in all subjects, and 24 Advanced Placement courses are offered in 20 disciplines.

The Lighthouse Point Academy Program presents elements of the same curriculum to students in Grades 2–12 of average to gifted intelligence with learning disabilities that require more specialized approaches. They participate with other students in enrichment and extracurricular activities and, upon attaining the necessary standards, have the opportunity to enter the mainstream program at any level.

College placement services begin as early as Middle School and intensify as students enter their junior year. In 2006, 94 percent of the NBPS seniors won acceptance to their first or second college choices. Recent graduates have enrolled in such institutions as Columbia, Cornell, Duke, Harvard, Massachusetts Institute of Technology, Princeton, and the Universities of Florida, Notre Dame, and Miami, among others.

STUDENT ACTIVITIES. Each class elects its own officers, and each English class elects a legislator/representative who serves in the 70-member student legislature. In addition, the entire student body elects a President, Vice President, Secretary, and Treasurer. The President officiates at meetings of the legislature every two weeks where the members consider policies and proposals to improve and sustain the quality of student life.

Students can choose among a variety of clubs and activities according to their interests. The National and National Junior Honor Societies and the Key Club provide many services to the community. The Cappies (The Critics and Awards Program for High School Theatre) is a team of student theatre critics who review performances of South Florida school productions for publication in local newspapers and participate in a year-end Tony Awards-style Gala. The Debate Team offers training in forensics and opportunities to compete in tournaments within the state and across the nation.

Musical ensembles, choirs, and theater groups perform throughout South Florida, often raising money for charities. Together with peers from their sister schools, band members tour Europe every year performing for the public and for sick children. In conjunction with the International Make-A-Wish Foundation, they grant a wish to a terminally ill child.

More than 320 boys and girls participate on Middle School, junior varsity, and varsity teams in interscholastic competition. NBPS is a member of the Florida High School Athletic Association and competes in football, cross-country, golf, swimming, lacrosse, volleyball, bowling, basketball, ice hockey, soccer, wrestling, baseball, crew, flag football, rugby, softball, tennis, track and field, and softball. Some teams have traveled to Mexico, Hawaii, and Europe to compete in Meritas tournaments. The Schools also offer opportunities for intramural competition.

ADMISSION AND COSTS. The Schools seek students of good character who have the academic potential and desire to be successful and contribute to the school community. A parent and student application, writing sample, previous school records, achievement test results, teacher and principal recommendations, a campus visit, and a personal interview are necessary to complete the process.

Day tuition ranges from $13,100 for Pre-Kindergarten to $18,500 for Grade 12. Extra fees are charged for boarding, books, activities, school uniforms, lunch, overnight trips, and a laptop computer. Tuition for Lighthouse Point Academy ranges from $24,950 to $28,950 with similar extra fees. Financial aid is available at all levels, and academic honors scholarships are offered in Grades 9–12 and in Grades 2–5 at the Coral Springs campus.

Headmaster: David V. Hicks
Assistant Headmaster of Academic Affairs: Peri-Anne Chobot
Assistant Headmaster of Institutional Advancement: Jeanne Korn
Director of Admissions, Coconut Creek Campus (PK–12): Jackie Fagan
Director of Admissions, Coral Springs Campus (PK–5): Joni Cowan
Director of College Counseling: Heidi Teplitz

Oak Hall School 1970

8009 SW 14th Avenue, Gainesville, FL 32607
Tel. 352-332-3609; Fax 352-332-4975
Web Site oakhall.org; E-mail agarwood@oakhall.org

Oak Hall School is a coeducational, college preparatory day school enrolling approximately 760 students in PreKindergarten–Grade 12. The School aims to challenge college-bound students to reach the limits of their academic ability as they prepare for college and future responsibilities. Facilities include a new performing arts center, a state-of-the-art Media Center, a Fine Arts Center, a theater, and a new Middle School Science Center. Community service, clubs, and athletics are principal cocurricular activities. Tuition: $6500–$10,100. Alice Garwood is Director of Admissions; Richard H. Gehman (Princeton University, B.A. 1975; University of Massachusetts, M.Ed. 1980) was appointed Headmaster in 1993.

The Out-of-Door Academy 1924

PK–Grade 6: 444 Reid Street, Sarasota, FL 34242
Tel. 941-349-3223; Admission 941-554-3400
Fax 941-349-8133
Web Site www.oda.edu; E-mail admissions@oda.edu
Grades 7–12: 5950 Deer Drive, Sarasota, FL 34240
Tel. 941-349-3223; Admissions 941-554-5954; Fax 941-907-1251

The Out-of-Door Academy is an independent, coeducational, college preparatory day school enrolling 600 students from

Sarasota, Manatee, and Charlotte Counties in PreKindergarten–Grade 12. The school's mission is to provide an environment in which students strive to achieve their highest academic goals and to build character through a balanced program of academics, athletics, and the arts. The traditional curriculum is

designed to prepare graduates for the most rigorous colleges and universities. The average class size is 16, with a 10:1 student-faculty ratio. Tuition: $12,100–$16,000. Financial aid is available. David V. Mahler is Head of School; Laura Murphy is Director of Admissions.

PACE-Brantley Hall School 1972

3221 Sand Lake Road, Longwood, FL 32779-5898
Tel. 407-869-8882; Admissions Ext. 221; Fax 407-869-8717
Web Site www.pacebrantleyhall.org; E-mail kshatlock@mypbhs.org

PACE-Brantley Hall School was founded 35 years ago with the mission of providing an atmosphere where all students can learn and advance in a safe and nurturing environment. Serving a student population of 175 children with diagnosed learning disabilities in Grades 1 to 12, the School offers a multisensory program designed to remediate and teach compensation skills while building confidence and self-esteem. The student-teacher ratio is maintained at 10:1. Tuition: $13,120–$13,580. Registration Fee: $500. Barbara Winter is Admissions Director; Kathleen Shatlock was named Principal in 2004.

Palm Beach Day Academy 2006

PK–8: 1901 South Flagler Drive, West Palm Beach, FL 33401
Tel. 561-832-8815; Fax 561-832-3343
Web Site www.palmbeachdayacademy.org
E-mail malbanese@palmbeachdayacademy.org
K–9: 241 Seaview Avenue, Palm Beach, FL 33480
Tel. 561-655-8349; Fax 561-665-5794

Palm Beach Day Academy was formed by the 2006 merger of two successful and respected elementary day schools: Palm Beach Day School (1921) and The Academy of the Palm Beaches (1981). The union of these two institutions maximizes the resources, programs, and opportunities available to 520 boys and girls age 2 through Grade 9. The cornerstone of the school program is educating the minds and spirits of its students in a challenging, vibrant community that prizes academic excellence. Palm Beach Day Academy prepares students for appropriate secondary school studies and endeavors to provide a foundation for a lifetime of enthusiastic learning. Course work centers on language arts, math, foreign language, history, and science, enriched by library, computer technology, art, music, drama, and physical education. Among the activities are Student Council, athletics, and community service. Tuition: $10,800–$19,900. Meghan Albanese is Director of Admission; Dr. Rebecca van der Bogert is Head of School.

Palmer Trinity School 1991

7900 SW 176th Street, Miami, FL 33157
Tel. 305-251-2230; Admissions 305-969-4208; Fax 305-251-0607
Web Site www.palmertrinity.org
E-mail dreynolds@palmertrinity.org

Palmer Trinity School, a coeducational, Episcopal day school, provides a rigorous college preparatory curriculum that engenders academic excellence and global awareness. An essential goal of the School's mission is to promote the ability to integrate knowledge, compassion, and social responsibility while honoring the unity of mind, body, and spirit. Palmer Trinity serves a community of 600 students in Grades 6–12; they come from a broad range of socioeconomic, ethnic, and religious backgrounds and represent 35 nations. Located on 55 acres in south Miami, the School features one of the first wireless laptop learning programs in the nation as well as competitive athletics, outstanding fine arts, and an extensive community service program. All graduating seniors attend four-year universities, with 80 percent matriculating outside of Florida. Tuition: $19,350–$20,050. Danny Reynolds is Director of Admissions & Financial Aid; Sean Murphy is Head of School. *Southern Association.*

Pine Crest School 1934

1501 Northeast 62nd Street, Fort Lauderdale, FL 33334-5116
Tel. 954-492-4100; Admission 954-492-4103; Fax 954-492-4188
Web Site www.pinecrest.edu; E-mail pcadmit@pinecrest.edu

Pine Crest, an all-faith, coeducational day school enrolling approximately 1650 students in Pre-Primary–Grade 12, seeks to develop each individual's character, independence, and academic proficiency. The challenging courses emphasize a college preparatory curriculum, including 30 Advanced Placement courses in the upper school. Computer technology, modern languages, leadership training, community service, and diverse offerings in the visual and performing arts enhance the core academic program. National Honor Society, aquatics, over 60 athletic teams, and a wide range of interest clubs and activities are among the extracurricular offerings. Tuition: $15,680–

$19,240. Financial aid and summer programs are available. Elena Del Alamo is Vice President for Admission; Lourdes M. Cowgill, Ph.D., is President. *Southern Association.*

Pine Crest School at Boca Raton 1987

2700 St. Andrews Boulevard, Boca Raton, FL 33434-3625
Tel. 561-852-2800; Admission 561-852-2801; Fax 561-852-2832
Web Site www.pinecrest.edu; E-mail jrobinson@pinecrest.edu

Pine Crest is a coeducational, college preparatory school enrolling approximately 900 day students in Pre-Primary (age 4)–Grade 8 on a beautiful 20-acre campus. Students continue their high school education at Pine Crest's Fort Lauderdale campus. The Boca Raton facilities include a 750-seat performing arts center; a 150-seat recital hall; state-of-the-art library/media center; a newly built Middle School complex with a professional TV production studio; fine arts studios; ensemble rehearsal rooms for orchestra, band, and chorus; acoustically engineered studios for private vocal and instrumental lessons; and a Student Activities Center with gym, dance studios, an 8-lane swimming pool, fitness facilities, and playing fields. After-school programs include many enrichment classes, Extended Day Care, USS Swim team and competitive sports, and private music lessons. Academic summer school, tennis camp, fine arts camps, and a summer sports camp are offered. Tuition: $15,680–$17,950. Joyce R. Robinson is Director of Admission and Financial Aid; Robert S. Goldberg is Head of School; Lourdes M. Cowgill, Ph.D., is President.

The Pine School 1969

1300 East Tenth Street, Stuart, FL 34996
Tel. 772-283-1222; Admission Ext. 2017; Fax 772-220-9149
Web Site www.thepineschool.org
E-mail blettengarver@thepineschool.org

The Pine School, a coeducational, college preparatory day school enrolling 485 students in Early Learning–Grade 11, opened a second campus on 140 acres in 2007 for its Middle and Upper Schools. The School's challenging yet nurturing environment promotes academic excellence, sound moral values, and the development of the whole child. Classroom studies include a traditional core curriculum, enhanced by programs in art, music, dance, computer science, Spanish, and Chinese/Asian studies. Physical education is an important part of The Pine School's program and spirit. Competitive sports include basketball, soccer, volleyball, cross-country, and lacrosse. Tuition: $8500–$17,000. Financial Aid: $500,000. Beth Lettengarver is Director of Admission; Dr. James Cantwell (Columbia, Ed.D.) is Headmaster.

Ransom Everglades School 1903

Upper School: 3575 Main Highway, Coconut Grove, FL 33133
Tel. 305-460-8800; Admission 305-250-6875
Fax 305-854-1846
Web Site www.ransomeverglades.org
E-mail admission@ransomeverglades.org
Middle School: 2045 South Bayshore Drive, Coconut Grove, FL 33133
Tel. 305-250-6850

The Adirondack-Florida School, founded in 1903, later became the Ransom School for Boys and merged with Everglades School for Girls in 1974 to form Ransom Everglades School, enrolling 1035 boys and girls in Grades 6–12. The School believes the pursuit of academic excellence should be complemented by a concern for each student's moral, physical, emotional, and aesthetic development. The curriculum encompasses visual and performing arts; activities include drama, sports, publications, and service groups. A summer academic program is offered. Ransom Everglades is a member of the National Association of Independent Schools. Tuition: $22,500. Financial Aid: $2,540,540. Elaine J. Mijalis-Kahn is Director of Admission and Financial Aid; Ellen Y. Moceri (Washington University, B.A., M.A.; Columbia University Teachers College, A.B.D.) is Head of School. *Southern Association.*

Riverside Presbyterian Day School 1948

830 Oak Street, Jacksonville, FL 32204
Tel. 904-353-5511; Admission 904-353-3459; Fax 904-634-1739
Web Site www.rpds.com; E-mail sfrancis@rpds.com

Riverside Presbyterian Day School, founded by the church bearing the same name, enrolls 500 boys and girls in Pre-

Kindergarten–Grade 6. The School's primary goals are to "educate the mind, nurture the spirit, and foster the development of the whole child while affirming the teachings of the Christian faith." Art, music, Bible, computer, library, Spanish, physical education, and weekly chapel services enrich the basic program of reading, language arts, math, science, and social studies. An extended-day program is available on a year-round basis and includes creative activities and field trips. Riverside Presbyterian Day School is accredited by the Florida Council of Independent Schools and the Florida Kindergarten Council. Tuition: $5535–$8980. Financial Aid: $166,446. Shirley W. Francis is Director of Admission and Head of Lower School; Robert W. Littell (Colorado College, A.B.; Johns Hopkins, M.S.) is Headmaster. *Southern Association.*

Saint Edward's School 1965

Lower School/North Campus: 2225 Club Drive, Vero Beach, FL 32963
Tel. 772-231-5357
Middle & Upper Schools/South Campus: 1895 Saint Edward's Drive, Vero Beach, FL 32963
Tel. (Middle School) 772-231-1677
Tel. (Upper School) 772-231-4136; Admissions Ext. 2360
Fax 772-231-2427
Web Site www.steds.org

Saint Edward's School in Vero Beach, Florida, is a coeducational, college preparatory day school enrolling 900 students in Pre-Kindergarten through Grade 12 on two campuses. Vero Beach, with a population of 17,705, is on Florida's mid-Atlantic coast, known as the Treasure Coast. Vero Beach is equidistant from Melbourne to the north and Stuart to the south and is located in Indian River Country, known for its pleasant climate, beautiful beaches, and abundant natural resources.

An independent school in the Episcopal tradition, Saint Edward's was founded in 1965 to empower students of many faiths and cultures to reach their full potential. In a community of advocacy, the School aims to challenge the whole child, cultivate moral courage and spiritual growth, and instill a lifelong passion for learning. Students adhere to an Honor Code designed to encourage responsible citizenship, ethical behavior, and an appreciation for diversity. Chapel services are attended by all students and led by the school chaplain.

A not-for-profit institution guided by a Board of 24 Trustees, Saint Edward's is accredited by the Florida Council of Independent Schools and holds membership in the National Association of Independent Schools, National Association of Episcopal Schools, Educational Records Bureau, Council for Religion in Independent Schools, and the Council for Advancement and Support of Education. The Parents Association and the Alumni Council support Saint Edward's in carrying out its mission.

THE CAMPUS. The Lower School campus was the original Riomar Country Club (1929), one of the first structures built on the barrier island. Bought by Saint Edward's in 1965, the 6-acre site was renovated in 1988, preserving the Old Florida, Mediterranean-influenced architecture still evident today.

A pre-kindergarten and kindergarten complex, fine arts center, and two state-of-the-art computer labs were added in 1996.

The 27-acre Upper and Middle School campus was opened in 1972 and occupies a unique location along the Indian River. The School has expanded, doubling the size of its south campus, to include a separate Middle School, an Activities Center, a fine arts center, the 780-seat Waxlax Center for the Performing Arts, and Oglethorpe Hall, which houses administrative services. The $20,000,000 expansion project includes a retrofit of Upper School classrooms, state-of-the-art lab spaces, computer labs, writing center, and athletic program enhancements.

THE FACULTY. Dr. Charles F. "Charlie" Clark became Saint Edward's sixth Head of School in 2003. A graduate of The Peddie School, Dr. Clark (St. Lawrence University, B.A., M.Ed.) earned his doctorate in Educational Leadership at the University of Delaware. Before assuming his present position, he held administrative and teaching posts at independent schools in Ohio, Indiana, and Delaware. He and his wife, Gail, have three children and four grandchildren.

The cornerstone of Saint Edward's is its 98-member faculty, the majority of whom hold advanced degrees. Their degrees represent colleges and universities such as Assumption, Ball State, Boston University, Bowling Green State, Brown, Central Michigan, Colgate, Columbia, Cornell, Duke, Fairleigh Dickinson, Florida Atlantic, Florida State, Harvard, Lehigh, Loyola, Middlebury, New York University, Nova, Ohio State, Quinnipiac College, Rollins, Southwest Texas State, Springfield College, Stanford, Susquehanna, Temple, Tufts, Vassar, Wesleyan, Wilkes, and the Universities of Florida, London, Maryland, Massachusetts, Michigan, North Carolina, Pennsylvania, Pittsburgh, San Francisco, Vermont, Washington, and Wisconsin.

The Richardson Wellness Program offers physical, emotional, and spiritual support programs and services, including student health education programs, faculty training programs, leadership workshops, and a student-led Spiritual Life Committee. The Wellness Team includes two guidance counselors, a chaplain, and two registered nurses. Emergency medical service for both campuses is readily accessible.

STUDENT BODY. In 2006–07, Saint Edward's enrolled 900 students in its Lower (Pre-Kindergarten–Grade 5), Middle (Grades 6–8), and Upper School (Grades 9–12) divisions. Students commute via carpool or by bus service provided by the School from Vero Beach and the tricounty area. They represent a wide cross-section of racial, ethnic, religious, and socioeconomic backgrounds.

ACADEMIC PROGRAM. The 175-day school year, from early September to early June, is divided into four marking periods, with a Thanksgiving recess, vacations in December and in the spring, and observances of several national and school holidays. Teachers provide the individual attention each student needs in classrooms with a class size average of 16. Courses are offered in Advanced Placement, college preparatory, and honors tracks, with special accommodations for gifted students with learning differences.

Students attend classes daily from 8:05 A.M. to 3:35 P.M. in the Lower School and from 8:05 A.M. to 3:27 P.M. in the Middle and Upper Schools. All students are required to select six academic classes, and many concentrate their efforts in Advanced Placement courses. The Advanced Studies Program at Saint Edward's is a comprehensive program specifically designed for highly motivated students in Grades 9–12.

The Lower School academic program provides a strong foundation in the traditional disciplines, beginning with reading and mathematics readiness in pre-kindergarten and building on mastery of those skills as students progress through the primary and intermediate grades. The schedule is departmentalized from Grade 4 on, with a major emphasis on language arts and math. The core academics are enhanced by mini courses in fine arts, music, computer science, ethics, foreign language, and physical education.

In the Middle School, the curriculum is designed to provide age-appropriate challenges in core subjects in readiness for the college preparatory course work of the Upper School. Students take full-year courses in English, history, mathematics, science, foreign language, and physical education/health, with one semester each year in the arts, research, writing, and technology. There are a number of noncredit enrichment courses, and students are exposed to numerous extracurricular activities. The Middle School implemented a 1:1 tablet computer program for the 2006–07 school year.

To graduate from the Upper School, students must complete a minimum of 24 credits as follows: 4 each in English, mathematics, and history; 3 or 4 in science and foreign language; and 1 each in religion, personal fitness, and life management, plus 4 credits of electives from any department. Saint Edward's does not provide class rank until graduation, and grades shown on transcripts are unweighted, although extra weight is awarded for Honors or Advanced Placement courses.

Among the academic offerings are English 9–12, Writing Lab, Creative Writing, Journalism; French 1–5, Spanish 1–5, Chinese 1–3; American Government, United States History, United States History Since 1865, World History, Economics, Sociology, Psychology; Algebra 1–2, College Algebra, Geometry, Pre-Calculus, Trigonometry; Biology, Chemistry, Physics, Anatomy and Physiology, Integrated Science, Environmental Science, Marine Biology; Character Education, Ethics, Introduction to the Bible, World Religion; Emerging Technology, Computer Programming, Computer Graphics; and Art History, Broadway Review, Chorus, Concert Choir, Modern Theatre, News and Broadcasting, Studio Arts, and Theatre Arts. Honors and/or Advanced Placement courses are available in all major departments.

College guidance begins in Grade 8 and continues throughout the entire planning, application, and admission process. Historically, all graduates pursue advanced education. Members of the Class of 2007 were accepted at such institutions as Auburn, Brown, Bucknell, Clemson, Colby, Columbia, Davidson, Elon, Florida State, Franklin and Marshall, McGill, Northwestern, Rollins, United States Naval Academy, Vanderbilt, Villanova, and the Universities of Florida, Miami, Notre Dame, and Pennsylvania.

Saint Edward's offers extensive summer programs, including EXCEL, the Educational Center for Exceptional Learners, which enrolls academically gifted students in Grades 2–6 in a three-week session. A six-week program offers remediation and enrichment to approximately 200 students; a seven-week water-oriented summer camp program and various sports camps are also available.

STUDENT ACTIVITIES. A diverse extracurricular program engages students in leadership roles, special-interest clubs, and athletics.

More than 30 Class 2A and 1A interscholastic teams are organized in football, baseball, softball, lacrosse, golf, volleyball, soccer, cross-country, swimming, basketball, tennis, and cheerleading.

As members of a greater community, students are encouraged to become active volunteers on and off campus. Two of the most successful student outreach programs are the Pals in Partnership for special-needs children and the Care to Share program for the elderly.

Among the special events on the school calendar are the annual Pirate Fall Festival, Fun Run, Poetry Readings, Living Museum, Science Fair, annual speech presentations, fall drama, spring musical, Lagoon Days, Saint Edward's Day, Christmas Concert, Homecoming Weekend, Alumni Holiday Reception, and the Lower School class plays.

ADMISSION AND COSTS. Saint Edward's welcomes students who are good citizens with a desire for a first-rate education. Acceptance is based on standardized test results, current transcripts, evaluations by the student's mathematics and English teachers, recommendations from the principal or guidance counselor, writing samples, and a personal interview. For first-round consideration at the Middle and Upper School level, applications are due by February 15. Subsequent applications will be considered on a space-available basis. Applications are acted on by the Admission Committee on March 1 of the year of intended enrollment. The nonrefundable application fee is $50.

For 2007–08, tuition ranges from $7400 to $19,775 and includes bus transportation, class trips, lunch for Grades 6–12, and the yearbook. Uniforms are additional. Tuition insurance is required for all new students. Annually, the School awards financial aid to students who have demonstrated need and academic ability.

Associate Head of School/Head of Upper School: Mr. Bruce R. Wachter
Head of Middle School: Dr. Kristine Alber
Head of Lower School: Mrs. Barbara Mohler
Director of Admission: Mr. Bob Gregg
Dean of Students/Upper School: Ms. Belinda Cummings
Dean of Students/Middle School: Ms. Kris Fojtik
Dean of Students/Lower School: Mrs. Ginger Topp
Curriculum Coordinator: Mrs. Barklie Eliot
Director of Academic & College Counseling: Mr. Darby Gibbons
Athletic Director: Mr. Doug Booth

St. Johns Country Day School 1953

3100 Doctors Lake Drive, Orange Park, FL 32073
Tel. 904-264-9572; Fax 904-264-0375
Web Site www.sjcds.net; E-mail bpargman@sjcds.net

St. Johns, enrolling 767 students in Pre-Kindergarten–Grade 12, furnishes an environment that encourages academic excellence at all levels. A challenging college preparatory curriculum, athletics, and fine arts prepare students for selective colleges. Advanced Placement and honors classes, extracurricular, and summer academic and camp programs are available. Computer, foreign language, and science labs; a swimming pool complex; a fine arts center; a 10,000-square-foot resource learning center; a 600-seat theater; and a Grades 6–8 educational center on the 26-acre suburban campus address the varied needs of St. Johns students. Tuition: $5600–$12,400. Financial Aid: $520,000. Brian Pargman is Director of Admissions; Gregory L. Foster is Headmaster. *Southern Association.*

St. John's Episcopal Parish Day School 1951

Grades 5–8: 240 South Plant Avenue, Tampa, FL 33606
Tel. 813-849-4200; Fax 813-849-1026
Web Site www.stjohnseagles.org; E-mail scox@stjohnseagles.org
Grades 1–4: 906 South Orleans Avenue, Tampa, FL 33606
Tel. 813-849-5200; Fax 813-258-2548
PreK–K: 1002 Rome Avenue, Tampa, FL 33606
Tel. 813-849-6200

Now in its 57th year, St. John's enrolls 515 boys and girls from diverse religious and cultural backgrounds in pre-kindergarten (4-year-olds) through eighth grade. St. John's Episcopal Parish Day School offers an academically rigorous program in a Christian and nurturing environment. Every day begins with a chapel service designed to inspire spiritual awareness and moral character. The curriculum centers on English, literature, writing, mathematics, science, and social studies and is enhanced by courses in Spanish, Latin, studio art, music, physical education, and a divinity program. Technology is woven throughout the curriculum with two computer labs, computers in all classrooms, SMART boards, and a high-speed Internet service providing a 21st-century education. Extracurriculars include clubs, National Junior Honor Society, drama productions, math team, Science Olympiad team, and, from Grade 5, competition in seven sports. Tuition: $7885–$8105. Financial aid is available. Cindy Fenlon is Director of Admissions; Gordon R. Rode is Headmaster.

Saint Joseph's School 1958

3300 South Seacrest Boulevard, Boynton Beach, FL 33435
Tel. 561-732-2045; Fax 561-732-1315
Web Site www.sjsonline.org; E-mail maperavich@sjsonline.org

This church-affiliated, coeducational day school welcomes 230 children from diverse faith backgrounds in PreKindergarten through Grade 8. Saint Joseph's School is committed to providing a rigorous education in mind, body, and spirit in a safe Christian environment. The college preparatory curriculum, designed to accommodate a variety of differences in learning styles, emphasizes the mastery of skills in core subjects. Sacred studies, Spanish, technology, and the Academy of the Arts round out the academic program. Students participate in community service and team sports. Tuition: $8450–$10,100; Financial aid is available. Mary Aperavich is Admission Director; Tami Pleasanton is Associate Head; Kay Johnson (Stetson University, B.A.; Lewis and Clark College, M.A.T.) is Headmistress.

St. Mark's Episcopal Day School 1970

4114 Oxford Avenue, Jacksonville, FL 32210
Tel. 904-388-2632; Admission Ext. 21; Fax 904-387-5647
Web Site www.stmarksdayschool.org
E-mail smeds@stmarksdayschool.org

St. Mark's Episcopal Day, enrolling 480 students in the Early Learning Program (age 1)–Grade 6, is dedicated to excellence within a Christian environment. Small class size and a dedicated faculty foster a personal connection between teachers and their students. A challenging academic curriculum provides an opportunity for high-quality learning and personal growth. Beginning in Pre-Kindergarten (age 3), enrichment resources include Spanish, computer, physical education, science, library, music, art, and Christian education. St. Mark's also offers an

Extended Day Program, after-school enrichment, and a summer day camp. Tuition: $2820–$8910. Financial aid is available. Susan Kwartler is Director of Admissions; Cathy Hardage is Head of School.

St. Mark's Episcopal School 1959

1750 East Oakland Park Boulevard, Fort Lauderdale, FL 33334
Tel. 954-563-4508; Admissions 954-563-1241; Fax 954-563-0504
Web Site www.saintmarks.com; E-mail gpalmer@saintmarks.com

St. Mark's is a coeducational, Episcopal day school enrolling 580 students in Pre-Kindergarten (age 3) through Grade 8. In a "unique learning environment within a solid Christian tradition," the School seeks to offer a superior academic program complemented by regionally recognized offerings in the arts, including band, chorus, drama, and studio art. The athletic program features teams for boys and girls at both varsity and intramural levels. Emphasizing a strong foundation in core subjects, the academic program includes Spanish language, computers, physical education, art, music, and guidance. Daily chapel services and the religion curriculum emphasize the Episcopal values of inclusion, open inquiry, and respect for all faiths. More than 40 percent of fourth and seventh graders qualify for the Duke Talent Search Program. After-school enrichment and summer camp programs are also offered on St. Mark's 10-acre campus. The challenging preparatory program ensures that graduates enroll in the independent secondary schools of their choice. Tuition: $7305–$12,840. Financial aid is available. Ms. Alice Hendrickson is Director of Admission; Fr. Dub Brooks is Head of School.

St. Mary's Episcopal Day School 1953

2101 South Hubert Avenue, Tampa, FL 33629-5648
Tel. 813-258-5508; Fax 813-258-5603
Web Site www.smeds.org; E-mail kathleen.lopez@smeds.org

St. Mary's Episcopal Day School, enrolling 436 girls and boys in Pre-Kindergarten–Grade 8, offers a well-balanced and challenging curriculum delivered by talented, enthusiastic teachers in a caring, Christian environment. Early grades emphasize comprehensive skills, including computer use and Spanish, leading to advanced levels in writing, algebra, and lab sciences by Grade 8. Grade 6 studies Latin; Grades 7–8 study Latin or Spanish. Religion, public speaking, music, and art are taught. Activities include competitive athletics, choir, publications, community service, student council, and drama. Before- and after-school care are offered. Tuition: $9500. Financial aid is available. Kathleen Lopez is Director of Admissions; Scott D. Laird (West Chester, B.S. 1978; Florida Atlantic, M.Ed. 1987, M.A. 1993) is Headmaster.

Saint Paul's School 1968

1600 Saint Paul's Drive, Clearwater, FL 33764
Tel. 727-536-2756; Admissions Ext. 238; Fax 727-531-2276
Web Site www.st.pauls.edu; E-mail hleiser@st.pauls.edu

Saint Paul's, enrolling 515 boys and girls in Preschool–Grade 8, is affiliated with the Episcopal Church and celebrates the rich diversity of its school community. Its mission is to provide an excellent education in a nurturing environment, laying the foundation for successful academic progress, and to create a desire for lifelong learning. Intellectual, spiritual, and physical development are stressed through a challenging curriculum, hands-on science, fine arts, interscholastic athletics, intramurals, foreign languages, a state-of-the-art technology center, summer programs, extracurriculars, and community service. Tuition: $6855–$14,190. Financial Aid: $308,599. Holly Leiser is Director of Admissions; Douglas C. Eveleth is Head of School.

Saint Stephen's Episcopal School 1970

315 41st Street West, Bradenton, FL 34209
Tel. 941-746-2121; Admissions Ext. 568; Fax 941-746-5699
Web Site www.saintstephens.org
E-mail saintstephen@saintstephens.org

A college preparatory day school, Saint Stephen's Episcopal School enrolls 755 boys and girls in Pre-Kindergarten 3–Grade 12. In a family-like environment, Saint Stephen's strives to encourage learning beyond the classroom walls. Chapel services help students of all religions understand the importance of spirituality in their lives. Fundamentals and theme-based units characterize the curriculum through Grade 8. Upper School students follow a traditional liberal arts course of studies with Advanced Placement classes in all disciplines. Academics are complemented by fine arts, clubs and activities, interscholastic sports, and the Service Learning Program. Tuition: $10,450–$14,550. Financial Aid: $390,000. Linda Lutz is Admission Coordinator; Janet S. Pullen is Head of School.

St. Thomas Episcopal Parish School 1953

5692 North Kendall Drive, Coral Gables, FL 33156
Tel. 305-665-4851; Admissions 786-268-3304; Fax 305-669-9449
Web Site www.stepsmia.org; E-mail vdouberley@stepsmia.org

St. Thomas, enrolling 425 students in Preschool–Grade 5, provides an atmosphere that is both challenging and affirming. The academic program is designed to develop the whole child, meet the demands of the information age, and prepare students with a solid basis for future learning. Grades 4–5 benefit from the use of laptops. Classes are small. The curriculum is enhanced by Spanish, dance, art, music, physical education, science, drama, library, and computers. An extended-day program provides enrichment, including sports. Summer programs are also offered. Tuition: $8800–$11,680. Need-based financial aid is available. Valerie Douberley is Director of Admission and Financial Aid; Kris Matteson Charlton (Southampton College of Long Island University, B.A.; Southern Connecticut State, M.S.) is Head of School.

San Jose Episcopal Day School 1954

7423 San Jose Boulevard, Jacksonville, FL 32217
Tel. 904-733-0352; Admissions 904-733-0355; Fax 904-733-2582
Web Site www.sjeds.com

San Jose Episcopal Day School enrolls more than 400 students in Pre-Kindergarten–Grade 6. The curriculum is designed to enhance natural abilities and, at the same time, teach new skills and habits that build a strong foundation for the future. Language arts, math, social studies, and science are enriched with Spanish, Latin, technology, art, music, media, and physical education. Religious education is enhanced by the Fruits of the Spirit character education program. Extended day, lunch, and after-school activities are offered. Tuition: $4300–$7500. Limited financial aid is available. Rev. Steph Britt is Rector; Rev. Jean C. Dodd is Head of School; Pamela C. Barry is Director of Admission.

Seacrest Country Day School 1983

7100 Davis Boulevard, Naples, FL 34104-5314
Tel. 239-793-1986; Fax 239-793-1460
Web Site www.seacrest.org; E-mail seacrest@seacrest.org

SEACREST COUNTRY DAY SCHOOL in Naples, Florida, is a coeducational, college preparatory school enrolling students in Prekindergarten through Grade 12. Naples (population 38,879) is on Florida's Gulf Coast between Fort Myers and Marco Island. A favorite destination for tourists because of its sunny climate and beautiful beaches, Naples offers a wealth of nature preserves, cultural and historic attractions, shopping, and outdoor recreation.

Seacrest Country Day School opened its doors in 1983 with 18 students. Today, this Outstanding Model School of America enrolls nearly 580 children. A $30,000,000 capital campaign has added 30 acres to the existing 10-acre campus and will provide state-of-the-art facilities to accommodate the Upper School campus.

The mission of Seacrest Country Day is to nurture the social, cognitive, and emotional development of every student. In the belief that learning has no boundaries, the School offers a challenging, well-rounded curriculum designed to unleash the unlimited potential that is in each child, balancing academic, aesthetic, and athletic opportunities with life skills, character development, and values education.

Guided by a 20-member Board of Trustees, Seacrest is accredited by the Florida Council of Independent Schools, the Southern Association of Colleges and Schools, and the Florida Kindergarten Council. It holds membership in numerous professional organizations including the National, Southern, and Florida Associations of Independent Schools.

THE CAMPUS. The Seacrest Country Day School campus is graced by mature trees, flowering shrubs, and gardens as well as a wetland preserve, outdoor learning laboratory, and playing fields. Grouped around the center courtyard are several buildings. The Lynne Marz Powell Student Services Center houses administrative and departmental offices, while the new Resource Center provides a 20,000-volume library, a media center, TV production equipment, six classrooms, and two computer labs. Networked computers are also located in every classroom. A Math and Science Challenge Lab provides Lego building blocks, gears, pulleys, levers, and other instruments to solve advanced math and physics problems. A regulation Gymnasium and Performing Arts Center is the setting for indoor sports and a wide range of programs and plays using the latest sound, lighting, and projection systems.

The high school campus includes a new modular village, a baseball stadium, soccer field, and track as well as a beach volleyball venue.

THE FACULTY. Lynne M. Powell, Ed.D., was appointed Head of School in 1993, having served as Seacrest's Academic Dean since 1987. She holds baccalaureate and master's degrees in Elementary Education and earned her doctorate in Educational Leadership from Nova University. Dr. Powell has also done postgraduate work at Boston University and the University of New Hampshire and taught in New Hampshire public schools for 20 years.

All 62 men and women on the teaching faculty hold bachelor's degrees from colleges and universities nationwide, and more than 60 percent have earned or are working toward advanced degrees; 5 hold doctorates.

STUDENT BODY. In 2007–08, Seacrest Country Day School enrolled nearly 580 boys and girls in Prekindergarten through Grade 12. The students come from communities in Collier and Lee Counties, including Marco Island, and represent a wide diversity of racial, ethnic, religious, and socioeconomic backgrounds.

ACADEMIC PROGRAM. The school year, from late August to early June, is divided into quarters, with a Thanksgiving recess and longer vacations in the winter and spring. Grades are issued at the midpoint and end of each quarter, and parent conferences are scheduled in November and April. Younger students receive evaluations ranging from Outstanding to Unsatisfactory; letter grades are issued beginning in Grade 4. Homework is assigned and checked on a regular basis and varies in amount according to grade.

A typical day begins at 8:30 A.M., with dismissal at 2:45 P.M. in the elementary division and 3:30 P.M. in the middle and high schools. Classes, with an 8:1 student-teacher ratio, are 30 to 90 minutes in length, depending on grade. Both the middle and high schools use an eight-day schedule rotation that includes time for club meetings and activities. Extended care, open to all Seacrest students, begins at 7:15 A.M. and ends at 5:30 P.M. There is no charge for before-school care; families can use the after-school program on a regular or as-needed basis for a fee.

The fully integrated, multisensory curriculum emphasizes the acquisition and mastery of strong skills in core subjects as the foundation for success in higher education and in life. In Prekindergarten through Grade 2, age-appropriate content and hands-on activities introduce children to key concepts in language arts, mathematics, science, social studies, Spanish, art, and the fine arts and music. The program is enriched by life skills, computer technology, media and learning strategies, and health and physical education.

As students progress through the grades, the curriculum increases in breadth and depth. In fourth grade, children create, plant, and maintain a garden that provides opportunities for the application of lessons in math and natural science. Fifth graders spend an overnight at Sea World; students in Grades 6–7 engage in biology research at Marinelab in Key Largo; and eighth graders may take part in outdoor education or travel to Washington, Philadelphia, or New York. Qualified Middle School students may take high school-level and advanced courses in math and Spanish, and each year, students in Grades 4 through 7 qualify for Duke University's Talent Identification Program.

The high school program features traditional college preparatory courses in the liberal arts and sciences. To earn a Seacrest diploma, students must complete 28 credits as follows: 4 each in language arts and history/social studies; 3 each in math, science, and foreign language; 1 each in humanities, technology, physical education/health; 1 elective each in math or science, studio arts, and music; and 5 additional electives.

Among the specific offerings are World Mythologies, World Literature, Writing Seminar/American Literature; Spanish I–IV, Latin, French I–IV; World Civilization I–II, U.S. History, Modern Government/Economics; Algebra I–II, Geometry, Pre-calculus, Calculus, Statistics, Discrete Mathematics, Fractal Geometry/Chaos; Biology, Marine Biology, Chemistry I, Applied Chemistry, Physics, Genetics, Introduction to Environmental Science, Oceanography, Ecology, Astronomy; and Fundamentals of Computer Science, Web Design, Architecture and Computers I–IV, and Computer Art. Advanced Placement and honors courses are open to qualified scholars in all major departments, and private instruction in art and musical instruments is available.

High school students participate in Seacrest Seminars related to topics in Ethics and Attributes of a Leader, Opposition and Solution, Leadership in a Global Context, and Effective Communication.

Although Seacrest will graduate its first high school class in May 2008, prior alumni have gone on to attend Auburn, Boston College, Duke, Emory, Florida Atlantic, Florida State, George Washington University, Harvard, Middlebury, Princeton, Rensselaer Polytechnic, Rollins, State University of New York (Purchase), Trinity, Tufts, United States Air Force Academy, Villanova, Virginia Polytechnic, Washington and Lee, Wellesley, Yale, and the Universities of Central Florida, Florida, Georgia, Miami, Notre Dame, South Carolina, and Vermont.

STUDENT ACTIVITIES. Seacrest's extracurricular program provides opportunities to develop leadership and social skills, form new friendships, and engage in wholesome, fun activities. School teams compete in Scholar Bowl and the National Geography Bee and, in 2003, 2006, and 2007, reached the World Finals in Odyssey of the Mind. In 2005, the high school robotics team took first place in a national competition. Students publish a newspaper, yearbook, and literary magazine as well as present plays and musicals for the public.

Service learning is valued as a means of reaching out to help others in the local community and well beyond. Students have sent shoes to Haiti, linen supplies to flood victims in North Dakota, and toys to be distributed by local firefighters. Middle Schoolers perform on-campus service in the form of visiting and working with younger students. High Schoolers host an annual event and donate to the charity of their choice.

The athletic program at Seacrest emphasizes fitness, fun, and sportsmanship, and the middle school's "no cut" policy ensures that each student can try any sport. Boys' and girls' interscholastic teams are organized at varsity and junior varsity levels in basketball, soccer, and volleyball. Tennis, golf, cross-country, track and field, and swimming are also offered.

Among the special traditions and events on the school calendar are Flag Ceremony, Red Ribbon Week, Halloween Costume Parade, Heritage Luncheon, Breakfast with a Buddy, Book Fair, Grandparents' and Special Friends' Day, Young Authors' and Young Artists' Week, Awards Evening, monthly seminars for parents and the community, and Graduation.

ADMISSION AND COSTS. Seacrest Country Day School welcomes students from all racial, ethnic, religious, cultural, and socioeconomic backgrounds who are willing and able to participate enthusiastically in its programs. Admission is based on prior school records, the results of standardized tests, teacher recommendations, and an interview. The application fee is $75; an initial payment fee of $1500, which includes a one-time $500 enrollment fee, is due when the enrollment agreement is submitted.

In 2007–08, tuition is $12,700 in Prekindergarten–Grade 5,

$13,400 in Grades 6–8, and $15,700 in Grades 9–12. Annual fees are $1300 per child. Payment plans and tuition insurance are available.

According to statistics from the National Association of Independent Schools, Seacrest awards 30 percent more in need-based financial aid than the national average for elementary day schools. In 2007–08, the School provided more than $800,000 in need-based financial aid to one-quarter of its students.

Head of School: Dr. Lynne M. Powell
Lower School Head: Dr. Jennifer Amico
Upper School Head: Erin Duffy
Dean of Student Life: Dr. Deb Merwin
Admission Officer: Caroline Randall
Chief Financial Officer: Helen Ruisi
Athletic Director: Mark Marsala

Shorecrest Preparatory School 1923

5101 First Street NE, St. Petersburg, FL 33703-3309
Tel. 727-522-2111; Admissions Ext. 106; Fax 727-527-4191
Web Site www.shorecrest.org; E-mail admissions@shorecrest.org

Shorecrest Prep, Florida's oldest independent day school, enrolls nearly 1000 boys and girls in Early Childhood–Grade 12. A strong college preparatory program, providing close faculty support and small classes, is enhanced by the arts, foreign languages, laboratory sciences, and state-of-the-art computer facilities. The Upper Division offers a full range of Advanced Placement courses and individualized college counseling. The School encourages participation in athletic competition, extracurricular activities, visual and performing arts, and community service. Transportation and extended care are available. Tuition: $10,400–$15,500. Extras: $500. Financial Aid: $500,000. Diana N. Craig is Director of Admissions; Michael A. Murphy is Headmaster. *Southern Association.*

Trinity Preparatory School 1968

5700 Trinity Prep Lane, Winter Park, FL 32792
Tel. 407-671-4140; Admission Ext. 523; Fax 407-671-6935
Web Site www.trinityprep.org; E-mail inquire@trinityprep.org

An Episcopal day school enrolling 830 students in Grades 6–12, Trinity seeks to provide the finest educational experience, guided by outstanding professionals in a safe, caring, and challenging environment. Its mission is to develop students who are able to excel in college and beyond, contribute to their communities, lead in a changing society, and grow spiritually. Trinity fosters spiritual awareness while respecting cultural and religious diversity. The program offers 25 AP courses, 51 teams in 14 sports, extensive fine arts and community service opportunities, and many clubs. Tuition: $14,300. Malone Scholars Program and financial aid are available. Sherryn M. Hay (Rollins College, B.A.) is Director of Admission; Craig S. Maughan (Washington University, B.A.; University of North Carolina [Chapel Hill], M.S.P.H.; University of Kansas, M.B.A.) is Headmaster.

GEORGIA

Brenau Academy 1928

500 Washington Street, SE, Gainesville, GA 30501
Tel. 770-534-6140; Admissions 770-534-6243; Fax 770-534-6298
Web Site www.brenauacademy.org; E-mail enroll@brenau.edu

BRENAU ACADEMY, located on the campus of Brenau University, the historic women's college in Gainesville, Georgia, is a college preparatory boarding and day school for girls in Grades 9 through 12 and Postgraduate. Gainesville/Hall County (population 170,000) is situated at the base of the Blue Ridge Mountains, 50 miles northeast of Atlanta just over an hour from the Atlanta Hartsfield International Airport.

Since Brenau Academy opened its doors in 1928, it has been a high school designed to prepare talented young women for college educations, successful futures, and fulfilling community involvement. Brenau offers students small classes, a college preparatory curriculum, and invested teachers whose priority is to see each young woman do her best. The Academy's staff, teachers, and house directors embrace a combination of support, structure, and freedom, allowing students opportunities for fun and individual growth.

With a student body of 80 and an average class size of 12, Brenau Academy students benefit from lively, discussion-based classes, individualized assistance, and the opportunity to build strong relationships with teachers, administrators, coaches, and residential staff. One hundred percent of Brenau Academy seniors are accepted to college each year and have successfully graduated from collegiate institutions across the nation and worldwide.

The Academy's unique affiliation with Brenau University allows students to make a confident transition into a college atmosphere. Academy students have full access to the University library, athletic facilities, cafeteria, and auditorium. Advanced students have the opportunity to get a head start by taking courses at Brenau University and earning credit toward their college education.

Brenau Academy holds dual accreditation from the Southern Association of Colleges and Schools and the Southern Association of Independent Schools and is approved by the Georgia Department of Education.

THE CAMPUS. The 56-acre campus on the grounds of Brenau Women's College includes an outdoor amphitheater, a $12,000,000 fine arts center, an athletic field, and a tennis center. The fitness center's indoor athletic facilities are housed in the gymnasium and in the natatorium, which offers an Olympic-size swimming pool, a sauna, a steam bath, a weight and exercise room, and ballet studios.

The Academy classrooms, library, post office, Campus Shop, tea room, auditorium, recreation room, administrative offices, laundry, kitchenette, and dormitories are in one central location. Dormitory life is supervised by adult house directors. Students' rooms are wired for full computer hookup and high-speed Internet, with personal phones and voice mail for easy parent communication. Other facilities available for Academy student use include a cafeteria, science laboratories, state-of-the-art microcomputer laboratories, language laboratories, a 150,000-volume library, and a Victorian fine arts auditorium. Campus security is managed by a competent, qualified security staff.

The combined facilities are valued at more than $28,000,000.

THE FACULTY. Timothy A. Daniel is Headmaster of the Academy, having previously served as a teacher and administrator at a number of other independent boarding and day schools including The Grand River Academy in Ohio, Memphis University School in Tennessee, Portsmouth Abbey School in Rhode Island, University Liggett School in Michigan, and Shattuck-St. Mary's School in Minnesota; he was also Headmaster at The Leelanau School in Michigan. A native of Ohio, Mr. Daniel is a graduate of Deerfield Academy in Massachusetts, Northwestern University, and the University of Tulsa.

There are 12 teachers, four house directors, and six administrators. Most full-time instructors hold advanced degrees.

STUDENT BODY. Brenau Academy enrolls 80 students, 85 percent residential and 15 percent day. The 2007–08 student body represents 12 states and ten countries.

ACADEMIC PROGRAM. The school year, from August to late May, is divided into semesters with a Thanksgiving recess, a two-week Christmas vacation, and a one-week spring vacation.

Classes are held five days a week. An average class enrolls 12 students, and the overall student-faculty ratio is 8:1. Grades are sent to parents or guardians and students every 6 weeks.

To graduate, students must complete four years of English, three of history, four of mathematics, three of science, two years of one foreign language, two of physical education, and two of Fine Arts as well as two additional elective credits.

Brenau Academy offers college preparatory courses in academic areas that include Grammar, Literature, Composition, United States Literature, British Literature; Spanish; United States History, American Government, Economics, World History; Algebra, Geometry, Pre-Calculus; Biology, Chemistry, Anatomy and Physiology, Environmental Science; Fine Art, Drama, Journalism, Dance; and Physical Education. The school's relationship with Brenau Women's College allows qualified Academy students to take college courses for advanced credit at no additional cost.

For college-bound students with diagnosed learning differences, the Learning Center, modeled after the Brenau University Learning Center, provides appropriate support as students attend regular Academy classes. The program offers a more structured learning environment as well as the opportunities to meet regular classroom expectations.

One hundred percent of Brenau Academy seniors are accepted into college. The school's college counselor works closely with each senior to select the college or university that best suits her needs and abilities. Students take PSAT, SAT, and/or ACT exams during their junior and senior years. Past college selections include Boston University, Clemson, College of Charleston, Eckerd, Emory, Furman, Florida State, George Washington, Georgia Institute of Technology, Georgia State, Indiana University, Purdue, Savannah College of Art and Design, Tulane, Vanderbilt, and the Universities of Alabama and California (Berkeley).

STUDENT ACTIVITIES. Students are encouraged to participate in a variety of organizations and extracurricular activities such as the Key Club, Student Environmental Association, Student Government, and student publications including a yearbook, literary magazine, and newspaper. The two-pronged Student Government Association, made up of the Judiciary Board and Student Council, plays an integral part in helping direct student life. Students also participate in dance, drama, chorus, visual art, and interscholastic varsity and intramural sports.

Brenau Academy teams compete within the Atlanta Athletic Conference against other small private schools. Competitive sports offered include tennis, basketball, cross-country, golf, and volleyball.

Each year, Academy students have the opportunity to participate in a 10-day educational trip to a foreign country. The Dean's trip occurs during spring vacation and is open to all Brenau students in Grades 9–12. Past excursions have been to such destinations as Ireland, Switzerland, Greece, England, Scotland, France, China, and Italy.

Educational and recreational outings are regularly made to points of interest in Atlanta. Brenau arranges school-sponsored activities including movies; hiking and skiing trips; visits to local attractions such as Lake Lanier, Six Flags, Stone Mountain, Atlanta Thrashers hockey, World of Coca-Cola, the Atlanta Aquarium, and Atlanta Braves games. Special school traditions include Halloween Ghost Court, Christmas Traditions, Parents Weekend, and the Senior Banquet.

Concerts, plays, and lectures are offered at the Academy and College and are incorporated into school activities regularly. Recent campus art exhibits include Jasper Johns, Robert Rauschenberg, and Roy Lichtenstein.

ADMISSION AND COSTS. Brenau Academy enrolls college-bound students who, through the application process, demonstrate the potential for success in the Academy's college preparatory program. The Brenau Admissions Committee carefully considers each student on the basis of a completed application, three letters of recommendation, previous school records, a medical examination, and an interview with the Director of Admissions. Early application is encouraged; however, applications are accepted for the school year through January. There is a $25 application fee.

Tuition for the 2007–08 school year is $23,950 for boarding students and $10,500 for day students. Additional expenses include books and supplies, which average $500 per year. A limited amount of financial aid is available each year to families who demonstrate financial need.

Headmaster: Timothy A. Daniel
Assistant Dean: Lenna Applebee
Director of Alumni Affairs: Debbie Thompson
Director of Admission: Laura Nicholson
Vice President for Institutional Advancement: Jim Barco
College Counselor: Tami English
Business Manager: Holly Reynolds
Director of Athletics: Tess Trueheart

Brookstone School 1951

440 Bradley Park Drive, Columbus, GA 31904-2989
Tel. 706-324-1392; Fax 706-571-0178
Web Site www.brookstoneschool.org
E-mail msnyder@brookstoneschool.org

Enrolling approximately 840 students in Pre-Kindergarten through Grade 12, Brookstone School is a coeducational, college preparatory day school that seeks to produce leaders, instilling in its students the wisdom, courage, skills, work ethic, selflessness, and moral and spiritual foundation to lead. It encourages excellence by helping students to develop a passion for learning as well as fostering an atmosphere that encourages and enables personal growth. The challenging academic program includes 13 Advanced Placement courses, an extensive computer network, and fine and performing arts in all grades. Eighteen varsity sports are offered. Extended care is available. Tuition: $6250–$11,800. Financial Aid: $835,000. Mary S. Snyder is Enrollment Director; Scott A. Wilson is Headmaster. *Southern Association.*

Cliff Valley School 1966

2426 Clairmont Road, Atlanta, GA 30329
Tel. 678-302-1302; Fax 678-302-1300
Web Site www.cliffvalleyschool.org
E-mail info@cliffvalleyschool.org

Cliff Valley School's integrated curriculum is designed to nurture the development of young children as they begin their educational journey. The School enrolls more than 200 students from age 2 through fifth grade. Its mission is to provide a child-centered learning environment in which students can grow academically, socially, emotionally, and physically. The preschool and primary programs focus on readiness in math, reading, language arts, science, and social studies, while the upper elementary level expands on acquired skills as students undertake more complex and challenging course work. Art, music, drama, foreign language, technology, and health education are integral to the Cliff Valley experience. Tuition: $12,600. Megan Vitale is Admissions Manager; Michael Edwards is Acting Head of School.

Frederica Academy 1969

200 Hamilton Road, St. Simons Island, GA 31522
Tel. 912-638-9981; Admissions Ext. 106; Fax 912-638-1442
Web Site www.fredericaacademy.org
E-mail admission@fredericaacademy.org

Frederica Academy is a coeducational, college preparatory day school with an enrollment of approximately 420 students in Pre-Kindergarten–Grade 12. Founded in 1969, the school strives to help each student become an independent, lifelong learner. Foreign language study begins in Pre-K. A rigorous college preparatory course of study is enhanced by Advanced Placement courses as well as instruction in the arts, physical education, and technology. Twenty-two athletic teams, service learning opportunities, and outdoor education activities enrich the total academic experience. Tuition: $5000–$13,100. Financial aid is available. Ellen E. Fleming (George Washington University, B.A.; Georgia State University, M.Ed.) was appointed Headmistress in 2004. *Southern Association.*

The Galloway School 1969

215 West Wieuca Road, NW, Atlanta, GA 30342
Tel. 404-252-8389; Admission Ext. 106; Fax 404-252-7770
Web Site www.gallowayschool.org

Founded by Headmaster Emeritus Elliott Galloway, this coeducational day school enrolls approximately 710 students in Preschool through Grade 12. The student-teacher ratio is 10:1. The goals of the Galloway philosophy are to develop in each student a value for learning as a lifelong process, to encourage engaged and active learning, and to teach all members of the Galloway community to respect the dignity of the individual. Extracurricular activities range from student government and service clubs to interscholastic sports and a variety of interest groups. Galloway also conducts after-school and summer programs. Tuition: $15,680–$16,720. Rosetta Gooden is Director of Admission; Tom Brereton is Headmaster. *Southern Association.*

George Walton Academy 1969

#1 Bulldog Drive, Monroe, GA 30655
Tel. 770-267-7578; Admission Ext. 234; Fax 770-267-4023
Web Site www.gwalton.com; E-mail cstancil@gwa.com

George Walton Academy, an independent, coeducational day school enrolling 990 students in Pre-Kindergarten–Grade 12, seeks to encourage young people to strive for excellence in everything they undertake. The Academy is dedicated to providing an environment in which students grow, learn, are challenged, and find success. The college preparatory curriculum, which emphasizes excellence, intellectual challenge, student responsibility, and hard work, is enhanced by Spanish, Latin, fine arts, computer, and Advanced Placement and honors courses. Students participate in a wide range of varsity sports and extracurricular activities. Tuition: $5200–$7200. Chris Stancil is Admission Director; William M. Nicholson is Headmaster. *Southern Association.*

The Heritage School 1970

2093 Highway 29 North, Newnan, GA 30263
Tel. 770-253-9898; Admissions 678-423-5393; Fax 770-253-4850
Web Site www.heritagehawks.org
E-mail jknott@heritagehawks.org

Situated on a 63-acre campus in the midst of a pecan grove, The Heritage School serves 400 day students from Coweta, Fayette, and the Southern Arc. Using an integrated curriculum, the Lower School features unique projects, re-enactments, role-playing, research topics, and field trips. The primary mission of the Middle School is to provide the bridge for maturing students. The curriculum addresses intellectual, social/emotional, creative, physical, and moral development. Heritage incorporates outdoor education into the Middle School curriculum through the use of the School's Alpine Climbing Tower as well as with off-campus experiences on outdoor adventure trips. The Upper School stresses the liberal arts and character education while preparing students for college entrance. Upper School students are bound by the Honor Code and benefit from the guidance of college counselors as they plan and carry out their course of college preparatory work. Computer, language, music, physical education, and art classes are offered in all grades. The foreign language sequence in Kindergarten requires students to study French, Spanish, and Latin. Tuition: $6210–$11,755. Financial aid is available. Julie Knott is Director of Admissions; Judith Griffith is Head of School. *Southern Association.*

The Lovett School 1926

4075 Paces Ferry Road, NW, Atlanta, GA 30327
Tel. 404-262-3032; Fax 404-479-8463
Web Site www.lovett.org; E-mail dlange@lovett.org

Lovett is a coeducational, college preparatory day school committed to developing the whole child. Enrolling 1550 students in Kindergarten–Grade 12, the curriculum includes a full range of honors and Advanced Placement courses as well as an Academic Resource Center for academic support. Programs in all the fine arts are available at every level, and a full athletic program provides an opportunity to experience teamwork and sportsmanship. Lovett operates within the Judeo-Christian tradition, with weekly chapel services. The School seeks students from all ethnic, cultural, racial, and religious backgrounds who can benefit from a challenging academic program. Tuition: $15,440–$18,410. Financial aid is available. Debbie Lange is Director of Admission; William S. Peebles IV is Headmaster. *Southern Association.*

Marist School 1901

3790 Ashford-Dunwoody Road NE, Atlanta, GA 30319-1899
Tel. 770-457-7201; Fax 770-457-8402
Web Site www.marist.com; E-mail admissions@marist.com

Founded and operated by the Society of Mary, this coeducational, Roman Catholic day school enrolls 1070 students in Grades 7–12. Marist School's mission is to provide spiritual and ethical guidance within a challenging college preparatory program. Religious studies, campus ministry, and retreats involve students from many faiths. The curriculum includes 20 Advanced Placement courses, and all graduates enter four-year colleges and universities. Activities include peer support and leadership programs, honor societies, award-winning student publications, Habitat for Humanity, a comprehensive music program, dramatic and visual arts, and 18 sports. Tuition: $14,225; Registration Fee: $450. Need-based Financial Aid: $1,000,000. James G. Byrne is Director of Admissions; Rev. Joel Konzen, S.M., is Principal; Rev. Richmond J. Egan, S.M., is President. *Southern Association.*

Oak Mountain Academy 1962

222 Cross Plains Road, Carrollton, GA 30116
Tel. 770-834-6651; Fax 770-834-6785
Web Site www.oakmountain.us
E-mail admissions@oakmountain.us

Oak Mountain Academy was founded in 1962 as a nondenominational school for students in Pre-Kindergarten (age 4)–Grade 12. Enrolling 273 students, the Academy offers a traditional college preparatory curriculum, including Advanced Placement courses in six disciplines. Qualified Upper School students may take joint enrollment courses at the State University of West Georgia for dual credit. Participation in extracurricular activities includes Student Council and team and individual sports as well as seasonal dramatic productions and competition in speech and debate. Tuition: $3255–$8890. Need-based financial aid is available. Susan Emmons is Director of Admissions; Ricky Parmer (University of Alabama, M.A., Ed. Spec.) is Headmaster.

Pace Academy 1958

966 West Paces Ferry Road, NW, Atlanta, GA 30327
Tel. 404-352-4516; Admissions 404-926-3710; Fax 404-240-9124
Web Site www.paceacademy.org; E-mail cstrowd@paceacademy.org

Enrolling 950 boys and girls in Pre-First–Grade 12, Pace Academy is a college preparatory day school committed to academic excellence within a framework of Judeo-Christian values. The school offers a strong foundation in liberal arts, math, science, and technology. A demanding curriculum includes honors and Advanced Placement courses and a wide variety of electives. Students participate in service learning and peer leadership programs. Activities include athletics, drama, debate, art, and leadership programs. Pace's ideal size creates opportunities for involvement and a sense of belonging. Tuition: $15,885–$18,545. Financial Aid: $850,000. Claire Strowd (Middle/Upper) and Susan Gruber (Lower) are Directors of Admissions; Frederick G. Assaf is Headmaster. *Southern Association.*

St. George's Episcopal School 1996

103 Birch Street, Milner, GA 30257
Tel. 770-358-9432; Fax 770-358-9495
Web Site www.sges.org; E-mail lfolds@sges.org

This coeducational, elementary day school was founded by families of St. George's Episcopal Church to develop the minds, hearts, spirit, and physical well-being of their children. Enrolling 190 students from diverse faiths in Pre-Kindergarten–Grade 8, the School aims to offer an educational experience that embodies its motto: To Learn, To Serve, To Live. Academic excellence shares equal importance with respect for others, community service, and social responsibility. The preparatory curriculum, taught in a nurturing environment that reflects the traditions of the Episcopal Church, emphasizes mastery of skills in core subjects. Students take part in team sports and a variety of extracurricular activities. Tuition: $4450–$7050. Financial Aid: $60,000. Donna Mallett is Acing Head of School. *Southern Association.*

St. Martin's Episcopal School 1959

3110-A Ashford Dunwoody Road, Atlanta, GA 30319
Tel. 404-237-4260; Admissions Ext. 709; Fax 404-237-9311
Web Site www.stmartinschool.org
E-mail bmarsau@stmartinschool.org

St. Martin's Episcopal School is a parish day school enrolling 585 boys and girls in PreKindergarten–Grade 8. The School seeks to offer a quality academic program based on a traditional curriculum within a Christian environment. Core instruction is supplemented by art, music, foreign language, drama, public speaking, physical and health education, computer, and religion. Small class size and individualized instruction characterize the three divisions within the School—Early Childhood, Elementary, and Middle School. There is a variety of extracurricular activities. Tuition: $8931–$13,775. Financial Aid: $300,000. Blythe Marsau is Director of Admissions; The Reverend Dr. James E. Hamner IV (University of the South, M.Div.; University of Oxford, M.Phil., D. Phil.) is Headmaster. *Southern Association.*

The Savannah Country Day School 1955

824 Stillwood Drive, Savannah, GA 31419
Tel. 912-925-8800; Fax 912-920-7800
Web Site www.savcds.org; E-mail barfield@savcds.org

Savannah Country Day, enrolling 1007 boys and girls in Pre-Kindergarten through Grade 12, offers a challenging college preparatory curriculum designed to empower students to reach their full personal and academic potential. Country Day provides an academic program based in the traditional liberal arts, sciences, and humanities, complemented by modern and classical languages, information technology, and honors and Advanced Placement courses. Each year, 100 percent of graduates enter four-year colleges. Activities include music and drama, publications, community service, and award-winning team sports. Tuition: $6940–$14,730. Financial aid is available. Terri Barfield is Director of Admissions; Thomas C. Bonnell is Headmaster. *Southern Association.*

Tallulah Falls School 1909

P.O. Box 249, Tallulah Falls, GA 30573
Tel. 706-754-0400, Ext. 5112; Fax 706-754-3595
Web Site www.tallulahfalls.org; E-mail admissions@tallulahfalls.org

TALLULAH FALLS SCHOOL in Tallulah Falls, Georgia, is an independent, coeducational, college preparatory boarding and day school enrolling 140 students in Grades 6 through 12. Tallulah Falls is 90 miles northeast of Atlanta and 100 miles west of Greenville, South Carolina. The area is served by U.S. Hwy 441, which connects to the interstate system. The 500-acre campus lies on the slopes of Cherokee Mountain in an area of great natural beauty. Students and faculty are encouraged to participate in outdoor activities and have easy access to nearby Tallulah Gorge State Park and its outdoor education center.

Mrs. Mary Ann Lipscomb, president of the Georgia Federation of Women's Clubs, led the Federation in founding the School to serve the mountain children of northeast Georgia. It opened with an enrollment of 21 students from Habersham and Rabun Counties and has expanded to encompass a diverse student body including nearly a third from other states and countries.

Tallulah Falls School strives to present a challenging curriculum, using traditional teaching methods in small-class settings that stimulate student engagement in the learning process. Every student has the benefit of close personal attention from teachers, advisors, and other members of the staff. The program aims to instill in young people the desire for success and the self-confidence that comes with achievement. Students participate in the day-to-day operation of the School and in the care of facilities through a work program where they have definite assignments and responsibilities.

The School is a nonprofit organization, owned and operated by the Georgia Federation of Women's Clubs and governed by a Board of 35 Trustees. It is accredited by the Southern Association of Colleges and Schools and holds membership in the Georgia Independent School Association and the National Association of Independent Schools as well as several professional educational organizations. The School's endowment currently exceeds $30,000,000.

THE CAMPUS. Approximately 120 acres of the School property has been developed as a campus encompassing 22 buildings. This includes the original property of 5 acres and two buildings that are listed on the National Historic Register.

Student activities are centered in a group of buildings in the middle of the campus. Most classes take place in the H.R. and C.R. Cannon Academic Building, which also houses the Briggs Computer Laboratory and the Passie Felton Ottley Library with a collection of more than 9000 catalogued volumes. The Young Matrons Circle Building is the venue for performing arts, visiting lecturers, and community events. It has a 300-seat theater and fine arts classrooms and studios as well as a gymnasium, and other physical education facilities. The two newest facilities are the Lettie Pate Evans Student Center and Federation Hall, where students dine.

Boarding students live in recently renovated two-story dormitories, Fitzpatrick Hall for boys and Westmoreland Hall for girls. Athletic fields and outdoor tennis courts are at the edge of the developed campus. The school buildings are valued in excess of $17,000,000.

THE FACULTY. Mr. Larry A. Peevy, a graduate of the University of Montevallo (B.S., Ed.S.) who has also undertaken advanced study at the University of Alabama is President of the School.

The teaching faculty includes 12 men and 13 women who hold 25 bachelor's degrees and 24 advanced degrees from Appalachian State, Brenau University, Centre College, Clemson 2, Eastern Illinois, Georgia State, Howard, Iowa State, Mars Hill, Marymount College, Mercer, North Georgia College & State University 6, Piedmont College 9, State University of West Georgia 3, Toccoa Falls College, Woman's College of Georgia, and the Universities of Central Florida, Georgia, New Mexico, and Phoenix.

A registered nurse is on duty at the School infirmary daily during the school day and is on call at other times.

STUDENT BODY. Tallulah Falls School enrolls 140 students, in even proportions of boys and girls in Grades 6–12. Forty of these are day students. Seventy percent are from Georgia and 15 percent from other states. Another 15 percent are international students. More than half receive financial aid.

ACADEMIC PROGRAM. The academic year, divided into semesters, begins in mid-August and ends in late May. Vacations are scheduled for nine days at Thanksgiving, two weeks at Christmas, one week at winter break in late February, and ten days in the spring. Faculty members serve as advisors to small groups of students who meet daily to discuss learning activities and other issues. Extra help is offered in 30-minute tutorials at the end of the school day, and a mandatory, staff-supervised study hall is held from 8:00 to 9:40 P.M. five nights a week. Grades are sent to parents four times a year.

Classes are scheduled in a six-period day beginning at 8:30 A.M. and ending at 3:10 P.M. with a 40-minute lunch break. After classes, students take on tasks related to the kitchen or school maintenance on assigned days as part of the mandatory work program, which fosters a sense of responsibility to the community.

To graduate, a student must complete a college preparatory curriculum earning a minimum of 21 credits. This curriculum requires 4 units of English, 3 of social studies, 4 of mathematics, 2 units of foreign language, 3 units of science (including 2 lab courses), 1 of physical education/health, and 4 electives. Students are encouraged to take additional electives, when possible, to improve their preparation.

Among the courses offered are English 7–12, with Honors courses provided in Grades 9–12; English as a Second Language 1–3; French 1–3, Spanish 1–3; World History, U.S. History, Women in History, Government, World Religion, Economics; Algebra 1–3, Geometry, Calculus; Physical Science, Biology, Chemistry, Human Anatomy and Physiology, Physics; Art 1–4, Handbells 1–2, Chorus, Piano, Drama, American Cultural Literacy, Creative Writing, Journalism; Computer Science 1–2; and Industrial Arts 1–2. Honors courses are offered in English, U.S. History, Geometry, Algebra 3, Biology, and Chemistry. Advanced Placement courses are available in Biology, and more are planned.

A school counselor assists students with planning for college and completing applications. Nearly all graduates attend postsecondary schools. Among the institutions accepting members of the Class of 2006 and 2007 were Berry College, Florida State, Georgia Southern, Georgia State, Liberty State, Mercer, Michigan State, North Georgia, Ohio State, Piedmont, Purdue, Western Carolina, and the Universities of Florida, Georgia, Illinois, Kentucky, and Washington.

STUDENT ACTIVITIES. Students elect one representative from each class and the President, Vice President, and Secretary/Treasurer to the Student Council, which presents student views to the adult community and strives to develop student activities and opportunities.

Some of the regular activities are the Yearbook, Chorus, National Honor Society, and clubs devoted to chess, foreign languages, astronomy, poetry, math, and science. Competitions are organized in several areas of interest including spelling and geography bees and singing, with trios, quartets, and soloists demonstrating their talents for their peers. Art students compete in a number of contests including the School Art Symposium sponsored by the University of Georgia.

Tallulah Falls School is a member of the Georgia High School Association and fields teams that compete interscholastically in volleyball, cross-country, basketball, baseball, tennis, soccer, and track and field. The voluntary intramural program offers competition in soccer, basketball, volleyball, and softball. A feature of the school year is Field Day when students are divided into four teams and compete in a wide range of sporting events. Hiking, camping, cycling, white-water rafting, skiing, and horseback riding are activities available in the appropriate seasons.

Several dances are organized throughout the year as well as weekend trips to Atlanta and other cities. Special events on the school calendar include Great Smoky Mountains Deep Creek Tubing/Outdoor Games/Picnic, Field Day, Ocoee White Water Rafting Trip, Halloween Carnival, Christmas Play, Christmas Dinner and Social, Spring Musical, Homecoming Day, Awards Day/Parents' Day, and the Junior-Senior Prom.

ADMISSION AND COSTS. Tallulah Falls School seeks to enroll boys and girls of average to above-average ability who have the desire to participate actively in the School's programs. Admission is selective, since space in each class is limited, and is offered on a rolling basis. Prospective students are strongly encouraged to submit their applications, with a $30 fee, by March 1 for fall entry and by December 1 for a midyear start. Prospective students are evaluated on the basis of the completed application, school transcripts, teacher and principal recommendations, standardized test scores, and parent questionnaires.

Tuition for 2007–08 is $8000–$8500 for day students; $19,000 for boarding students from Georgia; $21,000 for boarders from other states; and $24,000 for international students. The fees include meals and books for all students. For international students, there is an additional $1500 charge for a required ESOL week in August as well as a $1500 charge for annual ESOL support. Tuition payment plans are available, and financial aid of more than $1,000,000 is awarded annually on the basis of need. A completed Parents Financial Statement (PFS) and accompanying income tax forms are necessary for this purpose.

President: Larry A. Peevy
Principal: Kim Popham
Dean of Students: Mike Dale
Director of Admission: Susan Waldorf
Director of Financial Aid: Tish Roller
Director of Business Affairs: Steve Cannon
Director of Communications: Brian Boyd
Boarding Director: Jimmy Franklin
Director of Information Technology: Bryan Roller
Athletic Director: Allen Campbell

Trinity School 1951

4301 Northside Parkway, NW, Atlanta, GA 30327
Tel. 404-231-8100; Admissions 404-231-8118; Fax 404-231-8111
Web Site www.trinityatl.org; E-mail kbaty@trinityatl.org

Trinity School is a nondenominational day school enrolling 588 children in Pre-school–Grade 6. Established by Trinity Presbyterian, the School operates in the Judeo-Christian tradition. The challenging, developmentally appropriate program includes an integrated curriculum and cooperative learning methods. The child-centered atmosphere nurtures each student's positive self-image. Spanish, art, music, technology, and physical and outdoor education are vital parts of the curriculum. Every student in Grade 6 has a tablet PC for use at home and school. Many of the School's well-qualified faculty members hold advanced degrees. There is an after-school enrichment program. Tuition: $11,120–$16,200. Financial aid is available. Kristin Baty is Director of Admissions; Stephen Kennedy (University of Tulsa, M.A.) is Head of School. *Southern Association.*

The Walker School 1957

700 Cobb Parkway North, Marietta, GA 30062
Tel. 770-427-2689; Admission 678-581-6921; Fax 770-514-8122
Web Site www.thewalkerschool.org
E-mail mozleyp@thewalkerschool.org

The Walker School is a coeducational day school enrolling 1100 students in Pre-Kindergarten–Grade 12. The School seeks to provide quality education through the efforts of a caring faculty with the ability to motivate children to achieve. The major emphasis is a traditional college preparatory academic program that includes computer technology. In addition, there are programs in the visual and performing arts, publications, and physical education. Extracurricular activities include sports, clubs, music, and drama. Tuition: $8460–$15,140. Financial Aid: $500,000. Patricia H. Mozley is Director of Admission and School Relations; Donald B. Robertson (William and Mary, B.S. 1968; Rider University, M.A. 1974) was named Headmaster in 1985. *Southern Association.*

Wesleyan School 1963

5405 Spalding Drive, Norcross, GA 30092
Tel. 770-448-7640; Admissions Ext. 2254; Fax 770-448-3699
Web Site www.wesleyanschool.org
E-mail blencke@wesleyanschool.org

Wesleyan School aims to create a community that exemplifies Christian values through a liberal arts education that includes required language and Bible studies. Enrolling 1075 day boys and girls with a maximum class size of 20, Wesleyan offers a full range of sports, arts, and activities in Kindergarten through Grade 12. Adherence to an honor code, uniform requirements, and a Chapel program are integral to school life. Tuition: $13,915–$16,050. Mrs. Bobbie Lencke is Admission Director; Zach Young (University of Virginia, B.A.; Harvard, Ed.M.) is Headmaster.

The Westminster Schools 1951

1424 West Paces Ferry Road, NW, Atlanta, GA 30327-2486
Tel. 404-355-8673; Admission 404-609-6202; Fax 404-367-7894
Web Site www.westminster.net; E-mail admissions@westminster.net

A Christian, college preparatory day school for 1820 boys and girls of various backgrounds in Pre-First–Grade 12, Westminster seeks to develop each student's potential for sound values, continuing education, and community service. The academic program includes Advanced Placement courses in 28 subjects. Extracurricular activities include athletics, fine arts, performing arts, and an experiential education program. Graduates have attended 432 colleges and universities in 40 states and 8 countries. The 180-acre campus is valued at $79,000,000, and the endowment is $229,000,000. Tuition: $15,440–$18,000. Financial Aid: $2,600,000. Marjorie Mitchell is Director of Admission;

William Clarkson IV (A.B., M.Div., D.Min.) is President. *Southern Association.*

Westminster Schools of Augusta 1972

3067 Wheeler Road, Augusta, GA 30909
Tel. 706-731-5260; Admissions Ext. 2201; Fax 706-261-7786
Web Site www.wsa.net; E-mail amccallie@wsa.net

The Westminster Schools of Augusta offer a college preparatory education in a Christian setting with small classes, caring faculty, and many service opportunities and activities in athletics and the arts. Enrolling 510 day boys and girls in Pre-Kindergarten–Grade 12, Westminster provides Honors and Advanced Placement courses, foreign language, music, art, and drama. Among the activities are team sports, chorale, drama, and debate. Bible courses and weekly chapel services enrich the program. Graduates have been accepted at competitive colleges and universities nationwide. Tuition: $4856–$9476. Financial Aid: $320,000. Alex McCallie is Director of Admissions; James A. Adare is Headmaster. *Southern Association.*

Woodward Academy 1900

1662 Rugby Avenue, College Park, GA 30337
Tel. 404-765-4000; Admissions 404-765-4001; Fax 404-765-4009
Web Site www.woodward.edu; E-mail admissions@woodward.edu

Woodward Academy in College Park, Georgia, is a coeducational college preparatory school enrolling 2880 day students in Pre-Kindergarten through Grade 12. Woodward Academy is comprised of five divisions. The Primary School (Kindergarten–Grade 3), Lower School (Grades 4–6), Middle School (Grades 7–8), and Upper School (Grades 9–12) are located on the main campus in College Park, a suburban community 7 miles south of downtown Atlanta, and convenient to the Hartsfield-Jackson International Airport. Woodward North (Pre-Kindergarten–Grade 6), is located in North Fulton County along the Chattahoochee River.

Founded in 1900 as Georgia Military Academy by Col. John C. Woodward, the school was originally a secondary military academy for boys; an elementary division was subsequently added. In 1964, the Academy became coeducational, and in 1966, the Academy's charter was amended to discontinue the military program and to rename the school in honor of its founder. Colonel Woodward was succeeded by his son-in-law, Col. William R. Brewster, Sr.; Capt. William R. Brewster, Jr., served as President from 1961 until December 1978. Dr. Gary M. Jones was installed as Woodward's fourth President in January 1979 and retired in July of 1990. Mr. A. Thomas Jackson served as the fifth President of the Academy from 1990 to 1999. Dr. Harry C. Payne was named the sixth Academy President in 2000.

The Academy is incorporated as a nonprofit institution under a self-perpetuating Governing Board comprised of alumni and patrons of the school. Woodward Academy's productive endowments are valued at more than $100,000,000. Woodward is accredited by the Southern Association of Colleges and Schools; it holds membership in the National Association of Independent Schools, the Southern Association of Independent Schools, the Georgia Independent Schools Association, and the Atlanta Area Association of Independent Schools. The 7000 living graduates are served by an Alumni Association.

THE CAMPUS. The 80-acre College Park campus contains more than 50 buildings, practice fields, a football stadium, and a nine-court tennis center. Carlos Hall contains the administrative and business offices. West Hall contains Upper School offices and the infirmary, with Upper School classrooms located in the adjacent Brewster Hall. The Thalia N. Carlos Science Center contains 23,000 square feet of modern laboratories and classrooms. The Colquitt Student Center houses a snack bar, student lockers, and a recreation area. The George C. Carlos Library houses 25,000 volumes and includes an Academy archive, conference rooms, reading areas, and study carrels for both Middle and Upper School students. The 92,000-square-foot Richardson Fine Arts Center contains classrooms, offices, studios, a gallery, a 400-seat auditorium, and a closed-circuit television station. The Alumni Center houses the alumni and development offices. The Paget Gymnasium Complex contains five basketball courts, a weight room, wrestling loft, and physical education offices. Adjacent to the Paget Complex is the Kennedy Natatorium, housing an eight-lane Olympic-size pool. More than 5000 spectators can be seated in the lighted Colquitt Stadium. Upper School meals are served in Robert W. Woodruff Hall. The 600-seat Richard C. Gresham Chapel also contains a multipurpose conference room. Middle School offices, classrooms, laboratories, dining and art spaces, and study areas are located in Jordan Carlos Middle School Complex, constructed in 2003. Lower School offices, classrooms, a 15,000-volume library, computer lab, gymnasium, and cafetorium are located in Thomas Hall.

A new Primary School Building was completed in 2007. The $9,000,000 Primary School campus features a central complex containing administrative offices, classrooms, a library, and a cafetorium. The grounds also include an athletic field. The 36-acre Woodward North campus includes a facility containing administrative offices, a cafetorium, a library, adjacent athletic fields, nature trails, and a performing and visual arts center.

THE FACULTY. President of the Academy Dr. Harry C. Payne holds B.A. and Ph.D. degrees from Yale University. Vice President and Headmaster David R. McCollum is a graduate of Millsaps College (B.A.), Emory University (M.Div.), and the University of Georgia (M.Ed., Ed.S.).

The faculty include 350 full-time instructors and 110 academic support staff. Faculty and staff hold more than 225 master's or higher educational degrees, including 6 doctorates. Two or more degrees were earned at Agnes Scott, Auburn, Brenau, Cleveland State, Emory, Georgia Institute of Technology, Georgia Southern, Georgia State, Jacksonville State, LaGrange, Louisiana State, Mercer, Miami of Ohio, Michigan State, Milligan, Millsaps, Notre Dame College, Oglethorpe, Ohio State, Peabody, Purdue, Shorter, Wake Forest, West Chester State, West Georgia, West Virginia, William and Mary, and the Universities of Alabama, Arkansas, Central Florida, Georgia, Mississippi, North Alabama, North Carolina, South Carolina, South Florida, and Tennessee.

The Academy provides a salary schedule, supplements for extracurricular activities, merit pay, comprehensive major medical insurance, and a retirement program.

STUDENT BODY. Woodward Academy enrolls 2880 students, of whom 51 percent are boys and 49 percent girls. Students come from communities throughout the metropolitan Atlanta area.

ACADEMIC PROGRAM. The academic year, from mid-August to late May, is divided into two semesters and includes Thanksgiving, Winter Break, and Spring vacations. Classes begin at 8:30 A.M. and end at 3:05 P.M., depending on individual schedules.

A college preparatory curriculum is offered to all Upper School students; available electives include computer programming, television production, science fiction, astronomy, oceanography, satire, Shakespeare, and dance. Honors courses and Advanced Placement courses include English, European history, American history, mathematics, computer science, biology, chemistry, physics, French, Japanese, Spanish, music, and art. Report cards are mailed to parents at six-week intervals, and interim reports are sent to parents in cases of deficient or unsatisfactory work.

Middle School students are required to take Computer Science, Foreign Language, and Life Skills in addition to English, reading, mathematics, science, social studies, fine arts, and physical education. Honors and regular sections are offered in most departments; tutorials and study halls are available.

The Lower Schools offer a competitive program of instruction. The upper elementary grades are departmentalized, and reading and mathematics receive primary emphasis along with computer science, social studies, science, art, music, drama, and physical education. The main campus Lower School and Woodward North offer a Student Transition Education Program for above-average students with slight learning differences. Tutorials, interim reports, and parent-teacher conferences chart a student's progress.

The 253 members of the Class of 2007 attend such institutions as Agnes Scott, Appalachian State, Auburn, Boston University, Clemson, Cornell, Dartmouth, Duke, Florida State, Georgia Institute of Technology, Georgia Southern, Harvard, Louisiana State, Mercer, Miami (Ohio), Southern Methodist, Stanford, U.S. Air Force Academy, U.S. Military Academy, U.S. Naval Academy, Vanderbilt, Wellesley, Williams, and the Universities of Alabama, Colorado, Michigan, Mississippi, Pennsylvania, South Carolina, and Virginia.

STUDENT ACTIVITIES. The Academy offers a wide variety of activities to students. Lower School activities include Cub Scouts, chorus, band, patrols, intramural sports, cultural programs, and educational trips. Middle School activities include a Student Government, class activities, a Camera Club, an Art Club, and Honor Council. Dances are held periodically. Upper School activities include Student Government, Honor Council, the National Honor Society, French and Spanish honor societies, debate, newspaper, yearbook, Camera Club, cheerleaders, flag corps, Art Club, choruses, Drama Club, band, a dance ensemble, ten service clubs, and the WATV crew. Upper School students are required to fulfill a 20-hour work contract during the year by working on campus. All Upper School students are involved in small group sessions through the Peer Leadership and Teacher Advisory programs. These programs assist students in dealing with peer pressure, academic stress, and other pertinent issues.

Interscholastic and intramural sports include football, baseball, basketball, soccer, swimming and diving, tennis, track, wrestling, cross-country, volleyball, fast-pitch softball, lacrosse, ultimate frisbee, and golf. Social activities include formal and informal dances and weekend outings.

Frequent assemblies provide a forum for various speakers and school groups.

ADMISSION AND COSTS. It is Woodward Academy's policy to admit students from a variety of racial, ethnic, and economic backgrounds who desire to attend the Academy and who provide evidence of good character, conduct, and academic achievement. New students are accepted at all grade levels except Grade 12. An entrance examination, an interview, school records, teacher/principal evaluations, and evidence of extracurricular interests are required, especially for older students.

In 2007–08, tuition is $11,300 for Pre-Kindergarten, $15,600 for Kindergarten–Grade 6, and $18,100 for Grades 7–12. Additional charges for all students include textbooks

($300–$500) and uniforms (approximately $700). Additional fees may be levied for private lessons, private tutoring, developmental reading, the yearbook, and the diploma. An additional $8600 is required for students in the Transition Program to provide the small classes and individual tutoring such children require. More than $1,600,000 in financial aid is awarded annually to approximately 10 percent of the students in the Middle and Upper Schools.

Dean of Faculty: Mr. David R. McCollum
Dean of Students: Mrs. Elaine T. Carroll
Alumni Director: Ms. Amy Zarriello
Dean of Admission: Mr. Russell L. Slider
Director of Development: Mr. Robert F. Hawks
College Counselor: Mrs. Missy Sanchez
Business Manager: Ms. Barbara Egan
Director of Athletics: Mr. David H. Chandler

HAWAII

Hanahau'oli School 1918

1922 Makiki Street, Honolulu, HI 96822
Tel. 808-949-6461; Admission Ext. 107; Fax 808-941-2216
Web Site www.hanahauoli.org
E-mail ctakamine@hanahauoli.org

A coeducational, nonsectarian elementary school enrolling 200 children in Junior Kindergarten–Grade 6, Hanahau'oli's philosophy of "learning by doing" informs its curriculum while creating an environment in which students share experiences and cooperate as a large family. A multiage classroom system recognizes that children of the same age learn at different paces and allows team teaching and flexibility in instruction to support individual progress toward academic excellence. Specialists in music, visual arts, physical education, technology, physical world lab, and French integrate curricula with classroom programs. Tuition: $14,900. Carol Takamine is Director of Admission; Robert G. Peters (University of Massachusetts, B.A., M.A., Ed.D.) is Headmaster. *Western Association.*

Holy Nativity School 1949

5286 Kalanianaole Highway, Honolulu, HI 96821
Tel. 808-373-3232; Admissions Ext. 113; Fax 808-377-9618
Web Site www.holynativityschool.org
E-mail admissions@holynativity-hi.org

Holy Nativity School, an independent, coeducational, Episcopal day school, enrolls 180 students in Pre-Kindergarten–Grade 6. Holy Nativity provides students with an integrated, research-based curriculum, which is developmentally appropriate and aligned with national standards. Small group and individualized instruction in a nurturing environment contributes to the quality of the program. In addition to classroom teachers who provide a solid foundation in the core subject areas, students attend music, art, religion, computer technology, and physical education classes with specialist teachers weekly. Teachers work collaboratively, ensuring a seamless transition between grades, maximizing the cumulative effect of instruction, and thus preparing students for a successful trasition to seventh grade at Hawai'i's fine secondary schools. A summer program offers various subjects, activities, and field trips. Tuition: $10,600. Financial aid is available. Kelly Goheen is Director of Admission; Dr. Robert H. Whiting (University of Colorado [Boulder], Ph.D.) is Head of School. *Western Association.*

Iolani School 1863

563 Kamoku Street, Honolulu, HI 96826
Tel. 808-949-5355; Admissions 808-943-2222; Fax 808-943-2375
Web Site www.iolani.org; E-mail admission@iolani.org

In the tradition of the Episcopal Church, Iolani School provides academic, spiritual, athletic, and extracurricular programs that promote Christian values and personal excellence. The School's college preparatory day program enrolls 1830 students in Kindergarten–Grade 12. The curriculum features five languages, the fine arts, and Advanced Placement courses in most subjects. Students participate in 17 boys' and girls' interscholastic teams and more than 50 clubs and organizations, including four publications, service and leadership groups, theater, dance, and music. Financial aid and a summer session are available. Tuition: $14,000. Patricia Liu is Director of Admission; Val T. Iwashita (Brigham Young, Ed.D.) is Headmaster. *Western Association.*

LA PIETRA-Hawaii School for Girls 1962

2933 Poni Moi Road, Honolulu, HI 96815
Tel. 808-922-2744; Fax 808-923-4514
Web Site www.lapietra.edu; E-mail info@lapietra.edu

LA PIETRA-Hawaii School for Girls, an independent day school enrolling 249 students in Grades 6–12, is committed to small enrollment, low pupil-teacher ratio, a broad college preparatory curriculum, extensive college counseling, and the advantages of an all-girls' school. The creative instruction includes cooperative learning, expanded fine arts opportunities, and hands-on learning as well as Advanced Placement courses. A 1:1 student-computer ratio makes possible full integration of technology in all disciplines. Activities include athletics, peer leadership, drama, chorus, speech, and debate. Tuition: $13,675. Financial Aid: $600,000. Mahina Eleneki Hugo is Head of School. *Western Association.*

Le Jardin Academy 1961

917 Kalanianaole Highway, Kailua, HI 96734
Tel. 808-261-0707; Fax 808-262-9339
Web Site www.lejardinacademy.com
E-mail staylor@lejardinacademy.com

Le Jardin Academy is a coeducational, college preparatory day school enrolling 800 youngsters in Prekindergarten–Grade 12. Le Jardin seeks to enable students to develop in mind, body, and character. The curriculum provides a strong foundation in academic subjects while encouraging creative and critical thinking and effective decision making. The core program is enriched by Japanese, after-school sports, drama, band, and orchestra. Exchanges with schools in Japan and China and outdoor educational programs promote cultural understanding and appreciation for the environment. Extended-day care and a summer program are optional. Tuition: $12,596. Ms. Susan L. Taylor is Director of Admission; Mr. Adrian Allan (Leeds University, B.S.; University of Alabama, M.A.) is Headmaster. *Western Association.*

Parker School 1976

65-1224 Lindsey Road, Kamuela, HI 96743
Tel. 808-885-7933; Fax 808-885-6233
Web Site www.parkerschool.net; E-mail arenick@parkerschool.net

Set on a beautiful campus near the Big Island's Kohala Coast, Parker is by design a small, coeducational day school enrolling 298 students in Kindergarten through Grade 12, with separate facilities for its lower, middle, and upper school divisions. The School seeks and welcomes diversity and enrolls youngsters from a wide variety of racial, ethnic, religious, and socioeconomic backgrounds. The college preparatory curriculum emphasizes the traditional liberal arts, sciences, and humanities in a family-like environment where students develop academically while discovering their unique, individual talents. Spanish language instruction begins in Kindergarten and is offered at five ability levels through graduation. Honors and Advanced Placement courses are offered to qualified students in Grades 9–12, and all seniors are accepted by four-year colleges and universities. Activities include interscholastic sports in two athletic conferences. Bulls teams compete in cross-country, volleyball, swimming, paddling, golf, track, tennis, girls' soccer, and boys' wrestling and basketball. Parker's Middle School also offers an equestrian program. Tuition: $9600–$11,200. Ann Renick is Director of Admissions; Dr. Carl Sturges was appointed Headmaster in 2002. *Western Association.*

St. Andrew's Priory School for Girls 1867

224 Queen Emma Square, Honolulu, HI 96813
Tel. 808-536-6102; Admissions 808-532-2418; Fax 808-531-8426
Web Site www.priory.net; E-mail sawargo@priory.net

St. Andrew's Priory is an Episcopal day school enrolling 550 young women from many ethnic, cultural, and religious backgrounds in Kindergarten–Grade 12. It also has a coeducational preschool enrolling 150 children ages 2 to 5. Following traditions set by its founder, Hawaii's Queen Emma, the School offers a well-balanced college preparatory education that is designed to prepare young women to meet the challenges and opportunities of college and adult life. Extensive technology, athletics, and visual and performing arts complement the curriculum. Tuition: $11,385–$12,000. Sue Ann Wargo is Admissions Director; Ivan M. Lui-Kwan, Esq. (Rutgers University, J.D., M.S.), is Head of School. *Western Association.*

IDAHO

The Community School 1973

P.O. Box 2118, Sun Valley, ID 83353
Tel. 208-622-3955; Admissions Ext. 117; Fax 208-622-3962
Web Site www.communityschool.org
E-mail kraffetto@communityschool.org

The Community School is a college preparatory day school enrolling 300 students in Kindergarten–Grade 12. Located in Sun Valley in the Wood River Valley, the School integrates outdoor education with a challenging academic program while striving to achieve a sense of community. Numerous activities include skiing, tennis, soccer, basketball, drama, and camping. The summer program provides academic courses and recreation. Tuition: $18,300–$20,845. Financial Aid: $1,100,000. Katie Raffetto is Director of Admission; Andy Jones-Wilkins (Hamilton, B.A.; Villanova, M.A.) is Head of School.

ILLINOIS

The Ancona School 1962

4770 South Dorchester Avenue, Chicago, IL 60615-2023
Tel. 773-924-2356; Fax 773-924-8905
Web Site www.anconaschool.org; E-mail info@anconaschool.org

Ancona is a coeducational, elementary day school enrolling 260 children from a wide range of racial and ethnic backgrounds in Preprimary (age 3) to Grade 8. The School's diversity is valued as a means of promoting understanding, respect, and social justice. Based in the Montessori tradition, the School emphasizes a solid academic foundation in a joyful environment. Children learn in multiage classrooms, with small reading, writing, and math groups that enhance independently acquired learning. Research and organizational skills are emphasized in readiness for the challenges of selective secondary schools. Music and the arts are an integral component of child-centered curriculum. Tuition: $9970–$15,275. Financial Aid: $130,000. Carol Parham is Director of Admissions; Bonnie Wishne is Director.

The Avery Coonley School 1906

1400 Maple Avenue, Downers Grove, IL 60515-4897
Tel. 630-969-0800; Fax 630-969-0131
Web Site www.averycoonley.org; E-mail minicar@averycoonley.org

The Avery Coonley School, enrolling 372 day students in Early Childhood (age 3)–Grade 8, offers a challenging program designed to meet the needs of academically bright and gifted students. A student-teacher ratio of 11:1 allows each child to receive a high level of individual attention and to progress at an accelerated rate. The enriched curriculum is designed to nurture the development of students so that they will become critical thinkers and independent learners. The program also includes French, art, music, drama, physical education, technology, and character education. Student Council, fine arts, athletics, and many interest clubs are among the activities. Tuition: $4455–$15,230. Mr. Paul Barton (Loras College, B.A.; St. John's College, M.A.) is Head of School.

Baker Demonstration School 1918

201 Sheridan Road, Wilmette, IL 60091
Tel. 847-425-5800; Admission 847-425-5813; Fax 847-425-5801
Web Site www.bakerdemschool.org
E-mail dharrison@bakerdemschool.org

Founded by progressive education pioneer Clara Bell Baker in 1918, Baker Demonstration School serves nearly 400 students in Early Childhood through Grade 8. In the 21st century, Baker continues its mission as a demonstration school whose outstanding faculty study how children learn and mentor the next generation of teachers. A curriculum that promotes academic excellence is taught through innovative research-based best practices and assessment tools. Differentiated instruction is enhanced by full-time teaching associates in all classrooms. With over 50,000 square feet of green space, Baker boasts a sports field and two play areas including a dedicated Early Childhood yard. The 18,000-volume library, newly furnished technology/media lab, performance hall, dance studio, music studio, pool, and gym are used by students in PreK–Grade 8. Baker's inclusive community celebrates individual, family, and cultural differences. Baker graduates attend top public, private, and parochial schools throughout the Chicagoland area. Tuition: $6250–$15,200. Deirdre Harrison is Director of Admission; Robert Coombs is Interim Head of School.

Bernard Zell Anshe Emet Day School 1946

3751 North Broadway Street, Chicago, IL 60613
Tel. 773-281-1858; Admissions 773-572-1236; Fax 773-281-4709
Web Site www.bzaeds.org; E-mail admissions@bzaeds.org

The Bernard Zell Anshe Emet Day School is a fully accredited, independent, coeducational, Jewish day school with 492 students in nursery through eighth grade. Day School families represent a microcosm of Chicago's diverse Jewish community and span the continuum of practice and belief. Despite differences in observation of Jewish traditions at home, students share a common experience in school and develop a connection to universally respected values. The Day School's commitment to academic excellence is evident in both general and Jewish studies with small classes and innovative teaching methods creating an ideal learning environment. Students have many opportunities for enrichment and enjoyment in and out of the classroom. A new 45,000-square-foot athletic field is used by classes and teams, and after-school activities support various interests, including chess, band, science, Mandarin Chinese, digital video editing, art, and more. Faculty, committed parents, and seasoned administrators work together, creating a vibrant, caring, student-centered community. Students graduate well prepared for high school and for the world beyond. Tuition: $12,930–$20,925. Alyson K. Horwitz, Ed.D., is School Head; Pamela Popeil is Director of Admissions.

Brehm Preparatory School 1982

1245 East Grand Avenue, Carbondale, IL 62901-3600
Tel. 618-457-0371; Fax 618-529-1248
Web Site www.brehm.org; E-mail admissionsinfo@brehm.org

Carol Brehm founded Brehm Preparatory School to provide an appropriate educational setting for her son and other students with learning differences. Today, Brehm Prep is the Midwest's only boarding school specifically designed to help youngsters with complex learning disabilities and disorders such as ADD and ADHD. Enrolling 98 boys and girls ages 11–21, the School provides a full range of services to meet individual academic, social, and emotional needs. In a family environment, students undertake a college preparatory curriculum that implements Orton-Gillingham and other methodologies related to personalized education. Using a team approach, faculty address each student's areas of academic strength and weakness with the goal of empowering him or her to become an independent learner and self-advocate. In addition to academic course work, Brehm also focuses on the development of life skills such as time management and problem solving. Among the activities are Student Council, weekend field trips, physical fitness, outdoor pursuits, basketball, indoor soccer, and community service. Boarding Tuition: $53,600; Day Tuition: $33,080. Donna Collins is Director of Admissions; Richard G. Collins, Ph.D., is Executive Director.

The Catherine Cook School 1975

226 West Schiller Street, Chicago, IL 60610
Tel. 312-266-3381; Admissions Ext. 146; Fax 312-266-3616
Web Site www.catherinecookschool.org
E-mail admissions@catherinecookschool.org

The Catherine Cook School is an urban, coeducational, nondenominational day school that enrolls 460 children from Preschool through Grade 8. The liberal arts educational program includes core curriculum, math, science, literacy, and humanities as well as fine arts, music, physical education, foreign language, and character development. The School's approach incorporates hands-on, experiential learning designed to instill critical thinking and problem-solving strategies. Small classes and careful attention to individual learning patterns ensure that all students have the ability to reach their full potential. Student Government, interest clubs, and athletic programs enrich the core program. Extended day is optional. Tuition: $3200–$14,235. Need-based financial aid is available. Lindsey Valente is Director of Admission; Dr. Michael Roberts is Head of School.

The Chicago Academy for the Arts 1981

1010 West Chicago Avenue, Chicago, IL 60622
Tel. 312-421-0202; Fax 312-421-3816
Web Site www.chicagoartsacademy.org
E-mail generalinfo@chicagoartsacademy.org

The Chicago Academy for the Arts is the area's only private high school specializing in a combined academic and intensive arts education in visual arts, music, dance, theater, media arts, and musical theater. Enrolling approximately 160 students, the Academy strives to prepare talented youth in Grades 9–12 for educated choices about continued study at universities and conservatories as well as the pursuit of professional careers in the visual and performing arts. Admission is by audition and academic testing. Most graduates enter four-year colleges or are recruited by major dance, theater, film, and recording companies. Tuition: $15,860. Mark Taylor is Director of Admissions and Marketing; Pamela Jordan was appointed Head of School in 2002.

Chicago City Day School 1981

541 West Hawthorne Place, Chicago, IL 60657
Tel. 773-327-0900; Fax 773-327-6381
Web Site www.chicagocitydayschool.org

Founded in 1981 to provide high-quality education for city dwellers, the Chicago City Day School enrolls 283 boys and girls in Junior Kindergarten–Grade 8. Rigorous but nurturing education and the development of strong skills in reading, language arts, mathematics, and social studies are its aims. French, Spanish, science, art, music, drama, and physical education are offered at all levels; computer studies begin in Grade 1 and industrial arts in Grade 2. Sports, yearbook, and clubs are some of the activities. Tuition: $17,500–$19,150. Extras: $1000–$1175. Galeta Kaar Clayton (Northwestern, B.A. 1961; Loyola, M.Ed. 1965; Erikson Institute, M.Ed. 1974) is the founding Headmistress.

Elgin Academy 1839

350 Park Street, Elgin, IL 60120
Tel. 847-695-0300; Admissions 847-695-0303; Fax 847-695-5017
Web Site www.elginacademy.org; E-mail info@elginacademy.org

Elgin Academy, the oldest nonsectarian, coeducational college preparatory school west of the Allegheny Mountains, enrolls 480 students from diverse backgrounds in Preschool–Grade 12. The educational program gives students sound knowledge in the arts and sciences and the skills necessary to acquire and use that knowledge as lifelong learners. Students are active in the arts, athletics, and community service. World language study begins in Preschool; Advanced Placement-level courses and independent study are available in the Upper School. All seniors are college bound and attend universities throughout the United States. Tuition: $9900–$15,750. Financial Aid: $1,045,000. Erik C. Calhoun is Director of Admission; Dr. John W. Cooper (Syracuse, Ph.D.) is Head of School. *North Central Association.*

Fenwick High School 1929

505 Washington Boulevard, Oak Park, IL 60302
Tel. 708-386-0127; Admissions Ext. 115; Fax 708-386-3052
Web Site www.fenwickfriars.com
E-mail fcasaccio@fenwickfriars.com

Fenwick, a Catholic, coeducational, college preparatory school founded in 1929 by the Dominican Order of Preachers, draws 1160 students from more than 60 communities and a broad spectrum of cultural and socioeconomic backgrounds. Emphasizing academic excellence and participation in athletics, activities, and community service, Fenwick prepares its students for college, with a 100 percent college acceptance rate, and for life and leadership. Motivated students, qualified faculty, and a supportive community of parents and graduates result in Fenwick's recognition as an exemplary high school by the U.S. Department of Education. Tuition: $9400. Financial aid is available.

Francesca Casaccio is Director of Admissions; Rev. De Porres Durham, O.P., is President; James J. Quaid, Ph.D., is Principal.

Francis W. Parker School 1901

330 West Webster Avenue, Chicago, IL 60614
Tel. 773-353-3000; Admissions 773-797-5107 (JK–5); 773-797-5510 (6–12); Fax 773-549-0587
Web Site www.fwparker.org; E-mail admission@fwparker.org

Now in its 106th year, Francis W. Parker continues its commitment to enhancing the potential of each of the 910 boys and girls enrolled in Junior Kindergarten–Grade 12. Guided by a profound educational philosophy, Parker's distinction lies in its desire to foster the development of the individual so that graduates can flourish as active citizens in a diverse, democratic society and changing world. Through a variety of methods, teachers encourage students to think independently by developing their skills in making judgments and inferences based on what they have observed or experienced. Parker's goal is to develop students' confidence to learn throughout their lives and improve the quality of life for others. Tuition: $17,640–$22,600. Financial Aid: $2,200,000. Kate Pivinski (JK–5) and Cokey Evans (6–12) are Admission Directors; Dr. Daniel B. Frank (Amherst, B.A.; University of Chicago, M.A., Ph.D.) is Principal. *North Central Association.*

Lake Forest Academy 1857

1500 West Kennedy Road, Lake Forest, IL 60045-1047
Tel. 847-234-3210; Admissions 847-615-3267; Fax 847-295-8149
Web Site www.lfanet.org; E-mail info@lfanet.org

Lake Forest Academy is a coeducational, college preparatory school enrolling 390 students, about half of whom are boarders, in Grades 9–12. The school adheres to high academic standards, with challenging course work taught by dedicated faculty. Small classes, computer technology throughout the disciplines, and Advanced Placement courses are features of the curriculum. All-school meetings, a strong advisory system, and English as a Second Language for international students enrich the Lake Forest experience. Among the extracurricular options are drama, instrumental and vocal groups, interest clubs, and 23 interscholastic sports. Boarding Tuition: $36,300; Day

Tuition: $26,500. Financial Aid: $2,800,000. Loring Strudwick is Dean of Admission; John Strudwick is Head of School.

Lake Forest Country Day School 1888

145 South Green Bay Road, Lake Forest, IL 60045
Tel. 847-234-2350; Admissions Fax 847-234-8725
Web Site www.lfcds.org; E-mail nicoletc@lfcds.org

Lake Forest Country Day School enrolls 440 boys and girls in Preschool (age 3) to Grade 8. Education in basic skills is stressed, along with a substantial program in interdisciplinary studies and the arts to help students develop the capacity to think independently, achieve their full potential, and interact effectively with others. Included are art, music, drama, computer, outdoor education, athletics, and community service programs. French, Mandarin Chinese, and Spanish instruction begins at age 3. Summer offerings feature study skills, language arts, mathematics, and the arts, plus a computer and sports camp. Tuition: $11,000–$18,250. Financial Aid: $300,000. Christine R. Nicoletta is Director of Admission; Robert Bullard is Assistant Head of School; Michael Robinson was appointed Head of School in 2005.

North Shore Country Day School 1919

310 Green Bay Road, Winnetka, IL 60093-4094
Admissions 847-441-3313; Main 847-446-0674; Fax 847-446-0675
Web Site www.nscds.org; E-mail admissions@nscds.org

North Shore Country Day School, enrolling 475 boys and girls in Junior Kindergarten–Grade 12, provides a rigorous, college preparatory education within a supportive, ethics-based community. The School is committed to the highest quality of education, balanced with athletics, the arts, and service to others. North Shore also encourages its students to explore many extracurricular opportunities. The School has developed unique programs in languages, math, science, global consciousness, and technology; a state-of-the-art science center recently opened. Tuition: $11,564–$20,770. Financial aid is available. Dale L. Wentz is Director of Admissions and Financial Aid; W. Thomas Doar III is Head of School.

Quest Academy 1982

500 North Benton Street, Palatine, IL 60067
Tel. 847-202-8035; Fax 847-202-8085
Web Site www.questacademy.org
E-mail admission@questacademy.org

Quest Academy is a fully accredited, independent day school enrolling more than 300 academically gifted and talented students from Preschool through Grade 8. In the hands-on interdisciplinary curriculum, equal emphasis is placed on the academics and the arts. Students are encouraged to collaborate and share ideas. Enrichment classes for all students include visual arts, music, drama, physical education, French, technology, library, and science. Quest's character education program incorporates service learning experiences. Differentiation in all subject areas and a faculty trained in the needs of gifted students set Quest apart from other educational opportunities. Tuition: $16,000. Financial aid is available. Mary Cunningham is Director of Admission and Marketing; Ben Hebebrand is Head of School.

Roycemore School 1915

640 Lincoln Street, Evanston, IL 60201
Tel. 847-866-6055; Fax 847-866-6545
Web Site www.roycemoreschool.org
E-mail info@roycemoreschool.org

A college preparatory, coeducational day school with 250 students in Junior Kindergarten–Grade 12, Roycemore School nurtures students in an attentive, stimulating environment. A diverse student body with a variety of backgrounds, cultures, and interests, reflects the communities Roycemore serves. Small classes of 10–18 allow faculty to challenge students and to respond to individual learning styles. Roycemore's Upper School permits qualified students to take classes at nearby Northwestern University as well as Advanced Placement courses in most subjects and a three-week independent study project. Summer recreational and gifted programs are offered. Tuition: $6535–$20,475. Financial aid is available. Carolyn Coyne is Director of Admission; Joseph A. Becker is Headmaster.

Sacred Heart Schools 1876

6250 North Sheridan Road, Chicago, IL 60660-1799
Tel. 773-262-4446; Admissions 773-681-8401; Fax 773-262-6178
Web Site www.shschicago.org; E-mail admissions@shschicago.org

A Chicago landmark on Lake Michigan, Sacred Heart Schools enroll 652 day students. They are part of a Network of 130 Sacred Heart Schools in 22 countries. Kindergarten is coeducational; in Grades 1–8, girls attend the Academy, and boys attend Hardey Prep. French begins in Kindergarten, Spanish in Grade 6. In addition to a rigorous curriculum, Sacred Heart Schools are dedicated to a values-based program concerned with the education of the whole child. An active faith, critical thinking, personal responsibility, a global vision, and concern for others embody a Sacred Heart education. Financial, ethnic, and religious diversity is promoted. Tuition: $13,500. Financial Aid: $968,200. Judith Corrin is Director of Admissions; Sr. Susan Maxwell, RSCJ, is Director of Schools.

Saint Ignatius College Prep 1869

1076 West Roosevelt Road, Chicago, IL 60608
Tel. 312-421-5900; Admissions 312-432-8411; Fax 312-421-7124
Web Site www.ignatius.org; E-mail maura.maloney@ignatius.org

Founded in 1869 by members of the Society of Jesus to serve the "academically talented children of immigrants," Saint Ignatius College Prep today offers a demanding college preparatory curriculum to 1348 day boys and girls in Grades 9–12. The school, located in the heart of the City of Chicago in facilities designated as a national historic landmark, enrolls a religiously, racially, and ethnically diverse student body drawn from the city

and its suburbs. The core curriculum is enriched by Honors and Advanced Placement courses, electives, a complete athletic program, and 50 nonathletic clubs and activities. Tuition: $10,820. Financial Aid: $2,500,000. Maura Maloney is Director of Admissions; Dr. Catherine Karl is Principal. *North Central Association.*

The University of Chicago Laboratory Schools 1896

1362 East 59th Street, Chicago, IL 60637
Tel. 773-702-9450; Admissions 773-702-9451; Fax 773-834-1831
Web Site www.ucls.uchicago.edu; E-mail mveitch@ucls.uchicago.edu

Founded by John Dewey to test his educational theories, The University of Chicago Laboratory Schools enroll 1744 boys and girls in Nursery–Grade 12. The Schools offer a culturally and racially diverse community within which students actively engage in an academically rigorous, experience-centered education. The program challenges each student to think independently by encouraging the individual's natural curiosity and cultivating his or her love of learning. The college preparatory program includes Advanced Placement courses in most disciplines. Many extracurricular activities and a summer program are available. Tuition: $10,656–$20,445. Financial Aid: $1,000,000. D. Michael Veitch is Director of Admissions; David W. Magill, Ed.D., is Director. *North Central Association.*

INDIANA

Canterbury School 1977

Grades 9–12: 3210 Smith Road, Fort Wayne, IN 46804
Tel. 260-436-0746; Fax 260-436-5137
Web Site www.canterburyschool.org
E-mail admissions@canterburyschool.org
Early Childhood–Grade 8: 5601 Covington Road, Fort Wayne, IN 46804
Lower School: Tel. 260-432-7776; Fax 260-436-9069
Middle School: Tel. 260-436-7721; Fax 260-436-6665

Canterbury School in Fort Wayne, Indiana, is a coeducational, college preparatory day school enrolling students in Early Childhood (age 2) through Grade 12. The state's second-largest city, Fort Wayne (metropolitan population 565,606) is in northeastern Indiana, about 130 miles from Indianapolis. Once a bustling trading hub, today the city is an important commercial, industrial, and cultural center, home to the Fort Wayne Ballet, the Fort Wayne Philharmonic Orchestra, the Fort Wayne Museum of Art, Fort Wayne Children's Zoo, theater and fine arts groups, and several institutions of higher learning.

Founded in 1977, Canterbury School provides a challenging liberal arts education that places equal emphasis on academic excellence and character development. The curriculum is designed to promote intellectual curiosity and creativity at every level, encouraging students to reach their potential intellectually, artistically, and morally. Daily life is conducted according to an honor code, and acts of kindness, cooperation, and good citizenship receive community recognition. Community service, religion classes, and daily chapel in the Christian tradition are key factors in forming values.

Canterbury is a nonprofit, nondenominational school accredited by the Independent Schools Association of the Central States, the North Central Association of Colleges and Schools, and the State of Indiana. It holds membership in the National Association of Independent Schools, the Educational Records Bureau, The Cum Laude Society, and the College Board. The Parent Association and Alumni Association assist in fund-raising, recruitment, and other activities.

THE CAMPUS. The High School occupies a 70,000-square-foot building on the Smith Road campus, within a half-mile of the Covington Road campus that houses Early Childhood–Grade 8. The two campuses, totaling 71 acres, are intersected by the property of the Fort Wayne Country Club golf course. Together, they house two auditoriums, three libraries, four computer labs, six science labs, 14 classrooms dedicated to the fine arts, and two cafeterias. The extended-day care program is located on the Covington Road campus. Among the athletic facilities are three gyms, baseball and softball diamonds, five tennis courts, five soccer fields, and three playgrounds.

THE FACULTY. Jonathan M. Hancock has been Headmaster at Canterbury School since 1982, with a two-year interval (1988–90) as Director of Schools at Cranbrook Schools in Michigan. A graduate of St. John's College, Oxford (B.A., M.A.), he also holds an M.Ed. degree from Harvard University. In addition to his administrative responsibilities, Mr. Hancock teaches Middle School Latin. He is the former chairman of the Board of Directors of the Independent Schools Association of the Central States and a former president of the Indiana Association of Independent Schools. He and his wife, Alice, an English teacher at Canterbury, have three sons who are graduates of the School.

The faculty includes 109 teachers and administrators who all hold baccalaureate degrees or the equivalent and have earned 52 advanced degrees, including 5 doctorates. Among their representative colleges and universities are Ball State, Brandeis, Brigham Young, Carleton, Cornell, DePauw, George Washington, Hanover, Hillsdale College, Indiana-Purdue University, Miami University of Ohio, Middlebury, Northern Illinois, Ohio State, Saint Francis, St. Mary's, Stanford, Taylor, Vanderbilt, Wake Forest, Washington University, Wesleyan College, Xavier, and the Universities of Chicago, Iowa, Kentucky, Michigan, New Mexico, North Carolina, Notre Dame, Virginia, and Wisconsin.

STUDENT BODY. In 2007–08, Canterbury enrolled 925 students, including 298 in the High School, from a wide spectrum of racial, ethnic, religious, and socioeconomic backgrounds.

ACADEMIC PROGRAM. The school year runs from the end of August to early June, with Thanksgiving, winter, and spring breaks, and observances of national holidays.

The Early Childhood division includes Canterbury Kids for 2-year-olds, Cavaliers for age 3, and Junior Kindergarten. At all levels, the program emphasizes social and emotional development, language and motor skills, and a positive introduction to learning in key subject areas. Numerous special activities and field trips enhance and reinforce classroom instruction.

The curriculum in the Lower School (Kindergarten Prep–Grade 4) is designed to provide a strong foundation in language arts and literature, social studies, math, and science. French begins in Kindergarten Prep and by Grade 3, children may choose to study either French or Spanish. Computer technology, religion, music, art, and drama are also integrated into the academic program.

Students in Grades 5–12 have a faculty advisor who provides direction and guidance in academic and personal matters. In the fully departmentalized Middle School (Grades 5–8), students undertake increasingly challenging subject matter in readiness for the High School. Course work includes math through geometry and, beginning in Grade 7, Latin and Japanese are available as electives.

In Grades 9–12, all courses are considered to be honors level and carry one credit per semester except religion and physical education, which are not included in determining grade point average. Advanced Placement courses in 15 subject areas are weighted 1.2, advanced-level courses are 1.1, and honors courses taken on schedule, 1.05.

To graduate, students must complete four years of English; three years each of math, science, and history/social studies; three years of one foreign language or two years each of two languages; one year of fine/performing arts; four semesters of religion/community service; one semester of physical education; and one quarter each of health and computer technology.

Among the required and elective courses offered are Survey of Literature, American Literature, British Literature, Creative Writing; Algebra I–II, Geometry, Pre-Calculus, Statistics & Probability; Biology, Advanced Biology, Chemistry, Advanced Chemistry, Physics, Meteorology; World History, American History, American Government; French I–IV, Latin I–III, Spanish I–IV, Japanese I–III; Introduction to Computer Science, Java Programming; Photography, Studio Art; Theatre/Advanced Theatre, Public Speaking; and Introduction to World Religions.

Advanced Placement is offered in Calculus AB and BC, Statistics, English Language and Literature & Composition, Latin Literature, French and Spanish Language, Biology, Chemistry, Physics, Computer, American History, and European History. All students enrolled in Advanced Placement classes must take AP exams; typically, more than 90 percent earn scores of 3 or higher. Other special features include Senior Seminar, an introduction to college-level scholarship, analysis and discussion, and May internships for seniors. Between one quarter and one third of the High School graduating seniors are recognized by the National Merit Scholarship program.

While college preparation begins upon entrance to Canterbury, formal college counseling starts in Grade 11 and includes meetings with students and parents, College Night presentations, computer software, and visits from college admission counselors. Each year, juniors have the opportunity to participate in a school-sponsored college visit trip.

Members of the Class of 2007 are enrolled at such institutions as Bryn Mawr, California State, College of Charleston, Denison, DePauw, Emory, Furman, Indiana University, Manchester College, Massachusetts Institute of Technology, Miami University (Ohio), Michigan State, Mount Holyoke, Northwestern, Oberlin, Purdue, Southern Methodist, Taylor University, Tulane, Wabash College, Xavier University, and the Universities of California (Berkeley), Miami, and Michigan.

Canterbury offers summer academic camps for Early Childhood–Grade 6 and athletic camps for students of all ages.

STUDENT ACTIVITIES. Canterbury's extracurricular program is designed to meet the interests and needs of a diverse student body. Among the groups organized are elected Middle and High School Student Councils, Model United Nations, Amnesty International, Key Club, Junior Classical League, Mock Trial, and the Philosophy Club.

Community service includes peer tutoring, work crew, Habitat for Humanity, weekly visits to nursing homes, and Big Brothers/Big Sisters. Students in Grades 6, 10, and 11 are involved in required off-campus community service.

The fine arts are well represented as students of all ages stage concerts, band and orchestra performances, musicals, and dramas. Exhibits of artwork are displayed throughout the school, and students publish a newspaper, yearbook, and literary magazines.

Canterbury Cavaliers compete in interscholastic sports at the varsity and junior varsity levels. Girls' and boys' teams are formed in soccer, volleyball, cross-country, basketball, swimming, golf, track, and tennis. Boys also compete in baseball, while girls take part in softball and cheerleading. The athletic department's policy of inclusion ensures that appropriate levels of competition are available to all interested students.

ADMISSION AND COSTS. Canterbury welcomes students of strong academic ability, character, and motivation who show promise of benefiting from and contributing to the school community. Candidates in Kindergarten Prep through Grade 12 are assessed on the basis of the completed application, recommendations, previous school transcripts, an entrance exam, and an interview. Acceptance is offered without regard to race, color, religion, national origin, age, or gender.

In 2007–08, tuition is $11,655 for Kindergarten–Grade 9 and $11,905 for Grades 10–12. Extras include books and incidental fees ($705–$880) and a technology fee ($175). A nonrefundable deposit of 10 percent of the tuition is required with the enrollment contract. In 2006–07, financial aid in the amount of more than $840,000 was awarded to approximately one-quarter of the student body based on need, and a merit scholarship competition is held for incoming ninth graders.

Headmaster: Jonathan M. Hancock
Director of High School: Robert Schantz
Director of Middle School: Lars Kuelling
Director of Lower School: Judy Anderson
Director of Early Childhood & Early Childhood Admissions: Paula Pritchard
Director of Alumni Relations: Emily Kimbrough Roussel
Directors of Admissions: Krista Lohmar (KPrep–8) & Susan Johnson (9–12)
Director of External Relations: Susan Johnson
Director of School Development: Myrna Morgan
Director of Publications: Karen Belcher
College Counselor: Dennis Eller
Business Manager: Jerry Belcher
Athletic Directors: Ken Harkenrider (High School) & Connie Oberlin (Middle School)

Evansville Day School 1946

3400 North Green River Road, Evansville, IN 47715
Tel. 812-476-3039; Admission Ext. 205; Fax 812-476-4061
Web Site www.evansvilledayschool.org
E-mail bbaker@evansvilledayschool.org

Founded by parents, the Evansville Day School is a coeducational college preparatory school enrolling 320 students in Junior Pre-Kindergarten–Grade 12. The School provides a traditional curriculum stressing personal growth, academic excellence, and character education. The educational experience is enhanced by a wide range of learning and extracurricular activities including off-campus Intersession projects and a variety of athletic teams and clubs. A personal development program and a caring faculty provide a positive learning atmosphere. A block schedule for Grades 8–12 includes numerous Advanced Placement courses. Tuition: $1885–$11,290. Financial Aid: $250,000; Merit Scholarships: $50,000. Beth Baker is Admission Director; Mr. Kendell Berry is Head of School.

The Orchard School 1922

615 West 64th Street, Indianapolis, IN 46260
Tel. 317-251-9253; Admissions 317-713-5753; Fax 317-254-8454
Web Site www.orchard.org; E-mail khein@orchard.org

Orchard, a nonsectarian, coeducational, progressive school, enrolls 615 students in Preschool–Grade 8. The curriculum integrates learning through language arts, social studies, math, music, drama, science, Spanish, physical education, technology, and outdoor education. The Dignity Center, core values, problem solving, critical thinking, field trips, components of the "Responsive Classroom," and service learning are integral to the social and academic curriculum. Learning support, speech-language therapy, assessment and evaluation, and school counseling are available. Extended-day programs are offered. Tuition: $4085–$14,114. Financial Aid: $1,460,000. Kristen Hein is Admissions Director; Joseph P. Marshall (Franklin and Marshall, B.A.; Hofstra, M.Ed.) is Head of School.

Park Tudor School 1970

7200 North College Avenue, P.O. Box 40488, Indianapolis, IN 46240-0488
Tel. 317-415-2700; Admissions 317-415-2727; Fax 317-254-2714
Web Site www.parktudor.org; E-mail info@parktudor.org

Formed by the merger of two single-sex schools, Park Tudor enrolls 986 boys and girls from diverse backgrounds in Preschool through Grade 12. Its mission is to prepare students for positive college experiences and to instill in them a lifelong curiosity about their world. The traditional curriculum includes Spanish starting in preschool, Advanced Placement courses and a Global Scholars program in the Upper School, and music, the arts, and technology at all levels. Students participate in interest and academic clubs, publications, leadership groups, and varsity sports. Tuition: $9100–$16,090. More than $2,500,000 in financial aid is available annually. David Amstutz is Director of Admissions; Douglas S. Jennings (Lafayette, B.A.; Montclair State, M.A.; Columbia University, M.A.) is Head of School.

The Stanley Clark School 1958

3123 Miami Street, South Bend, IN 46614-2098
Tel. 574-291-4200; Fax 574-299-4170
Web Site www.stanleyclark.org; E-mail douglass@stanleyclark.org

The Stanley Clark School, a nationally recognized private elementary school accredited by the Independent School Association of the Central States, enrolls 435 day boys and girls in Preschool through Grade 8. A multifaceted curriculum, emphasizing academics, fine arts, athletics, and technology, provides the basis for continuing success in high school, college, and the workplace. In addition to traditional academics, there are foreign languages, dramatics, and optional minicourses. The preschool is based on the Reggio philosophy with an optional all-day program. Extended day is available before and after school. Tuition: $3200–$12,475. Financial Aid: $650,000. Barbara T. Beach is Director of Admissions; Robert G. Douglass (University of Bridgeport, B.A., M.A.) was appointed Headmaster in 1988.

Sycamore School 1985

1750 West 64th Street, Indianapolis, IN 46260
Tel. 317-202-2500; Admissions Ext. 110; Fax 317-202-2501
Web Site www.sycamoreschool.org
E-mail skarpicke@sycamoreschool.org

Parents and educators established this coeducational day school to provide intellectual stimulation for academically gifted children. Sycamore School enrolls 410 children from diverse racial, ethnic, and socioeconomic backgrounds in a preparatory curriculum that spans Early Childhood (2 years, 8 months) to Grade 8. Classroom instructors are either endorsed in gifted education or are candidates for endorsement. The School's environment encourages the acquisition of skills in core subjects through activities and materials appropriate to each child's abilities and interests. The Early Childhood program explores multidisciplinary thematic units that integrate language arts and basic math. Course work promotes critical thinking and problem solving, along with mastery of English, math, social studies, technology, sciences, modern languages, and the arts. Extracurricular activities revolve around academic competitions such as MathCounts and Knowledge Masters as well as leadership opportunities, publications, field trips, choir and symphonic bands, and interscholastic sports. Tuition: $4455–$11,985. Financial aid is available. Dr. Susan Karpicke is Director of Admissions; Leo P. Dressel is Head of School.

University High School 2000

2825 West 116th Street, Carmel, IN 46032-8730
Tel. 317-733-4475; Admission Ext. 102; Fax 317-733-4484
Web Site www.universityhighschool.org
E-mail nwebster@universityhighschool.org

University High School is an independent, nonsectarian, college preparatory day school that enrolls 175 girls and boys in Grades 9–12. The School's mission is "to expand the hearts and minds of students and to nurture excellence through academic, creative, and physical achievement." The School emphasizes critical thinking, character building, and intellectual stimulation. A formal mentoring program; 100 percent college placement; an intensive, one-subject January Term; competitive, inclusive sports; and small classes provide a personal and challenging approach to learning. Extracurriculars include community service, varsity sports, academic and special-interest clubs, publications, and theater. Tuition: $14,250. Extras: $600. Nancy Webster is Director of Admission; Chuck Webster is Head of School.

IOWA

Rivermont Collegiate 1884

1821 Sunset Drive, Bettendorf, IA 52722-6045
Tel. 563-359-1366; Admission Ext. 302; Fax 563-359-7576
Web Site www.rivermontcollegiate.org
E-mail info@rvmt.org

Rivermont Collegiate is dedicated to providing an environment that challenges each student to fulfill his or her maximum potential academically, creatively, and morally. This coeducational, college preparatory day school enrolls 240 students in Early School (age 3)–Grade 12 from the Greater Quad City area, consisting of Bettendorf and Davenport in Iowa, Rock Island and Moline in Illinois, and smaller surrounding communities. Academic diversity in Early and Lower School as well as discipline-specific teachers in science, foreign language, art, music, technology, and physical education allow for teaching one to two grades above grade level. Latin is required of all Middle School students who may also choose to study High School-level Spanish or French. Chinese language is an elective beginning in Grade 10. In addition, the school offers an accelerated math program in Lower School as well as AP, Honors classes, and independent study in the Upper School. Rivermont Collegiate was honored in 2006 and 2007 as #1 in the Iowa AP Index, with 58 percent of the Class of 2006 honored as AP Scholars or Scholars with Honor. Tuition: $4210–$9700. Financial aid is available. Stephanie Seals is Admission Assistant; Richard St. Laurent is Headmaster.

KENTUCKY

Louisville Collegiate School 1915

2427 Glenmary Avenue, Louisville, KY 40204
Tel. 502-479-0340; Admission 502-479-0377; Fax 502-454-8549
Web Site www.loucol.com; E-mail aaron-james@loucol.com

Louisville Collegiate, a coeducational, college preparatory day school enrolling 650 students in Kindergarten to Grade 12, prepares talented, diverse, global citizens to meet both college and lifelong learning with character, confidence, and imagination. Students may explore a potential career, perform community service, take part in a leadership development program, and investigate in depth an area of academic interest. Collegiate has the only K–12 Chinese Language Program in the State of Kentucky and offers a comprehensive college counseling program for Grades 9–12. Activities include athletics, clubs, drama, student government, and publications. Tuition: $11,700–$16,500. Financial Aid: $1,200,000. Robin Seiler is Associate Director of Admission; Tom Hobert is Head of School.

LOUISIANA

Academy of the Sacred Heart 1887

4521 St. Charles Avenue, New Orleans, LA 70115
Tel. 504-891-1943; Admission 504-269-1213; Fax 504-896-7880
Web Site www.ashrosary.org; E-mail ash@ashrosary.org

Affectionately known as The Rosary, this Catholic day school for girls is one of 21 Sacred Heart Schools in the United States. The Academy is committed to developing a personal and active faith in God, deep respect for intellectual values, social awareness that impels to action, building of community as a Christian value, and personal growth in an atmosphere of wise freedom. The school enrolls 770 girls from many faiths in Preschool–Grade 12, with an early learning center for toddler and nursery girls. The college preparatory program emphasizes mastery of skills in the arts, sciences, and humanities within the context of Catholic teaching and tradition. The core curriculum of English, math, religious studies, sciences, social studies, and languages is enriched by offerings in fine arts, technology, and AP and honors courses in the major departments. Community service and a senior speech are graduation requirements. Historically, 100 percent of Rosary students enter four-year colleges and universities. Among the activities are student governance, clubs, Diversity Team, National Honor Society, drama, music, publications, and sports. Tuition: $10,600–$11,750. Christy Sevante is Director of Admission; Timothy M. Burns, Ph.D., is Headmaster.

The Dunham School 1981

11111 Roy Emerson Street, Baton Rouge, LA 70810-1786
Tel. 225-767-7097; Fax 225-757-7056
Web Site www.dunhamschool.org; E-mail spearls@dunhamschool.org

The Dunham School was founded to provide "an education of the mind and the heart" for children from a wide diversity of backgrounds. Offering a challenging college preparatory program within a distinctively Christian context, Dunham's curriculum focuses on the mastery of strong skills in core academic subjects combined with chapel services, Bible studies, and counseling. The 23-acre campus in a residential area of South Baton Rouge accommodates 700 day boys and girls in Pre-Kindergarten–Grade 12. Teachers are chosen based on their instructional skills as well as their ability to serve as Christian role models and mentors. The student-teacher ratio is 9:1, and the average class enrolls between 14 and 16 students, allowing ample opportunity for participation, discussion, and individual support. English, math, science, social studies, modern language, and religious studies are at the heart of the academic program, with elective enhancements in art, music, drama, technology, and physical education. Field trips, school government, publications, plays, music groups, community service, and athletics are among the activities. Tuition: $5700–$9350. Linda Spear is Director of Admission & Financial Aid; Robert W. Welch is Headmaster. *Southern Association.*

Isidore Newman School 1903

1903 Jefferson Avenue, New Orleans, LA 70115-5699
Tel. 504-899-5641; Admission 504-896-6323; Fax 504-896-8597
Web Site www.newmanschool.org; E-mail jrosen@newmanschool.org

Since 1903, Isidore Newman School has been providing college preparatory education to the children of New Orleans. Newman enrolls 1008 boys and girls in Pre-Kindergarten through Grade 12 and enjoys a reputation for excellence and achievement in academics, athletics, and the arts. The curriculum includes sophisticated science programs in the Lower School as well as multiple foreign language offerings, computer, and Advanced Placement and honors courses. More than 60 team sports, publications, theater, fine arts, debate, community service, and other student clubs are available. Newman also provides extended-day care, after-school activities, and a summer session. Tuition: $13,335–$15,173. Need-based financial aid is available. Jennifer Rosen is Admission Director; T. J. Locke is Head of School.

Kehoe-France School 1962

720 Elise Avenue, Metairie, LA 70003
Tel. 504-733-0472; Fax 504-733-0477
Web Site www.kehoe-france.com; E-mail janet@kehoe-france.com
Northshore Campus: 25 Patricia Drive, Covington, LA 70433
Tel. 985-892-4415; Fax 985-875-7636
Web Site www.kehoe-francens.com
E-mail lori@kehoe-francens.com

Frank A. and Patricia Kehoe France founded this elementary school to provide an excellent educational experience directed toward the intellectual, spiritual, emotional, and social development of each child. Enrolling 1200 boys and girls age 2–Grade 8 on two campuses, Kehoe-France's curriculum emphasizes strong skills in core subjects to enable all students to realize their full personal and academic potential. A wide range of enrichment programs engages youngsters in community service, dramatic presentations, vocal and instrumental ensembles, team sports, and educational field trips. Extended day care is available before and after school, and there is a summer camp program. Tuition: $5800–$6400. Janet Pananos is Admissions Director; Frank A. France and his four sons direct the School.

Ridgewood Preparatory School 1948

201 Pasadena Avenue, Metairie, LA 70001-4899
Tel. 504-835-2545; Fax 504-837-1864
Web Site www.ridgewoodprep.com
E-mail mmontgomery@ridgewoodprep.com

Ridgewood Preparatory School is a day school enrolling 300 boys and girls in Pre-Kindergarten–Grade 12. Its aim is to prepare students for college and life through development of intellectual skills, awareness of the world and its beauties, participation in society, and preparation for a vocation. Beginning in Pre-Kindergarten, the School provides a traditional curriculum including art, music, and physical education. Student government, service and activity clubs, publications, band, and interscholastic sports are among the activities. Tuition & Fees: $4000–$5750. Jennifer Larmann is Director of Admissions; M. J. Montgomery, Jr. (Loyola, B.S. 1959, M.Ed. 1962), was appointed Headmaster in 1972. *Southern Association.*

St. Andrew's Episcopal School 1957

8012 Oak Street, New Orleans, LA 70118
Tel. 504-861-3743; Fax 504-861-3973
Web Site www.standrews.k12.la.us
E-mail admissions@standrews.k12.la.us

St. Andrew's Episcopal School, the oldest Episcopal day school in New Orleans, enrolls 145 boys and girls in Prekindergarten–Grade 7. Small classes promote a challenging learning environment where students interact with teachers and grow spiritually, socially, and intellectually. A strong academic program, enhanced by state-of-the-art technology, includes Spanish, music, chapel, fine arts, athletics, and library skills. Student publications, dramatics, intramurals, and community service round out the St. Andrew's experience. Tuition: $6950–$8950. Financial aid is available. Mary Ann Straub is Coordinator of Admission; Gary J. Mannina was appointed Headmaster in 1986.

St. Mark's Cathedral School 1953

908 Rutherford Street, Shreveport, LA 71104
Tel. 318-221-7454; Admission 318-226-4036; Fax 318-221-7060
Web Site www.stmarksschool.com
E-mail cwilkinson@stmarksschool.com

The Vestry of St. Mark's Cathedral founded this coeducational day school to provide quality education infused with Christian values. St. Mark's Cathedral School offers a lively, rigorous academic program designed to nurture the intellectual, spiritual, and social development of each child. Currently enrolling 354 children from diverse religious backgrounds in Preschool–Grade 8, St. Mark's emphasizes the mastery of skills in core subjects, enriched by modern and classical languages, theater, technology, and opportunities to earn high school credit in some course work. Students take part in services at the Cathedral and enjoy activities in school government and team sports. Tuition: $2500–$7300. Charlotte Wilkinson is Director of Admission; Pamela H. Byrd is Head of School.

St. Martin's Episcopal School 1947

5309 Airline Drive, Metairie, LA 70003
Tel. 504-733-0353; Admissions 504-736-9917; Fax 504-736-8802
Web Site www.stmsaints.com; E-mail susan.pansano@stmsaints.com

St. Martin's Episcopal School, founded in 1947, is a coeducational, college preparatory, diocesan-sponsored day school that welcomes 700 students from diverse backgrounds age 18 months–Grade 12. Based on the values of faith, scholarship, and service, St. Martin's seeks to nurture the whole child within the context of Christian community and a family environment. Regular chapel services, religion classes, and social outreach develop spiritual awareness in students of all faiths. The curriculum emphasizes strong skills in core subjects of English, math, science, and social studies, enriched by world languages, information technology, the visual and performing arts, and physical education. In the Upper School (Grades 9–12), qualified scholars may choose from 24 honors and AP courses. All students contribute numerous hours per year to community service projects related to Habitat for Humanity, soup kitchens, and food and clothing drives. Among the activities are school government, publications, and sports teams that involve 70 percent of the student body. Tuition: $7600–$15,600. Financial aid is available. Susan Pansano is Director of Admission; Dr. Jeffrey P. Beedy is Headmaster.

Southfield School 1934

1100 Southfield Road, Shreveport, LA 71106
Tel. 318-868-5375; Fax 318-869-0890
Web Site www.southfield-school.org;
E-mail ccoburn@southfield-school.org

Southfield was founded by a group of local residents to provide their children with the finest educational opportunity. The preparatory day school serves 452 boys and girls in Preschool through Grade 8. The School is accredited by the Independent Schools Association of the Southwest and the National Association for the Education of Young Children. The liberal arts curriculum challenges students while providing them the skills necessary to succeed. The application of technology is evident throughout the program. After-school care and summer programs are offered. Tuition: $2668–$8318. Financial aid is available. Clare Coburn is Admissions Director; Jeffrey Stokes (State University of New York, B.A.; University of North Carolina, M.A.T.) is Headmaster.

Trinity Episcopal School 1960

1315 Jackson Avenue, New Orleans, LA 70130
Tel. 504-525-8661; Admission 504-670-2506; Fax 504-523-4837
Web Site www.trinitynola.com; E-mail sderussy@trinitynola.com

Trinity Episcopal School was established by Trinity Church in 1960 as an elementary school for approximately 325 boys and girls from Preschool through Eighth Grade. The School is dedicated to fostering the academic, emotional, social, and spiritual growth of its students through a skills-based curriculum. Trinity students, faculty, and staff begin each day with Chapel, which establishes and reinforces the moral tone of the school community. Art, music, drama, foreign language, and physical education enhance the core subjects at each grade level. Child care is offered before and after school. Tuition: $7510–$13,440. Tuition assistance is available. Susie DeRussy is Director of Admission; The Reverend Dr. Michael C. Kuhn is Headmaster.

MAINE

Bridgton Academy 1808

P.O. Box 292, North Bridgton, ME 04057
Tel. 207-647-3322; Admissions Ext. 209; Fax 207-647-8513
Web Site www.bridgtonacademy.org
E-mail cwebb@bridgtonacademy.org

Bridgton Academy is the only college preparatory school in the nation exclusively devoted to a one-year postgraduate program for young men. The school aims to help approximately 180 boarding and day students develop the academic skills, study skills, self-discipline, and self-confidence to succeed in college and beyond. Students with the potential, motivation, character, and commitment to benefit from and contribute to the program are welcome. Both the student's academic program and college counseling are individualized and monitored closely. School government, athletics, publications, and clubs are among the activities. Room, Board & Tuition: $36,900; Day Tuition: $23,500. Financial Aid: $1,300,000. Chris Webb is Director of Admission; David N. Hursty is Headmaster. *New England Association.*

Foxcroft Academy 1823

975 West Main Street, Dover-Foxcroft, ME 04426
Tel. 207-564-8351; Fax 207-564-8394
Web Site www.foxcroftacademy.org
E-mail jay.brennan@foxcroftacademy.org

One of the oldest private schools in America, Foxcroft Academy serves a diverse coeducational population of 410 day and boarding students in Grades 9–12. The challenging college preparatory curriculum offers 135 courses including 30 Honors and 8 AP courses. The Academy's math and science program exceeds national standards and utilizes state-of-the-art technology, while the humanities program explores the culture of an era through a study of its history, literature, art, and music. In addition to traditional subjects, students may take courses in music composition, web design, art history, economics, computer-assisted drawing, personal finance, vocational subjects, ethics, and four levels of French, Latin, Spanish, and Chinese. For international students, there are three levels of ESL, including ESL Writing. The Academy fields 32 sports teams for boys and girls, and the school holds several regional and state titles. Foxcroft also provides more than 20 clubs and student organizations. Boarding Tuition: $29,400; Day Tuition: $9600. ESL:

$1500. Jay Brennan is Associate Head of School for Admissions and Residential Life; Raymond Webb is Head of School.

Hebron Academy 1804

Route 119, P.O. Box 309, Hebron, ME 04238-0309
Tel. 207-966-2100; Fax 207-966-1111
Web Site www.hebronacademy.org
E-mail admissions@hebronacademy.org

Inspiring and guiding students to reach their highest potential in mind, body, and spirit, Hebron Academy enrolls 255 girls and boys in Grade 6–Postgraduate, including 144 boarders from Grade 9 upward. The school provides a challenging educational experience designed to prepare graduates for success in college. Course work in the liberal arts and sciences is complemented by honors and Advanced Placement courses, English as a Second Language, and more than 20 electives. Activities include fine arts, student government, publications, drama, music groups, and 14 interscholastic sports. Boarding Tuition: $39,600; Day Tuition: $21,900. Joseph A. Hemmings is Director of Admissions; John J. King (Williams, B.A.) is Head of School. *New England Association.*

Lee Academy 1845

26 Winn Road, Lee, ME 04455
Tel. 207-738-2252; [Toll-free] 888-433-2852; Fax 207-738-3257
Web Site www.leeacademy.org
E-mail admissions@leeacademy.org

Lee Academy, a high school with boarding facilities for 75 students, enrolls a diverse group of 270 boys and girls in a college preparatory program. The renovated dormitories house international and domestic students at the high school and postgraduate levels from ten states and 12 countries. The curriculum emphasizes math, writing, problem solving, and personal development. Flexible scheduling, small class size, AP courses, and the Academic Learning Laboratory are designed to meet individual needs and ensure personal attention. Activities include Student Council, Civil Rights Team, Math Team, drama, music, and athletics. Boarding Tuition: $26,000; Day Tuition: $8500. Scholarships are available upon request. Jeffrey D. Wright is

Admissions Director; Bruce Lindberg is Head of School. *New England Association.*

North Yarmouth Academy 1814

148 Main Street, Yarmouth, ME 04096
Tel. 207-846-9051; Admissions 207-846-2376; Fax 207-846-8829
Web Site www.nya.org; E-mail admission@nya.org

North Yarmouth Academy, a coeducational, college preparatory day school enrolling 323 students in Grades 6–12, sets high expectations in an environment that emphasizes mutual respect, trust, and community. The Academy seeks to foster integrity, character, and intellect in young adults. A structured academic program, comprehensive advisor system, small classes, extra help and tutoring, and 13 Advanced Placement courses strengthen the core curriculum. Athletics or an afternoon program is required, and a two-week social service project is a graduation requirement. Wilderness trips, publications, and school government are among the activities. Tuition: $20,300. Financial aid is available. Joseph P. Silvestri is Director of Admission; Peter W. Mertz (Williams, B.A.; Barry, M.B.A.) is Headmaster. *New England Association.*

Washington Academy 1792

High Street, P.O. Box 190, East Machias, ME 04630
Tel. 207-255-8301; Admissions Ext. 207; Fax 207-255-8303
Web Site www.washingtonacademy.org
E-mail admissions@washingtonacademy.org

Washington Academy has a rich heritage focused on success for the individual. With college preparatory, career technology, and vocational programs for 385 coeducational day students in Grades 9–12 and 65 boarding students from around the world, students may choose course work consistent with their abilities and interests. Advanced Placement and Honors courses, ESL, Culinary Arts, Health Occupations, and instruction for students with special needs enhance the core curriculum. Marine Vocational Technology emphasizes skills and knowledge related to seafaring, and Environmental Studies provides experience in research and problem solving. Located in a safe, coastal community in Maine, the Academy has small classes with extensive offerings in art, music, math, science, digital video editing, carpentry, and marine mechanics. Sports include soccer, tennis, swimming, wrestling, football, basketball, golf, and others. Drama, music, and more than 50 extracurricular activities are also available. Host-Family Boarding: $27,780; Dorm Boarding: $29,780; Day Tuition: $12,000. Kim Gardner is Director of Admissions; Judson L. McBrine III is Headmaster. *New England Association.*

MARYLAND

The Academy of the Holy Cross 1868

4920 Strathmore Avenue, Kensington, MD 20895-1299
Tel. 301-942-2100; Admissions 301-929-6442; Fax 301-929-6440
Web Site www.academyoftheholycross.org
E-mail schooloffice@academyoftheholycross.org

This college preparatory high school, a Blue Ribbon School of Excellence, was founded to provide a Catholic education for young women. Sponsored by the Sisters of the Holy Cross, the Academy offers its 620 students a challenging curriculum of the liberal arts and sciences combined with opportunities for spiritual growth through religious studies, community prayer, and Christian service. Honors and Advanced Placement courses and internships enhance the program. Girls participate in a wide range of activities including publications, speech and debate team, Model U.N., drama and musical productions, and interscholastic teams in 15 sports. Tuition: $14,800. Extras: $900. Louise Hendon is Director of Admissions; Sr. Katherine Kase, CSC, is President. *Middle States Association.*

The Barnesville School 1969

21830 Peach Tree Road, Box 404, Barnesville, MD 20838-0404
Tel. 301-972-0341; Fax 301-972-4076
Web Site www.barnesvilleschool.org

The Barnesville School is a coeducational day school enrolling approximately 250 children in Pre-Kindergarten through Grade 8. It opened in what was then the Arabian Horse Museum and continues operation on that site today, with modern facilities on a quiet 11-acre campus. Small by design, the School seeks to provide a safe, joyous, and supportive environment in which all students can develop to their full academic, social, emotional, artistic, musical, and athletic potential. The Pre-Kindergarten program emphasizes personal and physical development as well as academic readiness in language, numeracy, listening skills, memory, and vocabulary. Spanish begins in Pre-K, and music, art, drama, and computer technology enrich the program. At all levels, hands-on activities enable children to maximize learning in and beyond the classroom. Students take part in interest clubs, plays, choral groups, service learning and community service, and sports. Parental involvement is vital to the fulfillment of the School's mission. Extended care and a summer camp are optional. Tuition: $7525–$13,950. Tuition assistance is available. Nicole Campbell is Director of Admissions; John J. Huber is Head of School.

The Barrie School 1932

13500 Layhill Road, Silver Spring, MD 20906-3299
Tel. 301-576-2800; Fax 301-576-2803
Web Site www.barrie.org; E-mail admissions@barrie.org

The Barrie School is a coeducational, independent day school serving approximately 390 students from Pre-Kindergarten through Grade 12. Founded in 1932, Barrie is one of the oldest progressive schools in the Washington area. The School is located on a beautiful, 45-acre wooded campus minutes from the nation's capital. The campus boasts athletic playing fields, an equestrian riding/jumping facility, and a state-of-the-art gymnasium complex. The Black Box theater gives Barrie students a unique opportunity to explore the world of music, visual arts, and the performing arts. Before- and after-school child care and transportation services are offered. Tuition: $10,750–$22,040. Need-based financial aid is available. Andrea Williams is Director of Admission; Timothy Trautman is Head of School. *Middle States Association.*

The Bryn Mawr School 1885

109 West Melrose Avenue, Baltimore, MD 21210
Tel. 410-323-8800; Admission Ext. 272; Fax 410-377-8963
Web Site www.brynmawrschool.org
E-mail admissions@brynmawrschool.org

A day school founded by five pioneering young women who believed in a challenging college preparatory education, Bryn Mawr School enrolls 800 girls in Kindergarten–Grade 12. In addition, the coeducational Little School enrolls 137 children. Coordinate classes with Gilman School for boys and Roland Park Country School for girls are available in Grades 9–12. French begins in Kindergarten and computers in Preschool. Activities include 47 teams in 15 sports, Dance Company, choral groups, art, drama, clubs, and community service. The School enjoys an excellent college placement record. Tuition: $20,280–$20,870. Financial Aid: $2,200,000. Patricia M. Nothstein is Director of Admission and Financial Aid; Maureen E. Walsh is Headmistress. *Middle States Association.*

The Calverton School 1967

300 Calverton School Road, Huntingtown, MD 20639
Tel. 410-535-0216, 301-855-1922; Admissions Ext. 108
[Toll-free] 888-678-0216; Fax 410-535-6934
Web Site www.CalvertonSchool.org
E-mail jsimpson@CalvertonSchool.org

The Calverton School offers a challenging, student-centered curriculum, complemented by athletics and the arts, to 400 day boys and girls in Preschool through Grade 12. A dedicated faculty and 10:1 student-teacher ratio promote the School's goal of producing well-balanced and well-educated students. A 33,000-square-foot Science/Art Center and a 100-acre expansion of the campus enhance Calverton's programs. Before- and after-care, transportation to five counties, and a summer day camp are optional. Tuition: $4210–$15,080. Financial aid and scholarship opportunities are available. Julie Simpson is Director of Admission; Daniel Hildebrand (University of Chicago, B.A., M.A.) is Head of School.

Calvert School 1897

105 Tuscany Road, Baltimore, MD 21210
Tel. 410-243-6054; Fax 410-243-0384
Web Site www.calvertschool.org; E-mail dfrey@calvertschool.org

Calvert School, enrolling 536 day students in Pre-Kindergarten–Grade 8, aims to develop solid fundamental skills, including the ability to read with comprehension, to write with style and discipline, and to use mathematical principles. The challenging curriculum includes English, science, math, history, French, Spanish, Latin, computers, astronomy, art, art history, music, and physical education. The Middle School (Grades 5–8) offers competitive athletics, state-of-the-art wireless technology and take-home laptop program, drama, clubs, and community service. The School also educates students through its home instruction division, Calvert Education Services, which offers homeschooling families complete curriculum for Pre-K–Grade 8, including lesson manuals, textbooks, workbooks, and supplies. CES supports those families with online instruction, education counselors, and correspondence testing, among other services, and assists over 180 private, public, charter, or virtual charter schools with curriculum, teacher support, and classroom implementation strategies. Tuition: $9100–$18,100. Financial Aid: $820,000. Deborah D. Frey is Admissions Director; Andrew D. Martire '83 (Princeton, A.B.; Johns Hopkins, M.L.A.) is Headmaster.

Chesapeake Academy 1980

1185 Baltimore-Annapolis Boulevard, Arnold, MD 21012
Tel. 410-647-9612; Fax 410-647-6088
Web Site www.chesapeakeacademy.com
E-mail srichburg@chesapeakeacademy.com

Chesapeake Academy, an independent day school serving 320 children age 3–Grade 5, is dedicated to educating each child in his or her best interest. The school believes that personal responsibility, care for others, and a zest for learning are as important as academic achievement. To provide a nurturing and challenging program, Chesapeake Academy offers instruction that is matched to fit each child's capabilities and level of development. Art, music, physical education, Spanish, computer, and library enhance the traditional curriculum. Before and After School care is available. Tuition: $5560–$11,355. Ms. Sue Richburg is Director of Admission; Mr. Jay Scheurle is Head of School.

Concord Hill School 1965

6050 Wisconsin Avenue, Chevy Chase, MD 20815
Tel. 301-654-2626; Fax 301-654-1374
Web Site www.concordhill.org

Four local educators founded this nondenominational school to provide young children with a positive primary experience. Opening with 20 students in Prekindergarten and Kindergarten, today Concord Hill School enrolls 100 boys and girls from age 3 to Grade 3. The School's mission is to create a joyful learning experience in an environment that nurtures each student's intellectual, social, emotional, physical, and ethical growth. Qualified teachers emphasize the mastery of basic skills in core subjects while respecting and responding to the individual child's unique patterns of learning and maturity. The curriculum centers on language arts, mathematics, social studies, and science, with enrichment classes in music, art, technology, and library skills. Special class projects and age-appropriate field trips in the Washington, D.C., region enliven and reinforce classroom instruction. Upon leaving Concord Hill, students matriculate at public and private schools such as Bullis, Holton-Arms, Landon, Maret, National Cathedral School, Potomac, Sheridan, and Sidwell Friends. A summer camp is available for children ages 3–5. Tuition: $12,050–$18,125. Denise Gershowitz is Director; Susan Arzt is Director of Admissions.

Connelly School of the Holy Child 1961

9029 Bradley Boulevard, Potomac, MD 20854
Tel. 301-365-0955; Fax 301-365-0981
Web Site www.holychild.org; E-mail admissions@holychild.org

Connelly School of the Holy Child is a Catholic, college preparatory day school enrolling 373 young women from diverse backgrounds in Grades 6–12. The School traces its origins to the first Holy Child school founded in 1846 by Cornelia Connelly, a nun and educational reformer. The School continues to value the philosophy of its foundress to nurture "the intellectual, spiritual, artistic, social and physical development of each student; to instill academic challenge and the joy of learning; and to educate women of faith and action for compassionate service to humanity." The curriculum, which includes honors and AP courses in most disciplines, centers on the liberal arts, sciences, and humanities. Community service, Campus Ministry, and shared liturgies deepen spiritual awareness in girls of all religious faiths. Activities designed to meet many interests include Student Council, language clubs, drama, vocal and instrumental music groups, yearbook, literary magazine, newspaper, overseas travel experiences, and interscholastic athletics. Tuition: $18,325–$19,600. Financial aid is available. Meg Mayo is Director of Admissions; Maureen K. Appel (Rosemont, B.A.; Long Island University, M.S.) is Headmistress. *Middle States Association.*

The Country School 1934

716 Goldsborough Street, Easton, MD 21601
Tel. 410-822-1935; Admissions Ext. 130; Fax 410-822-1971
Web Site www.countryschool.org; E-mail info@countryschool.org

The Country School, enrolling 300 boys and girls in Kindergarten–Grade 8, offers a challenging program in a nurturing environment with small classes, individual attention, and outstanding teachers as its hallmarks. A traditional and structured yet creative and child-centered curriculum serves a range of diverse students within a family context. The School creates an atmosphere of academic excellence designed to educate the whole child. It seeks to imbue students with a love of learning and provides sound preparation for secondary education. Activities include sports, fine and performing arts, community service, physical education, and life skills instruction. Tuition: $11,650. Financial Aid: $411,525. Kimerly C. Balderson is Admissions Director; Neil Mufson is Headmaster.

Friends School of Baltimore 1784

5114 North Charles Street, Baltimore, MD 21210
Tel. 410-649-3200; Admission 410-649-3211; Fax 410-649-3302
Web Site www.friendsbalt.org; E-mail kdates@friendsbalt.org

Friends School of Baltimore is a Quaker, college preparatory day school, located on 32 acres, enrolling 466 boys and 514 girls in Pre-Primary–Grade 12. Approximately 142 new students enroll each fall, the largest entry points being Kindergarten and Grades 1, 6, 7, and 9. Extracurricular activities include athletics, community service, Meeting for Worship, publications, vocal music, dramatics, and student government. A summer program includes academics, day camp, and sports. Tuition: $16,760–$19,325. Extras & Lunches: $500–$800. Financial Aid: $2,000,000+. Karen E. Dates is Director of Admission; Matthew Micciche (Amherst, B.A.; Tufts, M.A.T.; Middlebury, M.A.) was appointed Head of School in 2005. *Middle States Association.*

Garrison Forest School 1910

300 Garrison Forest Road, Owings Mills, MD 21117
Tel. 410-363-1500; Admission 410-559-3111; Fax 410-363-8441
Web Site www.gfs.org; E-mail admission@gfs.org

Garrison Forest's mission is to provide young women with a college preparatory program that inspires them to approach life with intellectual awareness, enthusiasm, and spirit. The School enrolls 700 girls in Preschool–Grade 12, with residential students from Grade 8 upward. The core curriculum is enriched by Advanced Placement courses in 12 subjects, an independent project in Grade 12, and English as a Second Language. The athletic program features 12 varsity sports: field hockey, tennis, cross-country, basketball, indoor and outdoor soccer, lacrosse, softball, badminton, horseback riding, and polo. Other activities are drama, service league, music, dance, publications, and interest clubs. Boarding Tuition: $29,900–$36,400; Day Tuition: $4500–$20,975. A. Randol Benedict '76 is Director of Admission and Financial Aid; Peter O'Neill is Head of School. *Middle States Association.*

Georgetown Preparatory School 1789

10900 Rockville Pike, North Bethesda, MD 20852
Tel. 301-493-5000; Fax 301-493-6128
Web Site www.gprep.org; E-mail admissions@gprep.org

Founded by Bishop John Carroll, Georgetown Preparatory School is America's first Catholic secondary school and its only Jesuit boarding school. Set on a 90-acre campus with tennis courts, a golf course, and playing fields, the School enjoys convenient access to the rich resources of the nation's capital. Prep enrolls 450 young men from diverse faiths in Grades 9–12; approximately 100 are resident students from 22 states and 13 countries. The rigorous college preparatory curriculum is infused with Christian ethics; boys of all religious beliefs adhere to a strict code of conduct, take part in liturgies, and perform social outreach. The academic program includes Advanced Placement courses, English as a Second Language, and off-campus internships. The average class enrolls 17, ensuring a personalized and participatory learning environment. Among the activities are Student Government, Model UN, Dramatics Society, Forensics Club, Math Team, and competition in 14 sports. Virtually all graduates enter four-year colleges and universities. Boarding Tuition: $34,740; Day Tuition: $19,640. Financial Aid: $1,100,000. Brian J. Gilbert is Director of Admissions; Jeffrey Jones is Headmaster; Rev. William L. George, S.J., is President. *Middle States Association.*

Gibson Island Country School 1956

5191 Mountain Road, Pasadena, MD 21122
Tel. 410-255-5370; Fax 410-255-0416
Web Site www.gics.org; E-mail admissions@gics.org

Gibson Island Country School is a coeducational day school enrolling more than 85 students in Pre-Kindergarten–Grade 5. The School's challenging, integrated curriculum emphasizes hands-on, experiential learning in a unique waterfront setting. The student-teacher ratio is 7:1, and the atmosphere is nurturing and attentive to individual needs. Science, foreign language, computer, library, music, art, and physical education are taught to all grades by specialists. Activities include student government, assemblies, community service, field trips, athletics, special theme days, and numerous environmental projects. GICS is a Maryland Green School. Bus service and after-school care are available. Tuition: $7500–$11,342. Financial aid is available. Jane C. Pehlke is Director of Admission; Merrill Hall (University of New Orleans, B.A., M.Ed.; Johns Hopkins University, M.L.A.) is Head of School.

Gilman School 1897

5407 Roland Avenue, Baltimore, MD 21210
Tel. 410-323-3800; Fax LS 410-864-2823, US 410-864-2825
Web Site www.gilman.edu
E-mail lsadmissions@gilman.edu; msusadmissions@gilman.edu

America's first country day school, Gilman offers a challenging liberal arts curriculum to 980 young men in Pre-First–Grade 12. Gilman seeks to produce men of character and integrity who have the skills and ability to make a positive contribution to the communities in which they live. The Upper School offers Advanced Placement in the major disciplines. All Gilman graduates go on to higher education, and 75 percent are accepted by the most competitive or highly competitive colleges and universities. Community service, Mock Trial, a radio station, publications, the arts, and athletics are among the activities. Tuition: $18,755–$20,265. Financial Aid: $2,500,000. William H. Gamper is Director of Admissions; John E. Schmick is Acting Headmaster.

Glenelg Country School 1954

12793 Folly Quarter Road, Ellicott City, MD 21042
Tel. 410-531-8600; Admission 410-531-7347; Fax 410-531-7363
Web Site www.glenelg.org; E-mail wootton@glenelg.org

Glenelg Country School, enrolling 805 day students in Pre-K–Grade 12, emphasizes academic growth and the development of the whole child. The School balances rigorous academics, creative arts, interscholastic sports, community service, and social activities. The faculty provides personal attention in classes of 12–18 students. The Upper School features 19 Advanced Placement courses and a Director of College Counseling. The School's 87 acres offer state-of-the-art classrooms, athletic facilities, tennis courts, and a swimming pool. Summer programs include a day camp and an academy for basics and enrichment. Tuition: $9920–$19,860. Financial Aid: $1,200,000. Karen Wootton is Director of Admission/Financial Aid; Gregory Ventre is Head of School.

Green Acres School 1934

11701 Danville Drive, Rockville, MD 20852
Tel. 301-881-4100; [Toll-free] 888-410-4152; Admissions Ext. 189
Fax 301-881-3319
Web Site www.greenacres.org; E-mail admissionoffice@greenacres.org

Green Acres is a coeducational, progressive day school enrolling 320 students in Pre-Kindergarten–Grade 8. Set on a 15-acre campus outside Washington, D.C., the School is dedicated to fostering the natural curiosity of students and engaging them actively in the joy of learning. The intellectually rigorous program is cognitively and creatively challenging. Green Acres values acceptance of a variety of viewpoints and diversity. The curriculum includes technology, visual/performing arts, and physical/outdoor education. Extended day and after-school classes are available, including interscholastic sports for Grades 5–8. A recreational summer camp is offered for ages 4–12. Tuition: $23,500. Susan Friend and Nina Chibber are Co-Directors of Admission; Louis Silvano is Head of School.

Gunston Day School 1998

911 Gunston Road, P.O. Box 200, Centreville, MD 21617
Tel. 410-758-0620; [Toll-free] 800-381-0077; Admission Ext. 104
Fax 410-758-0628
Web Site www.gunstondayschool.org
E-mail dhenry@gunstondayschool.org

Sam and Mary Middleton founded this school in 1911 at their home along the Corsica River. Gunston Day School today enrolls 140 motivated and capable young men and women in Grades 9–12. Students come from several counties on Maryland's Eastern Shore. Gunston's mission is to provide a supportive, challenging environment in which the art of learning is accompanied by critical thinking, creative expression, stewardship, and self-discipline. The school community adheres to high standards of academic excellence, with an equal emphasis on ethical behavior and physical well-being. Centered on the traditional liberal arts, sciences, and humanities, the challenging college preparatory curriculum includes honors and Advanced Placement courses. The School's Bay Studies program offers weeklong explorations of the Chesapeake aboard ship or in a canoe. Students are involved in activities such as school government, publications, drama, choral ensembles, and interest clubs. Gunston offers 15 team sports including sailing, crew, and swimming as well as five club sports. Tuition: $19,595. Financial Aid: $500,000. David Henry is Director of Admission; Jeffrey C. Woodworth (Boston College, B.A.; Harvard University, M.A.) is Head of School. *Middle States Association.*

The Harbor School 1972

7701 Bradley Boulevard, Bethesda, MD 20817
Tel. 301-365-1100; Fax 301-365-7491
Web Site www.theharborschool.org

The Harbor School offers a rich learning environment for 110 boys and girls in Preschool through Grade 2. The child-centered curriculum incorporates the best elements of early childhood educational methods to develop academic and personal potential. The preschool program emphasizes socialization as a means of promoting self-confidence. Classroom instruction focuses on the mastery of basic skills as a foundation for future learning, while specialists teach art, dance, library, music, physical education, reading, and Spanish. Small classes and individual attention maximize students' achievements.

Extended care and a summer program are optional. Tuition: \$8515–\$15,748. Financial aid is available. Carol Schabe is Associate Head of School/Director of Admission; Judy Dudley is Interim Head of School.

Harford Day School 1957

715 Moores Mill Road, Bel Air, MD 21014
Tel. 410-838-4848; Fax 410-836-5918
Web Site www.harfordday.org; E-mail info@harfordday.org

Located 20 miles northeast of Baltimore, Harford Day School enrolls 350 boys and girls in K-Prep–Grade 8. The School seeks to offer a program of challenging academics in a dynamic, empowering atmosphere. The student-teacher ratio is 9:1. Fundamental skills, reasoning, independent thinking, and character building are emphasized, and frequent field trips to Baltimore, Washington, and Delaware enrich classroom learning. French, Spanish, Latin, computer skills, music, art, drama, and athletics are offered at all levels. An Extended Day program is optional. Tuition: \$11,650. Financial Aid: \$380,000. Heidi K.L. Sprinkle is Director of Admissions and Parent Relations; Susan G. Harris (Bucknell University, B.S.) was appointed Head of the School in 1994.

The Holton-Arms School 1901

7303 River Road, Bethesda, MD 20817
Tel. 301-365-5300; Fax 301-365-6071
Web Site www.holton-arms.edu; E-mail admit@holton-arms.edu

Founded by Jessie Moon Holton and Carolyn Hough Arms in 1901, The Holton-Arms School is a college preparatory day school enrolling 660 girls in Grades 3–12. The School fosters a high standard of academic performance and a supportive environment where students from diverse backgrounds may cultivate that which is unique in each of them. Rigorous programs in academics, the arts, athletics, and opportunities for leadership allow students to develop their full potential. Advanced Placement courses are available. Tuition: \$25,425–\$26,650. Financial Aid: \$2,042,225. Sharron Rodgers is Director of Enrollment & Marketing; Susanna A. Jones (Princeton, A.B.; Columbia University, M.A., M.Phil.) is Head of School. *Middle States Association.*

The Ivymount School 1961

11614 Seven Locks Road, Rockville, MD 20854
Tel. 301-469-0223; Admission Ext. 107; Fax 301-469-0778
Web Site www.ivymount.org; E-mail jwintrol@ivymount.org

Founded to serve students with special needs such as developmental disabilities, speech/language deficits, and autism, Ivymount aims to maximize each student's intellectual, physical, and social potential. Ivymount enrolls more than 200 students (ages 4–21) in a day program offering speech/language services, occupational/physical therapy, clinical social work, and adaptive physical education. Specialized teachers use innovative strategies and technology to implement Individualized Education Plans that emphasize oral and written communication, visual motor skills, and independent living skills. Expressive Arts and a summer session complement the program. Basic Program (10-month): \$41,020; Autism Program (11-month): \$60,799; Asperger Program (11-month): \$52,283. Jan Wintrol is Director.

The Jemicy School 1973

Lower & Middle School Campus: 11 Celadon Road, Owings Mills, MD 21117-3009
Upper School Campus: 301 West Chesapeake Avenue, Towson, MD 21204
Tel. 410-653-2700; Fax 410-653-1972
Web Site www.jemicyschool.org; E-mail smorse@jemicyschool.org

The Jemicy School, a coeducational, college preparatory day school, enrolls 280 students with language-based learning differences in Grades 1–12. An Upper School Prep Program, for students needing a pre-high school year, emphasizes organizational strategies and study skills. Originally established as a summer camp for dyslexic children, the School seeks to emphasize self-confidence and respect for others in an effort to help students realize their intellectual and social potential. The sequential, flexible, and multisensory curriculum promotes ordered observation, problem solving, and critical thinking. All students follow a traditional liberal arts program, taking classes in English, mathematics, social studies, science, the arts, foreign languages, and physical education. Small classes and a student-faculty ratio of 3:1 guarantee individual attention to each student's unique learning style. Extracurricular options include the visual and performing arts, athletics, community service, and sports. Jemicy is located on 23 acres spread over two campuses. Tuition: \$26,850. Financial aid is available. Sarah Morse (Lower and Middle School) and Patricia Utz (Upper School) are Directors of Admission; Ben Shifrin is Head of School.

Kent School 1967

6788 Wilkins Lane, Chestertown, MD 21620
Tel. 410-778-4100; Fax 410-778-7357
Web Site www.kentschool.org; E-mail admissions@kentschool.org

A day school enrolling 190 girls and boys age 3–Grade 8, Kent seeks to foster intellectual, moral, and personal growth through a rigorous curriculum that engages students actively in their learning. Appreciation of the arts, use of language skills, critical thinking skills, and a strong sense of responsibility and involvement in the larger community are emphasized. Kent acknowledges the multiple talents of its students as it nurtures and celebrates each child's contribution to the School. Students leave Kent School ready for the challenges of college preparatory schools. Tuition: \$4345–\$10,985. Elizabeth Collins is Admissions Director; Michael Schuler (Washington and Lee, B.A.; College of Notre Dame of Maryland, M.A.) is Head of School.

The Key School 1958

534 Hillsmere Drive, Annapolis, MD 21403
Tel. 410-263-9231; Fax 410-280-5516
Web Site www.keyschool.org

Located in Annapolis, The Key School is a nonsectarian, college preparatory day school enrolling 720 boys and girls in Pre-Kindergarten–Grade 12. The School encourages intellectual rigor, independence of thought, curiosity, creativity, and openness to differing ideas and perspectives. The curriculum includes music, art, and modern and classical languages, with electives in African-American Literature, Dance, Estuarine Biology, and Music Theory. Theater, chorus, jazz and instrumental ensemble, debate, math team, and Model Congress are among the activities. Extensive field trips and outdoor education are integral to the program. Tuition: $10,525–$20,500. Financial aid is available. Jessie D. Dunleavy is Director of Admission;

Marcella M. Yedid (Indiana University, B.S.; Brown, M.A.) is Head of School.

Landon School 1929

6101 Wilson Lane, Bethesda, MD 20817
Tel. 301-320-3200; Fax 301-320-1133
Web Site www.landon.net; E-mail george_mulligan@landon.net

Landon School prepares talented boys for productive lives as accomplished, responsible, and caring men whose actions are guided by perseverance, teamwork, honor, and fair play. A college preparatory day school serving 675 boys in Grades 3–12, Landon is known for a rigorous academic program, a commitment to the arts, and daily athletic participation. The School places leadership and character education at the top of its educational goals. Landon's teacher-coach-mentor model allows faculty to get to know boys in every aspect of school life. Students administer their own Honor Code and serve as peer advisors, prefects, and class representatives. Tuition: $25,300–$27,100. Financial Aid: $1,850,000. George Mulligan is Admissions Director; David M. Armstrong (Princeton, B.A.; University of Denver, J.D.) is Headmaster. *Middle States Association.*

Loyola Blakefield 1852

500 Chestnut Avenue, Towson, MD 21204
Tel. 410-823-0601; Admissions 443-841-3680; Fax 443-841-3105
Web Site www.loyolablakefield.org
E-mail mbreschi@loyolablakefield.org

Loyola Blakefield, founded by the Society of Jesus, is a Roman Catholic, college preparatory day school enrolling 1000 boys in Grades 6–12. Its aim is to graduate young men who are intellectually competent, open to growth, religious, loving, and committed to justice. Core requirements include 20 course units in English, mathematics, modern language, science, and social studies. Fine arts, computer science, physical education, and religious studies are also required. Loyola Blakefield offers a variety of cocurricular activities. Tuition: $13,105; Fees: $715. Michael Breschi is Director of Admissions; Rev. Thomas A. Pesci, S.J. (Weston School of Theology [Cambridge, Massachusetts], M.Div.), is President.

Maryvale Preparatory School 1945

11300 Falls Road, Brooklandville, MD 21022
Tel. 410-252-3366; Admissions 410-560-3243; Fax 410-308-1497
Web Site www.maryvale.com; E-mail grahamm@maryvale.com

Maryvale, an independent, Catholic, girls' school founded by the Sisters of Notre Dame de Namur, provides an atmosphere in which each student can reach her academic, spiritual, physical, and civic potential. Enrolling 390 young women from many faiths as day students in Grades 6–12, Maryvale seeks to inspire excellence in all aspects of life in an environment of mutual respect. The academic program centers on the liberal arts and sciences, with AP and honors courses, religious studies, the arts, and computer technology as a learning tool throughout the disciplines. The student-teacher ratio is 9:1. Girls take part in community service, Student Council, four publications, drama, clubs, and nine sports. Tuition: $13,600. Monica C. Graham is Director of Admissions; Sr. Shawn Marie Maguire, SND, is Headmistress. *Middle States Association.*

Mater Dei School 1960

9600 Seven Locks Road, Bethesda, MD 20817
Tel. 301-365-2700; Fax 301-365-2710
Web Site www.materdeischool.net

Mater Dei School, enrolling 225 boys in Grades 1–8, is a Catholic day school serving the Washington, D.C., area. The School strives to mix daily work with a sense of fun, perspective, and morality. Although the curriculum is broad, emphasis is placed on the basics, particularly religion, language arts, mathematics, social studies, science, and physical education. A one-week District of Columbia Cultural Program and a one-week Outdoor Environmental Camp are part of the curriculum in the upper grades. Tuition: $11,800. Christopher S. Abell (Boston College, B.A. 1970; Georgetown, M.A. 1974; Catholic University, J.D. 1979) is President; Edward N. Williams (College of the Holy Cross, B.A. 1983; Harvard, M.Ed.) is Headmaster.

McDonogh School 1873

8600 McDonogh Road, Owings Mills, MD 21117-0380
Tel. 410-363-0600; Admissions 410-581-4719; Fax 410-998-3507
Web Site www.mcdonogh.org; E-mail admissions@mcdonogh.org

McDonogh School enrolls 1292 boys and girls in Kindergarten–Grade 12, including 80 five-day boarding students in Grades 9–12. Emphasizing academic excellence, moral character, responsibility, and leadership, McDonogh "offers students the opportunities of a large school plus the advantages of a smaller one." Class size averages 15, and 16 Advanced Placement courses are offered. Upper School students choose from 24 interscholastic sports and 50 clubs and activities. The campus is set on 800 acres northwest of Baltimore. Bus transportation and lunches are included in tuition. Boarding Tuition: $27,770; Day Tuition: $18,550–$20,640. Financial Aid: $2,600,000. Anita Hilson is Director of Admissions; Charles Britton is Headmaster.

McLean School of Maryland 1954

8224 Lochinver Lane, Potomac, MD 20854
Tel. 301-299-8277; Admissions 240-395-0698; Fax 301-299-8638
Web Site www.mcleanschool.org
E-mail admission@mcleanschool.org

Enrolling 495 students in Kindergarten–Grade 12, McLean seeks to make education accessible, stimulating, and meaningful for a broad range of learners. McLean serves students who thrive in a warm, supportive atmosphere and accommodates a variety of learning needs and styles. The college preparatory curriculum emphasizes the mastery of basic skills in the liberal arts and sciences. Students may be placed in classes according to their skill levels and academic strengths. All students engage in sports and in art, music, computer, and drama. Tuition: $22,350–$27,250. Financial aid is available. Judy Jankowski is Director of Admission; Darlene B. Pierro is Head of School.

The Montessori School 1962

10807 Tony Drive, Lutherville, MD 21093
Tel. 410-321-8555; Fax 410-321-8566
Web Site www.montessorischool.net
E-mail admissions@montessorischool.net

This coeducational day school seeks to provide a progressive, child-centered program in which students joyfully and actively engage in the learning process. The Montessori School enrolls 325 youngsters from diverse backgrounds in Pre-Kindergarten–Grade 6. Small, multiaged classes are grouped heterogeneously to encourage peer teaching, sharing, and natural social development. The core program focuses on language arts, math, science, and social studies, enhanced by art, music, French, physical education, outdoor education, and library skills. Before- and after-school care and a summer program are available. Tuition: $6400–$12,950. Financial Aid: $95,000. Beth Callahan is Admissions Director; Albert J. Swartz (St. John's,

B.A.; Long Island University, M.Ed.) is Head of School. *Middle States Association.*

The Newport School 1930

12101 Tech Road, Silver Spring, MD 20904-1915
Tel. 240-645-0145; Fax 240-645-0150
Web Site www.newportschool.org

The Newport School is a coeducational, college preparatory day school enrolling 125 students "with individual differences who are average to gifted in intelligence" in Preschool–Grade 12. The School emphasizes creative and analytical decision-making, compassion, responsibility, and self-expression. The average class size is 10, and the student-teacher ratio is 4:1. Younger students develop communication and problem-solving skills through a traditional curriculum and Spanish, art, and technology courses. High school students may take electives such as Graphic Design, Film Studies, Political Theory, Economics, Psychology, Chinese, Latin, and AP courses. Five credits of English; four credits of math, science, and social science; three credits of foreign language and fine arts; and one credit of technology are required for graduation. Athletics offered are soccer, basketball, baseball, wrestling, hockey, yoga, and figure skating. Extracurricular activities include student government, community service, and special-interest clubs. One hundred percent of graduates are accepted to colleges and universities. Tuition: $14,240–$22,355. Financial aid is available. Letty Rosen is Director of Admissions; Rachel Goldfarb is Head of School.

The Nora School 1964

955 Sligo Avenue, Silver Spring, MD 20910
Tel. 301-495-NORA; Fax 301-495-7829
Web Site www.nora-school.org; E-mail elaine@nora-school.org

The Nora School is a progressive, coeducational, college preparatory day school serving 60 students in Grades 9–12. Its mission is to nurture and empower bright students who have not realized their potential in larger, more traditional school settings. The School offers a challenging curriculum in an environment designed to develop and maintain a just community, communal decision-making, a high level of discourse, and attention to individual needs and concerns. At all levels, students study the traditional disciplines—English, social studies, mathematics, science, and foreign language—via thematic, engaging approaches. Tuition: $19,950. Elaine Mack is Director of Admissions; David Mullen (University of Maryland, M.S.Ed.) is Headmaster. *Middle States Association.*

Norwood School 1952

8821 River Road, Bethesda, MD 20817
Tel. 301-365-2595; Admission 301-841-2130; Fax 301-365-4277
Web Site www.norwoodschool.org
E-mail admission@norwoodschool.org

Norwood, a coeducational day school for 530 students in Kindergarten–Grade 8, seeks to offer individual attention and superior instruction. The School's mission is to help each child grow intellectually, morally, physically, and socially. Norwood provides training in fundamental skills, logical and analytical thinking, and independence of mind and self-expression. The curriculum emphasizes facility in both language and math. Art, music, French, Spanish, Latin, Chinese, science, social studies, technology, and physical education are integral parts of the program. Tuition: $22,370–$23,185. Financial Aid: $1,160,000. Mimi Mulligan is Director of Admission and Enrollment Management; Richard T. Ewing, Jr., is Head of School.

Notre Dame Preparatory School 1873

815 Hampton Lane, Towson, MD 21286
Tel. 410-825-6202; Admissions 410-825-0590; Fax 410-825-0982
Web Site www.notredameprep.com
E-mail admissions@notredameprep.com

Notre Dame is a Catholic, independent, college preparatory day school enrolling 760 girls in Grades 6–12. Under the leadership of the School Sisters of Notre Dame, it seeks to foster the spiritual, moral, and intellectual growth of each student in a warm, supportive atmosphere. A broad and extensive curriculum presented at four levels of challenge allows each student to work according to her ability. Facilities include a new Sports and Fitness Center, classroom and performing arts wings, wireless network, and state-of-the-art science labs and language center. Clubs and 15 varsity sports, including crew, supplement the curriculum. Social service complements school life. Tuition: $14,140. Katherine Goetz is Director of Admission; Sr. Patricia McCarron, SSND (College of Notre Dame of Maryland, B.A.; Loyola College, M.Ed.; Catholic University, Ph.D.), is Headmistress. *Middle States Association.*

Oldfields School 1867

1500 Glencoe Road, Glencoe, MD 21152
Tel. 410-472-4800; Fax 410-472-6839
Web Site www.oldfieldsschool.org
E-mail admissions@oldfieldsschool.org

Oldfields School in Glencoe, Maryland, is a college preparatory boarding and day school for girls in Grades 8 through 12 and a postgraduate year.

Oldfields was founded in 1867 by Mrs. John Sears McCulloch and continues to reflect her desire to provide young women with the opportunity to make the most of their academic and personal potential. The mission of Oldfields is to provide a family-like environment in which students can develop intellectually, ethically, and socially by learning the values of self-discipline and self-respect.

Oldfields is governed by a self-perpetuating Board of Trustees made up of alumnae and parents of current and past students. Oldfields is accredited by the Middle States Association of Colleges and Schools and holds membership in the National Association of Independent Schools and other organizations.

THE CAMPUS. The 230-acre campus lies in rolling hills and woodlands, 25 miles north of Baltimore, with convenient access to the cultural and recreational activities available there, as well as in Washington, D.C., Philadelphia, and New York. Old House, the original school building, is more than 200 years old. Other structures include Commons, which contains dining facilities, the school store, and recently renovated social activity areas (2004); a gymnasium; a dance studio; and five dormitories. A renovated and expanded academic building (2000) features updated classrooms, smartboards, a new library, five state-of-the-art science labs, and a fine arts facility.

THE FACULTY. George S. Swope, Jr., appointed Head of Oldfields in 2003, holds a B.A. degree in Slavic Studies from Lawrence University. He also earned an M.A. in Slavic Languages and Literature and an M.B.A., both from Northwestern University.

There are 29 full-time and 3 part-time faculty members, 4 of whom are men. Over 75 percent of the full-time faculty live on campus and serve as dormitory parents in one of the five dormitories. Faculty attend sporting events and art performances and participate in all areas of student life. Each faculty member has a group of approximately five students for whom he or she acts as an advisor and as a contact for parents.

Nurses have regular clinic hours in the health center and are on call 24 hours a day.

STUDENT BODY. Typically, Oldfields enrolls 135 boarders and 60 day students. The school size is limited to 195 girls in order to maintain its family-like atmosphere. Seventy percent of the students are boarders.

In 2007–08, the student body represented 17 states and seven countries.

ACADEMIC PROGRAM. The school year is divided into trimesters, with term exams given. Students carry at least five courses per semester, and classes meet in a combination of six 80-minute periods on a rotating, three-class-a-day schedule. Grades and comments from faculty members are sent home three times a year. The academic and social progress of each girl is reviewed at weekly faculty meetings. The average class enrolls 14 students, with a low student-teacher ratio. Extra help from teachers is available, and tutoring can be arranged when necessary.

Oldfields is committed to providing each student with the college preparatory course of study most appropriate to her needs and interests. In 2004, the entire faculty received training from the Schools Attuned program based on Dr. Melvin Levine's neurodevelopmental studies. Through ongoing training, faculty develop the pedagogical knowledge and skills required to meet the diverse learning needs of each Oldfields student. This professional development enables the School to provide a college preparatory curriculum tailored to the distinctive academic styles of girls in Grade 8 through Postgraduate. Technology is integrated into the curriculum through the use of five Smartboards, and each student is required to have a laptop computer.

Nineteen credits are required for graduation. Students must take four years of English, three years of mathematics, two years of laboratory science, three years of a foreign language (including two of the same language), three years of history (including one year of U.S. history), one year of Fine Arts, and physical education each semester. In addition, students in each grade level participate in the Oldfields Seminar Series. In Grade 9, the series focuses on study skills and time management; in Grade 10, financial literacy; in Grade 11, the college search and admission process; and in Grade 12 and Postgraduate, leadership. Qualified juniors and seniors may undertake an independent study in any academic discipline.

Students in Honors courses are encouraged to take the appropriate Advanced Placement examination/SAT II. Oldfields faculty prefer the curricular flexibility of an Honors course, while they also prepare students for advanced national exams; thus the AP designation will not appear on the student transcript.

During the two-week May Program in 2006–07, students traveled abroad to Peru and Costa Rica and completed community service projects in Appalachia and Baltimore. One-week trips included arts appreciation in New York and exploring Native American culture in New Mexico. On campus, students participated in courses including photography, yoga, quilting, driver's education, Spanish cuisine, Habitat for Humanity, equine management, and the study of local ecosystems in the Gunpowder River. Past Senior Projects have included working as a veterinary aide, on a Congressional campaign committee, at the Earthwatch Institute, and in surgical pathology at Johns Hopkins University.

College counseling and aptitude testing begin in the fall of the junior year. The college counselor coordinates on-campus visits from more than 60 college representatives and plans college fair evenings. College testing is conducted on campus.

Oldfields School's commitment to academic diversity is reflected in the colleges students attend. Among the colleges and universities attended by recent graduates are College of Charleston, Gettysburg, Howard, Ithaca, Johnson and Wales, Johns Hopkins, Lynchburg, Northwestern, Ohio State, Rhode Island School of Design, Smith, Virginia Polytechnical Institute, Washington College, and the Universities of Maryland and Michigan.

STUDENT ACTIVITIES. The Student Council, made up of 12 elected students, helps to formulate and implement school policy. Selected seniors also help enforce the spirit and letter of the School's rules by serving as Resident Assistants in dormitories.

Campus cocurricular activities are organized and run by students. In recent years, students have contributed their time and enthusiasm to FOCUS, Black Awareness Club, Global Awareness Club, Art Club, Environmental Awareness Club, and Tour Guides. Dubious Dozen and Images are a cappella choral groups that perform frequently for the Oldfields community. The school literary magazine and yearbook are produced entirely by students.

Competitive and noncompetitive sports are offered at the interscholastic and intramural level. Field hockey, cross-country, basketball, soccer, tennis, softball, volleyball, badminton, and lacrosse are played on the varsity and junior varsity levels. Third-squad intramurals are offered in many sports, depending on student interest. Varsity and junior varsity riding teams compete throughout the Middle Atlantic states. Dance (ballet, tap, jazz, and modern) and aerobics classes are offered each afternoon. The traditional school spirit competition, Green and White, lasts throughout the year.

Lectures, workshops, concerts, and movies are presented on campus, and students take trips to local and regional areas of interest. Plays, concerts, and dances with nearby boys' schools, as well as ski weekends and hiking trips, are scheduled regularly. All events are chaperoned by faculty members. Community service and excursions to theaters, museums, sporting events, shopping malls, and restaurants supplement the weekend activities.

ADMISSION AND COSTS. Oldfields seeks students who want to make the most of their potential, to work hard and play hard, and to contribute to a community in which honesty, social responsibility, and intellectual curiosity are emphasized. It welcomes motivated girls of average to superior ability who will take advantage of the personalized attention inherent in the curriculum, which accommodates students' needs for challenge and support.

The deadline for admission application is February 1. Admission is based on the application and essay, along with standardized test scores, a transcript and school recommendation, two teacher recommendations, and a personal interview on campus. Phone interviews are required when campus visits are not possible. International students must submit TOEFL and SSAT testing to determine English proficiency. An enrollment deposit of $3500 for boarders and $2500 for day students, applicable toward tuition, is required with a signed entrance contract.

The comprehensive fee for 2007–08 is $39,100 for seven-day boarders, $34,100 for five-day boarders, and $24,100 for day students. Additional expenses include textbooks, school supplies, and a laptop computer. Optional expenses include photography, music, and riding lessons.

Financial aid is available on the basis of need, and grants are reviewed and awarded annually. Oldfields awards more than $1,000,000 per year in grants to approximately 30 percent of the student body. All families applying for aid must complete the forms for the School and Student Service for Financial Aid and submit their last two tax returns.

Merit scholarships are available to new applicants. Candidates must complete the admission process and submit an essay of 300 to 500 words by February 1. The Admission Office provides detailed information on scholarship requirements.

Head of School: George S. Swope, Jr.
Director of Developmental Operations: Margaret Andrews
Director of Admission & Financial Aid: Kimberly C. Loughlin
Dean of Academic Life: Anne Weeks
Dean of Student Life: Wendy Skinner
Alumnae Affairs: Janine Brennan
College Counselor: Barbara Ahalt
Business Officer: Deborah Anderson
Athletic Coordinator: Stephanie Maycheck

The Primary Day School 1944

7300 River Road, Bethesda, MD 20817
Tel. 301-365-4355; Fax 301-469-8611
Web Site www.theprimarydayschool.org
E-mail j.mccaffery@theprimarydayschool.org

The Primary Day School offers an environment in which young children develop a strong foundation for future learning. Enrolling 152 girls and boys in PreKindergarten–Grade 2, Primary Day's traditional curriculum is based on the Phonovisual Method, a multisensory phonetic system that promotes comprehension and fluency in reading. Along with basic skills, students acquire sound work habits and an appreciation of the arts. Core subjects of language arts, math, science, and social studies are enriched by music, art, technology, creative writing, physical education, and library. Children take part in weekly assemblies that provide experience and poise in public speaking. Tuition: $10,900–$15,000. Financial aid is available. Julie A. McCaffery is Admission Director; Louise K. Plumb is Director.

Queen Anne School 1964

14111 Oak Grove Road, Upper Marlboro, MD 20774
Tel. 301-249-5000; Admissions Ext. 305; Fax 301-249-3838
Web Site www.queenanne.org; E-mail cpochet@queenanne.org

A college preparatory, coeducational day school enrolling 210 students in Grades 6–12, Queen Anne is located on 60 acres between Washington and Annapolis. Affiliated with St. Barnabas' Episcopal Church, the School offers a demanding, comprehensive program, including Advanced Placement courses, community outreach, and a biology of the Chesapeake Bay program. Fine arts, athletics, and other electives enhance the curriculum. Classes are small, and students are prepared to be critical thinkers and mature individuals. Tuition: $17,200–$18,850. Need-based financial aid is available. Courtney Pochet is Director of Admissions; J. Temple Blackwood (University of Hartford, B.S.; Washington College, M.A.) is Headmaster. *Middle States Association.*

Radcliffe Creek School 1995

201 Talbot Boulevard, Chestertown, MD 21620
Tel. 410-778-8150; Fax 410-778-8176
Web Site www.radcliffecreekschool.org
E-mail frontdesk@radcliffecreekschool.org

Radcliffe Creek School provides an ungraded, alternative education for learning-disabled youngsters of average to above-average intelligence. Enrolling 102 boys and girls from age 3 to 14, the School seeks to remediate weaknesses in writing, spelling, and math while building on individual strengths to promote success. Quality, rather than quantity, of work is emphasized in a stimulating environment free of time constraints and competition. Certified teachers, innovative instruction, small classes, and multisensory, hands-on methods of learning benefit students and facilitate the return to traditional classrooms. Daily job teams and a unique program of behavior management encourage children to assume personal responsibility and integrity. Tuition: $5500–$19,400. Molly Judge is Head of School.

Roland Park Country School 1901

5204 Roland Avenue, Baltimore, MD 21210
Tel. 410-323-5500; Fax 410-323-2164
Web Site www.rpcs.org; E-mail admissions@rpcs.org

A college preparatory day school for 700 girls in Kindergarten–Grade 12, Roland Park Country School offers comprehensive academic, arts, and athletic programs. The School seeks to aid the intellectual, aesthetic, physical, and moral development of all its students. The Lower School develops fundamental skills in reading, math, science, art, music, technology, and foreign languages, while the Middle School aims to bridge the transition between concrete and abstract study. The Upper School offers courses in all major subjects as well as electives in art, music, theater, computer science, and public speaking. The curriculum features Advanced Placement in all disciplines and eight languages including Russian, Chinese, and Arabic. Upper School coordination with Gilman School offers the option of coeducational classes. Strong school spirit and college placement, foreign exchanges, four honor societies, Model UN, student government, community service, senior internships, and academic and interest clubs enhance the program. Students also participate on athletic teams. A summer camp is offered. Tuition: $20,085. Financial Aid: $2,000,000. Peggy K. Wolf is Director of Admissions and Financial Assistance; Jean Waller Brune (Middlebury, B.A.; Johns Hopkins, M.A.) is Head of School.

Ruxton Country School 1913

11202 Garrison Forest Road, Owings Mills, MD 21117
Tel. 443-544-3000; Admission Ext. 221; Fax 443-544-3010
Web Site www.ruxton.org; E-mail rgarfield@ruxton.org

Enrolling 220 day boys and girls in Kindergarten–Grade 8, plus Pre-First, Ruxton believes that small classes provide maximum learning opportunities. Skilled teachers accommodate varied learning styles. Strong academics are based on the liberal arts. Reading and math specialists are on staff in the Lower and Middle Schools. Core subjects are enhanced by art, music, drama, physical education, computers, and Spanish. Enrichment classes are offered in Kindergarten–Grade 8. Tuition: $15,975–$18,340. Roberta Garfield is Director of Admissions; Stephen Barker (Harvard University, A.B., Ed.M.) is Head of School.

St. Andrew's Episcopal School 1978

8804 Postoak Road, Potomac, MD 20854
Tel. 301-983-5200; Admission Ext. 236; Fax 301-983-4620
Web Site www.saes.org; E-mail admission@saes.org

St. Andrew's Episcopal School, a coeducational, college preparatory day school, endeavors to provide a comprehensive program for students in Grades 6 through 12 in an inclusive environment that embodies the faith and perspective of the Episcopal Church. Only 16 miles from downtown Washington, D.C., the School's location enables students to take advantage of the educational, cultural, and historical resources of the nation's capital.

St. Andrew's strives to challenge and support all of its students in a balanced program that nurtures their academic, artistic, athletic, and spiritual growth. The School believes that developing intellect, character, and a sense of self-worth helps students live a creative and compassionate life. Because St. Andrew's values the benefits of a community, the School also encourages students to lead lives of responsibility to each other and to the larger community.

St. Andrew's is a nonprofit institution governed by a 22-member Board of Trustees, including a representative of the Bishop of Washington. The School is accredited by the Middle States Association of Colleges and Schools and holds membership in the National Association of Independent Schools and other organizations. St. Andrew's Parent Association is organized to promote, support, and enhance the total school program.

THE CAMPUS. Situated in a residential neighborhood, the 19.2-acre campus features state-of-the-art classrooms, science and technology laboratories, a two-story library, a media center, darkroom, and combined theater and assembly hall. The sports program is supported by two athletic fields, baseball and softball diamonds, four tennis courts, a weight-training room, girls' and boys' locker rooms, dance studio and wrestling room, a gymnasium, and an athletic medicine training room.

THE FACULTY. Robert Kosasky was appointed the fourth Headmaster of St. Andrew's in 2002. He earned his B.A. from Yale University and an M.A. from Columbia University.

There are 67 faculty and administrators who teach, 35 men and 32 women. They hold 67 baccalaureate degrees and 59 advanced degrees, including 6 doctorates. The School's faculty represents study at such colleges and universities as American, Amherst, Boston University, Bowdoin, Colby, Colgate, College of William and Mary, College of Wooster, Columbia, Cornell, Dartmouth, Davidson, Dickinson, Duke, George Washington, Johns Hopkins, Loyola, Middlebury, Northwestern, Princeton, Rhode Island School of Design, Rochester Institute of Technology, Syracuse, Tufts, Washington University of St. Louis, Wesleyan, Yale, and the Universities of Cambridge, Maryland, Massachusetts, Michigan, North Carolina, Tennessee, and Virginia.

Both a nurse and a certified athletic trainer are on duty full-time during school hours. Complete hospital facilities are approximately 6 miles from the School.

STUDENT BODY. In 2007–08, St. Andrew's enrolled 452 students, 246 boys and 206 girls, as follows: 22 in Grade 6, 49 in Grade 7, 55 in Grade 8, 78 in Grade 9, 99 in Grade 10, 84 in Grade 11, and 65 in Grade 12. They come from the Greater Washington metropolitan area and represent diverse racial, ethnic, religious, and socioeconomic backgrounds. Seventy-four percent of the student body is Christian, and 24 percent of those students are Episcopalian.

ACADEMIC PROGRAM. The school day begins at 8:25 A.M. with a morning meeting, followed by either seven 40-minute class periods or a modified block schedule and a lunch break. Dismissal is at 3:05 P.M. in the Upper School and 3:25 P.M. in the Middle School. The School's calendar, which extends from early September to early June, is divided into 12-week trimesters, with Thanksgiving, Christmas, and spring vacations and observances of national holidays.

The normal course load in both the Middle and Upper Schools is five academic courses in English, history, math, science, and foreign languages. Parents receive written evaluations of their child's progress in each course at the midway point and end of each trimester. Exceptional achievement is recognized on the Academic and Effort Honor Rolls.

In order to graduate, students in the Upper School must complete four years each of English, history, and physical education; three years of science and mathematics, including Algebra I and II or Algebra II/Trigonometry and Geometry, Geometry, and Trigonometry; two consecutive years of the same language; eight trimesters of art; three trimesters of religion; and two trimesters of health. A senior research paper and 120 hours of community service are also required.

Courses offered in the Upper School include English 9–12, Creative Writing, Journalism, Modern American Literature, World Literature: Global Visions; Art History, Economics, Globalization: A Non-Western Perspective, History of Non-Violence in the Twentieth Century, Latin American Studies, Race and Culture in the Modern World; French I–IV, Latin I–IV, Spanish I–IV; Algebra I–III, Calculus, Geometry, Intro to Computer Science, Multivariable Calculus, Statistics; Service Learning 9, World Religions, Ethics, Philosophy of Religion; Biology, Chemistry, Physical Geography, Physics I–II, Robotics; Ceramics, Digital Media as Fine Art and Design, Drawing, Painting, Photography I–III, Photo-Journalism, 3-D Art, Video I–III, Yearbook I–II, Acting I–II, Band I–III, Dance I–III, Guitar I–II, Improvisation I–III, Musical Theatre, Technical Theater I–II, Traveling Chorus, Orchestra I–III, Public Speaking, and Computer Graphics.

Advanced Placement courses are offered in all academic disciplines. Consortium courses are provided for juniors and seniors from St. Andrew's, Bullis, Connelly School of the Holy Child, Holton-Arms School, Landon School, and Stone Ridge Country Day School. Each seminar meets three times a week from 7:15 to 8:00 A.M.

All students are assigned a faculty advisor with whom they meet several times a week. For students who experience academic difficulties, the School offers tutoring space and a "clearing house" service to connect parents and tutors. There are four academic deans in the Upper School, and each dean monitors course selection and academic progress for an entire grade. Deans continue to monitor the same students until the class graduates.

In 2007, all seniors entered college, and 18 were admitted by "early decision." Students are attending such institutions as Art Institute of Chicago, Bates, Boston College, Boston University, Bucknell, Carnegie Mellon, College of Charleston, Dartmouth, Dickinson, Elon, Emory, George Washington, Georgia Institute of Technology, Gettysburg, Hamilton, Kenyon, Miami University of Ohio, Oberlin, Rhode Island School of Design, Syracuse, Tufts, Vanderbilt, Virginia Military Institute, Wake Forest, Yale, and the Universities of Maryland (College Park) and Wisconsin (Madison).

STUDENT ACTIVITIES. Clubs and organizations meet during the activity period on Mondays from 3:10 to 3:55 P.M. and on Wednesdays from 2:30 to 3:05 P.M. Students participate in activities such as Band, Black Student Alliance, Book Club, Bridge Club, Chorus, Dance, Debate Club, Diversity Club, drama and play productions, Gay-Straight Alliance, Improv Club, Jazz Band, Jewish Culture Club, Model United Nations, Orchestra, Recycling Club, Student Vestry and Clubs focusing on religion, women's issues, and service organization are also offered, along with student-published literary magazines, newspapers, and an annual yearbook. The Student Council and Student Government Association provide Middle and Upper School students, respectively, with a way to participate in school government and policies.

St. Andrew's athletic program is open to students in Grades 7–12. Athletics offered for girls and boys include aikido, basketball, cross-country, dance, equestrian team, fitness, golf, lacrosse, soccer, tennis, track, volleyball, and wrestling. Boys may also participate in baseball, and girls play softball. St. Andrew's is a member of the Independent School League and the Mid-Atlantic Conference.

St. Andrew's believes that community service is a vital part of a young person's education. Middle School activities occur periodically throughout the school year in small groups organized by grade level. Ninth graders participate in service learning during the school day as part of their trimester religion course. All students in Grades 10–11 must complete 20 hours of community service a year. During the senior year, students must select an approved project of at least 60 hours in which to participate during the final two weeks of school.

Field trips include visits to places in and around the Washington and Baltimore areas, and athletic, recreational, class, and curricular-related trips are planned during the school year and summer. The School also sponsors service learning opportunities as well as international and exchange trips. Countries visited have included Canada, China, Dominica, France, Greece, Honduras, Italy, Jamaica, South Africa, and Spain.

ADMISSION AND COSTS. St. Andrew's seeks students who have demonstrated academic ability, intellectual curiosity, motivation, and a desire to contribute to the community. Admission decisions are based on the candidate's individual strengths and talents and his or her potential to be successful at St. Andrew's. The application and all supporting materials must be received by February 1. After that deadline, admission is granted as space is available.

In 2007–08, tuition is $27,240 for Grades 6–8 and $28,265 for Grades 9–12. Textbooks are purchased online and cost approximately $400–$700 per year. Shuttle bus service is available for an additional fee. Financial aid is based solely upon demonstrated financial need, and tuition insurance and payment plans are offered. Financial aid applications and other materials must be submitted to the School by December 15 for current financial aid recipients and by February 1 for new applicants.

Headmaster: Robert Kosasky
Assistant Headmaster: John Holden
Upper School Head: Joanne Beach
Assistant Head of Upper School: David Brown
Middle School Head: Mark Segal
Dean of Upper School Students: Virginia Cobb
Dean of Middle School Students: Amanda Macomber
Director of Admission and Financial Aid: Julie Jameson
Directors of Athletics: Al Hightower & Joan Kowalik
Director of College Counseling: Randy Tajan
Director of Development: Linda Kiser
Chief Financial Officer: Walter Manning
Director of Summer Programs: Chris Polyak

Saint James School 1842

17641 College Road, St. James, MD 21781
Tel. 301-733-9330; Fax 301-739-1310
Web Site www.stjames.edu; E-mail admissions@stjames.edu

Saint James, the oldest Episcopal boarding school in the United States based on the English model, was founded by Bishop William Whittingham in 1842. The School offers a challenging college preparatory curriculum to 235 young men and women in Grades 8–12, including 158 resident students from 16 states, 9 countries, and diverse religious, racial, ethnic, and socioeconomic backgrounds. Students of all faiths take part in the spiritual life of the community including theology and scripture studies, daily worship, and shared prayer. The academic program emphasizes the liberal arts, sciences, and humanities, with Advanced Placement courses in the major disciplines. With an average enrollment of 12, students have personalized attention and support. Typically, all graduates go on to four year-colleges. Prefect and Honor Councils and Disciplinary Committee provide leadership experience, while required community service develops responsibility and sensitivity to others. Drama, music, publications, tour guides, interscholastic sports, and a variety of interest clubs are among the extracurricular activities. Boarding Tuition: $32,000; Day Tuition: $21,000. Lawrence Jensen is Director of Admissions; the Reverend Dr. D. Stuart Dunnan is Headmaster. *Middle States Association.*

St. John's Episcopal School 1961

3427 Olney-Laytonsville Road, Olney, MD 20832
Tel. 301-774-6804; Fax 301-774-2375
Web Site www.stjes.com; E-mail lori.backlund@stjes.com

St. John's Episcopal School was founded in 1961 by the Reverend James Valliant "to send forth well-balanced, disciplined, courteous, self-reliant students generously equipped with academic knowledge." The School's mission is to provide a structured and challenging academic program, an everyday focus on Christian values and moral character, and a community-centered approach to learning. St. John's currently enrolls 309 day students in Kindergarten–Grade 8. Challenging academics, weekly chapel, active family involvement, and social outreach are integral to the program. Extended-day care, interscholastic athletics, and summer programs are offered. Tuition: $13,520–$13,843. Financial aid is available. Lori Backlund is Director of Admissions and Marketing; John Zurn was appointed Headmaster in 1989.

St. John's Parish Day School 1965

9130 Frederick Road, Ellicott City, MD 21042
Tel. 410-465-7644; Fax 410-465-7748
Web Site www.stjohnspds.org; E-mail kmckee@stjohnsec.org

Founded by St. John's Episcopal Church, this coeducational school provides a rigorous education in a spiritual environment for 450 boys and girls from many ethnic, religious, and cultural backgrounds in Preschool through Grade 5. The curriculum is designed to prepare children for success in middle and secondary school and beyond while instilling high standards of personal ethics. Core subjects are complemented by science, music, art, media, technology, Spanish, and physical education, taught by specialist teachers. All students take part in regular chapel services. St. John's has been recognized for its innovative environmental, diversity, and community service programs. It has also been designated a Maryland Green School for its recycling program as well as for the development of a schoolyard habitat that features a meadow, a bluebird trail, and an alphabet garden. Parental involvement is valued as a means of bringing the school community together in various celebrations and spirit-building activities. After-school enrichment includes garden club, chess, sports, Chinese, Spanish, and tae kwon do. Tuition: $9500. Financial Aid: $240,000. Krista McKee (Abilene Christian, B.S.; Texas Woman's University, M.A.) is Head of School.

St. Paul's School 1849

P.O. Box 8100, Brooklandville, MD 21022-8100
Tel. 410-825-4400; Admissions Fax 410-427-0380
Web Site www.stpaulsschool.org; E-mail admissions@stpaulsschool.org

St. Paul's is an Episcopal, college preparatory day school for boys and girls in Kindergarten–Grade 4 and boys in Grades 5–12. Located on 95 acres, the School offers its 850 students the International Baccalaureate Diploma Program, honors and Advanced Placement courses, multilingual and computer experience in all grades, and a foreign exchange program. A chapel program, broad art and athletic programs, community service, and coordinate classes with the adjacent St. Paul's School for Girls complement the curriculum. Facilities include the 47,000-square-foot Athletic Center and the 32,000-square-foot Middle School Building. Tuition: $19,750. Financial Aid: $1,700,000. Amy Hall Furlong is Director of Admissions; Thomas J. Reid is Headmaster.

St. Paul's School for Girls 1959

Falls Road & Seminary Avenue, Brooklandville, MD 21022
Tel. 410-823-6323; Admission 443-632-1046; Fax 410-828-7238
Web Site www.spsfg.org; E-mail cdouglas@spsfg.org

A college preparatory school in the Episcopal tradition, St. Paul's School for Girls enrolls 463 day students in Grades 5–12. The program combines academics, athletics, the arts, and the spiritual, with opportunities for coed studies with young men at adjoining St. Paul's School. Faculty aim to teach girls "the way girls learn best." The Middle School curriculum centers on a team approach. The Upper School includes Advanced Placement and honors courses and a unique leadership program for young women. Technology is state-of-the-art, and technology tools such as laptops and tablets are routinely used in classrooms. Numerous clubs, community service outreach, and travel/study to Europe and Japan enhance the program. The School seeks to provide a secure, diverse community that challenges each student to strive for excellence. Tuition: $20,475. Financial Aid: $890,000. Charlotte Douglas is Director of Admission; Dr. Monica Gillespie is Head of School.

St. Timothy's School 1882

8400 Greenspring Avenue, Stevenson, MD 21153
Tel. 410-486-7400; Admission 410-486-7401; Fax 410-486-1167
Web Site www.stt.org; E-mail admis@stt.org

ST. TIMOTHY'S SCHOOL in Stevenson, Maryland, is a boarding and day school, affiliated with the Episcopal Church, enrolling young women in Forms 3 through 6 (Grades 9–12). The School's rural setting is 15 minutes from downtown Baltimore and an hour north of Washington, D.C. It is easily reached by Interstate 95 and from the Thurgood Marshall Baltimore-Washington International Airport. Students and faculty make excellent use of the rich cultural, historical, and recreational resources of the two cities and their environment as an extension of classroom learning.

St. Timothy's School was founded in 1882 by sisters Sally and Polly Carter, who shared a vision of a rigorous educational environment in which bright young women could stretch and expand their intellectual capabilities, without limitations, for their own enrichment and the betterment of their world. During the 1970s, the School consolidated with Hannah More Academy, the first Episcopal school for girls in the country.

St. Timothy's School seeks girls with energy, character, and high potential. Its mission is to build in its students the capability, confidence, and integrity they need to compete and contribute effectively and ethically throughout their lives. Challenging academics, based on the International Baccalaureate Diploma Program, are integrated with broad exposure to the arts, athletics, and service to the community. Girls live according to an Honor Code that has been developed and administered by students throughout the years.

Governed by a 25-member Board of Trustees, St. Timothy's School is accredited by the Middle States Association of Colleges and Schools and the Association of Independent Maryland Schools, and holds membership in the National Association of Independent Schools, the Association of Independent Maryland Schools, National Coalition of Girls' Schools, and the National Association of Episcopal Schools, among other organizations. An IB World School, St. Timothy's is also a member of the Council of International Schools, and a Cambridge University Center for International Education. Its $10,000,000 endowment is enriched by the $950,000 Annual Fund, which is supported by many of the School's approximately 2500 alumnae.

THE CAMPUS. St. Timothy's 22 buildings include the Hannah More Arts Center, which houses a 350-seat theater, scenery and costume shops, a spacious dance studio, music practice rooms, and a gallery. The Art Barn holds facilities for two- and three-dimensional studies including design, photography, and ceramics. Fowler House, the academic building, has science and computer laboratories and the 22,000-volume Ella R. Watkins Library containing computerized catalog search capabilities. Each classroom is equipped with an on-line computer. Girls live two or three to a room in a stately 1930s mansion and a more contemporary residence, each containing living rooms, faculty apartments, study areas, and computer labs. A health center, chapel, bookstore, student bank, and the Irvine Nature Science Center, an independent nature education and conservation foundation, are also on campus.

Athletic facilities include six all-weather tennis courts, an outdoor swimming pool, a gymnasium, and cross-country, hiking, and running trails. A state-of-the-art athletic complex (2003) houses basketball courts, locker rooms, a fitness center, and a training room. The School's extensive riding program, which involves students in interschool horse shows, is facilitated by indoor and outdoor riding rings, five fenced fields, and a 24-stall barn.

THE FACULTY. Randy S. Stevens, appointed Head of School in 2003, earned a B.A. from the University of South Carolina and a Master of Public Administration from Cornell University.

There are 38 full-time and 7 part-time members of the faculty and administration. Seventy-one percent have ten or more years' teaching experience; 59 percent of the faculty and administration hold advanced degrees; and 66 percent live on campus. They have graduated from colleges and universities such as Bowdoin, Brown, Colby, Columbia, Cornell, Dartmouth, Drake University, George Washington, Goucher, Harvard, Hobart and William Smith, Johns Hopkins, Lafayette, Maryland Institute College of Art, Middlebury, Princeton, Towson, Vassar, Washington College, Williams, Yale, and the Universities of California, Maryland, Massachusetts, North Carolina, South Carolina, Virginia, and Wisconsin.

STUDENT BODY. In 2007–08, St. Timothy's School enrolled 145 young women, 60 percent boarding and 40 percent day students, in Forms 3 through 6. They come from 12 states and 13 countries and represent a wide diversity of religious, ethnic, and racial heritages.

ACADEMIC PROGRAM. St. Timothy's curriculum is based on the International Baccalaureate Program, which is one of the most rigorous and advanced curricula for preparing students for the varied challenges they will confront throughout their lives. St. Timothy's offers a rich and highly individualized program with extensive resources in athletics, the arts, clubs, world affairs, and community service that capitalize on the talents and strengths of each student.

Each girl has an advisor who keeps track of her academic progress and personal growth and maintains a liaison with her parents. With a 5:1 student-teacher ratio, classes enroll, on average, 12 girls, ensuring each student individual attention and encouraging full participation in the learning process.

St. Timothy's curriculum currently offers the International General Certificate of Secondary Education (IGCSE) for Grades 9 and 10 in preparation for the International Baccalaureate (IB) program in Grades 11 and 12. IGCSE course offerings include French, Latin, Mandarin, Spanish; ESL (two levels), Coordinated Science I–II (chemistry, biology, physics); and Mathematics I–II. Students also undertake two years of humanities requirements and two years of visual and performing arts.

Juniors and seniors spend two years studying the IB curriculum, culminating in both internal and external exams for the IB diploma. IB course work in English draws on American and European literature, focusing on the different genres of fiction, non-fiction, poetry, and drama, including Shakespeare. In science, students may undertake comprehensive studies in their choice of biology or chemistry over a two-year period. Mathematics are offered at three ability levels ranging from practical applications to advanced college-level courses. World and European History provides a survey of world events in the 20th century with an emphasis on historiography and analysis of contemporary issues. The Foreign Language component intensifies French, Latin, Mandarin, or Spanish language studies in the context of history, culture, and daily living. IB Options enable students to round out their schedule with a choice of courses in visual arts, theater arts, economics, social and cultural anthropology, or a second foreign language or science. The Theory of Knowledge course involves girls in the pursuit of knowledge and truth utilizing their critical thinking and research skills.

College advising begins early and involves both the student and her parents. One hundred percent of St. Timothy's School girls attend college. In the last three years, graduates have been accepted at American University, Boston University, Brown, Bucknell, Carnegie Mellon, Columbia, Drexel, Goucher, Hamilton, Johns Hopkins, Lafayette, New York University, Peabody Conservatory, Pennsylvania State, Rutgers, Roanoke, Salve Regina, Smith, Swarthmore, Syracuse, Towson, Tufts, Vanderbilt, Washington and Lee, Wellesley, Wesleyan, Williams, and the Universities of California, Massachusetts, Pennsylvania, and Virginia, among other institutions.

STUDENT ACTIVITIES. St. Timothy's School provides a wide range of extracurricular opportunities that meet a variety of interests and abilities, involving students in leadership, community service, and social and athletic activities.

The riding program, headed by a professional horsewoman, is an integral component of the School's athletic offerings. Girls take part in competitive horse shows, fox hunting, combined training events, dressage, and trail and recreational riding. Varsity and junior varsity teams are formed in basketball, ice hockey, volleyball, squash, field hockey, cross-country, lacrosse, indoor soccer, softball, and tennis; fitness and dance are also available.

On-campus organizations include Amnesty International, Challenge 20/20, Choir, Bell Choir, two a cappella singing groups, Madrigals, literary magazine, yearbook, Dramat, Tour Guides, Chapel Club, Current Events, Model UN, Environmental Awareness, International Club, Equestrian, Shalom, and Social Services Clubs.

St. Timothy's School enjoys many time-honored traditions, among them the hard-fought Brownie-Spider basketball game that has been played just before Thanksgiving for over 100 years.

ADMISSION AND COSTS. St. Timothy's School welcomes girls who have high personal standards, leadership potential, and a good academic record. Candidates submit an application along with an essay. Acceptance is based on a personal interview, results of either the Secondary School Admissions Test or the Independent School Entrance Examination, personal recommendations from the student's math and English teachers and principal or advisor, a parent's statement, the student's transcript, a graded essay, and the completed application. The application fee is $45.

In 2007–08, boarding tuition is $39,000; day tuition is $23,000. Additional expenses include transportation, a $675 social activities fee, $400–$600 for books and academic supplies, approximately $250 for the required school uniform and $900–$2600 for the optional Riding Program. Financial aid of more than $1,500,000 is awarded to more than 40 percent of the student body.

Head of School: Randy S. Stevens
Academic Dean: Adam K. Man
Dean of Students: Jacqulyn Geter-Hunter
Director of Admission & Assistant Head of School: Patrick M. Finn
Associate Directors of Admission: Gina B. Finn, Robin DePaolis, & Leslie Lichtenberg
Director of College Counseling: Anne R. Mickle
Director of Advancement: B. Page Nelson
CFO & Business Manager: Anne Esposito
Director of Athletics: Kara Carlin

Sandy Spring Friends School 1961

16923 Norwood Road, Sandy Spring, MD 20860
Tel. 301-774-7455; Admissions Ext. 1; Fax 301-924-1115
Web Site www.ssfs.org; E-mail admissions@ssfs.org

Sandy Spring Friends School aims to offer a preeminent college preparatory program for pre-Kindergarten through Grade 12, with optional five- or seven-day boarding available in Grades 9 through 12. Sited on 140 wooded acres within 40 minutes of both Washington, D.C., and Baltimore, the School provides a stimulating and diverse environment that fosters leadership, promotes social awareness, and encourages intellectual and spiritual growth. Led by a dynamic faculty committed to inspiring high academic achievement, Sandy Springs Friends School provides a variety of opportunities for artistic expression in studio and performing arts housed in state-of-the-art facilities. The School's competitive athletic teams in both Middle and Upper School divisions follow a no-cut policy.

Founded in 1962 and under the care of the Sandy Spring Monthly Meeting of Friends, the School adheres to basic Quaker values, emphasizing stewardship of the environment, simplicity, and respect for the individual.

Sandy Spring Friends School is approved by the Maryland State Board of Education and is accredited by the Association of Independent Maryland Schools. It is a member of the Friends Council on Education and the National Association of Independent Schools.

THE CAMPUS. The 140-acre campus includes woods, a stream, a pond, meadows, and athletic fields. The plant includes a state-of-the-art science center; an expanded Lower School; a new Middle School building; a dormitory and dining hall; three major classroom buildings; an administration building; a new performing arts center with a fine arts wing; a new athletic complex that includes a fitness center, training room, and a 9000-square-foot gymnasium; a historic Meetinghouse (1881); and faculty housing. Yarnall Hall, a $1,750,000 resource center, houses a 25,000-volume library, another gymnasium, an observatory, classrooms, and computer lab.

THE FACULTY. Kenneth W. Smith, appointed Head of School in 1996, is a graduate of Trinity University (B.S.), Princeton Theological Seminary (M.Div., Th.M.), and Southern Methodist University (D.Min.).

There are 134 teachers and administrative staff. Approximately a dozen live on campus, most with their families. Faculty members hold baccalaureate degrees or higher. Faculty degrees were earned at such institutions as American, Bank Street College, Brown, Bucknell, Catholic University, Colgate, Dartmouth, Earlham, Florida Southern, Frostburg University, George Washington University, Georgia State, Harvard, Haverford, Hood, Kenyon, Longwood, Manchester College, Middlebury, Mount Holyoke, New York University, Pennsylvania State, Pierce, Princeton, Princeton Theological Seminary, Sarah Lawrence, Smith, Southern Methodist, Stanford, Swarthmore, Tufts, Virginia Polytechnic Institute, Williams, Yale, and the Universities of Chicago, London, Maryland, Minnesota, Oregon, Pennsylvania, and Wisconsin.

STUDENT BODY. In 2007–08, the School enrolled 558 students, with 187 in Lower School, 135 in Middle School, and 236 in Upper School. The boarding program enrolled 39 students from the Mid-Atlantic region as well as from several countries.

ACADEMIC PROGRAM. The curriculum at Sandy Spring Friends School is intended to prepare students not only for entering college, but also for being valuable citizens of the world. It stresses the challenge of Quaker values, academic excellence, and personal growth within a structured environment.

A typical Upper School daily schedule includes six academic periods, jobs, lunch, an activities period, and sports. The school day is from 8:00 A.M. to 3:20 P.M. with sports and activities after school. Boarding students are required to attend dinner at 6:00 P.M. and study hall from 7:30 to 9:30 P.M. The average class size is 15 with a faculty-to-student ratio of 1:8.

The Lower School encourages exploration and creativity and fosters caring interaction with others. Basic skills in reading and mathematics are taught sequentially, and children are encouraged to apply these skills to other life contexts, to think analytically, and to evaluate in both verbal and quantitative areas.

The Middle School (Grades 6–8) offers a curriculum of English, general mathematics and algebra, social studies, science, foreign language, art, music, and sports. The program encourages the development of academic skills, preparing students for the Upper School curriculum. Enrichment activities include field trips, art and music programs, and science activities.

The required academic load for an Upper School student is six courses. To graduate, students must earn 24 credits, including English 4, foreign language 3, history 3 (including

United States History), mathematics 3, science 3, electives 3, and fine arts 3. Additional noncredit requirements are participating in a physical activity each year and passing a semester course on Quakerism. Advanced Placement courses are available in Art History, Environmental Science, Music Theory, English, History, Calculus, Statistics, Chemistry, French, and Spanish. Full-year courses are English; French, Spanish; History; Algebra, Geometry, Pre-Calculus, Calculus, Statistics; Biology, Chemistry, Physics, Astronomy, Geology, Advanced Science; Art, Orchestra, Chorus; Theater; Modern Dance; and Wood Shop.

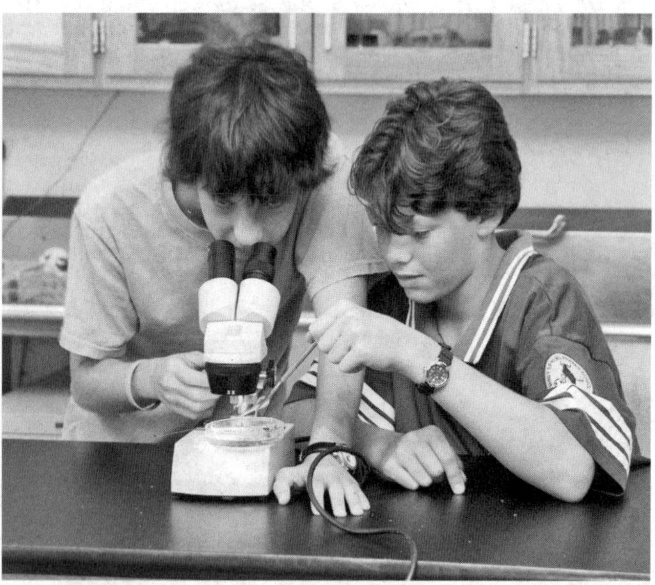

The English as a Second Language Program is open to students in Grades 9–12. Currently, 35 students are enrolled.

"Intersession" week in the spring gives students an opportunity to participate in off-campus activities that supplement the standard curriculum. Projects have included trips to Kenya, Brazil, and throughout Europe; a theater improvisation workshop; inner-city service projects in the District of Columbia, Baltimore, and New York; and numerous outdoor exploration activities.

In 2007, all of the 60 graduates entered college. They are attending such institutions as Bates, Bryn Mawr, Carleton, Colgate, Columbia, Drexel, Duke, Earlham, Frostburg, George Washington, Guilford, Harvard, Haverford, Hofstra, James Madison, Oberlin, St. Mary's College (Maryland), Spelman, Swarthmore, Tulane, Wesleyan, and the Universities of Delaware and Maryland.

STUDENT ACTIVITIES. A Town Meeting composed of students and faculty convenes regularly to discuss issues of importance to the school community. Students present many dramatic productions and perform in dance recitals and choral concerts. Involvement in some aspect of the sports program is mandatory. Interscholastic teams in baseball, lacrosse, soccer, tennis, golf, softball, track and field, cross-country, volleyball, and basketball compete with other preparatory schools in the Baltimore-District of Columbia area. Students may also participate in a variety of intramural sports.

Student participation in Quaker study centers and conferences is encouraged, and a community service requirement is part of the curriculum. Frequent trips are made to Washington, D.C., or Baltimore for shopping, films, and cultural events.

ADMISSION AND COSTS. The School accepts students whose backgrounds represent diverse social, economic, religious, and cultural experiences. Students should apply before January 15 to be considered for the following fall. Candidates must submit application forms, a school transcript, and a photograph (optional). A personal interview and academic references are also required, and there is a $60 application fee.

In 2007–08, tuition ranges from $16,900 to $18,250 in the Lower School, $20,200 in the Middle School, and $22,900 in the Upper School. Boarding tuition is $32,580 for five days and $39,750 for seven days. Tuition payment plans are available. In 2007, financial assistance was awarded to 25 percent of the student body.

Head of the Upper School: David Hickson
Head of the Middle School: Dana Harrison
Head of the Lower School: Lynn Darman
Assistant Head, External Relations: Karl Gedge
Dean of Students: Karen Cumberbatch
Coordinator of Admissions: Mary Mazzuca
Chief Financial Officer: Carmen Johnson
College Counselor: Victoria W. Garner
Director of Athletics: Stephen Powers

Severn School 1914

Water Street, Severna Park, MD 21146
Tel. 410-647-7700; Admissions 410-647-7701, Ext. 267
Fax 410-544-9451
Web Site www.severnschool.com; E-mail admissions@severnschool.com

Severn School, founded in 1914, is a coeducational day school for Grades 6–12, located 6 miles from Annapolis. Severn believes in educating the whole person in a student-centered school community and challenges its students to pursue excellence in character, conduct, and scholarship. The current enrollment is 594 students. Severn offers foreign languages, mathematics, science, English, history, fine and performing arts, Advanced Placement and honors courses, and independent study. There are over 20 sports teams and 35 clubs and activities for student participation. Severn's summer program includes academic study, computer training, SAT preparation, a day camp, and chess and sports camps. Tuition: $19,500. Financial Aid: $1,000,000. Molly M. Green '83 is Director of Advancement; Douglas H. Lagarde (College of William and Mary, A.B.; Harvard University, M.Ed.) was named Headmaster in 2006. *Middle States Association.*

Stone Ridge School of the Sacred Heart 1923

9101 Rockville Pike, Bethesda, MD 20814
Tel. 301-657-4322; Admission Ext. 321; Fax 301-657-4393
Web Site www.stoneridge.org; E-mail admissions@stoneridge.org

Stone Ridge is a Catholic, college preparatory day school serving 675 students, with girls in Junior Kindergarten–Grade 12 and boys in Junior Kindergarten–Kindergarten. As a member of the Network of Sacred Heart Schools worldwide, Stone Ridge commits itself to educate toward an active faith, respect for intellectual values, a social awareness, building of community, and personal growth. The School, known for its challenging curriculum, technology initiatives, competitive athletics, and community service, also offers publications and studio and performing arts to broaden students' academic experience. Extended-day and summer programs are offered. Tuition: $10,650–$20,320. Financial aid is available. Michelle McPherson is Director of Admission; Dr. Richard Barbieri is Interim Head of School. *Middle States Association.*

Thornton Friends School 1973

Upper School (Grades 9–12): 13925 New Hampshire Avenue, Silver Spring, MD 20904
Tel. 301-384-6672; Fax 301-879-8238
Web Site www.thorntonfriends.org
E-mail admissions@thorntonfriends.org
Middle School (Grades 6–8): 11612 New Hampshire Avenue, Silver Spring, MD 20904
Tel. 301-622-9033

Thornton Friends School is an intentionally small, progressive, college preparatory school in Silver Spring, Maryland. Thornton serves bright, creative students in Grades 6–12 who may be underachieving and seek a smaller, more nurturing environment in which to thrive. Classes average 8 students with a student-teacher ratio of 5:1. Guided by the Quaker values of integrity, community, diversity, respect, peace, simplicity, and service, Thornton's community-supported ambience makes study relevant and engaging. A required community service program enriches students, as do programs in music, art, and photography. Sports include soccer, tennis, basketball, and softball. Tuition: $19,750–$20,750. Financial Aid: $150,100. Norman Maynard (Upper School) and Marcy Seitel (Middle School) are Directors; Michael W. DeHart (University of Maryland, B.A.; Catholic University, M.S.W.) is Head.

Washington Waldorf School 1969

4800 Sangamore Road, Bethesda, MD 20816
Tel. 301-229-6107; Admissions Ext. 154; Fax 301-229-9379
Web Site www.washingtonwaldorf.org
E-mail llawson@washingtonwaldorf.org

One of more than 900 Waldorf (Rudolf Steiner) schools worldwide, this coeducational, nonsectarian school enrolls 275 students in Preschool–Grade 12. Students of various social, religious, and economic backgrounds comprise Washington Waldorf's diverse makeup. The rich curriculum and innovative instructional methods provide an education that addresses the needs of the whole child, working to develop clarity of thought, balance in feeling, and initiative in action. This academic, artistic, and practical program provides a continuum of education, in preparation for college, from the earliest grades through high school graduation. Interscholastic sports are offered for boys and girls. Tuition: $4000–$19,000. Lezlie Lawson is Enrollment Director; Natalie R. Adams is Faculty Chair. *Middle States Association.*

The Woods Academy 1975

6801 Greentree Road, Bethesda, MD 20817
Tel. 301-365-3080; Admissions Ext. 214; Fax 301-469-6439
Web Site www.woodsacademy.org
E-mail admissions@woodsacademy.org

A Catholic, coeducational day school enrolling 300 students from many faiths and nationalities, The Woods Academy has celebrated the education of mind, body, and spirit for over two decades. A Woods education begins in Montessori Preschool and concludes as graduating eighth-graders choose from a wide range of selective secondary schools. The academic program is enhanced by daily French or Spanish, technology, Chicago Math, hands-on laboratory science, computer labs, and an 8000-volume library. Activities include student government, sports, publications, theater arts, and community service. Extended care is offered. Tuition: $10,605–$16,180. Financial Aid: $25,000. Barbara B. Snyder is Director of Admission; Mary C. Worch (Trinity, B.A., M.A.) is Head of School. *Middle States Association.*

MASSACHUSETTS

The Academy at Charlemont 1981

The Mohawk Trail, 1359 Route 2, Charlemont, MA 01339
Tel. 413-339-4912; Fax 413-339-4324
Web Site www.charlemont.org; E-mail academy@charlemont.org

The Academy of Charlemont is a coeducational, college preparatory school enrolling 112 day students in Grades 7–12 and a postgraduate year. It is a closely knit community based on an honor code. The interdisciplinary curriculum is rigorous and challenging. Activities beyond the academic classroom include a full range of studio arts, choral and instrumental music, photography, performance and technical theater, computer studies, interscholastic and life sports, foreign exchanges, internships, and community service. Tuition: $17,900. Sandy Warren is Director of Admissions; Todd Sumner is Headmaster. *New England Association.*

Applewild School 1957

120 Prospect Street, Fitchburg, MA 01420
Tel. 978-342-6053; Fax 978-345-5059
Web Site www.applewild.org; E-mail admissions@applewild.org

Enrolling 290 day boys and girls from north central Massachusetts and southern New Hampshire in Kindergarten–Grade 9, Applewild celebrates its 50th year of academic excellence, the development of core values, and the social, physical, and emotional well-being of each student. The program is predicated on an understanding of children and offers an enriching and award-winning combination of traditional academic subjects coupled with "specials" such as art, wood shop, music, French, and physical education. The curriculum spirals in a well-planned way from Kindergarten to Grade 9. Students begin science with trained professionals in Kindergarten and choose French, Latin, or Spanish beginning in Grade 6. They can choose from interscholastic sports or fine or performing art mentor programs in Grade 7 and engage in developmentally appropriate community service options in K–9. Extended-day care is offered for all grades. Tuition: $13,761–$19,373. Financial aid is available. Terry Perlmutter is Director of Admission and Financial Aid; Christopher Williamson (Williams, B.A.; University of New Hampshire, M.A.) is Head of School. *New England Association.*

The Atrium School 1982

69 Grove Street, Watertown, MA 02472
Tel. 617-923-4156; Admissions Ext. 23; Fax 617-923-1061
Web Site www.atrium.org; E-mail sdean@atrium.org

Enrolling 115 boys and girls in Preschool through Grade 6, The Atrium School offers an integrated curriculum designed to blend and balance the intellectual, social, and creative needs of its students. Daily conduct is based on the principle of respect for self, for others, and for the environment. Small classes, each with two teachers, enable students to develop a sense of community while learning from one another. The School encourages and celebrates diversity, and strong parental and family involvement in the educational process is essential to the program. The after-school program is open to all students. Tuition: $16,500. Linda Echt is Director of Admissions; Stephen Middlebrook is Head of School.

Austin Preparatory School 1961

101 Willow Street, Reading, MA 01867
Tel. 781-944-4900; Admissions Ext. 17; Fax 781-942-0918
Web Site www.austinprepschool.org
E-mail kdriscoll@austinprepschool.org

Founded by the Augustinian Fathers, Austin Preparatory School is a coeducational, secondary day school in the Roman Catholic tradition, serving 700 young people from many religious, racial, and cultural backgrounds in Grades 6 through 12. In the Augustinian tradition of "one mind, one heart, intent on God," the Campus Ministry offers liturgies, communal prayer, days of recollection, and retreats to inspire spiritual growth in students of all faiths. The rigorous educational program is designed to equip students for success in higher education and in all other aspects of their lives. The curriculum is presented at five ability levels known as the Phase System, to accommodate students' varied college and career goals. Students who benefit from additional support are enrolled in Phase Two, while Phase Five features Advanced Placement and college-level courses. Among the activities are school government, academic honor societies, a literary magazine, a quarterly newspaper, theater, debate, chorus, band, language clubs, and 16 interscholastic athletics. Students are also involved in service outreach and assist in humanitarian efforts such as the World AIDS Project. Tuition: $12,300. Scholarships, financial aid, and sibling discounts are available. Kevin J. Driscoll is Director of Admission and Financial Aid; Paul J. Moran is Head of School. *New England Association.*

Bancroft School 1900

110 Shore Drive, Worcester, MA 01605
Tel. 508-853-2640; Admission Ext. 206; Fax 508-853-7824
Web Site www.bancroftschool.org; E-mail scranford@bancroftschool.org

Bancroft School is a coeducational, college preparatory day school enrolling 550 students in Kindergarten–Grade 12. Attracting families from nearly 60 Worcester-area cities and towns, Bancroft's mission is to provide a comprehensive, caring, and creative curricular and extracurricular program that fosters an experience of excellence for each student. Inspired students, a dedicated faculty, and engaged families thrive in Bancroft's diverse, safe, and supportive environment. Students have the opportunity to learn to embrace confidently and responsibly the moral and ethical challenges of being lifelong learners, teachers of others, and citizens of an increasingly complex global community. Tuition & Books: $11,700–$22,100. Financial Aid: $900,000. Susan Cranford is Director of Admission and Financial Aid; Scott R. Reisinger was appointed Headmaster in 1999. *New England Association.*

Belmont Day School 1927

55 Day School Lane, Belmont, MA 02478
Tel. 617-484-3078; Admissions Ext. 226; Fax 617-489-1942
Web Site www.belmontday.org; E-mail dbrissenden@belmontday.org

A few minutes from Boston, Belmont Day School offers a balance of strong academics, arts, athletics, and social competency skills to 265 children in Pre-Kindergarten–Grade 8. The challenging, supportive environment encourages the development of self-confidence, friendship, and mastery in an experientially based, individualized curriculum. The program emphasizes the joy of learning and integrates art, music, drama, woodworking, French, Spanish, technology, and physical education at all levels. After-school, extended-day, vacation, and summer session programs are offered. Financial aid is available to qualified applicants. Tuition: $16,000–$25,870. Deborah Brissenden is Director of Admissions; Lenesa Leana (Oberlin College, A.B.; University of Missouri, M.A.) is Head.

Belmont Hill School 1923

350 Prospect Street, Belmont, MA 02478-2662
Tel. 617-484-4410; Admissions Ext. 220; Fax 617-484-4688
Web Site www.belmont-hill.org; E-mail grant@belmont-hill.org

Belmont Hill School is a day and five-day boarding school enrolling 425 boys in Grades 7–12. In its effort to develop young men of character, the School seeks to combine a rigorous curriculum featuring traditional subjects taught by innovative faculty, with an outstanding art department and an extensive athletic program. Activities, many of which are coordinated with The Winsor School for Girls, include glee club, drama, debate, Student Council, and literary publications. A six-week, coeducational summer program is offered. Five-day Boarding Tuition: $35,410; Day Tuition: $29,530. Financial Aid: $2,300,000. Michael R. Grant is Director of Admission; Richard I. Melvoin (Harvard, A.B.; University of Michigan, M.A., Ph.D.) is Head of School. *New England Association.*

Berkshire Country Day School 1946

P.O. Box 867, Lenox, MA 01240
Tel. 413-637-0755; Admission Ext. 16; Fax 413-637-8927
Web Site www.berkshirecountryday.org
E-mail info@berkshirecountryday.org

Berkshire Country Day School seeks to provide a challenging and inspiring education in the finest liberal arts tradition. This coeducational school enrolls approximately 200 students, age 4–Grade 9. Steadfast in its commitment to learning in the spirit of inquiry and discovery, the school community encourages academic excellence, advancing each student's potential for well-rounded development and fostering responsive and responsible citizenship. The curriculum includes modern and classical languages, AP courses, visual and performing arts, and computer science. Among the activities are athletics, internships, community service, travel-study, and student government. Tuition: $9900–$18,700. Financial Aid: $600,000. Gray Jessiman is Director of Admission; Robert R. Peterson is Head of School. *New England Association.*

Berkshire School 1907

245 North Undermountain Road, Sheffield, MA 01257-9672
Tel. 413-229-8511; Admission 413-229-1003; Fax 413-229-1016
Web Site www.berkshireschool.org
E-mail admission@berkshireschool.org

Berkshire School in Sheffield, Massachusetts, is a coeducational, college preparatory school enrolling boarding and day students in Grades 9 through 12 and a postgraduate year. Sheffield lies in the Berkshire Hills, about 10 miles from the borders of New York State and Connecticut. The region is noted for its natural beauty and provides abundant opportunities for vigorous outdoor activities.

Berkshire School aims to provide students with the tools and skills needed to develop into mature, productive adults capable of achieving their best in college, in careers, and in all aspects of life. The academic and extracurricular programs are designed to guide and motivate each student intellectually, morally, and physically.

Berkshire School, a nonprofit, nondenominational institution guided by a 28-member Board of Trustees, is accredited by the New England Association of Schools and Colleges and holds membership in numerous educational organizations including the National Association of Independent Schools. Many of the 4100 alumni support the School through fund-raising, recruitment, and service on committees and advisory boards.

THE CAMPUS. The 500-acre campus, situated at the base of Mount Everett, offers woodlands, landscaped lawns, playing fields, and hiking trails.

Berkshire Hall, the primary academic facility built in 1930 and the centerpiece of the campus, is closed for renovations during the 2007–08 school year. Upon its reopening in the fall of 2008, Berkshire Hall will feature larger classrooms with state-of-the-art technology as well as new administrative offices, a two-story atrium, and a "great room" for student study and special functions. In the meantime, humanities classes will be held in modern, temporary modular classrooms wired for the most current technology. The science wing of Berkshire Hall has been refurbished and remains open. The James C. Kellogg Alumni Center, adjacent to the football field, houses administrative offices as well as a large meeting area used for half-time receptions and other events. Performing arts studios are housed in Memorial Hall, adjacent to Allen House, which contains the 430-seat Allen Theater and the radio station. The 43,000-volume Geier Library is fully computerized and provides additional classrooms and conference rooms. Other facilities include Dixon Observatory; the Thoreau House, an exact replica of the philosopher's cabin near Walden Pond; and the 18th-century Chase House, which contains the admission office.

The Athletic Center features full-size courts for basketball and volleyball, four international squash courts, and a fitness center. Scheduled to open in the fall of 2008 is the Multi-Purpose Indoor Athletic Facility, which includes two hockey rinks, one of which will also be used for performance space as well as training facilities and a fitness center. The Rovensky Field House, also used for indoor tennis and choral concerts, is the site of the current hockey rink. Other athletic facilities include new baseball and softball fields, an all-weather track, a lighted football field, and two synthetic-turf fields.

Students reside in single and double rooms in dormitories located in ten school buildings throughout the campus. Each room has its own phone line and direct access to the Internet.

THE FACULTY. Michael Maher was named Berkshire's 15th Head of School in 2004. Mr. Maher holds a bachelor's degree in political science from the University of Vermont and a master's degree in liberal studies from Wesleyan University. Before accepting his current position, he was a long-time administrator, teacher, and hockey coach. He and his wife, Jean, an admission officer and Spanish teacher at Berkshire, have three children.

The teaching faculty comprises 38 men and 23 women, the majority of whom live on campus. In addition to baccalaureates, they hold 25 master's degrees and 4 doctorates from such colleges and universities as Amherst, Bowdoin, Colby, College of the Holy Cross, Columbia, Connecticut College, Dartmouth, Georgetown, Harvard, Middlebury, Mount Holyoke, Rutgers, Tufts, Wesleyan, Yale, and the Universities of Connecticut, Massachusetts, Vermont, Virginia, and Washington.

Berkshire retains the services of four pediatricians, a nurse practitioner, four registered nurses, and two certified athletic trainers.

STUDENT BODY. In 2007–08, Berkshire School enrolled 336 boarding and 36 day students in Forms III–VI (Grades 9–12) and a postgraduate year. They come from 28 states and 23 countries.

ACADEMIC PROGRAM. The school year is divided into semesters, with vacations at Thanksgiving, in December, and in March. Marks are posted and sent to parents at the midpoint and end of each semester. Each student is paired with a faculty advisor who provides guidance, monitors academic progress, and serves as a liaison with the family. Classes, with an average of 12 students, are held six days a week, with abbreviated schedules on Wednesday and Saturday. Boarding students have two hours of study hall nightly.

Students typically carry five courses per semester. To graduate, they must complete four years of English; three years each of one foreign language, history including American and European History, and mathematics including Algebra I–II and Geometry; two years of laboratory science; and one year of visual or performing arts. Third and Fourth Formers must participate in two competitive sports a year; upperformers, in one. There are nonathletic alternatives that fulfill the competitive sport requirement. The community service program is integral to Berkshire life. Students must participate in on- and off-campus service options.

Among the required and elective courses are College Writing; Chinese I–IV, French I–IV, Latin I–IV, Spanish I–IV; Ancient and Medieval History, European History, American History, American Government, Economics, Constitutional Law; Comparative Religion, Mythology and Religion, Introduction to Philosophy, Ethics; Biology, Chemistry, Physics, Human Genetics, Environmental Science; Algebra I–II, College Algebra and Trigonometry, Precalculus I–II, Calculus AB/BC, Statistics I–II; 2-D Fundamentals, Drawing I–II, Ceramics I–III, Digital Art I–III, Music Synthesis I–III, Instrumental Ensemble I–III, and Chorus.

Advanced Placement courses are offered in 13 subjects, and upperformers in good standing may undertake independent study projects with faculty guidance. English as a Second Language is taught at the advanced level.

All students participate in a year-long program that underscores the School's core values: leadership, service, wellness, and conservation. All seniors and postgraduates take part in an intensive Leadership and Character Development program, while Fifth Formers engage in community service projects on and off campus. Fourth Formers devote the year to health and wellness, and Third Formers focus on conservation.

The 116 graduates of the Class of 2007 attend such four-year colleges or universities as American, Bard, Bates, Boston College, Boston University, Hamilton, Harvard, Lehigh, New York University, Northeastern, Syracuse, Trinity, Villanova, and the Universities of Massachusetts, New Hampshire, Vermont, and Virginia.

STUDENT ACTIVITIES. Their peers elect four representatives from each class to the student government, which provides a formal voice in school policy and in organizing school activities to benefit the entire Berkshire community.

Students publish a newspaper, a yearbook, and a biannual literary magazine; operate the School's FM radio station; and stage several major productions each year. Concert and choral groups, dance recitals, bands, and small ensembles are among other performing opportunities on campus.

Berkshire School competes in the Western New England Preparatory School Athletic Association. Forty-eight interscholastic teams in 27 sports include Division I boys' and girls' ice hockey, Division II crew, cross-country, soccer, basketball, alpine skiing, squash, golf, lacrosse, tennis, track and field, field hockey, softball, football, and baseball.

The Ritt Kellogg Mountain Program supports community, academic rigor, physical exercise, and learning in all aspects of school life. An experientially based education provides learning opportunities and activities that allow students to gain greater insight into themselves and the world around them. They have the opportunity to participate in canoeing, kayaking, rock/ice climbing, camping, snowshoeing, mountain biking, boat and bridge building, maple sugaring, and hiking on the Appalachian Trail, which abuts the campus.

ADMISSION AND COSTS. Berkshire welcomes young people of good character and ability who demonstrate the potential to benefit from and contribute to the academic and extracurricular opportunities offered at the School. Acceptance is based on previous school transcripts, a student essay, recommendations from math and English teachers, and results of standardized testing. A personal visit and interview are also required. Applications are accepted until January 31 for March 10 notification.

After that date, admissions are on a rolling basis, space permitting. The application fee is $50 for students residing in the U.S. and $100 for candidates living outside the U.S.

Boston University Academy 1993

One University Road, Boston, MA 02215
Tel. 617-353-9000; Fax 617-353-8999
Web Site www.buacademy.org; E-mail admissions@buacademy.org

Boston University Academy seeks to provide an exceptional education for students with genuine intellectual curiosity, strong academic abilities, and diverse interests. A coeducational day school of 150 students, the Academy is located on the Boston University campus and offers highly motivated students in Grades 9–12 an "unparalleled preparation for the college experience." Engaging with dedicated teachers in a caring community, students first immerse themselves in a classically based core curriculum and then continue their intellectual interests through course work at Boston University. Students take as many as two University classes a semester in Grade 11 and up to four in Grade 12. To graduate, all students much complete an independently researched senior thesis under the guidance of a university professor as well as 20 hours of community service each year. Activities include A Cappella, Art Club, competitive athletic teams, Chamber Orchestra, Literary Magazine, Model UN, robotics and science teams, and Student Council. Tuition & Fees: $25,849. Financial aid is awarded to 33 percent of families. Michelle M. Cannon is Director of Admission and Financial Aid; James Berkman (Harvard, A.B., J.D.; Oxford, M.A.) is Head of School.

Brimmer and May School 1939

69 Middlesex Road, Chestnut Hill, MA 02467
Tel. 617-566-7462; Admissions 617-738-8695; Fax 617-734-5147
Web Site www.brimmer.org; E-mail admissions@brimmer.org

Brimmer and May, enrolling 395 students in Pre-Kindergarten–Grade 12, is celebrating its 128th year as a college preparatory day school. Located 3 miles west of Boston, the School uses the city's cultural and educational resources to expand classroom experiences. Brimmer and May has opened a new Middle School/Upper School Academic Center, which includes a new library, classrooms, and state-of-the-art science labs. Strong academic programs, computer technology, creative arts, and physical education are emphasized at all levels; 8 Advanced Placement courses are offered in the Upper School. Middle and Upper School students participate in team sports. Community service is required. Extended-day care is available for Lower School students. Brimmer and May is a member of the Coalition of Essential Schools. Tuition: $15,900–$29,100. Financial Aid: $1,600,000. Barbara Shoolman is Director of Admissions; Anne C. Reenstierna is Headmistress. *New England Association.*

Brooks School 1926

1160 Great Pond Road, North Andover, MA 01845-1298
Tel. 978-686-6101; Admission 978-725-6272; Fax 978-725-6298
Web Site www.brooksschool.org; E-mail admission@brooksschool.org

Brooks School provides a coeducational, college preparatory program for 355 students on a 250-acre campus overlooking Lake Cochichewick. Small classes allow students to work closely with teachers, fostering a relationship that is at the core of the warm, close-knit community. With a challenging academic curriculum that includes 17 Advanced Placement courses, Brooks also offers opportunities to study abroad in Europe and Africa. A unique summer science program places juniors in labs at MIT and Harvard and on the coast of Canada in Labrador. On the stage and in the gallery, visual and performing arts are an integral part of school life, while in the athletic fields, numerous teams have won New England or league championships in recent years. Boarding Tuition: $40,730; Day Tuition: $30,200. Financial Aid: $2,700,000. Kevin Breen is Acting Director of Admission; Lawrence W. Becker is Headmaster. *New England Association.*

Brookwood School 1956

Brookwood Road, Manchester, MA 01944
Tel. 978-526-4500; Admissions Ext. 6203; Fax 978-526-9303
Web Site www.brookwood.edu; E-mail admissions@brookwood.edu

Brookwood, a coeducational day school enrolling 404 students in Prekindergarten–Grade 8, stands on two foundation stones: a demanding program of academics, athletics, and arts and a commitment to sociomoral and affective education designed to foster self-esteem, self-discipline, respect for others, and an appreciation of both competition and cooperation. Team sports, community service, student publications, field trips, multicultural assembly programs, and student government supplement the curriculum. There are before-school and after-school REACH programs. Tuition: $12,590–$20,045. Financial Aid: $1,026,500. Barbara W. DiGuiseppe is Admissions Director; John C. Peterman (Wittenberg, B.A.; Loyola University [Chicago], M.Ed.) was appointed Headmaster in 1992.

Buckingham Browne & Nichols School 1974

80 Gerry's Landing Road, Cambridge, MA 02138
Tel. 617-547-6100; Admissions 617-800-2136; Fax 617-547-7696
Web Site www.bbns.org; E-mail admissions@bbns.org

Formed by the merger of The Buckingham School (1889) and The Browne & Nichols School (1883), this college preparatory day school enrolls 966 boys and girls in Beginners–Grade 12. The School, through its rigorous academic program, concern for the individual, and wide array of artistic, athletic, and leadership activities, aims to produce creative, independent thinkers who will act responsibly in the larger world in which they will live. Students in Grade 12 may spend the spring term off campus on a special-interest project. Tuition: $17,040–$31,440. Financial Aid: $4,800,000. George Mitchell is Director of Enrollment Management; Rebecca Upham (Middlebury College, B.A.; Columbia University, M.A.) was appointed Head of School in 2001. *New England Association.*

Cambridge Friends School 1961

5 Cadbury Road, Cambridge, MA 02140
Tel. 617-354-3880; Admission Ext. 104; Fax 617-876-1815
Web Site www.cfsmass.org

Cambridge Friends is a Quaker coeducational day school serving 220 students in Pre-Kindergarten–Grade 8. Established by the Friends Meeting at Cambridge, it has a socioeconomically, racially, and culturally diverse student body and remains committed to social justice and equity. School goals are to promote critical thinking skills and individualized cooperative learning; integrate the arts, sciences, and mathematics; and nurture the spiritual and intellectual growth of students. Tuition: $19,000–$22,215. Tuition Assistance: $848,588. Merle Jacobs is Admission Director; Mary Newmann is Head of School.

Cape Cod Academy 1976

50 Osterville-West Barnstable Road, Osterville, MA 02655
Tel. 508-428-5400; Admissions Ext. 216; Fax 508-428-0701
Web Site www.capecodacademy.org
E-mail admissions@capecodacademy.org

Cape Cod Academy, a coeducational college preparatory school serving 400 day students in Kindergarten–Grade 12, offers a challenging education that emphasizes the liberal arts and sciences, underscored by the values of honesty, respect, and compassion. Small classes and an 8:1 student-teacher ratio provide personal support and encouragement from faculty. Interscholastic athletics, drama, chorus, music, and outdoor club are among the activities. A new Science Building houses six classroom/labs, project and conference rooms, a 65-seat auditorium, and an atrium with a Foucault pendulum. Tuition: $17,000–$19,900. Financial aid is available. Steve DiPaolo is Director of Admissions; Clark Daggett (Johns Hopkins, B.A.; Drew University, M.Litt.) is Head of School. *New England Association.*

The Carroll School 1967

25 Baker Bridge Road, Lincoln, MA 01773
Tel. 781-259-8342; Admissions Ext. 3023; Fax 781-259-8852
Web Site www.carrollschool.org; E-mail admissions@carrollschool.org

Encompassing Grades 1–8, The Carroll School provides education for 270 bright boys and girls with language-based learning differences. With only 6–8 children per class, qualified specialist instructors and tutors use proven teaching methods, specific strategies, and remedial support services to develop students' maximum potential and equip them for success in mainstream schools. Guest speakers and diverse enrichment activities, including Bounders, Carroll's modified version of Outward Bound, enhance classroom instruction. Extended-day activities and a summer program are offered. Tuition: $33,800. Sue Kingman is Director of Admission and Transition; Stephen Wilkins is Head of School. *New England Association.*

Charles River School 1911

6 Old Meadow Road, Box 339, Dover, MA 02030
Tel. 508-785-0068; Admissions 508-785-8213; Fax 508-785-8290
Web Site www.charlesriverschool.org
E-mail mearley@charlesriverschool.org

Charles River School, enrolling 215 children in Pre-Kindergarten–Grade 8, has a strong commitment to a balance of academic, creative, physical, and social growth within a progressive school environment that celebrates differences. The program engages children in active learning and encourages them to explore, assume responsibility, and gain self-awareness and respect for others. The interdisciplinary curriculum emphasizes critical thinking, writing, reading, and math skills as well as science, social studies, computer, world language and culture, art, music, and physical education. After-school sports and extended-day programs are offered. Tuition: $17,700–$25,900. Financial Aid: $550,000. Marion L. Earley is Director of Admissions; Catherine H. Gately (Boston University, B.A., M.Ed.) is Head.

The Chestnut Hill School 1860

428 Hammond Street, Chestnut Hill, MA 02467
Tel. 617-566-4394; Fax 617-738- 6602
Web Site www.tchs.org; E-mail admissions@tchs.org

The Chestnut Hill School, a coeducational day school located in a residential section of Newton, encompasses a preschool program for ages 3–4, an all-day Kindergarten, and Grades 1 to 6. More than 250 children are enrolled, with two sections at each grade level. Because of the comparatively small size and the favorable student-teacher ratio, Chestnut Hill is able to offer a rigorous academic program that embraces diversity and promotes community. Special subjects are art, computers, library, music, physical education, science, Spanish, and woodworking. Before- and after-school programs are optional. Tuition: $17,550–$24,750. Financial aid is available. Wendy W. Borosavage is Director of Admission; Steven Tobolsky (Princeton, A.B.; Columbia University Teachers College, M.A., Ph.D.) is Head.

The Clark School 1978

487 Locust Street, Danvers, MA 01923
Tel. 978-777-4699; Admissions Ext. 12; Fax 978-777-7116
Web Site www.clarkschool.com; E-mail clarkschool@clarkschool.com

The Clark School is a coeducational, preparatory school for 75 gifted and talented children in Kindergarten–Grade 10. The School seeks to encourage self-expression in academic and artistic endeavors and to foster creative problem-solving skills. In a multiage learning environment, each student pursues an individualized program. Additionally, science, history, geography, Spanish, and physical education are offered. Other activities include weekly electives and swimming lessons, skiing, drama, poetry, and field trips. Tuition: $14,000–$18,000. Heather Tripp is Director of Admissions; Jeffrey Clark is Head of School.

The Commonwealth School 1957

151 Commonwealth Avenue, Boston, MA 02116
Tel. 617-266-7525; Fax 617-266-5769
Web Site www.commschool.org; E-mail admissions@commschool.org

THE COMMONWEALTH SCHOOL in Boston, Massachusetts, is a day school enrolling boys and girls in Grades 9–12. The School is in the Back Bay area of Boston and is served by city and commuter buses and trains.

The School was founded in 1957 by Charles Merrill, who was Headmaster until his retirement in 1981. Commonwealth aims to give its students the ability to write forceful and effective English; a historical perspective on human nature and human affairs; well-grounded proficiency in mathematics and science; wide experience in literature and the art of reading; mastery of at least one foreign language; a rich field for creativity in the arts; and vigorous training in and enthusiasm for athletic endeavor.

The School is a nonprofit organization whose 31-member Board of Trustees includes faculty and alumni/ae members and nonvoting student and faculty representatives. The endowment includes more than $10,500,000 in productive funds.

Commonwealth is accredited by the New England Association of Schools and Colleges and is a member of the National Association of Independent Schools and other organizations.

THE CAMPUS. Commonwealth's location in the heart of Boston, two blocks from the Boston Public Library and a short distance from the Museum of Fine Arts, encourages students to take advantage of the city's resources. Two adjoining 19th-century townhouses accommodate classrooms; library; laboratories; art and ceramics studios; a darkroom; lunchroom/gymnasium; student lounge; and offices. The School uses nearby athletic facilities for squash, basketball, fencing, and dance as well as playing fields of the Metropolitan District Commission and the Community Boating Club.

THE FACULTY. William D. Wharton (Brown, B.A., M.A.) was appointed Headmaster in 2000. Since joining the Commonwealth faculty in 1985, Mr. Wharton has taught history, Latin, Greek, ancient philosophy, and world religions; he has also served as Faculty Trustee, College Advisor, Acting Head, and Director of Admissions. He has received grants from the Council for Basic Education and was a recipient of a Teacher-Scholar Grant from the National Endowment for the Humanities.

There are 23 full-time teachers and administrators who teach, 10 men and 13 women. They hold 26 baccalaureate, 18 master's degrees, and 13 doctorates from Barnard, Boston College, Boston University, Brown, Federal Institute of Technology (Switzerland), Harvard, Johns Hopkins, Massachusetts Institute of Technology, McGill, Mount Holyoke, New York University, Oklahoma State, Pitzer, Princeton, Radcliffe, Stanford, Swarthmore, Tufts, Wesleyan, Williams, Yale, and the Universities of California (Berkeley), Cambridge (England), Kentucky, Massachusetts, Minnesota, Oxford (England), Paris, and Washington. There are also 8 part-time instructors who teach history, theater, ceramics, dance, jazz music, English, Spanish, health, and photography and printmaking. Four of the 8 hold master's degrees; 2 hold doctorates.

Among the benefits for full-time faculty are health, dental, disability, and life insurance; a retirement plan; sabbaticals; professional development grants; tuition remission at Commonwealth for faculty children; and partial reimbursement for study undertaken to improve professional skills.

There are always several faculty members at Commonwealth who are trained in first aid; several hospitals are nearby.

STUDENT BODY. In 2007–08, Commonwealth enrolled 150 boys and girls as follows: 34 in Grade 9, 39 in Grade 10, 43 in Grade 11, and 34 in Grade 12. Most students come from Boston and surrounding communities. Those born abroad have come from as far away as Algeria, Chile, China, Colombia, Russia, and the Philippines.

ACADEMIC PROGRAM. The school year runs from early September to early June. There are two-week vacations in December and March and several long weekends. The average class size is 12 students. Grades, teachers' comments, and advisers' letters are sent to parents three times per year; for freshmen and for students in academic difficulty, a fourth grading period is observed.

The school day is divided into seven 40-minute periods. Full-credit courses meet four times a week and half-credit courses two to three times a week. On average, students carry five academic credits and two art credits. Free periods are intended for study. One-on-one conferences with teachers are a regular part of every student's experience. Additional tutorial help is available for an extra fee.

Students must complete a minimum of 16 academic credits for graduation, including four years of English, three of mathematics, three of science, three of foreign language, and three of history, one of which must be American history. Additional requirements each year include one course in the arts and participation in two of the three sports seasons. Freshmen and seniors also take half-credit courses with the Headmaster in Language and Ethics. Ninth-graders enroll in a City of Boston course for one term and health and community workshops for another. All students must perform 70 hours of community service before the beginning of their junior year.

Once a week, the entire School meets for an assembly, often with public figures. Each grade holds its own weekly meeting, and there is an all-school meeting each Tuesday.

Among the full-credit courses offered are English 9–12; Ancient History, Medieval World History, United States History, Modern European History, Philosophy, Economics, The Rise & Fall of Communism; French I–IV, Latin I–V, Spanish I–IV; Biology I–III, Chemistry I–II, Physics I–III; and Algebra II, Geometry, Calculus, Applied Calculus, and Theoretical Calculus.

Courses that receive half credit include Spacetime Physics, Abstract Algebra, Linear Algebra, Multivariable Calculus, Probability and Statistics; Chemistry III: Introduction to Organic Chemistry, Computer Programming I–III, Structural Mechanics; African Literature, Fiction Writing, Literature of the Bible, Modernism, Poetry, Short Story, The World of the Novel; China, Nationalism, African History, African-American History, Constitutional Law, Current History, History of Japan, Latin American History, Art History, City of Boston, Economics; Film Analysis, Reading in Ethics, Greek I–II, Philosophy, Chamber Music, Composition, Conducting, Jazz Theory I–II, and Music Theory I–III; and for art credit, Artists' Books, Drawing and Painting, Life Drawing, Printmaking, Jazz Ensemble, Acting 1–4, Advanced Dance, Ceramics, Photography, Chorus, Chorale, Orchestra, and Chamber Music.

Twice a year, the entire School adjourns to a camp in southern Maine for four days. Students and teachers take hikes, prepare meals, perform skits, play games and sports, and hold activities and discussion sections on subjects ranging from maskmaking to mushroom identification to foreign policy.

During Project Week, younger students can become involved in activities outside the scope of regular schoolwork. Students participate in projects ranging from hospital work to teaching to working in a senator's Washington office. In the spring, seniors engage in similar projects that last for a whole month.

Commonwealth participates in three-week exchange programs with schools in France and Spain. Financial aid is provided for all students demonstrating need.

The 36 graduates of the Class of 2007 are attending such institutions as Barnard, Bates, Boston College, Brown, Carleton, Carnegie Mellon, Harvard, Haverford, McGill, Oberlin, Occidental, Princeton, Reed, Rice, Sarah Lawrence, Smith, Trinity, Tufts, Vassar, Wesleyan, and the Universities of California (Berkeley, Davis, Santa Cruz), Chicago, Pennsylvania, Texas, and Toronto.

STUDENT ACTIVITIES. All students help clean up after lunch and recycle trash as part of the jobs program. Two nonvoting student representatives are elected to the Board of Trustees each year. Students tutor other students, give assemblies, publish the yearbook and literary magazine, and plan dances and the prom. They join the debate team, science team, chess club, Glee Club, Improv Club, Commonwealth Cares, and Model UN.

Commonwealth teams compete interscholastically in soccer, basketball, squash, sailing, fencing, and Ultimate Frisbee. All sports are open to all grades and to both boys and girls.

Traditional events include the Senior-Freshman Lunch, Ninth-Grade Cookout, New Parents' Evening, Parent-Teacher evenings for each grade, fall and spring Parents' Association meetings, Alumni/ae Reunions in various cities, Impromptu Day, Skate into Vacation, Fall Open House, Beach Day, two choral concerts, dance and jazz concerts, two theater productions, and a spring art show.

ADMISSION AND COSTS. Commonwealth seeks boys and girls of character and intelligence, without regard to race, color, religion, or national or ethnic origin, who are willing to work hard for a good education. Applicants are asked to submit recommendations, transcripts, and Secondary School Admission Test scores. An interview with the applicant and parents and a full-day visit by the applicant are also required. Applications for fall admission must be completed by January 1. The School accepts new students later in the year if places remain.

In 2007–08, tuition is $27,405, including lunches, with additional expenses of $640 for books, $370 for the two weekends in Maine, and a $740 activities fee. Scholarship aid of $904,700 was given to approximately 32 percent of the student body. A Technology Grant Program for students receiving financial aid helps in purchasing a computer. All grants are made on the basis of financial need.

Headmaster: William D. Wharton
Director of Admissions: Helene Carter
Director of Studies: Mallory Rome
Director of Student Life: Mary Kate Bluestein
College Counselor: Fern Nesson
Consulting Psychologist: Debbi Offner
Director of Athletics: Meagan Kane
Business Manager: Diane Morris
Director of Development: Tim Monroe
Director of Communications: Janetta Stringfellow

Cushing Academy 1865

39 School Street, P.O. Box 8000, Ashburnham, MA 01430-8000
Tel. 978-827-7000; Admission 978-827-7300; Fax 978-827-6253
Web Site www.cushing.org; E-mail admission@cushing.org

This coeducational, college preparatory school enrolls 450 students, primarily boarders, from 27 states and 27 nations. Encompassing Grade 9–Postgraduate, Cushing Academy's curriculum is designed to shape students' minds and character in a learning environment marked by friendliness, respect, and diversity. Advanced Placement in 12 subjects, challenging electives, the creative and performing arts, English as a Second Language, independent study, and off-campus internships enhance the program. Students take part in school government, honor societies, community service, musical ensembles, drama, dance, publications, and 23 competitive sports. Boarding Tuition: $39,950; Day Tuition: $28,100. Deborah A. Gustafson is Interim Director of Admission; Dr. James Tracy is Headmaster. *New England Association.*

Dana Hall School 1881

45 Dana Road, Wellesley, MA 02482
Tel. 781-235-3010; Admission Ext. 2202; Fax 781-235-0577
Web Site www.danahall.org; E-mail admission@danahall.org

Dana Hall is a college preparatory school enrolling 465 girls from around the globe in Grades 6–12, including 135 boarders from Grade 9 upward. The School's mission is to provide an excellent liberal arts education designed to accommodate the unique learning needs of young women. AP courses are offered in all disciplines, and college-credit courses are available at neighboring Wellesley College. Resources and special faculty assist students who benefit from additional support. A Senior Project and 20 hours of community service are required. Private instruction in voice and 13 musical instruments is optional. Girls take part in leadership groups such as Proctors, Peer Educators, and Senate as well as in a wide array of extracurricular opportunities including Amnesty International, gospel choir, Big/Little Sisters, newspaper, yearbook, Students Against Destructive Decisions, and new Latin American and Asian Clubs. Among the athletic offerings is a 22-member equestrian team. Travel-study exchanges bring Dana Hall girls to destinations in the U.S., Europe, and Australia. Boarding Tuition: $42,163; Day Tuition: $31,907. Financial Aid: $2,200,000. Wendy Sibert Secor is Director of Admission; Mrs. Blair Jenkins is Head of the School. *New England Association.*

Dedham Country Day School 1903

90 Sandy Valley Road, Dedham, MA 02026
Tel. 781-329-0850; Fax 781-329-0551
Web Site www.dedhamcountryday.org; E-mail etretter@dcds.net

Dedham Country Day School enrolls 245 boys and girls in Pre-Kindergarten–Grade 8. With close teacher-student rapport and an emphasis on excellence in traditional academics, the School seeks to develop independent thinking and personal responsibility. Art, music, drama, shop, and physical education, including team sports for upper grades, are offered at all levels. Spanish begins in Grade 4, Latin in Grade 6. Computer instruction is offered in all grades. Extended Day and summer camp are available. All-inclusive Fees: $17,540–$26,500. Financial Aid: $235,000. Ellen Tretter is Director of Enrollment Management; Nicholas S. Thacher (Yale University, A.B.; Balliol College [Oxford], M.Phil.) was appointed Head in 2005.

Derby Academy 1784

56 Burditt Avenue, Hingham, MA 02043
Tel. 781-749-0746; Admission Ext. 46; Fax 781-740-2542
Web Site www.derbyacademy.org; E-mail admissions@derbyacademy.org

Founded in 1784 to provide equal education for girls and boys, Derby Academy enrolls 315 students, ages 4–14, in Prekindergarten–Grade 8. The school's mission is to bring together motivated students, talented faculty, and a challenging program for a well-balanced education. The curriculum is designed to prepare students for the rigors of competitive secondary schools and allow them to develop individual strengths in the arts and athletics. Summer offerings include The Young Explorers Club for ages 4–6, a creative arts camp for ages 7–14, an academic program, and several sports camps. Tuition: $16,900–$22,500 (all-inclusive). Financial Aid: $645,000. Jay K. Sadlon is Director of Admission; Andrea Archer (Warwick University, M.Sc.; Oxford University, M.A.) was appointed Head of School in 2007.

Dexter School 1926

20 Newton Street, Brookline, MA 02445-7498
Tel. 617-522-5544; Fax 617-522-8166
Web Site www.dexter.org; E-mail admissions@dexter.org

Enrolling 434 day boys in Pre-Kindergarten–Grade 12, Dexter develops each student's mental and physical abilities and helps him form good social, moral, and spiritual attitudes and habits. Basic academic skills and traditional subjects, including Latin in Grades 6–12, are emphasized and enhanced by classes in science, computer, art, shop, and music. The Clay Center for Science and Technology offers comprehensive science programs and advanced study in astronomy using seven research-grade telescopes, including a 25-inch f/9.6 Ritchey-Chretian reflecting telescope similar in design to the Hubble telescope. Marine Science studies are held at the School's Briarwood Marine Science Center on Cape Cod. All students participate in athletics using the gym, indoor pool, two indoor ice rinks, and five playing fields. Interscholastic sports begin in Grade 7. Summer programs include day camp, hockey, sci-tech, and enrichment camps at Dexter and marine science and sailing programs at Briarwood. A sister school, Southfield, enrolls 368 girls on the same 36-acre campus. Tuition: $18,200–$28,880. Financial Aid: $2,666,000. Christopher Overbye is Director of Admissions; William F. Phinney is Headmaster.

Eaglebrook School 1922

Pine Nook Road, Deerfield, MA 01342
Tel. 413-774-7411; Admissions 413-774-9111; Fax 413-774-9119
Web Site www.eaglebrook.org; E-mail admissions@eaglebrook.org

Eaglebrook School, enrolling 281 boarding and day boys from 28 states and 18 countries in Grades 6–9, aims to help each boy develop his innate talents, to improve the skills needed for the challenges of secondary school, and to establish values that will allow him to become a thoughtful, compassionate person. The core curriculum places equal emphasis on academic excellence and character. English, math, science, history, and foreign languages are enhanced by technology, music, drama, and visual

arts. Boys take part in athletics, Student Council, Mountain Club, publications, and community service. English as a Second Language and a coeducational summer session are available. Boarding Tuition: $39,150; Day Tuition: $25,000. Theodore J. Low is Director of Admissions; Andrew C. Chase is Headmaster. *New England Association.*

The Eliot Montessori School 1971

Six Auburn Street, South Natick, MA 01760
Tel. 508-655-7333; Fax 508-655-3867
Web Site www.eliotmontessori.org
E-mail lbackman@eliotmontessori.org

The Eliot Montessori School enrolls 115 boys and girls as day students in Kindergarten–Grade 8 (ages 4.10–14). Montessori philosophy is the foundation of the School's approach and program. Specially trained teachers discern and nurture each child's strengths and talents. Eliot's carefully prepared, child-centered environment and unique learning materials help students develop on many different levels. Through the Eliot Montessori School's integrated, rigorous, and diverse program curriculum, children develop the knowledge, self-confidence, and curiosity about learning that will last a lifetime. Tuition: $16,400–$17,200. Laura Backman is Director of Admissions; Bill O'Hearn is Head of School.

Falmouth Academy 1977

7 Highfield Drive, Falmouth, MA 02540
Tel. 508-457-9696; Fax 508-457-4112
Web Site www.falmouthacademy.org
E-mail mearley@falmouthacademy.org

Falmouth Academy is a coeducational college preparatory school enrolling 210 day students in Grades 7–12. The rigorous core curriculum focuses on traditional liberal arts and sciences, with a strong emphasis on reading and writing in all subjects. Science classes utilize the resources of the nearby Woods Hole oceanographic and marine biology facilities, while the art-in-humanities program integrates the fine arts with course work across the disciplines. Students perform in drama and musical productions and engage in a wide range of activities from publications and landscaping to academic clubs and athletics. Tuition: $19,550. Financial Aid: $694,000. Michael Earley is Director of Admissions; David C. Faus was appointed Headmaster in 2005. *New England Association.*

Fayerweather Street School 1967

765 Concord Avenue, Cambridge, MA 02138
Tel. 617-876-4746; Admission Ext. 703; Fax 617-520-6700
Web Site www.fayerweather.org; E-mail info@fayerweather.org

Fayerweather Street School was founded by parents and educators to provide alternative schooling that affords child-centered, project-based education within a safe, supportive, stimulating environment. The School celebrates and promotes diversity in its student body of 205 boys and girls in Pre-Kindergarten–Grade 8. Mixed-age classes allow for a wider range of companions and learning partners. The curriculum is enriched by music, drama, library, Spanish, woodshop, art, resource room, physical education, field trips, and a weekly School Meeting. Extended care and vacation programs are optional. Tuition: $13,700–$21,925. Financial aid is available. Cynthia Bohrer is Admission Director; Edward Kuh is Head of School.

The Fenn School 1929

516 Monument Street, Concord, MA 01742-1894
Tel. 978-369-5800; Admission 978-318-3606; Fax 978-371-7590
Web Site www.fenn.org; E-mail lkugler@fenn.org

The Fenn School is a day school enrolling 300 boys in Grades 4–9. It seeks to offer sound academic training in an intellectually stimulating atmosphere tempered with an understanding of the emotional needs of the early adolescent. Students develop basic skills at the fourth- and fifth-grade levels and enter a fully departmentalized program in Grade 6. Spanish and Latin begin in Grade 6. The School has a long tradition of supporting its challenging academic program with extensive art courses and a competitive athletic program. Graduates are accepted at leading secondary schools nationwide. Tuition: $24,070–$28,710. Financial Aid: $706,300. Lori T. Kugler is Director of Admissions and Financial Aid; Gerard J.G. Ward (Boston University, B.A.; Harvard, Ed.M.) is Headmaster.

Gann Academy 1997

333 Forest Street, Waltham, MA 02452-4717
Tel. 781-642-6800; Fax 781-642-6805
Web Site www.gannacademy.org

Gann Academy is a Jewish, college preparatory day school enrolling 309 young men and women from diverse Judaic expressions in Grades 9–12. The school combines a rigorous liberal arts curriculum with intensive studies of the Jewish faith, history, culture, and Hebrew language. Its mission is to promote study of the Torah, to form a "sacred community" within the Jewish people, and to fulfill the Commandments and mend the world. The academic program develops critical thinking and a lifelong love of learning. General studies are infused with Judaic concepts and points of view centered on the rich intellectual, cultural, and historical legacies of the Jewish people. Juniors may spend a trimester in Israel to deepen their faith through first-hand encounters with Israelis and visits to Jerusalem, the Negev Desert, Galilee, and other Old Testament sites. English, math, lab sciences, social studies, and computer science form the core of the secular curriculum, while Jewish Studies courses are offered at several levels to accommodate students new to Hebrew as well as those more proficient. Students engage in numerous activities and compete in eight sports. Tuition: $24,650. Mindy Harris is Director of Admissions; Rabbi Marc Baker is Head of School.

Glen Urquhart School 1977

74 Hart Street, Beverly Farms, MA 01915
Tel. 978-927-1064; Admission Ext. 15; Fax 978-921-0060
Web Site www.gus.org; E-mail rnance@gus.org

Glen Urquhart School, enrolling 230 boys and girls as day students in Kindergarten–Grade 8, creates an environment where each student is encouraged to fully develop his or her knowledge, imagination, and character. The School believes that a combination of all three is essential in developing intelligent, creative people who are emotionally mature, socially involved, and well prepared for their future. Field trips, special events, and visiting artists are part of the program. Spanish is taught in all grades, and Latin is taught in Grades 7 and 8. Team sports begin in Grade 6. An extended-care program is available, and a summer camp emphasizing creative arts runs for six weeks. Tuition: $13,400–$20,050. Financial aid is available. Leslie Marchesseault is Director of Admission; Raymond Nance is Head.

Great Barrington Rudolf Steiner School 1971

35 West Plain Road, Great Barrington, MA 01230
Tel. 413-528-4015; Admission Ext. 106; Fax 413-528-6410
Web Site www.rudolfsteinerschool.org
E-mail info@rudolfsteinerschool.org

One of more than 1000 Waldorf schools worldwide, Great Barrington Rudolf Steiner School is committed to developing academic and personal excellence, a broad base of knowledge, and a depth of experience in every child. The coeducational day school enrolls 200 students in Nursery to Grade 8 in a classical education designed to prepare them for the challenges of higher learning. The arts and humanities are integrated with the sciences as students are encouraged to become independent thinkers capable of understanding the interrelationship among all disciplines. Modern languages, drama, outdoor education, and sports enrich the program. Tuition: $12,100. Financial Aid: $490,000. Ms. Kathi Weinstein is Director of Admission; Marilyn Ruppart is Faculty Administrator.

Groton School 1884

P.O. Box 991, Groton, MA 01450-0991
Tel. 978-448-3363; Admission 978-448-7510; Fax 978-448-9623
Web Site www.groton.org; E-mail admission_office@groton.org

Groton, a coeducational, college preparatory school affiliated with the Episcopal Church, enrolls 313 boarders and 40 day students from many religious, racial, and cultural backgrounds in Grades 8–12. Set on a 350-acre campus 40 miles from Boston, Groton offers a rigorous liberal arts program taught by a distinguished and dedicated faculty. A required laptop program, modern and classical languages, Advanced Placement courses, the arts, and diverse electives round out the curriculum. Among the numerous activities are men's and women's sports, drama, music, community service, and leadership groups. Boarding Tuition: $42,040; Day Tuition: $31,530. Financial Aid: $3,400,000. Ian Gracey is Director of Admission; Richard B. Commons is Headmaster. *New England Association.*

Hillside School 1901

Robin Hill Road, Marlborough, MA 01752-1099
Tel. 508-485-2824; Admissions 508-303-5731; Fax 508-485-4420
Web Site www.hillsideschool.net; E-mail admissions@hillsideschool.net

Hillside School in Marlborough, Massachusetts, an independent, nonsectarian school, has been enrolling boys as boarding and day students in Grades 5 through 9 for more than 100 years. Marlborough (population 37,444) is 30 miles west of Boston and 17 miles east of Worcester. The rural, wooded areas surrounding the School provide opportunities for many outdoor pursuits, while the nearby cities offer ample cultural, recreational, and historic attractions.

Hillside School offers a strong, fundamental education within a nurturing family environment. Caring, qualified faculty aim to instill core values of honesty, respect for others, compassion, and determination with the goal of developing each boy's academic strengths, civic and social awareness, and personal standards. Beginning in 1925, Hillside has been the recipient of generous assistance from the Daughters of the American Revolution, one of only six schools in the nation to be endowed by this organization.

A nonprofit institution since 1907, Hillside is guided by a 24-member, self-perpetuating Board of Trustees. It holds membership in the National Association of Independent Schools, the Independent School Association of Massachusetts, and other professional organizations. The Hillside Parents Association is instrumental in organizing special events and financial support for the School.

THE CAMPUS. The Assabet River flows through the Hillside School's 200-acre wooded campus, which has its own spring-fed pond, a working farm, and 6 acres of athletic fields. The academic hub of the School is centered in Stevens Hall, which contains 14 classrooms, WiFi computer access, and the science laboratory. Linked to Stevens Hall is the Tracy gymnasium/auditorium. The Student Center houses the dining room, school offices, and the state-of-the-art Wick Tutorial Center. Boys reside in five faculty-supervised dormitories. A new addition to the campus is the Academic and Health Center (March 2008). The center features fitness rooms, an infirmary, a wrestling/multipurpose room, nine classrooms, three of which are science labs, and offices for health and wellness and counseling programs.

THE FACULTY. David Z. Beecher was appointed Headmaster in 1998. An honors graduate of The Choate School, Mr. Beecher earned a B.A. degree in American Studies and Education from Lake Forest College, where he was named a Lila B. Frank Scholar. Prior to coming to Hillside, he served as Director of Admission & Financial Aid at Fay School and Wilbraham & Monson Academy, both in Massachusetts. Mr. Beecher also spent six years at Berkshire School as Dean of Students, teacher, dorm parent, coach, and member of the Admissions and Development departments. At Yale University, he served as Athletic Administrator and assistant men's varsity ice-hockey coach. Mr. Beecher and his wife, Carrie, have two daughters, Madeline and Haley.

In addition to Mr. Beecher, there are 70 staff members, including 30 teachers and administrators who teach. Faculty are chosen for their ability to motivate students through their teaching strategies and their commitment to helping young people reach their full potential. In addition to teaching, they are coaches, dorm parents, study hall supervisors, and advisors to the various clubs and campus groups.

A registered nurse staffs the Drinkwater Infirmary. Complete hospital facilities are available 3 miles away in Marlborough.

STUDENT BODY. In 2007–08, Hillside School enrolls 141 boys as boarders and day students in Grades 5–9. The boys come from 15 states and 10 foreign countries.

ACADEMIC PROGRAM. The school year is divided into trimesters, beginning in September and concluding in early June, with vacations at Thanksgiving, Christmas, and in the spring. Grades are mailed to parents each trimester, and two parent-teacher conferences are scheduled each year.

Students who require extra academic support take part in the tutorial program, with small groups working under the supervision of several learning specialists. Tutorials include organizational and study skills and language, math, and social skills development. On Sunday through Thursday, boarding students attend supervised evening study halls.

Hillside School embraces the four core values of honesty, compassion, respect, and determination as the guiding principles for overseeing student behavior and achievement. Shades of Hillside Blue, a system based on these values, is designed to give students and families comprehensive and timely feedback about a boy's overall performance at school. During a biweekly period, boys are evaluated in all areas of school life using three shades of blue. Royal blue, the school color, signifies that a boy consistently meets established expectations. Sky blue signifies that he meets expectations with some assistance, and navy blue indicates that he needs frequent guidance in attempting to meet expectations. Each student has an advisor who reviews this feedback with the boy and his family. The advisor works in conjunction with the Dean of Students and other faculty in helping boys to set and meet appropriate individual goals on an ongoing basis.

A typical school day begins at 6:30 A.M., with breakfast served for boarders at 7:15. Day students arrive on campus by 8:00 A.M. Classes are held five days a week, with seven 50-minute periods scheduled from 8:00 A.M. to 3:30 P.M., followed by athletic practices and the Outdoor Program. After dinner and evening study hall, students enjoy free time with open gym time, board games, an Open House with the Headmaster in his home, and other recreational activities. "Lights out" is between 9:00 and 10:00 P.M., depending on age and dorm "shade" level.

Hillside School recognizes the importance of committed faculty, small classes, and a highly structured program as factors in developing the student's self-confidence, self-esteem, individual thinking, and decision-making ability. Students in Grades 5 and 6 learn in self-contained classrooms, with a core curriculum consisting of mathematics, language arts, social studies, and reading, and specialized instruction in art, science, and music.

In Grades 7–9, the curriculum includes English, history, science, math, studio art, music, farming, and French, Latin, or Spanish.

The Honors Seminar Program at Hillside is for eighth and ninth graders. The boys are selected by faculty to challenge top students and to better prepare them for competitive secondary schools. In 2006, seminars were The Writing in Mathematics and The Myths of the Settling of the American West, for Grades 8 and 9 respectively.

The Leadership Training Program is required of all grades to learn teamwork and leadership skills. With the new low-ropes course, students are able to incorporate skills they have acquired, both by leading and listening to their peers.

Responding to concerns about school violence in America, a Peace Initiatives course allows students to review essays and ideas about how to promote peace within our society. Also, Hillside has incorporated a special health and wellness focus across the entire curriculum to enhance students' well-being and development.

Excellence in academics, athletics, citizenship, and self-improvement is recognized by several awards and named scholarships. Among these are the E. Sherwin Kavanaugh Memorial Sportsmanship Award, Mentor of the Year, the Moody Robinson Award for excellence in English, the Dorothy Willard Award for improvement in math, and the Warren I. and Marion F. Higgins Award for outstanding contributions to the farm program by a returning student.

Among past secondary school choices were Bancroft, Brewster Academy, Cambridge School of Weston, Concord Academy,

Cushing, Dublin, Eagle Hill, Hebron, The Hill School, Holderness, Lawrence Academy, Marvelwood, Middlesex, New Hampton, Noble and Greenough, Pomfret, Portsmouth Abbey, St. Andrew's, St. Mark's, St. Thomas More, Tabor, Tilton, Vermont Academy, and Wilbraham & Monson.

STUDENT ACTIVITIES. All students must take part in a sport or athletic activity in each trimester. Boys compete interscholastically in soccer, cross-country, basketball, hockey, wrestling, track and field, baseball, and lacrosse.

Boys selected to participate in the Farm Program live in their own dorm and take responsibility for rising early each morning to feed and water the animals.

The Outdoor Program features downhill skiing, snowboarding, hiking, canoeing, mountain biking, and sailing. On the weekends, students enjoy faculty-supervised activities including swimming, fishing, ice- and roller-skating, and sledding. The School also arranges trips throughout New England to high school and college sporting events, movies, museums, and bowling. Other groups include the newspaper, the Drama Club, the yearbook, Sudoku, and Chess Society.

ADMISSION AND COSTS. Hillside School welcomes boys of average to above-average intelligence who will benefit from a supportive, structured environment. Many applicants have not performed to their potential, either academically or socially. Candidates are admitted on the basis of past school transcripts, standardized test results, psychological/educational evaluations, and three teacher recommendations. The application fee is $50.

In 2007–08, boarding tuition is $39,950 for five days and $44,400 for seven days; tuition for day students is $25,650.

Head of School: David Z. Beecher
Associate Head: Arthur Goodearl
Dean of Academics: Rich Meyer
Director of Development: Emily Kent
School Counselors: Jena Adams, Abby Pettee, Nathan Boston & Alf Wilson
Chief Financial Officer: Ed Gotgart
Director of Athletics: Mike Foster
Dean for Parents: Harry Worrall
Director for Admission & Financial Aid: Kristen Naspo
Associate Dean of Faculty & Curriculum: Matthew Laliberte

Holy Name Central Junior/Senior High School 1942

144 Granite Street, Worcester, MA 01604
Tel. 508-753-6371; Fax 508-831-1287
Web Site www.holyname.net
E-mail jnorgren@worcesterdiocesek12.org

Holy Name is a coeducational day school founded by the Sisters of Saint Anne and operating under the auspices of the Roman Catholic Diocese of Worcester. Enrolling 742 students from many faiths and denominations in Grades 7 through 12, Holy Name provides a quality Catholic education combined with strong religious and ethical values within a structured, disciplined environment. Studies in theology focus on the Old and New Testaments, liturgy, the sacraments, and social justice. The college preparatory curriculum centers on a strong foundation in English, mathematics, sciences, French and Spanish, and social sciences. Business courses, including computer programming and technology, diverse offerings in the visual and performing arts, and a well-rounded extracurricular program are also key components of a Holy Name education. Graduates go on to selective colleges and universities nationwide. Among the activities are National Honor Society, student government, publications, dramatic productions, vocal and musical groups such as chorus and jazz band, and a wide range of interscholastic sports for men and women. Tuition: $6120; Extras: $160. Jackie Norgren is Director of Admissions; Edward Reynolds is Headmaster.

Lawrence Academy 1793

Powder House Road, Box 992, Groton, MA 01450
Tel. 978-448-6535; Fax 978-448-1519
Web Site www.lacademy.edu; E-mail admiss@lacademy.edu

Lawrence Academy's coeducational boarding and day program enrolls 395 students in Grades 9–12 from 14 countries and 14 states in a rigorous yet innovative college preparatory curriculum. Students are encouraged to assume leadership roles and value individual differences. Computers and the arts are integral to the program. Winterim, a two-week adventure term, promotes experiential learning. Daily advisor contact, Internet access, English as a Second Language, and state-of-the-art music recording studio, Sony language lab, athletic complex, a new 44-bed dorm, and a new academic building enhance the program. Boarding Tuition: $41,630; Day Tuition: $31,800. Financial Aid: $2,000,000. Tony Hawgood is Director of Admissions and Financial Aid; Scott Wiggins is Head of School. *New England Association.*

The Learning Project 1973

107 Marlborough Street, Boston, MA 02116
Tel. 617-266-8427; Fax 617-266-3543
Web Site www.learningproject.org; E-mail tlp@learningproject.org

Enrolling 112 day boys and girls in Kindergarten through Grade 6, The Learning Project seeks to promote in children a deep concern for others and a healthy respect for diversity. Character education shares equal emphasis with a strong foundation in core skills as vital tools for academic and personal excellence. Small and diverse by design, The Learning Project accommodates students of varying abilities and provides close personal attention and support to each youngster. Cross-grade programs encourage friendships with all ages and contribute to a familial environment. Many graduates attend Boston Latin and other independent secondary schools. After-school and extended day programs are available. Tuition: $15,700–$16,300. Financial aid is available. Michael McCord is Head of School; Pauline Hargreaves is Director of Enrollment and Academics.

Lesley Ellis School 1919

41 Foster Street, Arlington, MA 02474
Tel. 781-641-5987; Admission 781-641-1346; Fax 781-641-1052
Web Site www.lesleyellis.org; E-mail admission@lesleyellis.org

Lesley Ellis School enrolls 165 boys and girls in Preschool–Grade 5. In a safe, supportive, progressive environment, the School provides a strong academic program to promote cognitive, social, and creative development and to foster joy and enthusiasm in learning. A strong arts program is integrated into the curriculum. Small classes are grouped according to age and developmental level. A multicultural, antibias approach helps students to respect, appreciate, and celebrate diversity. Parental involvement is important to the mission of the School. Before and Afterschool, Vacation, and Summer Programs are offered. Financial aid is available to qualified applicants. Tuition: $7575–$16,680. Tricia Moran is Director of Admission; Deanne Benson (North Park University, B.A.; Lesley University, M.Ed.) is Head of School.

Lexington Christian Academy 1946

48 Bartlett Avenue, Lexington, MA 02420
Tel. 781-862-7850; Admissions Ext. 140; Fax 781-863-8503
Web Site www.lca.edu; E-mail admissions@lca.edu

Founded by leaders of Boston's business and professional community, Lexington Christian Academy is a college preparatory day school enrolling 345 boys and girls in Grades 6–12. A curriculum that integrates faith and learning in every subject includes courses in creative writing, music theory and composition, computer, and Christian studies. Drama, music, athletics, and a summer day camp are available. The Academy conducts

an Interim Program in March when students take week-long courses or trips that allow for concentrated study and experiential learning. Tuition: $16,950–$18,975. Financial Aid: $800,000. Jill C. Schuhmacher is Director of Admissions; Mark Davis is Headmaster. *New England Association.*

The Meadowbrook School of Weston 1923

10 Farm Road, Weston, MA 02493
Tel. 781-894-1193; Admissions Ext. 227; Fax 781-894-0557
Web Site www.meadowbrook-ma.org
E-mail salpert@meadowbrook-ma.org

Meadowbrook, a nationally recognized School of Excellence, enrolls 286 boys and girls in Junior Kindergarten–Grade 8. A mission-driven school, it seeks to help students achieve excellence in academics and to develop honesty, courtesy, and respect for others. The curriculum is challenging, innovative, and integrated. A second language begins in Junior Kindergarten, with added language choices starting in Grade 5. A wide range of arts and computer studies are offered at all levels. Leadership training, field trips, and an athletic program are among the activities. After-school and summer programs are available. Detailed information is offered on the web site. Tuition: $17,215–$24,970. Financial Aid: $616,085. Barbara T. Vincent is Director of Admissions; Stephen T. Hinds was appointed Headmaster in 1986.

Miss Hall's School 1898

492 Holmes Road, Pittsfield, MA 01201
Tel. 413-443-6401; Admission 800-233-5614; Fax 413-448-2994
Web Site www.misshalls.org; E-mail info@misshalls.org

Miss Hall's, enrolling 195 young women from 18 states and 19 countries in Grades 9–12, aims to inspire girls to pursue the highest standards of learning and character; to contribute to the common good; and to seek a purposeful life based on honor, respect, and authenticity. The college preparatory curriculum, including honors and Advanced Placement courses, is enhanced by two nationally recognized programs: Horizons, an off-campus community service/internship program, and the Girls' Leadership Project, an action research initiative. Additional resources include a learning center, ESL, athletics, the arts, and extracurriculars. Boarding Tuition: $39,800; Day Tuition: $23,500. Financial Aid: $1,700,000. Kimberly Boland '94 is Director of Admissions; Jeannie Norris is Head of School. *New England Association.*

Montrose School 1979

29 North Street, Medfield, MA 02050
Tel. 508-359-2423; Admissions Ext. 315; Fax 508-359-2597
Web Site www.montroseschool.org
E-mail pkeefe@montroseschool.org

Parents and educators founded Montrose School to provide a challenging academic program integrated with the Christian values that develop sound character and prepare students for life. Enrolling 140 day girls in Grades 6–12, the School offers a classical liberal arts curriculum, including selected Advanced Placement courses, options in Spanish and French, and Catholic theology and philosophy courses. Classes in the fine arts are also offered. Cocurricular activities include newspaper, yearbook, drama, chorus, speech team, Student Council, the National Honor Society, athletics, and other clubs. Tuition: $14,300–$16,500. Financial aid is available. Patricia M. Keefe is Director of Admissions; Heather Roy is Associate Director of Admissions; Dr. Karen E. Bohlin (Boston College, B.A.; Boston University, Ed.D.) is Head.

Nashoba Brooks School 1980

200 Strawberry Hill Road, Concord, MA 01742
Tel. 978-369-4591; Admission Ext. 129; Fax 978-287-6038
Web Site www.nbsc.org

Nashoba Country Day School (founded 1958) and The Brooks School of Concord (1928) merged in 1980 as an elementary day school. Enrolled are 154 boys and girls in Preschool–Grade 3 and 156 girls in Grades 4–8. The School strives to recognize each student's contributions to the community, whether they be academic, artistic, dramatic, or athletic. Art, music, physical education, Spanish, and Latin are included in the curriculum. Tuition: $16,670–$26,410. Jean Stahl Heaton is Director of Admission; E. Kay Cowan (Manhattanville College, M.A.) is Head of School.

The Newman School 1945

247 Marlborough Street, Boston, MA 02116
Tel. 617-267-4530; Fax 617-267-7070
Web Site www.newmanboston.org; E-mail pridge@newmanboston.org

THE NEWMAN SCHOOL in Boston, Massachusetts, is a college preparatory day school enrolling boys and girls in Grades 9–12. The School is situated in the city's Back Bay, within a few blocks of significant cultural and historic institutions, where students and faculty find special resources to enrich their academic work. With its downtown location, the School is easily accessible by subway, bus, or car.

Founded in 1945 as The Newman School for Boys and since transformed into a coeducational institution, the School shapes its program in harmony with the vision of Cardinal John Henry Newman, the 19th-century British cleric who emphasized the relationship between faith and reason and whose writings set standards for liberal education. The Newman School strives to provide a rigorous educational experience that encourages students to be open-minded, to grow intellectually, and to take an active role in their own cultural and moral development. The aim is to prepare students with a solid academic background and the confidence, flexibility, and integrity to succeed in a complex world.

The Newman School is governed by a Board of nine Trustees, including alumni and parents. It is accredited by the New England Association of Schools and Colleges and holds membership in the Association of Independent Schools of New England and other professional organizations.

THE CAMPUS. The main school building at 245–247 Marlborough Street houses classrooms, science labs, and some special facilities including a computer lab and a 2000-volume school library. The library collection consists mainly of reference materials and nonfiction carefully selected to support the curriculum. In addition, all students must hold a Boston Public Library card, and they are introduced as freshmen to the main library three blocks away. The School librarian teaches a course in Library Research Skills in which students learn to access databases provided through the Boston Public Library web site. Adjacent to the School's library is the Newman Computer Lab with 16 workstations. All classrooms are equipped with wireless capacity to enable teachers to use the computers without going to the Computer Lab. Twelve wireless laptops are available for student use on a daily basis.

Art classes and individual students take advantage of the nearby Gardner Museum and the Museum of Fine Arts as well as the Newbury Street art galleries to enrich their studies; The Newman School also maintains an affiliation with the Copley Society of Art. The entire school community attends a professional theater performance every year.

The School rents athletic fields and tennis and basketball courts from the city and private organizations for home games and practices.

THE FACULTY. J. Harry Lynch, a graduate of College of the Holy Cross (B.A.) and Northeastern (M.B.A.), is President and Headmaster.

The full-time teaching faculty includes 21 men and women. They all hold bachelor's degrees, and 7 hold advanced degrees from Berklee College of Music, Boston College 4, Boston State, Boston University 2, Bowdoin, Bucknell, Colby, Connecticut College, Dartmouth, Gordon, Harvard, John Paul II Institute,

Northeastern, St. Anselm, Simmons, State University of New York (Binghamton), Thomas Aquinas, Tufts 2, and the Universities of Massachusetts 2, New Hampshire 2, and Provence. Faculty members serve as mentors, coaches, and advisors to students and to their activity groups. Professional guidance counselors help students with a variety of issues.

STUDENT BODY. The Newman School enrolls approximately 240 boys and girls from all parts of Metropolitan Boston as well as students from 27 foreign countries such as Brazil, Germany, Indonesia, Italy, Morocco, Russia, Saudi Arabia, and others. The School admits students of any race, color, religion, and national or ethnic origin.

ACADEMIC PROGRAM. The academic year is divided into semesters, and each semester includes four marking periods. At the end of each quarter, grade reports are mailed home. Academic alert reports are mailed at any time when faculty observe poor performance by the student. Classes meet on a six-day rotating schedule with all classes meeting five times within the cycle. Most classes are 45 minutes in length, but some are double periods lasting 90 minutes. The day begins at 8:15 A.M. and ends at 2:40 P.M. A mandatory school meeting takes place at 9:50 A.M. when daily announcements are made and individual students, teachers, and staff members may address the community. Additional studies, athletics, activities, and extra help begin at 2:45 P.M. Freshmen and other new students have a monitored homework session daily from 2:45 to 3:30 P.M. to help them with the transition to Newman. This continues for about four weeks until the first academic progress reports are issued. Students in good standing at that time may be relieved of the obligation.

All students must complete a total of 22 credits, taking a five-course load in all semesters. These must include 4 in English, 4 in mathematics, 2 in foreign language, 3 in social studies, 3 in laboratory science, 1 in visual arts, and 5 electives. A demonstrated proficiency in computer science and completion of a technology portfolio are also necessary. International students take English as a Second Language at intermediate and advanced levels.

Among the courses are English 9–12, American Studies/Literature, Writing Workshop, Basic Literature, The Writing Process, Creative Writing, British Literature, Modern Drama and Poetry, The Bible as Literature, The Classical Tradition, The Study of Theater; French 1–4, Spanish 1–4, Latin 1–4; World Cultures, Western Civilization, American Studies/American History, U.S. History, Twentieth Century America, U.S. Government and Politics, African-American Studies, Anthropology, Law/Politics/Society; Moral Reasoning/Ethics, Political Science, Psychology, The History of Boston, The World's Religions; Algebra 1–2, Geometry, Trigonometry, Calculus; Biology, Chemistry 1–2, Physics, Ecology/Marine Biology, Field Biology, Conservation Biology, Anatomy and Physiology, Technology, Computer Science; and Art and Music Integration, Fine Arts, Studio Art, Gallery Methods, and Theater. Honors courses are available in most subjects, and Advanced Placement courses are offered in English, Government and Politics, Calculus, Biology, and Computer Science. Qualified students may enroll in courses at nearby colleges and earn credit for both high school and college records.

Guidance seminars for small groups are conducted on a monthly basis to help students with academic planning. In the junior and senior years, these seminars focus on the college application process and the transition to college. Nearly all students at Newman go on to further education. Members of the Class of 2006 are currently enrolled at Boston University 2, Brandeis, Bryant, Clark, Colgate, Dean, Emmanuel 2, Manhattan, Massachusetts College of Art, Mount Ida, Newbury 3, Northeastern, North Shore Community College, Oberlin, Parsons, Providence, R.J. Reynolds Community College, Rochester, Roger Williams, St. John's (New York) 2, Salem State, Simmons, Suffolk 2, Tufts, Wagner, Washington & Lee, Wentworth, Wheelock, Worcester Polytechnic Institute, and the Universities of Arkansas, British Columbia, Colorado, Massachusetts 8, Michigan, New England, Vermont 2, and Victoria. Two students are enrolled at Japanese universities.

STUDENT ACTIVITIES. Students elect eight of their peers to the Student Council, which organizes activities throughout the year and works to enhance the quality of student life.

Other activities include National Honor Society, Key Club, Peer Tutoring, Prom Committee, International/American Friends Club, Junior Achievement, Literary Magazine, Yearbook, Drama Workshop, Shakespearean Society, and Classic Film, Outdoor Adventure, Recycling, Science/Math, and Strategic Game Clubs.

The Newman School is a member of the Mass Bay Independent League and the Girls Independent League and fields teams for interscholastic competition in soccer, tennis, crew, boys' and girls' basketball, baseball, tennis, and girls' lacrosse.

ADMISSION AND COSTS. The Newman School seeks to enroll young men and women in Grades 9–12 who have the ability and motivation to be active participants in a rigorous educational program. Applicants are evaluated on the basis of prior school records, a personal essay, entrance examination or SSAT or PREP scores, and a teacher recommendation. A full-day visit to the School, with a parent, is recommended. A $40 fee payment should accompany the application.

Tuition for the 2007–08 school year is $12,400. International student tuition is $19,500. Scholarships and financial aid are available.

Dean of Administration: Karen Briggs
Dean of Studies: Daniel Ohman
Dean of Students/Director of Guidance: Tamara Walsh
Admissions Counselor: Jackie Glandon
Registrar: Patricia Lynch
Director of Development: Susan Hepler
Alumni Relations Officer: Louise Merrigan
Buildings Supervisor: Frank Hartigan

Newton Country Day School of the Sacred Heart 1880

785 Centre Street, Newton, MA 02458
Tel. 617-244-4246; Admission Ext. 4721; Fax 617-965-5313
E-mail admissions@newtoncountryday.org

Newton Country Day School is an independent, college preparatory, girls' day school enrolling 380 students in Grades 5–12. The school offers a rigorous curriculum, which includes a full honors and Advanced Placement program. In keeping with the

Sacred Heart tradition, the School educates to five goals: a personal and active faith in God, respect for intellectual values, social awareness, community building and service, and personal growth. Exchange programs with other Sacred Heart schools worldwide are available. Tuition: $29,375. Financial Aid: $1,580,000. Mary Delaney is Director of Admission; Sr. Barbara Rogers (Manhattanville, B.A. 1974; Yale, M.B.A. 1988) was appointed Headmistress in 1989. *New England Association.*

Noble and Greenough School 1866

10 Campus Drive, Dedham, MA 02026-4099
Tel. 781-326-3700; Admission 781-320-7100; Fax 781-320-1329
Web Site www.nobles.edu; E-mail admission@nobles.edu

Noble and Greenough is a coeducational college preparatory school enrolling 550 five-day boarding and day students in Grades 7–12. It aims to provide a rigorous program to stretch academic abilities and foster curiosity, involvement, self-reliance, honesty, and a commitment to others. Intellectual skills and the use of language and technology in effective communication are emphasized. All students participate in an afternoon program including athletics, performing arts, or community service. Boarding Tuition: $35,000; Day Tuition: $30,600. Financial Aid: $2,300,000. Jennifer Hines is Dean of Enrollment Management; Robert P. Henderson, Jr. (Dartmouth, B.A. 1980, M.A.L.S. 1989), was appointed Head of School in 2000. *New England Association.*

The Park School 1888

171 Goddard Avenue, Brookline, MA 02445
Tel. 617-277-2456; Fax 617-232-1261
Web Site www.parkschool.org

Park is a coeducational day school serving a diverse student body from the Boston metropolitan area. Located on a 25-acre wooded campus, Park enrolls 515 students in Nursery–Grade IX. Small classes, rigorous academics, and close contact with parents are emphasized. Three sections of 15–16 children at each grade level ensure individual attention. Music, art, and drama are integral to the program. Activities include interscholastic sports and service learning. Park offers a wide range of summer programs. Tuition: $15,870–$27,800. Financial Aid: $1,739,000. Cynthia A. Harmon is Director of Admission; Dr. Jerrold I. Katz (Harvard, Ed.D.) was appointed Head of School in 1993.

Phillips Academy 1778

180 Main Street, Andover, MA 01810-4161
Tel. 978-749-4000; Admission 978-749-4050; Fax 978-749-4068
Web Site www.andover.edu; E-mail admissions@andover.edu

Phillips Academy, known familiarly as Andover, was founded during the American Revolution by Samuel Phillips, Jr., to educate "youth from every quarter." Andover is a leading college preparatory school in the New England tradition, serving 1083 young men and women in Grade 9–Postgraduate as boarding and day students from the U.S. and over 30 world nations. The broad curriculum encompasses more than 300 courses in the liberal arts, sciences, and humanities, taught by faculty committed to both students and to the subjects they teach. AP and honors courses, independent study, overseas exchanges, state-of-the-art resources, and world-class facilities on a 550-acre campus are hallmarks of an Andover education. Students are involved in school government, community service, publications, drama and music groups, a wide range of special-interest organizations, and teams in 30+ sports. Andover is the only American secondary school to include two U.S. presidents

among its alumni. Boarding Tuition: $37,200; Day Tuition: $29,000. Financial Aid: $12,800,000. Jane F. Fried is Dean of Admission; Barbara Landis Chase is Head of School. *New England Association.*

Pine Cobble School 1937

163 Gale Road, Williamstown, MA 01267
Tel. 413-458-4680; Admission Ext. 15; Fax 413-458-8174
Web Site www.pinecobble.org; E-mail ljl.becker@pinecobble.org

Pine Cobble School, enrolling 165 boys and girls as day students in Nursery–Grade 9, provides a rigorous liberal arts curriculum designed to instill in each child a lifelong passion for learning. Within a caring environment, students of varying academic abilities acquire a firm foundation in core subjects in readiness for the challenges of higher education. Small classes, dedicated teachers, and enrichment activities such as community service, math and science fairs, and Latin and French studies are cornerstones of the program. Students participate in drama and sports, including skiing. A summer session is optional. Tuition: $10,600–$14,900. Financial Aid: $275,000. Linda J. L. Becker is Director of Admissions and Placement; Nicholas M. Edgerton (Brown, A.B.; Columbia, M.A.) is Headmaster.

The Rivers School 1915

333 Winter Street, Weston, MA 02493-1040
Tel. 781-235-9300; Fax 781-239-3614
Web Site www.rivers.org; E-mail info@rivers.org

A college preparatory day school enrolling 432 boys and girls in Grades 6–12, Rivers challenges its students with high academic standards, while also emphasizing personal development in a community atmosphere. The curriculum includes honors courses and 15 Advanced Placement courses across the disciplines. In addition to meeting academic requirements, students must give time to athletics, the arts, activities, and community service. Focus on the individual is augmented by the 1:8 faculty-student ratio and an average class size of 12. Tuition: $30,500. Financial Aid: $2,138,000. Gillian Lloyd is Director of Admission and Financial Aid; Thomas P. Olverson is Head of School. *New England Association.*

Riverview School 1957

551 Route 6-A, East Sandwich, MA 02537
Tel. 508-888-0489
Web Site www.riverviewschool.org

RIVERVIEW SCHOOL, a coeducational, residential school in East Sandwich, Massachusetts, provides a caring, structured setting for students with complex language, learning, and cognitive disabilities, scoring within the 70–100 range. The School is committed to developing student competence and confidence in academic, social, and independent living skills.

Located on Route 6-A on Cape Cod, Riverview is 60 miles from both Boston and Providence. The School's seaside location offers students extensive cultural, recreational, and environmental activities from which to choose.

Celebrating its 50th anniversary in 2007, Riverview School was founded in 1957 by William M. Janse with the aim of providing an academic, social, and residential environment for students with complex learning needs. The School continues to provide a structured and supportive program today in an effort to help students acquire the skills necessary to become self-sufficient adults who can contribute to society.

Governed by a 21-member Board of Trustees, Riverview was incorporated as a nonprofit institution in 1958 and holds the original License Number One from the Office for Children of the Commonwealth of Massachusetts. Accredited by the New England Association of Schools and Colleges and approved and licensed by the Massachusetts Department of Education, Riverview also holds membership in the National Association of Independent Schools and the Association of Independent Schools in New England. The Alumni Resource Center provides ongoing services to graduates and their families and, in the spring of 1989, The Parents Association was founded to offer support to other parents and help raise funds for the School.

THE CAMPUS. The 16-acre main campus contains 21 buildings and a lighted athletic field. The buildings include classrooms, three computer labs, science lab, greenhouse, fitness center, seminar rooms, industrial arts and photography lab; kitchen, dining room, and conferencing center; a health care center; gymnasium; an auditorium; and dormitories and apartments for older students.

THE FACULTY. Maureen Brenner, appointed Head of School in June 2001, holds a Bachelor of Arts degree and Higher Diploma in Education from University College in Dublin, a Master of Education degree from Bridgewater State College, and a Certificate of Advanced Graduate Studies from the University of Massachusetts. With more than 25 years of professional experience in education, Mrs. Brenner has worked as a high school teacher, school psychologist, special-education administrator, and assistant superintendent of schools. She and her husband, Richard, have two grown children.

The experienced School staff includes individuals holding degrees and licensure in the areas of special education, psychology, reading, social work, and speech and language. The staff also includes residential supervisors, dormitory coordinators, and dormitory assistants who participate in yearlong, specialized training. Each Riverview staff member is trained to understand learning challenges; all are committed to cultivating the potential of each student.

Registered nursing staff are on duty daily from 7:00 A.M. to 9:00 P.M. On-call registered nursing services are available. Local professional medical services and consultants are utilized as needed.

STUDENT BODY. Yearly, Riverview School's secondary program enrolls 115 students, divided almost equally between boys and girls, ages 12 through 18. The postsecondary program (GROW) enrolls approximately 85 students, ages 18 to 22.

ACADEMIC PROGRAM. The school year begins in early September and ends in early June with vacations at Thanksgiving, Christmas, and in the spring. The academics are designed around a quarterly schedule with comprehensive reports sent to parents four times yearly. Parent conferences are scheduled in the fall and spring. An Individual Education Service Plan is designed to meet each student's needs based on previous academic records and diagnostic testing in addition to ongoing assessment.

Academic instruction is provided via a unique thematic integrated curriculum. With an emphasis on high expectations and research-validated instructional approaches, students receive directed instruction for an hour daily in reading and an hour daily in writing. While maximum class size is eight students, many opportunities are available for small group and individualized instruction.

GROW (Getting Ready for the Outside World) is a unique, ten-month, postsecondary, three-year transitional program for students ages 18–22 who have completed high school. The academic and residential programs are closely linked and work together to foster critical social, academic, and independent living skills. The success-oriented, noncompetitive, individualized nature of the program helps to increase students' self-esteem, self-confidence, and their willingness to take risks. GROW emphasizes academic skill development, vocational training, and independent living skills. If appropriate, students have the opportunity to attend Project Forward, a vocational skills training program at Cape Cod Community College.

STUDENT ACTIVITIES. The structured, supportive residential component fosters independence and self-determination through the development of life skills, social skills, and self-esteem. The philosophy of the "whole child" guides the ongoing dialogue between academic and residential staff and ensures that student needs are addressed quickly and comprehensively. The Residential Program offers social and recreational opportunities that many Riverview students have not previously experienced. All secondary students may participate in the sports program, since there is a "no cut" system. The after-school and weekend activities program offers social, recreational, and athletic activities after classes during the week. Many weekend activities take advantage of the School's location, having easy access to the seashore, to Boston, and to other historic New England sites. A five-week summer program is also available for middle, secondary, and postsecondary students.

Annual school events include the Graduation and Benefit Gala and auction, the Parent Open House in October, and the prom. Riverview's active Parents Association is involved in a wide range of activities to benefit students, their families, and the School.

ADMISSION AND COSTS. Riverview School seeks to enroll learning-disabled students who will benefit from a structured, supportive, language-based, thematic-approach learning environment. Males and females ages 12 through 22 are considered for admission on the basis of their educational, psychological, and medical reports. After these reports are reviewed, a preliminary admissions decision is made. A positive decision results in extending an invitation to the candidate for a personal interview on campus and a two-day visit. Riverview School admits students without regard to race, color, and national or ethnic origin.

In 2007–08, tuition for a 244-day school year in the secondary program is $63,919. Limited financial aid is available.

Head of School: Maureen B. Brenner
Director of Admissions: Jeanne M. Pacheco
Admissions Assistants: Monica L. S. Lindo & Nancy Hopkins

The Roxbury Latin School 1645

101 St. Theresa Avenue, West Roxbury, MA 02132-3496
Tel. 617-325-4920; Admission Ext. 217; Fax 617-325-3585
Web Site www.roxburylatin.org; E-mail admission@roxburylatin.org

The Roxbury Latin School, the oldest school in continuous existence in North America, enrolls 286 day boys in Grades 7–12. This college preparatory school strives to develop intellectual excellence and personal values in a diverse socioeconomic community where every boy has the opportunity to occupy a leadership role. About one-third of the boys are on scholarships. An increasingly flexible curriculum includes programs in art, music, dramatics, and independent study. A variety of extracurricular activities is available. Tuition: $17,900. Financial Aid: $1,300,000. Thomas R. Guden is Director of Admission; Kerry P. Brennan (Amherst, A.B. 1977; Columbia, M.A. 1983) is Headmaster. *New England Association.*

St. John's Preparatory School 1907

72 Spring Street, Danvers, MA 01923
Tel. 978-774-1050; Admissions Ext. 301; Fax 978-774-5767
Web Site www.stjohnsprep.org; E-mail jdriscoll@stjohnsprep.org

St. John's Preparatory School is a Catholic, Xaverian Brothers-sponsored secondary school for young men. Founded in 1907, St. John's enrolls 1200 day students in Grades 9–12. The School offers an academically challenging college preparatory program emphasizing personal achievement, leadership, spiritual development, and commitment to service. The 175-acre wireless campus is a vibrant blend of old and new with a state-of-the-art library, six new science labs, Campus Ministry Center, center for the arts, and gymnasium. Students participate in a wide variety of extracurricular activities, travel programs, and athletics. Tuition: $15,400 (no fees). Tuition Assistance: $2,500,000. Albert J. Shannon, Ph.D., is Headmaster; Edward P. Hardiman, Ph.D., is Principal; John Driscoll '90 is Dean of Admission and Freshman Academic Programs. *New England Association.*

St. Sebastian's School 1941

1191 Greendale Avenue, Needham, MA 02492
Tel. 781-449-5200; Admissions 781-247-0125; Fax 781-449-5630
Web Site www.stsebastiansschool.org; E-mail admissions@stsebs.org

St. Sebastian's School is a Roman Catholic, independent day school enrolling 350 boys in Grades 7–12. Students participate in a structured and rigorous liberal arts curriculum, with carefully sequenced courses in English, mathematics, classical and modern foreign languages, science, and social studies. The School places heavy emphasis on verbal skills enrichment, and all freshmen take a required writing course. Upper School courses are taught on standard, honors, and Advanced Placement levels. The extracurricular program features 11 interscholastic sports and 22 nonathletic clubs. Tuition: $28,375. Financial Aid: $1,600,000. David M. Emond is Dean of Admission and Financial Aid; William L. Burke III (Middlebury College, B.A.; Boston College, M.A.) is Headmaster. *New England Association.*

School Year Abroad 1964

439 South Union Street, Lawrence, MA 01843
Tel. 978-725-6828; Fax 978-725-6833
Web Site www.sya.org; E-mail mail@sya.org

Established in 1964 and now a consortium of well-known American independent schools, School Year Abroad sends 50–60 students each year to schools in China, France, Italy, or Spain for their junior or senior year of high school. Programs in France and Spain have a two-year language requirement; the programs in China and Italy are open to beginners. Students live with a local family while earning U.S. graduation credits and preparing for selective colleges and universities nationwide. School Year Abroad provides a traditional liberal arts program, college counseling, and all standardized testing. English and math are taught in English by American faculty. Extracurricular activities and travel round out the educational program. See additional listings under specific countries. Tuition: $37,400. Financial aid is available. Roland Lemay is Director of Admissions; Woodruff W. Halsey II is Executive Director.

Shady Hill School 1915

178 Coolidge Hill, Cambridge, MA 02138
Tel. 617-868-1260; Admissions 617-520-5200; Fax 617-520-9387
Web Site www.shs.org; E-mail admission@shs.org

Professor and Mrs. William Ernest Hocking founded Shady Hill to offer a more liberal and imaginative alternative to the public education of the times. Situated in a quiet residential area, the School enrolls 500 boys and girls in four-year-old Pre-Kindergarten–Grade 8. The curriculum is designed to instill a zest for learning "within a rigorous intellectual and physical setting." Mastery of basic skills in the humanities, arts, and sciences and the interrelationship among the disciplines are emphasized. Music, art, woodworking, and drama are a regular part of the curriculum. An Afterschool Program is optional. Tuition: $16,900–$24,400. Financial aid is available. Amy Jolly is Director of Admission; Bruce A. Shaw (Macalester, B.A. 1967; Antioch, M.A.T. 1973) was named Director in 1994.

Southfield School 1992

10 Newton Street, Brookline, MA 02445-7498
Tel. 617-522-6980; Admissions 617-454-2721; Fax 617-522-8166
Web Site www.southfield.org; E-mail admissions@southfield.org

Southfield, serving 395 girls in Pre-Kindergarten–Grade 12, is a sister school to Dexter, founded in 1926 and enrolling 391 boys. Located on the 36-acre Dexter campus, Southfield emphasizes the same traditional academic subjects, including Latin in Grades 6–12, as its counterpart. Southfield has its own classroom complex and shares an administrative building, science and computer laboratories, the Clay Observatory, the gym, indoor pool, two ice rinks, five fields, and art, shop, and music studios. The Clay Center for Science and Technology and the Briarwood Marine Science Center on Cape Cod offer the same advanced areas of study as those of Dexter. All students participate in athletics, and interscholastic sports begin in Grade 7. Summer programs include day camp, hockey, sci-tech, and enrichment camps on campus and marine science and sailing programs at Briarwood. Tuition: $18,200–$28,880. Financial Aid: $2,570,700. Christopher Overbye is Director of Admissions; William F. Phinney is Head.

Stoneleigh-Burnham School 1869

574 Bernardston Road, Greenfield, MA 01301
Tel. 413-774-2711; Fax 413-772-2602
Web Site www.sbschool.org; E-mail admissions@sbschool.org

Stoneleigh-Burnham School in Greenfield, Massachusetts, is a college preparatory boarding and day school enrolling girls in Grades 7 through 12 and a postgraduate year. The School is 3 hours from New York, 2 hours from Boston, and an hour from Bradley International Airport in Hartford, Connecticut. Students have access to academic symposiums and cultural events at nearby Smith, Mount Holyoke, Williams, Hampshire, and the University of Massachusetts; the ski areas of Vermont and New Hampshire are nearby.

Stoneleigh-Burnham was formed in 1968 by the merger of the Mary A. Burnham School (1877) and the Stoneleigh-Prospect Hill School (1869). The School continues its 139-year tradition of encouraging girls to develop their interests to the best of their abilities, to enjoy the challenge and rewards of learning, and to gain self-confidence and independence. Stoneleigh-Burnham seeks to achieve these goals through programs and personnel who respect young women's voices and intellects and who understand how girls learn best.

The School is a nonprofit corporation directed by a Board of Trustees composed of alumnae, parents, and friends. There is an active Alumnae Association. Accredited by the New England Association of Schools and Colleges, Stoneleigh-Burnham holds membership in the National Association of Independent Schools, among other organizations.

THE CAMPUS. The School occupies more than 100 wooded acres. The entire campus is connected through a wireless technology network. The Main Building, with the addition of Mary Burnham Hall, houses classrooms, the technology center, the library, the infirmary, dorm rooms, student lounges and common rooms, and dining facilities. There are faculty apartments on the second floor as well as in Ferdon House. The Jesser Science Center for chemistry, biology, and physical science houses laboratories, lecture and discussion space, and a reading resource room. Emerson Hall has a gymnasium, a dance studio, and an auditorium. The Student Arts Center and The Geissler

Gallery contain teaching and studio facilities for drawing, painting, ceramics, photography, weaving, desktop publishing, computer graphics, film editing, other arts, and a renovated fitness area.

On campus are five tennis courts, an outdoor swimming pool, three playing fields, and cross-country ski trails. The School's state-of-the-art riding facilities include stabling for 60 horses, two indoor riding arenas, two outdoor riding rings, the McDonald Jumper Derby course, a cross-country riding course, and a hunt course.

THE FACULTY. Dr. Paul C. Bassett, Head of School, joined the Stoneleigh-Burnham faculty in 1981. Dr. Bassett holds a B.A. from Providence College and an M.Ed./C.A.G.S. and an Ed.D. in Educational Administration from the University of Massachusetts (Amherst). During his tenure at the School, Dr. Bassett has held a variety of key positions including Academic Dean, Dean of Faculty, faculty advisor to the Debate and Public Speaking Society, head coach for the varsity softball and cross-country teams, student advisor, and member of the English Department.

The 48 faculty and administrators hold baccalaureate and 32 advanced degrees from such institutions as Aberdeen, Aichi, Amherst, Bates, Boston University, Brown, Bryn Mawr, Colgate, Columbia, Hamilton, Harvard, Juilliard, Macalester, McGill, Middlebury, Mount Holyoke, Princeton, Providence, Smith, Stanford, and the Universities of Massachusetts and Michigan.

The Health Care Center staff includes the school physician, a gynecological nurse practitioner, an orthopedic/sports physician, and three registered nurses. Hospital facilities are located in Greenfield at the Bay State Franklin Medical Center less than a mile away.

STUDENT BODY. In 2007–08, the School enrolled 150 girls in Grades 7–12 and a postgraduate year, 100 boarders and 50 day students.

ACADEMIC PROGRAM. The school year is divided into trimesters from early September to early June, with Thanksgiving, winter, and spring vacations. Stoneleigh-Burnham's course offerings are designed to place each girl in classes most commensurate with her scholastic ability, and each discipline offers college preparatory, honors, and Advanced Placement courses. The Academic Skills Program supports students who need additional help in reading, writing, mathematics, and organizational skills. Faculty advisors monitor academic progress and assist with issues relating to general life at school. The student-faculty ratio is approximately 6:1. Evening study hall for boarding students is required from 7:30 to 9:30 P.M. five nights a week in addition to one daily 40-minute study hall five days a week are required. Progress reports and written teachers' comments are issued every three weeks to students; grades are mailed to parents at the end of each trimester.

In Grades 7–8 (Middle School), classes include humanities, math, science, foreign language, visual and performing arts, physical education, and health. All students may participate in the Upper School's athletic, riding, music, and dance programs.

To graduate, students must earn a minimum of 18 credits in Grades 9–12, including four years of English; two years of the same foreign language; three years each of mathematics and laboratory science; and three and one-third years of social studies, including one of United States History; two trimesters each year in the arts; and four years of physical education.

English courses in Grades 9–12 focus on vocabulary, grammar, writing, and literature. English electives are required of juniors and seniors in the spring semester. Stoneleigh-Burnham is recognized nationally for its science program for girls. Courses include Advanced Placement Environmental Science and Biology, plus Conceptual Physics, Biology, Chemistry, Physics, Equine Studies, Health, and several science electives. Other full-term and elective courses include French, Chinese, Spanish; Algebra I–II, Geometry, PreCalculus, Discrete Math, Calculus, Advanced Placement and Multivariable Calculus; World History, U.S. History, Advanced Placement U.S. History, Political Science, Gender Studies; Drawing I–II, Painting, Design and Color, Watercolor and Painting, Computer Art, Advanced Placement Studio Art, Desktop Publishing, Photography I–III, Papier Maché Sculpture, Ceramics I–III; and Music Theory, Music History, Chorus, Octet, and Acting. Honors classes are offered in each discipline. Private music lessons are available. There are several instrumental ensemble groups, a big band, a chamber group, a rock band, and a jazz combo, and instruction is offered in ballet, jazz, and modern dance at all levels.

English as a Second Language, available in English and history, provides help in basic English skills at three levels.

The Senior Project allows students to work in a yearlong project with regional colleges and other organizations to study or research a topic of their choice.

Graduates from the last three years are attending such colleges and universities as Bates, Boston University, Bowdoin, Carnegie Mellon, Colby, College of the Holy Cross, College of William and Mary, Columbia, Cornell, Davidson, Dickinson, Georgetown, George Washington, Massachusetts Institute of Technology, Middlebury, Mount Holyoke, Providence, Reed, Rhode Island School of Design, Skidmore, Smith, Syracuse, Texas A&M, Trinity, Tufts, Union, Wellesley, Wesleyan, Wheaton, Williams, William Smith, and the Universities of Colorado, Illinois, New Hampshire, North Carolina, Vermont, and Virginia.

STUDENT ACTIVITIES. The Student Council is divided into two areas. The Proposal Committee considers proposals submitted by students and forwards them to the Head of School. The Judicial Committee reviews school policy. Students may participate in many weekend social activities, and many volunteer in a variety of community organizations.

Clubs and activities include the Literary Society, Peer Tutors, Peer Mediation, Blue Key Guides, Student Activities, GSA, Pangea, MECCA, Riding and Community Service. Students publish a newspaper, yearbook, and literary magazine. The Stoneleigh-Burnham Debate Team competes nationally and is one of the top-ranked teams in New England.

Stoneleigh-Burnham athletes compete in the Western New England Prep School Association in soccer, field hockey, cross-country, basketball, volleyball, softball, lacrosse, and tennis. Recreational skiing and golf are also offered.

With one of the country's most extensive riding programs, Stoneleigh-Burnham has been national champion in the hunters interscholastic riding category. The School hosts numerous horse events each year for Stoneleigh-Burnham riders and the outside community.

Stoneleigh-Burnham offers three two-week sessions of the Bonnie Castle Summer Riding Camp for girls ages 9–17. Residential camps for girls in softball, debate, dance, math/English, and ESL are also held on campus.

ADMISSION AND COSTS. Stoneleigh-Burnham seeks girls with average to superior academic abilities who demonstrate a respect for learning and who will contribute positively to the School community. Candidates must submit academic transcripts, standardized test scores, a personal reference, references from the school counselor and English and math teachers, and the parent-guardian and student questionnaires. The application fee for 2007–08 is $40 for domestic students and $100 for international students. The application deadline is February 15.

In 2007–08, tuition for boarding students is $38,960 and $24,490 for day students. There are additional fees for the academic skills, ESL, and horseback riding programs.

Financial aid is available on the basis of need as determined by the School and Student Service for Financial Aid. In 2007, $904,000 was awarded to 62 students. There is an Honor Scholarship Program, and the Alumnae Association funds a scholarship to be awarded each year to the daughter of an alumna.

Director of Development: Mrs. Robin Johnson
Academic Dean: Mr. Scott Peeler
Dean of Students: Ms. Marje Monroe
Dean of Residential Life & Student Activities: Ms. Natalie de Reus
Director of Admissions: Ms. Sharon L. Pleasant
Director of International Programs & College Counselor: Mrs. Andrea Patt
Director of Finance & Operations: Ms. Leslie Brown
Director of Athletics: Mr. Jeremy Deason

Tenacre Country Day School 1910

78 Benvenue Street, Wellesley, MA 02482
Tel. 781-235-2282; Admission Ext. 204; Fax 781-237-7057
Web Site www.tenacrecds.org; E-mail sam_reece@tenacrecds.org

Tenacre Country Day School enrolls 191 girls and boys in Pre-Kindergarten–Grade 6. A well-rounded program focuses on basic skills, math, language arts, Spanish, social studies, science, music, art, computer, and physical education. Good citizenship and character development are also emphasized. Small classes, talented teachers, a challenging yet nurturing environment, a diverse population, and attention to the needs of each child prepare students for highly competitive secondary schools. Tenacre values the importance of team teaching, the strong partnership between parents and staff, and the meaningful participation of each child in daily school life. An After School Program is open to all grades. A summer day camp enrolls boys and girls ages 4–12. Tuition: $16,570–$23,230, depending on grade. Financial aid and limited transportation are available. Ms. Sam R. Reece is Director of Admission; Christian B. Elliot (Princeton, A.B. 1974) is Head of School.

Thayer Academy 1877

745 Washington Street, Braintree, MA 02184
Tel. 781-843-3580; Admission 781-664-2221; Fax 781-843-2916
Web Site www.thayer.org; E-mail admissions@thayer.org

Thayer Academy in Braintree, Massachusetts, is a coeducational, college preparatory day school enrolling 668 students in Grades 6 through 12. First colonized in 1625, historic Braintree (population 33,828) is a residential community 13 miles southeast of Boston in an area accessible to a myriad of educational, cultural, and recreational resources.

The School was founded in 1877 by Gen. Sylvanus Thayer, a distinguished soldier, engineer, and educator who is widely known as "The Father of the United States Military Academy." General Thayer established high standards of scholarship and instituted a performance evaluation process for each student with the goal of producing "worthy leaders of high character."

Today's Thayer Academy holds true to its founder's ideals by providing a rigorous learning environment designed to inspire in students "moral, intellectual, aesthetic, and physical excellence so that each may rise to honorable achievement and contribute to the common good." Faculty are chosen for their devotion to scholarship and their sincere interest in the development of their students.

Thayer Academy is accredited by the New England Association of Schools and Colleges and the Massachusetts Department of Education; it holds membership in the National Association of Independent Schools, The Cum Laude Society, Association of Independent Schools of New England, and the Secondary School Admission Test Board, among other professional affiliations.

THE CAMPUS. At the heart of the 25-acre suburban campus is Main Building, constructed in 1877 and featuring a recently renovated clock tower with bells. Glover Laboratory (1894, renovated in 1952 and 1986) contains math and science classrooms including 11 computer labs and 5 technology classrooms. The student-computer ratio is 2:1, and a campus-wide intranet features connections to computer workstations in faculty offices, labs, classrooms, administrative offices, and the Southworth Library, providing 21,000 volumes, 58 periodicals, and an art gallery. Students and faculty have access to file storage and printers as well as full-time Internet connectivity at each workstation and electronic mail across campus. Frothingham Hall houses the Academy's drama and music programs, while Cahall Observatory houses a 12-inch Schmidt Cassagrain telescope and three Newtonians for viewing the cosmos. Cahall Campus Center (1998) contains the dining hall for all students as well as meeting space and locker rooms. Thayer recently completed two state-of-the-art biology labs.

The Thayer Academy Middle School, accommodating 213 students in Grades 6–8, was expanded and upgraded to include a new satellite library and state-of-the-art technology.

A Center for the Arts, scheduled to open in 2008, will feature a 550-seat theater, dance studios, and art classes.

Among the athletic resources are a running track and cross-country trails, tennis and basketball courts, a ropes course, a two-story training and fitness facility, and four new synthetic grass playing fields for baseball, football, softball, and other sports.

THE FACULTY. W. Theodore "Ted" Koskores, a 1970 graduate of Thayer Academy, was appointed the school's ninth Headmaster in 2006. Mr. Koskores received a baccalaureate degree from Boston University and holds advanced degrees from Columbia University.

Of Thayer's 102 faculty members, 60 percent hold master's or doctoral degrees, and 17 teachers have been at the school for 25 or more years. Faculty have graduated from four-year colleges and universities such as Amherst, Ball State, Bates, Bowdoin, Brown, California Lutheran, Colby, College of Wooster, Connecticut College, Dartmouth, Hamilton, Harvard, Johns Hopkins, Kenyon, Laval, Marymount, Massachusetts College of Art, Massachusetts Institute of Technology, Middlebury, New England School of Law, New School for Social Research, Ohio State, Pepperdine, Purdue, Rhode Island School of Design, Simmons, Skidmore, State University of New York, Suffolk University, Tufts, Wesleyan, Wheaton, Williams, Worcester Polytechnic, Yale, and the Universities of Colorado, Massachusetts (Lowell), New Hampshire, North Carolina, Pennsylvania, Rhode Island, Rochester, Vermont, and Virginia.

STUDENT BODY. In 2007–08, Thayer Academy enrolled 668 young men and women—213 in Grades 6 through 8 and 455 in Grades 9–12. They come from widely diverse ethnic, racial, religious, and socioeconomic backgrounds.

ACADEMIC PROGRAM. The school year extends from September to June, with vacations at Thanksgiving, in December, and in the spring, along with observances of several national holidays. The student-teacher ratio is approximately 6:1, and the average class enrolls between 13 and 16 students.

Overall, Thayer offers 135 courses in addition to nearly 80 electives. The curriculum in the Middle School centers on English, history, math, modern languages plus required Latin in Grade 6, computer science/technology, the arts, and health. Students can receive additional academic support from teachers upon request.

To graduate, Thayer students must successfully complete 4 years of English; 3 years each of math and science; 2 years of a foreign language (Chinese, French, Latin, Spanish); 3 years of history (World, United States, and Modern European); 11 terms of physical education or interscholastic sports; ½ credit in an arts elective plus Foundation in the Arts; and a Senior Project.

Among the specific course offerings are English Language and Literature, English Language and Composition, American Masterworks, World Literature, Scene to Screen, Crossing Borders: Journeys and Transformations, African History and the African-American Experience, Sports Literature, Memoir and Biography: The Stories of Our Lives, Rag and Bone Poetry Workshop, Modern American Culture, Imaginative Literature, Philosophy and Literature; French I–V, Latin I–II, Spanish I–V, Hispanic History and Culture, Chinese I–II, Chinese Culture; World History, Australian Studies, Modern European History, United States History, Vietnam and the '60s, Contemporary Issues, Psychology, Hiroshima and the Holocaust, Sports and

Society; Algebra I–II, Geometry, Precalculus; Physics, Biology, Chemistry, Chemistry in Community; Environmental Science, Earth Science; Architectural Design, Photography, Pottery, Graphic Design, Acting, Choreography Workshop; and Health.

Thirty-seven honors and Advanced Placement courses for qualified students include Biology II, Chemistry II, Physics II, Calculus AB/BC, English Literature and Composition, French, Latin, Spanish, U.S. History, and Environmental Science. Thayer students consistently qualify as AP scholars, and over 90 percent earn scores of 3 or higher on their respective exams.

Thayer strongly believes that international travel and study abroad are important elements in a student's education and has developed rich cultural exchange programs with schools in France, Italy, Spain, Mexico, Costa Rica, England, and Canada.

Traditionally, 100 percent of Thayer graduates enter four-year colleges and universities. Members of the Class of 2007 have been accepted at such institutions as Boston Architectural Center, Boston College, Boston University, Brown, College of the Holy Cross, Cornell, Connecticut College, Dartmouth, Dickinson, Fairfield, Goucher, Hamilton, Harvard, Hobart and William Smith, Hofstra, Lafayette, Lake Forest, Macalester, Massachusetts Maritime Academy, McGill, New York University, Northeastern, Northwestern, Ohio Wesleyan, Providence College, Quinnipiac, St. Lawrence, Salve Regina, Stonehill, Trinity College (Dublin), Trinity (Connecticut), Wake Forest, Worcester Polytechnic Institute, and the Universities of Arizona, Chicago, Massachusetts, North Carolina, Pennsylvania, Richmond, South Carolina, Southern California, and Vermont.

Thayer Academy conducts a summer school program of enrichment, remediation, and advanced course work as well as sports camps and other recreational pursuits.

STUDENT ACTIVITIES. Thayer's extracurricular program is structured to meet the many diverse interests and abilities of its student body. Community Council offers students a voice in school decisions and policies and the opportunity to plan spirit-building activities.

Thirty-seven organizations include Mathletes, cultural enrichment, three yearly drama productions, seven jazz ensembles, three choirs, yearbook, and *Voice,* Thayer's award-winning student magazine.

Community service learning comprises a vital component of a Thayer education. Students, faculty, and staff tutor children as part of the local Head Start program; conduct food drives for the homeless and hungry; walk to raise money for cancer and AIDS research; advocate for human rights as members of Amnesty International; and visit residents of the Braintree Manor Nursing Home. Through these and many other outreach activities, the Thayer community experiences first-hand its potential to have a significant impact on the lives of others.

The athletic program is open to students at all levels, with 80 teams in 26 sports. Some sports are offered to both Middle and Upper School athletes. Among the offerings are baseball, basketball, cross-country, football, skiing, field hockey, softball, swimming, lacrosse, wrestling, tennis, golf, and ice hockey.

ADMISSION AND COSTS. Thayer Academy admits students of good character and academic potential as determined by past school transcripts, personal and teacher recommendations, standardized testing (ISEE or SSAT), a campus visit, and the completed application. Candidates are notified of admission decisions on or about March 10.

In 2007–08, tuition is $28,950. The school provides nearly $4,000,000 in need-based financial aid to approximately one-third of its student body.

Headmaster: W. Theodore Koskores '70
Upper School Director: Michael Clarke
Middle School Director: Nicole Wilkinson
Director of Admissions: Jonathan White
Director of Development: Mark Gutierrez
Director of Communications: David Casanave
Business Manager: William Stephenson
Director of Athletics: Matthew McGuirk '92

Tower School 1912

75 West Shore Drive, Marblehead, MA 01945
Tel. 781-631-5800; Admissions Ext. 203; Fax 781-631-2292
Web Site www.towerschool.org; E-mail admission@towerschool.org

Tower School, a day school enrolling 300 boys and girls in Prekindergarten–Grade 8, aims to spark a lifelong love of learning by providing a stimulating education in a supportive environment. High academic standards are sought within an atmosphere of trust and cooperation among students, teachers, and parents. Tower expects its students to be intellectually and socially competent, self-reliant, and respectful of the views and dignity of others. Interscholastic sports, publications, and clubs are among the activities offered. Arts and day camp summer programs are available. Tuition: $14,900–$20,950. Financial Aid: $560,000. Elizabeth Parker is Director of Admission; Peter S. Philip (Yale, B.A. 1985; Wesleyan University, M.A.L.S. 1996) was appointed Head of School in 2000.

Valley View School 1970

Oakham Road, P.O. Box 338, North Brookfield, MA 01535
Tel. 508-867-6505; Fax 508-867-3300
Web Site www.valleyviewschool.org; E-mail valview@aol.com

A clinical psychologist founded this residential school to help boys ages 11–16 who function below their academic and social potential. Typically, Valley View enrolls 56 students who may demonstrate attention difficulties, nonverbal learning disabilities, and often, associated depression and oppositional behavior, which interfere with their adjustment to the world around them. The structured, 12-month program offers intensive remediation and therapeutic help and a broad range of success-oriented experiences designed to motivate learning and promote the boy's self-esteem and confidence in himself. Travel in the United States and abroad affords special challenge and enrichment. Most students are mainstreamed after 2–3 years. Tuition: $58,600. Philip G. Spiva, Ph.D., is Founding Director.

The Williston Northampton School 1841

19 Payson Avenue, Easthampton, MA 01027
Tel. 413-529-3000; Admissions 413-529-3241; Fax 413-527-9494
Web Site www.williston.com; E-mail admissions@williston.com

Williston Northampton offers a rigorous academic curriculum for 550 day (Grade 7–Postgraduate) and boarding (Grade

9–Postgraduate) students in an educational setting designed to foster respect, independence, and responsibility. The beautiful 125-acre campus features a state-of-the-art Science Tech Lab and Technology Center, a 45,000-volume library, a theater, art studios, lighted turf field, and athletic complex. Enrichment offerings include college-level courses, advanced Photojournalism, and visiting Writers' Workshops. Students take part in leadership activities such as community and campus work service, travel abroad, tutoring, and clubs. Boarding Tuition: $39,500; Day Tuition: $28,000. Financial Aid: $3,000,000. Ann C. Pickrell is Director of Admission; Brian Wright, Ph.D., is Headmaster. *New England Association.*

The Winchendon School 1926

172 Ash Street, Winchendon, MA 01475
Tel. 978-297-1223; Admissions [Toll-free] 800-622-1119
Fax 978-297-0911
Web Site www.winchendon.org; E-mail admissions@winchendon.org

THE WINCHENDON SCHOOL in Winchendon, Massachusetts, is a college preparatory boarding and day school enrolling boys and girls in Grades 9 through 12 and a postgraduate year. The School is located in the town of Winchendon (population 7500) in north central Massachusetts, 65 miles from Boston, 35 miles from Worcester, and 20 miles from Keene, New Hampshire. Bus service to surrounding cities is available within walking distance of the campus.

The Winchendon School was founded by Lloyd Harvey Hatch in 1926 in Dexter, Maine, to create a structured and traditional atmosphere in which students of good character and good ability may reach their academic potential. After a period in Newport, Rhode Island, the School was moved in 1961 to its present location. Girls were first admitted in 1973.

The Winchendon philosophy is that most young people can succeed when surrounded by an atmosphere of caring attention to their individual needs. To that end, the School seeks to offer academic programs that are closely tailored to each student's strengths and weaknesses, in a traditional environment designed to encourage moral and spiritual growth. Small classes, a personalized approach, and excellent guidance and support systems are intended to stimulate an interest in learning and to teach students that they themselves are "the most valuable contributors to their own education."

The School is a nonprofit institution governed by a self-perpetuating 17-member Board of Trustees, which meets at least three times per year. At present, the Board includes several of Winchendon's 2500 alumni. The Winchendon School is accredited by the New England Association of Schools and Colleges and is affiliated with the National Association of Independent Schools.

THE CAMPUS. Winchendon's 236 acres include such outdoor facilities as a swimming pool, tennis courts, an 18-hole golf course, cross-country ski trails, and baseball, lacrosse, and soccer fields. Four academic buildings house science laboratories, a 20,000-volume library, a computer lab, and classrooms specially designed for the School's small classes. Ford Hall (1888) contains administrative offices, classrooms, a dormitory, the infirmary, and the dining hall. Other facilities include an art building, a performing arts building, seven dormitories, a gymnasium (1990), a student center, faculty residences, a golf pro shop, an ice arena, and the Headmaster's residence, Homewood (1921).

The plant, which is valued at $20,000,000, is owned by the School.

THE FACULTY. J. William LaBelle was appointed Headmaster in 1988. A native of Massachusetts, Mr. LaBelle attended the University of Massachusetts (B.S. 1958, M.S. 1968) and Massachusetts State College (M.Ed. 1967). After receiving his baccalaureate degree, he taught science at Trinity-Pawling School, where he also coached soccer, wrestling, and lacrosse and served as a dormitory master and Director of Athletics. For the 15 years immediately preceding his appointment at Winchendon, he was Associate Headmaster and Dean of the Academy at Wilbraham & Monson Academy. Mr. LaBelle's wife, Marilyn Peach LaBelle, is the Academic Dean.

There are 32 full-time faculty and administrators who teach, 20 men and 12 women. Of these, 29 live at the School, 15 with their families. Faculty members hold baccalaureate and advanced degrees from Allegheny, Assumption, Bates, Boston University, Brown, Colby, Colgate, College of the Holy Cross, Dartmouth, Franklin and Marshall, Hamilton, Harvard, Merrimack, Pennsylvania State, Union, and the Universities of California (Berkeley), Massachusetts, New Hampshire, and Vermont. Faculty benefits include insurance and retirement plans and financial assistance with further education.

The school infirmary is staffed by two full-time nurses, and other staff members are certified in first-aid, CPR, and sports training. A school physician is on call; hospitals and emergency rooms are nearby.

STUDENT BODY. In 2006–07, Winchendon enrolled 220 boarding students, 160 boys and 60 girls; 10 boys and 10 girls were admitted as day students. Boarding students came primarily from New England, with 38 states and 25 foreign countries also represented.

ACADEMIC PROGRAM. The school year runs from early September until early June, with vacations at Thanksgiving and Christmas and in the spring. Classes are held five days a week from 7:50 A.M. to 12:40 P.M. and are followed by a two-hour sports period and a conference period. A typical weekday for boarders begins at 7:00 A.M. and includes, in addition to classes, recreation, meals, a clean-up period, school meeting, evening study period, and "lights-out" at 10:30 P.M.

The Winchendon approach to education is based on highly personalized attention to each student. Classes have an average of six to eight students, and the student-faculty ratio is approximately 5:1. Following extensive testing in September, a process-based curriculum is created for each student, based on test scores, previous grades, and teacher recommendations. Placement in courses is determined by students' needs rather than their grade level; most students take five courses per term. Faculty-supervised study halls are held in the evening, with an additional conference period scheduled daily to allow for individual consultation between teachers and students. To help students monitor their progress, grade slips are issued daily in all classes and are reviewed with dorm parents during the evening study period. Parents are also sent grades and comments once a week by their child's teachers.

Winchendon offers remediation in mathematics, writing, and reading to help students with specific learning disabilities. To graduate, students must successfully complete four years of English, four of mathematics, three of social science (including United States History), and two years of science. The study of a foreign language is encouraged but not required.

Among the required and elective courses offered are English I–V, The Short Story/Poetry, Writing Workshop/Public Speaking, Drama; U.S. History, World History, Civics/World Geography, American Culture, Psychology, Modern American History/Contemporary Social Issues, Great American Biography; General Science, Biology, Chemistry, Physics, Contemporary Issues in Science; Integrated Math I–II, Advanced Mathematics, Calculus I–II; Latin, French, Spanish (various levels); Basic and Advanced Computer Science, Graphic Design; and Painting, Drawing, Ceramics, Photography, Art History, and Music History and Appreciation. SAT, ACT, and TOEFL preparation courses are also offered.

Winchendon offers English as a Second Language, focusing on reading, writing, and oral communications at beginning, intermediate, and advanced levels. Courses in other disciplines and preparation for the Test of English as a Foreign Language are designed to help international students strengthen academic skills and assist in their adjustment to American life and customs.

The members of the Class of 2006 were accepted at the following colleges and universities: Assumption, Bentley, Boston College, Bradford, Canisius, Clark, Connecticut College, Elmira, Gettysburg, Hartwick, Harvard, Hofstra, Manhattan, Merrimack, Northeastern, Norwich, St. Anselm, St. Lawrence, Salve Regina, Seton Hall, Siena, Temple, United States Military Academy, Wentworth, Wheaton, and the Universities of Maine, Maryland, Massachusetts, New Hampshire, Notre Dame, and Pittsburgh.

The School offers a six-week summer program for boys and girls in Grades 8 through 12, with remedial, make-up, and enrichment courses. The program also provides ESL at three levels of competency and recreational sports and field trips for relaxation and enrichment. The director is Elliot C. Harvey.

STUDENT ACTIVITIES. The Winchendon Student Council, with representatives from each class, plans student activities and special events, as does the Student Activities Committee. Students also sit on the Judiciary Board, which advises the Headmaster on major disciplinary cases.

Because Winchendon believes that a carefully crafted athletic program can complement and enhance students' growth in other areas, participation in athletic activities is required for each season. Varsity sports include soccer, basketball, lacrosse, ice hockey, baseball, golf, tennis, cross-country running, volleyball, and alpine skiing. Both boys and girls participate in intramural and recreational sports.

Students publish a yearbook (*Vestigia*), newspaper (*Progress*), and literary magazine (*Impressions*), and may join special-interest groups such as the Photography and Outing Clubs. There are performing arts activities in instrumental and choral music, theater, and dance. School-sponsored weekend trips to Boston and Worcester allow students access to the cultural and recreational resources there; closer to home, the School's location in the foothills of the Monadnock Mountains provides excellent skiing and hiking. Other local entertainment includes movies, bowling, and activities at colleges in the area. With parental permission, students may spend the weekend off campus.

ADMISSION AND COSTS. Winchendon welcomes students who have the potential to do successful college work, despite previous academic weakness. Admission is made to all grade levels, based on a recent Wechsler test, a transcript, teacher recommendations, and a personal interview on campus. Applications are accepted throughout the year on a rolling basis; the application fee is $50.

In 2007–08, boarding tuition is $36,900, and day tuition is $21,250. Additional expenses include a fixed fee ranging from $1250 for day students to $3400 for international boarding students to cover such items as bedding and linen, athletic supplies and services, arts and lab materials, and textbooks. There is an extra fee for Driver Education.

Financial aid is offered according to need as determined by the School Scholarship Service. Approximately 25 percent of the student body receives financial aid totaling $1,000,000.

Academic Dean: Marilyn P. LaBelle
Dean of Faculty: Pamela S. Blair
Dean of Students: Elliot C. Harvey
Director of External Affairs: C. Jackson Blair
Director of College Counseling: J. William LaBelle
Director of Athletics: Daniel P. Chrieten
International Student Advisor: Robert N. Harrington

The Winsor School 1886

Pilgrim Road, Boston, MA 02215
Tel. 617-735-9500; Fax 617-739-5519
Web Site www.winsor.edu; E-mail admissions@winsor.edu

Founded by Mary Pickard Winsor, The Winsor School is a college preparatory day school enrolling 434 girls in Grades 5–12. The School offers an academically challenging curriculum, features small classes, uses the cultural and scientific resources of Boston, and shares some activities with nearby boys' schools. Physical education and fine arts are integral parts of the program. Facilities include a renovated library with 27,000 volumes plus access to 850 periodicals, a multimedia language lab, 3 computer labs, 3 art studios, 8 science labs, acres of playing fields, tennis courts, and a gymnasium. Tuition: $29,000. Financial Aid: $2,000,000. Pamela Parks McLaurin is Director of Admission and Financial Aid; Rachel Friis Stettler was appointed Director in 2004. *New England Association.*

Worcester Academy 1834

81 Providence Street, Worcester, MA 01604
Tel. 508-754-5302; Fax 508-752-2382
Web Site www.worcesteracademy.org
E-mail admission@worcesteracademy.org

WORCESTER ACADEMY in Worcester, Massachusetts, is a college preparatory day and boarding school enrolling boys and girls in Grades 6 through 12 and a postgraduate year. One of New England's largest cities, Worcester (population 170,000) is home to ten colleges, a nationally known civic center, and museums, theaters, concert halls, and shopping malls. Boston and Springfield are about an hour away, and ski areas are nearby. The school is easily accessible by train and bus.

Founded in 1834, Worcester Academy was originally coeducational but became an all-boys school in 1882 before returning to coeducation in 1974.

The Academy seeks to prepare able, motivated students for college and later life through intensive engagement in academics, athletics, and the arts. It relies on a firm grounding in inquiry, honesty, hard work, and respect for others and strives to foster independence in students as they advance in age and learning. This approach prepares students to become responsible citizens in a global society of increased technological complexity.

Worcester Academy is a nonprofit corporation governed by a self-perpetuating Board of Trustees. About 6300 living alumni provide financial and other support. The Academy is accredited by the New England Association of Schools and Colleges and holds membership in the National Association of Independent Schools and other organizations.

THE CAMPUS. The Academy occupies a 12-acre campus on Union Hill. Six major buildings are listed in the National Register of Historic Places. Walker Hall (1890) houses administrative offices, classrooms, the Walker Art Gallery, the Ackerman Media Center, the Academy's art studios, and the Andes Performing Arts Center. Kingsley Hall (1897) holds classrooms, science laboratories, the Upper School office, a computer room, and the audiovisual room. The Megaron (1905) is a large room used for social events and as a student lounge; its basement contains art studios. Rader Hall (2000) is a four-story academic building that includes a two-story library, ten classrooms, and three multimedia labs. The recently renovated and updated Lewis J. Warner Memorial Theatre (1932) houses the music department and the Harvey S. Ross '47 Auditorium, used for plays, concerts, movies, and assemblies.

The Kellner Student Center contains the school store, mail room, and recreation rooms. Adams Hall (1893) holds the dining hall and kitchen. Dexter, Davol, and Heydon Halls are dormitories with faculty apartments. Stoddard Hall is a dormitory that also houses the infirmary and a weight-training room. Abercrombie House (1897) is the Head of School's home. The Alumni and Development Office is located in a newly renovated Victorian home two blocks from the main campus.

Daniels Gymnasium (1915) holds two basketball courts, a swimming pool, a weight-training room, a wrestling room, an indoor track, and support facilities. Gaskill Field, an 11-acre tract several blocks from the school, includes a six-lane, all-weather track; tennis courts; playing fields for football, soccer, baseball, and softball; and the Michael L. Gould Field House. The New Balance Fields cover a 37-acre tract about 4 miles from campus and provide additional baseball and softball diamonds and four fields for soccer, field hockey, and lacrosse.

THE FACULTY. Dexter Morse, former Head of the Upper School at Phoenix Country Day School, was appointed Head of School in 1997. He is a graduate of Phillips Academy, Bowdoin College (A.B.), and the University of Vermont (M.Ed.).

The full-time faculty, including administrators who teach, is comprised of 59 men and 46 women, who hold baccalaureate degrees and 50 advanced degrees, including 5 doctorates, 2 law degrees, a medical degree, and a master's of divinity, from such institutions as Babson, Bard, Bates, Berklee School of Music, Boston College, Boston University, Bowdoin, Brigham Young, Brown, Bryn Mawr, Carnegie Mellon, Clark, Colby, College of the Holy Cross, Cornell, Elmira, Harvard, Johns Hopkins, Middlebury, Princeton, Regis, St. Lawrence, Stanford, Syracuse,

Texas Christian, Trinity, Union, Wesleyan, Wheaton, Williams, Worcester Polytechnic, Yale, and the Universities of Chicago, Cincinnati, Maine, Maryland, Massachusetts, Michigan, New Hampshire, Pennsylvania, Toronto, and Vermont. Twenty-nine faculty live on campus.

Two nurses staff the infirmary, a physician is on call, and several major hospitals are nearby.

STUDENT BODY. In 2007–08, Worcester Academy enrolled 655 students, including 145 five- and seven-day boarders and 510 day students in Grades 6–12 and a postgraduate year. There are 34 in Grade 6, 61 in Grade 7, 57 in Grade 8, 106 in Grade 9, 119 in Grade 10, 126 in Grade 11, 128 in Grade 12, and 24 postgraduates. Boarding students come from 11 states, Canada, China, Haiti, Hong Kong, Japan, Kazakhstan, Korea, Romania, Russia, Rwanda, Spain, Taiwan, Thailand, and Vietnam.

ACADEMIC PROGRAM. The academic year, divided into trimesters, runs from early September to early June, with vacations of two weeks at Christmas and in March. Classes, averaging 15 students, are held five days a week and are scheduled in six 49-minute sessions between 8:00 A.M. and 3:15 P.M. Extra-help sessions, study halls, activity periods, and assemblies are scheduled into the regular school day. Resident students have a two-hour study period each evening. Grades, with written comments from teachers, are sent to parents up to three times a year.

In the Middle School (Grades 6–8), students earn 5 credits per year from a curriculum that includes English; French, Spanish, or Latin; Social Studies; Mathematics; Science; Music, Art, Drama; Computer Science; and Health and Human Development. To graduate from the Upper School, a student must complete 18 credits including four years of English; two of foreign language; two of history, including U.S. History; three of mathematics; two of science, including biology; one and one-third of studio art/music/drama; and at least one elective, in addition to satisfying physical education and community service requirements. Postgraduate students earn a Worcester Academy Diploma.

Among the courses offered in the Upper School are English 1–4 and a choice of more than 20 English course electives; English as a Foreign Language; Chinese 1, French 1–5, Latin 1–5, Spanish 1–5; World Civilization, Modern World History, U.S. History, European History, American Government, and a choice of 12 History course electives; Algebra I–II, Geometry, Pre-Calculus, Calculus, Multivariable Calculus; Environmental Science, Biology, Chemistry, Physics, Oceanography, Human Anatomy/Physiology; Studio Art I–II, Acting I–III, Experimental Theater Lab, Costume Design and Construction; Design for the Performing Arts, Directing, Instrumental Ensemble, Chorus, Music Study, Music Theory, Web Communications and Design, Intro to Computers and Programming, Computer Applications, Video and Multimedia Design; and Health and Wellness. Opportunities for independent study, 16 honors sections, and Advanced Placement study in 16 subjects are available.

All of the 147 seniors who graduated in 2007 went on immediately to higher education. The graduates are enrolled at 92 colleges including Amherst, Boston College, Boston University, Brown, Carnegie Mellon, Colby, College of the Holy Cross, Columbia, Cornell, Emory, George Washington, Georgia Institute of Technology, Johns Hopkins, New York University, Princeton, Purdue, Swarthmore, Syracuse, Tufts, Union, Villanova, Washington University (St. Louis), Wellesley, Wesleyan, and the Universities of Chicago, Pennsylvania, and Virginia.

STUDENT ACTIVITIES. There are many opportunities for student leadership. The Board of Monitors oversees all school activities and provides assistance and service to faculty and other students.

Other activities include the newspaper, literary magazine, yearbook, and many clubs including Amnesty International, a cappella groups, Ambassadors, Debate, Foreign Language, Habitat for Humanity, International Relations, International Students, Jimmy Fund, Law, Math Team, Model U.N., Photography, Robotics, and Science.

Middle School students have their own newspaper, yearbook, and athletic teams and stage their own school play.

All students participate in organized athletics or physical education classes. Boys' varsity teams in football, basketball, and baseball compete against Class A prep school schools of New England and college junior varsity teams; other boys' and girls' teams compete against independent and public schools of comparable size. Other varsity sports for boys are cross-country, ice hockey, lacrosse, soccer, skiing, swimming, tennis, track, water polo, and wrestling. Girls compete in field hockey, lacrosse, softball, basketball, volleyball, cross-country, soccer, skiing, swimming, tennis, track, and water polo. Golf and crew coeducational. Junior varsity sports include baseball, basketball, field hockey, football, ice hockey, lacrosse, soccer, softball, and volleyball.

Weekend dances with students from other schools, pool tournaments, and shopping and ski trips enhance campus life.

Parents and alumni may attend special events such as Homecoming, Winter Carnival Weekend, Parents Weekend, Grandparents' Day, Musical "Pops" Night, Alumni Day, and an annual golf tournament.

ADMISSION AND COSTS. Worcester Academy seeks students of diverse abilities, interests, and backgrounds who are willing to extend themselves to meet the challenges of a college preparatory program. Students are accepted on evaluation of a completed application, with a $50 fee, two essays, recommendations from English and math teachers, a complete transcript, and a personal interview. ISEE or SSAT exams are required for some applicants, while SAT I or ACT results are required for Grade 12 and postgraduate applicants. A TOEFL or SSAT score is required for international students. Priority consideration is given to applications completed by February 1.

Tuition for 2007–08 is as follows: Middle School, $21,360; Upper School day students, $22,560; five-day boarding, $35,650; and seven-day boarding, $39,900. International students pay an additional $3500 for health insurance, activities, and services. Tuition payment plans are offered, and tuition refund insurance is required. The Academy awards approximately $2,600,000 annually to about 35 percent of students based on need.

Assistant Head of School: Antonio Viva
Dean of Faculty: Joel B. Strogoff
Director of Upper School: Ronald Cino
Director of Middle School: John F. Fox
Director of Admission: Susanne C. Carpenter
Director of Development: Marillyn Earley
College Counselor: Michael Pina
Business Manager: William Toomey
Director of Athletics: Edward Reilly

MICHIGAN

Academy of the Sacred Heart 1851

1250 Kensington Road, Bloomfield Hills, MI 48304
Tel. 248-646-8900; Admissions Ext. 129; Fax 248-646-4143
Web Site www.ashmi.org; E-mail blopiccolo@ashmi.org

The Academy of the Sacred Heart, a member of the Network of Sacred Heart Schools, is Michigan's oldest independent school, founded in 1851. It is a Catholic, college preparatory day school enrolling approximately 600 girls, age 3 to Grade 12, and boys, age 3 to Grade 8. Students reflect many cultures and faiths from the Detroit area. Coeducational classes in Preschool–Grade 4 focus on the wide span of developmental needs in these formative years. The Academy offers a Middle School for boys, Kensington Hall, and Middle (Grades 5–8) and Upper (Grades 9–12) Schools for Girls. Each program adapts curriculum, student activities, retreats, and extracurricular programs to challenge and maximize the potential of each student. Tuition: $15,270–$17,950. Financial aid is available. Barbara Lopiccolo is Director of Admissions; Bridget Bearss, RSCJ (Maryville University, B.A.; Washington University, M.A.), was appointed Head of School in 2000.

Cranbrook Schools 1927

39221 Woodward Avenue, Bloomfield Hills, MI 48304
Tel. 248-645-3602; Admissions 248-645-3610; Fax 248-645-3025
Web Site www.schools.cranbrook.edu; E-mail admission@cranbrook.edu

Cranbrook Schools in Bloomfield Hills, Michigan, comprise three divisions on four adjoining campuses. Brookside Lower School is coeducational, serving day students in Pre-kindergarten through fifth grade. The Middle School (Grades 6–8), also enrolling day students, provides single-gender education on separate campuses, with girls on the Kingswood campus and boys on the Vaughan campus. The Upper School (Grades 9–12) accommodates boarding and day students, with boys' dormitories at Cranbrook and girls' dorms at Kingswood. Bloomfield Hills (population 4000) is a residential community about 25 minutes northwest of Detroit.

George Gough and Ellen Scripps Booth began the Cranbrook Educational Community in the early 1920s with Brookside, an independent, coeducational elementary school. Eliel Saarinen, the renowned Finnish architect, was commissioned to design the Cranbrook School for boys (1927) and the Kingswood School for girls (1931). After operating independently for more than a half century, the two schools merged in 1985.

Cranbrook's comprehensive college preparatory education commences when the child enters Pre-kindergarten and continues to offer challenge and opportunity through graduation. Teachers work to provide an environment that cherishes and challenges the individual, encourages creative, critical, and independent thinking from the earliest age, and offers a broad range of academic, artistic, and athletic options.

Cranbrook Schools are governed by a 26-member Board of Trustees. The nonprofit institution is accredited by the Independent Schools Association of the Central States and holds membership in numerous professional organizations.

THE CAMPUS. The beautiful 319-acre campus of the Cranbrook Educational Community has been called one of the masterpieces of American architecture. In 1989, it was designated a National Historic Landmark, an honor accorded only two other independent schools in the United States. Sharing the grounds with the Schools are the Cranbrook Academy of Art and Museum (1932) and the Cranbrook Institute of Science (1930), both considered preeminent in their fields. Cranbrook House, the home of the founders, is surrounded by 40 acres of gardens, lawns, and woodlands.

In 1996, Brookside created an additional wing to the Lower School and began the Vlasic Early Childhood Center. A new girls' middle school academic building and a boys' middle school field house are planned. Other buildings include St. Dunstan's Playhouse, the Greek Theatre, an Italian-style boathouse, a greenhouse, and Thornlea, the former home of the founders' son.

Athletic facilities include a football stadium, a newly renovated, 12-month, enclosed ice arena, three gymnasiums, 15 outdoor tennis courts, a new sport and fitness center, training rooms, playing fields for baseball and soccer, and the $12,000,000 Williams Natatorium (1999).

Boarding girls live in a three-story dormitory wing on the Kingswood campus, and boarding boys are housed in four dorms on the Cranbrook campus.

The total school plant is valued at more than $145,000,000.

THE FACULTY. The faculty includes 124 women and 82 men, 70 of whom live on campus. They hold baccalaureate and advanced degrees, including 126 master's and 20 doctoral degrees, representing study at such colleges and universities as Brown, Bucknell, Carnegie Mellon, Columbia, Cranbrook Academy of Art, Dartmouth, Denison, DePauw, Dickinson, Gallaudet, Hamilton, Harvard, Lafayette, Miami University, Middlebury, Oakland University, Oberlin, Ohio State, Princeton, Stanford, Syracuse, Temple, Trinity, Vanderbilt, Wayne State, Wesleyan, Xavier, and the Universities of Angers (France), Bridgeport, California (Los Angeles, Santa Barbara), Detroit, Illinois, Michigan, Minnesota, Nebraska, Vermont, and Wisconsin.

Registered nurses staff the Health Centers, a doctor visits the campus twice weekly, and hospital facilities are readily accessible. The Schools also employ the services of five consulting psychologists, two full-time counselors, and an athletic trainer.

STUDENT BODY. In 2007–08, Cranbrook Schools enrolled 1629 students as follows: 517 in the Lower School, 340 in the Middle School, and 772 in the Upper School, 258 of whom were boarders. They came from 17 states and 15 countries and reflected a diversity of races, ethnic origins, and religious beliefs.

ACADEMIC PROGRAM. The school year, from September to June, is divided into semesters, with Thanksgiving recess, winter and spring vacations, and observances of national holidays.

The program at Brookside has been carefully developed to introduce children to academic skills in a positive learning environment. Traditionally, Brookside has been a school with a strong commitment from parents, faculty, and administration. The teachers' careful and thoughtful instruction takes place in a nurturing way with special attention tailored to each child's specific needs and style of learning. The focus is on strong academics and a balance of the fine arts in a liberal arts education. Homework is introduced gradually and varies according to grade level. Students participate in art, music, drama, science, Spanish, computers, visual studies, health, physical education, and library classes with specialists. Grades 4 and 5 have a departmental system with one teacher for reading and language arts, another for mathematics and social studies, and specialists for all the additional classes.

The single-gender program on separate campuses in the middle schools accommodates the specific physical, emotional, and learning differences between boys and girls in the adolescent years. The Middle School schedule is divided into trimesters. The core curriculum consists of English, mathematics, science, and social science with particular emphasis on the basics of writing and math. In addition, students participate in fine and performing arts, foreign language, computers, and physical education. Grade 6 has a week of outdoor education programs, and Grades 7 and 8 travel to such places as Boston, Arizona, Toronto, West Virginia, and Washington, D.C.

Students in Grades 6–8 participate in interscholastic athletics that promote teamwork rather than competition. The Middle School schedule also incorporates time for photography, publications, games, and other pursuits.

Recognized nationwide for academic excellence, Cranbrook Kingswood Upper School has been named an Exemplary School by the U.S. Department of Education. The curriculum is college preparatory, offering a broad selection of courses in English, math, science, history and social science, foreign language, religion, computer science, and the performing and fine arts. To graduate, students must earn a minimum of 4 credits in English, 3 each in mathematics and science, 2.5 in history/social science, 2 in foreign language, and 1 each in religion and fine/performing arts. Most students carry at least five courses each semester. In addition, students in Grade 9 are required to take a health course.

Advanced Placement and/or honors-level courses are available in the following departments: English, History, Science, Mathematics, Foreign Language, and Computer Science. Among the semester and yearlong courses offered in the Upper School are English 9, Expository Writing, Western Literary Traditions, Shakespeare, Satire, Current Literature, Literature and Film, Modern Voices of Doubt, Writing Workshop; Algebra I–II, Geometry, Pre-Calculus, Introductory Calculus, Calculus AB, Advanced Calculus; Latin I–II, Cicero & Ovid, Vergil, French I–V, Spanish I–IV, German I–IV; Conceptual Physics, Biology, Chemistry, Physics, Anatomy and Physiology, Astronomy, Engineering, Environmental Science, Geology, Genetics, Botany; Patterns in Civilization, United States History, American Studies, Russia and Eastern Europe, Principles of Psychology, Great Decisions, Economics, Model UN, Great Books; History of Religion, Western Traditions, Eastern Traditions, Humanities, Ethics; Concert Choir, Madrigals, The MasterSingers, Concert Band, Symphony Band, Orchestra, Dance I–IV, Acting and Theatre, Speech; Basic Design, Drawing, Painting, Photography, Drawing Studio, Ceramics Studio, Sculpture, Weaving/Fibers, Metalsmithing/Creative Jewelry; and Computer Applications and Computer Science.

Many sophomores choose to go on a Wilderness Expedition, a two-week backpacking trip in Tennessee's Great Smoky Mountains.

Qualified seniors can explore career interests or acquire technical proficiency in a field of interest through the three-week Senior May Project.

One hundred percent of the 196 members of the Class of 2007 have enrolled in college. Their choices include Amherst, Barnard, Bates, Boston College, Boston University, Brown, Carleton, Carnegie Mellon, Columbia, Cornell, DePauw, Duke, Emory, George Washington, Harvard, Indiana University, Johns Hopkins, Macalester, Massachusetts Institute of Technology, McGill, Michigan State, Middlebury, New York University, Northwestern, Oberlin, Skidmore, Tufts, Washington University, Wellesley, Williams, and the Universities of Michigan, Pennsylvania, and Virginia.

STUDENT ACTIVITIES. Student Council is a coalition of Upper School students, faculty, and administrators formed to review school policies and plan special events. Dorm councils and the Dining Hall Committee work to improve student life; Cabinet organizes community outreach projects; and the All

Campus Activities Committee organizes events for boarders and day students.

Upper School students publish *Brook/Woodwinds* (yearbook) and the nationally honored *Crane-Clarion* (newspaper) and *Gallimaufry* (literary arts magazine). Other interest groups include African American Awareness Association, Amnesty International, Asian American Cultural Society, Ergasterion (drama support group), Forensics, Gold Key, Jazz Band, Varsity, SADD, Robotics, World, French, Spanish, German, and Latin clubs.

Seventy athletic teams (varsity, junior varsity, freshman) are formed, including soccer, tennis, track, cross-country, football, basketball, skiing, golf, hockey, swimming, lacrosse, and baseball for boys; and field hockey, soccer, basketball, volleyball, swimming, cross-country, softball, tennis, lacrosse, ice hockey, skiing, golf, and track for girls. Crew, fencing, biking, ice-skating, bowling, dance, martial arts, and strength and fitness are also available.

Special traditions are observed each year such as Convocation, the White Gifts Assembly, Parent's Weekend, Junior Ring Ceremony, and Commencement.

ADMISSION AND COSTS. Cranbrook Schools welcome students of sound academic ability, character, motivation, and, for those entering Middle and Upper school, participation in extracurricular activities.

In 2007–08, tuition for day students ranges from $9900 for half-day Prekindergarten to $23,900 for Grades 9–12. Boarding tuition is $32,900. Financial aid totaling more than $6,000,000 was awarded based on need, and tuition payment and tuition refund plans are offered.

Director of Schools: Arlyce Seibert
Head of the Lower School: Brian Schiller
Head of the Girls Middle School: Fran Dagbovie
Head of the Boys Middle School: Larry Ivens
Head of the Upper School: Charlie Shaw
Director of Administrative Services: Kurt Godfryd
Director of Athletics: Jeff Vennell
Dean of Admission: Drew Miller

Detroit Country Day School 1914

22305 West 13 Mile Road, Beverly Hills, MI 48025
Tel. 248-646-7717; Fax 248-203-2184
Web Site www.dcds.edu; E-mail jprosperi@dcds.edu

Detroit Country Day School in Beverly Hills and Bloomfield Hills, Michigan, is a college preparatory day school for boys and girls in Preschool through Grade 12. Preschool, Junior Kindergarten, Kindergarten, Grades 1 and 2 are on the Maple Road Campus at 3003 West Maple Road (Telephone 248-433-1050); Grades 3–5 are on the Village Campus at 3600 Bradway Boulevard (Telephone 248-647-2522); Grades 6–8 are on the Hillview Campus at 22400 Hillview Lane (Telephone 248-646-7985); and Grades 9–12 are on the 13 Mile Campus at 22305 West 13 Mile Road (Telephone 248-646-7717). Beverly Hills and Bloomfield Hills are suburban areas 5 miles from Detroit's northern boundary.

In 1914, F. Alden Shaw founded Detroit Country Day School as an all-boys' school located in the city. Girls were admitted to the Lower School in 1941, and the School became fully coëducational in 1972. The School moved several times before 1957, when the 13 Mile Campus was acquired. In 1975, the Village Campus was purchased, in 1986, the Maple Road Campus was added, and in 1991, the Hillview Campus opened on property adjoining the 13 Mile Campus. In 2000, a new Preschool Learning Village was built on the Maple Road Campus. Detroit Country Day School's mission is "to provide a superior college preparatory, liberal arts educational opportunity to young people of cultural and intellectual diversity. Within a supportive setting, the School promotes the academic, artistic, moral, character, leadership, and physical development of all students."

A nonprofit institution, Detroit Country Day School is directed by a 14-member self-perpetuating Board of Trustees, which includes parents. The School holds membership in the National Association of Independent Schools, among other professional affiliations.

THE CAMPUS. The 13 Mile Campus and the Hillview Campus are located on an 80-acre site within three miles of the 10-acre Maple Road Campus and the 3-acre Village Campus.

On the 13 Mile Campus, the main building contains administrative offices, a 750-seat performing arts center, classrooms, language and science laboratories, art studios, music and computer rooms, a library, two gymnasiums, and facilities for weight and fitness training. The adjacent Student Center provides a multipurpose area for study hall and dining. Ten all-weather tennis courts, an all-weather track, and athletic fields complete this campus.

On the Hillview Campus is a three-story building, which houses 20 classrooms, 5 science laboratories, art and music studios, computer rooms, a library, a dining room, and offices.

The Village Campus features a Tudor-style building containing classrooms, a science laboratory, a library, an art room, a music-dance studio, offices, a gymnasium, and kitchen facilities.

On the Maple Road Campus, a one-story building houses classrooms, a library, a gymnasium, and art, speech, French, science, music, and activities rooms. There are also offices, a clinic, and kitchen facilities. The Victorian-style Barbara Plamondon Earle Early Learning Village has six classrooms for three- and four-year-olds, a Junior Kindergarten, and an activity room.

THE FACULTY. Glen P. Shilling (B.A. Albion, M.Div. Harvard, J.D. University of Detroit) is Headmaster.

The Directors are Bradley M. Gilman (B.A. Dartmouth, M.A. Occidental) for the Upper School, Cynthia Goldberg (B.A. Central Michigan University, M.A. Michigan State) for the Middle School, Joseph D'Angelo (B.S. University of Detroit, M.A. Wayne State) for the Junior School, and Ruth Rebold (B.A. Michigan State, M.A.T. Oakland University) for the Lower School.

There are 202 full-time faculty members and administrators who teach, 59 men and 143 women. They hold 122 master's and 10 doctoral degrees from 95 colleges and universities. Among the schools attended are Albion, Amherst, Cambridge (England), Cornell, Dartmouth, Georgetown, Harvard, Princeton, Rutgers, and the Universities of Michigan and Notre Dame.

There are four full-time registered nurses. The School is located three miles from a hospital, and first-aid equipment is available on campus.

STUDENT BODY. In 2007–08, Detroit Country Day School enrolled 1620 students. There are 315 students in Lower School (Preschool–Grade 2), 246 in Junior School (Grades 3–5), 385 in Middle School (Grades 6–8), and 674 in Upper School (Grades 9–12).

The students, 3 to 18 years of age, reside in 55 nearby communities. A Cottage Boarding program enables a limited number of students to live on campus with faculty families.

ACADEMIC PROGRAM. The school year runs from early September to mid-June. The calendar includes Thanksgiving, winter, midwinter, and spring vacations.

The average class size is 15 pupils. Students have opportunities to take both art and music classes every year. The Middle and Upper Schools operate on a rotating schedule. Class periods are scheduled from 8:00 A.M. to 2:55 P.M. for the Middle School, with a late start of 8:35 on Thursdays, and 3:20 P.M. for the Upper School, followed by athletics for Grades 7–12. Grades 6–8 have several weekly assemblies and daily activity periods. Grades 9–12 have weekly assemblies and activities. Grades 11 and 12 may use the commons room at their discretion.

A computer-based learning program, one of only a few in the nation, requires all Middle and Upper School students and faculty to have laptop computers for class exercises, homework, tests, research, and other functions. Some 1200 notebook computers are networked to provide Internet resources and improve communication among students, faculty, and parents.

Grade reports are sent to parents every ten weeks in the Middle School and every eight weeks in the Upper School. Marks are posted quarterly in the Upper School and three times a year in the Middle School. All teachers participate in an adviser-advisee program and are available to give tutorial assistance.

The Lower and Junior schools foster early academic development and values through a broad-based, integrated, stimulating curriculum that includes basic instruction in language arts, math, social studies, science, French, the arts, movement education, and computer science. A PM program of enrichment activities is also held after school. The faculty are dedicated to meeting the needs of the whole child and developing character through exposure to time-honored values.

The Middle School curriculum offers basic subjects, supplemented with enrichment courses for qualified students. Among the courses are English, Writing, French, Spanish, Latin, History, Geography, Mathematics, Pre-Algebra, Algebra, Geometry, Computers, General Science, Chemistry, C.A.R.E. Program related to adolescent growth and development, Speech and Dramatics, Art, Music, and Physical Education. Interdisciplinary classes are also offered.

To graduate, students must complete requirements in three categories: academic, athletic, and activities. Academic credit requirements include English 4, foreign language 3, history 3, mathematics 3, science 2, and fine and performing arts 1. Students must also complete courses in Speech and Health Education. Additional requirements include interscholastic athletics and fitness and skill- and service-oriented activities.

Flexible scheduling allows Upper School students to take more than one class in a particular area of concentration. Among the courses are French, German, Latin, Spanish, Japanese; Ancient and Non-Western World, Modern European Civilization, Contemporary World History, American Studies, African-American Studies; Geometry, AB and BC Calculus, College Algebra; Advanced Biology, Advanced Physics, Advanced Chemistry, Anatomy and Physiology; World Literature, Literature and Law, Shakespeare and Modern Drama, Humanities, Modern Themes in Literature, Theory of Knowledge; and Advanced Harmony and Composition. Advanced Placement study is offered in 19 areas.

Typical semester electives are Human Genetics, Cell Biology; Speech; Theatre; American Legal System, Civil War, Economics; Discrete Mathematics; Art and Design, Media Exploration, Computer Graphics, Painting, Drawing, Ceramics, Photography, and Sculpture.

Honors courses are available at all levels. The Advanced Placement Program is designed for students who are progressing at a rapid pace in a particular subject. Qualified students are offered the opportunity to enroll in the demanding International Baccalaureate program. Graduates of this two-year liberal arts curriculum are eligible for admission to universities throughout the world or for sophomore standing in most American colleges and universities.

Detroit Country Day School and the local business and professional community cooperate in the Senior Project. Students in Grade 12 spend four weeks as observers and interns in such fields as architecture, advertising, medicine, law, and banking.

In 2007, all of the graduating seniors were accepted at four-year colleges and universities. They are attending such institutions as Albion, Columbia, Cornell, Dartmouth, Denison, Georgetown, Harvard, Johns Hopkins, Kalamazoo, Massachusetts Institute of Technology, Michigan State, Northwestern, Stanford, Yale, and the University of Michigan.

During the summer, Detroit Country Day School conducts both academic and recreational programs. The five-week academic program offers Enrichment and Tutorial classes for students in Kindergarten–Grade 12, a writing workshop, and a five-week Study Skills course for students in Grades 6–9. Recreational camps include tennis, soccer, baseball, lacrosse, field hockey, and basketball.

STUDENT ACTIVITIES. Participation in activities is required for graduation. Directed by students, with help from faculty advisers, these include the yearbook, literary magazine, and newspaper; the Student Government; the drama, photography, art, community service, computer, debate, and foreign language clubs; Contemporary Issues; the Model United Nations; Quiz Bowl; Academic Games; DCD–TV; and others.

Detroit Country Day School athletic teams compete with area public and private schools. Teams are formed in soccer, lacrosse, football, cross-country, basketball, hockey, baseball, tennis, track, field hockey, volleyball, skiing, swimming, softball, cheerleading, golf, and many others. Strength and conditioning is offered as an alternative to competitive sports.

Throughout the year, there are assemblies, dances, dramatic productions, concerts, lectures, and field trips. Extended trips include Space Camp in Huntsville, Alabama (Grade 5), science trip to Disney World, and Washington, D.C. (Grade 8). Traditional events for the school community include Auction, Homecoming, Parents' Night, an ice cream social, and the Alumni-Varsity Basketball and Ice Hockey games.

ADMISSION AND COSTS. Detroit Country Day School seeks students who show evidence of "ability, ambition, achievement, character, and discipline." The School has a policy of socioeconomic diversification, enrolling students "without regard for race, creed, or ethnic origin." Admission is highly competitive and is based on previous school records, entrance examinations, recommendations, and an interview. The entrance examinations, which are given by appointment only, consist of the Educational Records Bureau Assessment tests, and the Otis Lennon aptitude and intelligence test. New students are accepted for all grades. There is a $100 application and testing fee.

Tuition ranges from $15,080 for all-day Pre-Kindergarten to $23,110 for the Upper School. This basic fee covers lunches, athletic uniforms, tutoring and study skills, and reading evaluations. Among the additional expenses are books, laptop computers, transportation, personal athletic equipment, field trips, and school uniforms. Tuition payment plans and tuition insurance are available. Detroit Country Day, which subscribes to the Private School Aid Services, awarded financial aid to 179 boys and girls in 2007–08. Financial aid is given on the basis of financial need, citizenship, prior academic performance, and leadership.

Deans of Students: Eva M. Dodds, John Meyers, Joe Hansen & Betsy Moss (Upper School); Stan Chodun, Judy Leybourn & Lisa Zimmerman (Middle School), Lisa Morgan & Meredith Stone (Lower School), and Marlenn Maicki (Junior School)
Alumni Director: Kira Mann
Director of Admission: Jorge D. Prosperi
Director of Development: Scott C. Bertschy
Director of College Counseling: Anne Sandoval
Director of Athletics: Dan MacLean

The Grosse Pointe Academy 1885

171 Lake Shore Road, Grosse Pointe Farms, MI 48236
Tel. 313-886-1221; Admissions Ext. 146; Fax 313-886-4615
Web Site www.gpacademy.org; E-mail mmcdermott@gpacademy.org

THE GROSSE POINTE ACADEMY in Grosse Pointe Farms, Michigan, is an independent day school enrolling boys and girls in a Montessori Early School (ages $2^1/_2$–5), a Lower School (Grades 1–5), and a Middle School (Grades 6–8). Grosse Pointe Farms is a suburb located six miles northeast of downtown Detroit and is the central community of the five Grosse Pointes. The school makes extensive use of the museums and other cultural resources of southeastern Michigan.

The Grosse Pointe Academy was founded as the Academy of the Sacred Heart in 1885. It was operated by the Religious of the Sacred Heart as a day and boarding primary, middle, and upper school for girls. The Academy's coeducational Montessori Early School was built in 1887. In 1969, the school was reincorporated under the original charter as The Grosse Pointe Academy and ownership was transferred to the Academy Board of Trustees. In September of that year, The Grosse Pointe Academy opened as an independent, coeducational day school with 270 students from metropolitan Detroit enrolled in Pre-Kindergarten through Grade 8.

The Grosse Pointe Academy holds that learning is a continuous and highly personalized process extending throughout life and requires a strong intellectual, moral, and physical foundation. Moral values and Montessori principles, emphasizing attention to individual needs, govern the Early School and are sustained throughout the grades. Founded on Christian principles, the school has as its mission to respect all religious beliefs and cultures while honoring the value and growth of each individual child. It is within this framework that all life at the Academy is conducted.

The Academy is a nonprofit organization governed by a self-perpetuating Board of 19 Trustees, which meets eight times a year. There are 747 living alumnae of the Academy of the Sacred Heart and 1286 alumni of The Grosse Pointe Academy. The Academy, through its Parent Coordinating Council, operates an active parent volunteer program. Parents, alumni, and friends assist the school financially through Annual Fund and "Action Auction," a yearly fund-raiser involving the entire community.

The Grosse Pointe Academy is a member of the Independent Schools Association of the Central States, the National Association of Independent Schools, the Association of Independent Michigan Schools, the American Montessori Society, and the Educational Records Bureau.

THE CAMPUS. The Academy is situated on a stately, 20-acre campus overlooking Lake St. Clair. The historic facilities, which include a half-mile double row of maples known as the Nun's Walk, appear in local, state, and national registers of historic sites. Six tennis courts, two playgrounds, and fields for lacrosse and soccer are also located on campus.

The Lakeshore Building, completed in 1885 as the Academy and Convent of the Sacred Heart, now houses business, alumni, and advancement offices. It is also used for meetings and social functions. The Montessori Early School (circa 1887) has spacious classrooms. An additional classroom and a new gymnasium were added in 1987. The Academy's Main School Building (circa 1929) houses classrooms, a library, a cafeteria, an auditorium, and the school's original gymnasium. A newly refurbished, state-of-the-art building opened in September 2007. The Tracy Fieldhouse gymnasium/auditorium was dedicated in 1990. The Grosse Pointe Academy Chapel (circa 1899) is the site of many weddings and school chapel assemblies. The school-owned plant is valued at more than $10,000,000.

THE FACULTY. Phil Demartini (Columbia University, B.A.; Fordham University, M.Ed.) is the Head of School. He is the former Headmaster of St. Francis School in Goshen, Kentucky. Prior to that, Mr. Demartini was Lower School Principal at Metairie Park Country Day School in New Orleans, Louisiana, and Principal of the Upper School at Elisabeth Morrow School in Englewood, New Jersey.

The full-time faculty consist of 9 men and 35 women. They hold baccalaureate degrees from Albion, Baldwin-Wallace, Central Michigan, Chatham, College of St. Catherine, Columbia, Cortland State, Curry, Denison, Eastern Michigan, Hillsdale, Kalamazoo, Marygrove, Mercy, Michigan State, Nazareth, Northern Illinois, Oakland, Ohio State, Purdue, St. Joseph's, St. Lawrence, St. Mary's of Notre Dame, Sweet Briar, Trent, Wayne State, Western Michigan, and the Universities of Akron, Denver, Maryland, Michigan, and Windsor. They hold advanced degrees from Eastern Michigan, Fordham, Long Island University, Marygrove, Michigan State, Oakland, Ohio State, Wayne State, Xavier, and the Universities of Michigan and Toronto.

Faculty benefits include health and dental insurance, life insurance, long-term disability, a retirement plan, and Social Security. Leaves of absence are granted on approval of the Board of Trustees.

A school nurse is on duty at the Academy and three hospitals are located nearby.

STUDENT BODY. In 2006–07, the Academy enrolled 340 boys and girls, with 110 students in the Early School and 230 in Grades 1–8. Students came from the Grosse Pointes and 32 metropolitan Detroit communities and reflected a wide range of socioeconomic backgrounds.

ACADEMIC PROGRAM. The academic year, divided into semesters, begins in early September and ends in mid-June. Major vacations are scheduled in December and March. Classes are held five days a week between 8:30 A.M. and 3:20 P.M. In the Early School, students are taught on an individualized basis, using Montessori methods of education. No more than ten children are in the charge of each adult. Grades 1–3 are in self-contained classrooms and Grades 4 and 5 provide a transition to the fully departmentalized programs of Grades 6–8. The emphasis on individual attention is maintained throughout the Middle School years. Academy teachers pride themselves on enabling students to achieve in all areas and are available to assist students as necessary. Grades are sent to parents three times a year supplemented by regular conferences scheduled in October and February.

All students in Grades 1–5 take reading, language arts (including spelling, vocabulary, writing, grammar, and literature), French, Spanish, Chinese, social studies, mathematics, computers, science, religion, music, art, library/reference skills, and physical education. The emphasis is on mastery of basic skills. Multitexts and teacher-designed programs for reinforcement and enrichment are used so that each student can progress at his or her level. Computers, videotapes, and video disks are employed. Electives in music, art, the social sciences, and science supplement the regular program. Instruction in environmental education is also offered. A formalized leadership program is a hallmark of the eighth-grade year.

Before- and After-School Care programs are available, at an extra charge, for children ages 3 to 14 on a daily or occasional basis.

Students graduating from The Grosse Pointe Academy enroll at private, parochial, and public high schools. In recent years, graduates have attended the Academy of the Sacred Heart, Andrews School, Brother Rice, Cranbrook, DeLaSalle Collegiate, Detroit Country Day, Fay School, Grosse Pointe North, Grosse Pointe South, The Gunnery, Holderness, Hotchkiss, The Hun School of Princeton, Kingswood, Lake Forest Academy, Lawrenceville, The Leelanau School, Marian High School, Mercy, Miss Porter's, Pomfret, Portsmouth Abbey, Proctor, St. George's School, St. Mark's, University Liggett School, University of Detroit High School, and Woodberry Forest.

Academy Adventures, a summer program for boys and girls ages 10 to 15, offers a variety of learning opportunities.

STUDENT ACTIVITIES. Middle School students are elected to the Student Council. The Council operates a number of extracurricular programs.

Students are involved in school activities through the yearbook, crafts, and cooking. Grades 4–8 participate in volunteer services and Student Council activities. Grades 7 and 8 perform 20 hours of community service each year.

Middle School teams compete with other private schools in lacrosse, soccer, basketball, and tennis for boys; and tennis, basketball, volleyball, and soccer for girls. Both boys and girls participate in the cross-country team. Teams from Grades 4 and 5 play limited interscholastic schedules.

An intramural sports program for Grades 1–5 includes soccer, floor hockey, basketball, softball, and lacrosse.

Special events include the Back to School Picnic, Parents' Orientation Nights, Fall and Winter/Spring Sports Awards

Assemblies, Spirit Nights, Alumni Reunions, Book Fair, a tree-lighting ceremony, Alumni Scholarship Benefit, Dads' Day, Grandparents' Day, the Eighth Grade Play, and the William Charles McMillan III Lecture Series.

ADMISSION AND COSTS. The Grosse Pointe Academy seeks academically strong and motivated students. Students are admitted in all grades with available spaces on the basis of standardized tests, recommendations, and personal interviews. Applications, with a fee of $50, should be submitted before July 1. Students may be admitted during the school year under special conditions.

In 2007–08, tuition for half-day Early School is $9300; for full-day Early School, $13,400; the fees for Grades 1 through 8 range from $14,000 to $16,600, depending on grade. Tuition insurance and payment plans are available. The Grosse Pointe Academy subscribes to FACTS for Financial Aid and offers approximately $250,000 in financial aid annually to 13 percent of the students on the basis of need and academic standing.

Principal, Early School and Grades 1–3: Camille DeMario
Principal, Middle School: Scott Tily
Director of Admissions: Molly McDermott
Director of Finance & Operations: Angela Boyle

Kalamazoo Country Day School 1979

4221 East Milham Road, Kalamazoo, MI 49002
Tel. 269-329-0116; Fax 269-329-1850
Web Site www.kalamazoocountryday.org
E-mail sbridenstine@kalamazoocountryday.org

Kalamazoo Country Day School, founded by a group of families interested in providing quality education in the area, enrolls 200 boys and girls in Pre-School–Grade 8. It aims to provide a supportive environment that emphasizes active learning, enhancement of self-esteem, and promotion of individual talents and community responsibility. Spanish, computers, music, art, and drama complement the traditional subjects. Students with learning differences are accommodated. Science fair, speech festival, Student Council, ski club, and sports are among the activities. Tuition: $7723–$7853. Financial aid is available. Sheila Bridenstine (Saint Louis University, A.B.) is Director.

Kingsbury Country Day School 1953

5000 Hosner Road, Oxford, MI 48370
Tel. 248-628-2571; Fax 248-628-3612
Web Site www.gokingsbury.org
E-mail adibble@kingsburyschool.org

Founded by Carlton and Annette Higbie, the Kingsbury Country Day School enrolls 180 boys and girls in Junior Kindergarten–Grade 8. The School seeks to recognize individual needs and develop individual potential. In addition to core subjects, students are involved at every level in Spanish, music, environmental education, art, computers, and physical education. Grades 6–8 are fully departmentalized. Competitive and recreational sports are available all year round. A summer program offers nature, sports, art, and computer courses. Tuition: $11,950–$12,100. Financial aid is available. Audrey J. Smith-Dibble is Director of Admissions; Gil Webb is Head of School.

Notre Dame Preparatory School and Marist Academy 1994

1300 Giddings Road, Pontiac, MI 48340-2108
Tel. 248-373-5300; Fax 248-373-8024
Web Site www.ndpma.org; E-mail ndp@ndpma.org

NOTRE DAME PREPARATORY SCHOOL AND MARIST ACADEMY in Pontiac, Michigan, is a Roman Catholic, college preparatory day school enrolling young women and men in Grades 9 through 12. Marist Academy, Notre Dame Prep's middle school counterpart, enrolls students in Grades 6 through 8. A second campus housing Junior Kindergarten–Grade 5 is located in Waterford. Pontiac, an industrial city of 72,800 residents, is located 30 miles northwest of Detroit. Many students take private car pools to the campus, and the School maintains a fleet of eight buses.

At the request of the Archbishop of Detroit, the Marist Fathers and Brothers of the Boston Province founded Notre Dame Preparatory to provide an excellent college preparatory program with a strong Catholic identity. The School opened in 1994 with 183 high school students and 18 staff members and met with immediate success. The middle school was added a few years later, and today Notre Dame Prep and Marist Academy enroll 1150 young people with the support of 130 faculty and staff.

Notre Dame Prep's mission derives from the philosophy of Fr. Jean-Claude Colin, founder of the Marist Fathers and Brothers. The School seeks to train students as faithful and active disciples of Christ, to instruct them in "all virtues," and to teach them "letters and various branches of knowledge." Intended to develop "Christian people, upright citizens, and academic scholars," the rigorous curriculum encompasses a wide range of liberal arts and sciences while placing equal emphasis on moral conduct and the formation of spiritual values.

A not-for-profit institution, Notre Dame is operated by the Marist Fathers and Brothers, Boston Province. It is governed by a Board of Directors whose members are provincial councilors of the sponsoring congregation; the 28-member Board of Trustees is chosen from a slate presented to the Directors. The School is accredited by the North Central Association of Colleges and Schools and the Independent Schools Association of the Central States. It holds membership in the National Catholic Educational Association and is an IB candidate school.

THE CAMPUS. Notre Dame Prep and Marist Academy occupy nearly 100 wooded acres on the outskirts of Pontiac. The 150,000-square-foot main building contains all the School's classrooms, science and computer labs, and art and music studios as well as a chapel, guidance and counseling center, bookstore, cafeteria, gymnasium, and the 10,000-square-foot St. Peter Chanel Media Center.

Notre Dame Prep's rapid growth has necessitated a vigorous expansion of its facilities. The School plans to continue an equally aggressive expansion program over the course of the next several years. A ProGrass artificial turf surface and six new, state-of-the-art tennis courts are among the improvements to the athletic facilities. A new gym/band building opened in the fall of 2007.

The School proper is owned by the Marist congregation; the building is leased from the Archdiocese of Detroit.

THE FACULTY. In 1993, Rev. Leon M. Olszamowski, s.m., was appointed to organize the founding of Notre Dame Preparatory School. He serves as President of both Notre Dame and Marist Academy. A native of Detroit, Father Leon graduated from Notre Dame High School in Harper Woods, Michigan, where he was later Principal. He holds a B.A. from Boston College, an M.A. from the University of Notre Dame, an M.Div. from Weston School of Theology, and M.A. and Ph.D. degrees from The Catholic University of America. Rev. Joseph C. Hindelang, s.m. (Assumption College, B.A.; Weston School of Theology, M.Div.), became Principal in 2002. Mrs. Sandra Favrow (Wayne State University, B.A.; Saginaw Valley State University, M.A.) heads Marist Academy.

Notre Dame Prep and Marist Academy have a combined faculty and staff of 130, all but 6 of whom are full-time. In the Upper School, 75 percent hold advanced degrees, including 4 doctorates. Among their representative colleges and universities are Alma, Assumption, Central Michigan, Ferris State, Marygrove, Michigan State, Northern Illinois, Northern Michigan, Oakland University, Ohio University, Olivet College, Pennsylvania State, Rutgers, Saginaw Valley State, St. Mary's College, Temple, Trinity, Wayne State, Western Michigan, Siena, and the Universities of Arizona, Dayton, Detroit, Maryland, Massachusetts, Michigan, Notre Dame, and Washington.

STUDENT BODY. In 2007–08, 730 boys and girls are enrolled at Notre Dame and 416 at Marist Academy. While 85 percent are Roman Catholic, students from all faiths are welcome.

ACADEMIC PROGRAM. The school year, from late August to early June, is divided into semesters, with Thanksgiving, Christmas, Winter Break, and Easter vacations and several religious and national holidays. Grades are posted six times a year.

All students wear the school uniform throughout the day. The school day consists of nine periods between 7:30 A.M. and 2:45 P.M. Some students have a study hall. The average enrollment is 22–24 in core courses or as few as 5 in specialized courses. Members of the National Honor Society provide tutoring three days a week.

At Marist Academy, students in Grades 6–8 have a core curriculum of religion, English, mathematics including algebra, foreign language (French, German, Spanish), science, and social science. Band, chorus, and desktop publishing are also available.

To graduate, Upper School students must earn 28 credits including 4 each in religion and English; 3 each in mathematics, science, and social science; 2 in a modern language; 1 in health/physical education; and .5 each in fine and performing arts and computer applications. Ten hours of community service are required each year. These requirements meet or exceed the admission criteria of Michigan's state universities. The ACT composite is 26.

Among the Upper School courses are Old Testament, New Testament Studies 1–2, Foundations of Catholic Morality, Moral Issues and Lifestyles, History of the Church 1–2; Composition 1–2, Research and Speech, Introduction to the Classics, American and English Authors 1–2, World Literature 1–2, Theater, Public Speaking, Lincoln-Douglas Debate, Forensics; Algebra 1–2, Geometry 1–2, Trigonometry and Pre-Calculus, Probability and Statistics; five-year programs in French, German, Spanish; Biology 1–2, Chemistry 1–2, Astronomy 1–2, Human Anatomy and Physiology; World History and Cultures 1–2, United States History 1–2, American Government, The Modern World Since 1945, Economics, Current Issues, Law, Psychology, Sociology; Computer Applications, Computer Science Topics, BASIC Programming, C++ Programming; Accounting 1–2, Business Law; Exploration in Art, Drawing, Painting, Pottery, Commercial Art, Portfolio 1–2; Marching/Symphonic Band, Jazz Band 1–2, Concert Choir, Honors Choir; and Health/Physical Education 1–2, Weight Training, and Officiating.

Advanced Placement courses are available in Computer Science, Literature, Composition, Calculus, French, Spanish, German, American History, European History, Chemistry, Biology, Physics, Environmental Science, Psychology, and Art.

All 184 seniors in the Class of 2007 were accepted to college; 99 percent were accepted to four-year colleges and universities, and nearly all were admitted by "early decision." They were offered nearly $8,500,000 in scholarships. Michigan State, Oakland University, and the University of Michigan (Ann Arbor) were the graduates' three most popular choices; other schools included Art Institute of Chicago, Boston College, Bowling Green State, DePaul, George Washington University, Loyola, Purdue, School of Visual Arts, Syracuse, Western Michigan

University, Xavier, and the Universities of Colorado, Nevada, Notre Dame, Pittsburgh, Tennessee, and Wisconsin.

A summer program offers enrichment in language arts, mathematics, and computer science.

STUDENT ACTIVITIES. Extracurricular activities are designed to meet diverse student interests, provide leadership opportunities, and maintain school spirit and morale. Grades 9–12 elect eight representatives per class to the Student Council, which is responsible for overseeing the "life-giving" events of the School, such as dances, fund-raisers, games, and interaction with other schools.

Interscholastic sports are played at all grade levels and involve more than three-quarters of the student body. Marist Academy is a member of the Catholic Youth Organization; Notre Dame holds membership in the Detroit Catholic High School League and the Michigan High School Athletic Association.

Fighting Irish teams compete in football, soccer, golf, cross-country, basketball, ice hockey, wrestling, baseball, lacrosse, tennis, and track for boys, while girls' teams are organized in basketball, cross-country, tennis, swimming, volleyball, soccer, softball, pompon, lacrosse, and track. Notre Dame's cheerleading squads are an important addition to many varsity contests.

Among the various groups in which students are involved are a statewide Student Congress discussion tournament, the National Honor Society, forensics and debate, a drama and theater program, and the Optimist (community outreach), Computer, Modern Language, Students Against Drunk Driving, F.I.R.S.T. Robotics, and Chess Clubs. Students publish *The Legend* (yearbook) and *The Leprechaun* (newspaper). Other popular activities are musical performances in the fall and spring, band and chorus concerts, and a visual arts exhibit.

Throughout the year, the Campus Ministry plans retreats and special liturgies and provides pastoral counseling as a means of furthering spiritual development. Homecoming, a three-day celebration of school spirit enjoyed by students, parents, and alumni, features a pep rally, football game, and dance. The calendar also includes traditions such as Halloween Party, Thanksgiving Liturgy, Irish Week, Walk-a-Thon, sports banquets, Mothers' Mass and Brunch, Awards Night, senior prom, and graduation.

ADMISSION AND COSTS. Notre Dame Prep and Marist Academy welcome capable students of good character and ability, regardless of racial, ethnic, religious, or socioeconomic backgrounds. Students are accepted in Grades 6–11 and occasionally, depending on circumstances, in Grade 12. Admission is offered on the basis of the entrance exam, previous academic transcripts and testing, teacher and principal recommendations, and a personal interview. Acceptance letters are mailed on the fourth Friday in January. The application fee is $25.

In 2007–08, tuition is $9450, plus uniforms, books, and parking and retreat fees. Merit-based scholarships are awarded in the amount of $375,000, and need-based financial aid of about $100,000 is available. Students may earn money for some on-campus jobs.

President: Rev. Leon M. Olszamowski, s.m., Ph.D.
Vice-President & Principal: Rev. Joseph C. Hindelang, s.m.
Middle School Principal: Sandra J. Favrow
Elementary School Principal: Diana Atkins
Vice-Principal & Dean of Faculty: Donna A. Kotzan
Assistant Principal: Rev. James J. Strasz, s.m.
Assistant Principal: Kimberly Anderson
Assistant Principal: Jill Mistretta
Campus Ministers: Deacon Anthony Morici & Rev. Maciej Pawlowski
Director of Admissions: Gregory P. Simon
Director of Advancement: Andrew Guest
College Counselor: Justine Sciriha
Business Manager: Anthony Block
Directors of Athletics: Betty Wroubel, Marty Simmons & Megan Thayer

The Roeper School 1941

41190 Woodward Avenue, Bloomfield Hills, MI 48304
Tel. 248-203-7300; Admissions 248-203-7317; Fax 248-203-7350
Web Site www.roeper.org; E-mail admissions@roeper.org

The Roeper School is a coeducational day school for gifted children enrolling approximately 620 students in Pre-Kindergarten–Grade 12. Founded by George and Annemarie Roeper, it seeks to "provide an environment that fosters intellectual stimulation, independence, breadth of view, and compassion." The Lower School is in Bloomfield Hills; the Middle/Upper School is in Birmingham. A strong core curriculum is enhanced by a broad selection of classes and activities to meet the interests

of students. Tuition: $13,950–$19,500. Financial Aid: $500,000. Lori Zinser is Admissions Director; Randall Dunn (Brown University, A.B.; Harvard University, M.Ed.) was appointed Head of School in 2004.

University Liggett School 1878

1045 Cook Road, Grosse Pointe Woods, MI 48236
Tel. 313-884-4444; Fax 313-884-1775
Web Site www.uls.org; E-mail daxford@uls.org

University Liggett, a coeducational, college preparatory day school, enrolls 550 students in Pre-Kindergarten–Grade 12. Established by the merger of Grosse Pointe University School (1899) and the Liggett School (1878), the School occupies 30 residential acres. Combining high expectations with individual assistance, University Liggett challenges students to reach the highest levels of their ability. The School's goals support growth of self-reliance, self-respect, concern for others, and commitment to community service. Strong programs in athletics and the creative arts supplement the curriculum. Honors and Advanced Placement courses are available. Tuition: $7600–$18,200. Dan Axford is Director of Enrollment; Joseph P. Healey (Pontifica Universitas Gregoriana, A.B.; Catholic University of America, M.Div.; Harvard, Ph.D.) is Head of School.

MINNESOTA

The Blake School 1900

Northrop Campus (Upper School): 511 Kenwood Parkway, Minneapolis, MN 55403
Blake Campus (Lower/Middle School): 110 Blake Road South, Hopkins, MN 55343
Highcroft Campus (Lower School): 301 Peavey Lane, Wayzata, MN 55391
Tel. 952-988-3400; Admissions 952-988-3420; Fax 952-988-3455
Web Site www.blakeschool.org

Founded in 1900, The Blake School is an independent, coeducational, nonsectarian, college preparatory day school serving Pre-Kindergarten–Grade 12. Coming from more than 56 Twin Cities' communities, over 1375 students attend Blake on one of three campuses in Minneapolis, Hopkins, and Wayzata. The challenging liberal arts curriculum integrates academics, arts, and athletics. All graduates go on to four-year colleges. Blake is dedicated to creating a safe and inclusive environment that encourages risk-taking, recognizes effort, and provides opportunity for success for everyone. The School is committed to diversity, and community involvement is expected of every student. Tuition: $11,700–$19,900. Financial Aid: $3,000,000. Adaline Shinkle is Director of Admissions; John C. Gulla is Head of School.

Breck School 1886

123 Ottawa Avenue North, Minneapolis, MN 55422
Tel. 763-381-8100; Admissions 763-381-8200; Fax 763-381-8288
Web Site www.breckschool.org; E-mail info@breckschool.org

BRECK SCHOOL in Minneapolis, Minnesota, is a college preparatory day school enrolling boys and girls in Preschool through Grade 12. The School uses the cultural and educational resources of the Twin Cities metropolitan area (population 2,500,500) to offer a vigorous liberal arts curriculum. It is the only school in Minnesota to have all divisions—Lower, Middle, and Upper—honored by the U.S. Department of Education. The Lower School received the "School of Excellence" award in 1987. The Middle and Upper schools received the "Blue Ribbon" award in 1993.

Named for a pioneer missionary, the Reverend James Lloyd Breck, the School was established in 1886 in Wilder, Minnesota, to provide children with a top-quality education under the auspices of the Episcopal church. In 1916, Breck moved to St. Paul; in 1956, a new facility was built on the Mississippi River in Minneapolis; and in 1981, the School relocated to the present 50-acre campus just west of downtown Minneapolis.

Breck strives to create a supportive and caring environment where the emphasis is on building self-worth. Friendship, respect, and mutual support among all members of the school community are stressed in an academic setting. Breck aims to be warm and friendly, academically rigorous but not driven, competitive but not compulsive, and structured but not rigid. Mastering basic skills is emphasized in the lower grades, enabling students to take advantage of increased options—such as independent study, internships, and Advanced Placement courses—in the upper grades. Students are encouraged to participate in sports, community service, and on-campus extracurricular activities. Chapel attendance and religion courses are required.

A nonprofit institution, Breck is affiliated with the Episcopal Diocese of Minnesota, and the Bishop is Chairman of the Board. The School is directed by a 26-member lay Board of Trustees, which meets monthly and includes parents, past parents, alumni, and friends of the School.

Breck is accredited by the Independent Schools Association of the Central States; it holds membership in such organizations as the National Association of Independent Schools, the National Association of Episcopal Schools, and other professional organizations.

THE CAMPUS. Breck's campus, including two wildlife ponds, a stream, and woods, is located at the junction of Glenwood Avenue and Highway 100, just north of Interstate Highway 394, a main artery linking Minneapolis and St. Paul. Two football fields, three soccer fields, three baseball fields, and seven tennis courts are on site.

The School houses eight science laboratories, three gymnasiums, and a five-lane swimming pool. It also contains the Cargill Theatre (a 450-seat production theater with stage), 3 library/media centers, and many classrooms, interior courtyards, and commons areas. The Chapel of the Holy Spirit, seating 1300, is the focal point of the campus and the center of the School's spiritual life. In addition, Breck owns an ice arena for hockey and figure-skating programs. Campus renovations include state-of-the-art spaces for performing arts, several new classrooms, and a large field house.

THE FACULTY. Edward Kim, Head of School, is a graduate of Dartmouth College (A.B.) and Columbia University (M.Ed.) Prior to his appointment at Breck, Mr. Kim served as Assistant Headmaster at Delbarton School in Morristown, New Jersey.

The faculty include 108 teachers recruited on a national basis. Nearly 70 percent hold advanced degrees.

STUDENT BODY. In 2007–08, the School enrolls 615 girls and 594 boys as follows: 447 in the Lower School (Preschool–Grade 4), 344 in the Middle School (Grades 5–8), and 418 in the Upper School (Grades 9–12). Students come from 66 communities; approximately 10 percent are Episcopalian. Students of color represent 25 percent of the student body.

ACADEMIC PROGRAM. The school year, from late August to early June, is divided into two semesters. The Middle and Upper Schools are further divided into quarters, with a special May program in the Upper School. School vacations include Labor Day, Thanksgiving, Christmas, Martin Luther King Day, Presidents' Day, spring break, Good Friday, and Memorial Day. School convenes at 8:30 A.M.; students in the half-day Preschool and Kindergarten programs are dismissed at noon. For all other students, including full-day Preschool and Kindergarten students and afternoon-session Preschool students, the academic day concludes at 3:15 P.M.

Auxiliary services for students include two college placement counselors, a nurse, a health education counselor, an educational psychologist, consulting psychologists, mentors, and professional tutors.

The Preschool and Kindergarten programs introduce students to language arts, mathematics skills, science, creative arts, and physical education. Students attend chapel and take field trips to local businesses and museums. Lower School students study Chinese or Spanish beginning in Kindergarten.

The program in the Lower School (Grades 1–4) is designed to encourage basic skills, good study habits, and sound moral values. In addition to Chinese or Spanish, students have daily instruction in language arts, mathematics, science, social studies, and physical education as well as regularly scheduled classes in music, art, modern languages, and library skills. All classrooms have their own microcomputers for drill and enrichment activities. The Suzuki String Program offers instruction in violin, viola, and cello to students in Preschool–Grade 4. Parent volunteerism is strongly encouraged.

In the Middle School (Grades 5–8), the basic curriculum consists of English, modern language (Chinese, French, and Spanish), history, mathematics, science, and physical education, including Project Adventure. All grades have a social skills program, which includes religious study, health, and Skills of Adolescence. Electives for all Middle School students are band, orchestra, drama, art, dance, and chorus.

To graduate, students must accumulate the following full-year credits in Grades 9–12: English 4, mathematics 3, foreign language 3, science 3, history (including United States History) 3, visual and performing arts 1, religious studies 1/2, physical education 1 1/2, health science 1/2, and electives 3 1/2.

The Upper School curriculum includes English, Senior English, Shakespeare, British Literature, Creative Writing, American Literature, Advanced Composition, Advanced Placement English; French 1–5, Advanced Placement French, German 1–5, Advanced Placement German, Spanish 1–4, Advanced Placement Spanish, Chinese 1–4; Medieval World History, United States History, Advanced Placement United States History, Modern World History, Political Ideologies, The Constitution, Comparative Government, Utopia, Economics, The Middle Ages and the Emerging World; Senior Ethics, Comparative Religions, Philosophy, Spiritual Questions; Computer Literacy, Algebra, Geometry, Advanced Algebra, Pre-Calculus, Honor Advanced Algebra, Advanced Placement Calculus AB and BC; Physical Science, Biology 1–3, Chemistry 1–3, Physics 1–2, Advanced Placement Biology, Advanced Placement Chemistry, Advanced Placement Physics; Theater/Drama, Speech, Studio Art, Ceramics, Printing, Drawing, Jazz Ensemble, String Ensemble, Chorus, Dance, Band; Student Service; and Physical Education.

Through the Upper School's Wednesday Program, all Upper School students and faculty perform community service at more than 20 different sites in the Twin Cities. Twenty hours of service to the School are required for graduation.

During May, Upper School juniors and seniors may pursue a directed study in an academic or research area. Internships in the professions or business management may also be arranged. International study trips have included programs in China, France, Russia, Greece, Spain, Kenya, and Japan.

In 2008, all of the 95 graduates went on to college. Three or more are attending Colorado College, DePaul, Northwestern, St. Olaf College, Tulane, and the Universities of Colorado and Southern California.

STUDENT ACTIVITIES. Middle and Upper School class presidents and vice-presidents serve on the Student Councils. Students may join the staffs of the yearbook, newspaper, and literary journal; other activities are the Mock Trial, Math League, Destination: Imagination, and Quiz Bowl teams; and the Computer, Chess, and Science Clubs.

The after-school athletic program involves most students in Grades 7–12. There are interscholastic teams for boys in baseball and football; for girls in gymnastics, softball, and volleyball; and for boys and girls in basketball, tennis, swimming, cross-country running, golf, lacrosse, slalom and cross-country skiing, soccer, ice hockey, and track. Intramural programs (Grades 4–6) field coeducational teams in flag football, soccer, basketball, tennis, softball, skating, gymnastics, cross-country skiing, and track and field.

Separate dances are held each year for Grades 7–8 and Grades 9–12. In addition, there are overnight camping trips for Grades 6–12 and frequent field trips to The Guthrie Theater, the University of Minnesota, Orchestra Hall, the Minneapolis Art Institute, the Children's Theatre, the Science Museum, the Minnesota Zoological Gardens, and other places of interest. Traditional school events include Senior Weekend, Parents'

Nights, athletic awards banquets, graduation festivities, Grandparents' Day, alumni class reunions, and evening parent coffees.

ADMISSION AND COSTS. In evaluating candidates, Breck looks for motivation, evidence of sound character, and strong academic achievement or potential. Academic transcripts, letters of reference, and a personal interview are required. The School also requires achievement testing.

In 2007–08, tuition is $13,145 for half-day Preschool and Kindergarten and $18,360 for full-day Preschool and Kindergarten. Tuition is $18,500 for Grades 1–12. Fees ($1415–$2845) include the lunch program, student activities, and other items. In addition, transportation costs range from $650 to $1200.

In 2007–08, need-based scholarship aid was granted to 17.4 percent of the student body. Applicants for scholarship aid apply through the School and Student Service for Financial Aid.

Academic Dean, Upper School: Kimberly Peeples
Dean of Students, Upper School: Christopher Ohm
Director, Upper School: Linda Tapsak
Director, Middle School: Becky Farber
Director, Lower School: Peg Bailey
Director of Admissions: Warner T. (Jim) James, Jr.
College Counselor: Melissa Soderberg
Business Manager: Wendy Engelman
Director of Athletics: Brett Bergene

Convent of the Visitation School 1873

2455 Visitation Drive, Mendota Heights, MN 55120-1696
Tel. 651-683-1700; Admissions 651-683-1707; Fax 651-454-7144
Web Site www.visitation.net; E-mail vischool@vischool.org

Visitation enrolls 600 day students, with boys and girls in Preschool–Grade 6 and girls only in Grades 7–12. The School provides a challenging college preparatory program within a sound religious environment. The curriculum emphasizes the liberal arts and sciences, enhanced by theology, computers, and Advanced Placement courses in the Upper School. The school takes an individualized approach to educating young people, recognizing each one's unique gifts and talents. Seniors undertake a two-week service project, and service learning is incorporated into the curriculum at all levels. The school's philosophy is rooted in joyful optimism and the infinite worth of each individual. The athletic program begins in Kindergarten, with 13 varsity sports in Grades 7–12. Girls in Grades 7–12 collaborate with young men from Saint Thomas Academy, Visitation's brother school, in many areas. The school's fine arts program is nationally renowned. Leadership skills development is incorporated into the program. Tuition: $5815–$14,735. Katie Owens is Director of Admissions; Dawn Nichols, Ed.D., is Head of School.

Shattuck-St. Mary's School 1858

P.O. Box 218, 1000 Shumway Avenue, Faribault, MN 55021
Tel. 507-333-1500; Admissions 507-333-1618; Fax 507-333-1661
Web Site www.s-sm.org; E-mail admissions@s-sm.org

SHATTUCK-ST. MARY'S SCHOOL in Faribault, Minnesota, is a coeducational, college preparatory boarding and day school enrolling students in Grades 6 through 12. The School is located in Faribault (population 22,000), just 45 minutes south of the Twin Cities of Minneapolis/St. Paul.

Shattuck-St. Mary's was founded by Dr. James Lloyd Breck in 1858, with 45 white and Native American mission school students and 6 divinity school students. By the early 1900s, Shattuck-St. Mary's had grown into four separate schools: Shattuck School for boys, St. Mary's Hall for girls, St. James School for younger boys, and the Seabury Theological Seminary. In 1933, Seabury merged with Western Theological Seminary and moved to Illinois. The remaining three schools merged and formed the present Shattuck-St. Mary's School in 1972.

The School's rigorous academic, arts, and athletic programs foster excellence, self-confidence, and well-roundedness, all in the context of strong Midwestern values. Shattuck-St. Mary's is affiliated with the Episcopal Church and strives to educate the whole person—character, mind, body, and spirit. Weekly chapel services and course work in leadership, ethics, and values, plus a 20-hour-per-year community service requirement, help prepare students to become responsible, contributing members of society. At the beginning of the school year, students experience an integrated Bastian Student Leadership Development Program, which includes an outdoors adventure week, campus leadership positions, a speaker series, journal writing, and ropes course challenge elements.

Shattuck-St. Mary's, a nonprofit corporation, is governed by a 20-member Board of Trustees. There are more than 6000 alumni, many of whom are active in fund-raising and admissions.

THE CAMPUS. The 250-acre campus, with its collegiate Gothic buildings, has been designated a National Historic District. Athletic facilities include an 18-hole golf course, two indoor ice arenas for hockey and figure skating, an indoor domed soccer field, two outdoor soccer fields, a baseball diamond, tennis courts, indoor and outdoor tracks, a fully equipped weight room, and two gymnasiums.

Shumway Hall (1887) is the School's main academic and administrative building. Johnson Armory (1909) includes a gymnasium, a weight room and conditioning center, and the 25,000-volume Homer T. Hirst III Memorial Library. Dobbin Hall (1907) houses classrooms, a music center, the infirmary, the student center, and the Upper School office. The facilities of Kingham Hall include science laboratories as well as a music library and rehearsal hall. Other campus buildings include the Chapel of the Good Shepherd (1872), five dormitories, the Head of School's residence, and faculty homes. The School-owned plant is valued at $35,000,000.

THE FACULTY. Nicholas J.B. Stoneman, appointed Head of School in 2003, is a graduate of Bowdoin College and earned his master's degree at Columbia University's Teachers College. Prior to his appointment, he served as the Head of the Country Day School in Arlington, Texas.

There are 95 teaching faculty members, nearly all of whom live on campus. All teaching faculty hold baccalaureate degrees, 24 hold graduate degrees, and 3 have earned doctorates.

The Health Center is staffed by registered nurses as well as two full-time athletic trainers, and hospital and clinic facilities are less than a mile away.

STUDENT BODY. In 2007–08, the School enrolled 417 students, 300 boarders and 117 day students. Boarding students come from 34 states and 22 countries such as the Bahamas, Canada, China, the Czech Republic, England, Finland, Germany, Ghana, Hong Kong, Japan, Jordan, Korea, Latvia, Mexico, Mongolia, Russia, Saudi Arabia, Sweden, Taiwan, Thailand, and Vietnam.

ACADEMIC PROGRAM. The school year, which runs from late August to late May, is divided into trimesters. Classes are held from 8:00 A.M. to 3:45 P.M. Monday through Friday, with a nine-period, rolling block schedule. Class sizes average 15 students. Faculty-supervised study halls are held Sunday through Thursday from 8:00 to 9:30 P.M. Grades are available to parents online. Parents receive narrative comments at midterm and advisor letters at the end of each term.

Graduation requirements for Upper School (Grades 9–12) students include four years of English; three years of mathematics; three years of science, including one of physical science; three years of history; three consecutive levels of the same language in Grades 9–12; and one term of fine arts per year of attendance. An extensive Honors Program challenges students to explore course work above and beyond traditional high school-level work and offers honors classes as well as Advanced Placement courses in 14 areas of study.

The Performing Arts Department offers course work and select performance ensembles in vocal and instrumental music, dance, and drama. Extensive courses in these areas, plus numerous opportunities to perform on campus and to tour domestically and abroad,, make it possible for young artists to pursue conservatory training within a college preparatory program. The Pre-Conservatory Strings Program, inaugurated in the 2007–08 school year, is designed to offer serious string musicians ample practice time, weekly lessons with a private instructor, ensemble work, music theory, and performing opportunities as soloists and ensemble members. The School also offers English as a Second Language at five levels of proficiency and prepares students for the Test of English as a Foreign Language.

The School's Center for Academic Achievement includes an Academic Skills Program designed to recognize and enhance the potential of students with diagnosed mild learning disabilities and attention disorders. Each student enrolled receives an individualized education plan and concentrated course work specifically tailored to his or her educational needs.

In the past three years, virtually all graduating seniors were accepted by at least one college; 75 percent are accepted into their first-choice school. They are attending such institutions as Augsburg, Boston College, Brown, Carleton, Colorado College, Duke, Grinnell, Harvard, Johns Hopkins, Macalester, Massachusetts Institute of Technology, Northeastern, Northwestern, Rensselaer, Sonoma State, Wellesley, Wheaton, and the Universities of California (Berkeley), Chicago, Denver, Michigan, Minnesota, North Dakota, Rochester, Vermont, and Wisconsin.

Summer programs include drama, soccer, dance, figure skating, and ice hockey camps.

STUDENT ACTIVITIES. Students publish a yearbook. The Dramatic Association produces three full-length plays each year. Among the other student organizations are language clubs, Art Club, Student Vestry, Gold Key Club, Mathletes, and Crack Squad and Wooden Soldiers, the boys' and girls' drill teams.

The School fields interscholastic or intramural teams in soccer, tennis, volleyball, basketball, fencing, baseball, lacrosse, and a 5-K Running Club. Nine-month intensive training programs in ice hockey, soccer, and figure skating round out the competitive athletic offerings.

Students enjoy activities ranging from canoeing and camping trips to dances, museum visits, and shopping. Movies, lectures, and concerts are offered on and off campus. Weekends may be spent off campus, with appropriate permission.

ADMISSION AND COSTS. The School seeks "students of good character who are qualified to pursue a demanding college preparatory program." New students are accepted in Grades 6–12 on the basis of previous school records, the results of standardized tests, a personal interview, recommendations, and an aplicant questionnaire. Most students are accepted through late July until spaces are filled, with a priority application deadline of March 1. Applications, accompanied by a nonrefundable fee of $50 for U.S., Canadian, and Mexican applicants or $100 for international applicants, should be submitted as early as possible.

In 2007–08, tuition is $34,500 for boarding students and $21,200 for day students. Approximately $1500 is required for students' personal expenses. About 50 percent of the student body receives financial aid, which is based on need. In the current year, more than $1,800,000 was distributed in need-based grants. Tuition insurance and a tuition payment plan are available. Shattuck-St. Mary's subscribes to the School and Student Service for Financial Aid.

Headmaster: Nicholas J. B. Stoneman
Director of Studies: Matt Ruby
Dean of the Middle School: Beth Trout
Dean of Student Life: Scott Curwin
Director of Admissions & Communications: Amy Wolf
Director of Development: Lonnie Schroeder
Director of College Counseling: D. Lynn Redmond
Director of Student Services: Nate Payovich
Chief Financial Officer: Greg Engel
Director of Athletics: John LaFontaine

MISSISSIPPI

Chamberlain-Hunt Academy 1879

124 McComb Avenue, Port Gibson, MS 39150
Tel. 601-437-4291; Admission 601-437-8855; Fax 601-437-4313
Web Site chamberlain-hunt.com
E-mail admissions@chamberlain-hunt.com

Chamberlain-Hunt was founded by the Presbytery of Mississippi to provide a Christian education marked by strict discipline and high moral values. The school enrolls 125 young men as boarders and 5 day boys and girls in Grades 7–12. The school's college preparatory program features AP courses, support for learning differences, Biblical studies, and a Wilderness Program. In an atmosphere guided by military protocol and training, cadets learn in an environment that promotes academic, physical, and spiritual growth. Choir, a ropes course, a paintball arena, and athletics are among the activities. Boarding Tuition: $16,500; Day Tuition: $5000. Financial Aid: $250,000. MAJ Chris Blackwell is Director of Admission; COL Shane Blanton is Head of School. *Southern Association.*

Jackson Academy 1959

4908 Ridgewood Road, P.O. Box 14978, Jackson, MS 39236-4978
Tel. 601-362-9676; Fax 601-364-5722
Web Site www.jacksonacademy.org
E-mail mqdonnelly@jacksonacademy.org

JACKSON ACADEMY in Jackson, Mississippi, is the state's largest independent school, enrolling approximately 1400 boys and girls as day students in K3 through Grade 12. Located 180 miles north of New Orleans, the state capital (population 350,000) is home to five colleges, the Mississippi Arts Festival, Civil War battlefield sites, museums, and civic opera, theater, and the International Ballet Competition. Students and faculty enjoy frequent enrichment excursions to such attractions as a means of enlivening and reinforcing classroom learning.

Jackson Academy was established in 1959 to teach children to read by phonics. Today, the school continues its emphasis on reading and writing across the disciplines as it renews its commitment to provide a "superior academic program in every subject." Preparation for success in four-year colleges is a primary focus, and 100 percent of Jackson Academy graduates go on to higher education. In a nurturing, family-like environment, students are respected and challenged to become responsible citizens capable of achieving their highest intellectual, spiritual, social, emotional, and physical potential. The nonsectarian school, which promotes values and ethical conduct according to Judeo-Christian principles, welcomes students from diverse racial, ethnic, religious, and socioeconomic backgrounds.

Governed by an 11-member Board of Trustees, Jackson Academy is accredited by the Southern Association of Colleges and Schools and the Southern Association of Independent Schools. The Academy holds membership in the National Association of Independent Schools, among other organizations. In 2005, The Cum Laude Society installed a chapter at Jackson Academy. The school is aided in its mission by parent groups and the Alumni Association, which represents more than 2300 graduates.

THE CAMPUS. Jackson Academy's spacious campus is on the corner of Ridgewood Road and Sheffield Drive in the northeast area of the city. The 48 acres contain nine major academic buildings housing preschool, elementary, and junior and senior high divisions, each with its own library. In the Learning Center are upper school language, art, and social studies classrooms and the networked secondary library, equipped with an online database and 90-station computer labs to provide access to information technology. The entire campus is completely networked with Internet connections in every classroom and additional access through three labs, a multimedia training and presentation theater, and a teacher-training lab. Other academic facilities are science labs, art and music rooms for all grade levels, a multipurpose building, two fully equipped gymnasiums, and a band hall. Athletic resources include a lighted football stadium, and Raider Park, with lighted baseball and softball diamonds, a soccer field, and a dedicated track and field facility. Play areas for younger children are also on campus.

THE FACULTY. James Peter Jernberg, Jr., was appointed President and Head of School in 2005. He has earned bachelor's and master's degrees from Delta State University and completed additional graduate work at Mississippi State University and the Universities of Mississippi and South Carolina. Previously, Mr. Jernberg held administrative positions at Indianola Academy and is past president of the Southern Association of Independent Schools and a member of the Board of Trustees of the Southern Association of Colleges and Schools.

Dr. Pat Taylor took office as Headmaster in 2007. Previously, he spent 34 years at St. Paul's Episcopal School in Mobile, Alabama, where he served in several administrative and teaching positions. Dr. Taylor has also held leadership positions with SACS and SAIS.

The 150 faculty members hold baccalaureate degrees, and over 60 percent have earned advanced degrees. They are graduates of colleges and universities throughout the United States who participate regularly in opportunities for continued growth and professional development.

STUDENT BODY. In 2007–08, Jackson Academy enrolled 1400 students in K3 (age 3) to Grade 12.

ACADEMIC PROGRAM. The school year, from mid-August to late May, is divided into four nine-week grading periods, with Thanksgiving, Christmas, and spring recesses and several national holidays. A typical day, from 8:00 A.M. to 2:46 P.M., includes seven classes, lunch, and an activity break. Preschoolers are dismissed at 11:30 A.M. unless they are enrolled in the optional Lunch Bunch program.

Jackson Academy's preschool program is designed to promote a nurturing and loving learning environment where children acquire self-esteem and a positive approach to the educational experience. Basic concepts in core disciplines are introduced through reading, phonics, handwriting, story time, and library activities. Students work and play in small groups and rotate their activities every 20 minutes. Art, music, perceptual motor skills, and character/values are also integrated into the program. A highlight of the preschool program is an annual weeklong visit to the "World of Beatrix Potter" where children enjoy exploring the author's art and stories in an English-garden setting and then develop their own story-telling abilities.

Grades 1–6 feature a traditional curriculum centered on reading, writing, mathematics, science, social studies, and technology. Hands-on learning and age-appropriate materials provide students with a strong foundation on which to build academic competence. Music, Spanish, Italian, French, art, community service, and physical education, including Little Dribblers Basketball, round out the program.

The Upper School (Grades 7–12) offers a curriculum of more than 80 required and elective courses, including English 7–12, English Literature, World Literature, Forensics, Creative Writing, Speech; World History, American History, American Government/Politics, American Government/Economics; Bible; Biology, Chemistry, Physics, Anatomy and Physiology, Computer Programming, Computer Applications; Algebra I–III, Pre-Calculus, Calculus, Geometry; French I–V, Spanish I–V, Latin I–IV; and Art I–IV, Band, Film History, Select Choir, and Foundations of Music.

An Honors program in math, science, and English begins in Grade 7, and Advanced Placement courses for Grades 11–12 are available in English Language, English Literature, American History, American Government/Politics, Biology, Chemistry, Physics, Calculus, and Art. About 40 percent of juniors and seniors take these courses, which are weighted according to the subject's degree of difficulty. Of those sitting for AP exams, 80 percent score "3" or higher. In addition, over the last four years, approximately 10 percent of the senior class has been recognized as National Merit Semifinalists. The school has also graduated a Rhodes Scholar.

To receive a Jackson Academy diploma, students must earn at least 22 credits and successfully complete four years of English, math, science, and history/social studies; two years of a foreign language (Latin, French, or Spanish); four electives; and one-half unit of computer application.

All 97 graduates in the Class of 2007 went on to higher education. Seniors chose to attend colleges and universities around the country including such Mississippi schools as Belhaven, Delta State, Millsaps, Mississippi College, Mississippi State, and the Universities of Mississippi and Southern Mississippi. Other institutions attended by 2007 graduates included Auburn, Baylor, New York Institute of Technology, Samford, and the Universities of Miami and Virginia.

Jackson Academy's summer enrichment program provides courses for academic credit, leadership, reading and study strategies, art, driver education, cheerleading, and sports camps.

STUDENT ACTIVITIES. The extracurricular program is designed to develop new interests, promote leadership and service, and provide fun, socialization, and athletic and artistic opportunities. Qualified scholars may be invited to membership in the Junior and Senior National Honor Societies and Mu Alpha and Chi Alpha (math) Honor Societies. Jackson Academy is a chapter member of The Cum Laude Society. Academic clubs are organized in science, Latin, Spanish, French, math, forensics, pre-med, chess, and other areas. Students regularly achieve distinction in state and national tournaments and arts and music festivals.

In the fine arts, students perform in color guard, three bands, Encore show choir, and other vocal groups. They also stage music and dramatic productions and publish a yearbook, newspaper, and award-winning literary magazine. Leadership opportunities are found through such organizations as Junior and Senior High Student Councils, Earth Team, Students Against Destructive Decisions, Relay for Life (fund-raising for cancer research), Student Traffic Aides, Big Brothers/Sisters, Fellowship of Christian Athletes, scouting, and Key Club.

In all grades, students reach out to others through a variety of age-appropriate, service-oriented activities such as working for Habitat for Humanity and Toys for Tots, tutoring inner-city children, visiting the elderly, organizing food drives, and undertaking environmental improvement projects.

Jackson Academy athletics help develop sportsmanship, camaraderie, and physical fitness. Raider teams compete in the Mississippi Private School Association and at the AAA state level. Boys and girls compete in basketball, track, tennis, swimming, golf, soccer, and cross-country. Boys also play football and baseball, and girls play fast-pitch and slow-pitch softball. Junior High and varsity cheerleaders as well as the Accents and Silver Steppers, all-girl dance groups, provide lively entertainment and spirit-building at games throughout the season. Jackson Academy athletes have a long history of championship teams and currently hold a number of local, state, and regional titles. There are also elementary interscholastic teams in many sports.

Among the traditional events are preschool and first-grade tea parties, All-Sports Night, Homecoming, open houses, Fall Carnival, Winter Festival, Career Day, Features Pageant, awards days, and graduation. Other activities include canoe trips, the junior-senior prom, and national and overseas travel.

ADMISSION AND COSTS. Jackson Academy seeks to enroll students of good character and academic ability who are eager to excel and participate in the life of the school. It places strong emphasis on personal integrity, achievement, and growth and does not discriminate on the basis of race, color, or national or ethnic origin. Admission is based on standardized test scores, previous academic records, letters of recommendation from teachers and counselors, and a personal interview with the Academic Dean.

In 2007–08, tuition ranges from $4560 in Preschool to $9480 in Grades 9–12, plus registration fees of $250 to $500, depending on grade. Families of first-time students entering Grades 1–6 pay an Elementary Fund fee of $50 to $300. Discounts for siblings, tuition payment plans, and need-based financial aid are available.

President and Head of School: Peter Jernberg
Headmaster: Dr. Pat Taylor
Associate Headmaster: Keith Branning
Director of Alumni Relations: Becky Greer
Director of Admissions & Financial Aid: Linda Purviance
Director of Development: Tim McWilliams
College Admissions Counselor: Amy Bush
Dean of Financial & Legal Affairs: Clifton Kling
Athletic Director: Bobby West

MISSOURI

Andrews Academy 1979

888 North Mason Road, St. Louis, MO 63141
Tel. 314-878-1883; Fax 314-878-0759
Web Site www.hope-andrews.com/academy.htm

Andrews Academy is a coeducational day school enrolling 250 students in Junior Kindergarten–Grade 6. The philosophy of Andrews Academy is committed to the highest intellectual, physical, and social development of each child. The curriculum places emphasis on basic skills and individualized instruction. Computer instruction, Spanish, physical education, art, music, science laboratory, and library are offered at all levels. A summer camp, located on the Academy's 20-acre campus, offers numerous activities to approximately 200 campers. Extended-day care for working parents is offered at no extra fee. Tuition: $12,325–$12,900. Joseph C. Patterson (Washington University, B.S., M.Ed.) was appointed Headmaster in 1983.

The Barstow School 1884

11511 State Line Road, Kansas City, MO 64114
Tel. 816-942-3255; Admission 816-277-0307; Fax 816-942-3227
Web Site www.barstowschool.org

The Barstow School offers its 650 students a challenging, creative, and supportive environment where learning is constant, immersive, active, and exciting. The close-knit Preschool–Grade 12 community promotes independence and investigation to help develop forceful, compassionate thinkers, writers, and citizens. Classes stress individual attention and invite self-expression. A Barstow education encourages students and teachers to gather knowledge, seek inspiration, and articulate understanding while growing intellectually, ethically, and emotionally in an atmosphere as rigorous as it is nurturing. The curriculum includes 16 AP courses, a variety of offerings in the visual and performing arts, and an emphasis on technology. Athletics, student government, honor council, clubs, and service learning all teach leadership and the importance of commitment to the greater community. Tuition: $10,110–$15,190. Elizabeth Bartow is Director of Admission; Art Atkison is Head of School.

Chesterfield Day School 1962

1100 White Road, Chesterfield, MO 63017
Tel. 314-469-6622; Admission Ext. 254; Fax 314-469-7889
123 Schoolhouse Road, P.O. Box 78, St. Albans, MO 63073
Tel. 636-458-6688; Fax 636-458-6660
Web Site www.chesterfielddayschool.org
E-mail mcaldwell@chesterfielddayschool.org

Chesterfield Day, west of St. Louis, enrolls 400 boys and girls in two suburban neighborhoods: Chesterfield (Toddlers–Grade 6) and St. Albans (Toddlers–Grade 8). It seeks to provide "a personalized education of unparalleled excellence" for students of diverse backgrounds. As a student-centered, parent-supported independent school, Chesterfield Day aims to promote joy in learning, positive character development, and service to others. Montessori philosophy and methodology are used in preschool, kindergarten, and Grade 1 and more traditional approaches in Grades 2–8. Computers, Spanish, art, music, library science, and physical education are taught at all levels. Tuition: $3692–$17,262. Marjorie C. Caldwell is Director of Admission; Dennis Guilliams is President.

The College School 1963

1 Newport Place, Webster Groves, MO 63119
Tel. 314-962-9355; Admissions Ext. 111; Fax 314-962-5078
Web Site www.thecollegeschool.org
E-mail admissions@thecollegeschool.org

The College School, enrolling 260 day students in Preschool (age 3)–Grade 8, offers a challenging academic program designed to provide excellent preparation for further education and for life. The thematically integrated curriculum emphasizes hands-on learning using both traditional and innovative teaching methods. Students use the resources of cutting-edge technology in the classroom as well as the numerous historic and cultural opportunities in and around the city of St. Louis. Wilderness and urban adventures reinforce students' understanding of core subjects, which center on language arts, math, science, and social studies. An extensive summer program is available. Tuition: $6080–$12,400. Adrienne Rusbarsky is Director of Admissions; Sheila Gurley is Head of School.

Community School 1914

900 Lay Road, St. Louis, MO 63124
Tel. 314-991-0005; Admission Ext. 315; Fax 314-991-1512
Web Site www.communityschool.com
E-mail admissions@communityschool.com

Community School, located on a 16-acre campus in suburban St. Louis, is a coeducational day school enrolling 335 students age 3–Grade 6. The School provides a setting in which each individual can develop and emerge with positive attitudes and values and strong academic achievement. Basic skills are emphasized; French, linguistics, science, social studies, art, shop, band, drama, computer, and physical education are included in the curriculum. The After School Program includes Extended Day, Homework Club, and "mini" classes. A summer program for ages 3–5 is also offered. Tuition: $13,900. Financial aid is available. Dana Scott Saulsberry is Admission Director; Dr. Matthew A. Gould (Earlham College, B.A. 1990; University of Chicago, Ph.D. 1997) is Head of School.

Forsyth School 1961

6235 Wydown Boulevard, St. Louis, MO 63105
Tel. 314-726-4542; Fax 314-726-0112
Web Site ForsythOnline.com
E-mail admission@forsythonline.com

Forsyth, a coeducational elementary school with 386 students age 3–Grade 6, offers a challenging and engaging academic program, a commitment to diversity, 8:1 student-teacher ratio, team teaching, year-round programs, and before- and after-school classes and sports. Named a Blue Ribbon School by the U.S. Department of Education, Forsyth fosters a love of learning, self-confidence, and a sense of responsibility in a warm, supportive environment. In addition to a Director of Studies and a Learning Specialist, the School employs full-time specialists in science, art, music, French, Spanish, Latin, creative movement, physical education, outdoor education, and drama. The

Forsyth Adventure Center features a climbing wall, a high ropes course with platforms, and a high beam. The School recently completed $4,800,000 in campus improvements including a 9100-square-foot Arts Center, a Field Turf field and track, and a dedicated outdoor classroom, among other enhancements. Tuition: $13,886. Ann Babington is Director of Admission; Michael J. Vachow is Head.

John Burroughs School 1923

755 South Price Road, St. Louis, MO 63124
Tel. 314-993-4040; Admission Ext. 242; Fax 314-567-2896
Web Site www.jburroughs.org; E-mail clavigne@jburroughs.org

Burroughs, a coeducational, college preparatory day school, enrolls 590 students in Grades 7–12 in a curriculum balancing academics, arts, and athletics. Students are actively engaged in learning, and small classes promote respect among faculty and students. Community service and environmental awareness, objectives set by the founders, are integral to the mission. Burroughs emphasizes ethics, diversity, student government, and activities such as American Field Service and International Model UN. The 47.5-acre campus is enhanced by an outdoor facility in Missouri's Ozarks. Informality, challenging academics, and community spirit distinguish a Burroughs education. Tuition: $18,575. Tuition Aid: $1,510,000. Caroline LaVigne is Admission Director; Keith E. Shahan, Ed.D., is Head of School.

Mary Institute and Saint Louis Country Day School 1859

101 North Warson Road, St. Louis, MO 63124
Tel. 314-993-5100; Admission 314-995-7367; Fax 314-872-3257
Web Site www.micds.org; E-mail admissions@micds.org

Mary Institute and Saint Louis Country Day School, enrolling 1220 students in Junior Kindergarten–Grade 12, is a community where people strive to think critically, live virtuously and compassionately, and act responsibly. The rigorous college preparatory program is designed to foster academic excellence, leadership, and self-confidence; the coordinate Middle School balances single-gender classes in the core curriculum with coed classes and activities. MICDS offers fine arts activities, service learning opportunities, and athletics. Cutting-edge technology, including new foreign language labs, enhances teaching and

learning. A summer program is offered. Tuition: $15,540–$18,690. Financial Aid: $3,100,000. Peggy B. Laramie is Director of Admission; Lisa Lyle is Head of School.

Metropolitan School 1967

7281 Sarah Avenue, Maplewood, MO 63143
Tel. 314-644-0850; Fax 314-644-3363
Web Site www.metroschool.org; E-mail info@metroschool.org

Metropolitan School is a fully accredited, coeducational day school providing a special-educational program for adolescents who have learning disabilities, attention deficits, or other atypical learning styles. The School enrolls 63 students in Grades 5–12. The fully certified staff, with a 9:1 student-teacher ratio, provides a challenging academic curriculum with highly individualized instruction. Tuition: $19,715. Rita M. Buckley is Executive Director; Judi Thomas is Head of School; Nancy Smith is Director of Admissions.

Missouri Military Academy 1889

204 N. Grand Street, Mexico, MO 65265
Tel. 573-581-1776; Admissions Ext. 323; Fax 573-581-0081
Web Site www.mma-cadet.org; E-mail info@mma.mexico.mo.us

Now in its 119th year, this college preparatory school serves 300 young men as boarding cadets in Grades 6–12 and Postgraduate. Missouri Military Academy offers a traditional curriculum in the liberal arts and sciences within the structure and discipline of the Junior Reserve Officer Training Corps. Course work emphasizes the development of strong academic skills, with small classes, supervised study halls, and individual support from teachers. Technology, ESL, and the arts enhance the core program, while activities such as precision drill team, marching band and chorus, 11 varsity sports, and 30 clubs promote character, good citizenship, and leadership. Tuition & Fees: $28,000. Financial Aid: $750,000. Maj. Greg Seibert is Director of Admissions; Maj. Gen. Robert M. Flanagan is President.

The Pembroke Hill School 1910

400 West 51st Street, Kansas City, MO 64112
Tel. 816-936-1200; Admissions 816-936-1231; Fax 816-936-1218
Web Site www.pembrokehill.org; E-mail csullivan@pembrokehill.org

This coeducational day school enrolls 1190 students in Early Years (age 2)–Grade 12 in a college preparatory program designed to develop the unique intellectual, physical, and creative abilities of each youngster to full potential. In small classes taught by committed, qualified faculty, students undertake an academic curriculum that includes Advanced Placement classes in all departments. Among the activities are student government, publications, community service, and interscholastic teams in 20 sports. Extended care and a summer program of academics, recreation, and athletics are available. Tuition: $6515–$16,880. Carolyn Sullivan is Assistant Head for Admissions and Financial Aid; Steven J. Bellis (Kansas State, B.A.; University of Texas [Austin], M.B.A.; University of Kansas, Ed.D.) is Head.

Rohan Woods School 1937

1515 Bennett Avenue, St. Louis, MO 63122
Tel. 314-821-6270; Fax 314-821-6878
Web Site www.rohanwoods.org; E-mail spage@rohanwoods.org

Rohan Woods, enrolling up to 140 children age 3 through Grade 6, offers a challenging curriculum in a warm environment that emphasizes personal responsibility and respect for all individuals. Instruction is designed to reveal key concepts and encourage teachers to be assessors of learning. Specialist instruction includes science, computer, athletics, art, music, and foreign languages. Attention to scholastic success, values, and ethics are supported equally. Small-group work and multiage activities create a strong school community, which was recognized for excellence by the Department of Education. Rohan Woods was also the proud recipient of the 2007 Champions for Character Award for its outstanding service learning program. Extended care, enrichment programs, and summer camps are optional. Tuition: $13,450 (including lunch & supplies). Financial aid is available. Samantha Templin-Page is Admission Director; Kelly R. Horn is Headmaster.

Rossman School 1917

12660 Conway Road, St. Louis, MO 63141-8625
Tel. 314-434-5877; Fax 314-434-1668
Web Site www.rossmanschool.org; E-mail kmartin@rossmanschool.org

Rossman is an elementary day school featuring a challenging academic program for 230 boys and girls in Junior Kindergarten (age 4)–Grade 6. Seeking to maximize each child's potential, the School holds to a student-teacher ratio of 8:1. The curriculum focuses on the basics of mathematics and language arts and integrates computers, science, social studies, Spanish, Latin, music, art, library, and physical education. A cultural enrichment program, field trips, and athletics supplement the curriculum. After-school Enrichment and Extended Day are available. Tuition (including lunch): $14,420. Applications for financial aid are welcome. Katharine Martin is Director of Admission; Patricia A. Shipley (Webster University, B.A.) is Head of School.

Thomas Jefferson School 1946

4100 South Lindbergh Boulevard, St. Louis, MO 63127
Tel. 314-843-4151; Fax 314-843-3527
Web Site www.tjs.org; E-mail admissions@tjs.org

THOMAS JEFFERSON SCHOOL in St. Louis, Missouri, is a boarding and day school for boys and girls in Grades 7 through 12 and a postgraduate year. The campus is located in the suburban community of Sunset Hills (population 5000), 15 miles from the center of St. Louis.

Thomas Jefferson School was founded in 1946 by three Harvard alumni—Robin McCoy, Graham Spring, and Charles E. Merrill, Jr. After 25 years as a school for boys, it became coeducational in 1971, and girls now make up about one-half of the student body. A college preparatory school, it seeks "to provide thorough academic training under conditions that help a student develop the habit of hard work and a sense of responsibility for his own affairs."

The School is a nonprofit institution controlled by a self-electing Board of Trustees, the majority of whom must be active teachers at the School. Every full-time teacher becomes a Trustee within three years of joining the faculty.

Thomas Jefferson School holds membership in the National Association of Independent Schools, the Educational Records Bureau, The Association of Boarding Schools, the Small Boarding Schools Association, Midwest Boarding Schools, and the Independent Schools Association of the Central States.

THE CAMPUS. The school property, acquired in 1946, is a 20-acre former estate landscaped with lawns and many varieties of shade trees. The back part of the property includes an athletic field and track and five tennis courts.

The Main Building contains the Head's office, the business office, teachers' offices, classrooms, computers, the library, the common room, and the dining room. Boarders live in the Gables—a two-story building that is part of the original estate—and in six student houses of modern construction and design (1960, 1994). Each house has four double rooms with private baths and outside entrances, providing quiet, privacy, and independence for the students. Every room has telephone and Internet access. Sayers Hall (1992) contains state-of-the-art science labs, several classrooms, and a reference library. A new kitchen and dining hall was completed in 2001.

The gymnasium provides facilities for basketball and volleyball. The entire plant is valued at approximately $5,000,000.

THE FACULTY. William C. Rowe became the School's third Head in the summer of 2000, succeeding Lawrence Morgan. Mr. Rowe was born in St. Louis. He attended Thomas Jefferson School and Wesleyan University (A.B. 1967), and he holds a master's degree from Washington University. He has taught at the School for 38 years and was Director of Admissions for 20 years.

In addition to the Head, who also teaches, there are 12 full-time faculty members, five men and seven women. Six teachers live on campus. The faculty hold 12 baccalaureate and 10 master's degrees representing study at Columbia, Haverford, Kenyon, Rensselaer Polytechnic Institute, St. John's, Smith, Washington University, Webster, Wesleyan, and the Universities of Cincinnati, Missouri, and Wisconsin.

Two nearby hospitals and several doctors' offices are available as needed.

STUDENT BODY. In 2007–08, Thomas Jefferson School enrolled 23 boarding boys, 17 day boys, 21 boarding girls, and 21 day girls, ages 12–18, as follows: 8 in Grade 7, 11 in Grade 8, 16 in Grade 9, 13 in Grade 10, 16 in Grade 11, and 18 in Grade 12. Boarding students come from Illinois, Indiana, Kentucky, Missouri, Oregon, Pennsylvania, Hong Kong, Japan, Poland, and South Korea. Day students reside in St. Louis and its suburbs.

ACADEMIC PROGRAM. The school year, from early September to early June, includes 32 weeks of classes, a Thanksgiving recess, a 4-week vacation at Christmas, and a 4-week vacation in March.

Classes, which have an enrollment of 3 to 16, meet five days a week for Grades 7–11 and four days a week for Grade 12. The weekday schedule follows: 7:45–8:05 A.M., breakfast buffet; 8:30 A.M.–1:10 P.M., classes; 11:25 A.M.–1:10 P.M., lunch; 1:20–5:30 P.M., labs, athletics, other activities, and independent studies; 5:45 P.M., dinner; and 6:15–bedtime, study and leisure. Day students are on campus from 8:30 A.M. to 5:00 P.M.

The boys and girls may study anywhere on campus they wish; there are study halls only for those in academic difficulty. Boarders in Grades 7–10 have bedtimes according to their age and academic status; juniors and seniors are expected to use good judgment in determining their bedtimes. On Saturdays and Sundays, a student in good standing is free to plan his or her own schedule.

Discipline is handled through a demerit system, and penalties generally involve work around the School on weekends, such as cleaning jobs and yard work. An effort is made to keep supervision of as many disciplinary chores as possible in the hands of the students.

The curriculum for Grades 7–8 includes English, Latin, Mathematics, Science, and Social Studies. Students in Grades 9–12 take four years of English, two years each of two foreign languages (including Greek), two years of history (including United States History), four years of mathematics, and at least two years of laboratory science. In addition, each student has a choice of one or two more laboratory sciences, a third year of one foreign language, or a third year of history. Among the courses offered are English; French, Greek, Italian; Ancient History, European History, United States History; Algebra, Geometry, Advanced Algebra and Trigonometry, Precalculus, AB and BC Calculus; and Biology, Chemistry, and Physics. English courses usually include Shakespeare, selections from the Bible, and other classics of English and world literature. There is a strong emphasis on grammar, spelling, and writing skills as well as daily discussion of reading. English as a Second Language is offered to international students.

All students take either four (Grades 10–12) or five (Grades 7–9) academic courses per year, plus a fine arts class, which meets once a week. Alternatives include drawing, photography, ceramics, music appreciation, and art history.

Qualified students take Advanced Placement Examinations in English, United States History, European History, French, Biology, Physics, Chemistry, and Calculus. Some students prepare independently for other Advanced Placement exams in Latin, Government, Computer Science, and other subjects. There are frequent quizzes in most courses, one-hour quarterly examinations, and longer midyear and final examinations. Reports are sent home quarterly. In addition, juniors and seniors take SAT I and II examinations.

Thomas Jefferson School graduates are currently studying at Bentley, California Institute of Technology, Claremont–McKenna, Duke, Eckerd, Emory, Harvard, Haverford, Indiana University, Johns Hopkins, Loyola University, Northwestern, Pennsylvania State, Pitzer, Reed, Rensselaer, Rhodes, Saint Louis University, Smith, Stanford, Swarthmore, Truman State,

Tulane, Vanderbilt, Virginia Military Institute, Washington University, Wesleyan, and the Universities of Chicago, Illinois, and Missouri.

STUDENT ACTIVITIES. An active Student Council casts a vote in faculty meetings on any decision affecting student life.

Athletics are both intramural and interscholastic. Participation is required three or four days each week, and the program includes tennis, soccer, and other alternatives in the fall; basketball, aerobics, volleyball, and ice skating in the winter; and tennis, softball, and other alternatives in the spring.

In its social life, the School leaves the initiative with the students. Dances are held from time to time, and boarders in good standing may get permission to leave the campus on Friday or Saturday nights. Other weekend activities include leisure or study time, informal athletics, and off-campus trips to places of interest.

Thomas Jefferson School encourages use of the cultural facilities in St. Louis by securing tickets and providing transportation to ballets, concerts, and plays and by organizing trips to the Art Museum, the Botanical Garden, the zoo, and downtown St. Louis. The entire student body attends the six annual play productions at the Repertory Theater of St. Louis. The School often plans and supervises trips to Europe during vacations, most frequently to Florence and London in the summer. In Europe, the students visit museums and go to the theater and have free time to explore and shop.

ADMISSION AND COSTS. Requirements for admission include a school transcript from the applicant's previous school, entrance tests (SSAT, ISEE, or the School's own tests), a teacher recommendation, and an interview. "Natural ability, past performance, liveliness, ambition, and willingness to work hard" are important considerations in evaluating candidates. Thomas Jefferson School has a policy of admitting students "without regard to race, color, creed, or national or ethnic origin." New students are accepted in all grades, and applications will be considered for a postgraduate year.

For 2007–08, the annual fee is $32,250 for full-time boarding students, $30,500 for five-day boarders, and $19,300 for day students. Total yearly expenses for books, supplies, athletic clothes, and play and concert tickets (all available through the School bookstore) come to $1500 or more. Day students provide their own transportation. Financial aid totaling approximately $500,000 is awarded annually.

Alumni Secretary: Jane Pesek
Director of Admission: Marie DeJesus
Director of Development: Jane Pesek
College Counselor: William C. Rowe
Business Manager: William C. Rowe
Director of Athletics: Boaz Roth

Whitfield School 1952

175 South Mason Road, St. Louis, MO 63141
Tel. 314-434-5141; Fax 314-434-6193
Web Site www.whitfieldschool.org
E-mail admission@whitfieldschool.org

Whitfield's college preparatory curriculum challenges students while teaching them to work both independently and collaboratively. The demanding academic program and the support of a dedicated faculty prepare graduates for college and life beyond; the introduction of a 1:1 computing program, utilizing Linux and Citrix, complements the educational experience and sets the pace for school technology. With an average class size of 12 and a student enrollment of 470 day boys and girls in Grades 6–12, Whitfield seeks to develop and maintain a diverse community that values mutual respect and personal responsibility. Students are encouraged to take part in activities that include visual and performing arts, community service, student government and an honor council, and 42 athletic teams, clubs, and organizations. Tuition: $19,250. Financial aid is available. Cynthia Crum Alverson is Admission Director; Mark J. Anderson is President.

The Wilson School 1913

400 DeMun Avenue, St. Louis, MO 63105
Tel. 314-725-4999; Fax 314-725-5242
Web Site www.wilsonschool.com; E-mail lchartung@wilsonschool.com

This coeducational, elementary day school seeks to inspire "a confidence born of discovering and learning that is bred into the culture of The Wilson School." The supportive community is small, enrolling approximately 190 children age 3 through Grade 6. Students have the benefit of two teachers per classroom, one class per grade, and specialists who provide instruction in French, Latin, science, music, art, physical education, technology, and library. In the core programs of reading and writing, math, and science, Wilson students often rank nationally in the 90th to 99th percentile on standardized tests. Students are also recognized in regional, state, and nationwide competitions. A new, state-of-the-art gymnasium and a pro-turf soccer field enhance the curriculum. Tuition: $9300 (Pre-K); $13,885 (K–6). Laura C. Hartung is Director of Admission; Thad M. Falkner is Headmaster.

NEVADA

The Meadows School 1984

8601 Scholar Lane, Las Vegas, NV 89128
Tel. 702-254-1610; Fax 702-254-2452
Web Site www.themeadowsschool.org
E-mail cgoodman@themeadowsschool.org

The Meadows is a nonprofit, nonsectarian, coeducational, college preparatory day school serving 910 students in Preschool–Grade 12. Located on a 40-acre campus, the School offers accelerated academics and broad extracurricular, technology, arts, and athletic programs. It seeks to develop in students a love of learning and the desire to become knowledgeable, productive, and compassionate members of society. Standards of high academic achievement are supported by 26 AP and 45 Honors courses in all disciplines. The School offers 100 percent four-year college and university placement. The Spanish immersion program is mandatory in Kindergarten–Grade 8; Latin is required in Grades 6–8. Tuition: $8450–$18,780. Fees: $570–$1270. Financial Aid: $1,100,000. Carolyn G. Goodman is Head of School. *Pacific Northwest Association.*

Sage Ridge School 1998

2515 Crossbow Court, Reno, NV 89511
Tel. 775-852-6222; Admissions Ext. 503; Fax 775-852-6228
Web Site www.sageridge.org; E-mail cmurphy@sageridge.org

Sage Ridge School is a traditional, core-centered, college preparatory day school serving 229 boys and girls in Grades 5 through 12. The School provides an innovative educational experience that generates excitement for learning and discovery. The dynamic curriculum emphasizes a traditional approach in all grades, integrating technology with a variety of disciplines. Sage Ridge stresses the arts and challenges students to mature as excellent scholars, compassionate citizens, and self-confident adults. Small class sizes ensure individual attention and adequate time for the mastery of core skills and concepts. The School offers a wide range of performing arts and interscholastic athletics. Tuition: $13,090–$16,668 (laptop required). Financial aid is available to qualified families. Carol Murphy is Director of Admission; William Heim III is Headmaster.

NEW HAMPSHIRE

Cardigan Mountain School 1945

62 Alumni Drive, Canaan, NH 03741
Tel. 603-523-4321; Admissions 603-523-3548; Fax 603-523-3565
Web Site www.cardigan.org; E-mail admissions@cardigan.org

On a 500-acre lakeside campus near Dartmouth College, Cardigan provides small classes in which 200 boys in Grades 6–9 can develop skills, discipline, and self-confidence. Tracked classes allow students to learn alongside their academic peers. About 20 percent of the students are served by academic support programs. Interscholastic athletics are featured. Weekend activities are diverse at Cardigan, where over 90 percent of the students are boarders. Graduates enter such schools as St. Paul's, Lawrenceville, Exeter, Deerfield, Holderness, and Salisbury. A coed summer program is offered for Grades 4–8. Boarding Tuition: $38,275. Financial Aid: $850,000. Chip Audett is Director of Admissions; David J. McCusker '80 (Dartmouth College, B.A.) is Headmaster.

The Derryfield School 1964

2108 River Road, Manchester, NH 03104-1396
Tel. 603-669-4524; Fax 603-641-9521
Web Site www.derryfield.org; E-mail admission@derryfield.org

Located on 84 wooded acres, Derryfield values its distinctive role in southern New Hampshire as a college preparatory, coeducational day school. Teachers coach and mentor 383 students in Grades 6–12 in an informal, yet structured environment. Derryfield's ultimate goal is to foster intellectual growth, a passion for lifelong learning, and purposeful involvement in the local and global community. Participation in the fine arts and athletics is required. Offerings include Organic Chemistry, Chinese, Photography, HTML Web Design, Understanding the Middle East, and 11 Advanced Placement courses in six subjects. Tuition: $21,750. Financial Aid: $1,020,000. Allison M. Price is Director of Admission; Craig N. Sellers (Franklin and Marshall, A.B.; New York Law School, J.D.; New York Teachers College, M.A.) is Head of School. *New England Association.*

Hampshire Country School 1948

28 Patey Circle, Rindge, NH 03461
Tel. 603-899-3325; Fax 603-899-6521
Web Site www.hampshirecountryschool.org
E-mail hampshirecountry@monad.net

HAMPSHIRE COUNTRY SCHOOL in Rindge, New Hampshire, is a seven-day boarding school enrolling 20–25 high-ability boys who want and need a family-like school community and highly personalized learning environment in order to thrive. Most students are ages 9–15, but boys as young as 8 may be accepted, and a few students may remain through high school graduation. Rindge (population 5200) is situated in the southwestern part of the state, about 35 miles west of Nashua and 60 miles northwest of Boston, Massachusetts. The town is in the Monadnock Region, a predominantly rural area of historic small towns and a wealth of outdoor activities.

Hampshire Country School was founded at its present location in 1948, after being developed gradually by Henry and Adelaide Patey, a psychologist and teacher, respectively. In 1936, the Pateys had welcomed into their home a bright, sensitive young boy who was severely overreacting to the stresses of his own home and community. As other children and young adults joined the Pateys, their home expanded into a small school.

The special focus of the School has always been on nurturing and developing the abilities and interests of highly intelligent students whose sensitivities and, perhaps, idiosyncrasies, have made adapting to the more aggressive and competitive social climate of larger schools a major challenge. While these students are often labeled with such diagnoses as Asperger's Syndrome, nonverbal learning disabilities (NLD), or ADHD, it is the students' interests, abilities, and natural goodness that are the focus of the School, rather than their disabilities, which can usually be accommodated without undue concern in the small-school setting. Students benefit particularly from the personal attention they receive from approximately 15 faculty members who reside on campus as teachers, dorm parents, and activity instructors, and who work with students in classes of 4–6, dorm groups of 6–7, and activity groups of about 2–15.

Hampshire Country School is governed by a Board of Trustees, accredited by the New England Association of Schools and Colleges, and approved by the State Department of Education. It holds membership in the National Association of Independent Schools, The Association of Boarding Schools, the Small Boarding School Association, and the Independent Schools Association of Northern New England, among other affiliations.

THE CAMPUS. The School is set on the site of historic Cheshire Place, an experimental town established in the late 19th century. The rural area is removed from major traffic arteries and offers a quiet setting far from the distractions of city and suburbia. The School's 1700 acres are intersected by historic stone walls and foundations and feature meadows, woodlands, lakes, streams, beaver ponds, and abundant wildlife. The Wapack Trail crosses the School's wooded ridge, providing 50-mile views in all directions.

Students reside in four small dorms, each containing single and double rooms, a common living and play room, and a full kitchen for snacks or special occasions. Nutritious meals are served in the School dining room, where students and faculty join together for three family-style meals daily.

Three buildings house the academic facilities, which include six classrooms, a music room, science lab, theater, and a 3000-volume library. Several computers are available exclusively for school work.

THE FACULTY. William Dickerman was appointed Headmaster in 1996, after serving as a faculty member since 1971. A licensed psychologist, Mr. Dickerman holds a B.A. degree from Oberlin College and M.A. and Ph.D. degrees from the University of Wisconsin (Madison).

The 15 men and women of the faculty interact with students both in and out of class. Most have served in various roles during their years at the School. At any one time, 6 have classroom teaching as their primary responsibility; 5 serve as full-time dorm parents; and 4 carry administrative and supervisory responsibilities. All are involved in teaching or leading afternoon and weekend activities. All have been chosen not only for their scholastic and extracurricular expertise but also for their ability to enjoy and support boys who require an unusual amount of adult energy, personal interest, and accommodation.

Faculty and administrators hold bachelor's and advanced degrees from such institutions as Boston University, Bridgewater State, California State, College of the Holy Cross, Dickinson, Elmira College, Goddard, Grove City College, Houghton, New England Conservatory of Music, and the University of New Hampshire.

A registered nurse is on campus five days a week and on call at other times. Four pediatricians affiliated with a nearby hospital are available as needed.

STUDENT BODY. Small by design, Hampshire Country School enrolls 20–25 boys, primarily ages 9–15, in Grades 3–12. They typically come from about 15 states, well distributed throughout the continental United States, plus an occasional student from abroad.

ACADEMIC PROGRAM. The daily pace at Hampshire Country School is relaxed but purposeful. The 35-week academic year, divided into trimesters, runs from early September to the second week in June. Courses are taught in a traditional manner but with the extra support, attention, and personal interest that is possible in a class of 3–6 students.

On a typical day, students rise at 7:30 A.M., eat breakfast, and take six 55-minute classes beginning at 9:00 A.M. Course work focuses on the core subjects of English, mathematics, science, social studies, and a foreign language. Music, art, and physical education are scheduled as noncredit courses and activities after the school day and on weekends. Letter grades are issued every trimester and at the end of the year, along with written teacher comments. A student's participation in class, test and quiz results, special projects, completion of assignments, and effort determine his overall evaluation. Students are identified with a specific grade level, but youngsters from different grades are regularly grouped together in their courses.

Classes end at 3:30 P.M., followed by snack, afternoon activities, supper, a one-hour study period, and bedtime between 9:00 and 10:00 P.M., depending on age.

Courses in Grades 3–6 are designed to instill strong basic skills in English, reading, writing, history and geography, science, and math. Younger students are taught in a mostly self-contained, mixed-grade class that allows flexibility in both schedule and curriculum in order to take full advantage of the group's interests, needs, and teachable moments. As an example, a lesson that has the students fully engaged can easily be extended, while a period in which they are unduly restless can be modified to adapt to the mood of the class.

Seventh- and eighth-grade courses include English; U.S. History, World Geography; General Math, Pre-algebra, Algebra; Earth Science, Life Science, and General Science. Students in Grades 7 and 8 are in classes together, and the selection of courses taught each year depends on the educational needs of the particular group.

Among the courses for Grades 9–12 are Language Arts, Literature, Concepts in Literature; Ancient Civilizations to Medieval Europe, The Renaissance to the Twentieth Century, U.S. History to the Civil War, U.S. History from the Civil War, Civics; Practical Mathematics, Consumer and Career Math, Algebra 1, Algebra 2 with Trigonometry, Geometry; Biology, Environmental Science, Anatomy and Physiology, Chemistry, Physical Science; and a foreign language.

While classwork and courses provide the formal portion of the Hampshire Country School educational program, the learning process continues throughout the afternoons, evenings, and weekends, as students rehearse for theater productions; take music lessons; explore the School's ponds, streams, and natural environment; read for pleasure; play trivia games; listen to concerts or lectures; and engage in dinner-table discussions with teachers.

Students in all grades take the Stanford Achievement Test in the spring. They are also encouraged to take the SSAT, PSAT, and SAT at appropriate times. Students generally gain the most by spending three to five years at Hampshire Country School and transferring elsewhere during their early high school years. Many find that a medium-size boarding school is the best next step, and high school choices in recent years have included Buxton, Dublin, Gould, Putney, Virginia Episcopal School, and Wheeler.

STUDENT ACTIVITIES. Extracurricular activities and interests grow out of the School's rustic setting and the students' fertile imaginations, combined with the absence of television and video games. Active, spontaneous play is a major part of student life, and care is taken not to impose so much formal structure that natural playfulness is lost. Outdoors, students explore beaver ponds, build snow forts, play hide-and-seek, and chase imaginary dragons. Indoors, they build with Legos, race toy cars, paint miniature figures, and play a wide variety of strategy board games.

More formal activities include drama, woodshop, beginning and intermediate music lessons, canoeing, and sports such as soccer, softball, flag football, tennis, and floor hockey played for fun and recreation. Hiking, exploring, and camping are regular weekend activities. Occasional trips may include museums, classical concerts, live theater, skiing, and hiking. Each weekend ends with a jacket-and-tie dinner and Sunday Forum, a special lecture, concert, or presentation.

Family weekends in October and February bring families together to enjoy the School's outdoor resources, attend student performances, and meet formally with teachers and administrators. The last Sunday afternoon of each month is also open for casual visits by families who live close enough to attend.

ADMISSION AND COSTS. Hampshire Country School students are typically bright, sensitive boys who have had serious difficulty adapting to the complexities and social stresses of larger schools. They seek a school that can provide a solid education, interesting activities, and a peer group that shares their interests and abilities. Applicants are evaluated on the basis of educational and personal histories, a personal interview, and, when appropriate, medical and psychological evaluations.

For 2007–08, the fee for room, board, and most other expenses is $42,000. Clothing and personal supplies, ski rentals, and vacation transportation are additional.

Hampstead Academy 1978

320 East Road, Hampstead, NH 03841
Tel. 603-362-5814, 603-329-4406; Fax 603-329-7124
Web Site www.hampsteadacademy.org
E-mail lyn.kutzelman@hampsteadacademy.org

Founded in 1978, Hampstead Academy is a coeducational day school enrolling 268 students in Nursery–Grade 8. Blending hands-on experience with a solid academic curriculum in liberal arts, fine arts, and sciences, Hampstead Academy uses eclectic teaching styles to "educate the whole child." Designed to engender the love of learning, this approach embraces such values as discipline, perseverance, character, and ethical behavior. A new Arts and Early Childhood Center opened in January 2005, and a recently built gymnatorium enhances the school's sports, drama, and music programs. Students are actively involved in community service projects. Tuition: $4995–$12,995. Sibling discounts are available. Lyn E. Kutzelman (Lesley College, M.Ed. 1984) is Founder and Head of School. *New England Association.*

Kimball Union Academy 1813

57 Main Street, Meriden, NH 03770
Tel. 603-469-2000; Admissions 603-469-2100; Fax 603-469-2041
Web Site www.kua.org; E-mail admissions@kua.org

Founded in 1813, Kimball Union Academy is a coeducational boarding and day school serving 325 students in Grades 9 through 12 and a postgraduate year. Kimball Union's location in the heart of the Upper Connecticut River Valley and its proximity to Dartmouth College have long made it the choice for students seeking an educational experience that develops the whole person as scholar, athlete, artist, and global citizen. The scenic 800-acre campus includes state-of-the-art facilities and many opportunities to enjoy its rural village setting. Boarding Tuition: $39,600; Day Tuition: $25,500. Financial Aid: $1,900,000. Rachel Tilney is Director of Admissions; Michael J.

Schafer (Colby, B.A.; Harvard, M.Ed.) is Head of School. *New England Association.*

St. Paul's School 1856

325 Pleasant Street, Concord, NH 03301-2591
Tel. 603-229-4600; Admissions 603-229-4700; Fax 603-229-4771
Web Site www.sps.edu; E-mail admissions@sps.edu

Set on a beautiful, 2000-acre campus, St. Paul's is a college preparatory boarding school in the Episcopal tradition enrolling 525 young men and women from diverse backgrounds in Grades 9–12. Within a dynamic learning community, students undertake a curriculum that emphasizes communication, critical thinking, and problem solving of important global issues. Math, science, the humanities, technology, modern and classical languages, and the arts form the core program. Students are involved in school government, interest clubs, academic competitions, drama, music groups, and athletics. Tuition: $39,300. Tuition Support: $5,600,000. Jada K. Hebra is Director of Admissions; William R. Matthews, Jr., is Rector. *New England Association.*

The White Mountain School 1886

371 West Farm Road, Bethlehem, NH 03574
Tel. 603-444-2928; [Toll-free] 800-545-7813; Fax 603-444-5568
Web Site www.whitemountain.org
E-mail admissions@whitemountain.org

The White Mountain School strives to prepare young people for rigorous college studies and life beyond formal academics. By providing an environment for challenging academics and growth within a small, supportive community of 110 boarding and day students in Grade 9–Postgraduate, White Mountain helps encourage responsible and active young adults. Classes are discussion-based, and teachers use a variety of approaches to engage and motivate students. Small classes mean teachers can touch base with every student every day, allowing faculty to respond to individuals in a personal way. WMS offers an academic program balanced with studio arts, outdoor learning, and international community service. Outside the classroom, students have the special opportunity to develop wilderness skills with three Outdoor Learning Expeditions as well as seasonal sport choices including rock climbing, hiking, and backcountry skiing. English as a Second Language and learning assistance are available. Boarding Tuition: $39,100; Day Tuition: $18,000. Joanna Evans is Director of Admission; Brian Morgan is Head of School.

NEW JERSEY

Academy of Saint Elizabeth 1860

P.O. Box 297, Convent Station, NJ 07961-0297
Tel. 973-290-5200; Fax 973-290-5232
Web Site www.academyofsaintelizabeth.org; E-mail sea1860@aol.com

The Academy of Saint Elizabeth is the oldest high school for girls in the State of New Jersey. Under the direction of the Sisters of Charity of Saint Elizabeth, the Academy is a Catholic, college preparatory day school enrolling 250 girls in Grades 9–12. The mission of the school is to develop the full potential of each student in an atmosphere of educational excellence and moral responsibility. Honors, Advanced Placement, and college courses are included in the curriculum. Student Council, publications, sports, forensics, and performing arts highlight some of the activities. The Academy is located on a scenic 250-acre campus. Tuition: $11,000. Kathy Thomas is Director of Admissions; Sr. Patricia Costello, O.P., is Principal. *Middle States Association.*

Blair Academy 1848

2 Park Street, Blairstown, NJ 07825
Tel. 908-362-6121; Admissions 800-462-5247; Fax 908-362-7975
Web Site www.blair.edu; E-mail admissions@blair.edu

Blair Academy seeks to provide a dynamic coeducational experience in a nurturing environment. Since 1848, Blair has shaped the minds of young people in pursuit of excellence. Enrolling 340 boarding and 100 day students in Grade 9–Postgraduate, the Academy offers a liberal arts curriculum including 17 Advanced Placement courses, independent studies, aeronautics, and a comprehensive fine and performing arts program. Students participate in numerous activities including Model UN, community service, and the Society of Skeptics lecture series. Extensive facilities support Blair's award-winning programs and championship teams. Boarding Tuition: $39,200; Day Tuition: $28,400. Financial aid is available. Barbara Haase is Dean of Admission; T. Chandler Hardwick III is Headmaster. *Middle States Association.*

Collegiate School 1896

Kent Court, Passaic Park, NJ 07055
Tel. 973-777-1714; Fax 973-777-3255
Web Site www.collegiatenj.org

Collegiate School is a coeducational, college preparatory day school enrolling 115 students in Pre-Kindergarten–Grade 12. It aims to provide a traditional and classical academic program in a nurturing climate that will motivate students to think independently and to meet the future with industry and challenge. Collegiate School offers small classes and individual attention. Sports, clubs, and scholastic competitions are the principal extracurricular activities. Tuition: $4000–$6500. Paula Steele Grassie was appointed Headmaster in 2006. *Middle States Association.*

The Craig School 1980

10 Tower Hill Road, Mountain Lakes, NJ 07046
Tel. 973-334-1295; Fax 973-334-1299
Web Site www.craigschool.org; E-mail jday@craigschool.org

Enrolling approximately 160 day students in Grades 3–12, Craig is committed to meeting the educational needs of youngsters of average to above-average ability whose progress has been impeded by difficulties in speech and language, reading comprehension, information processing, and other key areas. In a structured environment, certified specialist teachers and professionals provide individualized instruction in classes of 8 or fewer. The college preparatory program focuses on developing strong written language skills, strategies for critical thinking, content acquisition and retention, and the social, behavioral, and self-advocacy skills that are vital to success in the extended community. After-school and summer programs are available. Tuition: $26,500–$32,500. Julie Sage Day is Director of Advancement; Janet M. Cozine is Lower School Director; Eric Caparulo is Upper School Director; David Dennen Blanchard is Headmaster. *Middle States Association.*

Delbarton School 1939

230 Mendham Road, Morristown, NJ 07960
Tel. 973-538-3231; Admissions Ext. 3019; Fax 973-538-8836
Web Site www.delbarton.org; E-mail admissions@delbarton.org

Founded by Benedictine monks, Delbarton School is a Roman Catholic, college preparatory day school enrolling 540 boys in Grades 7–12. The School places emphasis on academic achievement but seeks personal and social development in its students as well. A traditional, liberal arts curriculum emphasizes reading, writing, and critical thinking. Advanced Placement courses are offered in every subject. Athletics, publications, drama, music, and service groups are among the activities. Tuition: $23.600. Financial Aid: $1,050,000. Dr. David Donovan is Dean of Admission; Br. Paul Diveny, OSB (Catholic University, B.A.; Middlebury College, M.A.), was appointed Headmaster in 2007. *Middle States Association.*

The Elisabeth Morrow School 1930

435 Lydecker Street, Englewood, NJ 07631
Tel. 201-568-5566; Admissions Ext. 7212; Fax 201-568-2065
Web Site www.elisabethmorrow.org; E-mail mail@elisabethmorrow.org

A day school for 500 boys and girls age 3–Grade 8, The Elisabeth Morrow School pursues the highest educational standards in a supportive, creative environment. The program emphasizes strong values, hard work, creative problem-solving, and the attitude that learning is a lifelong experience. In an atmosphere of intellectual challenge, the School seeks to meet the individual needs of its students through a comprehensive educational program and close contact between home and school. Summer, after-school, and child-care programs are offered. Tuition: $10,800–$23,100. Blair Talcott Orloff is Director of Admissions and Financial Aid; David M. Lowry (Haverford College, B.A. 1967; Teachers College Columbia University, M.S. 1972, Ph.D. 1981) is Head.

Far Brook School 1948

52 Great Hills Road, Short Hills, NJ 07078
Tel. 973-379-3442; Fax 973-379-9237
Web Site www.farbrook.org; E-mail admissions@farbrook.org

Far Brook School in Short Hills, New Jersey, is a coeducational day school enrolling students in Nursery through Grade 8. The School is approximately 2 miles from the center of Millburn Township (population 19,765), a suburban community 21 miles west of New York City. Classroom studies are supplemented with field trips to such places of interest as the Cloisters, the Brooklyn Museum, The Franklin Institute, the Great Swamp, and Sterling Mines.

Far Brook School was founded in 1948 by a group of parents who wanted to provide an "education of uncommon quality" for their children. Emphasizing the development of creative thinking, self-assurance, and initiative, Far Brook strives for "academic excellence through the integration of the liberal arts and sciences with the creative arts." Central to the School's philosophy is the expectation that children are capable of intellectual depth and of meeting rigorous standards of achievement. The School provides a "supportive and challenging environment, where concern for each individual's dignity and growth is paramount."

Incorporated as a nonprofit institution, the School is governed by a parent-elected Board of Trustees. The Board is composed of up to 18 members, including a maximum of 6 nonparents. The Annual Fund, supported mainly by parents and many of the approximately 1187 alumni and their families, raised $446,559 for 2006–07. *The Campaign for Far Brook—Preserving Tradition and Securing the Future* has made possible the renovation and expansion of Winifred S. Moore Hall. Far Brook School holds membership in the National Association of Independent Schools, among other affiliations. It is accredited by The Middle States Association of Colleges and Schools Commission on Elementary Schools.

THE CAMPUS. Far Brook's 9-acre campus encompasses playing fields, woods, a wetlands habitat, a pond and brook, a schoolyard, and a pony paddock. The School's facilities include the Junior High Building; the Lower School Building, housing Nursery–Grade 2 as well as the woodshop and jewelry-making room; the Small Barn; Moore Cottage, providing living quarters for the caretaker; and the Gymnasium. Moore Hall is the setting for daily Morning Meetings of the entire school community as well as drama and music presentations; it also contains the School's kitchen and expanded drama facilities. Buildings financed through the last capital campaign include the Ruth and Max Segal Family Library; the Mary Margaret Wearn Wiener Middle School, with classrooms for Grades 3–6, the School's computer laboratory, and Middle School science laboratory; an administration building; and the Laurie Arts Center, which houses an expanded arts facility, vocal and orchestral rehearsal rooms, and individual lesson studios.

The plant is owned by the School and is valued at $6,600,000.

THE FACULTY. Murray E. Lopdell Lawrence was appointed Head of School in July 2006, after a yearlong, nationwide search for a successor to Mary Wearn Wiener, Director of Far Brook since 1979. A graduate of Victoria University in Wellington, New Zealand, Mr. Lawrence pursued a double major in English and Political Science and was awarded a postgraduate Diploma of Teaching from Wellington Teacher's College. In addition to administrative positions at *Highlights for Children* magazine and Children's Television Workshop, Mr. Lawrence has held teaching posts in San Francisco, London, and New Zealand. Most recently, he was Head of School at Marin Primary and Middle School in California. He has also served as Headmaster at St. Thomas Episcopal Parish School in Florida and Acting Headmaster at St. Thomas Choir School in Manhattan. Mr. Lawrence is the Vice President of the Board of Directors of the Elementary School Heads Association.

The 33 full-time teachers hold baccalaureate and graduate degrees from Bank Street Graduate School, Bard, Boston University, Brooklyn College, California State, Carleton, City University of New York, College of New Jersey, College of St.

Elizabeth, Columbia, Elizabethtown, Empire State College, Framingham State, Hamilton, Harvard, Indiana University, Kean College, Montclair State, Mount Holyoke, National University, New York University, Northwestern, Ohio State, Pratt Institute, Princeton, Purdue, Queens College, Rutgers, St. John's, Skidmore, State University of New York (Potsdam, Purchase), Syracuse, Temple/Tyler School of Art, Trenton State, Vassar, Vermont College, Williams, Yale, and the Universities of Kansas, Pennsylvania, Quebec, Virginia, and Western Ontario. There are 11 part-time faculty for dance, resource room, learning consulting, Lower School French, and music as well as teaching assistants in Lower School classrooms.

For emergencies, there is a full-time nurse; most faculty members have first-aid and CPR training. St. Barnabas Hospital is approximately one mile from the School.

STUDENT BODY. In 2007–08, Far Brook enrolled 120 boys and 114 girls. Students represent 38 local communities as well as a variety of racial, religious, and economic backgrounds.

ACADEMIC PROGRAM. The academic year, from mid-September to mid-June, includes Thanksgiving, December, winter, and spring vacations. The school day begins at 8:10 A.M. and ends at 3:00 P.M. on Monday through Thursday and at 2:00 P.M. on Friday. Each day begins with Morning Meeting at 8:25 A.M., when the students gather in the Hall to hear poetry, to see faculty and student presentations, and to sing the songs and rounds that have become an integral part of the Far Brook experience. Class size ranges from 12 to 26 students. Traditional grading begins in Grade 7. Instruction in instrumental music is available.

Lower School (Nursery–Grade 3) children experience the security of belonging to a community whose life and work they find challenging and stimulating. Through an enriched sensory-motor and language experience, the curriculum stresses the development of sound basic skills and problem-solving processes. Children master skills sequentially in reading, writing, and computation, and develop facility in the scientific process. In Grades 2 and 3, study focuses on the interrelatedness of various disciplines through a core curriculum. The second grade focuses on Child and Universe; the third grade on Native Americans. Classroom studies include language arts, literature and writing, social studies, science, mathematics, and art. In addition, specialists in art, music, drama, dance, library/research skills, woodworking, and physical education work with children in all grades. French and private instrumental lessons are offered as early as Kindergarten.

Beginning in Grade 4, classroom studies are centered on a history core curriculum. Each grade studies a civilization or historical period in depth, learning about its architecture, music, art, literature, scientific principles, agriculture, clothing, and everyday life. In Grade 4, students study Ancient Egypt; in Grade 5, Ancient Greece; and in Grade 6, Rome and the Middle Ages. Other Middle School studies include reading, creative writing, language arts; French; mathematics; laboratory science; minicourses in art, drama, computers, library, and woodworking; choir, orchestra; and team sports.

The Junior High School readies students for secondary school and college work. Core curriculum studies focus on the Renaissance in Grade 7 and on American History in Grade 8. Students study English, French, mathematics, laboratory life science, and laboratory physical science; students complete Algebra I or a further course in Advanced Algebra by the end of Grade 8. All students take minicourses in art, computers, drama, library, and woodworking and are members of the School choir and sports teams. Many are also in the orchestra and special vocal groups. Each fall, the Junior High embarks on a wilderness trip during which students and faculty spend a week living, working, and studying together as a community.

Of the 32 graduates in 2006 and 2007, 26 entered the following schools: Delbarton 3, Foxcroft, Groton, Kent Place 3, Lawrenceville 2, Montclair Kimberley 2, Morristown-Beard 3, Newark Academy 4, Peddie, Phillips Andover, Pingry 2, Seton Hall Prep, and Williston Northampton. Six entered area public high schools.

The campus is home to two summer programs: Mini-Camp, a seven-week program for ages 3–6, and "Fundamentals" Sports Camp. The Mini-Camp Co-Directors are Paula Levin, Director of the Lower School and Nursery teacher, and Bill Deltz, also a Nursery teacher. Fundamentals Sports Camp is run by Greg Bartiromo, the School's physical education teacher and Director of After School Programs.

STUDENT ACTIVITIES. Students with strong interests in particular fields or areas of study are given special opportunities to pursue these interests.

Interscholastic sports, beginning in Grade 5, include soccer and baseball for boys and field hockey and softball for girls. Touch football, basketball, volleyball, badminton, floor hockey, speedball, and coeducational softball are also included in the sports program. Complementing their study of Greece, Grade 5 students participate in a yearly "Greek Olympics," competing in the shot put, the discus throw, the broad jump, and running.

Traditional events include daily Morning Meeting, the Thanksgiving Processional, the Medieval Masque, the Class Plays, Pergolesi's *Stabat Mater,* and the eighth graders' performance of Shakespeare's *The Tempest* or *A Midsummer Night's Dream* at graduation.

ADMISSION AND COSTS. Far Brook School seeks students from varied economic, racial, and religious backgrounds who are intellectually curious, serious about learning, self-motivated, and disciplined." Students are accepted in all grades except Grade 8 when openings are available. Application may be made in the fall preceding the year of desired enrollment. A play-group screening for Nursery, both play-group and individual screenings for Kindergarten, and student visits and testing for Grades 1–7 are required as part of the application process. Application and testing fees are $100.

In 2007–08, tuition ranges from $19,625 for full-day Nursery to $23,550 for Grade 8. Financial aid is awarded on the basis of need as well as the academic or social contribution a student makes to his or her class. A number of endowed scholarships, not available each year, are awarded for a student's duration at Far Brook. The George Bartol Scholarship provides tuition and transportation to one economically disadvantaged student with academic promise. The Barbara Jordan Endowment provides modest tuition assistance for an economically disadvantaged student of color. The Koven Family Scholarship offers substantial, need-based assistance for one or more incoming students, preferably those entering in the young grades. Two junior high scholarships—The Mary Adams Scholarship for Mathematics and Science and The Edwin E. Finckel Scholarship for the Arts—are awarded to talented students who have shown potential in those fields. Awarded annually, the Hite Scholarship provides students with the necessities of Far Brook life that fall outside the normal range of tuition assistance.

In the current year, 26 students received financial aid, including scholarships, totaling $374,435. Far Brook School subscribes to the School and Student Service for Financial Aid.

Director of Admissions & Placement: Mary Lacey Murphy
Director of Advancement: Caroline L. Sargent
Director of Development & Public Relations: Pat Lawler
Business Manager & Transportation Supervisor: Donna Chahalis
Director of Athletics: Nancy Muniz

Gill St. Bernard's School 1900

St. Bernard's Road, P.O. Box 604, Gladstone, NJ 07934
Tel. 908-234-1611; Admissions Ext. 245; Fax 908-234-1611
Web Site www.gsbschool.org; E-mail admission@gsbschool.org

Gill St. Bernard's is a coeducational, nonsectarian, college preparatory day school enrolling 676 students in Pre-Kindergarten–Grade 12. The School's mission is to develop respectful, intelligent, capable young people who will succeed in higher education, who can think critically and analytically, who act with integrity and compassion, and who are responsible citizens. The program is based on academic excellence and the education of each student in mind, body, and character. GSB offers Honors and Advanced Placement courses in English, history, mathematics, world languages, and the sciences as well as a wide variety of extracurricular activities for Middle and Upper School students in the areas of the arts, community service, student government, academics, and athletics. Facilities include two gymnasiums and a new athletic center. Tuition: $12,800–$24,200 (including lunch). Financial Aid: $1,000,000. Karen A. Loder is Director of Admission and Financial Aid; S. A. Rowell (Trinity College, B.A., M.A.) is Headmaster. *Middle States Association.*

Haddonfield Friends School 1786

47 North Haddon Avenue, Haddonfield, NJ 08033-2476
Tel. 856-429-6786; Fax 856-429-6376
Web Site www.haddonfieldfriends.org

For 221 years, Haddonfield Friends School has sought to provide a liberal arts education conducted according to traditional Quaker values of peace, cooperation, and nonviolence. The School enrolls 160 girls and boys in Pre-Kindergarten–Grade 8 in a curriculum designed to enable each child to reach his or her highest intellectual and social potential. Strong academic skills are emphasized, and children are led to understand that there is "something of God" in everyone. In a nurturing environment, reading, language arts, science, math, Spanish, and social studies are enriched by music, the arts, library, and physical education. Weekly Meeting for Worship inspires spiritual awareness. A summer program is offered. Tuition: $7435–$10,990. Sandy Trezza is Director of Admissions; Sharon Dreese is Head of School. *Middle States Association.*

Hilltop Country Day School 1967

32 Lafayette Road, Sparta, NJ 07871
Tel. 973-729-5485; Admissions Ext. 225; Fax 973-729-9057
Web Site www.hilltopcds.org; E-mail ltsemberlis@hilltopcds.org

Hilltop Country Day School, enrolling approximately 200 children in Preschool to Grade 8, aims to provide a family-oriented, creative, nurturing, highly educational environment where children discover the excitement of learning, develop good study habits, accept responsibility, and meet personal challenges. Hilltop values the role of learner in the education process, boasting a low teacher-student ratio and a balanced approach to social, emotional, academic, and artistic/creative growth. Music, the arts, computer and information technology, drama, and physical education/field program complement traditional subjects. Foreign language begins in Preschool. Tuition: $4017–$12,922. Financial aid is available. Lisa Tsemberlis is Admissions Director; Joseph R. Stefani is Headmaster.

The Hudson School 1978

601 Park Avenue, Hoboken, NJ 07030
Tel. 201-659-8335; Admissions Ext. 107; Fax 201-222-3669
Web Site www.thehudsonschool.org
E-mail hudson@thehudsonschool.org

Founded to provide challenging academic and arts programs for gifted and talented students, The Hudson School enrolls more than 200 urban students from diverse racial, economic, and cultural backgrounds in Grades 5–12. The college preparatory curriculum, which emphasizes the creative and performing arts, classical and modern languages, science, and math, is enriched by Advanced Placement and honors courses, retreats, field trips, and student exchanges abroad. Electives include chess, chorus, instrumental music instruction, yoga, video production, dance, sports, theater, and community service. Tuition: $12,740–$13,700. Financial aid is available. Suellen Newman (Oberlin, B.A.; University of Chicago, M.Ed.) is Founding Director. *Middle States Association.*

The Hun School of Princeton 1914

176 Edgerstoune Road, Princeton, NJ 08540
Tel. 609-921-7600; Fax 609-279-9398
Web Site www.hunschool.org; E-mail admiss@hunschool.org

THE HUN SCHOOL OF PRINCETON in Princeton, New Jersey, is a coeducational, college preparatory school encompassing Grades 6 through 12 and a postgraduate program. Resident students are admitted from Grade 9 through postgraduate. Situated in central New Jersey, Princeton is home to 12,000 year-round residents and the 6500-member student body of Princeton University. The School is about 45 miles from New York and Philadelphia. Students benefit from the many cultural, historic, and recreational opportunities available at the University and elsewhere in the region.

The Hun School of Princeton was founded as a boys' boarding school in 1914 by Dr. John Gale Hun, a member of the Princeton faculty who sought to provide a dynamic learning environment in which students were free to exchange ideas and share their understanding of the world. Girls were first welcomed as day students in 1971 and later as boarders in 1975.

The Hun School offers a challenging liberal arts curriculum that places equal emphasis on lasting values and academic achievement. Faculty are united in the common purpose of preparing students from widely diverse backgrounds for success in college and for full, productive citizenship in today's global community. School life is conducted according to an Honor Code that stresses integrity, kindness, respect, trust, and commitment.

Hun is a nonprofit, nonsectarian institution governed by a 30-member Board of Trustees, 10 of whom are alumni. The School is accredited by the Middle States Association of Colleges and Schools and holds membership in the National and New Jersey Associations of Independent Schools and other professional organizations. The Alumni Association, which represents the School's 7300 graduates, and the Parents' Association are active in fund-raising, recruitment, and other supportive endeavors.

THE CAMPUS. Formerly a private estate, Hun's 45-acre campus is graced by wooded areas, open meadows, formal gardens, and a brook, with ample space to accommodate five athletic fields, a natural cross-country trail, and a 400-meter all-weather track.

Most Upper School classrooms are located in the Chesebro Academic Center, which contains the Dingman Science and Technology Center, Sellon Information Center, and Sharp ceramics studio. Together these facilities include 32 classrooms, 6 science labs, a wet lab, aquarium, greenhouse, a newly renovated 35,000-volume library with more than 45 on-line and CD-ROM databases, and three 20-work-station computer labs. The Alexander K. Buck '49 Student Activity Center provides Middle School classrooms, television and radio broadcast studios, a computer center, art and music studios, the student bookstore, and snack bar. Adjacent is the Nature Center used as an environmental resource laboratory that enables students to transform the campus into a wildlife sanctuary.

Russell Hall is a Tudor-style mansion that furnishes administrative offices, the health clinic, faculty apartments, and a boys' residence hall. Additional housing for boys is located in Poe Dormitory; girls reside across the quad in Carter Dormitory. Meals are served in the newly renovated Dining Hall adjacent to Poe. An athletic center and gymnasium complete the School's facilities.

A $14,000,000 capital campaign nearing completion provided funding for three major projects: a newly completed Athletic Center, a Fine Arts Building under renovation, and a faculty endowment that has provided increased opportunity for faculty recognition and development.

THE FACULTY. James M. Byer, Ed.D., a graduate of Hun's Class of 1962 and a Hun faculty member and Dean of Students from 1966 to 1972, was appointed Headmaster in 1994. He earned a baccalaureate in economics from Marietta College, a master's degree in guidance and counseling from Rider College, and Ed.S. and Ed.D. degrees from Nova University. Previously, Dr. Byer held administrative and teaching posts at independent college preparatory schools in Florida.

More than one-half of Hun's 105 full-time faculty and administrators hold advanced degrees, with 5 holding doctorates. Twenty-nine live on campus.

Two registered nurses staff the clinic during the day and are on call 24 hours. Complete medical services are within minutes of the campus.

STUDENT BODY. In 2007–08, the Upper School enrolled 91 boarding boys, 195 day boys, 59 boarding girls, and 153 day girls, including 15 postgraduate students. The Middle School enrolled 95 day students in Grades 6–8. Boarding students represent 15 states and 14 countries.

ACADEMIC PROGRAM. The school year, which is divided into semesters, includes 35 weeks of instruction, with Thanksgiving, winter, and spring recesses. Grades are mailed to parents four times per year, and progress reports are issued three or more times a year. Each Hun student has a faculty advisor with whom he or she confers weekly. The student-faculty ratio is 14:1. Teachers are available for consultation during the school day and daily after the last scheduled period.

A typical day for boarding students begins with breakfast in the Dining Hall. Classes from 8:00 A.M. to 2:30 P.M. are followed by the consultation period. Athletic activities, community service outings, and extracurriculars run until 5:50 P.M. Dinner for boarding students and resident faculty is served from 5:45 to 6:45 P.M. A required two-hour study hall follows, during which time the library and computer labs are open. After study hall, students enjoy free time until "lights out" at 11:00 P.M.

The Middle School (Grades 6–8) curriculum consists of English, French or Spanish, pre-algebra, algebra 1, science, social studies, computer instruction, health, and art/drama/music throughout the three years.

To graduate from the Upper School (Grades 9–12), students must earn at least 19½ credits, including the following: 4 in English; 3 each in history and mathematics; 2 each in science and a foreign language; and ½ in fine arts. Students must also participate in community service each year and satisfy a computer-literacy requirement.

The International Student Program uses field trips and the study of United States history to introduce international students to American life; English as a Second Language is taught at four levels. The Academic Learning Skills Program, limited to an enrollment of 25, offers support to students with specific, diagnosed learning differences. The postgraduate program allows students who have completed high school graduation requirements to take Advanced Placement courses in specific areas of interest. Additionally, all students can benefit from the resources of the Writing Center, which is staffed by peer tutors who assist classmates in the preparation and refinement of written assignments.

Members of the Class of 2007 matriculated at 79 institutions, with 2 or more attending American, Brown, Bucknell, Colgate, Connecticut College, Dartmouth, Fairfield, Franklin and Marshall, James Madison, Muhlenberg, New York University, Pennsylvania State, Princeton, Rutgers, Syracuse, and George Washington University.

The Hun School's summer session includes academic enrichment and credit courses, English as a Second Language, SAT preparation, theater production, and dance workshops.

STUDENT ACTIVITIES. Among the leadership groups formed are the Student Council, Honor Council, and the Resident Life and Resident Judiciary committees. Middle School students publish their own yearbook *(The Yearling)*, and Upper School students issue *The Mall* (newspaper) and *The Edgerstounian* (yearbook). All grades are welcome to contribute to the art and literary magazine, *The Hun Review*.

The School stages three dramatic productions and several dance performances annually. Students perform in music groups such as the chorus, pit and jazz bands, and an instrumental music ensemble.

Among the organizations on campus are the Model United Nations program, Mock Trial, Key Club (community service), Environmental Club, Speech and Debate Team, Philosophy Club, Outing Club, Art Club, Diversity Club, Hun TV and Radio Club, and The Janus Players.

More than 50 athletic teams compete interscholastically. Some sports are offered on a "no-cut" basis. Intramurals are also offered each season.

The resident life curriculum allows students to take advantage of the surrounding areas as well as the beautiful campus. A typical weekend involves athletic contests on campus, student performances, community service opportunities, and trips to Princeton, Philadelphia, and New York City.

ADMISSION AND COSTS. The Hun School seeks students who exhibit a willingness to work hard, a strength of purpose, and an excellent citizenship record. Admission is based on a personal interview, previous school performance, three academic recommendations, and the results of the Secondary School Admission Test. First-round admission decisions are made in early March. Applicants are urged to apply early in the year for the following fall. There is a $50 application fee ($100 for international applicants).

In 2007–08, tuition is $39,190 for residents and $26,960 for day students. The fee for the Academic Learning Skills program is $14,935; the fee for English as a Second Language is $8500. A $1000 deposit is due with the contract to secure a place. Other charges include $350–$550 for books and a $390 clinic fee for resident students. Tuition insurance is required. Twenty-five percent of the students receive financial aid, and approximately $2,000,000 is awarded each year. The Gerald G. Donaldson Scholarship awards full tuition to one entering ninth- or tenth-grade student. The remainder of financial aid is need-based.

Upper School Head: William R. McQuade
Middle School Head: Patricia A. McKenna
Dean of Students: William E. Long
Director of Admissions & Financial Aid: P. Terence Beach
Director of Business & Finance: Richard L. Fleck
Director of Institutional Advancement: James P. O'Boyle
Director of College Counseling: David C. McMillan
Director of Athletics: William H. Quirk, Jr.

Kent Place School 1894

42 Norwood Avenue, Summit, NJ 07902-0308
Tel. 908-273-0900; Admission Ext. 254; Fax 908-273-9390
Web Site www.kentplace.org
E-mail admission@kentplace.org

Founded in 1894, Kent Place School is New Jersey's largest independent nonsectarian, college preparatory day school for girls, enrolling more than 600 students in Nursery–Grade 12, with boys admitted only in Nursery–Preschool. Kent Place is committed to an overall program of excellence that allows each girl to achieve her maximum academic, physical, and creative potential. Small classes, a Women's Life Studies Program, individualized college counseling, state-of-the-art technology, and diverse options in the fine arts are hallmarks of a Kent Place education. Students live by an Honor Code and participate in community service, interscholastic athletics, and other activities. Tuition: $9034–$26,818. Nancy Humick is Director of Admission and Financial Aid; Susan C. Bosland is Head of School. *Middle States Association.*

The Lawrenceville School 1810

Main Street, Box 6008, Lawrenceville, NJ 08648
Tel. 609-896-0400; Admission [Toll-free] 800-735-2030
Fax 609-895-2217
Web Site www.lawrenceville.org; E-mail admissions@lawrenceville.org

Set on a historic 700-acre campus designed by Frederick Law Olmsted, The Lawrenceville School is a coeducational, college preparatory school enrolling 539 boarders and 258 day students from around the world in Grades 9–12. The academic curriculum provides more than 300 courses in 11 disciplines, including 22 Advanced Placement courses. Students may spend a term abroad, undertake independent research and study, and design individualized off-campus projects. Over 50 organizations provide activities such as leadership groups, music, drama, dance, debate, community service, and interscholastic, intramural, and lifetime sports. Boarding Tuition: $39,397; Day Tuition: $32,110. Financial Aid: $6,000,000. Gregg Maloberti is Dean of Admission; Elizabeth A. Duffy is Head Master. *Middle States Association.*

Moorestown Friends School 1785

110 East Main Street, Moorestown, NJ 08057
Tel. 856-235-2900; Admissions Exts. 226–228; Fax 856-235-6684
Web Site www.mfriends.org; E-mail admiss@mfriends.org

Moorestown Friends School operates under the care of the Moorestown Monthly Meeting of the Society of Friends. The college preparatory day school enrolls 727 girls and boys in Preschool–Grade 12 and provides a challenging liberal arts education consistent with Quaker practice. Students participate in athletic, dramatic, and musical activities. Community service projects are encouraged. Tuition: $13,800–$18,900. Financial Aid: $1,200,000. Karin B. Miller is Director of Admissions & Financial Aid; Laurence R. Van Meter (Hamilton, B.A.; Dartmouth, M.B.A.) was appointed Head of School in 2001.

Morristown-Beard School 1971

70 Whippany Road, Morristown, NJ 07960
Tel. 973-539-3032; Fax 973-539-1590
Web Site www.mobeard.org; E-mail admissions@mobeard.org

This day school was formed by the merger of two single-sex schools to provide a coeducational program for 505 college-bound students in Grades 6–12. Morristown-Beard School aims to nurture each young person's intellectual, social, creative, and athletic potential, instilling the skills and knowledge needed to sustain them throughout life. Sharing equal emphasis with the academic and cocurricular programs are character development and the Core Values of Respect, Responsibility, Integrity, Courage, and Compassion. Course work is tailored to each student's unique aptitudes and interests, with small classes and a 7:1 student-teacher ratio. Classes are available at standard, honors, and AP levels, and required service learning is integral to the Morristown-Beard experience. The Learning Center provides assistance from teaching specialists, and qualified students can earn credit from self-directed independent study. School government, publications, Quiz Bowl, Math League, language clubs, interest groups, and varsity sports for boys and girls are among the activities. Tuition: $24,850–$25,950. Financial Aid: $900,000. Tracey Wetmore is Director of Admissions; Dr. Alex C. Curtis is Head of School. *Middle States Association.*

Mount Saint Mary Academy 1908

1645 U.S. Highway 22 at Terrill Road, Watchung, NJ 07069
Tel. 908-757-0108; Admissions Ext. 4506; Fax 908-756-8085
Web Site www.mountsaintmary.org
E-mail dtoryak@mountsaintmary.org

Mount Saint Mary Academy, founded by the Sisters of Mercy, is a Roman Catholic, college preparatory day school enrolling 381 young women in Grades 9–12. The Academy features a rigorous curriculum for the average to above-average student in a nurturing, supportive environment. Honors and Advanced Placement courses, varied technology offerings, and in-depth college guidance are additional highlights. Student government, clubs, drama, music, and varsity sports are among the activities. Tuition: $15,300. Financial Aid: $90,000. Donna Venezia Toryak is Director of Admissions; Sr. Lisa Gambacorto, RSM (Georgian Court, B.A.; Seton Hall, M.A., Ed.S.), was appointed Directress in 2000. *Middle States Association.*

Newark Academy 1774

91 South Orange Avenue, Livingston, NJ 07039
Tel. 973-992-7000; Admission Ext. 323; Fax 973-992-8962
Web Site www.newarka.edu; E-mail admissions@newarka.edu

Newark Academy offers a college preparatory education to 555 young men and women from diverse backgrounds in Grades 6–12. In a dynamic community of learners and teachers, the curriculum is designed to provide a strong base of knowledge and understanding in the liberal arts and sciences. Advanced Placement courses are available in all disciplines, and selected scholars may earn the International Baccalaureate diploma. From middle school through graduation, students enjoy a wide range of opportunities in the visual and performing arts, leadership groups, more than 40 interest clubs, an award-winning newspaper, and interscholastic athletics. Tuition: $24,700. Financial aid is available. Willard L. Taylor, Jr., is Director of Admission; Donald M. Austin is Head of School. *Middle States Association.*

Newark Boys Chorus School 1967

1016 Broad Street, Newark, NJ 07102
Tel. 973-621-8900; Fax 973-621-1343
Web Site newark-boys-chorus-school.net

Enrolling 80 day students in Grades 4–8, Newark Boys Chorus School emphasizes a love for learning, the quest for excellence, and compassion for humanity. Created in order to provide boys with a full-time quality education and a unique choral experience, the School helps students develop the skills and talents needed to attend artistic and college preparatory high schools. Students from diverse backgrounds build a community of honor, responsibility, mutual respect, scholarship, creative expression, and civic involvement. Students develop repertoires and take classes on music theory, sight reading, instruments, and choral training. Reading, writing, Spanish, math, geography, history, civics, and physical, earth, and life science comprise the academic curriculum, and students in Grade 8 may take AP courses in literature and social studies, with a focus on critical thinking, problem solving, and hands-on learning. Older students participate in international choral tours and concerts. The School receives partial funding from the New Jersey State Council on the Arts Department of State, a partner agency of the National Endowment for the Arts. Tuition: $2600. Financial Aid: $50,000. Lawrence R. Emery (St. Vincent, B.A.; Seton Hall, M.A.) is Head of School. *Middle States Association.*

Oak Hill Academy 1981

347 Middletown-Lincroft Road, Lincroft, NJ 07738
Tel. 732-530-1343; Fax 732-530-0045
Web Site www.oakhillacademy.com
E-mail clarkins@oakhillacademy.com

Oak Hill Academy combines "the strongest possible academic atmosphere with a supportive caring environment" in which children can develop into confident, motivated students who have a love of learning. Enrolling 420 boys and girls in Pre-Kindergarten–Grade 8, Oak Hill emphasizes the mastery of basic skills in a curriculum that provides both standard and accelerated classes to accommodate different learning styles. In addition to traditional subjects in the liberal arts and sciences, students benefit from participation in school government, publications, music and band, drama, team sports, and interest clubs. Selective summer sessions are offered. Tuition: $13,400. Financial Aid: $157,000. Christina Larkins is Director of Development; Joseph A. Pacelli is founding Headmaster. *Middle States Association.*

The Pingry School 1861

Kindergarten–Grade 5: Country Day Drive, Short Hills, NJ 07078
Tel. 973-379-4550; Fax 973-379-1861
Web Site www.pingry.org
Grades 6–12: Box 366, Martinsville Road, Martinsville, NJ 08836
Tel. 908-647-5555; Fax 908-647-3703

Pingry is a coeducational, college preparatory, country day school on two campuses enrolling approximately 1000 students in Kindergarten–Grade 12. Since its founding by Dr. John F. Pingry in 1861, the School has earned a reputation for excellence in teaching, high moral standards, a student-driven Honor Code, and the development of integrity and character among its students by an enthusiastic and committed faculty. The School offers extracurricular opportunities including athletics, music, drama, art, special-interest activities, and community service. Specialized and general summer camps are offered. Tuition: $21,750–$26,100. Financial aid is available. Reena Kamins is Director of Admission; Nathaniel Conard is Headmaster. *Middle States Association.*

The Peck School 1893

247 South Street, Morristown, NJ 07960
Tel. 973-539-8660; Admissions Ext. 117; Fax 973-539-6894
Web Site www.peckschool.org; E-mail pdodge@peckschool.org

The Peck School, an independent, coeducational day school of approximately 315 students in Kindergarten–Grade 8, strives to prepare each child to succeed in secondary school and, ultimately, to lead a productive and healthy life. Since its founding, Peck has remained devoted to excellence in both teaching and learning. It offers an academically challenging curriculum focusing on the development of academic skills, character, and consideration of others. With a caring faculty and a supportive school environment, Peck provides a rigorous and well-balanced curriculum designed to develop students' curiosity, talents, and critical thinking skills. In addition to its academic reputation, the School's character development (InDeCoRe), athletic programs, and use of laptop technology are widely recognized. Peck embraces a variety of perspectives and ethnic and cultural backgrounds. A strong academic and moral foundation with a positive attitude toward learning make Peck graduates successful candidates for secondary school placement. Tuition: $21,750–$24,900. Patricia E. Dodge is Director of Admissions & Financial Aid; John J. Kowalik (Williams, B.A.; Columbia, M.A.Ed.Adm.) is Headmaster. *Middle States Association.*

Peddie School 1864

South Main Street, Hightstown, NJ 08520
Tel. 609-490-7500; Admission 609-490-7501; Fax 609-944-7901
Web Site www.peddie.org; E-mail admission@peddie.org

With a 230-acre campus and a history dating from 1864, Peddie enrolls 520 boys and girls as boarding and day students in Grade 9–Postgraduate. Mixing tradition and innovation, the School provides rigorous academics including 20 Advanced Placement courses. Students have opportunities in the arts, interscholastic sports, and Study Abroad. They must participate in the campus Work Program and the Community Service Program. In a friendly and supportive environment, faculty encourage students to reach for new levels of achievement. Tuition fees include a laptop computer. Boarding Tuition: $37,275; Day Tuition: $28,250. Raymond H. Cabot is Director of Admission; John F. Green (Wesleyan University, B.A.; Harvard, M.Ed.) was appointed Head of School in 2001. *Middle States Association.*

Princeton Day School 1965

The Great Road, P.O. Box 75, Princeton, NJ 08542
Tel. 609-924-6700; Admission Ext. 1200; Fax 609-279-2703
Web Site www.pds.org; E-mail admissions@pds.org

Princeton Day enrolls 900 college-bound girls and boys in Junior Kindergarten–Grade 12. It offers opportunity for intellectual growth and character development through high standards of academic excellence and caring, individualized teaching. The 105-acre campus includes a synthetic-turf field, an art gallery, woodshop, architecture drafting room, darkrooms, kiln room, three computer labs, three libraries, planetarium, greenhouse, enclosed skating rink, 400-seat theater, 100-seat amphitheater, science labs, and art, music, photography, and ceramics studios. More than 90 percent of graduates are accepted to "Most Difficult" or "Very Difficult" colleges and universities. Tuition: $21,400–$26,000. Financial Aid: $2,600,000. Kelly Dun is Director of Admission; Lila Lohr is Interim Head of School. *Middle States Association.*

Princeton Junior School 1983

Box 672, Princeton, NJ 08542
Tel. 609-924-8126; Admissions Ext. 103; Fax 609-924-7456
Web Site www.pjs.org; E-mail admissions@pjs.org

Taking pride in "its history, simple beauty, and rich curriculum," Princeton Junior School was founded in 1983 to provide academic excellence in a nurturing environment and to graduate students with a solid grounding in the skills necessary to excel throughout their academic careers. The journey for 125 boys and girls in Pre-school–Grade V is pivotal in cultivating a passion for learning and shaping character. It is a process that values high standards, creativity, and exploration, all finely balanced between work and play. The curriculum includes language arts, math, science, geography, social studies, Spanish, art, music, drama, sports, and computer education. The campus provides a stage on which to observe, analyze, and marvel at the mysteries of nature through the School's Learning Through Landscapes program. Princeton Junior School is also defined by its culturally diverse population and commitment to community service. Neighboring Princeton offers abundant cultural and educational opportunities. Before- and after-school care is provided. Tuition: $9100–$17,970. Deborah M. Agnew is Director of Admissions; Peter Y. Rapelye is Headmaster.

Princeton Montessori School 1968

487 Cherry Valley Road, Princeton, NJ 08540
Tel. 609-924-4594; Fax 609-924-2216
Web Site www.princetonmontessori.org; E-mail pmonts@pmonts.edu

This coeducational day school enrolls 302 children in five divisions: Infant (through 18 months), Toddler (to 3 years), Primary (through Kindergarten), Elementary (through Grade 5), and Middle School (through Grade 8). Princeton Montessori School is dedicated to the highest-quality education of children, parents, and teachers, according to the values and principles of the Montessori philosophy. Certified Montessori teachers nurture the individual child's innate abilities and self-exploration that provide the skills and foundation for leading full lives. The recruitment, training, and continued mentorship of talented faculty, along with the integrated curriculum and environments tailored to meet the developmental needs of the individual, are the School's priorities. The curriculum centers on language arts, math, social studies, and science, complemented by French, music, art, and fitness. Students learn in multiage classrooms and participate in activities such as percussion ensemble, public speaking, cooking, chorus, ceramics, ecology, chess, sewing, yearbook, and computer. Extended day care and an academic summer session are offered. Tuition: $19,500–$22,950. Mary Beth Evans is Director of Admission; Marsha Stencel is Head of School. *Middle States Association.*

Ranney School 1960

235 Hope Road, Tinton Falls, NJ 07724
Tel. 732-542-4777; Admissions Ext. 109; Fax 732-460-1078
Web Site www.ranneyschool.org
E-mail admissions@ranneyschool.org

Ranney School, enrolling 815 day students age 3–Grade 12, offers a college preparatory curriculum that nurtures intellectual inquiry, creative expression, and diversity. The School emphasizes basic and traditional learning skills, refined by the fine and performing arts, foreign languages, computer science, and athletic and extracurricular programs. Small classes allow students to become fully involved in their learning. All graduates attend college, with the majority enrolling at the most prestigious universities. The Middle and Upper School complex provides state-of-the-art technology and a college-style dining facility. Tuition: $10,550–$21,900. Heather Rudisi is Associate Head for Admissions & Marketing; Lawrence S. Sykoff (University of San Diego, M.Ed., Ed.D.) is Head of School. *Middle States Association.*

The Red Oaks School 1965

21 Cutler Street, Morristown, NJ 07960
Tel. 973-539-7853; Admissions Ext. 20; Fax 973-539-5182
Web Site www.redoaksschool.org
E-mail admissions@redoaksschool.org

A coeducational Early Childhood and elementary day school, The Red Oaks School, formerly Montessori Children's House, promotes a love of learning, self-confidence, and high achievement for 160 children ages 3–12. Red Oaks is fully accredited by the American Montessori Society and the National Association for the Education of Young Children. The educational approach is informed by leading thinkers and the latest validated research in education, psychology, and related disciplines, including the time-tested insights and methods of Dr. Maria Montessori. With mixed-age classes and a 9:1 student-teacher ratio, Red Oaks embraces a child-centered curriculum that allows students to learn deeply and at their own pace. Core values of respect, dignity, and social awareness are thoroughly imbedded into the culture of the School. Artist- and scientist-in-residence programs, environmental projects, music, drama, and technology enhance the program. The School benefits greatly from strong parental involvement and a gifted and caring faculty. Tuition: $10,100–$15,975. Rebecca Spence is Director of Admissions; Marilyn E. Stewart is Head of School. *Middle States Association.*

The Rumson Country Day School 1926

35 Bellevue Avenue, Rumson, NJ 07760
Tel. 732-842-0527; Admissions Ext. 112; Fax 732-758-6528
Web Site rcds.org; E-mail spost@rcds.org

THE RUMSON COUNTRY DAY SCHOOL in Rumson, New Jersey, is a coeducational, elementary day school enrolling students in Nursery–Grade 8. Rumson (population 7000) is a residential community situated on the Atlantic Ocean in Monmouth County. It is about an hour south of New York City via car, bus, and rail, and a high-speed ferry transports passengers across the bay to the southern tip of Manhattan.

The Rumson Country Day School was established in 1926 by local parents who sought a challenging independent education for their children. It opened with 23 students and five teachers on a 2.5-acre site that featured a 19th-century church building. Since its founding, the School has periodically undergone major renovations and expansions to the facilities, and adjoining properties have been acquired. Today, Rumson Country Day enrolls 395 children in the K–8 school, with triple sections in every class, and 55 children in the Pre-School.

The School's mission over the years has remained constant: to provide students from all communities with a challenging academic experience in a supportive environment; to nourish academic excellence, individual and social responsibility, civic awareness, and leadership skills; and to inspire graduates to become lifelong learners, able to thrive, contribute, and excel in a demanding secondary school environment and in tomorrow's society.

The Rumson Country Day School, named a Blue Ribbon School of Excellence in 1999, is a nonsectarian, not-for-profit institution governed by a 23-member, self-perpetuating Board of Trustees. The School is accredited by the Middle States Association Commission on Elementary Schools and holds membership in the National Association of Independent Schools and the Council for Advancement and Support of Education.

THE CAMPUS. Located in a residential area, The Rumson Country Day School's 14-acre campus accommodates a baseball diamond, three playing fields, two playgrounds, and two gyms. The main school building houses Beginners (Kindergarten) through Grade 8. Students have the use of three libraries: The main library contains 13,000 volumes, 45 periodicals, and a comprehensive collection of audiovisual and resource materials; the Pre-School and Beginners libraries each hold 1000 volumes. Students and teachers have the use of 200 computers; 17 of these are in a new computer/multimedia center, and the other 183 are in classrooms and offices. Three fully equipped science labs, arts and crafts studios, an observatory, a two-room music center, and a 200-seat auditorium for student productions complete the academic facilities. Students and faculty share a hot lunch in two spacious dining rooms. The Pre-School building also provides the Headmaster's residence.

The plant is owned by the School and valued at $20,000,000.

THE FACULTY. Chad B. Small was appointed Headmaster in 1989. A graduate of Millbrook School in New York, he holds a B.A. from Ohio Wesleyan (1976), an M.Ed. from the University of Virginia (1979), and a doctoral degree from Seton Hall University. Dr. Small has taught in public and private schools and, before assuming his present position, was Head of St. Richard's School in Indianapolis, Indiana. He and his wife, Susan, have three children, all of whom are RCDS graduates.

There are 60 full-time faculty members, 13 men and 47 women, and 5 part-time teachers. The average teaching experience is 16 years, with an average of 11 years spent at the School. All hold baccalaureate degrees or the equivalent; additionally, they have earned 28 advanced degrees from such colleges and universities as Bank Street College, Bloomsburg, Boston University, Columbia, Fordham, Jersey City State, Kean, Monmouth University, Montclair State, New York University, Rutgers, St. Peter's College, Seton Hall, State University of New York, Trenton State, Widener College, and the Universities of Colorado, Delaware, and Washington.

A full-time registered nurse is on campus, and several faculty members are trained in first aid; the nearest hospital is five minutes away.

STUDENT BODY. The Rumson Country Day School enrolls 450 students in Nursery through Grade 8. They come from 36 communities within a 20-mile radius of the School; approximately 10 percent are students of color.

ACADEMIC PROGRAM. The school year, which is divided into trimesters, begins after Labor Day and extends to early June. The calendar includes a Thanksgiving recess, vacations in December and March, and the observances of several national and religious holidays. Classes are held five days a week on a rotating basis, beginning at 8:00 A.M. and ending between 3:15 and 3:30 P.M., depending on grade level. Half-day classes are held for Nursery (age 3), while Pre-Kindergarten (age 4) is offered on a half- or full-day basis. From the Pre-School level through Grade 5, students are grouped heterogeneously.

The Lower and Upper School schedules incorporate a midday extra-help period for students requiring additional support, and after-school and summer tutoring are available from some teachers at extra cost. Every Upper School student has a faculty advisor. A special new individualized program is available for students in Grades 5–7 with language-based learning differences.

The core curriculum is centered on English literature and language arts, math, science, social studies/history, and Spanish or French. Art, shop, crafts, music, computer, health, and physical education are integrated into the weekly schedule. Students in Kindergarten–Grade 4 study French, with the choice of French or Spanish in Grades 5–8. An honors program is available for qualified Upper School students in English, math, and foreign languages. Latin is required for all students in Grades 7 and 8, and speed-reading instruction is offered in Grade 8. All students participate in community service as part of the curriculum.

On a typical day, Upper School students take three classes, then a 10-minute break, followed by three more classes, a conference or reading period, and lunch. There are three afternoon periods prior to dismissal.

Graduates in the Class of 2007 entered a variety of public and independent schools including American International School (South Africa), Brearley, Christian Brothers Academy, Colts Neck High, Dwight-Englewood, The Hill School, Hotchkiss, Lawrenceville, Marine Academy of Science and Technology, Middletown South High, Monsignor Donovan High, Peddie, Ranney, Red Bank Catholic, Rumson-Fair Haven, St. George's, and Warner-Robins High School.

STUDENT ACTIVITIES. The Rumson Country Day School offers extracurricular activities designed to provide leadership experiences as well as social, recreational, and enrichment opportunities. Upper School students elect officers and homeroom representatives to a Student Council that provides communication between the student body and the Administration and organizes social events.

Upper School students can choose from a variety of weekly minicourses and become involved in forensics, newspaper, and a Weekend Club. The Drama Club stages a musical, and individual grades present plays and concerts for schoolmates and families. There are also overnight class trips for Grades 5–8. Lower School activities include after-school games and crafts, Brownies, and Drama Club. After-school care is available on Monday through Thursday.

The athletics program, open to Grades 5–8, involves competition with other independent, parochial, and public schools. Boys compete in football, soccer, basketball, baseball, and lacrosse; girls' teams compete in soccer, field hockey, basketball, softball, and lacrosse.

Among the family events on the school calendar are Field Day, Halloween Party, Holiday Alumni Brunch and Program, Homecoming, Grandfriends' Day, Class Day, and Graduation.

ADMISSION AND COSTS. The Rumson Country Day School welcomes students from diverse racial, ethnic, and religious backgrounds who show evidence of good character and integrity and who are eager to participate fully in the School's academic and extracurricular offerings available. The application process for Beginners–Grade 8 includes on-site testing, teacher recommendations, and a classroom visit. Notification is rolling. No testing is required for Pre-School; early application is recommended, and the School's age cut-off date is September 1. The application fee is $50 for Pre-School and $75 for Beginners–Grade 8.

In 2007–08, tuition ranged from $8875 for four half-day Nursery (age 3) to $18,475 in Grade 8. Included in the tuition are all hot lunches, books, supplies, and lab fees. An activity fee of $150 in Pre-School, $350 in Beginners–Grade 4, and $500 in Grades 5–8 covers field trips, athletic trips, minicourses, testing, and other incidentals. There are additional charges for the wilderness education trips in Grades 5–8. Two payment plans are available. In the current year, 33 students received $330,000 in need-based financial aid.

Headmaster: Chad B. Small
Upper School Head: L. William Lamb, Jr.
Lower School Head: Jayne S. Carmody
Director of Admissions/External Affairs: Suzanne R. Post
Dean of Students: Elizabeth Luzio
Director of Development: Diana N. Flippo
Business Manager: Linda M. Schottland
Director of Support Services: Richard N. Shanley, Jr.
Lower School Curriculum Coordinator: Joy S. Rathemacher

Rutgers Preparatory School 1766

1345 Easton Avenue, Somerset, NJ 08873
Tel. 732-545-5600; Admissions Ext. 261; Fax 732-214-1819
Web Site www.rutgersprep.org

RUTGERS PREPARATORY SCHOOL in Somerset, New Jersey, is a coeducational day school for students in Pre-Kindergarten through Grade 12. Located in Somerset, the School enrolls students from diverse geographic, economic, social, and ethnic backgrounds. The metropolitan area of Central New Jersey, nearby Rutgers University, and accessibility to New York City offer students additional educational and cultural experiences. The School provides bus and van service to 39 communities.

The oldest independent school in New Jersey, Rutgers Preparatory School was founded in 1766 under the same charter as Queens College, now Rutgers—The State University of New Jersey. In 1957, the School adopted its own charter and moved to its present Franklin Township site. In 1993, the Council for American Private Education and the U.S. Department of Education named Rutgers Preparatory a Blue Ribbon School.

The School values intellectual curiosity and personal integrity and emphasizes a strong academic program, creative problem solving, cooperation and group interaction, appreciation of culture and beauty, and healthy emotional and physical growth.

Rutgers Preparatory School is a nonprofit institution governed by a Board of Trustees. The Parents' Association provides support through volunteer activities and fund-raising events. The School is accredited by the Middle States Association of Colleges and Secondary Schools and holds membership in the National Association of Independent Schools, among other organizations.

THE CAMPUS. The 35-acre campus is bounded by wooded areas and the Delaware and Raritan Canal. The 18th-century Elm Farm House, formerly the home of one of the School's founders, houses administrative offices. A campus-wide building program includes a new media and computer center, computer classrooms, and two physical education facilities. Seven additional buildings of pre-Revolutionary War and modern architecture lend themselves to age- and class-appropriate activities. Athletic facilities include playing fields, the field house, and tennis courts.

THE FACULTY. Steven A. Loy, appointed Headmaster in 1992, is a graduate of Princeton University (B.A. 1974), Stanford University (M.A. 1976), and the University of California, Los Angeles (Ed.D. 1979). He was previously Headmaster of Dunn School and Assistant Headmaster of Brentwood School, and has had teaching experience in England, Scotland, and Denmark.

There are 108 full-time faculty members, including administrators who teach. They hold 57 master's, and 10 doctoral degrees representing study at Bucknell, College of New Jersey, Columbia, Dickinson, Georgetown, Goucher, Hamilton, Harvard, Johns Hopkins, Lehigh, Middlebury, Princeton, Rutgers, Tufts, and the Universities of Massachusetts, Michigan, and Pennsylvania.

There is a full-time nurse on duty, and St. Peter's Hospital is located nearby.

STUDENT BODY. In 2007–08, Rutgers Preparatory School enrolled 720 students. There were 69 in the Primary School (PK3/JK4/K), 123 in the Lower School (Grades 1–4), 194 in the Middle School (Grades 5–8), and 334 in the Upper School (Grades 9–12). Students came from 81 communities in Central New Jersey.

ACADEMIC PROGRAM. The school year, divided into semesters, begins in early September and ends in mid-June. There are vacations in the winter and spring. Parent conferences are held in the fall, and grades are sent home quarterly. The school day begins at 8:20 A.M. and ends at 3:05 P.M. Before- and after-school programs are available beginning at 7:30 A.M. and ending at 6:00 P.M.

Lower School students are taught in self-contained classrooms. The basic skills of reading, writing, science, social science, mathematics, and computers are emphasized, and foreign language study begins in Grade 1.

The Middle School curriculum is departmentalized. These students take courses in English, foreign language, mathematics, social studies, science, art, drama, music, library skills, computer skills, and health/physical education.

To graduate from the Upper School, students must earn 20 credits, including 4 in English, 3½ in mathematics, 2 in world language, 2 in science, 3 in social studies, 1 in fine arts, and three years of physical education and health.

Advanced Placement courses are available in Biology, Chemistry, Computer Science, Calculus, English Language, English Literature, Environmental Science, European History, French Language, U.S. Government, Music Theory, Physics, Psychology, U.S. History, Spanish Language, and Statistics. Select students in Grade 12 participate in an Interpersonal and Group Communication Theory course and hold small group discussions with students in Grade 9.

Graduates in the Class of 2007 matriculated at such institutions as Brown, Bucknell, College of New Jersey, Connecticut College, Cornell, Emory, Georgetown, George Washington, Haverford, Johns Hopkins, Lehigh, Middlebury, New York University, Rutgers, Swarthmore, Syracuse, and the Universities of Colorado, Notre Dame, Virginia, and Wisconsin.

STUDENT ACTIVITIES. Each Middle School homeroom elects a representative to the Middle School Student Council. The Council is encouraged to assume responsibility for social activities in the Middle School. The Upper School Student Council, elected by the student body, discusses and acts on matters of student business, provides assembly time for club presentations, funds budget requests from clubs, and plans after-school social events. The Judiciary Board meets on cases involving rules infractions and makes recommendations to the administration. Senior prefects are elected to serve as role models to underclassmen.

Lower School students are introduced to a variety of clubs and community service projects and publish a newspaper, *40:32* (a literary magazine), and *Ye Dial* (a yearbook). All Lower School students participate in the Science Fair and a school-wide Writing Day. Music lessons are available in keyboard, strings, and wind instruments, and concerts are given in the winter and spring.

Middle School students publish *Ye Dial* (the yearbook). They present dramatic and musical productions each year and participate in field days in addition to cross-curricular, grade-level projects during a special project week.

Upper School activities include academic teams, Math League, Model Congress, Model United Nations, Maroon Stock Exchange, and the Chess, Computer, French, Spanish, and Video Clubs. There are dramatic and musical productions each year, and students publish *Argo* (a newspaper), *Excelsior* (the literary magazine), and *Ye Dial* (the yearbook).

Interscholastic competition begins in Grade 7. Boys compete in soccer, wrestling, basketball, lacrosse, baseball, and tennis. Girls' teams are organized in soccer, tennis, basketball, volleyball, lacrosse, and softball. There are coeducational teams in cross-country, swimming, and golf.

Traditional annual events include the Writing Fair, Ethnic Pride Festival, winter and spring music concerts, Spring Family Picnic, Book Fair, Career Day, Foreign Language Tea, Upper School Honors Convocation, Senior Retreat, College Night, Sports Award Dinner, Creative Arts Dinner, and Commencement.

ADMISSION AND COSTS. Rutgers Preparatory School seeks students who are able to apply themselves to a rigorous academic program and are willing to make a commitment to the school community. Applicants are urged to apply early in the school year. A personal interview is required. After receipt of an application, the School will notify the candidate of testing procedures and request the release of school transcripts and teacher recommendations.

In 2007–08, tuition is $12,730 for half-day Pre-/Junior Kindergarten, $15,320 for full-day Pre-Kindergarten, $16,750 for Kindergarten, $19,400 for Grades 1–5, $20,800 for Grades 6–7, and $22,900 for Grades 8–12 plus additional fees not included with tuition. A 10 percent deposit is due by mid-March.

Financial aid is available for applicants who demonstrate need and evidence of academic, social, and leadership promise.

Upper School Principal: Stephen Duffy
Middle School Principal: John Miller
Lower School Principal: Kathy Rusyn
Primary School Principal: Tara Klipstein
Co-Directors of Admission: Diane Glace (PK3–Grade 6) & Vincent Valenzuela (Grades 7–12)
Director of Development: James Ackerman
Director of Financial Aid: Patria Sullivan
Co-Directors of College Counseling: Sherry Riggi & Shelley Krause
Athletic Director: Mary Coyle Klinger

Saddle River Day School 1957

147 Chestnut Ridge Road, Saddle River, NJ 07458
Tel. 201-327-4050; Admission Ext. 1105; Fax 201-327-6161
Web Site www.saddleriverday.org
E-mail jdyszkiewicz@saddleriverday.org

Saddle River Day School in Saddle River, New Jersey, is a coeducational, college preparatory day school enrolling students in Kindergarten through Grade 12. The suburban town of Saddle River (population 7198) is located in the northeastern corner of the state. The School is 18 miles from New York City and benefits from the cultural opportunities available in the metropolitan area.

In 1957, founding Headmaster Douglas S. Ogilvie leased a site, formerly the Denison Estate, owned by John C. and Diane Alford. Together, they created Saddle River Day School to provide families with school choice and to create lasting educational value for the community. The School had its first graduate in 1959.

Saddle River Day School seeks to provide a safe, intellectually challenging environment where children are encouraged to learn, to question, and to grow as individuals while being part of a community. With its goal of helping students become caring, competent adults able to succeed in and contribute to society, the School best serves those who have the ability to thrive in a traditional, college preparatory curriculum. All students subscribe to the School's Honor Code.

A nonprofit institution, the School is governed by a 20-member Board of Trustees. An Alumni Association and a Parents' Guild sponsor programs and special events. The School is currently involved in a Long Range Plan designed to strengthen its mission in curriculum, faculty, admissions, marketing, funding, and a campus master plan. Accredited by the Middle States Association of Colleges and Schools, Saddle River Day holds membership in the National Association of Independent Schools, the Educational Records Bureau, and the Council for Advancement and Support of Education, among other organizations.

THE CAMPUS. The 26-acre campus provides a view of the Ramapo Mountains and includes two full-size soccer fields, a softball field, a baseball diamond, six all-weather tennis courts, an outdoor climbing wall, two playgrounds, and the Headmaster's House as well as formal gardens, lawns, and woods. The original estate mansion, now Main Hall, contains the Lower School and administrative offices. Alford Hall (1963) houses science and mathematics classrooms, the Athansia M. Tsoukas Biology Laboratory, the Performing Arts Center, two art studios, and the office of the Middle School Dean. The Connell Science Wing was added in 1986. North Hall (1971) holds classrooms, the Computer Center, an amphitheater, reading lab, dining rooms and kitchen, gymnasium and fitness room, the music room, the library-media center, and the Minton Library Wing (1986). The offices of the Upper School Dean, Dean of Students, and the Director of College Placement are also located here.

THE FACULTY. John T. O'Brien (Trinity College, B.A.; Dartmouth College, M.A.L.S.) was appointed Headmaster in 2005.

The 31 women and 18 men on the faculty hold baccalaureate degrees and 28 master's degrees. Each of the three school divisions has its own dean; each academic department has its own chairperson. Saddle River's teachers also coach, counsel, and conduct the extracurricular program. The School's registered nurse is trained in first-aid procedures.

STUDENT BODY. The School serves a diverse population of students, ages 5–18, drawn from 64 nearby communities in New Jersey and New York State. In the 2007–08 school year, 320 students are enrolled, including 161 boys and 159 girls, as follows: 78 in the Lower School (Kindergarten–Grade 5); 95 in the Middle School (Grades 6–8); and 147 in the Upper School (Grades 9–12).

ACADEMIC PROGRAM. The school year, which begins in early September and ends in early June, includes Thanksgiving, winter, and spring breaks. The Upper School year is divided into semesters of two marking periods each. In Grades 6–12, a midyear exam is given in January and a final exam in June.

The Lower School combines classroom learning with hands-on experiences in an integrated curriculum. Students are engaged in reading/language arts, mathematics, science, and social studies. Art, music, world language, physical education, and computer lab supplement the core curriculum. Extracurricular activities include field trips, special events, and a performance orchestra and chorus that is open to Grade 4 and higher. Students in Kindergarten–Grade 3 are instructed in self-contained classrooms, while Grades 4–5 take advantage of increasing departmentalization. Throughout the Lower School, there is only one section per grade level with an average of 16 per grade.

Middle School students follow a fully departmentalized curriculum. Core courses include literature, composition, research skills, mathematics, calculator skills, laboratory science, history and world cultures, and foreign language including Latin, French, and Spanish. Minor courses include art, computer, family life, and geography. Qualified students may move into Upper School courses in math and world language. Extracurricular opportunities include music, theater, orchestra, student government, publications, sports skills, art, computer, and community service. Annual events are a trip to Frost Valley and a Medieval Renaissance Festival.

Upper School courses include English I–IV, World Literature; Algebra I–III, Geometry, College Algebra, PreCalculus; Physical Science, Biology, Chemistry, Physics, Ecology; World History, Foundations of the 21st Century, U.S. History I–II; Latin I–III, French I–III, Spanish I–III; Desktop Publishing, Programming; Theater Arts, Drama, Tech Theater, Experiencing Art, Independent Art, Portfolio Art; and Experiencing Music, Advanced Music Literature, Music Theory, Concert Choir, and Concert Orchestra. All students write a research paper each year as part of their social science course. Most courses have Honors sections. Advanced Placement courses are offered in English, Calculus AB and BC, Biology, Chemistry, Physics, Computer Science, U.S. History, European History, Latin, French, and Spanish. Class size is small, with a teacher-student ratio of 1:8.

To graduate, students must complete four years of English; three years each of mathematics, laboratory science, and social sciences; three levels of a world language; and six credits of visual or performing arts. Graduates must be proficient in word processing and computers and are required to have completed four years of physical education. Independent study courses are offered for capable students wishing to pursue an area of interest not offered in the course catalog.

Qualified seniors may participate in a special project starting in May. The project, consisting of community service work, is designed to provide meaningful educational experience outside the classroom.

The academic day contains nine periods preceded by homeroom, lasting from 8:18 A.M. to 3:20 P.M. On Mondays, homeroom is replaced by an assembly or advisor period on a rotating basis.

The advisor program, designed to provide academic guidance as well as social and community awareness, assigns each Middle and Upper School student to a faculty member. Each advisor has 7–10 students in the same grade. Advisors and students are expected to keep in individual contact throughout the year.

College counseling is a four-year process involving the student, family, and counselor. More than 75 college representatives visit the School each year. Typically, 100 percent of the senior class matriculates at college. Graduates of the Class of 2006 and 2007 were accepted at such institutions as American University, Boston College, Colgate, Columbia University, Cornell, Dickinson, Drew, Emory, Fairfield, Franklin and Marshall, George Washington, Indiana University, Johns Hopkins, Lafayette, Lehigh, Muhlenberg, New York University, Princeton, Quinnipiac, Rensselaer Polytechnic Institute, School of the Museum of Fine Arts (Boston), Skidmore, State University of New York (Binghamton), Swarthmore, Trinity (Connecticut), Tufts, Union, Villanova, Washington University, Wheaton (Massachusetts), Yale, and the Universities of Colorado, Delaware, and Michigan.

STUDENT ACTIVITIES. Students may participate in a variety of activities: student government, judiciary committee, yearbook, newspaper, literary magazine, peer leadership, concert choir, orchestra, theatrical productions, student-sponsored dances, field days, and junior varsity and varsity sports. The School has chapters of Interact, SADD, the Spanish National Honor Society, the French National Honor Society, and The Cum Laude Society.

Middle and Upper School interscholastic teams in baseball, basketball, cross-country, golf, soccer, softball, tennis, track, and volleyball practice from 3:30 to 5:30 P.M. Student art exhibitions, three major theater productions, two levels of chorus, three orchestras, and individual instrument lessons highlight the arts program.

Students who maintain a 3.0 or higher grade-point average and who exhibit exemplary character and leadership ability may be nominated to the Zeta Chi fraternity to serve as in-house tutors and admissions ambassadors.

ADMISSION AND COSTS. Saddle River Day School admits students who show evidence of creative, analytical, and critical thinking and reasoning skills as well as those students who will make positive and meaningful contributions to the School. New students are accepted at all grade levels as space permits. Along with a $50 application fee, candidates must submit transcripts from the past two years, any standardized test scores, two teacher recommendations, and results of the Independent School Entrance Examination. An interview with parents and student is required. While admission is made on a rolling basis, families are encouraged to apply early.

In 2007–08, tuition is $17,270 for Kindergarten, $17,866 for Grades 1–5, $20,366 for Grade 6, $22,944 for Grades 7–8, and $23,900 for Grades 9–12. There is a technology fee of $350. Financial aid is available based upon merit as well as need. In 2007–08, approximately $437,500 in financial aid was awarded. The School offers a tuition payment plan and tuition insurance.

Headmaster: John T. O'Brien
Director of Admission & Financial Aid: Gretchen Lee
Dean of Students: Robert Waters
Head of the Upper Division: Andrew J. Rork
Head of the Middle Division: Kirk Effinger
Head of the Lower Division: Dr. Arlene Hartman
Dean of Academic Affairs: Evan C. Strager
Director of Development: Jane Wenning
Financial Officer: Judith Kuhlman
Director of College Placement: Mary Ellen Zittel
Director of Technology: Jennifer Davenport
Athletic Director: Joseph S. Augienello

St. Benedict's Preparatory School 1868

520 Dr. Martin Luther King, Jr., Boulevard, Newark, NJ 07102
Tel. 973-792-5800; Fax 973-643-6922
Web Site www.sbp.org; E-mail graybee@sbp.org

St. Benedict's is a Roman Catholic, college preparatory day school with a 75-student boarding program enrolling 554 boys in Grades 7–12. Founded by monks of the Order of St. Benedict at Newark Abbey, the School aims for academic and personal excellence in a student body that reflects the racial and cultural diversity of the city. A rigorous curriculum is supplemented by special projects, elective programs, and short-term exchanges with other schools. A full athletic program, publications, drama, choir, and clubs are among the activities. A six-week summer session is mandatory. Tuition: $5100–$7250; Boarding Fee: $5000. Financial aid is available. James Wandling, OSB, is Director of Admissions; Rev. Edwin D. Leahy, OSB (Seton Hall, A.B.; Woodstock College, M.Div.), is Headmaster. *Middle States Association.*

St. Mary's Hall/Doane Academy 1837

350 Riverbank, Burlington, NJ 08016-2199
Tel. 609-386-3500; Admission Ext. 15; Fax 609-386-5878
Web Site www.thehall.org; E-mail sgillespie@thehall.org

Situated on the banks of the Delaware River, St. Mary's Hall/Doane Academy is a coeducational, college preparatory day school. It enrolls 196 students of diverse religious and socioeconomic backgrounds in Pre-Kindergarten–Grade 12. The school's rigorous academic program is complemented by athletics and extracurricular activities that include art, music, drama, literary publications, and computers. The low student-faculty ratio and a strong sense of community encourage students to develop their full potential as individuals and as members of society. Tuition: $8730–$11,505. Financial Aid: $100,000. Susan Gillespie is Dean of Admission; John F. McGee (University of Notre Dame, B.A. 1967, M.A. 1970) was appointed Headmaster in 2000. *Middle States Association.*

Stuart Country Day School of the Sacred Heart 1963

1200 Stuart Road, Princeton, NJ 08540
Tel. 609-921-2330; Admission Ext. 235; Fax 609-497-2784
Web Site www.stuartschool.org; E-mail admissions@stuartschool.org

Stuart Country Day School of the Sacred Heart, which opened its doors in 1963, is an independent day school enrolling 505 students, with girls in Kindergarten through Grade 12 and boys and girls in the Pre-School and Junior Kindergarten. Stuart offers an education marked by a distinctive spirit that is founded in the goals and criteria of the Society of the Sacred Heart. While Stuart's academic rigor is emphasized, values are also placed on physical, social, and moral growth. Students are educated by a dedicated faculty in an atmosphere of love and trust with the goal to empower young women to make a difference in their world. In 2006–07, 145 students took a total of 512 Advanced Placement exams in 26 subjects and earned college credit by scoring a 3 or higher on 88 percent of them; they scored a 4 or 5 on 65 percent of the exams. Tuition: $13,800–$25,650. Average Financial Aid Award: $16,838. Stephanie Lupero is Director of Admission; Frances de la Chapelle, RSCJ, is Headmistress. *Middle States Association.*

The Wardlaw-Hartridge School 1882

1295 Inman Avenue, Edison, NJ 08820
Tel. 908-754-1882; Admission Ext. 110; Fax 908-754-9678
Web Site www.whschool.org; E-mail cdavis@whschool.org

Formed by the merger of two schools founded more than a century ago, The Wardlaw-Hartridge School is a coeducational, college preparatory day school enrolling 420 students in Pre-Kindergarten 3–Grade 12. It aims to provide a diverse humanistic environment in which students can achieve intellectual growth and moral development. Small classes, academically challenging Advanced Placement and honors courses, varied extracurricular activities, and a vigorous athletic program help each individual develop according to his or her potential.

Tuition: $13,280–$24,300. Charlotte Davis is Director of Admission and Financial Aid; Andrew Webster (Brown University, B.A.; University of Virginia, M.A.) is Head of School. *Middle States Association.*

The Willow School 2000

1150 Pottersville Road, Gladstone, NJ 07934
Tel. 908-470-9500; Admissions Ext. 1015; Fax 908-470-9545
Web Site www.willowschool.org
E-mail aworthington@willowschool.org

The Willow School is an independent, coeducational day school for Kindergarten through Grade 8, located on 34 wooded acres in Gladstone, New Jersey. The School is built on the belief that children thrive in a setting that embraces the joy of learning and the wonder of the natural environment. The curriculum maintains a deliberate balance of rigorous academics and creative projects and emphasizes the School's unique commitment to environmental sustainability. This program, in the hands of talented teachers, fans the flame of each child's natural curiosity and desire to learn. Small classes create an atmosphere of trust and allow teachers to focus on children's individual strengths and needs. Through The Willow School's virtues program, children become knowledgeable and wise, curious and creative, responsible and confident. Tuition: $18,136–$19,950. Annette Worthington is Director of Admissions; Kate Burke Walsh (American University, B.A.; Antioch University, M.A.) is Head of School.

The Wilson School 1909

271 Boulevard, Mountain Lakes, NJ 07046
Tel. 973-334-0181; Fax 973-334-1852
Web Site www.the-wilson-school.org

Wilson serves 70 boys and girls as day students in Pre-Kindergarten–Grade 8. Its mission is to create a nurturing environment in which children become independent, thoughtful, and confident learners. The curriculum emphasizes strong skills in key concepts. In the lower grades, subjects are presented thematically, while older students learn through interdisciplinary units that emphasize the relationships among the liberal arts, sciences, and humanities. French begins in Pre-Kindergarten, and computer technology is integrated throughout all disciplines. Activities include drama, music, community service, field trips, weekly swim lessons, and a variety of sports. An after-school program is optional. Tuition: $14,500–$17,500. Carolyn Borlo is Head of School. *Middle States Association.*

The Winston School 1981

100 East Lane, Short Hills, NJ 07078
Tel. 973-379-4114; Fax 973-379-3984
Web Site winstonschool.org; E-mail pbloom@winstonschool.org

The Winston School was established to meet the needs of intellectually capable boys and girls who were encountering problems in school due to language-based learning disabilities. Enrolling 62 day students ages 7–14, the School seeks to provide students with the strategies needed to achieve academic success. Each student's program is designed based on his/her academic profile. Classes, taught by certified specialists, are limited in size to ensure personalized attention and support. The program includes art, music, physical education, computers, and speech-language and occupational therapy. Tuition: $26,000–$33,500. Financial aid is available. Paula Lordy is Admissions Assistant; Pamela R. Bloom (George Washington, B.A.; Harvard, Ed.M.) was appointed Head of School in 1992. *Middle States Association.*

NEW MEXICO

Albuquerque Academy 1955

6400 Wyoming Boulevard, NE, Albuquerque, NM 87109
Tel. 505-828-3200; Admission 505-828-3208; Fax 505-828-3128
Web Site www.aa.edu; E-mail hudenko@aa.edu

Albuquerque Academy is a coeducational, college preparatory day school enrolling 1080 students in Grades 6–12. Emphasizing mastery of fundamentals and independent judgment, the Academy seeks the full academic, creative, moral, and physical development of each student. It offers a challenging curriculum with more than 20 Advanced Placement courses, requires participation in a wilderness experience, and provides exchange programs with schools in this country and abroad. Student Senate, debate, sports, clubs, and publications are some of the activities. A six-week summer school and day camp are available. Tuition: $15,510. Financial Aid: $3,364,000. Judy Hudenko is Director of Admission; Andrew T. Watson is Head of School.

Manzano Day School 1938

1801 Central Avenue, NW, Albuquerque, NM 87104-1197
Tel. 505-243-6659; Admission Ext. 401; Fax 505-243-4711
Web Site www.manzanodayschool.org
E-mail mprokopiak@manzanodayschool.org

Manzano Day School is an independent, nonsectarian elementary school enrolling students in Pre-Kindergarten through Grade 5. The School offers a strong core curriculum as well as six cocurricular areas of Spanish, art, music, physical education, technology, and library skills. Manzano is a member of the National Association of Independent Schools, a Blue Ribbon School, and a member of Exemplary Schools Attuned Network. It is one of only a few schools nationwide that offers a separate campus for environmental studies at the elementary level. Founded in 1938 in historic Old Town Albuquerque, Manzano remains true to its mission—*Joy in Learning*®. The student-teacher ratio is 10:1. An extended day program and summer school are offered. Tuition: $8990–$11,480. Madonna Prokopiak is Director of Admission; Neal Piltch is Head of School.

Rio Grande School 1978

715 Camino Cabra, Santa Fe, NM 87505
Tel. 505-983-1621; Admission Ext. 2002; Fax 505-986-0012
Web Site www.riograndeschool.org; E-mail info@riograndeschool.org

Rio Grande is an independent coeducational day school enrolling approximately 160 students in Pre-Kindergarten–Grade 6. The School offers an integrated curriculum that includes traditional academics, fine and performing arts, and outdoor activities. Small classes and personalized attention for each student are features of the program. Class activities are enlivened by field trips to study local cultures, overnight stays, and service learning projects. An extended-day program is available as well as a summer program. Tuition: $9950–$14,787. Extras: $300. Tuition assistance is available. Daniela Deluca is Director of Admission; Jay Underwood is Head of School.

Sandia Preparatory School 1966

532 Osuna Road, NE, Albuquerque, NM 87113
Tel. 505-338-3000; Fax 505-338-3099
Web Site www.sandiaprep.org; E-mail info@sandiaprep.org

Founded by Mrs. Albert G. Simms II, Sandia Prep is a college preparatory day school enrolling 670 students in Grades 6–12. The joy of learning and living is at the center of its college preparatory curriculum. Sandia Prep provides a well-balanced program based on the 5 A's: academics, arts, athletics, activities, and atmosphere. Sandia Prep has been recognized nationally for its rigorous academic program and has received awards for its advisory, community service, drama, and no-cut sports programs. Tuition: $14,000. Financial Aid: $754,100. Ester Tomelloso is Director of Admission; Richard L. Heath (Cornell, A.B. 1969; Colgate, M.A.T. 1972) was appointed Headmaster in 1986.

NEW YORK

Academy of Mount St. Ursula 1855

330 Bedford Park Boulevard, Bronx, NY 10458
Tel. 718-364-5353; Admission 718-364-2486; Fax 718-364-2354
Web Site www.amsu.org; E-mail bcalamari@amsu.org

Founded by the Ursuline nuns in 1855, Academy of Mount St. Ursula is a Roman Catholic, college preparatory day school enrolling 400 girls in Grades 9–12. This Blue Ribbon School aims to meet the needs of today's students in a context of unchanging spiritual and moral values. State-of-the-art science labs were constructed in 2002–03. Advanced Placement courses are given in five subjects. A wide range of activities includes championship sports teams. Tuition: $5775. Extras: $475 fee. Sr. Barbara Calamari is Admissions Director; Sr. Mary Beth Read (Catholic University of America, B.A.; Fordham University, M.S.) was appointed Principal in 1992; Jane Martinez Dowling (Georgetown University, A.B.) is President. *Middle States Association.*

Allendale Columbia School 1971

519 Allens Creek Road, Rochester, NY 14618-3497
Tel. 585-381-4560; Fax 585-249-0230
Web Site www.allendalecolumbia.org
E-mail acarroll@allendalecolumbia.org

Allendale Columbia, a coeducational day school, enrolls 450 students in a challenging college preparatory day program spanning Nursery to Grade 12. The academic program is designed to enable students to fulfill their intellectual potential and to develop as well-rounded citizens. Set on a 30-acre campus, the School offers a curriculum that includes Advanced Placement courses in 16 disciplines, extensive offerings in the arts, computer technology, and foreign languages. Students take part in school leadership groups, community service, drama, vocal and instrumental ensembles, interest clubs, and competitive sports. Tuition: $6000–$17,175. Alan Carroll is Director of Admission; Charles F. Hertrick is Head of School. *Middle States Association.*

The Allen-Stevenson School 1883

132 East 78th Street, New York, NY 10075
Tel. 212-288-6710; Fax 212-288-6802
Web Site www.allen-stevenson.org

Founded in 1883 to teach young men "intelligent habits of study and to develop straightforward, manly characters," Allen-Stevenson enrolls 407 day boys in Kindergarten–Grade 9. The traditional curriculum prepares students for entrance to challenging secondary schools. Courses include French, Spanish, language fundamentals, computers, shop, music, and art. Extracurricular activities include orchestra, Student Council, publications, and arts and drama groups. Facilities include a gymnasium, shop, art, and multipurpose room. Tuition: $31,450. Financial Aid: $1,200,000. Ronnie R. Jankoff is Director of Admissions; David R. Trower (Brown University, B.A. 1968; Union Theological Seminary, M.Div. 1973) was appointed Headmaster in 1990.

Bank Street School for Children 1915

610 West 112th Street, New York, NY 10025
Tel. 212-875-4420; Admissions 212-875-4433; Fax 212-875-4733
Web Site www.bankstreet.edu/sfc
E-mail schoolforchildrenadmissions@bankstreet.edu

Bank Street School for Children, enrolling 435 day boys and girls ages 3–13, is the demonstration school for the Bank Street College of Education. The School sees social, emotional, and intellectual growth as equally important and inseparable. Reading and writing skills are developed in the core social studies and language arts program. Science and mathematics are presented as methods of inquiry with skill acquisition related to concepts. Curricular activities include social studies trips, creative arts, music, and physical education. After-school and summer recreational programs are available. Tuition: $25,700–$28,450. Financial Aid: $1,600,000. Marcia Roesch is Director of Admissions; Reuel Jordan (University of Dayton, B.A.; Bank Street College of Education, M.S.) is Dean.

The Berkeley Carroll School 1982

181 Lincoln Place, Brooklyn, NY 11217
Tel. 718-789-6060; Admissions Ext. 6527; Fax 718-398-3640
Web Site www.berkeleycarroll.org; E-mail bcs@berkeleycarroll.org

Now celebrating its 121st anniversary, Berkeley Carroll enrolls highly motivated boys and girls from diverse backgrounds as day students in Pre-Kindergarten–Grade 12. The School was formed by the 1982 merger of The Berkeley Institute (1886) and The Carroll Street School (1966). There are currently 870 students in the School's Child Care Center and the Lower, Middle, and Upper divisions. The college preparatory program is designed to develop young adults capable of thinking critically and making informed decisions. Computer technology and a library media center provide state-of-the-art learning resources for all grade levels. Student leadership groups, academic honor societies, numerous interest clubs, community service, and interscholastic sports are among the activities. Summer programs emphasize athletics and the creative arts. Tuition: $12,500–$26,920. Financial aid is available. Colm MacMahon is Director of Admissions; Robert D. Vitalo (New York University, B.S.; Columbia Teachers College, M.S.) was appointed Head of School in 2006.

The Birch Wathen Lenox School 1916

210 East 77th Street, New York, NY 10075
Tel. 212-861-0404; Fax 212-879-3388
Web Site www.bwl.org; E-mail admissions@bwl.org

THE BIRCH WATHEN LENOX SCHOOL in New York, New York, is a college preparatory day school for students in Kindergarten through Grade 12. The School was founded in 1991 by the consolidation of The Birch Wathen School (founded 1921) and The Lenox School (founded 1916).

The School seeks to provide a challenging academic curriculum with a balance among traditional education, student achievement, and social development. Birch Wathen Lenox implements its curricular commitments with small classes, a student-faculty ratio of 6:1, and an emphasis on individual attention to students.

The Birch Wathen Lenox School is a nonprofit corporation directed by a self-perpetuating Board of Trustees, which includes alumni and parents. An active Alumni Association represents more than 3600 graduates. The School's program is accredited by the State University of New York and the Middle States Association of Colleges and Schools, and it is registered by the New York State Board of Regents. Birch Wathen Lenox is a member of the New York Guild of Independent Schools, the New York State Association of Independent Schools, the National Association of Independent Schools, the Association of College Admissions Counselors, The College Board, and the Educational Records Bureau.

THE CAMPUS. The entire School—Lower (Kindergarten–Grade 5), Middle (Grades 6–8), and Upper (Grades 9–12)—is housed in a traditional, spacious building on Manhattan's Upper East Side. Facilities include a gymnasium, library, computer center, science laboratories, auditorium, music and art studios, cafeteria/commons area, and a rooftop play area. A $19,000,000 renovation of the School's facility was completed in 2006.

THE FACULTY. Frank J. Carnabuci III, formerly Assistant Headmaster of The Dalton School, was appointed Headmaster in 1992. He holds a B.A. degree from Drew University and master's degrees in education from Columbia and Harvard.

There are 30 men and 85 women on the faculty. All faculty members hold baccalaureate degrees; 95 percent hold master's degrees or higher. The staff includes instructors of music and art, reading specialists, science and mathematics coordinators, a full-time nurse, a librarian, two computer specialists, a college guidance counselor, and two school psychologists.

STUDENT BODY. The Birch Wathen Lenox School enrolls 500 boys and girls, 5 to 18 years of age, from Kindergarten through Grade 12. The diverse student population is drawn from all parts of New York City.

ACADEMIC PROGRAM. The school year, from mid-September to mid-June, includes Thanksgiving recess, four religious and patriotic holidays, and two-and-one-half-week vacations at Christmas and in the spring. Classes meet on a five-day schedule. School begins at 8:15 A.M., with dismissal at 3:00 P.M. A typical school day includes five class periods, activity and athletics periods, lunch, and time for independent study and teacher conferences. Homework, assigned in all grades, ranges up to one hour per day in the Lower School and 20 to 30 minutes per subject per day in the Middle and Upper schools. There is standardized testing throughout the year in all three divisions.

The curriculum provides a program in English, composition, mathematics, science, and history. Foreign languages begin in Grade 4. Computer science, word processing, art, drama, speech, instrumental and vocal music, and woodworking are taught from Kindergarten through Grade 12. Advanced Placement course work is offered in all major curricular areas to eligible Upper School students.

A full, extended-day after-school program is available for Lower School students. There is a comprehensive physical education program. The full interschool athletic sports program includes soccer, softball, volleyball, tennis, basketball, swimming, modern dance, ice hockey, golf, and lacrosse.

Birch Wathen Lenox graduates have enrolled at such colleges and universities as Brown, Colgate, Columbia, Cornell, Duke, Harvard, Northwestern, Princeton, Tufts, Yale, and the University of Pennsylvania.

STUDENT ACTIVITIES. The Student Forum, headed by an elected speaker, meets periodically and plans assembly programs. The Student Council, composed of a president and class representatives, brings questions to the attention of the Forum and has responsibility for the annual Student Activity Budget. There is also a Student-Faculty Judiciary Committee.

The traditional academic curriculum is complemented by extensive cocurricular activities such as the School newspaper, the literary journal, and the yearbook; the Community Services Program and the Model U.N.; chorus; and Business, Foreign Language, Overseas Study Program, Photography, and Drama clubs.

ADMISSION AND COSTS. Birch Wathen Lenox has a policy of accepting students "without regard to race, creed, or nationality of applicants." Students are accepted in Kindergarten–Grade 12 on the basis of entrance examination results, previous school records, teacher recommendations, and an interview. Applicants may take either the Educational Records Bureau tests or the Secondary School Admission Test. Application should be made 9 to 12 months in advance of entrance. Applications should be received no later than November 30. The application fee is $50.

In 2007–08, tuition is $26,672 in Kindergarten, $28,462 in Grades 1–4, $28,930 in Grade 5, $29,148 in Grades 6–7, $29,309 in Grades 8–9, and $29,576 in Grades 10–12. Lunch and additional fees are approximately $1800. A tuition payment plan is available. The Harrison W. Moore Merit Scholarship Award is presented annually in the Upper School, and scholarship aid is available at all grade levels based on need, ability, and character.

Director of Admissions: Julianne Kaplan
Assistant Director of Admissions: Kyle Rattigan
Director of Development: Janine Hopley
College Counselor: Brad Battaglia
Business Manager: Ann Glickman
Director of Athletics: Todd DiVittorio

The Brearley School 1884

610 East 83rd Street, New York, NY 10028
Tel. 212-744-8582; Admission 212-570-8600; Fax 212-472-8020
Web Site www.brearley.org; E-mail sborbay@brearley.org

Founded in 1884, The Brearley School challenges girls of adventurous intellect to think critically and creatively and prepares them for active, responsible citizenship in a democratic society. A Brearley education is designed to provide every student with the competence and confidence to succeed in whatever pursuit she may choose, while promoting growth in kindness and conscience. Brearley's broad liberal arts curriculum combines tradition and innovation, giving students the foundational knowledge and versatility to excel in college and to become leaders and agents of progress in an increasingly borderless world. A college preparatory day school, Brearley enrolls 685 girls in Kindergarten through Grade 12. Tuition & Fees: $29,175–$29,700. Financial Aid: $3,448,000. Joan Kaplan and Winifred Mabley are Directors of Admission and Financial Aid; Dr. Stephanie J. Hull (Wellesley College, B.A.; Harvard University, A.M., Ph.D.) was appointed Head of the School in 2003.

The Brick Church School 1940

62 East 92nd Street, New York, NY 10128
Tel. 212-289-5683; Fax 212-289-5372
Web Site www.brickchurch.org/dayschool
E-mail lspinelli@brickchurch.org

Founded by and affiliated with The Brick Presbyterian Church, this coeducational day school offers a developmentally appropriate early childhood program for 160 children in Nursery/Kindergarten (ages 3–6). In an environment marked by warmth and mutual respect, students are introduced to literacy, mathematics, science, social studies, cooking, dramatic play, art, and music. Teachers, all of whom are certified in Early Childhood Education, use various activities and materials designed to inspire self-confidence, curiosity, and joy in learning and play. A weekly nondenominational chapel service involves the entire School. Tuition: $13,500–$17,300. Holly Burke and Kathy Flintoft are Admissions Directors; Lydia Spinelli (Tufts, B.A.; Teachers College, Columbia University, M.A., M.Ed., Ed.D.) is Director.

Brooklyn Friends School 1867

375 Pearl Street, Brooklyn, NY 11201
Tel. 718-852-1029; Fax 718-643-4868
Web Site www.brooklynfriends.org
E-mail jknies@brooklynfriends.org

Serving 630 boys and girls in Preschool through Grade 12, Brooklyn Friends School offers a challenging educational experience to meet the academic, social, and physical well-being of its students. The Upper School offers the International Baccalaureate Diploma program for juniors and seniors. The liberal arts curriculum aims to nurture young people at every stage of development while instilling independence and a love of learning. Quaker ideals guide school life, and global awareness and community service enrich the program. Students develop creative expression through offerings in dance, music, art, and drama. School government, Model UN, clubs, and interscholastic and intramural sports are among the extracurricular activities. Tuition: $13,000–$27,400. Financial aid is available. Jennifer Knies is Director of Admissions; Dr. Michael Nill is Head of School.

Brooklyn Heights Montessori School 1965

185 Court Street, Brooklyn, NY 11201
Tel. 718-858-5100; Admissions Ext. 20; Fax 718-858-0500
Web Site www.bhmsny.org; E-mail info@bhmsny.org

Brooklyn Heights Montessori School seeks to develop and educate the whole child, nurturing the social, physical, emotional, and intellectual well-being of each student in an environment marked by mutual trust and respect. Set in historic Cobble Hill, Brooklyn Heights Montessori School welcomes 257 boys and girls from varied backgrounds in Preschool (age 2) through Middle School (Grades 7–8). Children work independently or in small groups, using age-appropriate materials to understand key concepts in core subjects of reading and language arts, math, science, social studies, computer technology, and the arts. Students learn according to their own pace and style as they progress through the grades. Beginning in Grade 7, students develop portfolios and have special instruction to prepare them for success in high school. Community service and outreach is practiced at all levels in and beyond the school, while field trips in New York City and to Cape May, Long Island, Boston, and Washington, D.C., enhance classroom lessons. Soccer and basketball teams are open to students from Grade 6. Tution: $6500–$25,000. Need-based tuition assistance is available. Elise Mattia is Director of External Relations; Dane L. Peters is Head of School.

The Browning School 1888

52 East 62nd Street, New York, NY 10021
Tel. 212-838-6280; Fax 212-355-5602
Web Site www.browning.edu; E-mail jcasey@browning.edu

The Browning School is a college preparatory day school enrolling 389 boys in Pre-Primary–Grade 12. It seeks to provide an education that emphasizes self-discipline, student participation, and the achievement of academic excellence. The curriculum focuses on basic skills with an enrichment program in Language Arts and Computer Science. Foreign languages are introduced in Grade 5. Advanced Placement courses and diverse electives are offered in the Upper School. Drama, clubs, publications, and sports are among the activities. Tuition: $29,100. Financial aid is available. Jacqueline A. Casey is Director of Admissions; Stephen M. Clement III (Yale, B.A. 1966; Union Theological Seminary, M.Div. 1970; Harvard, M.Ed. 1975, Ed.D. 1977) is Headmaster.

Buckley Country Day School 1923

I. U. Willets Road, North Hills, Roslyn, NY 11576
Tel. 516-627-1910; Admissions Ext. 117; Fax 516-627-8627
Web Site www.buckleycountryday.com
E-mail aduffy@buckleycountryday.com

Buckley Country Day School is an independent, coeducational day school enrolling 335 children in Toddler–Grade 8. The School provides a superior elementary education to an intellectually capable and diverse student body. Emphasis is placed on core skills in reading, writing, and mathematics, using a broad repertoire of teaching techniques and technologies. Buckley believes in fostering integrity, hard work, kindness, personal and social responsibility, and mutual respect. The School's educational philosophy is centered on intellectual, physical, and artistic development. French and Spanish begin in Pre-Kindergarten, Latin in Grade 7. Tuition: $10,000–$21,000. Financial Aid: $561,250. Ann V. Duffy is Director of Admissions; Dr. Jean-Marc Juhel (University of Paris, B.A. 1983, M.A. 1988; Columbia University, M.A. 1997; Michel de Montaigne University, Ph.D. 1995) was appointed Headmaster in 2002.

The Buckley School 1913

113 East 73rd Street, New York, NY 10021
Tel. 212-535-8787; Fax 212-472-0583
Web Site www.buckleyschool.org
E-mail jlynch@buckleyschool.org

The Buckley School is a day school that enrolls 370 boys in Kindergarten through Grade 9. The goals of a Buckley education are that every boy learn fundamental skills, gain self-confidence through disciplined thought and action, develop personal integrity and respect for others, and discover the joy of learning and the satisfaction of pursuing excellence. The traditional curriculum—math, English, science, history, and foreign languages including Latin—is supplemented by field trips to museums, special exhibitions, and events in Manhattan. Sports are mandatory as are class plays, arts, and music, all of which contribute to a well-rounded education. Tuition: $30,500. Financial Aid: $800,000. Jo Ann Lynch is Admissions Director; Gregory J. O'Melia (Harvard, A.B., Ed.M.) is Headmaster.

Buffalo Seminary 1851

205 Bidwell Parkway, Buffalo, NY 14222-9904
Tel. 716-885-6780; Fax 716-885-6785
Web Site www.buffaloseminary.org
E-mail admissions@buffaloseminary.org

Buffalo Seminary is a college preparatory day school enrolling 175 girls in Grades 9–12. While the school has no religious affiliation, values are emphasized through the school's Honor Code. Buffalo Seminary aims to develop scholarship, leadership, sportsmanship, and a commitment to service through a rigorous academic curriculum, studio and performing arts programs, and activities including athletics, honor societies, self-government, music, and drama. Advanced Placement and honors courses are available by invitation. Tuition: $13,950. Financial aid is available. Carrie Auwarter is Director of Admissions; Jody Douglass (Bates College, B.A.; Middlebury College, M.A.) was appointed Head of School in 2007. *Middle States Association.*

The Caedmon School 1961

416 East 80th Street, New York, NY 10075
Tel. 212-879-2296; Admissions Ext. 306; Fax 212-879-0627
Web Site www.caedmonschool.org
E-mail admissions@caedmonschool.org

The Caedmon School, offering a program based on Montessori principles, enrolls 220 day boys and girls in Nursery–Grade 5. The school program provides high standards of academic excellence and personal attention to all students. In addition to language arts, math, science, and social studies, the curriculum includes courses in computer science, art, music, physical education, library, yoga, and Spanish. Extracurricular activities are offered in an extended-day program. Tuition: $11,856–$23,720. Financial Aid: $485,000. Erica L. Papir is Director of Admissions; Dr. Greg Blackburn (Hendrix College, B.A.; University of Arkansas, M.S.; University of Mississippi, Ph.D.) is Head of School.

The Cathedral School 1949

319 East 74th Street, New York, NY 10021
Tel. 212-249-2840; Fax 212-249-2847
Web Site www.cathedralschoolny.org

Located on Manhattan's Upper East Side, The Cathedral School provides a warm, nurturing, and family atmosphere to 120 day students in Nursery–Grade 8. With a 10:1 student-teacher ratio, an international student body, and placement of graduates in the city's best high schools, The Cathedral School continues its legacy of educating children in the tradition of The Classics. The curriculum emphasizes Ancient Greek in Grades 7–8, mythology in Kindergarten–Grade 4, and drama in Grades 4–8. In addition to the standard core classes of math, English, history, social studies, and science, The Cathedral School offers French, computer science, physical education, art, and music. Extracurricular activities include sports, music, foreign language, and drama. Tuition: $9000–$11,000. Athena Efter is Admissions Director; Sonia Celestin is Head of School.

The Cathedral School of St. John the Divine 1901

1047 Amsterdam Avenue, New York, NY 10025-1702
Tel. 212-316-7500; Admission 212-316-7510; Fax 212-316-7558
Web Site www.cathedralnyc.org; E-mail admission@cathedralnyc.org

The Cathedral School, an Episcopal day school, welcomes 266 boys and girls of all faiths in Kindergarten–Grade 8. It seeks to develop confident, open-minded students who accept responsibility as active citizens of their diverse community and the world. The School's setting, complete with outdoor playgrounds, gardens, and free-roaming peacocks, provides an oasis in Manhattan. The rigorous academic program offers a strong foundation of knowledge and skills, combining traditional and innovative teaching methods. Individualized attention and student engagement are ensured by a small class size of about 16 students. The award-winning foreign language program includes Latin studies for all seventh and eighth graders. Students participate in community service, sports, and school government and have the opportunity to sing in the choir of The Cathedral of St. John the Divine. Tuition: $27,000–$27,700 (including fees). Approximately 35 percent of students receive financial aid, the level of each grant determined according to need. Linda D. Mathews is Director of Admission; Marsha K. Nelson is Head of School.

The Chapin School 1901

100 East End Avenue, New York, NY 10028
Tel. 212-744-2335; Fax 212-535-8138
Web Site www.chapin.edu

Chapin, a college preparatory day school enrolling 660 girls in Kindergarten–Grade 12, is dedicated to preparing young women to thrive and lead in an increasingly complex, competitive world through the pursuit of academic excellence, personal integrity, and community responsibility. Personal growth and community involvement are fostered through the homeroom program. The rigorous curriculum is enhanced by a commitment to the arts and athletics. Course offerings may be enriched by independent study and off-campus programs. Numerous activities are offered in the Middle and Upper Schools. Tuition: $29,100. Financial Aid: $2,903,000. Tina I. Herman is Director of Admissions; Dr. Patricia Hayot was appointed Head of School in 2003.

The Churchill School and Center 1972

301 East 29th Street, New York, NY 10016
Tel. 212-722-0610; Fax 212-722-1387
Web Site www.churchillschool.com
E-mail wfederico@churchillschool.com

THE CHURCHILL SCHOOL in New York City is a coeducational K–12 day school enrolling students of average to above-average cognitive ability whose progress in a mainstream classroom is compromised by a learning disability.

In 1972, Harry S. Valentine III founded Churchill for elementary-age children with learning disabilities. In 1986, the program expanded to include students up to age 14. Relocation in 2001 to the present site permitted the addition of a high school.

The Churchill Center was established in 1981 to build upon and disseminate the expertise of The Churchill School. The Center's educational programs and professional development in the field of learning disabilities assist students, parents, teachers, and related service providers. Ongoing programs include courses in literacy instructions and multisensory techniques for teaching reading and writing. The Center School Advisory Service is an information, resource, and referral service for parents and professionals in choosing appropriate school and/or summer programs for students. The Referral Service recommends qualified tutors and other professionals with expertise in working with students who have diverse learning styles. Additionally, the Center's Reading Initiative provides a free, 27-week after-school program of multisensory reading instruction to children in Grades 1–3 in New York City who need to improve reading skills. The Center's 10-week Enhancing Social Skills Development program helps children ages 5–14 interact effectively with peers and handle social situations.

In educating students, the School seeks to identify and use their strengths, stimulate intellectual curiosity, and expand knowledge. Their progress may have been hindered in traditional classrooms by a language or reading disability, attention problems, or perceptual and/or motor weaknesses. Churchill addresses the academic, cognitive, social, and emotional needs of its students so that they may reach their full potential. Blending instruction and application in all areas, the flexible interdisciplinary program offers structured, multisensory experiences, learning-style strategies, a low student-teacher ratio, and numerous opportunities in which to succeed. Students are encouraged to manage their learning disabilities, becoming advocates for themselves as they prepare for the future.

A member of the New York State Association of Independent Schools and the National Association of Independent Schools, Churchill is chartered by the Board of Regents of the State of New York. In 2004, the Board of Regents also granted The Churchill High School full registration status. Churchill has been designated as an "approved non-public school" by the New York State Commissioner of Education since 1972. A 25-member Board of Trustees governs the School, and the Parents Association publishes a newsletter and sponsors informational, social, and fund-raising activities for the Churchill community.

THE CAMPUS. The School's site on East 29th Street features a seven-story, 72,000-square-foot building containing 36 classrooms, a multimedia library, an auditorium with stage and music room, a soundproof band room and recording studio, four science labs, two state-of-the-art computer labs with school-wide Intranet and Internet access, a television/video production studio, a radio station, and three art studios. Recreational facilities include a rooftop playground and a regulation-size gymnasium with bleachers, and a fitness center. Students eat lunch in a spacious cafeteria; a garden and greenhouse are used by the Churchill community and for environmental programs.

THE FACULTY. Kristine Baxter began her career at Churchill in 1973. She was appointed Head of the School and Center in 1988. Previously, she was an Elementary School teacher, Principal of the Middle School, Director of Admissions, and Director of Graduate Placement and School Advisory Service. She holds a B.A. from Tufts, an M.A. from Teachers College of Columbia University, and a Supervision and Administration License from Bank Street College of Education.

All head teachers are state-certified and hold a master's degree in Special Education. High School faculty members are certified in their content area. Specialists include speech and language personnel, occupational therapists, psychologists, social workers, and a registered nurse. Among their representative institutions are Bank Street College of Education, Teachers College at Columbia University, Fordham, Hunter College, and New York University.

STUDENT BODY. The Churchill School enrolls 396 boys and girls from Kindergarten age (5½) through Grade 12. The ratio of boys to girls is 60:40. Representing a diverse range of racial, ethnic, religious, and socioeconomic backgrounds, students come from New York City's five boroughs as well as Westchester County, Long Island, and New Jersey.

ACADEMIC PROGRAM. The 180-day school year begins in early September and ends in mid-June, with breaks at Thanksgiving, winter holiday, midwinter, and spring.

The school day runs from 8:15 A.M. to 2:45 P.M. Classes, which enroll up to 12 students, are formed on the basis of both performance level and learning style. Homework is an essential complement to the curriculum, providing opportunity for review and reinforcement of skills taught in the classroom. Middle and High School students may attend a faculty-monitored study hall from 3:00 to 5:00 P.M.

The Elementary School is an ungraded program for children age 5½ through the equivalent of Grade 5. Each class is led by a head teacher and an assistant teacher. Age, gender, cognitive and language abilities, management needs, reading and math levels, and social factors are all considered in making up a class. Reading and math skills are taught in smaller groups, while social studies and science are taught in a whole-class setting. The process-based writing curriculum is designed specifically for children with language-based learning disabilities. Art, music, health, library, computer, and physical education are integral parts of the program. Some students receive speech and language services and/or occupational therapy in small groups one to three times weekly, using a pull-out model. Three parent conference days are scheduled during the year, and in-depth reports by teachers are written in January and June.

The Middle School comprises Grades 6–8. Subject departmentalization begins at this level, and students learn the necessary organization and study skills. Direct teaching in language arts and math skills continues. Science and social studies curricula are project-based. Expository writing is emphasized, and research skills are taught. Once a week, through the pull-out model, some students in Grades 6 and 7 receive speech and language therapy in groups averaging six students. Students in Grade 8 receive this therapy through the collaboration model in the classroom once weekly. All Middle School students take part in Counseling/Health groups related to issues of adolescence, health, and learning disabilities. Quarterly reports to parents from all teachers and related service providers include formal grades.

The High School offers a four-year college/career preparatory program in Grades 9–12. Students may obtain a Regents, a Local, or an Individual Education Plan diploma and receive both college and career counseling. The core curriculum requires four credits, or years, of both English and history, three each of science and math, two of physical education, and one each in art and health. The language-based English curriculum emphasizes mastery of basic skills in reading, writing, listening, and speaking. Courses include surveys of American and English Literature. Other specific academic courses are Global History and Geography, U.S. History and Government; Biology, Earth Science, Chemistry, Environmental Science; Competency Math, Pre-algebra, Math A/B, Applications for Business and Science; Computer Technology, Graphics, Programming; Comparative Politics, Media Ethics, Native American Culture; and Photography, Music, Theater, and Electronics. Speech and language services continue for some students via the classroom collaboration model once weekly. Some short-term pull-out sessions are provided for those students who could benefit from more specific strategies and skills. Health and Human Relations classes meet once a week with a psychologist or social worker. Conferences with teachers, parents, and students are held three times a year.

A primary goal of the School is to prepare students to continue their education at appropriate mainstream schools. In the past several years, students have transferred to Birch Wathen Lenox, Brooklyn Friends, Dwight, The Ethical Culture Fieldston School, Forman, Friends Seminary, Hewitt, Kildonan, Pennington, PolyPrep, The School at Columbia University, Trinity-Pawling, and York Preparatory.

Churchill graduates have enrolled in such postsecondary schools as Adelphi, American, Clark, College of the Holy Cross, Concordia, Curry, Fordham, Guilford, Indiana University, Ithaca, Johnson and Wales, Lynn, Manhattanville, Mitchell, Marist, Savannah College of Art and Design, School of Visual Arts, State University of New York (Plattsburgh, Purchase), Suffolk, Trinity, and the Universities of New Hampshire, New Haven, and North Carolina (Greensboro).

STUDENT ACTIVITIES. On Friday afternoons, elementary-age children engage in activities such as newspaper, science, puppetry, cooking, sewing, and model building. Middle School students may participate in sketching and drawing, cooking, jewelry making, guitar, board games, and newspaper. High School students may express their interests in web design, radio broadcasting, digital art and photography, and portfolio creation. Middle and High School sports teams in cross-country, track, soccer, softball, baseball, basketball, and volleyball compete with other area independent schools. Required community service begins in the Middle School.

ADMISSION AND COSTS. Churchill accepts students with average to above-average intelligence who have specific learning disabilities and who could benefit from a small, individualized, and supportive learning environment. Along with a $50 fee, candidates must submit a completed application, a developmental history, educational and psychological testing, speech and language evaluation, and teacher questionnaires. High School applicants must also write a personal essay and submit school transcripts.

In 2007–08, tuition is $34,000. Under provisions of Section 4402 of the State Education Law, the tuition of some students classified as "learning disabled" or "speech/language impaired" may be reimbursed by New York State.

Director of Admissions: Wendy Federico
Director of the Churchill Center: Dr. Jane Gertler
Director of Development: L. J. Mitchell
Business Manager: Robert Roldan
Elementary School Principal: Meryl Schwartz
Middle School Principal: Susan Jackson
High School Principal: Glenn Corwin
Director of Technology Education: Ann Nitzburg
Athletic Director: Laura Henrich

City & Country School 1914

146 West 13th Street, New York, NY 10011
Tel. 212-242-7802; Admissions Ext. 217; Fax 212-242-7996
Web Site www.cityandcountry.org; E-mail lisah@cityandcountry.org

City & Country School, a coeducational, progressive day school enrolling 310 students ages 2 to 13, was founded in 1914 by Caroline Pratt. Believing that education is fundamentally a social process, City & Country strives to create a vital school environment that supports each child's innate passion for learning while also expanding his or her understanding of communities and cultures that exist beyond home and school. Social Studies, the core curriculum, is enriched by science, mathematics, literature, and the arts. Extended day, after-school classes, and a summer program are available. Tuition: $14,100–$26,200. Financial Aid: $600,000. Lisa Horner is Director of Admissions; Kate Turley is Principal.

Claremont Preparatory School 2005

41 Broad Street, New York, NY 10004-2513
Tel. 212-232-0266; Fax 212-232-0284
Web Site www.claremontprep.org
E-mail dhaddad@claremontprep.org

Claremont Prep, set in the heart of Manhattan's financial district, is a coeducational day school enrolling 250 students, with a capacity of 1000 students age 4–Grade 8. They come from New York City's five boroughs and from New Jersey and represent a wide diversity of racial, ethnic, and socioeconomic backgrounds. Centered in a 125,000-square-foot, newly refurbished building, the School offers state-of-the-art facilities including wireless computer technology, a 15,000-volume library, an indoor swimming pool, and an outdoor play roof. Claremont's mission is to develop independent thinkers, to instill a love of the arts, and to develop each child's physical skills in a dynamic learning environment. Community service is a vital part of the curriculum and involves students in age-appropriate activities related to the environment, migrant workers, the elderly, and urban planning. The curriculum emphasizes the traditional arts, sciences, and humanities and includes studies in Mandarin Chinese, French, and Spanish. Classroom instruction is enriched by a variety of field trips to New York's many cultural and educational attractions. Tuition: $25,500–$27,800. Financial aid is available. Dana Haddad is Director of Admissions; Irwin Shlachter is Headmaster.

Collegiate School 1628

260 West 78th Street, New York, NY 10024
Tel. 212-812-8500; Admissions 212-812-8553; Fax 212-812-8547
Web Site www.collegiateschool.org
E-mail jheyman@collegiateschool.org

The oldest independent school in the nation, this college preparatory day school enrolls 630 boys in Kindergarten–Grade 12. Collegiate School prides itself on an academically rigorous program. While classical in nature, the School recognizes developmental differences and offers an impressive array of electives, including Advanced Placement in ten fields and independent study. Service is a critical part of the School's program, as are opportunities in the visual and performing arts. Teams are fielded in seven sports. Tuition: $29,100. Financial Aid: $3,100,000. Joanne P. Heyman is Director of Admissions & Financial Aid; Lee M. Levinson (Amherst College, B.A.; Harvard University, M.A., Ed.D.) is Headmaster.

Columbia Grammar and Preparatory School 1764

5 West 93rd Street, New York, NY 10025
Tel. 212-749-6200; Fax 212-865-4278
Web Site www.cgps.org; E-mail admissions@cgpsmail.org

Columbia Grammar and Preparatory School in New York, New York, is a college preparatory day school for boys and girls in Pre-Kindergarten through Grade 12. The School has two divisions, each with its own director: Grammar School (Pre-Kindergarten–Grade 6); and Preparatory School (Grades 7–12). Located just off Central Park West, it allows students to take advantage of the city's many cultural and educational resources.

In 1764, Columbia Grammar School was founded by King George II as a boys' preparatory school for Kings College (now Columbia University). Closed when the British occupied the city during the Revolutionary War, the School reopened in 1784 as the Grammar School of Columbia University. It functioned under the auspices of the university until 1864, when it was transferred to private ownership. It became coeducational in 1956 and was renamed Columbia Grammar and Preparatory School in 1969.

The School endeavors to provide a warm yet structured environment in which the student may "grow intellectually, develop a strong sense of responsibility, and learn tolerance for the opinions of others." The Grammar School emphasizes an approach that replaces memorization with investigation and discovery in a step-by-step process designed to provide an understanding of the structure of a subject area. Learning skills and disciplined work habits are stressed throughout the School.

Columbia Grammar and Preparatory School is a nonprofit, nonsectarian institution governed by a self-perpetuating Board of Trustees that meets a minimum of six times per year. Board members include parents and alumni representatives. The School is accredited by the New York State Association of Independent Schools and is chartered by the New York State Board of Regents. It holds membership in the National Association of Independent Schools and other educational organizations.

THE CAMPUS. The School occupies eight buildings on West 93rd and 94th streets. One of these, at 5 West 93rd, houses an art studio, a swimming pool, the grammar school gymnasium and cafeteria, a computer room, a library, a science room, and classrooms for Grades 3 and 4. Five converted brownstones, at 20–28 West 94th Street, house Pre-Kindergarten–Grade 2. In addition to classrooms, these buildings contain music studios, an art studio, and the grammar school nurse's office. They are connected to the building at 5 West 93rd Street by a covered walkway. The facility at 4 West 93rd Street houses Prep School classrooms, six science labs, a library, writing center, the prep school nurse's office, music classrooms and practice space, and two gymnasiums as well as a state-of-the-art theater seating 200. The facility at 36 West 93rd Street houses classrooms for Grades 5–6, three science labs, two computer rooms, and a library, plus five art studios, a drama practice room, a theater, and a cafeteria. Central Park is used for outdoor activities, including tennis. Another brownstone, purchased in 2004, includes the admissions and development offices.

School facilities are valued at $100,000,000.

THE FACULTY. Richard J. Soghoian is the Headmaster. He is a graduate of the University of Virginia (B.A.) and Columbia University (Ph.D.).

The full-time faculty consists of 164 teachers, 47 men and 117 women. In addition to baccalaureate degrees from such colleges and universities as Brown, Columbia, Cornell, Harvard, New York University, Oberlin, Tufts, Williams, Yale, and the University of Michigan, faculty also hold 127 master's degrees and 2 doctorates. There are 28 part-time instructors, 5 men and 23 women, including administrators who teach.

Two registered nurses are on duty during school hours, and the School has a part-time consulting psychologist.

STUDENT BODY. In 2007–08, the School enrolled 1129 students in Pre-Kindergarten–Grade 12, 570 boys and 559 girls. Grade sizes are approximately 35 in Pre-Kindergarten, 80 in Kindergarten–Grade 6, and 90 in Grades 7–12. Most students reside in Manhattan, but other boroughs, Long Island, Westchester County, and New Jersey are also represented.

ACADEMIC PROGRAM. The school calendar, with major holidays at Christmas and in the spring, provides 36 weeks of instruction divided into two terms of approximately 18 weeks each. Grammar School students attend school from 8:15 A.M. to 3:10 P.M. Monday through Thursday and to 2:20 P.M. on Friday. Preparatory school students have homeroom at 8:00 A.M., and classes meet on a six-day cycle from 8:20 A.M. to 2:55 P.M. Monday through Friday.

There are 10–15 students in an average teaching section. At designated times before, during, and after school, the faculty are available for extra help. Quarterly grades are issued, and written reports are sent to the parents at the end of each semester. Supplementary progress reports may be sent as the need arises. There are two parent-teacher conferences each year at the middle of each semester.

In Grades 1–4, the curriculum focuses on establishing proficiency in reading, writing, and mathematics. Science, social studies, physical education, art, and music supplement the basic program. Departmentalization of instruction begins in Grade 5 to ensure a well-planned, sequential curriculum in language skills, social studies, modern and traditional mathematics, computer, science, music, and fine arts. Beginning in Grade 4, ensemble classes offer orchestral instruction on string, woodwind, and brass instruments. Physical education includes indoor athletic activities, gymnastics, swimming, and outdoor play.

An arts program for students in Grades 7–12 offers special semester electives. Students choose from among such courses as photography, beginning instrumental music, orchestra, chorus, filmmaking, ceramics, painting and drawing, printmaking, and three-dimensional art.

The curriculum for Grades 7 and 8 includes English, history and social sciences, mathematics, earth and natural sciences, and creative arts. A foreign language sequence for Grade 7 provides an introduction to French, Japanese, Spanish, and Latin; Grade 8 students may select one of those languages for in-depth, daily study. A drugs/sex education course is part of the program.

To graduate, Preparatory School students must complete four years of high school English, history, and math; three years each of a foreign language and science, and two semester courses in art, music, or theater history.

Full-year courses include English 9–10, History 9–10, French, Latin, Japanese, Spanish; an integrated mathematics curriculum beginning in Grade 7; and Biology, Chemistry, and Physics. Typical of the varied semester electives are Modernist Literature, Creative Non-Fiction, Nature Writing Workshop, New York Literature; Introduction to Philosophy, Introduction to Psychology, Latin American Studies, Law and Society, Modern Middle East; Meteorology, Evolution, Human Anatomy and Physiology; Computer Graphics, Music Technology, Programming for the Worldwide Web; Acting, Playwriting, Painting and Drawing, Jewelry, Photography, Filmmaking, Ceramics, Chorus, Orchestra; and Weight Training. Opportunities are provided for Advanced Placement study in all departmental areas.

Graduates of the Class of 2007 are attending Bard, Bates, Boston University, Bowdoin, Brown, Colgate, College of Charleston, Columbia, Connecticut College, Cornell, Dartmouth, Emory, Fordham, George Washington, Goucher, Hamilton, Hartwick, Ithaca, Kenyon, Lehigh, Lincoln, McDaniel, New York University, Northwestern, Oberlin, Princeton, Sarah Lawrence, Skidmore, State University of New York (Binghamton), Tufts, Union, Vanderbilt, Vassar, Wesleyan, Wheaton, Yale, and the Universities of the Arts, Chicago, Michigan, Pennsylvania, Rochester, Southern California, Toronto, Vermont, and Wisconsin.

STUDENT ACTIVITIES. Students in Grades 9–12 participate in a service program. Among the possible projects are tutoring fellow students, teaching in the Grammar School, working as hospital volunteers, and helping in political offices. One hundred hours of service must be performed during the student's high school years.

Student organizations vary according to expressed interest. In the upper grades, activities include student government, the yearbook, a newspaper, a literary magazine, Issues and Human Rights, Jazz Band, Prep School Chorus, Film Appreciation, Environmental Awareness, and chapters of SADD and the Coalition for the Homeless. Each year, students are chosen to attend A Presidential Classroom for Young Americans and the Model UN.

Varsity and junior varsity teams for boys are organized in basketball, baseball, track, golf, tennis, and soccer; girls' teams are formed in basketball, softball, volleyball, swimming, soccer, tennis, and track. There is also a coeducational cross-country team as well as an optional after-school sports program for Grades 5–8 involving both intramural and interschool games in basketball, baseball, soccer, and track.

Special activities are dances, movies, field trips, and ski trips. Annual events include a street fair, orchestra and chorus concerts, several student plays, Moving-Up Day, Field Day, and Graduation.

ADMISSION AND COSTS. The School enrolls students without discrimination "on the basis of race, color, and national or ethnic origin." Students are chosen for their emotional maturity, ability to work in a demanding program, talents, concern for others, and potential for growth. Depending upon grade level, requirements include an admission test, academic transcripts, written exercises, and a personal interview. Application for fall enrollment should be made in the preceding fall or winter. There is a $55 application fee.

In 2007–08, tuition and fees range from $29,300 (Pre-Kindergarten) to $31,050 (Grade 12), including a full lunch program. A tuition payment plan and tuition insurance are available.

Columbia Grammar and Preparatory School subscribes to the School and Student Service for Financial Aid and awards financial aid on the basis of need. In 2007–08, 23 percent of the students received aid totaling $4,222,655.

Deans of Students: Barrie Allen, Monica Markovits, David Morss, Margo Potter & Vic Puccio
Director of Admission: Simone Hristidis
Director of the Annual Fund: Sara Ziff
College Counselors: Nicolette Love and Mark Speyer
Business Manager: Peter Reynolds
Director of Athletics: Stephen Rybicki

Convent of the Sacred Heart 1881

1 East 91st Street, New York, NY 10128-0689
Tel. 212-722-4745; Fax 212-996-1784
Web Site www.cshnyc.org

The oldest independent college preparatory girls' school in New York City, Convent of the Sacred Heart enrolls 670 day students in Pre-Kindergarten–Grade 12 and offers a comprehensive, rigorous curriculum that promotes academic excellence and intellectual growth within a community of respect and trust. As one of 21 Sacred Heart schools in the United States and 155 worldwide, Convent of the Sacred Heart in New York offers extensive opportunities for educational exchange throughout the world. The education focuses on the development of the "whole child," building faith and respect for intellectual values while fostering community and providing opportunities for personal growth. In addition to its broad array in the humanities, arts, and sciences, programs in sports, community service, and extracurricular activities abound. Tuition: $15,975–$30,975. Barbara Root is Director of Admissions; Dr. Joseph Ciancaglini is Head of School.

Corlears School 1968

324 West 15th Street, New York, NY 10011
Tel. 212-741-2800; Fax 212-807-1550
Web Site www.corlearsschool.org; E-mail rorryr@corlearsschool.org

Corlears School specializes in the early childhood education of students ages 2½ to 9. Its commitment is to perpetuate a love of learning and to provide students with the academic, social, and emotional tools they need. Now enrolling 136 boys and girls, the School emphasizes problem solving and interdisciplinary learning in a supportive environment as the basis for mastery of skills in reading, writing, mathematics, science, and the visual and performing arts. Tuition: $15,913–$23,074. Financial Aid: $325,000. Rorry Romeo is Director of Admissions, Placement, and Tuition Aid; Thya Merz (Norwich University, B.A.; Johns Hopkins University, M.S.) is Head of School.

The Dalton School 1919

108 East 89th Street, New York, NY 10128-1599
Tel. 212-423-5200; Admissions 212-423-5452; Fax 212-423-5259
Web Site www.dalton.org

A coeducational, college preparatory day school enrolling 1280 students in Kindergarten–Grade 12, Dalton is recognized as a model of progressive education based on a rigorous academic curriculum. The "Dalton Plan" provides the structural foundation of the School's program, promoting self-reliance, independence, and a strong sense of community. The School is known for extensive visual and performing arts programs and innovative use of technology in the humanities and sciences. Required community service, athletics, publications, and internships are among the activities. Tuition: $30,650–$31,200. Financial Aid: $5,800,000. Elizabeth Krents, Ph.D., is Director of Admissions; Ellen C. Stein (University of Pennsylvania, B.A.; Columbia University, M.B.A.) is Head of School.

Doane Stuart School 1852

799 South Pearl Street, Albany, NY 12202
Tel. 518-465-5222; Fax 518-465-5230
Web Site www.doanestuart.org; E-mail admissions@doanestuart.org

Doane Stuart is an interfaith day school offering a rigorous college preparatory program to 278 students of diverse faiths. Encompassing Nursery–Grade 12, Doane Stuart seeks to prepare young people for higher education and life while providing a strong moral and spiritual foundation. Small classes with an average of 14 students and a 7:1 student-faculty ratio are taught by dedicated, highly qualified teachers, 80 percent of whom hold advanced degrees. Students contribute 5000 hours of community service yearly and take part in school government, team sports, publications, music, drama, the arts, and numerous interest clubs. Tuition: $10,000–$17,985. Eric G. Stahura is Director of Admission; Richard D. Enemark (Columbia, Ph.D.) was appointed Headmaster in 1998.

Dutchess Day School 1955

415 Route 343, Millbrook, NY 12545
Tel. 845-677-5014; Fax 845-677-6722
Web Site www.dutchessday.org

Located on 23 acres in the middle of rural Millbrook, New York, Dutchess Day School enrolls 174 boys and girls from Dutchess, Columbia, and Litchfield Counties. The comprehensive program encompasses preschool through eighth grade. The School seeks to create an environment where children thrive intellectually, emotionally, and physically. All grades take part in physical education, while students in Grades 5–8 may participate on interscholastic athletic teams. A well-balanced curriculum emphasizes the mastery of skills, excites a child's natural curiosity, and encourages responsible citizenship. Small class sizes allow students to take intellectual risks and pursue individual projects and interests. Respect for the individuality of each child and for human differences is fundamental to Dutchess Day School's tradition and philosophy. A strong partnership between parents and faculty adds to the success of educating the whole child. Tuition: $15,800–$18,300. Financial Aid: $233,280. Ellen Potter is Admissions Director; John Cissel (Wesleyan University, M.A.L.S. 1986) is Head of School.

The Dwight School 1880

291 Central Park West, New York, NY 10024
Tel. 212-724-6360; Admissions 212-724-7524; Fax 212-724-2539
Web Site www.dwight.edu; E-mail admissions@dwight.edu

The Dwight School is an International Baccalaureate, college preparatory day school enrolling 470 boys and girls in Nursery–Grade 12. Dwight formed a consortium with The Anglo-American School in 1993 and became the first in the United States to offer the International Baccalaureate program in Pre-Kindergarten–Grade 12. The School believes that every child has a "spark of genius" that will be discovered and nurtured. Spanish beginning in Nursery, French and Chinese in Kindergarten, and 17 other languages are featured as well as state-of-the-art technology, athletics, arts, a comprehensive after-school program, and numerous study-abroad opportunities. Tuition: $28,200–$30,300. New Student Registration Fee: $750–$1500. Alicia Janiak (K–8) and Marina Bernstein (9–12) are Directors of Admissions; Stephen H. Spahn is Chancellor. *Middle States Association.*

East Woods School 1946

31 Yellow Cote Road, Oyster Bay, NY 11771
Tel. 516-922-4400; Admissions Ext. 114; Fax 516-922-2589
Web Site www.eastwoods.org; E-mail admissions@eastwoods.org

East Woods School was founded to provide elementary preparatory education combining exemplary academics and character development. Enrolling 280 boys and girls in Nursery–Grade 9, the School seeks to instill a love of learning through a child-centered approach that develops the whole child academically, creatively, physically, and socially. It values integrity, citizenship, independence, cooperation, responsibility, compassion, and respect for others. East Woods provides a traditional program in a warm and supportive community. A unique Advanced Learning Program in science supplements the curriculum. Extended day, extended care, and a summer program are available. Tuition: $10,400–$19,900. Financial Aid: $595,000. Carol Rogers is Admissions Director; Dr. Nathaniel W. Peirce is Headmaster.

The Elmwood Franklin School 1895

104 New Amsterdam Avenue, Buffalo, NY 14216
Tel. 716-877-5035; Admissions Ext. 113; Fax 716-877-9680
Web Site www.elmwoodfranklin.org
E-mail eacker@elmwoodfranklin.org

Elmwood Franklin School provides its students with the unique experience of sophisticated academics in a nurturing, child-centered environment. The School enrolls 380 students, beginning with a two-year Prep division, moving to Lower School (Grades 1 to 4), and finishing in Upper School (Grades 5 to 8). There is a balance of traditional academic work, along with physical education, foreign language, technology, music, and arts instruction offered to all students. Summer and extended-day programs are available. Tuition: $12,000–$13,900. Financial Aid: $675,000. Elaine Acker is Director of Admissions; Anthony G. Featherston IV (Boston College, B.A.; Boston University, M.A.) is Headmaster.

Ethical Culture Fieldston School 1878

33 Central Park West, New York, NY 10023
Tel. 212-712-6220; Admissions 212-712-8451; Fax 212-712-8441
Web Site www.ecfs.org; E-mail admissions@ecfs.org
3901 Fieldston Road, Bronx, NY 10471
Tel. 718-329-7300/7310; Fax 718-329-7305/7304

Ethical Culture Fieldston School offers coeducational instruction to 1600 students at two locations. Ethical Culture (Pre-Kindergarten–Grade 5) is in Manhattan, and Fieldston Lower (Pre-Kindergarten–Grade 5) and Fieldston Middle (Grades 6–8) and Fieldston (Grades 9–12) are in the Riverdale section of the Bronx. The rigorous curriculum integrates arts, humanities, and sciences with ethical values. Community service is required. Activities include sports, the arts, and publications. After-school programs and a summer day camp are offered. Tuition & Fees: $30,440. Financial Aid: $7,419,335. Taisha Thompson is Assistant Head of School for Enrollment Management & Financial Aid; Beth P. Beckmann is Interim Head of School.

Friends Academy 1876

Duck Pond Road, Locust Valley, NY 11560
Tel. 516-676-0393; Admissions Ext. 244; Fax 516-393-4276
Web Site www.fa.org; E-mail patty_ziplow@fa.org

Founded for "children of Friends and those similarly sentimented," this Quaker, college preparatory day school enrolls 745 boys and girls, Pre-Nursery–Grade 12. The Quaker philosophy emphasizes values, while the liberal arts curriculum offers a broad range of courses in both classical and modern disciplines, including computer technology and 14 Advanced Placement courses. Cocurricular activities include the arts and athletics. The composition of the student body reflects the school's commitment to diversity. Community service is required. Summer day and sports camps are available. Tuition: $14,800–$25,000. Financial Aid: $2,000,000. Patty Ziplow is Director of Admissions; Bill Morris was appointed Head of School in 2003.

Friends Seminary 1786

222 East 16th Street, New York, NY 10003
Tel. 212-979-5030; Admissions Ext. 138; Fax 212-979-5034
Web Site www.friendsseminary.org
E-mail fsadmissions@friendsseminary.org

Friends Seminary, a Quaker school, is the oldest coeducational school in New York City. The original recommendation put forth by the Yearly Meeting expressed both a practical concern and a compelling vision; this companionship of reason and foresight continues to inform the school's mission "to prepare students not only for the world that is, but to help them bring about the world that ought to be." Friends Seminary serves 670 college-bound day students in Kindergarten–Grade 12. The academic program includes AP opportunities, course work at New York University, and international/travel study exchanges. The arts, community service, clubs, and athletics are among the activities. Tuition: $28,475. Harriet Burnett is Director of Admissions; Robert Lauder, M.A., is the Principal.

The Gow School 1926

P.O. Box 85, South Wales, NY 14139
Tel. 716-652-3450; Fax 716-687-2003
Web Site www.gow.org; E-mail admissions@gow.org

THE GOW SCHOOL in South Wales, New York, is a college preparatory boarding school, encompassing Grades 7 through 12 and a postgraduate year, for young men who have a specific language disability often referred to as dyslexia. South Wales, a rural community in the western portion of the state, is on New York Route 16. Located a short distance from Niagara Falls, it is approximately 30 miles southeast of Buffalo, New York, and 100 miles south of Toronto, Canada.

The Gow School was founded in 1926 by Peter Gow, Jr., an educator who wanted to develop better methods for teaching young men who were experiencing academic failure. His work plus his personal and professional friendships with Dr. Samuel T. Orton and Anna Gillingham led to the establishment of a program for students who have at least average ability but a developmental disability in one or more phases of language usage. Reconstructive Language training, reading, and other aspects of language development are stressed in a learning environment that is individualized as much as possible.

Gow, a nonprofit school, is governed by a self-perpetuating Board of Trustees, 23 in number. The Board, composed primarily of alumni, meets three times a year. The School is registered by the New York State Board of Regents; it holds membership in the National Association of Independent Schools, the New York State Association of Independent Schools, and the International Dyslexia Association.

THE CAMPUS. The 100-acre campus, which is traversed by a trout stream, includes hilly woodland, athletic fields, tennis courts, a ski/snowboard slope, and a ropes course.

The Main Building contains the business office, development office, ten classrooms, infirmary, and the Gow Bookstore. Orton Hall provides 12 classrooms including a tutoring room, a science laboratory, two computer classrooms, the computer writing lab, and a study hall. The Green Cottage furnishes living quarters for students and two masters' apartments. Other facilities include The Admissions Building and the School House, which contains the Art Department. Students and masters reside in Cornwall House, Templeton Dormitory, Brown House, Ellis House, Whitcomb Dormitory, and Warner House. The 49,000-square-foot Gow Center provides a student union, classrooms, two indoor tennis courts, two basketball courts, three squash courts, and a fitness center. The campus also provides housing for the Headmaster and 28 teachers and their families.

The Isaac Arnold Memorial Library, with a capacity of 10,000 volumes, contains a reading room, seven classrooms, a faculty room, and the Headmaster's office. The Reid Arts Center houses three classrooms, a technology workshop, and painting, drawing, and 3-D design studios. The Simms Family Theater is also located in the arts center.

The plant is valued at approximately $14,000,000.

THE FACULTY. M. Bradley Rogers, Jr., was elected Headmaster in 2004. He holds a B.A. degree from the University of Dayton in Ohio and a master's degree from Johns Hopkins University. Prior to assuming his present position, Mr. Rogers was Headmaster at The Odyssey School in Maryland. He and his wife reside on campus with their four sons.

The faculty consists of 43 teachers and administrators who teach, 28 of whom live in the dormitories or in other campus housing. They hold 34 baccalaureate degrees, 28 master's degrees, and a doctorate from Canisius, Catholic University of

America, Cornell, Duke, East Stroudsburg University, Hamilton, Hiram College, Hobart, Indiana, Johns Hopkins, Kenyon, Macalester, Medaille College, Nazareth, St. Bonaventure, Slippery Rock, Springfield College, State University of New York (Binghamton, Brockport, Buffalo, Cortland, Fredonia, Geneseo), Syracuse, Texas A&M, Texas Tech, Towson State, Union College, and the Universities of Colorado, Minnesota, New Hampshire, Rochester, Virginia, and Washington.

A local doctor serves as the School physician, and emergency facilities are minutes away. School nurses coordinate all medical activities.

STUDENT BODY. In 2007–08, The Gow School enrolled 143 young men, 12 to 19 years of age, as boarders in Grades 7–12. They came from 28 states, Austria, Bermuda, Canada, England, Grand Cayman, Hong Kong, Jamaica, Japan, Mali, the Netherlands, Oman, Sri Lanka, Switzerland, Taiwan, and Trinidad.

ACADEMIC PROGRAM. The school year, which is divided into semesters, extends from early September to mid-May, with Thanksgiving, winter, and spring breaks. Comprehensive written reports are sent to parents at the end of each marking period. Advisor reports, summarizing student performance in academics, athletics, and residential life, are written at the midpoint of each marking period. The student-teacher ratio of 4:1 ensures that each young man receives individualized attention and support.

Classes have an average enrollment of five students and meet six days per week. The weekday schedule begins with the rising bell at 7:00 A.M., followed by breakfast and house jobs. Classes, lunch, athletics, tutorials, and supervised study hall are scheduled between 8:00 A.M. and 6:00 P.M. After dinner, all Upper School students have a brief reading period and two hours of supervised study before quiet time in the dorm from 9:00 to 10:00 P.M. or, at times, to 11:00 P.M. Faculty members are available for individual help whenever necessary. Middle School students have a 90-minute study period in the evening.

The core of the Gow curriculum is based on Reconstructive Language, using a multisensory approach, as an effective tool in teaching dyslexic/language learning-disabled students to read and improve language skills, particularly with regard to the printed or written word. Study skills such as note taking, test preparation, and drill work are integrated into all disciplines. The School has a laptop program, and all classrooms and student rooms are wireless for Internet access.

Generally, a student takes five academic courses in addition to one Reconstructive Language course. The language course involves training in deriving meaning from reading, in vocabulary extension, and in oral and written expression. In mathematics courses, effective traditional methods are employed as well as teaching math concepts and applications with manipulative materials. Instruction begins with the most basic operations and proceeds to more advanced concepts. Daily oral and written work is assigned as a means of promoting accurate and immediate recall.

The curriculum is designed to prepare students to enter college. To graduate, each student must complete 21.5 academic credits in Grades 9–12, including English 4, mathematics 3, history 4, laboratory science 2, art/music, health, and computer 1, which includes keyboarding, word processing, and data design.

The core curriculum in Grades 7–12 includes Grammar, Literature, Composition, Shakespeare, American Literature; United States History, Global History I–II; Developmental Math, Pre-Algebra, Algebra 1–2, Plane Geometry, Pre-Calculus, Calculus; and Science 7, Earth Science, Environmental Science, Biology, Conceptual Physics, Chemistry, and Physics. Among the elective offerings are courses in music, art, drama, economics, computer, business seminar, and advanced biology.

Among the colleges at which recent graduates have been accepted are Bethany College, Boston College, Catholic University, Cornell, Elon, Embry-Riddle, Fairleigh Dickinson, George Washington, Landmark College, Loyola University (New Orleans), Marshall, Mount Allison University, Muskingum College, Northeastern, Regis University, Rochester Institute of Technology, Roger Williams, St. Lawrence, Savannah College of Art and Design, Southern Illinois, Trinity, Tulane, Virginia Institute of Technology, Western State College, Widener, Wilfred Laurier University (Canada), and the Universities of Arizona, Denver, Oregon, Toronto, Utah, Vermont, and Wisconsin.

STUDENT ACTIVITIES. Extracurricular activities vary from year to year in response to student interest. In student affairs, the young men are represented by a school council, resident assistants, and class officers. Typical groups are the newspaper and yearbook staffs, and the Photography, Instrumental Music, Golf, Roller Blading, Skiing, Mountain Biking, and Outing Clubs. All students are encouraged to participate in drama activities, which include the production of at least two major plays each year in conjunction with girls from neighboring schools.

Interscholastic teams are organized in soccer, squash, lacrosse, basketball, cross-country, tennis, rowing, and wrestling. School teams compete with nearby public and independent schools, including Nichols School and Park School of Buffalo. Weight training, winter camping, and intramural sports are among the activities offered on a noncompetitive basis.

The extracurricular program includes dances and trips to Buffalo, Toronto, and Niagara Falls. Students attend NFL and NHL games as well as concerts, theater, and visits to area museums.

ADMISSION AND COSTS. The Gow School admits young,

dyslexic men capable of college preparatory work who need language-based remediation. School records, completed student and parent questionnaires, math and English teacher recommendations, educational assessment including WIAT or Woodcock-Johnson battery, WISC-IV or WAIS test results, and a personal interview are required for admission. In addition, specific skill testing to determine class placement is required. Placement testing and an interview take place on campus and are completed in one day. New students are admitted in any grade, and late enrollment is permitted if vacancies exist. There is a nonrefundable $4300 registration/deposit fee, which is applied to the first year's tuition, and a $100 application fee.

Tuition, board, lodging, technology fee, and transportation for regular school activities are $44,400 for the 2007–08 school year. Books, supplies, laundry, athletic supplies, and personal expenses are additional. Twenty-six percent of the student body receive financial aid from the School.

Director of Upper School and Assistant Headmaster: Daniel F. Kelley
Director of Middle School: Jeffrey Sweet
Director of Admission: Robert Garcia
Director of Development: Gayle Hutton
Director of College Counseling: Charles Brown
Director of Finance: Rosemary Bastian
Director of Athletics: Mark Szafnicki

Grace Church School 1894

86 Fourth Avenue, New York, NY 10003
Tel. 212-475-5609; Fax 212-475-5015
Web Site www.gcschool.org; E-mail mhirschman@gcschool.org

Grace Church School is a coeducational day school with an enrollment of 405 students in Junior Kindergarten–Grade 8. The students are challenged by a rigorous curriculum that consists of a broad range of course offerings. Multisensory learning is a priority so that each student may use his or her strengths as an avenue to learning. This Episcopal school aims to balance academic competence with the development of character based on Judeo-Christian values. Teachers provide individual attention, allowing children to advance at their own pace. Student council, publications, sports, drama, arts, computer, School chorus, church choir, and an after-school program are among the activities. Tuition: $28,500. Financial aid is available. Martha Hirschman is Director of Admissions; George P. Davison is Headmaster.

Grace Day School 1955

23 Cedar Shore Drive, Massapequa, NY 11758
Tel. 516-798-1122; Fax 516-799-0711
Web Site www.gracedayschool.org

This coeducational Episcopal school aims to prepare highly motivated students for competitive secondary schools in an environment guided by Christian principles. Grace Day School enrolls approximately 235 students in Kindergarten–Grade 8 plus 195 pre-schoolers. The curriculum is based on high expectations and a strong foundation in core subjects, with small classes that focus on the individual student. The program is enriched by Regents Math and Science, French, computer, and religion. The Voorhees Fine Arts Center provides facilities for the visual arts and choral and instrumental music. A comprehensive physical education and athletic program and a summer camp are available. Tuition: $8300–$8600. Patricia Quinto is Director of Admissions; Rev. Stephen Peverly is Interim Head of School.

The Green Vale School 1923

250 Valentine's Lane, Old Brookville, NY 11545
Tel. 516-621-2420; Fax 516-621-1317
Web Site www.greenvaleschool.org; E-mail info@greenvaleschool.org

Green Vale is proud to be celebrating its 83rd year. Enrolling 480 day boys and girls in Nursery (age 3)–Grade 9, the School seeks to provide the critical skills, concepts, and analytical thinking abilities children will need to succeed and to instill moral values, tolerance, and compassion. The curriculum balances the liberal arts and sciences, enriched by art, music, crafts, computer, library, and physical education. Intramural and varsity sports and other activities enjoy wide participation. A strong partnership between faculty and parents adds to the success of the program. Tuition: $10,750–$21,800. Financial aid is available. Anne B. Watters is Director of Admission; Stephen H. Watters (Denison, B.A.; University of Massachusetts, M.A.T.) is Head of School.

Hackley School 1899

293 Benedict Avenue, Tarrytown, NY 10591
Tel. 914-631-0128; Admissions 914-366-2642; Fax 914-366-2636
Web Site www.hackleyschool.org; E-mail admissions@hackleyschool.org

Hackley School in Tarrytown, New York, is a nonsectarian, coeducational, college preparatory school enrolling day students in Kindergarten through Grade 12 and five-day boarding students in Grades 9 through 12. Tarrytown (population 12,000) is located in the heart of the scenic Hudson Valley, 25 miles north of Manhattan. The School is reached easily by bus, car, or train.

The School was founded in 1899 by Mrs. Caleb Brewster Hackley to provide an educational culture in which a deliberate approach to social relationships stimulates and supports the moral, intellectual, artistic, and athletic accomplishments of individuals. Hackley students encounter serious classes, demanding homework assignments, and a peer environment that respects commitment and unreserved effort. In the belief that students grow in character and responsibility through service to others, all grades commit energy, time, and imagination to assisting others beyond the spheres of home and school as they carry out Hackley's motto: "United We Help One Another."

A nonprofit institution, Hackley is governed by a 20-

member Board of Trustees. It is registered by the New York State Board of Regents and holds membership in the National Association of Independent Schools, the College Board, the Association of College Admissions Counselors, and the New York State Association of Independent Schools. The Parents Association enhances school life through volunteer activities and fund-raising. Hackley's Centennial Campaign raised $50,000,000.

THE CAMPUS. The School, situated on a hilltop overlooking the Hudson, is graced by rambling, turn-of-the-century buildings of English Tudor style. Among the facilities are a Performing Arts Center with a music conservatory, a new Lower School building, a new Middle School, a new Upper and Middle School science building, new international squash courts, an indoor swimming pool, several art studios, a photography lab, and a library containing over 33,000 volumes. There are computer labs in each division and Internet access in every classroom.

Boarders, who spend weekends and holidays at home, are housed in single or double rooms in the main building complex. Resident faculty supervise the boarding corridors.

The 285-acre campus offers six tennis courts, numerous playing fields, four international squash courts, and a 3.2-mile cross-country trail.

THE FACULTY. Walter C. Johnson was appointed Headmaster in 1995. He graduated *summa cum laude* from Amherst (B.A. 1974) and earned master's degrees in literature and educational administration from the University of Pennsylvania and Teachers College, Columbia University, respectively. Mr. Johnson has had educational and administrative experience at Trinity School and Collegiate School in New York City and at The American School in London.

Faculty, including assistants and administrators who teach, number 132. Forty-four percent of the full-time teachers live on campus. They hold 132 baccalaureate and 102 graduate degrees representing study at more than 100 colleges and universities.

The College Counseling office is staffed by three experienced, full-time professionals. Other support services include a full-time nurse, two full-time psychologists, and two learning specialists.

STUDENT BODY. In 2007–08, the School enrolled 409 day boys, 402 day girls, 10 boarding boys, and 15 boarding girls, as follows: 209 in Kindergarten–Grade 4, 245 in Grades 5–8, and 382 in Grades 9–12. Day students come from 96 communities throughout New York, New Jersey, and Connecticut.

ACADEMIC PROGRAM. The school year, from early September to early June, is divided into semesters, with breaks for Thanksgiving, winter, and spring vacations.

Average class size is 16 students. There are supervised study halls throughout the day for students in Grades 5–12. Boarders also have supervised evening study. Teachers provide extra help as necessary; long-term tutoring is offered for an hourly fee. Grades are issued and sent to parents four times yearly, with interim reports issued as required.

The curriculum for Kindergarten–Grade 3 emphasizes reading and oral and written expression. Starting in Grade 3, students write a weekly theme and begin to work on research papers. The mathematics program teaches the logical structure of the number system and fosters dexterity in computation. Also included in the program are history, science, art, music, computers, and physical education. Spanish is introduced in Grade 3. The Director of the Lower School is Ronald DelMoro.

The curriculum for Grade 4 and the Middle School (Grades 5–8) includes English, which focuses on grammar, oral expression, expository and creative writing, and literary analysis; American history (Grade 4), ancient history and world history (Grades 5–7), and Asian civilizations (Grade 8); mathematics (emphasizing the four basic operations and probability, graphing, statistics, pre-algebra, algebra I, and geometry); science including the physical world (Grades 5–6), life science (Grade 7), and chemistry in biology (Grade 8); and art, drama, and music. All Middle School students are required to take a computer curriculum and health education. They may choose to study Latin, Chinese, Spanish, or French in Grade 6. Alona Scott is Director of the Middle School.

To graduate, Upper School students must complete four years of English; three years of a foreign language (French, Spanish, Chinese, or Latin); three years of required history sequence; mathematics through algebra II and trigonometry; three years of science, one of which must be a laboratory course; and one year of performing or visual arts. The Upper School puts a major emphasis on writing. The Monday composition period assigns at least 20 additional essays during the academic year.

In addition to required courses, the Upper School offers

Advanced Placement courses in 20 subjects across the disciplines. Other courses include Surviving the Apocalypse/New York City: Imagination and Desire, Hyphenated Americans/ Satire, History of Western Theatre, Seminar in Creative Writing (print- and Web-based), Economics, Modern European History, Government and Politics: The U.S.A. and the World, Media & Culture, Italian, Computer Science, Ecology, Biology, Organic Chemistry, Chemistry, 9th Grade Physics, Advanced Physics, Marine Biology, Environmental Science, Calculus, Finite Math, Statistics, Music Theory, Jazz Improvisation, Art History, Studio Art, Advanced Ceramics, Photography, Computer Graphics, 3-D Sculpture and Design, and Architecture & Design. The Director of the Upper School is Beverley Whitaker.

In the past four years, the following colleges and universities have enrolled the greatest number of Hackley graduates: Amherst, Boston University, Columbia, Cornell, Dartmouth, George Washington, Harvard, Middlebury College, New York University, Princeton, Vanderbilt, Wesleyan University, Yale, and the University of Pennsylvania.

STUDENT ACTIVITIES. The Community Council, composed of student and faculty representatives from Grades 5–12, organizes social and service activities. Students also participate in Model Congress and a student-faculty judicial board. Students publish a yearbook, a newspaper, and a literary magazine. All Lower and Middle School students perform in grade-level dramatic and musical productions annually. Students may join chorus, orchestra, band, and jazz bands, performing major choral works, chamber music, and vocal recitals. The Hackley Music Institute provides individual instruction for preprofessional and other music students in both vocal and instrumental music. There is also a variety of student clubs and a Student Teacher program working in Lower School classrooms.

Hackley families attend the Americana Festival, Carnival, Spring Fair, school art shows, gym & swim nights, and parent dinners. Hackley also holds dances and coffee house evenings for students.

Annual trips include sixth-grade camping at the Delaware Water Gap, seventh-grade visit to Boston, the eighth-grade trip to Washington, and ninth-grade outdoor challenge experience. Students take trips supplementing their courses such as visits to the Metropolitan Museum and Ellis Island, zoology and marine biology studies on a research vessel in Long Island Sound, and field trips to sites in the Hudson River Valley.

In 2000, Hackley received a grant for an annual educational trip; students and faculty have visited Cuba, Vietnam, China, the Galapagos, Italy, and Greece. The School also sponsors student exchanges with a school in France during the spring recess.

Varsity sports for boys and girls include basketball, cross-country, fencing, indoor track, lacrosse, golf, soccer, squash, swimming, track and field, and tennis. Boys also compete in baseball, football, and wrestling, while girls play field hockey and softball. A member of the Ivy League of the metropolitan area, Hackley competes against league members and public and parochial schools. Physical education courses include noncompetitive activities such as fitness center and hiking. Swimming is required in Kindergarten–Grade 6.

ADMISSION AND COSTS. Hackley seeks students of diverse backgrounds who demonstrate quickness of intellect and resourcefulness in problem solving, tempered by curiosity and love of truth. Students are admitted on the basis of a personal interview and written essay, a campus visit, two teacher recommendations, previous transcripts and the results of the Independent School Entrance Examination or Secondary School Admission Test for Middle and Upper Schools. In the Lower School, candidates for Kindergarten and Grade 1 take Hackley's own admissions test. Candidates for Grades 2, 3, and 4 must undergo the early childhood evaluation of the Educational Records Bureau. The application deadline is December 15. There is a $55 application fee.

In 2007–08, tuition ranges from $25,600 for Kindergarten to $29,500 for Grade 12. The boarding charge is $9100. Tuition includes lunch but not the cost of Middle and Upper School books.

In the current year, a total of $2,700,000 in financial aid was awarded to 110 students on the basis of demonstrated need. Low-interest loans, an installment payment plan, and tuition insurance are also available.

Headmaster: Walter C. Johnson
Assistant Headmaster: Philip Variano
Director of Development: Katherine Valyi
Co-Directors of Admissions: Julie S. Core & Christopher T. McColl
Co-Directors of College Counseling: Julie D. Lillis, Peter Latson & Jean Nadell
Technology Director: Joseph E. Dioguardi
Director of Finance: Peter McAndrew
Director of Athletics: Robert Pickert

Harbor Country Day School 1958

17 Three Sisters Road, St. James, NY 11780
Tel. 631-584-5555; Fax 631-862-7664
Web Site www.harborcountrydayschool.org
E-mail cpryor@harborcountrydayschool.org

Founded by parents, Harbor Country Day School enrolls 195 boys and girls in Nursery–Grade 8. The enriched curriculum focuses on the basic academic disciplines of language arts, mathematics, social studies, and science, while fostering good work habits, self-esteem, and consideration of others. Foreign language and instruction in music, art, computer science, and physical education are offered at every level beginning in Kindergarten. Competitive sports, intramurals, and the performing arts are also part of the School's program. Summer programs are offered. Financial aid is available. Tuition: $3320–$10,540. Whit Knapp is Director of Admissions; Christopher C. Pryor (Roanoke College, B.A.; Teachers College, Columbia University, M.A.) was appointed Headmaster in 2007.

The Harley School 1917

1981 Clover Street, Rochester, NY 14618
Tel. 585-442-1770; Admissions Ext. 3010; Fax 585-442-5758
Web Site www.harleyschool.org; E-mail admissions@harleyschool.org

Housed in spacious, modern buildings on a 20-acre suburban campus, The Harley School is a coeducational, college preparatory day school enrolling 500 students in Nursery through Grade 12. Harley encourages involvement in all areas of school life: academic study, visual and performing arts, athletic competition, extracurricular activities, and community service. Harley offers a full range of Advanced Placement classes, arts and music classes, foreign languages, science laboratories, and various electives. Summer programs and extended day are also offered. Tuition: $13,800–$17,000. Financial aid is available. Valerie A. Mynnti is Director of Admissions; Dr. Timothy R. Cottrell was appointed Head of School in 2006.

The Harvey School 1916

260 Jay Street, Katonah, NY 10536
Tel. 914-232-3161; Admission Ext. 138; Fax 914-232-6034
Web Site www.harveyschool.org
E-mail romanowicz@harveyschool.org

Harvey, a coeducational college preparatory school, enrolls 340 day and five-day boarding students of varying ability in Grades 6–12. Teachers work with students as individuals, both in and out of the classroom, in a warm, supportive environment. Small classes promote academic achievement and personal growth. Two Internet-accessible labs and computer technology in most academic subjects provide information and resources to encourage excellence. Harvey offers ten Advanced Placement courses and varied activities, including a nationally recognized Model UN program and competitive athletics. Tuition: $27,000;

Boarding Fee: $7000. Financial aid is available. Ronald H. Romanowicz is Director of Enrollment; Barry W. Fenstermacher (Drew, B.A.) was named Headmaster in 1986.

Horace Mann School 1887

Grades 6–12: 231 West 246th Street, Riverdale, NY 10471
Tel. 718-432-4000; Admissions 718-432-4100
Fax 718-432-3610
Web Site www.horacemann.org; E-mail admissions@horacemann.org
Kindergarten–Grade 5: 4440 Tibbett Avenue, Riverdale, NY 10471
Tel. 718-432-3300
Nursery Division: 55 East 90th Street, New York, NY 10128
Tel. 212-369-4600

Horace Mann is a day school enrolling 1750 boys and girls from diverse backgrounds in Nursery–Grade 12. The college preparatory curriculum is designed to challenge the imagination and intellect of its students while developing moral character and a love of learning. The core program, which includes Advanced Placement in all disciplines, is enhanced by programs at the School's 200-acre nature laboratory in Connecticut. All graduates typically enroll in four-year colleges. Varsity sports, Model United Nations, instrumental and vocal groups, publications, and activity clubs meet a variety of student interests. Tuition: $22,100–$30,830. Financial Aid: $6,800,000. Lisa J. Moreira is Director of Admissions; Thomas M. Kelly, Ph.D., is Head of School. *Middle States Association.*

Iona Preparatory School 1916

255 Wilmot Road, New Rochelle, NY 10804
Tel. 914-632-0714; Admissions Ext. 215; Fax 914-632-9760
Web Site www.ionaprep.org; E-mail avs81@ionaprep.org

IONA PREPARATORY SCHOOL in New Rochelle, New York, is an independent, Roman Catholic, secondary, college preparatory day school enrolling young men from diverse religious backgrounds in Grades 9 through 12. The suburban community of New Rochelle (population 72,985) is situated on Long Island Sound 16 miles from the heart of New York City. Home to Iona College and the College of New Rochelle, the town offers easy access to the myriad educational, historic, and cultural resources of Manhattan and Westchester County. Students commute to the campus by train, bus, and private car pools.

Iona Prep is operated by members of the religious order of Christian Brothers, founded in 1802 by Blessed Edmund Ignatius Rice and known worldwide for its dedication to the education and character formation of teenage boys. Supported by parents and local clergy, the School opened in 1916 on the grounds of the Stern estate, staffed by three Brothers and enrolling 37 students. Steady growth through the years led to expansion and relocation to its present-day location on Wilmot Road.

A National School of Excellence, Iona Prep is dedicated to the development of the whole person, spiritually, intellectually, ethically, and physically. In a nurturing, family-like environment, high academic standards share equal emphasis with faith and morals in a challenging liberal arts curriculum that integrates values education and service to others in the American Roman Catholic tradition. School-wide liturgies, prayer services, and retreats unite students and faculty in Christian purpose.

Now in its 90th year, Iona Prep is guided by a Board of Trustees and accredited by the Middle States Association of Colleges and Schools and the New York State Board of Regents. It holds membership in the National Catholic Educational Association, Catholic School Administrators Association of New York State, and The College Board. The Mothers' Auxiliary and Fathers' Council, comprised of current parents, and the Alumni Association, representing nearly 10,000 graduates, are key components in carrying out the School's mission.

THE CAMPUS. Iona Prep occupies 27 acres in a pleasant residential area of New Rochelle. Among the campus facilities are the Paul Verni Fine Arts Center, the Jakeway Library Media Center, the Tully and Heffernan Gymnasiums, and the state-of-the-art Hughes Fitness Center. Also on the grounds are tennis courts, an eight-lane running track, a baseball complex, a football field, and playing fields for several other sports.

THE FACULTY. Maureen Kiers is President of Iona Preparatory. In 1994, after serving for six years as principal of St. Joseph's School in Bronxville, New York, Mrs. Kiers joined the Iona Prep faculty as a math teacher. She was appointed Assistant Head of School in 2004 and assumed the role of President in 2006. Mrs. Kiers received her undergraduate degree from Molloy College and her Master's Degree in Education from St. John's University in New York. She also participated in the School Administrator/Supervisor Program at Manhattan College, resulting in her permanent New York State certification as a school administrator.

The Iona Prep faculty, comprised of religious and lay teachers, hold baccalaureate degrees from a wide range of four-year colleges and universities nationwide. More than 80 percent of the instructors also hold at least one master's degree in their subject area. They are graduates of such institutions as Adelphi, Catholic University, Columbia, Dartmouth, Fordham, Hampton, Hunter, Iona College, New York University, Ohio State, St. John's, Temple, Wesleyan, and the University of Notre Dame.

A registered nurse is on the premises during the school day, and major medical facilities are nearby.

STUDENT BODY. In 2007–08, Iona Prep enrolled 750 young men in Grades 9–12. They come from communities throughout Westchester County, the Bronx, and western Connecticut and represent a broad spectrum of racial, ethnic, religious, and socioeconomic backgrounds.

ACADEMIC PROGRAM. The school year, from early September to early June, is divided into semesters, with breaks at Thanksgiving, Christmas, and Easter, and the observance of several holy days and national holidays. Grades are issued at the midpoint and conclusion of each semester. Upon entrance to the School, boys are assigned a guidance counselor who provides academic and personal support throughout the student's four years. The After School Study Center offers individualized tutoring with a teacher and members of the National Honor Society.

The Freshman Program is designed to provide a seamless transition from grade school to secondary school. Prior to their entrance to Iona Prep, incoming ninth graders and their parents attend a family orientation night to meet teachers and learn about the School's policies and procedures. In the summer, they spend time with classmates and peer counselors, followed by a two-day orientation in September.

Classes are held five days a week and rotate in an eight-day cycle, with eight periods scheduled between 8:25 A.M. and 2:41 P.M. The enriched college preparatory curriculum, which exceeds the requirements of the New York State Board of Regents, features High Honors, Honors, and Regents courses, including Advanced Placement courses as early as the sophomore year. Most students are placed in classes at all three levels, depending on individual aptitude and prior academic experience, and they may advance to higher levels although not placed there initially.

STEP (Superior Talent Enrichment Program) offers a maximum of 30 of the top incoming freshmen the opportunity to complete between 12 and 18 Advanced Placement college credits prior to graduation. Invitation to the program is based on character, outstanding academic achievement in elementary school, and a score at or above the 95th percentile on standardized entrance tests.

To graduate, students must complete four units each in Religious Studies, English, Social Studies, Mathematics, Science, and Physical Education; 3 units of the same foreign language (French, Italian, Latin, Spanish); 2 units in Computer Science; and 1 unit each in Humanities (art and music) and Health Education.

Among the elective courses available are Advanced Placement in Biology, Calculus, Statistics, Chemistry, Physics, English Language, English Literature, American History, European History, World History, Government, Psychology, Chinese, Italian, Latin, and Spanish. Other electives include Accounting, Anatomy & Physiology, Advanced Computer, Environmental Science, Criminalistics, French 4, Spanish 4, Italian 4, Political Science, Media Literacy, Music Topics, and Art Projects.

Christian outreach is a graduation requirement, and all boys in Grades 9–11 take part in a class day of service, while seniors contribute 50 hours of work for worthwhile causes within the school and local communities.

Laptop computers are used by all students, and a wireless network throughout the campus provides access to information across the disciplines and beyond the classroom.

Iona Prep is proud of the long tradition of academic excellence of its students, who have been recognized as National Merit Scholarship Finalists, Semifinalists, and Commended Scholars as well as National Hispanic and National Achievement Scholars. In 2007, the graduating class was offered a total of $7,980,000 in college academic scholarships.

Historically, 100 percent of Iona Prep seniors enroll in four-year colleges and universities. Among these are American University of Rome, Bentley, Boston College, Boston University, Catholic University of America, College of the Holy Cross, Columbia, Cornell, Fairfield, Georgetown, Gettysburg, Howard, Johns Hopkins, La Salle, Marquette, Massachusetts Institute of Technology, New York University, Northwestern, Princeton, Purdue, Rensselaer, State University of New York, Syracuse, Temple, Vassar, Virginia Polytechnic, Wake Forest, and the Universities of Connecticut, Illinois, Massachusetts, Michigan, Notre Dame, Pittsburgh, Southern California, and Vermont.

STUDENT ACTIVITIES. Iona Prep students take part in a lively extracurricular program that provides opportunity for personal growth, friendship, and fun. The Student Faculty Council serves as a liaison among students, teachers, and administrators in the planning and implementation of school events and the financing and supervision of extracurricular activities. Boys also serve on the Library Council and as peer ministers; qualified scholars are invited to join the National Honor Society and the National Foreign Language Honor Society.

Students publish *Gael Force* (newspaper), *Saga* (yearbook), and *Renaissance* (literary magazine). Opportunities in the visual and performing arts are provided by the concert band, Prep Players, stage crew, Music Ministry, rock ensemble, Art Club, and handbell, guitar, and bagpipes groups. Special-interest clubs are formed for astronomy, speech and debate, Math Team, Mock Trial, video games, Gaelic Society, skiing, rock climbing, web design, and weight training, among others.

The athletic program is an integral component of the overall Iona Prep experience as a means of developing skills and promoting teamwork, sportsmanship, and fair play. More than 80 percent of all team athletes are Honor Roll students, and currently 116 alumni are playing sports at the collegiate level. Gaels teams compete in Divisions I and II of the Catholic High School Athletic Association in baseball, basketball, bowling, cross-country, football, golf, ice hockey, lacrosse, pole vaulting, shot put, soccer, swimming, tennis, indoor and outdoor track and field, and volleyball. Intramural sports include floor hockey, badminton, and indoor soccer.

ADMISSION AND COSTS. Iona Prep welcomes young men of excellent character, motivation, and "strong average" or above ability who demonstrate the willingness and enthusiasm to benefit from the School's academic and extracurricular programs. Admission is offered based on the candidate's completed application and essay, his previous academic records with emphasis on Grades 7 and 8, and recommendations from his principal, teacher, or guidance counselor. The School also considers the applicant's achivement on the Test for Admissions to Catholic High Schools (TACHS) or the Independent School Entrance Exam (ISEE). A registration fee of $150 is required of all new students.

In 2007–08, tuition, fees, and books total $12,150. A required laptop is additional. The deadlines for applying for financial assistance are November 1 and April 1.

President: Maureen Kiers
Principal: George Teasdale
Dean of Academics: Susan Natale
Dean of Student Life: Kieran Daly
Director of Admissions: Ann Slocum
Director of Development: Barbara Robertson
Director of College Counseling: Joseph Klein
Director of Finance: Brian Terhune
Director of Athletics: Bernard Mahoney

The Kew-Forest School 1918

119-17 Union Turnpike, Forest Hills, NY 11375
Tel. 718-268-4667; Admissions Ext. 125; Fax 718-268-9121
Web Site www.kewforest.org; E-mail kgarcia@kewforest.org

The Kew-Forest School enrolls 350 day boys and girls in Kindergarten–Grade 12. Its mission is to provide an academically challenging liberal arts education that encourages students to "achieve their individual potential and strive for personal integrity and respect for others." The School, which is accredited by the NYSAIS, attracts a racially and ethnically diverse cross-section of young people from 40 towns. The faculty includes 35 full-time teachers, more than two-thirds of whom hold advanced degrees. The student-faculty ratio is 9:1. The rigorous curriculum is designed to instill a strong foundation in reading, writing, math, social studies, and science. It also emphasizes the traditional values in education that provide a strong foundation for higher education. Computer technology, music, the arts, and foreign languages complete the program. Typically, all graduates go on to college. Among the activities are publications, clubs, leadership groups, Model UN, Mock Trial, vocal and instrumental ensembles, service learning, and varsity sports. Tuition & Fees: $18,925–$21,575. Financial aid is available. Katherine Garcia is Associate Director of Admissions; Peter S. Lewis is Head of School. *Middle States Association.*

The Kildonan School 1969

425 Morse Hill Road, Amenia, NY 12501
Tel. 845-373-8111; Fax 845-373-9793
Web Site www.kildonan.org; E-mail bsattler@kildonan.org

Kildonan, a coeducational, college preparatory school for dyslexic students of average to above-average intelligence, enrolls boarders in Grade 7–Postgraduate and day students in Grade 2–Postgraduate. In addition to regular subjects, the highly structured program features daily one-on-one language tutoring designed to help students develop the necessary level of proficiency in academic skills to allow them to return to another school or enter college. Computer and word processing are an integral part of a full curriculum that includes art, woodshop, riding, and interscholastic/intramural athletics. Boarding Tuition: $46,000–$48,100; Day Tuition: $27,825–$34,550. Bonnie A. Wilson is Admission Director; Ronald A. Wilson was appointed Headmaster in 1986.

The Knox School 1904

541 Long Beach Road, St. James, NY 11780
Tel. 631-686-1600; Admissions Ext. 414; Fax 631-686-1650
Web Site www.knoxschool.org; E-mail mshort@knoxschool.org

Set on 30+ acres overlooking Stony Brook Harbor, Knox provides the opportunity for 120 motivated students in Grades 6–12 to excel within a liberal arts program in preparation for success in selective colleges and universities. Six Core Values—integrity, kindness, courage, respect, responsibility, and scholarship—guide the School's Principles of Action. Students benefit from small classes in a familial environment that fosters character and leadership. Faculty are available for extra support as needed during and after the school day. Clubs, a student exchange program in England, and athletic teams, including an equestrian program, are offered. Boarding Tuition: $34,285–$36,385; Day Tuition: $18,850–$20,450. Meg Short is Director of Admissions; David B. Stephens is Headmaster. *Middle States Association.*

Lawrence Woodmere Academy 1891

336 Woodmere Boulevard, Woodmere, NY 11598
Tel. 516-374-9000; Admissions Ext. 827; Fax 516-374-4707
Web Site www.lawrencewoodmere.org
E-mail cking@lwa.ny.k12.us.com

A 1990 merger between Lawrence Country Day School (1891) and Woodmere Academy (1912) created this coeducational, college preparatory school, the only independent school on Long Island's South Shore. The present-day Lawrence Woodmere Academy enrolls 360 students in Pre-Kindergarten (4) through Grade 12. Located on a 7-acre campus 20 miles from Manhattan, the school offers state-of-the-art facilities including three computer centers, an art studio, and gymnasium. The curriculum emphasizes the liberal arts, sciences, and humanities, including a science research symposium, AP and honors courses in the major departments, and numerous opportunities in the visual and performing arts. The Achievement Center provides guided studies in time management, individual learning styles, and organizational and study techniques for students in Grades

9–12 who benefit from additional support. Students take part in volunteer activities for Habitat for Humanity, clothing drives, soup kitchens, and other projects. Extracurricular options are publications, school government, Tech Team, Model UN, music, drama, and interscholastic sports. Tuition: $16,500–$24,750. Corinne M. King is Director of Admissions; Alan Bernstein is Headmaster.

Loyola School 1900

980 Park Avenue, New York, NY 10028
Tel. 212-288-3522; Admissions 646-346-8132; Fax 212-861-1021
Web Site www.loyola-nyc.org; E-mail admissions@loyola-nyc.org

Loyola, a Catholic, coeducational, college preparatory, urban secondary day school rooted in the Jesuit tradition, enrolls 205 students in Grades 9–12. It aims to combine the Jesuit and independent school tradition of academic excellence while committing to each student religiously, intellectually, socially, and physically. Loyola offers honors and Advanced Placement courses; independent studies and courses at area colleges are options to qualified seniors. Activities include student government, athletics, intramurals, community service, student newspaper, yearbook, speech, math league, chorus, ensembles, dramatics, and student-organized clubs. Tuition: $24,000; General Fee: $650. Lillian Diaz-Imbelli is Director of Admissions; Jim Lyness is Headmaster; Rev. Stephen N. Katsouros, S.J., is President. *Middle States Association.*

Manlius Pebble Hill School 1869

Jamesville Road, Dewitt, NY 13214
Tel. 315-446-2452; Admission Ext. 131; Fax 315-446-2620
Web Site www.mph.net; E-mail mphinfo@mph.net

Manlius Pebble Hill School is a coeducational, college preparatory day school enrolling 592 students in Pre-Kindergarten–Grade 12. Five-day boarding and Thirteenth Year programs are available. The School offers a strong academic program in a supportive atmosphere. Students participate in sports and extracurricular activities such as soccer, basketball, track and field, chess, theater arts, orchestral ensembles, Model United Nations, and publications. There are extensive summer programs for students ages 4 to 18. Tuition: $11,980–$16,200. Financial Aid: $1,000,000. Lynne Allard is Director of Admission; Baxter Ball, Jr. (Kenyon College, B.A. 1970; Bowling Green State, M.A. 1972), was appointed Headmaster in 1990. *Middle States Association.*

The Mary Louis Academy 1936

176-21 Wexford Terrace, Jamaica Estates, NY 11432
Tel. 718-297-2120; Admissions Ext. 228; Fax 718-739-0037
Web Site tmla.org

This Catholic, college preparatory day school enrolling 1025 young women in Grades 9–12 aims to provide an environment of encouragement for spiritual, physical, emotional, and social growth. In addition to diploma/Regents requirements, sequences are offered in art, language, mathematics, music, and science. Religious studies and physical education are required. Honors and Advanced Placement courses, a full technology program, and state-of-the-art labs in chemistry, physics, and earth science are available. Activities include athletics, forensics, journalism, performing arts, and many cultural clubs. Tuition: $6300. Sr. Filippa Luciano is Admissions Director; Sr. Kathleen McKinney, CSJ (St. Joseph's, B.A.; Adelphi, M.S.; St. John's, Ed.D.), is Principal. *Middle States Association.*

Mary McDowell Center for Learning 1984

20 Bergen Street, Brooklyn, NY 11201
Tel. 718-625-3939; Fax 718-625-1456
Web Site www.marymcdowell.org; E-mail info@mmcl.net

The Mary McDowell Center for Learning, enrolling 192 students ages 5–14, is a Friends school for children with learning disabilities. It provides a supportive and nurturing learning environment that enables students to use their full intellectual, social, and emotional potential to become successful learners. Through a serious academic curriculum, which is experiential and language-based in presentation, each student's work is highly individualized to encourage strengths while addressing areas of need. The Center offers speech/language and occupational therapy as well as a comprehensive enrichment program. Tuition: $36,445–$37,860. Financial aid is available. Deborah Edel is Director of Admissions; Debbie Zlotowitz is Head of School.

Marymount School 1926

1026 Fifth Avenue, New York, NY 10028
Tel. 212-744-4486; Admissions Ext. 152; Fax 212-744-0716
Web Site www.marymount.k12.ny.us
E-mail admissions@marymount.k12.ny.us

Founded by the Religious of the Sacred Heart of Mary, Marymount School is an independent, college preparatory, Catholic day school enrolling 565 girls in Nursery–Class XII. Located in four turn-of-the-century mansions on Fifth Avenue, Marymount's proximity to the Metropolitan Museum of Art provides numerous opportunities for partnerships between the School and the Museum. Marymount is part of an international network, with RSHM schools in Los Angeles, Rome, Paris, London, Lisbon, Fatima, Oporto, and Medellin. Central to the mission of the School is the academic enterprise—the acquisition of knowledge and the development of lifelong skills of critical thinking and clear expression. Emphasizing classic disciplines and scientific inquiry, the curriculum includes 18 Advanced Placement courses, 12 team sports including field hockey, fencing, and soccer, and a variety of aesthetic and performing arts. Tuition: $18,250–$29,735. Financial Aid: $1,600,000. Lillian Issa is Director of Admissions; Concepcion Alvar (Maryknoll College [Philippines], B.A.; Columbia Teachers College, M.A.) is Headmistress.

The Masters School 1877

49 Clinton Avenue, Dobbs Ferry, NY 10522
Tel. 914-479-6400; Admission 914-479-6420; Fax 914-693-7295
Web Site www.themastersschool.com
E-mail admission@themastersschool.com

THE MASTERS SCHOOL in Dobbs Ferry, New York, is a coeducational, college preparatory school enrolling students in Grades 5 through 12. Boarding students are admitted from Grade 9. Dobbs Ferry (population 10,000) is a historic village 20 miles north of New York City, with easy access to Manhattan's wealth of educational, cultural, and recreational resources. Known familiarly as "Dobbs," the School is reached via Newark, Kennedy, LaGuardia, or Westchester County airports, the Metro North railroad, and interstate highways.

The Masters School celebrated its 130th anniversary in 2007. Miss Eliza Bailey Masters, daughter of a Presbyterian clergyman, founded her school in 1877 to provide young women with a curriculum that included the study of Latin, mathematics, and astronomy—subjects that were not customarily available to females of that era. From the start, The Masters School attracted students from across the nation and abroad who responded to its founder's challenge to assume responsibility for their own education, to think independently and logically, and to develop an awareness of themselves and others. In 1995, The Masters School became fully coeducational.

A nondenominational, nonprofit institution, the School is governed by a 27-member Board of Trustees. The Dobbs Alumnae/i Association, one of the oldest in the country, and the Parents Association support the School through recruiting, fundraising, and other activities. The Masters School is accredited by the Middle States Association of Colleges and Schools and holds membership in numerous educational organizations.

THE CAMPUS. Overlooking the Hudson River on 96 scenic acres, the campus features woodlands, expansive lawns, and dramatic architecture ranging from Victorian and Gothic styles to contemporary designs. The academic center of the School is Masters Hall (1921). The Pittsburgh Library holds 30,000 items including books, 60 periodicals, videos, audiotapes, CD-ROMs, and a computer center with Internet and library networks. Morris Hall, the new, state-of-the-art Science and Technology Building houses computer, chemistry, physics, biology, and general science laboratories as well as a Middle School lab. Strayer Hall furnishes orchestra and chorus rooms, practice rooms, classrooms, 15 grand pianos, and an heirloom harpsichord. Among other facilities are the 450-seat Claudia Boettcher Theatre (1972), the Art Center, a photo lab with two fully outfitted darkrooms and exhibition space, and a dance studio.

Boarding students live in five dorms, each supervised by faculty members and student proctors. Meals are served in the Dining Hall, which also houses the Student Center.

The Dobbs athletic program makes use of a full-size gym with a batting cage and volleyball, badminton, and basketball courts. The Fitness Center contains Nautilus, Free Weight, Stairmaster, Nordic Trac, and other workout equipment. Outdoor facilities include eight clay tennis courts, five playing fields, and cross-country trails.

THE FACULTY. Dr. Maureen Fonseca (Fordham University, Ph.D.) became Head of School in July 2000. Prior to assuming this position, she had been founding head of St. Philip's Academy in Newark, New Jersey, and had taught French and Spanish at both the high school and college levels in the United States and Guyana. Dr. Fonseca and her husband, a clergyman, have four children and reside on campus.

The 89 faculty and administrators hold undergraduate degrees or equivalent certification; more than 70 percent have earned advanced degrees, including seven doctorates. Among their colleges are Assumption, Bard, Brandeis, Brown, Bucknell, Catholic University, College of New Rochelle, College of William and Mary, Colorado College, Columbia, Dartmouth, Franklin and Marshall, Harvard, Haverford, Hunter College, Johns Hopkins, Kent State, Massachusetts Institute of Technology, Purdue, Queens College, Reed, Rutgers, St. Lawrence, Skidmore, Smith, Springfield, Trinity, Tufts, Wake Forest, Wheaton, Williams, and the Universities of California (Berkeley), Chicago, Connecticut, Havana, Maryland, Massachusetts, Michigan, North Carolina, Oregon, the Pacific, Paris, and Pennsylvania.

A registered nurse is on duty in the Health Center during the day, and the School physician is on call. In addition, many prominent hospitals are nearby.

STUDENT BODY. In 2007–08, The Masters School enrolled 562 students in Grades 5–12. Students come from throughout the United States and the world, representing a wide range of racial, ethnic, cultural, religious, and socioeconomic backgrounds.

ACADEMIC PROGRAM. Divided into semesters, the school year extends from early September to the beginning of June. Major courses meet three times a week, with minor courses meeting once or twice weekly. Class periods are either 55 or 110 minutes in length, allowing for more in-depth learning and reflective study. Each student is assigned a faculty advisor; faculty are also available for extra support throughout the day.

A typical school day begins with breakfast between 7:00 and 8:00 A.M. for boarding students. Three days a week, students attend an 8:00 A.M. All School Meeting before starting classes; each Thursday, students have breakfast with their faculty advisor in lieu of Morning Meeting. Classes are held five days a week from 8:25 A.M. to 3:00 P.M., including a lunch break. Supervised academic study halls are required for all freshmen and sophomores unless they are on the Highest Honor Roll; evening study for boarders is held in the dorms and in the library. From 3:30 to 5:00 P.M., students participate in sports and cocurricular activities.

The challenging college preparatory curriculum features more than 100 different courses in English, history, religion, Latin, French, Spanish, mathematics, computer technology, science, and the visual and performing arts. Honors and Advanced Placement opportunities are available in all disciplines. The School offers intermediate and advanced English as a Second Language for international students.

To graduate, Upper School students who attend Masters for four years must complete four years of English and physical education; three years of foreign language and math; three years of history; two years of science; one year each of world religions and arts; and one term each of speech, computer, and health.

Each year, a select group of Masters students joins students from around the United States to participate in CITYterm, a single-semester program of urban studies that utilizes the resources of New York City as both lab and classroom. The content incorporates math, foreign language, and other traditional academic courses designed to probe issues on the nature of urban life. This program is distinct from The Masters School; admission is highly competitive. Students also have many opportunities to take part in travel-study programs such as The Oxbow School, Rocky Mountain School, and cultural, faculty-led trips abroad during the March vacation.

College counseling, which begins in Grade 9, accelerates in the junior year. Through individual meetings with members of the college counseling office, students select the colleges to which they will apply and become familiar with the application process. Members of the Class of 2007 enrolled at numerous colleges and universities including Barnard, Brown, Bryn Mawr, Columbia, Cornell, Dartmouth, Duke, Johns Hopkins, New York University, Oberlin, Princeton, Wesleyan, and Yale.

STUDENT ACTIVITIES. Students are encouraged to become involved in at least one of the many cocurricular activities offered at The Masters School as a means of developing confidence, leadership skills, and social interaction. The Community Government and the officers of the Executive Committee include representatives from every grade level. Their function is to plan and implement projects and to serve as a liaison between students and the administration.

Participation in some activities, such as Glee Club, Dobbs 16, Dohters, Dance Company, and Urban Connection, is based on auditions; other groups are open to any interested students. Representative organizations include French Club, International Club, Gold Key (tour guides), Orchestra, Masters Interested in Sharing and Helping, Onyx (African-American students), Pamoja (social justice), and Phoenix (drama). Students also publish a yearbook, art and literary magazine, and newspaper.

Community service is central to the mission and values of The Masters School. Students volunteer at hospitals, nursing homes, child care, Special Olympics, and many other outreach activities.

On weekends, boarding and day students enjoy special outings and events planned by the Student Activities Committee. These may include movies, dances, laser tag, ice skating, and trips to New York for concerts, plays, and professional ball games.

The Masters School participates in the Fairchester Athletic League. Thirty-eight boys' and girls' teams compete on an interscholastic level in baseball, basketball, cross-country, fencing, field hockey, lacrosse, soccer, softball, tennis, and volleyball.

ADMISSION AND COSTS. The Masters School welcomes students from diverse backgrounds who demonstrate evidence of good character and ability. Applicants are requested to visit the campus for a tour and interview. Acceptance is based on the completed application, previous transcripts, personal and academic recommendations, and the results of standardized entrance examinations. The deadline for submission of all required materials for the first round of admission is January 5 for day students and February 5 for boarders.

Tuition in 2007–08 is $38,450 for boarding students, $28,000 for Upper School day students, and $27,050 for Middle School students. Need-based financial aid is awarded to 29 percent of the student body, and tuition payment plans are available.

Head of School: Dr. Maureen Fonseca
Head of Upper School: Mr. Chris Frost
Academic Dean: Mr. Chris Goulian
Dean of Students: Mrs. Priscilla Hindley
Associate Head of School for Enrollment & Strategic Planning: Mrs. Mary Schellhorn
College Counselor: Ms. Christine Scott
Business Manager: Mr. Lew Wyman
Director of Athletics: Mr. Ray Lacen

The Melrose School 1963

120 Federal Hill Road, Brewster, NY 10509
Tel. 845-279-2406; Admission Ext. 1; Fax 845-279-3878
Web Site www.melrose.edu; E-mail admissions@melrose.edu

The Melrose School, a day school serving 185 boys and girls in Preschool–Grade 8, offers a challenging academic program to intellectually motivated students. The School seeks to foster in students the courage to take risks, the conviction to strive for excellence, and the compassion to help each other achieve common goals. In a nurturing community in the Episcopal tradition, all faiths are welcome, and all individuals are respected. Active collaboration among student, family, and staff is key. In Grades 5–8, accelerated and honors classes are offered in foreign language, language arts, and mathematics. French is taught in all grades, Spanish is offered in Grades 5–8, and Latin begins in Grade 7. Melrose is accredited by the National Association of Episcopal Schools and the New York State Association of Independent Schools. Tuition: $6825–$15,800. Tom Burns is Director of Admission; William Porter (Yale College, B.A.; Teachers College, Columbia University, M.A.) is Headmaster. *Middle States Association.*

Millbrook School 1931

School Road, Millbrook, NY 12545
Tel. 845-677-8261, Ext. 138; Fax 845-677-1265
Web Site www.millbrook.org; E-mail admissions@millbrook.org

Located on 800 acres 90 miles north of New York City, Millbrook is a coeducational boarding and day school that offers its 250 students in Grades 9–12 a rigorous college preparatory program integrating academics, service, athletics, arts, and leadership. Since its founding in 1931, students have been encouraged to develop as strong and healthy individuals as well as concerned citizens of their world and its environment. All participate in an on-campus community service program. A traditional liberal arts curriculum features Honors and AP courses in the major disciplines, independent study opportunities, a culminating experience for seniors, and a variety of electives including Zoo Research, Astronomy, Constitutional Law, Anthropology, Digital Art Video, and Aesthetics. Facilities include Holbrook Arts Center, Mills Athletic Center, and the AZA-accredited Trevor Zoo. A $12,000,000 LEED-certified math and science center will open in 2008. Boarding Tuition: $39,250; Day Tuition: $28,525. Financial Aid: $1,740,000. Cynthia S. McWilliams is Director of Admission; Drew Casertano is Headmaster. *Middle States Association.*

New York Military Academy 1889

78 Academy Avenue, Cornwall-on-Hudson, NY 12520
Tel. 845-534-3710; [Toll-free] 888-ASK-NYMA; Fax 845-534-7699
Web Site www.nyma.org; E-mail admissions@nyma.org

New York Military Academy is set on a 165-acre campus in the Hudson Valley, 60 miles north of New York City. Designated an "Honor Unit with Distinction" by the Department of the Army, the Academy is a coeducational college preparatory school for 200 students in Grade 7–Postgraduate. The Corps of Cadets participates in competitive academic and athletic programs and the Junior Reserve Officer Training Corps, which develops character and leadership. The Academy offers a structured environment, tutorial assistance, SAT Prep, computer, ESL, band, and an equestrian program. Boarding Tuition: $30,800; Day Tuition: $13,800. Financial aid is available. Maureen Kelly is Director of Admissions; Capt. Robert D. Watts, USN (Ret.), is Superintendent. *Middle States Association.*

Nichols School 1892

1250 Amherst Street, Buffalo, NY 14216
Tel. 716-875-8212; Admissions 716-332-6325; Fax 716-875-2169
Web Site www.nicholsschool.org; E-mail lyusick@nicholsschool.org

Nichols, a coeducational, college preparatory day school, enrolls 590 students. In a nurturing environment, the Middle School (Grades 5–8) provides a stimulating atmosphere and challenging curriculum vital for academic growth, personal development, and readiness for high school. In the Upper School (Grades 9–12), small classes, a rigorous curriculum, and extensive extracurriculars prepare students for higher education. The fine and performing arts, interscholastic athletics, and community service enhance the traditional, technology-integrated curriculum. A summer academic session is available. Tuition: $15,500–$16,800. Financial Aid: $1,400,000. Laura Lombardo Yusick '96 is Director of Admissions; Richard C. Bryan, Jr. (Trinity, A.B.; University of North Carolina, M.A.), is Headmaster.

The Nightingale-Bamford School 1921

20 East 92nd Street, New York, NY 10128
Tel. 212-289-5020; Admissions 212-933-6515; Fax 212-876-1045
Web Site www.nightingale.org; E-mail info@nightingale.org

Nightingale-Bamford, a day school serving 560 girls in Kindergarten through Class XII, provides rigorous college preparation in a community that prizes intellectual development and self-esteem. Commitment to diversity and substantial financial aid ensure a multicultural student body. A state-of-the-art Schoolhouse features advanced computer facilities. The classical curriculum, which focuses on the major disciplines and values the arts and athletics, is updated annually to meet the needs of its students. Advanced Placement in 11 disciplines, cocurricular activities, foreign study and travel, social service, publications, and clubs supplement the program. Tuition/Fees: $30,000–$30,900. Margaret Metz is Director of Admissions; Dorothy A. Hutcheson is the Head of School.

Oakwood Friends School 1796

22 Spackenkill Road, Poughkeepsie, NY 12603
Tel. 845-462-4200; Admissions [Toll-free] 800-843-3341
Fax 845-462-4251
Web Site www.oakwoodfriends.org
E-mail admissions@oakwoodfriends.org

OAKWOOD FRIENDS SCHOOL in Poughkeepsie, New York, is a coeducational college preparatory school enrolling day students in Grades 6–8 and both day and boarding students in Grades 9–12. It is located in a suburban setting 4 miles south of Poughkeepsie on Route 9, near Vassar College and historic Hudson River sites. The School is 75 miles from New York City, 80 miles from Albany, and 220 miles from Boston.

Founded in 1796 by the New York Yearly Meeting of the Religious Society of Friends, Oakwood Friends is an educational community committed to Quakers' deep respect for the worth of each person. It seeks students who demonstrate a genuine concern for their own growth—academic, spiritual, social, and physical—and who are intent on becoming complete persons—competent, creative, responsible, and sensitive to the world and its needs for a just and moral social order.

Oakwood Friends is a nonprofit corporation managed for the New York Yearly Meeting by a Board of Managers. The School holds membership in the Friends Council on Education and the National Association of Independent Schools. It is chartered by the Regents of the University of the State of New York and accredited by the New York State Association of Independent Schools.

THE CAMPUS. The 60-acre campus includes six tennis courts, three soccer fields, two baseball diamonds, and wooded areas.

Collins Library houses 11,000 volumes, microform materials, a computer laboratory, and classrooms. The Main Building, Crowley, Collins Library, and Stokes house classrooms, a ceramics studio, the meeting room, the art room, and offices. Lane Auditorium is used for theatrical performances, dance and music classes, and public events; Connor Gymnasium contains basketball courts, lockers, bathrooms with showers, and a weight room. Other facilities include the Dining Hall and a darkroom. The Turner Math and Science Building contains state-of-the-art laboratories.

Both dorms—Craig Hall and Reagan Hall—contain faculty apartments and recreation, laundry, and kitchen facilities. Craig Hall also houses the fully equipped photography darkroom.

THE FACULTY. Peter F. Baily, appointed Head of School in July 2000, is a graduate of Earlham College, Nasson College (B.A., M.E.), and Bryn Mawr College (M.A.). Prior to his last position as Interim Head of School of the Quaker School at Horsham, Mr. Baily served seven years as Head of School at Oak Lane Day School in Blue Bell, Pennsylvania.

There are 26 full-time teachers and 10 administrators. Of these, most live at the School. They hold 36 baccalaureate and 17 advanced degrees from such colleges and universities as Adelphi, American, Brandeis, Brooklyn College, Brown, Bryn Mawr, Bucknell, Central Michigan, Colgate, College of New Rochelle, College of William and Mary, Columbia, Cornell, Drew, Earlham, Fashion Institute of Technology, Georgetown, Hunter College, Manhattan School of Music, Manhattanville, Marist, Nasson, New York University, Ohio Wesleyan, Rutgers, St. John's, St. Lawrence, St. Michael's, Scarritt, Siena, Smith, State University of New York, Syracuse, Tufts, Universidad de Chile, Vassar, Wesleyan, and the Universities of Colorado, Colorado School of Medicine, Delaware, Denver, and Tennessee. There are 10 part-time instructors.

The infirmary is staffed by a Director of Health Services/School Nurse, and a doctor is on call.

STUDENT BODY. Oakwood Friends enrolls 173 students in Grades 6–12. The enrollment includes 59 day boys, 43 day girls, 42 boarding boys, and 29 boarding girls as follows: 5 in Grade 6, 9 in Grade 7, 12 in Grade 8, 39 in Grade 9, 39 in Grade 10, 40 in Grade 11, and 29 in Grade 12. Eighty-five percent come from New York State; five other states and four countries are also represented.

ACADEMIC PROGRAM. The school year includes Thanksgiving, Christmas, midwinter, and spring vacations and consists of trimesters of 11 weeks each. Grades are posted and reported to parents at midterm and at the end of each trimester, and written course evaluations are sent at the end of each term.

The daily schedule for all Oakwood Friends students from 8:00 A.M. to 3:30 P.M. includes classes, study, lunch, and work assignments. Between 3:30 P.M. and dinner, students participate in interscholastic, intramural, and lifetime sports. From 7:30 to 9:30 P.M., boarders study in their dormitories. Students whose performance is consistently responsible are exempt from evening study hall. As a Quaker school, Oakwood Friends does not rank students or grant academic honors.

Graduation requirements include four years of English and history; three of science; three of math; three of a foreign language; one and one-third in the arts; and one trimester each of health, Quakerism, and computer literacy. Satisfactory participation in sports/physical education and the work programs is required every trimester, as well as the completion of the senior program.

The curriculum in Grades 6–11 emphasizes mastery of important fundamental skills in writing, both creative and analytical; reading comprehension; and applied and theoretical mathematics and science. Emphasis is placed on the ability to analyze as well as understand information and to recognize the interrelationships of disciplines.

In addition, the School offers electives such as studio art, ceramics, photography, drama, drama tech, chorus, instrumental ensemble, voice, music theory, music appreciation, music history, musical production, current events, world history, philosophy, and computer. Students whose learning differences are documented receive support for at least one period every other day in the Academic Support Center, where they are given two-to-one and small group assistance with homework assignments; basic skills in reading, writing, and math; organizing study time; and academic counseling.

In Grade 12, the Senior/Core Program helps students succeed in the college admissions process. Throughout the year, a "core group" provides time for mutual reflection and discussion to help students integrate their varied experiences in the program. In addition to the required interdisciplinary course focusing on the social sciences, Advanced Placement courses are offered in English, biology, calculus, and foreign languages.

International students must meet a minimum proficiency in English to be admitted. Students may be required to take additional ESL classes to improve their proficiency in English.

Ninety-eight to 100 percent of Oakwood graduates continue on to colleges and universities. Graduates in the Class of 2007 are attending such institutions as Alfred, American, Bard, Boston University, Champlain College, Clark, Corcoran College of Art and Design, Cornell, Earlham, Franklin and Marshall, Guilford, Keuka, Laboratory Institute of Merchandising, Lasell, Lycoming, McDaniel, Mitchell, Moravian, Pennsylvania State, Purdue, Rensselaer Polytechnic Institute, Rochester Institute of Technology, Siena, State University of New York (Albany, Binghamton, Buffalo, Delhi), Syracuse, Wells, Wentworth Institute of Technology, Widener, and the Universities of Chicago, Hartford, and Vermont.

STUDENT ACTIVITIES. All students and faculty attend weekly community meetings, which are chaired by an elected student clerk, and Meetings for Worship. Much of daily school life is overseen by faculty-student standing committees chosen by the community. These include the judicial, academic, activities, student life, Friends concerns, and nominating committees. Each upper school student has a work assignment. Assignments include dining hall chores, housekeeping, library work, recycling effort, and clerical duties.

The physical education program offers interscholastic and life sports. Interscholastic teams are fielded in boys' and girls' soccer, tennis, and cross-country; coeducational Ultimate Frisbee and swimming; boys' baseball; and girls' softball and volleyball. Life sports include table tennis, running, martial arts, fitness club, aerobics, and yoga. Other activities include a literary magazine, yearbook, drama, choral and instrumental groups, and committees on Friends' concerns.

Weekend activities include faculty open houses, films, dances, sightseeing, trips to Vassar and other colleges for special events, visits to local museums, field trips to New York City, informal cooking, hiking, skiing, and snowboarding. Parents Weekend in the fall and Alumni Day in the spring are traditional events.

ADMISSION AND COSTS. Oakwood Friends welcomes applicants of all racial and religious backgrounds who are genuinely interested in participating in the life of the School and in taking responsibility for their growth and learning. Applicants must submit school records and personal references and arrange a campus interview. Secondary School Admission Test scores are recommended but not required.

Application should be made as early as possible and will be considered as long as spaces are available. New students are admitted in Grades 6–11 and occasionally in Grade 12.

In 2007–08, tuition, room, and board is $34,991 for seven days and $30,397 for five days; day tuition is $17,430 in Grades 6–8 and $20,186 in Grades 9–12. Tuition includes an infirmary fee, accident insurance, and normal art and laboratory fees. Additional expenses—estimated at $900—include books, spending money, school trips, and transportation. Focused Instruction is an additional $730 per term. The yearly surcharges for the Learning Skills Program and the International Student Program are $5171 and $1811, respectively. In 2006–07, $600,000 in financial aid was awarded to 38 percent of the student body. Aid is awarded on the basis of need; students who wish to be considered should apply through the School and Student Service for Financial Aid.

Upper School Head: Anna Bertucci
Middle School Head: Nancy Doolittle
Director of Admissions: Susan Masciale-Lynch
Upper School Dean: Jeremy Robbins
Coordinators, Academic Support Center: Pat Meade & Karen Butt
Athletic Director: Charles Butts
Director of Alumni & Development: Elaine Miles
Business Manager: Natalia Armoza
Dean of Residential Life: David Whiting

The Packer Collegiate Institute 1845

170 Joralemon Street, Brooklyn Heights, NY 11201
Tel. 718-875-6644, Admissions 718-250-0266; Fax 718-875-1363
Web Site www.packer.edu
E-mail viason@packer.edu/jcaldwell@packer.edu

Founded in 1845, Packer Collegiate is a coeducational, college preparatory day school enrolling approximately 960 students in

Preschool–Grade 12. A dedicated and capable faculty offers a rich and challenging curriculum that supports students' learning and nurtures their social and emotional growth. The academic program is enriched by an array of AP courses as well as a breadth of offerings in the fine and performing arts, world languages, and athletics. Extracurricular activities provide many opportunities for independent study, travel abroad, leadership, and community service. The School's historic commitment to diversity is reflected in its student body and its ongoing support for broad and inclusive programming. Packer's collection of landmark buildings benefited from extensive renovations in 2003, which created a dramatically expanded, dynamic campus. A school-wide wireless environment and meaningful curricular integrations of technology complement a comprehensive dual-platform laptop program in Grades 5–12. Tuition: $17,260–$25,350. Financial Aid: $3,000,000. Valorie Iason (Pre & Lower School) and Jason Caldwell (Middle & Upper) are Directors of Admission; Dr. Bruce Dennis is Head of School. *Middle States Association.*

The Park School of Buffalo 1912

4625 Harlem Road, Snyder, NY 14226
Tel. 716-839-1242; Admissions Ext. 107; Fax 716-839-2014
Web Site www.theparkschool.org
E-mail abilloni@theparkschool.org

The Park School of Buffalo is a college preparatory country day school enrolling approximately 250 boys and girls in PreK–Grade 12. It offers a comprehensive and challenging curriculum to give students the academic foundation necessary for success and to develop their sense of responsibility and commitment. There is an extended-day program and a six-week summer day camp, which utilizes the 15 buildings on the 32-acre suburban campus. Tuition: $5040–$16,750. Financial aid is available. Anthony G. Billoni is Director of Admissions; Donald H. Grace (Harvard College, B.A., M.A.T.; Fairfield University, C.A.S.) was appointed Headmaster in 2004.

Poly Prep Country Day School 1854

Upper/Middle School: 9216 Seventh Avenue, Brooklyn, NY 11228
Tel. 718-836-9800; Fax 718-238-3393
Web Site www.polyprep.org
Lower School: 50 Prospect Park West, Brooklyn, NY 11215
Tel. 718-768-1103; Fax 718-768-7890

Poly Prep Country Day, enrolling 983 students in Nursery–Grade 12 on two campuses, offers a rigorous, humanistic academic program that meets the needs of the whole child at every stage of development. The Lower School, located in historic Park Slope, seeks to balance intellectual development with important social and emotional growth. The Middle and Upper Schools, on a 25-acre campus, emphasize rigorous college preparation including Advanced Placement in 15 subjects, independent study, and extracurriculars such as athletics, performing and fine arts, and interest clubs. Tuition: $7925–$27,550. Financial Aid: $4,270,000. Lori W. Redell is Assistant Head of School for Admissions and Financial Aid; David B. Harman (Harvard, B.A., M.Ed.; Reed, M.A.T.) is Headmaster. *Middle States Association.*

Poughkeepsie Day School 1934

260 Boardman Road, Poughkeepsie, NY 12603
Tel. 845-462-7600; Fax 845-462-7602
Web Site www.poughkeepsieday.org
E-mail jlundquist@poughkeepsieday.org

Founded in 1934 by members of Vassar College child study department and parents from the surrounding community, Poughkeepsie Day enrolls 330 students in Pre-Kindergarten to Grade 12. The School features a challenging and creative academic curriculum that recognizes the strengths and talents of each child. Small multi-graded classes and dedicated teachers encourage students to love learning and to become independent, critical thinkers. Seniors must complete a four-week, off-campus internship program as well as four years of every academic subject. Community service is required; sports and varied cocurricular activities are offered. All graduates are admitted to college each year. Tuition: $14,560–$19,450. Financial aid is available. Jill Lundquist, M.S.W., is Director of Admissions; Josie Holford (University of Wales, B.A.; New York University, ABD, Ph.D.) is Head of School.

Rippowam Cisqua School 1917

Box 488, Bedford, NY 10506
Cisqua Campus (JPK–4): 325 West Patent Road, Mount Kisco, NY 10549
Tel. 914-244-1200; Admission 914-244-1204
Fax 914-244-1234
Web Site www.rcsny.org
E-mail betsy_carter@rcsny.org
Rippowam Campus (5–9): 439 Cantitoe Road, Bedford, NY 10506
Tel. 914-244-1250; Admission 914-244-1248
Fax 914-244-1245
E-mail ashley_harrington@rcsny.org

This coeducational day school enrolls 545 students in Junior Pre-Kindergarten–Grade 9. The Rippowam Cisqua faculty encourages students to believe in themselves, become independent thinkers, and explore their talents to the fullest. The dynamic program of academics, arts, and athletics features hands-on learning at all levels. In an atmosphere that promotes intellectual curiosity and a love of learning, the School strives to instill a strong connection to community and the larger world. Honesty, consideration, and respect for others are taught in classrooms, on playing fields, and through community service. Tuition: $18,000–$28,250. Financial Aid: $1,152,000. Betsy Carter (Cisqua) and Ashley Harrington (Rippowam) are Directors of Admission; Eileen F. Lambert is Head of School.

Riverdale Country School 1907

5250 Fieldston Road, Riverdale, NY 10471-2999
Tel. 718-549-8810; Admissions 718-519-2715
Fax 718-519-2793
Web Site www.riverdale.edu

Riverdale Country School in Riverdale, New York, is an independent, college preparatory day school enrolling students in Pre-Kindergarten through Grade 12. It is located on two spacious, wooded campuses one mile apart in the northwestern corner of New York City known as Riverdale. The country setting within a short distance of the vast cultural and educational resources of one of the world's great cities provides a wide range of learning and enrichment experiences that extend beyond the boundaries of the physical plant.

The present-day institution traces its origins to The Riverdale School for Boys, which was established in 1907 by Frank Sutliff Hackett. Mr. Hackett shared a deep commitment to "scholarly, intimate teaching; rigorous, uncompromising academic standards; abundant play in the open; and a care for the best influences." In 1920, the Neighborhood Elementary School was founded, followed in 1933 by the Riverdale Girls School. In 1972, the three schools combined to form a single educational community shaped by these same goals and ideals. Riverdale Country School aims to cultivate the unique talents of its students and to nurture their intellectual, creative, physical, moral, emotional, and social development.

A nonprofit, nondenominational institution, Riverdale Country School is governed by a 30-member Board of Trustees. It is chartered by the New York State Board of Regents and accredited by the New York State Association of Independent Schools. The Parents Association and the Alumni Association assist Riverdale through various activities. Riverdale Country School is a member of the National Association of Independent Schools, among other professional affiliations.

THE CAMPUS. Riverdale Country School is the largest independent school campus in New York City with a total of 27.5 acres. The 19.5-acre Middle and Upper School Hill Campus for Grades 6–12 is located between the Henry Hudson Parkway and Van Cortlandt Park at the junction of Fieldston Road and West 253rd Street. Hill Campus buildings include the William C.W. Mow Hall, with administrative offices, classrooms, and the John R. Johnson Student Center; Frank S. Hackett Hall, containing the Roger Brett Boocock Library and the Dale E. Mayo Computer Laboratory and classrooms; the Weinstein Science Center, which houses the Lisman Laboratories, each equipped for a specific scientific discipline, as well as the Jan Falk Carpenter '71 Science Technology Center; the 9/10 Building, providing classrooms and a computer laboratory; the Linda M. Lindenbaum Center for the Arts; the Jeslo Harris Theater; and Vinik Hall, which houses the Offices of Admission and Institutional Advancement. The Marc A. Zambetti '80 Athletic Center contains a state-of-the-art fitness center, an athletic training room, a basketball/volleyball court, and an Olympic-size swimming pool; other athletic facilities include three playing fields and tennis courts.

The 8-acre River Campus for Pre-Kindergarten–Grade 5, bordered by the Hudson River and Independence Avenue, is adjacent to the Wave Hill public garden, which is often used as a resource for the School. The Lower School comprises four separate buildings. The Junior Building houses the Admission Office, dining room, computer laboratory, and several music rooms. The Perkins Building holds classrooms for Grades 4–5 and Pre-Kindergarten, the library, and the Hahn Theater. The Senior Building contains art studios, band and chorus rooms, a foreign language laboratory, and Support Services specialists. The K–3 Building provides classrooms and the gymnasium, with a stage used for theatrical productions. Classes use the campus itself as part of the learning process, and children can explore the beautiful wetlands and participate in ecology and gardening projects.

THE FACULTY. Dominic A. A. Randolph assumed his duties as Riverdale's sixth Headmaster in 2007. Mr. Randolph holds A.B. and Ed.M. degrees from Harvard. He had previously been Assistant Head Master at The Lawrenceville School in Lawrenceville, New Jersey, and, prior to that appointment, Dean of Studies at Lawrenceville. He has also taught English literature and language and managed academic departments at several international schools, most recently at The American School of The Hague, a K–12 school in the Netherlands.

Riverdale's faculty is comprised of 185 teachers and administrators, of whom 115 hold advanced degrees, including 20 doctorates and 120 master's degrees. The average class size in the Upper School is 16, and the student-teacher ratio is less than 8:1.

STUDENT BODY. In 2007–08, Riverdale Country School enrolled 540 boys and 520 girls in Pre-Kindergarten–Grade 12. Students reside in the immediate Riverdale area as well as Manhattan, the Bronx, Queens, Westchester, and New Jersey. Approximately 20 percent of the students are of color.

ACADEMIC PROGRAM. The curriculum in the early childhood program is designed to develop basic academic concepts and social skills. Field trips, creative play, and hands-on activities in a warm, nurturing environment help the youngest students gain an early enthusiasm for learning. Math and reading readiness skills, nature study, and introduction to computers are integrated into the program, which also includes health and physical education, music, art, and library activities.

In Grades 1–5, a strong, sequential approach to skill development in reading and math is balanced with literature, writing, and math problem solving. Students are trained in textual analysis, revising and editing their writing, and research skills. All Lower School students engage in a major research project. Students are introduced to French and Spanish in Grades 3–4, after which they choose one for continued study. A Support Services team comprised of a learning specialist, a reading and mathematics specialist, and a psychologist works with teachers, students, and parents to pilot each child's progress in the Lower School. The ethics and values program (C.A.R.E.) is integral to the curriculum and the community.

The Middle School is housed in Frank S. Hackett Hall, but students use arts, science, athletic, and dining facilities in common with upper schoolers, and the schedules of the two divisions permit teachers to teach classes in both. The Grade 6 program retains some organizational features of the Lower School, but departmentalization is the rule in Grades 7 and 8. Latin and Japanese join Spanish and French as language options. The arts program strives for engagement with a full range of arts experiences for every student. Several options for after-school athletics exist for Grades 7 and 8, with intramural opportunities for Grade 6. There are special programs in information literacy, study skills, community service, and health as well as a range of activities and clubs suitable for early adolescents.

To earn a high school diploma, students in Grades 9–12 must complete 4 credits in English; 3 credits in a single foreign language or 2 credits in each of two languages; 3 in history; $2^1/_2$ to $3^1/_2$ in mathematics; 2 in science; and $1^1/_2$ in the arts. Seniors must also earn 1 credit in Integrated Liberal Studies, which features social philosophy, literature, history of science, and arts components. Each grade has a Dean of Students who coordinates academic programs and serves as a liaison between parents and school. Students in Grades 6–12 must complete from 10 to 18 hours of community service yearly, depending on age.

The Upper School features numerous elective courses for juniors and seniors, including honors courses in language and mathematics and Advanced Placement courses in all disciplines. Other electives include Masterpieces of Western Literature, Shakespeare, Law, Statistics, Molecular Biology, Psychology, and Urban Studies. Opportunities exist for semester or yearlong study abroad.

The 111 graduates in the Class of 2007 entered four-year colleges and universities. Six each matriculated at Columbia and the University of Pennsylvania; 5 each enrolled at Boston University and Bowdoin; 4 each are attending Brown, Cornell, George Washington University, and Yale; and 3 are at Johns Hopkins.

STUDENT ACTIVITIES. Middle and Upper School students elect representatives to the Student-Faculty Councils, which help establish principles and procedures for student life and serve as a conduit of student opinion. In the Lower School, Student Council members are elected by their peers beginning in Grade 3. Each year, the Lower School Student Council supervises a charity outreach program entitled "Children Helping Children." Field trips enrich the program at all levels. Overnight excursions ranging from one night to one week are offered in Grades 6–12.

Upper School activities include Amnesty International, Environmental Club, Model Congress, Mock Trial, the literary magazine, the school newspaper, and the yearbook. Students regularly stage plays and musicals and perform in orchestra, jazz band, chamber ensembles, several a cappella groups, and chorus. Interscholastic and intramural teams are fielded in baseball, basketball, fencing, field hockey, football, golf, gymnastics, lacrosse, soccer, softball, swimming, tennis, cross-country, volleyball, and wrestling.

ADMISSION AND COSTS. Riverdale Country School welcomes students of strong academic ability and good character. Admission is based on the applicant's academic record, teacher recommendations, an entrance examination, a writing sample, and a personal interview. The greatest number of students enter in Kindergarten, Grade 6, and Grade 9, but candidates are admitted through Grade 11 if vacancies exist.

Tuition for 2007–08 ranges from $27,600 in Pre-Kindergarten to $33,100 in Grades 6–12. The School awards financial aid grants to approximately 20 percent of the student body based on need. Tuition payment plans are available.

Director of Studies: Michael Michelson
Head of Upper School: Kent J. Kildahl
Head of Middle School: Milton J. Sipp
Head of Lower School: Sandy S. Shaller
Director of Middle & Upper School Admission: Jenna C. Rogers
Director of Lower School Admission: Sarah M. Lafferty
Director of Institutional Advancement: Duncan L. Marshall
Director of College Office: Kristi H. Marshall
Director of Finance & Operations: Kathleen A. Schoonmaker

Robert Louis Stevenson School 1908

24 West 74th Street, New York, NY 10023
Tel. 212-787-6400; Fax 212-873-1872
Web Site www.stevenson-school.org
E-mail info@stevenson-school.org

Enrolling 75 boys and girls in Grade 8–Postgraduate, Robert Louis Stevenson School seeks to prepare bright, underachieving adolescents academically and personally for college. Small but challenging classes are offered in a warm, caring milieu that includes personal therapeutic assistance and any required remedial help. The academic program focuses on the mastery of solid language and study skills and the achievement of realistic goals. Classes and advising groups average fewer than ten students. An academic summer session is offered. Tuition: $39,000. Financial Aid: $75,000. B.H. Henrichsen is Headmaster.

Rockland Country Day School 1959

34 Kings Highway, Congers, NY 10920
Tel. 845-268-6802; Admissions Ext. 201; Fax 845-268-4644
Web Site www.rocklandcds.org; E-mail lgreenwell@rocklandcds.org

The principal aim of Rockland Country Day is to provide an academic curriculum and intellectual environment suitable for 180 students in PreKindergarten (age 4)–Grade 12 who are preparing for advanced education in the arts and sciences. The humanistically oriented faculty embodies a compassionate, concerned view of life. Recognizing and rewarding students for intellectual, artistic, and moral effort and achievement, the faculty encourages them to reach beyond themselves, even at a certain risk, to engage in mutually beneficial relationships with the larger community, to reexamine values, and to shun complacency in a responsible, meaningful, and mentally disciplined context. Tuition: $11,500–$26,450. Lorraine Greenwell is Admissions Coordinator; Dr. E. Lee Hancock is Interim Head of School.

Rudolf Steiner School 1928

Lower School: 15 East 79th Street, New York, NY 10021
Tel. 212-535-2130; Admissions 212-327-1457; Fax 212-744-4497
Upper School: 15 East 78th Street, New York, NY 10021
Tel. 212-879-1101
Web Site www.steiner.edu
E-mail lowerschooladmissions@steiner.edu
E-mail upperschooladmissions@steiner.edu

Enrolling 360 day students in Nursery–Grade 12, Rudolf Steiner School believes that "education is an art." In each elementary school subject, presentations aim to speak to the students' experience, providing vivid images and allowing them to take part in what they hear. German, Spanish, music, and handwork begin in Grade 1 and are enriched by a sports program. In addition to strong college preparation, the high school offers exchange programs in Europe and provides opportunities in art, music, practical skills, community service, and sports. The School is one of 900 Waldorf or Steiner schools worldwide. Tuition: $18,800–$27,800. Scholarships: $1,600,000. Irene Mantel is Admissions Director.

Rye Country Day School 1869

Boston Post Road at Cedar Street, Rye, NY 10580
Tel. 914-967-1417; Admissions 914-925-4513; Fax 914-921-2147
Web Site www.ryecountryday.org
E-mail rcds_admin@rcds.ryecountryday.org

RYE COUNTRY DAY SCHOOL in Rye, New York, is a coeducational day school enrolling students in Pre-Kindergarten–Grade 12. Rye (population 18,000), a Westchester County suburb of New York City, is 45 minutes from the city by train and is easily accessible by car and public transportation from Westchester and Rockland Counties and Fairfield County in Connecticut.

The School was founded in 1869 as the Rye Female Seminary by parents who wanted to provide better educational opportunities for their daughters. The 1921 merger with Rye Country School, an all-boys' institution, led to the formation of Rye Country Day School, which enrolled girls in Kindergarten–Grade 12 and boys through Grade 8 only. In 1964, the School became entirely coeducational.

Rye Country Day School seeks to provide a superior education that "should encompass cultural, athletic, and communal experiences that stress the responsibility of each individual for the life and spirit of the whole community, resulting in a graduate able to face the world with confidence, to compete effectively, and to contribute meaningfully to society."

Rye Country Day School is directed by a 27-member Board of Trustees, including parents and alumni. The Parents' Auxiliary contributes to school life through volunteer service and fund-raising activities, and the Alumni Association represents the 3500 active graduates. Rye Country Day School is accredited by both the Middle States Association of Colleges and Schools and the New York Association of Independent Schools. It holds membership in the National Association of Independent Schools, among other affiliations.

THE CAMPUS. The 26-acre campus includes four artificial turf athletic fields and two play areas. Indoor athletic facilities include the Gerald N. La Grange Field House, which contains an ice rink, four tennis courts, and the Scott A. Nelson Athletic Center providing a two-court gymnasium, four squash courts, four locker rooms, and a fitness center.

Pre-Kindergarten is conducted in a classroom addition to the Administration Building. The Main Building houses classrooms for Kindergarten–Grade 8, two computer labs, four new science laboratories, three art studios, a Lower School library, a Lower School dining room, and the nurse's office. A major addition for Kindergarten–Grade 6 and a 200-seat dining room for Middle and Upper Schoolers opened in 2002. The Pinkham Building contains classrooms for Grades 9–12, offices, five science laboratories, studios for art and photography, and a college counseling center. A library for Grades 5–12 connects the Main and Pinkham Buildings. A 400-seat Performing Arts Center includes a woodworking shop and music practice rooms. Other facilities are the Administration Building, five faculty houses, and the Headmaster's residence. The School-owned plant is valued at $46,000,000.

THE FACULTY. Scott A. Nelson, appointed Headmaster in 1993, is a graduate of Brown University (A.B. 1977) and Fordham University (M.S. 1989).

The full-time faculty, including administrators who teach, number 108. In addition to baccalaureate degrees, they hold 96 master's and 11 doctoral degrees, 2 or more of which were earned at Bank Street, Bowdoin, Brown, City College of the City University of New York, College of New Rochelle, College of the Holy Cross, Columbia, Dartmouth, Fordham, Harvard, Haverford, Iona, Ithaca, Johns Hopkins, Lebanon Valley, Manhattanville, Miami (Ohio), Middlebury, New York University, Northwestern, Rollins, Saint John's, Smith, State University of New York, Syracuse, Wesleyan, Yale, and the Universities of Connecticut and Wisconsin. There is a full-time school nurse and a certified athletic trainer.

STUDENT BODY. In 2007–08, the School enrolled 439 boys and 432 girls as follows: 199 in the Lower School (Pre-Kindergarten–Grade 4), 284 in the Middle School (Grades 5–8), and 388 in the Upper School (Grades 9–12). Students come principally from Westchester County, New York City, and Connecticut's Fairfield County.

ACADEMIC PROGRAM. The school year, from early September to early June, includes Thanksgiving and midwinter recesses, winter and spring vacations, and national and religious holidays. The calendar is divided into semesters for the Lower, Middle, and Upper Schools. Upper School classes, with an average enrollment of 15, generally meet five times in a six-day rotation from 8:05 A.M. to 2:50 P.M. Pre-Kindergarten is dismissed at noon; Kindergarten–Grade 4 meet from 8:15 A.M. to 3:05 P.M.; Middle School classes meet from 8:05 A.M. to 3:20 P.M.

Supervised study halls are held throughout the day in the Upper School. Teachers are available to provide extra help at all grade levels. In the Middle School, progress reports are issued after the first six weeks of school; grades are recorded at midsemester and semester end. Interim reports are sent home whenever necessary. In Kindergarten–Grade 4, parent-teacher conferences are scheduled in the fall and winter, and a written narrative report is provided in June. In the Middle and Upper Schools, letter grades are issued twice each semester, with teacher comments accompanying the grades. Progress reports are issued for new Upper School students after the first six weeks of school. Each Middle and Upper School student has a faculty adviser. All students in Grades 7–12 have their own laptop computers.

The Lower School program fosters the acquisition of basic skills while teaching children how to think logically and creatively and manipulate symbols effectively. The program for Pre-Kindergarten emphasizes reading and mathematics readiness, communication skills, and science and social studies projects. The program in Kindergarten–Grade 4 is based in self-contained classrooms and focuses on reading, writing, mathematics, and social studies. Science, Spanish or French, music, studio art, physical education, and library skills instruction are integral to the Lower School program. There are computers in all classrooms, and a computer lab is available to Lower School students. Developing effective communication skills and appropriate social behavior are important components of the Lower School experience.

Classes in the Middle School are departmentalized. Latin is introduced in Grade 5. In Grade 6, students elect to study Latin, French, Spanish, or Mandarin Chinese. The equivalent of the first year of high school language study is completed by the end of Grade 8. Honors sections are available in mathematics and Grade 8 science. In Grades 7 and 8, art, vocal and instrumental music, ceramics, woodworking, drama, photography, digital photography, and computer are offered as electives. All Middle School students have daily physical education classes. Middle School deans provide a regularly scheduled guidance program for Grades 5–8.

To graduate, students in Grades 9–12 must complete four years of English, three years of a foreign language, two years of history (including United States history), three years of mathematics, two years of lab science, and two semester-length elective units or one full-year elective course. Art, music, and health are required in Grade 9 or 10, and physical education is required each year. An interdisciplinary lecture and seminar course for seniors is required.

Full-year Upper School courses include English 1–4; French 1–6, Greek 1–2, Latin 1–6, Spanish 1–5, Mandarin Chinese 1–2; World Civilization 1–2, United States History, Government, Modern European History, Humanism and the West: An Urban Perspective (an interdisciplinary course for seniors); Algebra 1–2, Advanced Algebra and Mathematical Analysis, Geometry, Calculus, Multi-Variable Calculus, Computer Programming 1–2; Biology, Chemistry, Physics; Studio Art 1–3, History of Art, Photography; and Music History, Choir, and Wind Ensemble. Among the partial-credit and semester electives are Philosophy, Forensics, Oceanography, Psychology, Art Survey, Concert Choir, Wind Ensemble, Jazz Ensemble, and Music Theory. The Drama Department offers elective courses in History of Theater, Film and Filmmaking, Acting Workshop, and Oral Interpretation and Public Speaking.

There are honors classes in all disciplines as well as 20 Advanced Placement courses. Independent study can be arranged in any academic area. Qualified juniors and seniors may receive credit for courses at local colleges. During the two-week June Term, students in Grade 12 participate in a service project.

In 2007, 91 members of the graduating class entered four-year colleges; 39 students were admitted "early." Over the past three years, 2 or more graduates have enrolled at Babson, Barnard, Boston College, Boston University, Brown, Bucknell, Colgate, College of the Holy Cross, Columbia, Connecticut College, Cornell, Dartmouth, Denison, Duke, Elon, Emory, Franklin and Marshall, Georgetown, George Washington, Hamilton, Harvard, Johns Hopkins, Manhattanville, McGill, Middlebury, New York University, Northwestern, Pomona, Princeton, Stanford, State University of New York (Purchase), Syracuse, Trinity, Tufts, Vanderbilt, Villanova, Wesleyan, Yale, and the Universities of Michigan, Pennsylvania, Vermont, and Wisconsin.

The School conducts a six-week review and enrichment summer session and offers tutorial work.

STUDENT ACTIVITIES. The Middle School Student Council, composed of elected representatives from Grades 5 through 8, provides a forum for discussions of school issues and is responsible for implementing social activities. In the Upper School, elected student-faculty Academic Affairs, Activities, Guidance, and School Life committees meet regularly and make recommendations to the administration.

Upper School students publish a yearbook (*Echo*), a newspaper (*Rye Crop*), a current-events magazine (*FORUM*), a literary magazine (*Omega*), a sports magazine (*Topcat*). Other extracurricular activities include the African-American Culture, Astronomy, Debate, Drama, Classics, Model United Nations, Community Action Organization, International, Chess, Peer Leaders, Modern Languages, Mock Trial, Spirit, Stock Market, Entrepreneurs', and Ecology Clubs. The Upper School's musical organizations participate in county and state festivals. An active Upper School community service program involves more than 100 students as volunteers in area community agencies. The Middle School has its own community service activities as well as a chorus and wind ensemble; beginning in Grade 4, private instrumental lessons are available for all students.

Rye Country Day athletic teams compete with other independent schools in the Fairchester League. Interscholastic competition begins in Grade 7 with boys' teams organized in basketball, football, ice hockey, soccer, baseball, lacrosse, tennis, and wrestling; girls compete in basketball, field hockey, softball, soccer, lacrosse, and tennis. There are boys' varsity and junior varsity teams in baseball, basketball, football, golf, hockey, lacrosse, soccer, squash, tennis, and wrestling; varsity and junior varsity girls' teams are organized in basketball, field hockey, golf, ice hockey, lacrosse, softball, soccer, and squash. There are also coeducational teams in cross-country, sailing, and fencing. Physical education classes for Upper School students not on interscholastic teams focus on fitness, lifetime sports, and dance.

Field trips complement the academic program at all grade levels; younger children visit area attractions such as the Rye Nature Center and The Bronx Zoo. Dances are scheduled for both the Middle and Upper schools. Traditional annual events include the fall "wilderness" camping trip for Grade 8, the Cape Cod trip in Grade 6, sports banquets, Wildcat Weekend and Fall Fair, music festivals, and the invitational Model United Nations/Congress.

ADMISSION AND COSTS. New students are admitted to all grades, although rarely to Grade 12, on the basis of previous academic records, the results of standardized tests, and a personal interview. Application should be made in the fall or winter prior to September entrance. There is a $50 application fee.

In 2007–08, tuition ranges from $17,000 in Pre-Kindergarten to $27,500 in Grades 11–12. Extras range from $320 in Kindergarten to $1000 in the Upper School. Tuition insurance is available. In the current year, the School awarded more than $2,900,000 in financial aid to 113 students. Rye Country Day subscribes to the School and Student Service for Financial Aid.

Associate Head of School: Corinne Grandolfo
Assistant Heads of School: Alexis Wright & Barbara Shea
Director of Admission: Matthew Suzuki
Director of Finance: Robert Brody
Development & Alumni Relations: Virginia B. Rowen
College Counselors: Rosita Fernandez-Rojo & Jeffrey Bates
Director of Athletics: Frank Antonelli

Saint Ann's School 1965

129 Pierrepont Street, Brooklyn Heights, NY 11201
Tel. 718-522-1660; Fax 718-522-2599
Web Site www.saintannsny.org

Saint Ann's School is an independent, college preparatory day school enrolling 534 boys and 549 girls in Preschool–Grade 12. It seeks to create an urban alternative to traditional education with teachers and students using novel approaches to learning. Classes are grouped by ability and each student's schedule is individualized. A broad curriculum accommodates special subjects through the use of tutorials. Sports, publications, performing arts, and field trips are some of the activities. Tuition: $17,850–$25,500. Financial aid is available. Diana Lomask is Director of Admission; Larry Weiss (Columbia College, A.B. 1971; Columbia University, M.A. 1974, Ph.D. 1981) was appointed Head of School in 2004.

St. Bernard's School 1904

4 East 98th Street, New York, NY 10029
Tel. 212-289-2878; Fax 212-410-6628
Web Site www.stbernards.org

St. Bernard's School is a day school enrolling 379 boys in Kindergarten–Grade 9. It presents a curriculum to which it refers as "traditional but not hide-bound," emphasizing language, mathematics, and foundations for science and computer science. Instruction in music, art, and carpentry is offered. A literary magazine is published, and a Shakespearean play is presented annually. The School also makes ample use of the cultural resources of the city. Interscholastic and intramural sports are organized. All-inclusive Tuition: $29,960. Financial aid is available. Heidi Gore and Anne Nordeman are Co-Directors of Admissions; Stuart H. Johnson III (Yale, B.A.) was appointed Headmaster in 1985.

Saint David's School 1951

12 East 89th Street, New York, NY 10128
Tel. 212-369-0058; Admission Ext. 401; Fax 212-369-5788
Web Site www.saintdavids.org; E-mail admissions@saintdavids.org

Saint David's is a day school with an enrollment of 390 boys in Pre-Kindergarten–Grade 8. The School seeks to engender intellectual curiosity, spiritual and moral development, appreciation for the arts, and skill and sportsmanship in athletics. A rigorous classical curriculum is offered within a nurturing environment. Art, music, and drama are an integral part of the program. Founded by a group of Catholic families, Saint David's now includes boys of all religious and ethnic backgrounds. The Saint David's Sports Center is located a short distance from the School. Tuition: $19,755–$29,635. Financial Aid: $670,000. Julie B. Sykes is Admission Director; P. David O'Halloran, Ph.D., was appointed Headmaster in 2004.

Saint Francis Preparatory School 1858

6100 Francis Lewis Boulevard, Fresh Meadows, NY 11365
Tel. 718-423-8810; Admissions Ext. 229; Fax 718-423-1097
Web Site www.sfponline.org; E-mail admissions@sfponline.org

Founded by the Franciscan Brothers, this coeducational, Catholic school has been named by the U.S. Department of Education as a School of Excellence. More than 2700 students are enrolled in Grades 9–12. Although located in an urban setting, the campus borders on parkland, providing ample athletic fields. To develop critical, responsible seekers of truth, the School provides a comprehensive, Christian education within a nurturing environment. Advanced Placement, Honors, and Regents courses, combined with music, art, 35,000 circulating and noncirculating books, and computers with full-text databases containing peer review or scholarly journals, complement the religious foundation. Tuition: $6000. Theodore Jahn is Dean of Men and Assistant Principal for Admissions; Br. Leonard Conway, OSF (Pratt Institute, M.S.), is Principal. *Middle States Association.*

Saint Gregory's School 1962

121 Old Niskayuna Road, Loudonville, NY 12211
Tel. 518-785-6621; Fax 518-782-1364
Web Site www.saintgregorysschool.org
E-mail marrao@saintgregorysschool.org

Saint Gregory's School was founded by parents to prepare their children for the challenges of competitive boarding schools and to instill in them the values and principles of the Roman Catholic faith. Enrolling 180 students, the School is coeducational in Nursery–Kindergarten and boys only in Grades 1–8. In addition to traditional academic subjects, computer science, Latin, and French or Spanish are required. Music, drama, physical education, and interscholastic athletics are strong components of the program. Recreational camps are conducted in the summer. Tuition: \$4400–\$11,600. Financial Aid: \$150,000. Francis X. Foley, Jr. (John Carroll, A.B.; Fairfield University, M.A.), is Headmaster.

St. Hilda's & St. Hugh's School 1950

619 West 114th Street, New York, NY 10025
Tel. 212-932-1980; Fax 212-531-0102
Web Site www.sthildas.org

St. Hilda's & St. Hugh's is a coeducational, Episcopal day school enrolling 380 students in Toddlers–Grade 8. The School reflects New York City's richly diverse community and values the Judeo-Christian heritage. A strong liberal arts curriculum promotes the developmental competencies of each child and readies students for leading secondary schools in New York City and nationwide. Studio Art is introduced in Junior Kindergarten; French, Spanish, or Mandarin Chinese in Nursery; technology in Grade 2; woodworking, drama, and English brass band in Grade 4; Shakespeare in Grade 6; and Latin in Grade 7. Extended Day Program for Nursery–Grade 8 is offered until 6:30 P.M. Tuition: \$7000–\$28,750. Kate Symonds is Director of Admission; Virginia Connor (Wheelock, B.S.; Columbia Teachers College, M.A.) is Head of School.

St. Luke's School 1945

487 Hudson Street, New York, NY 10014
Tel. 212-924-5960; Fax 212-924-1352
Web Site www.stlukeschool.org

St. Luke's is an Episcopal day school enrolling 200 boys and girls of all faiths in Junior Kindergarten–Grade 8. The structured, balanced curriculum promotes academic excellence and critical thinking built upon the solid basis of fundamental skills. Small by design, the School creates a climate of trust and understanding, communicating values and building community. The program includes science, computer, music, art, modern language, physical and outdoor education, and sports. Chapel, world religion, and service learning are included. Its enclosed campus has spacious outdoor facilities. An After-School program is offered. Tuition & Fees: \$23,735–\$26,100. Financial Aid: \$575,000. Carole Everett is Director of Admissions and Financial Aid; Bart Baldwin (University of Georgia, B.A.; College of William and Mary, M.A.) is Head of School.

Saint Thomas Choir School 1919

202 West 58th Street, New York, NY 10019-1406
Tel. 212-247-3311; Fax 212-247-3393
Web Site www.choirschool.org; E-mail admissions@choirschool.org

Saint Thomas Choir School, located in midtown Manhattan, is the only church-affiliated, boarding choir school in the United States. Its mission is to "house, educate, and nurture its boy choristers through superior musical, academic, and Christian foundations that benefit Church and School and enable its students to embrace life with hope, skill, and confidence." The Choir School enrolls 40 boys in Grade 3 through 8 who are taught by a dedicated faculty who understand their roles as educators and mentors in the classroom and beyond. The traditional academic curriculum includes course work in English, math, Latin, French, social studies, science, theology, and music theory. Students are members of the acclaimed boys choir that sings at five services a week and performs a concert series. The Choir has performed at the Vatican, Lincoln Center, and Carnegie Hall and has sung at festivals across the United Kingdom and Europe. Boarding Tuition: \$10,760. Financial aid is available. Ruth Cobb is Director of Admissions; the Reverend Charles F. Wallace is Headmaster.

Soundview Preparatory School 1989

272 North Bedford Road, Mount Kisco, NY 10549
Tel. 914-242-9693; Fax 914-242-9658
Web Site soundviewprep.org

Enrolling 75 day students in Grade 6–Postgraduate, Soundview provides a rigorous academic program while promoting self-esteem by enabling students to develop their unique talents. Small, ability-grouped classes allow dialogue and participation by all students. The School aims to establish ethical values, formulate and meet individual goals, and encourage students to be their own advocates. Students enjoy close relationships with teachers and respond to a structured, yet relaxed environment. Core college preparatory courses are enriched by an extensive fine arts program, debate, publications, soccer, and basketball. A summer program is available. Tuition: \$27,000–\$28,000. Financial Aid: \$240,000. Mary Ivanyi is Dean of Admissions; W. Glyn Hearn is Headmaster.

Staten Island Academy 1884

715 Todt Hill Road, Staten Island, NY 10304
Tel. 718-987-8100; Fax 718-979-7641
Web Site www.statenislandacademy.org
E-mail LShuffman@statenislandacademy.org

STATEN ISLAND ACADEMY on Staten Island, New York, is a college preparatory day school enrolling boys and girls in Pre-Kindergarten through Grade 12. It is the oldest private school and the only independent school in the borough.

The Academy finds its origins in the Methfessel Institute, a boys' school founded in 1862. Two years later, the name changed to Staten Island Latin School, and it became, in 1884, a nonsectarian, coeducational, college preparatory school. After a series of expansions, mergers, and separate locations, the Academy consolidated its divisions and its campus on the Todt Hill Road location in 1963.

Staten Island Academy is committed to educating the whole child while fostering intellectual, creative, social, and physical development. Students are encouraged to participate actively in an educational community that promotes ethical leadership, self-reliance, and critical thinking. The Academy strives to provide a supportive educational environment that cultivates student achievement as well as intellectual and personal growth.

The Academy is governed by an 18-member Board of Trustees, several of whom are graduates of the school and many of whom are parents of current Academy students. The Alumni Association promotes and maintains relationships between alumni and the school. The Parents' League supports the Academy with a variety of volunteer activities. Accredited by the Middle States Association of Colleges and Secondary Schools and the New York State Association of Independent Schools, Staten Island Academy is chartered and registered by the Board of Regents, University of the State of New York.

THE CAMPUS. The 12-acre campus is located in the bucolic neighborhood of Todt Hill near the highest point on the East Coast south of Maine. Of the school's seven buildings, the heart of the campus is the recently renovated Stanley Library, which has more than 16,000 volumes of print and nonprint materials and subscriptions to more than 50 magazines, newspapers, and on-line databases. It has an automated circulation and cataloguing system and 12 computers with Internet access. Other facilities include the Science and Technology Center with computer labs, science labs, and classrooms; a commons area with dining hall; an auditorium; music and art rooms; and a fitness center completed in 2003, a gymnasium, three tennis courts, two in-ground pools, ball fields, and playgrounds.

THE FACULTY. Diane J. Hulse became Head of School in July 2002. A graduate of Beloit College, Mrs. Hulse received her master's degree from New York University. Mrs. Hulse has been involved with New York City area independent schools for more than 25 years and is the author of *Brad and Corey: A Study of Middle School Boys*.

Of the 59 members of the faculty and staff, 42 hold advanced degrees. Their representative colleges include Amherst, Barnard, Baruch College, Boston College, Boston University, Brooklyn College, Columbia University, Cornell, Haverford, Hunter, Kenyon, Muhlenberg, New York University, People's University of China, Pratt, Rutgers, St. John's University, the Sorbonne, Stevens Institute of Technology, Swarthmore, Wesleyan University, and the Universities of California, Massachusetts (Amherst), Miami, Notre Dame, and Pennsylvania.

STUDENT BODY. Staten Island Academy enrolls approximately 400 students in its Lower, Middle, and Upper Schools. While most live on the Island, a number of students commute from Brooklyn, Manhattan, and New Jersey and reflect the ethnic and cultural diversity of Greater New York City.

ACADEMIC PROGRAM. The academic year begins in early September and ends in early June, with Thanksgiving, winter, and spring vacations. The school day begins at 8:10 A.M. and ends at 3:20 P.M. To accommodate family schedules, the Academy has extended hours from 7:00 A.M. to 7:00 P.M., which are included in the tuition for Pre-K through Grade 8.

In a nurturing and developmentally appropriate environment, children in the Lower School (Pre-Kindergarten through Grade 4) focus on basic and advanced skills in reading, writing, social studies, science, and mathematics taught by a cooperative team of teachers. Art, music, library, computer lab, and physical education complement the academic program.

In Middle School (Grades 5–8), students receive instruction from specialized teachers in all subject areas. The core curriculum emphasizes the language arts, mathematics, social studies, science, computer skills, and physical education. Writing workshops span the grade levels, and students in Grade 8 take algebra. Students are introduced to Latin in Grade 5 and may begin French or Spanish in Grade 6. They may study both Latin and a modern foreign language. Fine arts and elective offerings range from public speaking and book club to chorus and journalism.

The Upper School encompasses Grades 9–12 with an average class size of 17 students. To graduate, students are required to take four years of English; three years each of mathematics, science, and social science; three years of one modern foreign language; four years of physical education; and computer science, foundation of art, music history, and an additional music or art credit.

Among the courses offered are English 9 and 10, American Literature, Trial Theme in Literature, Journey Theme in Literature, Political Ideas in Literature, Fantasy & Realism in Literature, Junior/Senior Writing Seminar; French I–V, Latin I–III, Spanish I–V; Western Civilization, United States History, New York: History of a City, The American Presidency, Global Debate, The Empire that was Rome, U.S./World Events in the 20th Century, Western Art History, Contemporary Religious Convictions; Algebra I, Algebra II with Trigonometry, Geometry, Precalculus, Probability & Statistics; Biology, Chemistry, Physics, Healthful Living, Chemistry of Life, Psychology, Dimensions of Human Relations; Computer Skills, Web Page Design, Visual Basic Programming; Robotics, Music History, Foundations of Art, Orchestra, Concert Choir, Drawing/Painting, Photography, Advanced Photography, Color & Design, Introduction to Dance, Introduction to Theater, and Stagecraft. Nine Honors courses as well as Advanced Placement courses in Biology, Calculus (AB and BC), Chemistry, Computer Science, English, French, Latin, Modern European History, Psychology, Spanish, and U.S. History are available for qualified students. The Power Track program, which begins in Grade 8, is designed to accommodate the needs of superior students considering pursuing math or science in college. All students in Grade 12 must participate in the Senior Internship program involving two weeks of community service with such organizations as the Red Cross, Project Hospitality, Head Start, and the Staten Island Institute of Arts and Sciences.

The college guidance program begins in the ninth grade when students are assigned an advisor who will assist them with academic, personal, and social matters. In junior year, students are paired with college counselors in an 8:1 ratio as they work to meet the challenges of the college application process. The Classes of 2004–07 have matriculated at such colleges and universities as American University, Amherst, Boston College, Boston University, Brandeis, Brown, Columbia, Connecticut College, Dartmouth College, Cornell, Drew, Harvard, Haverford, Johns Hopkins, Lafayette College, McGill, Muhlenberg, Oberlin, Parsons School of Design, Princeton University, Skidmore College, Vassar, Villanova, Wagner College, Wellesley, Yale, and the University of Chicago.

All grades take part in The Character Education Program, which helps students develop self-reliance, initiative, responsibility, and courage through on-going discussions of ethical issues and the performance of community service projects.

A summer day camp program, from one to ten weeks, is available.

STUDENT ACTIVITIES. Many opportunities exist for students to broaden their horizons and enrich their lives. Lower School students publish a newspaper, *The Inkspot*. They may also enroll in the Afterschool Adventures Club, which provides arts and crafts, minisports clinics, music lessons, theater and dance workshops, and karate. Students in Grades 1–4 may participate in intramural sports.

Middle School students publish their own newspaper, *The Tiger*. They also take part in community service, student government, interscholastic athletics, plays, choral groups, orchestra, and the Junior National Honor Society. The Middle School has a continuing telecommunications project via the Internet with a school in Japan.

The Upper School Student Advisory Council sponsors dances and various activities and is involved in numerous school-wide initiatives. Other extracurricular activities include choral groups, orchestra, theatrical productions, community service, The Gay-Straight Alliance, Model United Nations, National Honor Society, and the Art, Asian, Environment, Film, and Spanish Clubs. Boys' and girls' varsity teams are sponsored in soccer, tennis, volleyball, and basketball. Girls also play softball and lacrosse; there are coeducational teams in golf, cross-country, fencing, and cheerleading.

Traditional events include the Welcome Back Barbecue, Auction, Poetry Recital, Grandparents and Special Friends Day, Book Fair, Academy Day, Founders Day, and Commencement.

ADMISSION AND COSTS. The Academy admits students who will benefit from the school's rigorous academic program. The application process includes an entrance examination, school visit, and interview.

In 2007–08, tuition ranges from $14,600 for half-day Pre-Kindergarten through Grade 5 to $23,700 for Grades 6 through 12. Extended Day, field trips, and most books are included. Approximately 20 percent of the student body receives financial aid totaling more than $1,000,000 annually.

Head of Lower School: Patricia Lynch
Head of Middle School: Eileen Corigliano
Head of Upper School: Donald Knies
Academic Dean: Frank Crane
Director of College Guidance: Michael Acquilano
Director of Operations: Taube Import
Director of External Affairs: Maureen McShane
Director of Admissions: Linda Shuffman
Director of Development: Michael Barret Jones
Director of Finance: Angela Artale
Director of Athletics: Darlene Crowe

The Storm King School 1867

314 Mountain Road, Cornwall-on-Hudson, NY 12520-1899
Tel. 845-534-7892; Admissions [Toll-free] 800-225-9144
Fax 845-534-4128
Web Site www.sks.org; E-mail admissions@sks.org

The Storm King School, founded in 1867, is an independent, coeducational school enrolling 80 boarders and 55 day students in Grades 7–12. Individual attention is offered to a multicultural student body by caring teachers. A traditional curriculum, enhanced by cocurricular programs with an emphasis on moral development, prepares students for higher education. The Learning Center offers additional academic support. The Mountain Center is for students with college potential and established learning disabilities. The curriculum includes five Advanced Placement courses, American Sign Language, and electives in the arts. Among the activities are National Honor Society, The Cum Laude Society, community service, drama, music, visual arts, and sports. Boarding Tuition: $34,700–$41,200; Day Tuition: $19,850–$26,000. Financial Aid: $330,000. Dr. Stephen T. Lifrak is Director of Admissions; Helen Stevens Chinitz is Head of School. *Middle States Association.*

The Town School 1913

540 East 76th Street, New York, NY 10021
Tel. 212-288-4383; Admissions 212-288-6397; Fax 212-988-5846
Web Site www.thetownschool.org; E-mail nsahadi@townschool.org

The Town School is a coeducational, nonsectarian school enrolling 390 day students in three divisions encompassing Nursery–Grade 8. In keeping with Hazel Hyde's founding philosophy, it encourages the joy of learning in an academic environment with creative expression through the arts and physical education. Child-centered teaching and a low faculty-to-student ratio, combined with innovative technology and community service, develop the whole child physically, emotionally, intellectually, and morally. The Town School offers extended care daily, an after-school program, and SummerSault, a summer camp. Tuition: $13,500–$29,200. Financial aid is available. Natasha Sahadi is Director of Admissions; Christopher Marblo is Head of School.

Trevor Day School 1930

Grades 6–12: 1 West 88th Street, New York, NY 10024
Tel. 212-426-3360; Admissions 212-426-3380
Fax 212-873-8520
Web Site www.trevor.org
Nursery–Grade 5: 11 East 89th Street, New York, NY 10128
Tel. 212-426-3355; Fax 212-410-6507

Founded as a nursery school called The Day School, the institution expanded its program through Grade 8 in 1960 and added a high school division in 1991. The School assumed its present name in 1997. Enrolling 786 boys and girls, Trevor maintains a low student-teacher ratio, allowing instructors to conduct courses seminar style. The program emphasizes critical thinking, time management, collaborative work, and student-centered learning. Ample opportunities in the arts and other areas include dance, drama, choral and instrumental ensembles, filmmaking, photography, student government, publications, and a full athletic program. Each student fulfills an 80-hour community service requirement in high school, and seniors may elect to undertake an independent project. An after-school program for younger children is available, and an outdoor education program serves Grades 2–12. All students in Grades 5–12 utilize laptop computers. Nursery–Grade 5 is housed in joint facilities at 11 East 89th Street and 4 East 90th Street, while Grades 6–12 are housed in a single facility at 1 East 88th Street. Tuition: $20,100–$30,700. Financial Aid: $2,750,000. Pamela J. Clarke is Head of School.

Tuxedo Park School 1900

Mountain Farm Road, Tuxedo Park, NY 10987
Tel. 845-351-4737; Fax 845-351-4219
Web Site www.tuxedoparkschool.com
E-mail kheard@tuxedoparkschool.com

Tuxedo Park School enrolls 224 day boys and girls in Pre-Kindergarten–Grade 9. The School is committed to nurturing and developing the natural joy of learning inherent in each child. Concern for traditional and modern skills is demonstrated by the inclusion of such courses as French, Spanish, Latin, and computer throughout the School. Art, music, and sports are an integral part of the curriculum at all levels. Interscholastic sports are offered in Grades 7–9. Tuition: $14,800–$24,000. Financial aid is available. Kristen J. Heard is Director of Admissions and Financial Aid; James T. Burger (Hamilton College, B.A.; Case Western Reserve, J.D.) was appointed Head of School in 1994.

United Nations International School 1947

24-50 FDR Drive, New York, NY 10010
Tel. 212-684-7400; Admissions 212-584-3071
Fax 212-685-5023
Web Site www.unis.org; E-mail admissions@unis.org
173-55 Croydon Road, Jamaica Estates, NY 11432

This international day school was founded by parents committed to the educational principles outlined in the UN Charter. Today, United Nations International School enrolls 1500 boys and girls from over 120 countries in Kindergarten–Grade 12 on two campuses. An equally diverse faculty teaches an international curriculum with a global perspective, leading to the International Baccalaureate. The Junior School emphasizes reading, writing, speaking, listening, foreign languages, experiments and observation, computers, and the arts. The Middle School, a period of growth, fosters self-discovery, peer-group identification, and intellectual adventure. Upper School students acquire appreciation of the diversity of persons and cultures while mastering key skills in English, art, computing, mathematics, music, science, humanities, and physical education. Eight languages and ESL are available. The School was the first in the U.S. to offer the IB, preparing graduates for higher education worldwide. Outreach, publications, outdoor education, field trips, theater, school government, sports, and academic, honor, and interest clubs are among the activities. Tuition: $20,000–$22,500. Amelia Rattew is Director of Admissions; Dr. Kenneth J. Wrye is Director.

The Ursuline School 1897

1354 North Avenue, New Rochelle, NY 10804
Tel. 914-636-3950; Fax 914-636-3949
Web Site www.ursuline.pvt.k12.ny.us
E-mail admin@ursuline.pvt.k12.ny.us

The Ursuline School in New Rochelle, New York, is a private, Catholic, college preparatory school for young women in Grades 6 through 12. The School is located at the north end of New Rochelle in lower Westchester County, affording easy access to the many educational and cultural resources of both Westchester and New York City.

Central to the philosophy of The Ursuline School is a concern for the student as an individual and a commitment to the education of the whole person—intellectually, emotionally, socially, and spiritually. As a young woman prepares to assume leadership in the 21st century, she needs both challenge and support to realize her potential. Ursuline recognizes these needs and, believing in the benefits of single-gender education, places its young women firmly at the center of its philosophy and its programs. The School is committed to providing an intellectually stimulating, student-centered environment in which academic and personal achievements are demanded.

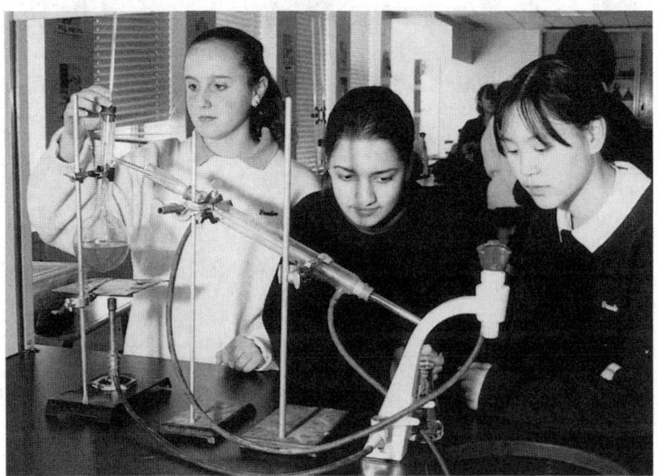

Ursuline also emphasizes the value of the total school community, fostering relationships among students and their families, faculty, and administration. Parent organizations, an alumnae association, and family and alumnae events are key elements in establishing the family atmosphere of the School.

Founded in 1897 by the Sisters of the Order of St. Ursula, the School is governed by a Board of Trustees comprised of Ursuline sisters and lay women and men. Designated a National Blue Ribbon School of Excellence three times by the United States Department of Education, Ursuline is accredited by the New York State Board of Regents and the Middle States Association of Colleges and Schools. It holds membership in the New York State Association of Independent Schools, the National Coalition of Girls' Schools, the National Catholic Educational Association, and other professional organizations.

THE CAMPUS. The 13-acre campus includes two academic buildings, a gymnasium, and a performing and fine arts center. The School's library houses more than 14,000 books, 60 periodicals, and numerous CD-ROMs and other electronic resources. The library, which has earned the designation of "Electronic Doorway Library" by the State Department of Education, is linked via a multipublic access system to public and college libraries in Westchester County. There are five state-of-the-art science laboratories for the study of biology, chemistry, and physics. Technological resources include a computer center and networked computers throughout the School as well as a schoolwide wireless network that students access using their laptops. The arts center houses a 300-seat theater, orchestra and chorus practice rooms, a dance studio, four art rooms, a darkroom, and classroom space. A small chapel provides a place for prayer, meditation, and small group liturgies.

Athletic facilities include a full-size gymnasium, a playing field, and four tennis courts. Ursuline also uses additional fields, tracks, and a swimming pool in the area.

THE FACULTY. Sr. Jean Baptiste Nicholson, OSU (Catholic University, M.A.), who became Principal in 1974 and President in 2005, led the School through its growth over the past 30 years. Eileen Davidson (Iona College, M.S.) became Principal in 2005. Three assistant principals and 80 faculty members, 90 percent of whom have master's or doctoral degrees, ensure a low student-faculty ratio and individual attention for students. A Catholic chaplain is a member of the staff. A registered nurse is on campus during the school day.

STUDENT BODY. In 2007–08, Ursuline enrolled 800 students in Grades 6–12. Ursuline students come from throughout Westchester County and the Bronx as well as from Manhattan and Connecticut. They represent a broad diversity of racial, ethnic, religious, and socioeconomic backgrounds. While a Catholic school, Ursuline welcomes students of all religions, and about 20 percent of students are non-Catholic.

ACADEMIC PROGRAM. Ursuline students are required to complete 24 credits for graduation, including four years of English, social studies, and religion; three years of science, mathematics, and foreign language; a year of Latin or art/music; and computer applications and health. Physical education is also required. More than 90 percent of students take four or more years of science, math, and foreign language. The traditional college preparatory program includes four modern foreign languages (French, Spanish, Chinese, and Italian), five years of Latin, a year of classical Greek, a broad range of fine arts courses, computer courses, and a variety of electives. Honors courses are available in all disciplines, and Advanced Placement courses are offered in art, French, Spanish, Italian, Latin, English, calculus, biology, physics, European and U.S. history, and U.S. government. The School also offers an Authentic Science Research program through which, in addition to their regular science courses, students engage in three years of directed independent research working with a mentor in a professional setting. Seventh- and eighth-grade students at Ursuline have the opportunity to earn high school credit in foreign language, mathematics, and science.

Technology is well integrated into the curriculum. In addition to the computers networked throughout the School, Ursuline implemented a "learning with laptops" program in 1997. Every student has her own laptop computer that she uses in class and homework activities for writing, accessing, analyzing and graphing data, and creating multimedia presentations. Interactive SMART Boards, a school-wide wireless network, an electronic learning community web site, Internet access, and e-mail ensure full integration of technology into the curriculum.

Ursuline's Reading and Language Development Program assists students who are challenged by learning differences but who are otherwise able to do college preparatory work. These students are enrolled in the regular college preparatory courses and attend additional sessions with a specialist to learn the compensatory strategies they need.

The Social Action Program provides a community service course available to juniors and seniors and a variety of volunteer experiences for the entire student body, including staffing meals at a local soup kitchen, tutoring and teaching religious education in parishes, and working in nursing homes and hospitals. "Make a Difference Day" and "Project Nicaragua" afford other opportunities for volunteer work.

Ursuline students broaden their experience through a school-sponsored European trip and networking opportunities with other Ursuline schools in the United States and abroad.

Recognizing the pressures and challenges that confront today's young women, Ursuline has in place extensive guidance and counseling services. Every student has a faculty advisor who meets with her regularly, helps her plan her schedule, and reviews her academic progress.

College guidance begins in the sophomore year and includes classes and individual meetings as well as programs and individual meetings with parents. One hundred percent of Ursuline students continue their education in college. Last year's graduates won over $5,500,000 in academic scholarships and were accepted at more than 150 colleges and universities, including Boston College, Carnegie Mellon, College of William and Mary, Columbia, Cornell, Dartmouth, Fordham, Georgetown, Harvard, Iona, Marist, New York University, Providence College, State University of New York, Syracuse, Yale, and the Universities of Michigan, Pennsylvania, and Scranton.

In addition to academic guidance, a staff of four provides individual counseling, organizes groups based on student need and interest, and arranges programs for parents. A Personal Development Education Program in Grades 6–9 helps students address issues such as self-esteem, relationships with peers and parents, conflict resolution, and physical, emotional, and social development. Juniors and seniors are trained as Peer Leaders and Peer Mediators to assist with the Personal Development Program and with mediation at any level.

As a Catholic school, Ursuline emphasizes the spiritual development of its students. In addition to religion classes, a retreat program at all grade levels gives students the opportunity to reflect on their relationship with God and with others. Juniors and seniors trained as Peer Ministers help direct these retreats. School liturgies are celebrated periodically throughout the year for the entire school community, and Masses and prayer services are held regularly in the chapel.

STUDENT ACTIVITIES. A broad range of activities, open to students of every grade level, provides opportunities for leadership and service. Student Council and clubs in language and culture, publications, forensics, chorus, band, drama, computer, math, and science are representative of the diverse organizations.

Ursuline belongs to the New York State Public High School Athletic Association and fields 32 interscholastic teams in swimming, tennis, field hockey, volleyball, cross-country, cheerleading, basketball, softball, soccer, golf, lacrosse, crew, and indoor and outdoor track. Competition is available at the varsity, junior varsity, freshman, modified, and sixth-grade levels.

Traditions are another important aspect of Ursuline life, bringing together students, parents, faculty and, often, alumnae. Among the most important events are Ring Day, the Father-Daughter Dance, the Mother-Daughter Communion Breakfast, the Fair, 8th Grade Moving Up Ceremony, Senior Mass, and Graduation.

ADMISSION AND COSTS. Ursuline welcomes students of above-average ability who choose the School for its philosophy, its programs, and its atmosphere. Ursuline does not discriminate on the basis of race, color, national or ethnic origin, or religion. Admission is based on the student's performance on standardized entrance examinations and her previous academic record. For admission to Grades 6–8 and for transfer students, a personal interview is required. Applicants for all grade levels are encouraged to attend Ursuline's Open House and to visit for a day.

Tuition in 2007–08 is $12,350. Academic scholarships are awarded to top-scoring applicants for Grade 9, and need-based student aid is available in Grades 9–12 only.

Assistant Principals: Deirdre Gaughan, Denise Moore & Sr. Joanne Safian, RSHM
Director of Advancement: Moira Prunty
Director of Guidance: Mary Scarella
Director of Counseling: Doretha Buster
Business Manager: Sr. Joan Woodcome, OSU
Athletic Director: Maureen Kern

Village Community School 1970

272-278 West Tenth Street, New York, NY 10014
Tel. 212-691-5146; Admissions Exts. 221 & 250; Fax 212-691-9767
Web Site vcsnyc.org; E-mail jtrano@vcs-nyc.org

Located in historic Greenwich Village, Village Community School serves 335 boys and girls in Kindergarten–Grade 8. The School offers a stimulating, challenging curriculum within a supportive environment that recognizes the developmental needs of the whole child. Students consistently gain admission to a variety of competitive high schools. The plant includes spacious, sunny classrooms, a large outdoor play yard, a free-standing woodshop, two science centers, a sky-lit library, and a computer lab. A five-story building that houses eight classrooms, a gymnasium, an auditorium, and a rooftop play area was added in 2003. A state-of-the-art kitchen was completed in 2007 to support the School's lunch program. Tuition: $26,000–$27,000. Judy Calixto is Director of Admissions; Eve Kleger (Wellesley, B.A.; Columbia, M.A.) is Director.

The Windsor School 1968

41–60 Kissena Boulevard, Flushing, NY 11355
Tel. 718-359-8300; Fax 718-359-1876
Web Site www.windsorschool.com
E-mail admin@thewindsorschool.com

The Windsor School is a coeducational, college preparatory day school enrolling approximately 100 boys and 100 girls in Grades 6–12. It is dedicated to providing individual guidance and a sense of identity for middle-range and gifted students. A coordinated program, including English as a Second Language, is arranged for international students. Students are programmed individually so that they can enroll in honors or accelerated programs in those subjects in which they excel. Extracurricular activities and teams and a summer school are available. Tuition (including books): $14,900–$16,900. Philip A. Stewart, Ph.D., is Director of Admissions; James L. Seery is Principal. *Middle States Association.*

Windward School 1926

Grades 1–4: Windward Avenue, White Plains, NY 10605
Grades 5–9: 40 Red Oak Lane, White Plains, NY 10604
Tel. 914-949-6968; Admissions Ext. 2225; Fax 914-949-8220
Web Site www.windwardny.org
E-mail jmetsch@windwardny.org

Windward School is a coeducational day school for students with language-based learning disabilities. The School serves 480 students of average to superior intelligence in Grades 1–9. Windward's curriculum emphasizes skills development in a multisensory, structured, language-based program. Activities include after-school programs, athletics, drama, student government, yearbook, and clubs. Tuition: $38,400. Financial aid is available. Maureen A. Sweeney is Director of Admissions; Dr. John J. Russell is Head of School.

The Winston Preparatory School 1981

126 West 17th Street, New York, NY 10011
Tel. 646-638-2705; Fax 646-638-2706
Web Site www.winstonprep.edu
E-mail admissions@winstonprep.edu

Winston Prep is a Middle and Upper School for 246 bright boys and girls with learning differences such as dyslexia, nonverbal learning disabilities, and attention deficit problems. The program offers assessment-driven, individualized instruction based on an understanding of each student's needs. Students are grouped according to learning profile and skill level and taught in small groups. "Focus," a daily 1:1 program, is taught by speech and language pathologists, reading specialists, and learning specialists who serve as primary remedial instructors, diagnosticians, and mentors. The arts, technology, sports, electives, after-school activities, a summer session, and visits to New York's cultural sites enhance the program. Tuition/Fees: $41,000. Courtney DeHoff is Admissions Director; Scott Bezsylko, M.A., is Executive Director; William DeHaven, M.A., is Head of School.

York Preparatory School 1969

40 West 68th Street, New York, NY 10023
Tel. 212-362-0400; Admissions Ext. 103; Fax 212-362-7424
Web Site www.yorkprep.org; E-mail admissions@yorkprep.org

This college preparatory day school enrolling 320 students in Grades 6–12 offers contemporary methods to enliven a challenging, traditional curriculum. York Prep's approach emphasizes independent thought, builds confidence, and equips graduates for entrance to selective colleges and universities. Facilities include a state-of-the-art computer lab, a large gym, a spacious art studio, two professionally equipped science labs, and a small concert hall. Numerous activities, including a winning Mock Trial Law Team and championship varsity basketball and soccer teams, enhance all aspects of school life. Tuition: $29,700–$30,200. Financial Aid: $750,000. Elizabeth Norton is Director of Enrollment; Ronald P. Stewart (Oxford, B.A., M.A., B.C.L.) is in his 39th year as Headmaster. *Middle States Association.*

NORTH CAROLINA

Cannon School 1969

5801 Poplar Tent Road, Concord, NC 28027
Tel. 704-786-8171; Admission 704-721-7164; Fax 704-788-7779
Web Site www.cannonschool.org; E-mail info@cannonschool.org

Cannon School's college preparatory program is designed to promote academic excellence, personal responsibility, athletic and artistic achievement, and respect for diversity. Serving over 900 day students in Junior Kindergarten–Grade 12, it is the first independent school in North Carolina to earn dual accreditation by the Southern Association of Independent Schools and the Southern Association of Colleges and Schools. Lower and Middle Schools supplement core subjects with art, music, foreign languages, and technology. The Upper School's wireless laptop learning environment offers a full range of AP courses, service learning, fine arts, and athletics. Tuition: $9020–$15,060. Financial aid is available. Matthew E. Gossage is Head of School. *Southern Association.*

Cape Fear Academy 1967

3900 South College Road, Wilmington, NC 28412
Tel. 910-791-0287; Admissions Ext. 1015; Fax 910-791-0290
Web Site www.capefearacademy.org; E-mail info@capefearacademy.org

Cape Fear Academy, a college preparatory day school serving 652 students in Pre-Kindergarten–Grade 12, emphasizes a sense of community and trust in a challenging academic program. Critical thinking, problem solving, and study skills are key elements of its strong interdisciplinary curriculum, which also includes a Marine Science program across all grades. Upper School offers numerous AP courses and a dedicated writing lab. Students perform community service at all grade levels. Participation in extracurricular activities in the Middle and Upper Schools is strongly encouraged. A summer enrichment program is offered. Tuition/Fees: $6650–$11,420. Financial aid is available. Susan Harrell is Director of Admission; John B. Meehl (Pomona College, B.A.; Stanford University, M.A.) is Headmaster. *Southern Association.*

Carolina Day School 1987

1345 Hendersonville Road, Asheville, NC 28803
Tel. 828-274-0757; Admissions Ext. 310; Fax 828-274-0756
Web Site www.cdschool.org; E-mail rgoertz@cdschool.org

Carolina Day School is a college preparatory school enrolling 670 boys and girls in Pre-Kindergarten–Grade 12. The School strives to develop within each student a strong academic foundation, personal ethics, and concern for community. The program includes 18 Advanced Placement courses, community service, athletics, outdoor education, computer science, and fine arts. Summer Quest offers enrichment in the arts, sciences, athletics, and outdoor education. The Key Learning Center, established in 1998, serves students with language-based learning disabilities. Tuition: $6900–$16,530. Robin Goertz is Director of Admissions; Beverly H. Sgro (Virginia Tech, Ph.D.) was appointed Head of School in 1999.

Cary Academy 1997

1500 North Harrison Avenue, Cary, NC 27513
Tel. 919-677-3873; Fax 919-677-4002
Web Site www.caryacademy.org

Cary Academy is a coeducational day school enrolling 710 students in Grades 6 through 12. Its commitment to "discovery, innovation, collaboration, and excellence" is carried out through a challenging college preparatory curriculum that combines new methodologies and technology with a traditional educational program. Small classes, creative teachers, and modern facilities enable students to acquire the knowledge and skills they need for productive citizenship in the 21st century. Course work emphasizes the mastery of skills in English, mathematics, social studies, laboratory sciences, and modern languages. A wireless, tablet PC environment enhances classroom learning. Students enjoy taking part in leadership activities, community service, the creative and performing arts, publications, and interscholastic team sports. All seniors historically enter four-year colleges and universities upon graduation. A summer program provides enrichment and recreation for students ages 6–18. Cary Academy is a recent No Child Left Behind/Blue Ribbon School winner. Tuition: $15,800. Financial Aid: $1,015,000. Denise Goodman is Director of Admissions; Donald S. Berger is Head of School. *Southern Association.*

Charlotte Country Day School 1941

1440 Carmel Road, Charlotte, NC 28226
Tel. 704-943-4500; Admissions 704-943-4530; Fax 704-943-4536
Web Site www.charlottecountryday.org

Charlotte Country Day School was founded in 1941 as a traditional college preparatory school. Continuing to maintain excellence in academic, athletic, and personal achievement, the coeducational program enrolls 1637 students in Junior Kindergarten–Grade 12. The curriculum includes Honors and Advanced Placement courses, independent study, English as a Second Language, and an International Baccalaureate program. Among the activities are publications, community service, clubs, and a wide variety of athletics. There is a summer program. Tuition: $12,900–$18,450. Financial aid is available. Nancy Ehringhaus is Director of Admissions; Margaret E. Gragg (Duke University, B.A.; University of North Carolina, M.A.T.) was named Head in 1992. *Southern Association.*

Charlotte Latin School 1970

9502 Providence Road, Charlotte, NC 28277-8695
Tel. 704-846-1100; Admissions 704-846-7207; Fax 704-846-1712
Web Site www.charlottelatin.org
E-mail admissions@charlottelatin.org

Charlotte Latin is an independent, coeducational, nonsectarian, college preparatory day school enrolling 1370 students in Transitional Kindergarten–Grade 12. Latin provides opportunities and challenges to nurture students' growth, leadership qualities, and lifelong love of learning. Instruction stresses academic excellence while meeting the developmental needs of the maturing child through an innovative pedagogy taught in a traditional environment. In-depth fine arts, athletics, and extracurricular activities are offered, including age-appropriate community service and an international exchange/study-abroad program. Enrichment and summer programs are also offered. Tuition: $13,500–$16,900. Financial Aid: $1,440,800. Kathryn B. Booe is Director of Admissions; Arch N. McIntosh, Jr., is Headmaster. *Southern Association.*

Christ School 1900

500 Christ School Road, Arden, NC 28704
Tel. 828-684-6232; Admission Ext. 106; [Toll-free] 800-422-3212
Fax 828-209-2003
Web Site www.christschool.org; E-mail admission@christschool.org

A college preparatory school for boys in Grades 8–12, Christ School enrolls 165 boarding and 50 day students. Affiliated with the Episcopal Church, the School prepares young men for success in college and beyond by providing a strong academic program, numerous athletic and outdoor opportunities, extensive offerings in the arts, and leadership opportunities for all students. Honors and Advanced Placement course work is available in all disciplines. All boys participate in chapel services, the work program, and community outreach. Boarding Tuition: $34,990; Day Tuition: $17,760. Financial Aid: $1,200,000. Merit-based Scholarships: $200,000. Denis Stokes is Director of Admission; Paul Krieger is Headmaster.

Durham Academy 1933

Pre-Kindergarten–Grade 4: 3501 Ridge Road, Durham, NC 27705
Tel. 919-493-5787; Fax 919-489-4893
Grades 5–8: 3116 Academy Road, Durham, NC 27707
Tel. 919-493-6181; Fax 919-489-9110
Grades 9–12: 3601 Ridge Road, Durham, NC 27705
Tel. 919-493-9595; Fax 919-489-7356
Web Site www.da.org; E-mail admissions@da.org

A college preparatory day school, Durham Academy enrolls 1135 students in Pre-Kindergarten–Grade 12. The Academy strives to prepare each student for a happy, moral, and productive life and to instill in each one an awareness of obligations to fellow students, community, and nation. The curriculum includes Advanced Placement courses in all disciplines and courses in computer, economics, music, art, dance, and drama. There is a full interscholastic sports program for Grades 7–12. A summer enrichment program is offered. Tuition: $10,920–$17,540. Financial Aid: $1,280,000. Victoria Muradi is Director of Admissions and Financial Aid; Edward R. Costello (Syracuse, A.B. 1970; Wesleyan, M.A.L.S. 1982) was appointed Headmaster in 1999. *Southern Association.*

Forsyth Country Day School 1970

5501 Shallowford Road, P.O. Box 549, Lewisville, NC 27023-0549
Tel. 336-945-3151; Admission Ext. 340; Fax 336-945-2907
Web Site www.fcds.org; E-mail cindykluttz@fcds.org

Forsyth Country Day School is a coeducational, college preparatory day school enrolling 1050 students in Junior Kindergarten–Grade 12. The School aims to educate students to become productive, responsible adults meeting the challenges of the future. The Lower and Middle Schools stress basic academic skills enriched with foreign languages, art, science, music, physical education, computer, and seminars. The Upper School curriculum includes advanced courses in all disciplines, a variety of electives, and athletics, fine arts, and clubs. The Johnson Academic Center provides additional support for students with a variety of learning styles. Tuition: $2700–$15,600. Financial aid is available. Cindy Kluttz is Director of Admission; Henry M. Battle, Jr., is Headmaster. *Southern Association.*

Greensboro Day School 1970

5401 Lawndale Drive, Greensboro, NC 27455
Tel. 336-288-8590; Fax 336-282-2905
Web Site www.greensboroday.org; E-mail dmorton@greensboroday.org

Greensboro Day School aims to meet the challenge of building relationships between caring adults and children of all ages within a dynamic environment. Enrolling 900 students in Transitional Kindergarten–Grade 12, Greensboro Day is the largest nonsectarian independent school in the Piedmont Triad of North Carolina and is known for its college preparatory program and its goal of excellence in education. The School emphasizes opportunities, honor and values, and dedication to each child and family. Advanced Placement, arts, athletics, leadership, experiential education, and small classes are featured. Financial aid and transportation are available. Tuition: $7155–$16,475. Danette Morton is Director of Admission & Financial Aid; Mark Hale (University of Washington, M.Ed. 1981) is Head of School.

Guilford Day School 1987

3310 Horse Pen Creek Road, Greensboro, NC 27410
Tel. 336-282-7044; Admission Ext. 4642; Fax 336-282-2048
Web Site www.guilfordday.org; E-mail tim@guilfordday.org

Guilford Day School is dedicated to preparing students with learning differences and/or attention deficit for academic success in traditional settings. Enrolling 150 boys and girls in Grades 1–12, Guilford Day's college preparatory curriculum is marked by small classes taught by certified special-education instructors. Individual education plans are tailored specifically to each student's abilities, goals, and learning style. The academic program emphasizes reading, English, math, history, science, and foreign language, with challenging electives, technology, and offerings in the arts. Student Council, community ser-

vice, field trips, athletics, music, and a summer session are available. Tuition: $16,550–$17,220. Tim Montgomery is Assistant Head of School/Admission Director; Laura Blackburn Mlatac is Head of School. *Southern Association.*

Kerr-Vance Academy 1968

700 Vance Academy Road, Henderson, NC 27537
Tel. 252-492-0018; Fax 252-438-4652
Web Site www.kerrvance.com; E-mail rirvin@kerrvance.com

Kerr-Vance Academy, a coeducational, college preparatory day school, enrolls more than 450 students in Pre-Kindergarten–Grade 12. The School also has a licensed Day Care Center with programs for 2- and 3-year-old children. The liberal arts curriculum emphasizes academic excellence as well as ethical values and concern for others. The program centers on reading and language arts, math, science, social studies, and modern languages. Computer technology is integrated throughout the disciplines. The arts are also integral components of an education at Kerr-Vance Academy. Advanced Placement courses are offered in most subjects, and high school students perform a minimum of 15 hours of community service per year. Other activities include school government, honor societies, vocal and instrumental ensembles, and athletics. Tuition: $6639–$7208. Rebecca Irvin is the Admissions Coordinator; Paul Villatico is Headmaster. *Southern Association.*

New Garden Friends School 1971

1128 New Garden Road, Greensboro, NC 27410
Tel. 336-299-0964; Admission Ext. 301; Fax 336-292-0347
Web Site www.ngfs.org; E-mail nfriendssc@aol.com

Guided by Quaker beliefs, New Garden Friends School is an inclusive, innovative educational community for 270 boys and girls in Preschool (age 3)–Grade 12. The curriculum, which emphasizes social justice and personal responsibility, includes reading, math, science, foreign language, music, art, and physical education. Faculty believe in children's ability to act responsibly and seek to develop their reliance more on inner conviction and less on opinions of others or the fashion of the day. Each person is nourished as a growing individual in his or her search for inward authority, integrity, and personal sense of rightness. Tuition & Fees: $5090–$12,360. Financial aid is available. Chris Winchester is Admission Director; Marty Goldstein and David Tomlin are Co-Heads.

The Oakwood School 1996

4000 MacGregor Downs Road, Greenville, NC 27834
Tel. 252-931-0760; Admission Ext. 223; Fax 252-931-0964
Web Site www.theoakwoodschool.org
E-mail info@theoakwoodschool.org

This coeducational day school was founded in 1996 by a group of parents looking for a challenging college preparatory program in a culturally diverse and secure setting. Currently enrolling 310 students in Kindergarten–Grade 11, The Oakwood School will add Grade 12 in 2008. Oakwood's mission is to ensure that all students develop the strength of character, creativity, and wisdom through which they can make a difference in the world. The curriculum accommodates students of average to high ability as well as those with mild learning differences. The 41-acre campus provides facilities for classrooms, media centers, science labs, fine arts, clubs, and sports teams. Extended care and summer programs are optional. Tuition: $8700–$9850. Financial aid is available. Emily Prokopowicz is Director of Admission; Dr. Parmalee Hawk is Interim Head of School. *Southern Association.*

The O'Neal School 1971

Airport Road, P.O. Box 290, Southern Pines, NC 28388
Tel. 910-692-6920; Admissions Ext. 103; Fax 910-692-6930
Web Site www.onealschool.org; E-mail adroppers@onealschool.org

O'Neal is a college preparatory school dedicated to the development of academic excellence, strength of character, and physical well-being of its students in an environment where integrity, self-discipline, and consideration for others are fundamental. There are 450 students in Pre-Kindergarten–Grade 12. The curriculum in Kindergarten–Grade 8 is based on the Core Knowledge Program, which emphasizes cultural literacy and content learning. Students take part in many athletic, extracurricular, and community service activities. There is also a specialized learning development program. Tuition: $6350–$13,150. Financial Aid: $565,000. Alice Droppers is Director of Admissions; John Neiswender (Furman University, B.S.; University of South Carolina, M.A.T.) is Headmaster.

The Patterson School 1909

P.O. Box 500, Patterson, NC 28661
Tel. 828-758-2374; Fax 828-758-9179
Web Site www.pattersonschool.org
E-mail headmaster@pattersonschool.org

The Patterson School is a nondenominational, college preparatory, coeducational boarding and day school for Grade 7–Postgraduate. Patterson offers an environment designed to stimulate the intellectual, ethical, physical, and social development of its approximately 100 students, about 25 percent of whom are international students representing over 20 nations. Small classes and an experienced, caring faculty allow young people to reach their maximum academic and creative potential. The 1400-acre campus offers a wide range of athletic, equestrian, and environmental activities. Academic Support and English as a Second Language (ESL) programs are available. Boarding Tuition: $23,500 plus fees; Day Tuition: $12,000 plus fees; Academic Support Program: $4500; ESL: $4500. Colin G. Stevens is Headmaster.

Providence Day School 1970

5800 Sardis Road, Charlotte, NC 28270
Tel. 704-887-6000; Admissions 704-887-7040; Fax 704-887-7520
Web Site www.providenceday.org
E-mail admission@providenceday.org

Providence Day, serving 1500 girls and boys in Transitional Kindergarten–Grade 12, has a reputation for high academic standards. Within a structured, yet nurturing environment, the college preparatory curriculum is designed to develop the intellectual, physical, social, and moral aspects of each student. Career exploration for seniors, a global studies program, and 24 Advanced Placement courses enrich the program. Students take part in honor societies, three publications, Student Council, clubs, and varsity athletics. An extensive summer program is available. Tuition: $13,015–$18,035. Financial Aid: $1,600,000. Scott Siegfried is Director of Admission; Dr. Jack E. Creeden (College of the Holy Cross, B.A. *[cum laude]* 1974; University of Wisconsin [Madison], M.A. 1976, Ph.D. 1984) is Headmaster. *Southern Association.*

Ravenscroft School 1862

7409 Falls of the Neuse Road, Raleigh, NC 27615
Tel. 919-847-0900; Admissions Ext. 2227; Fax 919-846-2371
Web Site www.ravenscroft.org; E-mail pjamison@ravenscroft.org

Ravenscroft, a Blue Ribbon School set on a spacious 125-acre campus, is a coeducational, college preparatory day school enrolling 1229 students in Pre-Kindergarten through Grade 12. Guided by its "legacy of excellence," the Ravenscroft community nurtures individual potential and prepares students to thrive in a complex and interdependent world. School programs emphasize experiential learning activities and community service while offering a comprehensive academic program that features Global Studies, Ethics and Leadership, and numerous Advanced Placement courses. A wide range of extracurricular opportunities includes an extensive Fine Arts program, competitive sports, student government, publications, and interest clubs. There is a summer program. Tuition: $9400–$15,600. Financial aid is available. Pamela J. Jamison is Director of Admissions; Doreen C. Kelly (University of Pennsylvania, B.A. 1985, M.S. 1985) was appointed Head of School in 2003. *Southern Association.*

Rocky Mount Academy 1968

1313 Avondale Avenue, Rocky Mount, NC 27803
Tel. 252-443-4126; Fax 252-937-7922
Web Site rmacademy.com; E-mail tstevens@rmacademy.com

This coeducational, college preparatory day school enrolls 451 students in PreKindergarten–Grade 12. Rocky Mount Academy seeks to prepare students for the challenges and responsibilities of life and college in a trusting, academically rigorous, and supportive environment. In addition to the core subjects, the curriculum includes Honors and Advanced Placement courses, guidance, art, physical education, foreign language, computers, and music. Sports, community service, drama, publications, field trips, and clubs enrich the program. Tuition: $3935–$9410. Financial Aid: $352,160. Millie H. Walker is Director of Enrollment Management; Thomas R. Stevens (Yale, B.A. 1973; Columbia, M.A. 1978) was appointed Headmaster in 1999. *Southern Association.*

Saint Mary's School 1842

900 Hillsborough Street, Raleigh, NC 27603-1689
Tel. 919-424-4000; [Toll-free] 800-948-2557
Admissions 919-424-4100; Fax 919-424-4122
Web Site www.saint-marys.edu; E-mail admiss@saint-marys.edu

Saint Mary's School in Raleigh, North Carolina, is an Episcopal, college preparatory, boarding and day school, dedicated to academic excellence and personal achievement for young women in Grades 9 through 12. Raleigh, the state capital and one of the largest cities in North Carolina, is located midway between the Great Smoky Mountains and the Atlantic Ocean. A center of historic and cultural attractions and high-tech industries, the area is also home to seven colleges and universities.

Founded in 1842, the School is dedicated to instilling the highest personal and academic standards in young women. Saint Mary's teachers and advisors work closely with each student to personalize and plan specifically for her future educational goals. Affiliated with the Episcopal Church, the School welcomes students from all denominations; a full-time chaplain is on staff, and chapel services are an integral part of the Saint Mary's experience.

Governed by a 26-member Board of Trustees, the School is accredited by the Southern Association of Colleges and Schools and holds membership in the National Association of Independent Schools and the Southern Association of Independent Schools.

THE CAMPUS. Saint Mary's scenic and historic 23-acre campus lies in the heart of North Carolina's Research Triangle. The front campus is listed on the National Register of Historic Places. While the campus buildings have been part of the School's 166-year history, they also serve as modern facilities in which students of the 21st century learn, play, perform, and live. Facilities include state-of-the-art science laboratories; a historic chapel built in 1856; the Sarah Graham Kenan Library, which contains 43,000 volumes, more than any other independent school library in North Carolina; and a newly renovated Smedes Hall, which houses two floors of dormitory rooms, a student center, administrative and academic offices, and the admission office. Athletic facilities include two athletic fields and the Bacon Gymnasium complex, which houses a basketball court, a swimming pool, six tennis courts, a state-of-the-art physical fitness center, and two dance studios.

Boarding students live in Smedes Hall, Penick Hall, and Cruikshank Hall, with faculty and senior prefects residing on every floor of each dorm. The dormitories are equipped with computer labs, lounges with large-screen cable televisions, laundry facilities, and mini-kitchens. There are two to three girls to a room, and each dorm offers suite or hall-style bathrooms. The rooms are wired for Internet access, and local phone service is provided.

THE FACULTY. Theo W. Coonrod became Head of School in 2000. She received baccalaureate and master's degrees in English from the University of Texas (Austin). Prior to coming to Saint Mary's, she held several administrative positions at St. John's School in Houston, Texas.

Of the 47 women and men on the faculty, 75 percent hold master's degrees or higher from colleges and universities in the United States and abroad, including American University, Campbell University, College of William and Mary, Duke, Emory, Florida Atlantic, Iowa State, North Carolina State, Northwestern, Ohio, Open University at Milton Keynes (England), Rutgers, Saint Louis, Seton Hall, Yale, and the Universities of Iowa, North Carolina, Phoenix, Provence (France), and South Carolina.

STUDENT BODY. In 2007–08, Saint Mary's School enrolled 294 girls from 16 states, 4 foreign countries, and the Raleigh area; 45 percent are boarders; 55 percent are day students.

ACADEMIC PROGRAM. The academic year, from mid-August through May, is divided into semesters, with fall, Thanksgiving, Christmas, spring, and Easter breaks. With a student-teacher ratio of 7:1 and an average class size of 13, faculty members have ample time inside and outside the classroom to assist students.

Each student is supported in a rigorous academic program by a faculty advisor who sees her daily and guides her in all areas of school life. She also receives support from an academic and college counselor who helps her throughout her high school career, from creating her achievement plan when she enters to guiding her through the college application process. Girls benefit from a writing center, staffed by English teachers, and a learning coordinator who teaches study skills and coordinates special services for learning-different students. Study halls are held during the class day and, for boarding students, for two hours in the evenings. The program boasts a 1:1 student-computer ratio, with each student having her own Tablet PC, and wireless locations.

To graduate, students must complete a total of 22 units with a cumulative grade-point average of at least 1.700. Students must complete course work in English, humanities and social sciences, science, mathematics, foreign language, physical education, fine arts, and electives, as well as 20 hours of community service each year. All courses are college preparatory; honors and Advanced Placement courses are offered in all core subjects and art. Upper-level students must take government and ethics/philosophy and may engage in independent study courses with school faculty or take courses at local colleges and universities. An innovative ninth-grade World Studies program focuses English and humanities courses on world cultures and voices.

Saint Mary's believes that educating a girl begins with knowing her in order best to enable each student's personal achievement. Central to this mission is each girl's MAP (My Achievement Plan), a carefully structured path through high school that allows each student, working with her teachers and advisors, to chart a personal course incorporating five core components. These elements are high-quality academic programs led by faculty who are experts in the teaching of girls; the COMPASS Curriculum; personal expression through arts, athletics, leadership, and other programs; experience with professionals, businesses and corporations, civic leaders, and universities in the Research Triangle; and relationships and responsibility in a community founded on honor.

The four-year COMPASS Curriculum is designed to act in tandem with the academic curriculum. Its mission is to equip young women with life skills that move them toward independence and enable them to navigate their world. Its focus is grade-level appropriate. In Grade 9, COMPASS focuses on identity, self-discovery, and character building. Tenth graders explore their worlds and learn to make connections. The 11th-grade programs emphasize challenges and taking responsibility; seniors focus on developing independence and voicing their views and concerns. These themes are carried out in ten subjects of study, ranging from ethics and spirituality to public speaking and adventure and travel.

Day-long programs focus on women's health and breast cancer awareness, financial literacy, leadership, and careers. In a variety of settings on and off campus, students learn about topics as diverse as stress management, the honor code, teamwork, nutrition, gender role socialization, cliques, toxic media messages, relationship cues, racial profiling, and managing money.

Typically, all Saint Mary's graduates go on to four-year colleges and universities. Members of the Class of 2007 are enrolled at Brown, Davidson, Duke, Elon, Meredith, North Carolina State, Rhodes, Rice, Wake Forest, Washington University, and the Universities of Alabama, Mississippi, North Carolina, Pennsylvania, the South, and Virginia.

STUDENT ACTIVITIES. Saint Mary's students enjoy a rich variety of activities such as athletics, dance, chorale, drama, clubs, organizations, internships, and community service. Students may participate in an in-house performing dance company, Orchesis; perform in drama productions; join the Chorale, string ensemble, or orchestra; or take music lessons in virtually every instrument. The visual arts program is designed to teach art history and appreciation and skills in various art disciplines from the beginning level to the most advanced. Field trips, slides, videos, Internet exploration, and community service projects enhance the students' classroom experiences.

The athletic program provides opportunities for each student to achieve her personal best in sports. Saint Mary's participates in the Triangle Independent Schools Athletic Conference and the North Carolina Independent School Athletic Association in cross-country, tennis, golf, volleyball, field hockey, basketball, swimming, soccer, fast-pitch softball, lacrosse, and track and field.

Traditional special events include the holiday Lighting O' the Grove, Spirit Week, Halloween festivities, the Spring Fling carnival and picnic, Founders Day, and the Junior-Senior Prom. Weekend activities feature movies, plays, the symphony and other musical performances, professional and collegiate sporting events, the State Fair, dining out, visits to museums, and shopping at some of the state's largest malls. Additional weekend adventures include trips to the mountains and beaches. Saint Mary's is a member of the Boarding Schools Activities Committee, which offers many opportunities to socialize with students at other independent schools such as Woodberry Forest and Christ School for boys. Students and faculty take trips to New York City, Washington, Boston, and Savannah to enrich and expand upon their classroom learning. Students travel to Australia, Greece, and Italy, and, in an exchange program, to France.

ADMISSION AND COSTS. Saint Mary's School admits students without regard to race, religion, sexual orientation, or national or ethnic origin. The application consists of a student personal statement, a parent statement, recommendations from teachers and a guidance counselor, standardized testing reports, previous transcripts, and a campus visit.

In 2007–08, day tuition is $15,488. Boarding tuition, room, and board is $32,448. The comprehensive fee for boarding and day students is $2500. Saint Mary's School offers financial assistance to eligible applicants. To apply for need-based financial aid, families must complete the Saint Mary's Financial Aid Form and the School and Student Service for Financial Aid Form available from the Admission Office. The School awards a limited number of merit scholarships, including the Blanche Robertson Bacon Honors Scholarships, to academically talented students.

Associate Head & Dean of Academics: Margaret Grissom
Associate Head & Dean of Students: Josette Huntress Holland
Alumnae Director: Emory Rogers Church '74C
Director of Admission: Catherine C. Leary
Associate Head of Institutional Advancement: Mary Moss '74HS
Academic & College Counselors: Scott Orvis & Melanie Lachance
Business Manager: Ken Troshinsky
Athletic Director: Seth Lieberman

St. Timothy's School 1958

4523 Six Forks Road, Raleigh, NC 27609
Tel. 919-781-0531; Admissions 919-781-0531; Fax 919-783-2399
Web Site www.sttimothys.org
E-mail admissions_director@sttimothys.org

St. Timothy's, an Episcopal, coeducational school, is North Carolina's oldest accredited nonpublic school and enrolls 490 students of all faiths in Kindergarten–Grade 8. The School is committed to academic excellence in an atmosphere that emphasizes traditional values, small classes, and a supportive environment. The academic curriculum is complemented by offerings in computer, library, science lab, Spanish, music, art, and physical education. Extracurricular activities include a full interscholastic sports program for Grades 6–8, student government, clubs, journalism, and the arts. Tuition: $9300–$12,000. Financial Aid: $375,000. Cathy Clement is Admissions Director; Michael S. Bailey (University of North Carolina, B.A.; East Carolina University, M.A.) is Headmaster. *Southern Association.*

Salem Academy 1772

500 Salem Avenue, Winston-Salem, NC 27108
Tel. 336-721-2646; [Toll-free] 877-40SALEM
Admissions 336-721-2643; Fax 336-917-5340
Web Site www.salemacademy.com; E-mail academy@salem.edu

SALEM ACADEMY in Winston-Salem, North Carolina, is a college preparatory boarding and day school for girls in Grades 9 through 12. Founded in 1772 by Moravian settlers, Salem Academy has been in continuous operation for more than 235 years. Initially a day school, it added boarding facilities in 1802. Postgraduate work was first offered in the 1860s, and Salem College was chartered in 1866. In 1930, the

Academy and Salem College were separated, with both schools remaining on the original campus.

Winston-Salem (population 200,000) is located in the Piedmont region of the state, approximately 90 miles from both Charlotte and Raleigh. It is served by two airports and Interstate highways 40, 77, and 85. The city's own activities and four colleges—North Carolina School of the Arts, Wake Forest University, Winston-Salem State University, and Salem College (the Academy's "sister school")—provide cultural and educational opportunities for Academy students.

Throughout its history, Salem Academy has maintained its original commitment to the education of women. It endeavors to provide "a thorough preparation for a continuing education and a fulfilling personal life, a spiritual and ethical climate in all phases of school life, and a program promoting mental and physical well-being." While the Academy retains its affiliation with the Moravian Church, students of various religious backgrounds are enrolled.

A nonprofit institution, Salem Academy is governed by a 30-member Board of Trustees, which serves as a common Board for the school and Salem College. Board members are chosen by the Synod of the Moravian Church, the Alumnae Association, and other organizations. Many of the school's 2500 living graduates lend it financial support and refer prospective students. Salem Academy is accredited by the Southern Association of Colleges and Schools. It holds membership in the National Association of Independent Schools, the North Carolina Association of Independent Schools, and The National Coalition of Girls' Schools.

THE CAMPUS. The 64-acre campus, which is shared with Salem College, adjoins the restored 18th-century Moravian village of Old Salem, a national historic landmark. It encompasses lawns and wooded areas as well as hockey fields, a softball field, an archery range, and 12 tennis courts.

Six buildings on the east side of the common campus constitute the self-contained portion of the Academy facilities. The main building provides administrative offices, reception rooms, and student recreation rooms as well as two dormitory wings, Shaffner and Bahnson. Weaver Building contains the library, the art studio, the admissions office, the dining room, and the school kitchen. Critz Hall houses classrooms, language and science laboratories, and faculty offices. Hodges Hall contains a music studio and library, an auditorium, a small meditation chapel, and dormitories for the upperclassmen. In addition, the school shares with Salem College the facilities of the Dale H. Gramley Library, Salem Fine Arts Center, gymnasium and indoor swimming pool, Blixt Fields, the Student Life and Fitness Center, the Student Commons Center, and the infirmary. The Academy plant is valued at $5,000,000.

THE FACULTY. Karl Sjolund, appointed Head of School in July 2007, is a graduate of Virginia Military Institute and Columbia University.

The full-time faculty, including administrators who teach, number 25. They hold 25 baccalaureate, 15 master's, and 1 doctoral degrees representing study at Agnes Scott, Appalachian State, Bob Jones University, Clemson, Columbia, Duke, D'Youville College, George Washington, Lehigh University, Presbyterian, Randolph College, Salem, Union, United States Naval Academy, Vanderbilt, Wake Forest, Western Illinois, and the Universities of Maryland, North Carolina (Chapel Hill, Greensboro), and Wyoming. Two part-time instructors teach Spanish and French. Eight House Counselors supervise the dormitories. Staff benefits include a health insurance plan, a retirement plan, and Social Security.

The Academy shares the services of physicians and a full-time infirmary staff with Salem College. Medical facilities are available nearby.

STUDENT BODY. In 2007–08, Salem Academy enrolled 87 boarding students and 95 day students, 14 to 18 years of age, as follows: 35 in Grade 9, 47 in Grade 10, 51 in Grade 11, and 49 in Grade 12.

The boarding students come from 12 states and China, Germany, Japan, Korea, Sweden, and Taiwan.

ACADEMIC PROGRAM. The school year, from late August to late May, is divided into two academic terms and a miniterm in January. There are two long weekends as well as vacations at Thanksgiving, Christmas, and in the spring.

Classes meet five days a week. A typical school day includes Assembly, five academic class periods, a recess, a study hall, and an assembly period. Language and science laboratories, study halls, music, studio art, physical education, and student activities are scheduled during four afternoon class periods. Boarding students have supervised study in the evening.

There are 12 to 14 students in an average class. Conference periods provide opportunities for individual help. The January miniterm also offers a concentrated tutorial program. Grades are discussed with the student and sent to parents every six weeks.

To graduate, a student must earn 20 academic credits, including English 4, Latin 2, a modern foreign language 2, history 3, mathematics 4, and science 3. Other required courses are Health in Grade 9, Religion in Grade 11 or 12, and Physical Education in Grades 9, 10, and 11. A course in art, drama, or music is required.

The curriculum includes English Composition and Literature 1–4, English as a Second Language Level 1, Communications; French 1–3, Spanish 1–3, Latin 1–3; United States History, Economics, Political Science, European History, Non-Western Cultures, Humanities 1–2; Algebra 1–2, Honors Algebra II, Geometry, Analytic Geometry, Pre-Calculus, Discrete

Mathematics; Biology, Chemistry, Conceptual Physics, Environmental Science; Biblical Narratives, World Religions; Studio Art; Theatre; and choral and vocal instruction. Private lessons are available in piano, organ, harp, flute, cello, violin, classical guitar, harpsichord, woodwind, and brass and percussion instruments. Advanced Placement courses are available in Latin, Spanish, U.S. History, World History, AB & BC Calculus, Statistics, Biology, Chemistry, and Physics. Advanced courses are offered to qualified juniors and seniors, who also have the opportunity to take courses for credit at Salem College. An intensive music program for qualified students is available in conjunction with the School of Music at Salem College.

The January miniterm provides each student an opportunity to choose her own educational experience. Programs both on and off campus provide a variety of ways for students to pursue individual interests. A school-sponsored trip is usually offered each year to such places as England, Greece, Germany, Australia, France, and Italy. Internships and independent studies in teaching, music, medicine, banking, and other fields may be pursued under faculty supervision. Teachers conduct intensive reviews and tutorials, introduce new topics, and assign and supervise independent projects.

In 2007, all 41 graduates were accepted by four-year colleges and universities. Typically, they attend such colleges and universities as Boston College, Brown, College of William and Mary, Cornell, Dartmouth, Davidson, Duke, Georgetown, New York University, North Carolina State, Southern Methodist, Wake Forest, Wofford, Yale, and the Universities of North Carolina and Virginia.

STUDENT ACTIVITIES. The student government is composed of two elected bodies. Within Salem's honor tradition, each girl is expected to be honest and considerate. The Honor Cabinet advises and guides through constructive counsel and leadership, and it may recommend disciplinary action. The Student Council, composed of the class presidents, a representative from each class, and the Honor Cabinet president, deals with student relations, activities, and concerns.

Students publish a newspaper, a yearbook, and an annual literary-art magazine. The Theatre Club stages two major productions a year, and the Glee Club performs both on and off campus. Since 1988, the Glee Club has performed at Carnegie Hall, in cathedrals throughout England, and in the Intermountain Youth Concert in Salt Lake City, Utah. In December 2001 and 2003, it performed in London at the invitation of the Queen's Charities. Among other student organizations is the Fellowship Council, which sponsors parties, campus activities, and community projects.

Varsity teams in field hockey, soccer, volleyball, basketball, softball, tennis, swimming, cross-country, golf, and track compete with other schools in the Triad Athletic Conference of the North Carolina Independent Schools Athletic Association. All girls participate in a friendly rivalry during the year, competing in team spirit as members of either the Purple or the Gold squad.

The Student Activities Directors plan trips to the theater, concerts, and to Wake Forest sporting events and cultural and social activities. They also plan outdoor activities such as rafting on the New River, camping, wilderness expeditions, and snow skiing. Dances and social events are scheduled with Christ School, McCallie, Woodberry Forest, and others. With written parental approval, boarding students in Grade 12 may have unlimited overnight permissions on weekends; students in Grades 9–11 are limited to 14 to 20 overnights per year. On three Sundays a month, boarding students are expected to attend the church or temple service of their choice. Transportation is provided.

Traditional annual events include Opening Assembly, Ring Banquet, Senior Bazaar, Parents' Weekend, Alumnae Day, Senior Vespers, Honors Banquets, and Recognition and Graduation Exercises.

ADMISSION AND COSTS. Salem Academy seeks to enroll academically motivated students who have personal integrity; a positive attitude toward work; potential for developing self-discipline, self-confidence, and self-esteem; and a strong desire to broaden their intellectual and cultural horizons. New students are admitted in Grades 9–11 and occasionally in Grade 12. Candidates must submit a transcript, academic and personal recommendations, and the results of the Secondary School Admission Test; a personal interview is also required. Application should be made during the year preceding desired entrance, but late entrance and midyear enrollment are sometimes possible. There is a $50 application fee.

In 2007–08, tuition, room, and board is $31,600; day-student tuition is $16,000, including lunches. Additional expenses are books ($450) and an activities fee ($125).

The Academy awards scholarships on the basis of merit and financial need, including the Medlin Scholarship, a full-merit award for a boarding student. One hundred students receive aid totaling $1,000,000 annually.

Director of Studies: Eileen Cahill
Dean of Students: Mary Lorick Thompson
Director of Admission: Lucia Uldrick
College Counselor: Kelen Walker
Chief Financial Officer: Dana Smith
Director of Athletics: Lorie Howard

Salisbury Academy 1993

2210 Jake Alexander Boulevard N., Salisbury, NC 28147
Tel. 704-636-3002; Fax 704-636-0078
Web Site www.salisburyacademy.org
E-mail admissions@salisburyacademy.org

Salisbury Academy provides a rich, child-centered education to a diverse student body in Grades 4K–8. The coeducational, nondenominational, independent day school welcomes approximately 200 students to the 10-acre campus. The Academy offers an integrated and challenging curriculum that provides a strong foundation in core subjects. Academic course work is balanced with hands-on learning activities and channels for creativity and self-expression. Numerous field trips afford the opportunity to contextualize and apply acquired knowledge. Enhancements include art, music, Spanish, media, and an active athletics program. Salisbury Academy encourages children to be intellectually curious and disciplined in work and study habits in an atmosphere that promotes kindness and personal and social responsibility. Known for close and supportive relationships among faculty and students, and a strong school community, the Academy provides an environment where children thrive and learn. Tuition: $6570–$7380. Marguerite Oestreicher is Admissions Director; Salvatore M. Trento (State University of New York, B.A.; Oxford University [England], DPL; University

of Massachusetts [Lowell], Ed.M.) was appointed Headmaster in 2007.

Summit School 1933

2100 Reynolda Road, Winston-Salem, NC 27106
Tel. 336-722-2777; Admission 336-724-5811; Fax 336-724-0099
Web Site www.summitschool.com
E-mail sadams@summitschool.com

Summit School is a day school enrolling 600 boys and girls in Pre-Kindergarten–Grade 9. The School strives to help students learn to respect their own beliefs, values, and achievements as well as those of others and encourages them to take responsibility for their own education. The traditional subjects are complemented by French (beginning in Pre-Kindergarten), Spanish, Latin, Chinese, art, music, drama, and computers. Other activities are sports and service groups. Field trips and student exchanges with other schools add variety to the program. Tuition: $9400–$16,560. Financial Aid: $866,000. Katherine Memory is Director of Admission; Sandra P. Adams (Wake Forest, B.A., M.A.; University of North Carolina, Ed.D.) was appointed Head in 1990.

Westchester Country Day School 1967

2045 North Old Greensboro Road, High Point, NC 27265
Tel. 336-869-2128; Fax 336-869-6685
Web Site www.westchestercds.org
E-mail admissions@westchestercds.org

Founded in 1967, Westchester Country Day School is an independent, nonsectarian institution established to provide a college preparatory education for 420 students in Kindergarten through Grade 12. An intellectually exciting environment enables students to excel in all areas associated with the classical liberal arts tradition—academics, athletics, and the arts—while simultaneously developing strong moral and ethical values. Advanced Placement courses are offered in 14 disciplines. The School's low student-teacher ratio and family-like atmosphere enhance the learning process. Located in a country setting on 53 acres in Davidson County, Westchester serves the Piedmont Triad of High Point, Greensboro, and Winston-Salem as well as neighboring communities throughout the state. Tuition: $7360–$11,515. Tuition assistance is available. Kerie Beth Scott is Director of Admissions; Charles Hamblet (Baldwin-Wallace College, B.S.; Rutgers, M.Ed.; Brown University, M.A.T.) is Interim Headmaster. *Southern Association.*

OHIO

Canton Country Day School 1964

3000 Demington Avenue, NW, Canton, OH 44718
Tel. 330-453-8279; Fax 330-453-6038
Web Site www.ccd-school.org; E-mail pmonks@ccd-school.org

This nonsectarian, coeducational day school enrolls 230 students in Pre-K (age 3)–Grade 8. Students develop a solid educational foundation in a culturally and socioeconomically diverse environment where scholarship, responsibility, and respect for others flourish along with creativity, enthusiasm, and self-respect. Field trips, lecturers, and community involvement support the curriculum. Core subjects are enhanced by art, computer, music, library, drama, creative movement, athletics, and service learning. The Nationally Recognized School of Excellence is accredited by the Independent Schools Association of the Central States, chartered by the State of Ohio, and a member of the NAIS. Tuition: $9890–$12,229. Financial Aid: $400,000. Paul Monks is Admission Director; Pamela Shaw is Head of School.

Cincinnati Country Day School 1926

6905 Given Road, Cincinnati, OH 45243-2898
Tel. 513-979-0220; Fax 513-527-7614
Web Site www.countryday.net; E-mail admission@countryday.net

This coeducational, college preparatory school enrolls more than 800 day students from 18 months (early childhood) through Grade 12. The School prides itself on academic excellence, close student-to-faculty relationships, involvement in the arts and athletics, and integrated technology programs. Students participate in numerous clubs, activities, and more than 15 varsity athletic teams on the 62-acre campus. All students in Grades 5–12 receive a Tablet PC to enhance their learning experience. A summer program is available. Tuition: $5220–$18,300. Merit- and Need-Based Financial Aid: $1,300,000. Aaron B. Kellenberger is Director of Admission; Dr. Robert P. Macrae (Wesleyan, B.A.; Stanford, M.A.; Columbia, M.A., Ed.D.) is Head of School.

The Columbus Academy 1911

Box 30745, 4300 Cherry Bottom Road, Gahanna, OH 43230
Tel. 614-475-2311; Admissions 614-337-4309; Fax 614-475-0396
Web Site www.columbusacademy.org
E-mail lou_schultz@columbusacademy.org

The Columbus Academy is a coeducational, college preparatory day school enrolling 1055 students in Pre-Kindergarten–Grade 12. The Academy, located on a 233-acre campus, first admitted girls in 1990 and achieved full coeducation in 1992. The school is committed to providing a balanced education of academics, arts, athletics, and activities, including a significant service component. Taught by 145 full- and part-time faculty, students are provided a liberal arts foundation in the five basic disciplines. Summer enrichment and remedial courses and a day camp are conducted. Tuition: $8750–$17,400. Financial Aid: $1,260,000. Louis A. Schultz is Admissions Director; John M. MacKenzie (Bowdoin College, A.B.; Columbia University, M.A.) is Headmaster.

Columbus School for Girls 1898

56 South Columbia Avenue, Columbus, OH 43209-1698
Tel. 614-252-0781; Fax 614-252-0571
Web Site www.columbusschoolforgirls.org

This college preparatory day school, serving 650 diverse students from age 3 to Grade 12, is committed to the value of a liberal arts education for women and to an academically excellent program that encourages each student to develop to her fullest capacity. The goal is to foster strong skills and a love of learning that will lead to lifelong intellectual curiosity, aesthetic understanding, desire for health and fitness, and commitment to social responsibility. Over 150 faculty and staff provide an ideal student-teacher ratio of 9:1. More than 65 percent of faculty hold advanced degrees. Facilities include modern science, math, and technology labs; "Smart" classrooms; an arts wing with a theater and a photo lab; and two libraries as well as two gyms, a 75-acre sports campus, and 95 wooded acres with a nature classroom to support the program. Activities include interscholastic and intramural sports, a variety of clubs, and theater productions. Summer programs, including a gifted program, are offered as well. Tuition: $15,490–$18,125. Financial aid is available. Donna Lindberg and Ann Timm are Directors of Admissions; Diane B. Cooper, Ed.D., is Head of School.

Gilmour Academy 1946

34001 Cedar Road, Gates Mills, OH 44040-9356
Tel. 440-442-1104; Admissions 440-473-8050; Fax 440-473-8010
Web Site www.gilmour.org; E-mail admissions@gilmour.org

Now in its 62nd year of college preparatory education in the Catholic tradition of Holy Cross and the University of Notre Dame, Gilmour Academy enrolls 740 students, with day students in Preschool–Grade 12 and boarders in Grades 7–12. By instilling a sense of self-worth through individual achievement, Gilmour helps students reach their personal best. Through a challenging curriculum that includes Socratic Seminars and 90-minute classes, students learn to think critically and solve problems in a project-oriented world. Athletic, artistic, dramatic, and civic activities are offered. Boarding Tuition: $32,750; Day Tuition: $8910–$22,045. Financial Aid: $2,000,000. Devin K. Schlickmann is Dean of Institutional Advancement; Steve M. Scheidt is Director of Middle and Upper School Admissions; Br. Robert E. Lavelle, CSC, is Headmaster. *North Central Association.*

Hathaway Brown School 1876

19600 North Park Boulevard, Shaker Heights, OH 44122
Tel. 216-932-4214; Admissions 216-320-8767; Fax 216-397-0992
Web Site www.hb.edu; E-mail admissions@hb.edu

Hathaway Brown, a college preparatory day school serving 860 students in a coeducational early childhood program and all-girls Kindergarten–Grade 12, seeks to maintain a tradition of excellence through a challenging program in a creative atmosphere. The School aims to equip young women for the future with knowledge, resolve, and imagination. The curriculum offers Advanced Placement in all fields as well as the arts, computer studies, and athletics. A Science Research course enables students to work on experiments in cutting-edge labs around the city. Adventure Learning is required in Middle School; Spanish begins in Kindergarten. Tuition: $3600–$21,950. Financial Aid: $2,700,000. Sarah L. Johnston is Director of Admission and Financial Aid; H. William Christ is Head of School.

Lake Ridge Academy 1963

37501 Center Ridge Road, North Ridgeville, OH 44039
Tel. 440-327-1175; Admissions Ext. 103; Fax 440-327-3641
Fax 440-353-0324/327-3641
Web Site www.lakeridgeacademy.org
E-mail admission@lakeridgeacademy.org

Lake Ridge Academy is the only independent, K–12, coeducational, college preparatory day school on Cleveland's west side. Enrolling 375 students, Lake Ridge offers a liberal arts curriculum that allows students to explore the sciences, the arts, drama, and international languages and travel in an open and diverse environment on the 88-acre campus. There are no bells or locks on lockers, and students are expected to take ownership of their learning, which serves them well as they pursue higher education. The Upper School offers 13 Advanced Placement courses, 15 Honors courses, and 3 courses in partnership with Oberlin College. Tuition: $15,650–$23,225. Financial Aid: $2,000,000. Alexa Hansen is Director of Admission; Carol Klimas (Alvernia College, B.A.) was appointed President in 2007.

Laurel School 1896

Lyman Campus: One Lyman Circle, Shaker Heights, OH 44122
Tel. 216-464-1441; Admission 216-464-0946; Fax 216-464-8996
Web Site www.laurelschool.org; E-mail mlgeppert@laurelschool.org
Fairmount Campus: 7420 Fairmount Boulevard, Russell, OH 44072

Now in its 112th year of educating young women, Laurel School offers a college preparatory program designed to foster intellectual excellence, leadership skills, and independent thinking. The School enrolls 610 students, with a coeducational preschool and girls only in Kindergarten–Grade 12. The traditional curriculum is enhanced by information technology, the creative and performing arts, and modern and classical languages. Academically qualified students may take honors and AP courses or cross-register at one of several area colleges. Community service and the preparation and delivery of a 10-minute speech to the school community are required for graduation. College counseling begins in Grade 9, and historically, all seniors are accepted to four-year colleges and universities. Members of the Class of 2007 enrolled in such institutions as Amherst, Boston College, Bucknell, Dartmouth, Ohio State (Honors), Princeton, and Spelman College. The extracurricular program enables girls to take part in student government, music, theater, dance, and sports. Tuition: $5000–$21,600. Financial Aid: $1,800,000. Mary Lisa Geppert is Director of Admission & Financial Aid; Ann Klotz is Head of School.

Magnificat High School 1955

20770 Hilliard Boulevard, Rocky River, OH 44116
Tel. 440-331-1572; Fax 440-331-7257
Web Site www.magnificaths.org; E-mail tcarney@magnificaths.org

The Sisters of the Humility of Mary founded this secondary day school, enrolling 875 young women, to promote growth and achievement within the context of a Christian philosophy. The college preparatory program, balancing the liberal arts and sciences, requires four years of theology and 30 hours of community service. Honors and Advanced Placement courses are available to qualified students, and an extensive tutoring program provides long- and short-term remediation. Girls participate in sports, band and choral concerts, academic teams, publications, drama, retreats, and interest clubs. Tuition: $8800. Financial Aid: $950,000. Terry Schabel Carney '80 is Director of Admission; Sr. Mary Pat Cook, H.M., '63 (Notre Dame College of Ohio, B.S.; Indiana University, M.S.Ed.), is Principal; Sr. Carol Anne Smith, H.M., is President. *North Central Association.*

Maumee Valley Country Day School 1884

1715 South Reynolds Road, Toledo, OH 43614
Tel. 419-381-1313; Admissions Ext. 3037; Fax 419-381-9941
Web Site www.mvcds.org; E-mail admissions@mvcds.net

Maumee Valley Country Day School enrolls 470 boys and girls in Preschool Age 3–Grade 12. Small classes and individual instruction are typical throughout; the Upper School is college preparatory, with focus on the liberal arts, critical thinking, and creative expression. Advanced Placement courses are available. The School offers programs in the fine arts and sports, and a month-long Winterim for independent study on or off campus, throughout the country, or abroad. Summer programs in mathematics, English, and computer studies are available. Tuition: $4210–$14,350. Financial Aid: $950,000. Vicki Koelsch is Director of Admissions; Gary Boehm is Head of School.

The Miami Valley School 1964

5151 Denise Drive, Dayton, OH 45429
Tel. 937-434-4444; Fax 937-434-1033
Web Site www.mvschool.com; E-mail admission@mvschool.com

The Miami Valley School, the only independent, college preparatory school in the Dayton region, enrolls 500 boys and girls in Early Childhood–Grade 12. The challenging curriculum, personalized attention, and outstanding faculty provide an enriching environment for students to think critically, communicate effectively, and nurture their unique talents. All students benefit from an extensive experiential learning philosophy that culminates in a four-week intensive immersion program for Upper School students. Advanced Placement, fine and performing arts, world languages, athletics, and summer enrichment programs for all ages are offered. Tuition: $6390–$15,170. Financial aid is available. Peter B. Benedict II is Headmaster.

Old Trail School 1920

2315 Ira Road, P.O. Box 827, Bath, OH 44210-0827
Tel. 330-666-1118; Admissions Ext. 312; Fax 330-666-2187
Web Site www.oldtrail.org; E-mail sholding@oldtrail.org

Old Trail School is a day school enrolling 540 boys and girls in Toddler–Grade 8. Situated on 57 acres within the boundaries of the Cuyahoga Valley National Park in north-suburban Akron, the School is also accessible to residents of south-suburban Cleveland and Medina County. It offers a personal, nurturing, and academically challenging environment. The traditional liberal arts curriculum places an emphasis on the visual and performing arts, foreign languages, computer literacy, and physical education. Summer academic and enrichment programs are offered. Tuition: $7050–$14,650. Financial Aid: $650,000. Susan Holding is Admission Director; John S. Farber (Trinity University, B.A. 1980; Antioch University, M.Ed. 1987) is Headmaster.

Olney Friends School 1837

61830 Sandy Ridge Road, Barnesville, OH 43713
Tel. 740-425-3655; Admissions Ext 3; [Toll-free] 800-303-4291
Fax 740-425-3202
Web Site www.olneyfriends.org; E-mail karen@olneyfriends.org

Olney Friends School celebrates intellectual vigor, provokes questions of conscience, and nurtures skills of living in community. A comprehensive college preparatory boarding and day school for Grades 9–12, Olney promotes traditional Quaker values such as integrity and simplicity while encouraging freedom of expression, creative thinking, and acceptance of individual differences. The 350-acre campus in the Appalachian foothills supports a sustainability program integrated into curricular and cocurricular activities. Fresh fruits and vegetables from Olney's farms and gardens are daily fare. Sixty to 70 students from countries around the world and from cities as close as Pittsburgh and Cleveland attend Olney each year. A high number enroll in AP classes in addition to fine arts and sports electives. Olney produces graduates who are self-possessed, confident, and capable of taking on college with zest. College visits and a dedicated college class for seniors focus on supporting each student's quest for their best-fit college. Olney is accredited by the Independent Schools Association of the Central States. Comprehensive Boarding Tuition: $25,200. Ela Jean Robertson is Director of Admissions; Richard Sidwell is Head of School.

Saint Ignatius High School 1886

1911 West 30th Street, Cleveland, OH 44113-3495
Tel. 216-651-0222; Fax 216-651-6313
Web Site www.ignatius.edu

Conducted by the Society of Jesus, this Roman Catholic day school, enrolling 1400 young men, emphasizes academic excellence and the development of the complete Christian person; students are encouraged to be open to growth, intellectually competent, loving, religious, and committed to work for peace and justice. The curriculum is enhanced by fine arts, technology, and Advanced Placement and honors courses. Religious education creates a basis for moral thought and action. Students are positively involved with inner-city life through structured activities; other extracurriculars include sports, speech and debate, publications, and student government. Tuition: $9970. Fees: $150. Financial Aid: $3,200,000. Rev. Timothy P. Kesicki, SJ, is President; Peter Corrigan, Jr., is Principal. *North Central Association.*

The Seven Hills School 1974

5400 Red Bank Road, Cincinnati, OH 45227
Tel. 513-271-9027; Fax 513-271-2471
Web Site www.7hills.org; E-mail admissions@7hills.org

Formed by the 1974 merger of schools whose roots date to 1906, Seven Hills seeks to offer college preparation of superior quality in a coeducational setting for 1055 students in Prekindergarten–Grade 12. Its mission is to prepare students to be successful, contributing citizens by emphasizing academic excellence, development of individual potential, participation, and service to school and community. Wireless network connectivity in all grades and laptops for teachers enhance learning. Advanced Placement and honors courses, the fine and performing arts, athletics, an outdoor program, and summer enrichment opportunities are offered. Year-long extended care is available through Grade 5. Tuition: $8520–$17,630. Financial Aid: $1,500,000. Peter C. Egan is Director of Admissions; Todd B. Bland is Interim Head of School.

Springer School and Center 1887

2121 Madison Road, Cincinnati, OH 45208
Tel. 513-871-6080; Admissions Ext. 210; Fax 513-871-6428
Web Site www.springer-ld.org; E-mail info@springer-ld.org

Springer School and Center, enrolling 206 boys and girls ages 6–14, empowers students with learning disabilities to lead successful lives. Small-group instruction and diagnostic teaching provide the strategies and skills students need to succeed in traditional schools. As well as a comprehensive academic program, students enjoy art, music, physical education, and activities that build social and leadership skills. Individualized programs may include language therapy, psychotherapy, and/or motor skills training. Students are enrolled an average of four years. The Center offers information, consultation, and programs for persons affected by learning disabilities. Tuition: $17,700. Financial aid is available. Jan Annett is Admissions Director; Shelly Weisbacher (Northwestern University, B.S., M.A.) is Executive Director.

The Summit Country Day School 1890

2161 Grandin Road, Hyde Park, Cincinnati, OH 45208
Tel. 513-871-4700; Fax 513-533-5373
Web Site www.summitcds.org; E-mail schiess_k@summitcds.org

Founded by the Sisters of Notre Dame de Namur, Summit is Cincinnati's only Catholic, coeducational school offering a college preparatory program in Preschool–Grade 12. Its 1080-member student body represents many racial, ethnic, religious, and socioeconomic backgrounds. The liberal arts curriculum includes a nationally recognized Educating for Character Program. Courses in core subjects are enhanced by the School's computer technology initiative. Each year, 20 percent of seniors receive National Merit Scholarship recognition, and 100 percent go on to college. Christian outreach, social and academic clubs, drama, publications, and athletics are among the activities. Tuition: $5360–$14,495. Kelley K. Schiess is Director of Admission; Gerald M. Jellig is Head of School.

University School 1890

Shaker Campus (K–8): 20701 Brantley Road, Shaker Heights, OH 44122
Tel. 216-321-8260; Fax 216-321-8317
Hunting Valley Campus (Grades 9–12): 2785 SOM Center Road, Hunting Valley, OH 44022
Tel. 216-831-2200; Fax 216-292-7810
Web Site www.us.edu

University School enrolls 860 talented young men as students in Kindergarten–Grade 12. The Shaker Campus offers a dynamic, theme-based, research-based curriculum coupled with high academic standards. The Hunting Valley Campus continues the boys' learning with a rigorous college preparatory curriculum. The traditional high school program includes Advanced Placement and college-level courses, endowed student fellowships, ecology programs, Greek, Chinese, and Latin studies, and numerous extracurricular offerings. A summer session is available. Tuition: $14,740–$21,080. Financial Aid: $2,500,000. Christopher S. Barton is Director of Enrollment; Stephen S. Murray (Williams College, B.A.; Harvard, M.Ed., M.A.) is Headmaster.

Western Reserve Academy 1826

115 College Street, Hudson, OH 44236
Tel. 330-650-4400; [Toll-free] 800-784-3776
Admissions 330-650-9717
Web Site www.wra.net; E-mail admission@wra.net

Western Reserve Academy in Hudson, Ohio, is a coeducational boarding and day school enrolling students in Grades 9 through 12 and a postgraduate year. The town of Hudson (population 25,000) retains the flavor of an 18th-century New England village and has been cited by the National Trust for Historic Preservation as "among the top 100 historic places in the nation."

Reserve was founded in 1826 as a college and preparatory academy by Hudson's earliest settlers. The college later moved to Cleveland and became Case Western Reserve University. After being closed for 13 years, James W. Ellsworth endowed the Academy with funding to permit its return to active operation in 1916. Mr. Ellsworth contributed an endowment that currently exceeds $111,000,000, enabling Reserve to offer substantial scholarship assistance. In May 2001, Reserve was highlighted as one of the nation's 13 outstanding coeducational boarding schools by *U.S. News and World Report.*

Western Reserve Academy is a close-knit community of teachers and students fully engaged in the process of education. Academics are foremost, but they are balanced by a spirit of discovery that extends beyond the classroom. Students are challenged to ask questions and to find answers in many different ways and places, including living with young people from different countries and cultures, planning team strategy in athletics, rehearsing for performances, and extending their efforts to participate in helping the community both within and outside of Reserve.

A nonprofit institution, Western Reserve Academy is governed by 30 Trustees, 23 of whom are alumni. The Alumni Association is actively involved in all aspects of the school. Western Reserve Academy holds membership in many educational associations and foundations, including A Better Chance, the

Naval Academy Foundation, the National Association of Independent Schools, School Year Abroad, and The Association of Boarding Schools. It is accredited by the Independent Schools Association of the Central States.

THE CAMPUS. The 190-acre campus features outstanding examples of Greek Revival architecture along with "Brick Row" buildings modeled after Yale University. Central to Western Reserve is Middle College, which is built on the Academy's cornerstone, laid in 1826. Five of the original seven buildings are still in use, including the David Hudson House, which is the oldest frame house in Ohio. The Loomis Observatory is the second-oldest structure of its kind in the United States. The 16,000-square-foot dormitory, Long House, opened in 2000 as did the 20,000-square-foot John D. Ong Library, which houses 45,000 volumes and an enlarged computer lab. In 2002, Cartwright House, a new girls' dormitory, was completed. The Knight Fine Arts Center houses studios for instruction in photography, digital imagery, the manual arts, dance, and a fine arts gallery. The fully equipped theater seats 400. The Academy's computers are connected through a fiberoptic network reaching dormitory rooms, classrooms, and offices, and students have full wireless Internet access as well as e-mail accounts. A state-of-the-art athletic complex includes a field house with a 200-meter track, varsity basketball court, and three practice courts.

Athletic facilities include a six-lane swimming pool with diving well, wrestling/multipurpose rooms, 12 tennis courts, squash courts, a state-of-the-art weight training/fitness center with new Nautilus equipment, a new 400-meter all-weather track, a new Pro-Turf all-weather field for football, soccer, lacrosse, and field hockey, a cross-country trail, a paddle tennis court, and 12 additional athletic fields. The ice-hockey team skates at Kent State University, while golf team members enjoy privileges at a local club.

More than 90 percent of Western Reserve's faculty live on campus with their families in Academy-owned homes or dormitories.

THE FACULTY. Henry E. Flanagan, Jr., was appointed Headmaster in 1982. He is a graduate of Rutgers College (B.A.), the University of Michigan (M.A., Ph.D.), and Harvard University (M.Ed.) and previously held teaching, coaching, and administrative positions at Avon Old Farms in Connecticut.

There are 68 full- and part-time faculty, 50 percent of whom hold advanced degrees. Most teachers continue their educational and professional growth through summer or full-year sabbaticals, writing workshops, marine biology projects, or graduate studies and seminars.

A full-time nurse heads the new Health Center and is supported by four staff members. A local doctor holds daily office hours and is on call at all times.

STUDENT BODY. In 2006–07, Reserve enrolled 152 boarding boys, 117 boarding girls, 75 day boys, and 62 day girls in Grades 9–12 and a postgraduate year. Boarding students represent 28 states and 25 countries. Day students are fully integrated into the residential experience, spending time on campus in the evenings and on weekends.

ACADEMIC PROGRAM. The school year, from September to June, is divided into four marking periods, with Thanksgiving, Christmas, and spring vacations. School begins at 8:00 A.M., with a morning meeting held three days a week, followed by academic classes, lunch, afternoon classes, activities, conferences, and athletics. "Lights out" for all classes but seniors is 11:15 P.M.

Reserve's academic program is designed to stretch each student to take full advantage of the Academy's offerings and to create an academic profile that builds on strengths and bolsters weaknesses. Classes are small, techniques are varied, and teachers are available for help outside the classroom during the day and evening. The Academic Enrichment Center is also available for students who need additional support. There is a mandatory quiet study period from 7:45 to 11:00 P.M. Sunday through Friday.

To graduate, students must complete four years of English, three years each of mathematics and foreign language, three years of science, two and one-half years of history, two years of fine arts, senior seminar (an interdisciplinary course focusing on humanistic topics), and a half-year of health.

The curriculum includes such courses as English I–IV, Creative Writing; French I–V, German I–V, Latin I–IV, Spanish I–V, Chinese I–IV; Algebra, Geometry, Pre-Calculus, Calculus, Advanced Topics in Mathematics; Biology, Zoology, Physics, Astronomy, Chemistry; United States History, Constitutional Law, Economics; Health/Ethics; Studio Art, Photography, Dance, Choir, Music Theory, String Orchestra; Public Speaking, Dramatic Performance; and Engineering Drawing, Web Publishing, and Architectural Design.

Honors classes are offered in Latin, geometry, pre-calculus, physics, intermediate algebra, and dance. Advanced Placement courses are formed in English, French, German, Latin, Spanish, U.S. History, European history, calculus, statistics, computer science, physics, chemistry, biology, and economics. Academic credit is also granted for independent study and special projects. Exchange programs are available through The English-Speaking Union, School Year Abroad, or the Ridley College Experience.

In 2007, the graduating seniors entered more than 80 colleges and universities including Amherst, Case Western Reserve University, Colgate, Columbia, Cornell, Dartmouth, Denison, Duke, George Washington University, Middlebury, Northwestern, United States Military Academy, United States Naval Academy, Vanderbilt, Wellesley, Yale, and the University of Pennsylvania.

Summer programs at the Academy include "Encore," an internationally recognized strings program affiliated with the Cleveland Institute of Music, and sports camps.

STUDENT ACTIVITIES. The Student Council is responsible for presenting student ideas and organizing activities. All students take part in Reserve's Service Program, which may involve working in the library or dining hall or acting as a laboratory assistant or teacher aide.

Reserve offers numerous extracurricular activities for students with a broad variety of interests including OpuS (theater), S.I.C.U. (Students for Intercultural Understanding), WWRA (student radio station), Student Affairs Committee, *The Reserve Record* (newspaper), *Hardscrabble* (yearbook), S.E.A.L. (Student Environmental Action League), R.E.A.C.H. (Reserve Ethically Advancing Community Health), and the Chess, Culinary, Debate, and Investment Clubs, among others.

The Western Reserve Academy athletic program is built around a history of strong teams, dedicated coaches, and enthusiastic parent and alumni supporters. Many student athletes have been named to All-American teams or become captains in college sports. Each student is required to participate in athletics at some level in order to balance academic and extracurricular life and provide exercise and an outlet from the rigors of the classroom. All sports have varsity squads, many have junior varsity teams and "C" squads. Boys compete in the Interstate Preparatory School League in football, soccer, basketball, cross-country, wrestling, hockey, swimming, diving, baseball, precision shooting, golf, lacrosse, and tennis. Girls compete in the Private School League in field hockey, soccer, volleyball, cross-country, swimming, diving, precision shooting, basketball, ice hockey, track, softball, lacrosse, and tennis. Students may also participate in a number of intramural activities including aerobics and weightlifting.

Dances, concerts, and trips are offered on weekends, and traditional annual events include Christmas Vespers, Winter Carnival, and the Dads Club Family Party.

ADMISSION AND COSTS. Most students enter Reserve in Grades 9 or 10, with a few admitted to the upper grades. The Academy admits students of any race, color, or national or ethnic origin. Applicants must submit scores from either the Secondary School Admission Test or the Independent School Entrance Examination; junior or senior applicants can submit Preliminary Scholastic Aptitude or Scholastic Aptitude Test results. Applications, accompanied by a $50 fee ($150 for international students), should be submitted by February 1 for boarders and January 15 for day students; families are notified by March 10 for boarders and February 10 for day students. Late applications will be considered as space permits.

In 2007–08, boarding tuition is $35,800; day tuition, including meals, is $25,500. Extras are approximately $500, with additional expenses for boarders of $1000. Tuition insurance and a payment plan are available.

In the current year, more than $3,315,000 was awarded in financial aid on the basis of need. Reserve uses the School and Student Service for Financial Aid to determine award amounts.

Headmaster: Henry E. Flanagan, Jr.
Academic Dean: John Haile
Dean of Faculty: Christopher Burner
Dean of Students: Brand Closen
Dean of Admission: Barbara Flanagan
Director of Enrollment & Financial Aid: Brendan Schneider
Director of Academy Advancement: Helen Tremaine Gregory
Director of College Guidance: E. Tariq Thomas
Business Manager: Leonard Carlson
Director of Athletics: Charles L. Schmitt

OKLAHOMA

Casady School 1947

9500 North Pennsylvania Avenue, P.O. Box 20390, Oklahoma City, OK 73120
Tel. 405-749-3100; Admissions 405-740-3185; Fax 405-749-3223
Web Site www.casady.org; E-mail admissions@casady.org

The Episcopal Bishop of Oklahoma and dedicated laypersons founded Casady School in 1947 to promote academic excellence and Christian principles. Now in its seventh decade of educating the mind, body, and spirit of young people, Casady enrolls 875 college-bound boys and girls in Pre-K (age 3)–Grade 12 in a liberal arts program designed to develop each child's mental, spiritual, and physical well-being. More than half the faculty hold master's degrees, and 9 have earned doctorates. The classical curriculum emphasizes a strong foundation in core subjects, enriched by AP courses in 12 departments. Historically, all Casady graduates enter four-year colleges and universities nationwide. Students enjoy a wide array of aesthetic, athletic, extracurricular opportunities, and electives. The spacious campus, centered around a 6-acre lake, provides facilities for student-produced publications, vocal and instrumental ensembles, academic tournaments, competitive team sports, peer tutoring, and service learning projects that introduce participants to meaningful work within the larger community. Tuition: $6275–$14,625. Aaron James is Director of Admission; David Gorham is Interim Headmaster.

Heritage Hall School 1969

1800 N.W. 122nd Street, Oklahoma City, OK 73120-9598
Tel. 405-749-3001; Fax 405-751-7372
Web Site www.heritagehall.com; E-mail dbolding@heritagehall.com

An independent day school founded in 1969, Heritage Hall enrolls 865 boys and girls in Preschool through Grade 12. Students come from many racial, ethnic, and socioeconomic backgrounds, creating a dynamic and diverse learning environment based on respect and understanding. In keeping with its school motto, "to learn, to lead, to serve," Heritage Hall offers a demanding college preparatory program at all levels, including Advanced Placement courses that culminate in preparation for AP exams in ten subjects. The Challenge Scholar Program for students of exceptional ability and the International Student Program, emphasizing American culture and English language fluency, enhance the core curriculum. Upon graduating, all seniors enter college. Students in Grades 7–12 contribute 20,000 hours of community service annually. School government, publications, Fellowship of Christian Athletes, honor societies, interest clubs, interscholastic sports, and award-winning speech, debate, drama, and music programs are among the

activities. Tuition: $9995–$12,655. Financial Aid: $400,000. Debbie Bolding is Director of Admissions; Guy A. Bramble (Amherst, B.A.; Harvard University, Ed.M.) is Head.

Holland Hall 1922

5666 East 81st Street, Tulsa, OK 74137-2099
Tel. 918-481-1111; Fax 918-481-1145
Web Site www.hollandhall.org

HOLLAND HALL in Tulsa, Oklahoma, is a coeducational, college preparatory, Episcopal-affiliated day school encompassing three-year-old PreSchool through Grade 12. The city (population 708,954) is home to The University of Tulsa and Oral Roberts University and enjoys cultural attractions including civic ballet, philharmonic, and opera companies; the Philbrook Museum of Art; and the Thomas Gilcrease Institute of American History and Art.

The city's first independent school, Holland Hall was founded in 1922 to provide an educational experience that prepares students to succeed in an ever-changing world. The program is designed to develop the talents and strengths of each individual within an environment informed by Judeo-Christian values. Holland Hall's affiliation with the Episcopal Church is reflected in religious studies, chapel services, and the presence of chaplains on campus. The school's core values include intellectual and open inquiry; mental, physical, and spiritual growth; inspiring and innovative teaching; trust, respect, and partnership; appreciation of diversity; and responsibility to self and others.

Holland Hall is governed by a Board of Trustees and accredited by the Independent Schools Association of the Southwest and the Oklahoma State Board of Education. It holds membership in the National Association of Independent Schools and the National Association of Episcopal Schools, among other organizations.

THE CAMPUS. Holland Hall's 162-acre campus is set amid two scenic wooded areas. The Primary, Middle, and Upper Schools are housed in separate buildings.

The spiritual hub of the school is All Saints Chapel, which serves all students regardless of religious affiliation. The 70,000-square-foot Pauline McFarlin Walter Arts Center provides a 1200-seat main theater, a studio theater, the Holliman Gallery, and studios and practice rooms. The Flint-Williams Gymnasium, serving the Upper School, includes basketball and volleyball courts; a weight-training facility is in an adjoining building. The 18,000-square-foot Duenner Family Science, Mathematics and Technology Center houses large, fully equipped biology and physics laboratories with flexibility to accommodate advancing technology; two seminar rooms; four math classrooms; a next-generation computer teaching facility designed for individual learning; faculty offices; and a student commons and study area. The Upper School also includes a state-of-the-art language lab.

The grounds include a pond, an eight-lane all-weather track, 12 tennis courts, hiking and cross-country trails, ten playing fields, and age-appropriate, game-specific playground areas.

The plant is valued at more than $50,000,000.

THE FACULTY. Mark D. Desjardins was appointed Headmaster in 2004. Dr. Desjardins holds an M.Ed. in Secondary School Administration and a Ph.D. in History of American Education from the University of Virginia. He also holds a B.A. in East Asian Civilizations from Bates College.

Holland Hall's 107-member faculty have an average of nearly 19 years of teaching experience. All hold baccalaureate degrees or the equivalent, and nearly one-half hold advanced degrees. Among their representative colleges and universities are Amherst, Boston College, Boston University, Brown, Carnegie Mellon, Clemson, Colgate, Cornell, Denison, Fordham, Harvard College, Indiana University, Lesley, Manhattanville, Northwestern, Oklahoma State, Pennsylvania State, Southern Methodist, Trinity, Tufts, Vanderbilt, Villanova, Williams, Xavier, Yale, and the Universities of California (Los Angeles), Chicago, Colorado, Illinois, Kansas, Michigan, Missouri, Oklahoma, Texas, Tulsa, and Wisconsin. Teaching assistants are in each classroom in Primary School and in each grade in Middle School.

STUDENT BODY. In 2007–08, Holland Hall enrolled 993 boys and girls in the Primary School (Age 3–Grade 3), Middle School (Grades 4–8), and Upper School (Grades 9–12). The student body reflects a broad diversity of racial, ethnic, religious, and social backgrounds.

ACADEMIC PROGRAM. The school year is divided into semesters with vacations at Thanksgiving, Christmas, and in the spring. Letter grades and written comments for students in Grade 6 and up are sent home four times a year, and written evaluations are provided for students through Grade 5. In the Middle and Upper Schools, each student has an advisor who works in concert with his or her parents to formulate a balanced educational program. Support service specialists in each division provide additional assistance and enrichment for students in time management, note taking, and other study skills. The student-teacher ratio schoolwide is 9:1.

In the Primary School, the child-centered, developmentally appropriate curriculum promotes a self-motivating approach to learning that engages students in exploration and discovery, decision making, and problem solving. Language arts, mathematics, science, social studies, and creative writing are emphasized, with enrichment classes in religion, library skills, the visual arts, music, foreign language, physical education, and computer education. Mobile, wireless computer technology is integrated throughout the Primary School curriculum.

Holland Hall's Middle School combines a rigorous curriculum with developmental, exploratory experiences to help students achieve their full potential. Middle School faculty are trained to understand emerging adolescents and to help them balance their new-found freedom with responsibility. The academic program builds on the foundations acquired in the Primary School as subject matter becomes appropriately more complex. Formal letter grades are not recorded until Grade 6 in keeping with the school's sensitivity to each child's development; parents receive written reports and attend conferences updating them on their child's achievement.

In addition to core studies in English/language arts, reading, mathematics, the sciences, and world culture and geography, Middle School students participate in Spanish, French, Latin, religion, computer class, fine arts, physical education, and library studies. Community service projects, student-faculty plays, ecology outings, and field trips provide opportunities for social, emotional, and intellectual growth.

Holland Hall's Upper School operates on a flexible, modular schedule. There are 18 22-minute modules each day, and each class varies from two to three modules, depending on the subject.

To graduate from the Upper School, a student must complete a minimum of 21½ credits as follows: 4 in English; 3 each in mathematics, laboratory science, the same foreign language, and social studies; 1 each in religious studies and fine arts; and 3½ in physical education. Honors and Advanced Placement courses carry additional weight in a student's grade-point average.

Upper School courses include English I and numerous English electives; French I–III, Latin I–III, Spanish I–III, Chinese I–IV; Algebra I–II, Geometry, Math Analysis, Probability and Statistics, Trigonometry; Biology, Chemistry, Conceptual Physics and Chemistry, Ecology, Geology, Physics, Physiology of Sports Medicine; Europe in the World: History, American Studies: History, Art History Survey, Culture of Pre-Modern East Asia, Democracy and Dissent, Global Issues, Vietnam and the American Experience; Community Service, Comparative Religion, Ethics; Introduction to Programming, Microsoft Office User; Advanced Art A, Advanced Art BC, Ceramics I–IV, Drawing I–II, Painting I–II, Basic Photography I–III; Choreography, Modern Dance I–IV, Repertory; Stagecraft, Theater Arts I–III, Theatrical Production; Chamber Orchestra I–IV, Concert Band, Concert Chorus I–IV, Jazz Ensemble I–IV, Holland Hall

Singers I–IV, Music Theory I–II; and Creative Writing. In addition, students may take facilitated studies in Web Page, Animation, Still Image, Digital Video, Page Layout, and Networking.

Advanced Placement courses are offered in 8 subjects. In 2007, 109 students took 245 Advanced Placement exams in 17 subjects. The Class of 2007 also produced 7 National Merit Finalists, and 5 Commended Students.

Twelfth graders are required to participate in a Senior Intern Program in which they work for a community agency or in a professional setting.

Members of Holland Hall's Class of 2007 are enrolled in colleges and universities across the nation and abroad such as DePauw, George Washington, Johns Hopkins, Massachusetts Institute of Technology, Princeton, Rice, Southern Methodist, Tulane, and the United States Military Academy.

STUDENT ACTIVITIES. Elected members of the Student Council promote school spirit and morale and serve as a liaison with the administration. Members of the Student-Faculty Honor Council in the Upper School make recommendations for action in cases of violation of school regulations.

Students publish a newspaper, yearbook, and creative writing and art magazine. Outstanding upperclassmen may be invited to join The Cum Laude Society; there are also chapters of national honor societies for French, Latin, Chinese, and Spanish.

Other groups include Academic Bowl, Holland Hall Singers, and the AFS, Art, French, Latin, Outing, Spanish, and Technology Clubs. Middle School clubs include Academic Bowl, MathCounts, Dutch for Christ, and Young Authors. Community service projects are ongoing in each division.

All students in Grades 6–12 compete on any of the school's 62 teams in cross-country, football, volleyball, soccer, track, field hockey, baseball, softball, basketball, tennis, and golf.

Among the special annual events are Field Day, School Out-of-Doors, Freshman Orientation, Service of Lessons and Carols, Dutch Weekend, a speaker series sponsored by the Kistler-Gilliland Center for the Advancement of Learning, ARTworks, Book Fair, Dutch Treat, Visiting Illustrator-Author Program, Auction, Fine Arts Festival, Baccalaureate, and Commencement.

ADMISSION AND COSTS. Holland Hall welcomes motivated students of good character and ability without regard to race, sex, religion, sexual orientation, national or ethnic origin, or physical handicap. Admission is based on previous school transcripts, teacher recommendations, and standardized test results.

In 2007–08, tuition is $3655–$8930 in the PreSchool, $11,050–$11,420 in Kindergarten–Grade 3, $13,210 in Grades 4–8, and $14,310 in Grades 9–12. Other expenses include required uniforms in Grades 1–12 ($300), books and supplies ($200–$400), an activity fee ($30–$100), and transportation ($340–$500 per semester). Tuition payment plans are offered. More than $1,600,000 in need-based assistance was awarded for the current school year.

Headmaster: Mark D. Desjardins, Ph.D.
Head of Upper School: Dennis Calkins
Head of Middle School: Richard Hart
Head of Primary School: Jo-An Vargo
Director of Admission & Financial Aid: Lori Adams
Assistant Head of School for Institutional Advancement & External Relations: Josh Wolman
Director of Communications: Mercedes Millberry
Director of Finance: Leslie Kelly
Director of Athletics: Steve Heldebrand

Riverfield Country Day School 1984

2433 West 61st Street, Tulsa, OK 74132
Tel. 918-446-3553; Fax 918-446-1914
Web Site www.riverfield.org; E-mail admissions@riverfield.org

Enrolling 500 children from 8 weeks of age to Grade 12, Riverfield offers an innovative program emphasizing small class size, personalized instruction, and academic excellence. Through varied teaching styles and multiage classrooms, the learning environment respects each pupil's pace. Riverfield, which is accredited by the Independent Schools Association of the Southwest, aims to develop strong readers, curious learners, and creative thinkers. The faculty and staff, whose first priority is the intellectual and personal growth of each student, are diverse in age and professional experience. A summer camp program is optional. Tuition: $6885–$8575. Financial aid is available. Britton Fox is Director of Admissions; Martha S. Clark (Principia, B.S.Ed.) is Head of School.

OREGON

The Delphian School™ 1974

20950 SW Rock Creek Road, Sheridan, OR 97378
Tel. 503-843-3521; Admissions [Toll-free] 800-626-6610
Fax 503-843-4158
Web Site www.delphian.org; E-mail info@delphian.org

The Delphian School is the founding, and only, day and boarding school in a network of nine schools dedicated to improving standards in education. The Delphi Program™ is designed to provide young people with a rich academic background, strong ethics, and a broad range of abilities to launch them successfully into higher education and life. Using the study methods developed by American educator L. Ron Hubbard, Delphi teaches students how to identify basic barriers that prevent understanding, to apply this knowledge to break through any problems with study, and to find true comprehension. Delphi, enrolling 270 boys and girls in Kindergarten–Grade 12, is set on an 800-acre campus overlooking Oregon's beautiful Willamette Valley. The comprehensive curriculum covers a wide spectrum of cultural, scientific, and social subjects. Reading, writing, and math are taken to a full mastery. Summer and ESL programs are available. Delphi is licensed to use Applied Scholastics™ educational services. Boarding Tuition: $32,224–$34,250; Day Tuition: $15,055–$18,685. Donetta Phelps is Director of Admissions; Rosemary Didear is Headmistress.

Oak Hill School 1994

86397 Eastway Drive, Eugene, OR 97405-9647
Tel. 541-744-0954; Fax 541-741-6968
Web Site www.oakhillschool.com; E-mail admissions@oakhillschool.com

Parents and interested citizens founded Oak Hill School to provide a solid college preparatory program for boys and girls in Kindergarten–Grade 12. Enrolling 130 day students from diverse racial, ethnic, and cultural backgrounds, Oak Hill emphasizes respect for others and stewardship of the environment in all aspects of its curriculum. Small classes enrolling 16–18 students, an 8:1 student-teacher ratio, and dedicated faculty, more than 75 percent of whom hold advanced degrees, promote academic excellence. In the lower grades, children discover key concepts in core subjects through an age-appropriate, differentiated, hands-on curriculum centered on reading and language arts, math, science, and social studies. Upper School students undertake a traditional liberal arts program, with honors and Advanced Placement offerings in 18 subject areas. There are also national and international travel-study opportunities. Community service is a graduation requirement; other activities include orchestral, choral, and classic string ensembles, chess club, and sports. All Oak Hill graduates have been admitted to four-year colleges and universities. Tuition: $9930–$16,000. Carrie Miller is Director of Admissions; Elliott Grey is Head of School. *Pacific Northwest Association.*

PENNSYLVANIA

Abington Friends School 1697

575 Washington Lane, Jenkintown, PA 19046
Tel. 215-886-4350; Fax 215-886-9143
Web Site www.abingtonfriends.net
E-mail mchristian@abingtonfriends.net

Abington Friends is the only school in the nation located on the same grounds and operating under the same management since its beginnings more than 300 years ago. Founded by Quakers, this college preparatory day school, enrolling 740 students in Preschool–Grade 12, emphasizes intellectual challenges, character development, interdisciplinary and intercultural studies, the arts, and moral, physical, emotional, social, and spiritual well-being. Lower School students learn to appreciate another culture through Spanish class, hone skills in reading and writing, and research, experiment, and solve problems in math and science courses. Middle and Upper School students prepare for future education by taking required core classes and studying specific topics through electives. An average class has 13–15 students. Ten sports teams, dance, orchestra, chorus, drama, and computer centers with high-speed Internet access enhance the curriculum. Community service is required, and foreign travel/study is encouraged. Extended-day and summer programs are offered. Tuition: $13,500–$21,900. Financial aid is available. Marnie Christian is Director of Admissions; Richard F. Nourie (Harvard Graduate School of Education, Ed.M.) is Head of School.

The Baldwin School 1888

701 West Montgomery Avenue, Bryn Mawr, PA 19010
Tel. 610-525-2700; Fax 610-581-7231
Web Site www.baldwinschool.org; E-mail admissions@baldwinschool.org

THE BALDWIN SCHOOL in Bryn Mawr, Pennsylvania, is a college preparatory day school enrolling girls in Pre-Kindergarten through Grade 12. The School is located 11 miles west of Philadelphia in the Main Line community of Bryn Mawr (population 8400). Bryn Mawr and Haverford Colleges are within walking distance. Nearby bus and rail services provide access to the historical, cultural, and recreational resources of Philadelphia.

Founded in 1888 by Florence Baldwin to prepare young women for admission to Bryn Mawr College, the School strives to provide a challenging academic program in a lively, creative environment. Emphasizing both scope and depth in learning, Baldwin hopes to endow each student with the ability and enthusiasm for a life of continuing growth as a scholar, a woman, and a human being.

The Baldwin School is a nonprofit institution governed by a 30-member, self-perpetuating Board of Trustees. The Alumnae Association maintains contact with approximately 3600 living graduates, helping with fund-raising and school events. The School has an endowment of $7,500,000. Accredited by the Middle States Association of Colleges and Schools and by the Pennsylvania Association of Private Academic Schools, Baldwin holds membership in the National Association of Independent Schools, among other organizations.

THE CAMPUS. The 25-acre campus includes three athletic fields, indoor and outdoor swimming pools, two playgrounds, three tennis courts, two gymnasiums, and an Early Childhood Center.

Listed on the National Register of Historic Places, the Residence (1896) houses administrative offices, a reception area, an assembly room, dining room, kitchen, bookstore, an arts facility, the Music Wing, the Middle School Music Room, and the Early Childhood Center. The Schoolhouse (1925, renovated 1998) contains Upper and Middle School classrooms, the library, and offices for the Head of the School as well as the Middle and Upper School directors. The Science Building provides a variety of laboratories. The Baldwin libraries have 30,000 volumes, online databases, and membership in a local consortium for resource sharing. Additional school facilities include the Mrs. Cornelia Otis Skinner Dramatic Workshop and Krumrine House, the residence of the Head of the School.

The School-owned plant is valued at $30,850,000.

THE FACULTY. Sally Powell was appointed as the seventh Head of Baldwin in 2006. A native of Great Britain, she was educated in England at the Perse School for Girls and the University of Cambridge, where she received both her bachelor's and master's degrees. Prior to coming to Baldwin, Mrs. Powell worked at the Dwight-Englewood School in New Jersey.

Faculty members include 70 full-time teachers and 16 part-time teachers. They hold 86 baccalaureate and 67 advanced degrees from such institutions as Curtis Institute of Music, Emory, French University of Beirut, Johns Hopkins, Rhode Island School of Design, Yale, and the University of Pennsylvania. Seen as role models, many faculty members serve as advisors to individual students, grades, or clubs. Faculty benefits include insurance, a retirement plan, and leaves of absence. Faculty turnover is low.

A wellness center is located on campus, and Bryn Mawr Hospital is approximately 5 minutes away.

STUDENT BODY. In 2007–08, the School enrolled 614 girls in Pre-Kindergarten–Grade 12 as follows: 17 in Pre-Kindergarten, 41 in Kindergarten, 42 in Grade 1, 37 in Grade 2, 40 in Grade 3, 41 in Grade 4, 45 in Grade 5, 52 in Grade 6, 43 in Grade 7, 45 in Grade 8, 60 in Grade 9, 49 in Grade 10, 49 in Grade 11, and 53 in Grade 12. Students represented a variety of ethnic, religious, socioeconomic, cultural, and racial backgrounds. Of the total school population, 31 percent are students of color.

ACADEMIC PROGRAM. The school year, which extends from early September to early June, is divided into trimesters and includes Thanksgiving, winter, and spring vacations. The school day begins at 8:15 A.M., when students meet with advisors to hear the daily announcements. For Grades 9–12, dismissal is at 3:30 P.M., Mondays through Thursdays, and at 2:45 P.M. on Fridays. Class periods vary in length from 42 to 75 minutes. Students in Grades 9–10 attend study hall during a free period; students in Grades 11–12 may choose how to spend their free time. A two-week rotating schedule permits club and class meetings as well as lengthened lab periods. The faculty-student ratio is about 1:7, and the average class size is 16. The math lab provides enrichment for those with exceptional ability; students needing supplemental work are recommended for the math or writing labs. Students have access to 250 computers on campus, and laptops are available for home use. Written reports are issued three times a year in Grades 5–12; parent/teacher conferences are interspersed with written reports for the younger students.

The Lower School (Pre-Kindergarten–Grade 5) program stresses self-expression, creativity, and the acquisition of basic skills. Computer science and Suzuki music instruction begin in Kindergarten; foreign language instruction begins in Grade 3. The Middle School (Grades 6–8) curriculum includes English, French, Latin, Spanish, social studies, mathematics, science, computer, music, art, drama, human development, physical education, and a library/media skills program.

Upper School (Grades 9–12) students take five units of credit each year in addition to physical education. Graduation requirements include four units of English, three units of one foreign language or two units each of two languages; three of history, consisting of one unit each in U.S. history, ancient history, and medieval history; three of mathematics; three of science; two of fine arts; one trimester course each of speech, health, and human development; and five units of electives.

Among the Upper School courses are English 1–4, Creative Writing, Poetry; Latin 1–3, Virgil, French 1–5, Spanish 1–5; Modern European History, Economics, Current World Issues; Algebra I, Algebra and Consumer Mathematics, Geometry, Algebra II and Trigonometry, Calculus, Logic, Topics in Advanced Mathematics; Environmental Science, Biology 1–2, Chemistry 1–2, Physics 1–2; and Art 1–4, Art History, Architecture, Ceramics, Design, Photography, Jewelry 1–4, Theatre 1–3, Instrumental Ensemble, Chorus, Handbell Choir, A Cappella Group, and Theory and Harmony. Advanced Placement courses, honors courses, and independent study are available.

The college placement process begins in the junior year when each girl and her parents meet with the college counselor to define interests, choices, and goals. The Class of 2007 had average SAT I scores of 610–720 verbal, 670–700 math, and 670–690 writing with 6 National Merit Semifinalists, 7 National Merit Commended Students, and 1 Presidential Scholar Semifinalist. Among the college choices for the Class of 2007 were Brown, Columbia, Cornell, Duke, Franklin and Marshall, Harvey Mudd, Northwestern, Pomona, Tufts, Washington University, and the Universities of Pennsylvania and St. Andrews (United Kingdom).

STUDENT ACTIVITIES. The Upper School Senate, composed of 12 elected student representatives, presents a forum for the expression of student opinions, implements the discipline system, and provides input on administrative issues. The Middle School Senate, which includes administrators, faculty, and elected student representatives, promotes school spirit, sponsors social functions, and helps with dining room and study hall supervision.

Extracurricular activities include the Maskers; a yearbook; a literary magazine; Lower, Middle, and Upper School newspapers; the Math Team; the Society of Latin Lovers; the Athletic Association; and the Investment, Film, Lamplighters, Ecology, Computer, Black Students' Union, Sci-Med, Amnesty International, and French Clubs. All Baldwin girls belong to the Service League, a community service organization.

Each season, girls choose between playing a team sport or joining a physical education class. Interscholastic teams are fielded in basketball, crew, cross-country, dance, field hockey, golf, lacrosse, soccer, softball, squash, swimming and diving, tennis, volleyball, and winter track. Lower School students receive swimming instruction once a week.

Social and traditional events include dances, plays, concerts, trips, art shows, music recitals, lecture series, Father/Daughter Phillies Game, Pumpkin Sale, Athletic Association Halloween Party, Café Internationale, Book Fair, Middle School Ski Trip, Marching-In Dinner, Alumnae Luncheon for Seniors, Class Night, and Ring Day. Proximity to historic and cultural sites in Philadelphia, elsewhere in Pennsylvania, and in New York City affords many opportunities for field trips.

ADMISSION AND COSTS. The Baldwin School seeks to admit girls with demonstrated academic motivation and achievement. Individual talents and diversity of background and interests are also valued. Students are admitted on the basis of a written application, standardized test scores, a personal interview and campus visit, previous school records, two recommendations, a letter to the Head of the School, and, for Grades 6–12, the results of an English placement test. There is an application fee of $50. Candidates are strongly encouraged to complete their applications prior to the February 1 deadline.

In 2007–08, tuition is $23,375 for Grades 9–12. Fees for lunch, books, labs, and uniforms are additional. A tuition insurance plan is available. In the current year, Baldwin awarded more than $1,484,536 in need-based financial aid to 19 percent of the student body. The Baldwin School subscribes to the School and Student Service for Financial Aid.

Assistant Head of School & Director of Middle School: Damaris South
Director of Upper School: Eric Benke
Director of Lower School: Baiba Vasys
Alumnae Director: Anne Plutzer Burns '96
Director of Admissions & Financial Aid: Sarah J. Goebel
Director of Development: Sue Houser Winant '78
College Counselor: Pamela Fetters
Director of Finance: John J. Berg
Director of Athletics: Deb Surgi

Carson Long Military Institute 1836

200 North Carlisle Street, P.O. Box 98, New Bloomfield, PA 17068
Tel. 717-582-2121; Fax 717-582-8763
Web Site www.carsonlong.org; E-mail clinfo@carsonlong.org

Theodore K. Long founded this college preparatory boarding school for young men as a memorial tribute to his son, William Carson Long. Enrolling 205 cadets in Grades 6 through 12, Carson Long Military Institute is committed to teaching boys "how to learn, how to labor, and how to live." Close interaction with faculty officers who serve as positive role models develops character and ethical conduct. All cadets are members of the JROTC and undertake training in military drills, marksmanship, orienteering, and related activities. Each school year begins with three weeks of intensive study skills development that enable each student to reach his academic potential. Small classes and supervised evening study hours enhance the educational experience, while standardized testing assists faculty in determining individual learning needs. The traditional liberal arts curriculum includes advanced courses, Spanish, computer science, and various electives. ESL is available for international students. Cadets participate in Scholastic Honor Society, publications, ski club, drill and rifle teams, drum and bugle corps, debate, and varsity sports including fencing and ice hockey. Tuition: $15,900. LTC David M. Comolli is Admission Director; COL Matthew J. Brown is President. *Middle States Association.*

Central Catholic High School 1927

4720 Fifth Avenue, Pittsburgh, PA 15213-2952
Tel. 412-621-8189; Admissions 412-621-7505; Fax 412-208-0555
Web Site www.pittcentralcatholic.org
E-mail admissions@pittcentralcatholic.org

Central Catholic High School was founded by the Diocese of Pittsburgh to prepare young men for college, for community leadership, and for life in today's complex world. It seeks to challenge its 850 students to reach their potential and to develop Christian values of justice, compassion, and respect. The program includes honors and Advanced Placement courses in all academic areas, and qualified students may earn college credit before graduation through dual enrollment at Duquesne or the University of Pittsburgh. Participation in interscholastic sports, publications, plays, concerts, clubs, community service, and foreign travel opportunities is encouraged. Tuition: $7050–$7750. Brian Miller is Director of Admissions; Bro. Richard Grzeskiewicz, FSC, is Principal. *Middle States Association.*

CFS, The School at Church Farm 1918

P. O. Box 2000, Paoli, PA 19301
Tel. 610-363-7500; Admissions 610-363-5347; Fax 610-280-6746
Web Site www.gocfs.net; E-mail bbronk@gocfs.net

CFS, THE SCHOOL AT CHURCH FARM, near Paoli, Pennsylvania, has been committed for more than 80 years to providing the best college preparatory education to qualified and deserving young men in Grades 7 through 12.

CFS was founded in 1918 by the Reverend Charles W. Shreiner, D.D., who dreamed of a college preparatory school for boys of ability and promise who otherwise might not have such an opportunity. The School's substantial endowment allows it to offer amenities that enhance the instructional program, including special dormitory faculty who do not teach in the classroom but serve as extracurricular tutors and advisers; well-equipped laboratories, library, and athletic facilities; and a computer-based Connected Learning Community. All students are issued personal laptop computers, and all facilities—desks, dormitories, library, and labs—are connected electronically to provide a new kind of academic environment that uses the World Wide Web as a classroom.

CFS is accredited by the Middle States Association of Colleges and Schools and holds membership in the National Association of Independent Schools, the National Association of Episcopal Schools, the Pennsylvania Association of Independent Schools, The College Board, and other professional organizations.

THE CAMPUS. Approximately 50 buildings, spread over a 350-acre campus, are used in the School's programs. The Administration Building holds electronically connected classrooms, offices, the multimedia center, recreation room, kitchen, and dining hall. The Science Building contains four sophisticated laboratories, six electronically equipped classrooms, a projection room, and the Art Department.

Ten cottage dormitories, all hard-wired for data transmission, house boarding students in small groups supervised by dorm faculty. Athletic facilities include soccer and baseball fields, a 400-meter track, six tennis courts, an indoor basketball court, a multipurpose field house, and an adjoining outdoor swimming pool.

Other buildings on campus are the School's chapel, an 8-bed infirmary, faculty homes, shop buildings, barns, and various outbuildings.

THE FACULTY. Charles W. Shreiner III, grandson of the founder, was appointed Headmaster in 1987. Under his leadership, the faculty has adapted to the idea that the role of the teacher is modified in the age of the Internet. Students work together on assignments that engage them in web-based activities, and faculty members do less lecturing and more coaching.

Teaching faculty also participate, with members of the administration, in admissions, curriculum revision, and staff development. The School is led academically by 30 men and women, of whom 70 percent have advanced degrees.

The School is committed to the Faculty Evaluation and Renewal System, a rigorous peer and departmental evaluation process developed by Independent School Management. The average tenure of faculty at CFS is 15 years.

STUDENT BODY. In 2007–08, the School enrolled 145 boarders and 35 day students. Because of its generous financial aid policy, the enrollment includes boys from diverse social, economic, and ethnic backgrounds. More than 40 percent of the students are from minority groups.

ACADEMIC PROGRAM. The academic year, beginning in early September and ending in early June, includes 36 weeks of instruction. Holidays are scheduled at Thanksgiving, Christmas, and in the spring. Parents receive grade reports with teachers' comments four times a year, in addition to midperiod progress reports that are increasingly transmitted by e-mail.

To graduate from CFS, a student must complete 23.1 credits distributed as follows: 4 in English, 2 in modern foreign language (French or Spanish), 4 in social studies, 3 in mathematics, 3.2 in laboratory science, 1 in fine art, 1 in technology education, .5 in religion, .4 in health, 1 in physical education, and 3 in free electives. Upper School students take at least five major courses each year. Several Advanced Placement and Honors courses are offered by the major academic departments.

Students in Grades 9–12 may choose from a variety of electives including British Literature, World Literature, Literature & Film, Journalism, Mythology, Shakespeare; African-American History, 19th & 20th Century United States History, Government, Medieval History, Modern European History, Evolution of Warfare, Advanced Placement United States History; Human Anatomy & Physiology, Environmental Studies, Advanced Placement Chemistry; Precalculus, Advanced Placement Calculus; Spanish III–IV, French III–IV; Two Dimensional & Three Dimensional Design, Clay, Weaving, Photography, History of Jazz, Music Theory, Music Technology, Choir, Instrumental Ensemble, and instrumental and voice lessons.

More than 90 percent of the young men who receive a CFS diploma go on to college. Recent graduates are enrolled at Carnegie Mellon, Emory, Franklin & Marshall, Haverford, Johns Hopkins, Pepperdine, Rutgers, Swarthmore, and the Universities of Chicago, Delaware, Illinois, Michigan, and Virginia, among other schools.

STUDENT ACTIVITIES. The School offers a wide variety of extracurricular activities to give each boy the chance to test and find himself. Students can work on *The Greystock News*, the school newspaper, and *The Griffin*, the yearbook, and participate in chorus, the audiovisual and science clubs, the student vestry, or other special-interest organizations. Those who qualify are elected to membership in the School's chapter of the National Honor Society.

CORE, the Challenge of Required Experience, is an important supplement to academic learning. Students are required to complete one Community Service Learning Experience and one Outdoor Experience each year. The School's Community Service Program maintains associations with some 30 local organizations and agencies that provide opportunities for student service. The Outdoor Experience Program offers many exciting activities on and off campus. These include backpacking, canoeing, caving/spelunking, cross-country and downhill skiing, fishing, hiking, sailing, white-water rafting, and wilderness survival.

Athletics are a major component of a CFS education, and participation is mandatory. Students limited by health or ability take part in less competitive programs.

ADMISSION AND COSTS. CFS, The School at Church Farm, seeks to enroll students who are aiming for higher education, enthusiastic about learning, interested in being involved, and willing to contribute to the welfare of the entire school community. Most openings for new students are in Grades 7, 8, and 9. Candidates are evaluated on the basis of previous academic records, school citizenship, standardized test results, teacher references, and a personal interview.

Every family is expected to be invested in its son's education, but no qualified applicant is turned away because of financial hardship. The family contribution to tuition ranges from $4000 to $12,500 a year for day students and $18,000 for boarders. Tuition assistance during the last five years has been in excess of $6,000,000 annually.

Headmaster: Charles W. Shreiner III
Director of Admissions: Bart Bronk

Chestnut Hill Academy 1861

500 West Willow Grove Avenue, Philadelphia, PA 19118
Tel. 215-247-4700; Admissions Ext. 1133; Fax 215-247-8516
Web Site www.chestnuthillacademy.org
E-mail admissions@chestnuthillacademy.org

Chestnut Hill Academy is an independent, college preparatory day school with an enrollment of 570 boys in PreKindergarten–Grade 12. Stressing high academic standards, Chestnut Hill offers a diversity of courses and opportunities, including a coordinate program in the Upper School in which courses are shared with Springside School, a neighboring school for girls. Performing arts, community service, sports, and publications comprise the school's extracurricular activities. Tuition: $13,100–$21,600. Financial Aid: $1,600,000. Andrew T. Weller is Director of Admissions; Francis P. Steel, Jr., '77 (Yale University, B.A.; University of Pennsylvania, M.A.) is Headmaster. *Middle States Association.*

The Crefeld School 1970

8836 Crefeld Street, Chestnut Hill, Philadelphia, PA 19118
Tel. 215-242-5545; Admissions Ext. 13; Fax 215-242-8869
Web Site www.crefeld.org; E-mail scunitz@crefeld.org

Crefeld, a school of new beginnings, is a coeducational, independent day school serving 100 students in Grades 7–12. Crefeld welcomes students seeking an alternative educational program—one that is progressive and college preparatory. Students seeking a safe, nurturing, and supportive environment benefit from the School's learning and emotional support, combined with a holistic, systemic approach to each young person. Students pursue high academic standards in a relaxed, intimate, and collaborative atmosphere while simultaneously promoting an appreciation for artistic creation and civic responsibility. This environment is marked by a culture that respects diversity and a staff that cares about every student. In class sizes of 8–14, students follow a hands-on, experiential curriculum designed to accommodate individual interests and learning styles. Crefeld offers weekly community service, visual and performing arts programs, and support for students who are gifted, sensitive, ADHD, mildly learning disabled, or who "march to the beat of a different drummer." Tuition: $20,750–$22,350. Financial aid is available. Stacey Cunitz is Director of Admissions; Dr. Mark Piechota is Head of School.

Delaware Valley Friends School 1986

19 East Central Avenue, Paoli, PA 19301
Tel. 610-640-4150; Admissions Ext. 2160; Fax 610-560-4336
Web Site www.dvfs.org; E-mail bowmj@fc.dvfs.org

Delaware Valley Friends is a coeducational day school for Grades 7–12 enrolling 205 college-bound students with learning differences and average to above-average intelligence. The School blends the Quaker mission with the mission to provide an environment that addresses individual learning needs while building upon a student's strengths. The School offers a structured program in a supportive, friendly setting. The core subjects of science, mathematics, history, and literature are enhanced by outdoor education, arts, and foreign language. All students take language arts, an individualized course designed

to improve skills. Interscholastic sports are offered at the end of the day. All-inclusive Tuition: $31,400. Financial aid is available. Jeannie Bowman is Admissions Director; Katherine Schantz is Head.

The Ellis School 1916

6425 Fifth Avenue, Pittsburgh, PA 15206
Tel. 412-661-5992; Fax 412-661-7633
Web Site www.theellisschool.org; E-mail admissions@theellisschool.org

As the Pittsburgh area's only independent school for girls, The Ellis School is committed to providing an educational experience in which young women can learn, lead, and be heard in a nurturing environment free of gender bias. Enrolling nearly 500 girls in Pre-Kindergarten through Grade 12, Ellis's challenging academic program is based on the traditional liberal arts, sciences, and humanities. Students "write across the curriculum," both on paper and online. French begins in Kindergarten, computers are integrated into all disciplines, and Advanced Placement is offered in 13 subject areas. Field trips to cultural, historic, and educational destinations throughout the Greater Pittsburgh area extend learning beyond the classroom. College counseling is intense and individualized, and all Ellis graduates enter four-year colleges and universities. Girls enjoy taking part in sports and activities such as publications, Student United Nations, a variety of interest clubs, and drama. Lower and Middle School students may enroll in the Extended Day program from 3:00 to 5:45 P.M., and a summer enrichment program is optional. Tuition: $12,500–$20,500. Financial aid is available. Sara E. Imbriglia is Director of Admissions; Dr. Mary H. Grant is Head of School. *Middle States Association.*

The Episcopal Academy 1785

Merion Campus: 376 North Latches Lane, Merion, PA 19066
Tel. 610-667-9612; Admission Ext. 3002; Fax 610-617-2262
Web Site www.ea1785.org; E-mail ea@1785.org
Devon Campus: 905 South Waterloo Road, Devon, PA 19333
Tel. 610-617-2273; Fax 610-293-9238

Founded in 1785, The Episcopal Academy blends its heritage and tradition with a rigorous, enriching curriculum and technology. Episcopal, a PreK–Grade 12 coeducational day school with more than 1600 students from diverse religious, racial, and economic backgrounds, seeks to cultivate the mind, body, and spirit of each student. Stimulating curricula, vibrant fine and performing arts, a competitive athletic program, inclusive Chapel services, and a commitment to community outreach define the core values of the school. Class and field trips enhance learning, and AP classes are offered in 15 subjects in Upper School. One hundred percent of graduates go on to four-year colleges and universities, many at the most selective level. A large variety of extracurricular offerings is available, including publications, debate, and political and creative opportunities. In 2008, Episcopal will open on a new site, currently

under construction in Newtown Square, and will close its Merion and Devon campuses. The 123-acre site will have state-of-the-art academic, arts, and athletic facilities including a black box theater, five basketball courts, and nine athletic fields. Tuition: $17,600–$23,940. Lynne Hay is Director of Admission; L. Hamilton Clark is Head of School *Middle States Association.*

Fox Chapel Country Day School 1948

620 Squaw Run Road, East, Pittsburgh, PA 15238
Tel. 412-963-8644; Fax 412-963-7123
Web Site www.foxchapelcountryday.com; E-mail fccdspa@city-net.com

Founded by parents seeking a local preschool alternative, Fox Chapel Country Day School serves 130 students in Pre-Kindergarten–Grade 5. The School shares an 18-acre site with the Fox Chapel Episcopal Church and boasts a $1,100,000 addition to its physical plant. Although its program is nonsectarian, children attend chapel once a week. With a balanced emphasis on academics and the arts, the School aims to develop each child's basic skills, creativity, and self-confidence through a positive, unhurried, nurturing environment and a traditional, yet flexible curriculum. Challenging academics are enhanced by outdoor play and the exploration of the School's natural setting. Tuition: $5350–$9950. Camille Wright is Head of School and Director of Admission. *Middle States Association.*

Friends' Central School 1845

Grades 5–12: 1101 City Avenue, Wynnewood, PA 19096
Tel. 610-649-7440; Fax 610-649-5669
Web Site www.friendscentral.org
E-mail admission@friendscentral.org
PK–Grade 4: 228 Gulph Road, Wynnewood, PA 19096
Tel. 610-642-7575; Fax 610-642-6983

Friends' Central School is a college preparatory day school enrolling 524 boys and 482 girls in Pre-Kindergarten–Grade 12. The School strives to maintain high academic standards and to treat its students with understanding and compassion. Friends' Central offers a demanding and broad program in academics, arts, and athletics and encourages students to participate and develop their minds, bodies, and spirits. All students assemble for the weekly Meeting for Worship in the tradition of the Society of Friends. Tuition: $15,000–$22,700. Financial Aid: $3,800,000. David M. Felsen (Haverford, B.A. 1966; University of Pennsylvania, M.A. 1971) was appointed Headmaster in 1988; Barbara Behar is Director of Admission and Financial Aid.

Friends School Haverford 1885

851 Buck Lane, Haverford, PA 19041
Tel. 610-642-2334; Admission 610-642-0354; Fax 610-642-0870
Web Site www.friendshaverford.org
E-mail fsh@friendshaverford.org

This coeducational, Quaker elementary school enrolls 165 students in Pre-School (age 3)–Grade 6. Friends School Haverford derives its strength from the emphasis it places on early childhood through preadolescent education. An experienced faculty and staff present a full academic curriculum emphasizing core concepts, clear and logical thinking, and the ability to communicate ideas. The School is a caring community based on Quaker values in which children receive abundant personal attention and gain the confidence to risk, stretch, and achieve. Art, music, technology, science, health, library, Spanish, and physical education enrich the program. The School is governed by the School Committee of Friends School Haverford under the care of Haverford Monthly Meeting of the Society of Friends. Tuition: $7745–$16,700. Financial Aid: $430,000. Beth Krick is Director of Admission; Martha Bryans (Bryn Mawr, B.A.; University of Pennsylvania, M.A., Ed.D.) is Head of School.

Germantown Academy 1759

P.O. Box 287, Fort Washington, PA 19034
Tel. 215-646-3300; Fax 215-646-1216
Web Site www.germantownacademy.net
E-mail admission@germantownacademy.org

Germantown Academy is a coeducational, college preparatory day school enrolling 592 boys and 530 girls in Pre-Kindergarten–Grade 12. It seeks to prepare students to think critically, communicate effectively, and understand the needs of others. The curriculum emphasizes a depth of analysis and offers a variety of electives and Advanced Placement courses in the Upper School, where students normally carry five courses. Independent study opportunities are available. Tuition: $16,040–$22,855. Financial Aid: $2,000,000. Barbara Serrill is Director of Admission; James W. Connor (Eckerd College, A.B. 1972; University of Pennsylvania, M.A. 1988) is Headmaster. *Middle States Association.*

Grier School 1853

Route 453, Tyrone, PA 16686
Tel. 814-684-3000; Fax 814-684-2177
Web Site www.grier.org; E-mail admissions@grier.org

GRIER SCHOOL in Tyrone, Pennsylvania, is a boarding school for girls in Grade 7 through Postgraduate, offering two levels of college preparatory education. It occupies a 300-acre campus in the hills of central Pennsylvania, 110 miles east of Pittsburgh, 200 miles from Philadelphia, and 25 miles from State College, where Pennsylvania State University provides many cultural and entertainment programs.

The School was founded in 1853 by residents of the nearby town of Birmingham to educate young women. It was acquired by Dr. Lemuel G. Grier in 1857 and since then has operated continuously under the direction of four generations of the Grier family.

Incorporated as a nonprofit foundation in 1957, Grier School is directed by a self-perpetuating Board of Trustees. The School is accredited by the Middle States Association of Colleges and Schools and holds membership in The National Association of Principals of Schools for Girls, the National Association of Independent Schools, the National Coalition of Girls' Schools, and the Pennsylvania Association of Independent Schools.

THE CAMPUS. The property, which rises as much as 300 feet from the entrance gate to the highest points on campus, is landscaped with white pine, Norway spruce, and hemlocks—many of which date back to Dr. Lemuel Grier's administration. The campus provides athletic fields, a modern gymnasium, outdoor pool, tennis courts, a tennis backboard, and complete facilities for the riding program, including winding trails, three paddocks, a dressage ring, stables for as many as 50 horses, an outdoor riding arena, and a large indoor riding hall.

The five principal buildings, which are connected, contain most of the residence facilities, the library, an assembly hall, the dining room, a computer resource center, recreational facilities, a dance studio, the main classrooms, laboratories, and audiovisual facilities. A Fine Arts building (2001) was followed in 2003 by a new Science Center. A new Performing Arts Center and an indoor Equestrian Center were completed in 2006.

THE FACULTY. Dr. Douglas A. Grier, who came to the School as Assistant Headmaster in 1968 and became Headmaster in 1969, was appointed Director in 1981; he is a graduate of The Hill School in Pennsylvania, Princeton University (A.B. 1964), and the University of Michigan (M.S. 1965, Ph.D. 1968). Headmaster Andrew Wilson and Headmistress Gina Borst became Co-Heads in July 2007.

There are 42 full-time teachers. Faculty colleges include Dartmouth, Duke, Georgetown, Hampshire, Indiana University (Pennsylvania), Juniata, Middlebury, Pennsylvania State, Temple, and the Universities of North Carolina, Pennsylvania, and Pittsburgh. Other staff members include 18 housemothers, office personnel, three riding instructors, and three grooms.

STUDENT BODY. In 2007–08, Grier enrolled 212 girls, 12 to 19 years of age, as follows: 17 in Grade 7, 12 in Grade 8, 36 in Grade 9, 44 in Grade 10, 56 in Grade 11, and 47 in Grade 12. The students represent many racial and religious backgrounds and come from 26 states and 10 countries.

ACADEMIC PROGRAM. The school year, from early September to early June includes 33 weeks of instruction, Thanksgiving recess, and Christmas and spring vacations. If she has written permission from home, a girl may leave school nearly any weekend during the year.

The school day begins at 8:00 A.M. with classes meeting Monday through Friday. There are five class or study periods before lunch and two in the early afternoon. Students may obtain individual help during a daily conference period. Beginning at 2:40 P.M., there are three athletic periods; dinner begins at 6:00 P.M., followed by 105 minutes of evening study Sunday through Thursday.

Grier offers a supportive, multitrack academic program. An Honors Program is designed to meet the needs of academically gifted students. "A" and "B" tracks aid in the placement of students who are not suitable for the Honors Program. For the underachieving student, Learning Skills support is offered. The Learning Skills Program is conducted by four specialists in the area of reading, writing, and mathematical skills. These specialists, working with the regular classroom teachers, provide guidance and tutorial support for the 40 students each year who require additional academic assistance.

The "hallmark" of all of Grier's academic programs is its small classes and nurturing faculty. Students are provided with the opportunity to grow in motivation and self-confidence by working closely with faculty members.

The curriculum includes English; French, Chinese, Spanish; Geography, United States History; Algebra, Geometry (Plane and Analytic), Advanced Mathematics (including Calculus), Computer Science; Physics, Chemistry, Ecology; Psychology; and Music Theory and Composition. Advanced Placement or honors work is available in most fields. An intensive English as a Second Language program is offered to students whose native language is not English.

Each girl chooses a half-credit course in the creative arts. Among the half-credit offerings are Dance (ballet, jazz, and tap dance), Piano, Voice, Studio Art, Drama, Weaving, Ceramics, Costume Design, Jewelry Making, and Photography. Electives are offered in equine studies, computer sciences, and other fields. Seniors spend a week in May engaged in community service projects.

In recent years, graduates entered such colleges and universities as Boston University, Bryn Mawr, Carnegie Mellon, Lynn University, Mount Holyoke, Pennsylvania State, Pratt Institute, and the Universities of Michigan and Wisconsin.

English as a Second Language is offered year-round. The summer program consists of eight weeks of intensive English on campus. At the same time, the Allegheny Riding Camp provides a recreational summer camp on Grier's campus to girls ages 7–15.

STUDENT ACTIVITIES. Active student groups include "Grier Dance," yearbook, literary magazine, Triple Trio, Women's Chorale, Athletic Association, and the Riding, Skiing, Dramatic, and Service Clubs. Outing Club activities include skiing, camping, backpacking, and sailing. Beginning and advanced instruction is available in studio art, photography, and dance.

Participation in the athletic program is required. "Green" and "Gold" intramural competition is carried on in such sports as soccer, volleyball, and basketball, and there is opportunity for such other sports as skiing and ice-skating. Varsity sports include soccer, tennis, basketball, and softball. The riding program is designed to provide girls with the technical points of equitation and with competition in horse shows. Riders may attend horse shows on weekends during the fall and spring terms. Each year, when qualified, Grier riders participate in the Nationals.

Entertainment programs at the School range from visiting speakers to sports festivals. Weekend activities include horse shows, movies, concerts, dances, shopping, skiing, skating, camping, and trips to Washington, Baltimore, and the local Amish country. Regularly scheduled assemblies dealing with current moral and ethical issues complement academic offerings. Longer School-sponsored excursions are conducted during the Thanksgiving recess and spring vacation; spring trips have been made to France, Ireland, and Spain.

ADMISSION AND COSTS. Grier seeks to enroll college-bound girls of average to above-average ability who possess interests in sports and the arts, as well as a desire to work in a challenging yet supportive academic atmosphere. Applicants are accepted in Grades 7–12, and occasionally for the Postgraduate year, on the basis of previous record, recommendations, and, if possible, an interview.

In 2007–08, the annual charge is $37,900 for tuition, room, and board. There are additional fees for ESL support ($3000), Learning Skills Program ($3000), Reading Program ($3000), private music lessons ($700), and horseback riding ($2000). The suggested monthly allowance is $100.

Scholarship aid, amounting to approximately $1,000,000 annually, is based on academic ability and financial need as determined by the School and Student Service for Financial Aid.

Headmistress: Gina Borst
Headmaster & Director of Admissions: Andrew Wilson
Alumnae Secretary: Sue Sorensen
Director of Development: Harriet Grier
College Counselor: Katie Kingera
Treasurer: Marlene Halbedl
Director of Athletics: Cherie Gates

The Hill School 1851

717 East High Street, Pottstown, PA 19464
Tel. 610-326-1000; Fax 610-705-1753
Web Site www.thehill.org; E-mail admission@thehill.org

The Hill School in Pottstown, Pennsylvania, is a college preparatory boarding and day school enrolling young men and women in Grades 9 through 12 (Forms Third–Sixth) and a postgraduate year. Pottstown (population 22,000) is 40 miles northwest of Philadelphia, easily accessible to New York City, Baltimore, and Washington, D.C., as well as the Pocono Mountains, the Amish country, and historic Valley Forge National Park.

Founded in 1851 by the Rev. Matthew Meigs, The Hill opened as the Family Boarding School for Boys and Young Men with an enrollment of 25 pupils. In the fall of 1998, the School became coeducational, enrolling 100 "First Girls." Although it is nondenominational, The Hill's philosophy is based on Christian principles, and all students are required to attend chapel services twice weekly.

The articles of the School's incorporation are held by the approximately 8000 alumni. There are 28 members of the Board of Trustees. The Hill School is accredited by the Middle States Association of Colleges and Schools and holds membership in the National Association of Independent Schools, among other affiliations. The School's endowment is $125,000,000.

THE CAMPUS. The Hill School campus consists of 200 acres overlooking the Schuylkill Valley. Among the 55 buildings are Alumni Chapel, Sweeney Gymnasium, the Harry Elkins Widener Science Building, the Center For The Arts, the John P. Ryan Library, and the Music House. The 50,000-square-foot Academic Center, completed in 1998, is home to administrative offices, classrooms, a student center, and the bookstore. Boarders live in 12 residences, including Dell Dormitory (1999).

The athletic facilities include an 18-hole golf course, 15 tennis courts, an ice-hockey rink, swimming pool, 10 sports fields, a fully equipped fitness center, an all-weather Olympic track, 9 squash courts, and the David H. Mercer Field House (2001), an indoor training facility.

The campus and facilities are valued at approximately $100,000,000.

THE FACULTY. David R. Dougherty was appointed Headmaster in 1993. A graduate of Episcopal High School in Virginia, he holds a baccalaureate degree in English from Washington and Lee University and a master's degree from Georgetown. Mr. Dougherty also earned an M.Litt. degree from Middlebury College's Bread Loaf School of English at Lincoln College, Oxford. His wife, Kay, is Senior Associate–Campaign for the Faculty at The Hill.

The 56 men and 38 women on the faculty hold 93 baccalaureate, 55 master's, and 6 doctoral degrees representing study at such institutions as Amherst, Boston University, Bowdoin, Brown, Bucknell, Clemson, Colgate, College of William and Mary, Columbia, Cornell, Dartmouth, Denison, Drexel, Duke, Duke Divinity School, Earlham, Fordham, Gettysburg, Harvard, Haverford, Hollins, Ithaca, Johns Hopkins, Kenyon, Lehigh, Mary Baldwin, Middlebury, Mount Holyoke, Muhlenberg, Ohio State, Princeton, Purdue, St. John's, St. Joseph's, Swarthmore, Temple, Trinity, Ursinus, Villanova, Washington and Lee, West Chester, Yale Divinity School, and the Universities of California, Connecticut, Delaware, Massachusetts, Michigan, New Hampshire, North Carolina, Notre Dame, Pennsylvania, Texas, Virginia, and Windsor.

The school physician holds regular hours in the Health Center, and Pottstown Memorial Medical Center is available for emergencies.

STUDENT BODY. In 2007–08, The Hill enrolled 285 boys and 210 girls, approximately 80 percent of whom are boarding students. Day students are required to live on campus for at least one year, as the boarding experience is integral to a Hill education. Students come from 35 states and 20 countries and represent a wide diversity of racial, ethnic, religious, and socioeconomic backgrounds.

ACADEMIC PROGRAM. The school year begins in early September and ends in early June, with three long weekends and vacations at Thanksgiving, Christmas, and in the spring. Interim grades are sent to parents every five weeks, and term grades are sent at the end of each trimester. There are parent conferences in the fall at Parents' Weekend. Classes, with an average class size of 12 girls and boys, are held six days a week, with half-days on Wednesday and Saturday when afternoons are reserved for athletics and other activities. Faculty live on campus and are readily available for extra help.

A typical day begins with the rising bell at 7:00 A.M., followed by breakfast and classes from 7:55 A.M. to 12:05 P.M., family-style lunch, more classes until 3:10 P.M., with sports scheduled until 5:30 P.M. Supervised evening study hours are conducted from 7:45 to 9:45 P.M. except on Saturday. "Lights out" is between 11:00 P.M. and midnight, depending upon grade.

To graduate, students must complete 17 scholastic units of credit, including 4 in English; 3 each in mathematics and foreign language; 2 each in history and a laboratory science (biology, chemistry, or physics); and 1 in theology or philosophy. Honors divisions and sequences leading to Advanced Placement examinations are available in mathematics, English, the sciences, history, foreign languages, art, and computer science.

Among the courses are American Literature, World Literature, Public Speaking; Algebra I–II, Geometry; Greek 1–4, Latin 1–6, French 1–5, Spanish 1–5, German 1–4, Chinese 1–4; American Studies, Modern European History, United States History, Economics, World Civilizations, The Civil War, World War II; Biology Research, Biology 1–2, Chemistry 1–2, Concepts of Physics, Physics 1–2; Judeo-Christian Roots, Religion in Literature, Psychology; History of Art and Music, Orchestra, Jazz Ensemble, Jazz Improvisation, Glee Club, Oral Communications, Drama Workshop, Studio Art I–II, and Photography. A two-year course in the humanities may be elected in place of English 3 and 4. Independent Study projects under faculty supervision further enrich the curriculum.

Study-travel opportunities include both a spring break and a summer humanities program in Italy as well as year-long programs in China, Italy, France, and Spain through School Year Abroad.

All seniors in the Class of 2007 entered college immediately after graduation. Numerous students are attending Bucknell, Colgate, College of William and Mary, Cornell, Dickinson, Georgetown, George Washington, Tufts, United States Naval Academy, Wellesley, and the Universities of Pennsylvania, St. Andrews (Scotland), Richmond, and the South.

STUDENT ACTIVITIES. A joint Student-Faculty Senate encourages boys and girls to develop leadership skills. In addition, select sixth formers act as dormitory prefects. Upperformers also supervise the Work Program in which all students contribute up to 30 minutes each day in school chores. Students fulfill a community service requirement and also initiate a variety of community-wide service projects.

All students participate in sports or exercise at some level. Girls' and boys' teams are fielded in cross-country, soccer, water polo, basketball, ice hockey, squash, swimming, track, golf, lacrosse, and tennis; girls also play field hockey and softball, while boys compete in football, wrestling, and baseball. Instructional-level teams are offered throughout the year in most sports and strength conditioning.

Students publish a yearbook, a newspaper, and a literary magazine. For students interested in music, there are numerous instrumental and vocal groups including the Chamber Ensemble, Jazz Band, and The Hilltones and Hilltrebles, select vocal ensembles. Other groups include the Hill Athletic Association, Student Activities and Reception committees, Ellis Theatre Guild, and numerous clubs.

The Bissell Forum has sponsored programs by a number of noted guests, many of whom are Hill alumni. These have included Secretary of State James A. Baker III '48, Lamar Hunt, and Tobias Wolff '64, Penn Faulkner Award winner.

Students play a major role in planning activities. Dances,

ski trips, on- and off-campus sporting events, and excursions to Philadelphia, New York, and Washington, D.C., provide a sampling of weekend activities.

Traditional Hill events include the Sixth Form Leadership Award presentation, Career Day, Junior Prize Day, Parents Weekend Music Concerts, the Spring Fling, and Alumni Weekends.

ADMISSION AND COSTS. The Hill, which maintains a nondiscriminatory policy regarding race, creed, and national or ethnic origin, seeks to enroll diverse young men and women most likely to succeed in, benefit from, and contribute to the School. Admission requirements include a student essay, transcripts from the current school, recommendations from a guidance counselor and English and mathematics teachers, an interview on campus, and the results of a standardized admission test. Application, with a $50 fee, should be made by January 31 for March 10 notification; late applications will be considered as space is available after April 10.

In 2007–08, tuition is $39,400 for boarders and $27,000 for day students. Books, transportation, lab fees, laundry, and social events are extra. Financial aid exceeding $4,252,000 is currently awarded on a need-only basis to approximately 40 percent of the enrollment. The Hill School subscribes to the School and Student Service for Financial Aid.

Director of Advancement: D. Andrew Brown
Assistant Head for Academics: Ryckman R. Walbridge
Assistant Head for Student Life: Christopher J. Hopkins
Dean of Students: Jennifer Lagor
Director of Admission: Tom Eccleston '87
Director of College Advising: Karen Walbridge
Director of Business Affairs/Treasurer & CFO: Don Silverson
Director of Athletics: Karl Miran

The Hillside School 1983

2697 Brookside Road, Macungie, PA 18062
Tel. 610-967-3701; Fax 610-965-7683
Web Site www.hillsideschool.org; E-mail office@hillsideschool.org

Encompassing Kindergarten through Grade 6, Hillside is a coeducational day school that provides a carefully structured program for 128 students of average to superior ability whose learning differences have prevented them from achieving their potential. The School strives to promote attitudes and abilities essential to academic success through remedial, developmental, and accelerated courses designed to meet each student's specific learning needs. Full-time specialists provide support services to parents and faculty, using a team approach to realize goals. Tuition: $16,100. Scholarships are available. Sue M. Straeter, Ed.D., is Head of School. *Middle States Association.*

Holy Ghost Preparatory School 1897

2429 Bristol Pike, Bensalem, PA 19020
Tel. 215-639-2102; Admissions 215-639-0811; Fax 215-639-4225
Web Site www.holyghostprep.org; E-mail rabram01@holyghostprep.org

Now in its second century of educating young men, this designated School of Excellence enrolls 505 young men in Grades 9–12 in an academic and cocurricular program formed by Catholic values and tradition. The School was founded by the Congregation of the Holy Ghost to nurture each boy's unique, God-given gifts and to develop spiritual, academic, and physical growth. Traditionally, 100 percent of graduates are accepted to college, with more than 80 percent receiving scholarships. Sports are offered at three levels; publications, bands, clubs, and a summer program are among the activities. Tuition: $13,400. Financial Aid: $500,000. Ryan T. Abramson '94 is Director of Admissions; Rev. Jeffrey T. Duaime, C.S.Sp. '76, is President; Michael O'Toole is Principal. *Middle States Association.*

Kimberton Waldorf School 1941

410 West Seven Stars Road, P.O. Box 350, Kimberton, PA 19442
Tel. 610-933-3635; Admissions Ext. 108; Fax 610-935-6985
Web Site www.kimberton.org; E-mail admissions@kimberton.org

Located in a semirural area near Philadelphia, Kimberton Waldorf, one of more than 900 Waldorf schools worldwide, is a coeducational day school dedicated to bringing forth the unique possibilities of each child. Enrollment is approximately 330 students in Pre-Kindergarten–Grade 12. Working within the Waldorf educational impulse founded by Rudolf Steiner, the School combines the arts and sciences to develop well-rounded intellectual, emotional, artistic, and practical capacities in each child. Foreign languages are introduced in Grade 1; music, drama, arts, and crafts are provided at every level. Varsity sports programs are offered. The School is a member of the Association of Waldorf Schools of North America. Tuition: $9900–$16,875. Financial aid is available. Danette Takahashi is Admissions Coordinator; Paula Moraine is Faculty Chair. *Middle States Association.*

Lancaster Country Day School 1908

725 Hamilton Road, Lancaster, PA 17603
Tel. 717-392-2916; Admissions Ext. 228; Fax 717-392-0425
Web Site www.lancastercountryday.org; E-mail admiss@e-lcds.org

Lancaster Country Day School, enrolling 500 boys and girls in Preschool–Grade 12, offers a broad, challenging course of study in an atmosphere characterized by caring and trust. The college preparatory curriculum is complemented by Advanced Placement opportunities and an extensive service learning program. Small classes encourage active participation and allow for personal attention. Activities include varsity and junior varsity sports, an after-school Enrichment Program, private music lessons, and special expeditions. Tuition: $2900–$17,400. Extras: $100–$400. Financial Aid: $1,100,000. Michelle O'Brien is Director of Admission; Michael J. Mersky is Head of School.

La Salle College High School 1858

8605 Cheltenham Avenue, Wyndmoor, PA 19038
Tel. 215-233-2911; Fax 215-233-1418
Web Site www.lschs.org; E-mail admissions@lschs.org

La Salle was founded by the De La Salle Christian Brothers to educate 1059 young men within a community in which all members share their experiences and values. The academic program emphasizes college preparation combined with extracurricular activities designed to add depth and dimension to the development of the individual. The curriculum includes Advanced Placement courses in 19 subjects, four years of religious studies, and diverse electives. Athletic teams are formed at three levels; students are also involved in publications, plays, musicals, debate, jazz band, chorus, and many regional, national, and international service projects. Tuition: $13,800. Br. James Rieck, FSC, is Director of Admissions; Joseph Marchese is Principal; Br. Richard Kestler, FSC, is President. *Middle States Association.*

Linden Hall 1746

212 East Main Street, Lititz, PA 17543
Tel. 717-626-8512; [Toll-free] 800-258-5778; Fax 717-627-1384
Web Site www.lindenhall.org; E-mail admissions@lindenhall.org

LINDEN HALL in Lititz, Pennsylvania, is a college preparatory boarding and day school enrolling students in Grades 6 through 12 and a postgraduate year. Historic Lititz (population 8000) is located on Route 501 between Harrisburg and Philadelphia. School vans and local bus service link the town to Lancaster (7 miles away), which is served by interstate bus lines, railroads, and major commercial airlines. The Lancaster airport is 3 miles from the campus.

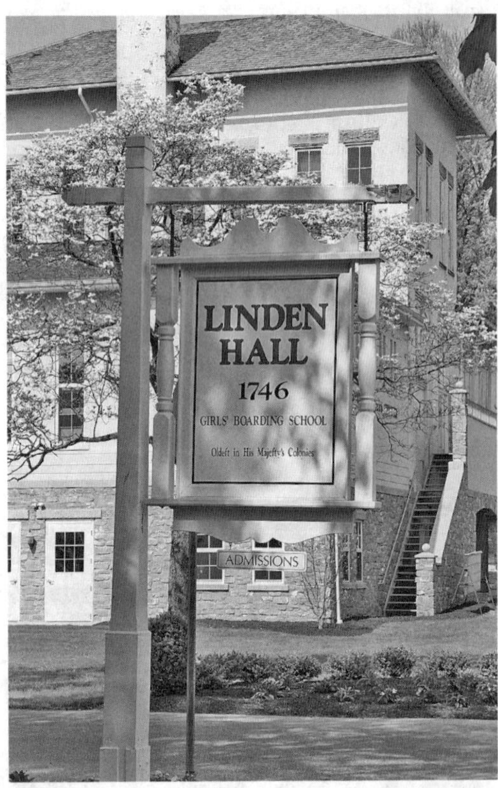

Linden Hall was established in 1746 by the Moravians, a Christian Protestant denomination. The School has more than 260 years of experience in the education and preparation of young girls for college and for life. Although Moravian in origin and tradition, the School operates independently. All religious activities, including the weekly chapel service, are nondenominational.

Founded in the belief that learning is not just for the classroom but for life, Linden Hall emphasizes the four Cs—Curriculum, Character, Culture, and Conditioning (fitness). The school offers a challenging academic program within a nurturing environment to best prepare women for the 21st century. Extensive arts and athletic programs ensure the education of the whole student. On weekdays, girls pursue rigorous academic schedules, electives, extracurricular activities, sports, and evening studies. Weekends are balanced with relaxation and socializing. Teachers serve as parents and chaperones for dorm life as well as for dances and special recreational and cultural outings.

A nonprofit institution, Linden Hall is directed by the Headmaster under the guidelines of a 24-member Board of Trustees. The School is accredited by the Middle States Association of Colleges and Schools and is approved by the Pennsylvania Department of Education. It holds membership in the National Association of Independent Schools, National Coalition of Girls' Schools, Secondary School Admission Test Board, the Pennsylvania Association of Independent Schools, The Association of Boarding Schools, Small Boarding Schools Association, Parents League of New York, and other organizations.

THE CAMPUS. Linden Hall occupies 47 fence-enclosed acres just two blocks from the town square of Lititz. The open, well-landscaped campus includes a modern 20-stall stable, indoor and outdoor riding areas, tennis courts, playing fields, and picnic areas. Indoor facilities include a new sports and fitness center with dance and exercise studios, and a new arts center with a theater, art gallery, art classrooms, a kiln room, a photography classroom, and a darkroom.

The School's physical plant includes historic structures and modern buildings—most connected by enclosed bridges. The dormitories stand between the main academic buildings and the dining room. All rooms are equipped with computer connections. Each dorm contains a student lounge and laundry facilities.

Other buildings on campus house the library, classrooms, an indoor swimming pool, and computer and science laboratories.

THE FACULTY. The teaching faculty consists of 22 full-time teachers/administrators. They hold 31 baccalaureate degrees, 16 master's degrees, and 3 doctorates representing study at American University, Carnegie Mellon, Cleveland Institute of Art, Dickinson, Norwich, Pennsylvania State, Queens College, State University of New York, Temple, Washington University, Wesleyan, and the Universities of Delaware, Pittsburgh, and Virginia.

There is a nurse and an infirmary on campus. A Lititz medical doctor is always on call; a new state-of-the-art hospital opened in Lititz in 2004.

STUDENT BODY. In 2007–08, Linden Hall enrolled approximately 85 boarding students and 40 day students, ages 11 to 19.

Boarding students came from five continents, nine states, and nine foreign countries: Australia, Bermuda, China, Dominican Republic, Ecuador, Mexico, Saudi Arabia, South Korea, and Taiwan.

ACADEMIC PROGRAM. The academic year, from late August

to late May, is divided into trimesters and includes 38 weeks of instruction with breaks at Thanksgiving and Easter and longer vacations in December and March.

Classes begin at 8:00 A.M. and average 8 to 10 girls per class. Each class meets daily in 48-minute sessions with an academic help session offered daily. The student-teacher ratio is 8:1. Teachers are also available for additional help during the postdinner leisure hour and after the evening study hall. Varsity teams practice after the academic day, from 3:40 to 5:40 P.M. Girls not involved in varsity sports must join in some type of physical activity from 3:30 to 4:15 P.M., Mondays through Thursdays. Every Sunday through Thursday from 7:30 to 9:00 P.M., there is supervised study for all girls in their rooms. Grades are posted and sent to parents six times annually; "midterm notices" are sent between each grading period.

The following courses are offered for Grades 6–12 and postgraduates: English, English as a Second Language, Literature; French I–V, Spanish I–V, Latin; Government, United States History, European History, World History, Art History, World Religions; Math, Pre-Algebra, Algebra I–II, Geometry, Pre-Calculus, Calculus, Statistics; Life Science, Biology, Anatomy & Physiology, Chemistry, Environmental Science/Marine Biology, Earth Science, Physics I–II, Conceptual Physics; Health, Physical Education; SAT Review, Composition; Ethics; and Voice Class, Studio Art, Foundation Art, Wearable Art, Mixed Media, Drawing, Ceramics, Painting, Theater, Drama, Film and Video, Equitation, and Photography.

Honor courses are offered in Social Studies, World History, Algebra I–II, English, Physical Science, and Conceptual Physics. Qualified students may take Advanced Placement courses in Art History, Biology, Calculus AB/BC, Chemistry, English Literature, Environmental Science, European History, French Literature, Government, Photography, Physics B/C, Spanish, Statistics, Studio Art: 2-D Design, and U.S. History.

A strong college counseling program ensures that virtually all Linden Hall graduates continue their education at the college level. Recent graduates are enrolled at American University, Boston University, Bryn Mawr, Case Western Reserve, George Washington, Lehigh, Massachusetts Institute of Technology, New York University, Northeastern Ohio Universities College of Medicine, Parsons School of Design, Penn State, Pratt Institute, Rensselaer, St. Joseph's, Washington University (St. Louis), and the Universities of Chicago, Michigan, and Virginia.

STUDENT ACTIVITIES. The Student Council contributes extensively to the life and administration of the School. Girls participate daily or weekly in numerous activities and organizations such as Photography, Journalism, Drama, Linden Hall Choir, Crafts, and Bell Choir. Music lessons and dance instruction are offered. Students also publish a newspaper, a literary magazine, and a yearbook, write for the local newspaper, and do all their own photography for these publications.

Linden Hall is a member of the Pennsylvania Interscholastic Athletic Association. Varsity teams compete with other independent and public schools in soccer, basketball, equitation, volleyball, softball, cross-country, and tennis. The School participates with the public school district for varsity lacrosse and swimming. Nonvarsity physical activities include aerobics, skiing, swimming, skating, bowling, running, and dance. Linden Hall hosts seven horse shows each year and participates in four varsity and other riding competitions off campus.

Special events include field trips related to school programs, dances with nearby boys' schools, all-school birthday party, school auction, lectures, movies, a "School Spirit" week, concerts, theater trips, and all-school day trips to New York City and Washington, D.C. Faculty members provide transportation to a variety of weekend activities. Traditional annual events include fall outings at nearby Mount Gretna, a school holiday party, Senior Class Night, the Lantern Walk, Parents' Weekends, International Night, Alumnae Weekend, and Graduation Day.

ADMISSION AND COSTS. Linden Hall seeks girls of average and above-average ability, without regard to geographical, racial, religious, national, ethnic, or social background. Applicants are chosen on the basis of personal interviews, school records, and letters of recommendation. Emphasis is placed upon the personal interview. If vacancies exist, students may enroll throughout the school year. There is a $45 application fee ($100 for applicants living outside the United States), and a $2000 deposit (deductible from the total fee) is required at the time of enrollment.

In 2007–08, tuition is $38,690 for seven-day boarders and $36,490 for five-day boarders. Day tuition is $16,950 for all grade levels. There is a required deposit of $1300 for the bookstore; uniforms are extra. Computers may also be leased from the School. A tuition payment plan is available. Merit scholarships are awarded to qualified applicants; no formal application is necessary. Financial aid is awarded on the basis of need as determined by the Linden Hall Financial Aid Committee and School and Student Service for Financial Aid. Full financial disclosure is required. In the current year, 30 percent of the student body received financial aid.

Head: Vincent M. Stumpo, Ph.D.
Assistant Head: Shaaron H. Lavery
Director of Admissions: Kate R. Rill
Business Manager: David J. Rainone

Meadowbrook School 1919

1641 Hampton Road, Meadowbrook, PA 19046
Tel. 215-884-3238; Admission Ext. 104; Fax 215-884-9143
Web Site www.themeadowbrookschool.org
E-mail kmosteller@themeadowbrookschool.org

Meadowbrook School is a coeducational, nonsectarian day school enrolling 151 students in PreKindergarten through Grade 6. Located on a beautiful 20-acre campus, the School offers strong basics, enrichment, and tradition within an intimate, family-oriented setting. The program includes French, art, music, library, computer, science, and physical education. The science center and greenhouse afford opportunities for hands-on learning. The ice-skating and waiter programs encourage mixed-age social situations that are basic to the philosophy. Teams are fielded in soccer, softball, baseball, and field hockey. After-school care is available. Tuition: $10,000–$16,200. Fees: $1100–$1800. Kelly Mosteller is Director of Admission; Robert Sarkisian (Colgate, B.A.; Beaver, M.Ed.) was appointed Headmaster in 1980.

MMI Preparatory School 1879

154 Centre Street, Freeland, PA 18224
Tel. 570-636-1108; Fax 570-636-0742
Web Site www.mmiprep.org; E-mail mmi@mmiprep.org

MMI Preparatory School, founded by Eckley B. Coxe to educate young miners, is a college preparatory day school enrolling 209 boys and girls in Grades 6–12. Emphasizing a strong, traditional academic program, the School seeks to develop its students into "well-rounded, broad-minded, self-disciplined individuals." Student Council, interest clubs, and ten interscholastic athletic teams comprise the School's extracurricular offerings. Every student must perform once annually in assemblies and present an Open House project for public exhibition. A summer program is available. Tuition: $8200–$10,950. Financial Aid: $425,000. Julie M. Lenio is Director of Admissions; William A. Shergalis (University of Pennsylvania, B.S.; Drexel, M.S.; Temple, Ph.D.) is President. *Middle States Association.*

Montgomery School 1915

1141 Kimberton Road, Chester Springs, PA 19425
Tel. 610-827-7222; Fax 610-827-7639
Web Site www.montgomeryschool.org
E-mail akeppler@montgomeryschool.org

Montgomery School is an independent, coeducational day school serving 305 students in Prekindergarten through Grade 8. The School is dedicated to the development of each child in mind and body through academics, fine and performing arts, and athletics in an enriching cultural and physical environment. Montgomery School is equally committed to the development of each child's character, emphasizing integrity, respect, responsibility, and service to others. Students benefit from small classes and an atmosphere that encourages intellectual curiosity and builds self-confidence. Tuition: $5000–$19,250. Amber K. Keppler is Director of Admission; Kevin R. Conklin is Head of School.

Moravian Academy 1742

Lower School: 422 Heckewelder Place, Bethlehem, PA 18018
Tel. 610-868-8571; Fax 610-868-9319
Middle School: 11 West Market Street, Bethlehem, PA 18018
Tel. 610-866-6677; Fax 610-866-6337
Upper School: 4313 Green Pond Road, Bethlehem, PA 18020
Tel. 610-691-1600; Fax 610-691-3354
Web Site www.moravianacademy.org

Moravian Academy in Bethlehem, Pennsylvania, is a coeducational college preparatory school enrolling day students in Pre-Kindergarten through Grade 12 on two campuses. Bethlehem and the greater Lehigh Valley (population 550,000) provide students with many educational resources including six area colleges. The community supports an art museum, a symphony orchestra, several historic museums, a repertory theater company, and community theater groups. The annual Bach Festival and Musikfest are special yearly events. Bethlehem is 50 miles from Philadelphia, 90 miles from New York, and 200 miles from Washington, D.C.

The Academy continues the educational commitment begun in 1742 by Countess Benigna von Zinzendorf and the early Moravian colonists. The school believes that "excellence is achieved when the needs of the whole child—body, mind, and spirit—are met." It seeks to provide a strong academic program for all students.

A nonprofit institution, the Academy is governed by a Board of Trustees, which meets quarterly.

Moravian Academy is a member of the Pennsylvania Association of Independent Schools, the National Association of Independent Schools, the Association of Delaware Valley Independent Schools, and the Council for Spiritual and Ethical Education among other organizations. It is accredited by the Middle States Association of Colleges and Schools and the Pennsylvania Association of Independent Schools.

THE CAMPUS. The buildings of the historic Lower School campus for Pre-Kindergarten–Grade 5 form a blend of past and present. They include the Old Chapel, a simple colonial structure built in 1751; the Main Building (1857), containing administrative offices, a library, classrooms, computer room, art room, and a nurse's room; the Helen de Schweinitz Building; the Gymnasium; the Devey Building, containing Kindergarten classrooms and the Lower School dining room; and the Christian Education Building, a multipurpose building with an auditorium and classrooms used cooperatively by the school and the nearby Central Moravian Church. The Middle School (Grades 6–8) is housed in two buildings, which include classrooms, two computer labs and a science laboratory, a library, an auditorium, a cafeteria, a gymnasium, and administrative offices.

The 120-acre Upper School (Grades 9–12) campus includes a pond, playing fields, tennis courts, and an outdoor swimming pool. Snyder House (1928) contains administrative offices, classrooms, and the music room. Art and photography studios are located in the Couch Arts Center. Walter Hall provides classrooms, administrative offices, lounges, an auditorium, a gymnasium, a library, a computer lab, and the dining room and kitchen. Science laboratories are located in the Heath House complex. A woodworking studio was completed in the spring of 2007. Benigna House and the Cottage are faculty/administrative residences.

THE FACULTY. George N. King, Jr., was appointed Headmaster in July 2007. He previously served as Head of Wooster School in Danbury, Connecticut. Mr. King received his B.A. from Murray State University in Kentucky and his Master of Science in Jazz Studies from the New England Conservatory of Music.

On the Academy faculty are 82 full-time teachers. All faculty members hold baccalaureate degrees and many have earned graduate degrees from such colleges and universities as Bucknell, Columbia, Dartmouth, Lehigh, Middlebury, Purdue, Temple, Villanova, and the Universities of Oxford (England) and Pennsylvania. There are also 17 part-time instructors.

A nurse is on staff for each division. Three hospitals are within a 15-minute drive of the school.

STUDENT BODY. In 2007–08, Moravian Academy enrolled 803 students, including 321 in the Lower School and 195 in the Middle School. In the Upper School, there are 287 students as follows: 77 in Grade 9, 74 in Grade 10, 70 in Grade 11, and 66 in Grade 12. The majority of the students are from Pennsylvania, but New Jersey is also represented.

ACADEMIC PROGRAM. The school year, from late August through early June, includes holiday recesses at Thanksgiving, Christmas, and Easter as well as a spring vacation. Classes are held five days a week in a schedule that varies according to grade level; the Upper School day, from 8:00 A.M. to 3:15 P.M., is divided into eight periods, with early dismissal on Thursday. A weekly chapel service is held.

The student-faculty ratio is 9:1. Generally, class sections range from 14 to 18 students. Supervised study halls are held regularly in the Middle and Upper Schools. Grades and reports are sent to parents regularly throughout the school year.

Lower School children are encouraged to develop sound work patterns and desirable social attitudes. In addition to traditional instruction, the program offers computers, French and Spanish, a vocal and instrumental music program using Suzuki techniques, art, a physical fitness program, and opportunities for creative play.

The Middle School curriculum includes English, French, Spanish, Latin, social studies, mathematics, science, music, instrumental music, art, drama, health, and physical education. The program is designed to reinforce basic learning and to provide opportunities for enrichment. Students participate in an elective period, and some serve on the Student Forum.

Minimum requirements for the diploma are four years of English; three years of a foreign language; Ancient History, World History, American History, World Religions; Algebra I–II, Geometry; Biology, Chemistry, and one other laboratory science; Music, Art; Physical Education; Health; and Community Service. Seniors must also participate in a post-term experience that focuses on community service and career exploration. Other Upper School courses include Twentieth Century Literature, British Literature, American Nonfiction, Drama, Film, Poetry; French I–V, Spanish I–V, Japanese I–III, Chinese I–II; Law, European History (Honors); Trigonometry, PreCalculus, Calculus, Probability and Statistics; Chemistry Honors, Physics and Advanced Physics Honors, Biology, Advanced Biology Honors, Ecology; and Introduction to Theatre, Chorale, MA Chamber Singers, Orchestra, Jazz Band, Bell Choir, Construction of Music, Photography, Portfolio Preparation, and Introduction to Woodworking. Attendance at weekly chapel services is also required.

Independent study is encouraged for superior students, and Advanced Placement study is offered in Contemporary Literature, Drama, Poetry, British Literature, French, Spanish, Advanced Chemistry, United States History, U.S. Government and Politics, and Calculus.

In 2007, 69 graduates were accepted at four-year colleges. Among the colleges and universities they are attending are Brown, Carnegie Mellon, Columbia, Drexel, Harvard, Haverford, Lehigh, Northwestern, Princeton, Smith, Vassar, and Wellesley.

STUDENT ACTIVITIES. The Student Council, consisting of officers, class representatives, and a faculty adviser, shares in decisions that concern student activities, privileges, and behavior. The Chorale, Instrumental Ensemble, and Drama groups present several performances each year. There is a newspaper, yearbook, and a literary magazine. Current groups include the Model United Nations, Model Congress, Pennsylvania Junior Academy of Science, Scholastic Scrimmage, Moravian Students for an Inclusive Community, and Ski, Environmental, International, and Photography Clubs. The school has a chapter of The Cum Laude Society.

Students at every level engage in community service. Many students work for local civic, church, and charitable organizations.

Varsity teams compete in soccer, basketball, field hockey, softball, cross-country, lacrosse, tennis, baseball, and golf.

The school sponsors dances, picnics, informal parties, and camping trips.

ADMISSION AND COSTS. Moravian Academy accepts boys and girls of high ability and potential. In the Upper School, students are admitted in Grades 9–11. A personal interview is required for all applicants but may be waived for international students or where distance is a factor. Applicants must supply a transcript from the current school and take school-administered tests. Upper School candidates also submit a formal application with four recommendations and a writing sample. Although admissions are normally completed by May, applications may be considered later if space is available.

In 2007–08, the comprehensive fee ranges from $7960 in Pre-Kindergarten to $18,460 for students in Grades 9–12. The comprehensive fee includes all tuition, local field trips, and Kindergarten snacks. The dining room fee ranges from $620 to $990 for lunch. Financial aid in the amount of $1,280,000 is awarded on the basis of need. Moravian Academy subscribes to the School and Student Service for Financial Aid and offers tuition insurance and a tuition payment plan.

Assistant Head: Ann S. Mindler
Director of Upper School: Carlton P. Chandler
Director of Middle School: Robert A. Bovee
Director of Lower School: Ella Jane Kunkle
Directors of Admissions: Suzanne H. Mason (Upper School), Christine L. Murphy (Middle School) & Ingrid Gerber (Lower School)
Director of Academic Counseling: Marilyn A. Albarelli (Upper School)
Dean of Students: Peyton Bray (Upper School)
Director of Financial Affairs: John F. Weber
Director of Athletics: James Tiernan

Mount Saint Joseph Academy 1858

120 West Wissahickon Avenue, Flourtown, PA 19031
Tel. 215-233-3177; Admission 215-233-9133; Fax 215-233-5887
Web Site www.msjacad.org; E-mail admiss@msjacad.org

Mount Saint Joseph Academy, a Roman Catholic day school founded by the Sisters of Saint Joseph, serves 563 girls in Grades 9–12. Academically challenging programs, which are teacher-directed and student-centered, provide a well-rounded, culturally enriched education that maximizes each student's personal and academic growth. The college preparatory curriculum includes Advanced Placement courses and College Scholars programs. Award-winning publications, varsity sports, the arts, and service organizations are among the diversified cocurricular activities. Tuition: $11,725. Carol Finney is Director of Admission; Sr. Karen Dietrich, SSJ (Villanova, M.S. 1977; Cappella University, Ph.D. 2003), is Principal; Sr. Kathleen Brabson, SSJ (Villanova, M.A. 1982), is President. *Middle States Association.*

Newtown Friends School 1948

1450 Newtown-Langhorne Road, Newtown, PA 18940-0848
Tel. 215-968-2225; Admissions Ext. 236; Fax 215-968-9346
Web Site www.newtownfriends.org
E-mail erendall@newtownfriends.org

Newtown Friends School is a day school enrolling 321 girls and boys in Pre-Kindergarten–Grade 8. Founded by the Newtown Monthly Meeting of the Religious Society of Friends, the School strives to provide a strong academic program that emphasizes critical and intellectual inquiry while fostering each student's sense of social responsibility. Art, music, computer instruction, and sports are integral to the curriculum. Students are involved in community service and participate in an intergenerational program with nearby Pennswood Village. Camping, field trips, and activities enrich the program. Tuition: $10,650–$14,300. Financial Aid: $300,000. Betsy N. Rendall is Director of Admissions; Steven R. Nierenberg (Earlham College, B.A.; Temple University, M.Ed.) is Head of School.

The Pen Ryn School 1946

235 South Olds Boulevard, Fairless Hills, PA 19030
Tel. 215-547-1800; Admission Ext. 12; Fax 215-946-2877
Web Site www.penryn.org; E-mail kbruno@penryn.org

The Pen Ryn School, a coeducational, elementary school, enrolls 225 day students in Pre-Kindergarten–Grade 8. The School aims to help each student develop individual academic talents in a caring, nurturing environment. The curriculum, which emphasizes reading, English, science, social studies, and math skills, is supplemented by programs in Spanish, art, music, health, physical education, computers, and experiences for social development. Activities include sports, leadership, student government, enrichment clubs, and annual school-wide events. Tuition: $8180–$8750. Kathy Bruno is Admission Director; Liz Morton is Head of School. *Middle States Association.*

Perkiomen School 1875

200 Seminary Avenue, Pennsburg, PA 18073
Tel. 215-679-9511; Admission 215-679-1174; Fax 215-679-1146
Web Site www.perkiomen.org; E-mail admissions@perkiomen.org

Perkiomen, a college preparatory boarding and day school, enrolls 280 boys and girls in Grade 5–Postgraduate. Its aim is to provide a strong basis in traditional academic subjects while offering study in areas of special interest. Advanced Placement and honors courses and English as a Second Language enrich the college preparatory curriculum. Twenty fine arts electives are offered in studio art, music, theater, and dance. Participation in three sports or activities a year is required. Among the activities are publications, drama, music, community service, and athletics. Boarding Tuition: $36,000; Day Tuition: $21,100. Financial Aid: $1,400,000. Carol Dougherty is Assistant Head of School; George K. Allison (Union, A.B. 1966; Trinity, M.A. 1974) is Headmaster. *Middle States Association.*

The Philadelphia School 1972

2501 Lombard Street, Philadelphia, PA 19146
Tel. 215-545-5323; Admissions Ext. 227/252
Fax 215-546-1798
Web Site www.thephiladelphiaschool.org
E-mail admissions@tpschool.org

The Philadelphia School, a coeducational, progressive school, enrolls 370 students in Preschool–Grade 8. The vigorous academic program is enriched by the use of cultural resources located close to the School's center-city facility and by use of a rural, outdoor environmental center. Students are encouraged to become inquisitive, creative, motivated, and self-reliant learners. After-school day care, instrumental music lessons, interscholastic sports, summer courses, and summer day camp are available. Tuition: $13,260–$18,540. Financial Aid: $800,729. Abigail S. Levner is Director of Admission and Financial Aid; Amy Purcell Vorenberg (University of New Hampshire, B.A. 1984; Wheelock College, M.S. 1986) was appointed Head of School in 2006.

The Quaker School—Horsham 1982

250 Meetinghouse Road, Horsham, PA 19044
Tel. 215-674-2875; Fax 215-674-9913
Web Site www.quakerschool.org; E-mail hmacinnes@quakerschool.org

The Quaker School enrolls 63 day students of average to gifted intelligence in Pre-First–Grade 9 whose learning differences have kept them from succeeding in traditional schools. Within a Friends environment, specialized faculty deliver curriculum based in the research of learning differences. The language arts program is designed to benefit the majority of the students with auditory processing and language challenges and to support them across the disciplines. With a 4:1 student-teacher ratio, the School seeks to develop children's gifts while remediating their challenges. Some depart after two or three years, while a few complete the entire lower and middle school programs. Extracurricular and summer programs are available. Tuition: $25,600–$28,455. Heather MacInnes is Director of Admission; Ruth S. Joray is Interim Head of School.

Rosemont School of the Holy Child 1949

1344 Montgomery Avenue, Rosemont, PA 19010
Tel. 610-922-1000; Admissions 610-922-1010; Fax 610-525-7128
Web Site www.rosemontsch.org; E-mail info@rosemontschool.org

Founded by the Society of the Holy Child Jesus, Rosemont School of the Holy Child is a Roman Catholic day school enrolling 150 girls and 164 boys in Nursery–Grade 8. It seeks to develop the whole child by combining sound religious training with vigorous intellectual and physical growth. Religion, Latin, computers, music, art, science, and physical education enrich the traditional curriculum; Spanish is introduced in Grade 5. Sports, musical recitals, clubs, and the annual school play are among the activities. Summer camp programs are offered. Tuition: $6540–$15,790. Financial Aid: $300,000. Jeanne Marie Blair is Director of Admissions; Sr. Mary Broderick, SHCJ (Villanova, B.A. 1972; Marywood, M.A. 1979), was appointed Head of the School in 1983.

Saint Basil Academy 1931

711 Fox Chase Road, Jenkintown, PA 19046
Tel. 215-885-3771; Admissions 215-885-6952; Fax 215-885-4025
Web Site www.stbasilacademy.org
E-mail admissions@stbasilacademy.org

Enrolling 420 day girls of diverse backgrounds in Grades 9–12, Saint Basil Academy, founded by the Sisters of Saint Basil the Great, is affiliated with the Byzantine Ukrainian Catholic Church and maintains its heritage through liturgies and language offerings. Within a community of faith, students undertake a college preparatory program that includes Advanced Placement courses, business and computer studies, music, and art. Students may also take courses at Manor College. Activities include Student Council, community service, language and drama clubs, publications, and athletics. Tuition: $8100. Academic Scholarships: $100,000. Mrs. Maureen McKeown Walsh is Director of Admissions; Sr. Carla Hernández, OSBM, is Principal. *Middle States Association.*

St. Joseph's Preparatory School 1851

1733 Girard Avenue, Philadelphia, PA 19130
Tel. 215-978-1950; Fax 215-765-1710
Web Site www.sjprep.org; E-mail jzazyczny@sjprep.org

St. Joseph's Prep, a Catholic high school in the Jesuit tradition, serves 980 young men from many religious, racial, and ethnic backgrounds. The School is dedicated to educating "the whole man," nurturing the moral, academic, spiritual, and social growth of each student. All boys take part in liturgies, retreats, and community service as a means of developing character and commitment to others. The college preparatory curriculum includes Advanced Placement courses in 16 areas. Students are involved in school government, publications, music and drama, and 14 interscholastic sports. Summer school and financial aid are available. Tuition: $14,300. Rev. William J. Byron, S.J., is President; Mr. Michael Gomez is Principal. *Middle States Association.*

St. Peter's School 1834

319 Lombard Street, Philadelphia, PA 19147
Tel. 215-925-3963; Fax 215-925-3351
Web Site www.st-peters-school.org; E-mail Tkyle@st-peters-school.org

This multidenominational day school enrolls 190 boys and girls from diverse backgrounds in Preschool–Grade 8. Within a safe, nurturing environment, students at St. Peter's School are encouraged to experience the joys of childhood while developing positive values and expanding their knowledge. Acquisition and mastery of strong skills in reading, language, and math are emphasized along with development of children's confidence in their thinking, creativity, and decision-making abilities. French and computer studies begin in Kindergarten. Field trips, music, physical education, and the arts enrich classroom learning. Sports, handbell chorus, and an art and literary magazine are among the activities. Tuition: $12,500–$17,100. Trish Kyle is Director of Admissions; David J. Costello is Head of School.

Sewickley Academy 1838

315 Academy Avenue, Sewickley, PA 15143
Tel. 412-741-2230; Fax 412-741-1411
Web Site www.sewickley.org; E-mail dgoodman@sewickley.org

The oldest independent school in Pittsburgh, Sewickley Academy is a coeducational, college preparatory day school enrolling 800 students in Pre-Kindergarten–Grade 12. Small classes, a challenging curriculum, and an emphasis on the arts and athletics characterize the Sewickley Academy experience. Students are taught to learn independently as well as cooperatively, reason clearly, communicate effectively, and respect themselves and others. Technology is fully integrated throughout the curriculum. Tuition: $11,900–$19,125. Financial aid is available. Douglas Goodman is Director of Admission; Kolia John O'Connor (Boston University, B.A.; Columbia Teachers College, M.A.; Université d'Avignon [France], M.A.) is Head of School. *Middle States Association.*

Shady Side Academy 1883

423 Fox Chapel Road, Pittsburgh, PA 15238
Tel. 412-968-3000; Admission 412-968-3206; Fax 412-968-3213
Web Site www.shadysideacademy.org
E-mail admissions@shadysideacademy.org

Shady Side Academy, the largest coeducational independent school in Pittsburgh, presently enrolls 516 boys and 422 girls as day students in Pre-Kindergarten–Grade 12 and 19 boys and 21 girls as five-day boarders in Grades 9–12. In a student-centered environment, the Academy provides extensive academic opportunities and encourages the moral, physical, and social development of each individual. Tuition: $12,750–$22,000. Boarding Fee: $8875. Katherine H. Mihm is Director of Enrollment Management and Marketing; Thomas N. Southard (University of South Carolina, B.A.; University of South Florida, M.A.) was appointed President in 2001. *Middle States Association.*

The Shipley School 1894

814 Yarrow Street, Bryn Mawr, PA 19010-3598
Tel. 610-525-4300; Admissions Ext. 4118; Fax 610-525-5082
Web Site www.shipleyschool.org; E-mail admit@shipleyschool.org

Now in its 114th year, Shipley is a coeducational, college preparatory day school located across the street from Bryn Mawr College. With its largest enrollment ever, 875 students in Pre-Kindergarten–Grade 12, Shipley remains committed to educational excellence and to developing in students "a love of learning and a compassionate participation in the world." Advanced Placement is offered in 18 subjects. French begins in Grade 2, Spanish in Grade 5, and Latin in Grade 6. Athletics are required in Middle School and strongly encouraged in Upper School. A Lower School Building and Gym opened in 2001. Community service is required. Tuition: $17,750–$25,100.

Financial Aid: $2,655,000. Gregory W. Coleman is Director of Admissions; Steven S. Piltch (Harvard, Ed.D.) is Head of School.

Springside School 1879

8000 Cherokee Street, Philadelphia, PA 19118
Tel. 215-247-7200; Admissions 215-247-7007; Fax 215-247-7308
Web Site www.springside.org; E-mail admissions@springside.org

The oldest girls' school in Philadelphia, Springside is a college preparatory school enrolling 660 students in Pre-Kindergarten–Grade 12, with a coeducational program with Chestnut Hill Academy in the Upper School. Springside offers an outstanding academic program and the advantages of small classes and individual attention. One-third of recent graduates have earned National Merit recognition. A rich extracurricular program includes 12 interscholastic sports, state-of-the-art technology, and an extensive variety of courses in the visual and performing arts. Early Bird and After-School programs are available. Tuition: $14,500–$22,100. Financial Aid: $1,500,000. Peggy Klein Mandell (Lower School) and Erin Corbett (Middle/Upper Schools) are Directors of Admissions; Priscilla G. Sands is Head of School.

The Swain School 1929

1100 South 24th Street, Allentown, PA 18103
Tel. 610-433-4542; Fax 610-433-8280
Web Site www.swain.org

Swain is a coeducational, independent day school enrolling 315 students ages 3 through Grade 8. The Swain School strives to maximize each student's potential through an education of exceptional quality accomplished by an enriched curriculum, small classes, and the reinforcement of ethical values and individual character development. The 11-year program includes the study of core subjects, enriched with experiences in the arts (visual, music, theater), library, technology, physical education, Latin, and Spanish. The "no-cut" athletics program begins in Grade 5, and there is a comprehensive character education program. The physical plant, housed on 20 wooded acres in the Lehigh Valley, includes a full complement of classrooms, science labs, full-size gym/performing arts center, two athletic fields, common areas, and an art gallery. Tuition: $5220–$14,490. Financial Aid: $757,000. Leah Papp is Director of Admissions; Todd P. Stansbery, M.A., was appointed Head of School in 2006.

Twin Spring Farm Educational Impressions 1953

1632 East Butler Pike, Ambler, PA 19002
Tel. 215-646-2665; Fax 215-646-4546
Web Site www.twinspringfarm.org; E-mail tsfinfo@mycomcast.com

Enrolling 300 day boys and girls in Toddler/Nursery–Grade 6, Twin Spring Farm Educational Impressions seeks to facilitate individual growth; cognitive, physical, social, and emotional discovery; and creative development. Children advance in a self-paced setting that is underscored by a traditional academic foundation. The Kumon program supplements the math curriculum. Multiweekly classes in music, art, and physical education are taught by specialists. Spanish instruction begins at the Nursery level; working with computers begins in Kindergarten. Students also participate in monthly field trips, sports, dance, computer, chess, and reading. Tuition: $2910–$8720. Financial Aid: $48,000. Lucia D'Andrea Hood is Director of Admission; Beatrice R. Hood is Headmistress and Founding Director.

Valley School of Ligonier 1947

Box 616, Ligonier, PA 15658
Tel. 724-238-6652; Fax 724-238-6838
Web Site www.valleyschoolofligonier.org
E-mail mkennedy@valleyschoolofligonier.org

Valley School of Ligonier, founded by Mrs. Richard King Mellon as an independent, elementary day school, enrolls 95 boys and 110 girls in Kindergarten–Grade 9. The School aims to build the strong academic foundation necessary to future scholastic success and personal fulfillment and to maintain a disciplined but friendly atmosphere in which energy and hard work can be productive. The traditional curriculum includes art, computer, music, physical education, and science for all grades. French begins in Grade 1, and Latin and Spanish begin in Grade 6. The School sponsors a summer day camp. Tuition: $9900. Financial Aid: $468,048. Johnette DeRose is Admission Director; Michael Kennedy (La Salle College, B.A.; University of Virginia, M.A.) is Headmaster.

West Chester Friends School 1836

415 North High Street, West Chester, PA 19380
Tel. 610-696-2962/2937; Fax 610-431-1457
Web Site www.wcfriends.org; E-mail admissions@wcfriends.org

West Chester Friends School is a coeducational day school enrolling 110 students in PreKindergarten (age 4)–Grade 5. Founded in 1836 by West Chester Friends Meeting and under its care, the School offers a comprehensive academic program rooted in the Quaker principles of respect, responsibility, community service, and peace. Small classes support individual academic growth and intellectual challenge in language arts and mathematics while encouraging a love of learning in all disciplines. Specialists teach art, computer, library science, music, physical education, Quakerism, science, and Spanish. Before- and after-school care and a summer program are offered. Tuition: $14,900. Tuition assistance is available. Barbara B. Rowe is Admissions Director; Matthew Bradley (University of Notre Dame, B.A.; Columbia, M.A.) is Head.

William Penn Charter School 1689

3000 West School House Lane, Philadelphia, PA 19144
Tel. 215-844-3460; Admissions Ext. 103; Fax 215-843-3939
Web Site www.penncharter.com; E-mail sbonnie@penncharter.com

This Quaker-affiliated, coeducational day school, chartered by William Penn, has an enrollment of 900 students in Kindergarten–Grade 12. The School strives to inspire students to think independently and to realize their full potential. A college preparatory curriculum is followed, and athletics, instrumental music, drama, chorus, service activities, and fine arts are offered as extracurricular activities. Summer courses are also available. Tuition: $14,250–$21,700. Extras: $1100–$3200. Financial Aid: $2,000,000. Dr. Stephen A. Bonnie is Director of Admissions; Dr. Darryl J. Ford (Villanova, B.A., B.S.; University of Chicago, M.A., Ph.D.) was appointed Head of School in 2007. *Middle States Association.*

Winchester Thurston School 1887

555 Morewood Avenue, Pittsburgh, PA 15213
Tel. 412-578-7500; Admission 412-578-7518; Fax 412-578-7504
Web Site www.winchesterthurston.org
E-mail admission@winchesterthurston.org

Winchester Thurston is an independent, coeducational, college preparatory school that serves more than 600 day students at the City Campus (Pre-K–Grade 12), located in the educational and cultural heart of Pittsburgh, and the North Hill Campus (Pre-K–Grade 5), situated on 7 acres of rolling farmland in the northern suburbs. The School offers rigorous academics complemented by competitive athletics, award-winning performing and visual arts, extracurricular programs and activities, and a strong commitment to community service. the Academic Enrichment and Challenge Program meets the needs of high-ability learners, while the City as Our Campus program links curriculum with the cultural and educational resources of Pittsburgh. Tuition: $14,300–$20,750. Financial Aid: $1,900,000. Karen Vella (Lower/Middle School) and Scot Lorenzi (Upper School) are Directors of Admission; Gary J. Niels is Head of School. *Middle States Association.*

The Wyndcroft School 1918

1395 Wilson Street, Pottstown, PA 19464
Tel. 610-326-0544; Admission Ext. 13; Fax 610-326-9931
Web Site www.wyndcroft.org; E-mail mschmidt@wyndcroft.org

Wyndcroft School, a coeducational, independent day school with 88 years of commitment to academic excellence, enrolls 250 students in Early Childhood (age 3) through Grade 8. The mission of the School is to provide a traditional and challenging academic program emphasizing basic skills in a secure and friendly environment. The curriculum includes French in PreSchool–Grade 8, Latin in Grades 5–8, and competitive sports in Grades 6–8. Special-area classes include art, music, library, computer, health, and physical education. Extended-day and afterschool care are available. Tuition: $4100–$14,500. Maureen K. Schmidt is Director of Admission; Gail L. Wolter is Assistant Head of School; Kathleen E. Wunner, Ph.D., is Head of School.

Wyoming Seminary 1844

Sprague Avenue, Kingston, PA 18704
Tel. 570-270-2100; Admissions 570-270-2160; Fax 570-270-2191
Web Site www.wyomingseminary.org
E-mail admission@wyomingseminary.org

Wyoming Seminary in Kingston, Pennsylvania, is a coeducational, college preparatory school enrolling day students in Preschool–Grade 12 and boarding students in Grades 9–12 and a postgraduate year. The Lower School campus is located in Forty Fort, approximately 3 miles from the Upper School campus. Kingston (population 14,500) is located in the Wyoming Valley, along the banks of the Susquehanna River (area population 353,000). Kingston is a 2.5-hour drive from New York City, 2.25 hours from Philadelphia, and 4 hours from the District of Columbia. The Wilkes-Barre/Scranton International Airport, 20 minutes from campus, is served by major airlines; bus service from Wilkes-Barre is also available. Five colleges, the Northeastern Pennsylvania Philharmonic, Steamtown National Historic Park, and the Kirby Center for the Performing Arts provide cultural opportunities. Skiing, biking, hiking, whitewater rafting in nearby state parks, and the Yankees AAA farm club baseball games are popular weekend activities.

Wyoming Seminary was founded in 1844 by leaders of the Methodist church to "prepare students for the active duties of life—for a course of professional or collegiate studies, or any degree of collegiate advancement." Today, Wyoming Seminary students and teachers challenge themselves and each other to reach their academic and personal goals. Students learn to manage their time, write and speak clearly and effectively, study efficiently, and work with others to achieve a common goal.

Wyoming Seminary is directed by a Board of Trustees elected by the Board itself, the Alumni Association, and the Wyoming Annual Conference of the United Methodist Church. Endowment for general operation and scholarships is valued at over $57,300,000. Wyoming Seminary is accredited by the Middle States Association of Colleges and Schools; it is approved by the University Senate of the United Methodist Church; and it is a member of the National Association of Independent Schools, among numerous professional affiliations.

THE CAMPUS. Wyoming Seminary Upper School occupies an 20-acre main campus including academic, athletic, performing arts, and residential facilities. Nesbitt Hall contains classrooms, state-of-the-art science laboratories, art studios, an art gallery, a darkroom, and a dance studio. Housed in the Stettler Learning Resources Center are the admission offices, a conference area, and the Kirby Library, with more than 20,000 volumes, CD-ROM towers, seminar rooms, and audiovisual facilities.

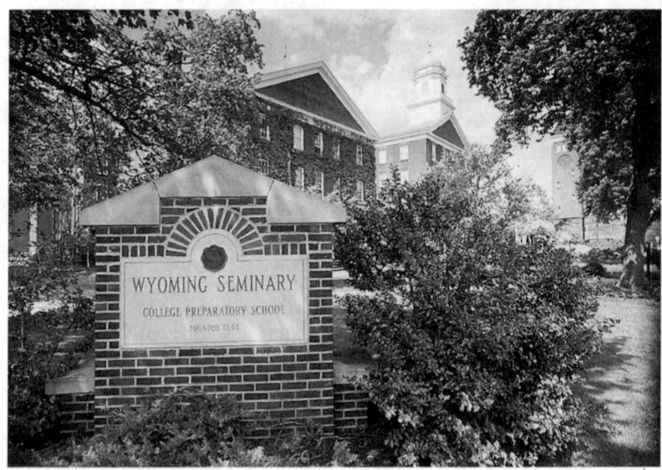

The Buckingham Performing Arts Center houses a 460-seat auditorium with high-tech stage equipment, music practice rooms and rehearsal studios, and a dramatics practice area and scenery construction shop. The Great Hall provides additional performance and classroom space.

Swetland, Fleck, and Darte Halls, erected in 1853, contain a girls' residence hall, a boys' residence hall, faculty quarters, a dining hall, and lounges. Carpenter Hall is a boys' dormitory with faculty apartments.

Carpenter Athletic Center houses a large gymnasium, a four-lane swimming pool, and exercise/weight and wrestling rooms. The adjoining Pettebone-Dickson Student Center incorporates an all-purpose gymnasium, the Antinnes Fitness Center, a climbing wall, a game room, lounge, club and publication rooms, and a darkroom. Nesbitt Memorial Stadium is equipped with a grandstand, a football field, a baseball diamond, four tennis courts, a fieldhouse, and an artificial-turf field (2006) for field hockey and lacrosse.

The Lower School (Age 3–Grade 8), on 6.5 acres, consists of a main building, which provides classrooms, administrative offices, and a gymnasium. The Sordoni Library, containing 12,500 volumes, is part of a 1995 addition featuring new classrooms and a cafeteria. The 450-seat Amato Auditorium was renovated in 2000. Athletic fields and a playground surround the school.

THE FACULTY. Dr. Kip P. Nygren was appointed the 11th President of Wyoming Seminary in July 2007. He holds a Ph.D. in Aerospace Engineering from Georgia Institute of Technology, a master's in Aeronautics & Astronautics from Stanford University, a master's in Industrial Engineering from Stanford University, and a bachelor's in General Engineering from the U.S. Military Academy. Prior to working at Sem, Dr. Nygren was Professor and Head of the Department of Civil & Mechanical Engineering at the United States Military Academy. He retired from the Army in 2007 and was advanced to the rank of Brigadier General.

The Upper School teaching faculty includes 27 women and 43 men; two-thirds of the faculty live on campus. There are 45 women and 9 men at the Lower School. Faculty hold baccalaureate and graduate degrees representing study at American University, Baylor, Bloomsburg, Brown, Bucknell, Catholic University, Central Michigan University, City University of New York, Clarion, Colgate, Columbia, Cornell, Denison, Dickinson, Drew, Drexel, Franklin and Marshall, Hartwick, Lehigh, Lock Haven, Lycoming, Marymount, Middlebury, Misericordia, Ohio State, Oregon State, Parsons School of Design, Pennsylvania State, Saginaw Valley State, St. Joseph's, Shippensburg, Skidmore, Smith, State University of New York, Susquehanna, Swansea (England), Syracuse, Trinity, Tulane, United States Military Academy, Washington and Lee, Wellesley, Westminster Choir College, Wilkes, Williams, Yale, and the Universities of California, Delaware, Georgia, Massachusetts, North Carolina, Pennsylvania, Pittsburgh, Richmond, Scranton, Virginia, and Wisconsin.

The infirmary facilities are staffed by two nurses, and a doctor is on call. Wilkes-Barre General Hospital is five minutes away.

STUDENT BODY. In 2007–08, Wyoming Seminary Lower School enrolled 349 day students in Pre-Kindergarten–Grade 8. The Upper School enrolled 193 boarders and 268 day students.

Students came from ten states and 20 foreign countries.

ACADEMIC PROGRAM. The school year, from September to late May, includes three terms, Thanksgiving, Christmas, and spring vacations, and long weekends at midterm. Classes meet five days per week, with an average of 14 students. A typical daily schedule in the Upper School (from 8:00 A.M. to 3:30 P.M.) includes four 45-minute class periods in the morning, lunch, three classes in the afternoon, and a conference period in addition to weekly school meetings and chapel. Students—with the exception of juniors, seniors, postgraduates, and honor students—are expected to attend supervised study hall during free periods. In addition, boarding students study in their rooms from 7:30 until 9:50 P.M. Sunday through Thursday. Faculty members give individual assistance as needed. Grades are distributed six times a year; advisors keep families apprised of academic progress throughout the year. All students in Grades 9–12 have individual phone and e-mail accounts, and every dorm room and classroom has Internet access.

To graduate, a student must accumulate a minimum of 19.33 credits; students earn .33 credit for a term course or 1 credit for a full-year course. Specific requirements are English 4, mathematics 3, foreign language 3, history/social science 3, laboratory science 3, physical education 4, health .33, religion .33, music history .33, art history .33, public speaking .33, and computer science .33.

The curriculum offers a variety of one-term, two-term, and full-year courses. Typical year courses or three-term sequences are freshman and sophomore English; French I–IV, Latin I–IV, Spanish I–IV, Russian I–IV; World Civilizations, U.S. History; Algebra I–II, Geometry, Advanced Algebra/Trig, Precalculus, Calculus AB&BC; Biology, Chemistry, Physics; and Drawing and Design. Among the term courses are Shakespeare, Women and Literature, Greek Legacy, Creative and Expository Writing, Best Sellers, Evil in Literature, Contemporary Drama, Public Speaking; 13 studio art electives; Art History, Masterpieces of Music; Contemporary American History, American Civil War, World War II, Mid-East History, Asian History, Economics, Classical History, Psychology, World Religions; Discrete Mathematics; Marine Biology, Ecology; Basic Computer Programming; Health; and Bible.

Advanced Placement courses are available in all disciplines including French, Latin, Russian, Spanish, American Seminar, European History, Government, Biology, Chemistry, Physics, Environmental Science, Calculus, Statistics, Computer Science, Art/Music History, Music Theory, and Studio Art.

Qualified students may enroll in advanced courses at nearby Wilkes University or King's College. With faculty approval, juniors and seniors may pursue independent study programs for one or more terms.

In 2007, 99 percent of the graduates entered college. Among the colleges accepting recent graduates are American University, Boston College, Brown, Carnegie Mellon, Colgate, Cornell, Duke, Georgetown, Hamilton, Harvard, Johns Hopkins, Kenyon, Lafayette, Lehigh, New York University, Pennsylvania State, Smith, Stanford, Susquehanna, Syracuse, United States Naval Academy, Villanova, Wesleyan, Williams, Yale, and the Universities of California, Delaware, and Pennsylvania.

STUDENT ACTIVITIES. The Seminary Upper School Government—composed of students, faculty, and administrators—is responsible for many nonacademic aspects of school life. There are four standing committees: spirit, activities, assemblies and programs, and finance.

Student activities include Peer Group, *The Wyoming* (yearbook), *The Opinator* (newspaper), *Pandemonium* (literary magazine), *Clio's Camera* (history journal), Chorale and Madrigal Singers, Drama, Dance, International Club, "W" Club, Blue Key, Mock Trial, Model United Nations, Rocket Club, Jazz Band, and Orchestra. Three plays are produced each year, and the chorus presents both formal and informal concerts. Involvement in community service is required.

Wyoming Seminary varsity and junior varsity athletic teams compete in the Pennsylvania Interscholastic Athletic Association and with independent schools in New York, New Jersey, Connecticut, and Pennsylvania. Sports for boys are football, basketball, tennis, lacrosse, baseball, wrestling, golf, ice hockey, soccer, cross-country, and swimming. Girls compete in field hockey, basketball, swimming, golf, softball, cross-country, ice hockey, lacrosse, soccer, and tennis.

Weekend activities take advantage of the school's proximity to major cities' sporting and cultural events as well as the hiking, skiing, and outdoor opportunities available in the Pocono Mountains.

ADMISSION AND COSTS. Wyoming Seminary seeks students who will challenge themselves and their peers to reach academic and personal goals. All applicants must submit school transcripts, letters of recommendation, and the application form, which includes a writing sample. Candidates should submit Secondary School Admission Test results; those applying for Grade 12 or the postgraduate year must submit SAT scores. An interview on campus is required. New students are accepted at all grade levels; late or midyear enrollment is sometimes possible. The application fee is $75 for domestic students and $100 for international students.

In 2007–08, Upper School tuition is $36,675 for boarding students and $18,525 for day students. Additional expenses include allowances, books, athletic clothing, a technology fee, and travel. A tuition payment plan is offered. Need-based financial aid is available. Presently, Wyoming Seminary awards over $5,500,000 in aid to about 51 percent of all students.

President: Kip P. Nygren, Ph.D.
Dean: John Gordon
Dean of Admission: John R. Eidam
Director of Admission: Anne Lew
Vice President of Advancement: John H. Shafer
Director of Development: A. Kay Young
College Counselor: Karen Mason
Business Manager: John T. Morris
Director of Athletics: Karen Klassner

Wyoming Seminary 1807

Preschool–Grade 8: 1560 Wyoming Avenue, Forty Fort, PA 18704
Tel. 570-718-6600; Admissions 570-718-6610; Fax 570-718-6649
Web Site www.wyomingseminary.org
E-mail admission@wyomingseminary.org

Wyoming Seminary's Lower School is an elementary day school enrolling 349 boys and girls in Preschool–Grade 8. The school's programs are child-centered, addressing individual learning styles in an environment that focuses on developing lifelong learning skills. Art, music, computer science, and athletic programs are a vital part of the curriculum. Students are introduced to the study of French and Spanish in Kindergarten; Latin is offered in Grades 7–8. Tuition: $4075–$15,075. Dawn Leas is Director of Admission; Dr. Kip P. Nygren (U.S. Military Academy, B.S.; Stanford University, M.S.; Georgia Institute of Technology, Ph.D.) is President; Patricia Summerhill (Shippensburg, B.S.; American University, M.Ed.) is Dean.

RHODE ISLAND

The Gordon School 1910

45 Maxfield Avenue, East Providence, RI 02914
Tel. 401-434-3833; Fax 401-431-0320
Web Site www.gordonschool.org; E-mail admission@gordonschool.org

This coeducational, independent day school enrolling 407 students in Nursery to Grade 8 offers a rigorous, integrated, and multicultural curriculum. The Gordon School encourages each student to develop as an individual, to be respectful of others, to work cooperatively, to contribute to the community, and to excel academically. Students learn by exploring connections, questioning assumptions, seeking new perspectives, and creating solutions. The School aims to produce confident leaders, creative thinkers, problem solvers, and involved citizens. The arts, music, sports, and a visiting-artist program are integral to the curriculum. Tuition: $6565–$20,710. Financial Aid: $828,000. Emily Anderson and Julie Cucchi are Co-Directors of Admission; Ralph L. Wales (Harvard, B.A., M.Ed.) is Head of School.

Lincoln School 1884

301 Butler Avenue, Providence, RI 02906
Tel. 401-331-9696; Admission Ext. 3157; Fax 401-751-6670
Web Site www.lincolnschool.org; E-mail jdevine@lincolnschool.org

Lincoln School, a college preparatory day school enrolling 385 students in Nursery–Grade 12, with girls only from Kindergarten up, is committed to its Quaker heritage, focusing on character and values as well as academic excellence. Advanced Placement courses are offered in addition to extensive programs in art, theater, sports, leadership, and music. Extracurricular activities and independent study enhance the curriculum. Tuition: $10,890–$23,360. Financial aid is available. Jennifer Devine is Director of Admission; Julia Russell Eells (Hobart and William Smith Colleges, B.A.; Wesleyan University, M.A.L.S.) is Head of School. *New England Association.*

Overbrook Academy 1984

836 Warwick Neck Avenue, Warwick, RI 02889
Tel. 401-737-2850; Fax 401-737-2884
E-mail information@overbrookacademy.org
Web Site www.overbrookacademy.org

OVERBROOK ACADEMY in Warwick, Rhode Island, is a Roman Catholic boarding school enrolling girls from the United States, Europe, and Central and South America in Grades 6 through 9. Warwick (population 85,427), located on Narragansett Bay, is 15 minutes south of Providence and within driving distance of Boston and New York City. The school plans many activities that take advantage of the physical and cultural resources found throughout New England and other parts of the Northeast.

Overbrook Academy was established by the Legion of Christ in Orange, Connecticut, in 1984 and moved to Dallas, Texas, for two years before relocating to its present site in 1991. The school is affiliated with Oak International, a Roman Catholic organization founded in Rome, Italy, in 1969 and committed to the integral formation of young people. It operates schools in Ireland, Switzerland, and the United States, including Everest Academy in Michigan and Oaklawn Academy in Wisconsin.

The harmonious development of each girl's intellectual, human, and spiritual potential is at the core of Overbrook's academic and extracurricular activities. Religious studies, moral training, and spiritual retreats are integral to an Overbrook education, and preparation for the sacrament of Confirmation is offered.

Overbrook Academy is approved by the Rhode Island Department of Education and holds membership in the Association of Independent Schools of New England.

THE CAMPUS. Overbrook Academy occupies a beautiful 90-acre campus of lawns and woodlands with sweeping views of Narragansett Bay. The focal point of the grounds is the imposing Romanesque chapel where the school community comes together for liturgies, celebrations, and other special gatherings. Two dormitory wings accommodate up to 185 girls in triple-occupancy rooms as well as 10–18 adult supervisors. The academic program is carried out in 13 classrooms; a library for student research; science, computer, and language labs; art and music rooms; a 300-seat auditorium for special events such as theater performances, cultural activities, and choir presentations; and an e-mail center.

The Academy's athletic facilities consist of a gymnasium with basketball and volleyball courts and fields for softball and hockey. Swimming, horseback riding, tennis, golf, and figure skating take place off campus.

THE FACULTY. Teachers are carefully selected as educators trained in the philosophy and methods of Oak International.

STUDENT BODY. Overbrook Academy enrolls 185 girls in an environment designed to foster friendship. To ensure personal attention, the student body is divided into sections, each with its own dean and team of assistants. Students come from the United States as well as Canada, Chile, Colombia, France, Guatemala, Italy, Mexico, Spain, and Venezuela. The presence of international students broadens the Overbrook experience with cultural enrichment.

ACADEMIC PROGRAM. The academic year, divided into three terms, begins in early September and extends to early June, with recesses at Christmas and Easter. Classes, enrolling between 15 and 25 students, meet five days a week; the student-teacher ratio is 19:1. Grades are issued five times a year, and personal progress reports are mailed to parents three times a year. Parents may also access academic and medical information through a password-secure page of the school's web site. Upon entering the Academy, each girl is assigned a guidance counselor who provides assistance in academic, spiritual, and personal matters.

On a typical weekday, girls attend classes from 9:00 A.M. to 3:30 P.M. Their classes include an extra emphasis on a foreign language. After classes, students participate in clinics and directed studies.

At Overbrook, a broad-based humanities program serves as the cornerstone of the academic curriculum, with an emphasis on the development of strong reading, writing, and language skills across the disciplines. Courses in English are offered to meet the needs of students at introductory, intermediate, and advanced levels of proficiency as well as for native speakers. Girls make use of the Language Laboratory to practice verbal communication skills, while reading classes foster an appreciation for American literature and British classics.

Other specific courses include Science, Physics, Biology, Health; Social Studies, History, Geography, Civics; Mathematics, Pre-Algebra, Algebra I–II, Computers; Religion, Confirmation Preparation; Spanish for native speakers; and Physical Education.

Following an initial language evaluation, girls may choose to study English, French, or Spanish as a second language at one of three ability levels, and international students are required to take the Test of English as a Foreign Language (TOEFL).

Throughout the year, girls have the opportunity to test their skills in language and mathematics competitions. Students in all English classes are encouraged to participate in regional, state, and national competitions including the Young Author's International Literary Contest, United States National Spelling Bee, and the National Language Arts Olympiad. Academy students have received top recognition for their participation in the Rhode Island Science Fair.

STUDENT ACTIVITIES. Overbrook believes that a balanced, comprehensive extracurricular program is essential to the overall health and well-being of the student. A variety of clinics enables girls to concentrate in an athletic or artistic area of particular interest, and all students are required to participate in two clinics a semester. Among their choices are tennis, swimming, figure skating, horseback riding, ballet, jazz, musical theater, and aerobics. Additionally, there are opportunities to engage in pursuits such as oil painting, piano, photography, etiquette, culinary arts, field hockey, golf, and softball. Girls are also encouraged to volunteer time to worthwhile community service projects both on and off campus.

Two trips are offered to the students during Christmas and Easter break. At Christmas, girls may visit Rome, with such highlights planned as a papal audience, Mass at St. Peter's Basilica, and excursions to Assisi, Florence, Tivoli, and Castelgandolfo. The Easter trip to Canada features a stop at Niagara Falls, sightseeing in Toronto, and a visit to the Ontario Science Centre. Other outings are planned to the Providence Theater, Mystic Seaport, downtown Boston, and New York's Radio City Music Hall.

Among the highlights on the school calendar are spiritual retreats, Christmas Pageant, Parents Weekend, Holy Week Activities, and Commencement Awards Ceremony.

ADMISSION AND COSTS. Overbrook Academy welcomes girls of good character and ability whose parents seek a quality education that emphasizes the spiritual, intellectual, and human dimensions of their daughter's natural gifts. Students are admitted to Grades 6 through 9.

In 2006–07, tuition for the academic year, including an enrollment fee, is $13,957; the boarding fee, which includes meals and laundry, is an additional $12,175. Enrollment in the autumn or spring term includes a fee; the tuition, room, and board cost is based on the yearly tuition. Other expenses include a personal allowance, optional travel, and fees for supplementary uniforms and special clinics. Some scholarships are available to meet special needs on an individual basis.

Director: Kristina Piñero
Dean of Studies: Jessica Snell
Director of Admissions: Adrienne Rolwes
Administrator: Mariela Lauría
Director of Development: Marco Rivera

The Pennfield School 1971

Little Slocum Farm, 110 Sandy Point Avenue, Portsmouth, RI 02871
Tel. 401-849-4646; Fax 401-847-6720
Web Site www.pennfield.org; E-mail kburke@pennfield.org

Founded as The New School by teachers, parents, and friends to provide a superior academic education, this country day school enrolls approximately 205 boys and girls in Three-Year-Old Nursery–Class VIII. Emphasizing concern for the individual, Pennfield aims to develop basic skills, resourcefulness, self-discipline, self-confidence, and responsibility in a supportive environment. Art, music, lab science, computer, and physical education begin in the early grades; French and Spanish are introduced in Kindergarten and are required through Grade 8. Tuition: $13,685–$15,645. Extras: $260–$645. Financial aid is available. Kathleen M. Burke is Director of Admissions; Robert A. Kelley (Tufts University, B.A., M.A.T.) was appointed Headmaster in 2005.

Portsmouth Abbey School 1926

285 Cory's Lane, Portsmouth, RI 02871
Tel. 401-683-2000; Admissions 401-643-1248; Fax 401-643-1355
Web Site www.portsmouthabbey.org
E-mail admissions@portsmouthabbey.org

PORTSMOUTH ABBEY SCHOOL in Portsmouth, Rhode Island, is a Roman Catholic, college preparatory school enrolling young men and women as boarding and day students in Forms III through VI (Grades 9–12). Founded by monks of the Benedictine Congregation, the School is situated on Narragansett Bay, providing opportunities for hands-on learning beyond the classroom as well as convenient accessibility to the cultural, historic, and recreational resources of Newport, Providence, and Boston.

Portsmouth Abbey School was established by Father John Hugh Diman, a Benedictine monk, in 1926. In keeping with Benedictine principles, the School's mission is to provide an excellent academic program based on reverence for God and man, respect for learning and order, and a responsibility for a shared experience of community life. The celebration of Mass, common prayer, and the presence of the monks on campus encourage spiritual development among students, and a monk serves as spiritual leader for every dorm.

The School is governed by a 23-member Board of Regents comprised of laypersons and members of the monastic community. Its current endowment is valued at approximately $35,000,000. Portsmouth is accredited by the New England Association of Schools and Colleges and holds membership in the National Association of Independent Schools and The Association of Boarding Schools, among other affiliations.

THE CAMPUS. The School and the Abbey share a 500-acre waterfront campus on Aquidneck Island in Narragansett Bay. Many of the buildings were designed by the distinguished architect Pietro Belluschi. The Cortazzo Administration Building, featuring a Winter Garden with a fountain, houses offices and the auditorium. Academic facilities include the Burden Classroom Building; the Science Building; the St. Thomas More Library, containing 30,000 volumes, and seminar rooms; a beachfront marine science laboratory; and a Victorian Manor House (1864). The McGuire Fine Arts Center, with studios, seminar rooms, a student/faculty gallery, a mechanical room, and a darkroom, opened in 2000. Mass and special programs and liturgies are held in the Church of St. Gregory the Great. Among the other buildings are the Student Center, Stillman Dining Hall, and the Nesbitt Infirmary.

Boarders reside in seven houses, four for girls and three for boys, each accommodating between 20 and 40 students and houseparents. Third-Form students live in their own houses, while the older students are mixed in the other houses. Each house has a lounge, a library and computer lab with wireless Internet access, a refrigerator, coin-operated laundry facilities, and vending machines.

The Portsmouth Abbey campus features excellent athletic facilities, including the Carnegie Abbey golf course. A state-of-the-art Squash & Fitness Center features eight international squash courts and a 3000-square-foot fitness center with weight-training stations and Cybex aerobic-conditioning equipment. There are also a six-lane, all-weather running track, six tennis courts, an indoor ice-hockey rink, two gymnasiums, multiple outdoor playing fields, and an equestrian center.

THE FACULTY. Right Reverend Dom Caedmon Holmes is Prior Administrator; Dr. James M. DeVecchi is Headmaster. Dr. DeVecchi earned his undergraduate degree at St. Francis College and his master's and doctoral degrees at the University of New Hampshire. Appointed to the School in 1973, he has served as Mathematics Department Head, Registrar, Academic Dean, Dean of Faculty, and Associate Headmaster during his tenure.

There are 54 faculty members, including 5 Benedictine monks. They hold 54 baccalaureate and 31 advanced degrees, including 7 doctorates.

Four registered nurses provide medical services on campus, and the School employs a physician, psychologist, and clinical social worker. Full hospital facilities are available in Newport.

STUDENT BODY. In 2007–08, Portsmouth Abbey School enrolled 359 students, two-thirds of whom are residents. They came from 21 states, the District of Columbia, and 16 countries and represented a wide cross-section of racial, ethnic, and religious backgrounds.

ACADEMIC PROGRAM. The school year is divided into trimesters, with grades issued twice during each term. The schedule includes vacations at Thanksgiving, Christmas, and in the spring and several long weekends. Each student's academic progress is monitored by an advisor. A learning specialist is available for students who need additional support in study, reading, writing, and time-management skills, and faculty are available for extra help during daily conference periods and supervised study hours.

On a typical day, classes are held from 8:15 A.M. to 2:50 P.M., with shortened hours on Wednesday and Saturday. Athletics are generally scheduled between 3:30 and 5:30 P.M. After the evening meal, students engage in activities and study, with "lights out" between 10:30 and 11:30 P.M., depending on grade.

The college preparatory curriculum includes 20 Advanced Placement courses. Students take Christian Doctrine and English each year of attendance. They must also earn 3 units each in mathematics and a modern or classical language, 2 units each in history and science, and 1 unit in the arts.

Among the specific courses offered are Basic Faith, Faith and Church, Faith and Life; English 1–5, Creative Writing; Latin 1–5, Greek 1–4, French 1–5, Spanish 1–5; Ancient History, European History, American History, World History, Political Science, Economics, International Relations, International Politics; Algebra 1, Geometry, Algebra 2/Introduction to Analysis, Precalculus, Statistics, Calculus, Computer Science; Physics 1–2, Chemistry 1–2, Biology 1–2, Marine Science, Medical Physiology; Art 1–3, History of Art, Photography; Music 1–3; and Drama Workshop.

College counseling begins formally in the winter of the junior year, with ongoing discussion among students, parents, and the School's College Counselors. Over the last five years, Portsmouth Abbey graduates have chosen to attend such colleges and universities as Bates, Boston College, Boston University, Brown, College of the Holy Cross, Columbia, Connecticut College, Cornell, Dartmouth, Emory, Fordham, Georgetown, Gettysburg, Harvard, Haverford, Johns Hopkins, Massachusetts Institute of Technology, New York University, Pomona College, Providence College, St. Anselm, Tufts, United States Naval Academy, Vanderbilt, Williams, Yale, and the Universities of California (Berkeley), Chicago, Notre Dame, Pennsylvania, and Vermont.

Portsmouth Abbey School conducts a coeducational summer session of academic course work for remediation and enrichment.

STUDENT ACTIVITIES. Extracurricular activities are designed to meet a variety of interests, from the elected Student Council and the Social Committee to sports teams and academic and special-interest clubs. Day students participate in all after-school and weekend activities as members of the resident houses to which they are assigned. They also are welcome to use the house for study.

On-campus groups include Student Council, Model United Nations, Amnesty International, debate club, Abbey Singers, and a cultural awareness club. The Abbey Players theater group stages major dramatic and musical productions; students publish a yearbook, a literary magazine, and a newspaper, and operate the School radio station.

Community service encompasses volunteer activities through Big Brother/Big Sister, peer tutoring, recycling, and other worthwhile endeavors on campus. Portsmouth Abbey remains committed to community action off campus as well. Students may assist in soup kitchens, relief organizations, and animal shelters, for which transportation is arranged by the School.

Portsmouth Abbey teams compete interscholastically in seasonal sports. Boys' and girls' teams are formed in soccer, cross-country, basketball, ice hockey, lacrosse, tennis, squash, golf, and track. Girls compete in field hockey and softball, while boys play football and baseball; there are also coed teams in swimming and sailing.

On weekends, boarding and day students enjoy a variety of activities such as dances, films, visits to art exhibits, student recitals, and whale-watching. The Dom Luke Childs lecture series attracts notable speakers to campus.

ADMISSION AND COSTS. Portsmouth Abbey School welcomes young people of above-average ability and excellent moral character who desire to benefit from the academic and cocurricular opportunities. Students are considered without regard to race, color, creed, or national or ethnic origin based on school records, test scores, an interview, and teacher recommendations. Candidates are required to take the Secondary School Admission Test. Applicants whose files are completed by January 31 are notified of admission decisions by March 10.

Tuition for boarding students in 2007–08 is $39,000; the fee for day students is $26,820. A four-year, full merit scholarship honoring the Reverend Hugh Diman is awarded on the basis of academic merit to a boarding student entering Grade 9. In addition, Portsmouth awards up to ten Abbey scholarships annually, each of which is a renewable merit grant that may supplement any need-based financial aid a student receives. The School annually makes available approximately $2,500,000 in financial aid based on demonstrated need. Tuition payment plans are offered.

Headmaster: Dr. James M. DeVecchi
Associate Headmaster: Daniel McDonough
Assistant Headmaster for Student Life: Nancy Brzys
Director of Admissions: Geri Zilian
Assistant Headmaster for Development: Patrick Burke '86
Director of College Placement: Mary McDonald
Athletic Director: Alfred Brown

The Providence Country Day School 1923

660 Waterman Avenue, East Providence, RI 02914-1714
Tel. 401-438-5170; Admissions Ext. 137; Fax 401-435-4514
Web Site www.providencecountryday.org
E-mail bailey@providencecountryday.org

The Providence Country Day School is a college preparatory, coeducational school for approximately 300 students in Grades 5–12. Students come from over 35 communities in Southeastern New England. The School seeks to foster confidence, respect, honesty, intellectual curiosity, and hard work. All students follow a traditional liberal arts curriculum, while older students enjoy Advanced Placement courses, electives, senior projects, and a two-week class in Ecuador. Reading analytically, writing logically, and persuasively, and making connections across disciplines are emphasized in all grades. The average class size of 12 students ensures individualized attention. The visual and performing arts are represented by chorus, musicals, theater productions, and film, music theory, ceramics, pottery, and photography classes. School government, Mock Trial, publications, and special-interest clubs are also offered. Athletes participate in baseball, golf, lacrosse, sailing, tennis, cross-country, wrestling, hockey, and soccer. Graduates historically attend the nation's most selective colleges and universities. Tuition: $23,880. Suzanne Bailey is Director of Admissions; Susan M. Haberlandt is Head of School.

St. Andrew's School 1893

63 Federal Road, Barrington, RI 02806
Tel. 401-246-1230; Fax 401-246-0510
Web Site www.standrews-ri.org; E-mail inquiry@standrews-ri.org

ST. ANDREW'S SCHOOL in Barrington, Rhode Island, is a college preparatory school enrolling boarding and day boys and girls in Grades 9–12 and day students only in Grades 6–8. Grades 3–5 will be added starting in the fall of 2008.

Founded in 1893 by the Reverend William Merrick Chapin, St. Andrew's served for many years as both home and school for young boys who needed the structure and support it provided. More than 100 years later, the School's mission has evolved but St. Andrew's remains a close-knit community, with small classes for a widely diverse student body and mindful of the needs of families who require financial assistance.

St. Andrew's students seek a school environment that is designed to help them discover and develop their unique talents. Students, faculty, and administrators are committed to the idea that individualized teaching can transform students' learning strengths into classroom success.

St. Andrew's is part of the Exemplary Schools Network, designated by learning expert Dr. Mel Levine and his Schools Attuned Program. The highly trained faculty is committed to the improvement of teaching and learning using a multisensory approach aimed at the different ways students learn. The goal for all students is to develop an understanding of the way they learn best and the tools they need to achieve in school and in life. The

95 percent of St. Andrew's graduates who enter four-year colleges attest to the efficacy of the School's programs.

St. Andrew's is accredited by the New England Association of Schools and Colleges. It holds membership in the National Association of Independent Schools and other organizations. The Learning Disabilities Program is certified by the State of Rhode Island.

THE CAMPUS. St. Andrew's 100-acre campus is reminiscent of a small New England college, with handsome stone, brick, and wooden buildings, ranging from modern to traditional, clustered around a central green. There are five academic buildings that house classrooms, a library, and two athletic buildings with a gymnasium and basketball courts. The Karl P. Jones Gymnasium is now home to the new Fitness Center, which includes a circuit-training room, an athletic trainer's office and workroom with a whirlpool. Also included are cardio/circuit machines equipped with individual TVs. Hardy Memorial Hall, which houses the Middle School, has been renovated to provide an addition for the new Lower School in 2008. Boys and girls reside in separate dormitories supervised by faculty houseparents; the Head Master's family occupies the 18th-century Rectory. The campus also includes playing fields, outdoor tennis courts, and a Project Adventure ropes course.

Emphasizing its strong commitment to math, science, the arts, and physical fitness, St. Andrew's School recently completed a $20,000,000+ effort to strengthen the School's program and infrastructure. The David A. Brown Science Center and a second gymnasium, the George M. Sage Gymnasium, were completed in 2000. The Norman E. and Dorothy R. McCulloch Center for the Arts, consisting of a theater, two art rooms, a music room, a theater classroom, and a graphic arts lab, opened in 2004. All students attend daily morning meetings in the 287-seat Les and Linda Keats Theatre, which is also used for plays, concerts, and assemblies.

The computer-networked campus provides access to outside library materials and the Internet. The Director of Technology coordinates all computer facilities for both students and staff. The Student Service Center houses the nurse's office, infirmary, classrooms, and additional office space. The Student Center provides a TV room, a game room, a lounge, and a school store.

THE FACULTY. John D. Martin assumed his duties as Head Master in 1996. A native of Chicopee, Massachusetts, he attended Northfield Mount Hermon School and earned a baccalaureate degree with honors in history from Tufts. Mr. Martin also holds an M.Ed. from American International College and an M.Div. from Yale University. His previous experience includes teaching at Tabor Academy and a chaplaincy and admissions work at The Peddie School and Sewickley Academy. The Head Master and his wife, Sheila, have three young sons.

There are 46 teachers on the faculty, many of whom live on campus. All hold baccalaureate degrees, and 26 have earned advanced degrees from such colleges and universities as Brown, Columbia, Harvard, Keene State, Mount St. Joseph, New Mexico State, Providence, Rhode Island College, Rhode Island School of Design, St. Cloud State, Simmons, Springfield College, Trinity College, Tufts, Vassar, Western Carolina, Worcester Polytechnic, and the Universities of Cheikh Anta Diop (Senegal), Colorado, Michigan, Oregon, and Rhode Island.

STUDENT BODY. In 2007–08, St. Andrew's School enrolled 216 students, 155 boys and 61 girls. Of these, 59 were boarders in Grades 9–12. They represent five states and four countries and come from diverse ethnic, racial, and religious backgrounds.

ACADEMIC PROGRAM. The school year, operated on a semester basis, runs from September to June and includes Thanksgiving, Christmas, winter, and spring breaks. The student-teacher ratio is 5:1, and all students have a faculty advisor with whom they meet twice daily for guidance in goal setting, self-monitoring, and developing strategies to become active learners. Parents, students, and advisors work together to create an academic program tailored to each child's own unique learning style. The learning process incorporates a multisensory approach, hands-on experiences, and computer instruction.

St. Andrew's offers an Honors Program, which allows students to excel in their areas of strength and challenges each to reach his or her potential. The Resource Program addresses the needs of students with diagnosed mild language-based disabilities, about 37 percent of the enrollment. Each student enrolled in Resource receives remedial assistance in the areas of reading, writing, and spelling. The Focus Program provides assistance for students with attentional disorders. ESL is required for international students.

To graduate, students must complete 26 credits as follows: 4 in English, 3 in social studies (including 1 in U.S. History), 3 in mathematics, 3 in science (including 2 in a lab science), 2 in physical education, and 1 credit in art. The study of a foreign language is strongly advised. Community Service is an additional requirement, ranging from 10 hours for freshmen to 40 hours for seniors.

Among the courses offered in the Upper School (Grades 9–12) are English I–IV, College Writing; Ancient History, European History, United States History, Ethics, Service Learning, Renaissance Florence (honors), The Middle East; Algebra I–II, Geometry, Pre-Calculus, Calculus, Advanced Placement Calculus, Trigonometry, Introduction to Probability and Statistics; Biology, Advanced Biology, Chemistry, Physics, Environmental Science, Human Physiology and Anatomy, Astronomy, Oceanography; Spanish I–III, Advanced Spanish, English as a

Second Language I–II; Art Fundamentals, Drawing with the Masters, Studio Art Painting, Studio Art 3-Dimensional Design, Jewelry Workshop, Ceramic Pottery and Sculpture, Printmaking; Theatre I–II, Oral Communications and Public Speaking; Computer Applications, Multi-Media, Computer Repair & Maintenance; and Music Theory, History of Jazz and Rock 'n' Roll, and Chorus. All ninth graders enroll in an Introduction to the Arts course, which includes one quarter each in music, theater, visual art, and computer graphics.

College counseling begins in the junior year and involves the student as well as parents, advisors, and other faculty. More than 95 percent of St. Andrew's seniors continue their education at the college level, with the majority entering four-year programs. Since 2004, graduates have matriculated at such institutions as Art Institute of Boston, Berklee College of Music, Boston College, Bryant, Colby-Sawyer, Curry, Dominican, Drew University, Emmanuel, Emory, Framingham State, Johnson and Wales, Lasell, Le Moyne, Longwood, Massachusetts College of Art, Mount Holyoke, New England College, Northeastern, Old Dominion, Parsons School of Design, Plymouth State, Pratt Institute, Providence College, Purdue, Rensselaer Polytechnic, Rhode Island College, Rhode Island School of Design, Roger Williams, Savannah College of Art and Design, Simmons, Southern New Hampshire, Suffolk, Syracuse, Wentworth Institute of Technology, Westfield State, Worcester State, and the Universities of Louisville, Massachusetts, Rhode Island, Southern California, Vermont, and Wisconsin.

STUDENT ACTIVITIES. Every weekend, the School provides extracurricular activities for boarders. The School's proximity to Providence, Newport, and Boston affords many opportunities to attend concerts, plays, and professional ballgames and visit museums and other attractions.

Athletic activity is considered an extension of classroom learning as it focuses on teamwork, sportsmanship, and interdependence among peers. There are boys' and girls' teams in soccer, basketball, tennis, cross-country, golf, and lacrosse. Examples of individual activities are weight training, biking, and walking club. Project Adventure is an on-campus ropes course designed to build self-esteem and encourage problem solving, trust, and collaboration among students and faculty.

ADMISSION AND COSTS. St. Andrew's seeks young men and women of good character who are willing to work hard to perform at or above grade level. Small classes of 8–12, individual attention from teachers and advisors, and a structured environment are the hallmarks of St. Andrew's. The School does not admit youngsters who exhibit behavioral or emotional problems. Students are admitted without regard to race, religion, sexual orientation, or national or ethnic origin. Admission is based on a campus visit and interview, letters of recommendation, previous transcripts, and standardized testing. Additional testing and information are required for participation in the Resource and Focus programs.

In 2007–08, boarding tuition is $37,300; day tuition is $24,200. The Resource and Focus programs are an additional $9400. Books cost approximately $400. Financial aid of $1,367,400 was awarded last year based on need.

Head Master: John D. Martin
Director of Admissions: R. Scott Telford
Assistant Director of Admissions: Bronwyn Roberts
Director of Academics: Michael Morin
Director of Learning Services: Dr. Dana E. Gurney
Director of Lower & Middle School: Nanci T. DeRobbio
Director of Student Life: Eric Hill
Director of Athletics: Michael Hart
College Counselor: Michael Raffa
Director of Finance & Physical Plant: James M. Meehan

St. Michael's Country Day School 1938

180 Rhode Island Avenue, Newport, RI 02840
Tel. 401-849-5970; Admissions Ext. 302; Fax 401-849-7890
Web Site www.stmichaelscountryday.org

Located on a 7-acre campus, St. Michael's is a nondenominational, coeducational school enrolling nearly 230 children in Pre-School–Grade 8. It aims to help students develop a strong, lifetime love of learning. Small classes, a supportive faculty, and a developmentally appropriate curriculum meet the academic needs of the youngest learners as well as those being prepared for the rigorous academic challenges beyond St. Michael's. French, Spanish, computer and science labs, a recently computerized library, a school-based publishing house, and lively music, drama, arts, and athletic programs are available to all students. Tuition: $8970–$17,850. Charles Laurent is Admissions Director; Whitney C. Slade (Tufts, B.A.; Harvard, M.Ed.) is Head of School.

The Wheeler School 1889

216 Hope Street, Providence, RI 02906
Tel. 401-421-8100; Fax 401-751-7674
Web Site www.wheelerschool.org

Wheeler, a college preparatory day school enrolling 729 girls and boys in Nursery–Grade 12, aims to provide a diverse academic experience, develop individual talents, and encourage involvement in School and world affairs. The traditional curriculum is enriched by electives, special-interest and computer center activities, and various sports. The Hamilton School at Wheeler, enrolling 69 boys and girls in Grades 1–8, serves high-potential, language-disabled students through a structured, multisensory approach applied to reading, spelling, and writing skills. Tuition: Wheeler—$11,140–$22,776; Hamilton—$32,095. Financial Aid: $1,697,630. Jeanette Epstein is Director of Admission; Dan B. Miller (Amherst, B.A.; Harvard, M.A., Ph.D.) is Head of School. *New England Association.*

SOUTH CAROLINA

Beaufort Academy 1969

240 Sams Point Road, Beaufort, SC 29907
Tel. 843-524-3393; Fax 843-524-1171
Web Site www.beaufortacademy.org
E-mail contact@beaufortacademy.org

Set in South Carolina's scenic Lowcountry, Beaufort Academy is an independent college preparatory day school enrolling 370 boys and girls from diverse backgrounds in Pre-Kindergarten–Grade 12. The Beaufort Academy experience is predicated on a "tripod philosophy" of education in which excellence in academics, the arts, and athletics is pursued. Equal with intellectual and personal achievement, the school honors and values high moral standards and good conduct. At all grade levels, programs are designed to meet individual goals, needs, and interests while promoting leadership, good citizenship, and service to others. Modern languages are introduced in Pre-K; Advanced Placement and honors courses are available in the Upper School to qualified scholars. More than 75 percent of students participate in multiple extracurricular activities. Among their options are student government, AWARE (inclusivity group), French and Spanish honor societies, Literary Meet, Math Team, publications, Academic Quiz Bowl, SADD, film club, an annual dramatic presentation, community service, and interscholastic sports. Tuition: $5300–$9400. Financial aid is available. Bethany Byrne is Director of Admissions; Timothy D. Johnston is Headmaster. *Southern Association.*

Charleston Collegiate School 1970

2024 Academy Drive, Johns Island, SC 29455-4437
Tel. 843-559-5506; Admission Ext. 224; Fax 843-559-6172
Web Site www.charlestoncollegiate.org
E-mail hburr@charlestoncollegiate.org

Set on a beautiful 30-acre campus in South Carolina's Low Country, Charleston Collegiate School serves 300 boys and girls as day students in Pre-Kindergarten through Grade 12. The enrollment is diverse, including African-Americans, Latinos, and descendants of the island's native and early white settlers. All are united in the desire to prepare for success in higher education and in adult life, able to meet the challenges of an ever-changing world. Now in its 38th year, Charleston Collegiate offers a traditional liberal arts program designed to qualify graduates for admission to four-year institutions nationwide. Advanced Placement courses are available in major subjects. Modern languages, information technology, and opportunities for enrichment in music, art, and drama enhance the core curriculum. The Learning Center provides services and resources to meet the individual needs of learning-different students. Boys and girls compete at varsity and junior varsity levels in nine team sports. Among the activities are service learning, school government, publications, vocal and instrumental music groups, and a variety of special-interest clubs. Tuition: $6800–$10,225. Hacker Burr is Admission Director; J. Robert Shirley, Ph.D., is Headmaster. *Southern Association.*

Charleston Day School 1937

15 Archdale Street, Charleston, SC 29401-1918
Tel. 843-377-0315; Admission Ext. 112; Fax 843-720-2143
Web Site www.charlestondayschool.org
E-mail sallie.barnes@charlestondayschool.org

Charleston Day School serves 186 boys and girls in Grades 1–8 on an urban campus located in the heart of historic Charleston, South Carolina. Founded in 1937, Charleston Day School provides a rigorous academic experience for its students. The school environment fosters scholarship, integrity, respect, and responsibility. In all grades, a core curriculum is enhanced by French, art, music, and physical education. Students in Grades 5–8 may take Spanish, and students in Grades 7–8 advanced math courses, including Honors Algebra I. Special academic programs, team sports, community service, and fine arts productions enrich learning. After-school programs are available. Tuition: $12,850. Sallie B. Barnes is Director of Admission; Brendan J. O'Shea is Headmaster.

Glenforest School 1983

1041 Harbor Drive, West Columbia, SC 29169
Tel. 803-796-7622; [Toll-free] 800-849-7312; Fax 803-796-1603
Web Site www.glenforest.org; E-mail glenforest@glenforest.org

Enrolling 120 boys and girls as day students in Kindergarten through Grade 12, Glenforest School meets the unique needs of students who have not reached their potential because of learning difficulties. The School teaches youngsters how to learn through individualized teaching methods. Special programs are designed for students with dyslexia, learning disabilities, Attention Deficit Disorders, and Attention Deficit Disorders with Hyperactivity. Small classes and multisensory instruction help youngsters acquire basic academic skills and develop self-confidence. Most students are mainstreamed, and 82 percent of graduates are accepted by the college or university of their choice. Glenforest School is a member of the Southern Association of Colleges and Schools (SACS). Tuition & Fees: $18,031–$18,655. Edith Bailey is Admissions Director; Dr. Gillian Barclay-Smith is Head of School; Paul Risinger is Associate Head of School.

Hammond School 1966

854 Galway Lane, Columbia, SC 29209
Tel. 803-776-0295; Fax 803-776-0122
Web Site www.hammondschool.org
E-mail admdirector@hammondschool.org

Hammond School in Columbia, South Carolina, is a college preparatory day school enrolling boys and girls in Pre-Kindergarten through Grade 12. The School is located in a residential district in the southeastern section of Columbia (metro area population 703,771). The city is the state's capital and the home of the University of South Carolina, and has a variety of cultural and educational resources that are enjoyed by students and faculty on field trips. In addition, the city affords access to both mountains and beaches within two-hour drives west or east. Public buses serve the area near the campus.

Hammond School was founded as Hammond Academy in 1966 by a group of parents interested in developing a college preparatory school to serve the Columbia area. It opened with an enrollment of 260. Since that time, it has more than tripled to its current enrollment of 998. In 1989, the Board of Trustees changed the name to Hammond School and voted to adopt "a global focus" to prepare students for the "larger" world they will be entering as adults.

The global focus begins in the earliest grades and is developed continuously in all subject areas. Each year, the School selects a country to study and gears its programs toward the people and culture of that land. In addition, members of Grade 11 travel to Belize, Central America, for a nine-day visit each spring. The School's mission is to provide students with the finest college preparatory curriculum, while inculcating in them an understanding of other peoples and cultures.

The School is a nonprofit organization governed by a self-perpetuating Board of 27 Trustees including parents, alumni, and community leaders. The Board meets monthly during the academic year. More than 2500 alumni provide financial support for the School.

Hammond is accredited by the Southern Association of Colleges and Schools and the National Association for the Education of the Young Child. It holds membership in the National Association of Independent Schools, among other professional organizations.

THE CAMPUS. The School occupies approximately 106 acres with six outdoor tennis courts, a football/baseball field complex, two practice fields, and a soccer/track and field complex that was completed in 1992.

The 17 principal buildings provide 85 classrooms, four laboratories, a primitive technology center, 2 music studios, four art studios, a college guidance center, two dining halls, two libraries containing more than 32,000 volumes, and a student center. Rutledge, Calhoun, and Bostic Halls were completed when the School opened in 1966, and the Gymnasium/Auditorium was added a year later. Lee and Marion Halls, which house the Lower School, were built in 1970; the Middle School facility was completed in 1988. In addition, a Fine Arts facility (2001), Wrestling Barn (2002), Fitness Center (2003), Theater (2004), Lecture Hall (2004), and Barks Hall and the Dorothy Walker Chapel (2007) were added.

The plant is owned by the School.

THE FACULTY. Adam de Pencier was appointed Headmaster in the fall of 2006. He has studied at the University of Chicago, Columbia, the University of Edinburgh, Queen's (Canada), and the University of Toronto. Prior to his appointment at Hammond, Mr. de Pencier had been Head of School at Madison Country Day School in Wisconsin. He has also taught and held administrative positions at Upper Canada College and Branksome Hall, both in Toronto, and at Trinity College School in Port Hope, Ontario. In 2004–05, Mr. de Pencier was a member of the Klingenstein Institute for Independent School Education at Teachers College, Columbia University.

One hundred fourteen men and women are full-time members of the faculty. All faculty members hold baccalaureate degrees, and the majority hold advanced degrees, including six doctorates.

A registered nurse provides health services on campus.

STUDENT BODY. In 2007–08, Hammond School enrolled 992 boys and girls in Preschool–Grade 12. The enrollments are distributed as follows: 50 in PK, 72 in Kindergarten, 81 in Grade 1, 82 in Grade 2, 77 in Grade 3, 68 in Grade 4, 74 in Grade 5, 73 in Grade 6, 73 in Grade 7, 78 in Grade 8, 63 in Grade 9, 58 in Grade 10, 65 in Grade 11, and 78 in Grade 12. The students come from Columbia and nearby communities. The School follows a nondiscriminatory admissions policy and has a minority component of approximately 12 percent. Most students are of various Christian denominations; however, Jewish, Muslim, and other faiths are also represented. Approximately 12 percent of the students receive financial aid.

ACADEMIC PROGRAM. The academic year, divided into semesters, begins in late August and ends in late May. Vacations are scheduled for two and a half weeks at Christmas and one week in the spring. Classes are held five days a week and are scheduled in seven 50-minute periods between 8:00 A.M. and 3:20 P.M. A 30-minute morning break is used for assemblies, advisor meetings, and activities. Free periods are used for special classes in the Lower School, supervised study halls in the Middle School, and free time in the Upper School. The average class size is 15. Students needing additional help use the Skills Centers or participate in tutorials after classes in the Middle and Upper schools, all at no extra charge. Grades are sent to parents at the end of each quarter.

The Lower School (Preschool–Grade 4) program presents a nontraditional learning environment in which teachers can employ new approaches. The curriculum includes English, language arts, Spanish, social studies, science, natural history, computers, art, music, drama, library, and physical education. The Middle School (Grades 5–8) seeks to build a sense of community and to develop individual self-esteem. Latin is studied in Grades 5 and 6. Students in Grades 7 and 8 may choose Latin or Spanish as their foreign language. The English and history sequences focus on important figures whose lives may serve as models of what students can become. Organized activities are an important complement to the program.

In the Upper School (Grades 9–12), the emphasis is on college preparation, personal development, and awareness. Studies of other peoples and cultures, which begin in the lower grades, culminate in discussions of world issues in the Upper School.

To graduate from the Upper School, a minimum of $23\frac{1}{2}$ credits must be earned including the following: English 4; foreign language 3; history 3, including World Cultures, United States History, and World History; mathematics 3, including Algebra 1–2 and Geometry; science 3, including Biology,

Chemistry, and Physics; Physical Education 2; Fine Arts 1; and electives $4^1/_2$.

Among the courses offered are American, British, and World Literature; French 1–5, Spanish 1–4; Algebra 1–2, Geometry, College Algebra, Statistics, Finite Math, Pre-Calculus, Calculus; Biology, Chemistry, Physics; Psychology, History of Religion, and Government/Economics. The Fine Arts curriculum includes a variety of courses in studio art, choral music, and drama. Technology courses are required in the Lower and Middle School and may be taken as electives in the Upper School. Advanced Placement courses are offered in most disciplines.

All 53 members of the Class of 2007 are attending college, and 87 percent of the class earned scholarships. Graduates are currently attending such colleges and universities as Clemson (Honors), College of Charleston, Columbia, Johns Hopkins, Kenyon, Southern Methodist, Washington, Washington and Lee, Wofford, and the Universities of California (Berkeley), Miami, Michigan, North Carolina, the South, South Carolina (Honors), and Virginia.

STUDENT ACTIVITIES. Students elect representatives from Grades 9–12 and a president and vice-president from the senior class to the Student Government, which serves as liaison to the administration and coordinates student services and other extracurricular events.

Other organized activities are: newspaper, yearbook, Civitans, Civinettes, Red Circle, Creative Writing, Outdoors, Astronomy, Community Service, Film, and Spirit clubs.

Hammond School is a member of the South Carolina Independent School Association and fields teams that compete against other private schools within the conference as well as some public school opponents in football, basketball, baseball, track, cross-country, soccer, swimming, tennis, wrestling, and golf for boys. Girls compete in volleyball, basketball, softball, track, cross-country, soccer, tennis, swimming, and golf. Intramural competition is offered in basketball and volleyball. Life sports and exercise programs are initiated through physical education classes, and the outdoor program provides canoeing, hiking, and rock climbing.

Special social events on the school calendar are Homecoming, Spirit Week, and the Junior-Senior Dance. Parents participate in the Hammond Parents Association, Skyhawk Club, and Dads Club. Various annual events are planned for prospective families and alumni including Open Houses, athletic events, and class reunions.

ADMISSION AND COSTS. Hammond School seeks boys and girls of above-average intelligence, with diverse interests and a willingness to work hard in a college preparatory program. Approximately 100 positions are available for new students each year, with most entering Pre-Kindergarten and Kindergarten. Some students are accepted in other classes if vacancies exist. Admissions are based on academic records, recommendations, a personal interview, and an entrance examination.

Tuition for 2007–08 is as follows: \$6800 in Half-day PK–K, \$9650 in Full-day K, \$11,470 in Grades 1–4, \$12,205 in Grades 5–8, and \$12,875 in Grades 9–12. Tuition payment plans are available. Hammond belongs to the School Scholarship Service and annually awards \$1,000,000 in financial aid, based on need.

Headmaster: Adam de Pencier
Director of Admission: Matt Radtke
Director of Development: Mahalie D. Moore
College Counselor: Rene C. Bickley
Chief Financial Officer: Tracie H. Ifkovits
Director of Athletics: J. Richard Edwards
Director of Operations: Karen Dickey
Upper School Head: Christopher B. Angel
Middle School Head: Blair Lowry
Associate Headmaster/Lower School Head: Robert E. Davis

Hilton Head Preparatory School 1968

8 Fox Grape Road, Hilton Head Island, SC 29928
Tel. 843-671-2286; Fax 843-671-7624
Web Site www.hhprep.org; E-mail lmarlis@hhprep.org

Hilton Head Preparatory School, enrolling 450 day students in Kindergarten–Grade 12, offers an academic program designed to challenge each individual to reach his or her highest potential. Learning and character are nurtured through a curriculum that integrates the liberal arts and sciences, technology, and ethical values. College Preparatory, Honors, and Advanced Placement courses are available, while a Learning Resource Program provides added academic support for all students. Diverse activities include music groups, drama, publications, service organizations, and Middle School and varsity athletics. Tuition: \$9500–\$14,360. Financial aid is available. Lauren R. Marlis is Admissions Director; Dr. Susan R. Groesbeck is Head of School. *Southern Association.*

Porter-Gaud School 1867

300 Albemarle Road, Charleston, SC 29407-7593
Tel. 843-556-3620; Admissions 843-402-4775; Fax 843-556-7407
Web Site www.portergaud.edu
E-mail eleanor.hurtes@portergaud.edu

Porter-Gaud School traces its origins to Holy Communion Church Institute, founded in 1867 by an Episcopal priest to educate children orphaned by the Civil War. The present-day Porter-Gaud was formed by the 1964 merger of three earlier schools. While adhering to its Episcopal heritage, Porter-Gaud today welcomes 920 day students from diverse faiths and backgrounds. Its mission is to nurture each student's faith, curiosity, talents, integrity, humanity, and dreams through a dynamic K–12 college preparatory curriculum. Academic course work centers on the traditional liberal arts and sciences including Latin, three modern languages, and honors and AP courses in all departments. The campus and buildings are designed to create an environment that maximizes the educational experience for both students and faculty. Among the facilities are The Science, Information and Technology Center with science and computer labs and a spacious library. All classrooms are connected to the campus network and the Internet. Students take part in community service, leadership groups, music, drama, debate, interest clubs, and 13 sports. Tuition: \$13,115–\$15,180. Eleanor W. Hurtes is Interim Director of Admissions; Dr. Christian Proctor is Head of School. *Southern Association.*

Trident Academy 1972

1455 Wakendaw Road, Mount Pleasant, SC 29464
Tel. 843-884-7046; Admissions 843-884-3494; Fax 843-881-8320
Admissions Fax 843-884-1483
Web Site www.tridentacademy.com
E-mail admissions@tridentacademy.com

Trident Academy, providing special education for learning-disabled students, enrolls approximately 100 day students in Kindergarten–Grade 12. A language-therapy program and a structured, individualized learning environment foster academic and personal development. The Upper School offers thorough preparation for postsecondary education. Sports, publications, Student Council, and clubs are offered. Participation in athletics or community service is encouraged. A summer day program provides tutoring. Restricted Boarding is offered. Tuition: $16,000–$21,620. Financial aid is available. Patty Held is Director of Admissions; Joe Ferber (George Washington University, B.A.; American University, M.Ed.) is Headmaster. *Southern Association.*

TENNESSEE

Battle Ground Academy 1889

P.O. Box 1889, Franklin, TN 37065-1889
Tel. 615-794-3501; Admissions 615-567-9014; Fax 615-567-8360
Web Site www.battlegroundacademy.org
E-mail sparrish@battlegroundacademy.org

Located 16 miles south of Nashville, Battle Ground Academy is a college preparatory day school enrolling 940 boys and girls in Kindergarten–Grade 12. Typically, 100 percent of the graduates enroll in four-year colleges and universities nationwide. College counseling and personal counseling assist Upper School students and their families. State-of-the-art facilities provide a setting for students and teachers to maximize the educational experience. Upper School course offerings include accelerated or Advanced Placement courses in each discipline. Student life in the Upper School is enriched by a broad and diverse range of activities, including required community service. Tuition: $11,500–$14,110; Extras: $300–$500. Financial Aid: $850,000. Scott Parrish is Vice President of Advancement; Dr. William Mott is President. *Southern Association.*

Brentwood Academy 1969

219 Granny White Pike, Brentwood, TN 37027
Tel. 615-373-0611; Fax 615-377-3709
Web Site www.brentwoodacademy.com
E-mail office@brentwoodacademy.com

Brentwood Academy is a coeducational, college preparatory school dedicated to nurturing and challenging the whole person—body, mind, and spirit—to the glory of God. Located 5 miles south of Nashville on a 49-acre campus, Brentwood Academy serves 780 students in Grades 6–12. Cocurricular activities include the Student Leadership Team, Fellowship of Christian Athletes, Winterim, Big Sisters-Big Brothers for new students, athletics, forensics, drama, chorus, band, Academy Singers, clubs, and publications. A summer program is available. Tuition: $14,450. Financial Aid: $1,010,000. Sue Gering is Director of Admission; Curtis G. Masters (Wheaton, B.A.; University of Puget Sound, M.S.) is Headmaster. *Southern Association.*

Christ Methodist Day School 1958

411 Grove Park, Memphis, TN 38117
Tel. 901-683-6873; Fax 901-761-5759
Web Site www.cmdsmemphis.org; E-mail office@cmdsmemphis.org

Established by Christ United Methodist Church, Christ Methodist Day School enrolls 400 boys and girls in Pre-Kindergarten through Grade 6. The School is committed to the task of helping each child develop to his or her potential academically, physically, socially, emotionally, and spiritually. The traditional curriculum is designed to provide a sound academic foundation supplemented by Bible, gifted education, Spanish, music, physical education, art, and computer studies. A complete recreational sports program, before- and after-school care, and a summer program are also available. Tuition: $3265–$8310. Alison Hinson is Admissions Director; Steven T. Jackson (Olivet College, B.A. 1982; University of Virginia, M.Ed. 1987) was appointed Headmaster in 2002. *Southern Association.*

Currey Ingram Academy 1968

6544 Murray Lane, Brentwood, TN 37027
Tel. [Toll-free] 866-507-3242; Admission 615-507-3173
Fax 615-507-3170
Web Site www.curreyingram.org
E-mail kathy.boles@curreyingram.org

Currey Ingram Academy is a coeducational, college preparatory school for students with learning differences. Small classes and a 6:1 student-teacher ratio ensure a personalized educational experience for each of the 304 students in Kindergarten through Grade 12. Using multisensory instruction, the highly trained faculty address all developmental areas (social, emotional, physical, moral, intellectual) and fully celebrate individual talents. On-staff speech-language pathologists and guidance counselors offer specialized tutorials, and college counselors have helped 100 percent of seniors in the last three graduating classes achieve college acceptance. Extracurricular activities include athletics, drama, art, music, videography, and outdoor education, among other options. Technology is extensive, with a 1:1 student-laptop computer ratio. Among the features of the 83-acre campus are five athletic fields, a gymnasium, and a recording studio. Tuition: $23,620–$27,634. Scholarships: $645,616. Kathy Harrigan-Boles is Director of Admission; Kathleen G. Rayburn is Head of School. *Southern Association.*

The Ensworth School 1958

211 Ensworth Avenue, Nashville, TN 37205
Tel. 615-383-0661; Fax 615-269-4840
Web Site www.ensworth.com; E-mail moseleyw@ensworth.com

Ensworth is a coeducational day school enrolling 1007 students in Pre-First–Grade 11. The high school opened in 2004 on a new 127-acre campus with Grade 9, adding a grade each year through 12. In small classes of 16, Ensworth promotes academic excellence and encourages students to be intellectually curious, to be people of integrity, to use their talents to the fullest, and to contribute to society. Programs include athletics, art, music, Chinese, Spanish, and community service. Latin is available in Grades 7–10. Summer camp and academic programs are offered. Tuition: $13,950–$16,950. Need-based financial aid is available. Rebekah Capps and Pascha Swett are Admissions Directors; William N. Moseley (Lake Forest, B.A.; Columbia Teachers College, M.A.) is Headmaster.

Episcopal School of Knoxville 1994

950 Episcopal School Way, Knoxville, TN 37932
Tel. 865-777-9032; Fax 865-777-9034
Web Site www.esknoxville.org; E-mail secor@esknoxville.org

Episcopal School of Knoxville is an independent elementary/middle school enrolling 251 boys and girls from many faiths in

Kindergarten–Grade 8. In the Episcopal tradition, the School offers a challenging academic curriculum underscored by character education, religious studies, and inclusive chapel services and liturgies. Courses emphasize the acquisition of strong skills and an understanding of basic concepts. They include language arts, math, science, and social studies, Middle School French and Latin, Middle and Lower School Spanish, art, music, computer technology on a networked campus, and physical education. Strong extracurricular offerings include a full sports program and interscholastic activities such as Youth Legislature and Destination Imagination. Tuition: $9850–$10,750. Financial aid is available. Peter Klekamp is Assistant Head of School and Director of Admissions; James Jay Secor III (Virginia Wesleyan, B.A.; James Madison, M.Ed.) is Headmaster.

Franklin Road Academy 1971

4700 Franklin Road, Nashville, TN 37220
Tel. 615-832-8845; Admissions Ext. 304; Fax 615-834-4137
Web Site www.franklinroadacademy.com
E-mail matthewsc@franklinroadacademy.com

Franklin Road Academy is an independent, Christian, coeducational day school enrolling 970 students in Prekindergarten 4–Grade 12. The school prepares students intellectually for higher levels of education while also providing programs and facilities for their total development. While emphasis is on traditional disciplines, arts, and physical education, students are encouraged to participate in sports, concert and pep bands, student government, publications, and interest clubs. Tuition: $12,120–$13,890. Jan Marshall and Alison Elliott are Associate Directors of Admissions; Dr. Margaret W. Wade (Vanderbilt, B.A.; Middle Tennessee State, M.Ed.; Peabody College of Vanderbilt University, Ed.D.) was appointed Head of School in 2001. *Southern Association.*

Grace-St. Luke's Episcopal School 1947

246 South Belvedere Boulevard, Memphis, TN 38104
Tel. 901-278-0200; Fax 901-272-7119
Web Site www.gslschool.org; E-mail ntaylor@gslschool.org

Grace-St. Luke's Episcopal, enrolling 500 boys and girls age 3–Grade 8, aims to motivate students academically within a nurturing community that reflects Christian values according to the Episcopal tradition. The curriculum is student-centered to address the changing needs of children as they enter new stages of development. Religious studies, foreign language, the fine arts, and physical education complement the core disciplines. In the Middle School, students are involved in Honor Council, Student Council, performance groups, yearbook, newspaper, a creative writing magazine, and athletics. Enrichment, afterschool, and summer programs are provided. Tuition: $6000–$10,500. Nancy Taylor is Director of Admissions and Financial Aid; Thomas A. Beazley (University of Pennsylvania, M.S.) is Headmaster. *Southern Association.*

Harding Academy 1971

170 Windsor Drive, Nashville, TN 37205
Tel. 615-356-5510; Fax 615-356-0441
Web Site www.hardingacademy.org
E-mail arnoldb@hardingacademy.org

A nonsectarian school, Harding Academy enrolls 475 boys and girls in Kindergarten–Grade 8. The Lower School (K–5) features extensive arts facilities and a Discovery Lab with an indoor creek in a greenhouse environment. The Middle School (6–8) places 97 percent of its students in their first-choice high schools. Library, reading, and computer specialists work with all students on the fully networked campus. Band, music, art, drama, and dance are showcased yearly, and varsity athletic teams compete in the Harpeth Valley Athletic Conference. Extended-day care and summer camps are offered. Tuition: $12,425. Financial aid and payment plans are available. Rebecca Arnold is Director of Admissions; Ian L. Craig (Syracuse University, B.A.; New York University, M.A.) is Head of School. *Southern Association.*

The Harpeth Hall School 1951

3801 Hobbs Road, Nashville, TN 37215-0207
Tel. 615-297-9543; Fax 615-297-0480
Web Site www.harpethhall.org; E-mail wild@harpethhall.org

Nashville's only independent school for girls challenges each student to develop her highest intellectual ability, to discover her creative talents, and to make a meaningful contribution to her community. Enrolling 633 students in Grades 5–12, Harpeth Hall integrates technology throughout all disciplines. Small classes and a 9:1 student-teacher ratio ensure that each girl participates actively in the learning process. The School's rigorous curriculum is complemented by athletics, arts, service learning, leadership opportunities, and innovative programs. A three-week opportunity for nontraditional studies, off-campus work/study, and academic travel enhance the Upper School program. Tuition: $17,645–$18,345. Dianne Wild is Director of Admissions and Financial Aid; Ann M. Teaff is Head of School. *Southern Association.*

Hutchison School 1902

1740 Ridgeway Road, Memphis, TN 38119
Tel. 901-761-2220; Admissions 901-762-6672; Fax 901-683-3510
Web Site www.hutchisonschool.org
E-mail ccovington@hutchisonschool.org

Miss Mary Grimes Hutchison began her school at the request of friends who wanted her to teach their children. Hutchison School today enrolls 893 young women in a college preparatory program encompassing Pre-Kindergarten–Grade 12. Hutchison is committed to offering a multidimensional education in a nurturing and inclusive community. The nondenominational school embraces Christian principles while welcoming girls from all backgrounds. Academic achievement shares equal emphasis with the social and moral growth of each student. Dedicated faculty encourage girls to develop a joy of learning, to sharpen intellectual curiosity, to cultivate artistic expression, and to strive for physical well-being. Qualified students may take AP courses in the major disciplines. Historically, all Hutchison seniors attend four-year colleges and universities nationwide. Girls take part in school government, honor societies, publications, dramatic and musical productions, instrumental and choral ensembles, community outreach, and 19 varsity and junior varsity sports teams. After-school and summer sessions are offered through Hutchison's Center for Excellence. Tuition: $4600–$14,500. Financial aid is available. Candy Covington is Director of Admissions; Dr. Annette C. Smith is Head of School. *Southern Association.*

Lausanne Collegiate School 1926

1381 West Massey Road, Memphis, TN 38120
Tel. 901-474-1000; Admission 901-474-1030; Fax 901-474-1010
Web Site www.lausanneschool.com

Enrolling 770 day boys and girls from diverse backgrounds in PreKindergarten–Grade 12, Lausanne Collegiate School is committed to preparing young people for success in higher education and in the global environment of the 21st century. Lausanne's rigorous curriculum includes honors and Advanced Placement courses, challenging electives, technology integration, modern languages, and the arts. One hundred percent of graduates enroll in four-year colleges and universities. Students follow a code of conduct that honors individuality and respects differences. Activities range from the arts and overseas travel to school government, Model UN, and sports. Tuition: $7900–$12,500. Financial aid is available. Molly B. Cook is Director of Admission; Stuart McCathie is Headmaster. *Southern Association.*

Memphis University School 1893

6191 Park Avenue, Memphis, TN 38119-5399
Tel. 901-260-1300; Fax 901-260-1355
Web Site www.musowls.org; E-mail danny.kahalley@musowls.org

Set on 94 acres, Memphis University School is a nondenominational, college preparatory day school for boys in Grades 7 through 12. With an enrollment of approximately 650 students, MUS is dedicated to academic excellence and the development of well-rounded young men of strong moral character. The academic program includes 18 Advanced Placement courses with 100 percent college attendance in an average year. The Class of 2007 received more than $9,200,000 in merit-based aid from universities. The School has many extracurricular offerings and fields athletic teams in 12 sports. Tuition: $14,350. Daniel Kahalley is Director of Admissions; Ellis L. Haguewood (Harding College, B.A.; Memphis State, M.A.) was appointed Headmaster in 1995. *Southern Association.*

Montgomery Bell Academy 1867

4001 Harding Road, Nashville, TN 37205
Tel. 615-298-5514; Admission 615-369-5311; Fax 615-297-0271
Web Site www.montgomerybell.edu
E-mail ferrelg@montgomerybell.edu

Montgomery Bell Academy, enrolling 680 day students in Grades 7 through 12, seeks to prepare young men for college and a lifetime of learning, enabling each to reach his full potential as "gentleman, scholar, and athlete." The rigorous liberal arts curriculum features 20 Advanced Placement and 30 honors courses as well as a variety of challenging electives. The Debate Program, exchange programs at Eton and Winchester Colleges, and publications offer further academic enrichment. Students take part in extracurricular activities such as chorus, jazz band, varsity sports, drama, leadership organizations, and community service. An academic session and sports camps are available in the summer. Tuition: $16,625. Greg Ferrell is Director of Admission and Financial Aid; Bradford Gioia is Headmaster. *Southern Association.*

Overbrook School 1936

4210 Harding Road, Nashville, TN 37205
Tel. 615-292-5134; Fax 615-783-0560
Web Site www.overbrook.edu; E-mail admissions-os@overbrook.edu

The Dominican Sisters of the St. Cecilia Congregation founded this coeducational day school to provide primary education in the Roman Catholic tradition. Enrolling 329 students in Pre-Kindergarten–Grade 8, Overbrook School seeks to "permeate students' entire day with Christ so that He will be the source of their strength, the goal of their actions, and the center of their lives." High standards of excellence dominate a curriculum that acknowledges and addresses individual differences and learning styles. In partnership with parents, dedicated teachers educate the whole child in all phases of intellectual, spiritual, athletic, aesthetic, personal, and social development. Good citizenship, responsibility, and character share equal emphasis with academic achievement. Classes in religion and special liturgies are open to children from all faith backgrounds. Activities include National Junior Honor Society, forensics (speech and debate), three choirs, three instrumental groups, MathCounts, soccer, basketball, cross-country, and more. The Class of 2007 raised $15,000 for scholarship purposes. Extended care and a summer program are available. Tuition: $9500. Financial Aid: $150,000. Ellen Fernández is Director of Admissions; Sr. Marie Blanchette, O.P., is Principal. *Southern Association.*

St. Agnes Academy–St. Dominic School 1851

4830 Walnut Grove Road, Memphis, TN 38117
Tel. 901-767-1356; Admission 901-435-5817; Fax 901-435-5866
Web Site www.saa-sds.org; E-mail tforsythe@saa-sds.org

This college preparatory day school enrolls 880 students, with boys in Pre-Kindergarten–Grade 8 and girls in Pre-K–Grade 12. Ecumenical by charter and Catholic in tradition, St. Agnes Academy–St. Dominic School seeks to develop academic excellence, spirituality, leadership, and morality in young people from diverse faith backgrounds. Classes are coeducational in early childhood and junior high and single-gender in lower and upper schools. This configuration helps provide the School's teachers with ways to individualize and customize curriculum to match the students' developmental and gender-specific needs. The classical curriculum, which includes Advanced Placement opportunities, is enriched by technology, three languages, and the arts. The School is a leader in the integration of technology into the curriculum and the first in the area to provide laptops to every student in Grades 1–12. Traditionally, graduates attend four-year colleges and universities. Among the activities are drama, chorus, newspaper, Key Club, and sports. Extended care and summer programs are available. Tuition: $5543–$10,490. Financial Aid: $530,000. Terry Forsythe is Dean of Admission; Barbara H. Daush is President. *Southern Association.*

St. Cecilia Academy 1860

4210 Harding Road, Nashville, TN 37205
Tel. 615-298-4525; Fax 615-783-0561
Web Site www.stcecilia.edu; E-mail info@stcecilia.edu

This college preparatory day school was founded by the Dominican Sisters of the St. Cecilia Congregation to meet the need for a Catholic secondary school for young women. St. Cecilia Academy takes pride in offering a strong college preparatory education, "rooted in faith, rich in excellence," that equips girls for learning and leadership in the 21st century. The curriculum emphasizes the liberal arts, sciences, and humanities, with 23 AP courses typically enrolling about 70 percent of the 228-member student body. Religious studies, world languages, information technology, and the fine and performing arts complement the core academic program. Classes enroll an average of 13 girls, with a 12:1 student-teacher ratio. Qualified students may cross-enroll at Aquinas College. Virtually all St. Cecilia graduates go on to challenging four-year colleges and universities such as Cornell, Massachusetts Institute of Technology, Princeton, and the University of Notre Dame. Activities include student government, drama, forensics, National Honor Society, Science Olympiad, and interscholastic sports. Tuition: $12,343. Financial Aid: $300,000. Betty Bader is Director of Enrollment Management; Sr. Mary Thomas, O.P., is Principal. *Southern Association.*

St. George's Independent School 1959

PK–5: 8250 Poplar Avenue, Germantown, TN 38138
Tel. 901-261-2300; Fax 901-261-2311
PK–5: 3749 Kimball Avenue, Memphis, TN 38111
Tel. 901-261-2200; Fax 901-261-2211
6–12: 1880 Wolf River Boulevard, Collierville, TN 38017
Tel. 901-457-2000; Fax 901-457-2111
Web Site sgis.org

St. George's Independent School is a coeducational, college preparatory school for 1192 students in Prekindergarten–Grade 12. The School's culture rests on its dedication to meaningful relationships, an appreciation for the individual, and a foundation for lifelong learning. The academically rigorous curriculum is designed to relate student learning with real-life experiences. Technology is woven into all subjects. Founded in the Episcopal tradition, St. George's maintains an ecumenical atmosphere that counts all students as children of God. Through regular chapel services and religious education, students learn traditional Judeo-Christian values. Among the cocurricular activities are Art Club, Band, Chorus, Drama, Engineering Club, Honor Council, Knowledge Bowl, Model UN, Student Senate, and Youth and Government. St. George's students also make meaningful contributions through community service and fellowship to others. Summer programs are optional. Tuition: $6839–$13,335. Jennifer Taylor (Germantown), Ginny Henderson (Memphis), and Jay Philpott (Collierville) coordinate admissions; William W. Taylor is President. *Southern Association.*

St. Nicholas School 1958

7525 Min-Tom Drive, Chattanooga, TN 37421
Tel. 423-899-1999; Fax 423-899-0109
Web Site www.stns.org; E-mail bdawkins@stns.org

St. Nicholas School, founded in 1958 in the Episcopal tradition, serves 230 day students age 4 through Grade 5. St. Nicholas addresses the whole, integrated development of the child and facilitates the unfolding of self-confident, independent learners. Its philosophy values diversity, fosters critical thinking among students, and uses age-appropriate approaches to meet the spiritual, intellectual, and physical needs of children. Extended school and summer camp programs are offered. Tuition: $8390–$11,290. Financial Aid: $200,000. Barbara B. Dawkins is Admissions Director; Mark Fallo is Head of School. *Southern Association.*

University School of Nashville 1915

2000 Edgehill Avenue, Nashville, TN 37212
Tel. 615-321-8000; Admissions 615-327-3812; Fax 615-321-0889
Web Site www.usn.org; E-mail jdouglas@usn.org

University School of Nashville, an independent, coeducational, nonsectarian day school enrolling 1007 students in Kindergarten–Grade 12, was established as the successor to Peabody Demonstration School. Learning is student-centered, active, and in-depth with a commitment to progressive ideals. The School's main campus is in the university area of the city, while the suburban 80-acre River Campus provides playing fields, a track, and a wetlands site for science research. One-third of the Class of 2006 has received National Merit recognition. Tuition: $13,784–$15,361. Financial aid is available. Juliet C. Douglas is Director of Admissions; Vincent W. Durnan, Jr. (Williams College, B.A.; Harvard, M.Ed.), was appointed Director in 2000. *Southern Association.*

Webb School of Knoxville 1955

9800 Webb School Drive, Knoxville, TN 37923
Tel. 865-693-0011; Admission 865-291-3830; Fax 865-691-8057
Web Site www.webbschool.org; E-mail terrie_balak@webbschool.org

This coeducational, college preparatory day school, enrolling 1048 students in Kindergarten–Grade 12, seeks to balance intellectual challenge within a broad-based liberal arts curriculum. Webb offers 25 Advanced Placement courses, 24 courses in the arts, and 66 interscholastic teams. Character development is a cornerstone of Webb's culture, and an honor code is the foundation of the Webb School experience. Students volunteer in numerous service learning projects including Habitat for Humanity and Boys and Girls Club. Webb has more than 650 networked computers located in nine labs. A summer day camp is available. Tuition: $12,184–$13,870. Financial Aid: $1,105,000. Terrie Balak is Director of Admission and Financial Aid; Scott L. Hutchinson (Duke, B.A.; College of William and Mary, M.Ed.) is President. *Southern Association.*

TEXAS

All Saints Episcopal School 1954

4108 Delaware, P.O. Box 7188, Beaumont, TX 77706
Tel. 409-892-1755; Fax 409-892-0166
Web Site www.allsaints-beaumont.org
E-mail sclark@allsaints-beaumont.org

All Saints is a day school enrolling 395 boys and girls age 3–Grade 8. The School's challenging program, which emphasizes the education and development of the whole child, mentally, physically, and spiritually, has earned statewide academic recognition through participation in the Private School Interscholastic Association. Spanish is taught at all levels; Latin is introduced in the middle school, piano in Kindergarten–Grade 3. High school credit may be earned for Algebra I, Integrated Physics and Chemistry, and Spanish. A 17,000-volume library, networked computers with Internet access, three science labs, a full-size gym, new athletic fields, and daily chapel are features of the program. Tuition: $2230–$6500. Financial Aid: $100,000. Kathy Fisher is Admissions Director; Catherine "Scootie" Clark is Head of School.

All Saints' Episcopal School 1951

9700 Saints Circle, Fort Worth, TX 76108
Tel. 817-560-5746; Fax 817-560-5720
Web Site www.aseschool.org; E-mail admissions@aseschool.org

All Saints' Episcopal School, a church-related, coeducational day school set on a spacious 103-acre campus, is one of the largest independent parish schools in the United States. Welcoming more than 800 students from many religious, ethnic, and racial backgrounds, the School offers a dynamic, values-based academic program encompassing Kindergarten through Grade 12. The college preparatory curriculum balances the arts, sciences, and humanities, combined with the development of moral values, character education, and ethical decision making. The Upper School program includes honors and Advanced Placement courses in all major departments. Students of all faiths attend chapel services in the Anglican tradition and take part in service outreach as a means of developing spiritual awareness. Among the activities are school government, honor societies, Students Against Drunk Driving, publications, dance, theater productions, instrumental and vocal ensembles, 15 men's and women's interscholastic sports, cheerleading, and interest clubs formed in such areas as business, chess, physics, and literature. Tuition: $11,790–$12,800. Financial aid is available. Linda Sherlock is Director of Admissions; Thaddeus B. Bird is Headmaster.

Annunciation Orthodox School 1970

3600 Yoakum Boulevard, Houston, TX 77006
Tel. 713-470-5600; Admissions 713-470-5611; Fax 713-470-5605
Web Site www.aoshouston.org; E-mail admissions@aoshouston.org

In addition to preparing students for their next academic steps, Annunciation Orthodox School works in partnership with parents to lay solid foundations for life. Founded to develop "the whole child," AOS offers a challenging academic curriculum within a nurturing Christian environment for 683 students in Preschool–Grade 8. Programs encompass a balance of academic, spiritual, physical, and social experiences that enrich students' lives and shape their hearts, bodies, and minds. Extracurricular activities include sports, student government, performing and visual art clubs, academic clubs, chess club, admissions club, and outreach service opportunities. Extended-day care and summer programs are available. Tuition: $10,500–$14,000; Fees: $500–$800. Financial Aid: $295,000.

Maria Newton is Advisor to the Head of School and Director of Admissions; Mark H. Kelly is Head of School.

The Awty International School 1956

7455 Awty School Lane, Houston, TX 77055
Tel. 713-686-4850; Fax 713-686-4956
Web Site www.awty.org; E-mail admin@awty.org

The Awty International School in Houston, Texas, is a coeducational, college preparatory day school enrolling 1180 students in Preschool through Grade 12. Situated in the fourth-largest city in the United States, the School was founded in 1956 by Kathleen Awty as a preschool. As demand increased, Lower, Middle, and Upper Schools were added by 1975. It became affiliated with the French School of Houston in 1979 through the efforts of the Mission Laïque Française. The School's name was changed in 1984 to reflect its multilingual character and international faculty and student body.

In addition to providing a strong basis in traditional academic subjects, The Awty International School strives to instill in its students an awareness of and appreciation for the diversity among nations. Learning to understand and respect other languages and cultures develops young adults who are prepared to lead and participate fully in today's global economy.

A nonprofit organization, The Awty International School is governed by a Board of Trustees comprised of parents, American and international business leaders, and representatives of the French Government. The School is accredited by the Independent Schools Association of the Southwest, the French Ministry of Education, and the Council of International Schools. It holds membership in the International Baccalaureate Organization, the National Association of Independent Schools, and the Houston Association of Independent Schools and is affiliated with the Mission Laïque Française.

THE CAMPUS. The Awty International School's urban campus occupies 15 acres. The School's facilities include a Preschool complex, three libraries, a science wing, a Middle/Upper School wing with computer and language labs, a gymnasium/auditorium, and a two-story classroom complex. The new home of the Lower School opened in the fall of 2003. There are 112 computers on campus for student use.

THE FACULTY. David Watson, Ph.D., born in Manchester, England, was appointed Head of School in July 2000. He comes to Awty from Kuala Lumpur, Malaysia, where he was

Head of The Garden International School. Dr. Watson holds Bachelor of Arts (with Honors) and Master of Science degrees from the University of Bristol, a *Licence ès lettres* from the University of Reims, and a doctoral degree from the University of Zagreb.

The faculty numbers 125. Because of the multilingual character of the School, many faculty members have earned their degrees and licenses from European universities. Among these are the Universities of Bordeaux, Lille, and Toulouse (France); the University of Hamburg (Germany); the Universities of Liverpool, London, and Nottingham (England); and Universidad Iberoamericana and Colegio La Florida (Mexico). American schools include Baylor, Boston College, Boston University, Bowdoin, Louisiana State, Princeton, Rice, Texas A&M, Tulane, Vanderbilt, and the Universities of Arizona, Houston, Michigan, and Texas.

Two registered nurses and two counselors serve on a full-time basis; two major medical centers are within 15 minutes of the campus.

STUDENT BODY. In 2007–08, The Awty International School enrolled 1180 students in three-year-old Preschool through Grade 12. The student body is comprised of young people from Houston and the surrounding communities and from most parts of the globe. Approximately 40 percent of the students are American citizens, followed by French and British citizens. In all, 50 countries are represented including Australia, Belgium, Brazil, Canada, Egypt, Germany, Holland, Japan, Mexico, Russia, and Switzerland.

ACADEMIC PROGRAM. Seeking to broaden understanding of diverse cultures, The Awty International School offers its students two academic programs: a traditional American college preparatory curriculum, leading to the International Baccalaureate, and a program, approved by the French Government, leading to the French *baccalauréat*. The American high school diploma is conferred on qualified candidates.

The school year, divided into three terms, begins in late August and extends through early June. Classes in all grades are held five days a week. Preschool through Lower School (Grades 1–5) begins at 8:15 A.M. and dismisses at 2:50 P.M., while the Middle (Grades 6–8) and Upper (Grades 9–12) Schools begin at 8:00 A.M. and dismiss at 3:30 P.M.

An average class has 15–18 students. Tutoring in the Awty Plus After-School Program is provided on a fee basis.

The Preschool offers a completely bilingual program in French and English or Spanish and English. All students are required to take a second language. For Secondary School students, French and Spanish are offered at a wide range of levels. In addition, Arabic, Dutch, German, Italian, Portuguese, Mandarin, and Norwegian are available under specific conditions. Secondary School students may also take a third language.

In the Upper School, students must complete a minimum of 26 credits as follows: 4 in English; 4 in a second language; 4 each in history, mathematics, and science; 1 in electives; 1 in fine arts; 2 in physical education; and 1 in computer science. In Grades 11–12, International Section students pursue the International Baccalaureate, which is accepted by most universities for Advanced Placement. Students have in-depth study and testing in six subjects, a course in Theory of Knowledge (1 credit), and the writing of an extended essay. A minimum of 150 hours of community service is also required.

French Section students may earn the French *baccalauréat* in a special concentration, including French literature, philosophy, mathematics, physics, biology, geography, physical education, foreign language, and history. Preparation for the *baccalauréat* is three years (Grades 10–12) and includes both compulsory and elective studies.

Awty graduates enroll in colleges and universities in the United States and throughout the world. Schools attended by recent graduates include American University, Carnegie Mellon, Columbia, Georgetown, Harvard, Johns Hopkins, McGill (Canada), New York University, Rice, Swarthmore, Texas A&M, Vassar, Williams, Yale, and the Universities of Bonn, Paris (all campuses), Pennsylvania, Texas, and Warwick (England).

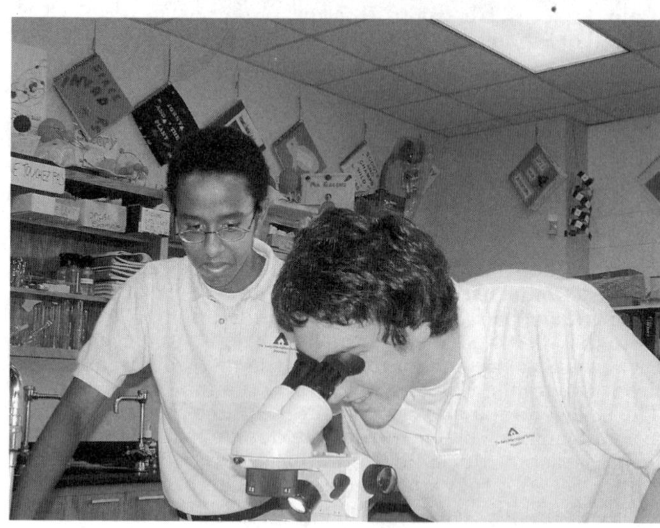

The Awty Plus After-School Program, operating from 2:50 to 6:00 P.M. daily, is provided for students seeking assistance in homework assignments or additional academic instruction in languages. Activities include dance, art, tennis, martial arts, and computer science.

STUDENT ACTIVITIES. Student Councils are elected in both the Middle and Upper Schools. Council members help with school events and serve on disciplinary and advisory committees. Extracurricular activities are organized according to student interest and include Model United Nations, choir, drama, cheerleading, yearbook, newspaper, robotics competition, band, a chamber music ensemble, and musical and dramatic productions.

The Athletic Department's goal is to enhance the student's physical, mental, emotional, and social development through a variety of extracurricular sports. Upper School athletic teams compete with members of the Texas Association of Private and Parochial Schools (TAPPS), while Middle School athletes compete with members of the Greater Houston Athletic Conference and other independent schools. Boys' varsity teams are formed in soccer, basketball, tennis, golf, cross-country, and track. Girls' varsity teams participate in soccer, volleyball, basketball, tennis, cross-country, and track. The school tennis team won the TAPPS state championship in 2002, 2003, and 2004.

New and returning students, their families, and faculty are welcomed each fall at a festive gathering. Homecoming dances and proms are held annually. Other scheduled events are open houses, a book fair, and an International Week.

ADMISSION AND COSTS. The Awty International School seeks college-bound students from the Houston area and around the world who are of above-average ability and good moral character. The application deadline is December 20. A completed application form with a nonrefundable $100 application fee, academic transcripts, test results, teacher recommendations, and a personal interview are required.

In 2007–08, tuition ranges from $11,485 for Preschool to $15,735 for the Upper School. Books ($400–$600), uniforms (required in Kindergarten–Grade 12), lunches, and bus transportation are extra; a tuition payment plan and limited financial aid are available.

Head of School: Dr. David Watson
Head, Bilingual French Section: Jean Stephan
Head, Upper School: Samuel P. Waugh
Head, Middle School: Thomas Beuscher
Head, Lower School: Lilian Mullane
Director of College Counseling: Rebecca Day
Director of Admissions: Beth Anne Gunn
Chief Financial Officer: Teresa La Bonte
Director of Athletics: Karen Waugh

The Canterbury Episcopal School 1992

1708 North Westmoreland Road, DeSoto, TX 75115
Tel. 972-572-7200; Fax 972-572-7400
Web Site www.thecanterburyschool.org
E-mail admissions@thecanterburyschool.org

The Canterbury Episcopal School, serving 306 boys and girls from diverse racial, religious, and ethnic backgrounds, offers a college preparatory curriculum encompassing Kindergarten through Grade 12. Set on a 37-acre campus, the School provides an academic program centered on the liberal arts, sciences, and humanities. Canterbury's Episcopal heritage is reflected in the School's ethnic, religious, and socioeconomic diversity, community service, chapel, and strong academics. English, math, history, science, modern and classical language, and the fine arts are integral to the curriculum, with honors and Advanced Placement courses in most subjects. Religious studies focus on the Hebrew Bible, New Testament, ethics, and theology. Students attend daily chapel, and an Episcopal chaplain conducts Eucharistic services on a regular basis. Middle (Grades 6–8) and Upper School (Grades 9–12) athletes compete interscholastically in eight sports. Other activities include the National Honor Society, publications, music and drama ensembles, academic and special-interest clubs, and community outreach. Tuition: $7360–$10,490. Financial aid is available. The Reverend C. Richard Cadigan is Head of School.

Cistercian Preparatory School 1962

3660 Cistercian Road, Irving, TX 75039
Tel. 469-499-5400; Admissions 469-499-5411; Fax 469-499-5440
Web Site www.cistercian.org; E-mail admissions@cistercian.org

Cistercian Preparatory School is a Roman Catholic, college preparatory day school enrolling 350 boys of all creeds in Grades 5 through 12. The curriculum is a fully integrated, eight-year honors program of English, theology, math, laboratory science, computer science, foreign language, and social studies, which is identical for all students. Electives, Advanced Placement, college-credit courses, and independent studies are offered in addition to athletics, activities, summer sports camp, and an academic summer school. Tuition: $11,900–$13,600. Need-based financial aid is available. Robert J. Haaser is Director of Admissions; Fr. Peter Verhalen is Headmaster.

Duchesne Academy of the Sacred Heart 1960

10202 Memorial Drive, Houston, TX 77024
Tel. 713-468-8211; Admissions Ext. 139; Fax 713-465-9809
Web Site www.duchesne.org; E-mail admissions@duchesne.org

Duchesne Academy was founded by the Religious of the Sacred Heart to educate young women to an active faith, a respect for intellectual values, and a commitment to service, community, and personal growth. Enrolling 670 girls in Pre-kindergarten through Grade 12, the school is part of a worldwide Sacred Heart Network. State-of-the-art technology is integrated throughout a college preparatory curriculum that includes Advanced Placement courses, spiritual formation, and a strong community service component. Fine arts, athletics, summer enrichment opportunities, an advisory program, and interest clubs enrich the core program. Tuition: $9500–$15,800. Financial Aid: $800,000. Beth Speck is Director of Admission; Sr. Jan Dunn is Headmistress.

Episcopal High School of Houston 1983

4650 Bissonnet, Bellaire, TX 77401
Tel. 713-512-3400; Admissions 713-512-3444; Fax 713-512-3603
Web Site www.ehshouston.org; E-mail akoehler@ehshouston.org

Founded in 1983 within the Episcopal Diocese of Texas, Episcopal High is a coeducational day school serving 630 students in Grades 9–12. The School's broad college preparatory program is comprised of four pillars that emphasize academic, religious, artistic, and athletic disciplines, nurtured by Christian values in a supportive environment. Daily chapel services reinforce the ethical and religious principles upon which the School was founded. The 35-acre campus is located in Bellaire, south of the Galleria. State-of-the-art buildings and wireless technology for the students' laptop computers enhance their total learning experience. Tuition: $19,260. Audrey Koehler is Director of Admission; C. Edward Smith (Princeton University, A.B.; Middlebury College, M.A.) is Headmaster.

The Episcopal School of Dallas 1974

4100 Merrell Road, Dallas, TX 75229-6200
Tel. 214-358-4368; Admissions 214-353-5827; Fax 214-353-5870
Web Site www.esdallas.org; E-mail admission@esdallas.org

The Episcopal School of Dallas was established to provide a strong classical education within the framework of Judeo-Christian principles. Its commitment places equal emphasis on character development and the acquisition of knowledge through a college preparatory curriculum centered on the liberal arts, sciences, and humanities. Enrolling 1100 day boys and girls from diverse backgrounds in Beginners (3)–Grade 12, the School aims to encourage the spiritual, intellectual, physical, and social well-being of its students through an academic program infused with enduring values. All students attend daily chapel and participate in social outreach. Core subjects are enhanced by world languages, computer technology, and the visual and performing arts. Students take part in school government, leadership committees, publications, dramas and musicals, vocal and instrumental ensembles, and interscholastic sports. Community service is required and may involve projects with local homeless shelters, nursing homes, Big Brothers/Sisters, and inner-city schools. Tuition: $8400–$20,500. Financial Aid: $1,400,000. Ruth Burke is Director of Admission and Financial Aid; the Reverend Stephen B. Swann is Founding Rector/Headmaster.

Fort Worth Academy 1982

7301 Dutch Branch Road, Fort Worth, TX 76132
Tel. 817-370-1191; Admission Ext. 603; Fax 817-294-1323
Web Site www.fwacademy.org; E-mail npalmer@fwacademy.org

Located in southwest Fort Worth, this nationally recognized prepreparatory day school enrolls 230 boys and girls in Kindergarten–Grade 8. In the belief that the curriculum is the catalyst to academic success, Fort Worth Academy offers a comprehensive program designed to develop strong skills in language arts, math, social studies, and science. One-to-one computing is a reality in the Academy's 21st Century School. All middle school (Grades 5–8) students are issued their own Tablet PC for classroom and home use. Lower school students have daily and immediate access to wireless laptop and desktop computers in their classrooms. Core subjects are complemented by enrichment courses and electives in foreign language, the visual and performing arts, and athletics. Small classes, inspiring teachers, shared values, and an active partnership with parents contribute to the success of the Academy's goals. Tuition: $11,690. Financial aid is available. Nancy Palmer is Director of Admission; William M. Broderick is Head of School. *Southern Association.*

Fort Worth Country Day 1962

4200 Country Day Lane, Fort Worth, TX 76109-4299
Tel. 817-732-7718; Admissions 817-302-3242; Fax 817-377-3425
Web Site www.fwcds.org; E-mail bjiongo@fwcds.org

Fort Worth Country Day enrolls 1115 students in Kindergarten–Grade 12 in a rigorous college preparatory program with required offerings in the fine and performing arts and athletics. Community service is an integral part of the program in all grades. An Honor Code is in place, and the School aims to prepare students for the academic and social challenges of most selective colleges. Each of the School's three divisions—lower, middle, and upper—has its own facility, division head, and faculty. The 100-acre campus includes 11 academic buildings, seven athletic fields, six tennis courts, a challenge ropes course, and a stadium/all-weather eight-lane track. Tuition: $13,910–$14,965. Financial Aid: $1,200,000. Barbara W. Jiongo is Admissions Director; Evan D. Peterson is Head of School.

Good Shepherd Episcopal School 1959

11110 Midway Road, Dallas, TX 75229-4119
Tel. 214-357-1610; Admission Ext. 230; Fax 214-357-4105
Web Site www.gseschooldallas.org; E-mail admissions@gsesdallas.org

Good Shepherd Episcopal School is a parish-affiliated school enrolling 600 boys and girls in Preschool–Grade 8. Its purpose is to equip students with Christian principles, a love of learning, a creative mind, and a giving spirit. In the lower grades, writing, language arts, social studies, math, science, and health are taught by classroom teachers, with specialized teachers for reading, art, music, Spanish, and physical education. In Grades 5–8, students take one class period each in core subjects and Spanish, and one semester each of art, music, and drama, all taught by specialists. Activities include Student Council, athletics, and Classroom of the Earth. Tuition: $8672–$11,970. Financial aid is available. Kathleen Whalen is Director of Admission; J. Robert Kohler is Head of the School.

The Hockaday School 1913

11600 Welch Road, Dallas, TX 75229-2999
Tel. 214-363-6311; Admissions 214-360-6526; Fax 214-265-1649
Web Site www.hockaday.org; E-mail jliggitt@mail.hockaday.org

The Hockaday School in Dallas, Texas, is an all-girls boarding and day school from Pre-Kindergarten through Grade 12 with a residence program for Grades 8–12. Situated in a residential neighborhood, the School's location affords students a secluded campus environment with exposure to many notable cultural and civic institutions. Hockaday is conveniently positioned minutes from downtown businesses, a renowned arts district, and an international airport.

Founded in 1913 by Miss Ela Hockaday, the School seeks to provide a college preparatory education to girls of strong potential and diverse backgrounds who may be expected to assume positions of responsibility and leadership in a rapidly changing world. Hockaday aims to foster a community of concern and friendship and to instill in every girl a love of learning and an appreciation of excellence in all its forms.

A nonprofit corporation, Hockaday is directed by a Board of Trustees that represents alumnae, parents, and the community. The School fosters relationships with approximately 6500 graduates and former students through the Hockaday Alumnae Association. Hockaday is accredited by the Independent Schools Association of the Southwest and holds membership in the National Association of Independent Schools, among other organizations.

THE CAMPUS. Located on 100 acres, the campus includes 16 buildings. The 52,000-square-foot Liza Lee Academic Research Center (2002) hosts two expansive libraries, several computer labs equipped with the latest technology, and a versatile hall that doubles as a lecture facility and audiovisual theater. In the academic area are classrooms; laboratories for languages, computers, and reading; and a study center. Recent renovations increased the size of all Middle and Upper School classrooms by 50 percent. The new classrooms are equipped with Smartboard™ technology for use in conjunction with the students' laptops, which are required for every girl in Grades 6–12. The campus is fully wireless. Eight computer labs are equipped with scanners, digital cameras, and a variety of software. The Fine Arts facilities include a 600-seat auditorium, instrumental and voice studios, practice rooms, a painting studio, ceramics facilities with outdoor kilns, a photography laboratory, printmaking facilities, and an electronic music studio. The Science Center contains a lecture hall, study lounges, classrooms, ten major laboratories, a computer lab, and a greenhouse powered by solar energy. Facilities for the Lower School include classrooms for Pre-Kindergarten–Grade 4, art and music rooms, two commons areas, and science labs. The new Wellness Center includes the 5000-square-foot Hill Family Fitness Center, an 1800-square-foot aerobics room with state-of-the-art aerobic and resistance equipment, and athletic training facilities fully equipped for the treatment of sports-related injuries.

The residence halls have lounges, kitchens, an exercise room, computer labs, and laundry facilities. The infirmary is adjacent to the living quarters. A large common lounge with a fireplace and recreational equipment leads to the outdoor pool.

Athletics facilities include two gymnasiums housing four basketball courts (convertible to three volleyball and indoor tennis courts), a climbing wall, two racquetball courts, a swimming pool, and a dance studio. On the grounds are six athletic fields, a softball complex, an all-weather track, a tennis center with ten courts and seating for 90, and 20 acres of open space.

THE FACULTY. Ms. Jeanne P. Whitman, the Eugene McDermott Headmistress, is a *magna cum laude* graduate of Wake Forest University. She earned a master's degree in English from the University of Virginia and a second master's degree in business from Wake Forest University.

The faculty is composed of 104 full-time teachers, most of whom have advanced degrees, with 12 holding doctorates. Hockaday instructors are recruited from around the world, providing a faculty that reflects the School's diverse student body. The average tenure is 10 years.

STUDENT BODY. In 2007–08, there were 1028 boarding and day students. The 62 boarding students come from 7 states and 11 foreign countries. Hockaday's residence program begins in Grade 8 upward. Day students are enrolled from Pre-Kindergarten to Grade 12. There are 443 girls in the Upper School, 308 in the Middle School, and 277 in the Lower School. Thirty percent are minority students.

ACADEMIC PROGRAM. Students are exposed to a rigorous academic curriculum that offers core educational subjects as well as unique offerings in technology, the arts, and leadership and personal development. Pre-Kindergarten girls are introduced to the basic elements of language, numerical reasoning, science, social studies, computers, art, music, and creative drama. An extended-day program is offered in the afternoons to provide cultural enrichment. In the full-day Kindergarten program, reading and mathematics become more structured, and emphasis is placed on a balanced reading program. In Grades 1–4, the program is divided into subject areas: language arts, mathematics, science, social studies, art, music, drama, and physical education, with Spanish or French introduced in Kindergarten.

Middle School (Grades 5–8) continues to strengthen and widen the foundation of the Lower School. In Grades 5–6, language arts, mathematics, science, social studies, art, music, Spanish or French, and physical education comprise the core curriculum. Students are taught and utilize their computer skills in all disciplines.

In Grades 7–8, the curriculum includes English, history, mathematics (pre-algebra in Grade 7 and algebra concepts in Grade 8), laboratory science, and foreign language choices in French, Spanish, Latin, or Chinese. Fine arts selections are photography, broadcast, drawing, painting, drama, speech, debate, dance, guitar, musical theater, and ceramics. The eighth-grade class produces a musical each year. Upper School credits may be earned in math and foreign languages by eligible students in Grade 8. Activities include athletics, beginning in Grade 7; Student Council; the literary magazine, *BANNER*; math, art, and science clubs; a school newspaper, *NEWSWAY*, the broadcast news class, *Daisy Days;* and chorus for Grades 5–8. There is a sixth-grade trip to Colonial Williamsburg and the District of Columbia and a seventh-grade environmental-education trip to Taos, New Mexico. The curriculum in Grades 5–8 is complemented by visits to museums, the opera, the ballet, the symphony, and other sites of interest.

The Upper School curriculum includes English at each grade level and such senior English seminars as "The Heroine's

Journey—The Search for Wholeness," "Stones of the Heart: Literature of War," and "Autobiography and Memoir." French, Spanish, Latin, Mandarin Chinese; United States History, World History, Criminal Law, Government, Consumer Economics and Media Literacy; Algebra I–II, Geometry, Pre-Calculus, Calculus and Analytical Geometry, Finite Math, Probability and Statistics, Multivariable Calculus; Web Design; Physics, Chemistry, Astronomy, and a multimester course in Biology, including Classical Genetics, Human Evolution, and Micro-Biology and Human Diseases; History of Art and Music; Video-Media Production, Acting Styles, Studio Art, Ceramics and Sculpture, Photography, Concert, Show and Madrigal Choirs, Orchestra, Dance; Debate, Journalism, Broadcast Journalism; and Physical Education and Health are also offered. Swiss Semester in Zermatt is available for Grade 10 and CITYterm in New York for Grades 11 and 12.

Advanced Placement courses are available in more than 18 subjects. A cooperative arrangement with St. Mark's School of Texas allows girls to select courses there. Some Hockaday courses are also open to St. Mark's boys.

An English as a Second Language program is offered on intermediate and advanced levels. Intensive language training in writing, reading, listening, and speaking skills is the focus. Students may continue at Hockaday after the first year, following acceptance into the regular academic program. First-year resident students take trips to Washington, D.C., Austin, and San Antonio, Texas.

Graduation credit requirements in years include English 4, mathematics 3, history 2.5, language 3, laboratory science 3, fine arts 1.5, physical education and health 4, and two additional academic courses from any department plus basic proficiency in computer usage.

Private lessons are available in piano beginning in Pre-Kindergarten; guitar beginning in Grade 1; flute, cello, violin, and brass from Grade 5; and voice beginning in Grade 7.

Hockaday has a 100 percent acceptance rate to colleges and universities nationwide. Graduates matriculated at such colleges and universities as Boston College, Cornell, Dartmouth, Emory, Georgetown, Harvard, New York University, Princeton, Rice, Southern Methodist University, Stanford, Vanderbilt, Wake Forest, Washington University, Yale, and the Universities of Southern California and Texas.

STUDENT ACTIVITIES. The conduct and activities of the older girls are regulated by the Student Council, elected by Upper School students. Special-interest organizations, publications, and honor societies augment the academic program. Community Service committees organize volunteer activities in the community and with nonprofit organizations. Students in Upper School must complete 15 hours of community service yearly, but most complete additional hours.

Each year, two alumnae memorial fellowships bring outstanding persons to spend extended time with the Hockaday community.

Festive occasions include class dances, retreats for Grades 9 and 12, all-school mixers, the Winter Formal, Senior Prom, a musical, and parent drop-ins.

Hockaday's program of health, physical education, and recreation begins in Pre-Kindergarten. Designed to meet each girl's needs and to encourage her to develop a permanent pattern of physical activity, it offers daily instruction in the Middle School. Swimming begins in Grade 1 and continues through Grade 11 lifeguarding. In Grades 7–8, Green and White intramural teams compete in field hockey, basketball, volleyball, lacrosse, soccer, tennis, gymnastics, flag football, softball, track and field, and swimming. Interscholastic athletics are available in Grades 7–12. Varsity and junior varsity teams in Grades 9–12 compete in swimming, golf, tennis, field hockey, softball, basketball, volleyball, cross-country, track, crew, lacrosse, and soccer.

ADMISSION AND COSTS. Applicants are accepted on the basis of previous school records, results of aptitude and achievement tests, recommendations, and a personal interview. Hockaday welcomes students of all nationalities, races, and creeds. Entrance tests are given at the School on specified dates.

In 2007–08, day tuition and fees range from $14,540 for Pre-Kindergarten to $19,730–$20,770 for Grades 8–12. For the residence program, the charge for tuition, room, and board is $36,945–$40,670. Optional expenses include allowances, transportation, and private lessons. Tuition payment plans and insurance are available. In 2005–06, Hockaday awarded a total of more than $2,000,000 in assistance based on need.

Eugene McDermott Headmistress: Jeanne P. Whitman
Assistant Head & Chief Financial Officer: Mary Pat Higgins
Assistant Head for Academic Affairs & Professional Development: Karen Drawz
Head of Upper School: Kirsten Adams
Head of Middle School: Linda Kramer
Head of Lower School: Lisa Holekamp
Dean of Students: Cathy Murphee
Director of Alumnae: Amy Spence
Director of Admissions: Jen Liggitt
College Counselor: Sara Lennon
Director of Athletics: Linda Morash
Director of Development & External Affairs: Susan Swan Smith

The John Cooper School 1988

One John Cooper Drive, The Woodlands, TX 77381
Tel. 281-367-0900; Admissions Ext. 308; Fax 281-298-5715
Web Site www.johncooper.org

Enrolling 940 boys and girls in Pre-K–Grade 12, The John Cooper School offers a challenging, traditional college preparatory curriculum designed to foster a lifelong love of learning and equip students for success in higher education. Core academic disciplines are supported by extensive visual and performing arts, technology, athletics, and community service. A full-time college counseling staff assists students throughout the college planning and admission process, and all graduates enter four-year institutions. Activities include interscholastic sports, student government, leadership organizations, drama and music, and community service, including an annual schoolwide commitment to build a Habitat for Humanity home. Tuition: $10,600–$15,650. Craig Meredith is Director of Admissions; Michael F. Maher is Head of School.

The Kinkaid School 1906

201 Kinkaid School Drive, Houston, TX 77024
Tel. 713-782-1640; Admissions 713-243-5035; Fax 713-243-5055
Web Site www.kinkaid.org; E-mail admissions@kinkaid.org

Kinkaid, the first coeducational, college preparatory day school in Houston, seeks to enable students to develop their talents and fulfill their potential through a balanced program of academics, arts, community service, and athletics. Enrolling 1350 students in Prekindergarten–Grade 12, The Kinkaid School offers a challenging liberal arts curriculum enhanced by special lecture series, off-campus career internships, and overseas travel/study. Students take part in school government, academic competitions, publications, interest clubs, arts, and athletics. A summer remedial and enrichment session is offered. Tuition: $11,900–$16,275. Financial Aid: $1,099,141. Iris Bonet is Admissions Director; Donald C. North (Vanderbilt, B.A.; Middlebury, M.A.) is Headmaster.

Lakehill Preparatory School 1971

2720 Hillside Drive, Dallas, TX 75214
Tel. 214-826-2931; Fax 214-826-4623
Web Site www.lakehillprep.org; E-mail sseitz@lakehillprep.org

A coeducational, college preparatory day school, Lakehill Prep enrolls 400 students in Kindergarten through Grade 12. Lakehill's tradition of excellence and service comes from its ability to cultivate a balance among academics, personal growth, and recognition of responsibility toward others. The traditional core curriculum, enhanced by numerous electives, focuses on liberal arts, science, and humanities. Advanced Placement is offered in all curricular areas. Community service is fundamental to the spirit of the School, and all seniors participate in a two-week career internship. Activities include theater, music, athletics, cheerleading, publications, and a variety of student clubs and organizations. Tuition: $9704–$13,199. Financial aid is available. Susanne Seitz is Director of Admissions; Roger L. Perry is Headmaster. *Southern Association.*

The Lamplighter School 1953

11611 Inwood Road, Dallas, TX 75229
Tel. 214-369-9201; Admission Ext. 347; Fax 214-369-5540
Web Site www.thelamplighterschool.org
E-mail mbrenner@thelamplighterschool.org

The Lamplighter School, enrolling 430 boys and girls in Preschool (age 3)–Grade 4, seeks to foster the love of learning and build a positive self-concept. A Blue Ribbon School of Excellence, it offers a highly integrated curriculum that merges the fine arts with language arts, math, environmental science, social studies, physical education, and Spanish. Innovative groupings provide a warm and supportive environment that fosters enthusiasm, self-confidence, and a sense of belonging. The north Dallas campus features a fine arts complex, a media center, a greenhouse, and a health and fitness facility. A summer program is available for 3- to 5-year-olds. Tuition: $9000–$15,500. Matt Brenner is Director of Admission and Community Services; Dr. Arnold S. Cohen (Ohio State, Ph.D.) is Head of School.

The Oakridge School 1979

5900 West Pioneer Parkway, Arlington, TX 76013
Tel. 817-451-4994; Admissions Ext. 704; Fax 817-457-6681
Web Site www.theoakridgeschool.org
E-mail lbroadus@theoakridgeschool.org

THE OAKRIDGE SCHOOL in Arlington, Texas, is a coeducational, college preparatory day school enrolling students in Preschool–Grade 12. Located east of Fort Worth, the School is accessible by car from the greater Dallas/Fort Worth Metroplex area. A variety of libraries, galleries, theaters, and museums as well as the cultural benefits of several universities are located in the Metroplex.

The Oakridge School was founded in 1979 by parents and educators concerned with offering a challenging college preparatory curriculum. Emphasizing personal development, the School aims "to provide . . . an education of highest quality to academically qualified students, to motivate each student to perform at his or her maximum potential, and to prepare students for a life of achievement and participation in a global society."

The Oakridge School is a nonprofit institution governed by an independent Board of Regents. The School is accredited by the Independent Schools Association of the Southwest and holds membership in the National Association of Independent Schools, among other organizations.

THE CAMPUS. The School's 83-acre campus consists of ten buildings. The Early Childhood Center houses Preschool, Pre-Kindergarten, and Kindergarten. The Lower and Middle School building contains classrooms and two computer labs. The Upper School building houses science labs, central commons area, and specialized classrooms. The Student Activities Center consists of two basketball courts, kitchen, eating area, locker rooms, weight room, training room, and offices. The Multipurpose Activity Center has been acoustically enhanced to serve as a performing arts facility as well as an additional gym. The Information Center houses the technology center, an expanded school library, and the offices of central administration. The Fine Arts Center features enhanced facilities for the visual and performing arts, including a 385-plus-seat multipurpose auditorium. The Parents Club Building provides meeting and work space for parent volunteers; the Maintenance Building accommodates the needs of the building and grounds staff. The Security Center is located at the main entrance of the campus and houses technology to monitor the entire campus. The campus includes two extensive playground areas; a restored Wetlands Park; a children's garden, greenhouse, and outdoor classroom; a new golf practice facility; and athletic fields, which border the Lake Arlington Golf Course.

THE FACULTY. Andy J. Broadus, appointed Headmaster in 1981, is a graduate of Jacksonville University (B.S.) and the University of North Florida (M.Ed.) and has done advanced graduate work at the University of Georgia and Columbia University. Jon Kellam, Associate Headmaster, is a graduate of Texas Christian University (B.S., M.Ed.). He has served Oakridge as administrator, English teacher, and varsity soccer coach. Betty Garton (Texas Tech, B.S.; Texas Christian, M.Ed.) is Head of the Early Childhood Center; Corliss Elsesser (Texas Christian, B.S., M.Ed.) has been with the School since its founding and is Head of the Lower School; Mike Cobb (University of North Texas, B.A.; Cambridge College, M.Ed.) is Head of the Middle School; Butch Groves (Southwest Oklahoma State, B.S.; University of Central Oklahoma, M.Ed.) is Head of the Upper School; Melissa Grubb (Austin College, B.A., M.A.) is Director of Studies.

The faculty include 95 teachers, 73 women and 22 men. They hold 95 bachelor's degrees, 50 master's degrees, and 4 doctoral degrees representing study at a variety of colleges throughout the United States and abroad.

First aid is provided by a full-time registered nurse with a fully equipped school infirmary. An emergency medical facility is located nearby.

STUDENT BODY. In 2007–08, the School enrolled 865 boys and girls, from 3 to 18 years of age. Students come from Arlington, Bedford, Burleson, Cedar Hill, Cleburne, Colleyville, Dallas, De Soto, Duncanville, Euless, Fort Worth, Grand Prairie, Grapevine, Hurst, Irving, Keller, Mansfield, Midlothian, Southlake, and Waxahachie. Also represented are ten foreign countries.

ACADEMIC PROGRAM. The school year is divided into four marking periods in all divisions. Parents are informed regularly of student progress through interim reports, parent conferences, and report cards, which are sent to parents at the end of each marking period. Classes range in size from 4 to 22 students with a student-teacher ratio of 9:1. Self-discipline and clear, concise rules are emphasized in "an atmosphere of mutual respect." Faculty members provide extra help as needed, and tutoring can be arranged.

The Early Childhood Center curriculum incorporates Mathematics, Language Arts, Science, Social Studies, Spanish, Computer, Visual Perception, Music, Art, and Physical Education. The entire curriculum is sequential from level to level. The Lower School (Grades 1–4) courses include Language Arts Enrichment, Social Studies, Math, Science, Spanish, Art, Music, Physical Education, Computer, and Library program. The Lower House of the Middle School (Grades 5–6) curriculum is as follows: Language Arts, French or Spanish, U.S. and World History, Latin, Math, General Science, Earth Science, Art, Music, Strings, Creative Dramatics, and intramural athletics. The Upper House of the Middle School (Grades 7–8) curriculum is as follows: English, Composition, French or Spanish, U.S. History, Pre-Algebra and Algebra I, Geometry, Life Science and Physical Science, Art, Choir, Drama, Strings, and Physical Education/Athletics. The Upper School (Grades 9–12) curriculum includes English, Creative Writing, Effective Writing; World History, U.S. History, American Government, Economics; Spanish, French, Chinese; Algebra I–II, Geometry, Pre-Calculus, Calculus, Statistics; Biology, Chemistry, Physics, Anatomy and Physiology, and Computer Science Programming; electives include Psychology, Anthropology/Archaeology, World Religions, Acting, Studio Art, Choir, Digital Production, and Yearbook.

Advanced Placement courses are offered in Language & Composition, Literature & Composition, Calculus, Statistics, Biology, Physics, U.S. History, European History, French, Spanish, Chinese, Computer Science, and Art.

Annual standardized testing includes the Stanford Achievement Test. The Otis-Lennon School Ability test is given every other year.

The College Counseling program is a four-year process. All students take the PLAN in 9th and 10th grade; the PSAT in 10th and 11th; and the SAT I, SAT II, and ACT in 11th and 12th. Oakridge hosts a number of college representatives on campus throughout the fall, and students attend an annual college fair. College advising is conducted on a one-to-one basis, particularly in the senior year, and includes financial aid counseling, computer resources, and field trips to nearby colleges. Oakridge students have been accepted at such colleges and universities as Arizona State, Baylor, Boston College, Cornell, Creighton, Duke, Emory, Georgetown, Harvard, Louisiana State, Massachusetts Institute of Technology, New York University, Northwestern, Ohio State, Rensselaer Polytechnic, Rice, Southern Methodist, Spelman, Stanford, Texas A&M, Texas Christian, Texas Tech, Trinity, and the University of Texas.

STUDENT ACTIVITIES. There are elected Student Council programs in the Middle and Upper schools. In the Upper School, the Student Council consists of elected officers and the officers of each class. Members of the Student Council are expected to serve as representatives, leaders, and good examples for the entire student body. A faculty sponsor advises and works with the Student Council.

The Middle and Upper School Inter-Scholastic Sports Program offers baseball, basketball, football, golf, soccer, tennis, cross-country, and track for boys, and basketball, soccer, tennis, golf, cross-country, softball, track, field hockey, and volleyball for girls. The Athletic Director schedules games with public and private schools in the Fort Worth/Dallas area. Other activities include the National Junior Honor Society, the National Honor Society, Math Teams, Computer Science Team, Youth and Government, Literary Magazine, cheerleading, and the Drama, French, Spanish, Art, and Whole Earth Clubs. Special social activities are scheduled on a monthly basis.

Special programs and events include Grandparents Day, New Parent Dinner, Book Fair, the Super Supper and Auction, Homecoming, Sports Banquets, Parent Orientation Night, Owlfest, Spring Fair, Living History Program, concerts, and awards programs.

ADMISSION AND COSTS. The Oakridge School seeks bright, college-bound students. Students are accepted in all grades, when openings exist, on the basis of an aptitude test, reading and math achievement tests, past academic and behavior records, recommendations, and an interview. Application should be made as early as possible; students who have recently moved to the Fort Worth/Dallas area may be admitted in midyear. There is an application fee of $50, a testing fee of $75 for Preschool–Grade 12, and, upon acceptance, a registration fee of $500, which is applied toward tuition. The Director of Admission handles applications.

In 2007–08, tuition ranges from $4860 for three-day Preschool to $13,675 for seniors. Monthly tuition payments are available. The Oakridge School subscribes to the School and Student Service for Financial Aid and provides limited financial aid to students who qualify.

Director of Admissions: Linda Broadus
Director of Development: Sharon LeMond
College Advisor: Sarah Kramer
Business Officer: Richard Horvath
Director of Finance: Kathy Gamill

Parish Episcopal School 1972

4101 Sigma Road, Dallas, TX 75244
Tel. 972-239-8011; Fax 972-991-1237
Web Site www.parishepiscopal.org; E-mail mmclean@parishepiscopal.org

Parish Episcopal School provides a college preparatory education within the Episcopal tradition. Currently enrolling 1100 boys and girls as day students in Pre-Kindergarten–Grade 12, Parish emphasizes academics and instills an awareness of obligations to fellow students and the community. All students attend daily chapel services, and religion is taught in Kindergarten–Grade 12. Extracurricular activities include community service, chorus, drama, publications, student vestry, student leadership opportunities, and a full range of athletics. Tuition: $6785–$16,610. Financial aid is available. Marci McLean is Director of Admission; Gloria Hoffman Snyder is Head of School.

Presbyterian School 1988

5300 Main Street, Houston, TX 77004
Tel. 713-520-0284; Admissions 713-620-6329; Fax 713-620-6390
Web Site www.pshouston.org; E-mail kbrown@pshouston.org

Presbyterian School, enrolling more than 500 day students in two-year-old Early Childhood–Grade 8, was founded to provide an environment in which family, school, and church unite in the education and support of each child. The School aims to maintain a healthy balance between a nurturing Christian learning experience and a challenging academic program that encourages each student to reach his or her full potential—intellectually, physically, emotionally, socially, and spiritually. Specialty classes are offered in music, art, computer, Spanish, motor skills, library, and chapel. Tuition: $6100–$13,800. Financial aid is available. Presbyterian School is fully accredited by the Independent Schools Association of the Southwest and the National Association for the Education of Young Children. Kristin Brown is Director of Admission; Ray Johnson (Alfred University, M.S.Ed.) is Head of School. *Southern Association.*

River Oaks Baptist School 1955

2300 Willowick, Houston, TX 77027
Tel. 713-623-6938; Fax 713-626-0650
Web Site www.robs.org; E-mail cbailey@robs.org

River Oaks Baptist School enrolls 830 day boys and girls in Two-Year-Olds through Grade 8. The academic environment, which balances high expectations with nurturing, encourages children to maximize their potential and cultivates creativity, critical thinking, initiative, respect for diversity, and the dignity of each individual. Extracurricular opportunities include Student Council, competitive sports and intramurals, publications, musical performances, theater arts, community outreach, and field trips. Tuition: $8765–$16,850. Financial Aid: $584,110. Cindy Bailey is Director of Admission; Nancy Heath Hightower (University of Texas, B.S. 1958; University of Houston, M.Ed. 1983, Ed.D. 1985) was appointed Head of School in 1989.

St. Agnes Academy 1906

9000 Bellaire Boulevard, Houston, TX 77036
Tel. 713-219-5400; Admission 713-219-5411; Fax 713-219-5499
Web Site www.st-agnes.org; E-mail ehoover@st-agnes.org

Founded by Dominican Sisters, St. Agnes Academy enrolls 848 girls as day students in Grades 9–12. The school strives to provide a demanding program in an atmosphere imbued with the values and principles of the Catholic faith. The college preparatory curriculum includes Advanced Placement courses and offerings in the arts. Some classes are shared with boys from Strake Jesuit Preparatory. Activities involve students in athletics, musical and theatrical productions, publications, debate, and community service. Tuition: $10,225. Extras: $300–$600. Financial Aid: $250,000. Deborah Whalen is Director of Admission; Sr. Jane Meyer (Dominican College, B.A.; Texas Woman's, M.S.) was named Principal in 1981 and is now Head of School. *Southern Association.*

St. Andrew's Episcopal School 1952

Lower/Middle School: 1112 West 31st Street, Austin, TX 78705
Tel. 512-452-5779; Fax 512-299-9822
Web Site www.sasaustin.org
E-mail dwilliams@sasaustin.org
Upper School: 5901 Southwest Parkway; Austin, TX 78735
Tel. 512-299-9700; Fax 512-299-9660
E-mail maycock@sasaustin.org

Encompassing Grades 1–12, St. Andrew's provides "an enriched academic program within a Christian environment" to more than 750 day students from various racial, national, and ethnic origins, creating a diverse and culturally rich atmosphere. The rigorous academic curriculum of this college preparatory school is balanced by daily chapel, fine arts, community service, and athletics. The Upper School was the first in Central Texas to set up a state-of-the-art wireless laptop system. After-school enrichment is offered. Tuition: $11,900–$16,200. Extras: $350–$1300. Financial aid is available. Diane Williams (Lower/Middle Schools) and Malia Aycock (Upper School) are Directors of Admissions; Lucy C. Nazro (University of Texas [Austin], B.A.; Episcopal Seminary of the Southwest, M.A.) is Head.

St. James Episcopal School 1946

602 South Carancahua Street, Corpus Christi, TX 78401
Tel. 361-883-0835; Fax 361-883-0837
Web Site www.sjes.org; E-mail pbell@sjes.org

St. James, a Blue Ribbon School of Excellence, enrolls 328 boys and girls in Preschool–Grade 8. Following its mission to provide a superior education that enables students to reach their full potential within a Christian community, the School integrates all learning activities around a "Central Theme." The early grades emphasize discovery activities in preparation for the mastery of specific academic skills in the Middle School. At all levels, classroom learning is enhanced by field trips and outdoor education beyond the campus, while fine arts and life skills, sports, drama, leadership opportunities, and regular chapel services support personal growth and achievement. Tuition: $2700–$6950. Sandra Gordon (Preschool/Lower School) and Darla Montano (Middle School) coordinate admissions; H. Palmer Bell was appointed Headmaster in 1996.

St. John's School 1946

2401 Claremont Lane, Houston, TX 77019-5897
Tel. 713-850-0222; Admissions Ext. 320; Fax 713-850-4089
Web Site www.sjs.org; E-mail msims@sjs.org

Founded by civic leaders interested in providing a school of exacting standards, St. John's School is a coeducational, college preparatory day school enrolling 1210 students in Kindergarten–Grade 12. Since its inception in 1946, the School has aimed to "yield self-disciplined graduates schooled to a pride in superior achievement and to an active understanding to the individual's responsibility to society." Athletics, arts, and community service are included among the extracurricular activities. Tuition: $13,390–$16,825. Financial aid is available. Myrtle Alice Sims is Director of Admissions; John Allman (Yale, B.A.; University of Virginia, M.A.) was appointed Headmaster in 1998.

St. Luke's Episcopal School 1947

15 St. Luke's Lane, San Antonio, TX 78209-4445
Tel. 210-826-0664; Fax 210-826-8520
Web Site www.saintlukes.net; E-mail admission@saintlukes.net

Now in its 60th year of providing quality education in a Christian context, St. Luke's Episcopal School enrolls 400 day boys and girls from many religious expressions in Pre-Kindergarten–Grade 8. Its mission is to provide a curriculum that nurtures the whole child intellectually, spiritually, physically, and socially. This Nationally Recognized 2005 Blue Ribbon School seeks to develop young people who contribute to their world and who possess the qualities of cooperation, good judgment, and leadership. Course work is based on the Core Knowledge Sequence featuring reading and language arts, math, science, history, and Spanish or Latin. Students adhere to an honor code and attend daily chapel services intended to nourish spiritual awareness and character development. Small classes, a 30,000-volume-capacity library, and state-of-the-art computers enhance the educational experience. Students may take part in the National Mythology Exam, national science fair competition, and declamation days. SLES participates in the Independent School Athletic League offering competitive sports such as volleyball, basketball, soccer, tennis, golf, and track. Tuition: $6870–$13,125. Margaret Ann Casseb is Director of Admission; Shirley Berdecio is Head of School.

St. Mark's School of Texas 1906

10600 Preston Road, Dallas, TX 75230-4000
Tel. 214-346-8000; Admissions 214-346-8700; Fax 214-346-8701
Web Site smtexas.org; E-mail admission@smtexas.org

St. Mark's is a nonsectarian, independent day school enrolling 830 boys in Grades 1–12. Since its founding in 1906, St. Mark's has prepared a diverse population of students for each successive step of their academic careers. It is the mission of the School to educate the "whole boy," providing him with the tools necessary to be successful in and out of the classroom. The rigorous academic program is balanced with opportunities to pursue varied interests including athletics, the arts, debate, community service, and school leadership. Tuition: $16,909–$21,580. Financial Aid: $1,600,000. David Baker is Director of Admission; Arnold E. Holtberg (Princeton, A.B.; Lutheran Theological Seminary, M.A.R.) is Headmaster.

Saint Michael's Academy 1972

2500 South College Avenue, Bryan, TX 77801
Tel. 979-822-2715; Fax 979-823-4971
Web Site www.st-michaels-academy.org; E-mail sma@txcyber.com

Saint Michael's Academy is a coeducational, Episcopal day school enrolling 190 children in Nursery through Grade XII. Saint Michael's strives to provide "intellectual challenge and personal attention in a moral atmosphere." The classical college preparatory curriculum includes Latin and modern languages, Sacred Studies, hands-on science, mathematics, honors-level and AP classes, and fine arts. Students attend daily Chapel and take part in extracurricular activities such as competitive sports, music ensembles, and an annual Gilbert and Sullivan operetta. Tuition: $4000–$7500. Limited financial aid is available. Ms. Patsy Cargill is Admissions Director; Mr. Charles (Chuck) Raymer (Trinity College, B.A.; University of Illinois, M.Ed.) is Head of School.

St. Pius X High School 1956

811 West Donovan Street, Houston, TX 77091-5699
Tel. 713-692-3581; Admission Ext. 137; Fax 713-692-5725
Web Site www.stpiusx.org; E-mail admissions@stpiusx.org

Founded by the Dominican Sisters, St. Pius X enrolls 707 young men and women. It is a Catholic school committed to developing students who reach their full intellectual, spiritual, social, and physical potential. The three-level college preparatory curriculum is designed to equip students for higher education and careers. Advanced Placement and honors courses are offered. Among the activities are 18 athletic teams for men and women, musical and theatrical productions, publications, Student Council, National Honor Society, clubs, and community service. A summer program is offered. Tuition: $8600. Extras: $400–$600. Financial Aid: $365,000. Susie Kramer is Admissions Director; Sr. Donna M. Pollard, OP (University of Houston, B.S.; Aquinas Institute, M.A.; Boston College, M.Ed.), is Head of School. *Southern Association.*

Shelton School and Evaluation Center 1976

15720 Hillcrest Road, Dallas, TX 75248
Tel. 972-774-1772; Fax 972-991-3977
Web Site www.shelton.org

Shelton School is a coeducational day school serving 840 students in Pre-school–Grade 12. The School focuses on the full development of "learning-different" students of average or above-average intelligence to enable them to succeed in conventional classroom settings. Services include an on-site Evaluation Center for diagnostic testing, a Speech, Language, and Hearing Clinic, and an Outreach Center. The curriculum is a multisensory program with a strong academic orientation. Tutoring, computer courses, intramural sports, and a summer session are offered. Shelton is accredited by the Independent Schools Association of the Southwest. Tuition: $9400–$16,250. Financial Aid: $150,000. Diann Slaton is Director of Admission; Joyce Pickering (Louisiana State, B.S.; Virginia Polytechnic, M.A.; Dallas Baptist, Hum.D.) is Executive Director.

Strake Jesuit College Preparatory 1961

8900 Bellaire Boulevard, Houston, TX 77036
Tel. 713-774-7651; Admissions 713-490-8113; Fax 713-774-6427
Web Site www.strakejesuit.org; E-mail admissions@strakejesuit.org

Strake Jesuit, a Catholic, college preparatory day school enrolling 893 boys in Grades 9–12, carries on the 450-year tradition of Jesuit education worldwide. The school prepares its graduates to be men in service to others as well as being ready to succeed in college; the curriculum allows 100 percent of the graduates to move directly into college. There is a closed-circuit TV system and electives in TV production as well as 11 varsity sports and many other extracurriculars. Some cross-registration is available at an adjacent Catholic girls' college prep. Summer remedial courses are available. Tuition: $12,100. Financial Aid: $1,000,000. Ken Lojo is Director of Admissions; Richard C. Nevle is Principal; Fr. Daniel K. Lahart, S.J., is President.

TMI — The Episcopal School of Texas 1893

20955 West Tejas Trail, San Antonio, TX 78257
Tel. 210-698-7171; Admission Ext. 6156; Fax 210-698-0715
Web Site www.tmi-sa.org; E-mail b.klaftenegger@tmi-sa.org

TMI, the oldest Episcopal college preparatory school in the Southwest, enrolls 363 boys and girls in Grades 6–12, with 40 boarders in Grade 9 upward. Its mission is to provide an excellent liberal arts education infused with the teachings of Jesus Christ. Daily chapel services for students of all faiths enable young people to explore and strengthen their relationship with God. The optional Corps of Cadets is one of the highest ranked Junior Reserve Officer Training Corps programs in the nation. Cadets adhere to military protocol and tradition and engage in efforts such as orienteering, cannon crew, color guard, drill team, rifle team, and saber guard. The school's curriculum, designed to develop each student's potential and to form compassionate, enlightened citizens of the world, centers on traditional course work in the liberal arts, sciences, and humanities, with Advanced Placement courses offered in all core areas. Classroom learning is enhanced by wireless computer technology and the use of laptops in all disciplines. Student government, publications, interest clubs, Panther teams in 15 sports, and numerous opportunities in the fine and performing arts complement the core offerings. Boarding Tuition: $27,740–$33,275; Day Tuition: $16,360–$16,450. Brenda Klaftenegger is Director of Admissions; Dr. James Freeman is Headmaster.

Trinity Valley School 1959

7500 Dutch Branch Road, Fort Worth, TX 76132
Tel. 817-321-0116; Fax 817-321-0105
Web Site www.trinityvalleyschool.org
E-mail tvs@trinityvalleyschool.org

Trinity Valley is a nondenominational, coeducational day school serving 950 young people in Kindergarten to Grade 12. Its mission is to develop in students high standards of scholarship, diverse and constructive interests, and intelligent citizenship. The curriculum in the lower grades focuses on mastery of strong skills in core subjects in readiness for the challenging college preparatory program in the Upper School. A Trinity Valley education is enhanced by Student Council, honor societies, a visiting-artist program, interest groups, music, drama, community service, and interscholastic athletics. Tuition: $13,245–$13,975. Financial Aid: $969,471. Judith S. Kinser is Director of Admissions; Dr. Gary Krahn is Head of School.

Vanguard College Preparatory School 1973

2517 Mount Carmel, Waco, TX 76710
Tel. 254-772-8111; Fax 254-772-8263
Web Site www.vanguard.org; E-mail fred_niell@vanguard.org

Vanguard College Preparatory School welcomes highly motivated students in Grades 7–12. The School offers a rigorous liberal arts curriculum and a challenging learning experience. The environment is one that prizes excellence and develops young community leaders. Enrolling 160 boys and girls from diverse racial, ethnic, religious, and economic backgrounds, Vanguard emphasizes a broad-based education centered in English, mathematics, science, technology, social studies, foreign language, and fine arts. Core offerings are complemented by Advanced Placement and honors courses as well as a wide variety of electives. Students are encouraged to participate in extracurricular activities such as service organizations, academic teams, student publications, special-interest groups, and athletics. Tuition: $10,500. Financial aid is available. Mary Helen George is Director of Admissions; Cindy Graves is Director of College Counseling; Bill Borg (Huntingdon College, B.A.; Jacksonville University, M.A.T.) is Head of School.

The Winston School 1975

5707 Royal Lane, Dallas, TX 75229
Tel. 214-691-6950; Fax 214-691-1509
Web Site www.winston-school.org

Winston, a coeducational, college preparatory day school, enrolls 230 *bright students who learn differently®* in Grades 1–12. Based on diagnostic testing and ongoing monitoring, the School formulates individual academic profiles to help students address learning problems. More than 95 percent of graduates enter college. Computers, the arts, and community service enrich the core curriculum, which emphasizes English, math, science, history, and Spanish. Activities include publications, sports, student government, honor societies, class trips, and clubs. Fees: Available upon request. Winston is accredited by the Independent School Association of the Southwest and is a member of the National Association of Independent Schools. Amy C. Smith is Director of Admission; Dr. Polly Peterson is Interim Head of School.

UTAH

Park City Academy 1989

3120 Pinebrook Road, Park City, UT 84098
Tel. 435-649-2791; Fax 435-649-6759
Web Site www.parkcityacademy.org; E-mail csachs@parkcityacademy.org

Frances Johnson and Patricia Russell founded the day school to provide eager students and enthusiastic teachers a learning environment marked by a relevant, challenging curriculum and Christian values. Park City Academy currently enrolls 140 children from diverse backgrounds in Preschool–Grade 9. The integrated program emphasizes relationships between ideas, blending of subjects, and project-based teaching methods. In a "safe, wonderfully happy, and stimulating" school community, small classes with a low student-teacher ratio allow individualized attention and participation in all aspects of classroom learning. The academic curriculum focuses on building a strong foundation in core subjects, complemented by outdoor education experiences in Utah's remarkable environment. Spanish language instruction begins in Preschool, and Middle School students may compete on interscholastic athletic teams. Tutorial assistance reinforces key concepts for students who need extra support. The school-wide community service program helps others while developing the students' sense of belonging, self-worth, and contribution. Tuition: $3780–$11,500. Susan Radtke is Director of Admission; Charles Sachs (Colgate, B.A.; Middlebury, M.A.) is Head.

Rowland Hall-St. Mark's School 1880

Upper School: 843 Lincoln Street, Salt Lake City, UT 84102
Tel. 801-355-7494; Fax 801-355-0474
Web Site www.rhsm.org; E-mail karenhyde@rhsm.org
Middle School: Tel. 801-355-0272; Fax 801-359-8318
Lower School: 720 Guardsman Way, Salt Lake City, UT 84108
Tel. 801-355-7485; Fax 801-363-5521
E-mail kathygundersen@rhsm.org

Founded in 1880, Rowland Hall-St. Mark's is an independent school enrolling 980 day students in Pre-Kindergarten–Grade 12. The traditional college preparatory program includes three languages and the study of ethics and world religion. Advanced Placement courses are offered in 17 subjects. Among the extracurricular activities are student government and a variety of athletics, including a ski academy. Tuition: $12,000–$15,040. Financial Aid: $1,300,000. Kathy Gundersen (Pre-K–Grade 5) and Karen Hyde (Grades 6–12) are Admissions Directors; Alan C. Sparrow (Brown, B.A.; University of Rochester, M.A.) is Headmaster. *Northwest Association.*

VERMONT

Long Trail School 1975

1045 Kirby Hollow Road, Dorset, VT 05251
Tel. 802-867-5717; Fax 802-867-4525
Web Site www.longtrailschool.org; E-mail ccallo@longtrailschool.org

Long Trail, a coeducational day school enrolling 165 students in Grades 6–12, offers an intellectually enriching college preparatory curriculum in a supportive, caring environment designed to foster in each student a lifelong commitment to excellence. A variety of teaching methods that address different learning styles, small-group instruction, and personalized course selection motivate students to their full potential. Art, activities, athletics, community service, computers, dance, drama, and music enrich the program and encourage social, ethical, and physical development. A summer academic and sports program is available. Tuition: $17,500; Homestay Program: $31,000. Courtney M. Callo is Director of Admissions; David D. Wilson (Indiana University, B.A.; Antioch, M.A.) is Headmaster. *New England Association.*

Maple Street School 1998

322 Maple Street, Manchester Center, VT 05255
Tel. 802-362-7137; Admissions Ext. 204; Fax 802-362-3492
Web Site www.maplestreetschool.com
E-mail efishman@maplestreetschool.com

Maple Street School, enrolling 97 boys and girls in Kindergarten–Grade 8, presents an exciting and challenging program in a learning environment designed to promote academic excellence, personal responsibility, and the desire to serve the school community and beyond. The core curriculum is enriched by art, music, and drama; French is introduced in Kindergarten, and technology is integrated into the program in the higher grades. A vigorous sports program includes snowboarding and skiing instruction at Bromley Mountain. A summer program emphasizes studio arts. Tuition: $12,350–$14,420. Financial Aid: $297,200. Esther Fishman is Director of Admissions; Dr. Fran Bisselle (Boston College, B.A.; Wesleyan University, M.A.; University of Vermont, Ed.D.) is Head of School. *New England Association.*

VIRGINIA

Alexandria Country Day School 1983

2400 Russell Road, Alexandria, VA 22301
Tel. 703-548-4804; Fax 703-549-9022
Web Site www.acdsnet.org; E-mail admissions@acdsnet.org

Alexandria Country Day School, a dynamic school community enrolling 250 students in Kindergarten to Grade 8, values academic excellence, character, independent thinking, citizenship, and respect for others. It seeks to inspire creativity, enthusiasm for learning, and confidence through a stimulating academic program, athletics, and the arts. The curriculum emphasizes a strong foundation in core subjects, while specialist instructors teach Spanish, music, computers, library skills, art, drama, and physical education. Student and Honor Councils, band, chorus, handbell choir, and clubs are among the activities. Middle School students take part in outdoor experiential learning; all students perform community service. Tuition: $17,950–$19,400. Rebecca Teti is Director of Admissions; Alexander "Exie" Harvey is Head of School.

Bishop Ireton High School 1964

201 Cambridge Road, Alexandria, VA 22314-4899
Tel. 703-751-7606; Admissions 703-212-5190; Fax 703-212-8173
Web Site www.bishopireton.org; E-mail hamerp@bishopireton.org

The Oblates of St. Francis de Sales operate this coeducational, diocesan school serving 800 students from Catholic and non-Catholic families. The Salesian tradition of excellence aims to develop the spiritual, aesthetic, intellectual, and physical potential of each young person while instilling a sense of responsibility and service to others. The curriculum is college preparatory, with Honors and Advanced Placement courses, computer technology, and required religious studies integral to the program. With 41 athletic teams, nearly 70 percent of students participate in at least one sport; other activities include a comprehensive music program, yearbook, drama, and special-interest clubs. Tuition: $9800–$14,350. Financial Aid: $272,000. Peter Hamer is Director of Admissions; Rev. Matthew J. Hillyard, OSFS, is Principal.

Bishop Sullivan Catholic High School 1949

4552 Princess Anne Road, Virginia Beach, VA 23462
Tel. 757-467-2881; Fax 757-467-0284
Web Site www.chsvb.org

Bishop Sullivan Catholic High School provides a college preparatory education, featuring Advanced Placement and accelerated courses in all disciplines, for more than 425 day students. Among the facilities are the state-of-the-art Shepherd Library/Media Center with graphic arts and computer labs, 65-seat presentation room, and the Barry-Robinson Theater Fine Arts Center housing a 270-seat auditorium, classrooms for visual and performing arts, and an art gallery. Liturgies, retreats, and required community service enrich students' lives. Students also take part in academic competitions, school government, National Honor Society, forensics, publications, clubs, and 36 athletic teams. Tuition: $9680. Dennis W. Price is Principal; Martin F. Campbell is Guidance Director. *Southern Association.*

Blue Ridge School 1909

273 Mayo Drive, St. George, VA 22935
Tel. 434-985-2811; Fax 434-985-7215
Web Site www.blueridgeschool.com
E-mail admission@blueridgeschool.com

Blue Ridge School in St. George, Virginia, offers a college preparatory boarding program for boys in Grades 9 through 12. Set in a region of great natural beauty, the School is a 5-minute drive from the Appalachian Trail, 25 minutes by car from Charlottesville, and less than 2 hours from Washington, D.C.

Blue Ridge began as an Episcopal mission school in 1909 to educate the children of local families. In 1962, it was reorganized as a college preparatory school dedicated to serving young men who thrive on personalized instruction that focuses on teaching students to learn and to reach their highest potential.

The School recognizes that every boy is unique, with different growth and development rates, learning styles, interests, objectives, and life paths. Responding to these differences, Blue Ridge focuses on individual needs to build success, self-confidence, and independence. With an average class size of 9 and a 5:1 student-teacher ratio, personalized academic support is a key element in empowering boys to achieve their goals.

While welcoming young men from all religious faiths, Blue Ridge is proud of its Episcopal heritage and requires school-wide participation in weekday and Sunday services. The Episcopal chaplain is committed to fostering the spiritual beliefs of students from Jewish, Buddhist, Islamic, and other world religions.

Life at Blue Ridge is guided by the Code of Conduct, which comprises the core values of the school community: being honorable and accountable, being willing to invest oneself and to try new things, persevering and maintaining a positive attitude, displaying mutual respect and tolerance, being a good citizen, and developing habits of mind, body, and spirit.

A nonprofit institution, Blue Ridge School is accredited by the Southern Association of Colleges and Schools and the Virginia Association of Independent Schools. The School holds membership in the National Association of Independent Schools, The Association of Boarding Schools, the Secondary School Admission Test Board, and other professional organizations.

THE CAMPUS. Adjacent to Shenandoah National Park, the School occupies 751 acres of ponds, streams, and woodlands in the eastern foothills of the Blue Ridge Mountains. The rural setting provides a learning environment free of the distractions of more populated areas.

Perkins Hall, which contains the David Brobeck Science Center, is the academic heart of the School, furnishing classrooms, study halls, laboratories, and the computer center. The science program is enhanced by the state-of-the-art, all-digital Blue Ridge Observatory, located on Flattop Mountain at an elevation of 3250 feet. Blue Ridge School has deployed fiber-optic cable within all of the major campus buildings, allowing for 100 MB connectivity to all desktops within the school network, and wireless access points within the library and computer lab. The newly renovated Academic Building houses the Fishburne Learning Center, Loving Hall classrooms, and the Hatcher C. Williams Library. The New York Auxiliary Student Center furnishes fine arts facilities, a game room, a viewing room with home theater, a snack bar, and space for dances and social events. Boys live in two dormitories staffed by resident house parents who are available *in loco parentis* on a 24-hour, seven-day-a-week basis.

The academic hub of the campus is supplemented by the Massey Athletic Complex, containing a basketball court and spectator seating as well as a field house with tennis and basketball courts and wrestling, training, and weight-lifting rooms. Outdoor facilities include a 400-meter all-weather track, a climbing tower, driving range, a swimming pool, and playing fields for football, baseball, soccer, and lacrosse.

The Turning Point Campaign has earmarked $3,000,000 for renovations and upgrades to the Academic Center, student residences, and the chapel, along with other improvements throughout the campus.

THE FACULTY. David A. Bouton, Ph.D., was appointed Headmaster in 2000. He holds undergraduate and master's degrees from the University of Notre Dame and earned his doctorate at Virginia Commonwealth University. Prior to coming to Blue Ridge, Dr. Bouton was head of Benedictine High School in Richmond and served as Academic Dean at the U.S. Army War College, where he spent 30 years. He and his wife, Sheila, are the parents of six grown children.

The 35 members of the teaching and professional staff hold baccalaureate degrees or the equivalent, and more than half have earned advanced degrees. Nearly all faculty live on campus.

Two full-time nurses staff the infirmary, and hospital facilities are located in Charlottesville.

STUDENT BODY. For the 2007–08 school year, 197 boys are enrolled in Grades 9–12 and actively engaged in life at Blue Ridge School. They come from 19 states and 12 countries and represent a wide spectrum of racial, ethnic, and religious backgrounds.

ACADEMIC PROGRAM. The school calendar, divided into trimesters, extends from early September to late May. Boys attend classes five days a week, with six 50-minute periods three days a week and three 75-minute periods on the other two. Saturday mornings feature a variety of fine arts productions, guest speakers, field trips, and other special programs.

The highly structured environment at Blue Ridge enables boys to focus on the mastery of skills fundamental to success in a challenging college preparatory curriculum. Professional staff at the Fishburne Learning Center work closely with faculty and students to ensure that every young man receives the appropriate level and range of support needed to achieve his academic objectives. Among the services provided are reviews of student files, consultation with teachers, and small-group instruction that emphasizes study strategies, reading comprehension, written expression, and math. Students can also utilize the Learning Center for help from classroom teachers with specific problems in core courses. With the approval of the Assistant Head for Administration and Academics, boys have the additional option of taking part in the Homework Assistance Program (HAP), which provides a focused, supportive environment in the Learning Center during evening study hours. Daily conference periods provide students with extra-help opportunities from classroom teachers, and two-hour supervised study halls are held each evening from Sunday through Thursday.

To graduate, boys must earn 4 credits in English; 3 credits each in social studies, math, science, and the same foreign language; 2 credits in physical education; and 1 in life skills. Students in Grade 9 and new 10th graders are also required to take a study skills program during their first trimester in attendance.

Among the core and elective subjects are Literary Genres and Composition 9–10, World Literature, American Literature; French I–V, Spanish I–V, Spanish Conversation and Culture; Algebra I–III, Geometry, Pre-Calculus, Calculus, Discrete Mathematics; Integrated Sciences, Biology, Chemistry, Physics, Astronomy, Environmental Science, Mountain Ecology; World History and Ancient Civilizations, Modern European History, United States and Virginia Government and History, U.S. History; and Studio Art, Advanced Art, Photography, Concert Choir, and Music Appreciation. Honors and advanced courses are available in all academic disciplines.

SAT/ACT Prep is integrated into English and math classes, with emphasis on format, content, and strategies to maximize student performance on these tests. Blue Ridge also offers SAT prep courses on campus.

The Outdoor Program provides opportunities for boys to earn credit by participating in leadership, environmental service projects, and activities such as mountain biking, skiing, canoeing, and outdoor living skills.

Typically, 100 percent of Blue Ridge graduates are accepted into four-year colleges and universities. Over the past four years, these have included such institutions as Auburn, Boston University, Brown, The Citadel, College of Charleston, College of William and Mary, Denison, Dickinson, Emory, George Mason, Georgia Southern, Gettysburg, Gonzaga, Hampden-Sydney, Hofstra, James Madison University, Johnson & Wales, Kansas State, Lynchburg, Manhattanville, Marist, Marymount, Mary Washington, Michigan State, New England College, Pace, Purdue, Rhode Island School of Design, Roanoke, Rollins, San Diego State, Trinity College, Tulane, Virginia Polytechnic, and the Universities of California, Houston, Maryland, Massachusetts, Mississippi, Notre Dame, Vermont, and Virginia.

STUDENT ACTIVITIES. Cocurricular activities at Blue Ridge, designed to promote leadership, growth, friendship, and recreation, reflect the trust and confidence the School places in its young men. Leadership opportunities include positions such as prefect, proctor, and member of the Honor Council and/or Disciplinary Committee. Qualified students may join the National Honor Society.

Community service involves students in altruistic endeavors such as food and fund drives, and they also volunteer with the American Heart Association, local elementary schools, nursing homes, and animal shelters.

Boys take part in clubs formed around interests in astronomy, chess, drama and the performing arts, publications, conservation, and other pursuits.

In the athletic program, Barons teams compete in cross-country, track and field, football, indoor and outdoor soccer, mountain biking, basketball, wrestling, baseball, golf, lacrosse, and tennis.

The Social Activities Committee coordinates events on and off campus, including dances and mixers with girls' schools in the area. Boys enjoy trips to amusement parks, collegiate and professional ballgames, and theaters in Charlottesville, Richmond, and the nation's capital.

ADMISSION AND COSTS. Blue Ridge seeks young men of good character and potential who will thrive in the School's structured program and close-knit community. Acceptance is based on the candidate's application, questionnaire and essay, teacher recommendations, previous transcripts, and the results of standardized tests.

In 2007–08, tuition, room, and board is $31,900. The School's innovative tuition plan is designed to make a Blue Ridge education more affordable. The tuition rate charged in the first year remains the same throughout a student's four years if the fee is paid in full before August 1 each year. The financial aid program assists approximately 30 percent of the student body based on demonstrated need and good academic and social standing.

Dean of Faculty: John Young IV
Dean of Students: Tony Brown
Director of Resident Life: Chris Rehm
Director of Alumni Relations: Dan Dunsmore
Assistant Headmaster for Enrollment & Marketing: William A. Darrin III
Assistant Headmaster for Advancement: Robert J. Murphy III
Assistant Headmaster for Academics & Administration: John O'Reilly, Ph.D.
College Counselor: Jill Perlmutter
Assistant Headmaster for Finance: Ronald Floor
Director of Athletics: Carl Frye

Browne Academy 1941

5917 Telegraph Road, Alexandria, VA 22310
Tel. 703-960-3000; Fax 703-960-7325
Web Site www.browneacademy.org
E-mail ssalvo@browneacademy.org

This coeducational day school enrolling 300 students in Preschool–Grade 8 is dedicated to the development of the individual child as an independent, lifelong learner who embraces the core values of excellence, diversity, character, and community. These values form the basis for preparing students for competitive secondary schools in the metropolitan area. Browne's academic environment features an interdisciplinary curriculum that emphasizes creative problem solving and critical thinking skills; 11 acres of fields and streams offer outdoor learning opportunities. The school also features a foreign language program from Preschool through Grade 8. Browne's new state-of-the-art Center for Athletics and Performing Arts provides a versatile space that not only allows students to engage in indoor athletic activities but also supplies a venue for musical performances, class plays, school assemblies, and community gatherings. Activities include competitive team sports, tae kwon do, soccer, choir, handbells, band, drama, publications, Scouts, and student council. Extended day and an 8-week summer camp program are available. Tuition: $7925–$19,050. Financial Aid: $350,000. Steve Salvo is Director of Admission; Margot Durkin is Head of School.

Burgundy Farm Country Day School 1946

3700 Burgundy Road, Alexandria, VA 22303
Tel. 703-960-3431; Admissions 703-329-6968; Fax 703-960-0800
Web Site www.burgundyfarm.org; E-mail info@burgundyfarm.org

Burgundy Farm Country Day School, enrolling 280 boys and girls in Junior Kindergarten through Grade 8, provides a family-friendly atmosphere in which children love to learn. The School occupies a 25-acre campus of forest, field, farm, and pond in a natural setting imbued with rich traditions and a unique history. Classrooms serve as laboratories where students undertake hands-on learning and a developmental curriculum. The innovative, student-centered academic program integrates fine arts, music, drama, French and Spanish, multicultural studies, and physical education throughout core subjects. Burgundy offers low student-teacher ratio, a 21,000-volume library, bus transportation, extended day programs, competitive sports, summer camps, and a 500-acre wildlife campus in West Virginia. Tuition: $17,770–$19,590. Financial Aid: $500,000. Kelsey Neal is Director of Admissions; Jeff Sindler is Head of School.

Cape Henry Collegiate School 1924

1320 Mill Dam Road, Virginia Beach, VA 23454
Tel. 757-481-2446; Fax 757-481-9194
Web Site www.capehenrycollegiate.org
E-mail richardplank@capehenry.org

Cape Henry Collegiate School is a coeducational, college preparatory day school enrolling more than 1000 students in Pre-kindergarten (age 3)–Grade 12. Emphasizing academic, social, and physical development, the balanced educational experience involves challenging academics, athletics, arts, community service, and extensive extracurricular activities. A year-round extended-day program is available for Lower School students. Tuition: $12,525–$14,535. Richard J. Plank is Director of

Admissions and Financial Aid; Dr. John P. Lewis (St. Peter's College, B.S., M.A.; Seton Hall University, Ed.D.) is Head of School.

Chesapeake Academy 1889

107 Steamboat Road, P.O. Box 8, Irvington, VA 22480
Tel. 804-438-5575; Fax 804-438-6146
Web Site www.chesapeakeacademy.org

Chesapeake Academy enrolls 167 day boys and girls in PreSchool through Grade 8. The school seeks to equip students for their current and future academic, moral, social, and physical endeavors by fostering honesty, respect, citizenship, and integrity in a nurturing, family-oriented atmosphere. The core curriculum is comprised of classes in English, reading, spelling, mathematics, science, Spanish, and social studies. Specials include art, music, study skills, forensics, technology, ethics, and physical education. Students in Grade 8 can receive high school credit for Algebra I and Spanish I. An average class size of 14 and a student-teacher ratio of 8:1 provide individual attention. Overnight field trips, week-long comparative ecosystem field studies in Florida, and community service enhance the curriculum. Choir, drama, and instrumental and vocal lessons are also offered, and athletes take part in soccer, volleyball, golf, basketball, and track and field. Traditional and athletic summer camps supplement the regular school year. The 10-acre campus holds nature trails, a library, and science, technology, and language labs. Tuition: $2675–$7375. Financial Aid: $163,000. Deborah M. Cook is Head of School.

Collegiate School 1915

North Mooreland Road, Richmond, VA 23229
Tel. 804-740-7077; Admission 804-741-9722; Fax 804-741-9797
Web Site www.collegiate-va.org
E-mail "firstinitial""lastname"@collegiate-va.org

Collegiate School enrolls 1554 boys and girls in Kindergarten–Grade 12 on a 55-acre campus, with an additional 150 acres devoted to athletic facilities. Collegiate seeks to admit students who have the academic and personal potential to meet the high standards of a college preparatory program, who have diverse abilities and backgrounds, and who will make positive contributions to the School. Math, sciences, foreign languages, art, music, physical education, economics, and computer literacy are required. A fine arts building features a 620-seat theater and art and music facility. Tuition: $14,660–$17,270. Financial Aid: $1,747,000. Amanda Surgner is Director of Admission; Keith A. Evans (Davidson, B.A.; Harvard University, Ed.M.; University of Tennessee, M.S.) is Head of School. *Southern Association.*

The Congressional Schools of Virginia 1939

3229 Sleepy Hollow Road, Falls Church, VA 22042-4311
Tel. 703-533-9711; Admissions Ext. 120; Fax 703-532-5467
Web Site www.congressionalschools.org; E-mail admissions@csov.org

Set on a 40-acre campus, The Congressional Schools of Virginia offer 375 day students in Preschool–Grade 8 an accelerated curriculum taught by fully certified teachers and designed to stimulate a love for learning. Children from different backgrounds form ties and learn to appreciate diversity. Parents, teachers, students, administrators, and advisors form a community committed to each student's intellectual, social, and ethical development. French or Spanish begins in Kindergarten, and Latin is offered in Grade 8. Technology is integrated into the curriculum at all levels. Age-appropriate community service involves food drives, a homeless shelter, recycling, and activities with senior citizens. Students may join the school choirs, band, ballet, the spring musical, newspaper, yearbook, team sports, and an equestrian program. The Schools' educational approach helps students discover their unique potential, become individuals valued by the world in which they live, and meet the challenges of the finest private high schools, AP classes, and International Baccalaureate programs. Extended hours, door-to-door transportation, and summer camps are available. Tuition: $15,000–$19,250. Karen Weinberger is Admissions Director; Seth Ahlborn is Head of School.

The Covenant School 1985

Pre-K–Grade 6: 1000 Birdwood Road, Charlottesville, VA 22903
Grades 7–12: 175 Hickory Street, Charlottesville, VA 22902
Tel. 434-220-7329; Admissions 434-220-7330; Fax 434-979-3204
Web Site www.convenantschool.org
E-mail dharris@covenantschool.org

The Covenant School is a nondenominational, coeducational, Christian day school enrolling 710 students in Pre-Kindergarten through Grade 12. The School fosters learning grounded in the best traditions of classical and Christian education. The central goal of its program is to cultivate young people who can think, communicate, and make wise decisions that honor Christ and serve the common interests of their community and society. The School offers a liberal arts, college preparatory education that seeks to instill the joy and discipline of learning in language arts, mathematics, history, science, fine arts, and physical education. Tuition: $6000–$12,300. Financial aid is available. Donna B. Harris is Director of Admission & Financial Aid; Dr. Ronald P. Sykes is Head of School.

Episcopal High School 1839

1200 North Quaker Lane, Alexandria, VA 22302
Tel. 703-933-3000; Admissions 703-933-4062
Fax 703-933-3016
Web Site www.episcopalhighschool.org
E-mail admissions@episcopalhighschool.org

Episcopal High School in Alexandria, Virginia, is a college preparatory boarding school for boys and girls in Grades 9 through 12. It is 15 minutes from the cultural and educational resources of Washington, D.C., and Washington's Ronald Reagan Airport. Alexandria (population 175,000) is situated in northern Virginia on the Potomac River. Once an 18th-century seaport, today it is a thriving business and residential area that offers a spectrum of cultural, social, and educational events.

Episcopal High School opened in 1839 as a school for boys. As the first high school in Virginia, it became known throughout the region as "The High School," a name by which it is still known today. Episcopal grew to accommodate more than 100 boys until May 1861, when the Civil War forced its closing. In continuous operation since reopening in 1866, the School became coeducational in 1991 and remains a fully residential community.

Episcopal is committed to the spiritual, intellectual, moral, and physical development of students. In addition to a challenging and dynamic academic program, there are regularly scheduled chapel services, an array of athletics and arts offerings, and community service programs.

Episcopal High School is a nonprofit corporation directed by a 30-member Board of Trustees, 17 of whom are alumni. There are approximately 4600 living graduates. The School is accredited by the Virginia Association of Independent Schools and the Southern Association of Colleges and Schools and holds membership in the National Association of Independent Schools, among other organizations. The School-owned plant is valued at $150,000,000, and the endowment is $150,000,000.

THE CAMPUS. Situated on 130 acres near the western boundary of Alexandria, Episcopal is surrounded by wooded areas. The principal buildings are situated on tree-shaded lawns in the middle of the campus.

The centerpiece of Episcopal's campus is Hoxton House, originally called Mount Washington when it was built in 1804 by Martha Washington's eldest granddaughter, Eliza Parke Custis Law. The original drawing room has been carefully restored and continues to be used as the main reception room on campus.

The School's academic facilities provide students with ample resources and state-of-the-art technology. The new 34,000-square-foot Baker Science Center (2005) includes laboratories for biology, chemistry, physics, and environmental science. The Computer Center houses a training center and a network operations center providing 20 servers. All students have laptops with wireless capability and access to the Internet via a T-1 line. Printers are distributed around the campus, including one in each dormitory. The Ainslie Arts Center (2003) provides extensive facilities for visual and performing arts. Other facilities include computer and science labs with Pentium-based Wintel computers; the art studio equipped with two computers with CD-ROM players, PhotoShop software, digital cameras, a high-resolution scanner, and two printers; a music lab with a MIDI digital interface linked to a Macintosh computer; Stewart Gymnasium Dance Studio; Auditorium and Performing Arts Center; a bookstore; Bryan Library Reception Center; and meeting rooms and offices.

Episcopal's outstanding athletic facilities include Hummel Bowl, a 2800-seat stadium for football and lacrosse; Flippin Field House with 3 tennis courts, 3 basketball courts, a 200-yard track, and a batting cage; Centennial Gymnasium with a basketball court and a newly renovated fitness center featuring a Cybex weight machine room and cardiovascular area; seven playing fields, including two new FieldTurf all-weather fields; Goodman Squash Center with 4 courts; Cooper Dawson Baseball Diamond; a wrestling cage; Shuford Tennis Courts (12 all-weather tennis courts); an outdoor swimming pool; and Hoxton Track, a six-lane, 400-meter outdoor track.

Residential facilities include eight dormitories with single, double, and triple rooms, common rooms, and laundry facilities; Patrick Henry Callaway Chapel, where students attend services on most weekdays and bimonthly Sundays; Laird Dining Room; Blackford Hall, the main coed student lounge with a snack bar, vending area, television, and CD jukebox; and the McAllister Health Center, which is staffed by a registered nurse and visited daily by a full-time resident physician. Alexandria Hospital, two blocks away, provides emergency treatment, if needed.

THE FACULTY. F. Robertson Hershey was appointed the School's 11th Headmaster in 1998. He attended Williams College (B.A. 1970) and the University of Virginia (M.Ed. 1975). Mr. Hershey had previously served as Headmaster at Durham

Academy from 1978 to 1988 and, most recently, at The Collegiate School in Richmond from 1988 to 1998.

The faculty of 77 men and women includes 58 who hold advanced degrees, including 6 doctorates. Nearly 90 percent of all full-time faculty members live on campus with their families.

STUDENT BODY. Episcopal High School's 435 boarding students—approximately 55 percent boys and 45 percent girls—come from 30 states, the District of Columbia, and 20 foreign countries.

ACADEMIC PROGRAM. The school year, from early September through late May, includes two semesters with vacations at Thanksgiving, Christmas, and in the spring.

Classes meet five days a week. A typical daily schedule, from 7:15 A.M. to 10:30 P.M., includes chapel, class periods, meals, a tutoring period, athletics and activities in the afternoon, and two hours of evening study.

There are 10 to 12 students in an average class, with a student-teacher ratio of 6:1. Homework is prepared during free periods in the morning and during the evening study halls, with these periods supervised by student leaders and faculty. Grades are issued and sent to families four times a year.

A minimum of 23 credits is required for graduation, with the following specific requirements: 4 credits in English, 3-3½ in mathematics, 2 in social studies, 3 in a foreign language, 2 in physical education, 2 in laboratory science, 1 in theology, and 1 in fine arts. Students also have the opportunity to experience Episcopal's unique Washington Program, which provides academic exposure to cultural and historical sites in Washington, D.C., and the surrounding area.

A wide variety of courses is available, including 40 honors and Advanced Placement courses. The curriculum offers courses in English, Chinese, Creative Writing, French, German, Latin, Spanish, U.S. and World History, Theology, Economics, Algebra, Geometry, Trigonometry, Pre-Calculus, AB and BC Calculus, Statistics, Ethics, Computer Studies, Electronic Publishing, Art History, Photography, Studio Art, Music Theory, Music History, and Theatre Arts.

Members of Episcopal's Class of 2007 will attend such colleges and universities as Brown, Davidson, Duke, Middlebury, Northwestern, Vanderbilt, Washington and Lee, Williams, and the Universities of North Carolina, Pennsylvania, and Virginia.

STUDENT ACTIVITIES. An enduring tradition is the Honor Code, which Episcopal pioneered among secondary schools. Faculty and students strongly support this concept, which asserts that students will not lie, cheat, or steal, and that, out of a genuine concern for and responsibility to the student who does, they are asked to report violators to the Honor Committee.

The student body is led by student monitors who are nominated to the Headmaster by the faculty and students and who are responsible for discipline and orderliness in the day-to-day life of the High School. A student-elected dorm council offers additional leadership opportunities.

Episcopal fields 45 teams in 15 sports for boys and girls, including junior, junior varsity, and varsity teams in many sports. Baseball, basketball, girls' crew, cross-country, field hockey, football, golf, lacrosse, soccer, squash, tennis, indoor and outdoor track, volleyball, and wrestling are offered. All students can participate in dance, and older students may choose aerobics, weight training, cross training, and an outdoor program during some seasons. Episcopal's teams play a full schedule with other independent schools located primarily in the Virginia, Maryland, and Washington, D.C., areas. Boys' teams participate in the Interstate Athletic Conference, and girls' teams compete in the Independent School League.

Activities include the Art Club, Choir, Community Service Program, Environmental Club, Honor Committee, International Relations Club, Model U.N., peer counseling, Quiz Bowl, Performing Arts Group, two literary magazines, newspaper, yearbook, Student Health Awareness Committee, Student Vestry, Tour Guides, and Service Council. In addition, the Activities Program involves students in cultural, historic, athletic, outdoor, and social activities throughout the Washington area. Qualified musicians may participate in the American Youth Philharmonic or Mount Vernon Youth Symphony orchestras. A formal Outdoor Program is also available.

Students present two full-length plays—a drama and a musical—and several one-act plays. Special events include dances and social events with other schools, winter weekend skiing in Pennsylvania, fall Homecoming, and Parents' Weekends in both the fall and spring.

ADMISSION AND COSTS. Qualified candidates are accepted without regard to race, creed, or family financial resources. Admission is highly selective, and applicants are evaluated on the basis of their academic record—previous grades, teacher comments, and testing—as well as intellectual curiosity, personal qualities, and extracurricular interests and talents.

Tuition is $38,200, and students must also purchase a laptop computer through the School. Tuition insurance and a tuition plan are available. In the 2006–07 academic year, 30 percent of the student body receive scholarship grants or low-interest loans totaling $3,300,000. Episcopal High School subscribes to the services and principles of the School and Student Service for Financial Aid.

Assistant Head for Academics: Jacqueline E. Maher
Assistant Head for Student Life: Timothy C. Jaeger
Director of Faculty Development: J. Mason New
Dean of Students: Leavenworth M. Ferrell
Director of Admissions: Emily Atkinson
Director of Development: Robert C. Eckert
Director of College Counseling: Robert M. Hedrick
Treasurer: William H. de Butts
Director of Athletics: Mark E. Gowin

Flint Hill School 1956

10409 Academic Drive, Oakton, VA 22124
Tel. 703-584-2300; Fax 703-242-0718
Web Site www.flinthill.org; E-mail admissions@flinthill.org

Flint Hill School, enrolling more than 1070 boys and girls in Junior Kindergarten–Grade 12, encourages both faculty and students to experience the joy of learning and growing in a diverse society. Academic excellence is engendered within a value-centered community where respect, responsibility, compassion, and honesty are fostered. The School consists of two campuses located on 50 acres, housing well-appointed library facilities, a state-of-the-art media center, learning centers, and

spacious science and computer labs. All faculty members teach in fully networked classrooms, integrating multimedia and technology into the curriculum, while an extensive experiential education program enhances classroom academics. Athletic facilities include two full-size gymnasiums, eight tennis courts, a 400-meter track, and playing fields. Fine arts facilities include a 300-seat theater and art, dance, and music studios. Tuition: $19,000–$24,550. Financial aid is available. Pat Harden is Director of Admission and Financial Aid; John M. Thomas is Headmaster.

Fork Union Military Academy 1898

Box 278, Fork Union, VA 23055
Tel. 434-842-4200; [Toll-free] 800-GO2-FUMA
Admissions 434-842-4205; Fax 434-842-4300
Web Site www.forkunion.com; E-mail maceks@fuma.org

FORK UNION MILITARY ACADEMY in Fork Union, Virginia, is a college preparatory, military boarding school for young men in Grades 6 through 12 and postgraduate. A limited number of day students are also enrolled. Affiliated with the Baptist General Association of Virginia but open to young men of all religious denominations, Fork Union's emphasis on Christian values and character development leads cadets to make good decisions for a lifetime of success and service. The military environment and traditions help them develop self-discipline, confidence, leadership, and pride.

The Academy's Middle School operates on a traditional six-period schedule and features small classes in a community learning environment. Fork Union's Upper School offers a unique "One-Subject Plan" of study under which students concentrate on a single major subject every seven weeks.

Fork Union is a small town 50 miles west of Richmond and 30 miles southeast of Charlottesville. The Academy was founded in 1898 by Dr. William E. Hatcher, a noted Baptist minister, and was originally a coeducational, "classical" school for day students who boarded in village homes.

The Academy is guided by a Board of Trustees that is responsible for the $34,000,000 plant and more than $15,000,000 in productive endowments. The school's primary goal is to help young men prepare for college in an environment that promotes their mental, spiritual, and physical development. The school is accredited by the Virginia Association of Independent Schools; it holds membership in the National Association of Independent Schools and the Association of Military Colleges and Schools of the United States.

THE CAMPUS. The Academy occupies 1305 acres, including extensive athletic fields, a new 400-meter all-weather track and cross-country course, and a 2500-seat stadium. There are also tennis courts, three gymnasiums, an indoor rifle range, a paved outdoor basketball/volleyball court, a 4-acre lake, and an airstrip.

Among the more prominent buildings, which are substantial brick and concrete structures surrounded by broad lawns, are the Guy E. Beatty Library, housing more than 19,000 volumes, with a new addition providing space for research, classrooms, and a conference center; Hatcher Hall, with offices and some classrooms; John J. Wicker Chapel, which seats 550; and the Dorothy Thomasson Estes Dining Hall, which seats 750. The Yeatman Infirmary is staffed 24 hours a day by a physician or nurse. The Estes Athletic Center is an 85,000-square-foot facility that includes a main floor with a 160-meter indoor track, three basketball courts, tennis courts, five air-conditioned racquetball courts, a squash court, a wrestling room, and a new Aquatic Center featuring an eight-lane, 25-meter indoor pool. There are also training and rehabilitation rooms, a lounge area, a weight-training room, a batting cage, and nine locker rooms.

THE FACULTY. The Academy's President is Lt. Gen. John E. Jackson, Jr., USAF (Ret.). General Jackson earned his baccalaureate degree from Alderson-Broaddus College and his master's degree from Central Michigan University. He is a graduate of the Senior Managers in Government course at Harvard University and was awarded an honorary doctorate in Public Administration by Alderson-Broaddus College.

The FUMA administrative staff includes a Chaplain, Chief Financial Officer, Director of Admissions, Academic Dean, Director of Development, Physician, and Athletic Director, as well as a Middle School Headmaster. Separate Commandants and Librarians serve in the Middle and Upper Schools. There are 43 full-time teaching faculty members. Faculty and administrators hold baccalaureate and graduate degrees from colleges and universities around the United States and abroad.

STUDENT BODY. The school enrolls a total of 530 boarders and 20 day students. The Middle School includes Grades 6–8; the Upper School is comprised of Grades 9–12 and postgraduates. Approximately 70 percent of the cadets come from states along the eastern seaboard; the remainder are from other parts of the United States and around the world, with a total of 31 states, the District of Columbia, and 13 foreign countries represented in the student body. Cadets represent more than 27 different religious backgrounds and denominations.

ACADEMIC PROGRAM. The school year runs from early September to the end of May, with a Thanksgiving leave, a two-week Christmas leave, and a Spring vacation. Weekend leaves are permitted approximately twice a month, subject to the cadet's passing grades and good behavior. Classes meet Monday through Friday and on approximately ten Saturdays during the year. A typical day, from Reveille at 6:15 A.M. to Taps at 10:00 P.M., includes classes from 8:00 A.M. to 2:00 P.M., Chapel three times a week, military drill (two 45-minute periods per week) in the early afternoon, sports and recreation until dinner, and personal inspection before the evening retreat formation, followed by clubs and activities and two hours of supervised evening study.

There are 10 to 15 students in an average class. Grades are reported to cadets every two weeks, and parents receive written reports monthly (more frequently for students experiencing difficulty). Testing for guidance, progress measurement, and college planning includes College Board Examinations, the American College Test, Preliminary Scholastic Aptitude Tests, TOEFL, aptitude and interest batteries, and a number of reading tests.

The Middle School curriculum includes Mathematics, English, Social Studies, Science, Reading, Spelling, and Writing, as well as exploratory courses in Art, Astronomy, Computer Science, Ethics/Leadership, and/or Music Appreciation. Each cadet receives a military grade based on tests, performance of duties, drill performance, and demerit record.

The Upper School curriculum includes English, Social Studies/History, Mathematics, Science, Foreign Language, Religious Studies, and Health/Driver Education.

Honors sections are offered in English, Science, World Cultures, Mathematics, and Foreign Language. Advanced Placement courses are offered in English, Calculus, U.S. History, U.S. Government, and Biology. Dual-enrollment college credit courses are available in English, Political Science, International Relations, Pre-Calculus/Trigonometry, Calculus, and Computer Science.

Each year, nearly 100 percent of graduating students are accepted at a college of their choice.

A nonmilitary summer school in July enrolls boarding and day boys in Grades 7–12. Many of the regular courses are offered, and the extracurricular emphasis is on intramural athletics. Class and athletic wear for the entire summer school is provided in the cost of tuition.

STUDENT ACTIVITIES. The Upper School battalion of more than 450 cadets is made up of five companies, a 65-piece marching band, an honor platoon of specialists in close-order drill, and the highest-ranking cadets who comprise the battalion staff. Cadet barracks are operated through the cadet chain-of-command, overseen by company advisors who are assigned by the Commandant. Under the standard disciplinary system, excessive demerits and regulation infractions can lead to loss of privileges or penalty tours.

Cadets enjoy involvement in more than 35 different clubs and activities based on student interest, including Weightlifting, Computer, Community Service, Debate, Fishing, Scuba, Woodworking, Equestrian, Paintball, Science, Chess, and Guidance clubs; the Fellowship of Christian Athletes; a yearbook; National Honor Society; and a Quadrille Club, which helps arrange all dances.

Music is an important part of the FUMA program. In addition to the Upper School marching band, which appears at athletic events, parades, and area festivals, there are various concert ensembles and a separate Middle School marching band. Two chorus groups participate in Chapel services and perform for various groups and churches throughout the Mid-Atlantic region.

Varsity (postgraduate), prep, junior prep, Middle School, and intramural teams in both schools compete in football, basketball, baseball, lacrosse, golf, orienteering, wrestling, indoor and outdoor track, cross-country, swimming and diving, rifle, tennis, and indoor and outdoor soccer. There are also junior and senior lifesaving programs. Interscholastic competition is held against teams from public and private schools, particularly against fellow members of the Virginia Prep League. Postgraduate teams generally play junior varsity squads from major colleges, as well as teams from junior and community colleges.

ADMISSION AND COSTS. Applicants are admitted in Grades 6–12 and as postgraduates on the basis of previous scholastic record, academic potential, and character; if testing is required, the school helps with arrangements. Qualified applicants are accepted "without regard to race, color, religion, or national origin." Application should be made by spring, but boys are often enrolled later when space permits.

In 2007–08, tuition, room and board, and fees total $24,700, with an additional charge for uniforms estimated at $3270. The day charge is $16,900 plus the cost of uniforms and books. A monthly payment plan is available. Financial aid includes certain standard reductions and a limited number of loans and grants.

Dean of Faculty: Col. Bob Miller
Commandant of Upper School Cadets: Lt. Col. Al Ivens
Commandant of Middle School Cadets: Maj. Bill Blanchetti
Director of Admissions: Lt. Col. Steve Macek
Director of Development: Lt. Col. Robert R. Cobb
College Counselor: Maj. Bob Grant
Chief Financial Officer: Sharon Higginbotham
Director of Athletics: Lt. Col. Micky Sullivan
Middle School Head: Lt. Col. Robert J. Feathers

Foxcroft School 1914

Route 626 North, Middleburg, VA 20118
Tel. 540-687-5555; [Toll-free] 800-858-2364; Fax 540-687-3627
Web Site www.foxcroft.org; E-mail admissions@foxcroft.org

FOXCROFT SCHOOL in Middleburg, Virginia, is a college preparatory boarding and day school enrolling girls in Grades 9 through 12. Situated in the countryside between the Blue Ridge and Bull Run Mountains, the School is an hour by car from Washington, D.C.; Dulles International Airport is 35 minutes away. Field trips to District of Columbia museums, theaters, concerts, and government agencies are offered to supplement classroom work.

Foxcroft School was founded in 1914 by Charlotte Haxall Noland, who directed the School until her retirement in 1955. From the beginning, Miss Noland stressed that "parents should require a great deal more of schools than just intellectual training." Accordingly, she sought to establish a school where the formation of character would be "a key aspect" of the educational program.

Foxcroft is governed by a 20-member Board of Trustees, which meets three times annually. The School endowment is $27,001,952, and the plant is valued at $38,000,000. Approximately 2880 graduates belong to the Alumnae Association, and 8 alumnae serve on the Board of Trustees. Foxcroft is accredited by The Virginia Association of Independent Schools; it is a member of the National Association of Independent Schools and other professional organizations.

THE CAMPUS. The School is situated on 500 acres of meadows and woodlands, part of which is used as a "Discovery Course" for survival games, group challenges, and similar outdoor activities. A swimming pool, four sports fields, eight tennis courts, three riding rings, and a jump course are adjacent to the main campus. There is an indoor riding arena in McConnell Stables; a gymnasium, a weight room, and dance studio are located in the Student Activity Center.

Foxcroft's brick and stone buildings are set among courtyards, orchards, and gardens. The restored 18th-century Brick House contains reception rooms, the development office, faculty apartments, and the dining room. The Schoolhouse has 14 classrooms, a studio art wing, music rooms, offices, and an auditorium. In addition, it houses science teaching facilities, including three laboratory/classrooms, an animal-plant room, and a computer-based laboratory. The Currier Library contains nearly 50,000 books and periodicals as well as information in 14 other formats including DVD, videocassette, microfiche, compact disk, and slides. The three-story facility provides two computer labs with e-mail and Internet access, an audiovisual/listening room, 85 study carrels, a classroom, study nooks, and the Foxcroft archives. The online web-based catalog serves as a gateway to thousands of resources, including several online research databases.

Girls live in Court, Dillon, Applegate, Orchard, and Reynolds dormitories. Dormitory common rooms have computer ports and e-mail access. Full-time housemothers facilitate residential life programs. Other facilities include faculty housing, the Head's home, the guest house, the Health Center, and an observatory.

THE FACULTY. Mary Louise Leipheimer was appointed Head of the School in 1989. She is a graduate of Indiana University of Pennsylvania with a B.S. degree in English. Ms. Leipheimer first came to Foxcroft in 1967 as an English teacher; she has also served as the School's Director of Admission, Assistant Head of External Affairs, and Director of Development.

Foxcroft has 50 full-time faculty and administrators. Thirty-five teachers and administrators live on campus, 22 with families. They hold 41 baccalaureate and 21 advanced degrees from such institutions as Colgate, College of William and Mary, Columbia, Denison, Duke, Fordham University, Georgetown, Harvard, Indiana University, Lawrence, Medical College of Virginia, New York Law School, Pennsylvania State, Skidmore, Wellesley, Wesleyan, and the Universities of California, Maryland, Massachusetts, Michigan, Pennsylvania, Vermont, and Virginia.

Two registered nurses live on campus and staff the infirmary; a doctor is on call.

STUDENT BODY. In 2007–08, Foxcroft enrolled 130 boarding students and 50 day students as follows: 41 in Grade 9, 50 in Grade 10, 47 in Grade 11, and 42 in Grade 12. Boarders represent 20 states, the District of Columbia, and 12 countries. Twenty-six students are from overseas.

ACADEMIC PROGRAM. The school year, from early September to early June, is divided into semesters, with Thanksgiving, Christmas, and spring vacations. Grades and comments are sent to parents four times yearly. Advisors, with a maximum of six advisees, maintain frequent contact with parents.

Classes, containing an average of ten students, meet Monday through Friday between 8:00 A.M. and 3:15 P.M. A campus-wide meeting is held three days a week. Athletics are scheduled after the regular academic day. Dinner is followed by free time, two and one-quarter hours of study, and "lights out" at 11:00 P.M. (10:30 P.M. for freshmen).

To graduate, a student must complete at least 18 credits. One credit (unit) is the equivalent of a full-year course. Minimum requirements are English 4, foreign language 3, history 3, mathematics 3, science 3, and fine arts 1.5. In addition, a student must take physical education or participate in riding, dance, or a varsity sport in all three seasons of the school year. Each girl also participates in community service on campus or in Middleburg.

The curriculum includes 83 full-year and term courses. Advanced Placement courses are offered in all disciplines. The Learning Center, the Math Lab, and the Writing Center offer students the opportunity to improve their study skills, to develop strategies for learning, to find special support when they encounter academic difficulty, and to take increasing responsibility for their own learning.

The Foxcroft academic program is further enriched by special events such as Interim Term, which offers two weeks of seminars, events, speakers, and trips as the entire school explores a single topic of current interest. The Goodyear Fellowship Program brings to Foxcroft each year a person distinguished in the arts, humanities, science, or public affairs to speak and conduct seminars with students. Past speakers include Barbara Walters, David McCullough, Andrei Codrescu, Aimee Mullins, Doris Kearns Goodwin, Maya Angelou, and Sally Ride. The English Department sponsors an annual two-day Poetry Festival, during which two published poets read from their work, lead workshops, and judge a student reading competition.

Students in the Class of 2007 received acceptances from a wide range of colleges and universities across the country including Boston University, College of Charleston, College of William and Mary, Cornell, Duke, George Washington University, Harvard, James Madison, Johns Hopkins, Princeton, Syracuse, Tulane, and the Universities of Colorado (Boulder), the South, and Virginia.

STUDENT ACTIVITIES. The School Council, including student, faculty, and administration representatives, is a clearinghouse for the proposal and implementation of new policies. Students also serve on the Judicial Council. Other organizations include three singing groups, CAPs tour guide program, the literary magazine, and the yearbook. There are clubs for girls interested in art, community service, drama, the environment, outdoor recreation, riding, photography, and astronomy.

All students compete in intramural sports as members of either the Fox or the Hound team; seven school teams compete interscholastically in the Washington, D.C., area. The athletic program includes field hockey, soccer, basketball, tennis, lacrosse, softball, volleyball, dance, cross-country, track, yoga, and riding. Approximately one-third of the students participate in the riding program, boarding their own horses on campus or riding one of the School's 31 horses. Equitation is the basic seat taught. Students may also participate in dressage, stadium jumping, cross-country riding, and fox hunting. Riders compete in interscholastic competition as part of the Tri-State Equitation League.

Special events—including dances, mixers, Outing Club events, picnics, movies, and horse shows—are scheduled each weekend. Regular trips to Middleburg and Washington, D.C., for shopping, movies, plays, opera, ballet, museums, and sporting events are also planned on weekends. Girls may attend worship services in local churches or participate in on-campus fellowship groups.

Foxcroft also has a Leadership Program designed to offer every student the opportunity to become a leader. Once students are elected, they must attend a spring retreat, complete specialized training to learn trust-building skills and conflict resolution, and return for additional training in the fall.

ADMISSION AND COSTS. Applicants are admitted on the basis of school records, recommendations, and results of the Secondary School Admission Test. A personal interview on campus is required, unless the distance is prohibitive. New students are admitted in Grades 9–11. There is a $50 application fee ($150 for international students).

In 2007, the tuition of $39,375 for boarding girls and $29,531 for day girls includes lodging, meals, tuition, lectures, and concerts held on campus.

In the current year, Foxcroft awarded more than $1,212,890 in financial aid. The School makes grants on the basis of financial need and offers a variety of programs to assist families with tuition and expenses.

Assistant Head of School: Sheila C. McKibbin
Dean of Faculty: Alexander O. Northrup
Dean of Students: Karen Gattuso
Director of Admission: Erica L. Ohanesian
Director of Advancement: Rebecca Gilmore
College Counselor: Paul W. Horgan
Business Manager: Richard Bettencourt
Director of Athletics: Katie Bryan Kantz
Director of Development: Marion Couzens
Director of Communications: Cathrine R. Wolf

Fredericksburg Academy 1992

10800 Academy Drive, Fredericksburg, VA 22408-1931
Tel. 540-898-0020; Fax 540-898-8951
Web Site www.fredericksburgacademy.org
E-mail admission@fredericksburgacademy.org

Fredericksburg Academy is a coeducational day school enrolling approximately 550 students in Prekindergarten through Grade 12. The Academy's curriculum utilizes both traditional and innovative approaches to reach its goals of preparing students for college, helping them become active citizens in the global community, and developing an appreciation for learning throughout their lives. Students benefit from a challenging core academic program that is balanced with exciting and rewarding opportunities in drama, music, art, computers, physical education, and community service. Upper School students participate in a wireless computer laptop program that is used in all disciplines. Parents are considered important and valuable partners in the educational process. Tuition: $12,190–$13,795. Financial aid and extended care are available. Jeffrey E. Eckerson is Director of Admission; Robert E. Graves is Head of School.

Hampton Roads Academy 1959

739 Academy Lane, Newport News, VA 23602
Tel. 757-884-9100; Admissions 757-884-9148; Fax 757-884-9137
Web Site www.hra.org; E-mail admissions@hra.org

Hampton Roads Academy, a nationally recognized Blue Ribbon school, was founded in 1959. It is an independent, coeducational, college preparatory day school enrolling 660 students in Prekindergarten–Grade 12, with a student-teacher ratio of 10:1. The school community works together to foster a safe environment for its students. One hundred percent of Hampton Roads graduates attend selective colleges across the nation. Hampton Roads Academy is committed to diversity and enrolls international students from several different countries. Tuition: $5600–$12,665. Mary Catherine Bunde is Director of Admissions; Thomas D. Harvey (St. Peter's College, A.B.; Wesleyan University, M.A.L.S.; Rockhurst College, M.B.A.; Klingenstein Fellow of Teachers College, Columbia) is Headmaster.

Hargrave Military Academy 1909

200 Military Drive, Chatham, VA 24531
Tel. 434-432-2481; [Toll-free] 800-432-2480; Fax 434-432-3129
Web Site www.hargrave.edu; E-mail admissions@hargrave.edu

Hargrave Military Academy in Chatham, Virginia, is a boarding and day school that combines a college preparatory curriculum with a comprehensive military program. Affiliated with the Baptist General Association of Virginia, the school encompasses Grades 7 through 12 and a postgraduate year, with boarding and day boys. The historic town of Chatham (population 1354) is in the Piedmont Region of the state, 15 miles north of Danville on U.S. Highway 29 and within reasonable driving distance of Roanoke, Lynchburg, and other larger cities.

Hargrave Military Academy traces its roots to the Chatham Training School, founded in 1909 by the Baptist clergyman Reverend T. Ryland Sanford, Mr. Jesse H. Hargrave, and his son, J. Hunt Hargrave. In 1911, Reverend Sanford became the first president of the school, which has enjoyed a close association with the Baptist General Association of Virginia since 1913. It was renamed in 1925 to honor J. Hunt Hargrave and to reflect its primary mission.

The Academy aims to provide a Christian environment that imbues all aspects of life. Through its academic, athletic, and religious programs, Hargrave seeks to develop cadets in mind, body, and spirit, and to challenge them through a well-rounded academic program that will motivate them to become lifelong learners. The military component of the curriculum provides discipline, training, and structure designed to prepare cadets for success in college and throughout life. Chapel services and Bible studies are regular components of the school schedule.

Hargrave Military Academy is governed by a Board of Trustees and accredited by the Virginia Association of Independent Schools and the Southern Association of Colleges and Schools. It holds membership in the National Association of Independent Schools, the Association of Military Colleges and Schools of the United States, and the Council for Advancement and Support of Education.

THE CAMPUS. Hargrave Military Academy is situated on a 214-acre campus of woodlands, lawns, and playing fields. Academic activities are centered in four main buildings housing classrooms, lecture rooms, photography darkrooms, and math, writing, computer, and science laboratories. The fully automated library is networked for academic research and curricular enhancement activities with 27 additional computers for research. The campus is equipped with more than 200 updated computers. The Science & Technology Building has a Distance Learning Center, and the school has a laptop computer program for all students in Grade 9–Postgraduate. The auditorium hosts musical productions and other events.

Cadets are housed two to a room on ten dormitory floors. Residents have the use of a recreation room, television lounge, and a student snack bar. Meals are served buffet style in an air-conditioned dining hall.

Among the athletic facilities are the Landon Tennis Complex, the Orlin Rogers-Dennis Fuller Baseball Field, an aquatic center with a 50-meter pool, two gymnasiums, a track, indoor rifle range, a skeet range, weight training and Nautilus equipment, tennis and basketball courts, and playing fields for football, baseball, soccer, and lacrosse.

THE FACULTY. Col. Wheeler L. Baker was appointed President of Hargrave Military Academy in 1999. Prior to assuming this position, Colonel Baker served as Provost at the Academy. He holds B.S. and doctoral degrees in economics and a master's degree in international affairs. He has spent nearly 40 years in the United States Marine Corps and was past chairman of the Naval Science Department at the University of New Mexico. He and his wife, Lynn, have four grown children.

There are 48 full-time faculty, 26 men and 22 women. They hold baccalaureate degrees and graduate degrees representing study at such colleges and universities as Appalachian State, Averett, Carson Newman, The Citadel, College of William and Mary, East Carolina University, Elon College, Furman, Greensboro College, Hampden-Sydney, Indiana University, James Madison, Liberty, Longwood College, Lynchburg, Old Dominion, Randolph-Macon Woman's College, Southern Baptist Theological Seminary, Virginia Military Institute, Virginia Polytechnic Institute and State University, Wake Forest, West Virginia University, and the Universities of Georgia, North Carolina (Chapel Hill, Greensboro), Richmond, South Carolina, and Virginia.

Registered nurses provide around-the-clock coverage in

the Academy infirmary, and a school doctor visits the campus on a daily basis.

STUDENT BODY. In 2006–07, Hargrave Military Academy enrolled 422 cadets. They came from 34 states, the District of Columbia, and five countries and reflect a diversity of racial, religious, ethnic, and economic backgrounds.

ACADEMIC PROGRAM. The school year, from August to June, includes Thanksgiving, Christmas, and spring vacations, plus overnight and weekend passes during the year. Each student has an advisor who serves as counselor, mentor, and friend on academic and personal issues throughout the year. The average student-teacher ratio is 11:1. A two-hour supervised study hall is held nightly from Sunday through Thursday.

On a typical day, cadets rise at 6:00 A.M. to eat breakfast and complete chores. Classes run from 7:30 A.M. to noon, including a 20-minute break. Lunch at noon is followed by an hour of military drills on Monday, Wednesday, and Friday, and extra-help sessions, known as Individualized Instruction Time (ITT), are held Monday through Thursday. Two hours of recreation and athletics precede dinner at 6:00 P.M. Evening study from 7:30 to 9:30 P.M. and "lights out" at 10:00 P.M. conclude the day.

Hargrave is committed to providing a strong, intensive Reading Program to students who wish to become better readers. Reading classes, taught by regular faculty, are scheduled as an integral part of the curriculum, and cadets may earn an elective credit upon completing the program. The curriculum is designed to strengthen students' comprehension of written material through explicit, direct instruction. Classes are intentionally small, and extra attention can be arranged outside of class.

To earn an Advanced Studies Diploma, 24 credits are required as follows: 4 in English, social studies, math, and science; 3 in a foreign language; 2 in physical education; 1 in religion; and 4 in electives. The curriculum also incorporates between 3½ to 4 hours of military training and classes per week. Students take six subjects scheduled on an alternating basis, with three subjects one day and three the next.

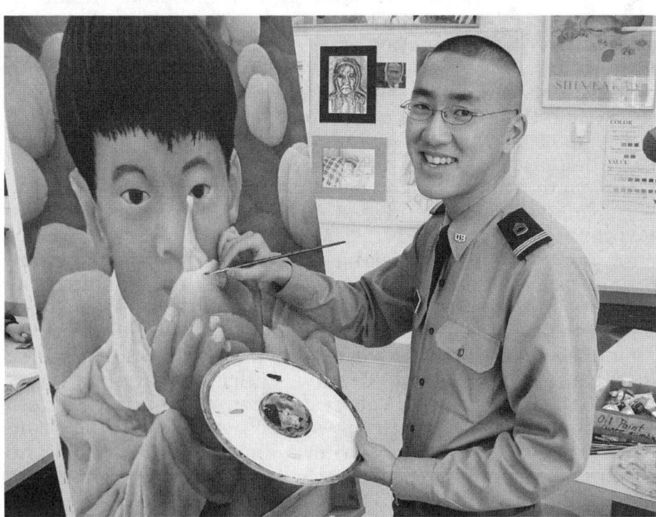

Academic courses in the Upper School include Introduction to the Old and New Testaments; English I-IV, American Literature and Composition, Critical Reading and Writing, Oral Communications, Journalism; French I–IV, Spanish I–IV; Algebra I & II, Intermediate Algebra, Advanced Algebra II, Modern Trigonometry, Geometry (Formal & Informal), Analytic Geometry, Pre-Calculus, Functions, Calculus; Physical Science, Earth Science, General Biology, Environmental Science, Astronomy, Meteorology, Chemistry, Physics; Civics/Economics, Sociology/Psychology, World Studies, Virginia/United States History, Virginia/United States Government; Health/Physical Education I & II; and Art I-IV. There are elective credit courses in SAT Preparation and Leadership & Ethics. Hargrave's How-to-Study Program is required for all new students.

For the past six years, 100 percent of graduates are enrolled at such institutions as Auburn, Charleston Southern, The Citadel, East Carolina University, Pennsylvania State, Purdue, Radford, United States Military Academy, United States Naval Academy, Virginia Military Institute, Virginia Polytechnic, Western Carolina, and the Universities of Alabama, Florida, Maryland, North Carolina (Chapel Hill), and South Carolina.

A four-week, relaxed, nonmilitary summer program allows students to earn academic credit in one new or two repeat subjects and participate in a sports program of their choice, including a High Adventure program.

STUDENT ACTIVITIES. The student body is organized in a battalion of six companies. Cadets may serve as members of the Drill Team, Precision Color Guard, Marching Band, Drum Corps, and Military Police. The Cadet Honor Code governs the conduct of daily life at the Academy, with infractions tried by the Honor Council, a nine-member committee chosen by their peers.

Students take part in numerous interest groups including the HMA Players (drama club), Boy Scouts, *Cadence* (yearbook), Beta Club, Art Club, Photography Club, Ski Club, jazz ensemble, and marching band.

Varsity teams are formed in 16 areas, with junior varsity and junior high teams in nearly every major sport. Among these are football, cross-country, soccer, basketball, golf, baseball, tennis, riflery, swimming, wrestling, and lacrosse.

On weekends, cadets are permitted to leave campus for excursions to downtown Chatham or visits to family and friends. Traditional festivities are planned for Parents' Weekend, Military Ball, Alumni Weekend, and Mother's Day.

ADMISSION AND COSTS. Hargrave Military Academy seeks young people of average to superior ability and good moral character who are purposeful in their desire to succeed in the school's challenging program. Acceptance is offered based on the candidate's previous academic record, standardized test results, teacher recommendations, and a personal interview and campus visit. Students are admitted in August, at mid-term, and at the start of the summer program. Decisions are rendered within 48 hours after the applicant's file has been completed.

In 2007–08, tuition, room and board, new-student uniforms, books, and sundry items total $26,500; expenses for a day student total approximately $12,500. Financial aid is available based on demonstrated merit and/or need, and several tuition payment plans are offered as well.

Dean of Faculty: Lt. Col. Walter Sullivan, USA (Ret.)
Director of Admissions: Commander Frank L. Martin III, USN (Ret.)
Director of Advancement: Mr. Roger Hill
College Counselor: Sgt. Maj. Mike Payne, USMC (Ret.)
Director of Athletics: Maj. Richard Motley
Dean of Students: Sgt. Maj. Harold Hofer, USMC (Ret.)

The Hill School of Middleburg 1926

130 South Madison Street, P.O. Box 65, Middleburg, VA 20118-0065
Tel. 540-687-5897; Fax 540-687-3132
Web Site www.thehillschool.org; E-mail thehillschool.org

The Hill School is a coeducational, elementary day school enrolling 236 students in Kindergarten–Grade 8. It seeks to prepare students for academic success in secondary schools through a strong curriculum, an excellent faculty, and small class sizes. Hill also offers a range of opportunities for intellectual, artistic, athletic, and interpersonal growth within its cocurricular program of art, music, drama, athletics, outdoor education, field trips, and community service. Tuition: $13,650–$18,000. Financial Aid: $500,000. Treavor Lord is Director of Admissions; Thomas A. Northrup (University of Pennsylvania, B.A. 1968, M.S.Ed. 1981) was appointed Headmaster in 1981.

The Langley School 1942

1411 Balls Hill Road, McLean, VA 22101
Tel. 703-356-1920; Admissions 703-848-2782; Fax 703-790-9712
Web Site www.langleyschool.org; E-mail admission@langleyschool.org

The Langley School, a coeducational day school enrolling 475 students in Preschool–Grade 8, strives to discover, amplify, and embrace the talents of every child every day through an engaging program of rigorous academics, fine arts, athletics, and community service. By nurturing, supporting, and academically challenging its students, Langley's inclusive community builds quietly confident, independent thinkers who flourish as learners and individuals. Situated on a 9.2-acre campus, the School's facilities include a 20,000-volume library, science and computer labs, a creative media studio featuring green screen technology, art studios, an athletic center, and a new arts center (2008). Langley offers a 7:1 student-teacher ratio, bus transportation, and extended day. Tuition: $12,300–$24,200. Financial aid is available. Kerry Moody is Director of Admission; Doris Cottam is Head of School.

Linton Hall School 1922

9535 Linton Hall Road, Bristow, VA 20136-1200
Tel. 703-368-3157; Fax 703-368-3036
Web Site www.lintonhall.com; E-mail lintonhall@aol.com

Founded by Benedictine Sisters, Linton Hall is a Catholic, coeducational day school enrolling 214 students in Pre-Kindergarten–Grade 8. The development of the student is based on Christian beliefs and a reverence for God, self, and others. The 120-acre campus includes tennis courts, soccer fields, track, baseball field, playgrounds, sport center, outdoor basketball courts, and a swimming pool. The curriculum consists of religion, reading, literature, English, mathematics, science, social studies, Spanish, music, art, physical education, technology, and OCEW (Outdoor, Conservation, Ecology, and Wildlife). Choir, Fife and Drum Corps, basketball, and soccer are among the activities. Tuition: $7860. Financial aid is available. Susan Barrett is Admissions Coordinator; Elizabeth A. Poole is Principal.

Loudoun Country Day School 1953

237 Fairview Street, NW, Leesburg, VA 20176
Tel. 703-777-3841; Fax 703-771-1346
Web Site www.lcds.org; E-mail info@lcds.org

Loudoun Country Day School, an independent, coeducational school enrolling 270 students in Prekindergarten–Grade 8, develops knowledge and skills in language arts, math, science, social studies, French, Spanish, physical education, athletics, computers, music, orchestra, and art. An 8:1 student-teacher ratio provides a nurturing environment and affords considerable individual attention. A character education program, which emphasizes respect, courtesy, kindness, cooperation, and consideration, permeates the School's culture and philosophy. Team sports, dramatic productions, and field trips are central to the program. Tuition: $9000–$14,500. Need-based financial assistance is budgeted each year. Pam Larimer is Admissions Coordinator; Dr. Randall Hollister is Headmaster.

Massanutten Military Academy 1899

614 South Main Street, Woodstock, VA 22664
Tel. 540-459-2167; [Toll-free] 877-466-6222; Fax 540-459-5421
Web Site www.militaryschool.com; E-mail admissions@militaryschool.com

Massanutten Military Academy in Woodstock, Virginia, is a coeducational, college preparatory school that seeks to offer a superior academic program combined with character, leadership, and athletic education for boarders and day students in Grades 7–12 and a postgraduate year. Woodstock (population 4200) is situated in Virginia's Shenandoah Valley about 90 minutes west of Washington, D.C., and 2 hours from Baltimore. Located off Interstate 81, Woodstock is a small, safe town that embraces the Academy.

The school was founded in 1899, and the military program was implemented in 1917. At Massanutten Military Academy, education is the priority, along with commitment to the development of character, integrity, and good citizenship. The Academy considers a structured, disciplined learning environment essential to the realization of these goals. All students are members of the Corps of Cadets, and high school students serve in the Academy's Junior Reserve Officers' Training Corps, which consistently earns the designation of Honor Unit with Distinction, the highest rating possible. An Honor Code and the *Cadet Handbook* outline criteria for personal conduct and discipline. Enrollment at MMA does not incur a military obligation.

Massanutten Military Academy is governed by a Board of Trustees and accredited by the Southern Association of Colleges and Schools and the Virginia Association of Independent Schools. It holds membership in the Association of Military Colleges and Schools of the United States, The Association of Boarding Schools, and other educational organizations.

THE CAMPUS. The 40-acre campus in the Northern Shenandoah Valley includes 12 buildings with 20 state-of-the-art classrooms, five computer labs, three science labs, more than 110 newly renovated two-person dorm rooms, six cadet lounge areas, the Cook and Kitchin Dining Hall, and a 300-seat chapel. The new Hayes Activity Center offers cadets a place to relax, enjoy themselves, and build friendships.

Up to 160 male cadets reside in Benchoff, Harrison, and Lantz Halls, and 61 female cadets live in Rosedrey Warehime Dormitory. Warehime Hall has a modern security system, and occupants enjoy their own computer lab, lounge, laundry, kitchen, and aerobics center.

Among the athletic resources are a 30,000-square-foot gymnasium, the Gordon D. Bowman Stadium for football and soccer, new baseball and softball facilities, the Harrison indoor pool, tennis and basketball courts, a cross-country course, a 440-yard track, practice fields, the Cook Weight Room, and aerobics center.

THE FACULTY. Col. Roy F. Zinser, USA (Ret.), was appointed President of Massanutten Military Academy in November 2001. Colonel Zinser is an alumnus of The Citadel where he earned baccalaureate and master's degrees in Business Administration and International Relations. He and his wife, Marty, have two sons, both U.S. Army officers.

The 30-member faculty includes 11 with master's degrees and 2 with doctorates. They are selected for their mastery of the subjects they teach as well as their ability to inspire young people. In addition to teaching, faculty members also serve as mentors, coaches, and student advocates.

The infirmary is staffed by nurses with more than 55 years of combined experience. Two live on the campus, and a nurse is on duty or on call at all times. Nearby Shenandoah Memorial Hospital is equipped for emergencies.

ACADEMIC PROGRAM. The college preparatory curriculum ensures that every student is equipped with the knowledge and skills necessary to succeed at college and in life. Individual student success is accomplished by dedicated teachers, daily tutorials, the Homework Assistance Program, and supervised study halls.

The school year is divided into semesters, each with two nine-week grading periods. Progress reports are issued every three weeks, and teachers keep parents apprised weekly of their cadet's academic progress through Edline, an online information program. Classes are small, averaging 10 per class, with a 7:1 student-teacher ratio to ensure individual attention and success. Afternoon tutorials benefit cadets who need extra assistance. Also, members of the National Honor Society are available for tutoring. The daily schedule provides structure to enable every cadet to attend classes, participate in one of the school's 24 sports programs, receive academic assistance, study, relax, and socialize.

The MMA Middle School is designed for the young learner, with emphasis on the acquisition of self-confidence and classroom skills. Cadets concentrate on building skills in English, math, science, and social studies while developing good study habits through organization and time management. Qualified cadets may take high school-level courses in foreign languages, math, and other subjects.

Cadets in Grades 9–12 follow one of two curricula: the Advanced College Preparatory diploma, which may include college credits earned at Shenandoah University, or the standard College Preparatory diploma, which qualifies applicants for entrace to major colleges and universities. Both diplomas meet the graduation criteria of the Commonwealth of Virginia. Also, junior and senior students may apply for honors course credit in their English, math, and social studies courses.

The Army Junior ROTC program's mission is to develop good citizens. The program provides 180 hours of instruction each year in such areas as leadership skills, American history, the Constitution, first aid, physical conditioning, technology awareness, and drill and ceremony.

Massanutten Military Academy offers the nation's only JROTC summer program for students from other public and private schools who wish to earn high school credit for JROTC. In 2007, nearly 25 percent of the MMA Summer School population enrolled in this program.

Cadets may take part in the JROTC color guard, drill team, and Raider programs. Because Massanutten is an Honor Unit with Distinction, the Academy can nominate qualified cadets to the U.S. Military, Naval, and Air Force Academies and provide assistance to cadets receiving ROTC scholarships to major universities.

The Academy's college placement officer personally works with each cadet to ensure acceptance at a college or university. College counseling begins in the junior year and continues until cadets have been accepted at the institution they will attend. As seniors, cadets must take the SAT or ACT at least once. The Academy conducts its own SAT prep course, which is 70 hours long. The program actively combines Kaplan Advantage Strategies with weekly guest speakers who help students hone their core math and English skills. The SAT course is a graduation requirement.

All MMA graduates in the last five years were accepted to colleges and universities of their choice such as The Citadel, George Mason University, Mary Baldwin College, Radford, United States Military Academy, United States Naval Academy, Virginia Military Institute, Virginia Polytechnic, and the University of Georgia. In addition, 53 graduates and postgraduates in 2007 received college scholarships in excess of $2,200,000.

STUDENT ACTIVITIES. The Corps of Cadets is organized into a battalion with six companies, led by cadets who have demonstrated exceptional leadership potential, discipline, and academic and extracurricular achievement. All cadets are expected to live by the rules and regulations outlined in the *Cadet Handbook* and by the Honor Code, which states, "A cadet will not lie, cheat, or steal nor tolerate those who do." Both academic and personal conduct are evaluated, and a system of rewards and punishments is administered depending on superior or substandard performance with a strong emphasis on rewards. Cadets in good standing may earn special privileges; cadets with demerits work off their tours, or punishment hours, during specified time periods.

Cadets publish a yearbook, take part in Boy Scouts (with three new Eagle Scouts in 2007), participate in vocal and instrumental groups, various interest clubs, and a community service club, which contributes more than 3000 hours of social outreach annually.

Every cadet plays at least one sport each season. The Academy competes interscholastically with boys' teams in football, baseball, cross-country, soccer, golf, rifle, swimming, basketball, lacrosse, rugby, track, softball, wrestling, and tennis. Girls' teams compete in swimming, cross-country, basketball, cheerleading, soccer, and volleyball. Other athletic opportunities include rifle, pistol, and weight lifting. A postgraduate basketball program is also available for young men.

On weekends, cadets may take the 5-minute walk to downtown Woodstock for shopping, dining, movies, or other diversions. The school also plans activity trips to amusement parks, paintball, nearby national and state parks, and cultural performances in Washington, D.C., as well as dances, professional sports competitions, fishing, and whitewater rafting. Cadets who remain on campus are encouraged to attend a church service of their faith; otherwise, they must attend Sunday morning character development classes.

ADMISSION AND COSTS. Massanutten Military Academy welcomes young men and women of average to above-average academic potential who show a willingness and determination to succeed in, and benefit from, a structured, disciplined program. Admission is based on previous transcripts, teacher and personal recommendations, and an interview. The school operates on a rolling admissions basis with no official deadline. A nonrefundable $50 fee is due with the completed application.

The 2007–08 tuition of $23,489 includes seven-day room and board, uniforms, haircuts, and basic infirmary needs.

President: Col. Roy F. Zinser, USA (Ret.)
Commandant of Cadets: Maj. Skip Anders, USA (Ret.)
Academic Dean: Rachael Hammond
Director of Admissions: Murali Sinnathamby
Director of Communications: Lt. Col. Jim DeLaney, USA (Ret.)
Director of Finance: Cheryl Funkhouser
Director of Operations: Steve Hollingsworth
Athletic Director: Richard Chiarolanzio
Director of Activities: Joseph D. Babcock
Director of Development: L. Stephen Jennings
Director of Technology: Matthew Klus
College Placement Officer: Lt. Col. Russ Burr, USA (Ret.)
Chief Nurse: Andi Avni, R.N.

Miller School 1878

1000 Samuel Miller Loop, Charlottesville, VA 22903
Tel. 434-823-4805; Fax 434-823-6617
Web Site www.millerschool.org; E-mail admissions@millerschool.org

Miller School in Charlottesville, Virginia, is a coeducational boarding and day school enrolling students in Grades 8 through 12 and Postgraduate. Historic Charlottesville lies in the foothills of the Blue Ridge Mountains, 74 miles northwest of Richmond and 122 miles southwest of Washington, D.C. The city is the site of the University of Virginia, Thomas Jefferson's "Monticello," and the homes of James Monroe and Patrick Henry. Founded in 1878, Miller School is one of the oldest coeducational boarding schools in America and the oldest one in Virginia.

The School's mission statement reads, in part: "With a unique emphasis on minds, hands, and hearts, Miller School prepares young women and men for success in college and life. Distinguished by a rigorous and supportive program, talented faculty and staff, meaningful leadership opportunities, and small classroom settings, our congenial community builds responsible citizens, insightful thinkers, and compassionate individuals." The faculty believes that young people learn best in a community of trust that seeks to educate a student's mind, hands, and heart through a challenging program of academics, athletics, service, and the arts.

A 16-member Board of Trustees oversees the operation of the School, which is accredited by the Virginia Association of Independent Schools and holds membership in the National Association of Independent Schools. Graduates are represented by the Miller School Alumni Association, and families may participate in the Parents' Auxiliary.

THE CAMPUS. Miller School is set on a 1600-acre campus, which includes woodlands, orchards, farmlands, and a 12-acre lake. Old Main, the Headmaster's residence, and the Arts Building are on the Virginia Landmarks Registry and provide excellent examples of High Victorian Gothic architecture. Old Main (1878) contains classrooms, administrative and admissions offices, chapel, dining hall, health center, the boys' dormitories, and the Flannagan Center for Innovative Technology, which houses state-of-the-art computer and support services. Old Main also contains the library, which is linked by computer to the University of Virginia's electronic library system, local public libraries, and all appropriate Internet research sites. Additional buildings on campus include The Arts Building (1882), with woodworking, music, photography, and art areas; the Science Building (1885); Wayland Hall and Haden-Hart Hall, the girls' dormitories; the Student Center, housing Sam's Bistro, the book store, and the launderette; Alumni Gymnasium, a fully equipped athletic center with basketball, wrestling, and weight training; and faculty residences.

The campus features an outdoor swimming pool, miles of cross-country running trails, tennis courts, and five athletic fields.

THE FACULTY. Lindsay R. Barnes, Jr., Esq., was appointed 11th Headmaster of Miller School in 1999. A graduate of Hampden-Sydney College and the University of Virginia School of Law, he holds a master's degree in journalism from the University of Georgia.

There are 53 faculty and professional staff, 27 women and 26 men. In addition to baccalaureates, they hold 26 advanced degrees. Faculty represent such schools as Auburn, Bates, Bridgewater, College of William and Mary, C.W. Post, Dartmouth, Denison, Florida State, Georgetown, Hofstra, Indiana University, James Madison, Mary Baldwin, Mary Washington, Middlebury, Pacific, Universidad Metropolitana de Caracas, Université Denis Diderot, Université Laval, Virginia Commonwealth, Virginia Polytechnic, Xavier, and the Universities of California, Colorado, North Carolina, Notre Dame, Pennsylvania, Tennessee, and Virginia.

STUDENT BODY. In 2007–08, Miller School enrolled 154 students, 106 boarding and 48 day, as follows: 12 in Grade 8, 23 in Grade 9, 37 in Grade 10, 39 in Grade 11, 41 in Grade 12, and 2 postgraduates. They came from diverse family backgrounds and cultures and represented ten states and 11 countries.

ACADEMIC PROGRAM. The school year, from early September until the end of May, is divided into semesters, with two grading periods in the fall semester and two in the spring. Vacations are scheduled at Thanksgiving, Christmas, and in the spring. Parents' Weekends are scheduled in the fall and spring. Each student takes six classes that meet five times a week. Class size averages 10 to 12, with a student-teacher ratio of 6:1 throughout the grades.

A typical day begins with breakfast at 7:00 A.M. Classes begin at 7:45 A.M. and run for 50 minutes. Students, faculty, and staff meet in the chapel daily for morning announcements on Monday, Wednesday, and Friday, and for a nondenominational chapel program on Tuesday and Thursday. Wednesday classes are shortened every other week to accommodate school-wide participation in community service programs. Each afternoon, all students are involved in athletics, theater, or other sanctioned activities. Required, faculty-supervised study periods are held each evening, Sunday through Thursday, from 7:30 to 9:30 P.M.

The Miller School diploma requires 23 credits, including four years each of English and history/social studies; three years of mathematics (at least through Algebra II), three years of laboratory science, three years of a foreign language (Latin, Spanish, or French), and two years of fine arts, plus electives. Qualified students may take Advanced Placement courses in a variety of disciplines.

The eighth grade offers a strong grounding in the foundational subjects of English (including spelling, grammar, and vocabulary building), mathematics, social studies, science, and the fine arts.

Miller School's Educational Support Services program ranges from educational assessment and support to specialized tutoring, SAT preparation, and, on a limited basis, a study skills class for students with certain identified needs. There is also an English as a Second Language program.

In 1998 through 2007, 100 percent of the graduates who sought to attend college were accepted at four-year colleges and universities including Colgate, College of William and Mary, Dartmouth, Dickinson, Drexel, Duke, Hampden-Sydney, James Madison, Johns Hopkins, Providence, Purdue, Rhodes, Roanoke College, St. Bonaventure, Seton Hall, Sewanee, Stanford, Syracuse, Tulane, Virginia Polytechnic, Wake Forest, and the Universities of Pennsylvania, Richmond, Southern California, Virginia, and Wisconsin, among others.

STUDENT ACTIVITIES. The student government is on the prefect model, where elected and appointed students and faculty members serve on the Honor Committee and the Disciplinary Review Board.

"Service to others" is a long-standing Miller tradition expressed in a multifaceted Community Service program. Students choose between on-campus and off-campus opportunities, and these groups, chaperoned by faculty, meet for two hours of service every other Wednesday afternoon. Off-campus groups become involved with various community agencies such as hospitals, retirement homes, local elementary schools, Parks and Recreation, the SPCA, and many others. On-campus groups include Environmental Projects, Library Assistance, and the Recycling Program.

Participation in athletics or other authorized activities is required of all. Students compete on varsity and junior varsity teams in the local Virginia Independent Conference or the Blue Ridge Conference. Fall offerings include girls' volleyball, boys' soccer, and girls' and boys' cross-country; winter term offers boys' and girls' basketball and wrestling; spring sports are boys' lacrosse and baseball, girls' soccer, and boys' and girls' tennis. Conditioning is offered as an alternative to team sports, drama is an option during the fall and winter seasons, and an equestrian program is available in the fall and spring.

On weekends, students engage in activities off campus ranging from white-water rafting and tubing to hiking and enjoying regional theme and water parks. Trips have included athletic and cultural events at the University of Virginia and other locations as well as Baltimore Orioles and Richmond Braves baseball games. Miller coordinates dances and social events with other boarding schools, and students shop and attend movies regularly.

ADMISSION AND COSTS. Miller School welcomes students of all cultural and racial backgrounds. International students should have a working knowledge of both spoken and written English. Miller seeks students who possess above-average to superior intelligence, high moral character, and a desire to improve and excel. Candidates are evaluated on their willingness to participate in the Miller School program, character and academic references, and the ability to handle challenging academic material. Acceptance is based on academic record and test scores, letters of recommendation from a current English and math teacher, completed applicant and parent questionnaires, and an interview in person or by phone, depending on distance. A $50 fee ($100 for international students) must accompany the application. Admission is on a rolling basis. First-round decisions are made in early March, and classes can fill any time thereafter. International applicants should allow enough time for processing the appropriate I-20 forms and student F-1 visas.

The cost in 2007–08 is $31,450 for seven-day boarding, $27,750 for five-day boarding (for families in Albemarle and surrounding counties), $36,745 for international students (including ESL), and $13,650 for day students. These fees include tuition refund insurance, room and board, and activities. There are additional charges for books ($200–$400), spending money for boarding students, and Educational Support Services when appropriate. Financial aid grants totaling $779,612 were awarded to 30 percent of the student body in the current year, with an average grant of $21,350 to boarding students and $5360 to day students.

Director of Academics: Rick France
Director of Admissions: Jay Reeves
Director of Development: Rita Ralston
Director of Finance: Gerri Stewart
Director of Operations: Dan Pugh
Director of College Placement: Hugh Meagher
Director of Athletics: Fred Wawner
Director of Student Life: Kathie Cason
Registrar: Cindy DeNome

Norfolk Academy 1728

1585 Wesleyan Drive, Norfolk, VA 23502
Tel. 757-461-6236; Admissions 757-455-5582; Fax 757-455-3199
Web Site www.norfolkacademy.org
E-mail fholcombe@norfolkacademy.org

NORFOLK ACADEMY in Norfolk, Virginia, is a coeducational, college preparatory day school enrolling students in Grades 1 through 12. Situated on the border of Norfolk (population 245,000) and Virginia Beach (population 450,000), the Academy enjoys the advantages and diversity of this major metropolitan area, known as Hampton Roads. Site of the world's largest naval base, Norfolk is also the home of Old Dominion University, Norfolk State University, the Regent University, Virginia Wesleyan College, and Eastern Virginia Medical School. The Academy is directly off Interstate 64 at Route 13 North and is easily accessible by car.

Founded in 1728, Norfolk Academy is the oldest independent secondary school in Virginia and the eighth oldest in the nation. At its founding, the Academy was a typical 18th-century classical school for boys. It became coeducational in 1966 when the Trustees of Norfolk Academy and the Board of the Country Day School for Girls in Virginia Beach merged the two schools and moved them to the present campus.

Norfolk Academy's program reflects the conviction that sound moral and spiritual values define the individual in a more significant way than academic success. The Academy's mission is to nurture each student's mind, body, artistic expression and appreciation, and sense of responsibility in accordance with the highest standards of excellence. Generations of Norfolk Academy students have exhibited intellectual and personal integrity, in large measure, through their ownership of and participation in the school's honor code. In its effort to develop responsible and productive citizens, the Academy provides leadership opportunities and encourages involvement in community activities, government, social service organizations, and cultural programs.

A nonprofit organization, Norfolk Academy is governed by a 30-member Board of Trustees that meets quarterly. The Alumni Association represents the more than 4350 living alumni, many of whom are active in school activities. The Academy has an endowment of approximately $36,000,000.

Norfolk Academy is accredited by the Southern Association of Colleges and Schools and the Virginia Association of Independent Schools. It holds membership in the National Association of Independent Schools and other educational organizations.

THE CAMPUS. The 64-acre campus includes 14 playing fields, 8 tennis courts, a 400-meter latex track, a football stadium, and an aquatic center. There are also seven single-family homes and one duplex housing administrators and senior faculty.

There are ten school buildings, which provide classrooms, science laboratories, computer centers, art and music rooms, a 375-seat auditorium, the refectory, the bookstore, and administrative offices. In addition, there are two libraries with a total of 50,000 volumes and an extensive collection of periodicals and audiovisual equipment.

Also on campus are two gymnasiums and an athletic pavilion (2005), which provides three additional basketball courts, a fully equipped fitness center, a wrestling room, and expanded locker areas. The 50,000-square-foot Tucker Arts Center (2006) houses the 575-seat Samuel C. Johnson Theater, rooms for choral and instrumental music, and dance, art, and sculpture studios.

The school plant is valued at $65,000,000.

THE FACULTY. Dennis Manning, appointed Headmaster in 2001, is a 1984 graduate of Wake Forest University (B.A., M.A.). Most recently, he was Headmaster of The American School in England. Previously, Mr. Manning had been a teacher, coach, and administrator at Woodberry Forest School; Dean of Freshmen and Residence Life and instructor in English at Washington and Lee University; faculty consultant to the Education Testing Service; consultant to the North Carolina Governor's Institute; and, from 1996 to 2000, a member of the Wake Forest University Board of Visitors.

The full-time faculty number 123—74 women and 49 men; 101 hold advanced degrees. Two or more degrees were earned at College of William and Mary, Dartmouth, Duke, George Washington, Harvard, James Madison, Johns Hopkins, Middlebury, Old Dominion, Princeton, United States Military Academy, United States Naval Academy, Vanderbilt, Washington and Lee, Wesleyan, and the Universities of Florida, Georgia, Maryland, Massachusetts, Michigan, North Carolina, Pennsylvania, the South (Sewanee), Texas, and Virginia.

Norfolk Academy offers health insurance, life insurance, and a retirement plan. Leaves of absence can be arranged.

Two school nurses and two trainers are available on campus. An emergency-care center and four major hospitals are within a 10-minute drive of the school.

STUDENT BODY. In 2007–08, Norfolk Academy enrolled 628 boys and 601 girls as follows: 530 in the Lower School (Grades 1–6), 355 in the Middle School (Grades 7–9), and 344 in the Upper School (Grades 10–12). The students live in Norfolk, Virginia Beach, and other communities in the region.

ACADEMIC PROGRAM. The school year, from late August to early June, is divided into semesters and includes a Thanksgiving recess, and Christmas and spring vacations. A typical school day, from 8:10 A.M. to 3:25 P.M., includes six 40-minute class periods, a morning break, lunch, a fine arts period, and an activities period. Sports, play practice, and the dance team are scheduled after the close of the school day.

Classes, which are held five days a week, have an average enrollment of 20 students. There are daily supervised study halls; some students may be required to attend a special study session held on Saturday mornings. A resource coordinator offers help to Lower School students; The Cum Laude Society provides tutorials for Middle and Upper School students who are having academic difficulties. Grades are issued every nine weeks; progress reports are sent to parents three times each semester.

The Lower School curriculum consists of reading, written and oral expression, spelling, handwriting, grammar, research skills, problem solving, listening skills, social studies, mathematics, science, and physical and health education. Spanish, computer education, art, music, and instruction in library skills further enrich the curriculum.

Core courses for Grade 7 are English, Introduction to the Social Studies, Latin I, Pre-Algebra, Life Science, and physical education. The Grade 8 curriculum consists of English, Latin II, Ancient History, Algebra, Physical Science, and health and physical education. Computer skills and library instruction are taught throughout the curriculum.

To graduate, students in Grades 9–12 must complete at least 20 credits, including 4 in English, 4 in mathematics, 3 in a foreign language, 3 in history, 2 in laboratory science, 3 in academic electives, and 1 in health and physical education. Seniors must also present an eight-minute speech to the student body and faculty.

Courses offered include English 1–4; French 1–4, German 1–4, Spanish 1–5, Latin 1–5, Italian 1–3, Homeric Greek; World Cultures, Modern European History, United States History, United States Government, Economics; Algebra 1–2, Geometry, Pre-calculus, Calculus, Statistics; Biology, Chemistry, Physics; Art History, Studio Art; Music Theory, Music History, Music Appreciation, Instrumental Music, Chorus; Dramatic Arts; Film Studies; and Dance. Advanced Placement courses are available in all major subject areas. All Upper School students participate in a seminar four times a year.

In 2007, 110 graduates entered such colleges and universities as Barnard, College of William and Mary, Columbia, Cornell, Dartmouth, Davidson, Duke, Georgia Institute of Technology, Hampden-Sydney, James Madison, Morehouse, Princeton, Stanford, United States Naval Academy, Virginia Polytechnic, Wake Forest, Wesleyan, and the Universities of North Carolina (Chapel Hill), Notre Dame, and Virginia.

Norfolk Academy offers special programs that include the Young People's Theatre, summer school, and sports and summer camps. Learning Bridge, a partnership between Norfolk

Academy and the Norfolk public schools, is an academic enrichment program for talented, motivated public school students who want to go to college but have limited educational opportunities. Learning Bridge is affiliated with Breakthrough National, which began at San Francisco University High School in 1978 as Summerbridge.

STUDENT ACTIVITIES. Each division has an elected student council, which, under the direction of a faculty advisor, helps to plan activities. The Honor Council, made up of students and faculty, reviews infractions of the Honor Code.

Students publish a newspaper for each division, a literary magazine, and a yearbook. Extracurricular activities include The Cum Laude Society, Honor Council, Student Council, Fine Arts Council, Key Club, Peer Counselors, Academy Singers, Dance, Orchestra, Theatre, and the Chess, Engineering, language, Science Fiction, Scientific Research, Forensics, Debate, and Cultural, Environmental, and Ethnic Awareness Clubs. Through Habitat for Humanity, the Happy Club, the Reach/Interact Club, Third World Grace, and tutoring programs, students take part in community service.

Norfolk Academy varsity teams compete with those of other schools in the Tidewater Conference of Independent Schools, the Virginia Prep League, and the League of Independent Schools. Girls' teams compete in basketball, crew, sailing, cheerleading, cross-country, field hockey, lacrosse, tennis, track, soccer, softball, swimming, and volleyball. Boys compete in baseball, basketball, crew, sailing, cross-country, football, golf, lacrosse, soccer, swimming, tennis, track, and wrestling. Weight training is encouraged for both boys and girls.

There are frequent theater and music productions by student groups as well as lectures and performances by guest speakers and artists. Traditional events include Field Day, Charter Day, Arts Festival Day, Grandparents' Day, the winter musical, Multicultural Day, Vespers, the Lower School Holiday Pageant, and Homecoming.

ADMISSION AND COSTS. Norfolk Academy seeks to enroll students from a variety of social, economic, religious, ethnic, and racial backgrounds who demonstrate intellectual curiosity and promise of accomplishment. New students are admitted to all grades on the basis of school-administered testing, interviews with school administrators, and previous school transcripts. Campus visits are encouraged. The application fee is $85 for Grade 1 and $35 for Grades 2–12.

In 2007–08, tuition and required fees for Grades 1–6 total $13,675; for Grades 7–12, costs total $15,575. Included in the total are lunches, supplies, athletics, publications, and laboratory fees. Additional costs include bus transportation ($1005) and driver education ($205). Textbooks are provided in the Lower School but are purchased by students in Grades 7–12.

In the current year, Norfolk Academy awarded $1,584,000 in financial aid to 185 students on the basis of need. A tuition payment plan is available. Norfolk Academy subscribes to the School and Student Service for Financial Aid.

Assistant Headmaster for Development: Herbert P. Soles
Assistant Headmaster for Business Operations: Sandra T. Kal
Director of the Upper School: Linda Gorsline
Director of the Middle School: Garrett C. Laws
Director of the Lower School: Michael Silva
Director of Communications: Vincent C. deLalla
Director of Admission: Frances C. Holcombe
Director of College Counseling: Paul M. Feakins
Director of Athletics: Sean P. Wetmore

Norfolk Collegiate School 1948

Grades 6–12: 7336 Granby Street, Norfolk, VA 23505
Tel. 757-480-2885; Admissions 757-480-1495; Fax 757-588-8655
Web Site www.norfolkcollegiate.org
E-mail bwaters@norfolkcollegiate.org
Kindergarten–Grade 5: 5429 Tidewater Drive, Norfolk, VA 23509
Tel. 757-625-0471

A coeducational, college preparatory school serving 918 students in Kindergarten–Grade 12, Norfolk Collegiate emphasizes academic excellence, integrity, individual expression and development, and service to school and community. The curriculum provides a foundation for the liberal arts and sciences, with travel/study opportunities, 18 Advanced Placement courses, the arts, technology, and foreign languages. Students take part in leadership groups, publications, drama, music, interest clubs, and 48 teams in 23 sports. The college counselor works with students and families in the college selection process. Summer

and extended-care programs are available. Tuition: $9150–$11,825. Financial Aid: $1,114,000. Brenda H. Waters is Director of Admissions; William W. King is President and Headmaster. *Southern Association.*

North Cross School 1960

4254 Colonial Avenue, SW, Roanoke, VA 24018
Tel. 540-989-6641; Admission Ext. 330; Fax 540-989-7299
Web Site www.northcross.org; E-mail cfunderburk@northcross.org

A college preparatory day school enrolling 500 students in Junior Kindergarten through Grade 12, North Cross School seeks to develop young men and women of intellect, curiosity, purpose, discipline, and patience. A rigorous academic program and accomplished, committed faculty afford all students unequaled opportunities to challenge, strengthen, and learn about themselves. The innovative curriculum includes broad offerings in the arts and community service; starting in sixth grade, 28 interscholastic teams; and student government and publications, as well as a student-run honor council and disciplinary system. As all of its graduates attend four-year colleges and universities, the school offers 13 Advanced Placement courses along with a full-time college counseling program. Tuition: $6375–$10,925. Need-based financial assistance is available. Carol Funderburke is Director of Admission and Financial Assistance; Paul Stellato (Hamilton College, B.A.; Columbia University, M.F.A.) was appointed Headmaster in 2001.

Notre Dame Academy 1965

35321 Notre Dame Lane, Middleburg, VA 20117
Tel. 540-687-5581; Admissions Ext. 3008; Fax 540-687-3552
Web Site www.notredameva.org; E-mail cstruder@notredameva.org

For more than 40 years, Notre Dame Academy has offered a challenging, coeducational, college preparatory program in the Catholic tradition of education. The program of studies encourages academic excellence. Enrolling 265 students in Grades 9–12, the Academy fosters an appreciation of teamwork with 18 interscholastic sports teams. Notre Dame Academy's visual and performing arts programs are recognized at regional and state levels. Judeo-Christian values and spiritual growth are emphasized through the study of theology and service to the community. Tuition: $17,085. Tuition assistance is available. Mrs. Cathy Struder is Director of Admission; Dr. George Conway is Interim CEO. *Southern Association.*

Oakcrest School 1976

850 Balls Hill Road, McLean, VA 22101
Tel. 703-790-5450; Fax 703-790-5380
Web Site www.oakcrest.org; E-mail admissions@oakcrest.org

Oakcrest School, in partnership with parents, challenges 209 girls in Grades 6–12 to develop their intellect, character, faith, and leadership potential to succeed in college and throughout their lives. As an independent school, Oakcrest weaves together a rich liberal arts curriculum, character development, one-on-one advising, and service to educate the whole person. Middle School students explore new interests and develop friendships through mini courses, field trips, and club activities. Upper School offers AP courses across the curriculum and comprehensive, individualized college counseling. In addition to classes in Catholic theology and Christian philosophy, students are free to attend daily Mass, seek spiritual advice from the School's chaplain, and take time for prayer and reflection in the chapel. Science, computer and language labs, team sports, and the fine arts complete the program. Tuition: $13,400–$14,600. Susan O'Connor is Director of Admissions and Enrollment Management; Holly Hartge is Director of Admissions; Ellen M. Cavanagh is Head of School.

Oak Hill Academy 1878

2635 Oak Hill Road, Mouth of Wilson, VA 24363-3004
Tel. 276-579-2619; Fax 276-579-4722
Web Site www.oak-hill.net; E-mail info@oak-hill.net

OAK HILL ACADEMY in Mouth of Wilson, Virginia, is a boarding and day school enrolling girls and boys in Grades 8 through 12. It offers both general and college preparatory curricula. The school is situated in the rural area of Grayson County among the Blue Ridge Mountains and near the scenic New River and Jefferson National Forest areas, which afford opportunities for recreation and exploration. The village of Mouth of Wilson is about 12 miles from the county seat of Independence. State Highway 16 and United States Highway 58 pass the entrance to the school. Interstate 77 is 37 miles southeast of the Academy, and Interstate 81 passes through Marion, which is 28 miles north of the campus. Marion is served by interstate bus lines, and taxi service to the school is available. The airport in Charlotte, North Carolina, offers the best flight scheduling, and taxi service is available for the 2.5-hour drive from Charlotte to the campus.

The Academy was founded in 1878 as a school for mountain girls and boys by the New River Baptist Association. The school is now supported by, and affiliated with, the Baptist General Association of Virginia. Oak Hill's mission is to provide a safe, secure, nurturing environment and a structured educational program to students in Grades 8–12 who need a change in school, peer, community, or family relationships. Oak Hill's curriculum challenges the brightest students and encourages those who are unmotivated, who are underachieving, or who are experiencing difficulty in their school setting. The Academy emphasizes the importance of student involvement in activities and the need to develop ethical and moral attitudes. One year of Religion is required, and attendance at Sunday service is required of all students.

Oak Hill Academy is a nonprofit organization governed by a Board of Trustees. Funds from the Baptist General Association of Virginia account for approximately 5 percent of the school's annual budget. The Academy is accredited by The Virginia Association of Independent Schools. It is a member of the Southern Association of Independent Schools, The Association of Boarding Schools, and the National Association for Foreign Student Affairs. It is approved by the United States government for the Teaching of Foreign Students.

THE CAMPUS. The Academy is situated on a campus of 400 acres of hills and woodlands with landscaped areas, playing fields, outdoor tennis courts, and riding arena. Administrative offices and the school cafeteria are located in the Vaughan Building at the center of the campus. All academic classes are held in the Louise Towles English Academic Building. This building also contains a library and computer center. A new Science Wing addition to the English Academic Building was dedicated in the spring of 2000. The Turner Building contains the gymnasium, training rooms, student activities center, and athletic director's office. The Rev. J. F. Fletcher Chapel provides an auditorium, music practice rooms, and a conference center. Male students are housed in four dormitories with a total capacity of 110. The Hough Dormitory accommodates 98 girls in two-room suites. Fourteen houses and apartments are provided on campus for faculty and staff members in addition to apartments in the dormitories.

The 50-acre Noonkester Park addition includes a picnic pavilion, lake, walking trails, and shower/bathroom facilities. The plant is owned by the school and is valued at $10,000,000.

THE FACULTY. Dr. Michael D. Groves was appointed President of Oak Hill Academy in July 2002. A native of West Virginia, he graduated from Marshall University (B.A.). Dr. Groves also received Master of Divinity and Doctor of Philosophy degrees from Southern Baptist Theological Seminary in Louisville, Kentucky, and has done additional study at Regent's Park College at the University of Oxford in England. At Oak Hill, he previously held positions as teacher of social studies, director of student affairs, and director of admissions.

The full-time faculty include 11 men and 7 women, 14 of whom live on campus. There are 2 part-time instructors. All faculty members hold baccalaureate or master's degrees from schools including Asbury College, Eastern Kentucky, Emory & Henry College, Fairfield, Gardner-Webb College, Marshall, North Carolina State, Radford University, Southern Baptist Theological Seminary, Virginia Polytechnic Institute, and the Universities of North Carolina (Chapel Hill, Charlotte) and Tennessee.

The Academy provides faculty with a retirement plan, health insurance, and life insurance.

STUDENT BODY. In 2007–08, the school enrolled 131 boarding students, 91 boys and 40 girls. Three were enrolled in Grade 8, 13 in Grade 9, 27 in Grade 10, 46 in Grade 11, and 42 in Grade 12. Students were from 22 states, the District of Columbia, Barbados, Canada, Korea, Senegal, and the United Kingdom.

ACADEMIC PROGRAM. The 2007–08 school year, divided into semesters, began on September 4 and extends to late May, with a vacation at Thanksgiving, a three-week vacation at Christmas and a two-week spring break in March. Classes are held five days a week plus some Saturday mornings. The average class has ten students. On a typical day, students rise at 6:45 A.M. Assembly begins at 7:50 A.M. and classes at 8:05 A.M. The class day concludes at 3:45 P.M. Activities and intramurals are held in the afternoon. Supervised study periods for all students are scheduled Sunday through Friday from 7:30 to 9:00 P.M. Extra-help sessions are also conducted each afternoon, and directed study sessions are held by individual teachers for their students throughout the week. Grades are mailed to parents four times a year.

The school offers a 23-unit diploma and a 26-unit diploma. The 23-unit diploma must include four years of English; one year each of World Geography, World History, Religion, U.S. History, and U.S. Government; two years of Health and Physical Education; three years each of Mathematics and Science; one year each of Fine Arts and a foreign language; and four elective subjects. Science courses include Earth Science, Biology I, Advanced Biology, Chemistry, and Physics. Mathematics courses include Business Math, Algebra 1 parts 1 and 2, Algebra I–II, Geometry, Advanced Algebra/Trigonometry, Advanced Math, and Pre-Calculus. Spanish I–V is offered. Dual-credit classes in College Composition, Pre-Calculus, Applied Calculus, U.S. History, and Keyboarding/Intro to Microcomputer Software are offered as well. In addition, students may elect from courses in World Geography, World History, Creative Writing, Yearbook, Psychology, Business Education, Keyboarding, Computer Applications, Men's Studies, Art, Chorus, and Musical Theater.

The campus is a site for PSAT/SAT and ACT testing.

Seniors in the Class of 2007 were accepted to such colleges and universities as College of Charleston, George Mason, North Carolina State, Ohio State, Pennsylvania State, Virginia Polytechnic Institute, and the Universities of Kentucky and Tennessee.

A five-week academic summer school is conducted from mid-June to late July for students in Grades 8–12 from Oak Hill and other private and public schools. Students may earn one new unit of credit or repeat two failed units of credit.

STUDENT ACTIVITIES. Oak Hill Academy offers extracurricular activities that include the Art Club, Campus Life, Drama Club, Ecology Club, Hiking Club, Horseback Riding Club,

International Students Club, Library Assistants, National Honor Society, *The Hilltopper* (yearbook), Outdoor Club, Ski Club, and Varsity Cheerleaders. Many students also are involved in church-related activities under the direction of a campus minister.

The school competes interscholastically in boys' and girls' basketball, boys' baseball, girls' volleyball, boys' and girls' tennis, track, and coeducational soccer. Intramural sports include basketball, softball, football, tennis, soccer, weightlifting, and running. Backpacking, swimming, and canoeing are also available as club activities.

Films, concerts, plays, and outings to the New River are part of the regular social life of the campus. Special events include the President's Picnic, Harvest Festival, Christmas Concert and Reception, Sweetheart Dance, Spring Formal, and Parents' Days in the fall and spring.

ADMISSION AND COSTS. The Academy selects students "who would most benefit from its special, but limited, program." Applications are accepted at any time for all grades, and students are evaluated on the basis of their previous academic record, references, and an interview. There is an application fee of $50 and a reservation deposit of $2413 due upon acceptance.

In 2007–08, the fee for boarders is $23,455, which includes $640 for allowance, $1500 for the student expense account, and $1515 for tuition insurance. The fee for day students is $6250. Tuition may be paid by the semester, by the month, or by the year. Financial aid is based on individual need, ability, resourcefulness, and character. Approximately $100,000 in scholarship aid is awarded each year.

President: Dr. Michael D. Groves
Director of Academic Affairs: Dr. Chris Mason
Director of Student Affairs: Mr. Henry Crede
Director of Girls Resident Life: Ms. Mary Thomas
Director of Boys Resident Life: Mr. Gary Crede
Director of Admissions: Dr. Michael D. Groves
Director of Development: Mr. Tim Henry
Director of Counseling: Mrs. Joy Groves
Business Manager: Mrs. Rhonda H. Bowen
Director of Athletics: Mr. Stephen A. Smith

The Potomac School 1904

1301 Potomac School Road, P.O. Box 430, McLean, VA 22101
Tel. 703-356-4100; Admission 703-749-6313; Fax 703-356-1764
Web Site www.potomacschool.org

The Potomac School is a day school enrolling 930 boys and girls in Kindergarten–Grade 12. Students come from throughout the Washington, D.C., metropolitan area utilizing the School's extensive bus service. Potomac's challenging college preparatory program encourages academic excellence, a love of learning, individual accomplishment, and diverse voices and ideas. The curriculum, designed to provide a substantial foundation in the liberal arts and sciences, includes elective and Advanced Placement courses in the Upper School. Students enjoy small classes, theatrical productions, weekly assemblies, character education and community service programs, and varsity athletics. Tuition: $22,535–$25,890. Financial Aid: $2,600,000. Charlotte H. Nelsen is Director of Admission; Geoff Jones is Head of School.

Powhatan School 1948

49 Powhatan Lane, Boyce, VA 22620
Tel. 540-837-1009; Admission Ext. 242; Fax 540-837-2558
Web Site www.powhatanschool.org
E-mail rea@powhatans.org

Enrolling 255 boys and girls in Kindergarten–Grade 8, Powhatan School emphasizes the mastery of the skills children need to succeed in challenging secondary programs and beyond. A 20-acre campus provides the setting for the School's liberal arts curriculum. Small classes with an 8:1 student-teacher ratio inspire active learning that maximizes each child's unique strengths and abilities. A strong foundation in language arts, math, and science is emphasized along with superior oral and written communication. Students learn to appreciate the arts and music with hands-on activities and excursions to related events throughout the area. Tuition: $11,975–$14,175. Amy M. Ré is Director of Advancement; John G. Lathrop (University of Pennsylvania, B.A.; Harvard, M.Ed.) is Headmaster.

Richmond Montessori School 1965

499 North Parham Road, Richmond, VA 23229-7217
Tel. 804-741-0040; Fax 804-741-5341
Web Site www.richmont.org; E-mail info@richmont.org

Based on teaching methods developed by Dr. Maria Montessori, Richmond Montessori School is a coeducational day school enrolling 320 students in Preschool–Grade 8. The School nurtures each student's fullest potential and emphasizes independence, self-assurance, self-motivation, and respect for others. Multiage classrooms allow younger students to learn by example, and older students develop leadership skills. Montessori-certified teachers introduce students to language arts, public speaking, physical and life science, mathematics, history, and geography individually or in small groups. Special areas include physical education, art, music, Spanish, and technology. The average student-teacher ratio is 11:1. Cultural feasts, basketball, soccer, gymnastics, yearbook, choir, and service projects enhance the academic curriculum. An after-school program offers activities in arts and crafts, drama, community service, and outdoor education. The 6-acre campus holds nature trails, athletic fields, a science center, classrooms that open to or look upon natural settings, art studios, theater, and a 7000-volume library. Tuition & Fees: $7550–$10,900. Financial aid is available. Amy Humphreys is Director of Admissions; Dr. Martha Mabey (University of Illinois, Ph.D.) is Head of School.

St. Andrew's Episcopal School 1946

45 Main Street, Newport News, VA 23601
Tel. 757-596-6261; Fax 757-596-7218
Web Site www.standrewsschool.com
E-mail standrews@standrewsschool.com

St. Andrew's offers a strong academic education within a Christian environment for approximately 200 children in Pre-Kindergarten–Grade 5. Each day begins with Chapel. The School provides a loving, caring atmosphere with small classes that assure individual attention by a qualified and dedicated faculty. Enrichment is provided by resource classes in art, music, French, physical education, and library as well as computer classes in the School's state-of-the-art lab. Pre-kindergarten and all-day and half-day kindergarten, extended-day, and summer programs are offered. St. Andrew's is fully accredited by the Virginia Association of Independent Schools. Tuition: $3950–$5850. Financial aid is available. Margaret Delk Moore is Head of School.

St. Anne's-Belfield School 1910

2132 Ivy Road, Charlottesville, VA 22903
Tel. 434-296-5106; Fax 434-979-1486
Web Site www.stab.org; E-mail admission@stab.org

St. Anne's-Belfield, a coeducational, college preparatory day school enrolling 838 students in Pre-school–Grade 12, offers five- and seven-day boarding and an ESL program in Grades 9–12. Required courses in fine arts and religion; a weekly, nonsectarian chapel service; and participation in community service and athletics complement the rigorous core curriculum. College counselors work individually with students and their families, and graduates attend select colleges and universities. The Upper School classrooms, library, dining facilities, and dormitories are newly renovated and expanded. Tuition: $17,850–$18,150 Boarding Fee: $12,750–$21,750. Financial aid is available. Jean Craig and Bo Perriello are Directors of Admission; David Lourie is Headmaster.

St. Catherine's School 1890

6001 Grove Avenue, Richmond, VA 23226
Tel. 804-288-2804; Admissions [Toll-free] 800-648-4982
Fax 804-285-8169
Web Site www.st.catherines.org; E-mail admissions@st.catherines.org

An Episcopal, diocesan day school for girls, St. Catherine's enrolls 862 college-bound students in Junior Kindergarten–Grade 12. Virginia Randolph Ellett, a pioneer in the education of women, founded the School to prepare girls for higher education and for leadership roles in life. The rigorous liberal arts curriculum is designed to develop each student intellectually, emotionally, physically, and spiritually. In the Upper School, qualified scholars may choose from 30 honors and 20 AP courses in all disciplines. Between the second and third trimesters, St. Catherine's offers a distinctive two-week program called Minimester. Students may choose a combination of interdisciplinary, experiential, or intensive courses; participate in a study or community service trip; or plan and execute an independent project. Coordination with St. Christopher's School, a boys' school three blocks away, presents the opportunity for coeducation and expands the course offerings. One hundred percent of St. Catherine's graduates are accepted to four-year colleges and universities. A coed summer session is available. Tuition: $13,050–$17,690. Kelly Jones Wilbanks is Director of Admission; Laura J. Erickson is Head of School. *Southern Association.*

St. Christopher's School 1911

711 St. Christopher's Road, Richmond, VA 23226
Tel. 804-282-3185; Fax 804-673-6632
Web Site www.stchristophers.com; E-mail admissions@stcva.org

St. Christopher's is an Episcopal day school enrolling 961 boys in Junior Kindergarten–Grade 12. The School offers a college preparatory curriculum, with a wide choice of electives, in an atmosphere stressing Christian ideals. Small classes foster close student/teacher relationships, with emphasis on bringing out the best in each boy. There is a program of coordinate education with St. Catherine's School. The athletic program features 16 varsity sports. Academic, recreational, and athletic camps are offered in the summer. Tuition: $13,925–$17,925. Financial Aid: $2,000,000. Anne D. Booker is Director of Admission; Charles M. Stillwell (Princeton, A.B. 1985; Brown, M.A. 1990) is Headmaster. *Southern Association.*

St. Margaret's School 1921

444 Water Lane, Tappahannock, VA 22560
Tel. 804-443-3357; Fax 804-443-6781
Web Site www.sms.org; E-mail admit@sms.org

Located on the banks of the Rappahannock River, St. Margaret's School has a rich tradition of educating young women for life. The college preparatory curriculum and small classes provide girls with an environment that nurtures intellectual curiosity. Experiential learning through the Minimester program, independent study projects, and international exchanges highlight St. Margaret's commitment to providing a diverse curriculum that empowers young women to succeed in an ever-changing society. The cocurricular program offers nearly 30 interscholastic sports, clubs, and after-school activities. St. Margaret's welcomes 158 students of diverse backgrounds from 18 states and 13 countries in Grades 8 through 12. Boarding Tuition: $36,000; Day Tuition: $14,000. Financial aid is available. Kimberly A. McDowell is Director of Admission; Margaret R. Broad is Head of School.

Saint Patrick Catholic School 2005

1000 Bolling Avenue, Norfolk, VA 23508-0246
Tel. 757-440-5500; Fax 757-440-5200
Web Site www.stpcs.org; E-mail info@stpcs.org

Saint Patrick Catholic School, set on a state-of-the-art 16.5-acre campus in Norfolk's historic Larchmont neighborhood, offers students from Pre-Kindergarten to Grade 8 an "exceptional education based on spiritual and character formation, leadership training, academic preparation, physical wellness, and service learning." Enrollment is limited to 400 students, which affords faculty and staff the time and resources to concentrate fully on each child. Saint Patrick Catholic School is open to youngsters from all faith traditions, Catholic and non-Catholic alike, and spiritual instruction is designed to help the student as well as the family as they continue along their own faith journey. An exciting feature in the academic program at Saint Patrick is the inclusion of resources to extend and enrich the curriculum at each grade level recognizing that students learn differently, learn at different paces, have different interests, and may need different resources, clubs, leadership groups, team sports, community outreach, and fine arts are among the after-school opportunities. Tuition: $3351–$6297. Stephanie DeSimone is Admissions Associate; Stephen Hammond is Principal.

St. Stephen's and St. Agnes School 1924

Upper School: 1000 St. Stephen's Road, Alexandria, VA 22304
Tel. 703-751-2700; Admissions 703-212-2706
Web Site www.sssas.org; E-mail info@sssas.org
Middle School: 4401 West Braddock Road, Alexandria, VA 22304
Tel. 703-751-2700; Admissions 703-212-2706
Lower School: 400 Fontaine Street, Alexandria, VA 22302
Tel. 703-751-2700; Admissions 703-212-2705

This college preparatory, Episcopal day school enrolls 1144 students in Junior Kindergarten–Grade 12. It seeks to instill a passion for learning, enthusiasm for athletics and the arts, and commitment to service. An honor code, chapel, and service learning are central to the program. Providing a global perspective enables the School to prepare students for a complex and changing world. Foreign language begins in Junior Kindergarten. The curriculum includes 24 Advanced Placement courses and varied electives. Student Government, sports, technology, drama, publications, music, and interest and multicultural clubs are among the extracurriculars. Single-gender math and science classes are unique to the Middle School. A summer program, transportation, and extended day are also provided. Tuition: $19,430–$24,810. Financial Aid: $3,249,700. Diane Dunning is Director of Admission; Joan G. Ogilvy Holden (Tufts, B.A.; Harvard, M.Ed.) is Head of School.

The Steward School 1972

11600 Gayton Road, Richmond, VA 23238
Tel. 804-740-3394; Admission 804-565-2315; Fax 804-740-1464
Web Site www.stewardschool.org
E-mail scott.moncure@stewardschool.org

The Steward School, serving 600 boys and girls in Kindergarten to Grade 12, offers a college preparatory curriculum designed to enable day students of varying abilities to reach their educational goals. Small classes, individual attention, extracurricular opportunities, and an optional in-school/one-on-one tutoring program are featured. Student activities include athletics, fine arts, community service, outdoor trips, and interest clubs. Extended care, summer sessions, and innovative minimesters with internships are offered. Tuition: $14,900–$16,670. Financial aid is available. A. Scott Moncure is Director of Admission; Kenneth H. Seward (Middlebury College, B.A.; Case Western Reserve University, M.A.) is Headmaster.

Sullins Academy 1966

22218 Sullins Academy Drive, Bristol, VA 24202
Tel. 276-669-4101; Admissions Ext. 224; Fax 276-669-4294
Web Site www.sullinsacademy.org
E-mail mmjustis@sullinsacademy.org

Founded in 1966, Sullins Academy is a fully accredited, independent, coeducational day school offering an accelerated program for 200 students in Pre-School through Grade 8. Academic excellence is created with a core curriculum of language arts, mathematics, social studies, foreign language, and computer instruction. Art, music, physical education, reading readiness, clubs, field trips, and athletics further support the nurturing of the whole child. Located on a beautiful 32-acre campus in southwest Virginia, Sullins Academy is committed to the development of minds and character. Tuition: $2940–$6490. Financial aid is available. Mary Margaret Justis is Director of Admissions; Ramona Harr is Head of School.

Trinity Episcopal School 1972

3850 Pittaway Road, Richmond, VA 23235
Tel. 804-272-5864; Fax 804-272-4652
Web Site www.trinityes.org; E-mail emilym@trinityes.org

A coeducational, college preparatory day school enrolling 445 students in Grades 8–12, Trinity Episcopal offers a strong academic program and a caring environment dedicated to the personal growth of each student. The International Baccalaureate program is offered in Grades 11–12. Advanced Placement courses are available in 13 disciplines, and electives include Computer Programming, American Foreign Policy, Creative Writing, Organic Chemistry, Computer Modeling, Art, Music, and Drama. Tuition: $14,880. Financial Aid: $750,000. Emily H. McLeod is Admissions Director; Thomas G. Aycock (Barton College, B.S.; University of North Carolina, M.A., Ph.D.) was appointed Headmaster in 1990.

Westminster School 1962

3819 Gallows Road, Annandale, VA 22003
Tel. 703-256-3620
Web Site www.westminsterschool.com
E-mail admissions@westminsterschool.com

Westminster School is a coeducational day school enrolling approximately 300 students of average to above-average ability in Kindergarten–Grade 8. Respect, integrity, responsibility, consideration for others, and perseverance are emphasized. All students take classes in reality-based mathematics, hands-on and laboratory science, classic literature, Western civilization, structure of societies and governments, different cultures, and the arts. Vocabulary, spelling, grammar, problem-solving, research methods, and observation and communication skills are studied. French begins in Kindergarten, and Latin starts in Grade 7. Eighth graders enjoy enrichment classes on creative writing, pop culture, and public speaking. Each course enrolls a maximum of 18 students. Community service, theatrical performances, orchestra, chorus, and art exhibitions enhance the academic curriculum. Athletic opportunities include softball, basketball, soccer, track, cross-country, and intramurals. The campus holds a library, athletic fields, theater, art studios, and computer labs. Tuition: $15,500. Financial aid is available. Nancy Schuler is Admissions Director; Ellis Glover is Headmaster.

WASHINGTON

The Bush School 1924

3400 East Harrison Street, Seattle, WA 98112
Tel. 206-322-7978; Admissions 206-326-7735; Fax 206-860-3876
Web Site www.bush.edu; E-mail elizabeth.atcheson@bush.edu

The Bush School enrolls 560 students in Kindergarten–Grade 12 on a 6-acre campus convenient to downtown Seattle and the Eastside. With a class size average of 16, the School provides a challenging, progressive educational program that balances rigor with close teacher relationships and experiential education opportunities. Programs emphasize high academic standards and the development of the whole child within a "culture of kindness" that values diversity; 24 percent are students of color and 15 percent receive financial aid. A full-time college counselor, an extended day program, and a wilderness/outdoor education program complement Bush's mission. Tuition: $16,180–$22,200. Elizabeth Atcheson is Director of Admissions and Financial Aid; Frank Magusin is Head of School. *Pacific Northwest Association.*

Charles Wright Academy 1957

7723 Chambers Creek Road West, Tacoma, WA 98467-2099
Tel. 253-620-8300; Admissions 253-620-8373; Fax 253-620-8431
Web Site www.charleswright.org
E-mail dyoung@mail.charleswright.org

A nonprofit, coeducational, college preparatory day school set on a 90-acre, wooded campus, Charles Wright Academy enrolls 730 students in Pre-Kindergarten–Grade 12. Advanced Placement, computer science, drama, art and music, outdoor education, and athletics are integral to the program. Each student's unique academic and artistic abilities, confidence, and sense of values are developed and nurtured by a carefully selected faculty within a community that respects and cares for the well-being of each member. Honesty, integrity, courage, and humor are essential to the school's individual and collective strength and growth. Tuition: $13,500–$18,580. Financial aid is available. Dori Young is Director of Enrollment Management; Robert Camner (Oberlin, B.A.; Ohio State, M.S.) is Headmaster. *Pacific Northwest Association.*

Epiphany School 1958

3710 East Howell Street, Seattle, WA 98122
Tel. 206-323-9011; Admissions 206-720-7663; Fax 206-324-2127
Web Site www.epiphanyschool.org; E-mail annes@epiphanyschool.org

Epiphany School is an independent, nonsectarian day school enrolling 195 boys and girls in Pre-School–Grade 5. It seeks to help students achieve academic excellence through a traditional, structured approach to learning with strong emphasis on fundamentals. Music, art, French, physical education, drama, library skills, science, and computers enrich the basic curriculum. The School also offers an intensive tutoring program for its students with learning disabilities. Tuition: $11,800–$14,900. Financial Aid: $225,000. Anne Sarewitz is Director of Admissions; George O. Edwards is Head of School. *Northwest Association.*

St. Thomas School 1951

P.O. Box 124, Medina, WA 98039
Tel. 425-454-5880; Fax 425-454-1921
Web Site www.stthomasschool.org
E-mail admissions@stthomasschool.org

St. Thomas School enrolls 198 boys and girls as day students in Preschool through Grade 6. St. Thomas School develops students' full potential in a challenging academic environment that builds a foundation of basic skills and integrates technology, language arts, social studies, science, mathematics, foreign language, fine arts, and physical education. Children develop proficient writing and speaking abilities and acquire solid technological skills. The daily community meeting in Chapel emphasizes character development. Through the curriculum, through school climate, and through service, St. Thomas students are encouraged to apply lessons from the classroom to the world around them. Tuition: $3615–$14,440. Financial aid is available. Lyn-Felice Calvin is Director of Admissions; Dr. Kirk Wheeler is Head of School. *Pacific Northwest Association.*

Seattle Academy 1983

1201 East Union Street, Seattle, WA 98122
Tel. 206-323-6600; Admissions 206-324-7227; Fax 206-676-6881
Web Site www.seattleacademy.org; E-mail jrupp@seattleacademy.org

Seattle Academy offers a demanding college preparatory program that incorporates academics with the arts, athletics, outdoor education, and community service. Enrolling 560 day boys and girls in Grades 6–12, the school provides a supportive environment that enhances the learning experience through hands-on activities and extensive use of classroom technology and Seattle's urban resources. The curriculum includes rigorous academic courses and the fine and performing arts, all of which prepare graduates to attend some of the country's most selective colleges, universities, conservatories, and art schools. Student government, sports, and travel to such locales as Alaska, Africa, Europe, and Latin America enrich the program. Tuition: $21,054–$22,116. Extras: $750. Financial aid is available. Jim Rupp is Director of Admission; Jean Marie Orvis (University of Washington, B.A., M.B.A.) is Founding Head of School.

Seattle Country Day School 1963

2619 Fourth Avenue North, Seattle, WA 98109
Tel. 206-284-6220; Admissions 206-691-2625; Fax 206-283-4251
Web Site www.seattlecountryday.org
E-mail kathymccann@seattlecountryday.org

Seattle Country Day School is an independent K–8 school serving 328 boys and girls of high intellectual and creative promise in the heart of Seattle. SCDS welcomes students of all races, religions, economic backgrounds, and ethnic origins. Experienced teachers, small class sizes, and an inquiry-based teaching model promote academic excellence and enthusiasm for learning. While the curriculum accentuates mathematics, science, and technology, every student's experience includes dynamic humanities, music, art, foreign language, and physical education programs. The learning environment is simultaneously challenging and developmentally age-appropriate. Students enjoy strong after-school and special programs including extended-day, athletics, alpine skiing, ice skating, clubs, and instrumental music classes. Tuition: $16,404–$19,182. Financial aid is available. Kathy McCann is Director of Admissions; Michael G. Murphy is Head of School. *Pacific Northwest Association.*

Seattle Waldorf School 1980

Main Campus: 2728 NE 100th Street, Seattle, WA 98125
Tel. 206-524-5320
Kinderhaus Kindergarten: 4919 Woodlawn Avenue North, Seattle, WA 98103
High School: 160 John Street, Seattle, WA 98109
Web Site www.seattlewaldorf.org
E-mail admissionsoffice@seattlewaldorf.org

Seattle Waldorf School serves 275 day students in Parent-Tot, Preschool/Kindergarten, and Grades 1–12. Through a core classical academic curriculum combined with fully integrated fine arts, world languages, movement, handwork, music, and gardening, Waldorf students are nurtured through the full development of their cognitive, emotional, social, intellectual, and spiritual capacities. They are guided by a classroom teacher who ideally stays with them through Grades 1–8 and develops with students and families a relationship of collaboration, understanding, and mutual trust. Specialist teachers enhance the classroom experience, bringing students genuine artistic and practical experience in alignment with the subject taught by the class teacher. The broad curriculum is structured to respond to and enhance the developmental phases of childhood. Based on the philosophy of Rudolf Steiner, Waldorf education views these developmental stages as basic to healthy learning: The First 7 Years–Imitation and warmth; The Second 7 Years–Imagination; the Third 7 Years–Truth, Discrimination, and Judgment. Tuition: $3450–$15,400. Financial aid is available. Meg Petty is Admissions Director; Geraldine Kline is Executive Director.

University Child Development School 1976

5062 9th Avenue, NE, Seattle, WA 98105
Tel. 206-547-8237; Fax 206-547-3615
Web Site www.ucds.org; E-mail admission@ucds.org

University Child Development School is centered on the lives of children and dedicated to the development of their intellect and character. Teaching is individualized and responsive to the talents of each student, and the curriculum is rigorous and integrates the concepts and skills embedded within the major disciplines. The School reflects and encourages the process of joyful discovery that is central to meaningful and responsible learning. University Child Development School enrolls 300 children in Preschool through Grade 5. Summer camp and before- and after-school care are available. Tuition: $10,977–$16,888. Financial Aid: $470,000. David Garrick is Director of Admission; Paula Smith is Head of School. *Pacific Northwest Association.*

University Prep 1976

8000 25th Avenue, NE, Seattle, WA 98115
Tel. 206-525-2714; Admission 206-523-6407; Fax 206-525-5320
Web Site www.universityprep.org
E-mail admission@universityprep.org

University Prep, a day school with more than 460 students in Grades 6–12, is committed to developing each student's potential to become an intellectually courageous, socially responsible citizen of the world. The curriculum is designed to inspire students' natural curiosity and to instill within them the desire for lifelong learning. Small classes, exceptional teachers, and innovative course work challenge students to develop creativity and critical thinking skills. University Prep students learn to solve problems and make mature decisions as well as learn to value diversity and give back to their community. Tuition: $21,045–$22,368. Financial Aid: $1,467,035. Kathy O'Neal is Director of Admission & Advancement; Erica L. Hamlin (Smith, B.A.; Wesleyan University, M.A.L.S.) is Head of School. *Northwest Association.*

WEST VIRGINIA

The Linsly School 1814

60 Knox Lane, Wheeling, WV 26003-6489
Tel. 304-233-3260; Admission 304-233-1436; Fax 304-234-4614
Web Site www.linsly.org; E-mail admit@linsly.org

The Linsly School, a coeducational, college preparatory boarding and day school, provides a structured, disciplined program in a community environment that challenges young people to achieve their greatest potential. Enrolling 444 students in Grades 5–12, with 99 boarders in Grade 7 upward, Linsly emphasizes the liberal arts and sciences, enriched by opportunities for overseas travel/study and a unique outdoor education program, The Linsly Outdoor Center. One hundred percent of graduates attend college. Campus activities include interest groups, community service, honor societies, musical productions, and interscholastic sports. Boarding Tuition: $23,900; Day Tuition: $11,740. Financial aid is available. Chad Barnett is Director of Admissions; Reno F. DiOrio is Headmaster. *North Central Association.*

WISCONSIN

Brookfield Academy 1962

3460 North Brookfield Road, Brookfield, WI 53045
Tel. 262-783-3200; Fax 262-783-3213
Web Site www.brookfieldacademy.org
E-mail admissions@brookfieldacademy.org

Founded in 1962 to provide a strong liberal arts education within a nurturing atmosphere, Brookfield Academy enrolls 765 day students in Pre-Kindergarten to Grade 12. The school's Five Star system emphasizes the moral principles of a free society, and patriotism and ethics are promoted at all levels. The college preparatory curriculum also includes classics, computers, music, art, and Advanced Placement opportunities. Upper School students experience a week of outdoor recreation and sports at the start of each academic year. Activities include yearbook, drama, and community service. Tuition: $7100–$13,600. Financial aid is available. Sharon Koenings is Director of Admissions; Robert Solsrud is Head of School.

Madison Country Day School 1997

5606 River Road, Waunakee, WI 53597
Tel. 608-850-6000; Admissions 608-850-6375; Fax 608-850-6006
Web Site www.madisoncountryday.org
E-mail jklug@madisoncountryday.org

Madison Country Day School offers an international liberal arts education to 270 boys and girls in Pre-Kindergarten through Grade 12. Set on a 75-acre lakeside campus, the School develops independent, motivated learners capable of meeting the challenges of higher education and citizenship in the 21st century. At the heart of the School's success is the delivery of academic excellence in an inspiring environment. The curriculum, which emphasizes academic skills in English, math, science, social studies, and foreign language, is heavily enriched by the arts. Students may take part in school publications, sports, and a variety of musical and theatrical experiences. At Lower, Middle, and Upper School levels, Madison Country Day's seamless blend of high academic standards in a supportive and nurturing environment enables students to meet high parental expectations. Tuition: $6500–$12,200. Jen Klug is Director of Admissions; Luke W. Felker is Head of School.

The Prairie School 1965

4050 Lighthouse Drive, Racine, WI 53402
Tel. 262-260-3845; Fax 262-260-3790
Web Site www.prairieschool.com

The Prairie School, serving 715 students in Early School through Grade 12, provides a progressive curriculum combining challenging academics, a comprehensive fine and creative arts program, and an exciting athletic program. Offerings include television/film production, and glass-blowing. The nontraditional campus, designed by Taliesin Associated Architects, houses the Student Research Center with computer labs and more than 400 computers, and the Johnson Athletic Center. Summer school and before- and after-school care are available. Tuition: $9500–$12,100. Molly Lofquist is Director of Admissions; Wm. Mark H. Murphy (Norwich, B.A.; State University of New York, M.A.) is Headmaster.

University Lake School 1956

4024 Nagawicka Road, Hartland, WI 53029
Tel. 262-367-6011; Admission Ext. 1455; Fax 262-367-3146
Web Site www.universitylake.org
E-mail dsmith@universitylake.org

University Lake School, a coeducational, college preparatory day school enrolling 324 students in three-year-old Pre-Kindergarten–Grade 12, is set on a 180-acre wooded campus 30 miles west of Milwaukee in the city of Delafield. The school features challenging academics in small class sizes averaging 14 students. Students participate in fine arts, athletics, and leadership-building classes. The student-teacher/advisor ratio is 9:1. University Lake offers a summer program of enrichment and recreation. Tuition: $7100–$13,365. Tuition assistance and scholarships are available. Debra H. Smith is Director of Admissions; Bradley F. Ashley is Head of School.

University School of Milwaukee 1851

2100 West Fairy Chasm Road, Milwaukee, WI 53217
Tel. 414-352-6000; Admission 414-540-3320; Fax 414-352-8076
Web Site www.usmk12.org; E-mail admissions@usmk12.org

University School of Milwaukee, an independent, college preparatory day school enrolling 1062 students in Prekindergarten (age 3) through Grade 12, is divided into three academic divisions: Lower, Middle, and Upper School. Class sizes are small, allowing teachers to know each student well and provide individual attention. A faculty-to-student ratio of 1:9 and an average class size of 15 promote an atmosphere that supports the academic, artistic, and athletic achievements of each student. The School offers preparation in a variety of AP courses, and the college guidance program assists students and families in finding the college that best matches a student's talents and interest. The 120-acre campus includes playing fields, an indoor ice arena, a new fitness center and state-of-the-art Science Center, a 395-seat theater, and facilities for band, orchestra, and chorus. Tuition: $4770–$17,802. Financial Aid. $2,200,000. Kathleen Friedman is Director of Admissions; Ward J. Ghory, Ed.D., is Head of School.

OTHER COUNTRIES AND UNITED STATES TERRITORIES

BERMUDA

The Bermuda High School for Girls 1894

19 Richmond Road, Pembroke HM 08, Bermuda
Tel. 441-295-6153; Fax 441-278-3017
Web Site www.bhs.bm; E-mail info@bhs.bm

Set on an 8-acre campus, The Bermuda High School for Girls enrolls 720 day students, predominantly young women, in Years 1–13. The School's rigorous college preparatory program is specially designed to enable young women to reach their potential in a safe, nurturing environment in which each is free to question, explore, and participate fully in the educational process. The island's first International Baccalaureate school, Bermuda High welcomes students from diverse racial, ethnic, religious, and economic backgrounds, including boys in Years 11–12 of the IB program. The core curriculum centers on English, math, sciences, world languages, and social studies. The arts, music, drama, and information technology complete the program. Students take part in school government, community service, publications, vocal and instrumental ensembles, dramatic productions, and a rigorous interscholastic sports program. Tuition: $14,500–$16,000. Financial aid, bursaries, and competitive scholarships are available. Tina Harris is Head of Primary Admissions; Levyette Robinson is Head of Secondary Admissions; Linda Parker is Head of School.

Saltus Grammar School 1888

P.O. Box HM-2224, HMJX Hamilton, Bermuda
Tel. 441-292-6177; Fax 441-295-4977
Web Site www.saltus.bm; E-mail admissions@saltus.bm

This coeducational school, established with funds left by Samuel Saltus, enrolls 1080 day students in Grades 1–12. Stressing "well-tried, traditional approaches" to education in a "lively and caring atmosphere," the School's goal is to prepare students mentally, spiritually, and physically to meet the demands of the modern world. A college preparatory year working toward Advanced Placement Exams is available. Activities include sports, drama, photography, music, and debate. A summer program is offered. Tuition: $15,286. Financial Aid: $350,000. Deputy Headmaster Malcolm Durrant (Oxford University, M.A., P.G.C.E.) coordinates admissions; N.J.G. Kermode (B.A. [Hons.], M.A., P.G.C.E.) was appointed Headmaster in 1999.

CANADA

Collingwood School 1984

70 Morven Drive, West Vancouver, BC V7S 1B2, Canada
Tel. 604-925-3331; Admissions 604-925-3016; Fax 604-925-3862
Web Site www.collingwood.org
E-mail judy.wilson-neil@collingwood.org

Collingwood, a coeducational, university preparatory day school set on two campuses, enrolls more than 1200 students in Junior Kindergarten–Grade 12. It has built a reputation as a dynamic and progressive educational environment. Collingwood's four-stranded approach to education emphasizes academics, arts, athletics, and service to provide the foundation for developing the whole child. The broad academic curriculum is enhanced with honors and AP courses across all subject areas. Among the School's innovative programs are Explore, a challenging outdoor educational and leadership course, and Key, a specialized program for children with learning disabilities. Collingwood is a member of The Round Square Conference, a worldwide association of schools whose students share a com

mitment, beyond academic excellence, to personal development and responsibility through service, challenge, adventure, and international understanding. In 2006, 48 percent of the 18th graduating class was offered more than $780,000 in scholarships to universities and colleges across Canada and the U.S. Tuition: $4595–$20,325 (CAD). Judy Wilson-Neil is Director of Admissions; Rodger Wright, M.Ed., is Headmaster.

The Country Day School 1972

13415 Dufferin Street, King, ON L7B 1K5, Canada
Tel. 905-833-1220; Fax 905-833-1664
Web Site www.cds.on.ca; E-mail admissions@cds.on.ca

Parents founded The Country Day School to provide a stimulating learning environment in which students achieve intellectual and personal potential. Following a challenging university preparatory curriculum, 725 boys and girls from Junior Kindergarten to Grade 12 are equipped for productive citizenship in the global community. Core courses are enriched by character development, exposure to the visual and performing arts, technology, and physical education. Activities include drama, publications, band, choir, sports, and the Duke of Edinburgh's Award. Graduates attend universities around the world. A recent expansion includes a performing arts center and a new gymnasium. Tuition: (Cdn.) $10,820–$19,670. Christopher White is Director of Admission; Paul C. Duckett is Headmaster.

Crescent School 1913

2365 Bayview Avenue, Toronto, ON Canada M2L 1A2
Tel. 416-449-2556; Admissions Ext. 238; Fax 416-449-7950
Web Site www.crescentschool.org; E-mail info@crescentschool.org

With 660 day students in Lower, Middle, and Upper School divisions (Grades 3–12), Crescent School aims to prepare motivated, self-directed young men for academic and personal success. The traditional curriculum includes computer technology, fine arts, music, and drama, with elective courses, Advanced Placement opportunities, and enrichment classes. Boys engage in a full range of cocurricular activities. Faculty and staff alike model Crescent's core values of respect, responsibility, compassion, and honesty as the School fosters the development of its graduates to men of character from boys of promise. Tuition: $21,685 (Cdn.). David Budden is Director of Admissions; Geoff Roberts is Headmaster.

Fraser Academy 1982

2294 West 10th Avenue, Vancouver, BC V6K 2H8, Canada
Tel. 604-736-5575; Fax 604-736-5578
Web Site www.fraser-academy.bc.ca; E-mail info@fraser-academy.bc.ca

Using a multisensory approach, Fraser Academy educates children with dyslexia and other language-processing challenges. Teachers teach in a multisensory way, and each student receives a block of Orton-Gillingham tutoring each day. With a school population of just over 200 students and no more than 10 students per academic class, Fraser Academy is centrally located in Vancouver's residential Kitsilano neighborhood. Facilities include computer labs, a library resource center, music and art studios, a woodwork shop, and a courtyard with a basketball court and play area. In addition, students have access to adjacent playing fields. The school is accessible by car and bus from throughout the Lower Mainland. Tuition: $20,750–$21,010 (Cdn.). Dr. Stephan Grasmuck is Head of School.

Glenlyon Norfolk School 1912

801 Bank Street, Victoria, BC V8S 4A8, Canada
Tel. 250-370-6800; Admissions 250-370-6801; Fax 250-370-6811
Web Site www.glenlyonnorfolk.bc.ca
E-mail admissions@glenlyonnorfolk.bc.ca

A day school for 700 students in JK–Grade 12, Glenlyon Norfolk is one of four schools in Canada accredited to offer all three of the International Baccalaureate (IB) programs: Primary Years, Middle Years, and Diploma. Facilitating critical thinking and breadth of study, the IB provides an inquiry-based, engaging, and demanding approach to learning. As a member school of the Round Square, Glenlyon Norfolk is committed to internationalism, democracy, environmental stewardship, outdoor adventure, leadership, and service. Participation in the fine arts, athletics, public speaking, and debating also enrich learning. The GNS motto, "Do your best through truth and courage," reflects the School's core values. Tuition: $9700–$12,575. Simon Bruce-Lockhart is Head of School; Deirdre Chettleburgh is Director of Admissions.

Halifax Grammar School 1958

945 Tower Road, Halifax, NS B3H 2Y2, Canada
Tel. 902-422-6497; Admissions 902-431-8550; Fax 902-423-9315
Web Site www.hgs.ns.ca; E-mail admissions@hgs.ns.ca

The Halifax Grammar School strives to educate "thoughtful, independent students prepared to take on the world." Located near Saint Mary's University, HGS is a leading IB World School where all graduating students study the full International Baccalaureate Program. Founded in 1958, this coeducational day school offers a challenging, balanced curriculum with enriched academics, competitive athletics, and vibrant arts programs. Since 2000, the School has expanded to two campuses, enrolling 540 students from Kindergarten to Grade 12. Students compete at the highest levels in soccer, basketball, and track and field and regularly win math league and debating honors. Scholarships and bursaries are available to qualified students. Tuition: $8805–$10,664. Ms. Doris Robbins is Admissions Officer; Dr. Paul W. Bennett is Headmaster.

Havergal College 1894

1451 Avenue Road, Toronto, ON M5N 2H9, Canada
Tel. 416-483-3519; Admissions 416-482-4724; Fax 416-483-6796
Web Site www.havergal.on.ca; E-mail admissions@havergal.on.ca

An independent university preparatory school in the Anglican tradition, Havergal College enrolls 910 girls in Junior Kindergarten–Grade 12, including 50 international boarders in Grade 9 upward. The school's academic and cocurricular programs are founded on the values of excellence, leadership, and diversity. Havergal's mission is to develop young women who are concerned, altruistic, and capable of effecting positive change in the world. The 22-acre campus offers access to the culture, art, and historic attractions of Toronto. Dedicated teachers and an enriched curriculum nurture a love of learning in an environment that is both supportive and caring. The academic program emphasizes the arts, sciences, and humanities, featuring traditional course work and the latest technology. Smartboards and laptops are utilized in many classroom and laboratory settings. Girls participate in a wide range of activities such as leadership groups, publications, orchestras, bands, vocal ensembles, special-interest clubs, and with 40 athletic teams, a comprehensive sports program. Boarding Tuition: $40,590 (Cdn.); Day Tuition: $20,295. Financial aid is available. Maggie Houston-White is Director of Admission; Dr. Susan J. Ditchburn is Principal.

The Mabin School 1980

50 Poplar Plains Road, Toronto, ON M4V 2M8, Canada
Tel. 416-964-9594; Admissions Ext. 251; Fax 416-964-3643
Web Site www.mabin.com; E-mail admissions@mabin.com

Enrolling 150 boys and girls as day students in Junior Kindergarten–Grade 6, The Mabin School is an educational leader committed to developing confident and independent learners through an innovative curriculum. The rich, hands-on program is organized around the learning needs of the students and set in an intimate and vibrant environment where children love to come because they feel known, respected, and effective. Teachers provide a strong academic foundation by promoting classroom themes that are of intrinsic interest to the students. Children are encouraged to inquire, investigate, develop theories, and build knowledge. French, music, art, science, computer technology, and physical education are taught by specialists and round out the program. A 6:1 student-faculty ratio and small class sizes enable teachers to know and understand each child. Students are engaged daily in leadership opportunities and the cultivation of conflict resolution skills, resulting in a thriving school and family community where respect for oneself and others is valued. Tuition: $18,270 (Cdn.). Monica Barden is Admissions Coordinator; Lynn Seligman is Principal.

The Priory School 1947

3120 The Boulevard, Montreal, QC H3Y 1R9, Canada
Tel. 514-935-5966; Admissions Ext. 24; Fax 514-935-1428
Web Site www.priory.qc.ca; E-mail admissions@priory.qc.ca

Founded on Catholic traditions, The Priory is an elementary day school that welcomes boys and girls of all faiths. An English school teaching French as a second language, with a well-rounded curriculum that includes specialists in art, music, physical education, and computers, The Priory provides a nurturing environment that encourages intelligent initiative, self-discipline, and creativity. An individualized reading program and small instructional groups promote self-esteem and success in all academic programs. The campus offers a renovated library, state-of-the-art computer room, multipurpose gym, a well-equipped art room, and a playground that includes an Astroturf soccer pitch, asphalt basketball court, and skating rink. Activities include interscholastic soccer and basketball, long-distance running, and an intramural sports program. An after-school program is also available. Because the School receives no government assistance, The Priory is able to accept students who may not otherwise be eligible for English education in Quebec. Tuition: (Cdn.) $10,110–$11,190 (including hot meals). Debra Merritt is Admissions Officer; Deborah Heuff is Principal.

Rosseau Lake College 1967

1967 Bright Street, Rosseau, ON, Canada P0C 1J0
Tel. 705-732-4351; Fax 705-732-6319
Web Site www. rosseaulakecollege.com; E-mail admissions@rlc.on.ca

Set on a beautiful campus in the Muskoka Lakes region, Rosseau Lake College enrolls 70 boarders and 70 day students in Grades 7 through 12. The school's philosophy and program are designed to enable each student to realize his or her "best of self" in all areas of endeavor. The university preparatory curriculum balances the arts, sciences, and humanities in a challenging program designed to equip graduates for successful postsecondary study at four-year institutions worldwide. English as a Second Language enables international students to mainstream into regular classroom learning while adapting to Canadian life and culture. Exciting outdoor education activities foster respect and concern for the environment, while travel abroad opportunities foster a global perspective and understanding. Extracurriculars focus on leadership, music, drama, community outreach, publications, and varsity and intramural athletics, including rugby, sailing, skiing, and snowboarding. Outtrips involve students and faculty in canoeing, kayaking, mountain biking, and other rugged pursuits. A four-week summer academic program is available. Boarding Tuition: $37,350–$40,050; Day Tuition: $16,425. Kara Ewart is Admissions Assistant; Joseph F. Seagram is Headmaster.

St. Andrew's College 1899

15800 Yonge Street, Aurora, ON L4G 3H7, Canada
Tel. 905-727-3178; Admission Ext. 303; [Toll-free] 877-378-1899
Fax 905-727-9032
Web Site www.sac.on.ca; E-mail admission@sac.on.ca

St. Andrew's, one of Canada's oldest and largest all-boys school for Grades 6–12, enrolls 550 students divided evenly between boarding and day. The school seeks well-rounded students who display intellectual curiosity, want to take part in its athletics programs, and have the ability to contribute to the arts, drama, or music curriculum. Activity-based learning offers an environment that challenges boys with an expanding AP program. The wireless laptop program allows students to take advantage of on-line daybooks, daily schedules, assignment calendars, and related websites. In fall 2006, St. Andrew's hosted the International Independent Schools' Public Speaking Competition. Model UN, photography, video editing, 53 teams in 23 sports, and community outreach are among the activities. Boys are encouraged to become involved at many different levels, all of which help to develop lifelong leadership and independent learning skills. All boys participate in the 102-year-old Cadet Corps, and 100 percent of graduates attend university in Canada, the U.S., and abroad. Boarding Tuition: (Cdn.) $39,500; Day Tuition: $23,500. Financial Aid: $1,200,000. Michael Roy '85 is Director of Admission; E.G. (Ted) Staunton is Head of School.

St. Clement's School 1901

21 St. Clements Avenue, Toronto, ON M4R 1G8, Canada
Tel. 416-483-4835; Admissions 416-483-4414, Ext. 259
Fax 416-483-8242
Web Site www.stclementsschool.ca; E-mail admissions@scs.on.ca

St. Clement's School, enrolling 440 day students in Grades 1–12, develops women of character by encouraging academic excellence, self-confidence, and independent thinking in an enriching, supportive environment. This approach provides success, as 100 percent of graduates gain university admission in Canada, the U.S., and abroad. St. Clement's opened a new facility (2006) that includes a theater-style performance and lecture hall, a dance/drama studio, a gymnasium, and science laboratories, reflecting the various activities of SCS students. The School has doubled in physical size but enrollment and spirit remain the same. SCS has received commendations for participation and performance in AP English Literature and Composition, as the top AP School in Ontario, and as the leading AP School Macroeconomics in the world. All girls take leadership roles in school government, the House system, service, clubs, and sports. Each student, staff member, alumna, parent, and friend in this close-knit community contributes to the vital St. Clement's spirit. Tuition: $19,500 (Cdn.). Financial aid is available. Martha Perry is Director of Admissions; Patricia D. Parisi is Principal.

Selwyn House School 1908

95 chemin Côte St. Antoine, Montreal, QC H3Y 2H8, Canada
Tel. 514-931-9481; Admission 514-931-2775
Admission Fax 514-932-8776
Web Site www.selwyn.ca; E-mail admission@selwyn.ca

Selwyn House, a day school for 570 boys in Kindergarten–Grade 11, strives to provide a thorough academic curriculum in preparation for university entrance. The School's challenging athletic and extracurricular programs include activities such as robotics, debating, public speaking, publications, community service, photography, art, chess, jazz ensembles, trips to Europe, and fine arts presentations. Elementary School (K–6) offers bilingual and French immersion programs. The School promotes the use of technology to support and enhance the educational experience. All secondary school students have their own laptops for use in school and at home. Tuition & Fees: $14,110–$17,849 (Cdn.). Scholarships and financial aid are available. Nathalie Gervais is Director of Admission; William Mitchell is Headmaster.

The Sterling Hall School 1987

99 Cartwright Avenue, Toronto, ON M6A 1V4, Canada
Tel. 416-785-3410; Admissions Ext. 238; Fax 416-785-6616
Web Site www.sterlinghall.com
E-mail shsadmissions@sterlinghall.com

The Sterling Hall School, situated on 6 acres in northwest Toronto, is a well-established, independent day school enrolling

300 boys in Junior Kindergarten–Grade 8. Founded to provide young boys with a balanced and well-rounded education as a foundation for the future, it offers small class size, constant and nurturing interaction between staff and students, a caring and supportive community, commitment to the development of self-confidence, and a comprehensive program. Academic and personal growth are supported by extensive cocurricular activities:

a house system, numerous clubs, intramurals, and more than 30 sports teams. Tuition: $19,800. Claire Reed coordinates admissions; Ian Robinson (University of London, B.A.; University of Keele, Cert.Ed.) is Principal.

Trafalgar Castle School 1874

401 Reynolds Street, Whitby, ON L1N 3W9, Canada
Tel. 905-668-3358; Admissions Ext. 227; Fax 905-668-4136
Web Site www.castle-ed.com; E-mail admin@castle-ed.com

Trafalgar Castle School, a day and boarding school established in 1874, educates university-bound young women in an environment that supports and challenges each individual to achieve her full potential. Trafalgar enrolls 240 students in Grades 6–12; 70 are boarders in Grades 7–12. The curriculum, featuring small classes, integrates the latest information technology across the disciplines. All classrooms are networked, and all girls are equipped with laptops. Field trips extend learning beyond the classroom, while the House System fosters a sense of community. Students take part in the arts, athletics, clubs, debate, robotics, and community service. Boarding Tuition: $36,000–$39,500 (Cdn.); Day Tuition: $17,000–$19,000. Irene Talent is Admissions Officer; Brian McClure is Principal.

Trinity College School 1865

55 Deblaquire Street North, Port Hope, ON L1A 4K7, Canada
Tel. 905-885-3217; Admissions 905-885-3209; Fax 905-885-7444
Web Site www.tcs.on.ca; E-mail rtraugott@tcs.on.ca

William A. Johnson opened Trinity College School in 1865 in Weston, Ontario, with a total of 9 students and faculty. Three years later, with enrollment growing steadily, the School relocated to Port Hope and now occupies a 100-acre campus overlooking Lake Ontario. Founded in the Anglican tradition, Trinity College School welcomes young men and women from all faiths, races, and cultures in a learning environment shaped by traditional values. The university preparatory curriculum serves 600 boys and girls in Grades 5–12, with 295 boarders in Grades 9–12. Daily life is conducted according to an Honour Code that reflects the TCS motto, "Blessed are the pure in heart." The curriculum emphasizes a liberal arts education, and laptop technology is used in all disciplines. ESL is offered to international students; indepth offerings in art and music and opportunities to travel and study internationally enhance the core program. Students enjoy cocurricular activities in the arts, community service, athletics on 24 interscholastic teams, and numerous recreational sports. Boarding Tuition: $39,990–$41,250; Day Tuition: $17,050–$22,980. Financial Aid: $1,150,000. Kathryn A. LaBranche is Director of Admissions; Stuart K.C. Grainger is Headmaster.

Upper Canada College 1829

200 Lonsdale Road, Toronto, ON M4V 1W6, Canada
Tel. 416-488-1125; Day Admission Ext. 4123
Boarding Admission Ext. 2221
Web Site www.ucc.on.ca; E-mail admissions@ucc.on.ca

Upper Canada College is one of the oldest and best-known boys' schools in Canada. Set on a spacious campus in the heart of Toronto, UCC enrolls approximately 1120 boys in K–IB2 (Grade 12) with boarders from Grade 9. One of the school's defining strengths centers on its commitment to excellence in educating boys and its willingness to pursue the highest possible academic standards. UCC is a vibrant community where motivated students are challenged to define and develop their unique talents. Igniting students' passion for lifelong learning is at the core of the school's goals. The College offers the opportunities and facilities of a big school along with the personal attention of a small school. Teachers use best practices in education to fulfill UCC's mission. Graduates receive both the International Baccalaureate Diploma and the Ontario Secondary School Diploma. Boarding Tuition: $43,150 (Cdn.); Day Tuition: $24,175. Financial assistance is available beginning in Grade 7. Chantal Kenny is Executive Director of Admission; Dr. James Power is Principal.

CHILE

Santiago College 1880

Lota 2465, Providencia, Casilla 130-D, Santiago, Chile
Tel. 56-2-751-3800; Fax 56-2-751-3802
Web Site www.scollege.cl
E-mail admiss@scollege.cl/master@scollege.cl

An American clergyman founded Santiago College to provide an education that reflects the values and traditions of the Chilean-American heritage. The mission of the College is to develop young people who will contribute to a democratic society in an interdependent world. Fluency in written and spoken English is a key goal for the coeducational school's 1800 students in Nursery–Grade 12. The integrated curriculum includes course work leading to the International Baccalaureate Diploma; 95 percent of graduates enter colleges and universities worldwide. Student Council, drama, debate, the creative arts, scouting, and interscholastic sports are among the activities. Santiago College is a member of the European Council of International Schools and the New England Association of Schools and Colleges. Tuition: $5730. Karen Thomas is Head of Admissions; Lorna Prado Scott is Headmistress.

CHINA

Chinese International School 1983

1 Hau Yuen Path, Braemar Hill, Hong Kong, China
Tel. 852-2510-7288; Admissions 852-2512-5915; Fax 852-2566-0239
Web Site www.cis.edu.hk; E-mail admissions@cis.edu.hk

Chinese International School was established as Hong Kong's first school teaching an international curriculum in English and Mandarin. With 1400 day students ages 4 to 18, the School aims to be a flagship institution for the region. A defining characteristic is that all students learn in English and Mandarin; however, prior knowledge of Chinese is not required for admission, and beginning Mandarin is available at many grade levels. Every Primary homeroom is headed by a pair of teachers, with native-language abilities in English and Chinese, who adopt a collaborative approach to planning and teaching the inquiry-based program. In the first three years, time devoted to each language is equal, with English gradually taking precedence by the Secondary years. All Secondary students pursue the International Baccalaureate Middle Years and Diploma Programs. Graduates continue on to leading universities around the world, with 40 percent studying in the U.S., 33 percent in the U.K., 15 percent in Canada, and 10 percent in Hong Kong. Tuition: HK$82,400–HK$130,700. Bonnie Chan is Admissions Officer; Dr. Theodore Faunce (Princeton, A.B., Ph.D.) is Headmaster. *New England Association.*

Hong Kong International School 1966

6 & 23 South Bay Close, Repulse Bay, Hong Kong, China
Tel. 852-3149-7000; Fax 852-2813-4293
Web Site www.hkis.edu.hk

Christian business leaders and members of the Lutheran Church Missouri Synod founded Hong Kong International School to nurture young people academically and spiritually. Situated on two campuses, the School enrolls approximately 2650 day students in Pre-School through Grade 12. More than 40 nationalities are represented in the American-style, English-language program, which includes religion, Mandarin, computer technology, and the arts. The curriculum is designed to prepare students for college, and 100 percent of graduates go on to higher education. Outward Bound, trips to mainland China, community service, drama, Student Council, athletics, and special-interest clubs are among the activities. Tuition: HK$66,700–HK$157,100. Richard W. Mueller is Head of School.

School Year Abroad 1994

BNU High School #2, 12, Xinjiekouwai Street, Beijing 100088, People's Republic of China
Tel. 8610-6235-4503; Fax 8610-6235-4505
Web Site www.sya.org; E-mail admissions@sya.org

School Year Abroad's mission is to teach self-reliance, responsibility, resourcefulness, and respect for other cultures. Through this program, approximately 60 students entering their junior or senior year of high school travel to China and live with a host family for nine months, gaining a life-changing experience outside the traditional preparatory school setting. Students travel extensively on school-led trips to both urban centers and rural areas throughout China, and a winter break during the Chinese New Year allows for an extended study in Tibet. All students enroll in $2^1/_2$ credits of Mandarin Chinese and develop speaking, listening, reading, and writing skills. Chinese History, Chinese Society and Culture, English, and mathematics classes through Calculus are taught in English. American and Chinese faculty teach an average of 12 students in each class. Numerous extracurricular activities involve athletics, music, dance, painting, and community service and are available through both BNU High School #2 and the Beijing community. Tuition: $37,400. Financial aid and China Merit Scholarships are available. Roland Lemay is Director of Admissions; Hope Staab is Executive Director.

ENGLAND

The ACS International Schools (formerly The American Community Schools) 1967

ACS Cobham International School: Heywood, Portsmouth Road, Cobham, Surrey KT11, 1BL, England
Tel. 44-1932-867251; Admissions 44-1932-869744
Fax 44-1932-869789
Web Site www.acs-england.co.uk
E-mail CobhamAdmissions@acs-england.co.uk
ACS Hillingdon International School: Hillingdon Court, 108 Vine Lane, Middlesex UB10 OBE, England
Tel. 44-1895-259771; Admissions 44-1895-818402
Fax 44-1895-818404
E-mail HillingdonAdmissions@acs-england.co.uk
ACS Egham International School: Woodlee, London Road (A30), Egham, Surrey TW20 OHS, England
Tel. 44-1784-430800; Admissions 44-1784-430611
Fax 44-1784-430626
E-mail EghamAdmissions@acs-england.co.uk

The ACS International Schools, founded in 1967 to serve the expatriate community, today educate over 2500 preschool through high school students from more than 70 nations on three suburban London campuses. The campuses are 30 minutes south and west of London, with easy access to excellent road and fast commuter rail links into the capital. All campuses accommodate day students, while ACS Cobham also offers boarding.

All ACS campuses are International Baccalaureate (IB) World Schools, offering the IB Diploma. In addition, ACS Egham is one of only two schools in the United Kingdom to also offer the IB Primary Years Programme (3–11) and the IB Middle Years Programme (11–16). All ACS campuses provide a traditional American high school diploma, with ACS Cobham and ACS Hillingdon also teaching Advanced Placement courses.

A proprietary institution, ACS International Schools are governed by a Board of Directors, accredited by the New England Association of Schools and Colleges, authorized by the Independent Schools Association UK, and hold membership in the Council of International Schools and the International Baccalaureate Organization.

THE CAMPUSES. Situated on a 128-acre country estate, ACS Cobham has purpose-built Lower, Middle, and High School buildings, a gymnasium and cafeteria complex, and a boarding house. The Early Childhood Village is located in an 1804 stable block, expanded by a new purpose-built classroom and office structure that provides classes and recreation areas for children ages 2½ to 5. Sports facilities include tennis courts, an Olympic-size track, a 6-hole golf course, separate adventure playgrounds for Early Childhood and Lower School students, and soccer, rugby, and baseball fields. The new Sports Centre houses a basketball/volleyball show court, 25-meter competition-class swimming pool, dance studio, fitness suite, and cafeteria.

The 11-acre ACS Hillingdon campus combines a stately mansion (1855), which is the setting for classes, concerts, art exhibitions, and receptions, with a modern, purpose-built wing housing classrooms, science laboratories, computer room, gymnasium, cafeteria, auditorium, and libraries. The campus also has off-site playing fields for soccer, rugby, and track. The facilities are augmented by a new music center, complete with digital recording studio, rehearsal rooms, practice studios, and a computer lab for music technology.

The 20-acre ACS Egham campus features a stately mansion house (1876) as well as purpose-built science and computer labs, gymnasiums, adventure playgrounds, classrooms, tennis courts, and landscaped gardens. The sports pitches have recently been improved and a new arts and design technology facility will open in 2008. The campus-wide wireless and cabled IT network makes working with laptop or desktop computers an integral part of the learning process.

THE FACULTY. ACS International Schools Superintendent Malcolm Kay holds a B.Sc. (Hons.) from Nottingham University and an M.A. from Bath University.

Thomas Lehman was appointed Head of School at ACS Cobham in 1992. Mr. Lehman holds a B.A. from Thiel College and a B.S. from Syracuse University.

Ginger G. Apple, Head of School at ACS Hillingdon, holds a B.S. from Miami University of Ohio and an M.Ed. from the College of New Jersey.

Moyra Hadley, Head of School at ACS Egham, is a graduate of the University of London and holds an M.A. from California State University.

The full-time faculty at ACS Cobham number 121. At ACS Hillingdon, there are 66 full-time teachers. There are 54 full-time teachers at ACS Egham. All teachers hold bachelor's degrees and are accredited; 112 have advanced degrees.

There are 13 part-time instructors; full-time nurses for each school provide health care.

STUDENT BODY. At ACS Cobham, enrollment is 1300—719 boys and 581 girls. The Boarding School has 54 boys and 43 girls. The student body at ACS Hillingdon numbers 600—310 boys and 290 girls. The ACS Egham campus enrolls 580 students—298 boys and 282 girls.

ACADEMIC PROGRAM. The school year, from late August to mid-June, is divided into two semesters with autumn, winter, midwinter, and spring recesses. The school day extends from 8:30 A.M. until approximately 3:10 P.M., followed by extracurricular activities.

Average class sizes range from 15 to 20 students. Teachers are available for extra-help sessions during and after school. School reports are issued every quarter (approximately every nine weeks). Regular parent-teacher conferences are scheduled twice per year and on an occasional basis as necessary.

Lower School students are in self-contained classes for their main academic areas; starting in the Middle School, students have separate subject-area teachers.

The academic program includes language arts, social studies, mathematics, science, art, music, library, information technology, and physical education. Modern foreign languages are studied on all campuses in the Lower, Middle, and High Schools. IB native language courses are offered as necessary on each campus. Starting in Grade 7, qualified students may take more advanced math classes.

Specialized learning support is available in all divisions for students with mild learning differences. English as an Additional Language (EAL) is offered on all campuses.

To graduate, High School students must complete 20 credits, including 4 in English, 6 in social studies and a foreign language, 6 in mathematics and science, 2 in art electives, and 2 in physical education in Grades 9–11. An Honours Diploma is awarded to graduates achieving additional requirements.

Among the full-year courses are English 9–12; French 1–4, German 1–3, Spanish 1–4; World History 1–2, United States History, Psychology, Economics; Algebra 1–2, Geometry, Algebra II, Precalculus; Biology, Chemistry, Physics; Drawing and Painting 1–3, Crafts, Ceramics and Sculpture, Advanced Art; Music, Chorus, Band, Drama; and Computer Science.

Semester or partial-credit courses include Advanced Composition, Journalism, Speech; Contemporary History, Economics, Psychology; Word Processing, Computer Sciences, Information Technology; and Photography. Courses vary slightly between campuses. The Schools reserve the right to add or delete courses according to student demand and staff availability.

At ACS Cobham in 2007, 58 students received the full International Baccalaureate Diploma, and 52 others also took some examinations. At ACS Hillingdon in 2007, 27 students achieved the full IB Diploma, with another 51 taking some exams. At ACS Egham, 22 students achieved the full IB Diploma, and 7 took certificates.

At ACS Cobham, Advanced Placement courses currently include English Literature and Composition, French Language and Composition, German Language and Composition, Spanish Language and Composition, U.S. History, European History, Calculus, Biology, Chemistry, Physics, Studio Art, Statistics, Psychology, Human Geography, Macroeconomics, and Microeconomics. At ACS Hillingdon, English Literature and Composition, French Literature and Composition, German Literature and Composition, Spanish Literature and Composition, Physics B, Chemistry, Biology, Calculus AB, Statistics, Microeconomics, Macroeconomics, U.S. History, Psychology, Comparative Government, Studio Art, and Music Theory are available.

Graduates attend such universities as Amherst, Baylor, Brown, Cornell, Dartmouth, Duke, Harvard, Johns Hopkins, Mount Holyoke, Stanford, Texas A&M, Tufts, and the Universities of California, Chicago, Michigan, Notre Dame, Pennsylvania, and Virginia. In the United Kingdom, graduates attend London School of Economics, Imperial College, and the Universities of Cambridge, Edinburgh, Oxford, and Warwick, among others.

ACS International Schools conduct various summer academic and recreational programs.

STUDENT ACTIVITIES. Lower School activities include arts and crafts clubs, scouts, choir, band, dance, chess, tennis, bowling, golf, and other sports. Middle School students enjoy a similar variety as well as cooking clubs, safe sitter programs, and a musical production. The High and Middle Schools also have student councils, peer counselors, cheerleaders, student newspapers, literary magazines, yearbooks, and recycling and environmental clubs. High School students may participate in three drama productions, math teams, Model UN, National Honor Society, International Schools Thespian Association, speech and debate competitions, quiz bowls, and service organizations such as Habitat for Humanity, The Duke of Edinburgh Award scheme, and World Challenge projects.

School teams compete with local American and British schools as well as international schools on the Continent. Middle School teams are fielded in baseball, basketball, soccer, swimming, tennis, track and field, and volleyball. Boys' and girls' varsity teams compete in basketball, cross-country, tennis, track and field, and volleyball. There are also boys' rugby and baseball teams, a girls' softball team, intramural sports, and noncompetitive physical activities.

Typical field trips include Stratford-upon-Avon; environmental or history centers in England; Outward Bound or pony-trekking in Wales; foreign language, ski, and arts trips in Europe; and community service in Africa and Asia. The Schools regularly host visiting artists, writers, and musicians and hold arts festivals, international celebrations, and a variety of community service events.

ADMISSION AND COSTS. ACS International Schools seek to enroll motivated students of all nationalities. New students are accepted in all grades throughout the year on the basis of the completed application form, previous school records, standardized test results, two recommendations from the previous school, and, in the Middle and High Schools, a student questionnaire. The School may administer diagnostic exams for new High School students; nonnative speakers may need to take an English proficiency test for entry. A nonrefundable £125 application fee must accompany each application.

Day tuition per semester for 2007–08 is £2690 for the half-day 2½-year-old program; £2935–£3975 for Pre-kindergarten half-day or full-day program; £6640–£7300 for Kindergarten–Grade 4; £7965–£8020 for Grades 5–8; and £8020–£8705 for Grades 9–12. Boarding fees per semester at ACS Cobham campus only are £4785 for five-day boarders and £6550 for seven-day boarders. Bus service per semester ranges from £415 for shuttle service to £1040 for door-to-door busing.

Superintendent: Malcolm J. Kay
Heads of School: Thomas Lehman (ACS Cobham), Ginger G. Apple (ACS Hillingdon) & Moyra Hadley (ACS Egham)
High School Principals: Stephen Baker (ACS Cobham), Joe McDonald (ACS Hillingdon) & Virginia McKniff (ACS Egham)
Deans of Admissions: Elizabeth Allis (ACS Cobham) & Julia Love (ACS Egham)
Head of Marketing: Fergus J. Rose

The American School in London 1951

One Waverley Place, London NW8 0NP, England
Tel. 020-7449-1200; Fax 020-7449-1350
Web Site www.asl.org; E-mail admissions@asl.org

The American School in London is a coeducational, college preparatory day school enrolling students in Pre-Kindergarten through Grade 12.

The mission of the School is to provide an American education of the highest quality. Students are challenged to achieve their full potential within a caring and supportive framework. As a richly diverse and international community, The American School in London fosters active citizenship in a changing world.

The School is situated in St. John's Wood, a residential area of Central London just north of Regent's Park and is convenient to the underground and bus routes. In addition, a School-administered door-to-door bus service covers a large area of the city. The School's location, within easy reach of the theaters and art galleries of the West End as well as many historic sites, makes field studies in London, the United Kingdom, and Europe a central part of the curriculum.

The American School in London was founded by Stephen L. Eckard in 1951 to provide the continuity of an American curriculum for children of U.S. business and government personnel on assignment in London. The American School in London is the oldest American-curriculum school in the United Kingdom and remains the only nonprofit American-curriculum school in London. The School is registered as a nonprofit organization in the United Kingdom and in the United States. It is governed by a Board of Trustees, with 19 full-time members of the educational, business, and professional communities.

The School is accredited by the Middle States Association of Colleges and Schools and the Council of International Schools. It holds membership in the National Association of Independent Schools, among other affiliations.

THE CAMPUS. The school building, located on a 3.2-acre site, houses all classes from Pre-Kindergarten through Grade 12. Eighty classrooms are supplemented with nine science laboratories, seven computer laboratories, five music rooms, five art studios, two theaters, a double gymnasium, craft shops, and two libraries containing 50,000 volumes and audiovisual and periodical departments. A major building program was completed in September 2001. The School's 21 acres of playing fields at nearby Canons Park include a baseball diamond, soccer fields, and rugby pitches as well as grass and all-weather tennis courts.

The School is committed to using technology to facilitate all aspects of education and has embarked on a long-term plan that combines the latest technology with innovative teaching strategies. A computer network with 1600 network outlets, a state-of-the-art, dedicated high-speed server, and a high-speed Internet connection links over 600 computers in the building.

THE FACULTY. Coreen R. Hester became the seventh Head at the American School in London in 2007. Most recently, Mrs. Hester served for 10 years as Head of The Hamlin School in San Francisco, California. Prior to that appointment, she was ASL's High School Principal from 1995 to 1997. Early in her career, Mrs. Hester taught English at University Liggett School in Grosse Pointe Woods, Michigan. Later, she spent 10 years at The Branson School as teacher, dean college counselor, Assistant Head, and Interim Head of School. Mrs. Hester is also a former Director of the Western Region of Independent Educational Services. She holds an A.B. in English and an A.M. in Education from Stanford University.

The full-time faculty consists of 51 men and 102 women. They hold 109 graduate degrees from schools and colleges such as Boston University, Brown, Columbia, Cornell, Harvard, Michigan State, Smith, State University of New York, and the Universities of California, Colorado, Hawaii, Illinois, Iowa, London, Massachusetts, Notre Dame, Oregon, Redlands, Sussex (England), and Wisconsin.

Two full-time nurses at the School attend to minor injuries and illnesses. Emergency medical services are available a few minutes from the campus.

STUDENT BODY. In 2007–08, the School enrolled 1337 day students, 689 boys and 648 girls, as follows: 409 in the Lower School (Kindergarten 1–Grade 4), 451 in the Middle School (Grades 5–8), and 477 in the High School (Grades 9–12). Although the majority of the students are American, more than 50 nationalities are represented.

ACADEMIC PROGRAM. The school year, divided into two semesters, begins in early September and extends to mid-June. Vacations are scheduled in October, November, December, February, and in the spring. The School is in session Monday through Friday from 8:05 A.M. to 3:05 P.M. The average class has 16–20 students.

The Lower School program is highly personal and attempts to encompass all traditional values of education as well as proven and effective modern methods. The basic skills of language arts and mathematics are complemented by social studies, art, music, technology, physical education, and library use. The Middle School (Grades 5–8) responds to the needs and characteristics of young people during the transition from childhood to adolescence. Team teaching and integrated study encourage mastery with a depth of understanding.

In the High School college preparatory curriculum, students fulfill major discipline requirements in English, mathematics, social studies, science, and modern language. Elective courses are offered, and advanced courses are offered leading to Advanced Placement examinations in more than 14 subjects.

To graduate, a student must complete at least 18 credits, including four years of English; two each of mathematics, visual and/or performing arts, and science; three of social studies and modern language; and one of physical education. One semester each of health and technology is also required. The School recommends at least an additional year of modern language, mathematics, and science. Students in Grades 9 and 10 must take five "solids" (English, modern language, history, mathematics, science) per year. Four "solids" are required in Grades 11 and 12; five are recommended.

The High School schedule is an eight-day rotating block schedule, with 80-minute periods divided over every two days. Because the periods rotate, classes meet at different times of the day over the course of an eight-day cycle. A full team of college counselors, grade-level deans, faculty advisors, and a personal counselor ensure that each student receives personal attention.

Grade reports are sent to parents twice yearly for Lower,

Middle, and High School students. The School has an "open-door" policy and communicates through parent conferences, the Parents' Newsletter, and the School magazine. Special events for ASL parents, sponsored by the Parent Teacher Organization, include an International Festival, a Book Fair, and a gala fund-raising auction.

Student support services include reading recovery, language development, and speech therapy in the Lower School. There are Lower and Middle School English as an Additional Language programs as well as a school-wide program for students with specific learning difficulties.

All 103 graduates of the Class of 2007 went on to college. Students are attending Brown, Cambridge, Columbia, Duke, Georgetown, Harvard, New York University, Oxford, Princeton, and Tufts.

The School runs a Summer Camp, which concentrates on athletic and recreational activities.

STUDENT ACTIVITIES. The Lower School After School Program organizes classes in crafts, sports, and other activities. Lower School students also participate in scouting and Little League.

Students in Grades 5–8 can take part in the Middle School After School Program, which offers them the opportunity to develop lifelong hobbies and pursuits and to make friends with students in other grades.

Students in the High School elect officers and class representatives to the Student Council, which brings their interests and concerns to the administration and organizes social activities. Regular student activities include the yearbook, newspaper, literary magazine, drama productions, National Honor Society, prom committee, Model United Nations, Mock U.S. Senate, instrumental and choral groups, math teams, Amnesty International, and the Robotics, Writers, and Debate Clubs. Volunteer student groups serve hospitals, schools, the elderly, and other groups in the local community.

The School's varsity teams compete against local British, American, and international schools as well as American and international schools on the continent in rugby, volleyball, basketball, wrestling, swimming, soccer, track, tennis, baseball, crew, golf, and cross-country for boys. Girls compete in volleyball, field hockey, soccer, basketball, track, tennis, softball, swimming, crew, golf, dance, cheerleading, and cross-country. Some interscholastic competition is arranged for Middle School teams. The physical education program is directed toward recreational and lifetime sports.

ADMISSION AND COSTS. The School welcomes American and international students who can meet its academic standards. Students are accepted in all grades throughout the year, provided vacancies are available, on the basis of a completed application, the previous academic record, standardized test results, a recommendation from the previous school, and payment of a £100 registration fee and a £1000 tuition deposit. Applications should be made up to one year before date of entry.

In 2007–08, tuition is £16,340 for Pre-Kindergarten–Grade 3, £16,630 for Grade 4, £18,700 for Grades 5–6, £19,510 for Grade 7, £20,020 for Grade 8, and £18,560 for Grades 9–12. Additional optional costs are £2200 per year for busing (per child) and £504 per year for food service in the Lower School. Approximately £456,000 in financial aid was awarded in 2006–07.

High School Principal: Gary Gruber
Dean of Students: Joe Chodl
Dean of Admissions: Jodi Coats
Director of External Affairs: Michael C. Miller
Director of College Counseling: Bill Mayher
Business Manager: Christopher Almond
Athletics Director: M. Frederick Koval

FRANCE

School Year Abroad 1967

5, Allée Sainte Marie, 35700 Rennes, France
Tel. 33-299-382-333; Fax 33-299-636-894
Web Site www.sya.org; E-mail admissions@sya.org

School Year Abroad's mission is to teach self-reliance, responsibility, resourcefulness, and respect for other cultures. Approximately 60 students entering Grades 11 and 12, who have had two years of French, travel to Rennes, France, for two semesters and immerse themselves in French language and culture. All students live with a local family for nine months. Courses in French language, French literature, English, history, art history, mathematics, and French society and culture are offered. Because only English and math classes are taught in English, prior knowledge of French is required. American and French faculty teach an average class size of 15 students. Extracurricular activities are abundant and organized by local schools and organizations, so students participate in athletics, the arts, and community service within the Rennes community. School Year Abroad also offers drama workshops and a chorus on campus. Trips with SYA take place on weekends and during regularly scheduled breaks and include school-led excursions to the Loire Valley, Paris, Normandy, and southern France. Tuition: $37,400. Financial aid is available. Roland Lemay is Director of Admissions; Denis Brochu is Executive Director.

GERMANY

Munich International School 1966

Schloss Buchhof, D-82319 Starnberg, Germany
Tel. 49-8151-366-0; Admissions 49-8151-366-120
Fax 49-8151-366-129
Web Site www.mis-munich.de; E-mail admissions@mis-munich.de

Founded in 1966, Munich International School enrolls 1300 day boys and girls from over 50 nationalities in Early Childhood (ages 4–5)–Grade 12. As an exemplary English-language, IB World School, MIS inspires students to be interculturally aware and achieve their potential within a stimulating, caring environment. The curriculum follows the framework of the International Baccalaureate Primary and Middle Year Programmes, culminating with the IB Diploma. MIS graduates enter such institutions as Brown, Cambridge, Columbia, Georgetown, Harvard, London School of Economics, Massachusetts Institute of Technology, Oxford, Princeton, and Yale. Competitive and noncompetitive sports with numerous teams participate in international tournaments. After-school activities include the fine arts, from painting, ceramics, and handicrafts to drama and dance, as well as school choirs, bands, and orchestral groups. Students take part in the International School Theatre Festival, Speech and Debate Team, math contests, and other international events. The 26-acre campus is 12 miles south of Munich. Tuition: €12,080–€14,790 + Entrance Fee. Ola Schmidt is Director of Admissions; Dr. Mary Seppala is Head of School. *New England Association.*

INDIA

American International School Chennai 1995

100 Feet Road, Taramani, Chennai 600 113, Tamil Nadu, India
Tel. 91-44-2254-9000; Fax 91-44-2254-9001
Web Site www.aisch.org; E-mail headofschool@aisch.org

This coeducational day school, enrolling 445 students in PreKindergarten–Grade 12, provides an American curriculum based on the California State Board and college preparatory program that incorporates an appreciation of other cultures, particularly that of India. The 10-acre campus on the Bay of Bengal features air-conditioned classrooms, a theater, a sports hall, a swimming pool, and tennis courts. The curriculum accommodates diverse learning styles, with Advanced Placement courses in ten subjects, French, Spanish, a Special Education component for learning-different students, and English as a Second Language. Classes have a 7:1 student-teacher ratio. Sports teams, drama, ballet, tae kwon do, and community service are some of the activities. American International School is accredited by The Council of International Schools and approved by the Association of Indian Universities. Tuition: $3350–$17,000. Josephine Ronald coordinates admissions; Barry Clough is Head of School. *Middle States Association.*

ITALY

St. Stephen's School 1964

3 Via Aventina, 00153 Rome, Italy
Tel. [3906] 5750605; Fax [3906] 5741941
Web Site www.ststephens-rome.com
E-mail ststephens@ststephens-rome.com
United States Office: 15 Gramercy Park, New York, NY 10003
Tel. 212-505-7409; Fax 212-505-7423

St. Stephen's School in Rome, Italy, is a nondenominational, coeducational college preparatory school enrolling boarding and day students in Grades 9 through 12 and a few postgraduates. Situated next to the Circus Maximus and a short distance from the Colosseum and the Roman Forum, St. Stephen's is easily reached by the city buses, streetcars, and Metro trains that run within a block of the School. Its location in the heart of the Eternal City offers students unique cultural, educational, and recreational advantages as well as frequent travel opportunities to other cities in Europe and the Mediterranean area.

Established by the late Dr. John O. Patterson, former Headmaster of Kent School in Connecticut, to "epitomize the best elements of the classical liberal arts education," St. Stephen's opened for classes in 1964; the first seniors graduated in 1966. Its founder chose Rome as the site because he believed the city to be "the symbol and repository of the enduring ethical, cultural, and religious values of the West," as well as "one of the most cosmopolitan international crossroads of the modern world."

The curriculum is based on the American model and also offers the International Baccalaureate, which prepares students for colleges and universities worldwide. The student body includes young people from many nations and diverse cultural backgrounds.

St. Stephen's School, a nonprofit corporation registered in Connecticut, is governed by a Board of Trustees composed of 25 members who reside in the United States and Italy. The approximately 4000 alumni provide financial assistance and offer other support. The School is accredited by the New England Association of Schools and Colleges and the European Council of International Schools.

THE CAMPUS. The campus of St. Stephen's School occupies 2.5 acres in the center of historic Rome. Constructed around a central courtyard in the traditional Roman style, the school building contains three science laboratories, new sculpture and art studios, an audiovisual facility, a photo lab, physical education facilities, and a renovated performing arts center/assembly hall on the lower floors. The two upper stories house 21 student dormitory rooms, faculty apartments, a computer room, classrooms, a library containing 14,300 volumes, CD-ROMs, and an extensive collection of videos, records, and English and foreign-language periodicals. Also on the premises are the dining hall, snack bar, and offices. The campus has gardens, a barbecue pit, and newly renovated tennis, volleyball, and basketball courts.

THE FACULTY. Philip Allen (Wesleyan University, B.A.; University of Chicago, M.A.) was appointed Headmaster in 1992. A former St. Stephen's faculty member, he was the Head of the Upper School at Friends Seminary in New York City before returning to Rome.

The faculty include 26 full-time and 11 part-time teachers, 25 of whom hold advanced degrees. They have attended Brooklyn College, Carlow College, Dartmouth, Harvard, Haverford, Indiana University, Mount Holyoke, New England Conservatory of Music, Northeastern, Oberlin, Princeton, Stanford, Temple, Tyler School of Art, Wellesley, Wesleyan, and the Universities of California, Chicago, Kansas, Massachusetts, Nebraska, Pennsylvania, Rhode Island, Santa Clara, and Tennessee in the United States; London Guild University, Warwick University, and the Universities of Cambridge, East London, Essex, Paisley, Sheffield, Sussex, and Westminster in the United Kingdom; Monash University and the University of Technology (Sydney) in Australia; Ecole Normale de Musique de Paris, the Sorbonne, and the University of Grenoble in France; the University of Rome in Italy; University Libanaise of Beyrouth; Bucharest Polytechnical University; and Université Libre in Belgium.

An infirmary is located on the school grounds, and a school psychologist is on staff. An American hospital is available for complete emergency medical care.

STUDENT BODY. In 2007–08, St. Stephen's enrolls 180 day and 38 boarding boys and girls as follows: 39 in Grade 9, 59 in Grade 10, 66 in Grade 11, and 54 in Grade 12. The diverse enrollment includes 91 students from the United States and Canada and 54 from Italy; 29 other countries are represented including Algeria, Australia, Bangladesh, Belgium, China, Denmark, France, Germany, Greece, India, Ireland, Japan, Korea, Macedonia, Mali, Mexico, Nepal, the Netherlands, Pakistan, the Philippines, Portugal, Romania, Russia, Spain, Sri Lanka, Sweden, Ukraine, the United Kingdom, and Uruguay.

ACADEMIC PROGRAM. The 39-week school year, which begins in early September and ends in mid-June, is divided into semesters, with a Thanksgiving break and vacations at Christmas and in the spring. All courses meet four periods per week, three of which are 45 minutes long, the fourth 90 minutes in length. Classes enroll 10 to 18 students to permit individual attention. In addition, each student selects a faculty advisor whose role is to offer guidance and support in personal and academic matters and to keep parents apprised regarding the student's progress. Tutorials in specific subjects and special counseling assistance are available upon request. On Sunday through Thursday evenings, supervised study halls are held in the library or in dormitory rooms.

The School's curriculum reflects the philosophy that "there

is no substitute for a balanced and comprehensive preparation" in each of the six major subject areas: English, foreign language, history, mathematics and computer studies, experimental science, and the arts. Each student is expected to carry five full-time courses. Nineteen credits are required for graduation as follows: four in English; three each in a foreign language, history, experimental science, and mathematics; two in electives; and one in the arts. In addition, noncredit physical education is a yearly requirement, and seniors must submit a research paper (senior essay). Approximately two-thirds of the upperclassmen participate in the International Baccalaureate program.

Among the courses offered are English I–IV; Italian I–VI, French I–V, Latin I–IV; Roman Topography, Renaissance and Baroque Rome, Medieval History, Classical Greek and Roman Studies, Art History, History of the United States, Islamic History and Civilization, Economics I–II, Contemporary History; Theory of Knowledge; Biology I–III, Chemistry I–III, Physics I–III; Algebra I–II, Geometry, Mathematical Studies, Precalculus, Calculus, Computer Studies; and Studio Art, Sculpture, Chorus, American Popular Music/Classical Music (alternate years), Drama, and Modern Dance. Special sessions are held for students who need assistance in English as a Second Language.

Recent graduates are attending such institutions as Bard, Barnard, Boston University, Brown, Columbia, Cornell, Dartmouth, Duke, Georgetown, Harvard, Haverford, New York University, Princeton, Purdue, Rhode Island School of Design, Sarah Lawrence, Scripps, Stanford, Swarthmore, Tufts, Tulane, Vassar, Wesleyan, Yale, and the Universities of California (Berkeley), Chicago, and Pennsylvania in the United States; McGill and the University of Toronto in Canada; Cambridge, Imperial College, King's College, London School of Economics, Oxford, School of Oriental and African Arts, University College London, and the Universities of Durham, Edinburgh, Glasgow, Kent, and Warwick in the United Kingdom; and Bocconi, LUISS, and the University of Rome in Italy.

STUDENT ACTIVITIES. The Student Council is comprised of representatives from each class, with juniors and seniors serving as elected officers. Members work with faculty representatives in the planning of social activities and serve as a liaison between students and the administration concerning all school matters. A variety of activities and clubs reflects the diversity of student interests and includes such groups as Model United Nations, Amnesty International, Community Service, Yearbook, Newspaper, Literary Magazine, and the Debate, Chess, Photography, Classics/Rome, Math, Computer, and Art Clubs.

St. Stephen's Physical Education Department offers track and field, soccer, softball, volleyball, basketball, tennis, yoga, and modern dance. Regularly scheduled games and meets bring St. Stephen's athletic teams into competition with other schools within the Rome community.

Weekly class-time field trips, weekend outings, and two mandatory excursions of three to seven days' duration are planned by faculty in the belief that Italy is an educational resource in itself and should be used accordingly. Students have visited historical and cultural sites in and around Rome, hiked in the Abruzzi, ascended Mount Vesuvius, and explored Etruscan sites. With parental permission, boarders may spend evenings or weekends with the families of day students.

St. Stephen's calendar of special highlights includes New Student Orientation and School Picnic, two Parent-Faculty Evenings, Treasure Hunt in Rome, and many student-organized events.

ADMISSION AND COSTS. St. Stephen's welcomes students of all races and religious backgrounds who are eager to undertake the School's academic challenges. Acceptance is based on the results of an admissions test, previous school records, and teacher recommendations. A personal interview with the prospective student and parents is recommended. Application should be accompanied by a fee of 100 Euros.

In 2007–08, day tuition is 17,900 Euros; tuition for boarders is 29,550 Euros. Additional charges include a capital assessment fee of 850 Euros for new students and 450 Euros for returning students, and a lunch fee of 1050 Euros for day students.

Headmaster: Philip Allen
Director of Studies: Deborah M. Dostert
Admissions Office: Alex Perniciaro
College Counselor: Alison Lewis
International Baccalaureate Coordinator: Lesley Murphy
Business Office: Alessandra Pisanelli
Director of Athletics: Duncan Pringle
Director of External Affairs: Michael Brouse

School Year Abroad 2001

Via Cavour 77, 01100 Viterbo, Italy
Tel. 39-0761-326-856; Fax 39-0761-304-529
Web Site www.sya.org; E-mail admissions@sya.org

School Year Abroad's mission is to teach self-reliance, responsibility, resourcefulness, and respect for other cultures. With SYA, 60 high school juniors and seniors travel to Viterbo, Italy, for nine months in order to live with an Italian family and embrace a different way of life. Courses in Latin, Greek, Italian, English, ancient history, art history, and mathematics are offered, with each class except Italian taught in English. Classes average 15 students. The intensive language courses allow students to learn Italian and Latin rapidly, while history courses address culture, philosophy, and politics during early civilization. School-led trips to Tuscany, Pompeii, and Greece occur during major breaks in the semester, and weekend trips bring students to ancient, medieval, Renaissance, and modern sites throughout Italy, including Sicily. Because most extracurricular activities are organized by local schools and organizations, students involve themselves in athletics, the arts, and community service within the Viterbo community. Students have participated in soccer, rugby, drama, music, sculpture, ceramics, and fresco restoration. Tuition: $37,400. Financial aid is avaialble. Roland Lemay is Director of Admissions; Patrick Scanlon is Executive Director.

JAPAN

St. Mary's International School 1954

1-6-19 Seta, Setagaya-ku, Tokyo 158-8668, Japan
Tel. 81-3-3709-3411; Fax 81-3-3707-1950
Web Site http://www.smis.ac.jp; E-mail jutras@inter.net

St. Mary's International School in Tokyo, Japan, is a Roman Catholic, college preparatory day school enrolling boys in Readiness Program through Grade 12. The School is located in a greenbelt section of Setagaya-ku, Tokyo's largest residential district, and is easily accessible from other areas of the city.

Founded in 1954 by the Brothers of Christian Instruction, St. Mary's International School first opened its doors to 59 foreign boys in Kindergarten–Grade 3. By 1971, the rapid growth of the international community and the demands for quality college preparatory education in Tokyo required the Brothers to expand. In that year, St. Mary's moved to a new campus at its current location, a 9-acre site in the Setagaya district in one of Tokyo's rare green residential areas. In September 2007, St. Mary's enrolled 975 students from its Readiness Program to Grade 12 and anticipates future development and expansion.

St. Mary's International endeavors to form free and responsible young men. As a Catholic school, it integrates the acquisition of knowledge, the establishment of responsible freedom, and the deepening of personal faith. Education is based on love and respect for the person in full recognition of the dignity of humankind, created in God's image and destined to live in union with Him.

Students are made aware of global issues as well as of the aspirations of people who work for peace, justice, freedom, and truth, in the hope that these may engender beliefs and actions conducive to the betterment of humanity. In this process, personal development is marked by empathy and mutual trust.

Academic programs are rigorous and challenging and are designed to prepare students for higher education within a safe, caring, and orderly atmosphere. The all-boy environment creates a place wherein positive self-esteem can fully develop and where learning is promoted at a pace appropriate for boys. A comprehensive and enriching cocurricular program is offered, which allows for individual expression to enhance self-worth. At St. Mary's, members of the international community in Japan can establish an identity respectful of both cultural and religious differences in an atmosphere that values diversity.

St. Mary's International School is a nonprofit institution operated by the Brothers of Christian Instruction. An active St. Mary's Association provides fund-raising support through various benefit events.

The School is accredited by the Western Association of Schools and Colleges and the Council of International Schools. It holds membership in the Japan Council of International Schools, the East Asia Regional Council of Overseas Schools, Council of International Schools, and other professional organizations.

THE CAMPUS. The School is situated on 9 acres including a multipurpose field covered in Astroturf and used for baseball, softball, and soccer and as a playground for students. Four tennis courts are also used for basketball and handball. A gymnasium and a 25-meter indoor pool are other major athletic facilities. The School also owns and operates a ski lodge in Tsumagoi, Gumma Prefecture, where students receive ski instruction on group outings. Local rinks are used for the hockey program.

The main building houses classrooms; biology, chemistry, and physics labs; a fully automated library containing 40,000 volumes; an audiovisual center with a closed-circuit television; and three computer centers. The School has 250 personal computers and a mainframe and is networked and Internet-accessible.

A major campus reconstruction will start in 2008 and end in 2010.

THE FACULTY. Br. Michel Jutras, a graduate of Laval University in Canada (B.Ed., B.A.), the University of Detroit (M.S.), and California State University at Northridge (M.A.), was named Headmaster in 1988. Brother Michel came to Japan in 1969 and served in other schools as teacher and administrator before accepting his present appointment.

There are 131 men and women on the faculty, 19 of whom teach part-time. Seven are Brothers of Christian Instruction. All hold baccalaureate degrees or the equivalent, and 52 have master's degrees. The average length of service of the entire teaching staff is 12 years, and the average teaching experience of faculty members is 19 years.

A nurse is on duty through the school day, and hospital facilities are nearby.

STUDENT BODY. In 2007–08, the School enrolled 975 boys in Readiness Program–Grade 12. Of these, 307 were in the high school grades, distributed as follows: Grade 9—79, Grade 10—76, Grade 11—78, and Grade 12—74. Students came from 59 countries, with the largest percentage from the United States.

ACADEMIC PROGRAM. The academic year, divided into semesters, begins in late August and ends in early June, with vacations at Christmas and one week in the spring. Classes are held 5 days a week between 8:30 A.M. and 3:15 P.M. Because the three school units share facilities, each operates on a different schedule, but, in the upper grades, a student normally has eight 45-minute classes. The library opens half an hour before the start of the class day and stays open for one hour after classes end to provide students ample study opportunities. Faculty members are involved in counseling and advising students. English as a Second Language support is available for students entering the School without full command of the language. Grades are issued four times a year.

The curriculum parallels the contemporary curricula of American schools. At the elementary level, homeroom teachers lead classes in English, Social Studies, Mathematics, Science, and Religion. Specialist teachers provide instruction in Computer, Art, Physical Education, Vocal and Instrumental Music, and Japanese language. Three religion programs are provided: one for Roman Catholics, another for other Christians, and a third for non-Christians.

Middle School (Grades 7–8) students take English, Japanese or French, World Geography of Social Studies, Mathematics, Life Science or Physical Science, Physical Education, and Religion/Ethics. Electives available are Latin, Study Skills, Journalism, Band, Mechanical Drawing, Computer, Choir, and Art, among others.

To graduate, a student must complete a minimum of 22 units of credit in Grades 9–12, with each unit representing a full-year course. These must include 4 of English, 3 of a second language, 2 of social studies, 3 each of mathematics and science, 1 of religion/ethics, 1 of physical education, 1/2 of fine arts, 1/4 each of computer skills and health, and 4 of electives. In Grades 11–12, students may take the International Baccalaureate curriculum to qualify for a diploma that usually affords advanced standing in American universities.

Among the courses offered are English 1–4; French 1–5, Japanese 1–9, Mandarin; Economics, World History, Contemporary World History, International Relations, U.S. History, East Asian Studies, Social and Cultural Anthropology; Algebra 1–3, Geometry, Pre-Calculus, Calculus, Advanced Topics in Mathematics; Earth Science, Biology 1–2, Chemistry 1–2, Physics 1–2; Fine Arts, Ceramics 1–2, Photography, Yearbook, Concert Band, Choir, Creative Music, Student Television, Architectural Design 1–2, Mechanical Drawing; SAT Preparation, Journalism, Theory of Knowledge, Computer Science; and Physical Education. In the major subject areas, International Baccalaureate courses are available.

All 54 seniors who graduated in 2007 went on to further their education at the college level. They are enrolled at such institutions as Boston University, Brown, Columbia, Waseda (Japan), and the Universities of British Columbia, Notre Dame, and Southern California.

A coeducational three-week Summer School Program offers review courses in English and Mathematics, various courses in the arts, and recreation for Elementary and Middle School students.

STUDENT ACTIVITIES. In the secondary school, students elect representatives to a Student Council, which organizes social activities with St. Mary's "sister" schools, Seisen and Sacred Heart (all-girls schools).

A variety of activities are offered to meet student interests. Among those currently functioning are the student newspaper, yearbook, literary magazine, National Honor Society, drama, musical, speech, debate, Boy Scouts, Leo Club, concert band, choir, and boosters.

The School competes in the Kanto Plains Association against other international and Department of Defense schools at both varsity and junior varsity levels in soccer, basketball, tennis, track and field, cross-country, baseball, swimming, and wrestling. Similar sports programs are provided in both the Elementary and Middle Schools.

From January through March, classes from Grades 4–6 take four- or five-day trips to the ski lodge in Tsumagoi to receive instruction in skiing and strengthen ties with classmates. Other student groups make use of the lodge as well.

Special events on the school calendar, including those sponsored by the SMA, are Back-to-School Day for Parents, New Mothers' Tea, Show Choir Dinner, Big Band Bash, Library Book Fair, Spring Luncheon, Christmas and Spring Band and Choir Concerts, Bingo, Musical, and Carnival.

ADMISSION AND COSTS. St. Mary's International School seeks students from the international community of Tokyo who will benefit from a college preparatory curriculum. Students are admitted on the basis of previous transcripts, standardized test results, and a personal interview with the student and parents. In some instances, an admissions test is administered. On acceptance, a registration fee of 300,000 yen must be paid and a medical certificate submitted.

In 2007–08, the tuition fee is 1,980,000 yen for all grades. Transportation and lunch fees are extra. Limited financial aid is available.

Headmaster: Br. Michel Jutras
High School Principal: Mr. Saburo Kagei
Middle School Principal: Mr. Stephen Wilson
Elementary School Principal: Br. Lawrence Lambert
Elementary Assistant Principal: Mr. Michael DiMuzio
Curriculum Coordinator: Ms. Linda Wayne
Elementary/Middle School Counselor: Ms. Julie Gordon
Middle/High School Counselor: Mr. Charles Stanislaw
College Counselor: Mr. Peter Hauet
Business Manager: Mr. Kunihiko Takamichi
Development Manager: Mr. Unryu Haku

KOREA

Seoul Foreign School 1912

55 Yonhi Dong, Seoul, Korea 120-113
Tel. 82-2-330-3100; Admissions 82-2-330-3120; Fax 82-2-330-1857
Web Site www.seoulforeign.org; E-mail sfsoffice@seoulforeign.org

Seoul Foreign School was founded by an association of parents, many of whom were missionaries, to provide excellence in education within "a caring environment centered in Christian values." The School serves nearly 1500 students in Preschool–Grade 12. British and American curricula are offered through middle school. The high school college preparatory curriculum provides both Advanced Placement courses and the International Baccalaureate diploma. Among the activities are student government, publications, debate, Korean crafts, drama, bands, choruses, and interscholastic sports. Tuition: $9820–$25,480. Esther Kim Myong is Director of Admissions; Harlan E. Lyso is Head of School. *Western Association.*

PUERTO RICO

Caribbean Preparatory School 1952

Upper School (Grades 7–12): Commonwealth Campus
Lower/Middle Schools (PPK–Grade 6): Parkville Campus
P.O. Box 70177, San Juan, PR 00936-8177
Tel. 787-765-4411; Admissions Exts. 32/33; Fax 787-764-3809
Web Site www.cpspr.org; E-mail jaranguren@cpspr.org

Caribbean Preparatory, a day school enrolling 725 boys and girls age 3–Grade 12, offers a program of academic vigor and varied activities including sports. With instruction in English, the School aims to prepare students for selective universities stateside and in Puerto Rico. It emphasizes interactive, hands-on experiences with exchange and travel programs abroad. The study of Spanish and Puerto Rican culture is required. Honors and Advanced Placement courses and a program for students with mild learning differences are offered. Summer program and camp are available. Tuition: $5250–$9250. Financial Aid: $75,000. Jo-Ann Aranguren is Admissions Director; Richard Marracino (University of Connecticut, B.A.; University of California [Los Angeles], M.P.A.) is Headmaster. *Middle States Association.*

SPAIN

The American School of Madrid 1961

Apartado 80, 28080 Madrid, Spain
Tel. 34-91-740-1900; Fax 34-91-357-2678
Web Site www.asmadrid.org; E-mail admissions@asmadrid.org

This college preparatory, coeducational day school enrolls over 850 students from more than 50 nations in K1 (3-year-olds)–Grade 12. Its primary objective is to provide a traditional U.S. curriculum consistent with that of the best American schools. Students may also opt to complete the Spanish *Programa Oficial* and the International Baccalaureate diploma. Electives and the arts enrich the program. Classes are taught in English; Spanish and French are offered as second and third languages. "Experience Spain" allows students in Grades 10–12 from other schools to attend the American School for a semester or a year while living with host families. Tuition: €5636–€17,320. Ms. Sholeh Farpour Arab is Admissions Head; William D. O'Hale is Headmaster. *Middle States Association.*

School Year Abroad 1964

Plaza de Aragón 12, Principal, 50004 Zaragoza, Spain
Tel. 34-976-239-208; Fax 34-976-235-220
Web Site www.sya.org; E-mail admissions@sya.org

School Year Abroad's mission is to teach self-reliance, responsibility, resourcefulness, and respect for other cultures. Approximately 60 rising juniors and seniors who have had at least two years of Spanish travel to Zaragoza, Spain, for the school year, live with a Spanish family, and immerse themselves in the country's language and culture. Spanish Language, Spanish Literature, English, History, Art History, Spanish Cinema, Spanish Journalism, Literature of the Theater, and math classes through Calculus are among the courses available. All classes except English and math are taught in Spanish. The average class size is 15 students. Student-exchange opportunities with schools in other cities are also offered. All students participate in over 20 days of school-led travel to Aragón, Navarra, Barcelona, Asturías, Valencia, and Andalucía and, with approval, are allowed to travel independently during breaks. Extracurricular activities are abundant and organized by local organizations or independent clubs. SYA Zaragoza is an authorized ETS test center so students can take appropriate tests, including APs, while abroad. Tuition: $37,400. Financial aid is available. Roland Lemay is Director of Admissions; Griffin Morse is Executive Director.

VIRGIN ISLANDS

The Good Hope School 1967

170 Estate Whim, Frederiksted, St. Croix, VI 00840
Tel. 340-772-0022; Fax 340-772-0951
Web Site www.ghsvi.org; E-mail mail@ghsvi.org

The Good Hope School is an independent, nonsectarian day school located on 32 acres on the Caribbean. Enrolling 278 boys and girls in Pre-Kindergarten–Grade 12, the School can offer visas to international students. A satellite campus serves ages 3–5 on the east end of the island. The rigorous college preparatory curriculum features honors and Advanced Placement courses, computer facilities, and a Resource Center. The School hosts an Intel-affiliated science fair. Activities include music, drama, dance, and sports teams. After-school and summer programs are available. Tuition: $6700–$10,000. Financial aid is awarded to 35 percent of the students. Richard Carter is Director of Admissions; Michael Mongeau (St. John's College, B.A.; Teachers College, Columbia University, M.A.) is Head of School. *Middle States Association.*

St. Croix Country Day School 1964

R.R. 1, Box 6199 Kingshill, St. Croix, VI 00850
Tel. 340-778-1974; Fax 340-779-3331
Web Site www.stxcountryday.com
E-mail bsinfield@stxcountryday.com

Founded in response to a demand for high-quality instruction in a nurturing environment, St. Croix Country Day enrolls 495 culturally diverse boys and girls in Nursery–Grade 12. This college preparatory school is a leader in technology in the U.S. Virgin Islands with computers in every classroom linked to the Internet. The curriculum includes advanced courses in physics, marine biology, calculus, French, computer science, and Spanish. Activities include sports, publications, dance, music, drama, fine arts, and special-interest clubs. After-school care and a summer day camp are offered. Tuition: $8200–$11,000. Tuition assistance is available. William D. Sinfield (Wilfred Laurier University, B.A.; Brock University, B.Ed.; Simon Fraser University, M.Ed.Ad.) is Headmaster. *Middle States Association.*

A

Ackerly, Rick, *Children's Day* (CA)
Acquavita, Fred, *St. Thomas's Day* (CT)
Adams, Dr. Albert II, *Lick-Wilmerding HS*(CA)
Adams, Dr. Sandra P., *Summit School* (NC)
Adams, Natalie R., *Washington Waldorf* (MD)
Adare, James A., *Westminster Schools/Augusta* (GA)
Ahlborn, Seth, *The Congressional Schools* (VA)
Allan, Adrian, *Le Jardin Academy* (HI)
Allen, Philip, *St. Stephen's School* (Italy)
Allio, Matt, *The Walden School* (CA)
Allison, George K., *Perkiomen School* (PA)
Allman, John, *St. John's School* (TX)
Alvar, Concepcion, *Marymount School* (NY)
Amadio, Paul, *Besant School/Happy Valley* (CA)
Anderson, Mark J., *Whitfield School* (MO)
Appel, Maureen K., *Connelly/Holy Child* (MD)
Archer, Andrea, *Derby Academy* (MA)
Armstrong, David M., *Landon School* (MD)
Ashley, Bradley F., *University Lake* (WI)
Assaf, Frederick G., *Pace Academy* (GA)
Atkison, Art, *Barstow School* (MO)
Austin, Donald M., *Newark Academy* (NJ)
Aycock, Thomas G., Ph.D., *Trinity Episcopal* (VA)

B

Babbs, Christopher, *Colorado Academy* (CO)
Bachmann, Peter, *Flintridge Prep* (CA)
Bailey, Michael S., *St. Timothy's School* (NC)
Baily, Peter F., *Oakwood Friends* (NY)
Baker, Rabbi Marc, *Gann Academy* (MA)
Baker, Col. Wheeler L., *Hargrave Military* (VA)
Baldwin, Bart, *St. Luke's School* (NY)
Ball, Baxter, Jr., *Manlius Pebble Hill* (NY)
Barbieri, Dr. Richard, *Stone Ridge/Sacred Heart* (MD)
Barclay-Smith, Dr. Gillian, *Glenforest School* (SC)
Barker, Stephen, *Ruxton Country School* (MD)
Barlow, Priscilla Winn, Ph.D., *Hamlin* (CA)
Barnes, Lindsay R., Jr., Esq., *Miller School* (VA)
Barone, Sr. Claire, *Santa Catalina School* (CA)
Barr, Kathryn W., *Highlands School* (AL)
Barrengos, John, *Independent Day* (CT)
Barrett, Peter A., *St. Patrick's Episcopal Day* (DC)
Barrows, Craig, *Berkeley Hall* (CA)
Barton, Paul, *Avery Coonley* (IL)
Bartow, Terry, *Jacksonville CDS* (FL)
Bassett, Dr. Paul C., *Stoneleigh-Burnham* (MA)
Battle, Henry M., Jr., *Forsyth CDS* (NC)
Battles, Una S., *Advent Episcopal* (AL)
Baxter, Kristine, *Churchill School/Center* (NY)
Bazemore, Timothy R., *New Canaan Country* (CT)
Bearss, Sr. Bridget, *Academy/Sacred Heart* (MI)
Beazley, Thomas A., *Grace-St. Luke's Episcopal* (TN)
Becker, Joseph A., *Roycemore School* (IL)
Becker, Lawrence W., *Brooks School* (MA)
Beckmann, Beth P., *Ethical Culture Fieldston* (NY)
Beecher, David Z., *Hillside School* (MA)
Beedy, Dr. Jeffrey P., *St. Martin's Episcopal* (LA)
Bell, H. Palmer, *St. James Episcopal* (TX)
Bellis, Steven J., Ed.D., *Pembroke Hill* (MO)
Benedict, Peter B. II, *Miami Valley* (OH)
Bennett, Dr. Paul W., *Halifax Grammar* (Canada)
Benson, Deanne, *Lesley Ellis* (MA)
Berdecio, Shirley, *St. Luke's Episcopal* (TX)
Beretta, Rev. J. Christian, OSFS, *Bishop Verot HS* (FL)
Berger, Donald S., *Cary Academy* (NC)
Berkman, James S., *Boston Univ. Academy* (MA)
Bernstein, Alan, *Lawrence Woodmere* (NY)
Berry, Kendell, *Evansville Day* (IN)
Bezsylko, Scott, *Winston Prep* (NY)
Biddulph, Karen, *The Mead School* (CT)
Bird, Thaddeus B., *All Saints Episcopal* (TX)
Bisgaard, Dennis, *Kingswood-Oxford* (CT)
Bisselle, Dr. Fran, *Maple Street School* (VT)
Blackburn, Greg, Ph.D., *Caedmon* (NY)
Blackwood, J. Temple, *Queen Anne School* (MD)
Blanchard, David Dennen, *The Craig School* (NJ)
Blanchette, Sr. Marie, O.P., *Overbrook* (TN)
Bland, Todd B., *Seven Hills* (OH)
Blanton, COL Shane, *Chamberlain-Hunt* (MS)
Bloom, Pamela R., *The Winston School* (NJ)
Blumenthal, Richard M, Ph.D., *Francis Parker* (CA)
Boehm, Gary, *Maumee Valley CDS* (OH)
Bohlin, Dr. Karen E., *Montrose School* (MA)
Bonnell, Thomas C., *Savannah CDS* (GA)
Borg, William, *Vanguard College Prep* (TX)
Borlo, Carolyn, *The Wilson School* (NJ)
Bosland, Susan C., *Kent Place* (NJ)
Bouton, David A., *Blue Ridge* (VA)
Bowers, Reveta, *Center for Early Education* (CA)
Bowers, Stephen L., *St. James Episcopal* (CA)
Brabson, Sr. Kathleen, SSJ, *Mount Saint Joseph* (PA)
Bracker, John W., *Watkinson School* (CT)
Bradley, Matthew, *West Chester Friends* (PA)
Bramble, Guy A., *Heritage Hall* (OK)
Branch, Peter M., *Georgetown Day* (DC)
Branigan, Br. James, CSC, *Notre Dame/West Haven* (CT)
Brennan, Kerry P., *Roxbury Latin* (MA)
Brenner, Maureen, *Riverview School* (MA)
Brereton, Tom, *Galloway* (GA)
Bria, Kris, *Long Ridge* (CT)
Bridenstine, Sheila, *Kalamazoo CDS* (MI)
Britton, Charles, *McDonogh School* (MD)
Broad, Margaret R., *St. Margaret's School* (VA)
Broadus, Andy, *Oakridge* (TX)
Brochu, Denis, *School Year Abroad* (France)
Broderick, Sr. Mary, SHCJ, *Rosemont/Holy Child* (PA)
Broderick, William M., *Fort Worth Academy* (TX)
Brooks, Fr. Dub, *St. Mark's Episcopal* (FL)
Brooks, Dr. Mark A., *Pilgrim School* (CA)
Brown, F. Graham, *Chatsworth Hills* (CA)
Brown, COL Matthew J., *Carson Long* (PA)
Bruce-Lockhart, Simon, *Glenlyon Norfolk* (Canada)
Brune, Jean Waller, *Roland Park Country* (MD)
Bryan, Dr. David, *New Roads School* (CA)
Bryan, Richard C., Jr., *Nichols School* (NY)
Bryans, Martha, Ed.D., *Friends/Haverford* (PA)
Buckley, Rita M., *Metropolitan* (MO)
Bull, Julian, *Campbell Hall* (CA)
Burger, James T., *Tuxedo Park* (NY)
Burke, William L. III, *St. Sebastian's* (MA)
Burns, Dr. Timothy M., *Academy/Sacred Heart* (LA)
Byer, James M., Ed.D., *Hun School/Princeton* (NJ)
Byrd, Pamela H., *St. Mark's Cathedral* (LA)
Byron, Rev. William J., SJ, *St. Joseph's Prep* (PA)

C

Cadigan, Rev. C. Richard, *Canterbury Episcopal* (TX)
Camner, Robert, *Charles Wright* (WA)
Campbell, Geoff, *Phoenix CDS* (AZ)
Canadas, Frédéric, *Ecole Bilingue* (CA)
Cantwell, Dr. James, *The Pine School* (FL)
Carnabuci, Frank J., *Birch Wathen Lenox* (NY)
Carreiro, Paula, *Beauvoir, Natl. Cathedral ES* (DC)

Casertano, Drew, *Millbrook School* (NY)
Cavanagh, Ellen M., *Oakcrest School* (VA)
Celestin, Sonia, *The Cathedral School* (NY)
Chamberlain, Judith, *Calmont School* (CA)
Chandler, Chisholm S., *Salisbury School* (CT)
Chapman, Paul D., Ph.D., *Head-Royce School* (CA)
Charlton, Kris Matteson, *St. Thomas Episc. Parish* (FL)
Chase, Andrew C., *Eaglebrook School* (MA)
Chase, Barbara Landis, *Phillips Academy* (MA)
Chinitz, Helen Stevens, *Storm King* (NY)
Christ, H. William, *Hathaway Brown* (OH)
Ciancaglini, Dr. Joseph, *Convent/Sacred Heart* (NY)
Cissel, John, *Dutchess Day School* (NY)
Clark, Catherine, *All Saints Episcopal* (TX)
Clark, Dr. Charles F., *Saint Edward's* (FL)
Clark, Jeffrey, *The Clark School* (MA)
Clark, L. Hamilton, *Episcopal Academy* (PA)
Clark, Martha S., *Riverfield CDS* (OK)
Clarke, Pamela J., *Trevor Day* (NY)
Clarkson, William IV, *Westminster Schools* (GA)
Clayton, Galeta Kaar, *Chicago City Day* (IL)
Clement, Stephen M. III, *Browning* (NY)
Clough, Barry, *American Intl./Chennai* (India)
Cohen, Arnold S., Ph.D., *Lamplighter* (TX)
Cohen, Murray, Ph.D., *College Prep* (CA)
Colb, Norman, *Menlo School* (CA)
Cole, W. Graham, Jr., *Westminster School* (CT)
Collins, Richard G., Ph.D, *Brehm Prep* (IL)
Commons, Richard B., *Groton School* (MA)
Conard, Nathaniel, *Pingry School* (NJ)
Conklin, Kevin R., *Montgomery School* (PA)
Connor, James W., *Germantown Academy* (PA)
Connor, Virginia, *St. Hilda's & St. Hugh's* (NY)
Conway, Br. Leonard, OSF, *Saint Francis Prep* (NY)
Conway, Dr. George, *Notre Dame Academy* (VA)
Cook, Deborah M., *Chesapeake Academy* (VA)
Cooke, Sr. Suzanne, *Carrollton /Sacred Heart* (FL)
Coombs, Robert, *Baker Demonstration* (IL)
Coonrod, Theo W., *Saint Mary's* (NC)
Cooper, Diane B., Ed.D., *Columbus School/Girls* (OH)
Cooper, John W., Ph.D., *Elgin Academy* (IL)
Corcoran, Andrew W, *Chinese American Intl.* (CA)
Costello, David J., *St. Peter's School* (PA)
Costello, Edward R., *Durham Academy* (NC)
Costello, Sr. Patricia, OP, *Academy/Saint Elizabeth* (NJ)
Cottam, Doris, *The Langley School* (VA)
Cottrell, Dr. Timothy R., *The Harley School* (NY)
Cowan, E. Kay, *Nashoba Brooks* (MA)
Cowgill, Lourdes M., Ph.D., *Pine Crest/Boca Raton* (FL)
Cowgill, Lourdes M., Ph.D., *Pine Crest School* (FL)
Craig, Ian L., *Harding Academy* (TN)
Creeden, Jack E., Ph.D., *Providence Day* (NC)
Cuddeback, Samuel M. III, *Drew School* (CA)
Curtis, Dr. Alex C., *Morristown-Beard* (NJ)
Cuzin, Alain, *Lycée Français* (CA)

D

Daggett, Clark, *Cape Cod Academy* (MA)
Dalton, The Rev. James E., OSFS, *Salesianum* (DE)
Daniel, Timothy A., *Brenau Academy* (GA)
Daub, Walt, *Lowell Whiteman* (CO)
Daush, Barbara H., *St. Agnes-St. Dominic* (TN)
David, Deborah, *Marymount/Santa Barbara* (CA)
Davis, Mark, *Lexington Christian* (MA)
Davis, Mark, *St. Luke's* (CT)
Davison, George P., *Grace Church School* (NY)
de la Chapelle, Sr. Frances, RSCJ, *Stuart CDS/Sacred Heart* (NJ)
de Pencier, Adam, *Hammond School* (SC)
DeHart, Michael W., *Thornton Friends* (MD)
Demartini, Phil, *Grosse Pointe Academy* (MI)
Dennis, Dr. Bruce, *Packer Collegiate* (NY)
Desjardins, Mark D., Ph.D., *Holland Hall* (OK)
DeVecchi, Dr. James M., *Portsmouth Abbey* (RI)
Diamonti, Dr. Michael, *San Francisco Univ. HS* (CA)
Diamonti, Dr. Nancy, *Ring Mountain Day* (CA)
Dickerman, William, Ph.D., *Hampshire Country School* (NH)
Didear, Rosemary, *Delphian* (OR)
Dietz, Philippe, *Intl. School of the Peninsula* (CA)
Dioli, Richard A., *Sacred Heart, Atherton* (CA)
DiOrio, Reno F., *The Linsly School* (WV)
Ditchburn, Dr. Susan J., *Havergal College* (Canada)
Diveny, Br. Paul, OSB, *Delbarton School* (NJ)
Doar, W. Thomas III, *North Shore CDS* (IL)
Dodd, Jean C., *San Jose Episcopal Day* (FL)
Dolven, Richard J, Ph.D., *The Canterbury School* (FL)
Dominguez, Jaime, *Stuart Hall for Boys* (CA)
Dooman, Michael D., *Mooreland Hill* (CT)
Dougherty, David R., *The Hill School* (PA)
Dougherty, Larry W., Ph.D., *The Buckley School* (CA)
Douglass, Jody, *Buffalo Seminary* (NY)
Douglass, Robert G., *Stanley Clark* (IN)
Dowling, Jane Martinez, *Academy/Mt. St. Ursula* (NY)
Dreese, Sharon, *Haddonfield Friends* (NJ)
Dressel, Leo P., *Sycamore School* (IN)
Drew, Richard, *Marin Academy* (CA)
Duaime, Rev. Jeffrey T., C.S.Sp. '76, *Holy Ghost Prep* (PA)
Duckett, Paul C., *Country Day School* (Canada)
Dudley, Judy, *The Harbor School* (MD)
Duffy, Elizabeth A., *Lawrenceville* (NJ)
Dunham, C. Dary, *The Foote School* (CT)
Dunn, Randall, *The Roeper School* (MI)
Dunn, Sr. Jan, *Duchesne/Sacred Heart* (TX)
Dunnan, Rev. Dr. D. Stuart, *Saint James School* (MD)
Durgin, Janet, *Sonoma Academy* (CA)
Durham, Rev. DePorres, *Fenwick HS* (IL)
Durkin, Margot, *Browne Academy* (VA)
Durnan, Vincent W., Jr., *Univ. School/Nashville* (TN)
Dworkoski, Dr. Robert J., *Viewpoint School* (CA)

E

Edgerton, Nicholas M., *Pine Cobble* (MA)
Edwards, George O., *Epiphany School* (WA)
Edwards, Margie, *The Gillispie School* (CA)
Edwards, Michael, *Cliff Valley* (GA)
Eels, Julia Russell, *Lincoln School* (RI)
Egan, Rev. Richmond J., SM, *Marist School* (GA)
Elam, Julie, *Marin Primary/Middle* (CA)
Elliot, Christian B., *Tenacre CDS* (MA)
Ely, W. Brewster IV, *Town School for Boys* (CA)
Emery, Lawrence R., *Newark Boys Chorus* (NJ)
Enemark, Richard D., Ph.D., *Doane Stuart* (NY)
Erickson, Laura J., *St. Catherine's* (VA)
Evans, Keith A., *Collegiate School* (VA)
Eveleth, Douglas C., *Saint Paul's School* (FL)
Ewing, Richard T., Jr., *Norwood School* (MD)

F

Falkner, Thad M., *The Wilson School* (MO)
Fallo, Mark, *St. Nicholas School* (TN)
Farber, John S., *Old Trail School* (OH)
Farmen, Thomas W., *Rumsey Hall* (CT)
Faunce, Dr. Theodore, *Chinese Intl. School* (China)
Faus, David C., *Falmouth Academy* (MA)
Fauvre, Mary, Ph.D., *The Oaks School* (CA)

Featherston, Anthony G. IV, *Elmwood Franklin* (NY)
Felker, Luke W., *Madison CDS* (WI)
Felsen, David M., *Friends' Central* (PA)
Fenstermacher, Barry W., *Harvey* (NY)
Ferber, Joe, *Trident Academy* (SC)
Ferreboeuf , Michael, *Cathedral School/Boys* (CA)
Finch, John, *Chandler School* (CA)
Fitzgerald, Richard P., *Bentley* (CA)
Fitzherbert, Gary L., *Glenholme School* (CT)
Fixx, John D, *Chase Collegiate* (CT)
Flanagan, Henry E., Jr., *Western Reserve* (OH)
Flanagan, Maj. Gen. Robert M., *Missouri Military* (MO)
Fleming, Ellen E., *Frederica Academy* (GA)
Foley, Francis X., Jr., *Saint Gregory's* (NY)
Fonseca, Dr. Maureen, *The Masters School* (NY)
Ford, Darryl J., Ph.D., *William Penn Charter* (PA)
Foster, Gregory L., *St. Johns CDS* (FL)
France, Frank A., *Kehoe-France* (LA)
Frank, Daniel B., Ph.D., *Francis W. Parker* (IL)
Freeman, Dr. James, *TMI-Episcopal School of Texas* (TX)
Freund, Mark J., *St. Mark's HS* (DE)
Frey, Graham D., *Crested Butte* (CO)
Frost, Les W., *St. Matthew's Parish* (CA)

G

Gambacorto, Sr. Lisa, *Mount Saint Mary* (NJ)
Garman, Dr. Bryan, *Wilmington Friends* (DE)
Gately, Catherine H., *Charles River School* (MA)
Gehman, Richard H., *Oak Hall School* (FL)
Geise, Paul G., *Pine Point* (CT)
George, Rev. William L., S.J., *Georgetown Prep* (MD)
Gershowitz, Denise, *Concord Hill* (MD)
Ghory, Ward J., Ed.D., *Univ. School/Milwaukee* (WI)
Gibbs, Debbie, *Lowell School* (DC)
Gilder, Thomas W., *Windward School* (CA)
Gillespie, Dr. Monica, *St. Paul's for Girls* (MD)
Gioia, Bradford, *Montgomery Bell* (TN)
Glass, Ruth Huyler, *Wesley School* (CA)
Glickman, Judith, Ph.D., *Sage Hill* (CA)
Glover, Ellis, *Westminster School* (WA)
Goldfarb, Rachel, *The Newport School* (MD)
Golding, Tim, *Wooster School* (CT)
Goldstein, Marty, *New Garden Friends* (NC)
Goodman, Carolyn G., *The Meadows School* (NV)
Gorham, David, *Casady School* (OK)
Gossage, Matthew E., *Cannon School* (NC)
Gould, Dr. Matthew A., *Community School* (MO)
Gozdecki, Dr. Mary Ellen, *Marymount HS* (CA)
Grace, Donald H., *Park School/Buffalo* (NY)
Gragg, Margaret E., *Charlotte CDS* (NC)
Graham, Susan G., *The Gunnery* (CT)
Grainger, Stuart K.C., *Trinity College* (Canada)
Grant, Douglas, *Convent/Sacred Heart HS* (CA)
Grant, Dr. Mary H., *The Ellis School* (PA)
Grasmuck, Dr. Stephen, *Fraser Academy* (Canada)
Grassie, Paula Steele, *Collegiate School* (NJ)
Graves, Robert E., *Fredericksburg Academy* (VA)
Green, John F., *Peddie School* (NJ)
Green, Landis, *Wildwood School* (CA)
Grey, Elliott, *Oak Hill School* (OR)
Grier, Dr. Douglas A., *Grier School* (PA)
Griffin, Barbara C., *Academy/Our Lady of Mercy (CT)*
Griffin, Stephanie D., *Mayfield Junior* (CA)
Griffith, Judith, *The Heritage School* (GA)
Groesbeck, Dr. Susan R., *Hilton Head Prep* (SC)
Groves, Dr. Michael D., *Oak Hill Academy* (VA)
Grzeskiewicz, Bro. *Richard, Central Catholic HS* (PA)
Guilliams, Dennis, *Chesterfield Day* (MO)
Gulla, John C., *The Blake School* (MN)
Gunther, Sr. Francine, SHCJ, *Cornelia Connelly* (CA)
Gurley, Sheila, *The College School* (MO)

H

Haberlandt, Susan M., *Providence CDS* (RI)
Haguewood, Ellis L., *Memphis Univ. School* (TN)
Hale, Mark, *Greensboro Day* (NC)
Hall, Merrill S., *Gibson Island* (MD)
Halsey, Woodruff W. II, *School Year Abroad* (MA)
Hamar, Rosalind, *Marin Horizon* (CA)
Hamblet, Charles, *Westchester CDS* (NC)
Hamlin, Erica L., *University Prep* (WA)
Hammond, Stephen, *Saint Patrick Catholic* (VA)
Hamner, Rev. Dr. James E. IV, *St. Martin's Episc.* (GA)
Hancock, Dr. E. Lee, *Rockland CDS* (NY)
Hancock, Jonathan M., *Canterbury School* (IN)
Hardage, Cathy, *St. Mark's Episcopal Day* (FL)
Hardwick, T. Chandler III, *Blair Academy* (NJ)
Harman, David B., *Poly Prep CDS* (NY)
Harr, Ramona, *Sullins Academy* (VA)
Harris, Susan G., *Harford Day* (MD)
Hartwell, Janet M., *Greens Farms Academy* (CT)
Harvey, Alexander, *Alexandria CDS* (VA)
Harvey, Thomas D., *Hampton Roads* (VA)
Hathaway, Dr. Laura, *Pegasus* (CA)
Hawk, Dr. Parmalee, *The Oakwood School* (NC)
Hayot, Dr. Patricia, *The Chapin School* (NY)
Healey, Joseph P., Ph.D., *University Liggett* (MI)
Hearn, W. Glyn, *Soundview Prep* (NY)
Heath, Richard L., *Sandia Prep* (NM)
Hebebrand, Ben, *Quest Academy* (IL)
Heim, William III, *Sage Ridge School* (NV)
Heller, Mark, *Academy at the Lakes* (FL)
Henderson, Robert P., Jr., *Noble and Greenough* (MA)
Henrichsen, B.H., *Robert Louis Stevenson (NY)*
Hermes, Michael, *Ojai Valley School* (CA)
Hernández, Sr. Carla, OSBM, *Saint Basil* (PA)
Hershey, F. Robertson, *Episcopal HS* (VA)
Hertrick, Charles F., *Allendale Columbia* (NY)
Hester, Coreen R., *American School/London* (England)
Heuff, Deborah, *The Priory School* (Canada)
Heus, James P., *Ridgefield Academy* (CT)
Hicks, David V., *North Broward Prep* (FL)
Hightower, Nancy Heath, Ed.D., *River Oaks Baptist* (TX)
Hildebrand, Daniel, *The Calverton School* (MD)
Hill, Frederick T., *Chadwick School* (CA)
Hillyard, Rev. Matthew J., *Bishop Ireton HS* (VA)
Hinds, Stephen T., *Meadowbrook of Weston* (MA)
Hobert, Tom, *Louisville Collegiate* (KY)
Hodges, Dr. Barbara, *Holy Comforter Episc.* (FL)
Holden, Joan G. Ogilvy, *St. Stephen's/St. Agnes* (VA)
Holford, Josie, Ph.D., *Poughkeepsie Day* (NY)
Hollister, Dr. Randall, *Loudoun CDS* (VA)
Holtberg, Arnold E., *St. Mark's of Texas* (TX)
Hood, Beatrice R., *Twin Spring Farm* (PA)
Horn, Kelly R., *Rohan Woods* (MO)
Horton, Holly, *Live Oak* (CA)
Horwitz, Alyson K., *Bernard Zell (IL)*
Huber, John J., *The Barnesville School* (MD)
Hudnut, Thomas C., *Harvard-Westlake* (CA)
Hugo, Mahina, *LA PIETRA-Hawaii for Girls* (HI)
Hull, Stephanie J., Ph.D., *Brearley* (NY)
Hulse, Diane J., *Staten Island Academy* (NY)
Hulsey, Dr. Byron, *Randolph School* (AL)
Hunter, Catherine, *San Francisco Friends* (CA)
Hursty, David N., *Bridgton Academy* (ME)
Hutcheson, Dorothy A., *Nightingale-Bamford* (NY)

Hutchinson, Scott L., *Webb of Knoxville* (TN)
Huybrechts, Jeanne, Ed.D., *Harvard-Westlake* (CA)
Hyslop, John R., *All Saints' Episcopal Day* (AZ)

I

Ireland, Patricia A., *The Independence School* (DE)
Iwashita, Dr. Val T., *Iolani School* (HI)
Izzo, Robert J., *Hamden Hall CDS* (CT)

J

Jablon, William W., *Maclay School* (FL)
Jackson, Lt. Gen. John E., Jr., *Fork Union Military* (VA)
Jackson, Steven T., *Christ Methodist Day* (TN)
Jacobson, Marvin, *Laurence School* (CA)
Jamieson, Kathleen O., *Natl. Cathedral School* (DC)
Jellig, Gerald M., *Summit CDS* (OH)
Jenkins, Blair, *Dana Hall* (MA)
Jennings, Douglas S., *Park Tudor* (IN)
Jernberg, James Peter, Jr., *Jackson Academy* (MS)
Johnson, Brian, *Alexander Dawson* (CO)
Johnson, Dale T., *The Field School* (DC)
Johnson, Kay, *Saint Joseph's School* (FL)
Johnson, Ray, *Presbyterian School* (TX)
Johnson, Stuart H. III, *St. Bernard's School* (NY)
Johnson, Thomas, *Bayside Academy* (AL)
Johnson, Walter C., *Hackley School* (NY)
Johnston, Timothy D., *Beaufort Academy* (SC)
Jonathan, Jeff, *Cold Spring* (CT)
Jones, Geoff, *The Potomac School* (VA)
Jones, Susanna A., *Holton-Arms* (MD)
Jones-Wilkins, Andy, *The Community School* (ID)
Joray, Ruth S., *Quaker School - Horsham* (PA)
Jordan, Pamela, *Chicago Academy for the Arts* (IL)
Jordan, Reuel, *Bank Street for Children* (NY)
Judge, Molly, *Radcliffe Creek* (MD)
Juhel, Dr. Jean-Marc, *Buckley CDS* (NY)
Jutras, Br. Michel, *St. Mary's Intl. School* (Japan)

K

Karl, Dr. Catherine, *Saint Ignatius College Prep* (IL)
Kase, Sr. Katherine, *Academy/Holy Cross* (MD)
Katsouros, Rev. Stephen N., SJ, *Loyola School* (NY)
Katz, Dr. Lucinda Lee, *Marin CDS* (CA)
Katz, Jerrold I., Ed.D., *The Park School* (MA)
Kaufman, Ilana, *Windrush School* (CA)
Kay, Malcolm, *ACS Intl. Schools* (England)
Kelley, Robert A., *The Pennfield School* (RI)
Kelly, Doreen C., *Ravenscroft School* (NC)
Kelly, Mark H., *Annunciation Orthodox* (TX)
Kelly, Thomas M., Ph.D., *Horace Mann* (NY)
Kennedy, Michael, *Valley School/Ligonier* (PA)
Kennedy, Stephen, *Trinity School* (GA)
Kennedy, W. Palmer, *St. Luke's Episcopal* (AL)
Kerby, Damon H., *Saint Mark's* (CA)
Kerins, Kristi, *Phillips Brooks* (CA)
Kermode, N.J.G., *Saltus Grammar* (Bermuda)
Kerns, Daniel M., J.D., *Georgetown Visitation Prep* (DC)
Kesicki, Rev. Timothy P., SJ, *Saint Ignatius HS* (OH)
Kestler, Br. Richard, FSC, *LaSalle College HS* (PA)
Kidd, Marie, *Crestview Prep* (CA)
Kiers, Maureen, *Iona Prep* (NY)
Kim, Edward, *Breck School* (MN)
King, George N., Jr., *Moravian Academy* (PA)
King, John J., *Hebron Academy* (ME)
King, Molly H., *Greenwich Academy* (CT)
King, William W., *Norfolk Collegiate* (VA)
Kleger, Eve, *Village Community* (NY)
Klimas, Carol, *Lake Ridge Academy* (OH)
Kline, Geraldine, *Seattle Waldorf* (WA)
Klotz, Ann, *Laurel School* (OH)
Kohler, J. Robert, *Good Shepherd Episcopal* (TX)
Kosasky, Robert, *St. Andrew's Episcopal* (MD)
Koskores, Theodore '70, *Thayer Academy* (MA)
Kowalik, John J., *The Peck School* (NJ)
Krahn, Dr. Gary, *Trinity Valley* (TX)
Krieger, Paul, *Christ School* (NC)
Kuh, Edward, *Fayerweather Street* (MA)
Kuhn, The Rev. Michael, *Trinity Episcopal* (LA)
Kutzelman, Lyn E., *Hampstead Academy* (NH)

L

LaBelle, J. William, *Winchendon* (MA)
Lagarde, Douglas H., *Severn School* (MD)
Lahart, Fr. Daniel K., SJ, *Strake Jesuit College Prep* (TX)
Laird, Scott D., *St Mary's Episcopal Day* (FL)
Lambert, Eileen F., *Rippowam Cisqua* (NY)
Landry, Jacqueline L., *Academy/Holy Names* (FL)
Larimer, Craig W., Jr., '69, *Fountain Valley* (CO)
Lathrop, John G., *Powhatan School* (VA)
Lauder, Robert, *Friends Seminary* (NY)
Lauer, Sharon, *Unquowa* (CT)
Lauria, Mark W., Ph.D., *Foothill CDS* (CA)
Lavelle, Br. Robert E., CSC, *Gilmour Academy* (OH)
Lawrence, Murray E. Lopdell, *Far Brook* (NJ)
Leahy, Rev. Edwin D., OSB, *St. Benedict's Prep* (NJ)
Leana, Lenesa, *Belmont Day* (MA)
Leipheimer, Mary Louise, *Foxcroft School* (VA)
Levinson, Lee M, Ed.D., *Collegiate School* (NY)
Lewis, Clayton W., *Washington Intl. School* (DC)
Lewis, John P., Ed.D., *Cape Henry Collegiate* (VA)
Lewis, Peter S., *The Kew-Forest School* (NY)
Libbon, Rosemary, *Bishop Montgomery* HS (CA)
Lindberg, Bruce, *Lee Academy* (ME)
Littell, Robert W., *Riverside Presbyterian Day* (FL)
Locke, T.J., *Isidore Newman* (LA)
Lohr, Lila, *Princeton Day* (NJ)
Lourie, David, *St. Anne's-Belfield* (VA)
Lowman, William M., *Idyllwild Arts Academy* (CA)
Lowry, David M., Ph.D., *Elisabeth Morrow* (NJ)
Loy, Steven A., Ed.D., *Rutgers Prep* (NJ)
Lui-Kwan, Ivan M., Esq., *St. Andrew's Priory* (HI)
Lutton, Joan D, Ed.D., *Cushman* (FL)
Lyle, Lisa, *Mary Inst./St. Louis CDS* (FL)
Lynch, J. Harry, *The Newman School* (MA)
Lyso, Harlan E., *Seoul Foreign* (Korea)

M

Mabey, Dr. Martha, *Richmond Montessori* (VA)
MacKelcan, Douglas, Jr., *Sanford School* (DE)
MacKenzie, John M., *The Columbus Academy* (OH)
MacMullen, William R. '78, *Taft* (CT)
Macrae, Dr. Robert, *Cincinnati CDS* (OH)
Magill, Dr. David W., *Univ. of Chicago Lab* (IL)
Magnetti, Sr. Joan, RSCJ, *Convent/Sacred Heart* (CT)
Maguire, Sr. Shawn Marie, SND, *Maryvale Prep* (MD)
Magusin, Frank, *The Bush School* (WA)

N

O

P

Phinney, William F., *Southfield School* (MA)
Pickering, Joyce, *Shelton School/Evaluation Ctr.* (TX)
Piechota, Dr. Mark, *The Crefeld School* (PA)
Pierro, Darlene B., *McLean School* (MD)
Piltch, Neal, *Manzano Day* (NM)
Piltch, Steven S., Ed.D., *Shipley* (PA)
Piñero, Kristina, *Overbrook Academy* (RI)
Plumb, Louise K., *Primary Day* (MD)
Plummer, C. Randall, *Sheridan School* (DC)
Pollard, Sr. Donna M., OP, *St. Pius X HS* (TX)
Pollina, Ann S., *Westover School* (CT)
Poole, Elizabeth A., *Linton Hall* (VA)
Porter, William, *The Melrose School* (NY)
Pottbecker, Scott E., *Marvelwood* (CT)
Powell, Lynne, Ed.D., *Seacrest CDS* (FL)
Powell, Sally, *The Baldwin School* (PA)
Power, Dr. James, *Upper Canada College* (Canada)
Powers, William, *The Country School* (CT)
Price, Dennis W., *Bishop Sullivan Catholic HS* (VA)
Proctor, Dr. Christian, *Porter-Gaud* (SC)
Pryor, Christopher, *Harbor CDS* (NY)
Pullen, Janet S., *Saint Stephen's Episcopal* (FL)

R

Randolph, Dominic A.A., *Riverdale Country School* (NY)
Rapelye, Peter Y., *Princeton Junior* (NJ)
Rayburn, Kathleen G., *Currey Ingram* (TN)
Raymer, Charles, *Saint Michael's Academy* (TX)
Rea, Charlotte L., *The Williams School* (CT)
Reed, Deborah, *Polytechnic School* (CA)
Reel, Kevin, *Colorado Springs School* (CO)
Reenstierna, Anne C., *Brimmer and May* (MA)
Regan, Dale, *Episcopal HS of Jacksonville* (FL)
Reid, Thomas J., *St. Paul's School* (MD)
Reisinger, Scott R., *Bancroft School* (MA)
Rench, Michele M., *All Saints' Episcopal Day* (CA)
Repsher, Stephen T., *Sacramento CDS* (CA)
Reynolds, Edward, *Holy Name Jr./Sr. HS* (MA)
Richards, Amy C., *Crystal Springs Uplands* (CA)
Richman, Deborah, *Turning Point* (CA)
Riley, Barbara Masters, *Hopkins School* (CT)
Roberson, Teresa, *Calvary Christian* (CA)
Roberts, Geoff, *Crescent School* (Canada)
Roberts, Michael, Ph.D., *Catherine Cook* (IL)
Robertson, Donald B., *The Walker School* (GA)
Robinson, Ian, *Sterling Hall* (Canada)
Robinson, Michael, *Lake Forest CDS* (IL)
Rode, Gordon R., *St. John's Episcopal Parish Day* (FL)
Rogers, M. Bradley, Jr., *The Gow School* (NY)
Rogers, Sr. Barbara, *Newton CDS/Sacred Heart* (MA)
Rohdie, Adam C., *Greenwich CDS* (CT)
Rosenberg, Diane, *The Nueva School* (CA)
Rowe, William C., *Thomas Jefferson Academy* (MO)
Rowell, S.A., *Gill St. Bernard's* (NJ)
Ruoss, Eric G., Ed.D., *The Tatnall School* (DE)
Ruppart, Marilyn, *Great Barrington Rudolf Steiner* (MA)
Russell, Dr. John J., *Windward School* (NY)

S

Sachs, Charles, *Park City Academy* (UT)
Salkind, Mark, *Urban School/San Francisco* (CA)
Sands, Priscilla G., *Springside School* (PA)
Sarkisian, Robert, *Meadowbrook* (PA)
Scanlon, Patrick, *School Year Abroad* (Italy)
Schafer, Michael J., *Kimball Union* (NH)
Schantz, Katherine, *Delaware Valley Friends* (PA)
Scheindlin, Rabbi Laurence, *Sinai Akiba* (CA)
Schell, Rev. Richardson W., *Kent School* (CT)
Scheurle, Jay, *Chesapeake Academy* (MD)
Schmick, John F., *Gilman School* (MD)
Schrader, Fr. Tom, *Crespi Carmelite HS* (CA)
Schuck, Christopher, *La Jolla CDS* (CA)
Schuler, Michael, *Kent School* (MD)
Scoble, Fran Norris, *Westridge School* (CA)
Scott, Lorna Prado, *Santiago College* (Chile)
Seagram, Joseph F., *Rosseau Lake* (Canada)
Secor, James Jay III, *Episcopal School/Knoxville* (TN)
Seery, James L., *The Windsor School* (NY)
Seibert, Arlyce, *Cranbrook Schools* (MI)
Seligman, Lynn, *The Mabin School* (Canada)
Sellers, Craig N., *Derryfield* (NH)
Seppala, Dr. Mary, *Munich Intl. School* (Germany)
Seward, Kenneth H., *The Steward School* (VA)
Sgro, Beverly H., Ph.D., *Carolina Day* (NC)
Shahan, Keith E., Ed.D., *John Burroughs* (MO)
Shanahan, Edward J., Ph.D., *Choate Rosemary Hall* (CT)
Shannon, Albert J., Ph.D., *St. John's Prep* (MA)
Shapiro, David, *Edmund Burke* (DC)
Sharafinski, Gordon, *Stuart Hall HS* (CA)
Shatlock, Kathleen, *PACE-Brantley Hall* (FL)
Shaw, Bruce A., *Shady Hill* (MA)
Shaw, Pamela, *Canton CDS* (OH)
Sheehy, Thomas J. III, *Canterbury School* (CT)
Shepardson-Killam, Martha, *Capitol Hill Day* (DC)
Shergalis, William A., Ph.D., *MMI Prep* (PA)
Sheridan, Rev. Paul, S.J., *Bellarmine College Prep* (CA)
Shifrin, Ben, *The Jemicy School* (MD)
Shilling, Glen P., *Detroit CDS* (MI)
Shipley, Patricia A., *Rossman School* (MO)
Shipp, Jane C., *Renbrook School* (CT)
Shirley, J. Robert, Ph.D., *Charleston Collegiate* (SC)
Shlachter, Irwin, *Claremont Prep* (NY)
Shreiner, Charles W. III, *CFS, School at Church Farm* (PA)
Sidwell, Richard, *Olney Friends* (OH)
Silvano, Louis, *Green Acres* (MD)
Sindler, Jeff, *Burgundy Farm CDS* (VA)
Sinfield, William D., *St. Croix CDS* (VI)
Singer, Paul M, *The Country School* (CA)
Sipus, Ronald G., Ph.D., *Village Christian* (CA)
Sjolund, Karl, *Salem Academy* (NC)
Skrumbis, Jim, *Sierra Canyon* (CA)
Slade, Whitney C., *St. Michael's CDS* (RI)
Small, Dr. Chad B., *Rumson CDS* (NJ)
Smiley, Alan, *St. Anne's Episcopal* (CO)
Smith, C. Edward, *Episcopal HS of Houston* (TX)
Smith, Dr. Annette C., *Hutchison School* (TN)
Smith, Kenneth W., *Sandy Spring Friends* (MD)
Smith, Paula, *University Child Development* (WA)
Smith, Sally L., *The Lab School* (DC)
Smith, Sr. Carol Anne, *Magnificat HS* (OH)
Snyder, Gloria Hoffman, *Parish Episcopal* (TX)
Soghoian, Richard J., Ph.D., *Columbia Grammar/Prep* (NY)
Solsrud, Robert, *Brookfield Academy* (WI)
Southard, Thomas N., *Shady Side* (PA)
Spahn, Stephen H., *Dwight School* (NY)
Sparrow, Alan C., *Rowland Hall-St. Mark's* (UT)
Speers, Elizabeth, *Ethel Walker* (CT)
Spinelli, Lydia, Ed.D., *Brick Church School* (NY)
Spiva, Philip G., Ph.D., *Valley View School* (MA)
Sprague, Shelley, *The Pine Brook School* (CT)
St. Laurent, Richard, *Rivermont Collegiate* (IA)
Staab, Hope, *School Year Abroad* (China)
Stansbery, Todd P., *The Swain School* (PA)
Staunton, E.G. "Ted", *St. Andrew's College* (Canada)
Steel, Francis P., Jr., '77, *Chestnut Hill Academy* (PA)
Stefani, Joseph R., *Hilltop CDS* (NJ)
Stein, Ellen C., *The Dalton School* (NY)
Stellato, Paul J., *North Cross School* (VA)
Stencel, Marsha, *Princeton Montessori* (NJ)
Stephens, David B., *The Knox School* (NY)

Stettler, Rachel Friis, *The Winsor School* (MA)
Stevens, Colin G., *The Patterson School* (NC)
Stevens, Randy S., *St. Timothy's* (MD)
Stevens, Thomas R., *Rocky Mount Academy* (NC)
Stewart, Bruce B., *Sidwell Friends* (DC)
Stewart, Marilyn E., *The Red Oaks School* (NJ)
Stewart, Ronald P., *York Prep* (NY)
Stillwell, Charles M., *St. Christopher's* (VA)
Stokes, Jeffrey, *Southfield School* (LA)
Stoneman, Nicholas J.B., *Shattuck-St. Mary's* (MN)
Straeter, Sue M., Ed.D., *The Hillside School* (PA)
Strudwick, John, *Lake Forest Academy* (IL)
Stumpo, Vincent M., Ph.D., *Linden Hall* (PA)
Sturges, Carl, *Parker School* (HI)
Suitor, John H., *Aspen CDS* (CO)
Sullivan, Christian, *Fairfield CDS* (CT)
Sumner, Todd, *Academy at Charlemont* (MA)
Swann, Rev. Stephen B., *Episcopal School/Dallas* (TX)
Swartz, Albert J., *The Montessori School* (MD)
Swarzman, Dr. Joyce Burick, *Independent Day* (FL)
Switzer, Stephen E., *Curtis School* (CA)
Swope, George S., Jr., *Oldfields School* (MD)
Sykes, Dr. Ronald P., *The Covenant School* (VA)
Sykoff, Lawrence S., Ed.D., *Ranney School* (NJ)

T

Talbott, Marjo, *Maret School* (DC)
Taplin, Nigel, *Tesseract School* (AZ)
Tavormina, Leonard, *Eagle Hill-Southport* (CT)
Taylor, William W., *St. George's Independent* (TN)
Teaff, Ann M., *Harpeth Hall* (TN)
Teitelman, Michael W., *The Bishop's School* (CA)
Temple Eric, *The Carey School* (CA)
Testacross, Joanne, *Barnhart School* (CA)
Thacher, Nicholas S., *Dedham CDS* (MA)
Thomas, John M., *Flint Hill School* (VA)
Thomas, Judi, *Metropolitan School* (MO)
Thomas, Sr. Mary, O.P., *St. Cecilia Academy* (TN)
Thompson, Douglas C., Ph.D., *Mid-Peninsula HS* (CA)
Tobolsky, Stephen, Ph.D., *Chestnut Hill* (MA)
Tomlin, David, *New Garden Friends* (NC)
Tracy, Dr. James, *Cushing Academy* (MA)
Trainer, Dr. John E., Jr., *Bolles* (FL)
Trautman, Timothy, *The Barrie School* (MD)
Trento, Salvatore M., *Salisbury Academy* (NC)
Trigaux, David, *Pear Tree Point School* (CT)
Trower, David R., *Allen-Stevenson* (NY)
Turley, Kate, *City & Country* (NY)

U

Underwood, Jay, *Rio Grande School* (NM)
Upham, Rebecca, *Buckingham Browne & Nichols* (MA)

V

Vachow, Michael J., *Forsyth School* (MO)
van der Bogert, Dr. Rebecca, *Palm Beach Day* (FL)
Van Meter, Laurence R., *Moorestown Friends* (NJ)
Ventre, Gregory, *Glenelg Country School* (MD)
Verhalen, Rev. Peter, *Cistercian Prep* (TX)
Villatico, Paul, *Kerr-Vance Academy* (NC)
Vitalo, Robert D., *Berkeley Carroll* (NY)
Vorenberg, Amy Purcell, *The Philadelphia School* (PA)

W

Wachter, Sr., Anne, RSCJ, *Convent/Sacred Heart ES* (CA)
Wade, Margaret W., Ed.D., *Franklin Road Academy* (TN)
Wagner, Barbara E., *Marlborough School* (CA)
Wales, Ralph L., *The Gordon School* (RI)
Wallace, The Rev. Charles F., *Saint Thomas Choir School* (NY)
Walsh, Kate Burke, *The Willow School* (NJ)
Walsh, Maureen E., *The Bryn Mawr School* (MD)
Ward, Gerard J.G., *The Fenn School* (MA)
Waskowitz, Bill, *Graland CDS* (CO)
Watson, Andrew T., *Albuquerque Academy* (NM)
Watson, David, Ph.D., *Awty International* (TX)
Watters, Stephen H., *The Green Vale School* (NY)
Watts, Capt. Robert D., USN (Ret.), *New York Military* (NY)
Webb, Gil, *Kingsbury CDS* (MI)
Webb, Raymond, *Foxcroft Academy* (ME)
Webster, Andrew, *Wardlaw-Hartridge* (NJ)
Webster, Chuck, *University HS* (IN)
Weigel, Russell H., Ph.D., *Loomis Chaffee* (CT)
Weisbacher, Shelly, *Springer School/Center* (OH)
Weiss, Joel, *Crane CDS* (CA)
Weiss, Larry, Ph.D., *Saint Ann's School* (NY)
Welch, Robert W., *The Dunham School* (LA)
West. John Thomas, *Mirman School/Gifted Children* (CA)
Wharton, William D., *Commonwealth* (MA)
Wheeler, Dr. Kirk, *St. Thomas School* (WA)
Whiteside, Sarah, *Altamont* (AL)
Whiting, Robert H., Ph.D., *Holy Nativity* (HI)
Whitman, Jeanne P., *Hockaday* (TX)
Wiggins, Scott, *Lawrence Academy* (MA)
Wilkins, Stephen, *The Carroll School* (MA)
Williams, Edward N., *Mater Dei School* (MD)
Williamson, Christopher, *Applewild School* (MA)
Wilson, David D., *Long Trail School* (VT)
Wilson, Ronald A., *The Kildonan School* (NY)
Wilson, Scott A., *Brookstone School* (GA)
Wilson, Vance, *St. Albans School* (DC)
Winn, Betty, *Abraham Joshua Heschel* (CA)
Wintrol, Jan, *The Ivymount School* (MD)
Wishne, Bonnie, *The Ancona School* (IL)
Woodworth, Jeffrey C., *Gunston Day* (MD)
Worch, Mary C., *The Woods Academy* (MD)
Wright, Brian, Ph.D., *Williston Northampton* (MA)
Wright, Camille, *Fox Chapel CDS* (PA)
Wright, Rodger, *Collingwood School* (Canada)
Wrye, Dr. Kenneth J., *United Nations Intl.* (NY)
Wunner, Kathleen E., Ph.D., *Wyndcroft* (PA)

Y

Yedid, Marcella M., *The Key School* (MD)
Young, James B., *The Benjamin School* (FL)
Young, Pat, *The Stanwich School* (CT)
Young, Zach, *Wesleyan School* (GA)

Z

Zaluski, Joseph, *Gulf Stream School* (FL)
Zank, Jerry, *Day School/Coral Springs* (FL)
Zeller, John E., Jr., *Community School/Naples* (FL)
Zeman, Mary, *The Montessori School* (CT)
Zinser, Col. Roy F., USA (Ret.), *Massanutten Mil.* (VA)
Zlotowitz, Debbie, *Mary McDowell Center* (NY)
Zurn, John, *St. John's Episcopal* (MD)

A

Abbiati, Julie W., *Pine Point School* (CT)
Abramson, Ryan T. '94, *Holy Ghost Prep* (PA)
Acker, Elaine, *Elmwood Franklin* (NY)
Adams, Lori, *Holland Hall* (OK)
Adams, Thomas W., *The Gunnery* (CT)
Agnew, Deborah M., *Princeton Junior* (NJ)
Albanese, Meghan, *Palm Beach Day Academy* (FL)
Allard, Lynne, *Manlius Pebble Hill* (NY)
Allis, Elizabeth, *ACS Intl. Schools* (England)
Almquist, Katherine, *Marvelwood* (CT)
Altshul, Laura O., *The Foote School* (CT)
Alvarez, Josie, *The Bishop's School* (CA)
Alverson, Cynthia Crum, *Whitfield School* (MO)
Amstutz, David, *Park Tudor School* (IN)
Anderson, Emily, *The Gordon School* (RI)
Annett, Jan, *Springer School/Center* (OH)
Anthony-Harris, Nettie, *College Preparatory* (CA)
Aperavich, Mary, *Saint Joseph's School* (FL)
Aquino, Lisa Lau '81, *Hamlin School* (CA)
Arab, Sholeh Farpour, *American School/Madrid* (Spain)
Aranguren, Jo-Ann, *Caribbean Prep* (PR)
Armenta, Gilbert Juan, *Windrush* (CA)
Arnold, Rebecca, *Harding Academy* (TN)
Arzt, Susan, *Concord Hill* (MD)
Atcheson, Elizabeth, *The Bush School* (WA)
Atkinson, Emily, *Episcopal HS* (VA)
Audett, Chip, *Cardigan Mountain* (NH)
Auwarter, Carrie, *Buffalo Seminary* (NY)
Axford, Dan, *University Liggett* (MI)
Aycock, Malia, *St. Andrew's Episcopal* (TX)

B

Babington, Ann, *Forsyth School* (MO)
Babior, Dan, *Marin Academy* (CA)
Backlund, Lori, *St. John's Episcopal* (MD)
Backman, Laura, *Eliot Montessori* (MA)
Bader, Betty, *St. Cecilia Academy* (TN)
Baigelman, Gayle, *Abraham Joshua Heschel* (CA)
Bailey, Cindy, *River Oaks Baptist* (TX)
Bailey, Edith, *Glenforest School* (SC)
Bailey, Suzanne, *Providence CDS* (RI)
Baker, Beth, *Evansville Day School* (IN)
Baker, David, *St. Mark's School of Texas* (TX)
Balak, Terrie, *Webb School/Knoxville* (TN)
Balderson, Kimerly C., *The Country School* (MD)
Barden, Monica, *The Mabin School* (Canada)
Barfield, Pam, *Independent Day School* (FL)
Barfield, Terri, *Savannah CDS* (GA)
Barker, Carinne M., *The Buckley School* (CA)
Barnes, Christena, *Walden School* (CA)
Barnes, Sallie B., *Charleston Day* (SC)
Barnett, Chad, *The Linsly School* (WA)
Barrett, Susan, *Linton Hall School* (VA)
Barry, Pamela C., *San Jose Episcopal Day* (FL)
Barton, Christopher S., *University School* (OH)
Bartow, Elizabeth, *The Barstow School* (MO)
Basch, Clarissa, *Ethel Walker* (CT)
Bastrenta, Brigitte, *Ecole Bilingue* (CA)
Battaile, Andrew C., *Gonzaga College HS* (DC)
Baty, Kristin, *Trinity School* (GA)
Beach, Barbara T., *The Stanley Clark School* (IN)
Beach, P. Terence, *Hun School/Princeton* (NJ)
Becker, Linda J.L., *Pine Cobble School* (MA)
Behar, Barbara, *Friends' Central* (PA)
Belton, Michelle, *Lowell School* (DC)
Benedict, A. Randol '76, *Garrison Forest* (MD)
Bernstein, Carol Inge, *Sage Hill School* (CA)
Bernstein, Marina, *The Dwight School* (NY)
Bertin, Randy, *Besant Hill School* (CA)
Billoni, Anthony G., *Park School/Buffalo* (NY)
Blackwell, MAJ Chris, *Chamberlain-Hunt* (MS)
Blair, Jeanne Marie, *Rosemont/Holy Child* (PA)
Blanchard, Dana L. '63, *Hopkins School* (CT)
Blankenship, Cecilia R., *Julie Rohr Academy* (FL)
Block, Patricia, *The Cushman School* (FL)
Bloedau, Lonna, *Sacramento CDS* (CA)
Bogardus, Andrew, *Berkshire School* (MA)
Bohrer, Cynthia, *Fayerweather Street* (MA)
Boland, Kimberly '94, *Miss Hall's School* (MA)
Bolding, Debbie, *Heritage Hall* (OK)
Bonaparte, Yvette, *San Francisco Friends* (CA)
Bonet, Iris, *The Kinkaid School* (TX)
Bonnie, Dr. Stephen A., *William Penn Charter* (PA)
Bonus, Sharman M., *Marin Horizon* (CA)
Booe, Kathryn B., *Charlotte Latin* (NC)
Booker, Anne D., *St. Christopher's* (VA)
Borden, Ann, *Marin CDS* (CA)
Borosavage, Wendy W., *Chestnut Hill* (MA)
Bowman, Jeannie, *Delaware Valley Friends* (PA)
Brechter, Claire, *The Independence School* (DE)
Breen, Kevin, *Brooks School* (MA)
Brennan, Jay, *Foxcroft Academy* (ME)
Brenner, Matt, *Lamplighter* (TX)
Breschi, Michael, *Loyola Blakefield* (MD)
Brissenden, Deborah, *Belmont Day* (MA)
Broadus, Linda, *Oakridge* (TX)
Bronk, Bart '96, *CFS, School at Church Farm* (PA)
Brown, Kristin, *Presbyterian School* (TX)
Bruno, Kathy, *The Pen Ryn School* (PA)
Budden, David, *Crescent School* (Canada)
Bunde, Mary Catherine, *Hampton Roads Academy* (VA)
Burke, Holly, *The Brick Church School* (NY)
Burke, Kathleen M., *The Pennfield School* (RI)
Burke, Ruth, *Episcopal School/Dallas* (TX)
Burnett, Harriet, *Friends Seminary* (NY)
Burns, Helen C., *Gulf Stream School* (FL)
Burns, Tom, *The Melrose School* (NY)
Burr, Hacker, *Charleston Collegiate* (SC)
Byrne, Bethany, *Beaufort Academy* (SC)
Byrne, James G., *Marist School* (GA)

C

Cabot, Raymond H., *Peddie School* (NJ)
Calamari, Sr. Barbara, *Academy/Mount St. Ursula* (NY)
Caldwell, Jason, *Packer Collegiate* (NY)
Caldwell, Marjorie C., *Chesterfield Day* (MO)
Calhoun, Erik C., *Elgin Academy* (IL)
Calixto, Judy, *Village Community* (NY)
Callahan, Beth, *Montessori School* (MD)
Callahan, Jennifer, *Ursuline Academy* (DE)
Callo, Courtney M., *Long Trail School* (VT)
Calvin, Lyn-Felice, *St. Thomas School* (WA)
Campbell, Martin F., *Bishop Sullivan HS* (VA)
Campbell, Nicole, *The Barnesville School* (MD)
Cannon, Michelle M., *BU Academy* (MA)
Capps, Rebekah, *The Ensworth School* (TN)
Cargill, Patsy, *Saint Michael's Academy* (TX)
Carney, Terry Schabel '80, *Magnificat HS* (OH)
Carpenter, Susanne C., *Worcester Academy* (MA)
Carroll, Alan, *Allendale Columbia* (NY)
Carter, Betsy, *Rippowam Cisqua* (NY)
Carter, Helene, *Commonwealth School* (MA)
Carter, Richard, *Good Hope* (VI)
Casaccio, Francesca, *Fenwick High School* (IL)
Casey, Jacqueline A., *The Browning School* (NY)
Casseb, Margaret Ann, *St. Luke's Episcopal* (TX)
Chan, Bonnie, *Chinese Intl. School* (China)

Chettleburgh, Deirdre, *Glenlyon Norfolk* (Canada)
Chibber, Nina, *Green Acres* (MD)
Chitjian, Jeanette Woo, *Marlborough School* (CA)
Christian, Marnie, *Abington Friends* (PA)
Clark, Taryn, *Nueva School* (CA)
Clement, Cathy, *St. Timothy's* (NC)
Clemons, Amy, *Renbrook School* (CT)
Coats, Jodi, *American School/London* (England)
Cobb, Ruth, *Saint Thomas Choir School* (NY)
Coburn, Clare, *Southfield School* (LA)
Coleman, Gregory W., *The Shipley School* (PA)
Collins, Donna, *Brehm Preparatory School* (IL)
Collins, Elizabeth, *Kent School* (MD)
Colucci, Bill, *Bellarmine College Prep* (CA)
Comolli, LTC David M., *Carson Long* (PA)
Conklin, Nancy, *Pegasus School* (CA)
Conner, Judy, *Francis Parker School* (CA)
Cook, Molly B., *Lausanne Collegiate* (TN)
Corbett, Erin, *Springside School* (PA)
Core, Julie S., *Hackley School* (NY)
Corrin, Judith, *Sacred Heart Schools* (IL)
Covington, Candy, *Hutchison School* (TN)
Cowan, Joni, *North Broward Prep* (FL)
Coyne, Carolyn, *Roycemore School* (IL)
Craig, Dr. Carolyn, *Graland CDS* (CO)
Craig, Diana N., *Shorecrest Prep* (FL)
Craig, Jean, *St. Anne's-Belfield* (VA)
Cranford, Susan, *Bancroft School* (MA)
Crisan, Anne, *All Saints' Episcopal Day* (CA)
Crosson, John J., *Watkinson School* (CT)
Cucchi, Julie, *The Gordon School* (RI)
Cunitz, Stacey, *The Crefeld School* (PA)
Cunningham, Mary, *Quest Academy* (IL)
Curran, Caitlin, *Convent/Sacred Heart HS* (CA)

D

Dale, Mary Jo, *Sonoma Academy* (CA)
Danish, Jennifer S., *St. Patrick's Episc. Day* (DC)
Darrin, William A. III, *Blue Ridge School* (VA)
Dates, Karen E., *Friends School/Baltimore* (MD)
Davis, Charlotte, *Wardlaw-Hartridge* (NJ)
Dawkins, Barbara B., *St. Nicholas School* (TN)
Day, Julie Sage, *The Craig School* (NJ)
DeHoff, Courtney, *Winston Prep* (NY)
DeJesus, Marie, *Thomas Jefferson* (MO)
Del Alamo, Elena, *Pine Crest School* (FL)
Delaney, Mary, *Newton CDS/Sacred Heart* (MA)
Deluca, Daniela, *Rio Grande School* (NM)
Denove, Verena, *Wesley School* (CA)
DeRose, Johnette, *Valley School/Ligonier* (PA)
DeRussy, Susie, *Trinity Episcopal* (LA)
DeSimone, Stephanie, *Saint Patrick Catholic* (VA)
Desmole, Isabelle, *Lycée Français La Pérouse* (CA)
Deveaux, Jon, *Westminster School* (CT)
Devine, Jennifer, *Lincoln School* (RI)
Diaz-Imbelli, Lillian, *Loyola School* (NY)
Diffley, Ray III, *Choate Rosemary Hall* (CT)
DiGuiseppe, Barbara W., *Brookwood* (MA)
DiPaolo, Steve, *Cape Cod Academy* (MA)
Dodge, Patricia E., *The Peck School* (NJ)
Donovan, Dr. David, *Delbarton School* (NJ)
Dos Remedios, Carl, *Sacred Heart, Atherton* (CA)
Douberley, Valerie, *St. Thomas Episc. Parish* (FL)
Dougherty, Carol, *Perkiomen School* (PA)
Douglas, Charlotte, *St. Paul's for Girls* (MD)
Douglas, Juliet C., *Univ. School/Nashville* (TN)
Douglas, Louise B., *Santa Catalina* (CA)
Downs, Christopher K., *Hotchkiss School* (CT)
Driscoll, John '90, *St. John's Prep* (MA)
Driscoll, Kevin J., *Austin Prep* (MA)
Droppers, Alice, *The O'Neal School* (NC)
Duffy, Ann V., *Buckley CDS* (NY)
Dun, Kelly, *Princeton Day* (NJ)
Dunleavy, Jessie D., *The Key School* (MD)
Dunning, Diane, *St. Stephen's and St. Agnes* (VA)
Durrant, Malcolm, *Saltus Grammar* (Bermuda)

E

Earley, Marion L., *Charles River School* (MA)
Earley, Michael, *Falmouth Academy* (MA)
Eblen, Leigh, *St. Luke's Episcopal* (AL)
Eccleston, Tom '87, *The Hill School* (PA)
Echt, Linda, *The Atrium School* (MA)
Eckerson, Jeffrey E., *Fredericksburg Academy* (VA)
Edel, Deborah, *Mary McDowell Center* (NY)
Efter, Athena, *The Cathedral School* (NY)
Egan, Peter C., *Seven Hills* (OH)
Ehringhaus, Nancy, *Charlotte CDS* (NC)
Eidam, John R., *Wyoming Seminary* (PA)
Elliott, Alison, *Franklin Road Academy* (TN)
Emmons, Susan, *Oak Mountain Academy* (GA)
Emond, David M., *St. Sebastian's* (MA)
Epstein, Catherine, *Head-Royce School* (CA)
Epstein, Jeanette, *The Wheeler School* (RI)
Escabar, Jeffrey, *Marin CDS* (CA)
Evans, Cokey, *Francis W. Parker School* (IL)
Evans, Joanna, *White Mountain* (NH)
Evans, Judy, *Community School of Naples* (FL)
Evans, Mary Beth, *Princeton Montessori* (NJ)
Everett, Carole, *St. Luke's School* (NY)
Everett, Laura Lee, *Pilgrim School* (CA)
Ewart, Kara, *Rosseau Lake College* (Canada)

F

Fagan, Jackie, *North Broward Prep* (FL)
Farquhar, Annie M., *Maret School* (DC)
Farrell, Anthony, *Stuart Hall HS* (CA)
Federico, Wendy, *Churchill School/Center* (NY)
Feeley, Susan F., *Lab School of Washington* (DC)
Fenlon, Cindy, *St. John's Episc. Parish Day* (FL)
Ferrell, Greg, *Montgomery Bell* (TN)
Fernández, Ellen, *Overbrook School* (TN)
Finley, Barbara, *Saint Mark's School* (CA)
Finn, Patrick M., *St. Timothy's School* (MD)
Finney, Carol, *Mount Saint Joseph* (PA)
Fisher, Becky Riley, *Mirman School/Gifted* (CA)
Fisher, Kathy, *All Saints Episcopal* (TX)
Fishman, Esther, *Maple Street School* (VT)
Fitzherbert, Kathi L., *Glenholme School* (CT)
Flanagan, Barbara, *Western Reserve* (OH)
Fleming, Alice, *Campbell Hall* (CA)
Flintoft, Kathy, *The Brick Church School* (NY)
Forsythe, Terry, *St. Agnes -St. Dominic* (TN)
Foster, Alan, *Bayside Academy* (AL)
Foulk, Margaretta, *Chase Collegiate* (CT)
Fowler, Lisa, *The Carey School* (CA)
Fox, Britton, *Riverfield CDS* (OK)
Fox, Peggy, *Episcopal HS of Jacksonville* (FL)
Francis, Shirley W., *Riverside Presbyterian Day* (FL)
Fredericks, Khadija, *St. Paul's Episcopal* (CA)
Frew, Peter A., *The Taft School* (CT)
Frey, Deborah D., *Calvert School* (MD)
Fried, Jane F., *Phillips Academy* (MA)
Friedman, Kathleen, *Univ. School/Milwaukee* (WI)
Friend, Susan, *Green Acres* (MD)
Fuchs, Dorrie, *Washington Intl. School* (DC)
Funderburke, Carol, *North Cross School* (VA)
Furlong, Amy Hall, *St. Paul's* (MD)

G

Gamper, William H., *Gilman School* (MD)
Garcia, Katherine, *The Kew-Forest School* (NY)
Garcia, Robert, *The Gow School* (NY)
Gardner, Kim, *Washington Academy* (ME)
Garfield, Roberta, *Ruxton* (MD)
Garrick, David, *Univ. Child Development* (WA)
Garwood, Alice, *Oak Hall School* (FL)
Gaudet, Samuel, *St. Luke's School* (CT)
George, Kai-Anasa, *Edmund Burke School* (DC)
George, Mary Helen, *Vanguard College Prep* (TX)
Geppert, Mary Lisa, *Laurel School* (OH)
Gerber, Ingrid, *Moravian Academy* (PA)
Gering, Sue, *Brentwood Academy* (TN)
Gersten, Tracey, *Live Oak School* (CA)
Gervais, Nathalie, *Selwyn House* (Canada)
Gilbert, Brian J., *Georgetown Prep* (MD)
Gilbert, Peter B., *Salisbury School* (CT)
Giles, Aimee, *Children's Day* (CA)
Gillespie, Susan, *St. Mary's Hall/Doane* (NJ)
Glace, Diane, *Rutgers Prep* (NJ)
Glandon, Jackie, *The Newman School* (MA)
Glassman, Lisa, *Wildwood School* (CA)
Goebel, Sarah J., *The Baldwin School* (PA)
Goertz, Robin, *Carolina Day* (NC)
Goetz, Katherine, *Notre Dame Prep* (MD)
Goheen, Kelly, *Holy Nativity School* (HI)
Goldman, Susanne, *Seven Hills* (CA)
Gooden, Rosetta, *The Galloway School* (GA)
Goodhill,Barbara, *Sinai Akiba Academy* (CA)
Goodman, Denise, *Cary Academy* (NC)
Goodman, Douglas, *Sewickley Academy* (PA)
Gordon, Sandra, *St. James Episcopal* (TX)
Gore, Heidi, *St. Bernard's School* (NY)
Gorecki, Michelle, *Academy of the Holy Names* (FL)
Gracey, Ian, *Groton School* (MA)
Graham, Monica C., *Maryvale Prep* (MD)
Grant, Michael R., *Belmont Hill* (MA)
Green, Molly M. '83, *Severn School* (MD)
Greenwell, Lorraine, *Rockland CDS* (NY)
Gregg, Bob, *Saint Edward's* (FL)
Gregory, Elizabeth, *Harvard-Westlake* (CA)
Groves, Dr. Michael D., *Oak Hill Academy* (VA)
Gruber, Susan, *Pace Academy* (GA)
Guden, Thomas R., *Roxbury Latin* (MA)
Gundersen, Kathy, *Rowland Hall-St. Mark's* (UT)
Gunn, Beth Ann, *The Awty Intl. School* (TX)
Gustafson, Deborah A., *Cushing* (MA)
Gutman, Anne, *National Presbyterian* (DC)

H

Haase, Barbara, *Blair Academy* (NJ)
Haaser, Robert J., *Cistercian Prep* (TX)
Haddad, Dana, *Claremont Prep* (NY)
Hamer, Peter, *Bishop Ireton HS* (VA)
Handalian, Linda, *St. Matthew's Episc. Day* (CA)
Hansen, Alexa, *Lake Ridge Academy* (OH)
Hansen, Suellen, *The Unquowa School* (CT)
Harden, Pat, *Flint Hill School* (VA)
Hargreaves, Pauline, *The Learning Project* (MA)
Harmon, Cynthia A., *The Park School* (MA)
Harrell, Susan, *Cape Fear Academy* (NC)
Harrigan-Boles, Kathy, *Currey Ingram* (TN)
Harrington, Ashley, *Rippowam Cisqua* (NY)
Harris, Donna B., *The Covenant School* (VA)
Harris, Jeffry, *Brunswick School* (CT)
Harris, Mindy, *Gann Academy* (MA)
Harris, Tina, *Bermuda HS for Girls* (Bermuda)
Harrison, Deirdre, *Baker Demonstration* (IL)
Hartung, Laura C., *Wilson School* (MO)
Hawgood, Tony, *Lawrence Academy* (MA)
Hawes, Janice, *Pear Tree Point School* (CT)
Hay, Lynne, *The Episcopal Academy* (PA)
Hay, Sherryn M., *Trinity Prep* (FL)
Heard, Kristen J., *Tuxedo Park School* (NY)
Heaton, Jean Stahl, *Nashoba Brooks* (MA)
Hebra, Jada K., *St. Paul's School* (NH)
Hein, Kristen, *The Orchard School* (IN)
Held, Patty, *Trident Academy* (SC)
Hemmings, Joseph, *Hebron Academy* (ME)
Henderson, Ginny, *St. George's Independent* (TN)
Hendon, Louise, *Academy/Sacred Heart* (MD)
Hendrickson, Alice, *St. Mark's Episcopal* (FL)
Henry, David, *Gunston Day School* (MD)
Herman, Tina I., *The Chapin School* (NY)
Hernandez, Ruth C., *Overbrook Academy* (RI)
Heyman, Joanne P., *Collegiate School* (NY)
Hilson, Anita, *McDonogh School* (MD)
Hines, Carolyn, *Aspen CDS* (CO)
Hines, Jennifer, *Noble and Greenough* (MA)
Hinson, Alison, *Christ Methodist Day* (TN)
Hirsch, Judy, *John Thomas Dye* (CA)
Hirschman, Martha, *Grace Church School* (NY)
Hodges, Nancy, *Randolph* (AL)
Hoeniger, Matthew S., *Rumsey Hall School* (CT)
Hoffman, Mary W., *Advent Episcopal* (AL)
Holcombe, Frances C., *Norfolk Academy* (VA)
Holding, Susan, *Old Trail School* (OH)
Holmgren, Andrew, *Fairfield CDS* (CT)
Holt, Gayle A., *The Williams School* (CT)
Holton, Keith R., *Canterbury School* (CT)
Honeywell, Ashley, *Episcopal Collegiate* (AR)
Hood, Lucia D'Andrea, *Twin Spring Farm* (PA)
Hopkins, Kathleen, *Wilmington Friends* (DE)
Hopper, Helen V., *Westridge School* (CA)
Horner, Lisa, *City & Country School* (NY)
Houston-White, Maggie, *Havergal College* (Canada)
Hristidis, Simone, *Columbia Grammar and Prep* (NY)
Hudenko, Judy, *Albuquerque Academy* (NM)
Hudnut, Deedie, *Center for Early Education* (CA)
Humick, Nancy, *Kent Place School* (NJ)
Humphreys, Amy, *Richmond Montessori* (VA)
Hurtes, Eleanor W., *Porter-Gaud School* (SC)
Hyde, Karen, *Rowland Hall-St. Mark's* (UT)

I

Iason, Valorie, *Packer Collegiate* (NY)
Imbriglia, Sara E., *The Ellis School* (PA)
Irvin, Rebecca, *Kerr-Vance Academy* (NC)
Issa, Lillian, *Marymount School* (NY)
Ivanyi, Mary, *Soundview Prep* (NY)
Izzo, Janet B., *Hamden Hall CDS* (CT)
Izzo, Pasquale G., *Notre Dame of West Haven* (CT)

J

Jacobs, Merle, *Cambridge Friends* (MA)
Jahn, Theodore, *Saint Francis Prep* (NY)
James, Aaron, *Casady School* (OK)
James, Warner T., Jr., *Breck School* (MN)
Jameson, Julie, *St. Andrew's Episcopal* (MD)
Jamison, Pamela J., *Ravenscroft School* (NC)
Janiak, Alicia, *The Dwight School* (NY)
Jankoff, Ronnie R., *Allen-Stevenson* (NY)
Jankowski, Judy, *McLean School* (MD)
Jensen, Lawrence, *Saint James* (MD)

Jessiman, Gray, *Berkshire CDS* (MA)
Jiongo, Barbara W., *Fort Worth Country Day* (TX)
Johnson, Susan, *Canterbury School* (IN)
Johnston, Sarah L., *Hathaway Brown* (OH)
Jolly, Amy, *Shady Hill School* (MA)
Jones, Jamie, *Ursuline Academy* (DE)
Jordan, John J., *Archmere Academy* (DE)
Justis, Mary Margaret, *Sullins Academy* (VA)

K

Kahalley, Daniel, *Memphis Univ. School* (TN)
Kamins, Reena, *The Pingry School* (NJ)
Kaplan, Joan, *Brearley* (NY)
Kaplan, Julianne, *Birch Wathen Lenox* (NY)
Karpicke, Dr. Susan, *Sycamore School* (IN)
Keefe, Patricia, *Montrose School* (MA)
Kellenberger, Aaron B., *Cincinnati CDS* (OH)
Keller, Janet D., *Georgetown Visitation Prep* (DC)
Kelly, Maureen, *New York Military* (NY)
Kelly, Rose, *St. Anne's Episcopal* (CO)
Kenny, Chantal, *Upper Canada* (Canada)
Keppler, Amber K., *Montgomery School* (PA)
Kindler, Karen N., *San Francisco Univ. HS* (CA)
King, Corinne M., *Lawrence Woodmere* (NY)
Kingman, Sue, *The Carroll School* (MA)
Kinser, Judith S., *Trinity Valley* (TX)
Klaftenegger, Brenda, *TMI* (TX)
Klekamp, Peter, *Episcopal/Knoxville* (TN)
Kluttz, Cindy, *Forsyth CDS* (NC)
Knapp, Whit, *Harbor CDS* (NY)
Knies, Jennifer, *Brooklyn Friends* (NY)
Knott, Julie, *The Heritage School* (GA)
Kodama, Robert, *Crespi Carmelite HS* (CA)
Koehler, Audrey, *Episcopal HS/Houston* (TX)
Koelsch, Vicki, *Maumee Valley CDS* (OH)
Koenings, Sharon, *Brookfield Academy* (WI)
Klug, Jen, *Madison CDS* (WI)
Kong, Patricia, *Pilgrim School* (CA)
Kramer, Susie, *St. Pius X HS* (TX)
Krents, Elizabeth, Ph.D., *The Dalton School* (NY)
Krick, Beth, *Friends Haverford* (PA)
Kroll, Ann, *The Stanwich School* (CT)
Kugler, Lori T., *The Fenn School* (MA)
Kwartler, Susan, *St. Mark's Episcopal Day* (FL)
Kyle, Trish, *St. Peter's School* (PA)

L

LaBelle, J. William, *Winchendon* (MA)
LaBranche, Kathryn A., *Trinity College* (Canada)
Ladden, Judy, *Highlands* (AL)
Lafferty, Sarah M., *Riverdale Country School* (NY)
Lange, Debbie, *The Lovett School* (GA)
Laramie, Peggy B., *Mary Inst./Saint Louis CDS* (MO)
Larimer, Pam, *Loudoun CDS* (VA)
Larkins, Christina, *Oak Hill Academy* (NJ)
Larmann, Jennifer, *Ridgewood Prep* (LA)
Laskey, Catherine, *Colorado Academy* (CO)
Laurent, Charles, *St. Michael's CDS* (RI)
Lavery, Nicole Demaray, *Marin Primary/Middle* (CA)
LaVigne, Caroline, *John Burroughs* (MO)
Lawson, Lezlie, *Washington Waldorf* (MD)
Layman, Will, *The Field School* (DC)
Leary, Catherine C., *Saint Mary's School* (NC)
Leas, Dawn, *Wyoming Seminary* (PA)
Lecky, Mason, *St. Albans School* (DC)
Lee, Gretchen, *Saddle River Day* (NJ)
Leiner, John, *Chinese American Intl.* (CA)
Leiser, Holly, *Saint Paul's School* (FL)
Lemay, Roland, *School Year Abroad* (China)
Lemay, Roland, *School Year Abroad* (France)
Lemay, Roland, *School Year Abroad* (Italy)
Lemay, Roland, *School Year Abroad* (MA)
Lemay, Roland, *School Year Abroad* (Spain)
Lemon, Thomas, *St. Mark's High School* (DE)
Lencke, Bobbie, *Wesleyan School* (GA)
Lenio, Julie M., *MMI Prep* (PA)
Lettengarver, Beth, *The Pine School* (FL)
Levner, Abigail S., *The Philadelphia School* (PA)
Lew, Anne, *Wyoming Seminary* (PA)
Lewis, Julie C., *Sheridan School* (DC)
Lifrak, Dr. Stephen T., *Storm King* (NY)
Liggitt, Jen, *Hockaday* (TX)
Lindberg, Donna, *Columbus School for Girls* (OH)
Liu, Patricia, *Iolani School* (HI)
Lloyd, Gillian, *The Rivers School* (MA)
Loder, Karen A., *Gill St. Bernard's* (NJ)
Lofquist, Molly, *The Prairie School* (WI)
Lohmar, Krista, *Canterbury School* (IN)
Lojo, Ken, *Strake Jesuit College Prep* (TX)
Lomask, Diana, *Saint Ann's School* (NY)
Loncar, Julia B., *Academy at the Lakes* (FL)
Lopez, Kathleen, *St. Mary's Episcopal Day* (FL)
Lopiccolo, Barbara, *Academy/Sacred Heart* (MI)
Lord, Treavor, *Hill School/ Middleburg* (VA)
Lordy, Paula, *The Winston School* (NJ)
Lorenzi, Scot, *Winchester Thurston* (PA)
Loughlin, Kimberly C., *Oldfields School* (MD)
Love, Julia, *ACS Intl. Schools* (England)
Low, Theodore J., *Eaglebrook* (MA)
Luciano, Sr. Filippa, *Mary Louis Academy* (NY)
Lundquist, Jill, *Poughkeepsie Day* (NY)
Lupero, Stephanie, *Stuart CDS/Sacred Heart* (NJ)
Lurie, Gretchen, *Chandler School* (CA)
Lutz, Linda, *Saint Stephen's Episcopal* (FL)
Lynch, Jo Ann, *The Buckley School* (NY)
Lynch, Patricia, *Bishop Montgomery HS* (CA)

M

Mabley, Winifred, *Brearley* (NY)
Mabry, Mark, *Ring Mountain Day* (CA)
Macek, Lt. Col. Steve, *Fork Union Military* (VA)
MacInnes, Heather, *Quaker School—Horsham* (PA)
Mack, Elaine, *The Nora School* (MD)
MacMahon, Colm, *Berkeley Carroll* (NY)
Madison, Catherine, *Cathedral for Boys* (CA)
Maloberti, Gregg, *Lawrenceville* (NJ)
Maloney, Maura, *Saint Ignatius College Prep* (IL)
Mandell, Peggy Klein, *Springside School* (PA)
Mantel, Irene, *Rudolf Steiner School* (NY)
Marchesseault, Leslie, *Glen Urquhart* (MA)
Marlis, Lauren R., *Hilton Head Prep* (SC)
Marsau, Blythe, *St. Martin's Episcopal* (GA)
Marshall, Jan, *Franklin Road Academy* (TN)
Martin, Cmdr. Frank III, USN (Ret.), *Hargrave* (VA)
Martin, Katharine, *Rossman School* (MO)
Masciale-Lynch, Susan, *Oakwood Friends* (NY)
Mason, Suzanne H., *Moravian Academy* (PA)
Mathews, Linda D., *Cathedral/St. John the Divine* (NY)
Mattia, Elise, *Brooklyn Heights Montessori* (NY)
Mattson, Libby, *Ridgefield Academy* (CT)
Mayo, Meg, *Connelly /Holy Child* (MD)
Mazzuca, Mary, *Sandy Springs Friends* (MD)
McAuliffe, Molly, *Mid-Peninsula HS* (CA)
McCaffery, Julie A., *Primary Day* (MD)
McCallie, Alex, *Westminster Schools /Augusta* (GA)
McCann, Kathy, *Seattle CDS* (WA)
McColl, Christopher T., *Hackley School* (NY)

McDermott, Molly, *The Grosse Pointe Academy* (MI)
McDowell, Kimberly A., *St. Margaret's* (VA)
McIlvaine, Janie, *Berkeley Prep* (FL)
McKannay, Lynn, *Town School for Boys* (CA)
McKenna, Pamela R., *Convent/Sacred Heart* (CT)
McKenna, Sally Jeanne, *Polytechnic School* (CA)
McLaurin, Pamela Parks, *Winsor* (MA)
McLean, Marci, *Parish Episcopal* (TX)
McLeod, Emily H., *Trinity Episcopal* (VA)
McPherson, Michelle, *Stone Ridge/Sacred Heart* (MD)
McWilliams, *Cynthia S., Millbrook* (NY)
Memory, Katherine, *Summit School* (NC)
Meredith, Craig, *The John Cooper School* (TX)
Merritt, Debra, *The Priory* (Canada)
Metz, Margaret, *Nightingale-Bamford* (NY)
Mihm, Katherine H., *Shady Side Academy* (PA)
Mijalis-Kahn, Elaine J., *Ransom Everglades* (FL)
Miller, Brian, *Central Catholic HS* (PA)
Miller, Carrie, *Oak Hill School* (OR)
Miller, Drew, *Cranbrook Schools* (MI)
Miller, Karin B., *Moorestown Friends* (NJ)
Miller, Maureen V., *National Cathedral School* (DC)
Miller, Nathalie, *Berkeley Hall* (CA)
Mitchell, Erby L., *Sidwell Friends School* (DC)
Mitchell, George, *Buckingham Browne & Nichols* (MA)
Mitchell, James Irwin, *Alexander Dawson* (CO)
Mitchell, Marjorie, *Westminster Schools* (GA)
Mobley, Erin, *Cornelia Connelly* (CA)
Moncure, A. Scott, *The Steward School* (VA)
Monks, Paul, *Canton CDS* (OH)
Montano, Darla, *St. James Episcopal* (TX)
Montgomery, Tim, *Guilford Day* (NC)
Moody, Kerry, *The Langley School* (VA)
Moore, Mary Beth, *Capitol Hill Day* (DC)
Moran, Tricia, *Lesley Ellis School* (MA)
Moreira, Lisa J., *Horace Mann* (NY)
Morse, Sarah, *The Jemicy School* (MD)
Morton, Danette, *Greensboro Day* (NC)
Mosteller, Kelly, *Meadowbrook School* (PA)
Moyer, Linda, *The Gillispie School* (CA)
Mozley, Patricia H., *The Walker School* (GA)
Mulligan, George, *Landon School* (MD)
Mulligan, Mimi, *Norwood School* (MD)
Muradi, Victoria, *Durham Academy* (NC)
Murphy, Carol, *Sage Ridge* (NV)
Murphy, Christine L., *Moravian Academy* (PA)
Murphy, Laura, *The Out-of-Door Academy* (FL)
Murphy, Mary Lacey, *Far Brook* (NJ)
Mynnti, Valerie A., *The Harley School* (NY)
Myong, Esther Kim, *Seoul Foreign* (Korea)

N

Naspo, Kristen, *Hillside School* (MA)
Neal, Kelsey, *Burgundy Farm CDS* (VA)
Nelsen, Charlotte H., *The Potomac School* (VA)
Newton, Maria, *Annunciation Orthodox* (TX)
Nicholson, Laura, *Brenau Academy* (GA)
Nicoletta, Christine R., *Lake Forest CDS* (IL)
Nielsen, Nan, *The Harker School* (CA)
Nordeman, Anne, *St. Bernard's School* (NY)
Norgren, Jackie, *Holy Name Central Jr./Sr. HS* (MA)
Norton, Elizabeth, *York Prep* (NY)
Nothstein, Patricia M., *Bryn Mawr* (MD)

O

O'Brien, Michelle, *Lancaster CDS* (PA)
O'Connor, Susan, *Oakcrest School* (VA)
O'Donnell, James E., *Kingswood-Oxford* (CT)
O'Neal, Kathy, *University Prep* (WA)
Oakes, Patricia F., *New Canaan Country School* (CT)
Obrecht, Michael, *Maclay School* (FL)
Oestreicher, Marguerite, *Salisbury Academy* (NC)
Ohanesian, Erica L., *Foxcroft School* (VA)
Olson, Jared, *Lowell Whiteman* (CO)
Orloff, Blair Talcott, *Elisabeth Morrow* (NJ)
Overbye, Christopher, *Dexter School* (MA)
Overbye, Christopher, *Southfield School* (MA)
Owens, Katie, *Convent/Visitation School*(MN)

P

Pacheco, Jeanne M., *Riverview School* (MA)
Palmer, Nancy, *Fort Worth Academy* (TX)
Pananos, Janet, *Kehoe-France* (LA)
Pansano, Susan, *St. Martin's Episcopal* (LA)
Papir, Erica L., *The Caedmon School* (NY)
Papp, Leah, *The Swain School* (PA)
Pargman, Brian, *St. Johns CDS* (FL)
Parham, Carol, *The Ancona School* (IL)
Parker, Elizabeth, *Tower School* (MA)
Parrish, Scott, *Battle Ground Academy* (TN)
Pearline, Sharon, *Windward School* (CA)
Pehlke, Jane C., *Gibson Island* (MD)
Perla, Amanda, *Phillips Brooks* (CA)
Perlmutter, Terry, *Applewild School* (MA)
Perniciaro, Alex, *St. Stephen's School* (Italy)
Perriello, Bo, *St. Anne's-Belfield* (VA)
Perry, Martha, *St. Clement's School* (Canada)
Peters, Julie, *The Canterbury School* (FL)
Petrie, Mimi, *Curtis School* (CA)
Petty, Meg, *Seattle Waldorf* (WA)
Phelps, Donetta, *Delphian* (OR)
Phillips, Clemmie, *Mayfield Senior/Holy Child* (CA)
Philpott, Jay, *St. George's Independent* (TN)
Pickrell, Ann C., *Williston Northampton* (MA)
Pivinski, Kate, *Francis W. Parker School* (IL)
Plank, Richard J., *Cape Henry Collegiate* (VA)
Pleasant, Sharon L., *Stoneleigh-Burnham* (MA)
Pochet, Courtney, *Queen Anne* (MD)
Popeil, Pamela, *Bernard Zell Anshe Emet Day* (IL)
Porter, Karen, *Idyllwild Arts Academy* (CA)
Post, Suzanne R., *Rumson CDS* (NJ)
Poteet, Michele, *Crestview Prep* (CA)
Potter, Ellen, *Dutchess Day School* (NY)
Price, Allison M., *Derryfield* (NH)
Primm, Mary Lou, *The Benjamin School* (FL)
Prokopiak, Madonna, *Manzano Day School* (NM)
Prokopowicz, Emily, *The Oakwood School* (NC)
Prosperi, Jorge D., *Detroit CDS* (MI)
Purviance, Linda, *Jackson Academy* (MS)

Q

Quattlebaum, Wendy, *Sacred Heart, Atherton* (CA)
Quinto, Patricia, *Grace Day School* (NY)
Quiring, A. Lee, *St. Matthew's Parish School* (CA)

R

Radtke, Matt, *Hammond School* (SC)
Radtke, Susan, *Park City Academy* (UT)
Raffetto, Katie, *The Community School* (ID)
Ramos, Bobby, *Urban School/San Francisco* (CA)

Rancourt, Dr. Regan E., *Holy Comforter* (FL)
Randall, Caroline, *Seacrest CDS* (FL)
Rattew, Amelia, *UN International School* (NY)
Ré, Amy M., *Powhatan School* (VA)
Redell, Lori W., *Poly Prep CDS* (NY)
Reece, Sam R., *Tenacre CDS* (MA)
Reed, Bradford L., *Bolles* (FL)
Reed, Claire, *Sterling Hall* (Canada)
Reeves, Jay, *Miller School* (VA)
Renda, Sara Lynn, *Westover School* (CT)
Rendall, Betsy N., *Newtown Friends* (PA)
Renick, Ann, *Parker School* (HI)
Reynolds, Danny, *Palmer Trinity School* (FL)
Richburg, Sue, *Chesapeake Academy* (MD)
Rieck, Br. James, FSC, *La Salle College HS* (PA)
Rill, Kate R., *Linden Hall* (PA)
Roach, Randy, *Fountain Valley School* (CO)
Robbins, Doris, *Halifax Grammar* (Canada)
Robertson, Ela Jean, *Olney Friends* (OH)
Robinson, Joyce R., *Pine Crest/Boca Raton* (FL)
Robinson, Levyette, *Bermuda HS for Girls* (Bermuda)
Rodgers, Sharron, *Holton-Arms* (MD)
Roesch, Marcia, *Bank Street School* (NY)
Rogers, Carol, *East Woods School* (NY)
Rogers, Jenna C., *Riverdale Country School* (NY)
Romanowicz, Ronald H., *The Harvey School* (NY)
Romeo, Rorry, *Corlears School* (NY)
Ronald, Josephine, *American Intl. Chennai* (India)
Root, Barbara, *Convent/Sacred Heart* (NY)
Rosen, Jennifer, *Isidore Newman* (LA)
Rosen, Letty, *The Newport School* (MD)
Rowars, Debra, *Day School/Coral Springs* (FL)
Rowe, Barbara B., *West Chester Friends* (PA)
Rowe, Kristin H., *Harbor Day* (CA)
Rowe, Vincent, *Georgetown Day School* (DC)
Roy, Michael '85, *St. Andrew's College* (Canada)
Roye, Ana J., *Carrollton of the Sacred Heart* (FL)
Rudisi, Heather, *Ranney School* (NJ)
Ruggiero, Jeffrey, *Eagle Hill-Southport* (CT)
Rupp, Jim, *Seattle Academy* (WA)
Rusbarsky, Adrienne, *The College School* (MO)
Ruth-Williams, Barbara, *Village School* (CA)

S

Sadlon, Jay K., *Derby Academy* (MA)
Sahadi, Natasha, *The Town School* (NY)
Salvatore, Carrie, *King & Low-Heywood Thomas* (CT)
Salvo, Steve, *Browne Academy* (VA)
Sarewitz, Anne, *Epiphany School* (WA)
Saulsberry, Dana Scott, *Community School* (MO)
Schabe, Carol, *The Harbor School* (MD)
Scheidt, Steve M., *Gilmour Academy* (OH)
Schellhorn, Mary, *The Masters School* (NY)
Schiavenza, Lisa, *Menlo School* (CA)
Schiess, Kelley K., *Summit CDS* (OH)
Schlickmann, Devin K., *Gilmour Academy* (OH)
Schmidt, Maureen K., *Wyndcroft* (PA)
Schmidt, Ola, *Munich Intl. School* (Germany)
Schuhmacher, Jill C., *Lexington Christian* (MA)
Schuler, Nancy, *Westminster School* (VA)
Schultz, Louis A., *The Columbus Academy* (OH)
Sckolnik, Eve, *Colorado Springs School* (CO)
Scott, Kerie Beth, *Westchester CDS* (NC)
Seals, Stephanie, *Rivermont Collegiate* (IA)
Secor, Wendy Sibert, *Dana Hall* (MA)
Seibert, Maj. Greg, *Missouri Military* (MO)
Seiler, Robin, *Louisville Collegiate* (KY)
Seitz, Susanne, *Lakehill Prep* (TX)
Serrill, Barbara, *Germantown Academy* (PA)
Sevante, Christy, *Academy/Sacred Heart* (LA)
Shelburne, Cathy, *Menlo School* (CA)
Sherlock, Linda, *All Saints' Episcopal School* (TX)
Shine, Kathleen, *Academy/Our Lady of Mercy* (CT)
Shinkle, Adaline, *The Blake School* (MN)
Shoolman, Barbara, *Brimmer and May* (MA)
Short, Meg, *The Knox School* (NY)
Shuffman, Linda, *Staten Island Academy* (NY)
Sicnolf, Andrew, *Bishop Verot Catholic HS* (FL)
Siegfried, Scott, *Providence Day* (NC)
Sills, Robin, *Westside Neighborhood* (CA)
Silvestri, Joseph P., *North Yarmouth Academy* (ME)
Simon, Gregory P., *Notre Dame Prep/Marist* (MI)
Simpson, Julie, *The Calverton School* (MD)
Sims, Myrtle Alice, *St. John's School* (TX)
Sinnathamby, Murali, *Massanutten Military* (VA)
Slaton, Diann, *Shelton School* (TX)
Slaughter, Steve, *The Montessori School* (CT)
Slider, Russell L., *Woodward Academy* (GA)
Slocum, Ann, *Iona Prep* (NY)
Smart, Patricia, *Village Christian* (CA)
Smith, Amy C., *The Winston School* (TX)
Smith, Debra H., *University Lake* (WI)
Smith, Nancy, *Metropolitan School* (MO)
Smith-Dibble, Audrey J., *Kingsbury CDS* (MI)
Snyder, Barbara B., *The Woods Academy* (MD)
Snyder, Mary S., *Brookstone School* (GA)
Southworth, Thomas D., *Loomis Chaffee* (CT)
Spear, Linda, *The Dunham School* (LA)
Speck, Beth, *Duchesne Academy* (TX)
Spence, Rebecca, *The Red Oaks School* (NJ)
Spencer, Leon, *The Tatnall School* (DE)
Sprinkle, Heidi K.L., *Harford Day Schoo*l (MD)
Stahura, Eric G., *Doane Stuart School* (NY)
Stancil, Chris, *George Walton Academy* (GA)
Stephens, Sharon, *Marymount HS* (CA)
Stetson, G. Arthur, *Flintridge Prep* (CA)
Stewart, Mary Lou, *Independent Day* (CT)
Stewart, Philip A., Ph.D., *The Windsor School* (NY)
Stokes, Denis, *Christ School* (NC)
Straub, Mary Ann, *St. Andrew's Episcopal* (LA)
Strowd, Claire, *Pace Academy* (GA)
Struder, Cathy, *Notre Dame Academy* (VA)
Strudwick, Loring, *Lake Forest Academy* (IL)
Sudmyer, Amy, *Cold Spring School* (CT)
Sullivan, Carolyn, *Pembroke Hill* (MO)
Sullivan, Colleen, *Gateway School* (CA)
Sullivan, Kathryn F. '94, *Kent School* (CT)
Surgner, Amanda, *Collegiate School* (VA)
Suzuki, Matthew, *Rye CDS* (NY)
Sweeney, Maureen A., *Windward School* (NY)
Swett, Pascha, *The Ensworth School* (TN)
Sykes, Julie B., *Saint David's School* (NY)
Sylvester, Tom, *Phoenix CDS* (AZ)
Symonds, Kate, *St. Hilda's & St. Hugh's* (NY)

T

Takahashi, Danette, *Kimberton Waldorf* (PA)
Takamine, Carol, *Hanahau'oli School* (HI)
Talent, Irene, *Trafalgar Castle* (Canada)
Taylor, Gary, *Wooster School* (CT)
Taylor, Jennifer, *St. George's Independent* (TN)
Taylor, Julie L., *St. Paul's Episcopa*l (AL)
Taylor, Mark, *Chicago Academy for the Arts* (IL)
Taylor, Nancy, *Grace-St. Luke's Episcopal* (TN)
Taylor, Susan L., *Le Jardin Academy* (HI)
Taylor, Willard L., Jr., *Newark Academy* (NJ)
Telford, R. Scott, *St. Andrew's School* (RI)
Templin-Page, Samantha, *Rohan Woods* (MO)
Teti, Rebecca, *Alexandria CDS* (VA)
Tew, Laurel Baker, *Viewpoint School* (CA)

Thielen, Averyl, *Mayfield Junior School* (CA)
Thomas, Karen, *Santiago College* (Chile)
Thomas, Kathy, *Academy/Saint Elizabeth* (NJ)
Thompson, Taisha, *Ethical Culture Fieldston* (NY)
Thorp, Pamela, *Convent/Sacred Heart ES* (CA)
Thorp, Pamela, *Stuart Hall for Boys* (CA)
Tilden, Elizabeth, *Drew School* (CA)
Tilney, Rachel, *Kimball Union* (NH)
Timm, Ann, *Columbus School for Girls* (OH)
Tomelloso, Ester, *Sandia Prep* (NM)
Toryak, Donna Venezia, *Mount Saint Mary* (NJ)
Travaglione, Vincent, *La Jolla CDS* (CA)
Tretter, Ellen, *Dedham CDS* (MA)
Trezza, Sandy, *Haddonfield Friends* (NJ)
Tripp, Heather, *The Clark School* (MA)
Tsang, Annie, *Bay School/San Francisco* (CA)
Tsemberlis, Lisa, *Hilltop CDS* (NJ)
Turekian, Roxanne, *St. Thomas's Day School* (CT)

U

Uldrick, Lucia, *Salem Academy* (NC)
Utz, Patricia, *The Jemicy School* (MD)

V

Valente, Lindsey, *The Catherine Cook School* (IL)
Valenzuela, Vincent, *Rutgers Prep* (NJ)
Veitch, D. Michael, *Univ. of Chicago Lab* (IL)
Vella, Karen, *Winchester Thurston* (PA)
Vincent, Barbara, *Meadowbrook of Weston* (MA)
Vitale, Megan, *Cliff Valley School* (GA)

W

Waage, Dan, *All Saints' Episcopal Day* (AZ)
Wachtel, Brooke, *The Mead School* (CT)
Wainio, Jason, *The Country School* (CT)
Waldorf, Susan, *Tallulah Falls* (GA)
Walker, Karen, *Telluride Mtn. School* (CO)
Walker, Millie H., *Rocky Mount Academy* (NC)
Wall, Kay, *The Stanwich School* (CT)
Walpole, Andrew R.N., *Sanford School* (DE)
Walsh, Maureen McKeown, *Saint Basil* (PA)
Wandling, James, *St. Benedict's Prep* (NJ)
Wargo, Sue Ann, *St. Andrew's Priory* (HI)
Warren, Sandy, *Academy at Charlemont* (MA)
Waters, Brenda H., *Norfolk Collegiate* (VA)
Watt, Virginia, *Barnhart School* (CA)
Watters, Anne B., *Green Vale* (NY)
Webb, Chris, *Bridgton Academy* (ME)
Webster, Nancy, *University High School* (IN)
Weinberger, Karen, *Congressional Schools* (VA)
Weinstein, Kathi, *Great Barrington Rudolf Steiner* (MA)
Weller, Andrew T., *Chestnut Hill Academy* (PA)
Wentz, Dale L., *North Shore CDS* (IL)
Wetmore, Tracey, *Morristown-Beard* (NJ)
Whalen, Deborah, *St. Agnes Academy* (TX)
Whalen, Kathleen, *Good Shepherd Episcopal* (TX)
White, Christopher, *Country Day* (Canada)
White, Jonathan, *Thayer Academy* (MA)
White, Nasi Maghsoudnia, *Bentley* (CA)
Whitney, Stephanie, *Greens Farms Academy* (CT)
Wilbanks, Kelly Jones, *St. Catherine's* (VA)
Wilcox, Rageshwar K., *Marymount Santa Barbara* (CA)
Wild, Dianne, *Harpeth Hall* (TN)
Wilder, Abby, *Crystal Springs Uplands* (CA)
Wilkinson, Charlotte, *St. Mark's Cathedral* (LA)
Williams, Andrea, *The Barrie School* (MD)
Williams, Debbie, *Crane CDS* (CA)
Williams, Diane, *St. Andrew's Episcopal* (TX)
Williams, Kirby, *Greenwich CDS* (CT)
Wilson, Andrew, *Grier School* (PA)
Wilson, Bonnie A., *The Kildonan School* (NY)
Wilson, Tracy, *Ojai Valley* (CA)
Wilson-Neil, Judy, *Collingwood School* (Canada)
Winchell, Mark '98, *Salesianum* (DE)
Winchester, Chris, *New Garden Friends* (NC)
Windsor, Janna, *Clairbourn School* (CA)
Winter, Barbara, *PACE-Brantley Hall* (FL)
Wiygul, Jimmy, *Altamont* (AL)
Wolf, Amy, *Shattuck-St. Mary's* (MN)
Wolf, Peggy K., *Roland Park* (MD)
Wolke, Lauren, *Laurence School* (CA)
Wolstan, Judith S., *Chadwick School* (CA)
Wong, Erwin T., *Calvary Christian* (CA)
Woodward, Ann B., *Greenwich Academy* (CT)
Wootton, Karen, *Glenelg* (MD)
Worthington, Annette, *The Willow School* (NJ)
Wright, Camille, *Fox Chapel CDS* (PA)
Wright, Jeffrey D., *Lee Academy* (ME)
Wright, Maggi, *Turning Point School* (CA)
Wu, Lisa, *Lick-Wilmerding HS* (CA)

Y

Young, Dori, Charles *Wright Academy* (WA)
Yusick, Laura Lombardo '96, *Nichols School* (NY)

Z

Zappelli, Al, *Woodside Priory School* (CA)
Zilian, Geri, *Portsmouth Abbey* (RI)
Zinser, Lori, *The Roeper School* (MI)
Ziplow, Patty, *Friends Academy* (NY)
Zondervan, Denise, *Foothill CDS* (CA)
Zucker, Jonathan, *College Preparatory* (CA)

Summer Programs 2008

What are you and your child looking for? A traditional summer camp? Creative and artistic opportunities? Hands-on computer and technology training? A sports clinic? Study in another country? Outdoor adventure opportunities? Do you want your child to learn about different cultures or to participate in community outreach? Perhaps your child needs support in an academic area or seeks college credit.

From coast to coast and overseas, the programs listed in these Yellow Pages offer a wide variety of ways to spend the summer in exploration, relaxation, growth, and renewal. Begin your search by reviewing the Yellow Pages Grid, which will help you prepare a list of appropriate offerings. Be sure, as well, to read the Blue Pages Grid, which references additional summer programs conducted by the schools in this book.

Time spent in summer learning, whether it's one week or two months, is exciting and rewarding. Make the summer count. Find the program of your choice in the Yellow Pages.

Bunting and Lyon, Inc.

238 North Main Street Wallingford, Connecticut 06492
1-203-269-3333 Fax 1-203-269-5697
E-mail: BuntingandLyon@aol.com
www.BuntingandLyon.com

MAKE YOUR SUMMER COUNT! CHOOSE FROM THESE OPPORTUNITIES IN 2008!

Academic Courses

enrichment
college credit
high school credit
computer technology
study skills & strategies
learning differences
English as a Second Language
SAT preparation

Fine & Performing Arts

drawing, painting & sculpture
photography & film
dance & movement
drama & theater production
vocal & instrumental ensembles

Travel & Adventure

cultural & language studies
foreign travel
leadership training
wilderness & survival training
oceanography & marine science

Sports & Recreation

skill-building & healthy competition
specialized clinics
archery to windsurfing
& every activity between

Field Trips

environmental/ecological excursions
college exploration
historical sites
cultural enhancement
sporting events & fun

GEOGRAPHICAL

DISTRIBUTION OF SCHOOLS

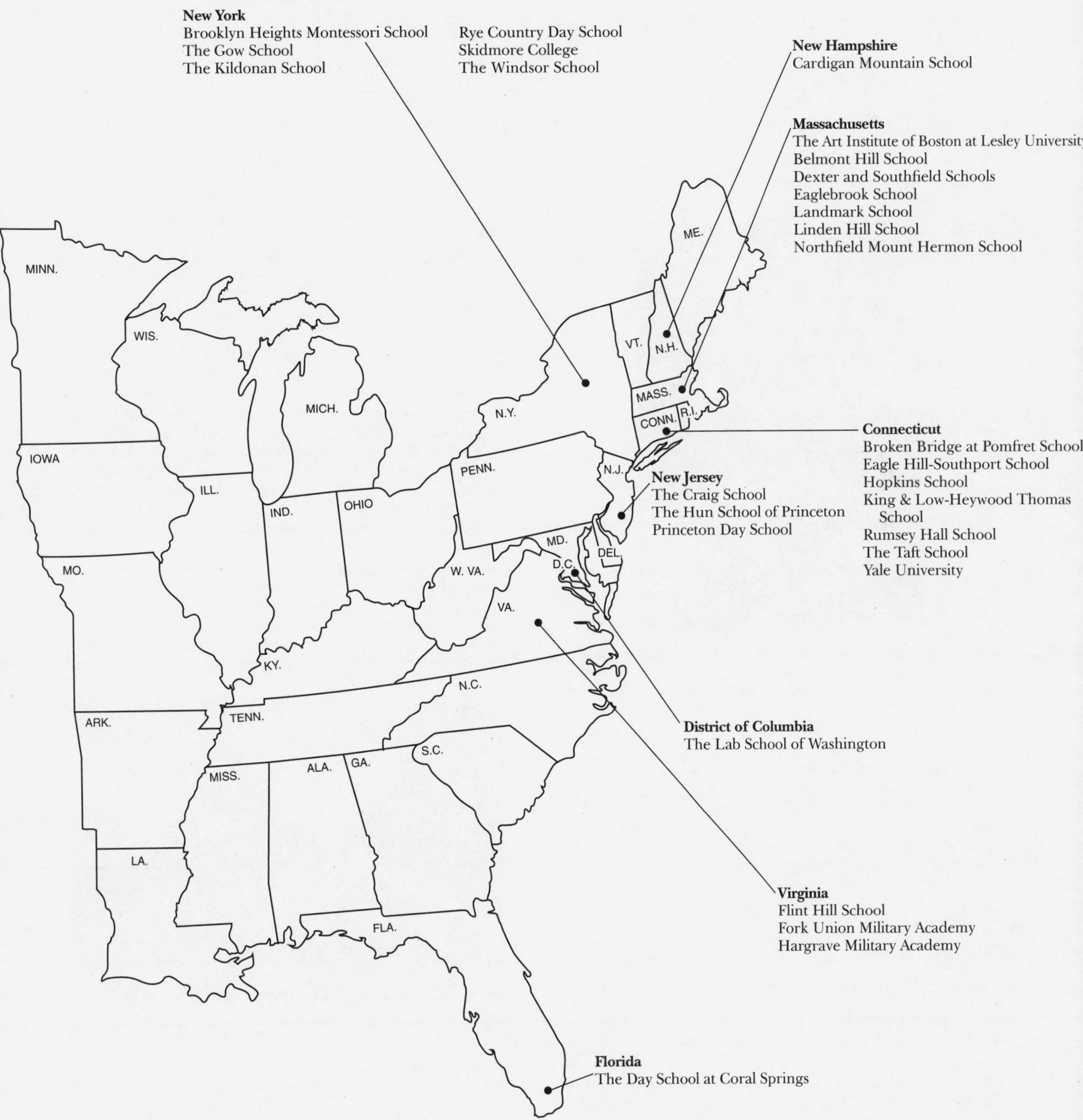

THE ART INSTITUTE OF BOSTON AT LESLEY UNIVERSITY

Young Artist Residency Summer Program 2007
Kerri Fisher, Coordinator

700 Beacon Street
Boston, Massachusetts 02215
Tel. 617-585-6724/6729; [Toll-free] 800-773-0494
Fax 617-585-6721
Web Site www.aiboston.edu
E-mail kfisher3@aiboston.edu

Day & Residential, Coeducational, Entering Grades 9–12

THE ART INSTITUTE OF BOSTON AT LESLEY UNIVERSITY PRE-COLLEGE SUMMER PROGRAM offers college courses for high school students in a university environment. Young artists expand their creative skills, work with a staff of professional artists, and build a unique portfolio. A limited number of students entering Grade 11 or 12 may live in the Lesley University residence halls while taking a full schedule of visual art courses. This intensive Young Artist Residency Program carries six college credits and includes museum visits, lectures, and tours of local professional artists' studios. The application deadline is May 10 for U.S. students and May 1 for international students.

Each Pre-College class, lasting three and one-half hours, meets seven times in July. Alternative Photographic Processes, Animation Festival, Art of the Handmade Book, Beginning Sculpture, Advanced Figure Drawing, Black and White Photography II, Color Photography, Drawing II, Experimental Figure Sculpture, Fashion Illustration, Figure Drawing Portfolio, Illustration, Animation, Graphic Design Techniques, Mural Painting, Video Production, and Digital Photography earn one college credit. Also offered are noncredit courses in Art Appreciation, Foundation in Drawing and Design, Portfolio Preparation, and Young Photographers' Workshop.

Participants gain experience using sophisticated equipment such as digital cameras, photo enlargers, computers, scanners, and printers. All materials are provided by AIB. The session culminates in a professional exhibit of students' work.

Contact The Art Institute for more details.

BELMONT HILL SCHOOL

Belmont Hill School Summer Programs
Colleen Kramer, Coordinator

350 Prospect Street
Belmont, Massachusetts 02478
Tel. 617-993-5215
Web Site www.belmont-hill.org/summer

Day, Coeducational

Summer School: 500 Students, Grades 6–12
Sport Camps: 800 Campers, Ages 6–16

BELMONT HILL SCHOOL SUMMER PROGRAMS offer academic courses for credit and enrichment as well as sport camps, music programs, and art programs for ages 6–18. The programs, which enroll private and public school students, extend from late June to early August.

Courses for Grades 6–12 feature small classes, with individual tutoring available. Classes meet for 50-minute periods, and students are encouraged to take several courses. Among the offerings are Expository Writing, Creative Writing, SAT English; Pre-algebra, Algebra I–II, Geometry, Trigonometry, Pre-calculus, Calculus, SAT Math; General Science, Physical Science, Biology, Chemistry, Physics; U.S. History, Western Civilization; and Chinese, French, Latin, and Spanish. There are also courses in ESL, Writing for the Internet and Programming, Robotics, Developmental Reading, Speech and Debate, and Study Skills.

The Art Program enables students to refine familiar skills or develop new interests through immersion in photography, theater, cartooning, jewelry making, woodworking, painting, drawing, sculpture, and pottery. Courses are taught by teachers proficient in their respective media. The music program for Grades 6–12 allows students to perfect skills in garage rock, jazz, and classical ensemble.

Sport camps engage students in training and competition in coed strength and conditioning and tennis; separate boys' and girls' basketball, lacrosse, and soccer; boys' baseball and wrestling; and girls' field hockey. Each camp is directed and staffed by experienced adult coaches.

Belmont Hill is located 5 miles west of Boston.

Contact Belmont Hill for more details; see listing on page 155.

BROKEN BRIDGE AT POMFRET SCHOOL

Broken Bridge Arts Workshops
Brad Davis, Director

398 Pomfret Street
Pomfret, Connecticut 06258
Tel. 860-963-5220
Web Site www.brokenbridge.us
E-mail brad@brokenbridge.us

Private Boarding School, Coeducational, Grades 9–12

BROKEN BRIDGE offers fine arts workshops for high school students from June 21 to June 30, 2008. Participants choose one of five programs: Writing Poetry, Writing Fiction, Acting, Drawing, or 3-Dimensional Art; the latter gears students toward an AP portfolio. Students board in dormitories, benefiting from interaction with others with the same ambition. All focus on the creative process, growth in writing and artistic skills, and empathetic critique.

Faculty members are an integral part of the program as they strive to help young artists realize their creative goals. Residential faculty, all of whom have graduated from Pomfret School, provide inspiration and guidance outside of the classroom experience. The visiting faculty consists of award-winning performers and artists and published writers who teach Broken Bridge's courses and workshops and facilitate idea generation and evaluation of work.

All students attend a master class each morning; workshops meet in the afternoon. Courses focus on peer- and self-evaluation, encouragement from faculty and students, and the ability to critique work honestly and effectively. The program's design encourages listening, conversation, and collaboration among the five workshops in an effort to foster out-of-the-box thinking. Each night students contribute to the Festival of the Arts, a program open to the public that features faculty and student work, readings, performances, and installations.

Located in northeast Connecticut, Pomfret's 500-acre campus supports extracurricular activities through athletic fields and facilities, a boathouse, observatory, library, chapel, and dance, woodworking, and art studios.

Contact Pomfret for more details.

BROOKLYN HEIGHTS MONTESSORI SCHOOL

Summer Camp
Molly Davis, Director

185 Court Street
Brooklyn, New York 11201
Tel. 718-858-5100, Ext. 19
Web Site www.bhmsny.org
E-mail mdavis@bhmsny.org

Day, Coeducational, Ages 3–12

BROOKLYN HEIGHTS MONTESSORI SCHOOL offers preschool and elementary programs for ages 3–12 from mid-June to early August. Students can enroll in one three-week session or two two-week sessions that include art, athletics, enrichment courses, and activities.

Students ages 3–5 may enroll in the Juniors Division, which meets five days a week from 9:00 A.M. to 3:00 P.M. All students participate in activities such as swimming, painting, mask-making, music, cooking, and learning about different animals and their habitats. Taking care of the environment is also emphasized; students plant and maintain a garden. Field trips to the beach, botanical gardens, and city parks enhance the program.

The Elementary Division is open to students entering Grades 1–6. Twice a week, students participate in games and athletics at Prospect Park, while swimming lessons are held on two days at St. Francis College and the neighborhood YMCA. Other activities include photography, water games, science experiments, workshops led by park rangers, painting, sculpture, ceramics, jewelry-making, drama, journalism, yoga, chess, dance, and cooking. Every Friday, students visit the New York Aquarium, Riis Park Beach, a wildlife preserve, or other city attractions.

In addition, a program for 3-year-olds who will be entering the School in September is provided. Students become accustomed to a school atmosphere and meet new friends and teachers.

An extended-day After Camp program is available in which students may arrive as early as 8:15 A.M. and leave as late as 6:00 P.M. The After Camp session includes arts and crafts, board games, movies, and free time.

Contact Brooklyn Heights Montessori for more details; *see listing on page 226.*

CARDIGAN MOUNTAIN SCHOOL

Cardigan Mountain Summer Session
Ryan Feeley, Director
Canaan, New Hampshire 03741
Tel. 603-523-3548; Fax 603-523-3565
Web Site www.cardigan.org
E-mail rfeeley@cardigan.org
Boarding, Coeducational, Grades 3–9

CARDIGAN MOUNTAIN SUMMER SESSION offers remedial and enrichment academic courses and a recreational program of land and water sports for students in Grades 3 through 9. The six-week session begins in late June and ends in early August. Classes meet six days a week.

The academic program focuses on the reinforcement or enrichment of fundamental skills in Reading, Language Arts, and Mathematics in small classes. Each student's strengths and weaknesses are carefully diagnosed and a curriculum is tailored to meet his or her individual needs. In addition, a number of students take Computer, Environmental Science, French, Latin, Spanish, Photography, accelerated courses in English, Mathematics, and Fine Arts, or sports clinics. A limited number of international students are accepted for study of English as a Second Language.

In each three-week period, a student chooses two activities for the afternoon recreation programs. These include tennis, soccer, flag football, baseball, softball, music, riflery, trapshooting, horseback riding, swimming, sailing, canoeing, art, rocketry, drama, and basketball, among others. In addition, three-day trail camping and canoeing trips to the White Mountains occur weekly.

The 525-acre lakeside campus has ten tennis courts (four indoor), a gymnasium, a rifle range, and five athletic fields. It is located 275 miles from New York City and 120 miles from Boston and is accessible by plane, car, or bus. Group transportation to and from Boston's Logan International Airport is provided.

Contact Cardigan Mountain for more details; see listing on page 204.

THE CRAIG SCHOOL

Summer Program
Niles Furlong, Director
Grades 3–8: 10 Tower Hill Road
Mountain Lakes, New Jersey 07046
Grades 9–12: 200 Comly Road
Lincoln Park, New Jersey 07035
Tel. 973-334-1295
Web Site www.craigschool.org
E-mail jday@craigschool.org
Day, 50 Boys & 30 Girls, Grades 3–12

THE CRAIG SUMMER PROGRAM provides morning academic sessions for Grades 3–12 and afternoon enrichment opportunities for ages 6–14 in a nurturing, relaxed environment.

Elementary school students, at the Mountain Lakes campus, improve study habits and reinforce previous classroom learning in four areas. Reading employs multisensory Orton-Gillingham methods and features comprehension strategies. Language Arts focuses on language processing and written expression. Math concentrates on problem solving and computation strategies, while Computer Skills includes word processing and Internet projects. High school students, at the Lincoln Park campus, also work in four areas. They increase their interpretation and comprehension abilities in Literature and acquire skill in process writing and thesis development in Writing Skills. Integrated Math focuses on concepts in pre-algebra, algebra, and geometry, while Science covers topics and methods in earth science, physical science, biology, and chemistry. Designed to reinforce and consolidate school year educational gains, all academic courses meet for 45 minutes four days a week for four weeks. Technology is integrated into the curriculum as appropriate.

An enrichment program, which meets for a two-week session in June and a four-week session in July, gives ages 6–14 hands-on, cooperative learning experiences in art, computers, drama, science, sports, and swimming. Students are encouraged to engage in positive social communication and creative expression. Trips may include the Jersey Shore, the Meadowlands, or Yankee Stadium.

Contact Craig for more details; see listing on page 207.

THE DAY SCHOOL AT CORAL SPRINGS

Camp Imagine
Eric Wilson, Director
9001 Westview Drive
Coral Springs, Florida 33067
Tel. 954-255-0020; Fax 954-255-1336
Web Site www.camp-imagine.com
E-mail info@camp-imagine.com
Day, Coeducational, Ages 3–14

CAMP IMAGINE offers traditional camp and career-themed activities for students ages 3–14. The program runs from the middle of June to the beginning of August in four two-week sessions.

The PreKindergarten program focuses on astronomy, earth science, cartooning, literature, and heroes and heroines. Children learn through creative movement, music, arts and crafts, sports, and indoor and outdoor activities.

The Junior Program, for ages 6–11, explores career choices in a fun environment. Examples of professions offered include actor, athlete, musician, author, scientist, chef, doctor, artist, and handyman. Every course follows a curriculum designed to show students what each job entails; authors focus on literature and creative writing; athletes learn basic skills in soccer, basketball, and baseball; and chefs cook and bake a variety of different ethnic foods. Field trips and guest speakers enhance the program.

The Senior Program is a mix of work and play. The two classes offered, Entrepreneurial Spirit and Job Skills 101, teach students how to run a business. Financing and banking, advertisement, and work safety are emphasized. The program also gives pointers on independence, interviewing, and résumés. Students can earn baby-sitting and pet-sitting certifications as well as learn how to develop and create a website.

Older students can volunteer as camp counselors; they develop leadership, organizational, and teaching skills.

One hour of early morning care and three hours of afternoon care are provided.

Contact the School for more details; see listing on page 98.

THE DELPHIAN SCHOOL™

Summer at Delphi™
Rosemary Didear, Headmistress
Sheridan, Oregon 97378
Tel. 800-626-6610; Outside the U.S. 503-843-3521
Web Site www.summeratdelphi.org
E-mail summer@delphian.org
Day and Boarding, Ages 5–18

SUMMER AT DELPHI, from June 23 to August 1, 2008, is an enrichment program for academically able students from many countries. Offered in four- to six-week sessions, advanced and make-up courses are complemented by activities, traditional camping, outdoor adventures, and computer classes. Upper School and older Middle School students may participate in intensive tennis, soccer, and volleyball camps.

Students learn how to study using the methods developed by educator L. Ron Hubbard. These methods allow them to progress at their own pace and apply what they have learned. The curriculum includes over 250 courses in math, science, language arts, the arts, humanities, health, and home economics. English as a Second Language is available.

In the afternoons, students enjoy crafts, archery, soccer, ceramics, art, basketball, volleyball, horseback riding, tennis, music, computers, and golf. Weekend activities can include white-water rafting, river floating, jet boat river tours, dune buggy riding, a beach trip and barbecue, camping, or hiking. There are trips for swimming, bowling, movies, and dinners out as well as an on-campus dance and jamboree. Excursions are made to Seattle and the Ashland Shakespearean Festival.

The campus, 50 miles southwest of Portland, is on 800 acres of rolling hills, meadows, forest, and croplands overlooking the Willamette Valley. Facilities include a library, computer center, career center, theater, athletic fields, riding stables and arena, a gym, lighted tennis courts, and studios for art, ceramics, and photography. The School's free video is offered by phone or online. The School is licensed to use *Applied Scholastics*™ educational services.

Contact Delphian for more details; see listing on page 279.

DEXTER AND SOUTHFIELD SCHOOLS

Briarwood Marine Science Camp
Jason Cassista, Director
Summer Office: 20 Newton Street
Brookline, Massachusetts 02445
Tel. 617-454-2725; Fax 617-522-8166
Web Site www.dexter.org
E-mail summer@dexter.org
Boarding, 30 Boys and 30 Girls, Grades 5–9

DEXTER AND SOUTHFIELD SCHOOLS' MARINE SCIENCE PROGRAM at Monument Beach on Cape Cod is designed to encourage young people to explore and appreciate the natural environment. In four one-week sessions, for boys and for girls separately, learning takes place through hands-on activities under the guidance of specialists in their fields.

Campers focus on several major areas of environmental study. In Marine Biology, they learn about deep- and shallow-water sea creatures; collect, examine, and photograph specimens; and manage a saltwater aquarium. In Ecology, they explore the food web and relationship among species; monitor water for pH, salinity, and temperature; study the effects of pollution and over-fishing; conduct a census of spawning horseshoe crabs; and screen plankton and benthic samples. By observing the weather, students learn to interpret signs, patterns, and prevailing winds as they come to understand how the atmosphere affects the marine world and the water cycle. Kayaking combines learning and recreation as campers explore the coastline, visit a nearby island, and learn the use of nautical charts and the compass. Shallow-water snorkeling is also part of various research studies.

A fully equipped marine laboratory contains saltwater tanks, sampling and collecting instruments, and microscopes. Other facilities include a pier, beach, dining hall and lodge, recreational areas, and heated cabins. The 8-acre property is adjacent to 90 acres of conservation land and has 2000 feet of shoreline and nature trails through the woods.

Contact the schools for more details; see listings on pages 161 and 172.

EAGLEBROOK SCHOOL

Eaglebrook Summer Semester
Andrew C. Chase, Headmaster
Karl J. Koenigsbauer, Director
Deerfield, Massachusetts 01342
Tel. 413-774-7411; Fax 413-772-2394
Web Site www.eaglebrook.org
Boarding, Coeducational, Ages 11–13

EAGLEBROOK SUMMER SEMESTER provides boys and girls ages 11, 12, and 13 a wide range of experiences in classroom, artistic, athletic, and social areas with the goal of developing academic proficiency, leadership skills, and personal success. The four-week program begins in July.

Students from diverse ethnic, racial, economic, and geographic backgrounds undertake a variety of activities designed to build confidence through achievement. Classes are taught by faculty chosen for their experience and commitment to children; faculty also serve as coaches and dormitory advisors.

Historic Deerfield and Eaglebrook's 640-acre campus provide natural areas that create an outdoor "classroom without walls" for discovery, exploration, and artistic inspiration. Courses are offered in English, reading, English as a Second Language, arithmetic, algebra, computer, science, history, drawing, photography, drama, and silkscreening.

Following morning classes and lunch, students participate in a wide range of sports; they also swim and play tennis with an emphasis on the development of physical fitness and athletic skills. Informal games of softball, volleyball, basketball, and indoor soccer are held after the evening meal.

Students reside in supervised dormitories and enjoy use of the School's extensive computer, athletic, and academic facilities. Among these are the Learning Center, the Schwab Family Pool, the Sports Center, and playing fields and hiking trails. On weekends, campouts, field trips, and on-campus activities provide students with an abundance of wholesome fun.

Contact Eaglebrook for more details; see listing on page 161.

EAGLE HILL-SOUTHPORT

Eagle Hill-Southport Summer Program
Jeffrey M. Ruggiero, Director
214 Main Street
Southport, Connecticut 06890
Tel. 203-254-2044; Fax 203-255-4052
Web Site www.eaglehillsouthport.org
E-mail info@eaglehillsouthport.org
Day, Coeducational, Ages 6–14

EAGLE HILL-SOUTHPORT SUMMER PROGRAM offers a five-week program beginning in late June that provides remedial assistance to help students maintain progress made during the school year while bolstering self-esteem. All students are immersed in success-oriented, language-based courses that are supportive, dynamic, and fun. Classes are taught by special educators who work creatively with the children to develop skills and confidence.

The Skills-Based Program, featuring five classes that meet daily from 8:15 A.M. until 12:15 P.M., is open to ages 6–12. This program includes math, handwriting, written expression, oral language, and study skills, along with daily tutorials geared toward each student's individual academic needs. With a 4:1 student-staff ratio, each child is able to become more proficient at mastering all subjects and study methods. The Learning Strategies Program for students ages 10–12 focuses on expanding study techniques and learning habits in preparation for the demands of middle school. The writing process, class discussion, research, test-taking, vocabulary, literary analysis, computation, and problem-solving skills are targeted in both programs.

Students ages 12–14 may take a two-week Study Skills class that emphasizes note-taking, reading comprehension, organization, and time management through small group and individualized activities, or they may enroll in a one-week Writing Skills Workshop that develops a solid foundation of practical writing strategies and skills. With a student-teacher ratio of 8:1, both courses are designed to introduce, improve, and enhance skills and habits that permit participants to maximize their learning potential.

Contact Eagle Hill-Southport for more details; see listing on page 61.

FLINT HILL SCHOOL

Summer on the Hill
Peggy Laurent, Director
3320 Jermantown Road
Oakton, Virginia 22124
Tel. 703-584-2392; Fax 703-242-0718
Web Site www.flinthill.org
E-mail plaurent@flinthill.org
Day, Coeducational, Ages 5–18

SUMMER ON THE HILL welcomes Flint Hill and other public and private school students to participate in up to six weeks of academics and enrichment, athletics, creative arts, and various specialty camps. The program, from mid-June to the end of July, includes counselor-in-training opportunities, fun field trips in the Baltimore/ Washington, D.C. area, and, for high school students, a three-week ecological trip to Ecuador, five-day river-rafting excursions, and backpacking in the American West.

Academic offerings range from reading and math clinics in Grades 2–6 and, for older participants, credit and refresher courses in Pre-Algebra Prep, Algebra I, Geometry, Art, Chemistry, Photography, and Ceramics. Students can also prepare for taking the SAT and brush up on skills such as note taking and active reading.

Among the options in the creative arts are drawing, painting, sculpting, Japanese art, acting, drumming, and dance.

Athletes interested in learning and developing skills and strategies may enroll in age-appropriate camps conducted by seasoned coaches. Girls play soccer, basketball, volleyball, lacrosse, tennis, weightlifting, and speed and agility training. Boys compete in most of these sports as well as in baseball and football.

Breakfast Club and Snack Pack offer extended care and activities for children in Kindergarten– Grade 8.

Summer on the Hill participants enjoy the use of Flint Hill's two campuses, extensive outdoor athletic facilities, two NCAA-regulation-size gyms, art and dance studios, theater, music halls, and computer labs.

Contact Flint Hill for more details; see listing on page 333.

FORK UNION MILITARY ACADEMY

Summer Programs
Maj. John DeVault, Director
P.O. Box 278
Fork Union, Virginia 23055
Tel. 434-842-4223
Web Site www.forkunion.com/summer
E-mail devaultj@fuma.org
Boarding, Boys, Grades 8–12

FORK UNION MILITARY ACADEMY'S SUMMER SESSION offers a fully accredited summer school program for young men in Grades 8 to 12.

The Academy's program features English; history; foreign language; math including Algebra, Algebra II, Geometry, and Trigonometry; science including Chemistry and Physics; and Computer Skills.

Students can take one new class (140 hours) and add a college preparatory course to their transcript with four weeks of intensive study. Alternatively, students seeking to improve their grade in a core course may repeat two classes (70 hours each). Small class sizes and individual attention can help a student turn a "C" to an "A" if he applies himself and practices good study habits.

Mini-Sports Camps meet 6 days a week and feature conditioning, basic skills review, strength training, and live scrimmages. Each camp follows the same structure as the full-year programs. Camps offered are football, swimming, distance running, baseball, basketball, weight lifting, tennis, and racquetball. All Mini-Camps have access to the school's state-of-the-art facilities and are coached by FUMA's regular staff.

The 1000-acre campus provides full athletic facilities, allowing students to improve athletic skills individually and practice teamwork. A technology center and 19,000-volume library provide access to computers and the Internet.

Contact Fork Union for more details; *see descriptive article on page 334.*

THE GOW SCHOOL

The Gow Summer Program
David Mendlewski, Director
Emery Road
South Wales, New York 14139
Tel. 716-652-3450
Web Site www.gow.org
E-mail summer@gow.org
Boarding, 100 Girls and Boys, Ages 8–16

THE GOW SUMMER PROGRAM was developed to allow children to benefit from summer academics without feeling as if they have lost their summer vacation. The five-week program, from late June to the end of July, provides solid academics with athletic, social, cultural, and recreational activities. The session includes morning academics, afternoon traditional camp, and weekend overnight trips. Gow strives to develop the skills and natural abilities of each camper while encouraging a sense of enthusiasm and positive self-image.

To best fit individual needs, camper-students and their families are assisted in the selection of four courses in the Academic Focus Programs. These programs, which enroll three to six students, meet five days per week. During a predinner period, camper-students have the option of reading for pleasure in the library, using the computer resource center, attending a film festival, playing challenging games such as chess and Trivial Pursuit, or attending a tutorial. Academics focus on reconstructive language, mathematics, organization and study skill development, humanities, studio art, computer literacy, and other courses offered according to student need.

Campers take part in afternoon camping and trip activities through Activity Instruction Clinics, Group Periods, and Focus Periods. There is also a Counselor in Training Program for older camper students.

The Gow Summer Program's 100-acre campus features a computer center, library, gymnasium/activities center, indoor-outdoor climbing walls, a challenging ropes course, and modern dormitories.

Contact Gow for more details; *see descriptive article on page 234.*

HARGRAVE MILITARY ACADEMY

Summer School
CDR Frank L. Martin, Director of Admissions
200 Military Drive
Chatham, Virginia 24531
Tel. 800-432-2480
Web Site www.hargrave.edu
E-mail admissions@hargrave.edu

Boarding and Day, 150 Boys, Grades 7–12

HARGRAVE MILITARY ACADEMY SUMMER SCHOOL is designed to provide a positive academic environment in which students can make up credits or earn new credits in the major subject areas while enjoying a diverse recreational program. The four-week program extends from late June to late July.

The summer school has two divisions: Middle School encompasses Grades 7 and 8; the Upper School serves Grades 9 through 12.

Upper School students may earn one academic credit for new course work or two credits for two repeated subjects. English 7–12, World Studies, Algebra I, Intermediate Algebra, and Geometry are offered for either new or repeat credit. Repeat credits only can be earned in Spanish I, Science 8–9, Math 8–9, Middle School History, Biology, and Algebra II. Students who repeat one course may earn a half-credit in electives such as Computer Applications, Leadership and Ethics, and Reading. In addition, a How to Study course aimed at the development of study and organizational skills is required of all students. There is also a strong English as a Second Language (ESL) course of instruction.

In the Middle School, students can take English, math, science, history, reading, and computer applications.

Classroom instruction is followed by afternoon sports such as swimming, soccer, football, weightlifting, tennis, and an adventure camp. On weekends, students are involved in paintball games, confidence courses, and visits to a water park. Attendance at chapel services twice a week is mandatory.

Contact Hargrave for more details; see descriptive article on page 338.

HOPKINS SCHOOL

Hopkins Summer School
Thomas Parr, Director
Ford Cole, Assistant Director
986 Forest Road
New Haven, Connecticut 06515
Tel. 203-397-1001, Ext. 540; Fax 203-392-0267
Web Site www.hopkins.edu
E-mail tparr@hopkins.edu

Day, 150 Boys, 130 Girls, Grades 3–12

HOPKINS SUMMER SCHOOL offers academic courses for credit and noncredit in a six-week program extending from late June to early August. A six-week sports camp is offered during the same period. It can be coordinated with the academic program.

Academic courses meet in 60-minute classes scheduled between 8:00 A.M. and 1:15 P.M., five days a week. Among the courses offered are Expository and Creative Writing, French 1–2, Latin 1–2, Spanish 1–2, Atlantic Communities, Arithmetic Review, Pre-Algebra, Algebra 1–2, Geometry, Functions, Statistics and Trigonometry, Pre-Calculus, Developmental Reading, SAT Preparation, and Study Skills. Credit courses require 90–180 hours of intensive study and noncredit courses 30–60 hours.

The elementary school program provides Developmental Reading, a Writer's Workshop, Mathematics and Computer, Science, and a sports camp.

The sports camp, meeting from 8:00 to 11:00 A.M. daily, includes six one-week coeducational sessions in fencing, swimming, and tennis for Grades 3–12.

Contact Hopkins for more details; see descriptive article on page 66.

THE HUN SCHOOL OF PRINCETON

The Hun School of Princeton Summer Session
Donna O'Sullivan, Director of Auxiliary Services
176 Edgerstoune Road
Princeton, New Jersey 08540
Tel. 609-921-7600; Fax 609-921-2565
Web Site www.hunschool.org
E-mail dosullivan@hunschool.org
Boarding, Ages 13–17; Day, Ages 12–17

THE HUN SCHOOL'S SUMMER SESSION offers five weeks of programs focusing on enrichment, refresher, and full-credit courses. In addition, Hun's American Culture and Language Institute provides international students a unique introduction to the way Americans speak and live through ESL classes and cultural trips.

Enrichment courses are designed for those who wish to get a head start on a class they intend to take in the fall. Preview or review courses (60 hours) are for students who need to complete credits or overcome a specific academic problem. Full-credit courses (120 hours) are given in Pre-Calculus, Chemistry, Algebra I, Algebra II, and Geometry. Students may take courses for enrichment in English, writing, mathematics, biology, chemistry, physics, and SAT prep. Middle school students may take math and English. Resident students participate in an afternoon activities program from 3:00 to 5:00 P.M. and follow an evening schedule that includes study hall and free time. All students enjoy a final off-campus party.

The American Language and Culture Institute combines intensive classroom study with frequent trips to museums, historical sites, and social events in the mid-Atlantic region including New York City, Philadelphia, Washington, D.C., and Hershey and Lancaster, Pennsylvania. In 2007, students prepared a picture CD-ROM and a collection of short stories and poetry.

Students use the School's facilities including an Athletic Center featuring a fitness center and gyms, air-conditioned classrooms, activity center, dining hall, snack bar, tennis courts, and playing fields. Resident students enjoy afternoon sports, organized group activities, weekend fun, and off-campus trips.

Contact Hun for more details; see descriptive article on page 210.

THE KILDONAN SCHOOL

Dunnabeck at Kildonan
Ronald A. Wilson, Headmaster
425 Morse Hill Road
Amenia, New York 12501
Tel. 845-373-8111
Web Site www.kildonan.org
Boarding, 85 Boys and Girls, Ages 8–16

DUNNABECK AT KILDONAN provides six weeks of intensive language training, from late June to mid-August, for students of average or above-average intelligence who have not succeeded academically due to difficulties in reading, writing, or spelling.

At the beginning of the program, each student is administered standard diagnostic tests to determine his or her areas of strength and weakness in language and communication skills. With a 2:1 student-teacher ratio, each participant is ensured individual attention and support, enabling each one to learn to study independently and develop self-confidence. Teachers are carefully selected for their maturity, imagination, and ability to work well with young people. Teaching methods based on the Orton-Gillingham approach integrate reading, writing, and spelling as different aspects of the language function. The program emphasizes correct expository writing, with attention to coherence, vocabulary, and clarity of expression. Typing and word processing are integral to the learning experience; math tutoring is also available.

A typical day begins with breakfast at 8:00 A.M., followed by an hour of one-on-one tutoring, a one-hour study hall, and a word-processing class. After lunch, students take part in a recreational program that includes ceramics, crafts, woodworking, photography, painting, horseback riding, water skiing, swimming, sailing, hiking, camping, softball, soccer, and canoeing.

Kildonan School is located on a 325-acre campus 90 miles north of New York City. Students reside in dormitories and have access to the School's athletic and fine arts facilities.

Contact Kildonan for more details; see listing on page 241.

KING & LOW-HEYWOOD THOMAS SCHOOL

2008 Summer Institute
Alex Weiner, Director
1450 Newfield Avenue
Stamford, Connecticut 06905
Tel. 203-322-3496; Fax 203-461-9988
Web Site www.klht.org; E-mail aweiner@klht.org

Day, Coeducational, Pre-K–Grade 12

THE KING & LOW-HEYWOOD THOMAS SCHOOL SUMMER INSTITUTE provides students from more than 45 private, parochial, and public schools a wide range of opportunities that combine fun and sports with academic acceleration, enrichment, and remediation. Programs run between one to six weeks, depending on grade level, from mid-June through early August.

Children in the Lower School (Pre-K–Grade 5) take classes from 8:00 A.M. to 2:30 P.M. Studies are related to such topics as story-telling, math, robotics, etiquette, crafts, and technology.

Students in Grades 6–8 may enroll in Introduction to Spanish, Pre-Algebra, Money Matters, Writer's Craft, Advanced Lego Robotics, Speaking With Confidence, and Explorations in Art, among others. Classes range from 50 minutes to 2 hours.

The King & Low-Heywood Thomas Summer Institute offers Upper School (Grades 9–12) courses that include honors-level classes and SAT preparation in Math and Verbal to facilitate the college application process. Students may also choose among Research Skills, Expository Writing, Chemistry, Physics, Algebra I, Algebra II/Trigonometry, Art Explorations II, and instruction in Spanish or French. Students may earn academic credit for work completed with prior approval from their home school.

Vikings athletic camps encourage children of all ages to develop a love of sports while acquiring specific skills and strategies in an atmosphere of teamwork, cooperation, and friendly competition. Among the sports offered are baseball, basketball, volleyball, lacrosse, and performance training.

Contact KLHT for more details; see descriptive article on page 70.

THE LAB SCHOOL OF WASHINGTON®

Summer Session
Sally L. Smith, Director
4759 Reservoir Road, NW
Washington, D.C. 20007
Tel. 202-965-6600
Web Site www.labschool.org

Day, 206 Boys, 104 Girls, Ages 5–18

THE LAB SCHOOL OF WASHINGTON SUMMER SESSION provides a six-week program for children, ages 5 to 18, of average to superior intelligence who have learning disabilities or are in need of remedial academic work. The session begins at the end of June and ends in late July. A five-week Summer Session is also held at Baltimore Lab, a division of The Lab School of Washington.

The Primary Program is for children ages 5–7½ who have been identified as "at risk" for learning disabilities. A multisensory approach focuses on auditory and visual perception, visual-motor coordination, sensory motor integration, language development, and intellectual stimulation. Small-group tutoring in reading, writing, and math skills takes place daily.

The Lower School Program is for children ages 7–12½ who have mild to severe learning disabilities. Individualized remedial instruction is given in all academic areas and through drama, music, woodworking, dance, and visual arts. Swimming and computer classes are optional.

The Junior High (Grades 7–8) and the High School (Grades 9–12) levels address students who have moderate to severe learning disabilities. Small-group instruction is offered in reading, spelling, written language, mathematics, science, computer skills, and study skills. Optional sports, computer, and arts programs are offered during the afternoon. High school students can receive credit.

Diagnostic services, individual tutoring, college counseling, occupational therapy, and speech/language therapy are available. Each summer's activities are built around a different program theme, such as "Green Summer at The Lab School" or a "Mediterranean Summer."

Contact the School for more details; see listing on page 90.

LANDMARK SCHOOL

Landmark Summer Programs
Carolyn Orsini Nelson, Director of Admission
429 Hale Street; P.O. Box 227
Prides Crossing, Massachusetts 01965-0227
Tel. 978-236-3000; Fax 978-927-7268
Web Site www.landmarkschool.org
E-mail admission@landmarkschool.org
Boarding and Day, Coeducational, Grades 1–12

LANDMARK SUMMER PROGRAMS offer academic skill development and recreation for students ages 7–20 in Grades 1–12 with diagnosed language-based learning disabilities. The typical student is of average to superior intelligence and socially adept with a history of healthy emotional development. A low student-faculty ratio ensures appropriate individualization within a program that concentrates on mastering reading, writing, spelling, and composition skills. Students may spend all day in an academic setting or split the day with recreational experiences.

The Standard Academic Program provides two 1:1 tutorials daily, reinforced by language arts classes. Small classes are also offered in mathematics, communication, and study skills.

The recreation component includes Adventure Ropes/Sea Kayaking for Grades 8–12; the course builds leadership, proglem-solving, and perseverance skills on high and low ropes courses as well as coastal navigation and safety techniques on the ocean. Musical Theater creates the opportunity to perform onstage or expand on technical theater skills behind-the-scenes. Exploration and Practical Arts programs enroll students in Grades 3–7 and combine a half-day of academics with various outdoor activities. Students in these programs attend one language arts tutorial daily and take classes from the Academic Programs.

All day students may choose a half-day, academic program in the morning.

High school programs are on the High School Campus in Prides Crossing; elementary and middle school programs are on the Elementary and Middle School Campus in Manchester, 3 miles away.

Contact Landmark for more details.

LINDEN HILL SCHOOL

Linden Hill Summer Program
James A. McDaniel, Headmaster
154 South Mountain Road
Northfield, Massachusetts 01360
Tel. 413-498-2906; [Toll-free] 888-254-6336
Fax 413-498-2908
Web Site www.lindenhs.org
E-mail admissions@lindenhs.org
Boarding, Coeducational, Ages 7–17

LINDEN HILL SUMMER PROGRAM offers academic enrichment and recreation for students with specific language differences, such as dyslexia. The program runs from June 30 to July 30. In a supportive environment, participants are encouraged to grow in confidence and self-esteem, to make lasting friendships, and to develop as individuals and athletes.

The program combines structure and focus with flexibility and choice. The carefully designed environment presents each participant with realistic and individualized challenges designed to increase self-confidence through real accomplishment. Classes of 1–6 students meet five days a week. Daily tutorials, drills, and written work are stressed, and all classes focus on motivation, a positive attitude, organization, study skills, social growth, and confidence. Courses include reading, computers, English, math, science challenges, language tutorials, journalism, technology, theater, art, and woodworking.

Afternoons feature traditional activities, selected by campers. Clinics include soccer, basketball, fishing, arts and crafts, paddle boating, archery, drama, and woodshop. Evenings feature team-building activities that improve self-esteem and communication skills. On weekends, campers enjoy canoeing, fishing, mountain biking, and overnight excursions. Past trips have included the Science Museum of Boston, Duck Tours, Pawsox baseball, Roger Williams Zoo, Mystic, and camping in Vermont.

The country campus at the tristate corner of Massachusetts, Vermont, and New Hampshire provides dorms, classrooms, a gym, student center, dining room, and a small farm.

Contact Linden Hill for more details.

NORTHFIELD MOUNT HERMON SCHOOL

NMH Summer Session
Debra J. Frank, Dean of Summer Admission
One Lamplighter Way
Mount Hermon, Massachusetts 01354
Tel. 413-498-3290; Fax 413-498-3112
Web Site www.nmhschool.org
E-mail summer_school@nmhschool.org

Boarding and Day, Coeducational, Entering Grades 7–12

NMH SUMMER SESSION welcomes committed students from the United States and abroad who want a challenging academic experience. College Prep and Middle School Programs as well as English as a Second Language provide five weeks of instruction with master teachers and interns.

College Prep is designed for students entering Grades 10–12 who seek credit or enrichment. Each student takes one major course that meets for three hours Monday through Saturday mornings, plus an afternoon lab or minor course and a sport. Major courses include American History, Economics, Algebra I, Algebra II, Geometry, Precalculus, Biology, Chemistry, Expository Writing, Literature and Composition, and Psychology. Among the minor courses are Art Studio, Community Service, Drama, Reading and Study Skills, and Public Speaking.

The Middle School Program develops skills and self-confidence for students entering Grades 7–9. Each student takes two major courses in the morning and a minor course and sports in the afternoon. Major courses include Drama Literature, Pre-Algebra, Algebra I, Beginning Spanish, Field Biology, Writing, and Skills in Literature.

Dances, movies, and talent shows complement field trips to Tanglewood, Red Sox baseball games, museums, amusement parks, and beaches. Students enjoy the use of the 40,000-volume library, a computer center, a language lab, a student center, and a gymnasium with fitness center.

Contact Northfield Mount Hermon for more details.

PRINCETON DAY SCHOOL

Summer Programs
Mark Adams, Director
P.O. Box 75, The Great Road
Princeton, New Jersey 08542
Tel. 609-924-6700, Ext. 1803
Web Site www.pds.org
E-mail summerprograms@pds.org

Day, Coeducational, Prekindergarten–Grade 12

PRINCETON DAY SCHOOL SUMMER PROGRAMS provide artistic, athletic, academic, and adventure classes from early June through early August. Most academic and artistic classes last for two weeks, while sports and adventure camps last for one week.

Students entering elementary school may take classes in digital photography, poetry, woodworking, robotics, nature, Spanish, French, acting, chess, puppetry, ancient Greece, problem-solving, dance, sewing, drawing and painting, graphic design, cooking, sculpture, mathematics, architecture, and meteorology. Students in Grades 5–8 may enroll in such courses as comics, creative writing, algebra, geometry, masks, filmmaking, knitting, photography, grammar, journalism, astronomy, choreography, and drama. Driver's education, SAT prep, writing the college essay, product design, web design, computer programming, mock trial, advanced photography, and electronics are some options for students in high school. Classes meet for three hours every day, with the morning session beginning at 8:30 A.M. and the afternoon session beginning at 12:30 P.M.

Overnight and adventure camps are offered in high and low ropes courses, leadership, indoor and outdoor rock climbing, canoeing, backpacking, hiking in the Adirondacks, and kayaking. Soccer, tennis, basketball, lacrosse, ice hockey, volleyball, baseball, ice-skating, martial arts, fencing, field hockey, and mountain biking are available in half- and full-day sports camps.

The 103-acre campus holds numerous athletic fields, tennis courts, theater, three libraries, greenhouse, architecture and science laboratories, and art, music, and ceramics studios.

Contact Princeton Day School for more details; see listing on page 214.

RUMSEY HALL SCHOOL

Rumsey Hall School Summer Session
Thomas W. Farmen, Headmaster
David Whiting, Director
Romford Road
Washington Depot, Connecticut 06794
Tel. 860-868-0535; Fax 860-868-7907
Web Site www.rumseyhall.org
E-mail admiss@rumseyhall.org
Coeducational
Grades 3–9 (Day), Grades 5–9 (Boarding)

RUMSEY HALL SCHOOL SUMMER SESSION is a five-week program of academic review and preview for students entering Grades 3–9. English as a Second Language is offered for international students. The program runs from the beginning of July to early August 2008 on a beautiful 147-acre campus bordering the Bantam River.

Academic courses are available for students who wish to review previous material or preview new material in English, mathematics, study skills, and computer skills. Average class size is ten students. Classes are available in language skills and developmental reading with trained specialists on a one-to-one basis. The schedule includes approximately four hours of coursework, with afternoon activities and recreation and evening study halls. Summer school participants spend at least an hour a day reading and must complete two book reports during the session. Parents receive biweekly progress reports and a comprehensive written report at the conclusion of the program.

English as a Second Language focuses on vocabulary and conversation in everyday situations. Students practice speaking skills with one another, keep journals, and discuss topics in American language and culture. Participants may also work with Language Skills faculty on a one-to-one basis.

Students live in dormitories and dine family style with their peers and faculty members. They enjoy swimming, various sports, hiking, mountain biking, and excursions to cultural events, historical sites, and amusement parks.

Contact Rumsey Hall for more details; see descriptive article on page 76.

RYE COUNTRY DAY SCHOOL

Rye Country Day School Summer Session
David M. Tafe, Director
Boston Post Road at Cedar Street
Rye, New York 10580
Tel. 914-925-4570
Web Site www.rcds.rye.ny.us
E-mail david_tafe@rcds.rye.ny.us
Day, 200 Boys and Girls, Grades 3–12

RYE COUNTRY DAY SCHOOL SUMMER SESSION offers a program of remedial and enrichment courses for students seeking to develop new areas of interest, earn course credits, or review subjects in which they need strengthening. The six-week session begins in late June and ends in early August.

Classes, enrolling 4–12 students, meet five mornings a week; normally, a student has one class and one study period, each 45 minutes long, for each course. The curriculum includes review courses in English, Mathematics, French, Latin, Spanish, United States History, Global Studies, Biology, and Chemistry; and enrichment courses in Reading and Study Skills, Summer Reading, Writing Clinic, SAT Review, and Art. The Performing Arts Center offers courses in Jazz Band and Electronic (MIDI) Music as well as private music lessons. Students wishing to take certain courses for advanced credit double the class time in each subject.

Some math and science courses provide preparation for the New York State Regents examinations.

Contact the school for more details; see descriptive article on page 251.

SHELTON SCHOOL & EVALUATION CENTER

Summer School and Shelton Scholars
Joyce S. Pickering, Director
15720 Hillcrest Road
Dallas, Texas 75248
Tel. 972-774-1772
Web Site www.shelton.org
E-mail webmaster@shelton.org
Day, Preschool–Grade 12 (Summer School)
835 Students

SHELTON SCHOOL & EVALUATION CENTER offers two distinct programs: Summer School and Shelton Scholars, each conducted for four weeks during the month of July.

The Summer School is designed to serve preschool through high school students of average to above-average intelligence who have learning differences. The multisensory curriculum focuses on perceptual motor and fine motor skills, Multisensory Structured Language Education, reading comprehension, handwriting, social and study skills, and language and speech. Course work is available in multisensory keyboarding, English, math, reading/spelling/handwriting, social skills, art, foreign language, and study skills. In addition, there is a half-day Early Childhood/Kindergarten component that addresses the learning needs of youngsters ages 3–7. Some high school classes can be taken for credit.

Enrichment classes are offered in art, drama, social skills, sports, music, and science.

Shelton Scholars is an outreach program emphasizing the improvement of reading, writing, and spelling skills for ages six to adult on Saturdays and during the summer. The program runs from 9:00 A.M. until noon and provides each student with two hours of one-on-one remediation tutoring based on the Sequential English Education Program and a one-hour auditory discrimination class.

Contact the school for more details; see listing on page 325.

SKIDMORE COLLEGE

Pre-college Program for High School Students at Skidmore
Dr. James Chansky, Director
815 North Broadway
Saratoga Springs, New York 12866
Tel. 518-580-5590; Fax 518-580-5548
Web Site www.skidmore.edu/summer
E-mail jchansky@skidmore.edu
Boarding and Day, 100 Women and Men
Rising Juniors and Seniors

THE PRE-COLLEGE PROGRAM FOR HIGH SCHOOL STUDENTS AT SKIDMORE is designed for academically talented young men and women with an interest in the liberal and studio arts and the desire to engage in college-level study. The five-week session runs from early July to early August and coincides with the peak summer season at Skidmore and in Saratoga Springs.

Through the combination of dormitory living, first-year college-level courses, and the rich and varied intellectual, cultural, artistic, and social life of the summer campus, the program offers high school students a true college experience. Pre-college students undertake two foundation-level courses that carry full credit usually transferable to other colleges and universities. Course offerings are drawn from those offered through the College's summer session in the humanities, social sciences, natural sciences, mathematics, and visual arts. Classes are taught by full-time members of the Skidmore community and are typically small, fast-paced, and informal.

In addition to course work, Pre-college students enjoy a wide variety of activities on campus. They have access to the resources of Skidmore's 850-acre wooded campus, including a swimming pool, tennis courts, an all-weather running track, and racquetball, squash, and basketball courts. Jazz concerts, fiction and poetry readings sponsored by the New York State Summer Writers Institute, the International Film Festival, gallery openings, and lecture-demonstrations are featured regularly on campus. In nearby downtown Saratoga Springs, students enjoy the rich variety and Victorian heritage of this summer resort town. Trips are also scheduled to concerts at The Saratoga Performing Arts Center, to museums in Manhattan, and to the Great Escape Amusement Park.

Contact Skidmore for more details.

THE TAFT SCHOOL

Taft Summer School
Stephen McCabe, Director
Watertown, Connecticut 06795
Tel. 860-945-7961
Web Site www.taftschool.org
E-mail summerschool@taftschool.org

Boarding and Day, 75 Boys, 75 Girls
Entering Grades 7–12

TAFT SUMMER SCHOOL provides an opportunity for motivated students to review course material, prepare for future courses, or enrich their school experiences by taking courses not available to them during the school year. High school students enroll in the Liberal Studies Program, which offers a broad selection in all academic disciplines. The Young Scholars Program, aimed at younger men and women who intend to take on the challenges of rigorous public and private secondary schools, focuses on building essential skills and on instilling students with confidence as they look ahead to Grades 7, 8, and 9, and, later, to the demands of a college preparatory program. Taft also offers programs in France and Spain.

The five-week, on-campus session runs from late June to late July. Classes meet six days a week; afternoons are reserved for athletics. Evening room study is supervised.

Offerings include Literature & Composition, Algebra, Geometry, Precalculus, Biology, Physical Science, French, Spanish, English as a Second Language, U.S. History, Creative Writing, Current Events, Public Speaking, Art History, Acting, Photography, Studio Art, SAT Preparation, SSAT Preparation, and Testing, Reading & Study Skills. Advisors report to parents at session's end with a description of work covered, a progress report, and achievement and effort grades.

Weekend activities are organized on campus, and trips to New York and Boston are planned. Taft's 220-acre campus includes a 53,000-volume library, a computer center, an arts/humanities building, a state-of-the-art modern language lab, and the Cruikshank Athletic Center. The School is located 55 miles from Hartford and 90 miles from New York City.

Contact Taft for more details; see listing on page 80.

VIEWPOINT SCHOOL

Summer Programs 2008
Dr. Robert J. Dworkoski, Headmaster
Paul Rosenbaum, Director of Summer Programs
23620 Mulholland Highway
Calabasas, California 91302
Tel. 818-340-2901; Fax 818-591-7354
Web Site www.viewpoint.org
E-mail prosenbaum@viewpoint.org

Day, Boys and Girls, Kindergarten–Grade 12

SUMMER PROGRAMS 2008 provide a wide array of academic and enrichment programs, athletics, and camp experiences for students in Kindergarten–Grade 6. Participants may enroll for all or part of the six-week session, which is conducted from late June through the end of July.

Camp Roadrunner, for children entering Kindergarten–Grade 6, consists of a morning program of workshops in activities such as art, cooking, science, and computer. Academic course work is available. Afternoons are devoted to recreation, special field trips, and performances by musicians, dancers, and puppeteers. Swimming lessons are provided by certified Red Cross instructors.

Contact Viewpoint for more details; see descriptive article on page 46.

THE WINDSOR SCHOOL

Summer School Program 2008
Dr. Philip A. Stewart, Director
Administration Building
136-23 Sanford Avenue
Flushing, New York 11355
Tel. 718-359-8300; Fax 718-359-1876
Web Site www.windsorschool.com
E-mail admin@thewindsorschool.com
Day, Coeducational, Grades 5–12

THE WINDSOR SUMMER SCHOOL PROGRAM 2008 gives students of middle and high school ages the opportunity to preview, enrich, repeat, or advance in academic subjects. Participants may earn credit in as many as four classes.

Students interested in preparing for the PSAT or SAT may enroll in classes that cover the math, verbal, and writing sections of these tests. Students applying to special high schools may take preparation classes for the entrance exams in both English and math. International students may take English as a Second Language and prepare for the Test of English as a Foreign Language (TOEFL).

Many courses are offered in the major disciplines. English selections include English 7–12, Remedial Reading, and Reading Skills. The math selections offered are Math A and B, Elementary and Intermediate Algebra, Geometry, Trigonometry, Precalculus, General Math, Business Math, and Advanced Placement Calculus. Social studies students may enroll in Government, Economics, United States History, Global Studies, or World History. Sciences include Biology, Living Environment, Environmental Science, Chemistry, Physics, and Earth Science. Each of these courses requires laboratory work. Other subjects include French, Health Education, Physical Education, Spanish, and required art or music. High school students take final examinations and the Regents Examinations at the end of the six-week program.

Classes in all subject areas are also offered at the middle or junior high school level.

Gifted students in Grades 5 and 6 may enroll in enrichment classes in all subjects.

Contact the school for more details; *see listing on page 259.*

YALE UNIVERSITY

Yale Summer Session
William T. Whobrey, Director
P.O. Box 208355
New Haven, Connecticut 06520-8355
Tel. 203-432-2430; Fax 203-432-2434
Web Site www.yale.edu/summer
E-mail summer.session@yale.edu
Boarding and Day, 250 Boys and Girls
High School Juniors and Seniors

YALE SUMMER SESSION offers an array of challenging, college-level academic courses for students who have completed their junior year. Most precollege students enroll in two courses in the 5-B session, from July 7 to August 8, 2008. They choose from Yale College courses in the humanities, social sciences, and sciences taught by regular Yale faculty or other qualified instructors.

Among the areas of study are anthropology, astronomy, archaeology, architecture, art, biology, chemistry, computer science, creative writing, drama, expository writing, film, history, history of art, literature, music, philosophy, political science, psychology, and religious studies.

Students are required to reside on campus in one of the Yale dormitories, called residential colleges, unless they live with their families within commuting distance of the University. The residential atmosphere provides precollege students with an introduction to college life and the opportunity to interact with other participants from across the country and around the world. Students enjoy a full range of recreational activities, many of which take advantage of Yale's relative proximity to New York, Boston, and the Atlantic coast.

All summer students have the use of Yale's academic and cultural resources including the 4,000,000 volumes housed in Sterling Memorial Library, the Yale University Art Gallery, Yale Center for British Art, and Peabody Museum of Natural History. During the summer, New Haven and Yale offer an abundance of activities including theater, concerts, and other cultural events.

Contact Yale for more details.

Summer Programs Grid

The Grid that follows is a quick reference to the summer opportunities in the Yellow Pages. Programs are arranged alphabetically by state or country, with a page number for locating the descriptive material. Summer programs are categorized in the following areas:

English/Reading

Mathematics

Science/Computers

History/Social Studies

Foreign Language

English as a Second Language

SAT Preparation/Study Skills

Dyslexia/Learning Differences

The Arts

Travel/Cross-Cultural Programs

Service/Outreach Programs

Wilderness/Survival Training

Sports Camps/Clinics

Summer Programs Grid

School	Location	Page	English/Reading	Mathematics	Science/Computers	History/Social Studies	Foreign Language	English as a Second Language	SAT Preparation/Study Skills	Dyslexia/Learning Differences	The Arts	Travel/Cross-Cultural Programs	Service/Outreach Programs	Wilderness/Survival Training	Sports Camps/Clinics
CALIFORNIA															
Viewpoint School	*Calabasas*	S22	X	X	X		X		X		X				X
CONNECTICUT															
Broken Bridge at Pomfret School	*Pomfret*	S9									X				
Eagle Hill-Southport	*Southport*	S13	X	X					X	X					
Hopkins School	*New Haven*	S15	X	X	X	X	X	X	X		X				X
King & Low-Heywood Thomas School	*Stamford*	S17	X	X	X		X		X		X				X
Rumsey Hall School	*Washington Depot*	S20	X	X	X			X		X					
The Taft School	*Watertown*	S22	X	X	X	X	X	X	X		X				
Yale University	*New Haven*	S23	X	X	X	X	X	X			X				
DISTRICT OF COLUMBIA															
The Lab School of Washington	*Washington*	S17	X	X	X	X	X		X	X	X				
FLORIDA															
The Day School at Coral Springs	*Coral Springs*	S10	X		X						X				X
MASSACHUSETTS															
The Art Institute of Boston at Lesley University	*Boston*	S8									X				
Belmont Hill School	*Belmont*	S8	X	X	X	X	X	X	X		X				X
Dexter and Southfield Schools	*Brookline*	S12			X										
Eaglebrook School	*Deerfield*	S12	X	X	X		X	X	X		X				
Landmark School	*Prides Crossing*	S18	X	X	X	X				X	X				
Linden Hill School	*Northfield*	S18	X	X	X			X		X	X				
Northfield Mount Hermon School	*Northfield*	S19	X	X	X	X	X	X	X						
NEW HAMPSHIRE															
Cardigan Mountain School	*Canaan*	S10	X	X	X		X	X	X	X	X				X
NEW JERSEY															
The Craig School	*Mountain Lakes/Lincoln Park*	S10	X	X	X					X					
The Hun School of Princeton	*Princeton*	S16	X	X	X	X	X	X	X		X				
Princeton Day School	*Princeton*	S19	X	X	X	X	X		X		X				X

Summer Programs Grid

	Page	English/Reading	Mathematics	Science/Computers	History/Social Studies	Foreign Language	English as a Second Language	SAT Preparation/Study Skills	Dyslexia/Learning Differences	The Arts	Travel/Cross-Cultural Programs	Service/Outreach Programs	Wilderness/Survival Training	Sports Camps/Clinics
NEW YORK														
Brooklyn Heights Montessori School *Brooklyn*	S9			X						X				
The Gow School *South Wales*	S14	X	X	X	X	X	X	X	X	X	X			X
The Kildonan School *Amenia*	S16	X	X	X				X	X					
Rye Country Day School *Rye*	S20	X	X	X	X	X	X	X		X				
Skidmore College *Saratoga Springs*	S21	X	X	X	X					X				
The Windsor School *Flushing*	S23	X	X	X	X	X	X	X						
OREGON														
The Delphian School™ *Sheridan*	S11	X	X	X	X	X	X	X		X				X
TEXAS														
Shelton School & Evaluation Center *Dallas*	S21	X	X	X	X	X		X	X	X				
VIRGINIA														
Flint Hill School *Oakton*	S13	X	X	X				X		X	X	X		X
Fork Union Military Academy *Fork Union*	S14	X	X	X	X	X		X		X				
Hargrave Military Academy *Chatham*	S15	X	X	X	X	X		X						

Classification Grid

These pages give the reader an outline of the schools described in our book. The schools are arranged alphabetically by state or country, together with a page number for locating more descriptive material on each school. Use it as a quick reference for categorizing schools in the following areas:

Boarding or Day

Boys, Girls, or Coed

Secondary or Elementary

Junior Boarding

Postgraduate Program

Summer Program

English as a Second Language

Learning Differences Program

Preprofessional Arts Training

Religious Affiliation

Military Program

The Classification Grid is the best place to begin your search for the right school. We find this section to be invaluable in our counseling sessions in the Bunting and Lyon offices.

Classification Grid

Boarding Boys	Boarding Girls	Day Boys	Day Girls	Elementary	Junior Boarding	Secondary	Postgraduate Program	Summer Program	English as a Second Language	Learning Differences Program	Preprofessional Arts Training	Religious Affiliation	Military Program	Page	School
															ALABAMA
		X	X	X								E		3	Advent Episcopal School *Birmingham*
		X	X	X		X		X						4	The Altamont School *Birmingham*
		X	X	X		X				X				5	Bayside Academy† *Daphne*
		X	X	X				X		X				5	Highlands School† *Birmingham*
		X	X	X		X		X						5	Randolph School *Huntsville*
		X	X	X				X				E		5	St. Luke's Episcopal School *Mobile*
		X	X	X		X		X		X		E		6	St. Paul's Episcopal School† *Mobile*
															ARIZONA
		X	X	X				X				E		7	All Saints' Episcopal Day School *Phoenix*
		X	X	X		X		X						8	Phoenix Country Day School *Paradise Valley*
		X	X	X										11	Tesseract School *Paradise Valley*
															ARKANSAS
		X	X			X		X				E		12	Episcopal Collegiate School *Little Rock*
															CALIFORNIA
		X	X	X								J		13	Abraham Joshua Heschel Day School *Northridge*
		X	X	X				X				E		13	All Saints' Episcopal Day School *Carmel*
		X	X	X				X						13	Barnhart School *Arcadia*
		X	X			X				X				13	The Bay School of San Francisco *San Francisco*
		X				X						RC		13	Bellarmine College Preparatory *San Jose*
		X	X	X		X		X						14	The Bentley School *Oakland*
		X	X	X										14	Berkeley Hall School *Los Angeles*
X	X	X	X			X			X					14	Besant Hill School of Happy Valley *Ojai*
		X	X			X		X				RC		16	Bishop Montgomery High School *Torrance*
		X	X			X		X				E		16	The Bishop's School *La Jolla*
		X	X	X		X								16	The Buckley School *Sherman Oaks*
		X	X	X										16	Calmont School *Calabasas*
		X	X	X				X				NC		17	Calvary Christian School *Pacific Palisades*
		X	X	X		X		X		X		E		17	Campbell Hall *North Hollywood*
		X	X	X										19	The Carey School *San Mateo*
		X		X				X		X		E		19	Cathedral School for Boys† *San Francisco*
		X	X	X				X						19	The Center for Early Education *West Hollywood*

NOTE: The dagger (†) denotes those schools with learning-differences programs that are cross-referenced in the Learning Differences Grid on page 421. Some elementary school classifications include Grade 9; secondary school classifications usually begin at Grade 9 although some commence at Grade 7. Junior Boarding indicates programs for middle school students and, in some instances, elementary school students. The following abbreviations designate formal religious affiliations or historical association: A—Anglican; B—Baptist; C—United Church of Christ Congregational; CSChristian Scientist; E—Episcopal; J—Jewish; L—Lutheran; NC—Nondenominational Christian; P—Presbyterian; Q—Quaker; RC—Roman Catholic; O—Other.

Classification Grid

Boarding Boys	Boarding Girls	Day Boys	Day Girls	Elementary	Junior Boarding	Secondary	Postgraduate Program	Summer Program	English as a Second Language	Learning Differences Program	Preprofessional Arts Training	Religious Affiliation	Military Program	Page	School
		X	X	X		X		X						19	Chadwick School *Palos Verdes Peninsula*
		X	X	X				X						20	Chandler School *Pasadena*
		X	X	X				X						20	Chatsworth Hills Academy *Chatsworth*
		X	X	X				X						20	Children's Day School *San Francisco*
		X	X	X				X	X					20	Chinese American International School *San Francisco*
		X	X	X				X				CS		21	Clairbourn School *San Gabriel*
		X	X			X				X				21	The College Preparatory School† *Oakland*
			X	X				X				RC		21	Convent of the Sacred Heart Elementary School *San Francisco*
			X			X						RC		21	Convent of the Sacred Heart High School *San Francisco*
			X			X						RC		22	Cornelia Connelly School *Anaheim*
		X	X	X						X				22	The Country School† *North Hollywood*
		X	X	X										22	Crane Country Day School *Santa Barbara*
		X				X						RC		22	Crespi Carmelite High School *Encino*
		X	X	X				X		X				22	Crestview Preparatory School† *La Cañada*
		X	X			X		X						22	Crystal Springs Uplands School *Hillsborough*
		X	X	X										23	Curtis School *Los Angeles*
		X	X			X		X	X	X				24	Drew School *San Francisco*
		X	X	X										24	Ecole Bilingue de Berkeley *Oakland*
		X	X			X								24	Flintridge Preparatory School *La Cañada Flintridge*
		X	X	X				X						25	Foothill Country Day School *Claremont*
		X	X	X		X		X						25	Francis Parker School *San Diego*
		X	X	X				X		X				25	Gateway School† *Santa Cruz*
		X	X	X				X						25	The Gillispie School *La Jolla*
			X	X				X						25	The Hamlin School *San Francisco*
		X	X	X										25	Harbor Day School *Corona del Mar*
		X	X	X		X		X						26	The Harker School *San Jose*
		X	X			X		X						26	Harvard-Westlake School *Los Angeles/North Hollywood*
		X	X	X		X		X						26	Head-Royce School *Oakland*
X	X	X	X			X	X	X	X	X	X			26	Idyllwild Arts Academy† *Idyllwild*
		X	X	X				X	X					28	International School of the Peninsula *Palo Alto*
		X	X	X				X						28	The John Thomas Dye School *Los Angeles*
		X	X	X		X				X				30	La Jolla Country Day School† *La Jolla*
		X	X	X				X		X				30	Laurence School† *Valley Glen*
		X	X			X								31	Lick-Wilmerding High School *San Francisco*
		X	X	X				X						31	Live Oak School *San Francisco*
		X	X	X		X		X	X	X				31	Lycée Français La Pérouse† *San Francisco*
		X	X			X								31	Marin Academy *San Rafael*
		X	X	X				X						31	Marin Country Day School *Corte Madera*
		X	X	X				X						32	Marin Horizon School *Mill Valley*
		X	X	X				X		X				32	Marin Primary & Middle School† *Larkspur*
			X			X								32	Marlborough School *Los Angeles*
			X			X		X				RC		32	Marymount High School *Los Angeles*
		X	X	X										32	Marymount of Santa Barbara *Santa Barbara*
		X	X	X				X				RC		32	Mayfield Junior School *Pasadena*
			X			X						RC		32	Mayfield Senior School of the Holy Child *Pasadena*
		X	X			X								33	Menlo School *Atherton*

Boarding Boys	Boarding Girls	Day Boys	Day Girls	Elementary	Junior Boarding	Secondary	Postgraduate Program	Summer Program	English as a Second Language	Learning Differences Program	Preprofessional Arts Training	Religious Affiliation	Military Program	Page	
		X	X			X		X		X				33	Mid-Peninsula High School† *Menlo Park*
		X	X	X						X				33	The Mirman School for Gifted Children† *Los Angeles*
		X	X	X										33	Mount Tamalpais School *Mill Valley*
		X	X	X		X		X	X	X				35	New Roads School *Santa Monica/Malibu/Los Angeles*
		X	X	X				X		X				37	The Nueva School† *Hillsborough*
		X	X	X										37	The Oaks School *Hollywood*
X	X	X	X	X	X	X			X					37	Ojai Valley School *Ojai*
		X	X	X				X		X				38	The Pegasus School† *Huntington Beach*
		X	X	X										38	The Phillips Brooks School *Menlo Park*
		X	X	X		X		X	X			C		38	Pilgrim School *Los Angeles*
		X	X	X		X		X						38	Polytechnic School *Pasadena*
		X	X	X				X						38	Ring Mountain Day School *Mill Valley/Tiburon*
		X	X	X		X		X	X	X				40	Rolling Hills Preparatory School† *San Pedro*
		X	X	X		X		X						40	Sacramento Country Day School *Sacramento*
		X	X	X		X		X				RC		41	Sacred Heart Schools, Atherton *Atherton*
		X	X			X		X						41	Sage Hill School *Newport Coast*
		X	X	X				X				E		41	St. James' Episcopal School *Los Angeles*
		X	X	X				X						41	Saint Mark's School *San Rafael*
		X	X	X								E		41	St. Matthew's Episcopal Day School *San Mateo*
		X	X	X				X				E		41	St. Matthew's Parish School *Pacific Palisades*
		X	X	X				X				E		42	St. Paul's Episcopal School *Oakland*
		X	X	X				X						42	Saklan Valley School *Moraga*
		X	X	X								Q		42	San Francisco Friends School *San Francisco*
		X	X			X				X				42	San Francisco University High School† *San Francisco*
	X		X			X						RC		42	Santa Catalina School *Monterey*
		X	X	X				X						44	The Seven Hills School *Walnut Creek*
		X	X	X		X		X						44	Sierra Canyon School *Chatsworth*
		X	X	X								J		45	Sinai Akiba Academy *Los Angeles*
		X	X			X								45	Sonoma Academy *Santa Rosa*
		X		X				X				RC		45	Stuart Hall for Boys *San Francisco*
		X				X						RC		46	Stuart Hall High School *San Francisco*
		X		X				X		X				46	Town School for Boys *San Francisco*
		X	X	X				X						46	Turning Point School *Culver City*
		X	X			X				X				46	The Urban School of San Francisco† *San Francisco*
		X	X	X		X		X		X				46	Viewpoint School† *Calabasas*
		X	X	X		X		X				NC		48	Village Christian Schools *La Tuna Canyon*
		X	X	X										48	Village School *Pacific Palisades*
		X	X	X										50	The Walden School *Pasadena*
		X	X	X				X						50	The Wesley School *North Hollywood*
			X	X		X		X						50	Westridge School *Pasadena*
		X	X	X				X						50	Westside Neighborhood School *Los Angeles*
		X	X	X		X								50	Wildwood School *Los Angeles*
		X	X	X				X		X				51	Windrush School† *El Cerrito*
		X	X			X								51	Windward School *Los Angeles*
X	X	X	X			X						RC		53	Woodside Priory School *Portola Valley*

Classification Grid

Boarding Boys	Boarding Girls	Day Boys	Day Girls	Elementary	Junior Boarding	Secondary	Postgraduate Program	Summer Program	English as a Second Language	Learning Differences Program	Preprofessional Arts Training	Religious Affiliation	Military Program	Page		
															COLORADO	
		X	X	X		X								54	Alexander Dawson School	*Lafayette*
		X	X	X										54	Aspen Country Day School	*Aspen*
		X	X	X		X		X						54	Colorado Academy	*Denver*
		X	X	X		X								54	The Colorado Springs School	*Colorado Springs*
X	X	X	X			X								54	Crested Butte Academy	*Crested Butte*
X	X	X	X			X			X	X				54	Fountain Valley School of Colorado†	*Colorado Springs*
		X	X	X										55	Graland Country Day School	*Denver*
X	X	X	X			X								55	The Lowell Whiteman School	*Steamboat Springs*
		X	X	X				X				E		55	St. Anne's Episcopal School	*Denver*
		X	X	X		X								56	Telluride Mountain School	*Telluride*
															CONNECTICUT	
			X			X		X				RC		57	Academy of Our Lady of Mercy, Lauralton Hall	*Milford*
		X		X		X								57	Brunswick School	*Greenwich*
X	X	X	X			X	X		X			RC		57	Canterbury School	*New Milford*
		X	X	X		X		X		X				57	Chase Collegiate School†	*Waterbury*
X	X	X	X			X	X	X						57	Choate Rosemary Hall	*Wallingford*
		X	X	X										59	Cold Spring School	*New Haven*
			X	X		X						RC		59	Convent of the Sacred Heart	*Greenwich*
		X	X	X										60	The Country School	*Madison*
		X	X	X		X		X		X				61	Eagle Hill-Southport†	*Southport*
	X		X			X								62	The Ethel Walker School	*Simsbury*
		X		X				X						62	Fairfield Country Day School	*Fairfield*
		X	X	X				X		X				62	The Foote School	*New Haven*
X	X	X	X		X	X	X	X	X	X				62	Glenholme School†	*Washington*
		X	X	X		X		X						63	Greens Farms Academy	*Greens Farms*
			X	X		X								63	Greenwich Academy	*Greenwich*
		X	X	X										63	The Greenwich Country Day School	*Greenwich*
X	X	X	X			X	X		X					63	The Gunnery	*Washington*
		X	X	X		X		X						64	Hamden Hall Country Day School	*Hamden*
		X	X			X		X						66	Hopkins School	*New Haven*
X	X	X	X			X	X	X						67	The Hotchkiss School	*Lakeville*
		X	X	X				X						68	The Independent Day School	*Middlefield*
X	X	X	X			X	X	X	X	X		E		68	Kent School†	*Kent*
		X	X	X		X		X						70	King & Low-Heywood Thomas School	*Stamford*
		X	X			X								72	Kingswood-Oxford School	*West Hartford*
		X	X	X										72	The Long Ridge School	*Stamford*
X	X	X	X			X	X							72	The Loomis Chaffee School	*Windsor*
X	X	X	X			X	X	X	X	X				72	The Marvelwood School†	*Kent*
		X	X	X				X						74	The Mead School	*Stamford*
		X	X	X							X			74	The Montessori School	*Wilton/Norwalk*
		X	X	X						X				75	Mooreland Hill School†	*Kensington*
		X	X	X										75	New Canaan Country School	*New Canaan*
		X				X				X		RC		75	Notre Dame of West Haven†	*West Haven*
		X	X	X						X				75	Pear Tree Point School	*Darien*

Boarding Boys	Boarding Girls	Day Boys	Day Girls	Elementary	Junior Boarding	Secondary	Postgraduate Program	Summer Program	English as a Second Language	Learning Differences Program	Preprofessional Arts Training	Religious Affiliation	Military Program	Page	School
		X	X	X										75	The Pine Brook School *Branford*
		X	X	X				X						76	Pine Point School *Stonington*
		X	X	X				X						76	Renbrook School *West Hartford*
		X	X	X				X						76	Ridgefield Academy *Ridgefield*
X	X	X	X	X	X			X	X	X				76	Rumsey Hall School† *Washington Depot*
		X	X	X		X								78	St. Luke's School *New Canaan*
		X	X	X								E		78	St. Thomas's Day School *New Haven*
X		X				X	X	X				E		78	Salisbury School *Salisbury*
		X	X	X										80	The Stanwich School, Inc. *Greenwich*
X	X	X	X			X	X	X		X				80	The Taft School† *Watertown*
		X	X	X										80	The Unquowa School *Fairfield*
		X	X			X	X	X		X	X			80	Watkinson School† *Hartford*
X	X	X	X			X	X							81	Westminster School *Simsbury*
	X		X			X		X			X			81	Westover School *Middlebury*
		X	X	X										81	Whitby School *Greenwich*
		X	X			X								81	The Williams School *New London*
		X	X	X		X		X	X			E		83	Wooster School *Danbury*

DELAWARE

Boarding Boys	Boarding Girls	Day Boys	Day Girls	Elementary	Junior Boarding	Secondary	Postgraduate Program	Summer Program	English as a Second Language	Learning Differences Program	Preprofessional Arts Training	Religious Affiliation	Military Program	Page	School
		X	X			X						RC		84	Archmere Academy *Claymont*
		X	X	X				X		X				84	The Independence School† *Newark*
		X	X			X						RC		84	St. Mark's High School *Wilmington*
		X				X				X		RC		84	Salesianum School† *Wilmington*
		X	X	X		X		X						86	Sanford School *Hockessin*
		X	X	X		X		X						86	The Tatnall School *Wilmington*
		X	X	X		X		X				RC		86	Ursuline Academy *Wilmington*
		X	X	X		X		X				Q		87	Wilmington Friends School *Wilmington*

DISTRICT OF COLUMBIA

Boarding Boys	Boarding Girls	Day Boys	Day Girls	Elementary	Junior Boarding	Secondary	Postgraduate Program	Summer Program	English as a Second Language	Learning Differences Program	Preprofessional Arts Training	Religious Affiliation	Military Program	Page	School
		X	X	X				X				E		88	Beauvoir, The National Cathedral Elementary School *Washington*
		X	X	X				X						89	Capitol Hill Day School *Washington*
		X	X			X		X						89	Edmund Burke School *Washington*
		X	X			X								89	The Field School *Washington*
		X	X	X		X				X				89	Georgetown Day School† *Washington*
			X			X				X		RC		90	Georgetown Visitation Preparatory School *Washington*
		X				X						RC		90	Gonzaga College High School *Washington*
		X	X	X		X		X		X				90	The Lab School of Washington† *Washington*
		X	X	X				X						90	Lowell School *Washington*
		X	X	X		X		X						90	Maret School *Washington*
			X	X		X						E		90	National Cathedral School *Washington*
		X	X	X				X				P		91	National Presbyterian School *Washington*
X		X		X		X		X				E		91	St. Albans School *Washington*
		X	X	X				X				E		91	St. Patrick's Episcopal Day School *Washington*
		X	X	X				X						91	Sheridan School *Washington*
		X	X	X		X		X				Q		92	Sidwell Friends School *Washington*
		X	X	X		X		X						92	Washington International School *Washington*

Classification Grid

FLORIDA

Boarding Boys	Boarding Girls	Day Boys	Day Girls	Elementary	Junior Boarding	Secondary	Postgraduate Program	Summer Program	English as a Second Language	Learning Differences Program	Preprofessional Arts Training	Religious Affiliation	Military Program	Page	School	Location
		X	X	X		X		X						93	Academy at the Lakes	*Land O' Lakes*
		X	X	X		X		X				RC		93	Academy of the Holy Names	*Tampa*
		X	X	X		X		X						93	The Benjamin School	*North Palm Beach/Palm Beach Gardens*
		X	X	X		X		X				E		93	Berkeley Preparatory School	*Tampa*
		X	X			X						RC		95	Bishop Verot Catholic High School	*Fort Myers*
X	X	X	X	X	X	X	X		X					95	Bolles	*Jacksonville*
		X	X	X		X		X						97	The Canterbury School	*Fort Myers*
			X	X		X						RC		98	Carrollton School of the Sacred Heart	*Miami*
		X	X	X		X		X						98	The Community School of Naples	*Naples*
		X	X	X				X		X				98	The Cushman School	*Miami*
		X	X	X				X						98	The Day School at Coral Springs	*Coral Springs*
		X	X			X		X			X	E		98	Episcopal High School of Jacksonville	*Jacksonville*
		X	X	X				X						99	Gulf Stream School	*Gulf Stream*
		X	X	X								E		99	Holy Comforter Episcopal School, Inc.	*Tallahassee*
		X	X	X				X						99	Independent Day School—Corbett Campus	*Tampa*
		X	X	X				X						99	Jacksonville Country Day School	*Jacksonville*
		X	X	X				X						99	Julie Rohr Academy	*Sarasota*
		X	X	X		X		X						99	Maclay School	*Tallahassee*
X	X	X	X	X		X				X				100	The North Broward Preparatory Schools	*Coconut Creek/Coral Springs*
		X	X	X		X		X						101	Oak Hall School	*Gainesville*
		X	X	X		X								101	The Out-of-Door Academy	*Sarasota*
		X	X	X		X		X		X				102	PACE-Brantley Hall School†	*Longwood*
		X	X	X										102	Palm Beach Day Academy	*Palm Beach/West Palm Beach*
		X	X			X		X	X			E		102	Palmer Trinity School	*Miami*
		X	X	X		X		X						102	Pine Crest School	*Fort Lauderdale*
		X	X	X				X		X				103	Pine Crest School at Boca Raton†	*Boca Raton*
		X	X	X		X								103	The Pine School	*Stuart*
		X	X			X		X						103	Ransom Everglades School	*Coconut Grove*
		X	X	X						X		P		103	Riverside Presbyterian Day School†	*Jacksonville*
		X	X	X		X		X		X		E		104	Saint Edward's School†	*Vero Beach*
		X	X	X		X		X						106	St. Johns Country Day School	*Orange Park*
		X	X	X								E		106	St. John's Episcopal Parish Day School	*Tampa*
		X	X	X								E		106	Saint Joseph's School	*Boynton Beach*
		X	X	X				X		X		E		106	St. Mark's Episcopal Day School†	*Jacksonville*
		X	X	X								E		107	St. Mark's Episcopal School	*Fort Lauderdale*
		X	X	X						X		E		107	St. Mary's Episcopal Day School†	*Tampa*
		X	X	X				X				E		107	Saint Paul's School	*Clearwater*
		X	X	X		X						E		107	Saint Stephen's Episcopal School	*Bradenton*
		X	X	X				X				E		107	St. Thomas Episcopal Parish School	*Coral Gables*
		X	X	X								E		108	San Jose Episcopal Day School	*Jacksonville*
		X	X	X		X		X						108	Seacrest Country Day School	*Naples*
		X	X	X		X				X				110	Shorecrest Preparatory School†	*St. Petersburg*
		X	X			X				X		E		110	Trinity Preparatory School†	*Winter Park*

GEORGIA

Boarding Boys	Boarding Girls	Day Boys	Day Girls	Elementary	Junior Boarding	Secondary	Postgraduate Program	Summer Program	English as a Second Language	Learning Differences Program	Preprofessional Arts Training	Religious Affiliation	Military Program	Page	School
	X		X			X	X			X				111	Brenau Academy† *Gainesville*
		X	X	X		X								112	Brookstone School *Columbus*
		X	X	X				X						112	Cliff Valley School *Atlanta*
		X	X	X		X								113	Frederica Academy *St. Simons Island*
		X	X	X		X		X						113	The Galloway School *Atlanta*
		X	X	X		X								113	George Walton Academy *Monroe*
		X	X	X		X								113	The Heritage School *Newnan*
		X	X	X		X								113	The Lovett School *Atlanta*
		X	X			X						RC		114	Marist School *Atlanta*
		X	X	X		X						NC		114	Oak Mountain Academy *Carrollton*
		X	X	X		X		X						114	Pace Academy *Atlanta*
		X	X	X								E		114	St. George's Episcopal School *Milner*
		X	X	X								E		114	St. Martin's Episcopal School *Atlanta*
		X	X	X		X		X						115	The Savannah Country Day School *Savannah*
X	X	X	X			X			X					115	Tallulah Falls School *Tallulah Falls*
		X	X	X										117	Trinity School *Atlanta*
		X	X	X		X		X						117	The Walker School *Marietta*
		X	X	X		X		X				NC		117	Wesleyan School *Norcross*
		X	X	X		X				X		NC		117	The Westminster Schools† *Atlanta*
		X	X	X		X				X		NC		118	Westminster Schools of Augusta† *Augusta*
		X	X	X		X				X				118	Woodward Academy† *College Park*

HAWAII

Boarding Boys	Boarding Girls	Day Boys	Day Girls	Elementary	Junior Boarding	Secondary	Postgraduate Program	Summer Program	English as a Second Language	Learning Differences Program	Preprofessional Arts Training	Religious Affiliation	Military Program	Page	School
		X	X	X										121	Hanahau'oli School *Honolulu*
		X	X	X				X				E		121	Holy Nativity School *Honolulu*
		X	X	X		X		X	X			E		121	Iolani School *Honolulu*
			X			X								121	LA PIETRA-Hawaii School for Girls *Honolulu*
		X	X	X		X		X						121	Le Jardin Academy *Kailua*
		X	X	X		X								122	Parker School *Kamuela*
			X	X		X		X	X			E		122	St. Andrew's Priory School for Girls *Honolulu*

IDAHO

Boarding Boys	Boarding Girls	Day Boys	Day Girls	Elementary	Junior Boarding	Secondary	Postgraduate Program	Summer Program	English as a Second Language	Learning Differences Program	Preprofessional Arts Training	Religious Affiliation	Military Program	Page	School
		X	X	X		X		X		X				123	The Community School† *Sun Valley*

ILLINOIS

Boarding Boys	Boarding Girls	Day Boys	Day Girls	Elementary	Junior Boarding	Secondary	Postgraduate Program	Summer Program	English as a Second Language	Learning Differences Program	Preprofessional Arts Training	Religious Affiliation	Military Program	Page	School
		X	X	X										124	The Ancona School *Chicago*
		X	X	X				X		X				124	The Avery Coonley School† *Downers Grove*
		X	X	X										124	Baker Demonstration School *Wilmette*
		X	X	X								J		124	Bernard Zell Anshe Emet Day School *Chicago*
X		X			X	X	X			X				124	Brehm Preparatory School *Carbondale*
		X	X	X										125	The Catherine Cook School *Chicago*
		X	X			X		X			X			125	The Chicago Academy for the Arts *Chicago*
		X	X	X										125	Chicago City Day School *Chicago*
		X	X	X		X								125	Elgin Academy *Elgin*
		X	X			X						RC		125	Fenwick High School *Oak Park*

Classification Grid

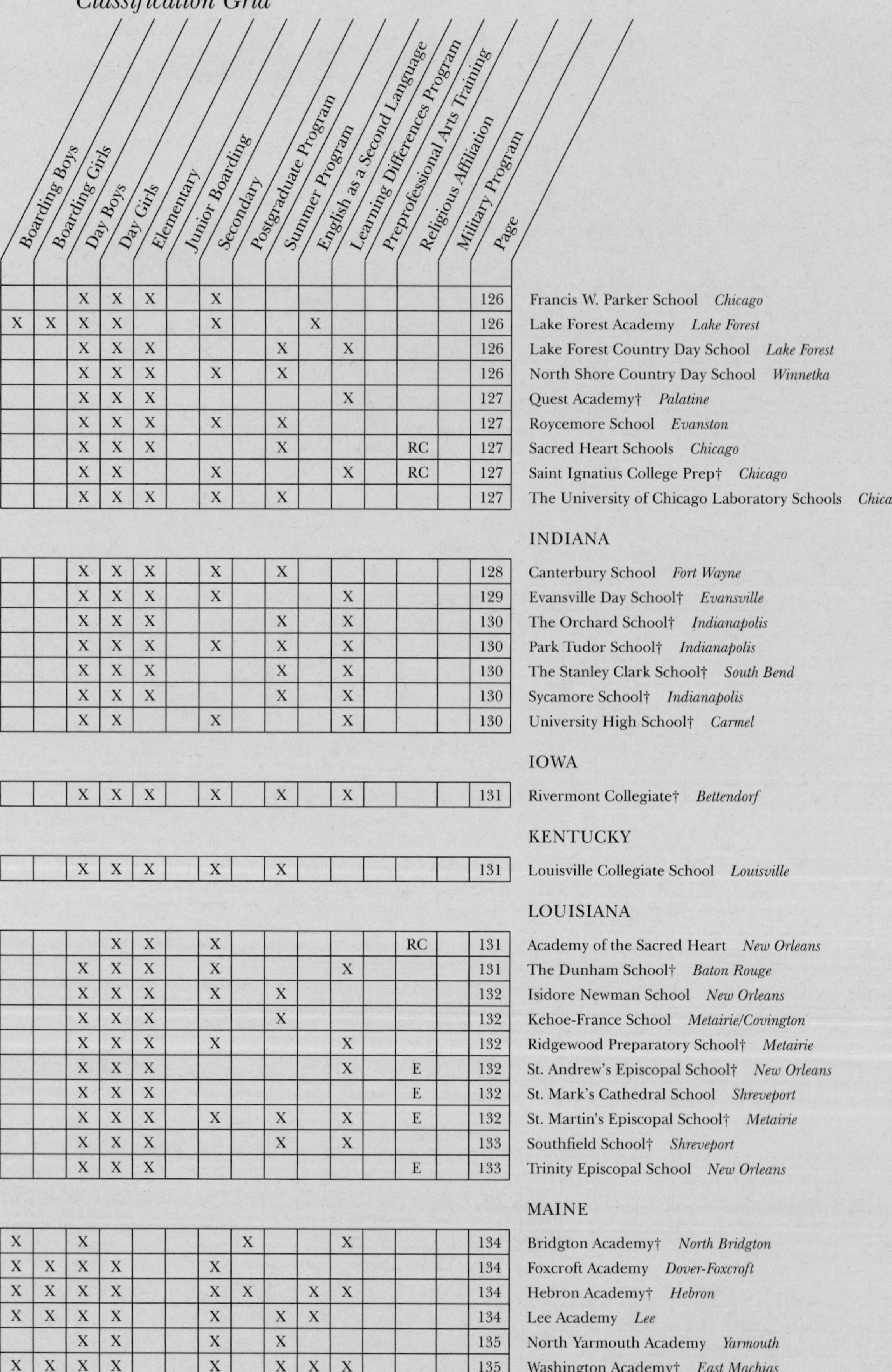

Boarding Boys	Boarding Girls	Day Boys	Day Girls	Elementary	Junior Boarding	Secondary	Postgraduate Program	Summer Program	English as a Second Language	Learning Differences Program	Preprofessional Arts Training	Religious Affiliation	Military Program	Page	School
		X	X	X		X								126	Francis W. Parker School *Chicago*
X	X	X	X			X			X					126	Lake Forest Academy *Lake Forest*
		X	X	X				X		X				126	Lake Forest Country Day School *Lake Forest*
		X	X	X		X		X						126	North Shore Country Day School *Winnetka*
		X	X	X						X				127	Quest Academy† *Palatine*
		X	X	X		X		X						127	Roycemore School *Evanston*
		X	X	X				X				RC		127	Sacred Heart Schools *Chicago*
		X	X			X				X		RC		127	Saint Ignatius College Prep† *Chicago*
		X	X	X		X		X						127	The University of Chicago Laboratory Schools *Chicago*
															INDIANA
		X	X	X		X		X						128	Canterbury School *Fort Wayne*
		X	X	X		X				X				129	Evansville Day School† *Evansville*
		X	X	X				X		X				130	The Orchard School† *Indianapolis*
		X	X	X		X		X		X				130	Park Tudor School† *Indianapolis*
		X	X	X				X		X				130	The Stanley Clark School† *South Bend*
		X	X	X				X		X				130	Sycamore School† *Indianapolis*
		X	X			X				X				130	University High School† *Carmel*
															IOWA
		X	X	X		X		X		X				131	Rivermont Collegiate† *Bettendorf*
															KENTUCKY
		X	X	X		X		X						131	Louisville Collegiate School *Louisville*
															LOUISIANA
			X	X		X						RC		131	Academy of the Sacred Heart *New Orleans*
		X	X	X		X				X				131	The Dunham School† *Baton Rouge*
		X	X	X		X		X						132	Isidore Newman School *New Orleans*
		X	X	X				X						132	Kehoe-France School *Metairie/Covington*
		X	X	X		X				X				132	Ridgewood Preparatory School† *Metairie*
		X	X	X						X		E		132	St. Andrew's Episcopal School† *New Orleans*
		X	X	X								E		132	St. Mark's Cathedral School *Shreveport*
		X	X	X		X		X		X		E		132	St. Martin's Episcopal School† *Metairie*
		X	X	X				X		X				133	Southfield School† *Shreveport*
		X	X	X								E		133	Trinity Episcopal School *New Orleans*
															MAINE
X		X					X			X				134	Bridgton Academy† *North Bridgton*
X	X	X	X			X								134	Foxcroft Academy *Dover-Foxcroft*
X	X	X	X			X	X		X	X				134	Hebron Academy† *Hebron*
X	X	X	X			X		X	X					134	Lee Academy *Lee*
		X	X			X		X						135	North Yarmouth Academy *Yarmouth*
X	X	X	X			X		X	X	X				135	Washington Academy† *East Machias*

MARYLAND

Boarding Boys	Boarding Girls	Day Boys	Day Girls	Elementary	Junior Boarding	Secondary	Postgraduate Program	Summer Program	English as a Second Language	Learning Differences Program	Preprofessional Arts Training	Religious Affiliation	Military Program	Page	School
			X			X		X				RC		136	The Academy of the Holy Cross *Kensington*
		X	X	X				X						136	The Barnesville School *Barnesville*
		X	X	X		X		X						136	The Barrie School *Silver Spring*
			X	X		X								136	The Bryn Mawr School *Baltimore*
		X	X	X		X		X						136	The Calverton School *Huntingtown*
		X	X	X						X				137	Calvert School† *Baltimore*
		X	X	X										137	Chesapeake Academy *Arnold*
		X	X	X				X						137	Concord Hill School *Chevy Chase*
			X			X						RC		137	Connelly School of the Holy Child *Potomac*
		X	X	X										137	The Country School *Easton*
		X	X	X		X		X		X		Q		137	Friends School of Baltimore† *Baltimore*
	X		X	X		X			X					138	Garrison Forest School *Owings Mills*
X		X				X			X			RC		138	Georgetown Preparatory School *North Bethesda*
		X	X	X										138	Gibson Island Country School *Pasadena*
		X		X		X		X						138	Gilman School *Baltimore*
		X	X	X		X		X		X				139	Glenelg Country School† *Ellicott City*
		X	X	X				X						139	Green Acres School *Rockville*
		X	X			X		X		X				139	Gunston Day School† *Centreville*
		X	X	X				X						139	The Harbor School *Bethesda*
		X	X	X										140	Harford Day School *Bel Air*
			X	X		X								140	The Holton-Arms School *Bethesda*
		X	X	X		X		X		X				140	The Ivymount School† *Rockville*
		X	X	X		X				X				140	The Jemicy School *Owings Mills/Towson*
		X	X	X										140	Kent School *Chestertown*
		X	X	X		X		X						140	The Key School *Annapolis*
		X		X		X								141	Landon School *Bethesda*
		X				X		X				RC		141	Loyola Blakefield *Towson*
			X			X						RC		141	Maryvale Preparatory School *Brooklandville*
		X		X								RC		141	Mater Dei School *Bethesda*
X	X	X	X	X		X		X						141	McDonogh School *Owings Mills*
		X	X	X		X		X		X				142	McLean School of Maryland† *Potomac*
		X	X	X				X						142	The Montessori School *Lutherville*
		X	X	X		X								142	The Newport School *Silver Spring*
		X	X			X				X				142	The Nora School† *Silver Spring*
		X	X	X				X		X				143	Norwood School† *Bethesda*
			X			X				X		RC		143	Notre Dame Preparatory School† *Towson*
	X		X			X	X							143	Oldfields School *Glencoe*
		X	X	X										145	The Primary Day School *Bethesda*
		X	X	X		X		X				E		145	Queen Anne School *Upper Marlboro*
		X	X	X						X				145	Radcliffe Creek School† *Chestertown*
			X	X		X		X						146	Roland Park Country School *Baltimore*
		X	X	X						X				146	Ruxton Country School† *Owings Mills*
		X	X	X		X		X				E		146	St. Andrew's Episcopal School *Potomac*
X	X	X	X			X				X		E		148	Saint James School† *St. James*
		X	X	X				X				E		148	St. John's Episcopal School *Olney*
		X	X	X								E		148	St. John's Parish Day School *Ellicott City*

Classification Grid

Boarding Boys	Boarding Girls	Day Boys	Day Girls	Elementary	Junior Boarding	Secondary	Postgraduate Program	Summer Program	English as a Second Language	Learning Differences Program	Preprofessional Arts Training	Religious Affiliation	Military Program	Page	
		X	X	X		X		X				E		148	St. Paul's School *Brooklandville*
			X	X		X						E		149	St. Paul's School for Girls *Brooklandville*
	X		X			X		X	X			E		149	St. Timothy's School *Stevenson*
X	X	X	X	X		X			X			Q		151	Sandy Spring Friends School *Sandy Spring*
		X	X			X		X						152	Severn School *Severna Park*
			X	X		X		X		X		RC		153	Stone Ridge School of the Sacred Heart† *Bethesda*
		X	X			X		X		X		Q		153	Thornton Friends School† *Silver Spring*
		X	X	X		X			X					153	Washington Waldorf School *Bethesda*
		X	X	X								RC		153	The Woods Academy *Bethesda*

MASSACHUSETTS

Boarding Boys	Boarding Girls	Day Boys	Day Girls	Elementary	Junior Boarding	Secondary	Postgraduate Program	Summer Program	English as a Second Language	Learning Differences Program	Preprofessional Arts Training	Religious Affiliation	Military Program	Page	
		X	X			X	X							154	The Academy at Charlemont *Charlemont*
		X	X	X										154	Applewild School *Fitchburg*
		X	X	X						X				154	The Atrium School† *Watertown*
		X	X			X						RC		154	Austin Preparatory School *Reading*
		X	X	X		X								154	Bancroft School *Worcester*
		X	X	X				X						154	Belmont Day School *Belmont*
X		X				X		X						155	Belmont Hill School *Belmont*
		X	X	X										155	Berkshire Country Day School *Lenox*
X	X	X	X			X	X		X					155	Berkshire School *Sheffield*
		X	X			X								157	Boston University Academy *Boston*
		X	X	X		X			X					157	Brimmer and May School *Chestnut Hill*
X	X	X	X			X						E		157	Brooks School *North Andover*
		X	X	X				X						157	Brookwood School *Manchester*
		X	X	X		X								157	Buckingham Browne & Nichols School *Cambridge*
		X	X	X								Q		158	Cambridge Friends School *Cambridge*
		X	X	X		X								158	Cape Cod Academy *Osterville*
		X	X	X				X		X				158	The Carroll School† *Lincoln*
		X	X	X				X						158	Charles River School *Dover*
		X	X	X				X						158	The Chestnut Hill School *Chestnut Hill*
		X	X	X		X				X				158	The Clark School† *Danvers*
		X	X			X								159	The Commonwealth School *Boston*
X	X	X	X			X	X	X	X	X				160	Cushing Academy† *Ashburnham*
	X		X			X								161	Dana Hall School *Wellesley*
		X	X	X				X						161	Dedham Country Day School *Dedham*
		X	X	X				X						161	Derby Academy *Hingham*
		X		X		X		X						161	Dexter School *Brookline*
X		X			X			X	X	X				161	Eaglebrook School† *Deerfield*
		X	X	X										162	The Eliot Montessori School *South Natick*
		X	X			X		X						162	Falmouth Academy *Falmouth*
		X	X	X										162	Fayerweather Street School *Cambridge*
		X		X										162	The Fenn School *Concord*
		X	X			X						J		162	Gann Academy *Waltham*
		X	X	X				X						163	Glen Urquhart School *Beverly Farms*
		X	X	X				X						163	Great Barrington Rudolf Steiner School *Great Barrington*
X	X	X	X			X						E		163	Groton School *Groton*

Boarding Boys	Boarding Girls	Day Boys	Day Girls	Elementary	Junior Boarding	Secondary	Postgraduate Program	Summer Program	English as a Second Language	Learning Differences Program	Preprofessional Arts Training	Religious Affiliation	Military Program	Page	School
X		X			X			X	X	X				163	Hillside School† *Marlborough*
		X	X			X						RC		165	Holy Name Central Junior/Senior High School *Worcester*
X	X	X	X			X		X	X					165	Lawrence Academy *Groton*
		X	X	X										165	The Learning Project *Boston*
		X	X	X				X						165	Lesley Ellis School *Arlington*
		X	X			X		X	X	X		NC		165	Lexington Christian Academy *Lexington*
		X	X	X				X		X				166	The Meadowbrook School of Weston† *Weston*
	X		X			X			X					166	Miss Hall's School *Pittsfield*
			X			X						RC		166	Montrose School *Medfield*
		X	X	X										166	Nashoba Brooks School *Concord*
		X	X			X	X	X	X			RC		167	The Newman School *Boston*
			X			X						RC		168	Newton Country Day School of the Sacred Heart *Newton*
X	X	X	X			X								169	Noble and Greenough School *Dedham*
		X	X	X				X						169	The Park School *Brookline*
X	X	X	X			X	X	X						169	Phillips Academy *Andover*
		X	X	X				X		X				169	Pine Cobble School† *Williamstown*
		X	X			X								169	The Rivers School *Weston*
X	X					X	X	X		X				170	Riverview School† *East Sandwich*
		X				X								171	The Roxbury Latin School *West Roxbury*
		X				X						RC		171	St. John's Preparatory School *Danvers*
		X				X						RC		171	St. Sebastian's School *Needham*
X	X					X								171	School Year Abroad *Lawrence*
		X	X	X										172	Shady Hill School *Cambridge*
			X	X		X		X						172	Southfield School *Brookline*
	X		X		X	X	X	X	X					172	Stoneleigh-Burnham School *Greenfield*
		X	X	X				X						174	Tenacre Country Day School *Wellesley*
		X	X			X		X		X				174	Thayer Academy† *Braintree*
		X	X	X				X						176	Tower School *Marblehead*
X					X	X		X		X				176	Valley View School† *North Brookfield*
X	X	X	X			X	X		X					176	The Williston Northampton School *Easthampton*
X	X	X	X			X	X	X	X	X				177	The Winchendon School† *Winchendon*
			X	X		X								179	The Winsor School *Boston*
X	X	X	X			X	X		X					179	Worcester Academy *Worcester*

MICHIGAN

Boarding Boys	Boarding Girls	Day Boys	Day Girls	Elementary	Junior Boarding	Secondary	Postgraduate Program	Summer Program	English as a Second Language	Learning Differences Program	Preprofessional Arts Training	Religious Affiliation	Military Program	Page	School
		X	X	X		X		X		X		RC		181	Academy of the Sacred Heart† *Bloomfield Hills*
X	X	X	X	X		X			X	X				181	Cranbrook Schools† *Bloomfield Hills*
		X	X	X		X		X						183	Detroit Country Day School *Beverly Hills*
		X	X	X				X				RC		185	The Grosse Pointe Academy *Grosse Pointe Farms*
		X	X	X				X		X				187	Kalamazoo Country Day School† *Kalamazoo*
		X	X	X				X						187	Kingsbury Country Day School *Oxford*
		X	X	X		X		X				RC		187	Notre Dame Preparatory School and Marist Academy *Pontiac*
		X	X	X		X		X		X				189	The Roeper School† *Bloomfield Hills*
		X	X	X		X				X				189	University Liggett School† *Grosse Pointe Woods*

Classification Grid

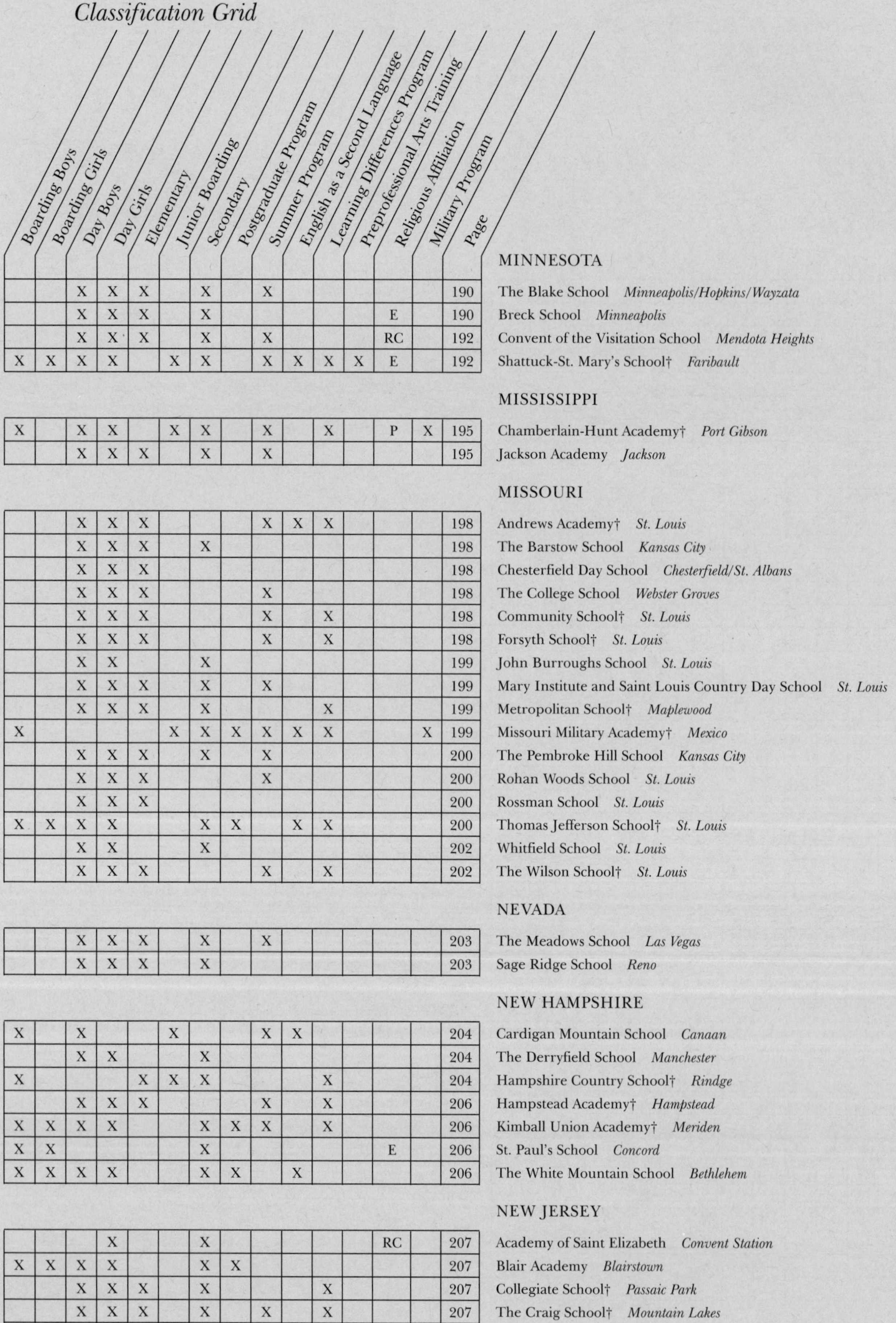

Boarding Boys	Boarding Girls	Day Boys	Day Girls	Elementary	Junior Boarding	Secondary	Postgraduate Program	Summer Program	English as a Second Language	Learning Differences Program	Preprofessional Arts Training	Religious Affiliation	Military Program	Page	School
															MINNESOTA
		X	X	X		X		X						190	The Blake School *Minneapolis/Hopkins/Wayzata*
		X	X	X		X						E		190	Breck School *Minneapolis*
		X	X	X		X		X				RC		192	Convent of the Visitation School *Mendota Heights*
X	X	X	X		X	X		X	X	X	X	E		192	Shattuck-St. Mary's School† *Faribault*
															MISSISSIPPI
X		X	X		X	X		X		X		P	X	195	Chamberlain-Hunt Academy† *Port Gibson*
		X	X	X		X		X						195	Jackson Academy *Jackson*
															MISSOURI
		X	X	X				X	X	X				198	Andrews Academy† *St. Louis*
		X	X	X		X								198	The Barstow School *Kansas City*
		X	X	X										198	Chesterfield Day School *Chesterfield/St. Albans*
		X	X	X				X						198	The College School *Webster Groves*
		X	X	X				X		X				198	Community School† *St. Louis*
		X	X	X				X		X				198	Forsyth School† *St. Louis*
		X	X			X								199	John Burroughs School *St. Louis*
		X	X	X		X		X						199	Mary Institute and Saint Louis Country Day School *St. Louis*
		X	X	X		X				X				199	Metropolitan School† *Maplewood*
X					X	X	X	X	X	X			X	199	Missouri Military Academy† *Mexico*
		X	X	X		X		X						200	The Pembroke Hill School *Kansas City*
		X	X	X				X						200	Rohan Woods School *St. Louis*
		X	X	X										200	Rossman School *St. Louis*
X	X	X	X			X	X		X	X				200	Thomas Jefferson School† *St. Louis*
		X	X			X								202	Whitfield School *St. Louis*
		X	X	X				X		X				202	The Wilson School† *St. Louis*
															NEVADA
		X	X	X		X		X						203	The Meadows School *Las Vegas*
		X	X	X		X								203	Sage Ridge School *Reno*
															NEW HAMPSHIRE
X		X			X			X	X					204	Cardigan Mountain School *Canaan*
		X	X			X								204	The Derryfield School *Manchester*
X				X	X	X				X				204	Hampshire Country School† *Rindge*
		X	X	X				X		X				206	Hampstead Academy† *Hampstead*
X	X	X	X			X	X	X		X				206	Kimball Union Academy† *Meriden*
X	X					X						E		206	St. Paul's School *Concord*
X	X	X	X			X	X		X					206	The White Mountain School *Bethlehem*
															NEW JERSEY
			X			X						RC		207	Academy of Saint Elizabeth *Convent Station*
X	X	X	X			X	X							207	Blair Academy *Blairstown*
		X	X	X		X				X				207	Collegiate School† *Passaic Park*
		X	X	X		X		X		X				207	The Craig School† *Mountain Lakes*

Boarding Boys	Boarding Girls	Day Boys	Day Girls	Elementary	Junior Boarding	Secondary	Postgraduate Program	Summer Program	English as a Second Language	Learning Differences Program	Preprofessional Arts Training	Religious Affiliation	Military Program	Page	School
		X				X		X				RC		207	Delbarton School *Morristown*
		X	X	X				X	X					208	The Elisabeth Morrow School *Englewood*
		X	X	X						X				208	Far Brook School† *Short Hills*
		X	X	X		X				X				210	Gill St. Bernard's School† *Gladstone*
		X	X	X				X				Q		210	Haddonfield Friends School *Haddonfield*
		X	X	X				X						210	Hilltop Country Day School *Sparta*
		X	X	X		X		X		X				210	The Hudson School† *Hoboken*
X	X	X	X			X	X	X	X	X				210	The Hun School of Princeton† *Princeton*
			X	X		X								212	Kent Place School *Summit*
X	X	X	X			X	X							213	The Lawrenceville School *Lawrenceville*
		X	X	X		X						Q		213	Moorestown Friends School *Moorestown*
		X	X			X								213	Morristown-Beard School *Morristown*
			X			X						RC		213	Mount Saint Mary Academy *Watchung*
		X	X			X		X						213	Newark Academy *Livingston*
		X		X										213	Newark Boys Chorus School *Newark*
		X	X	X				X						214	Oak Hill Academy *Lincroft*
		X	X	X										214	The Peck School *Morristown*
X	X	X	X			X	X							214	Peddie School *Hightstown*
		X	X	X		X		X						214	The Pingry School *Short Hills/Martinsville*
		X	X	X		X		X		X				214	Princeton Day School† *Princeton*
		X	X	X										215	Princeton Junior School *Princeton*
		X	X	X				X						215	Princeton Montessori School *Princeton*
		X	X	X		X		X						215	Ranney School *Tinton Falls*
		X	X	X				X						215	The Red Oaks School *Morristown*
		X	X	X										215	The Rumson Country Day School *Rumson*
		X	X	X		X					X			217	Rutgers Preparatory School *Somerset*
		X	X	X		X				X				219	Saddle River Day School† *Saddle River*
X		X				X		X				RC		221	St. Benedict's Preparatory School *Newark*
		X	X	X		X		X				E		221	St. Mary's Hall/Doane Academy *Burlington*
			X	X		X		X				RC		221	Stuart Country Day School of the Sacred Heart *Princeton*
		X	X	X		X		X						221	The Wardlaw-Hartridge School *Edison*
		X	X	X				X						222	The Willow School *Gladstone*
		X	X	X										222	The Wilson School *Mountain Lakes*
		X	X	X						X				222	The Winston School† *Short Hills*

NEW MEXICO

Boarding Boys	Boarding Girls	Day Boys	Day Girls	Elementary	Junior Boarding	Secondary	Postgraduate Program	Summer Program	English as a Second Language	Learning Differences Program	Preprofessional Arts Training	Religious Affiliation	Military Program	Page	School
		X	X			X		X						223	Albuquerque Academy *Albuquerque*
		X	X	X				X						223	Manzano Day School *Albuquerque*
		X	X	X				X						223	Rio Grande School *Santa Fe*
		X	X			X		X						223	Sandia Preparatory School *Albuquerque*

Classification Grid

Boarding Boys	Boarding Girls	Day Boys	Day Girls	Elementary	Junior Boarding	Secondary	Postgraduate Program	Summer Program	English as a Second Language	Learning Differences Program	Preprofessional Arts Training	Religious Affiliation	Military Program	Page	NEW YORK
			X			X						RC		224	Academy of Mount St. Ursula *Bronx*
		X	X	X		X		X						224	Allendale Columbia School *Rochester*
		X		X										224	The Allen-Stevenson School *New York*
		X	X	X				X						224	Bank Street School for Children *New York*
		X	X	X		X		X						224	The Berkeley Carroll School *Brooklyn*
		X	X	X		X								224	The Birch Wathen Lenox School *New York*
			X	X		X								226	The Brearley School *New York*
		X	X	X								P		226	The Brick Church School *New York*
		X	X	X		X						Q		226	Brooklyn Friends School *Brooklyn*
		X	X	X				X						226	Brooklyn Heights Montessori School *Brooklyn*
		X		X		X								226	The Browning School *New York*
		X	X	X				X						227	Buckley Country Day School *Roslyn*
		X		X										227	The Buckley School *New York*
			X			X								227	Buffalo Seminary *Buffalo*
		X	X	X										227	The Caedmon School *New York*
		X	X	X								O		227	The Cathedral School *New York*
		X	X	X								E		227	The Cathedral School of St. John the Divine *New York*
			X	X		X								228	The Chapin School *New York*
		X	X	X		X				X				228	The Churchill School and Center† *New York*
		X	X	X				X						230	City & Country School *New York*
		X	X	X										230	Claremont Preparatory School *New York*
		X		X		X								230	Collegiate School *New York*
		X	X	X		X								230	Columbia Grammar and Preparatory School *New York*
			X	X		X						RC		232	Convent of the Sacred Heart *New York*
		X	X	X										232	Corlears School *New York*
		X	X	X		X								232	The Dalton School *New York*
		X	X	X		X						RC/E		232	Doane Stuart School *Albany*
		X	X	X										232	Dutchess Day School *Millbrook*
		X	X	X		X		X	X	X				233	The Dwight School† *New York*
		X	X	X				X		X				233	East Woods School† *Oyster Bay*
		X	X	X				X		X				233	The Elmwood Franklin School† *Buffalo*
		X	X	X		X		X						233	Ethical Culture Fieldston School *New York/Bronx*
		X	X	X		X		X				Q		234	Friends Academy *Locust Valley*
		X	X	X		X		X				Q		234	Friends Seminary *New York*
X						X	X	X		X				234	The Gow School† *South Wales*
		X	X	X								E		236	Grace Church School *New York*
		X	X	X				X				E		236	Grace Day School *Massapequa*
		X	X	X										236	The Green Vale School *Old Brookville*
X	X	X	X	X		X								236	Hackley School *Tarrytown*
		X	X	X				X						238	Harbor Country Day School *St. James*
		X	X	X		X		X						238	The Harley School *Rochester*
X	X	X	X		X	X								238	The Harvey School *Katonah*
		X	X	X		X		X						239	Horace Mann School *Riverdale/New York*
		X				X						RC		239	Iona Preparatory School *New Rochelle*
		X	X	X		X								241	The Kew-Forest School *Forest Hills*

Boarding Boys	Boarding Girls	Day Boys	Day Girls	Elementary	Junior Boarding	Secondary	Postgraduate Program	Summer Program	English as a Second Language	Learning Differences Program	Preprofessional Arts Training	Religious Affiliation	Military Program	Page	School
X	X	X	X	X		X	X	X		X				241	The Kildonan School† *Amenia*
X	X	X	X		X	X			X	X				241	The Knox School† *St. James*
		X	X	X		X								241	Lawrence Woodmere Academy *Woodmere*
		X	X			X						RC		242	Loyola School *New York*
X	X	X	X	X		X	X	X	X					242	Manlius Pebble Hill School *Dewitt*
			X			X				X		RC		242	The Mary Louis Academy† *Jamaica Estates*
		X	X	X						X				242	Mary McDowell Center for Learning† *Brooklyn*
			X	X		X		X				RC		242	Marymount School *New York*
X	X	X	X			X			X					243	The Masters School *Dobbs Ferry*
		X	X	X				X				E		245	The Melrose School *Brewster*
X	X	X	X			X			X					245	Millbrook School *Millbrook*
X	X	X	X		X	X	X		X				X	245	New York Military Academy *Cornwall-on-Hudson*
		X	X	X		X		X						245	Nichols School *Buffalo*
			X	X		X								246	The Nightingale-Bamford School *New York*
X	X	X	X			X			X	X		Q		246	Oakwood Friends School† *Poughkeepsie*
		X	X	X		X								247	The Packer Collegiate Institute *Brooklyn Heights*
		X	X	X		X		X	X					248	The Park School of Buffalo *Snyder*
		X	X	X		X		X						248	Poly Prep Country Day School *Brooklyn*
		X	X	X		X		X			X			248	Poughkeepsie Day School *Poughkeepsie*
		X	X	X										248	Rippowam Cisqua School *Bedford/Mount Kisco*
		X	X	X		X								249	Riverdale Country School *Riverdale*
		X	X			X	X	X		X				250	Robert Louis Stevenson School† *New York*
		X	X	X		X								251	The Rockland Country Day School *Congers*
		X	X	X		X		X						251	Rudolf Steiner School *New York*
		X	X	X		X		X						251	Rye Country Day School *Rye*
		X	X	X		X		X						253	Saint Ann's School *Brooklyn Heights*
		X		X										253	St. Bernard's School *New York*
		X		X								RC		253	Saint David's School *New York*
		X	X			X			X		X	RC		253	Saint Francis Preparatory School *Fresh Meadows*
		X		X				X				RC		254	Saint Gregory's School *Loudonville*
		X	X	X								E		254	St. Hilda's & St. Hugh's School *New York*
		X	X	X								E		254	St. Luke's School *New York*
X				X	X					X	X	E		254	Saint Thomas Choir School† *New York*
		X	X			X	X	X						254	Soundview Preparatory School *Mount Kisco*
		X	X	X		X		X						254	Staten Island Academy *Staten Island*
X	X	X	X			X			X	X	X			256	The Storm King School† *Cornwall-on-Hudson*
		X	X	X				X						256	The Town School *New York*
		X	X	X		X								256	Trevor Day School *New York*
		X	X	X										257	Tuxedo Park School *Tuxedo Park*
		X	X	X		X			X					257	United Nations International School *New York/Jamaica Estates*
			X			X						RC		257	The Ursuline School *New Rochelle*
		X	X	X										259	Village Community School *New York*
		X	X			X	X	X	X	X				259	The Windsor School† *Flushing*
		X	X	X				X		X				259	Windward School† *White Plains*
		X	X			X				X				259	The Winston Preparatory School† *New York*
		X	X	X		X		X		X				260	York Preparatory School† *New York*

Classification Grid

NORTH CAROLINA

Boarding Boys	Boarding Girls	Day Boys	Day Girls	Elementary	Junior Boarding	Secondary	Postgraduate Program	Summer Program	English as a Second Language	Learning Differences Program	Preprofessional Arts Training	Religious Affiliation	Military Program	Page	School
		X	X	X		X								261	Cannon School *Concord*
		X	X	X		X		X						261	Cape Fear Academy *Wilmington*
		X	X	X		X		X		X				261	Carolina Day School† *Asheville*
		X	X			X		X						261	Cary Academy *Cary*
		X	X	X		X		X	X					261	Charlotte Country Day School *Charlotte*
		X	X	X		X		X						262	Charlotte Latin School *Charlotte*
X		X				X			X			E		262	Christ School *Arden*
		X	X	X		X		X		X				262	Durham Academy† *Durham*
		X	X	X		X		X		X				262	Forsyth Country Day School† *Lewisville*
		X	X	X		X		X	X					262	Greensboro Day School *Greensboro*
		X	X	X		X		X		X				262	Guilford Day School† *Greensboro*
		X	X	X		X								263	Kerr-Vance Academy *Henderson*
		X	X	X		X		X				Q		263	New Garden Friends School *Greensboro*
		X	X	X		X					X			263	The Oakwood School *Greenville*
		X	X	X		X				X				263	The O'Neal School† *Southern Pines*
X	X	X	X		X	X	X		X	X				264	The Patterson School† *Patterson*
		X	X	X		X		X		X				264	Providence Day School† *Charlotte*
		X	X	X		X		X						264	Ravenscroft School *Raleigh*
		X	X	X		X								264	Rocky Mount Academy *Rocky Mount*
	X		X			X				X		E		264	Saint Mary's School† *Raleigh*
		X	X	X						X		E		266	St. Timothy's School† *Raleigh*
	X		X			X		X	X			O		266	Salem Academy *Winston-Salem*
		X	X	X										268	Salisbury Academy *Salisbury*
		X	X	X				X		X				269	Summit School† *Winston-Salem*
		X	X	X		X		X		X				269	Westchester Country Day School† *High Point*

OHIO

Boarding Boys	Boarding Girls	Day Boys	Day Girls	Elementary	Junior Boarding	Secondary	Postgraduate Program	Summer Program	English as a Second Language	Learning Differences Program	Preprofessional Arts Training	Religious Affiliation	Military Program	Page	School
		X	X	X										270	Canton Country Day School *Canton*
		X	X	X		X		X		X				270	Cincinnati Country Day School *Cincinnati*
		X	X	X		X		X						270	The Columbus Academy *Gahanna*
			X	X		X		X		X				270	Columbus School for Girls† *Columbus*
X	X	X	X	X	X	X	X					RC		270	Gilmour Academy *Gates Mills*
			X	X		X		X						271	Hathaway Brown School *Shaker Heights*
		X	X	X		X		X		X				271	Lake Ridge Academy† *North Ridgeville*
			X	X		X								271	Laurel School *Shaker Heights/Russell*
			X			X		X		X		RC		271	Magnificat High School *Rocky River*
		X	X	X		X		X		X				271	Maumee Valley Country Day School† *Toledo*
		X	X	X		X		X		X				271	The Miami Valley School† *Dayton*
		X	X	X				X						271	Old Trail School *Bath*
X	X	X	X			X			X			Q		272	Olney Friends School *Barnesville*
		X				X		X				RC		272	Saint Ignatius High School *Cleveland*
		X	X	X		X		X						272	The Seven Hills Schools *Cincinnati*
		X	X	X				X		X				272	Springer School and Center† *Cincinnati*
		X	X	X		X				X		RC		273	The Summit Country Day School† *Cincinnati*

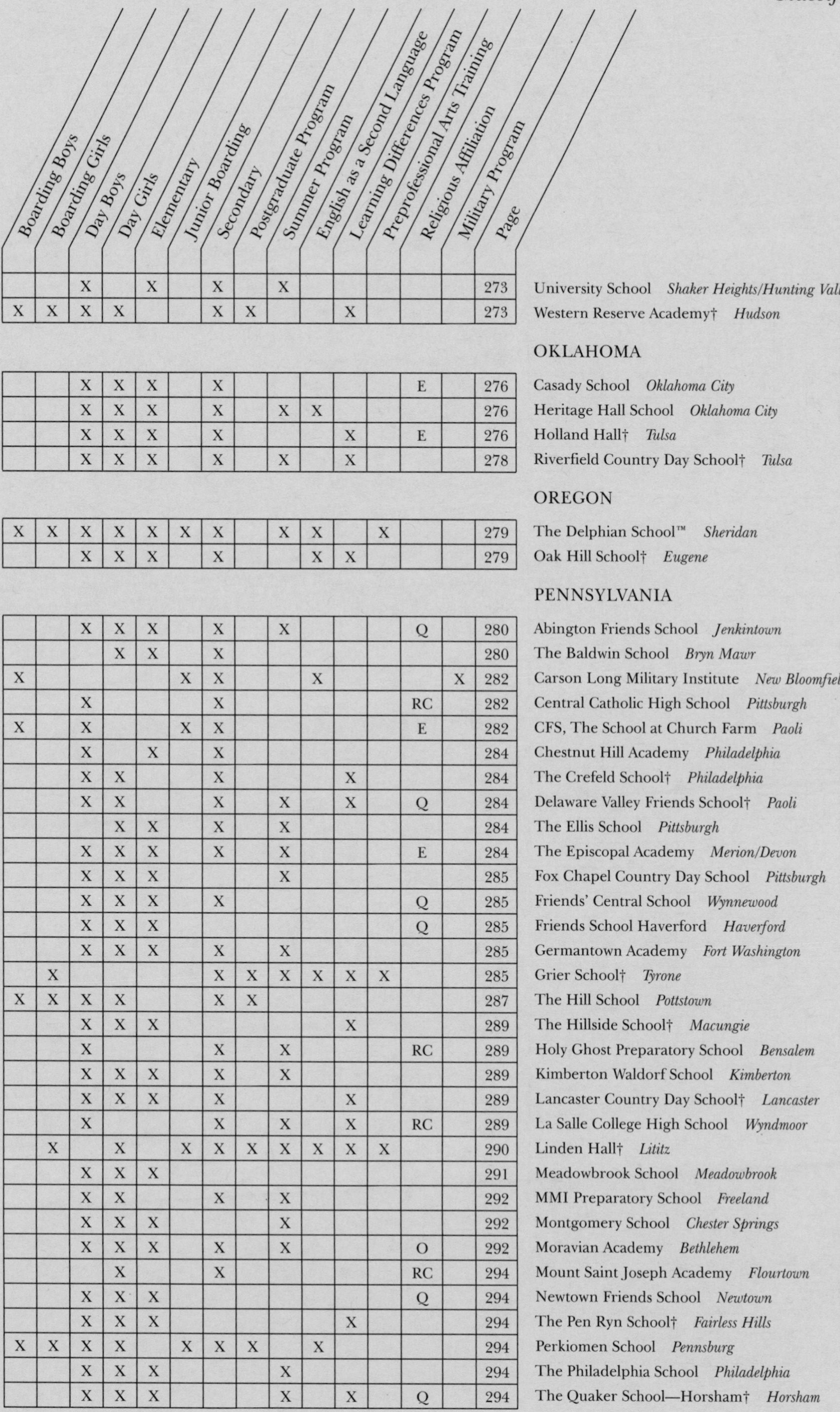

Boarding Boys	Boarding Girls	Day Boys	Day Girls	Elementary	Junior Boarding	Secondary	Postgraduate Program	Summer Program	English as a Second Language	Learning Differences Program	Preprofessional Arts Training	Religious Affiliation	Military Program	Page	School
		X		X		X		X						273	University School *Shaker Heights/Hunting Valley*
X	X	X	X			X	X			X				273	Western Reserve Academy† *Hudson*
															OKLAHOMA
		X	X	X		X						E		276	Casady School *Oklahoma City*
		X	X	X		X		X	X					276	Heritage Hall School *Oklahoma City*
		X	X	X		X				X		E		276	Holland Hall† *Tulsa*
		X	X	X		X		X		X				278	Riverfield Country Day School† *Tulsa*
															OREGON
X	X	X	X	X	X	X		X	X		X			279	The Delphian School™ *Sheridan*
		X	X	X		X			X	X				279	Oak Hill School† *Eugene*
															PENNSYLVANIA
		X	X	X		X		X				Q		280	Abington Friends School *Jenkintown*
			X	X		X								280	The Baldwin School *Bryn Mawr*
X					X	X			X				X	282	Carson Long Military Institute *New Bloomfield*
		X				X						RC		282	Central Catholic High School *Pittsburgh*
X		X			X	X						E		282	CFS, The School at Church Farm *Paoli*
		X		X		X								284	Chestnut Hill Academy *Philadelphia*
		X	X			X				X				284	The Crefeld School† *Philadelphia*
		X	X			X		X		X		Q		284	Delaware Valley Friends School† *Paoli*
			X	X		X		X						284	The Ellis School *Pittsburgh*
		X	X	X		X		X				E		284	The Episcopal Academy *Merion/Devon*
		X	X	X				X						285	Fox Chapel Country Day School *Pittsburgh*
		X	X	X		X						Q		285	Friends' Central School *Wynnewood*
		X	X	X								Q		285	Friends School Haverford *Haverford*
		X	X	X		X		X						285	Germantown Academy *Fort Washington*
	X					X	X	X	X	X	X			285	Grier School† *Tyrone*
X	X	X	X			X	X							287	The Hill School *Pottstown*
		X	X	X						X				289	The Hillside School† *Macungie*
		X				X		X				RC		289	Holy Ghost Preparatory School *Bensalem*
		X	X	X		X		X						289	Kimberton Waldorf School *Kimberton*
		X	X	X		X				X				289	Lancaster Country Day School† *Lancaster*
		X				X		X		X		RC		289	La Salle College High School *Wyndmoor*
	X		X		X	X	X	X	X	X	X			290	Linden Hall† *Lititz*
		X	X	X										291	Meadowbrook School *Meadowbrook*
		X	X			X		X						292	MMI Preparatory School *Freeland*
		X	X	X				X						292	Montgomery School *Chester Springs*
		X	X	X		X		X				O		292	Moravian Academy *Bethlehem*
			X			X						RC		294	Mount Saint Joseph Academy *Flourtown*
		X	X	X								Q		294	Newtown Friends School *Newtown*
		X	X	X						X				294	The Pen Ryn School† *Fairless Hills*
X	X	X	X		X	X	X		X					294	Perkiomen School *Pennsburg*
		X	X	X				X						294	The Philadelphia School *Philadelphia*
		X	X	X				X		X		Q		294	The Quaker School—Horsham† *Horsham*

Classification Grid

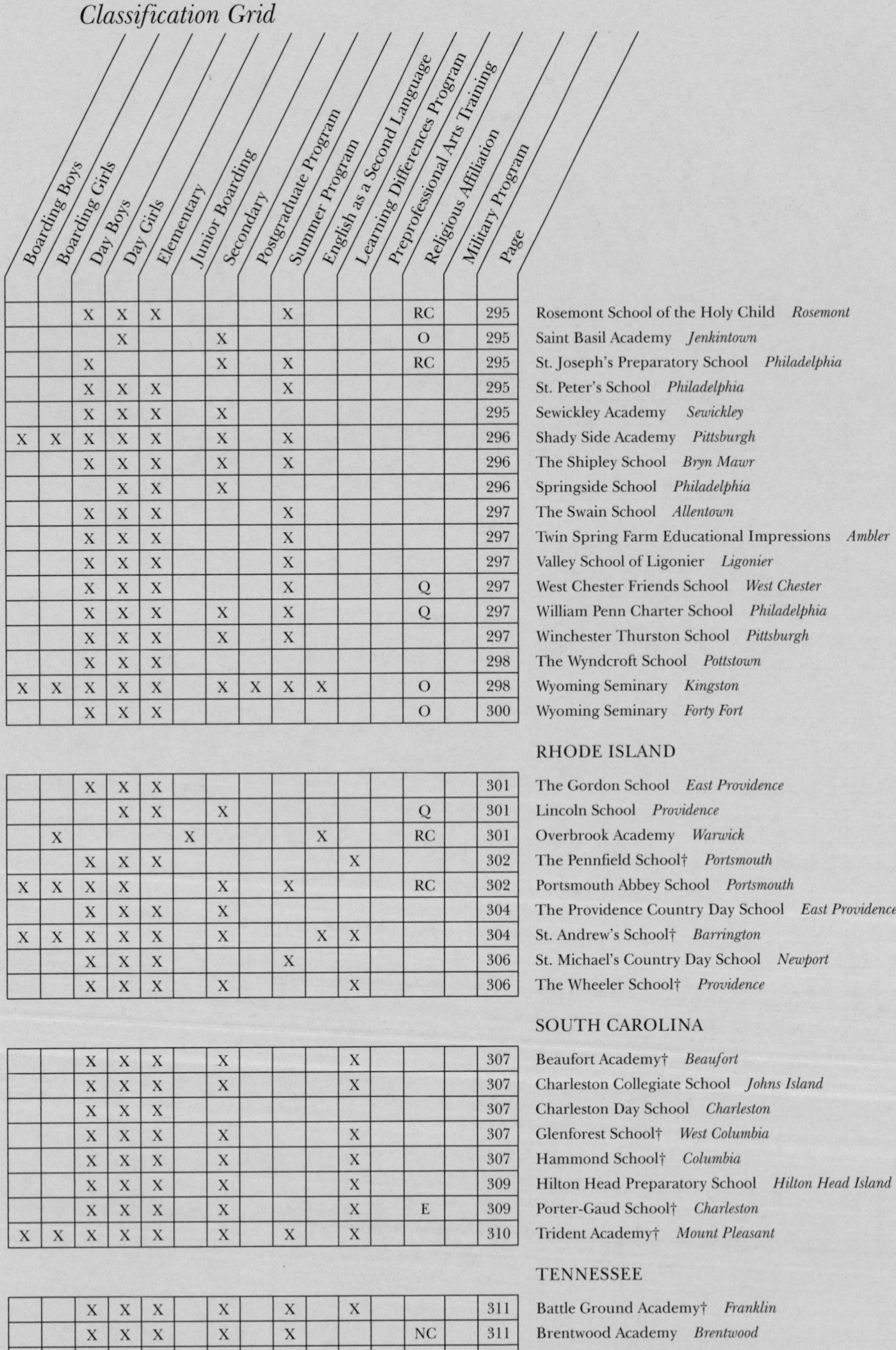

Boarding Boys	Boarding Girls	Day Boys	Day Girls	Elementary	Junior Boarding	Secondary	Postgraduate Program	Summer Program	English as a Second Language	Learning Differences Program	Preprofessional Arts Training	Religious Affiliation	Military Program	Page	School	Location
		X	X	X				X				RC		295	Rosemont School of the Holy Child	*Rosemont*
			X			X						O		295	Saint Basil Academy	*Jenkintown*
		X				X		X				RC		295	St. Joseph's Preparatory School	*Philadelphia*
		X	X	X				X						295	St. Peter's School	*Philadelphia*
		X	X	X		X								295	Sewickley Academy	*Sewickley*
X	X	X	X	X		X		X						296	Shady Side Academy	*Pittsburgh*
		X	X	X		X		X						296	The Shipley School	*Bryn Mawr*
			X	X		X								296	Springside School	*Philadelphia*
		X	X	X				X						297	The Swain School	*Allentown*
		X	X	X				X						297	Twin Spring Farm Educational Impressions	*Ambler*
		X	X	X				X						297	Valley School of Ligonier	*Ligonier*
		X	X	X				X				Q		297	West Chester Friends School	*West Chester*
		X	X	X		X		X				Q		297	William Penn Charter School	*Philadelphia*
		X	X	X		X		X						297	Winchester Thurston School	*Pittsburgh*
		X	X	X										298	The Wyndcroft School	*Pottstown*
X	X	X	X	X		X	X	X	X			O		298	Wyoming Seminary	*Kingston*
		X	X	X								O		300	Wyoming Seminary	*Forty Fort*

RHODE ISLAND

Boarding Boys	Boarding Girls	Day Boys	Day Girls	Elementary	Junior Boarding	Secondary	Postgraduate Program	Summer Program	English as a Second Language	Learning Differences Program	Preprofessional Arts Training	Religious Affiliation	Military Program	Page	School	Location
		X	X	X										301	The Gordon School	*East Providence*
			X	X		X						Q		301	Lincoln School	*Providence*
	X				X				X			RC		301	Overbrook Academy	*Warwick*
		X	X	X						X				302	The Pennfield School†	*Portsmouth*
X	X	X	X			X		X				RC		302	Portsmouth Abbey School	*Portsmouth*
		X	X	X		X								304	The Providence Country Day School	*East Providence*
X	X	X	X	X		X			X	X				304	St. Andrew's School†	*Barrington*
		X	X	X				X						306	St. Michael's Country Day School	*Newport*
		X	X	X		X				X				306	The Wheeler School†	*Providence*

SOUTH CAROLINA

Boarding Boys	Boarding Girls	Day Boys	Day Girls	Elementary	Junior Boarding	Secondary	Postgraduate Program	Summer Program	English as a Second Language	Learning Differences Program	Preprofessional Arts Training	Religious Affiliation	Military Program	Page	School	Location
		X	X	X		X				X				307	Beaufort Academy†	*Beaufort*
		X	X	X		X				X				307	Charleston Collegiate School	*Johns Island*
		X	X	X										307	Charleston Day School	*Charleston*
		X	X	X		X				X				307	Glenforest School†	*West Columbia*
		X	X	X		X				X				307	Hammond School†	*Columbia*
		X	X	X		X				X				309	Hilton Head Preparatory School	*Hilton Head Island*
		X	X	X		X				X		E		309	Porter-Gaud School†	*Charleston*
X	X	X	X	X		X		X		X				310	Trident Academy†	*Mount Pleasant*

TENNESSEE

Boarding Boys	Boarding Girls	Day Boys	Day Girls	Elementary	Junior Boarding	Secondary	Postgraduate Program	Summer Program	English as a Second Language	Learning Differences Program	Preprofessional Arts Training	Religious Affiliation	Military Program	Page	School	Location
		X	X	X		X		X		X				311	Battle Ground Academy†	*Franklin*
		X	X	X		X		X				NC		311	Brentwood Academy	*Brentwood*
		X	X	X				X				O		311	Christ Methodist Day School	*Memphis*
		X	X	X		X		X		X				311	Currey Ingram Academy†	*Brentwood*

Boarding Boys	Boarding Girls	Day Boys	Day Girls	Elementary	Junior Boarding	Secondary	Postgraduate Program	Summer Program	English as a Second Language	Learning Differences Program	Preprofessional Arts Training	Religious Affiliation	Military Program	Page	
		X	X	X		X		X						311	The Ensworth School *Nashville*
		X	X	X								E		311	Episcopal School of Knoxville *Knoxville*
		X	X	X		X		X				NC		312	Franklin Road Academy *Nashville*
		X	X	X				X				E		312	Grace-St. Luke's Episcopal School *Memphis*
		X	X	X				X		X				312	Harding Academy† *Nashville*
			X			X								312	The Harpeth Hall School *Nashville*
			X	X		X		X						312	Hutchison School *Memphis*
		X	X	X		X		X	X					313	Lausanne Collegiate School *Memphis*
		X				X		X						313	Memphis University School *Memphis*
		X				X		X						313	Montgomery Bell Academy *Nashville*
		X	X	X				X				RC		313	Overbrook School *Nashville*
		X	X	X		X		X		X		RC		313	St. Agnes Academy-St. Dominic School† *Memphis*
			X			X						RC		313	St. Cecilia Academy *Nashville*
		X	X	X		X		X				E		314	St. George's Independent School *Germantown/Memphis/Collierville*
		X	X	X				X		X		E		314	St. Nicholas School† *Chattanooga*
		X	X	X		X								314	University School of Nashville *Nashville*
		X	X	X		X		X						314	Webb School of Knoxville *Knoxville*

TEXAS

Boarding Boys	Boarding Girls	Day Boys	Day Girls	Elementary	Junior Boarding	Secondary	Postgraduate Program	Summer Program	English as a Second Language	Learning Differences Program	Preprofessional Arts Training	Religious Affiliation	Military Program	Page	
		X	X	X								E		315	All Saints Episcopal School *Beaumont*
		X	X	X		X						E		315	All Saints' Episcopal School *Fort Worth*
		X	X	X				X				O		315	Annunciation Orthodox School *Houston*
		X	X	X		X		X	X					315	The Awty International School *Houston*
		X	X	X		X						E		317	The Canterbury Episcopal School *DeSoto*
		X		X		X		X		X		RC		317	Cistercian Preparatory School† *Irving*
			X	X		X		X				RC		317	Duchesne Academy of the Sacred Heart *Houston*
		X	X			X						E		317	Episcopal High School of Houston *Bellaire*
		X	X	X		X		X				E		318	The Episcopal School of Dallas *Dallas*
		X	X	X				X						318	Fort Worth Academy *Fort Worth*
		X	X	X		X		X						318	Fort Worth Country Day *Fort Worth*
		X	X	X								E		318	Good Shepherd Episcopal School *Dallas*
	X		X	X	X	X		X	X					318	The Hockaday School *Dallas*
		X	X	X		X		X						320	The John Cooper School *The Woodlands*
		X	X	X		X		X						321	The Kinkaid School *Houston*
		X	X	X		X								321	Lakehill Preparatory School *Dallas*
		X	X	X				X						321	The Lamplighter School *Dallas*
		X	X	X		X		X						321	The Oakridge School *Arlington*
		X	X	X		X						E		323	Parish Episcopal School *Dallas*
		X	X	X								P		323	Presbyterian School *Houston*
		X	X	X								B		323	River Oaks Baptist School *Houston*
			X			X						RC		323	St. Agnes Academy *Houston*
		X	X	X		X						E		324	St. Andrew's Episcopal School *Austin*
		X	X	X						X		E		324	St. James Episcopal School† *Corpus Christi*
		X	X	X		X								324	St. John's School *Houston*
		X	X	X				X	X			E		324	St. Luke's Episcopal School *San Antonio*
		X		X		X								324	St. Mark's School of Texas *Dallas*

Classification Grid

Boarding Boys	Boarding Girls	Day Boys	Day Girls	Elementary	Junior Boarding	Secondary	Postgraduate Program	Summer Program	English as a Second Language	Learning Differences Program	Preprofessional Arts Training	Religious Affiliation	Military Program	Page	School
		X	X	X		X			X	X		E		324	Saint Michael's Academy *Bryan*
		X	X			X				X		RC		325	St. Pius X High School† *Houston*
		X	X	X		X		X		X				325	Shelton School and Evaluation Center† *Dallas*
		X				X		X				RC		325	Strake Jesuit College Preparatory *Houston*
X	X	X	X			X						E	X	325	TMI — The Episcopal School of Texas *San Antonio*
		X	X	X		X		X		X				325	Trinity Valley School† *Fort Worth*
		X	X			X								326	Vanguard College Preparatory School *Waco*
		X	X	X		X		X		X				326	The Winston School† *Dallas*

UTAH

Boarding Boys	Boarding Girls	Day Boys	Day Girls	Elementary	Junior Boarding	Secondary	Postgraduate Program	Summer Program	English as a Second Language	Learning Differences Program	Preprofessional Arts Training	Religious Affiliation	Military Program	Page	School
		X	X	X										327	Park City Academy *Park City*
		X	X	X		X								327	Rowland Hall-St. Mark's School *Salt Lake City*

VERMONT

Boarding Boys	Boarding Girls	Day Boys	Day Girls	Elementary	Junior Boarding	Secondary	Postgraduate Program	Summer Program	English as a Second Language	Learning Differences Program	Preprofessional Arts Training	Religious Affiliation	Military Program	Page	School
		X	X	X		X		X		X				327	Long Trail School† *Dorset*
		X	X	X				X						327	Maple Street School *Manchester Center*

VIRGINIA

Boarding Boys	Boarding Girls	Day Boys	Day Girls	Elementary	Junior Boarding	Secondary	Postgraduate Program	Summer Program	English as a Second Language	Learning Differences Program	Preprofessional Arts Training	Religious Affiliation	Military Program	Page	School
		X	X	X						X				328	Alexandria Country Day School† *Alexandria*
		X	X			X				X		RC		328	Bishop Ireton High School† *Alexandria*
		X	X			X				X		RC		328	Bishop Sullivan Catholic High School† *Virginia Beach*
X						X			X	X		E		328	Blue Ridge School† *St. George*
		X	X	X				X		X				330	Browne Academy† *Alexandria*
		X	X	X				X						330	Burgundy Farm Country Day School *Alexandria*
		X	X	X		X		X	X					330	Cape Henry Collegiate School *Virginia Beach*
		X	X	X				X						331	Chesapeake Academy *Irvington*
		X	X	X		X		X						331	Collegiate School *Richmond*
		X	X	X				X						331	The Congressional Schools of Virginia *Falls Church*
		X	X	X		X				X		NC		331	The Covenant School† *Charlottesville*
X	X					X				X		E		332	Episcopal High School† *Alexandria*
		X	X	X		X		X		X				333	Flint Hill School† *Oakton*
X		X				X	X	X	X	X		B	X	334	Fork Union Military Academy† *Fork Union*
	X		X			X				X				336	Foxcroft School† *Middleburg*
		X	X	X		X		X						337	Fredericksburg Academy *Fredericksburg*
		X	X	X		X		X						338	Hampton Roads Academy *Newport News*
X		X				X	X	X	X	X		B	X	338	Hargrave Military Academy† *Chatham*
		X	X	X										340	The Hill School of Middleburg *Middleburg*
		X	X	X				X						340	The Langley School *McLean*
		X	X	X								RC		340	Linton Hall School *Bristow*
		X	X	X										340	Loudoun Country Day School *Leesburg*
X	X	X	X		X	X	X	X	X			C	X	340	Massanutten Military Academy *Woodstock*
X	X	X	X		X	X	X		X					342	Miller School *Charlottesville*
		X	X	X		X		X						344	Norfolk Academy *Norfolk*
		X	X	X		X		X		X				346	Norfolk Collegiate School† *Norfolk*
		X	X	X		X		X						346	North Cross School *Roanoke*

Boarding Boys	Boarding Girls	Day Boys	Day Girls	Elementary	Junior Boarding	Secondary	Postgraduate Program	Summer Program	English as a Second Language	Learning Differences Program	Preprofessional Arts Training	Religious Affiliation	Military Program	Page	School
		X	X			X						RC		347	Notre Dame Academy† *Middleburg*
			X			X						RC		347	Oakcrest School *McLean*
X	X	X	X			X		X	X	X		B		347	Oak Hill Academy† *Mouth of Wilson*
		X	X	X		X		X						349	The Potomac School *McLean*
		X	X	X										349	Powhatan School *Boyce*
		X	X	X										349	Richmond Montessori School *Richmond*
		X	X	X				X				E		349	St. Andrew's Episcopal School *Newport News*
X	X	X	X	X		X		X	X			E		350	St. Anne's-Belfield School *Charlottesville*
			X	X		X		X				E		350	St. Catherine's School *Richmond*
		X		X		X		X				E		350	St. Christopher's School *Richmond*
	X		X			X			X			E		350	St. Margaret's School *Tappahannock*
		X	X	X								RC		350	Saint Patrick Catholic School *Norfolk*
		X	X	X		X		X				E		351	St. Stephen's and St. Agnes School *Alexandria*
		X	X	X		X		X	X					351	The Steward School *Richmond*
		X	X	X				X						351	Sullins Academy *Bristol*
		X	X			X						E		351	Trinity Episcopal School *Richmond*
		X	X	X										351	Westminster School *Annandale*

WASHINGTON

Boarding Boys	Boarding Girls	Day Boys	Day Girls	Elementary	Junior Boarding	Secondary	Postgraduate Program	Summer Program	English as a Second Language	Learning Differences Program	Preprofessional Arts Training	Religious Affiliation	Military Program	Page	School
		X	X	X		X								352	The Bush School *Seattle*
		X	X	X		X								352	Charles Wright Academy *Tacoma*
		X	X	X						X				352	Epiphany School† *Seattle*
		X	X	X								E		352	St. Thomas School *Medina*
		X	X			X								352	Seattle Academy *Seattle*
		X	X	X						X				352	Seattle Country Day School† *Seattle*
		X	X	X		X								353	Seattle Waldorf School *Seattle*
		X	X	X				X		X				353	University Child Development School† *Seattle*
		X	X			X				X				353	University Prep† *Seattle*

WEST VIRGINIA

Boarding Boys	Boarding Girls	Day Boys	Day Girls	Elementary	Junior Boarding	Secondary	Postgraduate Program	Summer Program	English as a Second Language	Learning Differences Program	Preprofessional Arts Training	Religious Affiliation	Military Program	Page	School
X	X	X	X	X	X	X				X				354	The Linsly School† *Wheeling*

WISCONSIN

Boarding Boys	Boarding Girls	Day Boys	Day Girls	Elementary	Junior Boarding	Secondary	Postgraduate Program	Summer Program	English as a Second Language	Learning Differences Program	Preprofessional Arts Training	Religious Affiliation	Military Program	Page	School
		X	X	X		X		X		X				355	Brookfield Academy† *Brookfield*
		X	X	X		X		X						355	Madison Country Day School *Waunakee*
		X	X	X		X		X	X					355	The Prairie School *Racine*
		X	X	X		X		X						355	University Lake School *Hartland*
		X	X	X		X		X						355	University School of Milwaukee *Milwaukee*

Classification Grid

OTHER COUNTRIES AND UNITED STATES TERRITORIES

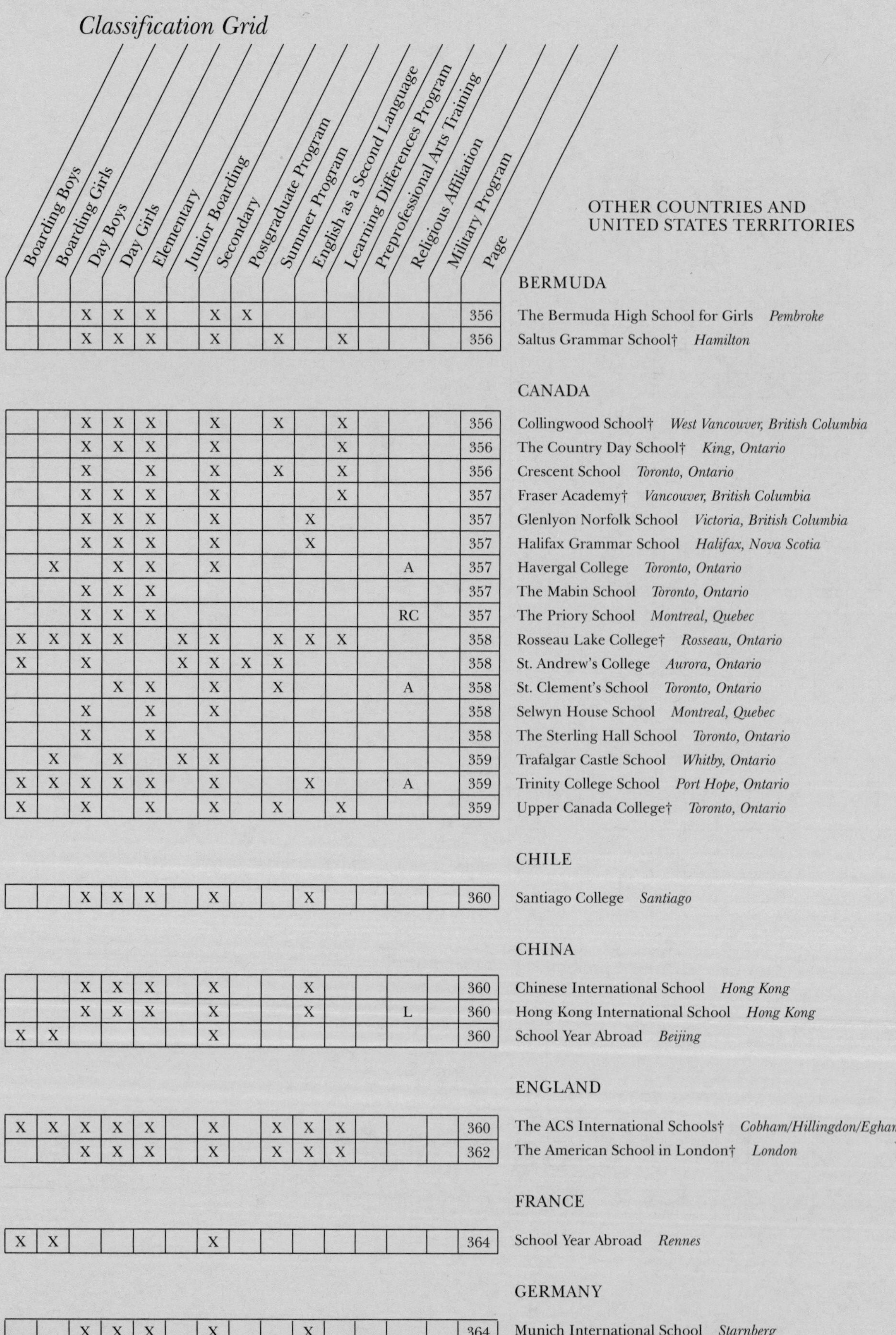

Boarding Boys	Boarding Girls	Day Boys	Day Girls	Elementary	Junior Boarding	Secondary	Postgraduate Program	Summer Program	English as a Second Language	Learning Differences Program	Preprofessional Arts Training	Religious Affiliation	Military Program	Page	School
															BERMUDA
		X	X	X		X	X							356	The Bermuda High School for Girls *Pembroke*
		X	X	X		X		X		X				356	Saltus Grammar School† *Hamilton*
															CANADA
		X	X	X		X		X		X				356	Collingwood School† *West Vancouver, British Columbia*
		X	X	X		X				X				356	The Country Day School† *King, Ontario*
		X		X		X		X		X				356	Crescent School *Toronto, Ontario*
		X	X	X		X				X				357	Fraser Academy† *Vancouver, British Columbia*
		X	X	X		X			X					357	Glenlyon Norfolk School *Victoria, British Columbia*
		X	X	X		X			X					357	Halifax Grammar School *Halifax, Nova Scotia*
	X		X	X		X						A		357	Havergal College *Toronto, Ontario*
		X	X	X										357	The Mabin School *Toronto, Ontario*
		X	X	X								RC		357	The Priory School *Montreal, Quebec*
X	X	X	X		X	X		X	X	X				358	Rosseau Lake College† *Rosseau, Ontario*
X		X			X	X	X	X						358	St. Andrew's College *Aurora, Ontario*
			X	X		X		X				A		358	St. Clement's School *Toronto, Ontario*
		X		X		X								358	Selwyn House School *Montreal, Quebec*
		X		X										358	The Sterling Hall School *Toronto, Ontario*
	X		X		X	X								359	Trafalgar Castle School *Whitby, Ontario*
X	X	X	X	X		X			X			A		359	Trinity College School *Port Hope, Ontario*
X		X		X		X		X		X				359	Upper Canada College† *Toronto, Ontario*
															CHILE
		X	X	X		X			X					360	Santiago College *Santiago*
															CHINA
		X	X	X		X			X					360	Chinese International School *Hong Kong*
		X	X	X		X			X			L		360	Hong Kong International School *Hong Kong*
X	X					X								360	School Year Abroad *Beijing*
															ENGLAND
X	X	X	X	X		X		X	X	X				360	The ACS International Schools† *Cobham/Hillingdon/Egham*
		X	X	X		X		X	X	X				362	The American School in London† *London*
															FRANCE
X	X					X								364	School Year Abroad *Rennes*
															GERMANY
		X	X	X		X			X					364	Munich International School *Starnberg*

Boarding Boys	Boarding Girls	Day Boys	Day Girls	Elementary	Junior Boarding	Secondary	Postgraduate Program	Summer Program	English as a Second Language	Learning Differences Program	Preprofessional Arts Training	Religious Affiliation	Military Program	Page	
															INDIA
		X	X	X		X			X	X				365	American International School Chennai *Chennai*
															ITALY
X	X	X	X			X	X							365	St. Stephen's School *Rome*
X	X					X								367	School Year Abroad *Viterbo*
															JAPAN
		X		X		X		X	X			RC		367	St. Mary's International School *Tokyo*
															KOREA
		X	X	X		X			X			NC		369	Seoul Foreign School *Seoul*
															PUERTO RICO
		X	X	X		X		X	X	X				370	Caribbean Preparatory School† *San Juan*
															SPAIN
		X	X	X		X		X	X					370	The American School of Madrid *Madrid*
X	X					X								370	School Year Abroad *Zaragoza*
															VIRGIN ISLANDS
		X	X	X		X		X		X				370	The Good Hope School† *Frederiksted*
		X	X	X		X		X		X				370	St. Croix Country Day School† *Kingshill*